# A Commentary on the LCIA Arbitration Rules 2014

# A Commentary on the LCIA Arbitration Rules 2014

## By

**Shai Wade,** Solicitor (England & Wales), Partner, International Arbitration Team, Stephenson Harwood LLP

**Philip Clifford,** Solicitor-Advocate (England & Wales), Partner at Latham & Watkins and former Global Co-Chair of Latham's International Arbitration Practice

**James Clanchy,** Solicitor (England & Wales), former Registrar and Deputy Director General of the LCIA

### With regional commentaries from:

**Robert Karrar-Lewsley,** Barrister (England & Wales), Senior Associate, Al Tamimi & Co, Dubai

**Ciccu Mukhopadhaya**, Senior Counsel, India

**Duncan Bagshaw,** Barrister (England & Wales), Registrar of the LCIA-MIAC Arbitration Centre (Mauritius)

SWEET & MAXWELL         THOMSON REUTERS

Published in 2015 by
Thomson Reuters (Professional) UK Limited
trading as Sweet & Maxwell
Friars House, 160 Blackfriars Road, Southwark, London, SE1 8EZ
(Registered in England & Wales, Company No 1679046.
Registered Office and address for service:
2nd Floor, Aldgate House, 33 Aldgate High Street, London, EC3N 1DL)

For further information on our products and services, visit www.sweetandmaxwell.co.uk

Typeset by LBJ Typesetting Ltd of Kingsclere
Printed and bound in Great Britain by CPI Group (UK) Ltd, Croydon, CR0 4YY
No natural forests were destroyed to make this product; only farmed timber was used and re-planted.

A CIP catalogue record for this book is available from the British Library.

ISBN 978-1-847-03560-8

Crown copyright material is reproduced with the permission of the Controller of HMSO and the Queen's Printer for Scotland.

All rights reserved. No part of this publication may be reproduced or transmitted in any form or by any means, or stored in any retrieval system of any nature without prior written permission, except for permitted fair dealing under the Copyright, Designs and Patents Act 1988, or in accordance with the terms of a licence issued by the Copyright Licensing Agency in respect of photocopying and/or reprographic reproduction. Application for permission for other use of copyright material including permission to reproduce extracts in other published works shall be made to the publishers. Full acknowledgment of authors, publisher and source must be given. Material is contained in this publication for which publishing permission has been sought, and for which copyright is acknowledged. Permission to reproduce such material cannot be granted by the publishers and application must be made to the copyright holder.

Thomson Reuters and the Thomson Reuters Logo are trademarks of Thomson Reuters. Sweet & Maxwell® is a registered trademark of Thomson Reuters (Professional) Limited.

IBA Guidelines on Conflicts of Interest in International Arbitration (2014), IBA Rules on the Taking of Evidence in International Arbitration (2010) and IBA Guidelines on Party Representation in International Arbitration (2013) are reproduced by kind permission of the International Bar Association, London, UK, and are available at: www.ibanet.org/Publications/publications_IBA_guides_and_free_materials.aspx.
© International Bar Association.

© 2015 Thomson Reuters (Professional) Limited

# PREFACE

This book sets out to provide arbitration practitioners and parties interested in LCIA arbitration with a practical and user-friendly, but also in-depth, guide to the LCIA and its new Arbitration Rules, which came into effect on October 1, 2014. The authors bring many decades of experience in international arbitration, as practising arbitrators, as Counsel to parties and as a former Registrar and Deputy Director General of the LCIA. This range of experience allows the authors to provide the reader with a balanced perspective and an understanding of the background and context needed to interpret the Rules in the situations that they may be faced with in practice. Where helpful, comparisons are drawn between the present Rules, their predecessors and other international arbitration rules.

Over the last few years there has been a wave of revisions to arbitration rules and, as a result, a great deal of discussion in the arbitration community as to what arbitration rules should contain and the best approaches to take. This has allowed those responsible for drafting the new LCIA Rules to fashion them in light of the views expressed, and has also provided a wealth of material for our commentaries. The result, we hope, is a comprehensive analysis of the issues of practical importance for those using, or considering, the LCIA Rules.

We extend our thanks to all those whose assistance and support has made this book possible, including: the authors of the chapters on the DIFC-LCIA (Robert Karrar-Lewsley), LCIA India (Ciccu Mukhopadhaya SC) and LCIA-MIAC (Duncan Bagshaw); LCIA staff who have kindly answered queries and provided information; our colleagues in the arbitration groups at Latham & Watkins, in particular, Oliver Browne and, for her secretarial support, Shelley Levett, and Stephenson Harwood; the publishing team at Sweet & Maxwell; and, for their long-suffering and patience, our families: Samantha, Lucy and Peter Clifford, Idit Albert, Ella, Tal and Mia Albert-Wade and Kate, Nicholas and Emma Clanchy.

We have sought to state the relevant law and LCIA practice as at October 1, 2014. All views expressed in this book are the authors' own, as are any errors which it might contain.

Finally, we dedicate this book to the memory of Stephen York, whose enthusiasm for the practice of international arbitration was an inspiration to his many friends and colleagues.

**Shai Wade, Philip Clifford and James Clanchy**
**December 2014**

# FOREWORD

In the best of all possible worlds, there would be no necessity for any arbitration rules. In such a world, however, there would be no disputes and no need for arbitration at all, still less an ancient arbitral institution such as the LCIA. Unfortunately, such a Panglossian world does not yet exist.

Today, for transnational parties to an arbitration operating in the real world, there remains a basic need for international arbitration rules so as to avoid the imposition of a paramount legal culture or repeated ad hoc studies in comparative legal procedures at the beginning of each arbitration. An institution's arbitration rules seek to provide a level playing-field for all users, practitioners and arbitrators, with settled expectations and, insofar as possible, no surprises.

From 1985 onwards, the LCIA's successive rules have attempted to meet this basic need. Under the guidance of the LCIA Court, comprising a majority of non-English specialists, the LCIA issued its New Rules on October 1, 2014. These New Rules retain the distinctive features of LCIA arbitration. The LCIA's emphasis remains on referring the parties' dispute to the arbitral tribunal as quickly as possible, with the early appointment of arbitrators, the immediate reference to the tribunal of any questions of jurisdiction or admissibility, and the fullest freedom of the parties to tailor their arbitration's procedure under the LCIA Rules to the particular characteristics of their dispute. These features are intended to avoid many of the delays that can often follow the commencement of an international arbitration. Thereafter, the conduct of the arbitration lies largely with the tribunal in consultation with the parties, subject to essential procedural safeguards and those rules governing the roles of the tribunal, the LCIA Court and the LCIA Registry. During the arbitration, the LCIA Court (with the LCIA Registry) operates "administration-lite" functions, save for the appointment (and removal) of arbitrators, the adjustment of time-limits and the interim payment of arbitral fees and expenses. At the end of the arbitration, the LCIA Court fixes the costs of the arbitration (i.e. the tribunal's fees and the LCIA's own administrative charges); but the LCIA Court plays no part in reviewing the tribunal's award.

There is by now much accumulated experience contained in the LCIA Rules. Each phrase bears the imprint of one or more forensic fables. Many are the result of one or more user's war-story. There is, however, no official LCIA commentary on the interpretation of the LCIA Rules; nor should there be. The LCIA Rules should stand alone. However, it has become increasingly useful for users, practitioners and arbitrators to study commentaries on the LCIA Rules as a guide to the different possibilities offered by these arbitration rules.

This work is the first to be published on the LCIA 2014 Rules. Its three authors are well qualified to explain the function of these rules: one the former LCIA Registrar and the other two well-known London arbitration practitioners. I am delighted to commend this work, as a useful and practical guide to LCIA arbitration. Of course, not all may agree with every aspect of this commentary. That, however, only demonstrates the flexibility of the LCIA Rules and the different choices available to parties in their application.

**V.V. Veeder QC**
**Essex Court Chambers, London**
**December 4, 2014**

# TABLE OF CONTENTS

*Preface* v
*Foreword* vi
*Table of Contents* ix
*Table of Cases* xvii
*Table of Statutes* xxiii
*Table of Protocols* xxv
*Table of Treaties and Conventions* xxxiii

## PART I—INTRODUCTION

Introduction 3
The LCIA's Growth and its Users 3
The Modern LCIA, its Aims and Organisation 4
Overview of the LCIA Rules 9
Underlying Theories 11
Other Characteristics of the LCIA Rules 17

## PART II—COMMENTARY ON THE LCIA RULES

Preamble 21

Article 1 – Request for Arbitration 26
    Sub-article 1.1 28
    Sub-article 1.2 36
    Sub-article 1.3 36
    Sub-article 1.4 37
    Sub-article 1.5 38

Article 2 – Response 39
    Sub-article 2.1 41
    Sub-article 2.2 47
    Sub-article 2.3 47
    Sub-article 2.4 48
    Sub-article 2.5 49

Article 3 – LCIA Court and Registrar 51
    Sub-article 3.1 51
    Sub-article 3.2 53
    Sub-article 3.3 54

| | |
|---|---|
| Article 4 – Written Communications and Periods of Time | 55 |
| Sub-article 4.1 | 57 |
| Sub-article 4.2 | 58 |
| Sub-article 4.3 | 59 |
| Sub-article 4.4 | 60 |
| Sub-article 4.5 | 60 |
| Sub-article 4.6 | 60 |
| | |
| Article 5 – Formation of Arbitral Tribunal | 63 |
| Sub-article 5.1 | 65 |
| Sub-article 5.2 | 66 |
| Sub-article 5.3 | 66 |
| Sub-article 5.4 | 73 |
| Sub-article 5.5 | 81 |
| Sub-article 5.6 | 82 |
| Sub-article 5.7 | 83 |
| Sub-article 5.8 | 83 |
| Sub-article 5.9 | 85 |
| Sub-article 5.10 | 86 |
| | |
| Article 6 – Nationality of Arbitrators | 87 |
| Sub-article 6.1 | 88 |
| Sub-article 6.2 | 89 |
| Sub-article 6.3 | 89 |
| | |
| Article 7 – Party and Other Nominations | 91 |
| Sub-article 7.1 | 92 |
| Sub-article 7.2 | 94 |
| Sub-article 7.3 | 94 |
| | |
| Article 8 – Three or More Parties | 96 |
| Sub-article 8.1 | 97 |
| Sub-article 8.2 | 97 |
| | |
| Articles 9A, 9B and 9C | 99 |
| Introduction | 102 |
| | |
| Article 9A – Expedited Formation of Arbitral Tribunal | 104 |
| Sub-article 9.1 | 104 |
| Sub-article 9.2 | 105 |
| Sub-article 9.3 | 110 |
| | |
| Article 9B – Emergency Arbitrator | 110 |
| Sub-article 9.4 | 112 |
| Sub-article 9.5 | 113 |
| Sub-article 9.6 | 116 |

| | |
|---|---|
| Sub-article 9.7 | 117 |
| Sub-article 9.8 | 119 |
| Sub-article 9.9 | 120 |
| Sub-article 9.10 | 121 |
| Sub-article 9.11 | 121 |
| Sub-article 9.12 | 122 |
| Sub-article 9.13 | 123 |
| Sub-article 9.14 | 124 |
| | |
| Article 9C – Expedited Appointment of Replacement Arbitrator | 124 |
| Sub-article 9.15 | 124 |
| Sub-article 9.16 | 124 |
| Sub-article 9.17 | 125 |
| | |
| Article 10 – Revocation and Challenges | 127 |
| Sub-article 10.1 | 130 |
| Sub-article 10.2 | 142 |
| Sub-article 10.3 | 147 |
| Sub-article 10.4 | 150 |
| Sub-article 10.5 | 150 |
| Sub-article 10.6 | 151 |
| Sub-article 10.7 | 152 |
| | |
| Article 11 – Nomination and Replacement | 154 |
| Sub-article 11.1 | 154 |
| Sub-article 11.2 | 155 |
| | |
| Article 12 – Majority Power to Continue Deliberations | 157 |
| Sub-article 12.1 | 158 |
| Sub-article 12.2 | 159 |
| Sub-article 12.3 | 159 |
| | |
| Article 13 – Communications Between Parties and Arbitral Tribunal | 161 |
| Sub-article 13.1 | 162 |
| Sub-article 13.2 | 164 |
| Sub-article 13.3 | 165 |
| Sub-article 13.4 | 165 |
| Sub-article 13.5 | 167 |
| | |
| Article 14 – Conduct of Proceedings | 169 |
| Sub-article 14.1 | 172 |
| Sub-article 14.2 | 172 |
| Sub-article 14.3 | 172 |
| Sub-article 14.4 | 175 |

Sub-article 14.5 176
Sub-article 14.6 178

Article 15 – Written Statements 179
   Sub-article 15.1 183
   Sub-article 15.2 183
   Sub-article 15.3 184
   Sub-article 15.4 186
   Sub-article 15.5 186
   Sub-article 15.6 187
   Sub-article 15.7 187
   Sub-article 15.8 187
   Sub-article 15.9 188
   Sub-article 15.10 188

Article 16 – Seat(s) of Arbitration and Place(s) of Hearings 190
   Sub-article 16.1 192
   Sub-article 16.2 192
   Sub-article 16.3 194
   Sub-article 16.4 195

Article 17 – Language(s) of Arbitration 198
   Sub-article 17.1 201
   Sub-article 17.2 201
   Sub-article 17.3 202
   Sub-article 17.4 203
   Sub-article 17.5 204

Article 18 – Legal Representatives 205
   Sub-article 18.1 208
   Sub-article 18.2 209
   Sub-article 18.3 210
   Sub-article 18.4 212
   Sub-article 18.5 213
   Sub-article 18.6 215

Article 19 – Oral Hearings 217
   Sub-article 19.1 218
   Sub-article 19.2 219
   Sub-article 19.3 221
   Sub-article 19.4 221

Article 20 – Witness(es) 223
   Sub-article 20.1 225
   Sub-article 20.2 226
   Sub-article 20.3 226

| | |
|---|---|
| Sub-article 20.4 | 227 |
| Sub-article 20.5 | 228 |
| Sub-article 20.6 | 229 |
| Sub-article 20.7 | 230 |
| Sub-article 20.8 | 230 |
| | |
| Article 21 – Expert(s) to Arbitral Tribunal | 232 |
| Sub-article 21.1 | 233 |
| Sub-article 21.2 | 234 |
| Sub-article 21.3 | 234 |
| Sub-article 21.4 | 234 |
| Sub-article 21.5 | 235 |
| | |
| Article 22 – Additional Powers | 236 |
| Sub-article 22.1 | 239 |
| Sub-article 22.2 | 255 |
| Sub-article 22.3 | 256 |
| Sub-article 22.4 | 258 |
| Sub-article 22.5 | 259 |
| Sub-article 22.6 | 259 |
| | |
| Article 23 – Jurisdiction and Authority | 260 |
| Sub-article 23.1 | 263 |
| Sub-article 23.2 | 264 |
| Sub-article 23.3 | 265 |
| Sub-article 23.4 | 267 |
| Sub-article 23.5 | 267 |
| | |
| Article 24 – Deposits | 269 |
| Sub-article 24.1 | 271 |
| Sub-article 24.2 | 272 |
| Sub-article 24.3 | 273 |
| Sub-article 24.4 | 273 |
| Sub-article 24.5 | 274 |
| Sub-article 24.6 | 275 |
| | |
| Article 25 – Interim and Conservatory Measures | 277 |
| Sub-article 25.1 | 281 |
| Sub-article 25.2 | 285 |
| Sub-article 25.3 | 286 |
| Sub-article 25.4 | 287 |
| | |
| Article 26 – Award(s) | 288 |
| Sub-article 26.1 | 289 |
| Sub-article 26.2 | 290 |
| Sub-article 26.3 | 292 |

| | |
|---|---|
| Sub-article 26.4 | 292 |
| Sub-article 26.5 | 293 |
| Sub-article 26.6 | 293 |
| Sub-article 26.7 | 294 |
| Sub-article 26.8 | 296 |
| Sub-article 26.9 | 297 |
| | |
| Article 27 – Correction of Award(s) and Additional Award(s) | 299 |
| Sub-article 27.1 | 300 |
| Sub-article 27.2 | 302 |
| Sub-article 27.3 | 302 |
| Sub-article 27.4 | 303 |
| Sub-article 27.5 | 304 |
| | |
| Article 28 – Arbitration Costs and Legal Costs | 305 |
| Sub-article 28.1 | 306 |
| Sub-article 28.2 | 309 |
| Sub-article 28.3 | 310 |
| Sub-article 28.4 | 311 |
| Sub-article 28.5 | 313 |
| Sub-article 28.6 | 314 |
| Sub-article 28.7 | 314 |
| | |
| Article 29 – Determinations and Decisions by LCIA Court | 315 |
| Sub-article 29.1 | 316 |
| Sub-article 29.2 | 317 |
| | |
| Article 30 – Confidentiality | 319 |
| Sub-article 30.1 | 320 |
| Sub-article 30.2 | 321 |
| Sub-article 30.3 | 322 |
| | |
| Article 31 – Limitation of Liability | 323 |
| Sub-article 31.1 | 324 |
| Sub-article 31.2 | 325 |
| | |
| Article 32 – General Rules | 327 |
| Sub-article 32.1 | 328 |
| Sub-article 32.2 | 329 |
| Sub-article 32.3 | 330 |
| | |
| **Annex to the LCIA Rules** General Guidelines for the Parties' Legal Representatives (Articles 18.5 and 18.6 of the LCIA Rules) | 332 |
| | |
| **Schedule of Arbitration Costs (LCIA)** | 341 |

## PART III—COMMENTARY ON THE LCIA RECOMMENDED CLAUSES

| | |
|---|---|
| Introduction | 361 |
| Future disputes | 364 |
| Existing disputes | 370 |

## PART IV—DIFC-LCIA ARBITRATION CENTRE by Robert Karrar-Lewsley

| | |
|---|---|
| Introduction | 375 |
| Background | 375 |
| The DIFC-LCIA and its Rules | 381 |
| Conclusion | 385 |

## PART V—LCIA INDIA by Ciccu Mukhopadhaya, SC

| | |
|---|---|
| Introduction | 389 |
| Background—The Indian arbitration market | 389 |
| Legal framework for arbitration in India: the (Indian) 1996 Act | 390 |
| LCIA India | 394 |
| LCIA India Rules | 394 |
| Notes for Arbitrators | 396 |

## PART VI—LCIA-MIAC ARBITRATION CENTRE by Duncan Bagshaw

| | |
|---|---|
| Mauritius | 399 |
| The arbitration environment in Africa | 400 |
| The development of the Mauritius infrastructure | 401 |
| The LCIA-MIAC Arbitration Centre and the LCIA-MIAC Arbitration Rules | 404 |
| The future | 407 |

## APPENDICES

| | |
|---|---|
| Appendix 1 – LCIA Arbitration Rules 2014 | 411 |
| Appendix 2 – Schedule of Arbitration Costs (LCIA) | 440 |
| Appendix 3 – Constitution of the LCIA Arbitration Court | 445 |
| Appendix 4 – LCIA Arbitration Rules 1998 | 449 |
| Appendix 5 – LCIA Mediation Rules | 467 |
| Appendix 6 – Recommended Clauses | 473 |
| Appendix 7 – Arbitration Act 1996 (1996 Chapter 23) | 475 |
| Appendix 8 – The DAC Reports on the Arbitration Bill 1996 | 548 |
| Appendix 9 – New York Convention 1958 | 624 |

Appendix 10 – UNCITRAL Model Law on International
Commercial Arbitration 1985 (with amendments as adopted
in 2006)   629
Appendix 11 – UNCITRAL Arbitration Rules (as revised in 2010)   673
Appendix 12 – IBA Rules on the Taking of Evidence in
International Arbitration   696
Appendix 13 – IBA Guidelines on Conflicts of Interest in
International Arbitration 2014   710
Appendix 14 – IBA Guidelines on Party Representation in
International Arbitration   728

*Index*   741

# TABLE OF CASES

A v B [2011] EWHC 2345 (Comm); [2011] 2 Lloyd's Rep. 591; [2011] Arb. L.R.
43; (2011) 161 N.L.J. 1291 ............. 5–030, 5–031, 5–040, 10–003, 10–017,
10–042, 29–005, 29–007
A v B (Costs) [2007] EWHC 54 (Comm); [2007] 1 All E.R. (Comm) 633; [2007]
1 Lloyd's Rep. 358; [2007] 2 C.L.C. 203; [2007] Bus. L.R. D59 .......... III–005
ABB Lummus Global Ltd v Keppel Fels Ltd [1999] 2 Lloyd's Rep. 24 QBD
(Comm) .................................................... 16–005
Aggeliki Charis Compania Maritima SA v Pagnan SpA (The Angelic Grace)
[1995] 1 Lloyd's Rep. 87 CA (Civ Div) ............................ III–005
Agrimex Ltd v Tradigrain Ltd [2003] EWHC 1656; [2003] 2 Lloyd's Rep 537. . 29–002,
34–033
Al Hadha Trading Co v Tradigrain SA [2002] 2 Lloyd's Rep. 512 QBD (Merc)..... 27–006,
27–007
Ali Shipping Corp v Shipyard Trogir [1999] 1 W.L.R. 314; [1998] 2 All E.R.
136; [1998] 1 Lloyd's Rep. 643; [1998] C.L.C. 566 CA (Civ Div) ......... 30–002
Andrews (t/a BA Contractors) v Bradshaw [2000] B.L.R. 6 CA (Civ Div) ...... 10–018
Angelic Grace, The. See Aggeliki Charis Compania Maritima SA v Pagnan SpA
Aoot Kalmneft v Glencore International Ag [2001] EWHC 464 (Comm) ....... 10–022
Arasmeta Captive Power Co v Lafarge India Pvt Ltd (2014) 4 Arb. L.R. 439 .... V–009
Arsanovia Ltd v Cruz City 1 Mauritius Holdings [2012] EWHC 3702 (Comm);
[2013] 2 All E.R. (Comm) 1; [2013] 1 Lloyd's Rep. 235; [2013] 1 C.L.C.
1040 ................................................ 16–016, 23–012
AT&T Corp v Saudi Cable Co [2000] 2 All E.R. (Comm) 625; [2000] 2 Lloyd's
Rep. 127; [2000] C.L.C. 1309; [2000] B.L.R. 293 ..................... 5–032
Barnwell Enterprises Ltd v ECP Africa FII Investments LLC [2013] EWHC
2517 (Comm); [2014] 1 Lloyd's Rep. 171..................... 25–016, 25–027
Berezovsky v Abramovich [2012] EWHC B15 (Ch) ....................... 20–002
Bharat Aluminium Co v Kaiser Aluminum Technical Services Inc (2012) 9
S.C.C. 552 Sup Ct (India) ................................. V–012, V–013
Bhatia International v Bulk Trading SA 6 (2002) 4 S.C.C. 105 Sup Ct (India) ... V–012,
V–013
Blackdale Ltd v McLean Homes South East Ltd [2001] All E.R. (D) 55 (Nov)... 27–006
Bremer Vulkan Schiffbau und Maschinenfabrik v South India Shipping Corp Ltd
[1981] A.C. 909; [1981] 2 W.L.R. 141; [1981] 1 All E.R. 289; [1981] 1
Lloyd's Rep. 253; [1981] Com. L.R. 19; [1981] E.C.C. 151; (1981) 125 S.J.
114 HL.................................................. 14–018
C v D [2007] EWCA Civ 1282; [2008] 1 All E.R. (Comm) 1001; [2008] Bus.
L.R. 843; [2008] 1 Lloyd's Rep. 239; [2008] C.P. Rep. 11; [2007] 2 C.L.C.
930; 116 Con. L.R. 230 ................................ 16–014, III–018
Compass Group UK and Ireland Ltd (t/a Medirest) v Mid Essex Hospital Services
NHS Trust [2013] EWCA Civ 200; [2013] B.L.R. 265; [2013] C.I.L.L.
3342...................................................... 14–018
Conquer v Boot [1928] 2 K.B. 336 KBD .............................. 26–012
Dallah Real Estate & Tourism Holding Co v Pakistan [2010] UKSC 46; [2011] 1
A.C. 763; [2010] 3 W.L.R. 1472; [2011] 1 All E.R. 485; [2011] 1 All E.R.
(Comm) 383; [2011] Bus. L.R. 158; [2010] 2 Lloyd's Rep. 691; [2010] 2
C.L.C. 793; 133 Con. L.R. 1; (2010) 160 N.L.J. 1569 ........... 23–003, III–006
Darley Main Colliery Co v Mitchell (1886) 11 App. Cas. 127 HL............. 26–012
Department of Economic Policy and Development of the City of Moscow v
Bankers Trust Co [2004] EWCA Civ 314; [2005] Q.B. 207; [2004] 3 W.L.R.

xviii TABLE OF CASES

533; [2004] 4 All E.R. 746; [2004] 2 All E.R. (Comm) 193; [2004] 2 Lloyd's Rep. 179; [2004] 1 C.L.C. 1099; [2004] B.L.R. 229; (2004) 148 S.J.L.B. 389 .................................................................. 30–002
Dhir v Waterfront Property Investment Ltd 8 CFI 011/2009 [2006-09] DIFC CLR 12. .................................................................. IV–018
Donohue v Armco Inc [2001] UKHL 64; [2002] 1 All E.R. 749; [2002] 1 All E.R. (Comm) 97; [2002] 1 Lloyd's Rep. 425; [2002] C.L.C. 440. ............. III–005
Dozco India Pvt Ltd v Doosan Infracore Co Ltd (2011) 6 SCC 179. ........... V–013
El-Farargy v El-Farargy [2007] EWCA Civ 1149; [2007] 3 F.C.R. 711; (2007) 104(46) L.S.G. 26; (2007) 151 S.J.L.B. 1500 ..................... 10–018
Emirates Trading Agency LLC v Prime Mineral Exports Private Ltd [2014] EWHC 2104 (Comm) ............................... 1–001, 1–002, 23–006
Enercon (India) Ltd v Enercon GmBH (2014) 5 S.C.C. 1 Sup Ct (India)........ V–015
Esso Australia Resources Ltd v Plowman [1995] 183 C.L.R. 10 .............. 30–002
Ethiopian Oilseeds Pulses Export Corp v Rio Del Mar Foods Inc [1990] 1 Lloyd's Rep. 86 .......................................................... III–010
Exmar BV v National Iranian Tanker Co [1992] 1 Lloyd's Rep 169 ........... 25–018
Findlay v United Kingdom (22107/93) (1997) 24 E.H.R.R. 221 ECHR. ......... 5–012
Fiona Trust & Holding Corp v Privalov; Premium Nafta Products Ltd v Fili Shipping Co Ltd [2007] UKHL 40; [2007] 4 All E.R. 951; [2007] 2 All E.R. (Comm) 1053; [2007] Bus. L.R. 1719; [2008] 1 Lloyd's Rep. 254; [2007] 2 C.L.C. 553; 114 Con. L.R. 69; [2007] C.I.L.L. 2528; (2007) 104(42) L.S.G. 34; (2007) 151 S.J.L.B. 1364. ........................... 23–006, 23–008, 23–010, III–011
First Investment Corp v Fujian Mawei Shipbuilding Ltd et al, United States District Court, Eastern District of Louisiana, US No.765; First Investment Corp v Fujian Mawei Shipbuilding Ltd et al, US District Court, Eastern District of Louisiana, 09-3663 Section I, 12 March 2012 ................ 12–002
Fletamentos Maritimos SA v Effijohn International BV (No.2) [1997] 2 Lloyd's Rep. 302. .................................................................. 10–018
Francis Travel Marketing Pty Ltd v Virgin Atlantic Airways Ltd (1996) 39 N.S.W.L.R. 160 .......................................................... III–010
Furness, Withy & Co Ltd v J&E Hall Ltd (1909) 25 T.L.R. 233. ................ 26–012
George Mitchell (Chesterhall) Ltd v Finney Lock Seeds Ltd [1983] 2 A.C. 803; [1983] 3 W.L.R. 163; [1983] 2 All E.R. 737; [1983] 2 Lloyd's Rep. 272; [1983] Com. L.R. 209 HL ............................................ 22–018
Gibbs v Cruikshank (1872–1873) L.R. 8 C.P. 454 ........................ 26–012
Gujarat NRE Coke Ltd v Coeclerici Asia (PTE) Ltd [2013] EWHC 1987 (Comm) .................................................................. 14–008, 14–012
Gulf Petro Trading Co, Inc (US) v Nigerian National Petroleum Corp (Nigeria), Bola Ajibola (Nigeria), March 15, 2006 US District Court, Eastern District of Texas, Beaumont Div, ............................................ 31–002
Habas Sinai Ve Tibbi Gazlar Istihsal Endustrisi v VSC Steel Co Ltd [2013] EWHC 4071 (Comm); [2014] 1 Lloyd's Rep. 479 ....... P–004, 16–017, 23–019
HEP v Slovenia (2008) (ICSID Case No.ARB/05/24) ..................... 10–017
Hiscox v Outhwaite (No.1) [1992] 1 A.C. 562; [1991] 3 W.L.R. 297; [1991] 3 All E.R. 641; [1991] 2 Lloyd's Rep. 435 HL. ..................... 16–013, 26–005
HPCL v Pink City Midway Petroleum 2003 (6) S.C.C. 503 .................. V–009
Hrvatska Elektroprivreda d.d. v Republic of Slovenia (ICSID Case No.ARB/05/24 (2008)) ICSID Tr18–014, 18–015
HSBC PI Holdings (Mauritius) Ltd v Avitel Post Studioz Ltd (Manu/MH /0050/2014) .................................................................. V–013
Jilken v Ericsson AB (Case No.T 2448-06) November 19, 2007 Sup Ct (Sweden) ... 5–009
Jivraj v Hashwani [2011] UKSC 40; [2011] 1 W.L.R. 1872; [2012] 1 All E.R. 629; [2012] 1 All E.R. (Comm) 1177; [2011] Bus. L.R. 1182; [2011] 2 Lloyd's Rep. 513; [2011] 2 C.L.C. 427; [2012] 1 C.M.L.R. 12; [2011]

## TABLE OF CASES

I.C.R. 1004; [2011] I.R.L.R. 827; [2011] Eq. L.R. 1088; [2011] Arb. L.R.
28; [2011] C.I.L.L. 3076; [2011] 32 E.G. 54 (C.S.).............. 1–016, 6–002,
16–010, 16–011, 17–004
JJ Ryan & Sons Inc v Rhone Poulenc Textile SA, 863 F.2d 315, 321 (4th Cir
1988) .......................................................................... III–010
Kastner v Jason [2004] EWCA Civ 1599; [2005] 1 Lloyd's Rep. 397; (2004) 148
S.J.L.B. 1436; [2004] N.P.C. 181...................................... 9–005
Kaverit Steel & Crane Ltd v Kone Corp (1992) 87 D.L.R. (4th) 129 CA (Alberta).... III–010
KFTCIC (Kuwait Foreign Trading Contracting and Investment Co) v Icori
Estero SpA June 28, 1991 Cour d'Appel, Paris........................ 10–017
Konkan Railways Corp Ltd v Rani Construction Pvt Ltd (2002) 2 S.C.C. 388 ... V–010
Laker Airways Inc v FLS Aerospace Ltd [2000] 1 W.L.R. 113; [1999] 2 Lloyd's
Rep. 45; [1999] C.L.C. 1124 QBD (Comm).................... 10–017, 18–017
Lawal v Northern Spirit Ltd [2003] UKHL 35; [2004] 1 All E.R. 187; [2003]
I.C.R. 856; [2003] I.R.L.R. 538; [2003] H.R.L.R. 29; [2003] U.K.H.R.R.
1024; (2003) 100(28) L.S.G. 30; (2003) 153 N.L.J. 1005; (2003) 147
S.J.L.B. 783 ................................................................ 10–017
Lesser Design & Build v University of Surrey [1993] 56 B.L.R. 57 ............. 1–010
Lorand Shipping Ltd v Davof Trading (Africa) BV (The Ocean Glory) [2014]
EWHC 3521 (Comm) .................................................... 26–003
Lord Warden and Admiral of the Cinque Ports v HM in his Office of Admiralty,
&c (In the matter of a Whale) (1831) 2 Haggard 438 166 E.R. 304 ........ 10–026
Manistaumunaigaz Oil Production Association v United World Trade Inc [1995]
Lloyd's Rep. 619 .................................................... III–002, III–007
Mantovani v Carapelli SpA [1978] 2 Lloyd's Rep. 63 QBD (Comm) .......... III–005
Maxtel (Judgment 156 of 2013) Dubai Ct of Cassation ..................... IV–010
Maxtel International FZE v Airmec Dubai LLC 5 (Cassation Appeal No. 132 of
2012) Dubai Ct of First Instance .......................... IV–009, IV–023
Michael Wilson & Partners Ltd v Emmott [2008] EWCA Civ 184; [2008] 2 All
E.R. (Comm) 193; [2008] Bus. L.R. 1361; [2008] 1 Lloyd's Rep. 616;
[2008] C.P. Rep. 26; [2008] B.L.R. 515 ................................ 30–002
Milutinovic PIM v Deutsche Babcock AG (Case No. 5017 (1987) ICC Ct of
Arbitration ................................................................ 12–002
Mitsubishi Motors Corp v Soler Chrysler-Plymouth Inc 473 U.S. 614, 628
(1985)..................................................................... I–029
N Radhakrishnan v Maestro Engineering (2010) 1 S.C.C. 72............ V–015, V–016
National Insurance Co Ltd v Boghara Polyfab Pvt Ltd (2009) 1 S.C.C. 267 ..... V–009
New Regency Productions Inc v Nippon Herald Films Inc CA(CAL.), 2007 US
Ct of Appeals, 9th Cir ..................................................... 5–009
Norbrook Laboratories Ltd v Tank [2006] EWHC 1055 (Comm); [2006] 2
Lloyd's Rep. 485; [2006] B.L.R. 412 .......... 9–040, 10–024, 10–025, 13–012
O Ltd (Cyprus) v M Corp (formerly A, Inc) (US), September 3, 2008, 3Ob35/08f,
XXXIV Y.B. COM. ARB. 409 (2009) Sup Ct (Austria) .................. 26–019
Ocean Glory, The. See Lorand Shipping Ltd v Davof Trading (Africa) BV (The
Ocean Glory)
ONGC v Saw Pipes Ltd (2003) 5 S.C.C. 705 ............................ V–014
Oxford Shipping Co Ltd v Nippon Yusen Kaisha (The Eastern Saga) (No.2)
[1984] 3 All E.R. 835; [1984] 2 Lloyd's Rep. 373 QBD (Comm) ......... 30–002
Petroleum Development (Trucial Coast) Ltd and the Sheikh of Abu Dhabi,
Arbitration between [1952] I.C.L.Q. 247 ............................ IV–005
Phulchand Exports Ltd v OOO Patriot Sup Ct (India) 13 (2011) 10 S.C.C. 300 .. V–014
Polanski v Condé Nast Publications Ltd [2005] UKHL 10; [2005] 1 W.L.R. 637;
[2005] 1 All E.R. 945; [2005] C.P. Rep. 22; [2005] E.M.L.R. 14; [2005]
H.R.L.R. 11; [2005] U.K.H.R.R. 277; (2005) 102(10) L.S.G. 29; (2005)
155 N.L.J. 245 ........................................................ 20–003

xx                    TABLE OF CASES

Porter v Magill [2001] UKHL 67; [2002] 2 A.C. 357; [2002] 2 W.L.R. 37; [2002]
    1 All E.R. 465; [2002] H.R.L.R. 16; [2002] H.L.R. 16; [2002] B.L.G.R. 51;
    (2001) 151 N.L.J. 1886; [2001] N.P.C. 184................... 10–015, 10–018
Premium Nafta Products Ltd v Fili Shipping Co Ltd. *See* Fiona Trust &
    Holding Corp v Privalov
Property Concepts FZE v Lootah Network Real Estate & Commercial Brokerage
    Unreported 2012(Dubai)............................... IV–014, IV–023
PT First Media TBK v Astro Nusantara International BV [2013] SCGA 57 CA
    (Singapore) ........................................... 22–027, 22–028
Publicis Communication v True North Communication Inc, 206 F.3d. 725
    (2000)............................................. 9–005, 9–042
R. v Lashley (Angela) [2005] EWCA Crim 2016; [2006] Crim. L.R. 83........ 10–018
R. v Momodou (Henry) [2005] EWCA Crim 177; [2005] 1 W.L.R. 3442; [2005]
    2 All E.R. 571; [2005] 2 Cr. App. R. 6; (2005) 169 J.P. 186; [2005] Crim.
    L.R. 588; (2005) 169 J.P.N. 276; (2005) 149 S.J.L.B. 178............... 20–015
Reliance Industries Ltd v UOI (2014) 7 S.C.C. 603 ................. V–011, V–013
Renusagar Power Co v General Electric Co (1994) Supp (1) S.C.C. 644........ V–014
République de Pologne c Eureko BV et Schwebel Stefen M (RG No.2007/
    AR/70) Cour d'Appel de Bruxelles, 17èmme Chambre,................. 5–009
Rompetrol Group NV v Romania (ICSID Case No. ARB/06/3) ICSID Tr....... 18–015
Rotenberg v Sucafina SA [2012] EWCA Civ 637; [2012] 2 All E.R. (Comm)
    952; [2013] Bus. L.R. 158; [2012] 2 Lloyd's Rep. 54; [2012] 2 C.L.C. 203 . 26–003
Royal & Sun Alliance Insurance Plc v BAE Systems (Operations) Ltd [2008]
    EWHC 743 (Comm); [2008] 1 Lloyd's Rep. 712; [2008] 1 C.L.C. 711;
    [2008] Bus. L.R. D127...................................... 26–022
Sanders v Hamilton (1907) 96 L.T. 679.................................. 26–012
SBP v Patel Engineering Ltd (2005) 8 S.C.C. 618 Sup Ct (India) ............. V–009
Serbia v Imagesat International NV [2009] EWHC 2853 (Comm); [2010] 2 All
    E.R. (Comm) 571; [2010] 1 Lloyd's Rep. 324 ..................... 2–010
Shell Egypt West Manzala GmbH v Dana Gas Egypt Ltd (formerly Centurion
    Petroleum Corp) [2010] 2 All E.R. (Comm) 442..................... III–013
Shri Lal Mahal Ltd v Progetto Grano Spa (2014) 2 S.C.C. 433 ............... V–014
Singh v Paswan – AIR1954SC340 = [1955] 1 S.C.R.117. ................... V–013
SL Sethia Liners v Naviagro Maritime Corp (The Kostas Melas) [1981] 1 Lloyd's
    Rep. 18; [1980] Com. L.R. 3 QBD (Comm) ........................ 10–018
Société Nationale des Pétroles du Congo et République du Congo v Société Total
    Fina Elf E&P Congo, April 29, 2003 Cour d'appel de Paris............... 9–005
Société Tecnimont SpA v J&P Avax SA February 2, 2009 CA (Paris) ........... 5–032
Sociétés BKMI et Siemens v Société Dutco January 7, 1992 Cour de Cassation... 8–001
State of West Bengal v Associated Contractors September 10, 2014 Sup Ct
    (India)................................................ V–016
Sulamérica Cia Nacional de Seguros SA v Enesa Engenharia SA [2012] EWCA
    Civ 638; [2013] 1 W.L.R. 102; [2012] 2 All E.R. (Comm) 795; [2012] 1
    Lloyd's Rep. 671; [2012] 2 C.L.C. 216; [2012] Lloyd's Rep. I.R. 405...... 16–016
Supplier (US) v State Enterprise (Belarus), III ZB 14/07 May 21 Bundesgerichtshof ... 12–002
Swiss Timing Ltd v Organising Committee 2010 Olympic Games (2014) 6
    S.C.C. 677 Sup Ct (India) ..................................... V–016
Titan Corp v Alcatel CIT SA, in A.J. van den Berg (ed), *Yearbook Commercial
    Arbitration* (Kluwer Law International, 2005), Vol.30, pp.139–143........ III–019
TSG Building Services Plc v South Anglia Housing Ltd [2013] EWHC 1151;
    [2013] B.L.R. 484; 148 Con. L.R. 228 ........................... 14–018
U&M Mining Zambia Ltd v Konkola Copper Mines Plc [2013] EWHC 260
    (Comm) ................................................ 25–026
Venture Global Engineering v Satyam Computers Services Ltd Unreported Sup
    Ct (India) .......................................... V–012, V–013
Videocon Industries Ltd v UOI (2011) 6 S.C.C. 161....................... V–013

Walker v Rowe [1999] 2 All E.R. (Comm) 961; [2000] 1 Lloyd's Rep. 116;
 [2000] C.L.C. 265 QBD (Comm Ct) .................................. 1–014
Wealcan Enterprises Inc v Banque Algerienne du Commerce Exterieur SA
 [2012] EWHC 4151 ................................................ 25–025
Weissfisch v Julius [2006] EWCA Civ 218; [2006] 2 All E.R. (Comm) 504;
 [2006] 1 Lloyd's Rep. 716; [2006] 1 C.L.C. 424 ............... 5–007, 14–012
West Tankers Inc v Allianz SpA (The Front Comor) [2012] EWCA Civ 27;
 [2012] 2 All E.R. (Comm) 113; [2012] Bus. L.R. 1701; [2012] 1 Lloyd's
 Rep. 398; [2012] C.P. Rep. 19; [2012] 1 C.L.C. 312; 140 Con. L.R. 45;
 [2012] I.L.Pr. 19; (2012) 109(6) L.S.G. 21 ........................... I–026
World Sport Group (Mauritius) Ltd v MSM Satellite (Singapore) Pte Ltd 2014
 (1) A.R.B.L.R. 197 ................................................ V–015

# TABLE OF STATUTES

**United Kingdom**

1996 Arbitration Act (c.23) . . . . I–030,
P–003, 2–010, 2–026, 5–008,
5–050, 7–010, 10–015, 11–004,
14–003, 14–011, 14–013,
16–003, 16–017, 17–001,
22–031, 25–005, 25–006,
25–023, 26–011, 30–002,
32–005, 34–033, IV–012,
Appendix 7
- Pt I. . . . . . . . . . . . . I–025
- s.1 . . . . I–025, I–030, **32–008**
  - (b) . . . . . . 9–040, **32–008**
- s.2 . . . . . . . 16–003, 16–018
- s.3 . . . . . . . . . . . . . 16–003
  - (1) . . . . . . . . . . . 10–022
- s.4 . . . . . . . 14–003, 16–018
  - (5) . . . . . . . . . . . 16–018
- s.5 . . . . P–003, P–004, 14–007
- s.7 . . . . . . . . . . . . . 23–009
- s.9 . . . . . . . . . . . . . III–004
- s.14(1) . . . . . . . . . . . . 1–005
- s.15 . . . . . . . . . . . . . 5–050
- s.16 . . . . . . . . . . . . . 9–004
  - (5)(a) . . . . . . . . . . 2–026
- s.17 . . . . . . . . 7–002, 7–010
- s.18 . . . . . . . . 5–002, 7–002
- s.24 . . 5–008, 10–001, 10–003,
10–025, 14–008, 29–002,
29–005, 29–007
  - (1)(c) . . . . . . . . . . 10–010
  - (d) . . . 10–021, 10–022
  - (2) . . . . . . . . . . . 29–007
  - (3) . . . . . . . . . . . 10–036
- s.27 . . . . . . . . . . . . 11–004
  - (5) . . . . . . . . . . . 11–004
- s.28 . . . . . . 29–002, 34–033
- s.30 . . . . . . . . . . . . 23–001
  - (1)(c) . . . . . . . . . . 1–010
- ss.30–32 . . . . . . . . . . III–006
- s.31(2) . . . . . . . . . . . 2–010
- s.33 . . . . . . . . I–030, I–032,
5–006, 14–014
  - (1) . . . . 10–022, 14–011,
14–012, 19–012
    - (a) . . . . . . . . . . 10–017
- s.34(1) . . . . . . . . . . . 14–007
  - (2)(b) . . . . . . . . . . 17–001

- (f) . . . . . . . . . . . 22–017
- s.35 . . . . . . 22–033, 22–034
- s.37(1) . . . . . . . . . . . 21–004
- s.38 . . . . . . . . . . . . 25–005
  - (1) . . . . 22–002, 25–005
  - (2) . . . . . . . . . . . 25–005
  - (3) . . . . . . . . . . . 25–023
  - (4) . . . . . . . . . . . 22–012
  - (5) . . . . . . . . . . . 20–019
- s.39 . . . . . . 10–018, 25–005
  - (1) . . . . . . . . . . . 25–006
  - (2) . . . . . . . . . . . 25–018
  - (4) . . . . . . . . . . . 25–006
- s.41(3) . . . . . . . . . . . 15–021
  - (4) . . . . . . . . . . . 15–021
  - (b) . . . . . . . . . . 24–011
  - (6) . . . . . . . . . . . 25–024
- s.44 . . . . . . . . . . . . 25–014
- s.48 . . . . . . . . . . . . 22–021
  - (5)(b) . . . . . . . . . . 22–022
  - (c) . . . . . . . . . . 22–002
- s.52 . . . . . . . . . . . . 26–009
- s.53 . . . . . . . . . . . . 26–005
- s.56 . . . . . . . . . . . . 24–004
- s.57 . . . . . . 27–006, 27–007
  - (3) . . . . . . . . . . . 27–001
- s.59 . . . . . . . . . . . . 28–019
- s.60 . . . . . . . . . . . . **28–019**
- s.61(2) . . . . . . . . . . . **28–015**
- s.63(1) . . . . . . . . . . . 28–018
  - (3) . . . . . . . . . . . 28–018
  - (b) . . . . . . . . . . 28–013
  - (5)(a) . . . . . . . . . . 28–018
  - (b) . . . . . . . . . . 28–018
- s.67 . . . . . . 16–016, 26–001,
III–006
- s.68 . . . 14–003, 14–011, 26–001
  - (2)(c) . . . . . . . . . . 10–020
- s.69 . . . . . . 26–001, III–013
- s.70(2) . . . . . 27–002, 27–006
  - (3) . . . . . . . . . . . 26–018
- s.73 . . . . . . **32–003**, 32–004
  - (1)(d) . . . . . . . . . . 5–037
  - (3) . . . . . . 2–010, 27–006
- s.76 . . . . . . . . . . . . 4–004
  - (3) . . . . . . . . . . . 4–006
- s.80(5) . . . . . 27–007, 27–010
- s.103 . . . . . . . . . . . 14–011
  - (2)(e) . . . . . . . . . 10–020

## Other jurisdictions

### Bahrain
2009 Decree No.30 . . . . . . . IV–004

### Belgium
Judicial Code
art.1679 . . . . . . . . . III–004

### Dubai
2004 Law No.12 of 2004 . . . . IV–014

### France
Nouveau Code de Procédure
Civile
art.1502 . . . . . . . . . . I–034
Code de Procédure
Civile. . . . . VI–004, VI–008
art.1448 . . . . . . . . . VI–010

### India
1937 Arbitration (Protocol and
Convention) Act . . . . V–006
1940 Arbitration Act . . . . . . V–006
1961 Foreign Awards (Recognition
and Enforcement) Act . . . V–006
1996 Arbitration and Conciliation
Act . . . . . . . V–004, V–006,
V–007, V–008
Pt I . . . . V–006, V–008, V–012,
V–013
s.5 . . . . . . . . . . . . . V–008
s.8 . . . . . . . . . . . . . V–009
(3) . . . . . . . . . . V–009
s.9 . . . . . . . . V–012, V–013
s.11 . . . 5–002, V–010, V–016
s.16 . . . V–009, V–010, V–015
s.34 . . . . . . . V–013, V–014
s.45 . . . . . . . . . . . III–004
s.48 . . . . . . . . I–034, V–014
Pt II . . . . . . . . . . . . V–006
Pt III. . . . . . . . . . . . V–006

### Mauritius
1965 Arbitration Act . . . . . . VI–005
2008 International Arbitration
Act . . . . . . VI–008, VI–009,
VI–010, VI–011,
VI–012, VI–019, VI–020
s.5 . . . . . . . . . . . . . VI–010
s.10 . . . . . . . . . . . . VI–019
s.16(1). . . . . . . . . . . VI–020
s.42(1A). . . . . . . . . . VI–012
(1B). . . . . . . . . . VI–012
(a). . . . . . . . . VI–012

### Netherlands
1986 Arbitration Act
art.1063 . . . . . . . . . . I–034

### Russian Federation
1993 Law 5338-1
art.8(1) . . . . . . . . . III–004

### Singapore
2012 International Arbitration
(Amendment) Act (No.12
of 2012) . . . . . 9–040, 9–42

### Sweden
1999 Arbitration Act
s.9 . . . . . . . . . . . . . 5–030

### Switzerland
1987 Federal Statute on Private
International Law
art.194. . . . . . . . . . . I–034

### United Arab Emirates
1992 Civil Procedure Code
(Federal Law No.(11) of
1992). . . . . IV–007, IV–009
art.216(1)(c). . . . . . . IV–009

# TABLE OF PROTOCOLS

1976 United Nations Commission on International Trade Law (UNCITRAL) Arbitration Rules . . . . . 10–016, 31–003
    art.5 . . . . . . . . . . . . . 5–046
    art.6.4 . . . . . . . . . . . . 6–009
    art.10.1 . . . . . . . . . 10–016
1985 London Court of International Arbitration (LCIA) Arbitration Rules . . . . . 3–005
    art.3.6 . . . . . . . . . . **10–026**
    art.3.8 . . . . . . . . . . . 10–017
    art.5.2 . . . . . . . . . . . **I–032**
    art.11.1 . . . . . . . . . **20–007**
1987 International Bar Association (IBA) Rules of Ethics for International Arbitrators
    art.1 . . . . . . . . . . . . . 5–009
    art.3.1 . . . . . . . . . . . **5–009**
    art.5.2 . . . . . . . . . . . **13–014**
1998 London Court of International Arbitration (LCIA) Arbitration Rules . . I–001, P–001, P–008, P–009, 1–007, 3–001, 3–005, 3–007, 8–001, 9–002, 9–004, 9–019, 9–055, 13–007, 15–003, 16–008, 17–005, 19–004, 19–008, 21–003, 21–004, 21–005, 21–006, 21–008, 24–010, 24–016, 26–001, 26–020, 28–019, 29–005, 32–007, 33–010, IV–020, IV–021, V–019, V–020
    Preamble . . . . . P–009, P–011
    art.1 . . . . . . . . . . . . . 4–002
    art.2 . . . . . . . . . . . . . 4–002
    art.4.5 . . . . . . . . . . . . 5–041
    art.5.3 . . . . . . . . . . . VI–019
    art.5.6 . . **5–050**, 7–010, V–020
    art.8 . . . . . . . . 8–001, 8–002
    art.9 . . . . . . . . 9–018, 9–033
    art.10.2 . . . . . . . . . . 10–026
    art.10.3 . . . . . . . . . . 10–017
    art.10.4 . . . . 10–003, 10–017
    art.14.1 . . . . . . . . . . 14–008
    art.18 . . . . . . . . . . . 18–003
    art.22.1(h) . . . . . . . . IV–024
    art.24 . . . . . . . . . . . 24–005
    art.24.3 . . . . . . . . . 24–013
    art.25.1(a) . . . . . . . . 25–022
    (c) . . . . . . . . . **25–020**
    art.26.1 . . . . . . . . . 26–009
    art.26.2 . . . . . . . . . 26–015
    art.26.3 . . . . . . . . . 26–013
    art.26.5 . . . . . . . . . 26–018
    art.26.6 . . . . . . . . . 26–012
    art.26.7 . . . . . . . . . 26–003
    art.26.9 . . . . . . . . . 26–021
    art.27.1 . . . . . . . . . 27–003
    art.32 . . . . . . . . . . 32–011
2004 American Bar Association Code of Ethics for Arbitrators in Commercial Disputes . . . . . . . . . 5–019
2004 Dubai International Financial Centre (DIFC) Arbitration Law (No.8 of 2004) . . IV–002
2004 International Bar Association (IBA) Guidelines on Conflicts of Interest in International Arbitration . . 5–010
2005 Qatar Financial Center Regulation No.8 of 2005 . . . . . . . . III–003
2006 United Nations Commission on International Trade Law (UNCITRAL) Model Law on International Commercial Arbitration . . . . . I–025, I–030, P–003, P–004, 9–040, 11–004, IV–002, IV–003, IV–007, IV–012, IV–013, V–006, VI–009, VI–011, Appendix 10
    art.2A . . . . . . . . . . 14–018
    art.3 . . . . . . . . . . . 4–004,09
    art.3.1(a) . . . . . . . . . . 4–006
    art.4 . . 5–037, **32–004**, 32–005
    art.6 . . . . . . . . . . . VI–009
    art.7 . . . **P–003**, P–004, 1–008
    art.7.3 . . . . . . . . . . . P–004
    art.7.5 . . . . . . . . . . . P–004
    art.8 . . . . . . . . . . . III–004
    art.9 . . . . . . . . . . . 25–013
    art.11.4 . . . . . . . . . . . 5–002
    art.12 . . . . . . . I–031, 5–008
    art.13 . . . . . . . . . . 10–036
    (3) . . . . . . . . . . 10–001
    art.16 . . . . . 23–001, 23–002, III–006

## TABLE OF PROTOCOLS

  (2) . . . . . . 2–010, 23–013
 art.17 . . . . . . . . . . . 25–005
 art.17A(1) . . . . . . . . 25–007
 art.17E. . . . . . . . . . . 25–021
 art.18 . . . . . . . . . . . . I–032
 art.19 . . . . . . . . . . . **22–001**
  (1) . . . . . . . . . . 14–006
 art.20(1) . . . . . . . . . III–020
 art.23 . . . . . . . . . . . 23–001
 art.25 . . . . . . . . . . . 15–021
 art.34 . . . . . . . . . . . 14–011
  (2)(a) . . . . 14–003, 19–012
   (ii) . . . . . . . . . 14–003
   (iv) . . . . . . . . . . 8–005
 art.36 . . . . . . I–034, 14–011
  (1)(iii) . . . . . . . . . 4–004
2008 Dubai International Financial
  Centre – London Court of
  International Arbitration
  (DIFC–LCIA) Arbitration
  Rules. . . . . . . . . . . . IV–001,
      IV–020, IV–026
 art.3.3 . . . . . . . . . . . IV–020
 art.4.1 . . . . . . . . . . . IV–020
 art.9 . . . . . . . . . . . . . IV–026
 art.16.1 . . . . IV–018, IV–022
 art.22.1(h) . . . . . . . . III–024
2008 Dubai International Financial
  Centre (DIFC) Arbitration
  Law (No.1 of 2008) . . IV–003,
       IV–024
 arts 42–44 . . . . . . . . . I–034
2009 China International Economic
  and Trade Arbitration
  Commission (CIETAC)
  Arbitration Rules
 art.9 . . . . . . . . . . . . . I–029
2010 International Bar Association
  (IBA) Rules on the taking
  of Evidence in International
  Arbitration . . . . . . . 14–016,
20–005, 20–006, 20–014, Appendix 12
 art.3(12)(d) . . . . . . . 17–015
 art.4 . . . . . . . . . . . . . 20–005
 art.4.4 . . . . . . . . . . . 20–010
 art.4.7 . . . . . . . . . . . 20–012
 art.8 . . . . . . . . . . . . . 20–005
 art.8.2 . . . . . . . . . . . 20–010
 art.8.4 . . . . . . . . . . . **20–011**
 art.8.5 . . . . . . . . . . . 20–013
 art.9.2 . . . . . . . . . . . 20–010
2010 London Court of International
  Arbitration (LCIA) India
  Arbitration Rules. . . . V–001,
    V–017, V–018, V–019,
      V–020, V–021
 art.5.3(b) . . . . . . . . . V–020

 art.5.6 . . . . . . . . . . . V–020
 art.5.7 . . . . . . . . . . . V–020
2010 London Court of International
  Arbitration (LCIA) India
  Mediation Rules . . . . V–001,
       V–017
2010 Singapore International
  Arbitration Centre (SIAC)
  Arbitration Rules. . . . . I–029,
       IV–026
 art.6 . . . . . . . . . . . . . 5–044
 art.12 . . . . . . . . . . . . 10–033
 art.14.3 . . . . . . . . . . 10–007
 art.16 . . . . . . . . . . . . I–029
 art.26 . . . . . . . . . . . . 9–005
 art.30.2 . . . . . . . . . . 24–007
 Sch.1 . . . . . . . . . . . . 9–005
 art.3. . . . . . . . . . . . . 9–037
 art.5. . . . . . . . . . . . . 9–039
2010 Stockholm Chamber of
  Commerce (SCC)
  Arbitration Rules. . . . . I–034
 art.15 . . . . . . . . . . . . 10–033
 art.19(2) . . . . . . . . . . I–029
 art.32 . . . . . . . . . . . . 9–005
 art.47 . . . . . . . . . . . . I–034
 Appendix I . . . . . . . . 9–026
 Appendix II art.4 . . . . 9–026
  (3) . . . . . . . . . . . 9–037
2010 United Nations Commission
  on International Trade Law
  (UNCITRAL) Arbitration
  Rules . . . . . . . I–014, I–017,
  I–020, 5–002, 5–046, 5–050,
   10–016, 15–005, 20–008,
   21–004, 31–003, IV–003,
      Appendix 11
 art.6 . . . . . . . . . . . . . 5–002
 art.6.7 . . . . . . . . . . . 6–009
 art.7 . . . . . . . . . . . . . 5–046
 art.7.1 . . . . . . . . . . . 5–050
 art.9 . . . . . . . . . . . . . 5–030
 art.10(1) . . . . . . . . . . 10–017
 arts 11–13 . . . . . . . . . I–031
 art.12.1 . . . . . I–032, 10–016
 art.13 . . . . . . . . . . . . 10–033
 art.16 . . . . . . . . . . . . **31–003**
 art.18 . . . . . . . . . . . . 16–008
 art.18.2 . . . . . . . . . . VI–019
 art.23 . . . . . . . . . . . . 23–002
 art.23.2 . . . . . . . . . . 23–013
 art.26.3 . . . . . . . . . . 25–007
 art.29 . . . . . . . . . . . . 21–003
 art.30 . . . . . . . . . . . . 15–021
 art.32 . . . . . . . . . . . . **32–005**
 art.42(1) . . . . . . . . . . **28–016**
 art.43(1) . . . . . . . . . . 24–007

| | |
|---|---|
| (4) . . . . . . . . . . 24–011 | art.16.2 . . . . . . . . . VI–019 |
| 2012 Dubai International Financial Centre – London Court of International Arbitration (DFIC–LCIA) Mediation Rules . . . . . . . . . . III–025 | 2012 London Court of International Arbitration –Mauritius International Arbitration Centre (LCIA–MIAC) Mediation Rules . . . . . VI–015, VI–018, VI–020 |
| 2012 International Chamber of Commerce (ICC) Arbitration Rules. . . . . I–020, I–029, P–006, 1–018, 5–008, 5–012, 5–050, 15–002, 15–005, 18–010, 20–004, 20–008, 21–004, 23–004, 23–005, 30–002, IV–026 | 2012 Paris Arbitration Rules . . . 9–040 |
| | 2012 Qatar International Centre for Commercial Arbitration Rules . . . . . . . . . . IV–003 |
| | 2012 Swiss Rules of International Arbitration . . . . . . . . 9–040 |
| Foreword . . . . . . . . . I–029 | art.5 . . . . . . . . . . . . 5–044 |
| art.3(1) . . . . . . . . . **13–010** | art.12 . . . . . . . . . . 10–007 |
| art.4.5 . . . . . . . . . . . 4–005 | art.15.7 . . . . . . . . . . I–029 |
| arts 4–6 . . . . . . . . . . I–020 | art.43 . . . . . . . . . . 9–005 |
| art.5 . . . . . . . . . . . . 9–039 | art.43.6 . . . . . . . . . . 9–039 |
| art.5.4 . . . . . . . . . . . 4–005 | 2013 International Bar Association (IBA) Guidelines on Party Representation in International Arbitration . . . . . . . 10–015, 13–015, 18–004, 18–009, 18–023, 18–027, 20–014, 33–003, 33–004, 33–011, Appendix 14 |
| art.6.4 . . . . . . . . . . 23–004 | |
| art.6.8 . . . . . . . . . . 15–021 | |
| art.7.2 . . . . . . . . . . . 5–030 | |
| art.8(2) . . . . . . . . . . 5–046 | |
| art.11 . . I–031, 5–048, 10–027 | |
| art.12 . . . . . . . . . . . 5–044 | |
| (4) . . . . . . . . . . . 5–050 | |
| art.13 . . . . . . . . . . . 5–044 | |
| art.14 . . . . . . I–032, 10–033 | Preamble . . . . . . . . 33–008 |
| (1) . . . . . . . . . . . 5–012 | Guideline 4 . . . . . . . 18–009 |
| art.15.2 . . . . . I–031, 10–007 | Guideline 5 . . . . . . . 18–016 |
| art.15.4 . . . . . . . . . 11–002 | Guideline 6 . . . . . . . 18–016 |
| art.18 . . . . . . . . . . 16–008 | Guideline 7 . . 13–002, 13–011 |
| art.25 . . . . . . . . . . 20–004 | Guideline 8 . . 13–002, 13–011 |
| art.25.4 . . . . . . . . . 21–003 | (b) . . . . . . . . . . 13–015 |
| art.26(3) . . . . . . . . . 30–002 | Guidelines 12–17 . . . . 18–025, 33–015 |
| art.29 . . . . . . . . . . . 9–005 | |
| art.29.5 . . . . . . . . . . 9–026 | Guideline 21. . . . . . . 20–014 |
| art.29.6 . . . . . . . . . . 9–026 | Guideline 24. . . . . . . 20–017 |
| art.35(2) . . . . . . . . . 27–002 | Guideline 26(d) . . . . . 33–020 |
| art.36(2) . . . . . . . . . 24–007 | 2014 American Arbitration Association/ International Centre for Dispute Resolution (AAA/ICDR) International Arbitration Rules |
| (5) . . . . . . . . . . 24–011 | |
| art.37(4) . . . . . . . . . **28–016** | |
| art.39 . . . . . . . . . . **32–005** | |
| art.40 . . . . . . . . . . **31–002** | |
| art.41 . . . . . . . . . . **32–009** | art.37 . . . . . . . . . . . 9–005 |
| Appendix V art.1(5). . . . 9–026 | 2014 Grain and Feed Trade Association (GAFTA) Arbitration Rules |
| art.7(1) . . . . . . . . 34–037 | |
| 2012 London Court of International Arbitration – Mauritius International Arbitration Centre (LCIA–MIAC) Arbitration Rules | |
| | r.16.1 . . . . . . . . . . 18–002 |
| | r.16.2 . . . . . . . . . . 18–002 |
| | 2014 International Bar Association (IBA) Guidelines on Conflict of Interest . . . 5–011, 5–036, 14–012, Appendix 13 |
| art.7.1 . . . . . . . . . . VI–016 | |
| art.11.3 . . . . . . . . . VI–020 | |
| art.14.4(i) . . . . . . . . VI–018 | |
| art.16.1 . . . . . . . . . VI–019 | |

| | |
|---|---|
| General Standard 7(b) . . | 18–013 |
| para.8 . . . . . . . . . . . | 5–010 |

2014 International Centre for Dispute Resolution (ICDR)
Arbitration Rules. . . . . I–029

2014 London Court of International Arbitration (LCIA)
| | |
|---|---|
| Arbitration Rules. . . . . | I–001, I–007, I–015, P–008, 1–003, 1–004, 1–018, 1–022, 9–013, 14–003, 17–005, 21–009, 33–001, 33–003, 33–010, 33–021, 34–003, III–001, III–009, III–013, III–014, III–016, III–017,III–020, III–022, III–026, IV–001, IV–020, IV–026, IV–027, IV–028, V–001, V–020, VI–015, VI–016, VI–018, VI–019, VI–020, Appendix 1 |
| Preamble . . . . . | **P–001**, P–011, 1–008, III–002, III–013 |
| art.1 . . . | I–020, P–003, 1–001, 1–002, 1–027, 2–021, 2–026, 3–006, III–016 |
| art.1.1 . . . | I–035, **1–001, 1–004,** 1–005 |
| (1) . . . . . . . . . . . | **1–006** |
| (i) . . . . . . . . . | 18–009 |
| (i)–(iv) . . . . . . . | 1–004 |
| (ii) . . . . . | **1–008,** 2–007 |
| (iii) . . . . | **1–009,** 1–010, 1–014 |
| (iv) . . . . | **1–016,** 2–013, 16–006, 17–009 |
| (v) . . . . . . . . . | **1–018** |
| (vi) . . . . | **1–020,** 34–004 |
| (vii) . . . . . | **1–020,** 1–021 |
| art.1.2 . . . | **1–001,** 1–021, **1–023** |
| art.1.3 . . | **1–001, 1–024,** 9–011, 9–029, 9–056 |
| art.1.4 . . . . . . . | **1–001, 1–025** |
| art.1.5 . . . . . . . . | **1–001, 1–026** |
| art.2 . . . . | I–020, 2–001, 2–002, 2–004, 2–026, 2–029, 5–004, 9–011, 9–023, 15–014, III–016 |
| art.2.1 . . | 1–025, **2–005,** 2–006, 2–020, 3–002 |
| (i) . . . . . . . | **2–007,** 18–009 |
| (ii) . . . . . . | **2–008,** 2–010 |
| (iii) . . . . . . . . . . . | **2–008** |
| (iv) . . | **2–013,** 2–015, 2–016,, 16–006, 17–009 |
| (v) . . . . . . . . . | **2–018** |
| (vi) . . . . . . . . . . . | **2–021** |
| art.2.2 . . . . . . . . . . . | **2–022** |
| art.2.3 . . | 2–004, 2–010, **2–023,** 5–050, 9–011, 9–029, 9–056 |
| art.2.4 . . | 2–002, **2–024,** 2–025, 15–014 |
| art.2.5 . . . . . . . . . . . | **2–028** |
| art.3 . . . . | I–013, I–020, 3–001, 10–031 |
| art.3.1 . . | I–015, **3–002,** 10–030, 29–006 |
| art.3.2. . . | **3–004,** 34–006, 34–030 |
| art.3.3 . . | **3–010,** 9–051, 10–030 |
| art.4 . . . . . . . . | I–035, 1–021, 4–001, 4–003 |
| art.4.1 . . . | **4–005,** 4–006, 4–007 |
| arts 4.1–4.3 . . . | 4–001, 4–004, 4–012, 4–014 |
| art.4.2 . . . | 1–006, **4–008,** 4–009 |
| art.4.3 . . | 1–006, 1–023, 2–022, **4–010,** 20–014 |
| art.4.4 . . . . . . . | **4–012,** 4–013 |
| arts 4.4–4.6 . . . . | I–020, 4–011 |
| art.4.5 . . . . . . . | **4–012,** 4–014 |
| art.4.6 . . . | **4–012,** 4–013, 4–014 |
| arts 4–12. . . . . . . . . | I–020 |
| art.5 . . . . | I–013, I–035, P–010, 1–016, 1–018, 1–019, 2–014, 2–019, 3–002, 3–006, 5–001, 5–003, 5–051, 7–001, 7–006, 7–010, 8–005, 9–002, 9–006, 9–037, 13–004, 29–001 |
| art.5.1 . . | 1–027, 2–029, **5–004,** 9–023, 9–035, 17–015 |
| art.5.2 . . | **5–005,** 5–011, 5–017, 5–018, 5–020 |
| art.5.3 . . . | I–020, **5–006,** 5–007, 5–020, 5–021, 9–036, 10–014, 13–005, 18–017 |
| arts 5.3–5.5 . . . . . . . . | 7–007 |
| art.5.4 . . . | I–031, **2–024,** 5–001, 5–012, 5–021, 5–024, 5–027, 5–031, 5–043, 9–036, 10–026, 10–027, 34–017, V–020 |
| art.5.5 . . | 5–006, 5–027, 5–031, **5–040,** 7–003, 7–004, **7–005,** 9–036 |
| arts 5.5–5.10. . . . . . . . | I–020 |
| art.5.6 . . . . . . . | I–017, **5–041** |
| art.5.7 . . . | 1–018, **5–044,** 9–035 |
| art.5.8 . . | 5–**045,** 5–046,III–015 |
| art.5.9 . . . | I–020, 1–012, 1–013, 1–017, 2–017, **5–049,** 5–050, 9–035 |
| art.5.10 . . . . . . | **5–051,** 9–035 |
| art.6 . . . . | I–031, 6–001, 6–002, 6–003, 6–004, 6–008, 9–035 |
| art.6.1 . . . . . . . | 6–004, **6–005** |

art.6.2 . . . . . . . . 6–004, **6–006**
art.6.3 . . . 6–004, **6–007,** 6–008
arts 6–11. . . . . . . . . . . 5–001
art.7 . . . . . . . 1–016, 1–018,
    I–020, 2–014, 3–002,
    7–003, 13–004, 13–005
art.7.1 . . . I–031, 1–018, 5–012,
    5–030, 5–044, **7–004,**
    7–006, 7–007, 7–008
art.7.2 . . . 1–003, 1–019, 2–020,
    **7–009,** 9–023
art.7.3 . . . . . . . . . . . . **7–010**
art.7.4 . . . . . . . . . . . . 2–002
art.8 . . . 1–016, 2–014, 3–002,
    8–001, 8–003, 29–001,
    III–017
art.8.1 . . . **8–003,** 8–004, 8–005
art.8.2 . . . . . . . . . . . . **8–005**
art.9 . . . . I–020, 3–002, 5–002,
    9–001, 9–018, 9–021
art.9.1 . . . . . . . . . . . . **9–006**
art.9.2 . . . . . . **9–009,** III–019
art.9.3 . . . . . . . **9–022,** 9–023
art.9.4 . . . . . . 9–026, **9–027**
arts 9.4–9.12. . . . . . . . 5–001
art.9.5 . . . 9–026, 9–027, **9–028,**
    9–030, 9–034, 34–037
art.9.6 . . 3–003, **9–035,** 34–037
art.9.7 . . . . . . . . . . . . **9–038**
art.9.8 . . **9–041,** 9–042, 34–037
art.9.9 . . . 9–042, **9–043,** 9–044
art.9.10 . . . . . . . . . . . **9–045**
art.9.11 . . 9–042, 9–043, **9–046**
art.9.12 . . . . . . . . . . . **9–049**
art.9.13 . . . . . . . . . . . **9–051**
art.9.14 . . . . . . . . . . . **9–052**
art.9.15 . . . . . . . . . . . 9–054
art.9.16 . . . . . . . . . . . **9–055**
art.9.17 . . . . . . . . . . . **9–057**
art.9A . . . 1–024, 2–006, 3–002,
    9–002, 9–007, 9–009,
    9–010, 9–011, 9–024,
    9–025, 25–004
art.9B . . . P–008, 1–024, 3–002,
    9–002, 9–018, 9–024, 9–026,
    9–027, 9–029, 9–031, 9–040,
    9–049, 9–052, 34–002, 34–004,
    34–037, V–011
art.9B.14 . . . . . . . . . VI–015
art.9C . . 1–024, 9–035, **9–053,**
    9–056, 25–004
art.10 . . . I–031, 3–002, 5–006,
  6–009, 9–035, 9–037, 10–005,
  12–004, 13–013, 14–008, 14–011,
    23–016, 29–007, 34–010
art.10.1 . . . . . 5–007, 10–005,

    **10–006,** 10–007,
    10–016, 10–027
(ii) . . . . . . . . . . 10–010
art.10.2 . . . . . . I–030, I–033,
    5–012, 5–031, 5–032,
    5–039, 10–005, 10–007,
    10–012, 10–013, **10–019,**
    18–029, 30–005
(ii) . . . . . . . . . . 23–016
art.10.3 . . . . . 5–031, **10–029,**
    10–032, 10–037
arts 10.3–10.6 . . I–020, 10–005,
    10–029
art.10.4 . . . . **10–038,** 18–017
art.10.5 . . . . 10–030, **10–039**
art.10.6 . . . . 10–030, **10–040,**
    29–004
art.10.7 . . . . **10–043,** 10–044,
    34–011, 34–023
art.11 . . . I–031, 1–016, 2–014,
  3–002, 9–053, 9–054, 10–006,
    11–001, 11–004, 12–004
art.11.1 . . . . . 5–012, **11–002**
art.11.2 . . . . . . I–020, **11–003**
art.12 . . I–020, I–030, 12–002,
    12–003, 30–005
art.12.1 . . . . 10–008, **12–004,**
    30–005
art.12.2 . . . . . . . . . . **12–005**
art.12.3 . . . . . 3–002, **12–007**
art.13 . . . I–021, 4–002, 4–007,
    13–001, 13–002,
    13–009, 18–022
art.13.1 . . . . . 7–007, **13–004,**
    13–005, 13–006, 13–007,
    13–008, 13–011, 24–007
arts 13.1–13.4 . . . . . . . 9–051
art.13.2 . . . . . . . . . . **13–009**
art.13.3 . . . . **13–010,** 15–010
art.13.4 . . . . **13–011,** 13–012,
    33–015, 33–016
art.13.5 . . . . . 7–007, 13–002,
    13–004, 13–005, 13–011,
    **13–014,** 13–015
arts 13–25 . . . . . . . . . . I–021
art.14 . . I–021, 5–012, 14–001,
    14–004, 22–005, 24–014
art.14.1 . . . . 10–009, **14–005,**
    15–022, 17–014
art.14.2 . . . . . . I–027, **14–006,**
    14–007, **15–008,** 16–006,
    17–014
art.14.3 . . . . **14–006,** 14–007
art.14.4 . . . . . . I–027, 9–051,
    10–014, 10–022, 14–002,
    14–006, 14–007, **14–011,**

|  |  |  |  |
|---|---|---|---|
|  | 14–012, 14–014, 14–015, 19–011, 20–010, 20–012, 33–005 | art.18 | . . . I–003, I–021, 1–007, 5–040, 9–051, 14–003, 18–004, 18–005, 18–008 |
| (i) | . . . . . . . . I–031, I–032, 14–011, 19–012, 33–019 | art.18.1 | . . . . **18–006**, 33–009 |
| (ii) | . . . . . . . I–029, I–032, 14–011, 19–002, 33–019 | art.18.2 | . . . . 18–007, **18–010** |
|  |  | art.18.3 | . . . . **18–013**, 18–017 |
| (iii) | . . . . . . . . . . 21–005 | art.18.4 | . . . . 16–006, 18–007, 18–013, 18–017, **18–019**, 18–021, V–020 |
| art.14.5 | . . . . . . I–029, 9–051, **14–015**, 14–017, 33–010 |  |  |
|  |  | art.18.5 | . . . . **18–022**, 33–001, 33–004, 33–009, 33–015, 33–017 |
| art.14.6 | . . . . . . . . . **14–019** |  |  |
| art.15 | . . . . . . . I–021, I–027, 4–015, 14–003, 15–001, 15–003, 15–004, 15–007, 15–009, 15–010, 15–012, 15–019, 15–022 |  |  |
|  |  | art.18.6 | . . . . **18–029**, 28–017, 33–004, 33–017, 33–018, 33–019, 33–020 |
|  |  | art.19 | . . . . . . I–021, 14–015, 14–015, 19–001, 20–007, 34–020 |
| art.15.1 | . . . . . . . . . **15–008** |  |  |
| art.15.2 | . . . . . 1–011, 13–006, 15–003, **15–009**, 15–011, 15–013 | art.19.1 | . . . . . . . . . **19–004**, 19–005, 19–006 |
|  |  | art.19.2 | . . . . 9–038, **19–007**, 19–008, 19–009, 19–010, 19–011 |
| arts 15.2–15.8 | . . . . . . 15–008 |  |  |
| art.15.3 | . . . . . 2–012, 4–015, 4–016, 15–003, **15–014**, 15–015, 15–016 | art.19.3 | . . . . . . I–035, 9–038, **19–012** |
|  |  | art.19.4 | . . . I–037, 9–038, **19–013** |
| art.15.4 | . . . . 15–003, **15–017** | art.20 | . . . . . . I–021, 15–004, 15–019, 20–001, 20–005, 20–006, 20–013, 21–002 |
| art.15.5 | . . . . 15–003, **15–018** |  |  |
| art.15.6 | . . . . . . . . **15–019** |  |  |
| art.15.7 | . . . . 15–018, **15–020** | art.20.1 | . . . . **20–007**, 20–011 |
| art.15.8 | . . . . 14–014, **15–021**, **24–011** | art.20.2 | . . . . . . . . . **20–009** |
|  |  | art.20.3 | . . . . **20–010**, 20–011, 21–008 |
| art.15.9 | . . . . . P–010, **15–022** |  |  |
| art.15.10 | . . . . 15–007, **15–022**, 15–023 | art.20.4 | . . . . **20–011**, 20–012, 20–013 |
|  |  | art.20.5 | . . . . **20–014**, 20–015, 20–021, 33–014, 33–015 |
| arts 15–21 | . . . . . . . . 14–003 |  |  |
| arts 15–22 | . . . . . . . . 14–001 |  |  |
| art.16 | . . . I–027, P–010, 1–016, 2–014, 9–051, 14–003, 14–015, 16–002, 16–003, 16–009 | art.20.6 | . . . . . . . . . **20–018** |
|  |  | art.20.7 | . . . . . . . . . **20–019** |
|  |  | art.20.8 | . . . . . . . . . **20–020** |
|  |  | art.21 | . . . . . . I–021, 14–003, **21–001**, 21–002 |
| art.16.1 | . . . . . . . . . **16–005** |  |  |
| art.16.2 | . . . . . 9–035, 16–006, **16–007**, 16–009, 16–011 | art.21.1 | . . . I–031, **21–004**, 21–005 |
|  |  | art.21.2 | . . . . . . . . . **21–006** |
| art.16.3 | . . . . . 9–038, **16–013**, 19–008 | art.21.3 | . . . . . . . . . **21–007** |
|  |  | art.21.4 | . . . . . . . . . **21–008** |
| art.16.4 | . . . . **16–014**, III–018, III–024 | art.21.5 | . . . . . . . . . **21–009** |
|  |  | art.22 | . . . I–021, I–030, 4–001, 14–003, 22–001, 22–002 |
| art.17 | . . . I–021, 1–016, 2–014, 3–002, 9–051, 14–003, 17–001, 17–002, 17–007 |  |  |
|  |  | art.22.1 | . . . . **22–005**, 22–006, 23–006 |
| art.17.1 | . . . . **17–008**, 17–013 | (i) | . . . . . . 1–010, **22–007** |
| art.17.2 | . . . . **17–011**, 17–012, 29–002, 29–003 | (ii) | . . . 4–001, **22–008**, 23–016, 27–003, 27–005, 27–008, 27–009, 27–011 |
| art.17.3 | . . . . . . . . . **17–013** |  |  |
| art.17.4 | . . . . . . . . . **17–014** | (iii) | . . . . . . . . . **22–010** |
| art.17.5 | . . . . . . . . . **17–015** | (iv) | . . . . 22–003, **22–012** |

# TABLE OF PROTOCOLS

| | |
|---|---|
| (v) . . | 15–003, 22–003, **22–013** |
| (vi) . . . . . . . . . . | **22–017** |
| (vii). . . . . | **22–021**, III–009 |
| (viii) . . . . . | I–037, 22–003, 22–006, **22–023** |
| (ix) . . . . . | **22–039**, 22–053 |
| (x) . . . . . | **22–041**, 22–053 |
| (xi) . . . . . . . . . . | **22–045** |
| (g) . . . . . . . . . . | 22–001 |
| (h) . . . . . | 22–003, III–024 |
| art.22.2 . . . . . | 10–034, **22–046** |
| art.22.3 . . . . . | I–027, **22–047** |
| arts 22.3–22.4 . . . . . . . | 9–051 |
| art.22.4 . . . . . . . | **22–052** |
| art.22.5 . . . . . | 2–004, 2–025, 3–002, 5–041, 9–022, 9–041, 9–057, **22–053**, 27–004, 27–005, 27–009, 27–011, 29–002 |
| art.22.6 . . . . . | 3–002, 22–003, **22–043**, 22–053, 23–006, 29–003 |
| art.23 . . . | I–021, I–030, I–035, 9–051, 23–001, 23–004, 26–003, III–003, III–012 |
| art.23.1 . . . . | **23–007**, 23–008, III–006 |
| art.23.2 . . . . . . . . . | **23–009** |
| art.23.3 . . . . . | 5–004, 15–015, **23–013**, 23–016 |
| art.23.4 . . . . . . . . . | **23–017** |
| art.23.5 . . . . . | I–035, 23–002, **23–019** |
| arts 23–25 . . . . . . . . . . | I–021 |
| art.24 . . . . . . . | I–017, I–021, I–030, 3–002, 3–006, 13–009, 14–005, 23–018, 24–001, 25–014, 26–006, 26–017, 28–001, 29–001, 34–001, 34–025 |
| art.24.1 . . . . . . | 9–034, 19–008, **24–005**, 24–007, 24–011, 25–023, 34–005, 34–007, 34–031 |
| art.24.2 . . . . | **24–009**, 28–021 |
| art.24.3 . . . . . | I–039, 13–008, **24–010**, 25–024, 26–006, 26–008, 28–007 |
| art.24.4 . . . . | 24–007, **24–010**, 24–011, **24–012**, 24–014, 24–016 |
| art.24.5 . . . . | 24–007, **24–013** |
| art.24.6 . . . . . | 24–013, **24–014**, 34–025 |
| art.25 . . . . . . | I–021, 25–001, 25–009 |
| art.25.1 | 25–005, **25–009**, 25–021 |
| (i) . . . . . | 25–001, **25–011** |
| (ii) . . . . | 25–001, **25–015**, 25–017, 25–020 |
| (iii) . . . . | 25–001, 25–006, **25–017**, 25–018, 25–020, 25–024, 26–003 |
| art.25.2 . . . . | 25–001, 25–005, **25–023**, 25–026 |
| art.25.3 . . . . . | 9–005, 9–049, 25–002, 25–014, **25–026** |
| art.25.4 . . . . . | 9–005, 25–002, **25–028** |
| art.26 . . . . . | 3–006, 26–001, 30–005 |
| art.26.1 . . . . | **26–003**, 26–017 |
| art.26.2 . . . . . | 9–043, 24–004, **26–004**, 26–009, **26–017**, 28–010 |
| arts 26.2–26.7 . . . . . . | 27–005, 27–010, 27–012, 30–005 |
| art.26.3 . . . . . . . . . | **26–010** |
| art.26.4 . . . . | **26–011**, 26–012 |
| art.26.5 . . . . | **26–013**, 26–014, 30–005 |
| art.26.6 . . . . . . . . . | **26–014** |
| art.26.7 . . . . . | 3–002, 24–024, 26–006, 26–016, **26–017**, 26–020, 28–008, 34–007, 34–036 |
| art.26.8 . . . . . | I–035, 26–001, **26–021**, 26–022, 31–004 |
| art.26.9 . . . . | 26–022, **26–024**, III–013 |
| arts 26–28 . . . . . . . . . | I–022 |
| art.27 . . . . . | 26–018, 27–001, 27–002, 27–003, 30–005 |
| art.27.1 . . . . | **27–003**, 27–007, 27–009, 27–010, 27–012 |
| art.27.2 . . . . | **27–008**, 27–011 |
| art.27.3 . . . . . . . . . | **27–009** |
| art.27.4 . . . . . . . . . | **27–011** |
| art.27.5 . . . . | 27–005, 27–010, **27–012** |
| art.28 . . . | I–017, 3–002, 3–006, 9–042, 9–051, 10–044, 21–009, 24–003, 24–005, 26–017, 28–001, 29–001, 29–002, 34–001, 34–025 |
| art.28.1 . . . . . . | I–039, 9–045, 10–044, 13–001, 23–018, 24–005, 25–025, 26–024, **28–002**, 28–007, 28–009, 28–020, 34–008, 34–021, 34–031, 34–034 |

art.28.2 . . . . . 9–045, 26–006, 26–007, 26–024, **28–009**, 28–010, 34–005, 34–034
art.28.3 . . . . . 9–045, 10–044, **28–011**, 28–013
art.28.4 . . . . 18–029, 28–009, **28–015**, 28–017
(b) . . . . . . . . . . V–020
art.28.5 . . . . 28–009, 28–012, **28–019**
art.28.6 . . . . **28–020**, 34–004
art.28.7 . . . . . . . . **28–021**
art.29 . . . . . . 9–013, 9–051, 10–042, 29–001
art.29.1 . . . . **29–003**, 29–004
art.29.2 . . . . . 3–002, 29–002, **29–006**, 29–007
arts 29–32 . . . . . . . . . I–022
art.30 . . . . . . I–037, 9–051, 19–013, 30–002
art.30.1 . . . . 30–002, **30–003**
art.30.2 . . . . 26–014, 30–002, **30–005**
art.30.3 . . . . 30–002, **30–006**
art.31 . . . . . . 9–051, 31–001
art.31.1 . . . . **31–002**, 31–003, 31–004, 32–007
art.31.2 . . . . . . . . . **31–004**
art.32 . . . . . . 9–051, 32–011
art.32.1 . . . . . I–035, **32–002**, 32–003, 32–005
art.32.2 . . . . . . I–034, I–035, 1–022, 11–004, 14–017, 18–020, **32–007**, 32–009
art.32.3 . . . . . . . . . **32–011**
Annex (General Guidelines for the Parties' Legal Representatives). . . . . . I–007, I–022, P–002, P–011, 9–051, 10–002, 18–022, 33–001, 33–003, 33–004, 33–007. 33–008, 33–010, 33–011, 33–014, 33–016, 33–019, 33–020
para.1 . . . . 33–004, **33–006**, 33–009, 33–010
para.2 . . . . 33–004, **33–012**, 33–013

paras 2–6 . . . . . . . 33–004
para.3 . . . . . . . . . **33–013**
paras 3–5 . . . . . . . 33–004
para.4 . . . . **33–014**, 33–015
para.5 . . . . . . . . . **33–015**
para.6 . . . . 13–002, 13–011, 33–004, **33–016**
para.7 . . . . 33–004, **33–017**
Recommended Clauses . . . . 17–008, III–001
Schedule of Arbitration Costs . . . . . . . I–007, I–022, P–002, P–011, 28–002, **34–001**, 34–003, 34–037
s.1(i) . . . . . . . . . **34–004**
(iii) . . . . . . . . **34–010**
(iv) . . . . . . . . **34–012**
(v) . . . . . . . . . **34–013**
(vi) . . . . . . . . **34–014**
s.2(i) . . . . 24–008, 28–004, 34–010, **34–016**
(ii) . . . . . . . . **34–019**
(iii) . . . 19–003, **34–020**
(iv) . . . . . . . . **34–021**
(v) . . . . . . . . . **34–022**
(vi) . . . 10–044, **34–023**
s.3 . . . . . 34–001, **34–025**
(i) . . . . . I–039, **34–025**
(ii) . . . . . . . . 28–021
s.4 . . . . . 24–008, 34–031, 34–032, 34–035
s.5 . . . . . . . . . . . . . . .
(i) . . . . 24–007, 24–008, 24–011, **34–030**
(ii) . . . . . . . . **34–031**
(iii) . . . 34–031, **34–032**
(iv) . . . 24–008, **34–033**
s.6 . . . . . . . . . 34–034
(i) . . . . 28–002, 34–034
(ii) . . . . . . . . **34–035**
(iii) . . . 28–008, **34–036**
s.7 . . . . . . . . . . 34–002
(i) . . . . . . . . . **34–037**
(ii) . . . . . . . . **34–037**
(iii) . . . . . . . . **34–038**
(iv) . . . . . . . . **34–039**
(v) . . . . . . . . . 34–037, **34–040**

# TABLE OF TREATIES AND CONVENTIONS

1948 Universal Declaration of
Human Rights
art.10 . . . . . . . . . . . 5–008
1950 Convention for the Protection
of Human Rights and
Fundamental Freedoms
(European Convention on
Human Rights)
art.6 . . . . . . . 5–008, 10–015
1958 Convention on the Recognition
and Enforcement of Foreign
Arbitral Awards (New York
Convention) . . . . . . . I–034,
I–035, 1–022, P–003, P–004,
P–008, 4–004, 9–047,
25–017, 26–019, 26–021,
26–024, III–005, III–019,
IV–003, IV–009,
IV–010, IV–011, IV–012,
IV–016, V–006, V–014,
VI–008, VI–011,
Appendix 9
art.II . . . . . . P–004, , **III–004**
(1) . . . . . **III–004**, III–009
(2) . . . . . . **P–003**, P–004
(3) . . . . . . . . . . **III–004**
art.IV . . . . . 26–005, 26–019
(1)(a) . . . . . . . . . . 26–019
art.V . . . . . . . I–034, 14–011,
23–003, 26–019
(1)(a) . . . . . I–035, 23–003,
III–006
(b) . . . . . I–035, 1–006,
2–007, 4–005, 4–007,
13–007, 14–003,
17–013, 19–005,
19–012

(c) . . . . . . . . . . I–035
(d) . . . . . I–035, 8–005,
10–020, 14–003,
14–006, 14–008,
16–004, III–019
(e) . . . . . I–035, 9–047,
16–004, III–019
(2) . . . . . . . . . . . I–035
(a) . . . . . . . . . III–009
(b) . . . . . . . . 22–051
1961 European Convention on
International Commercial
Arbitration . . . . . . . III–005
art.IX(1) . . . . . . . . . . I–034
1965 Convention on the Settlement
of Investment Disputes
Between States and
Nationals of Other
States (Washington
Convention) . . . . . . III–005
1972 Convention on the Settlement
by Arbitration of Civil Law
Disputes Resulting from
Relations of Economic and
Scientific-Technical
Cooperation (Moscow
Convention) . . . . . . III–005
art.V . . . . . . . . . . . I–034
1975 Inter-American Convention on
International Commercial
Arbitration (Panama
Convention) . . . . . . III–005
art.5 . . . . . . . . . . . I–034
1987 Arab Convention on
Commercial Arbitration
(Amman Convention) . III–005
art.35 . . . . . . . . . . . I–034

# PART I—INTRODUCTION

## Introduction

This book provides a commentary on the LCIA (London Court of International Arbitration) Arbitration Rules 2014, which came into effect on October 1, 2014. For readers familiar with the previous (1998) Rules, it highlights the differences and innovations in the new Rules and discusses their implications. For the same readers, and also for those who have not previously encountered the LCIA, it puts the Rules in context, explains the background to their various provisions and what makes them distinctive and attractive to commercial users worldwide, and discusses issues that can arise in interpreting and implementing them.

I-001

## The LCIA's Growth and its Users

The LCIA's increasing popularity as an institution administering international commercial disputes has itself been the subject of commentary in the legal and financial press in recent years. Its growth is confirmed by the LCIA's published statistics: its annual caseload more than doubled between 2007 and 2009,[1] in the wake of the global financial crisis, and it has remained well above 200 ever since, exceeding 300 for the first time in 2013.[2]

I-002

This growth has come from many quarters. The LCIA is not an elite institution or the playground of a clique of prosperous London law firms and their favourite arbitrators. As its statistics demonstrate, the LCIA is used by parties from all over the world: in 2013, only 18.6 per cent of parties in LCIA arbitrations were British, whilst 7 per cent were from the US, 27 per cent from other countries in Europe, not including Russia (3 per cent), 8.5 per cent were from the Middle East and 10 per cent from Africa.[3] One third of claims set out in Requests for Arbitration were for sums less than US$1 million, whilst 20 per cent were for sums over US$20 million.[4]

Parties are represented by a wide variety of law firms of different shapes and sizes and from many different jurisdictions; they can, and do, represent themselves as well.[5] Around a third of arbitrators appointed to Arbitral Tribunals by the LCIA Court (including parties' nominees) do not have UK nationality.[6] The LCIA maintains a large database of arbitrators, for which there are no entry criteria, and the LCIA Court regularly selects arbitrators for appointment who have never

I-003

---

[1] From 137 cases referred in 2007 to 285 in 2009 (includes mediation and other ADR): Director General's Reports for those years in the LCIA's Newsletter and on the LCIA's website *http://www.lcia.org* [Accessed 4 December, 2014].

[2] 290 arbitrations and 11 mediations and other ADR: Registrar's Report for that year.

[3] Registrar's Report in the LCIA's Newsletter and on the LCIA website *http://www.lcia.org* [Accessed 4 December, 2014]

[4] Registrar's Report in the LCIA's Newsletter and on the LCIA website *http://www.lcia.org* [Accessed 4 December, 2014].

[5] See the commentary on Article 18 below.

[6] 179 out of 502 appointments in 2009, and 120 out of 372 in 2013: Director General's and Registrar's Reports for those years, respectively.

before served on LCIA Arbitral Tribunals. In 2013, 214 different arbitrators were appointed and 16.5 per cent of appointments were of arbitrators not previously appointed by the LCIA.[7]

Other legal commentaries on the LCIA Rules have focused on comparisons with the rules of other international arbitral institutions, particularly the ICC (International Chamber of Commerce),[8] but, as the LCIA's growth in recent years has confirmed, its users come to the LCIA with various different experiences of commercial dispute resolution, whether in the courts of their home jurisdictions or in ad hoc or trade association arbitration. The commentary in this book therefore draws comparisons with a range of relevant rules and practices in other types of arbitration and court proceedings.

I–004   There are many different reasons why parties choose arbitration under the LCIA Rules. Users should not assume that their own reasons are shared by everybody else. Likewise, they should not assume that their own criticisms of the institution or of its Rules are shared.

Thus, for example, a complaint that not enough arbitrators from outside London are appointed to LCIA Arbitral Tribunals for it to be a truly international institution will not be shared by numerous international commercial parties, e.g. from Russia and the CIS, who choose the LCIA precisely in order to have their disputes decided under English law by English lawyers, with the added benefits of confidentiality, speed and efficiency, as well as the international enforceability of awards which proceedings in the Commercial Court in London cannot offer.

This commentary seeks to draw attention to features of the Rules that are of particular interest or benefit to users whose reasons for choosing LCIA arbitration may be new to the reader. Above all, it seeks to provide practical guidance on the interpretation and operation of the 2014 Rules, and on the conduct of LCIA arbitrations.

**The Modern LCIA, its Aims and Organisation**

I–005   Widely recognised as one of the leading international arbitration institutions, the LCIA has, since its 1985 relaunch, established a firm reputation for excellence and innovation in the administration of private justice.

Internationally, the institution plays an increasingly important role in the development and study of international arbitration law and practice. It holds ever-popular symposia for members of its regional Users' Councils, as well as other conferences and seminars, and sponsors a leading journal in the field.[9] Its publication in 2011 of decisions of the LCIA Court on challenges to arbitrators[10] has thrown light on an area of arbitral jurisprudence and practice which many other institutions still regard as best kept private.

I–006   In practical terms, having committed to at least three regional centres, including the Dubai International Financial Centre (DIFC-LCIA), LCIA India, and most

---

[7] Registrar's Report 2013.
[8] See, for example, P. Turner and R. Mohtashami, *A Guide to the LCIA Arbitration Rules* (Oxford: Oxford University Press, 2009).
[9] *Arbitration International*.
[10] (2011) 27(3) Arbitration Int.

recently the LCIA Mauritius International Arbitration Centre (LCIA-MIAC), the LCIA is at the forefront in transferring knowledge and the internationalisation of best arbitral practices.

These factors alone justify a careful study of the LCIA's work and successes. However, from a practitioner's point of view, it is the steady increase in the LCIA's caseload,[11] as well as the considerable body of experience and expertise that has developed along with it, that merit a close and dedicated study of the LCIA procedures in a book such as this.

In this introductory Part, the authors review the aims and organisational structure of the LCIA and provide a thematic overview of the LCIA Rules, the legal theories underlying them, and the significant characteristics of LCIA arbitration proceedings. Then follows a sequential, detailed review of each Article of the LCIA Rules and its operation in practice. The authors also comment on the new Annex to the Rules, containing General Guidelines for the Parties' Legal Representatives, and on the Schedule of Costs. Finally, separate Parts are devoted to the LCIA's international offices and the arbitration rules which operate there.

I–007

*Administration of arbitrations*

The LCIA has described itself as "a thoroughly international institution, providing efficient, flexible and impartial administration of dispute resolution proceedings for all parties, regardless of their location, and under any system of law".[12]

I–008

The LCIA's stated purpose of providing "administration of dispute resolution proceedings for all parties" is what distinguishes it from other arbitration service providers in London, whether they be (a) associations of arbitrators, such as the London Maritime Arbitrators' Association (LMAA), which have rules but do not provide administration, or (b) trade associations, such as the Grain and Feed Trade Association (GAFTA) and the London Metal Exchange (LME), which provide both rules and administration but whose services are generally restricted to their own members or to disputes arising under their own contract forms.

I–009

The administration of arbitration is the core function of all of the major international arbitration institutions, of which the LCIA is one. Parties used to ad hoc arbitration can be wary of the institutions, considering that they add a layer of bureaucracy and cost. In a jurisdiction such as England, where the courts are supportive of arbitration and can intervene relatively quickly to appoint arbitrators, determine challenges or assess costs, the services of an institution can appear unnecessary.

It is one of the LCIA's achievements that, in recent years, it has persuaded many commercial parties and law firms to adopt its Rules in place of ad hoc terms for the resolution of their disputes. Such parties have realised that administered arbitration has a number of advantages, and can even reduce costs.

I–010

The LCIA itself promotes the case for administered arbitration by highlighting the following factors[13]:

---

[11] As noted above, the LCIA's annual caseload more than doubled between 2007 and 2009 and has remained at well over 200 ever since: see its annual reports on its website.
[12] See the description of the LCIA on *http://www.difcarbitration.com* [Accessed November 3, 2014].
[13] LCIA website: *http://www.lcia.org* under "Dispute resolution services" [Accessed November 4, 2014].

- certainty in drafting: saving the need to draft a detailed arbitration clause;
- taking care of the fundamentals: appointments of arbitrators, determining challenges, and resolving interlocutory and procedural issues without recourse to state courts;
- managing cost and delay: the LCIA Secretariat does not scrutinise arbitration awards (as the ICC does) but it scrutinises arbitrators' fee notes and it monitors proceedings, raising questions about timing with arbitrators, which the parties and their lawyers might be reluctant to do themselves; and
- fundholding: securing payment of the arbitrators' fees, monitoring their budgets, keeping the parties informed, and arranging to have sufficient funds to pay the arbitrators' final invoices in order to release the award.

The LCIA has three constituent organs: the LCIA Company, the LCIA Court and the Secretariat.

*The LCIA Company*

I–011   The not-for-profit LCIA Company supervises the development, management and smooth operation of the institution and its business, but is not directly involved in the administration of cases or in the interpretation of the Rules. Its Board of Directors (the Board) is "made up largely of prominent London-based arbitration practitioners".[14]

The Directors have included partners in international law firms, barristers with specialist arbitration practices, in-house Counsel and full-time independent arbitrators. The internationalisation of the Board and its opening up to in-house lawyers reflect the importance of the LCIA's ventures outside the UK and its concern to remain relevant to its commercial users.

I–012   The aims of the LCIA Company are described in its Memorandum of Association as including the following:

- encouraging and promoting the use of arbitration in the settlement of commercial disputes of all kinds, particularly those of an international nature;
- publishing and revising rules for the conduct of arbitration;
- appointing of members to an Arbitration Court Committee;
- making and maintaining lists of arbitrators qualified and willing to sit as such;
- appointing arbitrators and providing administration and advisory services in connection with arbitrations; and
- promoting professional, academic and social gatherings and the publication of learned papers, journals and books.[15]

---

[14] LCIA website: *http://www.lcia.org* under "Organisation" [Accessed November 4, 2014].
[15] Memorandum of Association of the London Court of International Arbitration.

There is a certain amount of overlap in the functions of the LCIA Court and the  I–013
Company's Board. The Chairman of each sits on the other. As a matter of practice, as described below in relation to Articles 3 and 5, the appointment of arbitrators is overseen by the LCIA Court, not the Board. Likewise, the revision of the Arbitration Rules is handled by a committee of the LCIA Court. On the other hand, the publication of the Rules is a matter for the Company. The basic division of tasks is between the business of the LCIA, for which the Board is responsible, and the operation of the LCIA Rules, for which the LCIA Court is responsible.

Arguably the most important independent function of the Board of the LCIA Company is the appointment of the Registrar, and the Deputy Registrar(s), whose pivotal role is considered below.[16] The Board is also responsible for the appointment of the members of the LCIA Court, and of its President and Vice Presidents but, under the Constitution of the LCIA Court (the "Constitution"), those appointments are made "on the recommendation of the Court".[17]

## *The LCIA Court*

The LCIA Court comprises up to 35 members from around the world, including  I–014
no more than six English members. In addition to the President, the LCIA Court's officers include up to seven Vice Presidents who may be invited to perform his functions. Former presidents retain a lifelong right to be invited to attend meetings of the LCIA Court and to vote in the capacity of Honorary Vice Presidents and to be appointed to determine challenges to arbitrators.[18]

The LCIA Court is directly involved in some important aspects of the conduct of arbitrations. Under Article D of its Constitution, the functions of the LCIA Court include:

(a) acting as appointing authority under the LCIA Rules or other rules (such as UNCITRAL) and in any other case where an agreement provides for appointments by the LCIA;

(b) performing any other functions conferred on it by any applicable rules of arbitration, mediation or conciliation, including deciding on challenges to arbitrators under the LCIA Rules and other rules, such as the UNCITRAL Rules, where the LCIA is designated as the appointing authority;

(c) keeping the LCIA Rules under review;

(d) making recommendations to the Board as appropriate concerning the introduction of new general or specialist rules; and

(e) promoting the objectives of the LCIA and of international commercial arbitration generally.

---

[16] Article C of the Constitution of the LCIA Court; see the commentary on Article 3 of the Rules below.
[17] See, respectively, Articles A1 and B1 of the Constitution (Appendix 3). In practice, the LCIA Court sets up a committee to propose new candidates.
[18] Article B3 of the Constitution (Appendix 3).

**I–015** The functions of the LCIA Court under paragraphs (a) and (b) above, namely the appointment of arbitrators and determination of challenges to arbitrators, are perhaps most significant, from the practitioner's point of view, to the conduct of most arbitral references. The 2014 LCIA Rules have expanded the role of the LCIA Court generally in circumstances where the Arbitral Tribunal cannot function.[19] The administrative functions of the LCIA Court, and how and by whom they are performed, are described in more detail in the commentary on Article 3.1 below.

In performing their functions under Article D of the Constitution, the LCIA Court and its members must act independently of the Board.[20] Individual members of the LCIA Court must not participate in or influence any decision relating to a case in relation to which they have any connection.[21]

**I–016** The LCIA Court meets in person twice a year at the LCIA's symposia at Tylney Hall. It also deals with policy decisions, amendments to the Schedule of Costs, and other such matters by way of debates and votes conducted by email.

*The Secretariat*

**I–017** Headed by the Registrar,[22] the LCIA Secretariat is based in London. It is responsible for the administration of all disputes (arbitration and other forms of dispute resolution) referred to the LCIA. In the case of arbitrations, this responsibility extends from the filing of the Request for Arbitration until the issue of the award under the institution's seal.

Its most significant involvement arises at the outset of the proceedings when it assists the LCIA Court in the selection and appointment of arbitrators. The process is described in the commentary on Article 5.6 below. The LCIA Secretariat also performs a deposit-taking and fundholding function, for both LCIA arbitration proceedings and, when requested, for other arbitration proceedings (normally ad hoc, such as under the UNCITRAL Rules). Deposits are taken in respect of the costs of the arbitration, more particularly the arbitrators' fees, and are held in interest-bearing accounts pending the conclusion of the proceedings or earlier awards on costs. The manner in which deposits are dealt with, and arbitration costs determined, in LCIA arbitrations is set out in the commentary on Articles 24 and 28 below. Similar procedures will be followed for the fundholding service provided in other arbitrations, except that the LCIA Court will not determine the amount of the arbitrators' fees, which will be a matter for the arbitrators themselves.

By having the LCIA Secretariat look after the funds, the arbitrators are able to have security in place for the amount of their fees. At the same time, the parties have the comfort of knowing that their arbitrators will not be remunerated until the Secretariat is satisfied that they should be.

The Registrar's and the Secretariat's roles and their dealings with the LCIA Court are described more fully in the commentary on Article 3 below.

---

[19] See 3–002 below.
[20] Article D5 of the Constitution (Appendix 3).
[21] Article D6 of the Constitution (Appendix 3).
[22] Article G of the Constitution (Appendix 3).

## *Users' Councils*

Although not forming part of the "constituent organs" of the LCIA, also worthy of note are the five regional Users' Councils.[23] These Councils are established by the LCIA Court with a view to maintaining the links between the LCIA and its users, and to ensure that the LCIA's arbitration and ADR services remain "relevant, cost effective, efficient and consistent with current best practice".[24] The Councils' role also involves promoting confidence in the LCIA's dispute resolution process through conferences, meetings, publications and personal contacts.

Membership of the Users' Councils is open to virtually any person with an interest in international arbitration,[25] and the LCIA has used the Councils' symposia and other meetings effectively to promote the use of its services as well as international arbitration more generally.

I–018

## **Overview of the LCIA Rules**

The first port of call for any party or counsel contemplating the commencement of an LCIA arbitration, or upon the receipt of an LCIA Request for Arbitration, will be to turn to the LCIA Rules themselves. Designed with the principles of efficiency and party autonomy firmly in mind, the Rules set out only to delineate the limits of the parties' freedoms, and the Arbitral Tribunal's procedural discretion. These outer limits are set by the mandatory rules with which all who are involved in the reference must comply in order to preserve the integrity of the arbitral process, and the quality of LCIA awards. Thus the broadly drafted and relatively short (32) Articles set out a robust framework within which detailed aspects of the process can be agreed upon by the parties or determined by the Arbitral Tribunal on a case by case basis.

I–019

Although not clearly organised by reference to subject matters,[26] the Articles of the LCIA Rules do loosely follow the likely chronological progress of an LCIA arbitral reference.

I–020

Thus, Articles 1 and 2 deal with the content and delivery of the Request for Arbitration and the Response. The functions of the LCIA Court and Registrar, to whom the Request and Response must be addressed, and who are closely involved in the constitution of the Arbitral Tribunal, are considered in Article 3. Other matters that often arise at the start a reference are dealt with in Articles 4–12, including: calculating time limits[27]; rules relating to the formation of the Arbitral Tribunal and the underlying duties of LCIA arbitrators to be and remain

---

[23] Councils are established for European Users, Arab Users, North American Users, Latin American and Caribbean Users, Asia-Pacific Users and African Users.
[24] Constitution of the LCIA's Users' Councils Article A.
[25] Each Users' Council also has a President, up to four Vice Presidents, up to four Councillors and a Secretary.
[26] The articles of some of the other well-established arbitration rules, such as the UNCITRAL Arbitration Rules and the ICC Rules of Arbitration, are grouped by categories denoted by subject matter-related title headings in the text of the rules. For example, the articles in the ICC Rules relating to the filing of a Request for Arbitration, the Answer and the effect of the arbitration agreements (Articles 4–6) are preceded by the title heading "Commencing The Arbitration".
[27] Articles 4.4–4.6.

impartial and independent[28]; rules governing the nomination,[29] selection,[30] appointment,[31] challenge[32] and replacement[33] of arbitrators; emergency procedures,[34] and the power of the majority of an Arbitral Tribunal to continue the proceedings.[35]

I-021 Articles 13–25 follow the chronological progress of the reference and deal with stages in which the parties present the case to the Arbitral Tribunal. These provisions relate to such matters as communications between the parties and the Arbitral Tribunal[36]; the parties' right to agree on the conduct of the proceedings[37]; default provisions concerning the presentation of legal argument and evidence[38]; the language of the proceedings[39]; the conduct of parties and their representatives[40]; the right to be heard[41]; and the default additional powers of the Arbitral Tribunal and LCIA Court to organise the conduct of the reference.[42]

Arguably out of strict logical or chronological sequence, but still closely related to the conduct of the proceedings by the Arbitral Tribunal, Articles 23–25 then deal with the jurisdiction of the Arbitral Tribunal,[43] the power of the LCIA Court to direct the parties to pay deposits,[44] and the powers of the Arbitral Tribunal to order interim relief and conservatory measures.[45]

I-022 Articles 26–28 concern the powers of the Arbitral Tribunal to render awards and the roles of the LCIA Court and Registrar in relation to the determination of the arbitration costs, the delivery of awards, and any corrections that might be required. These provisions therefore deal in effect with the final part of the arbitration and relate to the conduct of the proceedings after the parties have concluded the legal and evidential presentations.

The Rules conclude with Articles 29–32, which deal with various miscellaneous, if important, matters including the force of decisions taken by the LCIA Court, the confidentiality of LCIA arbitration, exclusion of liability, waiver of objections by the parties and the duty of all parties in relation to the conduct of the arbitration.

Finally, the Rules are supplemented by an Index of defined terms, an Annex providing General Guidelines for the Conduct of Legal Representatives, and a Schedule of Costs.

---

[28] Article 5.3.
[29] Article 7.
[30] Article 5.9.
[31] Articles 5.5–5.10.
[32] Articles 10.3–10.6.
[33] Article 11.
[34] Article 9.
[35] Article 12.
[36] Article 13.
[37] Article 14.
[38] Articles 15, 20, 21 and 22.
[39] Article 17.
[40] Article 18.
[41] Article 19.
[42] Article 22.
[43] Article 23.
[44] Article 24.
[45] Article 25.

Whilst the LCIA Rules could therefore be classified into five or six roughly delineated chronological groups of related Articles, or other groupings related more closely to the subject matter of specific Articles, that is unnecessary in practice and, in fact, given the relationship between the provisions which would find themselves in different groups, could even be misleading.  I–023

**Underlying Theories**

Substantively, the LCIA Rules are underpinned by a number of theories, the influence of which is evident throughout the Articles. They include the principles of party autonomy, efficiency, fairness, neutrality/impartiality of arbitrators and the enforceability of LCIA awards. Arbitration practitioners will immediately recognise these as fundamental tenets of international arbitration law and practice generally and it is therefore hardly surprising that the LCIA Rules should be guided by these principles, as are the rules of many other arbitral institutions.  I–024

However, the balance struck in the LCIA Rules between these potentially conflicting notions differs in some regards from that struck in other rules, which perhaps accounts for some of the popularity of the LCIA in recent years. Understanding these principles and appreciating the interplay between them, both as a matter of general principle as well as in the Articles of the LCIA Rules, will greatly assist the practitioner's comprehension of the Rules and ability to influence the conduct of an LCIA arbitration.

The main principles and their application in the LCIA Rules are considered below.

*1) Party autonomy*

Reflecting the doctrine of freedom of contract and the contractual basis of the arbitral process, the principle of "party autonomy" has been described as "the guiding principle in determining the procedure to be followed in an international commercial arbitration".[46] The operation of the principle in the arbitral context was succinctly explained by the English Departmental Advisory Committee on Arbitration Law (DAC), Report on the Arbitration Bill 1996 (the "DAC Report") as stipulating "that the parties must be free to choose for themselves what procedures they and the arbitrator shall be required to follow, subject only to a few very circumscribed rules of public policy".[47] The significance of the principle is stated by the UNCITRAL Secretariat in the Explanatory Note to the UNCITRAL Model Law (as amended in 2006) as follows:  I–025

"Autonomy of the parties in determining the rules of procedure is of special importance in international cases since it allows the parties to select or tailor

---

[46] Alan Redfern et al., *Law and Practice of International Commercial Arbitration*, 4th edn (London: Sweet & Maxwell, 2004), p.265 at para.6–03.
[47] The DAC Report, para.94, and s.1 of the English Arbitration Act 1996 regard party autonomy as a fundamental principle of English arbitration, in accordance with which the provisions of Part I of the English Arbitration Act 1996 (governing the conduct of arbitration seated in England) should be construed.

the rules according to their specific wishes and needs, unimpeded by traditional and possibly conflicting domestic concepts, thus obviating the earlier mentioned risk of frustration or surprise".[48]

I–026 The principle of party autonomy extends beyond pure procedural matters to matters of substance, such as the parties' choice of the governing law, the seat of arbitration and remedies. As Lord Hoffmann stated in the English reference to the European Court of Justice (ECJ) in *West Tankers v Ras Rinnione and Generali (The Front Comor)*:

> "17. People engaged in commerce choose arbitration in order to be outside the procedures of any national court. They frequently prefer the privacy, informality and absence of any prolongation of the dispute by appeal which arbitration offers. Nor is it only a matter of procedure. The choice of arbitration may affect the substantive rights of the parties, giving the arbitrators the right to act as amiables compositeurs, apply broad equitable considerations, even a lex mercatoria which does not wholly reflect any national system of law. The principle of autonomy of the parties should allow them these choices.
>
> 18. Different national systems give support in different ways and an important aspect of the autonomy of the parties is the right to choose the governing law and seat of the arbitration according to what they consider will best serve their interests".[49]

I–027 The principle of party autonomy is expressed in various places in the LCIA Rules, but primarily in Article 14.2, which permits the parties to agree upon the conduct of the proceedings, subject to the Arbitral Tribunal's overriding duty to conduct them fairly and efficiently (Article 14.4). The parties' right to choose the seat of arbitration is reserved in Article 16, and their right to choose the substantive law of the dispute is provided for in Article 22.3.

There is a common misconception that the LCIA Rules, as a whole, are prescriptive, and that they circumscribe party autonomy.[50] As noted above, the parties' rights to make their own agreements in relation to the conduct of their arbitration is a consistent theme throughout the Rules. Where there are detailed provisions, as in Article 15 ("Written Statements"), they will often apply only if the parties have not made another agreement.

## 2) *Efficiency*

I–028 The efficiency of international arbitration, and particularly its speed, procedural flexibility and financial economy, have long been lauded as major advantages of

---

[48] Explanatory Note, at para.35. The principle of party autonomy is enshrined in Article 19 of the Model Law.
[49] [2005] EWHC 454 (Comm) per Lord Hoffmann (Lords Steyn, Rodger, Mance and Nicholls concurring), at [17]–[18]. The House of Lords in that case referred to the ECJ the question of whether the English court's power to order anti-suit injunctions in aid of international arbitration proceedings fell within the arbitration exception to the Brussels Convention.
[50] Turner and Mohtashami, *A Guide to the LCIA Arbitration Rules* (Oxford: Oxford University Press, 2009), speak of the "prescriptive approach of the Rules to procedural matters" (para.5.30).

international arbitration over litigation in national courts. Writing in 1892, Edward Manson famously noted of the newly established City of London Chamber of Arbitration (the LCIA's predecessor):

> "This Chamber is to have all the virtues which the law lacks. It is to be expeditious where the law is slow, cheap where the law is costly, simple where the law is technical, a peacemaker instead of a stirrer-up of strife."[51]

Whether the modern practice of international arbitration fulfils these expectations is a matter of debate,[52] which cannot easily be resolved by reference to empirical data.[53] However, enhancing the efficiency of the process remains one of the stated aims of arbitration under the LCIA Rules and one of the consistent features of its provisions.

I–029

Thus, Article 14.4(ii) lists the adoption of a tailor-made, swift and inexpensive procedure "so as to provide a fair, *efficient and expeditious*"[54] procedure, as one of the Arbitral Tribunal's overarching duties, and Article 14.5 of the Rules charges the parties themselves with the duty to "do everything necessary in good faith for the fair, *efficient and expeditious* conduct of the arbitration" (emphasis added). Parties to LCIA arbitration are personally responsible for ensuring that the proceedings are conducted efficiently and expeditiously. Although it is unclear whether this unique provision[55] could in practice form the basis for independent liability,[56] its inclusion in the Rules nevertheless underlines procedural efficiency as one of the overriding aims of LCIA arbitration.

The principle that LCIA arbitration should be conducted in an efficient manner is consistent with the spirit of the UNCITRAL Model Law,[57] and the English Arbitration Act 1996.[58] It is reflected in many other Articles of the LCIA Rules, including, amongst others, Article 10.2 (power of the LCIA Court to remove an arbitrator who does not efficiently conduct the proceedings); Article 12 (power of the majority to

I–030

---

[51] (1893) IX L.Q.R. 86.
[52] See, for example, *Mitsubishi Motors Corp v Soler Chrysler-Plymouth Inc* 473 U.S. 614, 628 (1985), a party agreeing to arbitration "trades the procedures and opportunity for review of the courtroom for the simplicity, informality, and expedition of arbitration"; P. Karrer, "Arbitration Saves! Costs: Poker and Hide-and-Seek" (1986) 3(1) J. Int. Arb. 35; Kerr LJ, "International Arbitration v. Litigation" (1980) J.B.L. 164.
[53] A 2006 survey of corporate Counsel from around the world conducted by PricewaterhouseCoopers in association with the School of International Arbitration, Queen Mary, University of London, revealed that the flexibility of the arbitration procedure is one of two significant advantages cited by corporate Counsel for preferring international arbitration to transnational litigation; whilst expense and time were actually perceived as two of the inherent disadvantages of international arbitration.
[54] Emphasis added.
[55] Although the principle of efficiency is inherent in the arbitral rules of other institutions (see, for example, the Foreword to the ICC Rules; Article 16 of the SIAC Rules; and Article 19(2) of the SCC Rules), the direct party obligation appears to be unique. The good faith obligation provided for in some other arbitral rules (e.g. the CEITAC Rules, Article 9 do require the parties to "proceed with the arbitration in bona fide cooperation"; Article 15.7 of the Swiss Rules requires the parties to act in "good faith") might be said to cover similar ground, but probably fall short of the positive obligation imposed by the LCIA Rules. Other Institutional Rules, such as the Rules of the ICDR, ICC and SIAC, express no equivalent obligation at all, even if the obligation to arbitrate in good faith may be implied by the law of the seat. See also V.V. Veeder, the 2001 Goff Lecture, "The Lawyer's Duty to Arbitrate in Good Faith" (2002) 18(4) Arbitration Int. 431.
[56] The appropriate remedy would appear to lie in the sphere of an award on costs.
[57] General Assembly Resolution 40/72 (1985), para.4 of the Preamble.
[58] Sections 1 (general principles) and 33 (general duty of the Tribunal).

continue deliberations in the absence of a recalcitrant arbitrator); Articles 22 and 25 (providing for various of the Arbitral Tribunal's powers); and last, but not least, Article 23, which incorporates the doctrine of *Kompetenz-Kompetenz*,[59] which significantly curtails national court interference in the proceedings.

*3) Neutrality, impartiality and independence*

I–031  The principle of neutrality is expressed in the obligation that LCIA arbitrators shall be impartial and independent of the parties. This continuing duty binds all LCIA arbitrators both generally[60] and specifically in relation to the conduct of the proceedings.[61] The principle of impartiality and independence is further protected through the arbitrator disclosure process[62] and the rules concerning the nationality of arbitrators.[63] The LCIA Court's powers to veto party nominations,[64] and to revoke an arbitrator's appointment,[65] serve as the ultimate safeguards of this principle.

The LCIA Rules adopt the internationally recognised standard of "impartiality and independence"[66] for its arbitrators, for experts appointed by the Arbitral Tribunal,[67] as well as for the exercise of the powers of the LCIA Court,[68] and by extension to the Secretariat and Registrar.

*4) Fairness*

I–032  Closely related to the principle of neutrality, Article 14.4(i) also requires LCIA arbitrators to "act fairly and impartially as between all parties", and to afford each party a reasonable opportunity to state its case and to deal with that of its opponents. The requirement that procedures must be fair is further emphasised in Article 14.4(ii). Ensuring that the parties are treated fairly is another of the overarching duties of the Arbitral Tribunal, from which the parties cannot derogate by agreement.

Article 14.4(i) follows the language of s.33 of the English Arbitration Act 1996, but could arguably be said to be less strict or more flexible than the requirements of Article 12.1 of the UNCITRAL Arbitration Rules or indeed Article 18 of the Model Law, which require arbitrators to treat parties "with equality" and to give each party a "full opportunity" to present its case.[69] The more flexible language in s.33 of the 1996 Act was adopted to avoid the perceived unintended consequence that might flow from the language of Article 18 of the UNCITRAL Model Law; namely, that reluctant parties would use the right to be treated *equally* and to be afforded a *full* opportunity to present

---

[59] The power of the Tribunal to rule on its own jurisdiction. See the commentary on Article 23.
[60] Article 5.3.
[61] Article 14.4(i).
[62] Article 5.4.
[63] Article 6.
[64] Article 7.1.
[65] Articles 10 and 11.
[66] See UNCITRAL Rules, Articles 11–13; UNCITRAL Model Law, Article 12; ICC Rules, Articles 11, 15.2 and others.
[67] Article 21.1.
[68] Paragraph D.6 of the LCIA Court's Constitution (Appendix 3) provides: "No member or former member of the Court who has a connection with an arbitration in relation to which the LCIA exercises any functions of any kind may participate in or influence any decision of the Court relating to such arbitration".
[69] Although Article 14 of the ICC Rules adopts a similar standard.

their case to delay the expeditious progress of the proceedings.[70] In adopting Article 14.4(i), the LCIA Rules appear to have accepted this rationale.[71]

Opting for a flexible substantive duty to conduct the proceedings fairly, over mechanical notions of equal treatment, may increase the efficiency of the process and in some jurisdictions, such as England, reduce the scope for challenge of LCIA awards on technical grounds. However, in practice, the arbitration law of the seat of the arbitration continues to delimit the scope of the discretion which arbitrators may exercise in procedural matters.

I–033

The principle of fairness is further reflected and protected in Article 10.2, which lists failing to act fairly as one of the grounds upon which the LCIA Court may revoke the appointment of an arbitrator.

## 5) *Enforceability of awards*

The cross-border enforceability of international awards under the New York Convention is credited by many as the cornerstone of international arbitration,[72] and one of the significant advantages international arbitration has over national litigation.[73] It is not surprising therefore that the enforceability of awards should feature as a principle, which should guide arbitrators and parties in the conduct of the proceedings. In fact, by imposing a positive obligation on the LCIA Court, the Arbitral Tribunal *and* the parties, to "make every reasonable effort to ensure that any award is legally recognised and enforceable",[74] the LCIA Rules go further in this regard than the rules of most other arbitral institutions.[75]

I–034

The LCIA Rules also positively deal with the issues that are likely to arise in the enforcement context. The most commonly provided for grounds for challenging the enforcement of foreign awards under enforcement conventions[76] and national laws[77]

---

[70] Paragraph 164–5 of the DAC Report on the Arbitration Bill.
[71] Under the title "Conduct of the Proceedings", Article 5.2 of the 1985 LCIA Rules provided: "In the absence of procedural rules agreed by the parties or contained herein, the Tribunal shall have the widest discretion allowed under such law as may be applicable to ensure the just, expeditious, economical, and final determination of the dispute."
[72] See, for example, A.J. van den Berg, *The New York Convention of 1958: Towards a Uniform Judicial Interpretation* (Kluwer Law International, 1994), p.1; Jacques Werner, "Should the New York Convention be Revised to Provide for Court Intervention in Arbitral Proceedings?" (1989) 6(3) J. Int. Arb. 113; Yves Derains and Eric A. Schwartz, *A Guide to the New ICC Rules of Arbitration* (Kluwer Law International, 1998), p.353. Felix Weinacht, "Enforcement of Annulled Foreign Arbitral Awards in Germany" (2002) 19(4) J. Int. Arb. 313; Earl McLaren, "Effective Use of International Commercial Arbitration: A Primer for In-house Counsel" (2002) 19(5) J. Int. Arb. 473.
[73] Julian D.M. Lew et al., *Comparative International Commercial Arbitration* (Kluwer Law International, 2003), paras 20.6–20.8; Emmanuel Gaillard and John Savage (eds), *Fouchard Gaillard Goldman on International Commercial Arbitration* (Kluwer Law International, 1999), p.137.
[74] Article 32.2.
[75] Some institutional rules impose a similar obligation on the Tribunal alone, or institution and the Tribunal, some do not contain such a positive obligation at all, whilst the latest edition of the Stockholm Chamber of Commerce Arbitration Rules has been amended to widen the obligation to cover the parties as well as the Tribunal (see Article 47).
[76] New York Convention Article V; Panama Convention Article 5; The 1961 European Convention Article IX(1); The 1972 Moscow Convention Article V; 1987 Amman Convention Article 35.
[77] UNCITRAL Model Law Article 36; the English Arbitration Act 1996 s.103; French *Nouveau Code de Procédure Civile* Article 1502; DIFC Arbitration Law 2008 Articles 42–44; The Indian Arbitration and Conciliation Act 1996 Article 48; The Netherlands Arbitration Act 1986 Article 1063; Swiss Federal Statute on Private International Law 1987 Article 194.

are well known and need not be repeated in full. Nevertheless, even a cursory review of the LCIA Rules reveals that each of the grounds is addressed in one or more of the Articles of the LCIA Rules. The point is simply demonstrated in tabular form, using the New York Convention grounds for challenges as a point of reference:

I–035

| New York Convention Grounds for Challenge | LCIA Rules Article addressing the issue |
|---|---|
| Article V.1(a) invalidity of arbitration agreement under the law applicable to it or failing such designation under the law of place of arbitration, or the incapacity of either party. | Article 23 – Arbitral Tribunal's power to determine its own jurisdiction and decide upon the scope and validity of the arbitration agreement. |
| | Article 32.1 – failure promptly to raise any known objection before the Arbitral Tribunal constitutes waiver of right to object. |
| Article V.1(b) insufficient notice of the proceedings, or either party unable to present its case. | Articles 1.1, 4 and 19.3 deal with the issue of notice. |
| | The principle of fairness and the Articles noted above in that context ensure that each party has a reasonable opportunity to present its case. |
| Article V.1(c) award exceeds the Tribunal's jurisdiction. | Article 23 – Arbitral Tribunal's power to determine its own jurisdiction and decide upon the scope and validity of the arbitration agreement.[78] |
| Article V.1(d) composition of the Tribunal not in accord with arbitration agreement, or failing such agreement with the law of the place of arbitration. | Article 5 – LCIA Court appointment of Arbitral Tribunals allows it to ensure that the parties' agreement and laws of the seat are respected. |
| Article V.1(e) award not yet binding or set aside or suspended by courts of the seat. | Article 26.8 – All awards (including partial awards) are final and binding on the parties. |
| | To the extent that it is lawful to do so, the parties waive any right to appeal or seek review or any other recourse against the award. |

Thus, together with the general requirements of Article 32.2, the provisions of the LCIA Rules provide a code which, if followed, should prevent many potential

---

[78] A party's right to challenge an award on jurisdictional grounds may not be entirely excluded, as acknowledged in Article 23.5.

issues arising on enforcement (with the exception, perhaps, of challenges that arise under the law of the place of enforcement).[79]

## Other Characteristics of the LCIA Rules

For completeness, a number of further characteristics of arbitration under the LCIA Rules are briefly noted.

I–036

### *Privacy and confidentiality*

Privacy and confidentiality are also often quoted as distinctive attractions of international arbitration over national judicial proceedings. But whilst the LCIA Rules nominally protect both rights,[80] neither protection is absolute,[81] and it is not clear whether traditional remedies would always be practical or effective in the case of a breach. Nor in any event could the confidentiality or privacy of the proceedings always be protected in the context of challenge or enforcement proceedings in national courts.[82]

I–037

### *Administration*

LCIA arbitration is an administered procedure. This aspect of the process is reflected throughout the Rules, but features particularly highly in connection with the appointment and replacement of arbitrators. Thus, whilst the legal responsibility for the smooth conduct of the arbitration rests primarily with the Arbitral Tribunal and parties, the LCIA Court assists with the framework, appointing the Arbitral Tribunal, dealing with challenges and determining the amount of the arbitrators' fees. The personal and efficient service afforded by members of the Secretariat to the parties' Counsel tends, in the authors' experience, to increase the confidence of the parties in the process and overall serves to increase its efficiency and thus justify its cost to the parties.

I–038

### *Cost*

The costs associated with the process will be a major concern for the parties to any dispute. Disputes referred to international arbitration give rise to the additional expense of paying for the Tribunal's fees and expenses and, where the proceedings are administered, for the services provided by the institution. Under the LCIA Rules, arbitrators may charge for the work done on an hourly basis at rates set by the LCIA Court in accordance with the institution's Schedule of Costs.[83]

I–039

---

[79] Such as arbitrability or public policy (e.g. New York Convention Article V(2)).
[80] Respectively, Articles 19.4 and 30. Note that no such protection is given by various other rules, such as those of the ICC.
[81] Under Article 22.1(viii), a third party may be joined to the proceedings over the objections of one of the parties, and under Article 19.4 the Arbitral Tribunal may order that third parties may attend the proceedings.
[82] Although some national laws do provide for such protections.
[83] Article 28.1.

The Schedule of Costs, which is revised periodically, stipulates a maximum hourly rate, allowing the LCIA Court to agree rates with arbitrators that reflect the complexity of the matter and the amount in dispute. The Secretariat and LCIA Court also charge the parties for work done on an hourly basis. Arbitral Tribunals should not proceed with any arbitration unless the Secretariat confirms that it is holding sufficient funds to cover the expected costs (Article 24.3). Deposits on costs are normally collected by the Secretariat on a regular basis,[84] thus reducing the difficulties of having to fund very large amounts at the outset of the proceedings, which parties might experience under the rules of some other arbitral institutions.

## Institutional culture

I-040 Whilst the LCIA describes itself as being "thoroughly international",[85] the organisation is perceived by some of its users as predominantly if not "quintessentially" English. The history of the organisation and its culture are closely linked to the history and culture of the City of London. The organisation is based in England and its management is based there. Its staff have been predominantly English, though since 2008 a number of other nationalities have been represented, particularly amongst the ranks of Counsel.[86] Arbitrations conducted under its Rules are administered in London (wherever the legal seat), and at least some of the Rules are influenced by English statute and jurisprudence.

At the same time, by recognising the predominance of the mandatory laws of the legal seat of each arbitration,[87] the LCIA Rules do provide for effective arbitral proceedings in the vast majority if not all jurisdictions around the world. Further, since 1985, none of the LCIA's presidents have been English and the majority of the LCIA Court members are from other jurisdictions as well. Finally, the composition of any particular panel of arbitrators will influence the legal culture and "style" of the proceedings to a far greater extent than the institutional culture of any organisation.

It is unclear whether more users are deterred by London's reputation as an expensive venue than those who are attracted by England's reputation for fair play, and cultural and political ties with the US, Europe, the Middle East and the Commonwealth. Whether or not such perceptions shift as the LCIA centres in Dubai, India and Mauritius establish themselves further, it is clear that in the meantime the LCIA's popularity amongst lawyers and business people continues to grow along with its caseload.

---

[84] LCIA Schedule of Costs Article 3(i).
[85] LCIA website, FAQs.
[86] In 2014, a non-English Director General was appointed for the first time.
[87] William W. Park, "*The Lex Loci Arbitri* and International Commercial Arbitration" (1983) 32(1) I.C.L.Q. 21–52, F.A. Mann, "England Rejects Delocalised Contracts and Arbitration" (1984) 33(1) I.C.L.Q. 193–198, Pierre Mayer, "Mandatory Rules of Law in International Arbitration" (1986) 2(4) Arbitration Int. 274–293 at 275.

# PART II—COMMENTARY ON THE LCIA RULES

# PREAMBLE

**Where any agreement, submission or reference howsoever made or evidenced in writing (whether signed or not) provides in whatsoever manner for arbitration under the rules of or by the LCIA, the London Court of International Arbitration, the London Court of Arbitration or the London Court, the parties thereto shall be taken to have agreed in writing that any arbitration between them shall be conducted in accordance with the LCIA Rules or such amended rules as the LCIA may have adopted hereafter to take effect before the commencement of the arbitration and that such LCIA Rules form part of their agreement (collectively, the "Arbitration Agreement"). These LCIA Rules comprise this Preamble, the Articles and the Index, together with the Annex to the LCIA Rules and the Schedule of Costs as both from time to time may be separately amended by the LCIA (the "LCIA Rules").**

P–001 The Preamble to the Rules sets out the pre-conditions for their application, and defines what they comprise. In doing so, it includes the important definitions of "Arbitration Agreement" and of "LCIA Rules".

The text of the Preamble has been expanded from the version in the 1998 Rules, which had contained the curious provision that they would apply whenever the parties had agreed to arbitration by "the Court of the LCIA ("the LCIA Court")". That provision has been removed, no doubt because no agreements are in fact made in those precise terms. The functions of the LCIA Court are explained in the commentary on Article 3; they are principally supervisory and do not extend to the actual conduct of arbitrations.[1] However, experience shows that parties have adopted various names and terminology to refer to the LCIA. It was therefore prudent to capture the various attempts to refer to the LCIA where the words "London", "court" and "arbitration" are used in naming it. The Preamble seeks to do this.

P–002 In addition to the Schedule of Costs, the Rules now include an Annex and an Index. These are all brought within the definition of "LCIA Rules".

**"Where any agreement, submission or reference howsoever made or evidenced in writing (whether signed or not)...".**

P–003 Arbitration requires the prior consent of both or all parties to the dispute. As noted in the commentary on Article 1 below, their agreement must be evidenced in

---

[1] For a description of the composition of the LCIA Court and of its wider role, see Part I, Introduction, I–014, and the commentary on Article 3.1.

writing. This is a requirement of the New York Convention[2] and Part I of the English Arbitration Act 1996.[3]

The UNCITRAL Model Law (Article 7) defines an arbitration agreement as:

> "an agreement by the parties to submit to arbitration all or certain disputes which have arisen or which may arise between them in respect of a defined legal relationship, whether contractual or not. An arbitration agreement may be in the form of an arbitration clause in a contract or in the form of a separate agreement."

The parties' written agreement may, then, be a clause in a contract or a stand-alone agreement (made before or after the dispute has arisen). The agreement could also be contained in another contract (perhaps between different parties) and incorporated in the contract in dispute by reference.

P–004   In *Habas Sinai Ve Tibbi Gazlar Isthisal Endustri AS v Sometal SAL*,[4] a judge in the English Commercial Court, on an application to set aside an interim final award made by an Arbitral Tribunal appointed under the LCIA Rules, had to decide whether a contract incorporated a particular arbitration clause which was contained in some, but not all, of the parties' previous 14 contracts, the words of incorporation being *"all the rest will be same as our previous contracts"*. Christopher Clarke J upheld the Arbitral Tribunal's decision that it had jurisdiction, finding the words apt to incorporate the relevant clause.[5]

Less frequently, but not uncommonly, an arbitration agreement may be found in a separate, ad hoc, document exclusively devoted to the parties' agreement to submit certain disputes to arbitration (sometimes called a "submission agreement"). Such stand-alone arbitration agreements tend to be longer and more often than not concern the submission of pre-existing disputes to arbitration. Stand-alone arbitration agreements are also useful in the context of multi-party projects involving chains of contracts in which not all parties sign all contracts, but where the parties believe that a single forum for resolving disputes is appropriate. In that context they are sometimes referred to as "Umbrella" agreements.

The only formal requirement which is consistently cited, including in the New York Convention (Article II), Option I of Article 7 of the UNCITRAL Model Law

---

[2] Article II(2) of the New York Convention 1958 (Appendix 9) provides: "The term "agreement in writing" shall include an arbitral clause in a contract or an Arbitration Agreement, signed by the parties or contained in an exchange of letters or telegrams". However, the UNCITRAL Recommendation Regarding the Interpretation of Article II, Paragraph 2, and Article VII, Paragraph 1, of the New York Convention 1958, adopted by the United Nations Commission on International Trade Law on July 7, 2006, recommended that in light of the growth in electronic commerce, the circumstances set out in Article II(2) of the convention should be construed as non-exhaustive, and that the convention should be interpreted in the light of more permissive national legislation so as to permit enforcement of arbitral awards rendered pursuant to arbitration agreements that are valid under the law of the place of enforcement.
[3] English Arbitration Act 1996 s.5.
[4] [2010] EWHC 29 (Comm).
[5] The clause did not refer expressly to the LCIA and is unlikely to have been held to incorporate the LCIA Rules, even with the wider wording of the new version of the Preamble. It read: "All disputes, or controversies, or differences, which may arise between buyer and seller under this contract, shall be settled in London, according to London arbitration rules, by the United Kingdom Law." The parties agreed that if this clause formed part of their contract, then the dispute between them was to be resolved by an LCIA arbitration.

and the arbitration laws of many jurisdictions, is that an arbitration agreement "shall be in writing". Under the Model Law definition, an arbitration agreement is in "writing" if its contents are recorded in any form, even if the agreement was concluded orally (Option I Article 7.3) and the requirement is met by an electronic communication that can be accessed for subsequent reference. An arbitration agreement is also "in writing" if it is alleged by one party in formal pleadings and not subsequently denied by the other (Option I Article 7.5).

The Model Law's Option II definition omits any reference to the formal requirement of writing. Under that definition, and under the laws of some countries (e.g. English common law and New Zealand statute) oral arbitration agreements are enforceable. However, for the foreseeable future at least, expressing an arbitration agreement in a written contractual document remains the safest course—if only due to the requirements of the New York Convention.

The requirement is for writing, not necessarily for signatures, as confirmed by the new words in parentheses. The agreement can be contained in an exchange of emails. The terms "howsoever made" and "evidenced" suggest that it can also be contained in a single email recording an agreement made orally, though this may not be regarded as sufficient for the purposes of the New York Convention.[6]

P–005 The LCIA has published Recommended Clauses which, if adopted, constitute written agreements for the submission of disputes to LCIA arbitration, both before and after the disputes have arisen. These are reproduced, with commentary, at Part III. They both state that the disputes "shall be referred to and finally resolved by arbitration under the LCIA Rules".

**"... provides in whatsoever manner for arbitration under the rules of or by the LCIA, the London Court of International Arbitration, the London Court of Arbitration or the London Court ...".**

P–006 The agreement does not have to refer to the LCIA by name. It could refer, for example, to arbitration by the London Chamber of Commerce and Industry whose bye-law 6.01 provides that disputes referred to the chamber for arbitration are deemed to be references to the LCIA. However, it should be noted that the reference has to be explicitly to the London Chamber and not, for example, to the London branch of the International Chamber of Commerce (ICC), which would be a reference to arbitration under the ICC Rules.

The LCIA was previously known as the "London Court of Arbitration", so references using that name will be treated as references to the LCIA.

P–007 If "the London Court", in an arbitration clause, is intended to be a reference to the LCIA, it is obviously helpful to have confirmation in the Preamble that this foreshortened wording will suffice. However, the reference must be to "arbitration" and not to some other (or unidentified) form of dispute resolution by "the London Court".

Confusion can arise with translations of arbitration clauses into English. For example, the Russian "*Арбитражный Суд*" is sometimes translated as "Arbitration

---

[6] Article II(2) of the New York Convention 1958 (Appendix 9) refers to an "exchange of letters or telegrams". Section 5 of the English Arbitration Act 1996 allows an agreement to be "evidenced" in writing if it has been recorded in writing by one party with the authority of all parties.

Court" whereas its usual meaning is "Commercial Court".[7] In a contract with parallel texts in English and Russian, the dispute resolution clause might, in the English version, refer to the submission of disputes to "the Arbitration Court in London". If the English version is to prevail, this could be interpreted, in accordance with the Preamble, as a reference to the LCIA. On the other hand, if the Russian version is to prevail, the reference might instead be to the Commercial Court in London.[8]

**"... the parties thereto shall be taken to have agreed in writing that any arbitration between them shall be conducted in accordance with the LCIA Rules or such amended rules as the LCIA may have adopted hereafter to take effect before the commencement of the arbitration ...".**

P–008   The publication of the revised LCIA Rules in 2014 may raise doubts in the minds of practitioners as to whether the new Rules, or the version existing at the date of a particular contract, should govern an arbitration. The Preamble suggests that it is the date of the commencement of the arbitration which should determine which version of the Rules will apply, not the date of the contract.[9]

By operation of this wording and the earlier "in whatsoever manner", a reference to the 1998 Rules (or even the 1985 Rules) should be treated as a reference to the new version of the Rules.[10] Similar language in the Preamble to the 1998 version of the Rules confirms that those Rules continue to apply in arbitrations commenced prior to October 1, 2014.

P–009   There has been a useful change to the previous wording of the Preamble (in the 1998 Rules) with the replacement of "the arbitration shall be conducted" with "any arbitration between them shall be conducted". This should serve to dispel arguments about the scope of the Arbitration Agreement, as defined in the Preamble, in circumstances where a Respondent challenges whether an arbitration is validly afoot or whether a Claimant is entitled to commence a second arbitration under the same contract.

**"... and that such LCIA Rules form part of their agreement (collectively, the "Arbitration Agreement")".**

---

[7] Depending on the context, these Russian words may also mean "Court of Arbitration" in the sense of the "court" of an arbitration institution, such as the ICC or the LCIA. To make it clear that a reference to international arbitration is intended, Russian adjectives for "international" and "commercial" will generally be added. The confusion arises not only in translations of Russian into English but even into Ukrainian: see Dmytro Marchukov and Oleksandr Volkov, "Ukraine: Arbitrazh courts and arbitration – what's in a name?" (2013) 8(5) G.A.R.

[8] This situation arose in an LCIA consolidated arbitration, in which the LCIA Court decided that the wording was sufficient to allow it to proceed to the appointment of an Arbitral Tribunal (comprising a sole arbitrator). In his first letter to the parties, the arbitrator took the initiative of asking the parties about their dispute resolution clause and about some related wording in another clause of the contract. The Respondent instructed lawyers who confirmed the jurisdiction of the LCIA.

[9] Although Article 9B requires that parties to Arbitration Agreements entered into before October 1, 2014 must expressly consent to the application of the "Emergency Arbitrator" procedures in order for them to apply. See 9–052.

[10] Ultimately, the Rules that have been selected by the parties is a matter to be determined by the construction of their arbitration agreement and, in principle, it remains possible to select an earlier version of the Rules if that is truly intended and provided for in clear enough terms. However, there are practical and administrative considerations which the LCIA Secretariat will draw to the parties' attention in such a case.

This wording was not present in the Preamble to the 1998 Rules. It serves the dual purpose of incorporating the LCIA Rules into the parties' arbitration agreement and of defining that agreement in such a way as to include the Rules.

The express incorporation of the Rules into the Recommended Clause for future disputes is discussed at Part III. Whether the "reverse" incorporation of the Rules into the parties' arbitration agreement by way of this wording in the Rules themselves is effective will depend on the law governing the parties' arbitration agreement. However, the wording should at least overcome any doubts that there might be in the absence of specific provisions in the Arbitration Agreement, for example, about the role and authority of the LCIA Court in appointing arbitrators (Article 5) or about the default seat being London (Article 16). **P–010**

As a result of the new definition of "Arbitration Agreement", those two words appear in the Rules in place of the "Rules" themselves. For example, Article 15.9 now prescribes that, following the exchange of submissions, the Arbitral Tribunal shall proceed "in such manner as has been agreed in writing by the parties or pursuant to its authority under the Arbitration Agreement" (previously "under these Rules"). The authority conferred on the Arbitral Tribunal is thus located both in the parties' written agreement and in the Rules themselves.

**"These LCIA Rules comprise the Preamble, the Articles and the Index, together with the Annex to the LCIA Rules and the Schedule of Costs as both from time to time may be separately amended by the LCIA (the "LCIA Rules")".**

The Preamble is itself stated to form part of the Rules, the full contents of which are defined here.[11] The Schedule of Costs is revised from time to time when the arbitrators' maximum fee rates and/or the LCIA's administrative charges are increased. The Index and Annex are new to the 2014 version of the Rules. The Index appears at the end of the main body of the Rules. It is not a comprehensive index, but a list of certain terms used in the Rules, and of where they are defined or explained in them (e.g. "Arbitration Agreement" and "LCIA Rules" in the Preamble). The Annex is entitled "General Guidelines for the Parties' Legal Representatives" and is discussed below.[12] **P–011**

---

[11] The Preamble to the 1998 Rules had merely provided that the Rules "include" the Schedule of Costs.
[12] See 33–001 et seq.

## Article 1—Request for Arbitration

1.1 Any party wishing to commence an arbitration under the LCIA Rules (the "Claimant") shall deliver to the Registrar of the LCIA Court (the "Registrar") a written request for arbitration (the "Request"), containing or accompanied by:

(i) the full name and all contact details (including postal address, e-mail address, telephone and facsimile numbers) of the Claimant for the purpose of receiving delivery of all documentation in the arbitration; and the same particulars of the Claimant's legal representatives (if any) and of all other parties to the arbitration;

(ii) the full terms of the Arbitration Agreement (excepting the LCIA Rules) invoked by the Claimant to support its claim, together with a copy of any contractual or other documentation in which those terms are contained and to which the Claimant's claim relates;

(iii) a statement briefly summarising the nature and circumstances of the dispute, its estimated monetary amount or value, the transaction(s) at issue and the claim advanced by the Claimant against any other party to the arbitration (each such other party being here separately described as a "Respondent");

(iv) a statement of any procedural matters for the arbitration (such as the arbitral seat, the language(s) of the arbitration, the number of arbitrators, their qualifications and identities) upon which the parties have already agreed in writing or in respect of which the Claimant makes any proposal under the Arbitration Agreement;

(v) if the Arbitration Agreement (or any other written agreement) howsoever calls for any form of party nomination of arbitrators, the full name, postal address, e-mail address, telephone and facsimile numbers of the Claimant's nominee;

(vi) confirmation that the registration fee prescribed in the Schedule of Costs has been or is being paid to the LCIA, without which actual receipt of such payment the Request shall be treated by the Registrar as not having been delivered and the arbitration as not having been commenced under the Arbitration Agreement; and

(vii) confirmation that copies of the Request (including all accompanying documents) have been or are being delivered to all other parties to the arbitration by one or more means to be identified specifically in such confirmation, to be supported then or as soon as possible thereafter by documentary proof satisfactory to the

LCIA Court of actual delivery (including the date of delivery) or, if actual delivery is demonstrated to be impossible to the LCIA Court's satisfaction, sufficient information as to any other effective form of notification.

1.2 The Request (including all accompanying documents) may be submitted to the Registrar in electronic form (as e-mail attachments) or in paper form or in both forms. If submitted in paper form, the Request shall be submitted in two copies where a sole arbitrator is to be appointed, or, if the parties have agreed or the Claimant proposes that three arbitrators are to be appointed, in four copies.

1.3 The Claimant may use, but is not required to do so, the standard electronic form available on-line from the LCIA's website for LCIA Requests.

1.4 The date of receipt by the Registrar of the Request shall be treated as the date upon which the arbitration has commenced for all purposes (the "Commencement Date"), subject to the LCIA's actual receipt of the registration fee.

1.5 There may be one or more Claimants (whether or not jointly represented); and in such event, where appropriate, the term "Claimant" shall be so interpreted under the Arbitration Agreement.

**Introduction**

Article 1 outlines the formal requirements for commencing LCIA arbitration proceedings. These centre on the filing of a Request for Arbitration at the LCIA and delivery of the Request to all other parties.

1–001

It is important to check, before a Request is delivered, that any contractual preconditions to arbitration, such as an agreement to undertake negotiations or mediation, have been complied with.[1] In some cases, a party may also wish to consider whether it wants to be the Claimant (for example, to drive the matter forward) or whether it would prefer to wait for the other party to commence proceedings and so make it the Respondent.

Once the arbitration has been commenced under Article 1, this should suffice for the purposes of limitation periods in relation to the claims made, making the "Commencement Date" of potentially vital importance.

1–002

The start of any arbitration represents an opportunity to set the tone and course of the proceedings. The Request is a valuable opportunity to present the case and identify the issues to be resolved. A strongly drafted Request can sometimes be a trigger for settlement discussions, as the Respondent(s) realise that formal

---

[1] The controversial decision of Teare J in *Emirates Trading Agency LLC v Prime Mineral Exports Private Ltd* [2014] EWHC 2104 (Comm) may mark a turning point in the enforcement of pre-arbitration ADR clauses under English law. It was held in that case that an obligation to enter into "friendly discussion" was an enforceable term of the parties' contract.

proceedings have been commenced and can see the case to be met. On the other hand, if the arbitration continues there will be a further opportunity to set out the claims in more detail, and in many cases parties prefer to draft a short Request, both to save costs and to keep further details in reserve for later, after the Respondent(s) makes its position clearer. The Respondent will, in turn, entertain similar considerations as to the strategy and tone it adopts in its Response. Indeed, a Respondent may wish to consider whether to deliver a Response at all.

**1-003** An arbitration is sometimes commenced without an immediate intention that it should be pursued. This can happen, for example, in a situation where a party is a defendant in litigation and, in order to protect itself, commences arbitration against a third party from which it will claim an indemnity, under a contract which contains an arbitration clause. In that situation, whilst there may be contractual, legal and/or tactical reasons to commence the arbitration, the claim may not have crystallised. The Request should explain what the Claimant is looking for and, if appropriate, the other side's agreement could be obtained to a delay in the formation of the Arbitral Tribunal.

The default position under the LCIA Rules is that the LCIA Court will select the Arbitral Tribunal. If the parties have agreed that they may make their own nominations, the Request must contain the Claimant's nomination of a co-arbitrator, failing which the LCIA Court may proceed to appoint the Arbitral Tribunal without regard to later nomination.[2]

The LCIA now has an optional, online form Request for Arbitration on its website (see Article 1.3 below). This is an innovative move that could, in appropriate cases, where the Claimant or its lawyers are not familiar with LCIA arbitration, serve to simplify and reduce the cost of commencing the arbitration. The online Request for Arbitration can be converted into a pdf document for delivery to the Respondent(s).

**1.1 Any party wishing to commence an arbitration under the LCIA Rules (the "Claimant") shall deliver to the Registrar of the LCIA Court (the "Registrar") a written request for arbitration (the "Request"), containing or accompanied by: . . .**

**1-004** Article 1.1 sets out the requirements with which Claimants should comply in order to commence arbitration under the LCIA Rules.

The first requirements are purely formal: the Request should be in written form and it should be delivered to the Registrar of the LCIA Court. Apart from that, however, and as long as the information required by Articles 1.1(i)–(vii) is provided, there is no particular form which the Request should follow.

Delivery to the Registrar is the method by which an arbitration is commenced under the LCIA Rules. It is the timing of this delivery which should determine when the arbitration was commenced under the law governing the arbitration.

**1-005** Section 14(1) of the English Arbitration Act 1996 confirms that the parties are free to agree when arbitral proceedings are to be regarded as commenced for the

---

[2] See Article 7.2.

purposes of that Act and also for the purposes of the Limitation Acts. Article 1.1 of the Rules contains such an agreement.

Claimants will sometimes arrange for copies of the Request to be hand-delivered to the LCIA. The Registrar, or another member of the Secretariat on the Registrar's behalf, should then stamp, sign and date one copy and/or a copy of the covering letter to acknowledge receipt. In all cases, whatever the method of delivery, receipt should be acknowledged by email and/or letter on the date of delivery.

The LCIA's formal letter to the parties, confirming precisely what has been filed, raising any relevant questions and confirming the next steps, should usually follow on the same day or on the following day. It should always confirm when the Request was received. That letter may be drafted by the Counsel in the Secretariat who will be in charge of the management of the arbitration through to its conclusion.

**(i) the full name and all contact details (including postal address, e-mail address, telephone and facsimile numbers) of the Claimant for the purpose of receiving delivery of all documentation in the arbitration; and the same particulars of the Claimant's legal representatives (if any) and of all other parties to the arbitration;**

The required inclusion in the Request of the full names, addresses and contact details of each party and each party's respective legal representatives (if any), for the purposes of receiving communications and delivery of documents in the arbitration,[3] serves an obvious practical purpose. However, since the enforcement of an award against a party who has not received proper notice of the arbitration proceedings or of the appointment of an arbitrator may be refused under Article V(1)(b) of the New York Convention, the provision also serves an important legal function.

1–006

Accordingly, if addresses and methods for delivering documents have been contractually stipulated, such details should be recorded in the Request, together with any other addresses regularly used in practice. In some cases, the names of the legal representatives of the opponents will be known, but even where such data is not known, this should be made clear.

The 1998 edition of the Rules had simply "addresses" and did not specify that "contact details" had to be supplied. Claimants would sometimes provide only registered office addresses, which might not be business or correspondence addresses but the addresses of lawyers or company secretarial services in offshore jurisdictions. Whilst that practice was unhelpful from the point of view of ensuring that communications reached the parties, it did at least have the virtue that the registered office addresses were made known. These can be essential for the purposes of identifying a party: separate but associated companies of precisely the same name (even including "Ltd") can be based in more than one jurisdiction,

1–007

---

[3] See also Articles 4.2 and 4.3, which govern the delivery of communications (including the Request and Response).

e.g. the British Virgin Islands and the Republic of Ireland. It must be best practice to include registered office addresses as well as contact details in the Request.

Legal representatives will include barristers. English solicitors have sometimes filed a Request, accompanied by a Statement of Case with a barrister's name at the foot, but without identifying the barrister or his or her chambers in the body of the Request. Solicitors should note that barristers will be regarded by the LCIA Court as legal representatives (see e.g. Article 18) and they should, when instructed, be identified to the LCIA Secretariat and to the other parties.[4]

> **(ii) the full terms of the Arbitration Agreement (excepting the LCIA Rules) invoked by the Claimant to support its claim, together with a copy of any contractual or other documentation in which those terms are contained and to which the Claimant's claim relates;**

1–008  Article 1.1(ii) provides that the terms of the Arbitration Agreement (in most cases the text of a clause contained in a longer "underlying" contract) relied upon by the Claimant should be reproduced in the Request (but not the LCIA Rules incorporated into the Arbitration Agreement); and that a copy of any contractual or other document in which the Arbitration Agreement is contained and to which the claim relates should be provided with (or exhibited to) it.

The provision of copies of the relevant contractual documentation serves three main purposes: it provides evidence of the jurisdiction of the LCIA over the dispute; it sets the legal foundation for recognition and enforcement of the ultimate award; and it identifies the contract which is claimed to have given rise to the dispute.

Examination of these documents also assists the Registrar to confirm the correct parties to the proceedings and provides relevant background that will assist with the selection and appointment of arbitrators.[5]

> **(iii) a statement briefly summarising the nature and circumstances of the dispute, its estimated monetary amount or value, the transaction(s) at issue and the claim advanced by the Claimant against any other party to the arbitration (each such other party being here separately described as a "Respondent");**

1–009  Article 1.1(iii) lists the substantive matters that should be recorded in the Request, including:

- the nature and circumstances of the dispute;
- the estimated monetary value of the dispute;

---

[4] See the commentary on Article 18 regarding Legal Representatives generally and 10–017 regarding challenges to arbitrators on grounds of lack of independence.

[5] The 1998 edition of this Article required the Claimant to include in the Request a copy of the "written" arbitration clause or agreement. This is no longer required, and although the Preamble to the Rules clarifies that the Arbitration Agreement must be evidenced in writing, both as a matter of English common law and under Option II of Article 7 of the UNCITRAL Model Law 2006, an oral arbitration agreement may be recognised and enforced by national courts.

- the transaction(s) at issue; and
- the claims advanced by the Claimant against each Respondent.

*The nature and circumstances of the dispute*

Whilst Article 1.1(iii) encourages brevity, and this stricture should be followed when it is possible to do so, on occasion it will be wise to set out the nature and circumstances of the dispute in some detail. At the very least, sufficient background information should be provided in order to enable the LCIA's Secretariat, Registrar and Court to reach well-founded decisions in connection with the appointment of arbitrators and other preliminary decisions.  1–010

It is also important to identify "the dispute" properly as the issues identified in the Request for Arbitration could serve to limit the jurisdiction of the Arbitral Tribunal if narrowly drafted[6] and subsequent permission to introduce new claims might not be granted.[7] Equally, if the statement describing the nature and circumstances of the disputes is too brief or vague, there may be doubts as to the scope or existence of a dispute, and the Respondent may be able to challenge the jurisdiction of the Arbitral Tribunal appointed on the grounds that no such dispute has arisen.

It should be noted that the requirement is to summarise "the dispute", not only the claim. The Claimant is expected to set out why it knows or believes its claim to be rejected or resisted. In this respect, the Request is more onerous than a simple notice of arbitration as might be delivered, for example, under the Centrocon arbitration clause in a charterparty.[8]  1–011

Where the Claimant intends to elect to have its Request treated as its Statement of Case, pursuant to Article 15.2 of the LCIA Rules, the requirements of that Article should be complied with; in which case a brief summary of the nature and circumstances of the dispute might not be sufficient.

*The estimated monetary value of the dispute*

The requirement that estimations of the value of the claims be included in the Request for Arbitration is new. Some institutional rules provide for the fees of the Tribunal and the institution to be charged according to the amount in dispute (the "ad valorem" basis). However, the LCIA does not charge on that basis, but rather according to hourly rates. Nonetheless, the amount in dispute may be relevant to the hourly rates to be fixed and the selection of arbitrators under Article 5.9 of the LCIA Rules.[9]  1–012

---

[6] *Lesser Design & Build v University of Surrey* [1992] 56 B.L.R. 57; s.30(1)(c) of the English Arbitration Act 1996.
[7] See Article 22.1(i). See 22–007.
[8] "Any claim must be made in writing and Claimant's Arbitrator appointed within three months of final discharge and where this provision is not complied with the claim shall be deemed to be waived and absolutely barred."
[9] The value of the claims is expressly stated as a matter to which the LCIA Court will have regard in the selection and appointment of arbitrators. See the commentary at 28–001—28–008 and 34–016—34–018.

*The transaction(s) at issue*

**1–013** Another new requirement is that the Claimant should summarise the transactions at issue in the Request. This will also assist the LCIA in the selection and appointment of arbitrators with relevant professional background and experience.[10]

*The claims advanced by the Claimant against each Respondent*

**1–014** Finally, Article 1.1(iii) requires the Claimant to specify the claims advanced against each Respondent. The heads of claim may be stated in general terms at this juncture, and made expressly subject to revision in due course, but the claims should be set out clearly.

It is not necessary to quantify damages claims precisely at this time,[11] but where the quantum is known it should be stated in order to provide the Respondent and the LCIA Court with a proper understanding of the dispute. Claims for costs, interest and interest on costs,[12] should also be made at this juncture.

**1–015** There should be no need to reserve rights to revise or supplement the summary of the claim. Indeed, there is no provision in the Rules for any amendment to a Request. The Request is not a pleading. It is only if the Request is itself to be treated as a Statement of Case, and an election is made in that respect after the appointment of the Arbitral Tribunal, that any amendment could be appropriate. Should a Claimant wish to draw the Registrar's, and the other parties', attention to a change in its case before the Arbitral Tribunal is appointed, this can be done by way of ordinary correspondence.

Finally, it should not be forgotten that even within the constraints of a brief statement, the Request and Response represent the parties' first opportunity to impress the Arbitral Tribunal with the strength of their respective positions on the merits and any special features of the case, and engage in some preliminary written advocacy of their positions.

> **(iv) a statement of any procedural matters for the arbitration (such as the arbitral seat, the language(s) of the arbitration, the number of arbitrators, their qualifications and identities) upon which the parties have already agreed in writing or in respect of which the Claimant makes any proposal under the Arbitration Agreement;**

**1–016** A well-drafted Arbitration Agreement will deal with the principal procedural aspects of the arbitration. It will designate the seat of the arbitration, the language of the proceedings and the number of arbitrators; normally a choice between one or three arbitrators. Less frequently, the Arbitration Agreement might contain agreements on the qualifications (e.g. seniority or areas of expertise) or even the

---

[10] See Article 5.9.
[11] The position is different in proceedings conducted pursuant to institutional rules that calculate the arbitration fees by reference to the amount in dispute.
[12] In *Walker v Rowe* [2000] 1 Lloyd's Rep 116, no application had been made for interest on the Tribunal's fees. Post-award interest was refused by Aikens J on enforcement.

identity of the arbitrators.[13] Where the Arbitration Agreement is silent, the parties are in many cases still able to reach an agreement on such matters prior to the commencement of the arbitration. Any such agreements on procedural matters that have been reached between the parties should be recorded in the Request for Arbitration. Where they have not been agreed in advance, it will fall to the LCIA Court to decide on matters such as the selection of the arbitrators[14] and the number of arbitrators.[15] The Rules provide that, absent provision by the parties, London, England will be the seat of arbitration pending any determination by the Arbitral Tribunal[16] and the language of the arbitration will normally be that of the Arbitration Agreement.[17] In such circumstances, the Claimant should seize the opportunity afforded by Article 1.1(iv) to make reasoned proposals with regard to the relevant matters in order to assist the LCIA Court in identifying the issues and making appropriate decisions.

Even where an arbitration agreement expressly confers the power to make certain decisions on the LCIA Court, it is still open to the parties to make proposals. In particular, where the LCIA Court is to select a sole or presiding arbitrator, the Request and Response are an opportunity to address matters that the LCIA Court should take into account; for example, the nature of the transaction, the nature and circumstances of the dispute, and the nationality, location and languages of the parties. It is not unusual for parties to propose specific individuals, if they are agreed by all parties, or to list desired qualifications. Claimants should note, however, that nominating a presiding arbitrator, without the Respondents' agreement, will result in that name being discarded by the LCIA Court.

Where the LCIA Court has discretion as to the number of the arbitrators (usually one or three) the Request should state the wishes of the Claimant and reasons for the position taken. **1–017**

Equally, where the parties have agreed that the nominated arbitrators should choose the third arbitrator, this should be stated in the Request and Response. Again it is good practice to indicate any desired qualifications. Article 5.9 of the Rules provides that the LCIA Court will appoint arbitrators with "due regard" for any particular method or criteria of selection agreed in writing by the parties.

**(v) if the Arbitration Agreement (or any other written agreement) howsoever calls for any form of party nomination of arbitrators, the full name, postal address, e-mail address, telephone and facsimile numbers of the Claimant's nominee;**

The ability to nominate an arbitrator is viewed by many parties as one of the great advantages of international arbitration over court proceedings where a judge is **1–018**

---

[13] Requirements as to qualifications, memberships of professional organisations, religion or nationality could fall foul of equality and anti-discrimination legislation in certain jurisdictions, as was initially found by the Court of Appeal in *Jivraj v Hashwani* [2010] EWCA Civ 712 before being overturned by the Supreme Court [2011] UKSC 40.
[14] Articles 5, 7, 8 and 11.
[15] Article 5.
[16] Article 16.
[17] Article 17.

simply allocated. Parties have an opportunity to ensure that the persons deciding their dispute have the appropriate experience and attributes, and can therefore have more confidence in the process. It is undeniable that the identity of an arbitrator could significantly impact on the conduct and outcome of the arbitration.

Parties are therefore sometimes surprised to discover that the default position under the LCIA Rules is not party-nomination of arbitrators (rather the arbitrators are selected by the LCIA Court). This default position has many advantages, which are discussed in relation to Articles 5 and 7 below and which have been amongst the major attractions of the LCIA Rules, particularly for new users from developing jurisdictions. The LCIA's default regime certainly provides comfort that the Arbitral Tribunal will be entirely neutral, and it places trust in the LCIA Court to select appropriate persons for this dispute.[18] If the parties want the right to select arbitrators in an LCIA arbitration, they must simply agree to adopt such a procedure either in their Arbitration Agreement or subsequently, e.g. by way of an exchange in the Request and Response.[19]

**1–019**   The nomination of arbitrators is a decision over which parties and their legal representatives will sometimes deliberate extensively. Factors ranging from experience to availability, from personal conflicts of interest to previously expressed views on pertinent legal or procedural matters, and even personality traits of prospective arbitrators, may all become the subject of careful scrutiny. Interviews with prospective arbitrators are also sometimes conducted in an attempt to ascertain such matters and to allow the client to gain a certain measure of the arbitrator to be selected.[20]

The nominee's contact details must be set out in full so that the LCIA Secretariat may contact the nominee, in due course, to ascertain his or her availability and suitability for the purposes of appointment under Article 5. Not infrequently, this approach from the LCIA will be the first time that the candidate arbitrator has heard anything about the case. Many parties and lawyers will nominate an arbitrator without contacting him or her first, leaving it to the LCIA to conduct the necessary checks under Article 5 and knowing that, should the nomination fail, they are likely to be offered further time to make a re-nomination.

If the Request for Arbitration does not contain a nomination by the Claimant where there is an agreement that the Claimant is to nominate an arbitrator, the LCIA Court may appoint the arbitrator without regard to any late nomination.[21]

> **(vi)   confirmation that the registration fee prescribed in the Schedule of Costs has been or is being paid to the LCIA, without which actual receipt of such payment the Request shall be treated by the Registrar**

---

[18] The default position under the 2012 ICC Arbitration Rules is for the parties to nominate two of a panel of three arbitrators, with the President being selected by the ICC Court.

[19] Note, however, that under Articles 5.7 and 7.1, the LCIA Court alone may appoint arbitrators, and the LCIA Court must decline to appoint any proposed arbitrator who does not meet the standards set out in Article 5.

[20] But see comments at 5–018, 13–004—13–008 and 13–014—13–015 below in relation to the interviewing of prospective arbitrators.

[21] Article 7.2.

as not having been delivered and the arbitration as not having been commenced under the Arbitration Agreement; and

(vii) confirmation that copies of the Request (including all accompanying documents) have been or are being delivered to all other parties to the arbitration by one or more means to be identified specifically in such confirmation, to be supported then or as soon as possible thereafter by documentary proof satisfactory to the LCIA Court of actual delivery (including the date of delivery) or, if actual delivery is demonstrated to be impossible to the LCIA Court's satisfaction, sufficient information as to any other effective form of notification.

Articles 1.1(vi) and (vii) deal with important administrative matters. **1–020**
Article 1.1(vi) provides that the arbitration is only deemed to commence once the prescribed registration fee has been paid. The fee is non-refundable, even if the arbitration proceeds no further than the Request stage, and it is paid only by the Claimant. Failure to make this payment may have significant consequences where statutory limitations of actions or contractual time bars are relevant. The Request must contain a confirmation that the payment has been or is being made.

In practice, the registration fee is normally paid by electronic transfer directly **1–021** into the LCIA's account either with or shortly before or after the transmission of the Request. Parties intending to file Requests should contact the Registrar and request the LCIA's bank account details, providing their names and any other brief details which might assist in identifying the payment and linking it to the Request to be filed. Less frequently, payment is made by cheque submitted with the Request, for which the Registrar can provide a receipt.

Article 1.1(vii) requires that the Claimant deliver the Request directly to the Respondent as well as to the Registrar, and confirm to the Registrar the methods by which delivery was effected.[22] The 1998 edition spoke of "service" of the Request, which caused confusion and unnecessary burdens on Claimants, who would sometimes resort to using sheriffs and other judicial officers entitled to "serve" court documents in their home jurisdictions. Delivery is far simpler and the relevant methods (to be considered alongside any contractual modes of delivery and any law or rule applicable at the place of delivery) are set out in Article 4.

Under the LCIA Rules, arbitration is commenced once the Request is delivered **1–022** to the LCIA Registrar (and the fee paid), but this alone might not be sufficient to stop time running under any applicable limitations or contractual time bars,[23] nor could delivery to the Registrar alone be sufficient for the purposes of the New York Convention to secure enforcement of the ultimate award.

The Claimant must also, as soon as possible, provide the LCIA Court with proof of actual delivery to all other parties to the arbitration. If actual delivery is not possible, this fact must be established to "the LCIA Court's satisfaction". This is a new requirement and, at the time of writing, it is not known what proof the LCIA Court might require, although common sense suggests that the LCIA Court

---

[22] Article 4 sets out the permitted methods of delivery of documents.
[23] See Article 1.4.

will wish to be satisfied that the party delivering the Request has engaged in reasonable measures in the circumstances of the case to ensure that the Request has actually been delivered.

The Arbitral Tribunal will also note the position in due course and will decide if any other particular steps should be taken to bring the proceedings to the attention of a non-participating Respondent, having regard to its obligations under Article 32.2 in relation to rendering an enforceable award.

**1.2 The Request (including all accompanying documents) may be submitted to the Registrar in electronic form (as e-mail attachments) or in paper form or in both forms. If submitted in paper form, the Request shall be submitted in two copies where a sole arbitrator is to be appointed, or, if the parties have agreed or the Claimant proposes that three arbitrators are to be appointed, in four copies.**

1–023 The Request and accompanying documents may be submitted to the Registrar by email[24] and/or in paper form.

If the Claimant chooses to deliver the Request in paper form, then it must provide:

- two copies where a sole arbitrator is to be appointed; or
- four copies where three arbitrators are to be appointed (or the Claimant proposes that three arbitrators should be appointed).

The additional paper copies will be forwarded to the arbitrator(s) by the LCIA when they are appointed.

**1.3 The Claimant may use, but is not required to do so, the standard electronic form available on-line from the LCIA's website for LCIA Requests.**

1–024 This new provision reflects the introduction of a new, optional, service offered by the LCIA for filing Requests, Responses and applications to the LCIA Court under Articles 9A (expedited formation of the Arbitral Tribunal), 9B (appointment of an Emergency Arbitrator) and 9C (expedited replacement of an arbitrator).

Where online filing is chosen, the party or its legal representative is required to register an online account with the LCIA's Online Filing website, after which the process for filing a Request involves the completion of an online form comprised of the following eight sections (each a webpage):

Section A: Claimant(s) details, including the name(s), address(es), contact information and similar information for any legal representative(s) of the Claimant(s).

---

[24] Note, however, that under Article 4.3, delivery of documents by email between the parties is only permitted if expressly agreed upon by the parties or ordered by the Arbitral Tribunal.

Section B: Respondent(s) details, including the details of any legal representative(s).

Section C: The Arbitration Agreement. This section of the form facilitates the uploading of electronic copies (such as MS Word or pdf documents) of the Arbitration Agreement, the contractual documents and other supporting evidence. The size of each file uploaded must be less than 64 Megabytes, but there appears to be no limit on the number of documents that can be uploaded.

Section D: Nature and circumstances of the dispute. This section consists of a text window (with limited formatting options) in which the Claimant should set out the background to the dispute, and a space for indicating the monetary value (and currency) of the dispute and whether declaratory relief is sought.

Section E: Statement of procedural matters. The Claimant is asked to confirm procedural matters that have been agreed upon in writing. Separately the Claimant has an opportunity to make proposals in respect of other procedural matters.

Section F: Nomination of arbitrators. This section allows the Claimant to provide details of any arbitrator nominated by it (if nomination has been agreed).

Section G: Service of the Request. The Claimant is asked to confirm the names of the parties to whom the Request has been delivered and the method of delivery.

Section H: Payment. Finally the form concludes with a payment section. Online submission of the Request is conditional on successful online payment by credit card of the Registration Fee (plus VAT where applicable).

The introduction of an online filing system is an innovative development that could, in appropriate cases, serve to streamline the process of commencing LCIA arbitration. However, in cases involving complex, factual or legal issues, experienced parties or counsel might not consider that the benefits of online filing justify a departure from the trusted methods of compiling, presenting and delivering Requests in LCIA arbitration proceedings.

**1.4 The date of receipt by the Registrar of the Request shall be treated as the date upon which the arbitration has commenced for all purposes (the "Commencement Date"), subject to the LCIA's actual receipt of the registration fee.**

Subject to the receipt by the LCIA of the registration fee, the date of receipt by the Registrar of the Request is treated as the date on which the arbitration has commenced (the "Commencement Date").

    This is of course important in the context of limitation periods and contractual time limits. In addition, the "Commencement Date" is the date from which the

1–025

Respondent's time to deliver the Response starts running, even when the Request has not yet been delivered to the Respondent.[25]

Nevertheless, the burden remains on the Claimant to make sure that the Respondent(s) has been properly notified under all applicable laws. Failure to notify the Respondent of the commencement of an arbitration and the appointment of an Arbitral Tribunal could result in an eventual award not being enforced by national courts.

**1.5 There may be one or more Claimants (whether or not jointly represented); and in such event, where appropriate, the term "Claimant" shall be so interpreted under the Arbitration Agreement.**

1–026   In some cases a number of parties seek to commence the arbitration proceedings as co-Claimants (for example, where there are disputes under multi-party contracts or a suite of related contracts). Article 1.5 recognises the possibility of co-Claimants, and provides that in such cases references to the Claimant in the LCIA Rules should be read as a reference to all co-Claimants.

The basis upon which each Claimant asserts that it has the right to commence the arbitration should be stated in the Request.

**Saving provision**

1–027   For the reasons explained above, full compliance with the provisions of Article 1 and, where appropriate, the utilisation of the Request for advocacy purposes is recommended. However, Article 5.1 of the LCIA Rules contains a saving provision which permits the LCIA Court to proceed with the formation of the Arbitral Tribunal even where the "Request is incomplete . . .".

Article 5.1 does not distinguish between matters that are fundamentally required, so that the Request is regarded as effective, and those which may be left incomplete. Nevertheless, Claimants should always endeavour to deliver a fully articulated Request (within the context explained above) and only seek to rely on Article 5.1 where required information is unavailable.

---

[25] See Article 2.1.

## Article 2—Response

2.1 Within 28 days of the Commencement Date, or such lesser or greater period to be determined by the LCIA Court upon application by any party or upon its own initiative (pursuant to Article 22.5), the Respondent shall deliver to the Registrar a written response to the Request (the "Response"), containing or accompanied by:

(i) the Respondent's full name and all contact details (including postal address, e-mail address, telephone and facsimile numbers) for the purpose of receiving delivery of all documentation in the arbitration and the same particulars of its legal representatives (if any);

(ii) confirmation or denial of all or part of the claim advanced by the Claimant in the Request, including the Claimant's invocation of the Arbitration Agreement in support of its claim;

(iii) if not full confirmation, a statement briefly summarising the nature and circumstances of the dispute, its estimated monetary amount or value, the transaction(s) at issue and the defence advanced by the Respondent, and also indicating whether any cross-claim will be advanced by the Respondent against any other party to the arbitration (such cross-claim to include any counterclaim against any Claimant and any other cross-claim against any Respondent);

(iv) a response to any procedural statement for the arbitration contained in the Request under Article 1.1(iv), including the Respondent's own statement relating to the arbitral seat, the language(s) of the arbitration, the number of arbitrators, their qualifications and identities and any other procedural matter upon which the parties have already agreed in writing or in respect of which the Respondent makes any proposal under the Arbitration Agreement;

(v) if the Arbitration Agreement (or any other written agreement) howsoever calls for party nomination of arbitrators, the full name, postal address, e-mail address, telephone and facsimile numbers of the Respondent's nominee; and

(vi) confirmation that copies of the Response (including all accompanying documents) have been or are being delivered to all other parties to the arbitration by one or more means of delivery to be identified specifically in such confirmation, to be supported then or as soon as possible thereafter by documentary proof satisfactory to the LCIA Court of actual delivery (including the date of delivery) or, if actual delivery is demonstrated to be impossible to the LCIA Court's satisfaction, sufficient information as to any other effective form of notification.

**2.2** The Response (including all accompanying documents) may be submitted to the Registrar in electronic form (as e-mail attachments) or in paper form or in both forms. If submitted in paper form, the Response shall be submitted in two copies where a sole arbitrator is to be appointed, or, if the parties have agreed or the Respondent proposes that three arbitrators are to be appointed, in four copies.

**2.3** The Respondent may use, but is not required to do so, the standard electronic form available on-line from the LCIA's website for LCIA Responses.

**2.4** Failure to deliver a Response within time shall constitute an irrevocable waiver of that party's opportunity to nominate or propose any arbitral candidate. Failure to deliver any or any part of a Response within time or at all shall not (by itself) preclude the Respondent from denying any claim or from advancing any defence or cross-claim in the arbitration.

**2.5** There may be one or more Respondents (whether or not jointly represented); and in such event, where appropriate, the term "Respondent" shall be so interpreted under the Arbitration Agreement.

**Introduction**

2–001   The Respondent may, but is not required to deliver a written Response to the Request for Arbitration, usually within 28 days of the filing of the Request for Arbitration with the Registrar. Article 2 sets out what the Response should contain and/or be accompanied by, including an indication of any cross-claim. As such, Article 2 provides a useful checklist of the matters to be addressed. As with the Request, there is no particular form which the Response is required to follow. The LCIA now has an online Response form which may be submitted over the internet. However, the use of the form is not compulsory. As long as the information required by Articles 2.1(i)–(vi) is provided, there is no particular form which the Response should follow.

2–002   A Response can be as short as one page, and there is usually no difficulty in filing and delivering it within 28 days.

Article 2 uses mandatory language, requiring a Response to be provided, and stating that a Respondent should confirm or deny "all or part of the claim advanced by the Claimant in the Request". However, Article 2.4 notes that the main potential consequence of failing to provide a Response is the loss of an opportunity to nominate an arbitrator. If the parties had agreed that the Respondent(s) was to nominate a co-arbitrator, but the Respondent did not file any Response, or did not make any nomination (in the Response or separately), the LCIA Court would proceed to appoint the Arbitral Tribunal (without regard to later nominations).[1]

2–003   Failure to send a Response does not preclude the Respondent from denying any claim or from advancing a cross-claim in the arbitration.

---

[1] See Articles 2.4 and 7.2.

Nevertheless, Respondents do generally deliver a Response. This affords an opportunity to influence the tone and course of the proceedings, which should not normally be missed.

Article 2 has changed in a number of respects from its predecessor under the 1998 Rules, in particular in shortening (from 30 to 28 days) the basic time limit for the delivery of the Response and (where relevant) nominating an arbitrator. The time period also now runs from the "Commencement Date" rather than from delivery of the Request to the Respondent. The Commencement Date is when the Request is received by the Registrar and not, necessarily, by the Respondent (although they will usually coincide). This shortening of the period for the Response is potentially mitigated by the newly introduced power of the LCIA Court to extend the time for the delivery of a Response where appropriate,[2] although it is not expected this power will be exercised frequently in practice.

2–004

The LCIA now has an optional, draft, electronic form Response (see Article 2.3 below) available on its website. This is an innovative move that could, in appropriate cases, serve to simplify and reduce the cost of providing a Response for parties (and their advisers) unfamiliar with LCIA arbitration.

**2.1 Within 28 days of the Commencement Date, or such lesser or greater period to be determined by the LCIA Court upon application by any party or upon its own initiative (pursuant to Article 22.5), the Respondent shall deliver to the Registrar a written response to the Request (the "Response"), containing or accompanied by: ...**

Article 2.1 sets out the time within which a Response should be delivered and the matters which should be addressed in it.

2–005

The Response should be delivered to the Registrar within 28 days of the Commencement Date.[3]

As the Commencement Date is when the Registrar receives the Request and not, necessarily, when the Respondent receives it (although this may coincide in practice), the Respondent may have less than 28 days to deliver the Response. However, Article 2.1 permits the LCIA Court to shorten or extend the time for delivery of the Response if appropriate, even if the 28 days provided for have already expired.[4]

2–006

In practice, the most common motivation for seeking an extension of the time limit for serving a Response is likely to be a concern to preserve any contractual right to nominate an arbitrator in the Response, since this is the only right that is irrevocably waived by a party who fails to deliver a Response within the time limit. Accordingly, where the Respondent needs more time (perhaps because it received the Request late), it can now request an extension from the LCIA Court for delivering the Response, together with its nomination of an arbitrator. The

---

[2] See Article 22.5.
[3] This is a shorter period than under the 1998 LCIA Rules, which allowed 30 days from the date of service of the Request on the Respondent, which could potentially be more than 30 days after the date of filing with the Registrar.
[4] See below and Article 22.5.

Claimant may apply to the LCIA Court to shorten the time for filing a Response, pursuant to Article 9A.[5]

(i) **the Respondent's full name and all contact details (including postal address, e-mail address, telephone and facsimile numbers) for the purpose of receiving delivery of all documentation in the arbitration and the same particulars of its legal representatives (if any);**

2–007  Article 2.1(i) requires the Respondent to confirm its contact details (and those of its legal representatives) for the purpose of receiving documents. However, as the enforcement of awards against a party who has not received proper notice of the arbitration proceedings or of the appointment of an arbitrator may be refused under Article V(1)(b) of the New York Convention, in practice the burden initially remains on the Claimant to ensure that the Request is properly delivered and that the contact information contained in it is correct.[6]

As noted above in relation to the Request, the Respondent should take the opportunity to ensure that its registered office address, as well as its contact details, is put on the record. This could become important for it at a later stage. For example, on enforcement of an award (e.g. on a counterclaim and/or for costs), a local court might require that its address as it appears in the award should correspond to the registered office address appearing, for the purposes of identification, on its application to that court. Contact details might be practical for communications in an arbitration but regard also needs to be had to the more formalistic requirements of state courts which might have an involvement at a later stage.

(ii) **confirmation or denial of all or part of the claim advanced by the Claimant in the Request, including the Claimant's invocation of the Arbitration Agreement in support of its claim;**

(iii) **if not full confirmation, a statement briefly summarising the nature and circumstances of the dispute, its estimated monetary amount or value, the transaction(s) at issue and the defence advanced by the Respondent, and also indicating whether any cross-claim will be advanced by the Respondent against any other party to the arbitration (such cross-claim to include any counterclaim against any Claimant and any other cross-claim against any Respondent);**

2–008  The Response is an opportunity to correct any factual errors and answer the allegations made by the Claimant in the Request. It is a chance to "set the record straight" and to narrow or widen the issues to be determined. This goes in hand with the decision whether to make any cross-claims against other parties (the LCIA Rules adopt the term "cross-claim" as encompassing both claims against

---

[5] See 9–006—9–023.
[6] See Article 1.1(i).

the Claimant and any other Respondent). Articles 2.1(ii) and (iii) are therefore considered together.

There is no prescribed form of pleading which Respondents must adopt in the Response, and it will be for each party to decide upon the best approach for the case in hand, having considered, for example, the level of information available to it, the strengths and weakness of a particular case and the likely composition of the Arbitral Tribunal (which will generally not have been constituted at the time of drafting the Response).

Although in some cases bare denials and/or admissions may be appropriate,[7] from the perspective of an Arbitral Tribunal, it is often more helpful if a Respondent answers the allegations contained in the Request with a fuller summary of its position on the issues in dispute. Article 2.1(iii) states that where the Claimant's allegations are contested, the Response should contain a summary of the nature and circumstances of the dispute, including:

2–009

- the amount in dispute;
- the nature of the transactions involved; and
- whether any cross-claims will be advanced.

Article 2.1(ii) also calls for comment on the applicability or otherwise of the Arbitration Agreement invoked by the Claimant as the basis for the jurisdiction of the Arbitral Tribunal. Accordingly, the Respondent should carefully consider whether the claims set out in the Request fall within the scope of the Arbitration Agreement that is relied upon by the Claimant. To the extent possible, any objections to the jurisdiction of the Arbitral Tribunal to be appointed under the Arbitration Agreement should be set out in the Response.[8]

2–010

*Cross-claims*

The Respondent must indicate whether it is advancing any cross-claims against the Claimant and/or any other party. If it does intend to do so, then it should address the same issues as addressed by the Claimant in the Request, namely:

2–011

- the nature and circumstances of the dispute;
- the estimated monetary value of the dispute; and
- the transaction(s) at issue;

as well as setting out the cross-claims themselves.

A Respondent should strive to avoid any unnecessary duplication, whilst effectively using the opportunity briefly to set out its view of the dispute and the issues falling to be determined by the Arbitral Tribunal.

2–012

---

[7] As is the pleading custom in some legal systems.
[8] Under Article 23.3 of the LCIA Rules, any objection to jurisdiction should be made as soon as possible, but no later than in the Statement of Defence (Article 16(2) of the UNCITRAL Model Law is to the same effect).

Where the Respondent intends to elect to have the Response stand as its Defence and (where applicable) cross-claim, pursuant to Article 15.3 of the LCIA Rules, the requirements of that Article should be complied with; in which case a *brief* summary of the nature and circumstances of the dispute is less likely to be sufficient. If the Claimant has filed a Statement of Case with its Request, or has indicated that it intends to elect to have its Request stand as its Statement of Case, there is no obligation on a Respondent to deal with its Defence in the same way: it is open to it to file a brief Response at this stage and to deliver a full Statement of Defence in due course after the appointment of the Arbitral Tribunal.

> (iv) **a response to any procedural statement for the arbitration contained in the Request under Article 1.1(iv), including the Respondent's own statement relating to the arbitral seat, the language(s) of the arbitration, the number of arbitrators, their qualifications and identities and any other procedural matter upon which the parties have already agreed in writing or in respect of which the Respondent makes any proposal under the Arbitration Agreement;**

2–013 Article 2(iv) addresses procedural aspects of the conduct of the arbitration. It calls upon the Respondent to reply to the statements and proposals made in the Request (in relation to the matters set out in Article 1.1(iv)), in respect of which the parties have reached agreement, in relation to which the Claimant has made separate proposals or to make its own proposals. Such matters include:

- the seat of the arbitration;
- the language of the arbitration;
- the number of arbitrators;
- the qualifications of potential arbitrators; and
- any other matters pertaining to the conduct of the arbitration.

2–014 A well-drafted Arbitration Agreement will have addressed these issues and a well-drafted Request for Arbitration might be expected to confirm the relevant details. Similarly, a well-drafted Response should re-confirm, correct any inaccuracies stated in the Request and set out any details omitted.

Equally, where the Arbitration Agreement is silent on any issue that will consequently fall to be decided by the LCIA Court or Arbitral Tribunal (such as the selection and appointment of arbitrators,[9] the number of arbitrators,[10] the seat of the arbitration[11] and the language or primary language of the arbitration where two languages are designated),[12] the Response should contain the Respondent's

---

[9] Articles 5, 7, 8 and 11.
[10] Article 5.
[11] Article 16.
[12] Article 17.

proposals in relation to such matters and any comments the Respondent has on the proposals made by the Claimant in the Request.

Even where the Arbitration Agreement expressly confers certain decisions on the LCIA Court, it is still open to the parties to make submissions and proposals. For example, where the LCIA Court is to select and appoint a sole or presiding arbitrator, the Response is an opportunity for the Respondent to highlight the matters which it considers that the LCIA Court should take into account in making its decision. Such matters might include the nature of the transaction, the nature and circumstances of the dispute and the nationality, location and languages of the parties. 2–015

It is unusual for parties to propose specific individuals, and Article 2.1(iv) is not intended to encourage this. In the absence of a framework for agreeing nominations, proposals made in a Request or Response are sometimes regarded with suspicion by the opposing party and named individuals are automatically objected to. As a general rule, the LCIA Court will not select an arbitrator unilaterally nominated by one party where there has been no prior agreement for nominations: the effect of proposing a candidate in these circumstances will likely be to have that candidate excluded.

On the other hand, it is not unusual for it to be stated in a Request that the parties have agreed on the identity of a sole arbitrator and for the Response to confirm the name. This confirmation is the "Respondent's own statement" relating to the "identity" of the arbitrator for the purposes of Article 2.1(iv). 2–016

Where the LCIA Court has discretion as to the number of arbitrators (usually one or three) the Response should state the wishes of the Respondent and reasons for the position taken, so that the LCIA Court can take them into account.

Equally, where the Arbitration Agreement states that the nominated arbitrators should agree upon the third arbitrator, this should be stated in the Request and confirmed in the Response. Again, it may well be appropriate to indicate any desired qualifications for the third arbitrator and perhaps to propose a method by which a list of candidates could be submitted to the two nominees or to the LCIA Court (e.g. a list of 10, comprising five names from each side, without any indication as to which party had chosen any of the 10 candidates). Article 5.9 provides that the LCIA Court will appoint arbitrators with "due regard for any particular method or criteria of selection agreed in writing by the parties". 2–017

(v) **if the Arbitration Agreement (or any other written agreement) howsoever calls for party nomination of arbitrators, the full name, postal address, e-mail address, telephone and facsimile numbers of the Respondent's nominee; and**

The default position under the LCIA Rules is that the LCIA Court, not the parties, will choose the arbitrator(s). The ability to have a sole arbitrator, in particular, selected and appointed quickly by a neutral body is perceived to be one of the major advantages of LCIA arbitration. 2–018

However, as noted in relation to the Request, the ability to nominate an arbitrator is often viewed by parties as one of the great advantages of international arbitration, and the choice of an arbitrator may significantly impact on the conduct and outcome of the arbitration. It is therefore a decision over which parties and counsel are sometimes inclined to deliberate extensively. Whilst a Respondent might very well take a different view from the Claimant as to the qualities that are required of an arbitrator in any given case, matters such as experience, availability, conflicts of interest, previously expressed views on pertinent legal or procedural matters, and even the personality traits of prospective arbitrators, are often considered. Interviews with prospective arbitrators may also be conducted in an attempt to ascertain such matters and to allow the nominating party to gain a certain measure of the arbitrator to be selected.[13]

2–019 The selection of an arbitrator to nominate can be very quick. Parties and their lawyers will often have candidate arbitrators in mind as soon as they become aware of a dispute and before a Request is filed. Indeed, variations on the LCIA recommended clauses, to introduce procedures for party nominations, are often made precisely because the parties on both sides do have ideas as to particular arbitrators they would like to deal with any dispute.

Once an arbitrator is selected, the Response should identify the name, address, fax number and email address (if known) of the Respondent's nominee. These contact details will be used in due course by the LCIA Secretariat when the nominee is approached for the purposes of appointment under Article 5.

2–020 If the Response does not contain a nomination by the Respondent where there is an agreement that it should do so, the LCIA Court may instead proceed to appoint an arbitrator, without regard to any late nomination.[14]

Finally, although not directly addressed by Article 2.1, the Respondent should also consider whether it wishes to object to the appointment of any arbitrator nominated by the opposing party or to any proposals for the appointment of a sole arbitrator made by the Claimant in the Request. Whilst the right to challenge an arbitrator under the LCIA Rules only arises following the "formation of the Arbitral Tribunal",[15] an objection made by the Respondent to a nominated arbitrator at an earlier stage might lead the Claimant to withdraw the nomination, to the arbitrator withdrawing his consent to the appointment, or indeed to the LCIA Court declining to make the appointment.[16]

> (vi) **confirmation that copies of the Response (including all accompanying documents) have been or are being delivered to all other parties to the arbitration by one or more means of delivery to be identified specifically in such confirmation, to be supported then or as soon as possible thereafter by documentary proof satisfactory to the LCIA Court of actual delivery (including the date of delivery) or, if actual delivery is demonstrated to be impossible to the LCIA Court's satisfaction, sufficient information as to any other effective form of notification.**

---

[13] But see comments at 5–018, 13–004—13–008 and 13–014—13–015 below in relation to the interviewing of prospective arbitrators.
[14] Article 7.2.
[15] Any objection must be made within 14 days of the formation of the Arbitral Tribunal; see Article 10.3.
[16] The LCIA Court may refuse to appoint a nominated arbitrator who fails to comply with the requirements of Article 5.3, including, in particular, those relating to independence and impartiality.

Article 2.1(vi) deals with the delivery of the Response to the relevant parties. It requires the Respondent to deliver the Response and all accompanying documents to all other parties (the Claimant(s) and any other Respondent(s) who are serving a separate Response) as well as to the Registrar.  **2–021**

The Respondent must also confirm to the Registrar the methods by which delivery was effected and, as soon as possible, provide the LCIA Court with proof of actual delivery. If actual delivery is not possible, this fact must be established to "the LCIA Court's satisfaction". This is a new requirement and it is not clear at this time what level of proof the LCIA Court might require, although common sense suggests that copying the Claimant's legal representatives into the covering email to the LCIA Secretariat should suffice.

The wording of Article 2 mirrors that of Article 1, but the provisions of the latter designed to deal with defaulting/non-participating Respondents will usually be inappropriate when a Response comes to be delivered. There have been cases where a Claimant has disappeared within weeks of filing a Request but the Respondent has been quite content not to locate it.

**2.2 The Response (including all accompanying documents) may be submitted to the Registrar in electronic form (as e-mail attachments) or in paper form or in both forms. If submitted in paper form, the Response shall be submitted in two copies where a sole arbitrator is to be appointed, or, if the parties have agreed or the Respondent proposes that three arbitrators are to be appointed, in four copies.**

Article 2.2 provides that the Respondent must deliver the Response (in the required number of copies for the Arbitral Tribunal and LCIA) to the Registrar by email[17] and/or in paper form.  **2–022**

If the Respondent chooses to deliver the Response in paper form, then it must provide:

- two copies where a sole arbitrator is to be appointed; or
- four copies where three arbitrators are (or are proposed) to be appointed.

The additional paper copies provided will be forwarded to the arbitrator(s) by the LCIA when they are appointed.

**2.3 The Respondent may use, but is not required to do so, the standard electronic form available on-line from the LCIA's website for LCIA Responses.**

As with the Request (see 1–024 above) the LCIA now offers an optional service for filing the Response online. If the Respondent chooses to use this service  **2–023**

---

[17] Note, however, that under Article 4.3 delivery of documents by email between the parties is only permitted if expressly agreed upon by the parties or ordered by the Arbitral Tribunal.

(which is not compulsory, whether or not the online service has been used by the Claimant for the Request), the Respondent(s) or its legal representative(s) are required to register an online account and will then have to complete a seven section online form, dealing with the following matters: The details of the parties and their respective legal representatives (Sections A and B); a confirmation or denial of the claims advanced by the Claimant(s) (Section C); if the claim is not fully confirmed, the nature and circumstances of the dispute, its monetary value, and whether the Respondent(s) advances any cross-claims (Section D); procedural agreements and/or proposals and supporting documents (Section E); nomination of an arbitrator (if relevant) (Section F); and confirmation of the delivery of the Response (Section G).

> **2.4 Failure to deliver a Response within time shall constitute an irrevocable waiver of that party's opportunity to nominate or propose any arbitral candidate. Failure to deliver any or any part of a Response within time or at all shall not (by itself) preclude the Respondent from denying any claim or from advancing any defence or cross-claim in the arbitration.**

2–024　Article 2.4 ensures that any failure to provide, or delays in the delivery of, a Response will not prevent the timely constitution of the Arbitral Tribunal or progress of the proceedings,[18] and does not on its own preclude the Respondent from relying on any defence or asserting any cross-claim.

Thus, Article 2.4 creates a significant disincentive for any Respondent considering the postponement of the delivery of a Response as a delay tactic where it has a right to nominate an arbitrator in the Response: failure to send a Response within the time allowed constitutes an irrevocable waiver by the Respondent of its "opportunity"[19] to make the nomination but will not stop the arbitration.

2–025　As the time for the delivery of the Response is measured from the Commencement Date of the arbitration, rather than from the date of receipt by the Respondent(s) of the Request, it is possible that the Respondent might have insufficient time from receiving the Request for delivering a Response and (where the right exists) for nominating an arbitrator. This potential difficulty, which is likely to be rare in practice given the obligation to deliver the Request directly to the Respondent at the same time that it is filed with the Registrar, might be ameliorated by the power of the LCIA Court to extend the time for the delivery of the Response where

---

[18] See also Article 5.1 which states: "The LCIA Court may also proceed with the arbitration notwithstanding that the Request is incomplete or the Response is missing, late or incomplete."
[19] Notably, Article 2.4 refers to an "opportunity" to nominate an arbitrator rather than a "right" to do so, which serves as a reminder to parties that under the LCIA Rules the LCIA Court alone has the right to appoint arbitrators (see Article 5.7). There is no equivalent provision to the effect that a Claimant that fails to nominate an arbitrator in a timely manner (i.e. in the Request) should lose the opportunity to do so. Presumably the drafters assumed that a Claimant would have no incentive *not* to nominate an arbitrator, and that this was in any event less likely to cause delay. In practice, Claimants will occasionally expressly decline to make a nomination, leaving the selection of an arbitrator, on their behalf, to the LCIA Court. Others who simply omit to make a nomination when they have a right to do so will usually be invited to do so by the deadline for the filing of the Response.

appropriate.[20] This is a new provision and it is not clear how such applications for further time for the Response will be dealt with by the LCIA Court. In cases where the Respondent has no right to nominate an arbitrator (because that has not been agreed), the LCIA Court may be more reluctant to extend the deadline for the delivery of the Response because the Respondent's ability to present its case and answer the case made against it need not be prejudiced by the lack of a Response.

The most important potential issue is the preservation of any right to nominate an arbitrator. In practice, Respondents sometimes make any nomination of an arbitrator separately from (or without) submitting any Response. Whilst the language of Article 2.4 could be read as preventing a Respondent from making a nomination of an arbitrator if it does not file a Response, it is doubted that this was the intention, or is the proper interpretation of, the Article. Rather, article 2.4 should be read as potentially waiving any right to nominate where such nomination was to be in the Response but no Response or separate nomination is provided.

2–026 The LCIA's recommended clauses do not include provisions for nominations. When these are added, a timetable for the nominations may be included and it will not necessarily correspond to the timetable under Articles 1 and 2. Sometimes the deadlines can be extraordinarily generous, e.g. three months for the Respondent's nomination. More frequently they are tighter, e.g. 14 days from delivery of the Request. Parties are free to agree or vary timetables at any time, including after the filing of the Request.

It should be borne in mind, in cases with a London seat, that the default timetable under the English Arbitration Act 1996 requires the Respondent's appointment of an arbitrator to be made within 14 days of the service of a request by the Claimant.[21] The LCIA's much longer period for a nomination has been described by certain commercial arbitrators in London as "leisurely" and "stately". It has surprised some London practitioners that the opportunity was not taken in the 2014 Rules to bring the LCIA's timetable in line with the speedier ad hoc timetable under the English Arbitration Act 1996, bearing in mind the improvements in communications technology and the criticisms levelled at international arbitration over the speed of proceedings.

2–027 There will, of course, be cases in which the interests at stake, and such matters as security and confidentiality concerns, will dictate a longer timetable for selecting appropriate arbitrators. However, in ordinary commercial arbitrations, practitioners should note that 28 days will be seen, in many quarters, as more than enough time for filing a Response and nominating an arbitrator. Very good reasons can be expected to be required to obtain an extension of time for a Response in the absence of an agreement with the Claimant.

**2.5 There may be one or more Respondents (whether or not jointly represented); and in such event, where appropriate, the term "Respondent" shall be so interpreted under the Arbitration Agreement.**

---

[20] See below and Article 22.5.
[21] Section 16(5)(a) of the English Arbitration Act 1996.

**2-028** In some cases, the Claimant(s) may commence arbitration against a number of Respondents. This typically, but not exclusively, occurs in disputes arising in connection with multi-party contracts or a suite of related contracts. Often the interests of such Respondents will coincide, but in some cases their interests will not be aligned in all respects (or at all) and independent cross-claims might also be advanced between them. Article 2.5 recognises the possibility of multiple Respondents and provides that in such cases references to the Respondent in the LCIA Rules should be read as a reference to all the Respondents.

**Saving provision**

**2-029** For the reasons explained above, full compliance with the provisions of Article 2 and the utilisation of the Response for advocacy purposes are usually to be recommended. However, Article 5.1 of the LCIA Rules contains a saving provision which permits the LCIA Court to proceed with the formation of the Arbitral Tribunal and the arbitration even where the "Response is missing, late or incomplete...".

Article 5.1 does not distinguish between matters that are fundamentally required, so that the Response is regarded as effective, and those which may be left incomplete. Nevertheless, Respondents should generally deliver a fully articulated Response (within the context explained above) and be aware that, under Article 5.1, where required information is unavailable the arbitration will nevertheless continue.

## Article 3—LCIA Court and Registrar

**3.1 The functions of the LCIA Court under the Arbitration Agreement shall be performed in its name by the President of the LCIA Court (or any of its Vice-Presidents, Honorary Vice-Presidents or former Vice-Presidents) or by a division of three or more members of the LCIA Court appointed by its President or any Vice-President (the "LCIA Court").**

**3.2 The functions of the Registrar under the Arbitration Agreement shall be performed under the supervision of the LCIA Court by the Registrar or any deputy Registrar.**

**3.3 All communications in the arbitration to the LCIA Court from any party, arbitrator or expert to the Arbitral Tribunal shall be addressed to the Registrar.**

**Introduction**

Article 3 deals with administrative arrangements pertaining to the functions of the LCIA Court and Registrar. Their general functions are set out in the Constitution of the LCIA Court and are discussed in the Introduction at Part I above. Those that are relevant to arbitrations under the LCIA Rules, in particular, are outlined below.

The text of Article 3 is based on the 1998 edition of the LCIA Rules, but expands the class of people who may act in the name of the LCIA Court if the President is unavailable. In line with the new definition in the Preamble, it refers to the functions of the LCIA Court and Registrar under the "Arbitration Agreement" rather than, as previously, the LCIA Rules. This change makes it clearer that the LCIA Court and Registrar are operating under the regime contractually agreed by the parties, whereby their arbitration will be administered by the LCIA under the supervision of its Court.

3–001

**3.1 The functions of the LCIA Court under the Arbitration Agreement shall be performed in its name by the President of the LCIA Court (or any of its Vice-Presidents, Honorary Vice-Presidents or former Vice-Presidents) or by a division of three or more members of the LCIA Court appointed by its President or any Vice-President (the "LCIA Court").**

Article 3.1 provides for the delegation of the functions of the LCIA Court to the President or a Vice President of the Court (or former Presidents, known as Honorary Vice Presidents[1] or former Vice Presidents, or (in particular, in

3–002

---

[1] Article B.3 of the Constitution of the LCIA Court (Appendix 3).

the case of challenges to arbitrators) to a "Division" of three or more members of the LCIA Court. The functions of the LCIA Court under the Rules include:

- determining applications for shortening or extending the time for the delivery of the Response—Article 2.1;

- appointments and replacements of arbitrators and Arbitral Tribunals—Articles 5, 7, 8, 9 and 11;

- determining applications for expedited formation of an Arbitral Tribunal—Article 9A;

- determining applications for the appointment of an Emergency Arbitrator—Article 9B;

- revocation of arbitral appointments—Articles 10 and 12.3;

- in circumstances where the parties have agreed that the arbitration should be conducted in two or more languages, determining which shall be the "initial" language of the arbitration—Article 17;

- abridging or extending periods of time—Article 22.5;

- consolidating two or more arbitrations—Article 22.6;

- directing the parties in relation to the payments of deposits on costs—Article 24;

- transmitting final awards to the parties—Article 26.7;

- determining the Arbitration Costs—Article 28; and

- deciding whether to continue the arbitral proceedings in the event of a challenge or appeal by a party to a national court—Article 29.2.

3–003 The exercise of the functions of the LCIA Court in practice is considered in greater detail in the commentary to the relevant Articles of the Rules.

As a general rule, though, the administrative decisions which are taken in the exercise of the functions listed above will be taken by the President or a Vice President acting alone. An exception is the hearing of challenges (Article 10), which may be submitted to a Division.

Except in relation to the appointment of Emergency Arbitrators[2] there is no set timetable or schedule for such decision-making. The Registrar, or other member of the LCIA Secretariat, under the Registrar's supervision, will contact the President or a Vice President (usually by email) as soon as a matter is ready to be referred. It is users' experience that a quick response can normally be expected from the LCIA Court.

The pool of available LCIA Court officers was extended in 2011, by an amendment to the Constitution, to include former Vice Presidents. This was done in order to make the formation of Challenge Divisions easier, reducing the incidence

---

[2] See Article 9.6 and the commentary at 9–035 below.

of conflicts and ensuring that experienced LCIA practitioners could be appointed to chair Divisions.

## 3.2 The functions of the Registrar under the Arbitration Agreement shall be performed under the supervision of the LCIA Court by the Registrar or any deputy Registrar.

Article 3.2 provides for the supervision by the LCIA Court of the performance of the Registrar's functions and the delegation of those functions to a Deputy Registrar. 3–004

According to the Constitution, the functions of the Registrar and Deputy Registrars are (a) to carry out in the name of the LCIA Court such day-to-day operations of the Court and administrative functions as are required under the Rules, and (b) to service the Court and any division of the Court.

In practice, the Registrar is responsible for the administration of all LCIA arbitrations, from acknowledging and processing the filing of a Request for Arbitration, through the appointment of the Arbitral Tribunal by the President or a Vice President of the Court, to the delivery of an award at the conclusion of the proceedings. In the early days of the modern LCIA, many of the tasks required by the 1985 and 1998 Rules were performed directly by the Registrar himself on all cases. The growth of the LCIA's caseload in recent years has been such that a Deputy Registrar has been appointed, together with several Counsel.[3] The day-to-day handling of cases is often delegated to the Deputy Registrar and/or to one of the Counsel. Fundholding and accounting matters on cases are dealt with by casework administrators and accounting staff. 3–005

In a typical LCIA arbitration, the Registrar should receive and review the Request (Article 1) and might then arrange for the Deputy Registrar or Counsel to acknowledge it and to take charge of the case. The Registrar will be consulted when the Arbitral Tribunal is to be selected (Article 5), which is usually the first point at which the LCIA Court, in the person of the President or a Vice President, will be informed of the arbitration. The Notice of Appointment, attaching the Form of Appointment, signed by the President or a Vice President, will usually be signed by the Registrar. The Notice or a subsequent email will contain a direction for a deposit (Article 24), as to which the Registrar has delegated authority up to standard limits set from time to time by the LCIA Court. 3–006

During the course of the proceedings, a casework administrator will keep an eye on the funds deposited and will liaise with the arbitrators, the assigned Counsel, and the Registrar in relation to deposits and in relation to the dossier which will be submitted to the President or a Vice President at the conclusion of the arbitration for the purposes of the Court's determination of the Arbitration Costs (Article 28). At the end of the proceedings, the Registrar or Deputy Registrar will sign the LCIA's stamps on the copies of the award and will sign the letter under which the award is sent to the parties (Article 26).

---

[3] The number of Arbitral Tribunals appointed by the LCIA rose from 88 in 2007 to 220 in 2009, subsequently settling at annual totals between 151 (2011) and 174 (2013): see the Director General's and Registrar's Reports for those years.

3–007　The Registrar, together with the Secretariat, is thus involved in the administration of each and every arbitration submitted to the LCIA and in the communications with the Arbitral Tribunal and with the LCIA Court. These functions require a high level of expertise and hands-on case management.

However, the functions assumed by the Registrar in practice are often even more involved. As the drafter of the 1998 and a co-drafter of the 2014 editions of the LCIA Rules noted,[4] in an article introducing the 1998 edition:

> "... the informal contact between the LCIA Registrar and the parties [in relation to the nomination and appointment of arbitrators] can work effectively to oil the wheels of the arbitral machinery, which are of course absent from an ad hoc arbitration."

3–008　He continued:

> "All questions of competence and procedure are decided by the tribunal, in default of the parties' agreement. Nonetheless, the LCIA Registrar performs a hugely important informal role; and the parties' legal representatives are not in practice slow to inform him of what may be going wrong with an LCIA arbitration."

3–009　In addition to the formal responsibilities, the Registrar has assisted parties and Arbitral Tribunals with the delivery of documents, questions relating to procedure, information regarding accepted practices, the administration of proceedings, the organisation of hearings and a wide range of other requests and queries.

Thus the LCIA Registrar provides users with a highly valued informal interface between the parties, the arbitrators and the LCIA Court. The user-friendly yet professional approach adopted by the Registrar in dealings with the parties provides a valuable service to parties of varying experience in the conduct of international arbitration proceedings, and is regarded by many as a major benefit of selecting the LCIA as an administering arbitral institution.

### 3.3 All communications in the arbitration to the LCIA Court from any party, arbitrator or expert to the Arbitral Tribunal shall be addressed to the Registrar.

3–010　Article 3.3 clarifies that communications with the LCIA Court (for example, in relation to the challenge of an arbitrator or for the abridgement or extension of any time period) are to be made through the Registrar.

---

[4] V.V. Veeder, "London Court of International Arbitration – The New 1998 LCIA Rules" in A.J. van den Berg (ed.), *Yearbook of Commercial Arbitration* (Kluwer, 1998), Vol.XXIII, pp.366–368.

## Article 4—Written Communications and Periods of Time

4.1 Any written communication by the LCIA Court, the Registrar or any party may be delivered personally or by registered postal or courier service or (subject to Article 4.3) by facsimile, e-mail or any other electronic means of telecommunication that provides a record of its transmission, or in any other manner ordered by the Arbitral Tribunal.

4.2 Unless otherwise ordered by the Arbitral Tribunal, if an address has been agreed or designated by a party for the purpose of receiving any communication in regard to the Arbitration Agreement or (in the absence of such agreement or designation) has been regularly used in the parties' previous dealings, any written communication (including the Request and Response) may be delivered to such party at that address, and if so delivered, shall be treated as having been received by such party.

4.3 Delivery by electronic means (including e-mail and facsimile) may only be effected to an address agreed or designated by the receiving party for that purpose or ordered by the Arbitral Tribunal.

4.4 For the purpose of determining the commencement of any time-limit, a written communication shall be treated as having been received by a party on the day it is delivered or, in the case of electronic means, transmitted in accordance with Articles 4.1 to 4.3 (such time to be determined by reference to the recipient's time-zone).

4.5 For the purpose of determining compliance with a time-limit, a written communication shall be treated as having been sent by a party if made or transmitted in accordance with Articles 4.1 to 4.3 prior to or on the date of the expiration of the time-limit.

4.6 For the purpose of calculating a period of time, such period shall begin to run on the day following the day when a written communication is received by the addressee. If the last day of such period is an official holiday or non-business day at the place of that addressee (or the place of the party against whom the calculation of time applies), the period shall be extended until the first business day which follows that last day. Official holidays and non-business days occurring during the running of the period of time shall be included in calculating that period.

## Introduction

**4–001** Article 4 deals with two related issues: the delivery of written communications (Articles 4.1–4.3) and the calculation of periods of time for their delivery.

Article 4 underwent a number of cosmetic and substantive changes in the 2014 edition of the LCIA Rules. The power of the Arbitral Tribunal to extend or truncate time limits was removed and is now dealt with in Article 22.[1] In addition, there has been a move away from the "last known address" rule to a focus on addresses that have been regularly used by the parties.

**4–002** Although relatively mundane, these provisions are of significant importance, particularly for the Claimant in relation to delivery of the Request for Arbitration, when the parties are likely to be less amenable to reaching agreement on procedural matters, and when any applicable limitation period might be near to expiry.

It should be noted that Article 4 does not mention "service" of documents. Articles 1 and 2 of the 1998 edition of the Rules had required that the Request for Arbitration and the Response, respectively, be "served", but the Rules did not specify what constituted "service". This lacuna has been corrected in the 2014 edition by eliminating any suggestion, in the Rules, that any particular formalities must be followed before notices or documents are deemed "delivered" under the Rules. This is a welcome amendment but, as noted below, local courts, in which enforcement or remedies are sought, may have more stringent requirements linked to their own notions of service of judicial proceedings.

**4–003** After an Arbitral Tribunal is constituted, it may establish modes and channels of communication that are suitable for the particular circumstances of the case.[2] Before then, however, Article 4 provides rules to which the parties should adhere, so as to ensure that any limitation period is respected, in order to avoid unnecessary arguments over delivery, and so as to ensure that the enforceability of the award is not jeopardised because proper notice was not given of the Request or of the appointment of the Arbitral Tribunal by the LCIA Court.

Unless and until the Arbitral Tribunal has made other directions, the provisions of Article 4 will apply to all written communications in the arbitration, regardless of their procedural significance.

Article 4 should be read alongside Article 13, headed "Communications between Parties and Arbitral Tribunal", which contains provisions relating to the involvement of the LCIA Secretariat in such communications and the need to copy the Secretariat in.

*Relationship with national laws*

**4–004** National arbitration laws generally contain provisions that govern the service or delivery of written communications relating to arbitration proceedings. Generally, such provisions only apply in the absence of other agreement between the parties.[3]

---

[1] See Article 22.1(ii) ('Power of the tribunal') and Article 22.5, which empowers the LCIA Court to extend or truncate time limits.
[2] See Article 13.
[3] See, for example, Article 3 of the UNCITRAL Model Law (Appendix 10) and s.76 of the English Arbitration Act 1996 (Appendix 7).

Thus in many jurisdictions, the first effect of Articles 4.1–4.3 of the LCIA Rules is to displace the default arrangement contained in national arbitration laws in relation to the service or delivery of communications.[4]

Nevertheless, attention must still be paid to the provisions of any relevant mandatory laws relating to the service or delivery of documents in arbitral proceedings, both in the place of arbitration and (if known) in potential enforcement jurisdictions. Failure to comply with any relevant mandatory laws in relation to the service of the Request or of the Notice of Appointment of the Arbitral Tribunal could result in the proceedings being deemed not to have been properly commenced; and/or constitute a ground for resisting the enforcement of the award under the New York Convention.[5]

**4.1 Any written communication by the LCIA Court, the Registrar or any party may be delivered personally or by registered postal or courier service or (subject to Article 4.3) by facsimile, e-mail or any other electronic means of telecommunication that provides a record of its transmission, or in any other manner ordered by the Arbitral Tribunal.**

*Scope*

Article 4.1 concerns written communications by the LCIA Court, the Registrar or any of the parties in the course of an LCIA arbitration. Significantly, communications falling within this article include the Request for Arbitration and Response, which unlike under some other arbitration rules, must be delivered by the parties and not by the administering institution.[6] Compliance with Article 4 with regard to the Request for Arbitration is of added importance, because failure to give "proper notice" of the commencement of the arbitration proceedings could render an award unenforceable under Article V(1)(b) of the New York Convention.

4–005

*Modes of delivery*

Article 4.1 prescribes the acceptable modes of delivery. Of the traditional methods, by hand delivery, and by "registered postal or courier service", are expressly permitted. Electronic methods of communication are only permitted subject to Article 4.3 (which in summary requires there to be an agreed or designated address for electronic communications). These methods may include facsimile, e-mail "or any other electronic means of telecommunication that

4–006

---

[4] In many civil law jurisdictions, "service" is an exclusively judicial function carried out by officers of the court or of the ministry of justice. "Service" in the English sense, as set out in s.76 of the English Arbitration Act 1996 (Appendix 7), which even allows service by ordinary post, would be regarded as mere delivery in those jurisdictions.
[5] Article V(1)(b) (Appendix 9). See also Article 36(1)(ii) of the UNCITRAL Model Law (Appendix 10).
[6] By contrast, under Articles 4.5 and 5.4 of the ICC Rules, the ICC Secretariat is charged with serving the Request for Arbitration as well as the Answer on the opposing parties.

provides a record of its transmission". This proviso was clearly intended to capture new, perhaps yet undeveloped, methods of communications.[7]

However, the emphasis on the sender's ability to prove "transmission" rather than *receipt* might fall short of the service or notification requirements in some jurisdictions, in which proof of delivery may be required.[8] Because the decision as to whether a communication was properly served or delivered may fall to an enforcement court in another jurisdiction, parties will be well advised to deliver all important communications in accordance with the laws of the place where they are delivered, having additional regard to the laws of any known potential enforcement jurisdictions, and in hard copy in addition to any copies transmitted electronically.

4–007 Parties should likewise, and for the same reasons, inform the LCIA if there is a particular method of delivery, e.g. courier service (with a signature to acknowledge receipt), which they would like to see used. Unless such a request is made, the Registrar might send the Notice of Appointment of the Arbitral Tribunal, for example, to the parties by fax and/or email only, which in some jurisdictions may not be deemed "proper" notice for the purposes of Article V(1)(b) of the New York Convention 1958.

The final proviso of Article 4.1 recognises that, once constituted, the Arbitral Tribunal might establish other methods for written communications.[9] Parties should take the opportunity of a case management hearing and/or of the first procedural order to make any appropriate suggestions to the Arbitral Tribunal as to methods of communication and delivery of certain notices and documents.

In practice, the Secretariat's own communications with the parties and their representatives are likely to be by email. The first letter to the parties acknowledging the filing of a Request for Arbitration will generally be sent in hard copy by courier as well, but subsequent communications might not be sent in hard copy and few might be on the LCIA's headed paper. As noted above, it is up to the parties to inform the Secretariat if they would like other methods of communication used.

> **4.2 Unless otherwise ordered by the Arbitral Tribunal, if an address has been agreed or designated by a party for the purpose of receiving any communication in regard to the Arbitration Agreement or (in the absence of such agreement or designation) has been regularly used in the parties' previous dealings, any written communication (including the Request and Response) may be delivered to such party at that address, and if so delivered, shall be treated as having been received by such party.**

---

[7] An arguably more flexible provision was adopted by s.76(3) of the English Arbitration Act 1996, which in the absence of alternative agreement by the parties permits service of documents "on a person by any effective means" (Appendix 7).

[8] As, for example, do the default provisions of the UNCITRAL Model Law in Article 3.1(a) (which does not apply where the parties have agreed alternative procedures), under which proof of delivery or attempted delivery is required (Appendix 10).

[9] See Article 13.

*Address for delivery of communications*

Article 4.2 provides rules regarding the place or address at which communications may be delivered under the Rules. Unless ordered otherwise by the Arbitral Tribunal (and certainly prior to its constitution), delivery may be effected on: 4–008

- the address agreed or designated for service of notices in relation to the Arbitration Agreement (for example, in a "Notices" clause in the underlying agreement in which the Arbitration Agreement is contained); or
- if no such agreement was concluded or designation made, then to the address that has been used regularly by the parties in their previous dealings.

Communications delivered to such addresses, including the Request for Arbitration and Response, are deemed to have been received under Article 4.2 of the LCIA Rules.

Article 4.2 represents a departure from the position under the 1998 edition of the LCIA Rules, which referred to the "last known residence or place of business". 4–009

In contrast to Article 3 of the UNCITRAL Model Law, which places the burden on the party delivering the notice to make reasonable enquiries as to the current address of the party to whom delivery is being made, under Article 4.2 the burden is on the party who changes its address from one regularly used in previous dealings to notify the other parties to the Arbitration Agreement, the Arbitral Tribunal and the LCIA Secretariat of its new address for the receipt of written communications.

**4.3 Delivery by electronic means (including e-mail and facsimile) may only be effected to an address agreed or designated by the receiving party for that purpose or ordered by the Arbitral Tribunal.**

Article 4.3 states that delivery by electronic means is only valid if made to an address agreed or designated by the receiving parties, or ordered by the Arbitral Tribunal. 4–010

The fact that the parties have regularly used email or facsimile communications in their dealings prior to the arbitration is not relevant, unless the email address or facsimile number were specifically agreed or designated as an address for the delivery of documents by the receiving party, or the Arbitral Tribunal orders that it may be used.

In cases in which the parties have not had regular communications in the past, a general email address for the Respondent might be identified, e.g. from its website. Typically, such an address would be of an "info@xyz.com" type. Emails sent to such addresses might not be picked up on a daily basis. The addresses might no longer be in use. Before providing such email addresses to the LCIA, parties should make enquiries about them and should consider whether any particular email address can be said to have been "designated".

**Time periods**

Articles 4.4–4.6 deal with the calculation of time periods and compliance with time limits. The prevalent practice amongst Arbitral Tribunals of setting time 4–011 periods by reference to specified calendar dates will, in many cases, render these provisions largely redundant; but they remain important in all cases in relation to the steps taken prior to the constitution of the Arbitral Tribunal, for example, following the receipt of the Request for Arbitration by the Registrar.

> **4.4** For the purpose of determining the commencement of any time-limit, a written communication shall be treated as having been received by a party on the day it is delivered or, in the case of electronic means, transmitted in accordance with Articles 4.1 to 4.3 (such time to be determined by reference to the recipient's time-zone).
>
> **4.5** For the purpose of determining compliance with a time-limit, a written communication shall be treated as having been sent by a party if made or transmitted in accordance with Articles 4.1 to 4.3 prior to or on the date of the expiration of the time-limit.
>
> **4.6** For the purpose of calculating a period of time, such period shall begin to run on the day following the day when a written communication is received by the addressee. If the last day of such period is an official holiday or non-business day at the place of that addressee (or the place of the party against whom the calculation of time applies), the period shall be extended until the first business day which follows that last day. Official holidays and non-business days occurring during the running of the period of time shall be included in calculating that period.

**4–012** Article 4.4 and the first proviso of Article 4.6 provide rules for determining the date on which the counting of a time period commences.

Article 4.5 and the second and third sentences of Article 4.6 set rules for determining when a time period concludes and whether it has been met by the party required to abide by it.

These provisions relate back to the rules for delivery of written communications provided for in Articles 4.1–4.3. It is convenient to consider their effect together, out of strict numerical order.

*Commencement of time periods*

**4–013** Article 4.4 provides that for the purpose of determining when a time period commences, a communication is deemed to have been received:

- on the day on which it was delivered, if delivered personally or by registered post or by courier service; or
- on the day it was transmitted (according to the recipient's time zone) if sent by electronic means.

The first sentence of Article 4.6 provides that the counting of any time period commences on the day after the day on which the communication triggering the time period was deemed to have been received.

*End of/compliance with time period*

The rest of Article 4.6 provides that if a time period ends on a non-business day or official holiday at the place of business of the addressee or of the party against whom the calculation of time applies (i.e. the party itself, rather than the person to whom the communication is sent), the period shall be extended until the next working day.[10] However, non-business days and holidays occurring in the course of the time period are counted as normal days.

Article 4.5 provides that a written communication will be treated as having been sent if "made or transmitted" (in accordance with Articles 4.1–4.3) on or before the day on which the time period expires. This provision applies equally to post and courier as it does to electronic means of transmission.

4–014

*Illustrations*

The combined effect of these provisions is conveniently illustrated by reference to an example based on Article 15 of the LCIA Rules (the default timetable for delivery of written statements). Article 15.3 requires a Respondent to serve a Statement of Defence within 28 days of the receipt of the Claimant's Statement of Case.
Thus:

4–015

- if a Statement of Case is sent by courier on March 1;
- is delivered on the following day, namely March 2;
- the 28-day time period for the delivery of the Statement of Defence commences on March 3;
- the Statement of Defence must be delivered or transmitted electronically by the Respondent on or before March 30, i.e. 28 days counted from (and including) March 3; save that
- if March 30 falls on a weekend or is a public holiday at the place of business of the Respondent (or its legal representative), the Statement of Defence could be delivered or transmitted on the next working day.

On the other hand:

4–016

- if electronic means are permitted and the Statement of Case is sent by electronic means on March 1;
- the 28-day time period for the delivery of the Statement of Defence under Article 15.3 would commence on March 2;

---

[10] Thus, whilst the time for the delivery of the Response under Article 2.1 is within 28 days of receipt by the Registrar of the Request for Arbitration, so that the Registrar is the "addressee" of the Request under Article 1.1, if there is a national holiday at the place of business of the Respondent the deadline for the Response will still be extended.

- the Statement of Defence must be delivered or transmitted on or before March 29 (i.e. 28 days later, counting from the day after the Statement of Case was transmitted); save that

- if March 29 falls on a weekend or is a public holiday at the place of business of the Respondent (or its legal representative), the Statement of Defence could be delivered or transmitted on the next working day.

ARTICLE 5—FORMATION OF ARBITRAL TRIBUNAL

5.1 The formation of the Arbitral Tribunal by the LCIA Court shall not be impeded by any controversy between the parties relating to the sufficiency of the Request or the Response. The LCIA Court may also proceed with the arbitration notwithstanding that the Request is incomplete or the Response is missing, late or incomplete.

5.2 The expression the "Arbitral Tribunal" includes a sole arbitrator or all the arbitrators where more than one.

5.3 All arbitrators shall be and remain at all times impartial and independent of the parties; and none shall act in the arbitration as advocate for or representative of any party. No arbitrator shall advise any party on the parties' dispute or the outcome of the arbitration.

5.4 Before appointment by the LCIA Court, each arbitral candidate shall furnish to the Registrar (upon the latter's request) a brief written summary of his or her qualifications and professional positions (past and present); the candidate shall also agree in writing fee-rates conforming to the Schedule of Costs; the candidate shall sign a written declaration stating: (i) whether there are any circumstances currently known to the candidate which are likely to give rise in the mind of any party to any justifiable doubts as to his or her impartiality or independence and, if so, specifying in full such circumstances in the declaration; and (ii) whether the candidate is ready, willing and able to devote sufficient time, diligence and industry to ensure the expeditious and efficient conduct of the arbitration. The candidate shall furnish promptly such agreement and declaration to the Registrar.

5.5 If appointed, each arbitral candidate shall thereby assume a continuing duty as an arbitrator, until the arbitration is finally concluded, forthwith to disclose in writing any circumstances becoming known to that arbitrator after the date of his or her written declaration (under Article 5.4) which are likely to give rise in the mind of any party to any justifiable doubts as to his or her impartiality or independence, to be delivered to the LCIA Court, any other members of the Arbitral Tribunal and all parties in the arbitration.

5.6 The LCIA Court shall appoint the Arbitral Tribunal promptly after receipt by the Registrar of the Response or, if no Response is received, after 35 days from the Commencement Date (or such other lesser or greater period to be determined by the LCIA Court pursuant to Article 22.5).

5.7 No party or third person may appoint any arbitrator under the Arbitration Agreement: the LCIA Court alone is empowered to appoint arbitrators (albeit taking into account any written agreement or joint nomination by the parties).

5.8 A sole arbitrator shall be appointed unless the parties have agreed in writing otherwise or if the LCIA Court determines that in the circumstances a three-member tribunal is appropriate (or, exceptionally, more than three).

5.9 The LCIA Court shall appoint arbitrators with due regard for any particular method or criteria of selection agreed in writing by the parties. The LCIA Court shall also take into account the transaction(s) at issue, the nature and circumstances of the dispute, its monetary amount or value, the location and languages of the parties, the number of parties and all other factors which it may consider relevant in the circumstances.

5.10 The President of the LCIA Court shall only be eligible to be appointed as an arbitrator if the parties agree in writing to nominate him or her as the sole or presiding arbitrator; and the Vice Presidents of the LCIA Court and the Chairman of the LCIA Board of Directors (the latter being ex officio a member of the LCIA Court) shall only be eligible to be appointed as arbitrators if nominated in writing by a party or parties – provided that no such nominee shall have taken or shall take thereafter any part in any function of the LCIA Court or LCIA relating to such arbitration.

## Introduction

5–001  Article 5 sets the basic framework for the constitution of an LCIA Arbitral Tribunal. It is closely related to, and should be read together with, Articles 6 through to 11, which provide for particular aspects of the process.

These provisions, including the primacy of the LCIA Court's selection and appointment of a sole arbitrator and its power to veto nominations of the parties under Article 5.4, are hallmarks of LCIA arbitration. The new "Emergency Arbitrator" procedure introduced in Articles 9.4–9.14 is bound to attract significant interest and could bring about a change in the manner in which parties engage in LCIA arbitrations.

5–002  The effective and supervised process of forming the Arbitral Tribunal is central to parties' choice of institutional arbitration over an ad hoc or statutory process. In an ad hoc arbitration, a recalcitrant Respondent might, by refusing to participate in the process of appointing an Arbitral Tribunal, be able to delay the arbitral process to a far greater extent than if the parties had chosen institutional arbitration. The Claimant's ability to constitute an ad hoc or statutory Tribunal where the Respondent refuses to comply with the contractual process will depend on the efficiency of the legal framework and courts of the place or seat of the arbitration.[1] Where the parties have chosen to arbitrate under the UNCITRAL Arbitration Rules, the default appointment procedures could also be complex.[2]

The potential for difficulties under such procedures stands in stark contrast to the regime under Article 5 of the Rules and with the procedures available under Article 9 for the expedited formation of the Arbitral Tribunal and for the appointment of an Emergency Arbitrator.

Article 5 confirms that the LCIA Court alone is empowered to appoint arbitrators, a principle which is central to LCIA arbitration. Parties may agree to nominate arbitrators for appointment[3] but the primary procedure consists in the selection and appointment of the Arbitral Tribunal by the LCIA Court. Around one half of Arbitral Tribunals in LCIA arbitrations comprise a sole arbitrator, who is usually chosen by the LCIA Court, not the parties.[4]

5–003

Article 5 has undergone a noticeable degree of editorial revision from the 1998 version. This includes re-organising the sub-paragraphs in a (largely) more coherent order and reformulation of some of the language. By and large, however, the substance of the provisions remains unchanged.

### 5.1 The formation of the Arbitral Tribunal by the LCIA Court shall not be impeded by any controversy between the parties relating to the sufficiency of the Request or the Response. The LCIA Court may also proceed with the arbitration notwithstanding that the Request is incomplete or the Response is missing, late or incomplete.

Article 5.1[5] provides that claims by either party that the Request or Response are defective or lacking in some respects will not delay the appointment of an Arbitral Tribunal in the arbitration. It expressly empowers the LCIA Court to proceed with the formation of the Arbitral Tribunal even where (a) the Request is incomplete, or (b) the Response is either missing, late, or incomplete.

5–004

Thus difficulties or delays resulting from the Claimant's failure fully to appreciate the requirements of Article 1, or the Respondent's failure to comply in full or in part with Article 2, are avoided. In light of this provision, the risk to a Respondent who seeks to rely on such arguments in order to delay or avoid submitting a Response is that by doing so he may, pursuant to Article 2.4, lose any right he might have had to nominate an arbitrator. On the other hand, it would be

---

[1] See Article 11.4 of the UNCITRAL Model Law (Appendix 10). See also s.18 of the English Arbitration Act 1996, which allows the court upon the application of a party: (a) to give directions as to the making of any necessary appointments; (b) to direct that the Tribunal shall be constituted by such appointments (or any one or more of them) as have been made; (c) to revoke any appointments already made; (d) to make any necessary appointments itself (Appendix 7). Another example is s.11 of the Indian Arbitration and Conciliation Act 1996, by which default appointments are entrusted to the Chief Justice of India or any person or institution designated by him.

[2] Under Article 6 of the UNCITRAL Rules, where the parties have failed to designate an appointing authority, it will be designated by the Secretary-General of the Permanent Court of Arbitration in The Hague (Appendix 11).

[3] Article 7.

[4] In 2013, 46% of Arbitral Tribunals comprised a sole arbitrator, but in 2012 the proportion was 54%.

[5] The current text is new but Article 5.4 of the 1998 version dealt substantively with the concerns now addressed in Article 5.1.

open to such a Respondent to raise any genuine objections to jurisdiction before the Arbitral Tribunal itself (once constituted), in accordance with Article 23.3.

Arguments about issues foreshadowed in the Request and Response, such as jurisdiction, the validity of the contract, standing, the sufficiency of pre-arbitration attempts at settlement, and the nature of relief claimed, will all be matters which can be referred to the Arbitral Tribunal.[6] It is pointless to seek to engage the LCIA Secretariat or LCIA Court in such controversies before the Arbitral Tribunal has been appointed.

### 5.2 The expression "the Arbitral Tribunal" includes a sole arbitrator or all the arbitrators where more than one.

5–005  Article 5.2 clarifies that references in Article 5, as well as in the LCIA Rules generally, to the "Arbitral Tribunal" include references to a sole arbitrator as well as a panel of arbitrators. Elsewhere in the LCIA Rules, and in the case of a panel of arbitrators, the term "Arbitral Tribunal" is used to refer to all members of the panel together, whereas the terms "presiding arbitrator" or "remaining arbitrators"[7] are used when it is necessary to distinguish between the individual members of a panel.

The 1998 version of Article 5.1 concluded with another rule of construction, that references in those Rules to an arbitrator included the masculine and feminine and that references to other officers of the LCIA should be similarly understood. That stipulation is now found at the foot of the Index to the Rules.[8]

### 5.3 All arbitrators shall be and remain at all times impartial and independent of the parties; and none shall act in the arbitration as advocate for or representative of any party. No arbitrator shall advise any party on the parties' dispute or the outcome of the arbitration.

5–006  Article 5.3 is directed primarily at the arbitrators and states the basic requirements of an LCIA arbitrator, namely that the arbitrator shall:

(a) be and remain impartial and independent of the parties;

(b) not act in the arbitration as an advocate of any party; and

(c) not advise either party on the merits or outcome of the dispute, either before or after the appointment.

Although directed at arbitrators, the obligations set out in this article bind the parties as well. Thus, in principle at least, the article imposes standards from which parties who choose to arbitrate under the LCIA Rules cannot derogate by

---

[6] Article 23 confirms that the Arbitral Tribunal will decide issues relating to its jurisdiction or authority.
[7] See, for example, Articles 5.10 and 12.1 respectively.
[8] See Appendix 1.

agreement. Although of earlier origin,[9] Article 5.3 is similar in that respect to s.33 of the English Arbitration Act 1996 which imposes a mandatory duty on the Tribunal (not the parties) to act fairly and impartially as between the parties. Commenting on the apparent conflict between that obligation and the principle of party autonomy, the DAC Report explains that the parties should be "free to agree upon anything to do with the arbitration, subject only to such safeguards as are necessary in the public interest."[10] Although not concerned with the public interest per se, by imposing duties on the arbitrators, Article 5.3 nevertheless prevents parties from agreeing to deviate from standards set by the LCIA Rules.[11]

Article 5.3 is concerned with the formation of the Arbitral Tribunal. Nevertheless, the lower standard for challenges to arbitrators applicable under Article 10.1[12] and the related decisions of the LCIA Court are likely to offer parties better guidance as to the viability of any contemplated arbitral nomination.[13] Any temptation to nominate an arbitrator who might not comply with these standards should be avoided, even if the nomination is consented to by all parties.[14]

5–007

The appointment of an arbitrator who does not comply with, or conduct himself in accordance with, the standards of Article 5.3 could provide a ground for challenging the award as well as grounds for challenging the appointment as arbitrator itself. If such an arbitrator is a member of a panel of three arbitrators, he will likely find that his influence in the course of deliberations is diminished even if his appointment is not formally challenged.

The specific standards set out in Article 5.3 are considered below.

*(a) To be and remain impartial and independent*

The arbitrator's duty to be and remain impartial and independent is widely acknowledged as "a fundamental and universally recognised principle of international arbitration"[15] and as a "fundamental principle in mainstream international commercial arbitration".[16] Indeed, as already noted,[17] the duty, which continues throughout the term of the reference, meets the internationally accepted standard propounded by Article 12 of the UNCITRAL Model Law, and is comparable with the rules of all other major international arbitration institutions.[18] It is stricter than

5–008

---

[9] Article 3.1 of the 1985 Rules was substantially the same.
[10] Departmental Advisory Committee on Arbitration Law, Report on the Arbitration Bill (February 1996) para.155 (Appendix 8).
[11] Under Article 5.5, the LCIA Court alone appoints arbitrators and, under Article 10, has powers to oversee compliance with these standards.
[12] Whether "circumstances exist that give rise to justifiable doubts" in relation to the arbitrator's impartiality and independence.
[13] See para.10–016 et seq. below.
[14] See *Weissfisch v Julius and Ors* [2006] EWCA Civ 218: protracted litigation arising from an agreement to appoint an arbitrator who had previously acted as a solicitor for each of the parties.
[15] Julian D.M. Lew et al., *Comparative International Commercial Arbitration* (The Hague: Kluwer Law International, 2003), p.256, para.11–4, citing Article 6 of the European Convention on Human Rights and Article 10 of the Universal Declaration of Human Rights.
[16] Alan Redfern et al., *Law and Practice of International Commercial Arbitration*, 4th edn (London: Sweet & Maxwell, 2004), p.236, para.4–52.
[17] Part I, 1–131 above.
[18] Even the ICC Rules, which historically required arbitrators only to remain "independent of the parties involved in the arbitration", because independence could be verified objectively, now adopts the standard formula of impartiality and independence.

the requirements of the English Arbitration Act 1996, which makes no reference to lack of independence as a ground for removing an arbitrator in s.24; nor is independence listed as one of the duties of the arbitrator in s.33(1), which requires arbitrators to act "fairly and impartially" as between the parties, even if in substance there is no difference at all.[19]

Various attempts have been made to define the duty of impartiality and independence, some of which are gaining acceptance in the international arbitration community including, in some cases, by Divisions of the LCIA Court. Thus, for example, Fouchard, Gaillard and Goldman define impartiality of an arbitrator as amounting to "the absence of risk of bias on the part of the arbitrator towards one of the parties",[20] a statement that was adopted by a Division of the LCIA Court in at least one challenge decision.[21]

**5–009** The work of the Arbitration Committee of the International Bar Association (IBA) is of particular note.[22] In recent years the IBA has produced two non-binding codes touching upon the arbitrator's duties of impartiality and independence. Article 1 of the 1987 Rules of Ethics for International Commercial Arbitrators ("Rules of Ethics") frames the duty as a requirement "to be and remain free from bias". Article 3.1 elaborates:

> "The criteria for assessing questions relating to bias are impartiality and independence. Partiality arises when an arbitrator favours one of the parties, or where he is prejudiced in relation to the subject-matter of the dispute. Dependence arises from relationships between an arbitrator and one of the parties, or with someone closely connected with one of the parties."

---

[19] The intention of the English legislator was stated at paras 100–104 of the Departmental Advisory Committee's Report (see fn.10 above), which conclude with the statement: "We should emphasize that we intend to lose nothing of significance by omitting reference to independence". And see many commentators to the same effect, for example, Lord Steyn, "England: The Independence and/or Impartiality of Arbitrators in International Commercial Arbitration", "Independence of Arbitrators" special supplement (2007) *ICC International Court of Arbitration Bulletin*; finally, see the analysis of the LCIA Court Division in LCIA Reference No. 81160, August 28, 2009 (2011) 27(3) Arbitration Int. 442 at para.3.5 citing V.V. Veeder QC, "England", in supplement 23, *International Handbook on Commercial Arbitration* (Kluwer Law International, 1997), p.27, to the effect that the wording of the Act only excluded non-biased dependence and that dependence could still constitute evidence of bias, or the appearance of bias.

[20] Emmanuel Gaillard and John Savage (eds), *Fouchard Gaillard Goldman on International Commercial Arbitration* (Kluwer Law International, 1999), p.566, para.1033.

[21] LCIA Reference No. 5660, August 5, 2005 (2011) 27(3) Arbitration Int. 371.

[22] The work of the IBA's Arbitration Committee is continuously gaining recognition and acceptance in the eyes of international arbitration practitioners. Arbitrators do in practice refer to its work in considering whether or not to accept appointments; and practitioners increasingly refer to the Code of Ethics and Guidelines in challenge submissions to the LCIA Court. Although not accepted as binding by the LCIA, both the Guidelines and Code of Ethics have been considered in some of the recent challenge decisions of the LCIA Court Divisions, e.g: LCIA Reference No. 81224, March 15, 2010 (2011) 27(3) Arbitration Int. 461 at para.3.6; LCIA Reference No. 81160, August 28, 2009 (2011) 27(3) Arbitration Int. 442 at para.3.6, citing United States Court of Appeals, Ninth Circuit, *New Regency Productions Inc v Nippon Herald Films Inc* CA(CAL.), 2007; *Cour d'Appel de Bruxelles, 17èmme Chambre, République de Pologne c. Eureko BV et Schwebel Stefen M*, RG No. 2007/AR/70; Swedish Supreme Court, Judgment of November 19, 2007, *Anders Jilken v Ericsson AB*, Case No. T 2448-06; and LCIA Reference No. UN7949, December 12, 2007 (2011) 27(3) Arbitration Int. 420 at para.3.4.

The IBA's subsequent much vaunted Guidelines on Conflicts of Interest in  5–010
International Arbitration (the "IBA Guidelines")[23] consider the practical aspects of
the arbitrator's obligations. The IBA Guidelines propose that an arbitrator must not
serve if he has *any* doubts as to his ability to be and remain impartial and independent, or in circumstances where an objective and informed person would conclude
that "there is a likelihood that the arbitrator may be influenced by factors other than
the merits of the case as presented by the parties in reaching his or her decision".[24]

The IBA Guidelines state that justifiable doubts as to an arbitrator's independence (and therefore his impartiality) necessarily arise where there is "an identity"
between a party and the arbitrator, if the arbitrator is a manager or director of a
legal entity that is a party in the arbitration, if the arbitrator has a significant financial or personal interest in the matter at stake, or if the arbitrator or his or her firm
regularly advises the party.[25]

The General Standards of the IBA Guidelines are supplemented by three[26] lists  5–011
of examples of situations which may be regarded as giving rise to questions
concerning the independence, and in some cases the impartiality, of an arbitrator.
The colour-coded lists (Red, Orange and Green) provide an indication of the
committee's views as to whether a particular relationship or set of circumstances
gives rise to: insurmountable concerns (Non-Waivable Red List); or whether a
potential conflict of interest could be cured by a disclosure to and an express
waiver by the parties (Waivable Red List); or the need for the disclosure to see if
any party objects (Orange List); or whether the arbitrator may freely accept an
appointment (Green List).[27]

The IBA Guidelines have not been endorsed by the LCIA but have been considered useful by Divisions of the LCIA Court, which have considered challenges to
arbitrators.[28] Common themes that can be gleaned from the above definitions
suggest that the Article 5.3 duty would require an arbitrator to be able, throughout
the conduct of the reference, to consider the arguments presented by each party
without having formed any prior opinion as to the merits of the particular case, or
of the arguments of any of the parties; and to be able to exercise his own independent judgement, free of external pressures or financial or other personal
interest in the outcome of the arbitration.

---

[23] These IBA Guidelines were first published in 2004 and have just been revised at the time of going to press. A copy of the 2014 IBA Guidelines appears at Appendix 13. Paragraph 8 of the introduction to the 2014 IBA Guidelines provides that the Guidelines "supersede the *Rules of Ethics* as to the matters treated here". The primary concern of the IBA Guidelines is with the duty of arbitrators to disclose to the parties circumstances that could in their eyes give rise to justifiable doubts as to the impartiality or independence of the arbitrator, which is narrower than the scope of the Rules of Ethics. Nevertheless, and although not relevant for the purposes of this work, it should be noted that the IBA Guidelines do to an extent at least replace the Rules of Ethics as the IBA's most recent view on the duty of impartiality and independence.

[24] IBA Guidelines, General Standard 2(c) (Appendix 13). It is submitted that the proviso "as presented by the parties" was not intended to limit the arbitrator's ability to bring his own expertise to bear by, for example, raising issues for the consideration of, and comment by, the parties, but highlights the inappropriateness of coming to a case with preconceived notions without regard to the submissions of the parties.

[25] IBA Guidelines, Non-Waivable Red List (Appendix 13).

[26] Note that the Red List is subdivided into a "Non-Waivable" Red List and a "Waivable" Red List.

[27] See discussion under Article 9 below.

[28] For example, the abstract of the decision in Arbitration No. 81160, August 28, 2009 (2011) 27(3) Arbitration Int. 449.

*Impartiality and independence*

5–012   It is often said that whilst the impartiality of an arbitrator is a question of his subjective state of mind, his dependence arises from a relationship between the arbitrator and one of the parties, and is therefore capable of objective measurement.[29] Independence is therefore believed by some to be the only true measure of an arbitrator's impartiality.[30] Some influential authors have suggested that the requirements of impartiality and independence have blurred in recent years, and that the distinction between them no longer serves any practical purpose.[31] With the inclusion of the "lack of impartiality" as a ground for challenging arbitrators in the ICC Arbitration Rules 2012[32] it might be hoped that the importance of the distinction will indeed diminish.

Nevertheless, although the "concepts of independence and objective impartiality are closely linked",[33] references in the LCIA Rules to impartiality "or" independence,[34] and other references in the Rules to the duty of impartiality alone,[35] suggest that at least in the context of LCIA arbitration, a distinction between the terms remains. Indeed, Lew, Mistelis and Kröll explain the utility of the distinction in the following terms:

> "While impartiality is needed to ensure that justice is done, independence is needed to ensure that justice is seen to be done."[36]

5–013   The decision of the Division of the LCIA Court in LCIA Reference No. 1303[37] provides a practical illustration of the distinction. A sole arbitrator was challenged on the grounds of lack of independence because the Respondent and he were members of the same professional organisation. The arbitrator reacted to the challenge in strong terms, claiming that the challenging party's lawyer was acting maliciously and that the challenge was "fictitious, false and malevolent". The Division rejected the challenge based on the arbitrator's alleged lack of independence, but upheld the challenge because the arbitrator's reaction to the challenge did give rise to justifiable doubts as to his impartiality.

One Division of the LCIA Court, deciding a challenge under the UNCITRAL Arbitration Rules,[38] adopted the following explanation of the distinction from Alan Redfern et al.:

---

[29] It is understood that this was the reason why the ICC adopted the standard of independence from the parties as the appropriate test for the challenge of an arbitrator.

[30] See, for example, Dominique Hascher, "A Comparison between the Independence of State Justice and the Independence of Arbitration", "Independence of Arbitrators" special supplement (2007) *ICC International Court of Arbitration Bulletin* 83.

[31] Redfern et al. (2004), p.238, para.4–54.

[32] ICC Arbitration Rules 2012, Article 14(1). In previous versions of the Rules, lack of impartiality was not an expressly stated ground for challenges, although lack of independence was regarded in practice as covering the same grounds.

[33] *Findlay v the UK,* Case No. 110/1995/616/706 (1997) 24 E.H.R.R. 221.

[34] See Articles 5.4 (duty of disclosure); 7.1 (grounds upon which the LCIA Court may decline to appoint a party-nominated arbitrator); and 10.2 (grounds for challenging the appointment of an arbitrator). A similar distinction is repeated in Article 11.1.

[35] See, for example, Article 14.

[36] Lew et al., *Comparative International Commercial Arbitration* (2003), p.261, para.11–19.

[37] (2011) 27(3) 342.

[38] LCIA Case No. UN 7949, at para.77 (available at *http://italaw.com/sites/default/files/case-documents/italaw1171.pdf* [Accessed November 5, 2014]).

"[i]t is generally considered that 'dependence' is concerned exclusively with questions arising out of the relationship between an arbitrator and one of the parties, whether financial or otherwise. This is considered to be susceptible to an objective test, because it has nothing to do with an arbitrator's (or prospective arbitrator's) mind. [. . .] By contrast the concept of 'impartiality' is considered to be connected with actual or apparent bias of an arbitrator – either in favour of one of the parties or in relation to the issues in dispute. Impartiality is thus a subjective and more abstract concept than independence, in that it involves primarily a state of mind".[39]

Another Division, deciding a challenge under the LCIA Rules, held in a well–reasoned decision that:  5–014

"3.8 . . . the test of independence was an objective one, in that it was a test for the appearance of bias, not for its actual presence; noting that independence required that 'there should be no such actual or past dependent relationship between the parties and the arbitrators which may or at least may appear to affect the arbitrator's freedom of judgment'."

Impartiality, however, was subjective in nature, implying a test not for the appearance of bias, but for its actual presence, to be inferred from the facts and circumstances surrounding the arbitrator's exercise of his arbitral functions. As the same authors had put it:  5–015

"Impartiality requires that an arbitrator neither favours one party nor is predisposed as to the question in dispute. Insofar as it is a state of mind it is a fairly abstract and subjective standard."[40]

Challenges to arbitrators made to the LCIA Court also reflect the distinction in other ways, with some challenges being based solely on allegations of lack of impartiality,[41] others solely on an alleged lack of independence[42] and some citing both as grounds.  5–016

Accordingly, it is not enough for an LCIA arbitrator to satisfy himself that he is impartial as between the parties, he must also satisfy himself, and be able to demonstrate to the parties and LCIA Court, that he is independent. Parties nominating arbitrators should also continue to bear both standards in mind.

---

[39] Redfern et al., *Law and Practice of International Commercial Arbitration* (2004), para.4–55.
[40] LCIA Reference No. 81160, August 28, 2009 (2011) 27(3) Arbitration Int. 442. Citing M. Scott Donahey, "The Independence and Neutrality of Arbitrators" in (1992) 9(4) J. Int. Arb. 31; Lew et al., *Comparative International Commercial Arbitration* (2003), pp.258, 261.
[41] See, for example, LCIA Court decisions dated: October 1, 2002 LCIA Reference No. 1291 (challenge based on the conduct of proceedings by the Chairman); August 5, 2005 LCIA Reference No. 5660 (challenge based on an alleged predisposition of the arbitrator towards Middle Eastern culture); and June 16, 2008 LCIA Reference No. 81007/81008/81024/81025 (challenge based on dissenting opinion of the arbitrator relating to an interim award).
[42] See, for example, LCIA Court decisions dated: May 29, 1996 LCIA Reference No. UN96/X15, 27(3) Arbitration Int. (the challenge in an UNCITRAL arbitration was based on the arbitrator's law firm's relationship with one of the parties and its involvement in the disputed transaction); June 5, 1997 LCIA Reference No. UN97/X11 (the arbitrator was challenged because one party's barrister was from the same set of chambers); October 23, 1997 LCIA Reference No. WO97/X27 (the arbitrator had previously been appointed in unrelated proceedings as expert witness by a party's solicitors); and September 30, 1998 LCIA Reference No. 8086 (challenge to an arbitrator based on nationality), 27(3) Arbitration Int.

*(b) No arbitrator shall act in the arbitration as advocate for any party*

5–017  The second duty expressly articulated in Article 5.2 requires arbitrators not to act in the arbitration as an advocate for any party. To many civil law lawyers this statement might seem rather obvious, but in the common law context the obligation does serve to clarify that the practice, customary in some arbitration fora,[43] of party-appointed arbitrators advocating the case of the party appointing them, is unacceptable in the context of LCIA arbitration.

*(c) No arbitrator, whether before or after appointment, shall advise either party on the merits or outcome of the dispute.*

5–018  This final requirement of Article 5.2 deals with another aspect of the requirement of independence and impartiality. It clarifies that, having advised on the merits of the dispute, an arbitrator will no longer be considered to be impartial or independent. The rule, which will appear self-evident to many, might have particular relevance in jurisdictions with a split legal profession. In such jurisdictions (such as England) members of the bar might in certain respects be considered to be independent of a party, even if they have provided it with a legal opinion concerning a dispute.

The rule might also be relevant to the conduct of arbitrator interviews. The practice of parties interviewing prospective arbitrators prior to nomination or appointment is not prohibited by the LCIA Rules and continues to gain acceptance and support in the arbitration community as allowing parties to maintain a level of confidence in the arbitral process.[44] Nevertheless, concerns have been expressed about the practice and possible scope for abuse, leading the Practice and Standards Committee of the Chartered Institute of Arbitrators to publish a Practice Guideline on interviewing prospective arbitrators.[45] The Chartered Institute Guidelines provide:

"(9) The following may not be discussed either directly or indirectly:

(i) the specific circumstances or facts giving rise to the dispute

(ii) the positions or arguments of the parties

---

[43] For example, in certain shipping and commodities arbitrations in England and in other jurisdictions (e.g. traditionally in the US) in other domestic arbitrations. For background on such practices see Murray L. Smith, "Impartiality of the Party-Appointed Arbitrator" (1990) 6(4) Arbitration Int. 320; Jacques Covo, "Commodities, Arbitrations and Equitable Considerations" (1993) 9(1) Arbitration Int. 57. In 2004, the AAA/ABA Code of Ethics for Arbitrators in Commercial Disputes adopted a presumption that all arbitrators appointed under its rules would be "neutral", with special considerations applicable to cases where the arbitrators were to be "non-neutral". On the history of US practice and the effect of the 2004 change see Ben Sheppard Jr, "A New Era of Arbitrator Ethics for the United States: The 2004 Revision to the AAA/ABA Code of Ethics for Arbitrators in Commercial Disputes" (2005) 21(1) Arbitration Int. 91.

[44] R. Doak Bishop, Lucy Reed, "Practical Guidelines for Interviewing, Selecting and Challenging Party-Appointed Arbitrators in International Commercial Arbitration" (1998) 14(4) Arbitration Int. 395; and see LCIA Reference No. UN96/X15, Decision Rendered May 29, 1996, (2011) 27(3) Arbitration Int. 317, in which the LCIA Court held that a pre-appointment interview for a role as partner at the Respondent's law firm did not give rise to justifiable doubts as to impartiality or independence.

[45] Chartered Institute of Arbitrators, Practice and Standards Committee, Arbitration Sub-Committee, Practice Guideline 16: The Interviewing of Prospective Arbitrators.

(iii) the merits of the case."

The 2004 American Bar Association's Code of Ethics for Arbitrators in Commercial Disputes[46] states:

5–019

"When the appointment of a prospective arbitrator is being considered, the prospective arbitrator ... should not permit [the parties] to discuss the merits of the case."

The LCIA has (quite sensibly) not developed special rules concerning the conduct of arbitrator interviews, but the final proviso in Article 5.3 of the LCIA Rules has the effect of limiting discussion of the merits of the case with prospective arbitrators during the interview process.

5–020

The final words of Article 5.3 state that arbitrators must not advise the parties on the outcome of the dispute. Whilst it might appear unlikely that an arbitrator would do so, in one LCIA case an arbitrator was successfully challenged after revealing the outcome of the arbitration to the party that appointed him prior to the publication of the award.[47]

**5.4 Before appointment by the LCIA Court, each arbitral candidate shall furnish to the Registrar (upon the latter's request) a brief written summary of his or her qualifications and professional positions (past and present); the candidate shall also agree in writing fee-rates conforming to the Schedule of Costs; the candidate shall sign a written declaration stating: (i) whether there are any circumstances currently known to the candidate which are likely to give rise in the mind of any party to any justifiable doubts as to his or her impartiality or independence and, if so, specifying in full such circumstances in the declaration; and (ii) whether the candidate is ready, willing and able to devote sufficient time, diligence and industry to ensure the expeditious and efficient conduct of the arbitration. The candidate shall furnish promptly such agreement and declaration to the Registrar.**

Article 5.4 is, like Article 5.3, directed predominantly at the arbitrators not the parties. It requires the arbitrator to provide to the Registrar information concerning his Curriculum Vitae (CV), his fees, his independence and impartiality, and his availability to devote the required time and care to ensure that the proceedings are progressed expeditiously.

5–021

In practice, following the nomination of an arbitrator by a party, or his selection by the LCIA Court, the LCIA Secretariat, acting through the Registrar, Deputy Registrar or one of its Counsel, will write an appointment letter to the prospective arbitrator requesting him to confirm that he is willing and able to serve. The appointment letter contains a brief summary of the nature of the dispute, normally distilled from the Claimant's Request for Arbitration and the Response, if filed, which are attached to the letter. The letter also sets out the text of the Arbitration

---

[46] Canon III para.B(1)(b).
[47] LCIA Reference No. 0252, July 1, 2002 (2011) 27(3) Arbitration Int. 351.

Agreement and the governing law clause (where applicable) and provides the prospective arbitrator with confirmation of the number of arbitrators and of the seat of the arbitration.

5–022   The letter reminds the arbitrator that if he accepts the appointment he must abide by the LCIA's fee scale,[48] and requests him to:

- indicate how much he intends to charge in the particular dispute;
- provide a copy of his résumé (unless already held by the LCIA); and
- return a signed copy of the Statement of Independence and Consent to Appointment, attached to the letter.

*Fees*

5–023   The fees of LCIA arbitrators are calculated by reference to the time actually spent working on the matter. That contrasts with the ad valorem fees charged by a number of other arbitral institutions, such as the ICC.[49]

The current fee scale adopted by the LCIA permits arbitrators to charge no more than £450 (pounds sterling) per hour.[50] In practice, even this maximum is lower than the hourly rates of many well–regarded arbitration lawyers, particularly those affiliated with international law firms or barristers' chambers. As a result, in many cases, arbitrators do seek to adopt the highest permissible fee rate. However, arbitrators who do so in relatively low value claims may be approached by the LCIA with requests to reduce their hourly rate and, in practice, experience does not suggest that parties have been driven to nominate "cheaper" (but perhaps less experienced) arbitrators in their cases. The LCIA Court will propose an appropriate maximum rate when approving a nomination or selecting arbitrators.

*Résumé and Statement of Impartiality and Independence*

5–024   Article 5.4 requires a prospective arbitrator to provide the LCIA Court with a brief written summary of his or her qualifications and professional positions, which in most cases is provided in the form of a résumé, or CV. A copy of the CV will be attached to the Notice of Appointment of the Arbitral Tribunal, which is sent to the parties with the Form of Appointment signed by the President or Vice President of the LCIA Court.[51] In communicating arbitrators' CVs to the parties, the Registrar historically performed an information-providing function, which is largely irrelevant in an era when parties are able to download arbitrators' CVs from the internet.

CVs can vary enormously in length. Academics and lawyers with academic inclinations will sometimes include lists of published articles which can extend to

---

[48] The fee scale is set out in the Schedule of Arbitration Costs. See the commentary on the Schedule of Arbitration Costs in Part II at p.337 and Appendix 2. At the time of writing, the applicable maximum is £450.
[49] SIAC, SCC, Swiss Chambers, DIAC and others, see Louis Flannery and Benjamin Garel, "Arbitration Costs Compared: The Sequel" (2013) G.A.R.
[50] Section 2(i), Schedule of Arbitration Costs, Appendix 2 and *http://www.lcia.org/Dispute_Resolution_Services/schedule-of-costs-lcia-arbitration.aspx* [Accessed November 5, 2014].
[51] See the commentary on Article 3 above and on Article 5.6 below.

several pages, a practice which is disliked by some commercial parties expecting arbitrators instead to demonstrate an understanding of their business and its practices. On the other hand, retired English judges, for example, sometimes use CVs as short as half a page.

The requirement to provide a summary of "qualifications" is new in the 2014 Rules. No particular, formal, qualifications are, in fact, required of arbitrators in LCIA arbitrations. Nor are there any specific criteria for entry on the LCIA's database of arbitrators.  **5–025**

As noted below in relation to Article 18, there is a new assumption in the 2014 Rules that lawyers will represent parties in LCIA arbitrations. It would be unfortunate if the requirement to list qualifications was seen as a requirement for arbitrators to be legally qualified too. The LCIA's database includes engineers, surveyors and accountants who act as arbitrators.

The candidate arbitrator must also sign "a declaration to the effect that there are no circumstances known to him likely to give rise in the mind of any party to any justified doubts as to his impartiality or independence, other than any circumstances disclosed by him in the declaration."  **5–026**

In practice, each prospective arbitrator is required to sign a Statement of Independence and Consent to Appointment[52] attached to the appointment letter sent to him by the LCIA. The statement contains five sections:

(a) a formal consent to the appointment in the arbitration;

(b) an undertaking to act in accordance with the LCIA Rules applicable to the arbitration;

(c) a declaration of impartiality and independence;

(d) an express agreement to assume a continuing duty to disclose any circumstances that are likely to cast doubt in the mind of the parties over the arbitrator's impartiality or independence; and[53]

(e) an express confirmation of their willingness and ability to devote sufficient time, diligence and effort in order to progress the matter expeditiously.

Points (a) and (b) are self-explanatory. Any prospective arbitrator may decline to accept a nomination by a party or an invitation from the LCIA Court. The most common reasons for declining are a perceived conflict of interest with one of the parties and, less frequently, unavailability. Where an arbitrator consents to being appointed by the LCIA Court, the undertaking to act in accordance with the LCIA Rules naturally follows. Should the arbitrator fail to do so the proceedings would be open to jurisdictional and other challenges.[54]  **5–027**

Points (c) and (d) reflect the arbitrator's disclosure requirement in Articles 5.4 and 5.5 in respect of current and future potential conflicts of interest, and the corresponding requirement in Article 7.1 of the Rules that every nominated

---

[52] For the text of declarations, see 5–028 and 5–029 below.
[53] See Article 5.5 below.
[54] A deliberate failure to comply with this undertaking also constitutes a ground for the revocation of the appointment under Article 10.2 of the LCIA Rules.

arbitrator must comply with the requirements of Articles 5.3–5.5 prior to appointment by the LCIA Court.

5–028   The arbitrator's declaration form, which is attached to the appointment letter, provides two options: Statement A or Statement B. "Statement A", by which the arbitrator declares that he has no conflict of interest and is free to accept the appointment, provides as follows:

> "Statement A: I am impartial, and independent of each of the parties, and I intend to remain so, and there are no circumstances known to me likely to give rise to any justified doubts as to my impartiality or independence."

5–029   "Statement B", on the other hand, is used when the arbitrator considers that, whilst in his view he is able to serve as an independent and impartial arbitrator, circumstances nevertheless exist which should be brought to the attention of the LCIA Court and the parties because they are *"likely* to give rise to justified doubts" as to his impartiality and independence. Statement B provides as follows:

> "Statement B: I am impartial, and independent of each of the parties, and intend to remain so, but I wish to disclose certain circumstances for the consideration of the LCIA Court prior to my appointment, whether or not any such circumstance is likely to give rise to any justified doubts as to my impartiality or independence (use separate sheet). Other than such circumstances here disclosed by me, there are no circumstances known to me likely to give rise to any justified doubts as to my impartiality or independence."

5–030   The duty to disclose potential conflicts of interest is also provided for in all other significant international arbitration rules, and has even been adopted into at least one national arbitration law.[55] It is recognised in the literature[56] and judicially[57] for its importance for the integrity of the arbitral process.

The information provided in the arbitrator's résumé and/or disclosure will inform the parties of the arbitrator's background and any relationships he may have with the parties or their advisers. The rationale for providing such information is to enable the LCIA Court to assess the suitability of the candidate.[58] The parties are also able in the light of such information to determine whether they wish to challenge an appointment or waive any objections if invited to make any prior to an appointment.

---

[55] Article 11 of the UNCITRAL Rules (Appendix 11); Articles 11.2–11.3 of the ICC Arbitration Rules; Article 7 of the AAA International Rules. Section 9 of the Swedish Arbitration Act 1999, which provides that a "person who is asked to accept an appointment as arbitrator shall immediately disclose all circumstances which, pursuant to sections 7 or 8, might be considered to prevent him from serving as arbitrator", represents the exception rather than the rule.

[56] For example, Karel Daele, *Challenge and Disqualification of Arbitrators in International Arbitration* (Kluwer Law International, 2012), Ch.1, and the references there; Gary B. Born, *International Arbitration: Law and Practice* (Amsterdam, Kluwer Law International, 2012), pp.132–133, and the references there.

[57] For example, *A v B* [2011] EWHC 2345 (Comm).

[58] Pursuant to Article 7.1, the LCIA Court will only appoint a party-nominated arbitrator if the arbitrator has complied with Article 5.3. Even if he has complied, the LCIA Court retains the discretion not to appoint an unsuitable arbitrator. See 7–007 below.

The duty of every arbitral candidate and arbitrator to make a disclosure under  5–031
Articles 5.4 and 5.5 of any matter likely to give rise in the minds of any party to
any justifiable doubts as to the arbitrator's impartiality and independence arises in
relation to circumstances that would not necessarily constitute grounds for a
successful challenge under Article 10.3 of the LCIA Rules.[59] As the commentary
on the IBA Guidelines on Conflicts of Interest 2014 explains in relation to their
own "General Standards":

> "(a) The arbitrator's duty to disclose under General Standard 3(a) rests on the principle that the parties have an interest in being fully informed of any facts or circumstances that may be relevant in their view. Accordingly, General Standard 3(d) provides that any doubt as to whether certain facts or circumstances should be disclosed should be resolved in favour of disclosure. ... As reflected in General Standard 3(c), a disclosure does not imply that the disclosed facts are such as to disqualify the arbitrator under General Standard 2. The duty of disclosure under General Standard 3(a) is ongoing in nature."[60]

From time to time parties have sought to challenge an arbitrator, or to annul  5–032
an award, due to an arbitrator's failure to make full disclosure of past or
existing circumstances concerning his relationship with one of the parties.
However, whilst the LCIA Rules do contemplate the revocation of an arbitrator's
appointment for the *deliberate* breach of the LCIA Rules,[61] it appears to be
settled that an inadvertent failure to disclose circumstances that do not impeach
the arbitrator's independence or impartiality (even if they might have been or
were *likely to* have given rise to justified doubts), should not form the basis for the
revocation of an appointment or a successful challenge to an arbitrator[62] or to an
award.[63]

Questions can and often do arise as to whether circumstances exist that
are likely to give rise to justified doubts as to the arbitrator's independence or

---

[59] One of the grounds for challenging an arbitrator under Article 10.1 of the Rules is that "circumstances *exist* that *give rise* to justifiable doubts" as to his impartiality or independence, whereas the arbitrator's duty to disclose arises where the circumstances exist that "*are* likely *to give rise* in the mind of any party *to justified doubts*" etc. However, in *A v B* [2011] EWHC 2345 (Comm) at [88], Flaux J held: "...Article 5.3 [of the LCIA Rules 1998] is imposing an obligation on the arbitrator to disclose circumstances likely to give rise to any justified doubts as to his impartiality or independence, that is only an obligation to disclose matters which amount to apparent bias i.e. where there is a 'real possibility'. Whilst arbitrators may indeed make wider disclosure out of caution, they are under no obligation to do so...". Further, the IBA Guidelines Waivable Red and Orange lists both contemplate that parties may waive certain circumstances that would otherwise give rise to justifiable doubts as to the arbitrator's impartiality and independence, and do not require disclosure of Green List circumstances that do not give rise to a conflict.
[60] IBA Guidelines on Conflicts of Interest in International Arbitration 2014, "Explanation to General Standard 3", para.(a), Appendix 13.
[61] See Article 10.2.
[62] See *AT&T Corp v Saudi Cable Co* [2000] EWCA Civ 154; LCIA Reference No. 81160, August 28, 2009 (2011) 27(3) Arbitration Int. 442, where the LCIA Court Division held that although the absence of disclosure or incomplete disclosure did not, as such, constitute sufficient grounds for removal, such failures may in some cases be taken into account in assessing whether there is apparent bias.
[63] *Société Tecnimont SpA v J&P Avax SA* (Paris Court of Appeal, February 12, 2009), RG 07/164; although the position in the US is less clear, see Mark Kantor, "Arbitrator Disclosure: An Active But Unsettled Year" (2008) 11 Int. A.L.R. 20.

impartiality. Whilst the legal test for independence and impartiality is objective,[64] the arbitrator is required to exercise his personal or "subjective" judgement in relation to the extent of his obligation to disclose particular circumstances or a particular relationship. There can be little doubt that different views as to whether a given set of circumstances give rise to justified or justifiable doubts can be honestly maintained by different individual arbitrators and parties.

5–033   Recognising that arbitrators are "often unsure about the scope of their disclosure obligations",[65] and aiming to increase consistency and reduce unnecessary challenges, the IBA Guidelines provide General Standards with Explanations to the Standards, as well as three lists of situations (red, orange and green) which in the view of the IBA's Conflicts of Interest Subcommittee do or do not trigger the disclosure obligation. Whilst not strictly binding, and not specifically endorsed by the LCIA, the Guidelines have been successful in creating a widely accepted point of reference for practitioners from different jurisdictions and are referred to in practice by arbitral institutions, arbitrators and practitioners alike. The three lists of circumstances are considered below:

The first list, referred to as the "Red List", is split into two parts, the "Non-Waivable Red List" and the "Waivable Red List". The former sets out four circumstances in which the IBA recommends that a potential arbitrator should always decline an appointment:

- There is an identity between a party and the arbitrator, or the arbitrator is a legal representative or employee of an entity that is a party in the arbitration.

- The arbitrator is a manager, director or member of the supervisory board, or has a controlling influence on one of the parties or an entity that has a direct economic interest in the award to be rendered in the arbitration.

- The arbitrator has a significant financial interest in one of the parties, or the outcome of the case.

- The arbitrator or his or her firm regularly advises the party, or an affiliate of the party, and the arbitrator or his or her firm derive a significant financial income therefrom.

5–034 The Waivable Red List includes circumstances that are serious, and in respect of which the Guidelines consider that disclosure is compulsory, but in which the arbitrator could serve if the parties, having been appraised of the relevant facts, "expressly state" that they have no objection. For example:

- The arbitrator has given legal advice, or provided an expert opinion, on the dispute to a party or an affiliate of one of the parties. The arbitrator had a prior involvement in the dispute.

---

[64] See 10–014 below.
[65] IBA Guidelines, Introduction (Appendix 13).

- The arbitrator holds shares, either directly or indirectly, in one of the parties (or an affiliate), being privately held.

- A close family member of the arbitrator has a significant financial or personal interest in one of the parties (or an affiliate) or has a significant financial interest in the outcome of the dispute.

- The arbitrator currently represents or advises one of the parties (or an affiliate) or the lawyer or law firm acting as counsel for one of the parties.

- The arbitrator is a lawyer in the same law firm as the counsel to one of the parties.

- The arbitrator's law firm had a previous but terminated involvement in the case without the arbitrator being involved himself or herself, or currently has a significant commercial relationship with one of the parties (or an affiliate).

- The arbitrator regularly advises one of the parties (or an affiliate) but neither the arbitrator nor his or her firm derives a significant financial income therefrom.

- The arbitrator has a close family relationship with one of the parties, or with a manager, director or member of the supervisory board, or any person having a controlling influence in one of the parties (or an affiliate), or with a counsel representing a party.

The Orange List includes situations which (in the view of the IBA Guidelines' authors) might give rise to justifiable doubts as to the independence and impartiality of an arbitrator. Disclosure in such circumstances is considered obligatory, but (unlike the Waivable Red List) the arbitrator may serve if the parties do not raise an express objection. For example: **5–035**

- The arbitrator has, within the past three years, advised or acted for one of the parties making the appointment (or an affiliate) in an unrelated matter, but the arbitrator and the party (or affiliate), have no ongoing relationship.

- The arbitrator has, within the past three years: (a) served as counsel against one of the parties (or an affiliate) in an unrelated matter; or (b) been appointed as arbitrator on two or more occasions by one of the parties (or an affiliate); or (c) served as arbitrator in another arbitration involving one of the parties (or an affiliate).

- The arbitrator's law firm has, within the past three years, acted for or against one of the parties (or an affiliate) in an unrelated matter without the involvement of the arbitrator, or is currently rendering services to them without creating a significant commercial relationship for the law firm and without the involvement of the arbitrator.

- The arbitrator and another arbitrator are lawyers in the same law firm or chambers.

- The arbitrator was, within the past three years, a partner of, or otherwise affiliated with, another arbitrator or any of the counsel.

- A close personal friendship (or enmity) exists between an arbitrator and a counsel or officer of a party.

- The arbitrator has, within the past three years, been appointed on more than three occasions by the same counsel, or the same law firm.

- The arbitrator and another arbitrator, or counsel, currently act or have acted together within the past three years as co-counsel.

- The arbitrator's law firm is currently acting adversely to one of the parties (or an affiliate).

- The arbitrator has publicly advocated a position on the case, whether in a published paper, or speech, or otherwise.

5–036  Finally, the Green List sets out situations which do not give rise to any appearance of a conflict of interest and which consequently would not require any disclosure. For example:

- The arbitrator has previously expressed a legal opinion (such as in a law review article or public lecture) concerning an issue that also arises in the arbitration (but this opinion is not focused on the case).

- The arbitrator has a relationship with another arbitrator, or with the counsel for one of the parties, through membership in the same professional association, or social or charitable organisation, or through a social media network.

- The arbitrator and counsel for one of the parties have previously served together as arbitrators.

- The arbitrator holds an insignificant amount of shares in one of the parties, or an affiliate of one of the parties, which is publicly listed.

*Duty to make disclosure and challenges to arbitrators under Article 10*

5–037  Disclosure by arbitrators to the LCIA Court of any circumstances that are likely to cast doubt over the arbitrator's impartiality or independence *in the mind of any party*, allows the LCIA Court to decide whether to proceed with the appointment and the parties to assess whether there are any grounds for challenging an arbitrator who has been appointed or for objecting to the appointment of an arbitrator if the LCIA Court decide that a disclosure should be brought to the parties' attention prior to appointment (which is a matter for the LCIA Court's discretion).

Parties receiving a "qualified" Statement of Independence in the form of Statement B, or subsequent disclosure from an arbitrator, should therefore pay careful attention to the details of the disclosure and decide quickly whether they intend to make any challenge or raise an objection. Under Article 10.3[66] of the Rules, any challenge must be brought within 14 days of the appointment of the Arbitral Tribunal or (if later) within 14 days of becoming aware of the circumstances giving rise to the challenge.[67]

*Devoting sufficient time, diligence and industry*

It has always been a requirement of LCIA arbitrators that they should conduct the proceedings so as to avoid unnecessary delay or expense; a failure to do so being a potential ground for challenge.[68] Nevertheless, the 2014 LCIA Rules introduce the newly formulated requirement that an arbitrator should confirm he is willing and able to devote "time, diligence and industry" to ensure the expeditious conduct of the proceedings.  5–038

The new rule was introduced against the backdrop of increasing concerns and complaints about delays to arbitration proceedings as a result of arbitrators with a full diary accepting new appointments. A similar requirement was first imposed by the 2012 version of the ICC Rules.[69]

The LCIA has had a relatively good reputation for the speed of its proceedings. Around one half of arbitrations which go to a final award are concluded within a year of the filing of the Request for Arbitration.[70] This is partly because around one half of LCIA arbitrations are conducted by a sole arbitrator and partly because the LCIA Court, with assistance from the LCIA Secretariat, is careful to select arbitrators with good availability. As the LCIA's statistics demonstrate, the LCIA Court selects a diverse range of arbitrators from numerous jurisdictions. Parties and their legal advisers will have more restricted lists of arbitrators, so their nominees are likelier to be busier.  5–039

Under Article 10.2 of the LCIA Rules, an arbitrator who does not conduct or participate in the arbitration with "reasonable efficiency, diligence and industry", may be challenged.[71]

**5.5 If appointed, each arbitral candidate shall thereby assume a continuing duty as an arbitrator, until the arbitration is finally concluded, forthwith to disclose in writing any circumstances becoming known to that arbitrator after the date of his or her written declaration (under Article 5.4) which are likely to give rise in the mind of any party to any justifiable doubts as to his or her impartiality or independence, to be**

---

[66] See 10–029 below.
[67] Under s.73(1)(d) of the English Arbitration Act 1996, a party that has continued to participate in an arbitration without raising an objection to any irregularity affecting the Tribunal within the time provided for in the arbitration agreement, may not later raise an objection before the Tribunal or courts unless he can show that he was unaware of the relevant circumstances (Appendix 7). See also, Article 4 of the UNCITRAL Model Law (Appendix 10).
[68] Under Article 10.2 of the 1998 LCIA Rules, an arbitrator could be challenged if he did not "... conduct or participate in the arbitration proceedings with reasonable diligence, avoiding unnecessary delay or expense ...".
[69] Article 11 of the ICC Rules.
[70] See FAQs on the LCIA website.
[71] See 10–026—10–028 below.

> delivered to the LCIA Court, any other members of the Arbitral Tribunal and all parties in the arbitration.

5–040   Article 5.5 provides that, once appointed, an arbitrator's duty to disclose in writing any circumstances that arise, or of which he becomes aware, which are likely to give rise in the mind of any party to justifiable doubts as to his impartiality or independence, continues until the conclusion of the arbitration.[72]

Such additional disclosures might arise following the discovery of circumstances previously unknown, or indeed if new circumstances arise. Some common examples of changes in circumstances that could lead to disclosures in the course of the arbitration might include the introduction of new counsel by a party (although this is now subject to the approval of the Arbitral Tribunal pursuant to Article 18), changes in the ownership of a party, or the arbitrator moving from one law firm to another.

> **5.6 The LCIA Court shall appoint the Arbitral Tribunal promptly after receipt by the Registrar of the Response or, if no Response is received, after 35 days from the Commencement Date (or such other lesser or greater period to be determined by the LCIA Court pursuant to Article 22.5).**

5–041   Returning to the technicalities of the formation of the Arbitral Tribunal, Article 5.6 deals with the timeframe for the appointment of the Arbitral Tribunal by the LCIA Court. It provides that the LCIA Court shall appoint the Arbitral Tribunal promptly after the receipt of the Respondent's Response, or after the expiry of 35 days[73] following the delivery of the Request for Arbitration on the Respondent if no Response is filed.

In a parenthetical reference to Article 22.5,[74] Article 5.6 clarifies that the LCIA Court may also proceed with the appointment of the Arbitral Tribunal within a shorter period of time, fixed by the LCIA Court in specific cases.

5–042   The procedure for appointment contemplated in Article 5.6 will include the selection of the arbitrator(s) by the LCIA Court if no agreement has been reached by the parties on nominations for appointment.

In practice, in the selection phase, as outlined in the FAQs on the LCIA's website, the Counsel in the LCIA Secretariat with responsibility for the case will consider the information contained in the Request and Response, enter relevant criteria in a search of the LCIA's database, and consult the Registrar, as appropriate, about possible candidates. A shortlist of recommendations, together with a

---

[72] Article 5.5 was carved out of the 1998 version of Article 5.3, the provisions of which (now in the 2014 version of Article 5.4) were expanded to include the arbitrator's duty to conduct the arbitration with industry. *A v B* [2011] EWHC 2345 (Comm) concerned a challenge prompted by a late disclosure.

[73] Under Article 5.4 of the 1998 version of the Rules, the LCIA Court had only 30 days from the delivery of the Request.

[74] Article 22.5 provides that, subject to any order by the Arbitral Tribunal, the LCIA Court may abridge or extend any timetable. In the context of the constitution of the Arbitral Tribunal, the abridgement of the 35-day period under Article 9A is perhaps most likely.

summary of the dispute, will be submitted to the President or a Vice President of the LCIA Court, who will select candidates either from the list or from his or her own knowledge.

The candidates are then contacted as outlined above in relation to Article 5.4. As soon as they have all provided their statements of independence, the LCIA Court will be ready to appoint the Arbitral Tribunal. The LCIA Secretariat will prepare a Form of Appointment reciting their names and details, which is submitted to the President or a Vice President for signature.

5–043

The length of time required to appoint the Arbitral Tribunal will depend on the number of arbitrators and on any difficulties that there might be with possible conflicts, including the communication of candidates' disclosures to the parties, should the President or Vice President decide that they should be invited to raise any objections. The selection and appointment of a sole arbitrator can often be extremely quick, being made within a matter of days of the filing of the Response.

**5.7 No party or third person may appoint any arbitrator under the Arbitration Agreement: the LCIA Court alone is empowered to appoint arbitrators (albeit taking into account any written agreement or joint nomination by the parties).**

Article 5.7 states that the LCIA Court alone shall have the power to appoint arbitrators under the LCIA Rules, whilst taking any agreement by the parties relating to the nomination of arbitrators into account.[75] This is in line with the practice of other international arbitration institutions.[76]

5–044

Article 7.1 further provides that any agreement between the parties to the effect that either of them or any other third party shall "appoint" an arbitrator will be read as an agreement that the party in question shall nominate the arbitrator, with the appointment being made by the LCIA Court.[77]

**5.8 A sole arbitrator shall be appointed unless the parties have agreed in writing otherwise or if the LCIA Court determines that in the circumstances a three-member tribunal is appropriate (or, exceptionally, more than three).**

Article 5.8 provides for the appointment of a sole arbitrator as the primary procedure in all LCIA arbitrations, unless:

5–045

(a) the parties have agreed otherwise in writing; or

(b) the LCIA Court determines that in view of all of the circumstances of the case a three-member Arbitral Tribunal should be appointed.

---

[75] See Article 5.9 below.
[76] Articles 12 and 13 of the 2012 ICC Rules; rule 6 of the SIAC Rules; Article 5 of the Swiss Rules.
[77] See para.7–004 below.

**5–046** The primary position under the LCIA Rules may be thought to contrast with the expectations of parties who harbour a belief (often coupled with a strong sense of an entitlement) that each party should be allowed to appoint one of a panel of three arbitrators. That is the default position under the UNCITRAL Rules, under which three arbitrators are appointed unless, in appropriate circumstances, the designated appointing authority considers that the appointment of a sole arbitrator would be more suitable.[78] However, it should be appreciated that one of the reasons some parties choose arbitration under the LCIA Rules is precisely because they want to avoid the time and expense associated with three-member panels in disputes which they consider would be appropriate for resolution by a sole arbitrator chosen by the institution.

The rationale for the appointment of a panel of three arbitrators where the parties have agreed so in writing does not require elaboration. On the other hand, the power of the LCIA Court to appoint a panel of three where the Arbitration Agreement is silent is only exercised infrequently. This is because the parties usually reach agreement on the number of arbitrators in post filing correspondence or by way of a proposal made in the Request which is accepted in the Response. In cases in which the Respondent is unresponsive, the Claimant is often content with the appointment of a sole arbitrator.

**5–047** When the question has been submitted for determination by the LCIA Court in the past, relevant circumstances have included such matters as:

- cost and proportionality;
- whether more than one applicable law was in play;
- whether some particular expertise should be brought onto the Arbitral Tribunal; and
- the value of the dispute and its complexity.

**5–048** On the final point there is certainly a good argument that if a case appears to be factually or legally difficult or complex, then three minds would be better than one, although experience suggests that it is not common for the LCIA Court to appoint a panel of three rather than a sole arbitrator.

It should also be noted that arbitration agreements will sometimes specify that the Tribunal is to comprise three arbitrators, but without providing for party nominations. It is the LCIA Court which will then select all three arbitrators.

In those cases, the agreements will sometimes also specify particular qualifications which one or more of the arbitrators should have, e.g. currently working in a particular industry, speaking a particular language, being a practising accountant. The institution is well placed to form a bespoke three-member Arbitral Tribunal of this kind, which would be far more difficult to achieve in an ad hoc arbitration,

---

[78] See Article 7 of the UNCITRAL Rules 2010 (Appendix 11). Note that Article 5 of the UNCITRAL Rules 1976 did not afford the Appointing Authority with discretion to appoint a sole arbitrator. On the other hand, Article 12(4) of the 2012 ICC Rules is similar in effect to Article 5.8 of the LCIA Rules.

in which the parties themselves, appointing an arbitrator each, would be more likely to choose lawyers as their arbitrators.

**5.9 The LCIA Court shall appoint arbitrators with due regard for any particular method or criteria of selection agreed in writing by the parties. The LCIA Court shall also take into account the transaction(s) at issue, the nature and circumstances of the dispute, its monetary amount or value, the location and languages of the parties, the number of parties and all other factors which it may consider relevant in the circumstances.**

Article 5.9 deals with the manner in which selections of arbitrators are to be made by the LCIA Court.   5–049

In its appointment of arbitrators, the LCIA Court is required to pay "due regard" to any method of selection or criteria agreed by the parties, but it is not strictly bound by the parties' agreement. Article 5.9 further provides that in selecting arbitrators, the LCIA Court must also consider the nature of the transaction and the nature of the dispute, as well as other practical considerations, including the nationality and languages of the parties. In practice, the LCIA Court will, where possible, rely in this regard on the information provided by the parties in the Request and Response in relation to the nature of the contract and the disputes. Article 5.9 therefore serves to highlight the practical importance of these early submissions.[79]

Article 5.9 further highlights that the parties do not have an automatic right to nominate an arbitrator. This must be agreed to by the parties. In this respect the LCIA Rules are distinguished from the default procedures for the appointment of arbitrators in ad hoc statutory proceedings under the English Arbitration Act 1996[80] as well as from the default position under the 2010 UNCITRAL Rules,[81] and 2012 ICC Rules.[82] These provide that each party has a right to appoint (UNCITRAL) or nominate (ICC) an arbitrator. Indeed, parties often regard the right to do so as being a rule of general application, and (mistakenly) assume that each party has such right under the LCIA Rules, whether or not they have provided for it in the Arbitration Agreement.[83]   5–050

Unlike its predecessor in the 1998 edition of the Rules, Article 5 does not refer to the nationality of the parties as a matter to which the LCIA Court may have regard in connection with appointments or to arrangements for the appointment of the presiding arbitrator.[84] Both issues are, however, dealt with in Article 6.

---

[79] See the commentary on the Request and Response (Articles 1 and 2).
[80] Section 15 and following (Appendix 7).
[81] Article 7.1 of the 2010 UNCITRAL Rules (Appendix 11).
[82] Article 12(4).
[83] Notably, Article 2.4 of the LCIA Rules refers to the "opportunity to nominate an arbitrator".
[84] Article 5.6 of the 1998 version of the LCIA Rules provided: "In the case of a three-member Arbitral Tribunal, the chairman (who will not be a party-nominated arbitrator) shall be appointed by the LCIA Court" (Appendix 4).

**5.10 The President of the LCIA Court shall only be eligible to be appointed as an arbitrator if the parties agree in writing to nominate him or her as the sole or presiding arbitrator; and the Vice Presidents of the LCIA Court and the Chairman of the LCIA Board of Directors (the latter being ex officio a member of the LCIA Court) shall only be eligible to be appointed as arbitrators if nominated in writing by a party or parties – provided that no such nominee shall have taken or shall take thereafter any part in any function of the LCIA Court or LCIA relating to such arbitration.**

5–051   Article 5.10 deals with the appointment of the President, the Vice Presidents of the LCIA Court and the Chairman of the LCIA Board of Directors, who is also an ex officio member of the LCIA Court, in LCIA arbitrations. It prescribes the circumstances in which the President, Vice Presidents and the Chairman may be appointed to serve as LCIA arbitrators. In the case of the President, she or he is only eligible if all parties agree in writing to nominate him or her as a sole or presiding arbitrator. In other words, the President could never serve as a party nominee, or be appointed by the LCIA Court as a co-arbitrator. In the case of vice presidents and the Chairman of the LCIA Board, they may only serve as arbitrators if nominated by a party or parties, and provided that the nominated individual has had no involvement in LCIA Court decisions relating to the proceedings.

Although this article is another addition to the 2014 iteration of Article 5 of the LCIA Rules, neither the text nor the rule it embodies are new to the LCIA Court. Both have formed part of the Constitution of the LCIA Court since at least 2002.[85]

---

[85] See Article F of the Constitution of the LCIA Court 2011 and 2002 respectively (although Article 5.10 extends the rule to the Chairman of the Board of Directors) (Appendix 3).

ARTICLE 6—NATIONALITY OF ARBITRATORS

6.1 Where the parties are of different nationalities, a sole arbitrator or the presiding arbitrator shall not have the same nationality as any party unless the parties who are not of the same nationality as the arbitral candidate all agree in writing otherwise.

6.2 The nationality of a party shall be understood to include those of its controlling shareholders or interests.

6.3 A person who is a citizen of two or more States shall be treated as a national of each State; citizens of the European Union shall be treated as nationals of its different Member States and shall not be treated as having the same nationality; a citizen of a State's overseas territory shall be treated as a national of that territory and not of that State; and a legal person incorporated in a State's overseas territory shall be treated as such and not (by such fact alone) as a national of or a legal person incorporated in that State.

**Introduction**

Article 6 forms an important limb of the framework of impartiality and independence. It provides for the national neutrality of the presiding arbitrator or sole arbitrator in cases in which the parties are not of the same nationality. Arguably, the notion of national neutrality harks back to days when the substantive nationality of individuals or companies was easier to identify and times when national affiliations were perhaps of greater significance. Nowadays, it might also be said that the notion appears to address the prejudice of some commercial parties, and cannot be supported by any sound legal analysis.[1]

6–001

Indeed, it is a matter of plain logic that national neutrality affords no real guarantee as to the impartiality and independence of the Arbitral Tribunal. On the one hand, the nationality of the parties, particularly corporations, affords little indication of their closest national affiliation, or indeed of their influence in other countries. On the other hand, the national neutrality of an arbitrator says little of any personal prejudices. Further, the requirement can and does in practice

---

[1] For a comprehensive review of the academic debate and practical implications (with the exception of the potential human rights issue—see below), see Ilhyung Lee, "Practice and Predicament: The Nationality of the International Arbitrator (With Survey Results)" (2007) 31(3) *Fordham International Law Journal*, article 1. For comment, see Ned Beale, "Are contract clauses stating religion of arbitrator discriminatory? Challenge to Supreme Court decision in Jivraj v Hashwani has been launched in Europe", *Guardian,* October 3, 2012.

serve to limit the field of available arbitrators, and may create a number of anomalies.[2]

6–002　Finally, the validity of the nationality requirement of Article 6 (and similar arbitration clauses) under the EU promulgated Employment Equality (Religion or Belief) Regulations 2003 (the "2003 Regulation") was brought into question as a result of the English Court of Appeal's decision in *Jivraj v Hashwani*.[3]

In 2011, the English Supreme Court ruled that the 2003 Regulation did not apply to arbitrators because they are not "employees" within the meaning of the legislation and, further, that even if the 2003 Regulation did apply, the parties' requirement that their dispute be resolved by an arbitrator of particular nationality or religion was a "genuine occupational requirement" with the effect that it was exempted from the 2003 Regulation.[4] However, in September 2012 a complaint was made to the European Commission by Mr Hashwani, alleging that the decision of the Supreme Court was in breach of the Treaty on the functionality of the European Union, creating further uncertainty over the validity of the national neutrality rule.

6–003　Nevertheless, the national neutrality rule stated in Article 6 remains of significant importance to many of the users of international arbitration generally, and of LCIA arbitration in particular. Justified or not, parties do in practice take comfort from the national neutrality rule, perhaps because a person of neutral nationality is instinctively perceived as being less likely to be predisposed in favour of either party.

### *Structure of Article 6*

6–004　The structure of Article 6 is straightforward. The substantive principle is stated in Article 6.1, whilst Articles 6.2 and 6.3 provide definitions.

> **6.1 Where the parties are of different nationalities, a sole arbitrator or the presiding arbitrator shall not have the same nationality as any party unless all parties who are not of the same nationality as the arbitral candidate all agree in writing otherwise.**

6–005　Article 6.1 provides that a sole arbitrator or the presiding arbitrator of a panel of three arbitrators in an LCIA arbitration between parties of different nationalities shall have a different nationality to that of any party unless all parties with a different nationality from the arbitrator candidate agree otherwise in writing.[5] This agreement may be included in the Arbitration Agreement but is more often

---

[2] For example, pursuant to Article 6, an English arbitrator might be prevented from serving as a presiding or sole arbitrator in an LCIA arbitration with a London seat, even though the governing law of the contract is English law and the language of the proceedings might be English. See further discussion by Ilhyung Lee, fn.1 above.

[3] [2010] EWCA Civ 712 and see P. Clifford and H. Haeri, "Jivraj v Hashwani: Arbitrator Nationality and the Law of Unintended Consequences" (2011) 8 *Berkeley Journal International Law: Publicist*.

[4] [2011] UKSC 40.

[5] It is not unusual for such a waiver to be given, see for example LCIA Reference No. 7990, May 21, 2010 (2011) 27(3), Arbitration Int. 471; and LCIA Reference No. 1303, November 22, 2001, (2011) 27(3) Arbitration Int. 342.

made in correspondence with the LCIA Secretariat after filing of the Request for Arbitration.

### 6.2 The nationality of a party shall be understood to include those of its controlling shareholders or interests.

Article 6.2 provides that the nationality of a party includes the nationality of its controlling shareholders or interests. This provision recognises that international business is often conducted through subsidiaries and shell companies that might not reflect the substantive nationality or affiliations of the parties to a business relationship. For example, a British Virgin Islands (BVI) registered company owned by a Russian citizen would be treated by the LCIA Secretariat and LCIA Court as having both those nationalities.  6–006

### 6.3 A person who is a citizen of two or more States shall be treated as a national of each State; citizens of the European Union shall be treated as nationals of its different Member States and shall not be treated as having the same nationality; a citizen of a State's overseas territory shall be treated as a national of that territory and not of the State; and a legal person incorporated in a State's overseas territory shall be treated as such and not (by such fact alone) as a national of or a legal person incorporated in that State.

The first part of Article 6.3 provides that holders of dual citizenship will be regarded as a national of both States.  6–007

The second proviso clarifies that citizens of the European Union shall be regarded only as nationals of the Member State of which they are a citizen (not the European Union as a whole or all its Member States). The provisions of Article 6.3 would presumably apply, with the necessary changes, to companies as well as to natural persons.

The remainder of Article 6.3 concerns the treatment of citizens of overseas territories of States and to companies registered in such territories, and confirms that the nationality of such persons or companies shall be regarded as that of the relevant overseas territory rather than the State. The provision recognises, however, that the place of registration might not be the only factor determining the nationality of a company.  6–008

The provisions regarding overseas territories are new to the 2014 Rules. Previously, a company registered, for example, in the BVI, was treated as British. This could produce the anomalous result that two Russian-owned businesses, one incorporated in the BVI and one in Cyprus, would be precluded from having a British sole arbitrator to hear their English law dispute at a London seat, unless the Cypriot party agreed in writing otherwise for the purposes of Article 6. The revision is an important one which brings the Rules in line with the expectations of international parties. It should have the effect of increasing the number of British sole and presiding arbitrators appointed to LCIA Arbitral Tribunals.

## LCIA Court challenge decisions

**6–009** In a number of cases, the nationality of an arbitrator has formed the basis of a challenge to his appointment under Article 10 of the LCIA Rules. In LCIA Reference No. 8086,[6] the LCIA Court Division accepted that an arbitrator may, through a long and meaningful association with a particular country, attain a "de facto"'nationality, but that a long-term residence in a country is not on its own sufficient to give rise to such an inference. In LCIA Reference No. UN9155,[7] a challenge arising from an UNCITRAL Rules arbitration,[8] the LCIA Court held that the fact that the arbitrator was of the same nationality as the counsel of one of the parties did not give rise to justifiable doubts as to the independence or impartiality of the arbitrator.

---

[6] LCIA Reference No. 8086, September 30, 1998 (2011) 27(3) Arbitration Int. 328.
[7] LCIA Reference No. UN9155, November 10, 1999 (2011) 27(3) Arbitration Int. 332.
[8] The UNCITRAL Rules do not contain a rule similar to Article 6, but do caution appointing authorities to consider the "advisability of appointing an arbitrator of a nationality other than the nationalities of the parties." See Article 6.4 of the 1976 UNCITRAL Rules and Article 6.7 of the 2010 UNCITRAL Rules (Appendix 11).

## Article 7—Party and Other Nominations

**7.1 If the parties have agreed howsoever that any arbitrator is to be appointed by one or more of them or by any third person (other than the LCIA Court), that agreement shall be treated under the Arbitration Agreement as an agreement to nominate an arbitrator for all purposes. Such nominee may only be appointed by the LCIA Court as arbitrator subject to that nominee's compliance with Articles 5.3 to 5.5; and the LCIA Court shall refuse to appoint any nominee if it determines that the nominee is not so compliant or is otherwise unsuitable.**

**7.2 Where the parties have howsoever agreed that the Claimant or the Respondent or any third person (other than the LCIA Court) is to nominate an arbitrator and such nomination is not made within time or at all (in the Request, Response or otherwise), the LCIA Court may appoint an arbitrator notwithstanding any absent or late nomination.**

**7.3 In the absence of written agreement between the Parties, no party may unilaterally nominate a sole arbitrator or presiding arbitrator.**

**Introduction**

As noted above in relation to Article 5 ("Formation of the Arbitral Tribunal"), it is the LCIA Court which appoints the Arbitral Tribunal. In summary, the primary procedure is that the LCIA Court will select the arbitrator(s), taking account of any agreed method or criteria for selection and any representations made to it, including as to relevant criteria, in the Request and Response and in any other correspondence. In practice, the selection is made by the President or a Vice President upon receipt of a summary of the case, and recommendations, from the Secretariat.

7–001

The selection and appointment of the Tribunal by the institution is one of the distinctive features of institutional arbitration. It is one of the major attractions of the Rules. In appropriate cases, or where the parties have so agreed, the LCIA Court will appoint a sole arbitrator, who will often be able to deal with the case faster and more cost effectively than a three-member panel.

In ad hoc arbitrations with London seats, the appointment of a sole arbitrator may be the result of a failure by one party to make its own appointment, so that the initiating party's arbitrator becomes the sole arbitrator (s.17 of the English Arbitration Act 1996), with consequences in terms of perceptions of bias and enforceability, or it may be the result of an application to court (s.18), with consequences in terms of expense and possible loss of confidentiality.

7–002

The regime under the Rules, on the other hand, allows for a swift and independent appointment. Generally, around one half of Arbitral Tribunals in LCIA arbitrations comprise a sole arbitrator (almost always selected by the LCIA Court rather than on a joint nomination by the parties).[1]

7–003   Jan Paulsson, former President of the LCIA Court, provoked a lively debate with his 2010 lecture, "Moral Hazard in International Dispute Resolution",[2] in which he challenged the notion of a "fundamental right" to name one's arbitrator, and proposed that "any arbitrator, no matter the size of the tribunal, should be chosen jointly or selected by a neutral body". Even his opponent in this debate, Alexis Mourre, has acknowledged that the LCIA has an "impeccable reputation" for institutional appointments.[3]

Nevertheless, consistent with the flexibility and pragmatism that characterise the Rules, nominations of arbitrators, made by the parties or by others on their behalf, are permitted. If the parties agree, the primary procedure can be displaced. The power of appointing the Arbitral Tribunal rests with the LCIA Court (Article 5.5) but the parties are entitled to agree that they will select the arbitrators themselves or will invite another person or institution to do so. Common additions to the LCIA Recommended Clauses are discussed below and in Part III.

Article 7 confirms how such agreements will be treated and how and when the LCIA Court will intervene if there has been a failure to nominate.

> **7.1 If the parties have agreed howsoever that any arbitrator is to be appointed by one or more of them or by any third person (other than the LCIA Court), that agreement shall be treated under the Arbitration Agreement as an agreement to nominate an arbitrator for all purposes. Such nominee may only be appointed by the LCIA Court as arbitrator subject to that nominee's compliance with Articles 5.3 to 5.5; and the LCIA Court shall refuse to appoint any nominee if it determines that the nominee is not so compliant or is otherwise unsuitable.**

7–004   The LCIA's recommended arbitration clause leaves the selection of the Arbitral Tribunal to the LCIA Court but allows the parties to choose whether it should comprise a sole or three arbitrators. If party nomination of arbitrators is contemplated, the LCIA's website confirms that the Secretariat will be pleased to discuss modifications.

In practice, arbitration clauses providing for the appointment of a three-member Arbitral Tribunal will usually provide that each side should appoint an arbitrator, and that the two so appointed should select the third and presiding arbitrator.[4] This language is often found in conjunction with the incorporation of the LCIA Rules.

---

[1] In 2013, 46% of Arbitral Tribunals comprised a sole arbitrator; in 2012, the proportion of appointments of sole arbitrators was 54%; in 2011, 42%, and in 2010, 50%.

[2] Inaugural lecture as holder of the Michael R. Klein Distinguished Scholar Chair, University of Miami School of Law, April 29, 2010.

[3] "Are unilateral appointments defensible? On Jan Paulsson's Moral Hazard in International Arbitration", Kluwer Arbitration Blog, October 5, 2010. See also *http://www.youtube.com/watch?v=DeTK-rUb6fU* [Accessed November 12, 2014], LSE debate, November 24, 2010, "Unilaterally Appointed Arbitrators – A Good Idea?"

[4] The LCIA's statistics confirm that the majority of arbitrators appointed to three-member LCIA Arbitral Tribunals are selected either by the parties or by their nominees.

The first sentence of Article 7.1 reconciles such wording with the mandatory provisions of Article 5.5. It does so by rectifying the parties' agreement so that the word "appoint" is replaced by the word "nominate".

As the LCIA's regime has become better known and understood, so more carefully tailored arbitration clauses have been introduced in some contracts, providing for "nominations" rather than "appointments". Difficulties have arisen where the drafting has been imperfect and has provided, for example, for two party nominations but for the co-arbitrators to "appoint" the presiding arbitrator. It has been suggested by some parties that a distinction has been made in their agreement and that the power to appoint the presiding arbitrator lies with the co-arbitrators, and not with the LCIA Court. However, the first sentence of Article 5.5 is clear and unequivocal. Accordingly, the verb "appoint" will always be rectified to "nominate" if the subject of the verb is anybody other than the LCIA Court.  7–005

In practice, the LCIA Court appoints all the members of an Arbitral Tribunal at the same time, even where there is a gap between their respective nominations. When providing for the two party-nominated arbitrators to select the presiding arbitrator, some parties have stipulated that such selection should take place within a certain number of days of the appointment of the second party-nominated arbitrator. This has, therefore, also been treated in practice as a reference to the date of nomination of the second party-nominated arbitrator rather than the date of his or her appointment. However, best practice must be to provide expressly for the selection of the presiding arbitrator within a certain number of days of the nomination of the second party-nominated arbitrator.

As the LCIA's role in selecting arbitrators has become more widely known and respected, arbitration clauses incorporating the Rules, but providing for "appointments" by other neutral bodies, have become rarer. Such provisions invariably delay the constitution of the Arbitral Tribunal. They can also lead to extra costs being incurred, as institutions and associations will often charge a fee for the nomination they are asked to make.  7–006

The second sentence of Article 7.1 confirms that nominees must comply with the same pre-appointment requirements as arbitrators chosen by the LCIA Court. In practice, nominating parties will often provide their arbitrator's CV at the time the nomination is made, whether in the Request or Response or with other correspondence. However, there is no obligation to do so: the LCIA Secretariat will contact the nominee for the purposes of Article 5.3 and will ask for a CV and/or any other relevant information missing from the CV (e.g. previous experience of institutional arbitration). It will invite the nominee to complete a Statement of Independence and consent to appointment. The process is described in more detail in the commentary to Article 5 above.

At this stage, after the nomination has been made, but before the Arbitral Tribunal has been appointed, communications with the nominee will take place through the Secretariat. This was expressly provided in the 1998 version of the Rules but remains implicit in the new version of Article 13.1, subject to the new provision, in Article 13.5, permitting communications with a nominated arbitrator for the purpose of consulting on the selection of a presiding arbitrator.[5]  7–007

---

[5] It was accepted practice under the 1998 Rules that, by derogation from Article 13.1, the parties may

The third sentence of Article 7.1 confirms that, as with an arbitrator it might itself have selected, the LCIA Court will not appoint a nominee if, on completion of the formalities, it transpires that the candidate is not compliant with the requirements of Articles 5.3–5.5, i.e. is not independent or impartial or will not be able to devote sufficient time to the arbitration. A third criterion is added in relation to nominees: suitability. This is not an additional obstacle. Had the LCIA Court made the selection, suitability would have been an essential prerequisite.

**7–008** The wording of Article 7.1 reflects the reality that the LCIA Court will refrain from appointing arbitrators who it considers will not be able to fulfil their mission. No particular qualifications are required of candidates and the LCIA Court is always ready to appoint non-lawyers, for example, in suitable cases. However, the Court will wish to be satisfied that a candidate has relevant knowledge and experience. If he or she is not already on the LCIA's database, the Secretariat may raise questions with the candidate.

**7.2 Where the parties have howsoever agreed that the Claimant or the Respondent or any third person (other than the LCIA Court) is to nominate an arbitrator and such nomination is not made within time or at all (in the Request, Response or otherwise), the LCIA Court may appoint an arbitrator notwithstanding any absent or late nomination.**

**7–009** This provision sets out what will happen if there has been a failure to nominate within the agreed timeframe, namely that the LCIA Court may step in and select an arbitrator itself. It should be noted that the LCIA Court has discretion in this matter. In practice, if a nomination is received by the Secretariat before the appointment of the Arbitral Tribunal, it will usually be accepted.[6]

If the arbitration clause provides for nominations, but without a timetable, the Claimant's nomination should be made in the Request for Arbitration (Article 1.1(e)). However, the LCIA Court will usually accept a nomination made later, particularly if it is made before the Respondent makes its own nomination in its Response.

**7.3 In the absence of written agreement between the Parties, no party may unilaterally nominate a sole arbitrator or presiding arbitrator.**

**7–010** This is a new addition in the 2014 Rules. It replaces Article 5.6 in the 1998 version, which had caused considerable confusion because it did not belong there.[7]

> agree that communications may take place direct with their nominees for the purpose of consultations in relation to the selection of the presiding arbitrator. Such a derogation is no longer required. Any such discussions should only be undertaken after the parties have received confirmation from the Secretariat that the nominations have been accepted upon completion of the formalities under Article 5.3.
>
> [6] In the 1998 version of the Rules, the court could appoint "without regard to" any late nomination, which suggested that such a nomination could be ignored (Appendix 4). The new wording suggests that the nomination should be considered but that the Court could, if appropriate, proceed to appoint an arbitrator it selected itself.
>
> [7] Article 5.6 had provided that the Chairman of the Arbitral Tribunal could not be a party-nominated arbitrator and would be appointed by the LCIA Court. The apparent intention of the Article was to

This new wording confirms that a sole arbitrator or presiding arbitrator must either be selected by the LCIA Court (under Article 5) or nominated jointly by agreement between the parties, unless the parties have agreed that such a nomination may be made by only one of them.

In practice, such agreements are extremely rare. They have occasionally arisen, in LCIA arbitrations, in disputes under shipping-related contracts, in which an arbitration clause provides for a three-member Arbitral Tribunal but for the appointment of the Claimant's nominee as sole arbitrator if the Respondent fails to make a nomination within time.[8] Such agreements are now expressly endorsed by the new Article 7.3 but they may nevertheless face obstacles in some seats and upon enforcement in certain jurisdictions.

---

disallow unilateral nominations of chairmen, but the wording could also be interpreted to mean that only the LCIA Court could select chairmen, which was not the case and was not intended. As all arbitrators are appointed by the LCIA Court in any event, the final provision was otiose.

[8] Such an agreement would reflect the wording of s.17 of the English Arbitration Act 1996 and would, therefore, be considered reasonable by London-based practitioners (see Appendix 7). The regime under the LCIA Rules, as set out in Articles 5 and 7, departs from the procedure under the 1996 Act and, as noted here, requires an express written agreement between the parties if the Claimant's nominee is to be appointed as sole arbitrator in this way.

ARTICLE 8—THREE OR MORE PARTIES

**8.1 Where the Arbitration Agreement entitles each party howsoever to nominate an arbitrator, the parties to the dispute number more than two and such parties have not all agreed in writing that the disputant parties represent collectively two separate "sides" for the formation of the Arbitral Tribunal (as Claimants on one side and Respondents on the other side, each side nominating a single arbitrator), the LCIA Court shall appoint the Arbitral Tribunal without regard to any party's entitlement or nomination.**

**8.2 In such circumstances, the Arbitration Agreement shall be treated for all purposes as a written agreement by the parties for the nomination and appointment of the Arbitral Tribunal by the LCIA Court alone.**

**Introduction**

8–001    Article 8 is concerned with the appointment of Arbitral Tribunals in cases involving three or more parties. Article 8 was introduced into the 1998 LCIA Rules in response to the decision of the French Supreme Court in the well-known case of *Sociétés BKMI et Siemens v Société Dutco (Cour de Cassation*, January 7, 1992). The underlying dispute in that case arose from a tripartite construction contract which contained an arbitration agreement providing for ICC arbitration by a panel of three arbitrators. The Claimant commenced a single arbitration against the remaining two parties, in circumstances where the claims brought against each party were distinct and the commercial and legal interests of the two Respondents were not aligned. In accordance with its normal practice at the time, the ICC Court invited both Respondents to make a joint nomination of an arbitrator. The Respondents initially challenged the Request for Arbitration, but when that challenge was rejected by the ICC Court they jointly nominated an arbitrator under protest.

The Tribunal rendered an award upholding the validity of the manner in which it was constituted, but eventually the *Cour de Cassation* annulled the award, holding that the Tribunal had not been properly constituted because the parties did not receive equal treatment in relation to the appointment of the Tribunal. According to the *Cour de Cassation*, this was a fundamental right of the parties that could not be waived in advance:

"Whereas, the principle of equality of the parties in the designation of arbitrators is a matter of public policy; it can be waived only after the dispute has arisen."[1]

---

[1] Eric A. Schwartz, "Multi-Party Arbitration and the ICC in the Wake of Dutco" (1993) 10(3) J. Int. Arb. 5, 14, author's own translation.

The decision of the *Cour de Cassation* had a profound effect on the world of  8–002
international arbitration, resulting in revisions to the arbitration rules of the major
international arbitral institutions of the time,[2] including the introduction of Article
8 into the 1998 version of the LCIA Rules.

> **8.1 Where the Arbitration Agreement entitles each party howsoever to nominate an arbitrator, the parties to the dispute number more than two and such parties have not all agreed in writing that the disputant parties represent collectively two separate "sides" for the formation of the Arbitral Tribunal (as Claimants on one side and Respondents on the other side, each side nominating a single arbitrator), the LCIA Court shall appoint the Arbitral Tribunal without regard to any party's entitlement or nomination.**

Unlike some other institutional arbitration rules, the primary position under the  8–003
LCIA Rules is that no party has an automatic right to nominate an arbitrator.[3]
Article 8 therefore only applies to cases in which there are three or more parties
*and* the Arbitration Agreement contains provision for party-nomination of
arbitrators.

The effect of Article 8.1 in those circumstances is that the parties will forfeit the
right to nominate an arbitrator completely, unless they have agreed in writing that
the parties in dispute represent two (and no more) separate sides for the purposes
of the formation of the Arbitral Tribunal. The reference to "disputant parties"
leaves open the question whether, under the LCIA Rules, such agreement must be
reached after the dispute has arisen (as suggested by the *Cour de Cassation* in the
*Dutco* case), although in practice parties often make this agreement in advance in
their arbitration agreement, and such agreements have been respected by the
LCIA Court.

In cases in which there is a multi-party contract and/or two or more Respondents  8–004
are named in the Request, and if the Arbitration Agreement provides for party
nominations without also providing for this kind of alignment, the LCIA
Secretariat should draw the parties' attention to Article 8.1 and will invite all the
Respondents to confirm in writing that they (now) agree that they form one side
for the purpose of the formation of the Arbitral Tribunal. If they fail to provide this
confirmation, Article 8.1 will come into operation and the Claimant will be
informed that its own nomination will be disregarded.

> **8.2 In such circumstances, the Arbitration Agreement shall be treated for all purposes as a written agreement by the parties for the nomination and appointment of the Arbitral Tribunal by the LCIA Court alone.**

---

[2] See Ricardo Ugarte and Thomas Bevilacqua, "Ensuring Party Equality in the Process of Designating Arbitrators in Multiparty Arbitration: An Update on the Governing Provisions" (2010) 27(1) J. Int. Arb. 9.
[3] See Articles 5.6–5.8.

**8–005** Where the parties have not reached an agreement regarding nominations for the purposes of Article 8.1, the Arbitration Agreement is treated as a written agreement to the effect that all arbitrators will be nominated and appointed by the LCIA Court alone, i.e. without regard to any party nomination.[4]

Article 8.2 has been described as "an especially cautious approach" that is not justified[5]; however, the rationale is clearly to prevent any potential jurisdictional objection or objection to the enforcement of an award on the grounds that the Arbitral Tribunal was not constituted in accordance with the agreement of the parties.[6]

---

[4] The 2014 Rules have added the word "nomination" in Article 8.2. Whilst this was no doubt intended to deal with the point that, under Article 5, all Arbitral Tribunals are "appointed" by the LCIA Court in any event, "nomination" is not appropriate here and must be considered an error in the revision of the Rules: the scheme of the Rules is that parties "nominate" and the Court "selects" (there being no other body to whom a nomination should be made by it).

[5] Ugarte and Bevilacqua, "Ensuring Party Equality in the Process of Designating Arbitrators in Multiparty Arbitration: An Update on the Governing Provisions" (2010) 27(1) J. Int. Arb. 20, and the texts referred to there.

[6] For example, pursuant to Article 34(2)(iv) of the UNCITRAL Model Law (Appendix 10) and Article V(1)(d) of the New York Convention (Appendix 9).

## Articles 9A, 9B and 9C

### Article 9A Expedited Formation of Arbitral Tribunal

9.1 In the case of exceptional urgency, any party may apply to the LCIA Court for the expedited formation of the Arbitral Tribunal under Article 5.

9.2 Such an application shall be made to the Registrar in writing (preferably by electronic means), together with a copy of the Request (if made by a Claimant) or a copy of the Response (if made by a Respondent), delivered or notified to all other parties to the arbitration. The application shall set out the specific grounds for exceptional urgency requiring the expedited formation of the Arbitral Tribunal.

9.3 The LCIA Court shall determine the application as expeditiously as possible in the circumstances. If the application is granted, for the purpose of forming the Arbitral Tribunal the LCIA Court may abridge any period of time under the Arbitration Agreement or other agreement of the parties (pursuant to Article 22.5).

### Article 9B Emergency Arbitrator

9.4 Subject always to Article 9.14 below, in the case of emergency at any time prior to the formation or expedited formation of the Arbitral Tribunal (under Articles 5 or 9A), any party may apply to the LCIA Court for the immediate appointment of a temporary sole arbitrator to conduct emergency proceedings pending the formation or expedited formation of the Arbitral Tribunal (the "Emergency Arbitrator").

9.5 Such an application shall be made to the Registrar in writing (preferably by electronic means), together with a copy of the Request (if made by a Claimant) or a copy of the Response (if made by a Respondent), delivered or notified to all other parties to the arbitration. The application shall set out, together with all relevant documentation: (i) the specific grounds for requiring, as an emergency, the appointment of an Emergency Arbitrator; and (ii) the specific claim, with reasons, for emergency relief. The application shall be accompanied by the applicant's written confirmation that the applicant has paid or is paying to the LCIA the Special Fee under Article 9B, without which actual receipt of such payment the application shall be dismissed by the LCIA Court. The Special Fee shall be subject to the terms of the Schedule of Costs. Its amount is prescribed in the Schedule, covering the fees and expenses of the Emergency Arbitrator and the administrative fees and expenses of the LCIA, with additional charges (if any) of the LCIA Court. After the appointment of the Emergency Arbitrator, the amount of the Special Fee payable by the applicant may be increased by the LCIA Court in accordance with the Schedule. Article 24 shall not apply to any Special Fee paid to the LCIA.

9.6 The LCIA Court shall determine the application as soon as possible in the circumstances. If the application is granted, an Emergency Arbitrator shall be appointed by the LCIA Court within three days of the Registrar's receipt of the application (or as soon as possible thereafter). Articles 5.1, 5.7, 5.9, 5.10, 6, 9C, 10 and 16.2 (last sentence) shall apply to such appointment. The Emergency Arbitrator shall comply with the requirements of Articles 5.3, 5.4 and (until the emergency proceedings are finally concluded) Article 5.5.

9.7 The Emergency Arbitrator may conduct the emergency proceedings in any manner determined by the Emergency Arbitrator to be appropriate in the circumstances, taking account of the nature of such emergency proceedings, the need to afford to each party, if possible, an opportunity to be consulted on the claim for emergency relief (whether or not it avails itself of such opportunity), the claim and reasons for emergency relief and the parties' further submissions (if any). The Emergency Arbitrator is not required to hold any hearing with the parties (whether in person, by telephone or otherwise) and may decide the claim for emergency relief on available documentation. In the event of a hearing, Articles 16.3, 19.2, 19.3 and 19.4 shall apply.

9.8 The Emergency Arbitrator shall decide the claim for emergency relief as soon as possible, but no later than 14 days following the Emergency Arbitrator's appointment. This deadline may only be extended by the LCIA Court in exceptional circumstances (pursuant to Article 22.5) or by the written agreement of all parties to the emergency proceedings. The Emergency Arbitrator may make any order or award which the Arbitral Tribunal could make under the Arbitration Agreement (excepting Arbitration and Legal Costs under Articles 28.2 and 28.3); and, in addition, make any order adjourning the consideration of all or any part of the claim for emergency relief to the proceedings conducted by the Arbitral Tribunal (when formed).

9.9 An order of the Emergency Arbitrator shall be made in writing, with reasons. An award of the Emergency Arbitrator shall comply with Article 26.2 and, when made, take effect as an award under Article 26.8 (subject to Article 9.11). The Emergency Arbitrator shall be responsible for delivering any order or award to the Registrar, who shall transmit the same promptly to the parties by electronic means, in addition to paper form (if so requested by any party). In the event of any disparity between electronic and paper forms, the electronic form shall prevail.

9.10 The Special Fee paid shall form a part of the Arbitration Costs under Article 28.2 determined by the LCIA Court (as to the amount of Arbitration Costs) and decided by the Arbitral Tribunal (as to the proportions in which the parties shall bear Arbitration Costs). Any legal or other expenses incurred by any party during the emergency proceedings shall form a part of the Legal Costs under Article 28.3 decided by the Arbitral Tribunal (as to amount and as to payment between the parties of Legal Costs).

9.11 Any order or award of the Emergency Arbitrator (apart from any order adjourning to the Arbitral Tribunal, when formed, any part of the claim for emergency relief) may be confirmed, varied, discharged or revoked, in whole or in part, by order or award made by the Arbitral Tribunal upon application by any party or upon its own initiative.

9.12 Article 9B shall not prejudice any party's right to apply to a state court or other legal authority for any interim or conservatory measures before the formation of the Arbitration Tribunal; and it shall not be treated as an alternative to or substitute for the exercise of such right. During the emergency proceedings, any application to and any order by such court or authority shall be communicated promptly in writing to the Emergency Arbitrator, the Registrar and all other parties.

9.13 Articles 3.3, 13.1-13.4, 14.4, 14.5, 16, 17, 18, 22.3-22.4, 23, 28, 29, 30, 31 and 32 and the Annex shall apply to emergency proceedings. In addition to the provisions expressly set out there and in Article 9B above, the Emergency Arbitrator and the parties to the emergency proceedings shall also be guided by other provisions of the Arbitration Agreement, whilst recognising that several such provisions may not be fully applicable or appropriate to emergency proceedings. Wherever relevant, the LCIA Court may abridge under any such provisions any period of time (pursuant to Article 22.5).

9.14 Article 9B shall not apply if either: (i) the parties have concluded their arbitration agreement before 1 October 2014 and the parties have not agreed in writing to 'opt in' to Article 9B; or (ii) the parties have agreed in writing at any time to 'opt out' of Article 9B.

## Article 9C Expedited Appointment of Replacement Arbitrator

9.15 Any party may apply to the LCIA Court for the expedited appointment of a replacement arbitrator under Article 11.

9.16 Such an application shall be made in writing to the Registrar (preferably by electronic means), delivered (or notified) to all other parties to the arbitration; and it shall set out the specific grounds requiring the expedited appointment of the replacement arbitrator.

**9.17** The LCIA Court shall determine the application as expeditiously as possible in the circumstances. If the application is granted, for the purpose of expediting the appointment of the replacement arbitrator the LCIA Court may abridge any period of time in the Arbitration Agreement or any other agreement of the parties (pursuant to Article 22.5).

## Introduction

9–001  It is not uncommon for parties engaging in litigation or arbitration to seek interim relief in an attempt to ensure that the ends of justice are not frustrated through, for example, the destruction of property or evidence or the dissipation of assets. The importance of measures that provide a "remedy or a relief that is aimed at safeguarding the rights of parties to a dispute pending its final resolution" is recognised across common law and civil law systems around the world.[1]

The practical difficulty that is addressed by Article 9 of the LCIA Rules is that, in international arbitration proceedings, the constitution of an Arbitral Tribunal can take a number weeks or months from the delivery of the Request for Arbitration. Most experienced practitioners will have had cases in which to "simply wait for tribunal formation in the normal course of events would [. . .] be problematic".[2] Indeed, without any form of preliminary relief, a recalcitrant Respondent could very well use the time during which the Arbitral Tribunal is constituted to frustrate the ultimate award, for example by destroying evidence or by dissipating assets.

9–002  Article 9A of the LCIA Rules seeks to overcome such difficulties by reducing (sometimes dramatically) the time within which the Arbitral Tribunal can be constituted.

Article 9B provides an alternative solution, namely the appointment of an Emergency Arbitrator to serve on an interim basis and award interim relief, pending the formation of the Arbitral Tribunal. If appointed, the Emergency Arbitrator has the power to make any order or award that the Arbitral Tribunal could make, albeit that this is subject to review by the Arbitral Tribunal once constituted.

9–003  An expedited formation procedure was first introduced in the 1998 edition of the LCIA Rules. At the time, it represented an early bid by an arbitral institution seeking to provide a practical answer to the questions being raised regarding the adequacy of arbitral interim relief at the commencement of proceedings.[3] The

---

[1] See Ali Yesilirmak, *Provisional Measures in International Commercial Arbitration* (Kluwer Law International, 2005), pp.3–4, including the texts referred to at fn.9, in particular Collins (1994) and Kessedjian (1998).
[2] Jeff Waincymer, *Procedure and Evidence in International Arbitration* (Kluwer Law International, 2012), Ch.8, p.667; also see Patricia Shaughnessy, "Pre-arbitral Urgent Relief: The New SCC Emergency Arbitrator Rules" (2010) 27 J. Int. Arb. 337.
[3] According to Simon Nesbitt, "LCIA Arbitration Rules, Article 9 [Expedited formation]", in Loukas A. Mistelis (ed.), *Concise International Arbitration* (Kluwer Law International, 2010) p.418, Article 9 of the 1935 edn of the London Court of Arbitration Rules contained a similar provision. However, in modern times, an early version of the Emergency Arbitrator procedure now contained in Articles 9.3–9.7 was rejected from the Rules because it was too controversial. See V.V. Veeder "The Draft New 1998 LCIA Rules", Biennial IFCAI Conference, October 24, 1997, Geneva, Switzerland, http://www.wipo.int/amc/en/events/conferences/1997/october/veeder.html [Accessed November 12, 2014].

expedited formation procedure has proven to be popular amongst the users of LCIA arbitration, with 128 applications for expedited formation being made between February 1998 and October 2013, of which 49 were granted, 28 were not decided for various reasons,[4] and 51 rejected.[5] For the reasons considered below, this distinctive feature of the LCIA Rules, as now improved in the 2014 version, may ultimately remain the primary path for parties seeking urgent relief within the arbitration process (as distinct from seeking it from national courts, in support of the arbitration).

It is worth noting that the LCIA Court's selection and appointment of a sole arbitrator, in the ordinary course under Article 5 (which is what happens in around half of LCIA arbitrations), is itself a relatively speedy procedure: the appointment will usually be made within one or two weeks of the delivery of the Response and will often be made within a matter of days.

One of the reasons that parties opt to have their dispute submitted to a sole arbitrator, chosen by the LCIA Court, is precisely the ability to secure a swift appointment and an early hearing date. Sole arbitrators are well placed to make interim and conservatory orders at short notice, which is a factor influencing this choice of Arbitral Tribunal. **9–004**

The situation where three arbitrators are to be appointed can be more complex and time-consuming, particularly where the parties have provided for party nominations of arbitrators. However, there has been an important change in the 2014 Rules: the LCIA Court now has the power to abridge periods of time under the Arbitration Agreement. This includes periods of time specified in an arbitration clause for the party nomination of arbitrators (or the nomination of a third arbitrator by the parties' nominees). Previously, under the 1998 Rules, if the parties had agreed their own timetable for nominations, the LCIA Court had, in principle, no power to disturb it. Thus, if the parties had, for example, agreed in their arbitration clause that the Respondent's nomination should be made within 15 days of delivery of the Request, the LCIA Court should have had no power to abridge that period.[6] The possibility of applying for the expedited appointment of an Arbitral Tribunal is now open to all parties, whatever the terms of their arbitration agreement.

The introduction of the additional, Article 9B Emergency Arbitrator, procedure in the 2014 LCIA Rules has brought them into line with the procedures adopted in recent years under many other major institutional arbitration rules.[7] **9–005**

The Expedited Formation and Emergency Arbitrator procedures together go a long way towards resolving the difficulties traditionally associated with obtaining effective urgent interim relief at the outset of arbitration proceedings. Nevertheless,

---

[4] Of which 19 were withdrawn by the party making the application and nine not decided for other reasons.

[5] Of which two were held to be inadmissible.

[6] Such a stipulation is not uncommon because the period of 28 days for the Respondent's nomination under Article 2 is regarded as too slow in many quarters. For example, it is slower than the procedure contemplated by s.16 of the English Arbitration Act 1996. It was ironic that the parties' attempt, by contract, to speed up the LCIA process for the appointment of the Arbitral Tribunal should have had the effect of depriving them of the availability of Article 9. This has been cured by the new wording.

[7] See Article 29 of the ICC Rules, Article 26 and Schedule 1 of the SIAC Rules, Article 43 of the Swiss Rules and Article 32 of the SCC Rules and Article 37 of the AAA/ICDR Rules, amongst others.

concerns over the enforceability of interim measures ordered by an Emergency Arbitrator, or even an Arbitral Tribunal, against third parties and under the New York Convention generally,[8] as well as the lack of an ex parte procedure under the LCIA Rules, suggest that in many cases parties will continue to seek pre-arbitral measures of protection from national courts.[9] In that regard the position under the LCIA Rules is similar to the position under the rules of many other institutions, as well as under many national international arbitration laws, virtually all of which expressly permit parties to seek preliminary relief from national courts.[10]

### Article 9A Expedited Formation of Arbitral Tribunal

**9.1 In the case of exceptional urgency, any party may apply to the LCIA Court for the expedited formation of the Arbitral Tribunal under Article 5.**

9–006  Article 9.1 provides that in cases of "exceptional urgency" any party may apply for the expedited formation of the Arbitral Tribunal, under Article 5 of the LCIA Rules.

The reference to Article 5 confirms that an Arbitral Tribunal and arbitrators appointed under the Article 9A procedure are in all other respects equal and subject to the same rules and requirements as any other arbitrators appointed under the LCIA Rules. Thus, notwithstanding the expedited appointment process, arbitrators appointed under Article 9A must comply with the requirements of Article 5 with regard to independence and impartiality and related statements and disclosures to the parties. Further, subject to any revocation or challenge in the normal way under Article 10 of the LCIA Rules, the appointment is final.

9–007  The procedure for making an application under Article 9A and the grounds that constitute exceptional urgency are considered under Article 9.2 below.

In cases in which an application for expedited formation was granted, Arbitral Tribunals were appointed in some cases within as little as 48 hours.[11]

---

[8] See the decision of the Paris Court of Appeal dated April 29, 2003 in *Société Nationale des Pétroles du Congo et République du Congo v Société Total Fina Elf E&P Congo, Cour D'appel de Paris* (1re Ch.C), April 29, 2003, reproduced in (2003) 21(3) ASA Bull. 662–666 which held that the "order" of an ICC Emergency Arbitrator was not a final award and could not therefore be subject to annulment proceedings (nor, it follows, would such an order be susceptible to enforcement proceedings). See also Bernard Hanotiau, "The ICC Rules for a Pre-arbitral Referee Procedure" (2003) 6 Int. A.L.R. 75). However, in *Publicis Communication v True North Communication Inc*, 206 F.3d. 725 (2000), the Federal Court of the 3rd District of the US enforced an "order" of a tribunal because the court considered that in substance the order was equivalent to final award.

[9] See Waincymer, *Procedure and Evidence in International Arbitration* (2012), Ch.8, p.671, under the heading: "Enforceability", and the references provided there, as well as *Kastner v Jason* [2004] EWCA Civ 1599, referred to in Sutton et al., *Russell on Arbitration*, 23rd edn (London: Sweet & Maxwell, 2007), p.217. Seeking such preliminary relief from national courts prior to (and in some circumstances after) the appointment of the Arbitral Tribunal or an Emergency Arbitrator is permitted under Article 25(2) of the LCIA Rules.

[10] See Articles 25.3 and 25.4.

[11] According to LCIA statistics, the fastest time within which an Arbitral Tribunal was appointed under the expedited procedure was two days from the time of the application, but in many other cases it took between 4 and 13 days between the date of the application and the date of appointment. The time required can depend on the adequacy or otherwise of the application and on objections being invited from and submitted by Respondents.

Whilst the reference to "any party" clearly encompasses Respondents, and there are cases in which it is the Respondent who wishes to see the proceedings move quickly, applications by Respondents have been rare. The simple reason for this is that it is open to a Respondent to deliver its Response quickly, thereby, in the ordinary course, securing a faster appointment of the Arbitral Tribunal than if it waited until the end of the 28-day period allowed under Article 2. The LCIA Court is then required, according to Article 5.6, to appoint the Arbitral Tribunal "promptly". Respondents have usually been content to let the LCIA Court deal with the appointment promptly, rather than distract it with an application under Article 9. However, there are cases in which the parties' agreement, in their arbitration clause or elsewhere, provides for a longer timetable, which extends beyond the deadline for the Response. The new wording of Article 9.3 will now allow such contractual timetables to be abridged, giving Respondents reason to make applications for expedited formation in appropriate cases.

9–008

**9.2 Such an application shall be made to the Registrar in writing (preferably by electronic means), together with a copy of the Request (if made by a Claimant) or a copy of the Response (if made by a Respondent), delivered or notified to all other parties to the arbitration. The application shall set out the specific grounds for exceptional urgency requiring the expedited formation of the Arbitral Tribunal.**

Article 9.2 sets out the procedure and grounds for making an Article 9A application for the expedited formation of the Arbitral Tribunal.

9–009

*Making an application*

An application for the expedited formation of the Arbitral Tribunal must be made to the Registrar,[12] and as Article 9 does not permit ex parte applications for relief,[13] it must always be delivered to all parties and/or potential parties to the proceedings.

9–010

Article 9.2 states that the application for expedited formation should be made in writing, and be submitted by email or other form of electronic communication (which includes the LCIA's online application form) together with a copy of the Request (if made by the Claimant) or a copy of the Response (if made by the Respondent).

Article 9.2 does not prevent an application being made where new, exceptionally urgent circumstances have arisen after the Request or Response have been delivered, but it does clarify than an Article 9A application cannot be made before the arbitration has formally been commenced and the Request delivered by the Claimant. Of course, an application for expedited formation of the Arbitral Tribunal can, and often is, made at the same time as delivering the Request.

9–011

---

[12] See Article 3.
[13] On the debate over the desirability of ex parte relief in international arbitration see para.9–040 below.

Where a Respondent seeks expedited formation of the Arbitral Tribunal, a copy of the Response should be delivered with the application. If the time for delivering the Response under Article 2 of the LCIA Rules has not yet expired, the Response should obviously be delivered early.

Although not referred to in the Rules, the LCIA now offers an optional service for filing an Article 9A application online (in addition to the optional online filing of Requests and Responses, which are provided for respectively in Articles 1.3 and 2.3). A party or Legal Representative wishing to utilise this optional service is required to register an account with the LCIA Online Filing website, and will then have to complete a three-section online form. In section A of the form the applicant must indicate whether the application is submitted with or after the Request, and confirm the arbitration number (if available) and the applicant(s) name(s). In section B, the applicant must set out the specific grounds of exceptional urgency alleged, and is afforded an opportunity to upload electronic copies of documents (each less than 64 MB in size) in support of the application. In section C, the applicant is required to confirm that the application and all supporting documents have been delivered to all parties, and to confirm how such delivery was effected.

**9–012** To assist the LCIA Court in expediting the consideration of the matter, counsel for a party planning an application for the expedited formation of the Arbitral Tribunal might consider the following steps:

(a) Giving the LCIA Secretariat advance warning of an impending application on a confidential basis (but not crying "Wolf!") so that it can make arrangements and ensure that members of the LCIA Court are available to deal with it.

(b) Filing the application by email or online as well as by paper copies to ease transmission to the LCIA Court.

(c) Checking the other party's contact details are correct and up to date as the LCIA Court will invariably invite comments from all other parties.

(d) Making proposals as to the order sought (e.g. how much time for filing the Response, making nominations (if any) and any other appropriate orders).

(e) Enclosing a (draft) application for any urgent interim relief that will be sought from the Arbitral Tribunal if the Article 9 application is granted.

### *The application process*

**9–013** The LCIA Court does not render reasoned decisions in response to Article 9 applications.[14] Its decisions are based on the submissions of the parties without an oral hearing. Parties who provide insufficient information or evidence may be asked by the LCIA Court to provide further information, evidence or argumentation within a very short period of time (possibly within hours).

Where an application is granted, the parties can also expect the LCIA Court to order a truncated timetable for the delivery of a Response and possibly the

---

[14] See Article 29.

nomination of an arbitrator, taking into account the overall circumstances of the dispute. Indeed, historically, the abridgment of time for the delivery of the Response has frequently been the main direction made by the LCIA Court. Under the 2014 Rules, the LCIA Court can also order the abridgement of time periods agreed for the nomination of arbitrators.

In one case at least, the LCIA Court rendered a decision granting expedited formation of the Arbitral Tribunal, which was then reconsidered, reviewed and overturned following receipt of submissions from the Respondent.

*Grounds: "Exceptional urgency"*

The application for expedited formation of the Arbitral Tribunal must set out the specific grounds, or circumstances, which the applicant claims give rise to "exceptional urgency". Absent a finding of exceptional urgency, the application will be rejected. **9–014**

The phrase "exceptional urgency" is not defined in the LCIA Rules. Each case will be examined on its own specific merits. However, in practice the standard the applicant must meet is similar to the requirements for "urgency" in connection with applications for interim relief generally, i.e. the applicant must show that there exists a threat of imminent, irreparable harm.[15] Thus, exceptional urgency is unlikely to exist if the threatened harm is not expected to occur within a very short period of time (measured in days rather than weeks or months), or if such threatened harm can be readily compensated by an award of damages.[16]

Indeed, applications for expedited constitution of the Arbitral Tribunal are commonly accompanied by a copy of the application for preliminary urgent interim relief pursuant to Article 25 of the LCIA Rules,[17] which the applicant intends to make to the Arbitral Tribunal when it is constituted.[18] **9–015**

A review of a collection of sanitised summaries of Article 9 application decisions by the LCIA Court indicates, above everything else, that each decision turns on its specific facts and circumstances. There are no fixed categories of circumstances that will give rise to an automatic finding of exceptional urgency. For example, in some cases a threatened transfer of Intellectual Property (IP) was accepted as justifying the expedited formation of the Arbitral Tribunal, but in other cases applications based on similar facts were rejected. It would, therefore, be perilous to suggest that some particular types of threats are more likely than others to establish exceptional urgency.

---

[15] Yesilirmak, *Provisional Measures in International Commercial Arbitration* (2005), Ch.4, pp.113–158; and Georgios Petrochilos, "Interim Measures under the Revised UNCITRAL Arbitration Rules" (2010) 28(4) ASA Bull. 878.

[16] Obviously, an award of damages will not adequately compensate the applicant in cases where there is a risk of dissipation of assets.

[17] Indeed, an application for the appointment of an Emergency Arbitrator pursuant to the provisions of Article 9B *must* be accompanied by an application for the urgent relief sought.

[18] Although delivering such an application for interim measures with the application for expedited formation is not required, in one case the Vice President's decision rejecting an Article 9 application expressly referred to the fact that no emergency relief was sought that would justify the need for expedited formation. In another case, the applicant was asked by the Secretariat to state the nature of the interim relief it intended to seek from the Arbitral Tribunal if the application was successful.

**9–016** Nevertheless the following grounds might, amongst others, constitute "exceptional urgency" justifying the granting of expedited formation of an Arbitral Tribunal:[19]

- the threat of imminent dissipation of assets from which an award could be satisfied;

- the threat of imminent destruction, transfer or dissipation of the subject matter of the dispute (e.g. shares in a company, or the right to use a business name);

- the threat of continuing disclosures of confidential IP;

- an injunction was sought to restrain the Respondent from manufacturing and/or selling the Claimant's products and harming its reputation;

- a scheduled Extraordinary General Meeting of a company in which prejudicial business was to be conducted;

- the Respondent's conduct would have resulted in irreversible disruption to the management and/or operation of a business or company which is the subject matter of the underlying agreement between the parties;

- goods held in port storage were degrading and losing value pending relief from the Arbitral Tribunal;

- a pending national court hearing would undermine arbitral proceedings or render them moot;[20]

- deadlines under guarantees or other financial securities were due to expire.

**9–017** On the other hand, the LCIA Court rejected Article 9 applications for expedited formation because, in the circumstances of the cases considered, the following events complained of did not give rise to "exceptional urgency"[21]:

- the Claimant had a "reasonable apprehension" or was "concerned" that the Respondent intended to sell its assets in order to escape liability;

- there was a risk of the Respondent becoming insolvent, resulting in assets being unavailable to satisfy an award;

- it was alleged that the applicant would suffer irrecoverable damage if the award was delayed;

---

[19] The circumstances are stated in summarised non-specific terms in order to maintain confidentiality and, further, to avoid repetition in relation to circumstances that were relied on in a number of different cases.

[20] It is not necessary for the court proceedings to have been brought in breach of an arbitration agreement. In one case, court proceedings between the Respondent and third party guarantors would have rendered the arbitration between a tenant and landlord moot.

[21] The circumstances are stated in summarised non-specific terms in order to maintain confidentiality and, further, to avoid repetition in relation to circumstances that were relied on in a number of different cases.

- the Respondent commenced national court proceedings in breach of an arbitration agreement;
- the Arbitration Agreement called for a very short arbitral procedure;
- it was alleged that the long-term relationship of the parties would be damaged by a protracted arbitration;
- the Respondent had acknowledged or admitted a debt; and
- it was alleged that the dispute was simple/involved a discrete issue.

*New standard of review?*

The above review of decisions made under the 1998 version of Article 9 of the LCIA Rules suggests that the LCIA Court has applied a high bar to the test of "exceptional urgency". The introduction of the Emergency Arbitrator procedure in the 2014 LCIA Rules,[22] which may be applied for in cases of "emergency", raises the question of whether going forward a less stringent test might be applied to Article 9A applications. Whilst it is certainly arguable that the "emergency" standard is stricter than "exceptional urgency", the primary focus of the distinction appears to be the immediacy of the relief required rather than, for example, the impact of the circumstances complained of.

9–018

*Rejection on grounds of inadmissibility*

In a number of cases, Article 9 applications have been rejected on the grounds of admissibility, where the arbitration clause provided a specific procedure or timetable for the constitution of the Arbitral Tribunal. Such clauses were, in a number of decisions, regarded under the 1998 edition of the LCIA Rules as excluding the power of the LCIA Court to expedite the constitution of the Arbitral Tribunal. As noted above, this exclusion no longer applies, now that the LCIA Court has the power to abridge periods of time contained in the Arbitration Agreement.

9–019

*Prejudice to the Respondent to the application*

One of the other factors which might be relevant to expedited formation is the extent to which the Respondent to the application will be prejudiced by the expedited formation of the Arbitral Tribunal. The authors are not aware of any cases in which an application was rejected on these grounds, but the absence of prejudice to the Respondent, for example, because the Respondent had been actively engaging in the proceedings, or the Respondent had not objected to the expedition of the formation of the Arbitral Tribunal, or the parties had in any event agreed on the appointment of a sole arbitrator by the LCIA Court would militate in favour of expedition.

9–020

---

[22] See Article 9B below.

## Interim relief from national courts

**9–021** In a number of cases, the LCIA Court also had regard to the availability of interim relief from national courts.[23] In some cases where the applicant had sought and obtained interim relief from national courts, or where the applicant has indicated that it intended to seek relief from a national court pending the constitution of the Tribunal, the LCIA Court concluded that there was no exceptional urgency justifying the expedited constitution of the Arbitral Tribunal. Conversely, a long period of delay without seeking relief from a national court might also indicate a lack of urgency.

> **9.3 The LCIA Court shall determine the application as expeditiously as possible in the circumstances. If the application is granted, for the purpose of forming the Arbitral Tribunal the LCIA Court may abridge any period of time under the Arbitration Agreement or other agreement of the parties (pursuant to Article 22.5).**

**9–022** Article 9.3 regulates the manner in which the LCIA Court must deal with applications under Article 9A of the LCIA Rules and the relief available to them. The first part of Article 9.3 provides that the LCIA Court must respond as quickly as possible in the circumstances of the case but there is no fixed time within which an application must be determined.

The second part of Article 9.3 sets out the power of the LCIA Court to abridge[24] any time period applicable under the LCIA Rules or any written agreement between the parties as required in order to expedite the appointment of the Arbitral Tribunal in cases in which an Article 9A application is successful.

**9–023** Typically, the LCIA Court may, under this provision, abridge the time for the delivery of the Response under Article 2, which often automatically abridges the corresponding time limit for any nomination of an arbitrator. As noted above, if a different timetable for party nominations has been agreed, the wording of Article 9.3 now allows the LCIA Court to abridge such contractual time limits as well.

If a party (typically the Respondent) fails to comply with the abridged time limit, the LCIA Court may then proceed to appoint the Arbitral Tribunal pursuant to Article 5.1 or Article 7.2 if the parties have agreed on a procedure for the nomination of arbitrators.

### Article 9B Emergency Arbitrator

*Introduction*

**9–024** Article 9B heralds the introduction of an LCIA Emergency Arbitrator procedure. This was introduced to the LCIA Rules only after a number of similar procedures

---

[23] Under Article 25.3, any party has the right to apply to a state court or other legal authority for interim or conservatory relief prior to the formation of the Arbitral Tribunal (and, in limited circumstances, afterwards as well); see 25–026—25–027.

[24] In accordance with Article 22.5, see 22–053.

had been adopted by other major institutional arbitration rules,[25] and reflects at least to some degree an element of "keeping up with the Joneses".[26]

In circumstances where, under the LCIA Rules, an Arbitral Tribunal can be constituted and appointed on an expedited basis within as little as 48 hours,[27] under Article 9A, the alternative, and arguably more problematic, Emergency Arbitrator option might be viewed as superfluous (all the more so given the ability in many LCIA arbitrations to seek urgent relief from the English courts because the seat of the arbitration is in England). However, a number of useful distinctions can be drawn between the expedited formation (9A) and Emergency Arbitrator (9B) procedures:

- First, Article 9B applies in cases of "emergency", i.e. where a serious, unexpected and often perilous situation requires *immediate* action;[28] whilst expedited formation under Article 9A is available for cases of "exceptional urgency", in which although exceptional and important, the circumstances or concerns that have arisen can be ameliorated by a *swift* response.[29]

- Secondly, which follows, whereas a successful Article 9B application should result in the *immediate* appointment of an Emergency Arbitrator, a successful Article 9A application results in the *shortening* (or abridgment) of otherwise applicable time periods relating to the constitution of the Arbitral Tribunal (such as the time for a Respondent to nominate an arbitrator or deliver a Response).

- An additional potential advantage of the Emergency Arbitrator procedure is that it might allow access to arbitral emergency relief, without depriving the parties of any agreed procedure for the nomination or constitution of the Tribunal, thereby avoiding potential objections to its ultimate constitution.

The extent to which the availability of the separate procedures overlap in practice will become clearer with time. It stands to reason that where circumstances exist in which an Article 9B application would be accepted, the apparently less strict standard applicable in relation to expedited formation applications under Article

9–025

---

[25] ICDR/AAA in 2006; SCC in 2010; ACICA in 2011; Swiss Rules in 2012; ICC in 2012 (following a less successful opt-in Pre-Arbitral Referee procedure adopted in 1990); SIAC in 2013; HKIAC in 2013; Finnish Arbitration Rules in 2013. If the provision of Emergency Arbitrator procedures reflects a need, parties might be expected to seek to make use of the LCIA Emergency Arbitrator process on a regular basis. This remains to be seen. The ICC Secretariat reports that within the first 24 months from the introduction of the ICC Emergency Arbitrator Procedure, 12 applications were made (although, as with the LCIA provisions, the procedure is not generally available where the arbitration agreement was made before the ICC Rules came into force, so some time lag is to be expected). Within the first 12 months of the introduction of the SCC procedure in 2010, four applications were made, see Johan Lundstedt, *SCC Practice: Emergency Arbitrator Decision Rendered 2010*, http://www.sccinstitute.com/filearchive/4/41504/Emergency%20arbitration%20final.pdf [Accessed June 13, 2013]. On the other hand, the SIAC procedure has proved more popular.

[26] Influential voices within the LCIA Court argued that without the adoption of such a procedure the LCIA Rules would become regarded as outmoded and would be spurned by users in regions in which Emergency Arbitrator procedures were an expected feature of arbitration rules.

[27] Raja Bose and Ian Meredith, "Emergency Arbitration Procedures: A Comparative Analysis" (2012) 5 Int. A.L.R. 186.

[28] The *Oxford Dictionary* defines an "emergency" as a "serious, unexpected, and often dangerous situation requiring immediate action".

[29] "Urgency" is defined by the *Oxford Dictionary* as of "importance requiring swift action".

9A may also be met. It cannot at present be said that the opposite is also true. In the meanwhile, it must be expected that parties which make applications under Article 9B will often make Article 9A applications in the alternative.

*Threshold procedure*

9–026   The first two Articles of Article 9B, namely Articles 9.4 and 9.5, constitute a gateway review process, apparently designed to prevent the unmeritorious use of the Emergency Arbitrator procedure. The scope of the review available to the LCIA Court places it amongst the institutions with the greatest exclusionary powers.[30] As the LCIA Court has no power to grant any form of relief itself, it might be fairly argued that the burden, or standard of proof, in an application under Articles 9.4 and 9.5 as to the urgency of the relief required, should be lower than the standard of proof required to secure the actual relief sought from the Emergency Arbitrator. It might even be argued that the determination of the LCIA Court should proceed on the assumption that matters alleged in the application are established. The review of decisions made by the LCIA Court on expedited formation applications[31] suggests that the LCIA Court has not generally adopted such an approach in that context.[32]

**9.4 Subject always to Article 9.14 below, in the case of emergency at any time prior to the formation or expedited formation of the Tribunal (under Articles 5 or 9A), any party may apply to the LCIA Court for the immediate appointment of a temporary sole arbitrator to conduct emergency proceedings pending the formation or expedited formation of the Tribunal (the "Emergency Arbitrator").**

9–027   Article 9.4 provides that any party to an arbitration may apply to the LCIA Court for the immediate appointment of an Emergency Arbitrator, in accordance with the procedures set out in Articles 9.4 and 9.5.

A number of points arise from Article 9.4:

---

[30] For example, the Board of Directors of the Arbitration Institute of the Stockholm Chamber of Commerce may only decline to appoint an Emergency Arbitrator if the SCC "manifestly lacks jurisdiction over the dispute"; Article 4 of Appendix II to the SCC Rules. The President of the ICC Court may only disallow the appointment of an Emergency Arbitrator if he concludes that the parties against whom emergency relief is sought are not parties to the arbitration agreement relied upon, or if the arbitration agreement was concluded before the Rules came into force, or if the parties have opted out of the Emergency Arbitrator procedure; Articles 29.5, 29.6 and Article 1(5) of Appendix V to the ICC Rules. The Arbitration Court of the Swiss Chambers' Arbitration Institution may decline to appoint an Emergency Arbitrator if there is "manifestly no agreement to arbitrate" under the Swiss Rules, or if it considers that it would be more appropriate to constitute the Tribunal and refer the application for emergency relief to it; Article 43.2 of the Swiss Rules. The President of the Court of Arbitration of SIAC may decline to appoint an Emergency Arbitrator if he determines that SIAC should not accept the application; Article 2 of Appendix 1 to the SIAC Rules. The application process and review conducted under the HKIAC Rules, however, is similar to the review conducted under the LCIA Rules.
[31] See paras 9.016–9.021 above.
[32] However, the context is different from that under the previous LCIA Rules. In an Article 9A application, the LCIA Court now has the power to abridge time limits relating to the constitution of the Arbitral Tribunal potentially impacting on the rights of parties to nominate arbitrators and participate in the constitution of the Arbitral Tribunal.

- The Emergency Arbitrator procedure can be excluded by the parties.[33]

- An application can be made by any party.

- An application can only be made in cases of "emergency". The meaning of "emergency" in the context of Article 9B is considered under Article 9.5 below.

- An application under Article 9.4 may only be made prior to the formation of the Arbitral Tribunal, whether in the normal course under Article 5, or under the Article 9A expedited formation procedure, but not after the appointment of the Arbitral Tribunal.

- The appointment of the Emergency Arbitrator is temporary and the proceedings conducted by him or her (and relief granted)[34] are undertaken pending the appointment of the Arbitral Tribunal.

- Finally, the Emergency Arbitrator is always a sole arbitrator.

**9.5 Such an application shall be made to the Registrar in writing (preferably by electronic means), together with a copy of the Request (if made by a Claimant) or a copy of the Response (if made by a Respondent), delivered or notified to all other parties to the arbitration. The application shall set out, together with all relevant documentation: (i) the specific grounds for requiring, as an emergency, the appointment of an Emergency Arbitrator; and (ii) the specific claim, with reasons, for emergency relief. The application shall be accompanied by the applicant's written confirmation that the applicant has paid or is paying to the LCIA the Special Fee under Article 9B, without which actual receipt of such payment the application shall be dismissed by the LCIA Court. The Special Fee shall be subject to the terms of the Schedule of Costs. Its amount is prescribed in the Schedule, covering the fees and expenses of the Emergency Arbitrator and the administrative fees and expenses of the LCIA, with additional charges (if any) of the LCIA Court. After the appointment of the Emergency Arbitrator, the amount of the Special Fee payable by the applicant may be increased by the LCIA Court in accordance with the Schedule. Article 24 shall not apply to any Special Fee paid to the LCIA.**

Article 9.5 sets out the procedure and grounds for making an Article 9B application for the appointment of an Emergency Arbitrator.  9–028

*Making an application*

An application for the appointment of an Emergency Arbitrator must be made in writing and be addressed to the Registrar, together with copies to all other parties  9–029

---

[33] See Article 9.14 below and the commentary at 9–052.
[34] Any award rendered or order made by the Emergency Arbitrator is also subject to revision by the Arbitral Tribunal once constituted. See Article 9.11 below.

(ex parte applications are not permitted). To save time, the application should (preferably) be communicated by email or other form of electronic communication (including by utilising the LCIA's online application form) and be accompanied by copies of the Request (if made by the Claimant) or the Response (if made by the Respondent).

Thus a Claimant cannot make an application for the appointment of an Emergency Arbitrator under the LCIA Rules prior to the formal commencement of the arbitration proceedings. An application can, of course, be made simultaneously with the delivery of the Request. Equally, a Respondent cannot make an application before the delivery of a Request, but it is open to the Respondent to deliver the Response earlier than otherwise provided for under the LCIA Rules.

Although not referred to in the Rules, the LCIA now offers an optional service for filing an Article 9B application online (in addition to the optional online filing of Requests and Responses, which are provided for respectively in Articles 1.3 and 2.3). A party or Legal Representative wishing to utilise this optional service is required to register an account with the LCIA Online Filing website and will then have to complete a four-section online form. In section A of the form the applicant must indicate whether the application is submitted with or after the Request, and confirm the arbitration number (if available) and the applicant(s) name(s). In section B, the applicant must set out the specific grounds requiring the appointment of an Emergency Arbitrator and the claim for emergency relief with reasons. The applicant may also upload electronic copies of documents (each less than 64 MB in size) in this section in support of the application. In section C, the applicant is required to confirm that the application and all supporting documents have been delivered to all parties, and to confirm how such delivery was effected. Finally, payment of the Emergency Arbitrator fee is made in Section D of the online form. An online application for the appointment of an Emergency Arbitrator is only transmitted to the Registrar if the payment is successfully processed by the website.

### Content of the application

9–030   The second part of Article 9.5 lists the matters that should be stated within an application for the appointment of an Emergency Arbitrator. These include:

(a) the specific grounds for requiring, as an emergency, the appointment of an Emergency Arbitrator; and

(b) the specific claim, with reasons, for emergency relief.

### Grounds

9–031   The application for the appointment of an Emergency Arbitrator must set out the specific grounds, or circumstances, which the applicant relies upon as the "emergency" requiring the appointment of the Emergency Arbitrator. It must be assumed that, unless it is satisfied that there is an "emergency", the LCIA Court will reject the application.

The word "emergency" is not defined in the LCIA Rules and at the time of writing there is no current practice as to the meaning of the term within the context of Article 9B. The *Oxford Dictionary* explains the meaning of the word "emergency" as a serious, unexpected and often dangerous situation requiring immediate action. In the context of an Article 9B application, the focus of the enquiry is likely to be on the seriousness of the consequences of any circumstances (including conduct by the other party or parties) as well as the immediacy and nature of the action required to prevent or ameliorate those consequences.

Where the circumstances are unlikely to give rise to harm that cannot be compensated by a monetary award, or to harm that will occur within a matter of days rather than weeks, it is predicted that an application for the appointment of an Emergency Arbitrator will be declined.

9–032

As with applications for the expedited formation of the Arbitral Tribunal pursuant to Article 9A, it must be expected that the standard the applicant will be required to meet will be akin to the requirements for "urgency" in connection with applications for interim relief generally, i.e. the applicant will at least have to show that a threat exists of imminent, irreparable harm.[35]

Indeed, applications for the appointment of an Emergency Arbitrator must be accompanied by a copy of the claim for urgent interim relief that the applicant seeks from the Emergency Arbitrator.

9–033

Whilst a review of the circumstances in which applications for expedited formation of Arbitral Tribunals under the 1998 version of Article 9 of the LCIA Rules[36] have been granted might provide some guidance as to the approach taken by the LCIA Court in certain circumstances, it is suggested that the test for the appointment of an Emergency Arbitrator under Article 9B of the LCIA Rules will be more stringent in relation to the immediacy of the interim relief sought in order to prevent the conduct complained of.

*Special Fee*

Article 9.5 provides that an application for the appointment of an Emergency Arbitrator must contain a confirmation that the additional fee referred to as the "Special Fee", prescribed in the Schedule of Costs,[37] has been paid by the applicant. The fee, which is required to cover the fees of the Emergency Arbitrator, the LCIA Secretariat's charges and any charges of the LCIA Court in respect of the Emergency Arbitrator reference, consists of a fixed, non-refundable application fee (currently £8,000) and an Emergency Arbitrator's fee (currently £20,000) which can subsequently be increased (but not decreased) where appropriate in the circumstances. If the application for the appointment of an Emergency Arbitrator is refused, the Emergency Arbitrator's fee will be treated as a deposit made by the applicant on account of the Arbitration Costs. The payment of deposits on costs

9–034

---

[35] Yesilirmak, *Provisional Measures in International Commercial Arbitration* (2005), Ch.4, pp.113–158; and Georgios Petrochilos, "Interim Measures under the Revised UNCITRAL Arbitration Rules" (2010) 28(4) ASA Bull. 878.
[36] See paras 9.016–9.021 above.
[37] See Appendix 2 and the commentary at 37–037.

pursuant to Article 24 of the LCIA Rules is not required in connection with the Emergency Arbitrator procedure itself.

The timely payment of the entire special fee (currently £28,000) by the applicant is crucial: if payment is not received, the application will be dismissed by the LCIA Court.

> **9.6** The LCIA Court shall determine the application as soon as possible in the circumstances. If the application is granted, an Emergency Arbitrator shall be appointed by the LCIA Court within three days of the Registrar's receipt of the application (or as soon as possible thereafter). Articles 5.1, 5.7, 5.9, 5.10, 6, 9C, 10 and 16.2 (last sentence) shall apply to such appointment. The Emergency arbitrator shall comply with the requirements of Articles 5.3, 5.4 and (until the emergency proceedings are finally concluded) Article 5.5.

9–035    Article 9.6 provides that the LCIA Court must determine applications for the appointment of an Emergency Arbitrator as quickly as possible in the circumstances of the case. If the application is granted, the LCIA Court must appoint an Emergency Arbitrator within three days of the application being made, or as soon as possible thereafter.[38]

The following articles of the LCIA Rules are specifically identified as applying to the appointment of the Emergency Arbitrator:

- 5.1—the appointment of the Emergency Arbitrator will not be delayed by arguments that the Request or Response are incomplete or missing;[39]

- 5.7—Emergency Arbitrators are appointed by the LCIA Court alone;

- 5.9—Emergency Arbitrators are to be appointed with due regard for any method or criteria of selection agreed in writing by the parties and taking into account the nature and circumstances of the transactions and dispute;

- 5.10—restrictions on the appointment of the President of the LCIA Court, Vice Presidents and Chairman of the Board;

- 6—nationality requirements for arbitrators;

- 9C—expedited appointment of replacement arbitrators;

- 10—challenges to and revocation of appointments of arbitrators; and

- 16.2—power of Emergency Arbitrator to determine seat of arbitration in the absence of agreement.

9–036    The Emergency Arbitrator must also comply with the requirements of the following Articles:

---

[38] The proposed three-day timeframe can be expected to be met in most cases but could, in any event, be extended by the LCIA Court pursuant to Article 22.5, see 22–053.
[39] See 5–004.

- 5.3—impartiality and independence;

- 5.4—disclosure letter concerning qualifications, fees and circumstances that might give rise to justifiable doubts regarding impartiality or independence; and

- 5.5—continuing duty to disclose any conflict of interest (until the conclusion of the Emergency Arbitrator procedure).

Thus, like any other arbitrator appointed under the LCIA Rules, Emergency Arbitrators must be and remain impartial and independent of the parties.[40] Notwithstanding the short timetable for their appointment, Emergency Arbitrators are expected to comply with the provisions of Article 5 relating to disclosures to the parties. They are subject to the challenge procedures of Article 10 of the LCIA Rules.[41] It will be for the LCIA Court to deal with any such challenges with the dispatch that is appropriate in the context of an Emergency Arbitrator procedure.[42]

9–037

**9.7 The Emergency Arbitrator may conduct the emergency proceedings in any manner determined by the Emergency Arbitrator to be appropriate in the circumstances, taking account of the nature of such emergency proceedings, the need to afford to each party, if possible, an opportunity to be consulted on the claim for emergency relief (whether or not it avails itself of such opportunity), the claim and reasons for emergency relief and the parties' further submissions (if any). The Emergency Arbitrator is not required to hold any hearing with the parties (whether in person, by telephone or otherwise) and may decide the claim for emergency relief on available documentation. In the event of a hearing, Articles 16.3, 19.2, 19.3 and 19.4 shall apply.**

Article 9.7 sets out the framework within which the Emergency Arbitrator must conduct the emergency proceedings. The Emergency Arbitrator is afforded the widest discretion over the procedure he adopts, provided that he balances the need for speed in an application for urgent, potentially temporary, relief with the need to ensure that each party has, "if possible", an "opportunity to be consulted" in relation to the claim for emergency relief, the claim generally and any further submissions. The Emergency Arbitrator is not required to convene any form of hearing and may decide the application on a "documents only" basis.

9–038

---

[40] For the meaning of "impartial and independent" see Article 5 and the commentary at 5–008—5012 above, and Article 10 and the commentary at 10–016—10–018 below.
[41] By contrast, Article 4(3) of Appendix II of the SCC Rules provides that any challenge to an Emergency Arbitrator must be made within 24 hours of his appointment; Article 3 of Schedule 1 of the SIAC Rules provides that any challenge to an Emergency Arbitrator must be made within one business day of his appointment; and Article 43(4) of the Swiss Rules provides that challenges must be made within three days.
[42] The power of the LCIA Court to extend or truncate time limits is set out in Article 22.5.

If a hearing is held, Articles 16.3 (hearings may be held at any convenient venue),[43] 19.2 (organisation and conduct of the hearing),[44] 19.3 (reasonable notice of hearings)[45] and 19.4 (hearings in private)[46] will apply.

9–039 The phrase "opportunity to be consulted" represents a departure from the terminology traditionally employed in arbitral rules as regards the right to be heard,[47] and will serve as an indication that parties may not insist on a right to adduce a fully reasoned written submission, counter-submission and/or evidence before the Emergency Arbitrator makes an order or renders an award. The reference to consultation suggests a less formal, more speedy procedure. The Emergency Arbitrator may carry on with the emergency proceedings and make a determination even if a party does not avail itself of the opportunity afforded.

## No ex parte arbitral applications

9–040 Whilst the utility of ex parte relief is widely recognised,[48] including by the drafters of the 2006 revisions to the UNCITRAL Model Law,[49] the question of whether ex parte measures (i.e. without notice to the party against whom relief is sought) should be available in international arbitration has been a matter of some considerable debate.[50] In the past few years, the notion that ex parte relief should be available within the arbitral context is increasingly gaining acceptance. Thus ex parte relief granted by emergency arbitrators is now available under the rules of a number of arbitral institutions[51] and would be recognised under the arbitration law in certain jurisdictions,[52] including "in theory" where the parties had agreed to this, under English law.[53]

---

[43] See 16–013 below.
[44] See 19–007—19–011 below.
[45] See 19–012 below.
[46] See 19–013 below.
[47] By contrast, many arbitration rules provide that arbitrators must "consult" with parties before making purely procedural decisions. Article 5 of the ICC Emergency Arbitrator Rules states that the Emergency Arbitrator must ensure that each party has a "reasonable opportunity to present its case"; Article 43.6 of the Swiss Rules provides that the Emergency Arbitrator must ensure that each party has a "reasonable opportunity to be heard on the application"; Article 5 of Schedule 1 of the SIAC Rules provides that the Emergency Arbitrator must give all parties a "reasonable opportunity" to be heard.
[48] Donald Francis Donovan, "The Scope and Enforceability of Provisional Measures in International Commercial Arbitration A Survey of Jurisdictions, the Work of UNCITRAL and Proposals For Moving Forward", in A.J. van den Berg (ed.), *International Commercial Arbitration: Important Contemporary Questions* (ICCA Congress series) (The Hague: Kluwer Law International, 2003), p.82.
[49] See Articles 17B and 17C (Appendix 9).
[50] Hans van Houtte, "Ten Reasons Against a Proposal for Ex Parte Interim Measures of Protection in Arbitration" (2004) 20(1) Arbitration Int. 85.
[51] For example, the WIPO arbitration rules have long permitted ex parte relief, as do the Swiss Rules 2012 and the Paris Arbitration Rules 2012.
[52] The Singapore International Arbitration (Amendment) Act 2012 (No. 12 of 2012) recognises the validity of ex parte relief.
[53] In *Norbrook Laboratories Ltd v 1. A. Tank and 2. Moulson Chemplant Ltd* [2006] EWHC 1055 (Comm) (at [139]) Mr Justice Colman recognised that "it would in theory be possible for both parties" to agree to the conduct of ex parte procedures. At the same time, the principle of party autonomy (s.1(b) of the English Arbitration Act 1996 and the parties' freedom, under s.58 of the same Act, to determine what constitutes an "award", also suggests that an ex parte preliminary award should be enforceable in England.

However, the requirement that each party be afforded an opportunity to be consulted if possible all but rules out the possibility of ex parte proceedings under Article 9B of the LCIA Rules.

**9.8 The Emergency Arbitrator shall decide the claim for emergency relief as soon as possible, but no later than 14 days following the Emergency Arbitrator's appointment. This deadline may only be extended by the LCIA Court in exceptional circumstances (pursuant to Article 22.5) or by the written agreement of all parties to the emergency proceedings. The Emergency Arbitrator may make any order or award which the Tribunal could make under the Arbitration Agreement (excepting Arbitration and Legal Costs under Articles 28.2 and 28.3); and, in addition, make any order adjourning the consideration of all or any part of the claim for emergency relief to the proceedings conducted by the Tribunal (when formed).**

Article 9.8 deals with the timeframe within which the Emergency Arbitrator must conduct the emergency proceedings, as well as with his powers to render orders and awards. 9–041

Under this article, the Emergency Arbitrator is required to render a decision, order or award on the claim for emergency relief within 14 days of being appointed. The 14-day deadline may only be extended by the LCIA Court pursuant to Article 22.5 in exceptional circumstances. Reports of emergency arbitrator procedures conducted under the SIAC Arbitration Rules suggest that such deadlines are certainly achievable,[54] even if not in every case.[55]

### *Powers of the Emergency Arbitrator and effect of decisions*

Article 9.8 also deals with the Emergency Arbitrator's decision-making powers. The Emergency Arbitrator may render any order or award which the finally constituted Arbitral Tribunal could make. Alternatively, the Emergency Arbitrator may also decide to refer the application to the finally constituted Arbitral Tribunal. The form of an Emergency Arbitrator's decision can impact on its international enforceability. With few exceptions,[56] arbitral orders are generally regarded as unenforceable by national courts under the New York Convention, whereas arbitral awards are enforceable. Article 9.9 (below) sets out the formal 9–042

---

[54] See Raja Bose and Ian Meredith, fn.27 above—case studies from SIAC confirm that the first reference was decided within eight days, but the following three were decided within less than two days.
[55] See Johan Lundstedt, fn.25 above, with regard to the experience in the first four SCC Emergency Arbitrator references, which were reached respectively within 12, 5, 6 and 5 days of the application.
[56] Such as Singapore, pursuant to the Singapore International Arbitration (Amendment) Act 2012 (No. 12 of 2012) or Switzerland, see Georg von Segesser and Christopher Boog, Chapter 6 "Interim Measures", in Elliott Geisinger and Nathalie Voser (eds), *International Arbitration in Switzerland: A Handbook for Practitioners,* 2nd edn (Kluwer Law International, 2013), pp.115–117; but see US Federal Court decision in *Publicis Communication v True North Communication Inc.*, 206 F.3d. 725 (2000), in which a different approach was taken.

requirements with which the Emergency Arbitrator must comply in rendering his decision.

With one exception, the Emergency Arbitrator has the same powers as the Arbitral Tribunal enjoys under the LCIA Rules to make such orders and awards as he deems appropriate. The exception is that decisions on the award of the legal costs of the emergency proceedings and the costs of the Emergency Arbitrator himself are reserved for the Arbitral Tribunal under Article 28 of the LCIA Rules. However, the effect of the orders and/or awards made by an Emergency Arbitrator may be of temporary duration; they may be confirmed, modified, discharged or revoked, pursuant to Article 9.11.

**9.9 An order of the Emergency Arbitrator shall be made in writing, with reasons. An award of the Emergency Arbitrator shall comply with Article 26.2 and, when made, take effect as an award under Article 26.8 (subject to Article 9.11). The Emergency Arbitrator shall be responsible for delivering any order or award to the Registrar, who shall transmit the same promptly to the parties by electronic means, in addition to paper form (if so requested by any party). In the event of any disparity between electronic and paper forms, the electronic form shall prevail.**

**9–043** Article 9.9 sets out the formal requirements for the Emergency Arbitrator's orders and awards. On the whole, they are self-explanatory. An order must be made in writing and contain reasons. An Emergency Arbitrator's award must comply with the requirements of Article 26.2 of the LCIA Rules and so be in writing, generally with reasons, and contain an indication of the date of the award and the seat of the arbitration. Under Article 26.2, an unreasoned award could be rendered if all the parties have agreed to this in writing.

The second sentence of Article 9.9 states that an award rendered by an Emergency Arbitrator shall have the same force and effect as any award made by a fully constituted Arbitral Tribunal. Whilst this provision should aid a party seeking to enforce an award of an Emergency Arbitrator under the New York Convention, the award is ultimately subject to review by the Arbitral Tribunal when constituted pursuant to Article 9.11 of the LCIA Rules. This may give rise to difficulties in enforcement which are considered under Article 9.11 below.

**9–044** Article 9.9 provides that the Emergency Arbitrator is responsible for delivering his decision, whether an order or an award, to the Registrar, who will transmit it promptly to the parties by electronic means and, if requested, in paper form. If any discrepancies exist between the two versions, then unlike the position with an award of the Arbitral Tribunal, the electronically communicated version prevails.[57] Unlike awards rendered by the Arbitral Tribunal, the award of an Emergency Arbitrator does not need to be "authenticated" by the LCIA Registrar. Both of these provisions appear to be aimed at expediting the delivery and enhancing the

---

[57] Article 26.7 provides that the paper version of awards by the Arbitral Tribunal shall prevail. See 26–020.

certainty and finality of the Emergency Arbitrator's decision, in circumstances where speed is likely to be crucial. However, the authentication (stamping, sealing and signing) of an award by the Registrar is not time-consuming and there can be no reason why parties should not request this, should they feel the need for it for enforcement or other reasons.

> **9.10** The Special Fee paid shall form a part of the Arbitration Costs under Article 28.2 determined by the LCIA Court (as to the amount of Arbitration Costs) and decided by the Arbitral Tribunal (as to the proportions in which the parties shall bear Arbitration Costs). Any legal or other expenses incurred by any party during the emergency proceedings shall form a part of the Legal Costs under Article 28.3 decided by the Arbitral Tribunal (as to amount and as to payment between the parties of Legal Costs).

Article 9.10 ties the Special Fee into the general costs regime of LCIA arbitration. Thus the Special Fee forms part of the overall Arbitration Costs, i.e. the costs of the arbitration proceedings other than the costs of legal representation incurred by the parties, and will be included in the determination of the LCIA Court of such costs. The Arbitral Tribunal will decide the proportions in which each party will bear such costs as part of its (or one of its) final awards.[58]

9–045

The legal costs incurred by the parties in connection with the Emergency Arbitrator proceedings form part of the wider Legal Costs (as defined in Article 28.3) of the Reference, and so might also form part of an award of the Arbitral Tribunal.

> **9.11** Any order or award of the Emergency Arbitrator (apart from any order adjourning to the Arbitral Tribunal, when formed, any part of the claim for emergency relief) may be confirmed, varied, discharged or revoked, in whole or in part, by order or award made by the Arbitral Tribunal upon application by any party or upon its own initiative.

By its nature, any urgent interim relief that is granted by a national court is subject to continuing review and, if appropriate, to modification, or even discharge or revocation by the court as facts become clear, the circumstances develop or parties modify their positions (for example, by offering security or other assurances to the court). Without such supervision and flexibility there would be a serious risk that an interim relief measure continued beyond the circumstances justifying it.

9–046

It is appropriate that any interim relief granted by an Emergency Arbitrator should also be subject to supervision and review even after the Emergency Arbitrator proceedings terminate. Continuing supervision is afforded under

---

[58] See Articles 28.1 and 28.2.

Article 9.11 of the LCIA Rules, which provides that the Arbitral Tribunal shall have the power to confirm, vary, discharge or revoke any relief (order or award) granted by the Emergency Arbitrator.

9–047 Whilst welcome and necessary, this power of the Arbitral Tribunal highlights the inherent difficulty with Emergency Arbitrator relief, namely its potential unenforceability under the New York Convention, which applies to final, binding, awards. An Emergency Arbitrator's decision, whether designated as an order or award, that is subject to review by the Arbitral Tribunal, faces potential objections to enforcement under the New York Convention on the grounds that it has not yet become binding on the parties.[59]

This may place the burden on the successful applicant to seek a confirmation of the measure granted by the Emergency Arbitrator if enforcement through national courts is to be sought.

9–048 There are no specific provisions regarding the termination of the Emergency Arbitrator proceedings, but he will effectively become "functus officio" as soon as he has ruled upon the applications submitted to him, and as soon as an Arbitral Tribunal has been appointed, it should address any further issues.

> **9.12 Article 9B shall not prejudice any party's right to apply to a state court or other legal authority for any interim or conservatory measures before the formation of the Arbitration Tribunal; and it shall not be treated as an alternative to or substitute for the exercise of such right. During the emergency proceedings, any application to and any order by such court or authority shall be communicated promptly in writing to the Emergency Arbitrator, the Registrar and all other parties.**

9–049 Some parties will prefer to seek urgent interim relief from national courts rather than an Emergency Arbitrator. For example, since arbitral relief will only ever bind parties to the Arbitration Agreement, the introduction of the Emergency Arbitrator procedure does not obviate the need in some cases to seek preliminary interim relief from a state court or authority with the power to bind third parties: an interim order freezing assets held by a third-party bank will only be effective if it is made by a court that exercises jurisdiction over the bank.

Thus, Article 9.12 of the LCIA Rules provides that the availability of Emergency Arbitrator relief under Article 9B of the LCIA Rules does not prejudice any party's right to apply to seek interim relief from any state court or other legal authority.[60]

9–050 Any party seeking interim relief from a state court whilst Emergency Arbitrator proceedings are pending must promptly notify the Emergency Arbitrator, the Registrar and all parties. However, unlike the position after the Arbitral Tribunal

---

[59] Article V(1)(e) of the New York Convention (Appendix 9).
[60] This is also in line with Article 25.3, which preserves the right of any party to seek interim relief from a state court.

has been constituted, a party seeking such a remedy need not obtain the Emergency Arbitrator's prior authorisation for seeking such relief.[61]

**9.13 Articles 3.3, 13.1-13.4, 14.4, 14.5, 16, 17, 18, 22.3-22.4, 23, 28, 29, 30, 31 and 32 and the Annex shall apply to emergency proceedings. In addition to the provisions expressly set out there and in Article 9B above, the Emergency Arbitrator and the parties to the emergency proceedings shall also be guided by other provisions of the Arbitration Agreement, whilst recognising that several such provisions may not be fully applicable or appropriate to emergency proceedings. Wherever relevant, the LCIA Court may abridge under any such provisions any period of time (pursuant to Article 22.5).**

Issues of speed and urgency aside, the Emergency Arbitrator's proceedings might be expected to resemble any other LCIA proceedings. In addition to the provisions applicable to the appointment of the Emergency Arbitrator, the following Articles of the LCIA Rules are stated as applying to the Emergency Arbitrator procedure:

9–051

- 3.3—communications with the LCIA Court;
- 13.1–13.4—communications between the parties and the Arbitral Tribunal;
- 14.4—the duty of the Arbitral Tribunal to act fairly and impartially between the parties and adopt suitable procedures for the dispute;
- 14.5—powers of the Arbitral Tribunal to discharge its functions, and duty of the parties to co-operate in good faith;
- 16—seat of arbitration and place of hearing;
- 17—language of the arbitration;
- 18—right to legal representation;
- 22.3–22.4—determination of dispute in accordance with the applicable law or *ex aequo et bono*;
- 23—jurisdiction and authority;
- 28—Arbitration Costs and Legal Costs;
- 29—determinations and decisions by the LCIA Court;
- 30—confidentiality;
- 31—limitation of liability of the Arbitral Tribunal and LCIA;
- 32—general rules; and
- Annex—general guidance for the parties' Legal Representatives.

---

[61] See Article 25.3.

**9.14 Article 9B shall not apply if either: (i) the parties have concluded their arbitration agreement before 1 October 2014 and the parties have not agreed in writing to 'opt in' to Article 9B; or (ii) the parties have agreed in writing at any time to 'opt out' of Article 9B.**

9–052   Article 9.14 provides that the Emergency Arbitrator proceedings will only apply where the Arbitration Agreement was entered into on or after October 1, 2014 or if the parties agree in writing to the application of Article 9B. Conversely, parties may agree in writing to disapply Article 9B. They may choose to do so, for example, if they have concerns that relevant national courts might refuse to entertain applications for emergency relief on the grounds that an emergency arbitrator procedure is available to the parties under the Rules they have agreed, and it should have priority.

### Article 9C Expedited Appointment of Replacement Arbitrator

**9.15 Any party may apply to the LCIA Court for the expedited appointment of a replacement arbitrator under Article 11.**

9–053   Article 9C empowers the LCIA Court to make an expedited appointment of a replacement arbitrator under Article 11.

Article 11 concerns the appointment of replacement arbitrators in circumstances where an appointed arbitrator has resigned, is unable to serve for any reason, or the LCIA Court has determined upon challenge or its own motion (under Article 10) that justifiable doubts exist as to his fitness to act, independence or impartiality.

9–054   Article 9.15 provides that, in such circumstances, any party to an LCIA arbitration may apply for the expedited appointment of a replacement arbitrator. The provision is a curious one and is likely rarely to be invoked. The LCIA Secretariat is copied into correspondence and will be aware of the circumstances in the proceedings. It will normally liaise with the LCIA Court in order to appoint a replacement arbitrator promptly and, in doing so, it will take account of representations made to it in ordinary correspondence from the parties' legal representatives. Cases in which the parties' arbitration agreement contains a timetable for nominations are covered by Article 11. It is open to the LCIA Court not to follow the original nominating process. Urgency is obviously a reason for not doing so. However, in the 16 replacements effected in the two years to November 2014, the original nominating process was followed in every case.

**9.16 Such an application shall be made in writing to the Registrar (preferably by electronic means), delivered (or notified) to all other parties to the arbitration; and it shall set out the specific grounds requiring the expedited appointment of the replacement arbitrator.**

Article 9.16 sets out the formal requirements for making an application under Article 9.15, which are similar to those applicable in the case of any other application for expedited appointment, namely: the application must be made in writing to the Registrar and notified to all other parties. The notification of the application should preferably be made by email or other form of electronic transmission.

9–055

The application must state the grounds on which it is made. Article 9.16 does not list possible grounds for an application, and just as the replacement of arbitrators is not a common occurrence under the LCIA Rules, applications for the expedited replacement of arbitrators are also uncommon.

Although not referred to in the Rules, the LCIA now offers an optional service for filing an Article 9C application online (in addition to the optional online filing of Requests and Responses, which are provided for respectively in Articles 1.3 and 2.3). A party or Legal Representative wishing to utilise this optional service is required to register an account with the LCIA Online Filing website and will then have to complete a three-section online form. In section A of the form the applicant must indicate whether the application is submitted with or after the Request and confirm the arbitration number (if available) and the applicant(s) name(s). In section B, the applicant must set out the specific grounds of exceptional urgency alleged and is afforded an opportunity to upload electronic copies of documents (each less than 64 MB in size) in support of the application. In section C, the applicant is required to confirm that the application and all supporting documents have been delivered to all parties, and to confirm how such delivery was effected.

The authors are aware of only one application for the expedited replacement of an arbitrator under the 1998 Rules, in circumstances where, around a month prior to a preliminary issues hearing, a Chairman of an Arbitral Tribunal offered to resign if either party had lost confidence in him. One of the parties accepted his offer, and applied to the LCIA Court for his expedited replacement. The other party reluctantly joined in the application in order to avoid a vacancy on the date of the hearing. Ultimately, the LCIA Court directed that the agreed co-arbitrator nomination process should be followed applying a truncated timetable.

9–056

Thus circumstances giving rise to exceptional urgency in relation to the appointment of a replacement arbitrator might include such issues as fast-approaching procedural deadlines or an urgent need for final relief that can only be granted by a fully constituted Arbitral Tribunal. The circumstances surrounding the replacement of an arbitrator, including for example the conduct of the parties in the course of the arbitration, might also be relevant.

**9.17 The LCIA Court shall determine the application as expeditiously as possible in the circumstances. If the application is granted, for the purpose of expediting the appointment of the replacement arbitrator the LCIA Court may abridge any period of time in the Arbitration Agreement or any other agreement of the parties (pursuant to Article 22.5).**

9–057   Article 9.17 provides that the LCIA Court must deal with an application for the expedited replacement of an arbitrator as quickly as possible in the circumstances of the case. If the application is granted, the LCIA Court may exercise its powers under Article 22.5 to shorten (or abridge) any time limit set out in the Arbitration Agreement or any other agreement between the parties regarding the appointment of the arbitrator.

ARTICLE 10—REVOCATION AND CHALLENGES

10.1 The LCIA Court may revoke any arbitrator's appointment upon its own initiative, at the written request of all other members of the Arbitral Tribunal or upon a written challenge by any party if: (i) that arbitrator gives written notice to the LCIA Court of his or her intent to resign as arbitrator, to be copied to all parties and all other members of the Arbitral Tribunal (if any); (ii) that arbitrator falls seriously ill, refuses or becomes unable or unfit to act; or (iii) circumstances exist that give rise to justifiable doubts as to that arbitrator's impartiality or independence.

10.2 The LCIA Court may determine that an arbitrator is unfit to act under Article 10.1 if that arbitrator: (i) acts in deliberate violation of the Arbitration Agreement; (ii) does not act fairly or impartially as between the parties; or (iii) does not conduct or participate in the arbitration with reasonable efficiency, diligence and industry.

10.3 A party challenging an arbitrator under Article 10.1 shall, within 14 days of the formation of the Arbitral Tribunal or (if later) within 14 days of becoming aware of any grounds described in Article 10.1 or 10.2, deliver a written statement of the reasons for its challenge to the LCIA Court, the Arbitral Tribunal and all other parties. A party may challenge an arbitrator whom it has nominated, or in whose appointment it has participated, only for reasons of which it becomes aware after the appointment has been made by the LCIA Court.

10.4 The LCIA Court shall provide to those other parties and the challenged arbitrator a reasonable opportunity to comment on the challenging party's written statement. The LCIA Court may require at any time further information and materials from the challenging party, the challenged arbitrator, other parties and other members of the Arbitral Tribunal (if any).

10.5 If all other parties agree in writing to the challenge within 14 days of receipt of the written statement, the LCIA Court shall revoke that arbitrator's appointment (without reasons).

10.6 Unless the parties so agree or the challenged arbitrator resigns in writing within 14 days of receipt of the written statement, the LCIA Court shall decide the challenge and, if upheld, shall revoke that arbitrator's appointment. The LCIA Court's decision shall be made in writing, with reasons; and a copy shall be transmitted by the Registrar to the parties, the challenged arbitrator and other members of the

Arbitral Tribunal (if any). A challenged arbitrator who resigns in writing prior to the LCIA Court's decision shall not be considered as having admitted any part of the written statement.

**10.7** The LCIA Court shall determine the amount of fees and expenses (if any) to be paid for the former arbitrator's services, as it may consider appropriate in the circumstances. The LCIA Court may also determine whether, in what amount and to whom any party should pay forthwith the costs of the challenge; and the LCIA Court may also refer all or any part of such costs to the later decision of the Arbitral Tribunal and/or the LCIA Court under Article 28.

**Introduction**

10–001  Many institutional arbitration rules contain provisions governing the removal and replacement of arbitrators, upon challenge and for other reasons. The procedure commonly envisages a challenge by a party, or a request or proposal by co-arbitrators or the institution, followed by an opportunity for the challenged arbitrator(s) and remaining parties to respond by accepting the challenge or objecting to it, in which case the final decision rests with the governing body of the institution or an independent panel designated by it. The LCIA is unusual in providing written reasons for challenge decisions to the parties.

The availability of a challenge procedure helps to ensure that the parties' faith in the arbitration process and the enforcement of the ultimate award are not undermined by the actual or perceived bias, or other form of misconduct, of an arbitrator. The importance of such procedures is recognised in national arbitration laws, many of which contain a statutory challenge procedure from which the parties cannot contract out.[1] The LCIA website regards the mechanism for determining challenges to arbitrators as one of the fundamental safeguards of the arbitral process.[2]

10–002  Regrettably, it has become common practice among some parties and counsel to bring tactical challenges by making "unwarranted objections"[3] to the other party's nominated arbitrator. Such challenges might be made with the intention of causing delay and expense or in the hope of obtaining some other forensic or procedural advantage, and even with a view to intimidating the arbitrator appointed by the other side.[4] It is an unavoidable reality that even if such challenges are doomed to fail, some disruption to the proceedings and wasted costs are bound to occur.

---

[1] Article 13(3) of the UNCITRAL Model Law (Appendix 10) and s.24 of the English Arbitration Act 1996 (Appendix 7) are both mandatory provisions.
[2] http://www.lcia.org/Dispute_Resolution_Services/The_Case_for_Administered_Arbitration_.aspx [Accessed November 14, 2014].
[3] William W. Park, "Arbitration's Discontents: Of Elephants and Pornography" (2001) 17(3) Arbitration Int. 263.
[4] See Julian D.M. Lew et al., *Comparative International Commercial Arbitration* (The Hague: Kluwer Law International, 2003) p.302; Nigel Blackaby and Constantine Partasides, *Redfern and Hunter on International Arbitration* (Oxford: Oxford University Press, 2009), pp.4–91. Howard M. Holtzmann et al., "I Conduct by a Party to Disrupt Establishing the Tribunal and Starting the Arbitral Proceedings" in A.J. van den Berg (ed.), *Preventing Delay and Disruption of Arbitration* (ICCA Congress series) (Kluwer Law International, 1991), pp.131–159.

The issue of costs can now be dealt with directly by the LCIA Court deciding the challenge. Furthermore, the new General Guidelines for the Parties' Legal Representatives in the Annex to the 2014 Rules include the following at paragraph 2: "A legal representative should not engage in activities intended unfairly to obstruct the arbitration or to jeopardise the finality of any award, including repeated challenges to an arbitrator's appointment or to the jurisdiction or authority of the Arbitral Tribunal known to be unfounded by that legal representative."[5]

Under the LCIA Rules it is the LCIA Court that is empowered both to appoint arbitrators and to consider challenges and revoke appointments. In practice, the determination of challenges is delegated to the President or a Vice President (or former Vice President) of the LCIA Court acting alone or to a Division composed of three members of the LCIA Court.[6] It is for the members of the LCIA Court in making challenge determinations to ensure that the challenge procedures are not abused and that they will be able to draft their written decisions promptly after the close of submissions.

Challenge procedures are followed closely by the Registrar and by Counsel in the Secretariat responsible for the administration of the particular case. The Secretariat is able to act quickly to provide the LCIA Court with the necessary information, documents and correspondence, and to respond to queries about the proceedings, because it is copied into all communications between the parties and the Arbitral Tribunal.[7] The Registrar will be able to advise the President of the LCIA Court on the relative urgency of the matter and on other factors to be taken into account in the selection of a Division or of a sole Vice President to determine the challenge.

**10–003**

Under the mandatory provisions of s.24 of the English Arbitration Act 1996, a party in an English seated arbitration, whose challenge is rejected by the LCIA Court, can apply to the English High Court for the removal of the arbitrator. Such an application was made in *A v B*, in which the judge upheld the decision of the former Vice President of the LCIA Court who had rejected the challenge.[8] The application under s.24 was combined with one under s.68 to have the sole arbitrator's partial award set aside for serious irregularity. The case concerned an arbitrator who practised as a barrister in England and who disclosed, shortly before making his award, that he had just realised that he was instructed as an advocate in recently revived court proceedings by a law firm which was representing one side in the arbitration. His award, issued 14 days after his disclosure, was in favour of that law firm's clients. The challenge under Article 10 was filed with the LCIA on the next day (the deadline under Article 10.4 of the 1998 Rules).

The judge noted the following in relation to the challenge and the LCIA Court's decision:

**10–004**

"After the claimants launched that challenge under the LCIA Rules, they invited X to resign as arbitrator, which he declined to do in a letter of

---

[5] See the commentary on Article 18.5 and on the Annex.
[6] See the commentary on Article 3.
[7] See the commentary on Article 13.
[8] [2011] EWHC 2345 (Comm).

31 December 2010. The President of the LCIA Court of Arbitration, Professor William W Park then appointed one of the members of the Court, Mr Gerald Aksen, a US attorney to determine the claimants' challenge to the arbitrator. He received written submissions from the parties as well as X's letter of 15 February 2011 and then issued his written Decision on Challenge to Sole Arbitrator dated 11 March 2011 in which he denied the challenge.

It is not necessary to refer to that Decision in detail as it is not in any sense binding on me, given that I have to decide the present application de novo. However, it is interesting to note that Mr Aksen, in ruling that there were no circumstances that gave rise to justifiable doubts as to X's impartiality and independence, focused on the fact that a barrister in England does not "represent" the solicitors who instruct him, but the lay client."

**10–005** By a joint decision of the LCIA Court and Board in May 2006, the LCIA resolved to publish abstracts of the LCIA Court's decisions on challenges to arbitrators. Motivated by a desire to provide an important source of information for parties, practitioners and arbitrators alike,[9] the subsequent publication of redacted challenge decisions[10] has not only distinguished the LCIA from other arbitral institutions, but has shed light on the standards adopted by LCIA Court Divisions in resolving challenges and in dealing with abusive challenges.[11]

Finally, whilst the 2014 version of Article 10 of the LCIA Rules introduced significant textual revisions, few substantive changes were made. The re-drafting of Article 10 served predominantly to clarify and organise the provisions in logical sequence, and the current wording is clearer and represents a significant improvement on the 1998 version. Thus, Articles 10.1 and 10.2 set out the grounds for revocation of an arbitral appointment; Articles 10.3–10.6 set out the procedure for challenging an arbitrator; and Article 10.7 deals with the question of the fees to be paid to an arbitrator whose mandate has been revoked, as well as with the allocation of the costs of any challenge. Article 11 deals with the replacement of an arbitrator whose appointment has been revoked.

> **10.1 The LCIA Court may revoke any arbitrator's appointment upon its own initiative, at the written request of all other members of the Arbitral Tribunal or upon a written challenge by any party if: (i) that arbitrator gives written notice to the LCIA Court of his or her intent to resign as arbitrator, to be copied to all parties and all other members of the Arbitral Tribunal (if any); (ii) that arbitrator falls seriously ill, refuses or becomes unable or unfit to act; or (iii) circumstances exist that give rise to justifiable doubts as to that arbitrator's impartiality or independence.**

---

[9] See "LCIA Court Decisions on Challenges to Arbitrators: A Proposal to Publish", Geoff Nicholas and Constantine Partasides (2007) 23(1) Arbitration Int. 1.

[10] "Challenge Digests" (2011) 27(3) Arbitration Int.

[11] For example, by making appropriate costs orders, see LCIA Court Decision on Challenge to Arbitrator, LCIA Reference No. 0252 (2011) 27(3) Arbitration Int. 358.

Article 10.1 sets out the circumstances in which the LCIA Court may exercise its  **10–006**
power to revoke an arbitrator's appointment.[12] These include:

- resignation;
- serious illness;
- refusal to act;
- inability to act;
- unfitness to act; and
- circumstances that give rise to justifiable doubts as to that arbitrator's impartiality or independence.

If any of the above grounds are established, the LCIA Court may revoke the  **10–007**
appointment of an arbitrator, on its own initiative,[13] at the request of the remaining arbitrators or upon a challenge by a party.

There is no prescribed form for a resignation, request by co-arbitrators for the revocation of the appointment of a fellow arbitrator[14] or for a challenge of an arbitrator.

It is notable that both under Article 10.1 and Article 10.2 the LCIA Court retains discretion, even when the grounds for revocation are established, as to whether or not to revoke the arbitral appointment.

**Grounds for revocation**

*Resignation*

Prima facie it appears uncontroversial that the resignation of an arbitrator should  **10–008**
lead to the revocation of his appointment and his replacement with another arbitrator. However, attempts by arbitrators in a number of infamous cases to frustrate the conduct of a reference by resigning from their post shortly before the award was rendered demonstrates that an unchecked right to resign could be abused by a partisan arbitrator (although if an arbitrator on a three-person Arbitral Tribunal refuses to participate in deliberations, it would be possible for the remaining arbitrators to continue with the arbitration and render a majority award pursuant to Article 12.1). Indeed, the resignation of an arbitrator, particularly at the later stages of an arbitration reference, can result in significant disruption to the proceedings and wasted costs while an arbitrator is replaced or if substantive

---

[12] The replacement procedure is set out in Article 11 of the LCIA Rules.
[13] Under the 1998 version of the LCIA Rules, the power of the LCIA Court to revoke an appointment on its own initiative was less clearly stated, but understood by the LCIA Court to be embodied in the language of the 1998 version of Article 10.2 (LCIA Court Decision on Challenge to Arbitrator, LCIA Reference No. 3431, July 3, 2003, December 18, 2003 and February 18, 2004 (2011) 27(3) Arbitration Int. 358). The current version of the Rules is in line with other modern institutional arbitration rules. See Article 15.2 of the ICC Rules; Article 14.3 of the SIAC Rules and Article 12 of the Swiss Rules.
[14] The authors are not aware of any case in which such a request was made.

hearings need to be repeated.[15] Thus the LCIA Court has a discretion whether to accept the resignation of an arbitrator (although the authors are not aware of any cases in which a resignation has been rejected by the LCIA Court).[16]

Although there is no prescribed form, an arbitrator's resignation must be made in writing, addressed to the LCIA Court and be copied to the parties and co-arbitrators (if any). Whilst neither the parties nor co-arbitrators are afforded an express right to respond to a resignation, such a right may be implied from the right to receive a copy and, if so, it would seem to follow that the LCIA Court would be required to consider any submissions made.

**10–009**   Another issue that arbitrators face from time to time is a request that they resign from a party that did not nominate them. Such requests, citing (for example) an alleged lack of confidence in the individual arbitrator, are sometimes made in circumstances where there are no grounds for making a formal challenge. An arbitrator faced with such a request at the outset of proceedings might be tempted to consider resignation in order to avoid wasting the time and cost associated with a challenge procedure, or because the arbitrator considers that having the full trust of all the parties is more important than staying in office. However, a strong argument can be made to the contrary; that arbitrators should not resign if they consider the grounds for the request to be insufficiently strong to form the basis for a formal challenge. Such circumstances might suggest that the request is being made solely for dilatory or other tactical purposes,[17] as an arbitrator resigning is likely to result in delay and disruption to the proceedings. In this regard, the arbitrator may consider that his duty under Article 14.1, to conduct the proceedings in a manner that avoids unnecessary delay and expense, militates against resigning where a request is not fully justified.

### Serious illness

**10–010**   The LCIA Court may revoke the appointment of an arbitrator who falls seriously ill or becomes unable to act as an arbitrator.

It is presumed that serious illness could only properly form the basis for the revocation of an appointment if the condition prevents the arbitrator from fulfilling his duties under the LCIA Rules, or at the very least if it gives rise to justifiable doubt as to his ability to perform his functions for the duration of the reference.[18] Although such a reading might render "serious illness" otiose as a stand-alone ground for revocation, it would be patently unfair if an arbitral appointment could be revoked in circumstances where an arbitrator's illness, however serious, does not give rise to justifiable concerns as to his ability to perform his functions.

---

[15] Howard M. Holtzmann et al., "III Conduct by a Party-Appointed Arbitrator during the Arbitral Proceedings" in A.J. van den Berg (ed.), *Preventing Delay and Disruption of Arbitration* (ICCA Congress series) (1991), pp.269–289.

[16] But see the examples given by Yves Derains and Eric A. Schwartz in *A Guide to the ICC Rules of Arbitration*, 2nd edn (Kluwer Law International, 2005), Ch.4, pp.115–207.

[17] See Derains and Schwartz, *A Guide to the ICC Rules of Arbitration* (Kluwer Law International, 2005), p.195.

[18] Under s.24(1)(c) of the English Arbitration Act 1996 (a mandatory provision), an arbitrator may be removed from office if he is physically or mentally incapable of conducting the proceedings or there are justifiable doubts as to his capacity to do so (Appendix 7).

of the challenge" may be limited to the fees and expenses of the members of the Division and the LCIA's administrative charges. However, the lack of a definition in the Rules will allow parties to argue that the power extends to all types of costs. It remains to be seen how this power will be used in practice.

Alternatively, the LCIA Court may defer the decision on all or part of such costs for determination pursuant to Article 28 of the LCIA Rules.

The costs of a challenge can be relatively high, particularly if a three-member Division is appointed and delicate and complex issues are raised. The requirement that a reasoned written decision be rendered, one which may be published in due course in the form of an abstract, imposes a burden on the Division, which could translate into many recorded hours of work.   **10–045**

successful challenge to the enforcement of any award rendered by them.[16] The arbitrators must consider procedural agreements reached by the parties in the light of the particular circumstances of the case before them. For example, a procedural agreement to the effect that one party shall have no right to raise defences or make submissions to the Arbitral Tribunal may not normally be acceptable to an Arbitral Tribunal, but could legitimately be adopted in an arbitration arising from an undertaking to pay an admitted debt, backed up by an express irrevocable agreement that upon breach the Claimant would be immediately entitled to a consent award.[17]

*The potential for disagreements*

**14–009** The freedom to agree on procedural matters also far too often entails the potential for disagreements between the parties over procedural matters, most commonly perhaps when their respective counsel are from different legal traditions. There will often be a temptation for parties represented by lawyers less accustomed to the practice of international arbitration to seek to replicate, to some extent at least, certain familiar procedures over any proposals put forward by the opposing party. A party's own domestic rules of procedure are, to them, "tried and tested", whereas its opponent's may well be unknown and perceived as conferring an advantage on the other side.

The differing approaches to procedure in international arbitration are often particularly apparent where one party is from a common law jurisdiction and the other a civil law jurisdiction, but significant differences can also be found between one common law jurisdiction and another as well as between one civil law jurisdiction and another.[18]

**14–010** It should be remembered that an international arbitration, under the LCIA Rules or otherwise, is quite different from domestic court litigation. One of the advantages of arbitration is the ability of the parties, or in the absence of agreement, the Arbitral Tribunal, to tailor the proceedings to the requirements of the dispute and of the parties to it.[19] International arbitration should not, therefore, blindly seek to replicate the domestic court procedure of any of the parties or of any of the arbitrators' home jurisdictions, and care should be taken, in particular, to avoid the extremes of any national legal system.[20]

---

[16] Under Article V(1)(d) of the New York Convention an enforcing court may refuse recognition and enforcement of an award if the arbitration procedure adopted was not in accordance with the agreement of the parties (Appendix 9).

[17] *Gujarat NRE Coke Ltd v Coeclerici Asia (PTE) Ltd* [2013] EWHC 1987 (Comm).

[18] There is no "one size fits all" in either common or civil law systems. For example, the approach to disclosure and the use of evidence in the US is significantly different to the approach adopted in England and Wales, notwithstanding that both are common law jurisdictions. Nor is an identical approach guaranteed in all civil law systems.

[19] See DAC Report at para.151 (Appendix 8).

[20] See *Redfern and Hunter on International Arbitration*, 5th edn (Oxford University Press, 2009), p.363 at at para.6.02. "The only certainty [in the conduct of international arbitration] is that the parties' counsel should not bring the rule books from their home courts with them."

conducted at the arbitral seat and any order or award as having been made at that seat.

Article 16.3 confirms that the venue both for hearings (involving all participants or at least the Arbitral Tribunal and the parties' representatives) and for deliberations (involving only the arbitrators) may be at a location other than the seat of the arbitration. It also confirms that an award signed in a different place, or perhaps circulated to different places for signature by three arbitrators, will be treated as having been made at the seat. This overcomes the problem which arose in an English case in which an otherwise English award was held to be French because it was signed in Paris.[15]

16–013

Hearings in LCIA arbitrations have been held in many different locations around the world, including, for example, New York, Washington DC, Geneva, Budapest, Dubai and Singapore.

The LCIA Rules do not require all participants in a hearing to attend physically at the relevant location. Initial procedural hearings, for example, are frequently conducted over the telephone.

**16.4 The law applicable to the Arbitration Agreement and the arbitration shall be the law applicable at the seat of the arbitration, unless and to the extent that the parties have agreed in writing on the application of other laws or rules of law and such agreement is not prohibited by the law applicable at the arbitral seat.**

Article 16.4 provides useful confirmation that both (i) the governing law of the Arbitration Agreement (which may or may not be the same as the governing law of the contract in which it is contained) and (ii) the procedural law of the arbitration (the *"lex arbitri"*) will be the law of the seat unless the parties have expressly agreed otherwise.

16–014

This provision overcomes the problem that arose, for example, in an English ad hoc arbitration under an insurance policy which was itself governed by New York law.[16] The Court of Appeal held in that case that the parties' choice of London as the seat for the arbitration "must be a choice of forum for remedies seeking to attack the award", as well as a choice of procedural law for the conduct of the arbitration, and that the English Arbitration Act 1996 would apply to a challenge to the award.

Longmore LJ considered (obiter) whether, in the absence of an express choice, the law governing the Arbitration Agreement was the law of the underlying contract or the law of the seat. He found that it would be rare for the law of the (separable) Arbitration Agreement to be different from the law of the seat, explaining:

16–015

"an agreement to arbitrate will normally have a closer and more real connection with the place where the parties have chosen to arbitrate than with the place of the law of the underlying contract in cases where the parties have

---

[15] *Hiscox v Outhwaite (No.1)* [1992] 1 A.C. 562 HL.
[16] *C v D* [2008] 1 Lloyd's Rep. 239.

**Tribunal, the Arbitral Tribunal may order any or all of the following sanctions against the legal representative: (i) a written reprimand; (ii) a written caution as to future conduct in the arbitration; and (iii) any other measure necessary to fulfil within the arbitration the general duties required of the Arbitral Tribunal under Articles 14.4(i) and (ii).**

18–029　Having made the new Guidelines part of its Rules, the LCIA is able to give Arbitral Tribunals the power to impose sanctions for breach of those Guidelines. Of course, such sanctions will only be imposed after the parties have been given an opportunity to comment. Once again, arbitrators will be conscious of the need to act fairly in exercising these new powers and to avoid holding themselves open to challenges.

The sanctions are somewhat muted and do not include the exclusion of a legal representative or the reporting to a legal representative's professional body, both of which had been proposed in drafts of the revisions.

It remains to be seen what sorts of sanctions will be applied as "any other measure necessary to fulfil within the arbitration the general duties required of the Arbitral Tribunal under Articles 14.4(i) and (ii)." Those duties are to act fairly and impartially as between the parties, but also to adopt procedures to provide an efficient and expeditious means for the final resolution of the parties' dispute. According to the new wording of Article 10.2, the LCIA Court may determine that an arbitrator is unfit to act if he or she does not act fairly or impartially or does not conduct the arbitration "with reasonable efficiency, diligence and industry". The balance between fairness and efficiency can be a difficult one.

It should be noted that, in making decisions on costs under Article 28.4, the Arbitral Tribunal may take into account the parties' conduct, which could, no doubt, include their legal representatives' compliance with the new Guidelines and with any measures taken under Article 18.6.

applicant party have consented to such joinder in writing following the Commencement Date or (if earlier) in the Arbitration Agreement; and thereafter to make a single final award, or separate awards, in respect of all parties so implicated in the arbitration;

(ix) to order, with the approval of the LCIA Court, the consolidation of the arbitration with one or more other arbitrations into a single arbitration subject to the LCIA Rules where all the parties to the arbitrations to be consolidated so agree in writing;

(x) to order, with the approval of the LCIA Court, the consolidation of the arbitration with one or more other arbitrations subject to the LCIA Rules commenced under the same arbitration agreement or any compatible arbitration agreement(s) between the same disputing parties, provided that no arbitral tribunal has yet been formed by the LCIA Court for such other arbitration(s) or, if already formed, that such tribunal(s) is(are) composed of the same arbitrators; and

(xi) to order the discontinuance of the arbitration if it appears to the Arbitral Tribunal that the arbitration has been abandoned by the parties or all claims and any cross-claims withdrawn by the parties, provided that, after fixing a reasonable period of time within which the parties shall be invited to agree or to object to such discontinuance, no party has stated its written objection to the Arbitral Tribunal to such discontinuance upon the expiry of such period of time.

22.2 By agreeing to arbitration under the Arbitration Agreement, the parties shall be treated as having agreed not to apply to any state court or other legal authority for any order available from the Arbitral Tribunal (if formed) under Article 22.1, except with the agreement in writing of all parties.

22.3 The Arbitral Tribunal shall decide the parties' dispute in accordance with the law(s) or rules of law chosen by the parties as applicable to the merits of their dispute. If and to the extent that the Arbitral Tribunal decides that the parties have made no such choice, the Arbitral Tribunal shall apply the law(s) or rules of law which it considers appropriate.

22.4 The Arbitral Tribunal shall only apply to the merits of the dispute principles deriving from "ex aequo et bono", "amiable composition" or "honourable engagement" where the parties have so agreed in writing.

22.5 Subject to any order of the Arbitral Tribunal under Article 22.1(ii), the LCIA Court may also abridge or extend any period of time under the Arbitration Agreement or other agreement of the parties (even where the period of time has expired).

- principles of conflicts of laws widely adopted in national laws and international instruments such as the Rome I Regulation (Regulation (EC) No. 593/2008; and

- likely enforcement venues.

The extent to which any such factors will take precedence over other factors will ultimately depend on the nature and circumstances of the case at hand.

*Mandatory rules*

22-051    Whether or not the parties have made an express choice of law, the Arbitral Tribunal needs to consider the application of mandatory rules of law. Mandatory laws are rules of law which parties cannot contract out of. Mandatory laws that are relied upon in arbitral proceedings may have a number of different sources, for example: the proper law of the contract; the law of the seat or place of arbitration; the legal order of a third country; a supranational order, such as resolutions of the UN Securities Council or EU competition laws or other norms of international public policy; or the legal order governing at the place or potential places where enforcement of the award might be sought.[52]

Where mandatory laws form part of the applicable law (as agreed by the parties or, in the absence of agreement, selected by the Arbitral Tribunal pursuant to Article 22.3 of the LCIA Rules), they must be applied by the Arbitral Tribunal, even if, ultimately, the parties' choice of law could mean that the award might be set aside at the seat of arbitration,[53] or enforcement of the award be denied at the place of enforcement.[54]

**22.4    The Arbitral Tribunal shall only apply to the merits of the dispute principles deriving from "ex aequo et bono", "amiable composition" or "honourable engagement" where the parties have so agreed in writing.**

22-052    Rather infrequently in practice, parties agree that the Arbitral Tribunal should decide the dispute between them not by reference to any particular rules of law, but by reference to the arbitrators' own sense of fairness and justice.

Article 22.4 of the LCIA Rules serves two functions. On the one hand it confirms that the parties may confer on the Arbitral Tribunal the power to act *ex aequo et bono*.[55] On the other hand, it restricts the power of the Arbitral Tribunal to act in this manner to cases in which the parties have so agreed in writing.

---

[52] Marc Blessing, "Mandatory Rules of Law versus Party Autonomy in International Arbitration" (1997) 14(4) J. Int. Arb. 23.
[53] See Article 34(2)(iv) of the UNCITRAL Model Law (Appendix 10) and s.68 of the English Arbitration Act 1996 (Appendix 7).
[54] See Article V(2)(b) of the New York Convention (Appendix 9).
[55] The expressions *"ex aequo et bono"*, "amiable composition" and "honourable engagement" are all taken to confer the power on an arbitrator to decide a dispute in accordance with principles of fairness and justice without reference to the rules of any national or other law. See the discussion at Gary B. Born, *International Commercial Arbitration* (2014), Ch.19 "Choice of Substantive Law in International Arbitration", para.19.07.

However, there is also an important distinction to be made between, on the one 25–003
hand, conservatory measures intended to ensure that the final award will be
enforceable, by way of preserving property or requiring security, and, on the other
hand, interim measures, allowing one party to obtain, on a provisional basis, part
of the relief that it has claimed.

Both types of measures carry the possibility of making it commercially worthwhile for the parties to continue with the arbitration, whether by "holding the ring" or, for example, by allowing one party to collect a debt before dealing with a complaint about performance or quality. Likewise, the possibility of obtaining security for the costs of defending a claim can give a Respondent financial comfort to participate in the arbitration, allowing it to conduct a full defence.

The commercial good sense of these provisions makes them attractive to 25–004
parties. They have often been used in conjunction with the expedited formation of
an Arbitral Tribunal (now Article 9A), which is another special feature of the
Rules,[1] and will now also be used in connection with applications to an Emergency
Arbitrator, provision for which is made in Article 9B of the 2014 Rules.

There are two questions that arise in relation to the grant of any interim or conservatory measures by an Arbitral Tribunal, which must be answered before any order is made; namely whether the Arbitral Tribunal has the power to grant the relief sought and, if so, whether it should exercise its power.

Whether an Arbitral Tribunal can exercise the powers conferred on it by Articles 25–005
25.1 or 25.2 may depend on the law of the seat. The arbitration laws in many
jurisdictions recognise that arbitrators may exercise such powers unless agreed
otherwise by the parties.[2]

In England, the Arbitration Act 1996 sets out in s.38 powers which the Tribunal will have to make certain orders in relation to the preservation of property and in relation to security for costs. However, the parties can agree not to confer these powers on the Tribunal (s.38(2)) and/or to agree on other powers "exercisable by the arbitral tribunal for the purposes of and in relation to the proceedings" (s.38(1)). In the case of an LCIA arbitration with a seat in England, Article 25.1 confirms that the parties have agreed on the specific powers set out in it.

In relation to provisional measures, s.39(1) of the English Arbitration Act 1996 25–006
confirms that parties are free to agree that "the tribunal shall have power to order on
a provisional basis any relief which it would have power to grant in a final award".
Section 39(4) states that unless the parties do so agree, the Tribunal has no such

---

[1] It is interesting to note, in the context of Article 25 and the debates about Emergency Arbitrator procedures, that the draftsmen of the 1998 Rules had contemplated inserting an article entitled "Exceptional Provisional Measures", which would have allowed the LCIA Court to make provisional orders prior to the formation of the Arbitral Tribunal. Objections on the LCIA Court to the notion of a non-arbitrator making orders of this kind were overwhelming, and the proposal was abandoned at the LCIA's Selsdon conference in May 1997. See V.V. Veeder "The Draft New 1998 LCIA Rules", Biennial IFCAI Conference, October 24, 1997, Geneva, Switzerland, *http://www.wipo.int/amc/en/events/conferences/1997/october/veeder.html* [Accessed November 12, 2014].

[2] See Article 17 of the UNCITRAL Model Law (Appendix 10). The power afforded by Article 25.1(iii) of the LCIA Rules to order on a provisional basis any remedy that would be available to it in the final award is provided for in s.39 of the English Arbitration Act 1996 (Appendix 7) but is not reflected, for example, in the UNCITRAL Model law. There is some debate as to the law that should govern this issue: the law of the seat, of the underlying contract or general principles of law. See Gary B. Born, *International Commercial Arbitration*, 2nd edn (Kluwer Law International, 2014), Ch.17 "Provisional Relief in International Arbitration", pp.2424–2563 at p.2546, and the references there.

In practice, arbitrators who fall seriously ill, and consider that they will be unable to conduct the reference properly, are likely to tender their resignation (Article 10.1(i)). If they are so ill that they cannot write a letter of resignation, Article 10.1(ii) comes into operation.

### *Inability to act*

The fact that "inability to act" is listed as a ground for revocation separately from "refusal" and "unfitness" to act (both considered below) clarifies that the LCIA Court may revoke an appointment even in circumstances where the inability to act is not deliberate or intentional and where there is no failure or culpability on the part of the arbitrator. Such circumstances may, for example, include a legal prohibition such as a national court order restraining the arbitrator from participating in the arbitration. 10–011

At the same time, inability to act can be distinguished from circumstances where the arbitrator is attempting in good faith to perform his duties but failing to meet the standards required under the LCIA Rules.

### *Refusal to act*

Whilst a refusal to act is a separate ground for the revocation of an arbitrator's appointment, as will become apparent in the context of Article 10.2 (below), an arbitrator who refuses to act may also fall within the definition of an arbitrator who is "unfit to act" either because he acts "in deliberate violation of the Arbitration Agreement" or because he does not "conduct or participate in the arbitration with reasonable diligence and industry". Because a challenge on the grounds of lack of fitness to act does not require proof of an actual "refusal" to act, but only an objective failure to do so, it may be used where the arbitrator's "refusal" could only be implied (for example, by reason of his inaction). 10–012

### *Unfit to act*

Circumstances in which the LCIA Court may declare an arbitrator unfit to act are set out in Article 10.2, which is considered below. 10–013

### *Circumstances exist that give rise to justifiable doubts as to the arbitrator's impartiality or independence*

This is the most commonly relied upon ground for removal of an arbitrator by parties in challenge proceedings. It safeguards the arbitrator's duties under Article 5.3 of the LCIA Rules to "be and remain at all times impartial and independent of the parties". It may also come into play where breaches of the duty under Article 14.4 of the LCIA Rules "to act fairly and impartially as between all parties" are alleged to give rise to justifiable doubts as to the arbitrator's independence and impartiality. The duty of impartiality and independence is a fundamental principle of international arbitration and is widely equated with the absence of bias. 10–014

The legal test of whether "justifiable doubts" exist as to the impartiality and independence of an arbitrator is an objective one and does not require actual bias to be established:[19]

> "Doubts are justifiable if a reasonable third person, having knowledge of the relevant facts and circumstances, would reach the conclusion that there is a likelihood that the arbitrator may be influenced by factors other than the merits of the case as presented by the parties in reaching his or her decision".

10–015 To date, all but one of the published challenge decisions by the LCIA Court pertained to arbitration proceedings with a seat in England,[20] and English law was often applied.[21] The leading English judicial authority is *Porter v Magill*,[22] in which the House of Lords phrased the English law test for bias in the following terms (at [103]):

> "The question is whether the fair-minded and informed observer, having considered the facts, would conclude that there was a real possibility that the tribunal was biased."

Thus it is apparent that English law on this subject is broadly in line with the IBA Guidelines, as well as with the jurisprudence of many other jurisdictions in Europe and beyond.[23]

### *LCIA Court challenge decisions concerning impartiality and independence*

10–016 A number of the LCIA Court challenge decisions referred to below were made in respect of arbitrators appointed in UNCITRAL arbitrations, in which the LCIA

---

[19] See the IBA Guidelines on Conflicts of Interest, General Standard 2(c) at Appendix 13; LCIA Court challenge decision in LCIA Case No. UN7949, *http://italaw.com/sites/default/files/case-documents/italaw1171.pdf* [Accessed November 14, 2014]; NB this was a decision in relation to a challenge brought in an arbitration conducted under the UNCITRAL Arbitration Rules 1976, pursuant to which the grounds for challenge were identical to Ground (d) of Article 10.2 of the 1998 version of the LCIA Rules; *Country X v Company Q*, challenge decision, January 11, 1995, A.J. van den Berg (ed.), *Yearbook Commercial Arbitration* (Kluwer Law International, 1997), pp.22–242.

[20] LCIA Court challenge decision in LCIA Case No. UN7949, *http://italaw.com/sites/default/files/case-documents/italaw1171.pdf* [Accessed November 14, 2014], was made pursuant to a special agreement between the parties to a Bilateral Investment Treaty arbitration under the UNCITRAL Rules. The parties agreed that the challenge should be referred to the LCIA Court rather the ICC Court, which was the designated appointing authority in the arbitration. The seat of the arbitration is not set out in the challenge decision, and whilst at least one of the parties did refer in submissions to the English Arbitration Act 1996 and related authorities, the decision does not expressly make reference to the application of any national laws. The decision is unusual because it is available in full: most other challenge decisions can only be read in abstract form in the special edition of *Arbitration International*.

[21] See, for example, LCIA Reference Nos 81209 and 81210, November 16, 2009 (2011) 27(3) Arbitration Int. 455, at paras 3.1–3.2; or LCIA Reference No. 7932, June 17, 2008 (2011) 27(3) Arbitration Int. 433, also at paras 3.1–3.2.

[22] [2002] 2 A.C. 357.

[23] *Porter v Magill* brought English law into line with the jurisprudence of the European Court of Human Rights (ECHR) in relation to Article 6 of the ECHR, and similar tests apply in relation to arbitration in Hong Kong, Malaysia, Australia, New Zealand and Brunei. See Sam Luttrell, *Bias Challenges in International Commercial Arbitration: The Need for a "Real Danger" Test* (Kluwer Law International, 2009), Ch.5. In the US, the remedy for arbitrator bias is vacatur of the award rather than the removal of an arbitrator in the course of the arbitration proceedings, and many US Circuits take a pro-enforcement approach, arguably requiring a higher standard of proof of bias than set out in Article 2 of the IBA Guidelines or English law—see Sam Luttrell (above), Ch.4, and Mark Kantor "Arbitrator Disclosure: An Active But Unsettled Year" (2008) 11(1) Int. A.L.R. 21.

Court served as appointing authority. However, as the relevant grounds for challenge under both the 1976 and 2010 versions of the UNCITRAL Rules are the same as the ground under Article 10.1 of the LCIA Rules,[24] the reasoning in such cases is instructive as regards Article 10.1 of the LCIA Rules.

Most of the decisions fall into one of the two obvious broad categories, namely cases concerning the arbitrator's independence and cases concerning the arbitrator's impartiality.

*Independence*

- **LCIA Reference No. UN96/X15**, decision rendered on May 29, 1996: the arbitrator appointed in an UNCITRAL arbitration was a partner in a law firm that had previously acted for associated companies of the Respondent. The arbitrator had not been personally involved in the representation, and the Respondent argued that, applying the test set out in the UNCITRAL Rules 1976, no justifiable doubts arose as to the arbitrator's independence or impartiality. The LCIA Court Division held that when considering a possible lack of impartiality or independence of an arbitrator, or potential arbitrator, in an international arbitration, a partner in a law firm must be identified with his partners. On the facts of the case, the involvement of the firm with the Respondent's associated companies did give rise to justifiable doubts as to the arbitrator's independence or impartiality (although the Division concluded that the arbitrator's pre-appointment interview by a director of the Respondent was appropriate and did not itself give rise to justifiable doubts as to his independence or impartiality).[25]

10–017

- **LCIA Reference No. UN97/X11**, decision rendered on June 5, 1997[26]: a challenge brought in an UNCITRAL arbitration in which the LCIA acted as the appointing authority. The Division of the LCIA Court rejected the Claimant's challenge, which was based on the fact that the arbitrator and opposing party's counsel practised from the same barristers' chambers (noting, however, that the Claimant and its counsel were considered to be familiar with the organisation of English barristers in chambers). The courts of England and France have reached similar conclusions.[27]

- **LCIA Reference No. 97/X27**, decision rendered on October 23, 1997[28]: a challenge brought pursuant to Article 3.8 of the 1985 LCIA Arbitration Rules in which the sole arbitrator, who had been selected and appointed by the LCIA Court and who was a barrister, disclosed that the Claimant's

---

[24] Article 10.1 of the UNCITRAL Rules 1976 and Article 12.1 of the UNCITRAL Rules 2010.
[25] LCIA Reference No. UN96/X15, Decision Rendered May 29, 1996 (2011) 27(3) Arbitration Int. 317.
[26] LCIA Court Decision on Challenge to Arbitrator, LCIA Reference No. UN97/X11, June 5, 1997 (2011) 27(3) Arbitration Int. 320.
[27] *Laker Airways Inc v FLS Aerospace Ltd* [1999] EWHC B3 (Comm); *KFTCIC (Kuwait Foreign Trading Contracting and Investment Co) v Icori Estero SpA, Cour d'Appel*, Paris, decision of June 28, 1991, Rev. Arb. (1992) 568; and most recently, *A v B* [2011] EWHC 2345 (Comm).
[28] Decision on Challenge to Arbitrator, LCIA Reference No. 97/X27, October 23, 1997 (2011) 27(3) Arbitration Int. 322.

counsel (a London firm of solicitors) had, 10 years earlier, instructed him as an expert in unrelated proceedings in the English High Court. The Division found that the circumstances of a barrister working with solicitors for one of the parties many years earlier on an unrelated case did not give rise to any justifiable doubts as to the arbitrator's impartiality or independence. The Division further noted that if the challenge were accepted in these circumstances it would create "an entirely novel precedent", which would prevent any barrister or former barrister, including virtually all English judges, from serving as arbitrators in LCIA proceedings in which leading London commercial solicitors were acting for one of the parties.

- **LCIA Reference No. 8086**, decision rendered September 30, 1998[29]: in a challenge brought under Article 10.4 of the 1998 Rules based on Articles 6.1 (nationality) and 5.3 (declaration), the LCIA Court Division accepted that an arbitrator, through a long and meaningful association with a particular country, could be regarded as a "de facto" national of that country. However, a long-term residence in a country on its own was not enough to give rise to such a de facto nationality on the facts of this case, when the arbitrator had maintained a strong affiliation with his home State.

- **LCIA Reference No. UN9155**, decision rendered on November 10, 1999[30]: an UNCITRAL arbitration where the Respondent challenged an arbitrator selected and appointed by the LCIA Court on the grounds that he had the same nationality as the Claimant's counsel (not the parties). The President of the court, who presided over the challenge proceedings alone, held that the fact that the arbitrator and Claimant's counsel were of the same nationality did not give rise to any justifiable doubts as to his impartiality or independence.

- **LCIA Reference No. UN3476**, decision rendered on December 24, 2004[31]: an UNCITRAL arbitration, in which the LCIA was designated as appointing authority by the Permanent Court of Arbitration in The Hague for the purpose of rendering a decision on the challenge brought under Article 10(1) of the UNCITRAL Rules, where the dispute arose from a joint operating agreement of an oil field. The arbitrator appointed by the Respondent had for a short period in 1999 worked for the then law firm of the Respondent and advised on some engineering contracts pertaining to the project under dispute. He met with the Respondent to discuss aspects of the engineering in the course of a two-day trip. He had left that firm within a few months of joining and had severed all ties with the Respondent. The LCIA Court Division held that the arbitrator's association with the Respondent in 1999 and its then counsel did not give rise to any justifiable doubt as to his independence and impartiality.[32]

---

[29] LCIA Reference No. 8086, September 30, 1998 (2011) 27(3) Arbitration Int. 328.
[30] Decision on Challenge to Arbitrator, LCIA Reference No. UN9155, November 10, 1999 (2011) 27(3) Arbitration Int. 332.
[31] Decision on Challenge to Arbitrator, LCIA Reference No. UN3476, December 24, 2004 (2011) 27(3) Arbitration Int. 367.
[32] In light of the wide acceptance of the IBA Guidelines on Conflicts of Interest (in particular, Article 3.1.1 of the "Orange List"), it is questionable whether the challenge in this apparently borderline case would have been decided in the same way today.

- **LCIA Reference No. 81132**, decision rendered on November 15, 2008[33]: the Respondent challenged the Claimant's nominated arbitrator, who had previously been instructed by the Claimant's law firm in small matters. He also challenged the Chairman, who had been nominated by the co-arbitrators, on the grounds that the Chairman's own law firm had on numerous occasions instructed the Claimant's nominated arbitrator as a barrister (including in matters led by the Chairman). The President of the LCIA Court, deciding alone, concluded that previous low value instructions of an arbitrator (in his capacity as barrister) by the Claimant's law firm did not give rise to justifiable doubts as to his independence or impartiality, holding that:

  "It was commonplace for lawyers, who act both as advocate and as arbitrator, and particularly for English barristers, to take instructions from firms of solicitors, who, in entirely unrelated matters, appear before them as representatives of parties in an arbitration".

  By contrast, the President of the Court invited the Chairman of the Arbitral Tribunal to withdraw without having to consider the merits of the challenge.

- **LCIA Reference No. 81160**, decision rendered on August 28, 2009[34]: the arbitrator, who was a QC specialising in the London reinsurance market, disclosed that:

  —He had previously accepted instructions to act as counsel for and against each of the five Co-Respondents that had nominated him. At the time of the commencement of the arbitration he was instructed on behalf of the one of the Respondents and against another of the Respondents. Earlier in the year he had served as President of a Tribunal in a dispute between two of the nominating Respondents.

  —Over the years he received a number of instructions from the Respondents' counsel, representing 11 per cent of all his instructions in the previous five years, and 5 per cent of all instructions over the last 12 months, as well as two instructions out of 25 in the previous two to three months.

  —Due to the nature of his practice (in the London insurance market with numerous syndicates at Lloyds and other underwriters involved in different combinations, different percentage risks assumed and different roles), he was not always aware of the identities of the ultimate clients to whom he provided legal opinions and would not therefore be able to provide full disclosure at the commencement of the proceedings or on an on-going basis.

  —He intended to continue to accept such instructions in the future, including in the course of the arbitration.

---

[33] LCIA Court Decision on Challenge to Arbitrator, LCIA Reference No. 81132, November 15, 2008, (2011) 27(3) Arbitration Int. 439.
[34] LCIA Reference No. 81160, August 28, 2009 (2011) 27(3) Arbitration Int. 442.

The arbitrator stated that he did not consider that any of his disclosures gave rise to any justified doubts as to his independence or impartiality. The Respondents similarly objected to the challenge, arguing that the Claimant's counsel would have explained to their client the nature of the legal market serving the London reinsurance market, in the context of which there could be no doubts as to the arbitrator's independence or impartiality.

The Division had regard to Article 10.3 of the 1998 LCIA Rules (ground (d)), s.33(1)(a) of the English Arbitration 1996 and the 2004 IBA Guidelines on Conflicts of Interest, as well as to the "traditions and cultural norms of the London insurance market, and the local lawyers that served it". However, in a carefully reasoned decision, the Division concluded that in an international arbitration under the LCIA Rules:

"... *it did not follow* that a fair-minded and informed observer (through whose eyes, the circumstances of the case were to be examined) should be as fully attuned with local traditions and culture as a member of the community, *or wholly uncritical of it*"[35] [emphasis added].

The Division therefore assessed the facts of the case through the eyes of a reasonable, fair-minded and informed bystander who was *not* accustomed to the norms, standards and working relationships of the English Bar and solicitors. In that light, the arbitrator's current instruction by one of the Respondents could reasonably be said to give rise to a real possibility or justifiable doubts as to the arbitrator's independence or impartiality.

The Division considered that: the significant financial relations between the solicitors of Respondents and the arbitrator; the arbitrator's failure to make full disclosure of his ties to the parties at the outset; and his refusal to disclose new retainers from parties in the course of the arbitration or to confirm that he would turn such retainers down in the course of the arbitration, were further factors that gave rise to reasonable doubt as to the arbitrator's independence and impartiality.[36]

In light of the more recent English High Court decision in *A v B*,[37] which arose from an LCIA arbitration in which a challenge had already been heard and rejected by the LCIA Court, and in which the traditional view of the independence of the English Bar was affirmed, it remains to be seen whether this LCIA Court decision heralds a wider change of approach towards the ability of barristers to sit as arbitrators in cases in

---

[35] Id. para.4.2.
[36] The Division noted that a London insurance barrister might not consider it desirable to turn down future retainers but this was what a proper balance between independence and impartiality, on the one hand, and the characteristic of a niche market, on the other, demanded. The decision caused some surprise in the small group of barristers' chambers with strong insurance practices but there has also been a recognition that their niche market needs to be aware of, and learn about, the expectations of practitioners and international arbitrators in institutional arbitration.
[37] [2011] EWHC 2345 (Comm).

which barristers from the same chambers have been appointed as counsel, or involving solicitors who are instructing them in unrelated matters.[38]

*Impartiality*

- **LCIA Reference No. UN0239**, decisions rendered on June 22, 2001,[39] **10–018** July 3, 2001 and October 3, 2001: the Respondent in an UNCITRAL arbitration, in which the LCIA was appointing authority and appointed a sole arbitrator, advanced three separate challenges, each containing numerous complaints concerning aspects of the conduct of the proceedings as well as relating to the content of procedural directions and a jurisdiction award, which were said to evidence partiality in favour of the Claimant. However, two Divisions and a Vice President, who considered the separate challenges, concluded that the arbitrator had properly determined his jurisdiction and conducted the proceedings correctly so that none of the complaints gave rise to justifiable doubts as to the arbitrator's impartiality or independence.

- **LCIA Reference No. 1303**, decision rendered on November 22, 2001[40]: a sole arbitrator selected and appointed by the LCIA Court was challenged by the Claimant on the grounds that he had failed to disclose that he was the President of a national Trade Court; that the Respondent was a member of a national chamber of commerce which was said to have close links with the Trade Court; and that there were shortcomings in the fairness of the Trade Court. The challenged arbitrator responded to the Claimant's allegations in strong terms, describing the allegations as "fictitious", "false", "malevolent" and "vicious". The LCIA Court Division concluded that the factual circumstances relied upon by the Claimant did not give rise to justifiable doubts as to the arbitrator's impartiality or independence. However, the tension and ill feeling between the arbitrator and Claimant evidenced by his comments in response to the challenge did give rise to justifiable doubts as to his ability to remain impartial in this particular case.

- **LCIA Reference No. 0252**, decision rendered on July 1, 2002[41]: the Claimant's counsel contacted its nominated arbitrator on an ex parte basis to enquire about the Arbitral Tribunal's progress in rendering an award. The arbitrator indicated that an award was imminent and confirmed the outcome

---

[38] In *HEP v Slovenia* (2008) (ICSID Case No. ARB/05/24), a party's barrister-counsel, who was instructed in the course of the proceedings a relatively short time before the hearing, was excluded from the proceedings because he was a member of the same chambers as the Chairman of the Tribunal. The Tribunal reasoned that, as the guardian of the legitimacy of the arbitral process, it was to make every effort to ensure that the award was soundly based and not affected by procedural imperfection. It concluded that a reasonable independent observer may very well form the apprehension of bias, in a case in which a barrister from the same chambers as the Chairman of the Tribunal represents one of the parties. The House of Lords' acknowledgment in *Lawal v Northern Spirit* [2003] UKHL 35 at [22], that "the administration of justice requires higher standards today than was the case even a decade or two ago" might also serve as an indication of changing times.
[39] LCIA Reference No. UN0239, June 22, 2001, July 3, 2001 and October 3, 2001 (2011) 27(3) Arbitration Int. 336.
[40] LCIA Reference No. 1303, November 22, 2001 (2011) 27(3) Arbitration Int. 342.
[41] LCIA Reference No. 0252, July 1, 2002 (2011) 27(3) Arbitration Int. 351.

of the arbitration, information which was then used by the Claimant in ancillary court proceedings. The Respondent's challenge was aimed against the entire Arbitral Tribunal, claiming that such conduct gave rise to justifiable doubts as to the impartiality of the Arbitral Tribunal. The LCIA Court Division said that such ex parte communications were never acceptable under the LCIA Rules[42] and that the conduct of the Claimant's nominated arbitrator did give rise to justifiable doubts as to his impartiality; and his appointment was revoked. The remaining members of the Arbitral Tribunal were not implicated in such conduct, however, and the challenges against them were rejected.

- **LCIA Reference No. UN3490**, decision rendered on October 21, 2005 and December 27, 2005[43]: a sole arbitrator appointed by the LCIA in an UNCITRAL arbitration accepted a private meeting with one of the parties' counsel in his hearing breakout room. During the meeting, which was held behind closed doors, matters pertaining to the dispute between the parties were discussed. When the other party's counsel objected, the arbitrator accused her of entering his breakout room without permission and stealing grapes. He maintained the accusations notwithstanding the counsel's denials. The arbitrator then sought to have the verbal exchange relating to these matters deleted from the hearing transcript. The LCIA Division held that the arbitrator's conduct was incompatible with the behaviour expected of an arbitrator and gave rise to justifiable doubts as to his impartiality.

- **LCIA Reference No. 5665**, decision rendered on August 30, 2006[44]: the challenge against the Chairman was made on numerous grounds and has already been referred to above. One aspect of the challenge related to an email message which the Chairman intended to send to the co-arbitrators but which he erroneously also sent to the parties in the arbitration as well. Referring to a procedural application made by the Claimants, the message stated (amongst other things) as follows:

    "What do we do about this? . . .

    . . . it reads to me as [if][Claimants' counsel] gets his pleasure in abusing us and when it comes to a crunch he does not want any particular orders now. I do not like his floating threats. All we may do is give him lashings of fair procedure."[45]

    The Claimants contended that the comments in the misdirected email evidenced prejudgment and bias, as well as revealing antagonism and an intention to punish the Claimants for the reservation of their rights. Relying

---

[42] Article 13.4 of the Rules forbids unilateral contact with arbitrators: see the commentary to that Article, which includes discussion of this case.
[43] LCIA Court Decision on Challenge to Arbitrator, LCIA Reference No. UN3490, October 21, 2005 and December 27, 2005 (2011) 27(3) Arbitration Int. 377. Notably, this was a 1976 UNCITRAL Rules arbitration, where the only challenge available is on the grounds of lack of impartiality or independence. Had the arbitration been conducted under the LCIA Rules a challenge under ground (ii) (failure to act fairly and impartially as between the parties) might also have been available.
[44] LCIA Reference No. 5665, August 30, 2006 (2011) 27(3) Arbitration Int. 395.
[45] (2011) 27(3) Arbitration Int. 398.

on English judicial precedent,[46] the Division found that a distinction can be drawn between an arbitrator's view of a party's legal representative and bias against that representative's client. The fact that an arbitrator forms a particular view of a party's counsel or other representative cannot without more be sufficient to give rise to justifiable doubts as to the impartiality of the arbitrator. The Division accepted that inappropriate antagonism or personal animosity towards a counsel could evidence a lack of impartiality,[47] but concluded that the Chairman's email in this case evidenced no more than a growing degree of impatience with the Claimants' counsel and did not give rise to justifiable doubts as to his impartiality.

- **LCIA Reference No. 3488**, decision rendered on July 11, 2007[48]: the primary ground of challenge was that a procedural order of the Arbitral Tribunal contained a reference to the "undisputed" ownership of shares by a joint-venture holding company. The Claimant challenged the Chairman or majority of the Arbitral Tribunal on the grounds of apparent bias, alleging that they had pre-judged an issue in the arbitration. The Division reviewed the impugned reference and concluded that, when read in context, it was clear that the Arbitral Tribunal had not prejudged the issue but was merely expressing a tentative view, subject to receiving submissions from the parties.

- A similar conclusion was reached by the Division appointed in **LCIA Reference No. UN7949**, decision rendered on December 3, 2007[49]: where the Respondent complained that a particular comment made by an arbitrator evidenced his pre-judgment and bias with regard to liability. When the arbitrator's comments were read in full, it was clear that concerns as to the arbitrator's impartiality and independence could not reasonably be entertained.

- The challenge in **LCIA Reference No. 81007/81008/81024/81025**, decision rendered on June 16, 2008, followed the Arbitral Tribunal's ruling on an application by the Claimant for provisional relief under Article 25.1(c) of the LCIA Rules 1998. Under that provision (now contained in Article 25.1(iii)),[50] which mirrors s.39 of the English Arbitration Act 1996, an LCIA Arbitral Tribunal has the power to order on a provisional basis, subject to final determination in a final award, any relief which it could grant in a final award.

The Claimant applied for a provisional order for the payment of 90 per cent of the amount claimed on the grounds that, under the scheme of the

---

[46] *Fletamentos Maritimos SA v Effjohn International BV (No.2)* [1997] 2 Lloyd's Rep. 302.
[47] The Division referred to *R. v Lashley* [2005] EWCA Crim 2016.
[48] Decision on Challenge to Arbitrator, LCIA Reference No. 3488, July 11, 2007 (2011) 27(3) Arbitration Int. 413.
[49] LCIA Reference No. UN7949, December 12, 2007 (2011) 27(3) Arbitration Int. 420, and see the full decision at *http://www.italaw.com/sites/default/files/case-documents/italaw1171.pdf* [Accessed November 14, 2014], which contains a well-reasoned analysis of the applicable legal standards in a challenge to an arbitrator in an UNCITRAL arbitration, commenced under a bilateral investment treaty. See also fn.19 above.
[50] See the discussion of this case in the commentary on that Article below.

contracts between the parties, the Respondent was obliged to pay first and claim later. The majority of the Arbitral Tribunal declined to make the order (although they acknowledged that they had the power to do so). However, the arbitrator appointed by the Claimant rendered a dissenting opinion, stating that the Arbitral Tribunal should have made the order requested, subject to appropriate cross-undertakings by the Claimant. The dissenting arbitrator stated that, in line with English authority with regard to the exercise of the power to grant provisional orders,[51] he felt a high degree of assurance that the Claimant was entitled under the contract to 90 per cent of the amount claimed.

The Division noted that Article 25.1(c) of the LCIA Rules was an enabling provision, allowing Arbitral Tribunals to exercise powers under s.39 of the English Arbitration Act 1996, and that it was impossible to exercise powers under that provision without forming a provisional view as to the merits. In this case the dissenting arbitrator had noted that his view was subject to receiving the parties' submissions and evidence regarding the merits. The Division therefore concluded that no justifiable doubts arose as to the arbitrator's impartiality or independence.

- **LCIA Reference No. 81224**, decision rendered on March 15, 2010[52]: the Respondent alleged that the arbitrator had expressed strong views regarding the parties' respective positions in the course of the hearing on the merits, made a number of comments regarding India, which were perceived as offensive, and exhibited towards the Respondent's counsel "impatience through his body language which is ultimately the reflection of his mind".[53] The LCIA Court's Vice President had regard to the English law test for bias,[54] as well as to other English law authorities regarding the conduct of arbitrators and judges in the course of a hearing[55] and acknowledged that rudeness and antagonism by an arbitrator towards counsel, and comments of a racist nature, can constitute evidence of bias. The Vice President found that, in this case, there was no evidence of racism.

Further, although the transcript suggested that the arbitrator had come to the hearing having formed a preliminary view of the merits, and that he expressed himself in a manner that could have been perceived as rude, the Vice President did not consider this sufficient to hold that he had a closed mind to the issues in question and concluded that the evidence did not establish justifiable doubts as to the arbitrator's independence or impartiality.

## 10.2 The LCIA Court may determine that an arbitrator is unfit to act under Article 10.1 if that arbitrator: (i) acts in deliberate violation of

---

[51] *SL Sethia Liners Ltd v Naviagro Maritime Corp (The "Kostas Melas")* [1981] 1 Lloyd's L.R. 18.
[52] LCIA Reference No. 81224, Decision Rendered on March 15, 2010 (2011) 27(3) Arbitration Int. 461.
[53] (2011) 27(3) Arbitration Int. 464.
[54] Applying *Porter v Magill* (above).
[55] *El-Faragy v El Faragy* [2007] EWCA Civ 1149 and *Andrews v Bradshaw* [2000] B.L.R. 6.

the Arbitration Agreement; (ii) does not act fairly or impartially as between the parties; or (iii) does not conduct or participate in the arbitration with reasonable efficiency, diligence and industry.

Article 10.2 sets out grounds on which the LCIA Court may find that an arbitrator is "unfit to act under Article 10.1", and consequently revoke his appointment. Whilst the grounds are set out separately in Article 10.2 and (as part of the 1998 Rules) have been treated as separate grounds in challenges by parties, a degree of overlap exists.   10–019

It is also noteworthy that, even where one or more of the grounds is established, the LCIA Court retains the discretion as to whether or not to make a finding that an arbitrator is "unfit to act as an arbitrator" and whether to revoke his appointment. This is illustrated, for example, by the two challenge decisions referred to under the *deliberate violation* ground below.[56]

### (i) Deliberate violation of the Arbitration Agreement

Under article V(1)(d) of the New York Convention,[57] the enforcement of an award may be refused by a national court if "the arbitral procedure was not in accordance with the agreement of the parties". National legislation generally contains provisions permitting courts to set aside awards or to refuse recognition of awards on similar grounds.[58] Under such provisions, even an unintentional failure to conduct a reference in accordance with the Arbitration Agreement can have serious consequences for the parties and the enforcement of the award. It follows that the appointment of an arbitrator who deliberately violates the Arbitration Agreement should generally be revoked.   10–020

The term "Arbitration Agreement" is not limited to the express terms of the contractual arbitration clause. Under the new Preamble to the Rules, the entire body of the LCIA Rules is deemed to be incorporated by reference into the arbitration clause, and therefore form part of the Arbitration Agreement.

In LCIA Reference No. 0256,[59] a sole arbitrator was challenged by the Claimant, after holding a hearing on one day's notice, on the ground that he had deliberately violated the duty to give the parties reasonable notice of a hearing.[60] The Claimant's counsel, who could not attend on short notice, was furnished with a copy of the transcript of the hearing and invited to comment. The arbitrator believed that he was complying with the LCIA Rules and the Division of the LCIA Court held that his conduct did not give rise to justifiable doubts as to his independence and impartiality. However, the Division found that the arbitrator had violated the LCIA Rules and that the violation was *deliberate*, because the   10–021

---

[56] See challenge decisions in LCIA Reference No. 0256 and in LCIA Arbitration Reference No. 5665 below.
[57] See Appendix 9.
[58] See also ss.68(2)(c) and 103(2)(e) of the English Arbitration Act 1996 (Appendix 7) and Articles 34(2)(a)(iv) and 36(1)(iv) of the UNCITRAL Model Law 2006 (Appendix 10).
[59] LCIA Court Decision on Challenge to Arbitrator, LCIA Reference No. 0256, February 13, 2002 (2011) 27(3) Arbitration Int. 345.
[60] Pursuant to the provisions of Article 19.2 of the 1998 LCIA Rules (Appendix 4).

arbitrator was deemed to have known of his duty to give reasonable notice of the hearing. The Division therefore concluded that had the arbitration gone forward the arbitrator's appointment should have been revoked,[61] and that the arbitrator's outstanding fees should not be paid.

However, a deliberate violation of an Arbitration Agreement alone will not always justify the removal of the arbitrator. In LCIA Arbitration Reference No. 5665,[62] a challenge to the Chairman of the Arbitral Tribunal was advanced on a number of grounds, including that he had deliberately violated the parties' Arbitration Agreement by publishing the names of the parties and the fact that he was appointed as arbitrator in a dispute between them in his CV, which was available on the internet. Having received submissions on the application of Article 10.2 of the LCIA Rules by reference to s.24(1)(d) of the English Arbitration Act 1996, the Division of the LCIA Court acknowledged that, under Article 10.2,[63] a deliberate violation of the Arbitration Agreement could occur without a substantial injustice being suffered by either party.[64] The Division concluded that the nature of the violation and its consequences must be considered. The Division expressed doubts as to whether the breach of the LCIA Rules in this case was deliberate and, in any event, found that it was not, on its own, of a nature that would justify the revocation of the arbitrator's appointment. The very limited disclosure of relevant information was unlikely to have caused significant prejudice or injustice to either party, and no evidence had been adduced by the challenging party in this regard.

### (ii) Failure to act fairly and impartially as between the parties

10–022 This ground reflects the duty of the Arbitral Tribunal pursuant to Article 14.4 of the LCIA Rules "to act fairly and impartially as between all parties, giving each a reasonable opportunity of putting its case and dealing with that of its opponent(s)". It is established when the conduct of the arbitrator is shown to be unfair to a party or biased. The interaction between ground (ii) and Article 14.4 of the LCIA Rules reflects the connection between s.24(1)(d)(i) of the English Arbitration Act 1996 (court's power to remove an arbitrator who has failed properly to conduct the proceedings) and s.3(1), which sets out the arbitrators' statutory duty (under English law) to "act fairly and impartially as between all parties. . .".[65]

---

[61] In the circumstances of the case it was clear that the arbitration would not proceed further, and there was therefore no point in revoking the appointment and replacing the arbitrator simply in order to terminate the arbitration. See paras 4.11–5.1 of the decision.
[62] LCIA Court Decision on Challenge to Arbitrator, LCIA Reference No. 5665, August 30, 2006 (2011) 27(3) Arbitration Int. 395.
[63] The decision was made in respect of the 1998 version of Article 10.2 of the LCIA Rules, which was for these purposes the same as the current provision.
[64] By contrast, s.24(1)(d) of the English Arbitration Act 1996 (removal of an arbitrator for failure properly to conduct the arbitral proceedings) requires the challenging party to prove that he has suffered substantial injustice as a result of the arbitrator's conduct (Appendix 7).
[65] In *Aoot Kalmneft v Glencore International Ag* [2001] EWHC 464 (Comm), the English Court of Appeal reflected on the relationship between ss.24(1)(d) and 33(1) of the English Arbitration Act 1996 and held that an arbitrator should only be removed under s.24(1)(d) where the conduct complained of consisted of such procedural unfairness that would permit a successful challenge of the ultimate award and there was a serious risk that the arbitrator's conduct would again breach s.33(1). The LCIA Court has not adopted such a restrictive view of its power under Article 10.2, and it is not suggested that it should.

This ground is also closely related to the final ground for challenge in Article 10.1; that circumstances exist that give rise to justifiable doubts as to the impartiality or independence of the challenged arbitrator. Thus challenges on both grounds are often made in the same case, where the alleged unfair or biased acts or conduct of the arbitrator are also relied on as evidence of circumstances which give rise to justifiable doubts as to his impartiality or independence.

The reports of some challenge decisions suggest that a challenge based on this ground can only succeed where there are circumstances that give rise to justifiable doubts as to the independence or impartiality of the challenged arbitrator.[66] However, other decisions illustrate that an arbitrator *can* be found to have acted unfairly, in a manner justifying his removal, without doubts arising as to his impartiality or independence. For example, in LCIA Reference No. 0256,[67] the Division of the LCIA Court found that the arbitrator had acted unfairly when he re-scheduled a substantive hearing with less than 24 hours' notice and then sent the transcript of the hearing to the lawyers of the party who were unable to attend inviting comments in writing. Nevertheless, the Division concluded that, in the circumstances of the case, the conduct of the arbitrator did not give rise to justifiable doubts as to his independence or impartiality. **10–023**

Most challenge decisions in relation to Article 10.2(ii) are heavily fact dependent and do not contain generally applicable statements of legal principle. Further, in the majority of these cases, the challenge has been rejected.

The LCIA Court Divisions have found that arbitrators failed to act fairly and impartially in the following circumstances: **10–024**

- As discussed above, where an arbitrator gave less than 24 hours' notice that a cancelled hearing would be reinstated and continued to hold the hearing in the absence of one party. Providing the absent party with a transcript of the hearing for comments was not enough.[68]

- Where an arbitrator accepted an ex parte communication from one party and provided that party with information about the award prior to its publication.[69]

---

[66] See, for example, LCIA Court Decision on Challenge to Arbitrator, LCIA Reference No. 3431, July 3, 2003, December 18, 2003 and February 18, 2004 (2011) 27(3) Arbitration Int. 358.

[67] LCIA Court Decision on Challenge to Arbitrator, LCIA Reference No. 0256, February 13, 2002 (2011) 27(3) Arbitration Int. 345.

[68] Ibid. In *Norbrook Laboratories Ltd v 1. A. Tank and 2. Moulson Chemplant Ltd* [2006] EWHC 1055, the English High Court reached a similar conclusion in relation to an arbitration conducted under other institutional rules, in which an arbitrator who held ex parte meetings with one party's witnesses was removed from office. Mr Justice Colman held [139]: "...An Arbitrator in contact with a factual witness in the absence of one or both parties may be exposed to information which consciously or unconsciously influences his judgement on a matter in dispute. It is therefore absolutely axiomatic that the parties should at the very least have the opportunity of access to what the witness or potential witness has said to the Arbitrator so as to enable that party to refute any statement adverse to its case or to rely upon any statement supportive of its case."

[69] LCIA Court Decision on Challenge to Arbitrator, LCIA Reference No. 0252, Decision Rendered July 1, 2002 (2011) 27(3) Arbitration Int. 351. Ex parte communications were prohibited even after the Arbitral Tribunal had concluded its deliberations.

10–025  On the other hand, challenges have been rejected where the conduct alleged not to be fair or impartial included: an arbitrator's mistake resulting from a "procedural mishap";[70] regrettable comments and an unfavourable demeanour towards a party;[71] refusal to grant further time extensions in the face of a party's numerous delays;[72] the exclusion of a letter from counsel to a third party;[73] failing to consult with both parties before making procedural decisions;[74] and declining to grant procedural orders applied for.[75] In most of these cases, however, the factual circumstances leading up to the challenge were difficult and the challenging party's own conduct and perceived motives may have been counted as a factor in the decision-making process. Parties might very well find that future challenges based on similar complaints could be upheld, if the surrounding circumstances differed.[76]

### (iii) Failure to conduct the arbitration with reasonable efficiency, diligence and industry

10–026  This ground has been revised with each new version of the LCIA Rules. In the 1985 version, if the LCIA Court concluded that an arbitrator had failed to "conduct the proceedings with reasonable diligence. . ." it would have been required to find him unfit to act.[77] The 1998 version gave the LCIA Court a discretion as to whether to find the arbitrator unfit to act and added the avoidance of unnecessary delay and expense to the requirement to proceed "with reasonable diligence".[78] The avoidance of unnecessary delay or expense has now been replaced with the requirement for "reasonable efficiency, diligence and industry".

Whilst each of the components of the phrase "reasonable efficiency, diligence and industry" requires little explanation, it is not a phrase commonly used in legal texts.[79] Questions may therefore arise as to the choice of this phrase over the previous formulations in the Rules. Article 5.4 of the LCIA Rules links the application of "sufficient time, diligence and industry" with ensuring "the

---

[70] LCIA Reference No. 7932, Decision Rendered June 17, 2008 (2011) 27(3) Arbitration Int. 433–438.
[71] LCIA Court Decision on Challenge to Arbitrator, LCIA Reference No. 81224, March 15, 2010 (2007) 27(3) Arbitration Int. 461–470.
[72] LCIA Reference Nos 81209 and 81210, Decision Rendered November 16, 2009 (2007) 27(3) Arbitration Int. 455–460.
[73] LCIA Reference No. 5665, Decision Rendered August 30, 2006 (2007) 27(3) Arbitration Int. 395–412.
[74] Ibid.
[75] Ibid.
[76] *Norbrook Laboratories Ltd v 1. A. Tank and 2. Moulson Chemplant Ltd* [2006] EWHC 1055 illustrates the approach of the English High Court to similar challenges to an arbitrator pursuant to s.24 of the English Arbitration Act 1996.
[77] Article 3.6 of the 1985 LCIA Rules: "If in the opinion of the Court an arbitrator acts in manifest violation of these Rules or does not conduct the proceedings with reasonable diligence he will be considered unfit."
[78] Article 10.2 of the 1998 LCIA Rules (Appendix 4).
[79] The expression "diligence and industry" was occasionally used in older English case law, to refer to the work of highly regarded legal scholars—see, for example, *The Lord Warden and Admiral of the Cinque Ports v H.M. in his Office of Admiralty, &c. (In the matter of a Whale) (1831)* 2 Haggard 438 166 E.R. 304; and in more recent times, but no more commonly, has been employed by judges referring to the efforts of counsel appearing in court.

expeditious and efficient conduct of the arbitration" and it may be that the new wording is a more practical and positive way of saying much the same as before.

There have been relatively few challenges to arbitrators based on this ground (as previously formulated under the 1998 Rules). Apart from the obvious overlap with the other grounds of challenge, parties considering a challenge are immediately faced with evidential difficulties in establishing that, in the course of the proceedings, an arbitrator has failed to meet the standard of reasonable diligence, at least until an award has been rendered. Even where evidence as to the care and skill employed by an arbitrator is available in the form of a partial final award, the LCIA Court has made it clear that it does not have the power to review an arbitrator's award to determine whether the factual or legal conclusions have been reached properly.[80] Although no such cases are known, it might be easier for the LCIA Court to conclude that an arbitrator is unfit under this ground upon a request made by the remaining arbitrators pursuant to Article 10.1.

10–027

The issue of delay as a result of the unavailability of arbitrators has been a cause for serious concern among arbitration users and institutions in the past few years. This led the ICC to require prospective arbitrators to confirm their availability prior to appointment by the ICC Court.[81] Article 5.4 of the LCIA Rules now also requires prospective arbitrators to confirm that they are ready, willing and able to devote sufficient time, diligence and industry to ensure the expeditious and efficient conduct of the arbitration.

When it falls to the LCIA Court to select an arbitrator, availability is a primary factor. Not only should the Secretariat be aware of a candidate's current LCIA arbitrations, if any, it should also know his or her response times in those arbitrations and be able to advise the LCIA Court accordingly. The submission of the selection of an arbitrator to the LCIA Court can, therefore, be a way of reducing the risk of delay.

10–028

**10.3 A party challenging an arbitrator under Article 10.1 shall, within 14 days of the formation of the Arbitral Tribunal or (if later) within 14 days of becoming aware of any grounds described in Article 10.1 or 10.2, deliver a written statement of the reasons for its challenge to the LCIA Court, the Arbitral Tribunal and all other parties. A party may challenge an arbitrator whom it has nominated, or in whose appointment it has participated, only for reasons of which it becomes aware after the appointment has been made by the LCIA Court.**

**Introduction**

Articles 10.3–10.6 deal with the procedural aspects of making a challenge to the appointment of an arbitrator. Article 10.3 deals with the time limit within which a

10–029

---

[80] LCIA Reference No. 96/X22, Decision Rendered July 22, 1998 (2007) 27(3) Arbitration Int. 325–327.
[81] Article 11 of the 2012 ICC Rules.

challenge must be brought, who must be notified of the challenge, and the limitation on a party challenging an arbitrator who it nominated.

### *Notification and appointment of the President, Vice President or Division*

10–030  The process of challenging an arbitrator is commenced by sending a notice containing a statement of the reasons for the challenge to the LCIA Court, the Arbitral Tribunal and the other parties to the arbitration. Pursuant to Article 3.3 of the LCIA Rules, any communications to the LCIA Court must be addressed to the Registrar.

Subject to the other parties' agreement to the challenge within 14 days (Article 10.5), or the arbitrator's resignation within the same 14 days (Article 10.6) the next step is the appointment (by the President or a Vice President of the LCIA Court) of the President, a Vice President or a Division of three or more members of the LCIA Court to deal with the challenge in the name of the LCIA Court, pursuant to Article 3.1 of the LCIA Rules.

10–031  Article 3 of the LCIA Rules is reflected in Article D of the 2011 version of the Constitution of the LCIA Arbitration Court (the "LCIA Constitution"),[82] which provides for the functions of the LCIA Court in relation to challenges to be performed in the name of the LCIA Court by the President or a Vice President (or an Honorary or former Vice President appointed by them) or a three or five member Division of the Court appointed by the President or a Vice President.

10–032  Neither Article 10.3, nor the LCIA Constitution, sets out the criteria for determining whether a particular challenge decision shall be determined by the President, Vice President (or Honorary or former Vice President) or by a Division of the Court. However, published abstracts indicate that challenges have most commonly been decided by a three-member Division. Such Divisions are chaired by the President or by a Vice President and might include at least one member of the Court with experience in determining arbitrator challenges. The relevant geographic and cultural characteristics of the parties involved might also play a part in who is selected for the Division.[83]

Urgent challenges (e.g. shortly before a hearing) may be heard by the President, a Vice President or a former Vice President.

The Registrar should consider the matter and its urgency and make appropriate recommendations to the President, including the names of possible members of a Division.

### *Time limits*

10–033  An arbitrator cannot be formally challenged until after he has been appointed by the LCIA Court. Nevertheless, where there are party-nominations, parties might be in a position to identify any objections and communicate them to the nominating party and the LCIA Court prior to the appointment of the arbitrator. This

---

[82] See Article D of the LCIA Constitution at Appendix 3.
[83] See Geoff Nicholas and Constantine Partasides,"LCIA Court Decisions on Challenges to Arbitrators: A Proposal to Publish" (2007) 23(1) Arbitration Int. 5.

could result in the withdrawal of the nomination, or even cause the LCIA Court to decline to confirm the nomination.

Once appointed, an arbitrator may be challenged within 14 days of the later of: (a) the date of appointment; and (b) the date on which the challenging party became aware of the circumstances giving rise to the challenge. The 14-day time limit imposes a stringent time constraint, shorter than the time period adopted by some arbitral institutions, such as the ICC,[84] but similar to the time adopted in some other rules.[85]

Failure to bring a challenge within the time limit could result in the loss of the right to challenge.[86] However, under Article 22.2 of the LCIA Rules, the LCIA Court has the power to extend any time limit provided for in the Arbitration Agreement (which includes the Rules). That power, which includes the time limit for a challenge, is subject only to the Arbitral Tribunal's power to extend or truncate any such limits itself.

10–034

## *Form*

There is no prescribed form for challenging the appointment of an arbitrator. Challenges are often made in the form of a memorial or statement of case document, but can also be made and responded to in the form of correspondence directed to the LCIA Court and sent to the Registrar.

10–035

Whatever the form used, the challenge document should include a "written statement" of the reasons for the challenge. Such statements should normally be supported by the evidence upon which the challenging party relies but do not have to include a full pleading out of the issues or to be accompanied by copies of any relevant legal authorities. The parties should have an opportunity to file submissions after the Division has been appointed and has made directions.

It is noted that the commencement of a challenge procedure does not suspend the arbitrator's authority over the underlying arbitral proceedings, including his power to continue to participate in or conduct on-going proceedings and make an award.[87] In LCIA Reference Nos 81209 and 81210, a challenge was filed less than four weeks before a hearing on the merits.[88] The Secretariat moved quickly and a Vice President was appointed to determine the challenge before the date of the hearing. Nevertheless, and despite strong protest from the non-challenging party, the Arbitral Tribunal decided to postpone the hearing. The Vice President rendered his decision, dismissing the challenge, six days after his appointment, which was also the day on which the hearing had been due to commence. Had the hearing not been postponed, he would have rendered it one or two days earlier, which would

10–036

---

[84] ICC Rules, Article 14; similarly see Article 15 of the SCC Rules and Rule 12 of the SIAC Rules (providing for a 14-day time limit).
[85] UNCITRAL Arbitration Rules, Article 13 (Appendix 11).
[86] Decision on Challenge to Arbitrator, LCIA Reference No. 5665, August 30, 2006 (2011) 27(3) Arbitration Int. 395, para.4.8.
[87] See Challenge Decision in LCIA Reference No. 3431, July 3, 2003, December 18, 2003 and February 18, 2004 (2011) 27(3) Arbitration Int. 358, and s.24(3) of the English Arbitration Act 1996 (a mandatory provision relating to challenges in the High Court) and Article 13 of the UNCITRAL Model Law (in relation to both challenges under agreed procedures and under national court procedures).
[88] (2011) 27(3) Arbitration Int. 455.

have allowed it to proceed. In the event, the hearing was postponed for several months.

*Challenges to party-nominated arbitrators*

10–037   Article 10.3 provides that a party may only challenge an arbitrator nominated by him, or in whose appointment he participated, for reasons he was not aware of at the time of the appointment. A party participates in the appointment of an arbitrator when he nominates or jointly nominates an arbitrator and, depending on the circumstances, possibly also when he is consulted about the identity of the person to be nominated or appointed.

Given that any appointment takes place later than a nomination, or participation in the appointment, it is possible that relevant facts may come to light between that nomination or participation and the appointment being made. In such event, a party would need to withdraw its nomination (or, in the case of participation other than by nomination, raise the issue) before the appointment was made in order to try to avoid falling foul of Article 10.3.

> **10.4** The LCIA Court shall provide to those other parties and the challenged arbitrator a reasonable opportunity to comment on the challenging party's written statement. The LCIA Court may require at any time further information and materials from the challenging party, the challenged arbitrator, other parties and other members of the Arbitral Tribunal (if any).

10–038   Article 10.4 deals with the procedure applicable in the course of the challenge procedure. It provides that the LCIA Court must allow the other parties and challenged arbitrator a reasonable opportunity to comment on the challenging party's written statement.

Indeed, unless the challenge is accepted (see below), it is common for the opposing party to object to any challenge made, by delivering written submissions. The LCIA Court does not hold hearings. A challenged arbitrator may also respond to the challenge, if only to refute the allegations made by the challenging party and/or to provide information which may be relevant to the issues raised.

Under Article 10.4, the LCIA Court also has the power to order any of the parties, the challenged arbitrator and/or other members of the Arbitral Tribunal to provide further information and materials.

> **10.5** If all other parties agree in writing to the challenge within 14 days of receipt of the written statement, the LCIA Court shall revoke that arbitrator's appointment (without reasons).

10–039   Article 10.5 envisages that the parties to the arbitration may agree to the challenge. Although such agreement is rare, one possible motivation for agreeing to a challenge could be to save the time and cost that might otherwise be spent on the challenge procedure, particularly if the challenge is raised at an early stage.

If all parties do agree to the challenge in writing within 14 days of receipt of the written statement, the LCIA Court has no discretion and must revoke the arbitrator's appointment without reasons.

The LCIA Secretariat should remind the parties of this 14-day period for an agreement when it acknowledges receipt of the notice of challenge. The non-challenging party is invited to indicate as soon as possible, and in any event within 14 days, whether or not it agrees to the challenge.

**10.6 Unless the parties so agree or the challenged arbitrator resigns in writing within 14 days of receipt of the written statement, the LCIA Court shall decide the challenge and, if upheld, shall revoke that arbitrator's appointment. The LCIA Court's decision shall be made in writing, with reasons; and a copy shall be transmitted by the Registrar to the parties, the challenged arbitrator and other members of the Arbitral Tribunal (if any). A challenged arbitrator who resigns in writing prior to the LCIA Court's decision shall not be considered as having admitted any part of the written statement.**

Article 10.6 provides that the LCIA Court shall decide upon a challenge to the appointment of an arbitrator unless the parties agree (in which case Article 10.5 applies) or the arbitrator resigns within 14 days of receiving the written Statement of Challenge. An arbitrator who resigns prior to the LCIA Court's decision on the challenge is not taken to have admitted any of the allegations made against him. Again, the LCIA Secretariat, when acknowledging receipt of the notice of challenge, should ask the challenged arbitrator to advise within 14 days whether or not he will resign. 10–040

Article 10.6 provides that the decision of the LCIA Court on a challenge shall be a reasoned decision, given in writing. This approach, which has been the practice of the LCIA Court for many years,[89] as well as the decision of the LCIA Court to publish summaries of challenge decisions, contrasts with the practice of many other arbitral institutions, in which no reasons are given.[90]

In practice, the LCIA Court's decision sets out the circumstances and grounds of the challenge, and sets out the reasons why the Court has decided to accept or reject the challenge. As stated on the LCIA website: 10–041

"the Court considers that the parties (particularly the party bringing the challenge) and the arbitrators (particularly the arbitrator who has been challenged) should be made aware of the LCIA Court's view of the matters said to give rise to doubts as to the arbitrator's independence or impartiality."[91]

Under Article 29 of the LCIA Rules, the parties to LCIA arbitrations are deemed, to the extent permitted by applicable laws, to have waived the right to appeal from 10–042

---

[89] But not expressly provided for in the LCIA Rules or LCIA Constitution.
[90] For example, the ICC.
[91] See http://www.lcia.org [Accessed November 14, 2014].

or challenge any LCIA Court decision or determination before any national court or state organ. Under s.24 of the English Arbitration Act 1996, as well as under Article 13.3 of the UNCITRAL Model Law, the right to challenge an arbitrator in the national courts cannot be contracted out of.[92]

> **10.7** The LCIA Court shall determine the amount of fees and expenses (if any) to be paid for the former arbitrator's services, as it may consider appropriate in the circumstances. The LCIA Court may also determine whether, in what amount and to whom any party should pay forthwith the costs of the challenge; and the LCIA Court may also refer all or any part of such costs to the later decision of the Arbitral Tribunal and/or the LCIA Court under Article 28.

10–043 The LCIA Court determines the amount of compensation due to an arbitrator whose appointment has been revoked. It should be noted that this is a decision on the amount only: apportionment of liability for the fees so determined will fall on the Arbitral Tribunal or replacement arbitrator in due course pursuant to Article 28.3. The decision might commonly be decided by reference to the amount of work done by the arbitrator, but the LCIA Court may take into account the circumstances and (in practice) the timing of the revocation.[93]

Thus, in LCIA Reference No. 0256,[94] the LCIA Division concluded that the arbitrator had "acted unfairly and in deliberate breach of the LCIA Rules" and decided that he would not be paid his outstanding fees or any associated expenses, particularly as the deposit held by the LCIA had been paid solely by the challenging party.

**Costs of the challenge**

10–044 A new proviso in the 2014 edition of Article 10.7 provides that the LCIA Court may also render a decision directing either party to pay the costs of the challenge forthwith. This new power appears to be intended as a potential sanction to deter frivolous challenges.

The expression "costs of the challenge" is not defined in Article 10.7 or elsewhere in the LCIA Rules. By comparison, Article 28.1 defines "Arbitration Costs" as the costs of the arbitration other than legal or other expenses incurred by the parties themselves. The costs and expenses of the parties themselves are referred to in Article 28.3 as the "Legal Costs". By analogy, and having regard to the split between the "costs and expenses generated by the challenge" and the "legal fees related thereto" in a number of the LCIA Court's challenge decisions,[95] the "costs

---

[92] As noted above, in *A v B* [2011] EWHC 2345, the English Commercial Court effectively reheard a challenge in an LCIA arbitration, which had already been decided by a former Vice President.
[93] See para.2(vi) of the Schedule of Arbitration Costs, Appendix 2.
[94] LCIA Court Decision on Challenge to Arbitrator, LCIA Reference No. 0256, February 13, 2002 (2011) 27(3) Arbitration Int. 345.
[95] For example, LCIA Reference No. 81160 and LCIA Reference No. 81224.

## Article 11—Nomination and Replacement

**11.1 In the event that the LCIA Court determines that justifiable doubts exist as to any arbitral candidate's suitability, independence or impartiality, or if a nominee declines appointment as arbitrator, or if an arbitrator is to be replaced for any reason, the LCIA Court may determine whether or not to follow the original nominating process for such arbitral appointment.**

**11.2 The LCIA Court may determine that any opportunity given to a party to make any re-nomination (under the Arbitration Agreement or otherwise) shall be waived if not exercised within 14 days (or such lesser or greater time as the LCIA Court may determine), after which the LCIA Court shall appoint the replacement arbitrator without such re-nomination.**

### Introduction

11–001   Article 11 provides the LCIA Court with the flexibility to depart from the original nominating process in the event that it needs to replace an arbitral candidate or appointed arbitrator. The provisions of the Article are short and straightforward, but as discussed below leave some questions to be determined by the Arbitral Tribunal or in accordance with the law of the seat.

**11.1 In the event that the LCIA Court determines that justifiable doubts exist as to any arbitral candidate's suitability, independence or impartiality, or if a nominee declines appointment as arbitrator, or if an arbitrator is to be replaced for any reason, the LCIA Court may determine whether or not to follow the original nominating process for such arbitral appointment.**

11–002   Although parties may agree upon a nomination process for the arbitrators, this is always subject to the LCIA Court agreeing to appoint the nominated arbitrators. In the vast majority of cases, the LCIA Court will appoint the candidates that have been nominated. However, if it decides that justifiable doubts exist as to the candidate's suitability, independence or impartiality, it may decline to do so. Also, some nominees may decline to be appointed (for example, because of a conflict of interest). Even once appointed, an arbitrator may need to be replaced. In such circumstances Article 11.1 permits the LCIA Court to decide whether to follow the original nominating process agreed by the parties or some other method.

Article 11.1 does not provide guidelines as to when the LCIA Court should or should not follow the originally agreed nomination process, but the discretion can be expected to be exercised where appropriate to expedite an unduly slow process or to prevent an abuse of process.[1]

For example, in the challenge decision in LCIA Reference No. 0252,[2] rendered on July 1, 2002, in which an arbitrator was successfully challenged after having disclosed the outcome of the arbitration to his nominating party prior to the publication of the award, the Division of the LCIA Court recommended that the LCIA Court should appoint a replacement arbitrator directly rather than repeat the agreed nomination process.

**11.2 The LCIA Court may determine that any opportunity given to a party to make any re-nomination (under the Arbitration Agreement or otherwise) shall be waived if not exercised within 14 days (or such lesser or greater time as the LCIA Court may determine), after which the LCIA Court shall appoint the replacement arbitrator without such re-nomination.**

Article 11.2 provides that where a party is allowed to make a re-nomination, the LCIA Court may require this to be made within 14 days (or such other period as the LCIA Court determines), failing which the right to re-nominate may be considered waived and the LCIA Court may simply make the appointment without regard to any re-nomination.

11–003

**Unanswered questions**

The replacement of an arbitral candidate may have little impact upon the proceedings beyond causing some delay. However, the replacement of an arbitrator during the course of an arbitration may lead to more difficulties. Article 11 does not deal with the issues that might arise following the replacement of an arbitrator, leaving this to the Arbitral Tribunal and the parties to resolve, guided as appropriate by the applicable procedural law. For example, it may be appropriate to repeat some of the proceedings before the new or newly constituted Arbitral Tribunal. Under the English Arbitration Act 1996, if the replaced arbitrator was involved in the appointment of a chairman (in the LCIA context, this would equate to the nomination of a presiding arbitrator), that appointment is not to be affected by the replacement of the arbitrator.[3] Other national arbitration laws may differ. The UNCITRAL Model Law simply provides that where an arbitrator is to be substituted the contractual appointment procedure shall be followed.

11–004

---

[1] See Yves Derains and Eric A. Schwartz, *A Guide to the ICC Rules of Arbitration*, 2nd edn (Kluwer Law International, 2005), at p.200 in relation to the equivalent provision in the ICC Rules (Article 12.4—now 15.4 in the 2012 ICC Rules).

[2] LCIA Reference No. 0252, July 1, 2002 (2011) 27(3) Arbitration Int. 351.

[3] See s.27 of the English Arbitration Act 1996 generally, and 27(5) in relation to the appointment of the Chairman or umpire.

Under Article 32.2 of the LCIA Rules, the Arbitral Tribunal must decide any matter not expressly dealt with by the LCIA Rules in good faith and with respect for the "spirit" of the Arbitration Agreement, and with the aim of preserving the enforceability of the award at the seat.

# Article 12—Majority Power to Continue Deliberations

**12.1** In exceptional circumstances, where an arbitrator without good cause refuses or persistently fails to participate in the deliberations of an Arbitral Tribunal, the remaining arbitrators jointly may decide (after their written notice of such refusal or failure to the LCIA Court, the parties and the absent arbitrator) to continue the arbitration (including the making of any award) notwithstanding the absence of that other arbitrator, subject to the written approval of the LCIA Court.

**12.2** In deciding whether to continue the arbitration, the remaining arbitrators shall take into account the stage of the arbitration, any explanation made by or on behalf of the absent arbitrator for his or her refusal or non-participation, the likely effect upon the legal recognition or enforceability of any award at the seat of the arbitration and such other matters as they consider appropriate in the circumstances. The reasons for such decision shall be stated in any award made by the remaining arbitrators without the participation of the absent arbitrator.

**12.3** In the event that the remaining arbitrators decide at any time thereafter not to continue the arbitration without the participation of the absent arbitrator, the remaining arbitrators shall notify in writing the parties and the LCIA Court of such decision; and, in that event, the remaining arbitrators or any party may refer the matter to the LCIA Court for the revocation of the absent arbitrator's appointment and the appointment of a replacement arbitrator under Articles 10 and 11.

## Introduction

As Schwebel J remarked in 1998, the problem of a biased arbitrator who declines to participate in the arbitration or in the deliberations of the Tribunal in an attempt to frustrate the proceedings or undermine an award:

**12–001**

"... has been notorious in public international law since the inception of modern arbitration late in the eighteenth century. In this century, it has reared its ugly head in international commercial arbitration as well."[1]

---

[1] Stephen M. Schwebel, "The Authority of a Truncated Tribunal", in A.J. van den Berg (ed.), *Improving the Efficiency of Arbitration Agreements and Awards: 40 Years of Application of the New York Convention* (ICCA Congress series) (Kluwer Law International, 1999), pp.314–318.

**12-002** The international arbitration community has, on the whole, recognised that when a partisan arbitrator engages in such "guerrilla tactics"[2] the arbitral proceedings should not be frustrated. Nevertheless, in a number of well-publicised cases the enforcement of awards rendered by truncated Tribunals has been refused, even in "arbitration-friendly" jurisdictions, predominantly where the rules under which the award was rendered did not expressly permit the two remaining arbitrators to proceed to make an award without seeking the replacement of the recalcitrant arbitrator.[3]

Article 12 provides arbitrators appointed under the LCIA Rules with the power, in certain circumstances, to continue with the proceedings and render a valid award, notwithstanding the lack of co-operation of one of the arbitrators.

**12-003** The previous version of this Article (under the 1998 Rules) was only very rarely used. However, the very existence of a provision dealing with the problem of a recalcitrant arbitrator perhaps helps to concentrate minds and to improve efficiency: arbitrators know that behaviour which delays and/or undermines the process could lead to their exclusion without frustrating the arbitration as a whole.

The emphasis of Article 12 suggests that it is only intended to be used in exceptional circumstances, and that it should have no application in "run of the mill" cases of slow arbitral progress.

> **12.1 In exceptional circumstances, where an arbitrator without good cause refuses or persistently fails to participate in the deliberations of an Arbitral Tribunal, the remaining arbitrators jointly may decide (after their written notice of such refusal or failure to the LCIA Court, the parties and the absent arbitrator) to continue the arbitration (including the making of any award) notwithstanding the absence of that other arbitrator, subject to the written approval of the LCIA Court.**

**12-004** Where one member of an Arbitral Tribunal refuses or persistently fails to participate in deliberations with his co-arbitrators, Article 12.1 authorises the remaining arbitrators to continue with the reference and render an award. The power to do so may only be exercised in "exceptional circumstances" (for example, where it would be inappropriate to replace the arbitrator under Article 10 or 11 of the LCIA Rules) and when the remaining arbitrators acting jointly have:

---

[2] G.J. Horvath, "Guerrilla Tactics in Arbitration, an Ethical Battle: Is There Need for a Universal Code of Ethics" in Klausegger et al. (eds), *Austrian Yearbook on International Arbitration 2011* (Manz'sche Verlags, 2011), pp.297–313 at p.311.

[3] See, for example, *Swiss Federal Court, Ivan Milutinovic PIM v Deutsche Babcock AG – the ICC Court of Arbitration in Case No. 5017 (1987)* reported in S. Schwebel, "The Authority of a Truncated Tribunal", reprinted in S. Schwebel, *Justice in International Law: Further Selected Writings* (Cambridge: Cambridge University Press, 2011); *First Investment Corp v Fujian Mawei Shipbuilding Ltd et al., United States District Court, Eastern District of Louisiana, US No. 765, First Investment Corp v Fujian Mawei Shipbuilding Ltd et al., United States District Court, Eastern District of Louisiana, 09-3663 Section I, 12 March 2012* in A.J. van den Berg (ed.), *Yearbook Commercial Arbitration* (Kluwer Law International, 2012), Vol.37, pp.377–380); *Supplier (US) v State Enterprise (Belarus), Bundesgerichtshof [Federal Supreme Court] III ZB 14/07, 21 May 2007* in A.J. van den Berg, *Yearbook Commercial Arbitration* (Kluwer Law International, 2009), Vol.34, pp.504–509.

- informed the parties, the arbitrator and the LCIA Court of their intention to proceed; and

- the LCIA Court has granted its written approval for them to do so.

**12.2 In deciding whether to continue the arbitration, the remaining arbitrators shall take into account the stage of the arbitration, any explanation made by or on behalf of the absent arbitrator for his or her refusal or non-participation, the likely effect upon the legal recognition or enforceability of any award at the seat of the arbitration and such other matters as they consider appropriate in the circumstances. The reasons for such decision shall be stated in any award made by the remaining arbitrators without the participation of the absent arbitrator.**

Article 12.2 sets out the matters which arbitrators considering whether to proceed with the reference without another arbitrator's participation must take into account, namely: **12–005**

- the stage of the arbitration;

- the reasons given for the refusal or non-participation;

- the likely effect of continuing without the other arbitrator on the recognition or enforceability of the award at the seat of arbitration; and

- such other matters as they consider appropriate.

The arbitrators must state their reasons for continuing the reference with a truncated Arbitral Tribunal in any award made without the participation of the other arbitrator. **12–006**

**12.3 In the event that the remaining arbitrators decide at any time thereafter not to continue the arbitration without the participation of the absent arbitrator, the remaining arbitrators shall notify in writing the parties and the LCIA Court of such decision; and, in that event, the remaining arbitrators or any party may refer the matter to the LCIA Court for the revocation of the absent arbitrator's appointment and the appointment of a replacement arbitrator under Articles 10 and 11.**

Article 12.3 permits the participating arbitrators to decide subsequently not to continue the arbitration in a truncated Arbitral Tribunal form. It might, for example, be appropriate for a truncated Arbitral Tribunal to reach such a decision if the remaining arbitrators are unable to reach a unanimous opinion on the facts or merits of the dispute. **12–007**

If the arbitrators do decide not to continue without another arbitrator, they must notify the parties and the LCIA Court in writing, and either the parties or the remaining arbitrators may refer the matter to the LCIA Court so that it may revoke the absent arbitrator's appointment and appoint a replacement so that the arbitration may proceed.

## Article 13—Communications between Parties and Arbitral Tribunal

13.1 Following the formation of the Arbitral Tribunal, all communications shall take place directly between the Arbitral Tribunal and the parties (to be copied to the Registrar), unless the Arbitral Tribunal decides that communications should continue to be made through the Registrar.

13.2 Where the Registrar sends any written communication to one party on behalf of the Arbitral Tribunal or the LCIA Court, he or she shall send a copy to each of the other parties.

13.3 Where any party delivers to the Arbitral Tribunal any communication (including statements and documents under Article 15), whether by electronic means or otherwise, it shall deliver a copy to each arbitrator, all other parties and the Registrar; and it shall confirm to the Arbitral Tribunal in writing that it has done or is doing so.

13.4 During the arbitration, from the Arbitral Tribunal's formation onwards, no party shall deliberately initiate or attempt to initiate any unilateral contact relating to the arbitration or the parties' dispute with any member of the Arbitral Tribunal or any member of the LCIA Court exercising any function in regard to the arbitration (but not including the Registrar), which has not been disclosed in writing prior to or shortly after the time of such contact to all other parties, all members of the Arbitral Tribunal (if comprised of more than one arbitrator) and the Registrar.

13.5 Prior to the Arbitral Tribunal's formation, unless the parties agree otherwise in writing, any arbitrator, candidate or nominee who is required to participate in the selection of a presiding arbitrator may consult any party in order to obtain the views of that party as to the suitability of any candidate or nominee as presiding arbitrator, provided that such arbitrator, candidate or nominee informs the Registrar of such consultation.

### Introduction

13–001 Arbitrations under the LCIA Rules are administered by the institution. Parties submit their dispute for determination by the Arbitral Tribunal which will be appointed by the LCIA Court. By adopting the Rules, they agree that the LCIA Court, and the LCIA Secretariat, by delegated authority, shall perform certain functions for the purposes of the formation of the Arbitral Tribunal and also during the course of the proceedings, notably in relation to the funding of the arbitration and issuing of the award. In order to follow the progress of the arbitration, to be alert to incidents which might require its own or the LCIA Court's intervention, and to keep up to date about the Arbitration Costs,[1] it is essential that the LCIA Secretariat remain in touch with the parties and the Arbitral Tribunal throughout the proceedings.

Article 13 sets out how the LCIA Secretariat should be involved in communications and confirms the well-known rule, common to all international arbitrations, that all communications with the Arbitral Tribunal should be copied to the other parties.

13–002   There have been important changes to the wording of Article 13 in the 2014 Rules. The emphasis in the 1998 version was on the role of the Registrar in communications with the Arbitral Tribunal. In the new version, direct communication between the parties and the Arbitral Tribunal is given primacy and ex parte communications with candidate arbitrators, prior to the formation of the Arbitral Tribunal but solely in connection with the selection of the presiding arbitrator, is expressly permitted.[2]

Paragraph 6 of the Annex to the LCIA Rules prohibits Party Representatives from deliberately contacting any member of the Arbitral Tribunal (once constituted) or LCIA Court in connection with the reference on a unilateral or ex parte basis. The IBA's Guidelines on Party Representation in International Arbitration contain similar provisions[3] which may be adopted and followed in an LCIA arbitration if the parties so agree, or the Arbitral Tribunal so orders after consultation.[4]

13–003   However, it is important not to lose sight of one of the primary benefits of institutional arbitration as administered by the LCIA: the neutrality and independence of the Registrar and the Secretariat, who are able to conduct communications with arbitrators on the parties' behalf, thereby avoiding perceptions of bias and misconduct that the IBA Guidelines seek to address.

> **13.1 Following the formation of the Arbitral Tribunal, all communications shall take place directly between the Arbitral Tribunal and the parties (to be copied to the Registrar), unless the Arbitral Tribunal decides that communications should continue to be made through the Registrar.**

---

[1] As defined in Article 28.1, i.e. the costs of the arbitration other than the legal or other expenses incurred by the parties themselves. It is these costs (essentially the arbitrators' fees and disbursements and the LCIA's administrative charges) which the LCIA Court will determine at the conclusion of the arbitration. Rather than wait until then to raise any queries, the Secretariat monitors the costs incurred during the proceedings. The Registrar, Deputy Registrar or Counsel in charge of the file will peruse the correspondence, which is copied to the LCIA, and will liaise, as appropriate, with the LCIA's casework administrator in relation to funding and billing.
[2] Article 13.5.
[3] Articles 7 and 8 of the Guidelines provide that, unless the parties have agreed otherwise, parties and their representatives should not hold ex parte communications with members of the Arbitral Tribunal except that party representative may conduct limited pre-appointment interviews of prospective arbitrators to determine their suitability for the appointment (Appendix 14).
[4] Guideline 1 (Appendix 14). See also the commentary on Article 18 below.

Arbitrators are appointed by the LCIA Court (Article 5). Prior to appointment, they  **13–004**
may more properly be called "candidates" or "nominees" (see Article 7). The 1998
version of Article 13.1 required all pre-appointment communications between parties
and candidate arbitrators to be made through the Registrar.[5] This has changed: the
requirement is no longer express and there is now, in Article 13.5, an exception for
direct and unilateral consultations between candidate arbitrators and parties without
the involvement of the Registrar. Nevertheless, it may still be implied from the
confirmation in the closing words of new Article 13.1 that the usual pre-appointment
procedure is for communications to be made through the Registrar.

Although less prominent than it was, this should remain, then, one of the
distinctive features of the LCIA Rules, which has made LCIA arbitration attractive to newcomers. It has provided comfort to those parties who might be
concerned that their opponents had superior knowledge of the process and/or of
the arbitrators who might be appointed. It has ensured equality of arms in the pre-appointment phase and has ensured that the appointments are completed quickly
without interference.

As discussed in relation to Article 13.5 below, there was no absolute ban on  **13–005**
pre-appointment consultations, under the 1998 version of the Rules: if all parties
and the Registrar were informed, such consultations could proceed for the
purposes of selecting the third and presiding arbitrator. However, the absence of a
written rule permitting such derogation had the effect of maintaining the primacy
of the procedure for channelling all pre-appointment communications through the
Registrar. It remains to be seen how the change of emphasis in Article 13.1 and the
new exception in Article 13.5 will alter perceptions and modify relations amongst
parties, the candidate arbitrators and the LCIA Secretariat.

As mentioned above in relation to Article 7, it is the LCIA Secretariat which
will contact nominees for the purposes of Article 5.3. This includes a presiding
arbitrator, whether selected by the parties themselves or by their nominees. Of
course, it would be usual for a prospective presiding arbitrator to be contacted, by
one or both of the other two nominees, with an informal enquiry as to availability
before the LCIA Secretariat is notified of the joint nomination. However, the
LCIA Secretariat has the burden of sending the Statement of Independence and
Consent to Appointment to the nominee presiding arbitrator for signature, together
with copies of the Request and Response and any other relevant documents.

The new wording of Article 13.1 makes it clear that, after the parties have been  **13–006**
notified of the appointment of the Arbitral Tribunal by (or on behalf of) the
Registrar, communications should, in principle, no longer be channelled through
the Secretariat but should instead be sent direct to the Arbitral Tribunal (and
copied to the Secretariat). The Notice of Appointment (Article 15.2) should
contain the arbitrators' contact details for this purpose.

Of course, the communications covered by Article 13.1 are those which concern
the Arbitral Tribunal directly, most particularly any communications about the
conduct of the proceedings and the timetable. Communications about matters for
which the LCIA, and not the Arbitral Tribunal, is responsible, e.g. deposits under

---

[5] It read: "Until the Arbitral Tribunal is formed, all communications between parties and arbitrators shall be made through the Registrar" (LCIA Rules 1998, Appendix 4).

Article 24, or applications to the LCIA Court should be sent direct to the Secretariat. Communications with the Secretariat should generally also be copied to the other side (exceptions include the communication of bank account details).

13–007   Article 13.1 allows an Arbitral Tribunal to decide that communications with it should take place not directly but through the Registrar.[6] Arbitral Tribunals have made such directions in cases in which there is a concern that issues relating to proper notice[7] could be raised on enforcement. The Secretariat is able to assist arbitrators by despatching their orders and other communications on their behalf, and by keeping records of this correspondence, including the methods of communication and as to whether receipt has been acknowledged or can be evidenced in another way.[8]

It is fairly common practice in arbitrations administered by trade associations in London for all communications to be channelled through the trade association's secretariat from beginning to end. This has benefits in terms of consistency and security, and it allows the relevant body to maintain a full procedural record. However, it can also give rise to delays. Most arbitrators in LCIA arbitrations prefer to communicate direct with the parties' representatives once the arbitration is under way.

13–008   Arbitral Tribunals will sometimes feel constrained, by the provisions of Article 24.3, from communicating directly with the parties until the first payment of a deposit has been made by one of the parties. If, for example, a Claimant has requested extensions of time both for filing a Statement of Case and for paying the initial deposit (a not unusual occurrence), an Arbitral Tribunal may wish to limit criticism, and/or avoid an accusation of misconduct, by not yet becoming involved in correspondence itself (and recording billable time for it), but by having the Registrar advise the parties, on its behalf, that an extension for the filing is granted.

As should be clear from the comments made above, and the words in brackets in Article 13.1, keeping the LCIA Secretariat informed of the proceedings, by copying it into correspondence, is an essential feature of LCIA arbitration.

**13.2 Where the Registrar sends any written communication to one party on behalf of the Arbitral Tribunal or the LCIA Court, he or she shall send a copy to each of the other parties.**

13–009   It is curious that Article 13 does not expressly provide that the Arbitral Tribunal must copy all parties into its (direct) communications, but this is perhaps so obvious that such confirmation is not needed. On the other hand, Article 13.2 does impose such an express obligation on the Registrar when communicating on the Arbitral Tribunal's behalf.

Despite the title of the article, the new wording also extends this obligation to communications on behalf of the LCIA Court which it is useful to have confirmed. An example of such a communication is a reminder to pay a share of a deposit under Article 24.

---

[6] In contrast, Article 13.2 of the 1998 Rules required the Arbitral Tribunal to make a direction if it decided to displace the presumption in favour of communications through the Registrar (Appendix 4).
[7] Article V(1)(b) of the New York Convention (Appendix 9).
[8] See Article 4 above in relation to methods of communication.

There has been a minor change in the 2014 Rules to recognise expressly that the Registrar may be female ("he or she"). The note at the foot of the Index attached to the Rules also confirms that "All references to any person or party include both masculine and feminine".

**13.3 Where any party delivers to the Arbitral Tribunal any communication (including statements and documents under Article 15), whether by electronic means or otherwise, it shall deliver a copy to each arbitrator, all other parties and the Registrar; and it shall confirm to the Arbitral Tribunal in writing that it has done or is doing so.**

Communications with the Arbitral Tribunal should be copied to the LCIA Secretariat and the other side. This is easily achieved by email by way of the "cc" line. Letters sent to the LCIA or the Arbitral Tribunal may likewise be marked "cc [parties], LCIA Registrar". This is sufficient confirmation for the purpose of the last part of Article 13.3.

13–010

The ICC Rules contain a similar provision at Article 3(1):

"All pleadings and other written communications submitted by any party, as well as all documents annexed thereto, shall be supplied in a number of copies sufficient to provide one copy for each party, plus one for each arbitrator, and one for the Secretariat. A copy of any notification or communication from the arbitral tribunal to the parties shall be sent to the Secretariat."

In principle, all documents sent to the Arbitral Tribunal should also be copied to the LCIA Secretariat. However, it should be borne in mind that the purpose is to keep the LCIA Secretariat informed of the progress of the arbitration. The Registrar or case handler will not be concerned to read all of the witness statements or expert reports. If hard copies are to be exchanged, it is worth checking with the LCIA Secretariat whether it will need those or whether a copy of the covering letter will suffice. The LCIA Secretariat will not usually require its own copies of hearing bundles.

**13.4 During the arbitration, from the Arbitral Tribunal's formation onwards, no party shall deliberately initiate or attempt to initiate any unilateral contact relating to the arbitration or the parties' dispute with any member of the Arbitral Tribunal or any member of the LCIA Court exercising any function in regard to the arbitration (but not including the Registrar), which has not been disclosed in writing prior to or shortly after the time of such contact to all other parties, all members of the Arbitral Tribunal (if comprised of more than one arbitrator) and the Registrar.**

Article 13.4 has been newly introduced in the 2014 version of the Rules. Similar wording also appears at para.6 of the new General Guidelines for the Parties' Legal Representatives, which appears as an Annex to the Rules.

13–011

The prohibition on unilateral communications conforms to generally expected international practice. It appears in paragraph 6 of the Annex to the LCIA Rules and in Guideline 7 of the IBA Guidelines on Party Representation. The exceptions to the rule relate to pre-appointment communications, which are discussed above in relation to Article 13.1 and below in relation to Article 13.5.

**13–012** Unilateral contact can have consequences for the arbitration and could justify a challenge to the Arbitral Tribunal as a whole or to the particular member concerned, as well as to the ultimate award(s) of any impugned Arbitral Tribunal.[9] In LCIA Arbitration No. 0252, an arbitration commenced in 2000, a Division of the LCIA Court considered a challenge by the Respondents to all three members of an Arbitral Tribunal after the Claimants' nominated arbitrator had taken a call from Claimants' counsel and had disclosed to him that the final award was being prepared and was partially favourable to his clients.[10] The Claimants used this information in US proceedings before the award had been rendered. The Division noted that it would have been acceptable for Claimants' counsel to have written to the Chairman of the Arbitral Tribunal (with a copy to his co-arbitrators and Respondents' counsel) after the hearing to enquire as to progress towards publication of the award, any such enquiry being transparent to all concerned. The Claimants' nominated arbitrator should have declined to answer the question posed by Claimants' counsel. His excuse that the proceedings were no longer pending was factually incorrect. The Division unanimously concluded that the challenge should be upheld and the Claimants' nominated arbitrator should be removed.

Parties and their representatives may be embarrassed to address to the Arbitral Tribunal an enquiry about the timing of a delayed award, as the Division suggested they should do in the decision cited above. They may be concerned not to irritate the arbitrators at this critical juncture. Their preference could be for an informal approach. This can be accommodated by the LCIA Secretariat, which is generally content to receive telephone calls from party representatives, enquiring as to when an award might be expected. If the answer is known, the Secretariat may say that it will send a message to all parties to advise them of this. If the enquiry will have to be passed on to the presiding arbitrator, the Secretariat is able to communicate it but without indicating which party has raised it. The answer should then be communicated to all parties.

Such an informal approach to the Registrar is expressly excluded from the ban on unilateral communications in Article 13.4.

**13–013** On the other hand, the ban extends to members of the LCIA Court who have exercised functions in regard to the arbitration. This would include, for example, the President or Vice President who appointed the Arbitral Tribunal and any Division established to consider a challenge to an arbitrator under Article 10. The ban concerns only communications relating to the arbitration or the dispute, and should not, therefore, prevent the parties or their lawyers from having ordinary professional contact with arbitrators and LCIA Court members in other contexts.

---

[9] For example, *Norbrook Laboratories Ltd v A Tank and Moulson Chemplant Ltd* [2006] EWHC 1055 (Comm).

[10] An abstract of the decision dated July 1, 2002 appears in (2011) 27(3) Arbitration Int. The Division comprised Prof. Emmanuel Gaillard, David W. Rivkin and John Beechey.

Communications with one arbitrator should always be copied to (or, in the case of oral communications, be made at the same time to) the other members of the Arbitral Tribunal. As noted above, the Registrar should also be copied into all such communications. The exception will be during the course of any hearings: neither the Registrar nor any member of the Secretariat will generally attend hearings (although it does happen on occasion).

Disclosure "shortly after the time of such contact" allows for the possibility that simultaneous contact is for some reason impossible. This could arise, for example, in an arbitration in which the Respondent is not participating. If the Respondent does not have a functioning email address, it may be necessary for printed copies of emails between the Claimant and the Arbitral Tribunal to be sent by post. This wording is new to the 2014 version of the Rules, and the extent of the indulgence permitted by "shortly after" remains to be tested.

**13.5 Prior to the Arbitral Tribunal's formation, unless the parties agree otherwise in writing, any arbitrator, candidate or nominee who is required to participate in the selection of a presiding arbitrator may consult any party in order to obtain the views of that party as to the suitability of any candidate or nominee as presiding arbitrator, provided that such arbitrator, candidate or nominee informs the Registrar of such consultation.**

The tradition in ad hoc commercial arbitrations in London is that, in those cases in which two sides have each appointed an arbitrator, the two so appointed will proceed quickly (often within one or two days) to choose a third and presiding arbitrator without further consultation and, therefore, without any suggestion of interference in their selection. However, this London tradition has been developed (or eroded) in recent years as a "jury vetting" approach has taken hold, permitting the parties' nominees to consult with the parties who nominated them in relation to the selection of the presiding arbitrator.[11]

The IBA's Rules of Ethics for International Arbitrators permits this practice; Rule 5.2 states:

"If a party-nominated arbitrator is required to participate in the selection of a third or presiding arbitrator, it is acceptable for him (although he is not so required) to obtain the views of the party who nominated him as to the acceptability of candidates being considered."

The practice is also endorsed by the new IBA Guidelines on Party Representation, in which it appears as one of the exceptions to the general rule that it is improper for a party representative to engage in ex parte communications with arbitrators (Guideline 8(b)).[12]

13–014

13–015

---

[11] Whilst this process allows the parties greater participation in the process of the constitution of the Arbitral Tribunal, difficulties can arise if the parties agree complex procedures and criteria for the selection and consultation, leading to delay in the constitution of the Arbitral Tribunal.

[12] Appendix 14.

Article 13.5, which is new to the 2014 Rules, expressly permits ex parte communications of this kind in the pre-appointment phase of LCIA arbitrations. It should be noted that it is worded in such a way as to suggest that it should be the candidate arbitrator, and not a party, who initiates such consultations, but that is not always the case in practise, where parties or their Legal Representatives sometimes initiate the consultations. Paragraph 6 of the Annex to the Rules does not appear to prohibit this type of contact by parties with nominated arbitrators who have not yet been appointed and so are not yet part of the "Arbitral Tribunal" (which will typically be the case where consultations concern the selection of the presiding arbitrator).

It has always been good practice for parties' representatives to notify the LCIA (with a copy to the other side) before contacting the nominees direct. The Secretariat will wish to ensure that the other side is aware that it has the opportunity to contact its own nominee, as well as an opportunity to raise any objection it might have. The closing words of Article 13.5 impose an obligation on nominees to ensure that the Registrar is informed if such consultations are going to take place.

Nominees will sometimes ask the Registrar to assist with their selection process by communicating a joint letter to the parties containing, for example, a list of candidates to be ranked by them. The parties or their representatives will be asked to communicate their response to the Registrar. Depending on the method of selection, the Registrar might carry out the ranking calculations on behalf of the two nominees, thereby ensuring that the nominees themselves receive only the blended results and are unaware of the parties' individual preferences.

ARTICLE 14—CONDUCT OF PROCEEDINGS

14.1 The parties and the Arbitral Tribunal are encouraged to make contact (whether by a hearing in person, telephone conference-call, video conference or exchange of correspondence) as soon as practicable but no later than 21 days from receipt of the Registrar's written notification of the formation of the Arbitral Tribunal.

14.2 The parties may agree on joint proposals for the conduct of their arbitration for consideration by the Tribunal. They are encouraged to do so in consultation with the Arbitral Tribunal and consistent with the Arbitral Tribunal's general duties under the Arbitration Agreement.

14.3 Such agreed proposals shall be made by the parties in writing or recorded in writing by the Arbitral Tribunal at the parties' request and with their authority.

14.4 Under the Arbitration Agreement, the Arbitral Tribunal's general duties at all times during the arbitration shall include:

(i) a duty to act fairly and impartially as between all parties, giving each a reasonable opportunity of putting its case and dealing with that of its opponent(s); and

(ii) a duty to adopt procedures suitable to the circumstances of the arbitration, avoiding unnecessary delay and expense, so as to provide a fair, efficient and expeditious means for the final resolution of the parties' dispute.

14.5 The Arbitral Tribunal shall have the widest discretion to discharge these general duties, subject to such mandatory law(s) or rules of law as the Arbitral Tribunal may decide to be applicable; and at all times the parties shall do everything necessary in good faith for the fair, efficient and expeditious conduct of the arbitration, including the Arbitral Tribunal's discharge of its general duties.

14.6 In the case of an Arbitral Tribunal other than a sole arbitrator, the presiding arbitrator, with the prior agreement of its other members and all parties, may make procedural orders alone.

**Introduction**

Article 14 sets out the fundamental ground rules for the conduct of LCIA arbitration, with the emphasis on party autonomy, flexibility and consultation.

**14–001**

Articles 15–22 set out in greater detail specific steps and default procedures that parties might expect to encounter in LCIA arbitration proceedings, which are always subject to the principles set out in Article 14.

Whilst the Arbitral Tribunal bears the ultimate responsibility to determine how the arbitral proceedings shall be conducted, Article 14 contains repeated reminders that the arbitration "belongs" to the parties. The parties are therefore expressly encouraged to take an active role in establishing the procedure that will govern the reference.

**14–002** Procedural matters can be highly significant and should be considered and addressed early on. Parties can suffer a material disadvantage in the pursuit, or defence, of a claim simply by overlooking, or paying scant regard to, the conduct of their arbitration.

The procedural flexibility that is inherent in the arbitral process is circumscribed by the Arbitral Tribunal's duties under Article 14.4 to give each party "a reasonable opportunity of putting its case and dealing with that of its opponent", "avoiding unnecessary delay or expense" and "to provide a fair and efficient means for the final resolution of the parties' dispute".

In practice, if the parties cannot agree on the applicable procedures amongst themselves, the Arbitral Tribunal will consider the circumstances of the case, including the issues in dispute (as set out in the Request for Arbitration and any Response) and the value of the claim in determining how the arbitration should be administered and, consequently, the procedural steps that should apply. How the Arbitral Tribunal determines what those appropriate steps will be may depend on what information is available to the Arbitral Tribunal at the time. The Arbitral Tribunal will be heavily reliant on input from the parties and any agreements that are reached between the parties will generally be gratefully received.

*Procedural law*

**14–003** It does not automatically follow that the Arbitral Tribunal's procedural powers are governed by the law that the Arbitral Tribunal will use to determine the underlying substantive dispute. The procedural powers of the Arbitral Tribunal derive from a number of different sources, which may be entirely unrelated to the substantive dispute. The primary sources are:

- **The Arbitration Agreement**. If the parties to a dispute incorporated the LCIA's recommended arbitration clause, either in the underlying contractual document or specifically in relation to a particular dispute, then, in addition to incorporating the LCIA Rules into their agreement, they should also have already reached an agreement on certain important aspects of the arbitration, namely the number of arbitrators, the seat or legal place of the arbitration (which will determine the national procedural law that will apply to the arbitration), the language of the arbitration and the substantive law governing the contract. Arbitration Agreements occasionally also make provision for procedural matters, such as the location for hearings, matters concerning evidentiary discovery or the powers of the Arbitral Tribunal to grant certain types of relief.

- **The LCIA Rules**. Articles 15–21 of the LCIA Rules provide, in greater detail than some other comparable rules, a basic procedural framework which may guide the parties and the Arbitral Tribunal as to the procedural issues which need to be determined or which may apply by default, if a particular issue is not agreed by the parties and no direction is given by the Arbitral Tribunal. There are specific provisions dealing with the submission of written statements (pleadings) and supporting evidence (Article 15), the seat and place of hearings (Article 16), the language of the arbitration (Article 17), party representation (Article 18), the format of hearings (Article 19) and witness and expert evidence (Articles 20 and 21). Article 22 sets out the additional procedural powers enjoyed by Arbitral Tribunals, including the power to direct or permit amendments to statements of case, to extend or curtail time limits, to adopt an inquisitorial approach in the proceedings and to order the inspection of documents and specific disclosure.

- **The law of the "seat" of the arbitration**. The "seat" is the juridical place of the arbitration, which forms the link between the arbitral proceedings and a national legal system.[1] If the Arbitration Agreement and the Rules fail to address a particular procedural issue, the provisions of the applicable procedural law under the national legislation of the seat will apply by default. Under the LCIA Rules, London is the default seat or legal place of arbitration, in which case, the provisions of the English Arbitration Act 1996 will apply. There are a number of mandatory provisions in the 1996 Act[2] to which both the Arbitration Agreement and the Rules will be subject.[3] Any provision in the Arbitration Agreement or the Rules that is inconsistent with the mandatory provisions of the 1996 Act will be ineffective. For the most part, however, the procedural provisions in the Act provide non-mandatory guidance as to how the arbitration should be conducted. The LCIA Rules were written against the backdrop of the 1996 Act and are consistent with it.

An Arbitral Tribunal that purports to make procedural directions outside the remit of its powers, or in contradiction of mandatory applicable laws, risks having an otherwise valid award set aside under the law of the seat,[4] or recognition and enforcement of the award refused by an enforcing court in another jurisdiction.[5]

*Structure of Article 14*

Although the 2014 edition of the LCIA Rules changed the structure of Article 14,[6] few if any substantive changes were made that might be expected to impact significantly on the conduct of proceedings.

**14–004**

---

[1] See Article 16 below.
[2] That is, provisions that cannot be changed or excluded by agreement of the parties.
[3] See s.4 of the English Arbitration Act 1996 (Appendix 7).
[4] For example, under Article 34.2(a)(ii) of the UNCITRAL Model Law (Appendix 10) or s.68 of the English Arbitration Act 1996 (Appendix 7).
[5] Under Article V(1)(d) of the New York Convention (Appendix 9).
[6] From three sub-Articles to six.

**14.1 The parties and the Arbitral Tribunal are encouraged to make contact (whether by a hearing in person, telephone conference-call, video conference or exchange of correspondence) as soon as practicable but no later than 21 days from receipt of the Registrar's written notification of the formation of the Arbitral Tribunal.**

14–005　Article 14.1 outlines an expectation that the Arbitral Tribunal and parties should establish contact soon after the formation of the Arbitral Tribunal. The Article is framed in permissive language of "encouragement"; it imposes no obligations on either the parties or the Arbitral Tribunal. A procedural ("case management"/"directions") meeting in person or by teleconference call, to consider the procedural conduct of the proceedings, is encouraged. Otherwise, there should at least be an exchange of correspondence between the Arbitral Tribunal and the parties. In either case, it is suggested that this take place within 21 days of notice of the constitution of the Arbitral Tribunal. This should normally be enough time for the initial deposit to be directed and paid, so that the LCIA is in funds and the Arbitral Tribunal is in a position to incur fees and expenses.[7]

The text of Article 14.1 and the suggestion that such a meeting should be held within a specific 21-day time period are new additions to the LCIA Rules. They respond to a concern that in many cases meetings prior to the merits hearing would be useful, if only to allow the parties to become acquainted with their arbitrator. However, it is also recognised that early procedural directions are not appropriate or even possible in every case, and that meetings can be disproportionately expensive, hence the tone of "encouragement" and the alternative suggestion of contact by way of telephone conference call or correspondence.

**14.2 The parties may agree on joint proposals for the conduct of their arbitration for consideration by the Arbitral Tribunal. They are encouraged to do so in consultation with the Arbitral Tribunal and consistent with the Arbitral Tribunal's general duties under the Arbitration Agreement.**

**14.3 Such agreed proposals shall be made by the parties in writing or recorded in writing by the Arbitral Tribunal at the parties' request and with their authority.**

14–006　One of the principal benefits of international arbitration in resolving disputes stems from the parties' freedom, or autonomy, to agree flexible procedures, which can be tailored to fit the specific circumstances of their dispute. Within certain mandatory requirements imposed by the law of the seat, parties may agree on any aspect of the procedure for their arbitration.[8]

---

[7] Article 24.
[8] Article 19(1) of the UNCITRAL Model Law: "Subject to the provisions of this Law, the parties are free to agree on the procedure to be followed by the arbitral tribunal in conducting the proceedings" (Appendix 10); s.4 of the English Arbitration Act 1996: "The mandatory provisions of this Part . . . have effect notwithstanding any agreement to the contrary" (Appendix 7).

Consistent with Article V(1)(d) of the New York Convention,[9] the presumption in Article 14.2 of the LCIA Rules is in favour of the adoption by the Arbitral Tribunal of the procedures that have been agreed and proposed by the parties. The parties are encouraged to make proposals that are agreed in consultation with the Arbitral Tribunal and which are consistent with its general duty to conduct a fair and efficient procedure.[10]

The express encouragement in Article 14.2 of the Rules to agree proposals on procedural matters *in consultation* with the Arbitral Tribunal also makes good practical sense. Consultation with the Tribunal will allow the arbitrators to ensure, as they are required to do under Article 14.4 of the Rules, that the procedures adopted are indeed consistent with its general duties of fairness and efficiency. The Arbitral Tribunal will also be able to ensure that the arbitrators are available to deal with the procedural steps proposed by the parties including, not least, to attend any hearings the parties wish to schedule.

14–007

Article 14.3 requires such agreed proposals to be recorded in writing either by the parties or by the Arbitral Tribunal having been authorised to do so by the parties. Unless recorded in writing, agreements over procedural matters might not be regarded as effective under the law of the seat.[11] The requirement of writing may be effected through correspondence (including email correspondence) between the parties and the Arbitral Tribunal. Producing a separate written document (whether or not signed by the parties) might be helpful, but is not required.

*Whose arbitration?*

The reference to the joint "proposals"[12] of the parties for the conduct of their arbitration, for "consideration" by the Arbitral Tribunal, is reminiscent of the well-rehearsed debate over who should have the ultimate power to direct the conduct of the arbitration: the parties acting by agreement, or the Arbitral Tribunal.[13] The reference to *proposals* might suggest it is the arbitrators who are expected to assume a greater degree of control over the proceedings.[14]

14–008

However, arbitrators who ignore agreements concluded by the parties on procedural matters potentially risk a challenge to their appointment,[15] or worse, a

---

[9] Under Article V(1)(d) of the New York Convention the enforcement court may refuse recognition and enforcement of an award if the arbitration procedure adopted was not in accordance with the agreement of the parties (Appendix 9).

[10] Which is set out in Article 14(4).

[11] See, for example, ss.5 and 34(1) of the English Arbitration Act 1996.

[12] Previous editions of the Rules contained no reference to proposals, only to the right of the parties to agree upon the conduct of their arbitration, subject to the general duties of the Arbitral Tribunal (see Article 14.1 of the 1998 edition of the LCIA Rules).

[13] V.V. Veeder, "Whose arbitration is it anyway: the parties' or the arbitration tribunal's—an interesting question?" in Lawrence Newman and Richard Hill (eds), *The Leading Arbitrators' Guide to International Arbitration*, 2nd edition (Juris Publishing, 2008).

[14] The DAC Report, at paras 157–159, indicates that it reached the conclusion that it was not desirable to allow the Tribunal the power to override the agreement of the parties in relation to procedural matters. According to the DAC, the nature and value of arbitration is that it is consensual and it is ineffective to try to impose on the parties a procedure to which they did not agree. The DAC Report points out that a Tribunal that is unable to persuade the parties to adopt a different agreement is free to resign.

[15] See Article 10 and s.24 of the English Arbitration Act 1996 (Appendix 7).

**14.4 Under the Arbitration Agreement, the Arbitral Tribunal's general duties at all times during the arbitration shall include:**

**(i) a duty to act fairly and impartially as between all parties, giving each a reasonable opportunity of putting its case and dealing with that of its opponent(s); and**

**(ii) a duty to adopt procedures suitable to the circumstances of the arbitration, avoiding unnecessary delay and expense, so as to provide a fair, efficient and expeditious means for the final resolution of the parties' dispute.**

Articles 14(4)(i) and (ii) guarantee basic procedural standards that the parties are entitled to expect from the Arbitral Tribunal, and to which the Arbitral Tribunal must adhere. Thus, any arbitral directions or order relating to procedural matters or procedure otherwise adopted that contravenes the principles of fairness and impartiality set out in these provisions could potentially give rise to challenges being made to the Arbitral Tribunal pursuant to Article 10 of the LCIA Rules; and might even provide the grounds for challenging any award rendered.[21]

**14–011**

The LCIA Rules were drawn up against the background of the English Arbitration Act 1996 and are consistent with it. Nowhere is this more obvious than in respect of the overriding duties of the Arbitral Tribunal (and the parties) in Articles 14(4)(i) and (ii) of the Rules, which are expressed in near identical terms to s.33(1) of the English Arbitration Act 1996:

"(1) The Tribunal shall

(a) act fairly and impartially as between the parties, giving each party a reasonable opportunity of putting his case and dealing with that of his opponent, and

(b) adopt procedures suitable to the circumstances of the particular case, avoiding unnecessary delay or expense, so as to provide a fair means for the resolution of the matters falling to be determined".

In light of the similarities between these provisions, parties might reasonably expect an Arbitral Tribunal exercising its procedural powers to have regard to jurisprudence concerning s.33(1) of the English Arbitration Act 1996, even when this is not directly applicable to the arbitration proceedings at hand.

**14–012**

As with the English Arbitration Act 1996, the fundamental duties of the Arbitral Tribunal under Article 14.4 of the LCIA Rules are to act fairly and impartially, and to give each party a reasonable opportunity to put its own case and answer the case(s) put forward by the opponent. However, these duties (and corresponding rights of the parties) are not absolute. As to impartiality, the parties may agree to waive an arbitrator's disclosed connections with the parties or circumstances that might otherwise give rise to justifiable doubts as to the impartiality of the Arbitral

---

[21] Article V of the New York Convention (Appendix 9); Articles 34 and 36 of the UNCITRAL Model Law (Appendix 10) ss.68 and 103 of the English Arbitration Act 1996 (Appendix 7).

Tribunal;[22] just as they are free to expressly agree to adopt procedures that might otherwise appear unfair.[23]

**14–013** The duty to afford the parties an opportunity to present their case is further moderated by the reference to reasonableness. This is not an absolute duty. As Merkin and Flannery note in their commentary on the English Arbitration Act 1996:[24]

> "Complying with this duty does not, however, entail giving each side endless chances to make arguments and respond to arguments put by the other side.... [T]he Tribunal is empowered to manage the proceedings actively ... and it is arguable that, to comply with its duty under section 33, a tribunal will be required to curtail submission at some point."

**14–014** Nor does the duty to give each party a reasonable opportunity to present its case (whether under Article 14.4 of the LCIA Rules or under s.33 of the English Arbitration Act 1996) allow a non-participating party to delay the proceedings ad infinitum or to avoid the consequences of an award rendered in LCIA arbitration proceedings commenced with proper notice.[25]

**14.5 The Arbitral Tribunal shall have the widest discretion to discharge these general duties, subject to such mandatory law(s) or rules of law as the Arbitral Tribunal may decide to be applicable; and at all times the parties shall do everything necessary in good faith for the fair, efficient and expeditious conduct of the arbitration, including the Arbitral Tribunal's discharge of its general duties.**

**14–015** The Arbitral Tribunal enjoys the widest discretion to decide the most appropriate procedure for the conduct of the arbitration. Provided its powers have not been curtailed by the parties, and that it complies with Article 14.4 and any applicable mandatory laws, it can adopt any procedures it deems appropriate.

It is for the Arbitral Tribunal to determine which law(s) or rules of law govern procedural matters, although this will inevitably involve at least the mandatory procedural law of the seat.[26] The power of the Arbitral Tribunal will also be subject to any written agreement between the parties, including the remaining

---

[22] See *Weissfisch v Julius* [2006] EWCA Civ. 218 and the IBA Guidelines on Conflicts of Interest in International Arbitration (Appendix 13).

[23] See, for example, *Gujarat NRE Coke Ltd v Coeclerici Asia (PTE) Ltd* [2013] EWHC 1987 (Comm), para.22 in particular: "If the Tribunal had been considering a new case in which NRE sought to put forward its defences to a claim then the procedure adopted [the Respondent was not allowed to make submissions] would of course have been irregular and unfair. But that is not this case.... Facing an imminent arbitration hearing NRE entered into another contract, the Payment Agreement, and then again failed to pay the money it had promised to pay. In the Payment Agreement "NRE and the Guarantor expressly and irrevocably agree that Coeclerici will be entitled to an immediate consent award, without the need for any pleadings or hearings".

[24] R. Merkin and L. Flannery, *Arbitration Act 1996,* 5th edn (Informa Law, 2014), p.129.

[25] See Article 15.8 below.

[26] Under Article 16, the parties may agree upon the seat of the arbitration, failing which the default seat is London, unless the Arbitral Tribunal determines that another seat is more appropriate. See 16–007 et seq.

provisions of the LCIA Rules. Thus, for example, under Article 19 of the LCIA Rules the Arbitral Tribunal can only conduct a documents-only arbitration if the parties have agreed to this in writing.

The approach that is taken on procedural matters in any given case will very much depend on the identity of the individual arbitrators appointed to determine the dispute who, in turn, may well be guided or influenced by soft law sources, such as the IBA Rules on the Taking of Evidence in International Arbitration, the procedural rules of other arbitral institutions and the procedural laws applicable in their home jurisdictions. 14–016

The approach that the Arbitral Tribunal takes to procedural issues could have a material impact on its assessment of the merits (for example, the weight to be given to witness testimony). Parties would therefore be wise to raise their procedural expectations and concerns with the Arbitral Tribunal at the earliest opportunity and seek to ensure that these are taken into account.

*Arbitrating in good faith*

The second half of Article 14.5 concerns the parties' conduct in the course of the arbitral proceedings. In particular, the provision requires parties to do "everything necessary in good faith for the fair, efficient and expeditious conduct of the arbitration, including the Arbitral Tribunal's discharge of its general duties". 14–017

The requirement that parties engage in "good faith" in the conduct of the proceedings is new to the 2014 edition of the LCIA Rules. A similar requirement was also introduced into Article 32.2 of the LCIA Rules.

In contrast to the position in many other jurisdictions, English law does not recognise a generally applicable duty of good faith in the performance of contracts or as a generally applicable principle of procedural law.[27] Nevertheless, English judges have long recognised that parties to a reference are under an implied obligation to "cooperate with the other[s] in taking appropriate steps to keep the procedure in the arbitration moving".[28] Equally, under s.40 of the English Arbitration Act 1996, parties to English seated arbitrations must "do all things necessary for the proper and expeditious conduct of the arbitral proceedings" and must (inter alia) comply "without delay with any determination of the tribunal as to procedural or evidential matters, or with any order or directions of the tribunal". These provisions are bolstered by s.41, under which arbitrators have the power to deal with recalcitrant parties by issuing peremptory orders, dismissing the claims of non-compliant parties or rendering awards against them.[29] 14–018

---

[27] In some recent cases, the English courts have indicated that, where the parties have expressly elected to include such a duty in commercial contracts, the courts should seek to enforce it; although not in the face of express provisions to the contrary. See, for example, *Mid Essex Hospital Services NHS Trust v Compass Group UK and Ireland Ltd (Trading as Medirest)* [2013] EWCA Civ 200; *TSG Building Services PLC v South Anglia Housing Ltd* [2013] EWHC 1151.

[28] *Bremer Vulkan Schiffbau und Maschinenfabrik v South India Shipping Corp Ltd* [1981] A.C. 909 HL at 983 per Lord Diplock.

[29] Article 2A of the UNCITRAL Model Law provides that its provisions must be construed and applied in a manner that promotes the observance of good faith (Appendix 10).

It remains to be seen how the express requirement of good faith will impact the conduct of LCIA arbitration proceedings in practice.[30]

**14.6 In the case of an Arbitral Tribunal other than a sole arbitrator, the presiding arbitrator, with the prior agreement of its other members and all parties, may make procedural orders alone.**

14–019   In appropriate cases, the power to permit the presiding arbitrator to make procedural orders alone can be a useful way of saving time and costs because it avoids the need for all three arbitrators to have to consider the parties' submissions on all, even minor, procedural issues or to attend all procedural hearings.

Unless all parties and arbitrators agree, the presiding arbitrator must consult with the co-arbitrators on all matters and every order must be rendered by the Arbitral Tribunal as a whole, even if it is communicated to the parties by only one of them.

---

[30] Notably, although forcefully advocated by a Vice President of the LCIA Court, and a co-drafter of the 2014 edition of the LCIA Rules (see V.V. Veeder, "The Lawyer's Duty to Arbitrate in Good Faith" (2002) 18(4) Arbitration Int. 431) and contemplated in an early draft of the 2014 Rules, the final version imposes no duty of good faith on the legal representatives and advocates of the parties in LCIA arbitrations.

## Article 15—Written Statements

15.1 Unless the parties have agreed or jointly proposed in writing otherwise or the Arbitral Tribunal should decide differently, the written stage of the arbitration and its procedural time-table shall be as set out in this Article 15.

15.2 Within 28 days of receipt of the Registrar's written notification of the Arbitral Tribunal's formation, the Claimant shall deliver to the Arbitral Tribunal and all other parties either: (i) its written election to have its Request treated as its Statement of Case complying with this Article 15.2; or (ii) its written Statement of Case setting out in sufficient detail the relevant facts and legal submissions on which it relies, together with the relief claimed against all other parties, and all essential documents.

15.3 Within 28 days of receipt of the Claimant's Statement of Case or the Claimant's election to treat the Request as its Statement of Case, the Respondent shall deliver to the Arbitral Tribunal and all other parties either: (i) its written election to have its Response treated as its Statement of Defence and (if applicable) Cross-claim complying with this Article 15.3; or (ii) its written Statement of Defence and (if applicable) Statement of Cross-claim setting out in sufficient detail the relevant facts and legal submissions on which it relies, together with the relief claimed against all other parties, and all essential documents.

15.4 Within 28 days of receipt of the Respondent's Statement of Defence and (if applicable) Statement of Cross-claim or the Respondent's election to treat the Response as its Statement of Defence and (if applicable) Cross-claim, the Claimant shall deliver to the Arbitral Tribunal and all other parties a written Statement of Reply which, where there are any cross-claims, shall also include a Statement of Defence to Cross-claim in the same manner required for a Statement of Defence, together with all essential documents.

15.5 If the Statement of Reply contains a Statement of Defence to Cross-claim, within 28 days of its receipt the Respondent shall deliver to the Arbitral Tribunal and all other parties its written Statement of Reply to the Defence to Cross-claim, together with all essential documents.

15.6 The Arbitral Tribunal may provide additional directions as to any part of the written stage of the arbitration (including witness statements, submissions and evidence), particularly where there are multiple claimants, multiple respondents or any cross-claim between two or more respondents or between two or more claimants.

15.7 No party may submit any further written statement following the last of these Statements, unless otherwise ordered by the Arbitral Tribunal.

15.8 If the Respondent fails to submit a Statement of Defence or the Claimant a Statement of Defence to Cross-claim, or if at any time any party fails to avail itself of the opportunity to present its written case in the manner required under this Article 15 or otherwise by order of the Arbitral Tribunal, the Arbitral Tribunal may nevertheless proceed with the arbitration (with or without a hearing) and make one or more awards.

15.9 As soon as practicable following this written stage of the arbitration, the Arbitral Tribunal shall proceed in such manner as has been agreed in writing by the parties or pursuant to its authority under the Arbitration Agreement.

15.10 In any event, the Arbitral Tribunal shall seek to make its final award as soon as reasonably possible following the last submission from the parties (whether made orally or in writing), in accordance with a timetable notified to the parties and the Registrar as soon as practicable (if necessary, as revised and re-notified from time to time). When the Arbitral Tribunal (not being a sole arbitrator) establishes a time for what it contemplates shall be the last submission from the parties (whether written or oral), it shall set aside adequate time for deliberations as soon as possible after that last submission and notify the parties of the time it has set aside.

## Introduction

15–001 Article 15 provides a default framework and timetable for the "written stage" of the arbitration, namely the submission of statements of case (also referred to as submissions or pleadings). It will apply unless the parties agree (or the Arbitral Tribunal orders) otherwise.

Whilst some may regard the procedure as overly "prescriptive", or perhaps as following too closely the process for the service of pleadings in the English Commercial Court, it is generally accepted that it provides a predictable, sensible and timely process for many cases. It is one of the distinctive features of the Rules, and one of its attractions for many commercial users. The tight timetable is without doubt one of the main reasons why LCIA arbitration has established a reputation for speed.

15–002 The provision of such a default procedure may be contrasted with many other arbitration rules, such as the 2012 ICC Rules, which leave it to the Arbitral Tribunal to fix the procedure to be followed for the substantive submissions.

The written submissions are perhaps the most important part of any arbitration—very often they constitute the primary statement of each party's case both on the facts and the law. They allow each party to set out its arguments before any hearing, thereby identifying at an early stage the issues that the Arbitral Tribunal has to determine. This should remove any element of surprise, and should ensure that the parties do not introduce new arguments at the last minute without the permission of the Arbitral Tribunal. It also assists in keeping the length of expensive hearing time required to a minimum.

Each written statement is to be accompanied by "all essential documents" which, in the 1998 Rules, were such documents "on which the party concerned relies and which have not previously been submitted by any party". It is unlikely that the new, shorter, wording is intended to increase the burden on the parties. Instead, it can be assumed that, in line with the previous wording and with common practice in international arbitration, each party would still only be required to adduce the essential documents upon which it relies. In many (but not all) cases the Arbitral Tribunal will afford the parties an opportunity to adduce further documents either in support of witness statements or in response to requests for production by the other party (see Article 22.1(v)). **15–003**

The default timetable for delivery of written submissions under Article 15 is summarised below:

| Written Submission | Party | Date for delivery | Article |
| --- | --- | --- | --- |
| Statement of Case | Claimant | Within 28 days of receipt of written notification from Registrar of the formation of the Arbitral Tribunal | 15.2 |
| Statement of Defence and any Cross-claim | Respondent | Within 28 days of receipt of Statement of Case, or written notification of election to treat Request as Statement of Case | 15.3 |
| Statement of Reply and Defence to Cross-claim | Claimant | Within 28 days of receipt of Statement of Defence and Cross-claim | 15.4 |
| Statement of Reply to Defence to Cross-claim | Respondent | Within 28 days of receipt of Statement of Reply and Defence to Cross-claim | 15.5 |

Under the default procedure, no party is allowed to submit further written submissions,[1] following the final submission under Article 15, without further order of the Arbitral Tribunal. Thus the default procedures and timetable provided for in Article 15 envisage a swift exchange of pleadings—completed within four months of the constitution of the Tribunal. Where this procedure is adopted, the written submissions will often be followed by a disclosure phase, then the exchange of witness statements and expert reports before a final hearing. **15–004**

---

[1] Article 20 makes a separate provision for the production of witness statements.

In practice, the Article 15 default timetable will not always be appropriate (or complete the exchange of written submissions) in complex arbitrations and/or where jurisdictional or other preliminary issues arise for determination at an early stage. Parties and their legal representatives will have a strong practical incentive to agree upon an appropriate timetable or seek directions from the Arbitral Tribunal for those cases at an early stage. Indeed, in many cases the Arbitral Tribunal will take the initiative and discuss the appropriate procedure to be followed with the parties shortly after being appointed.

**15–005** Whether agreed or directed by the Arbitral Tribunal at the outset or later in the proceeding, additional written submissions (or skeleton arguments) shortly before and/or after an evidentiary hearing (in place of lengthy oral opening and closing statements) are also common.

In a growing minority of cases parties expressly agree a procedure whereby written submissions are accompanied by all the documentary, witness and expert evidence relied upon (commonly referred to as "memorials"). This is the "memorials procedure" commonly adopted in arbitrations under some other rules of arbitration, notably the ICC, UNCITRAL and ICSID Rules. Where such a procedure is adopted, the parties will typically need much longer to produce each round of submissions than under the LCIA default procedure because they will also need to prepare the witness and expert evidence in parallel. It is common for the parties to seek three or four months (and sometimes longer) for the production and delivery of a memorial. However, there is then no need for separate rounds of witness and expert reports.

Where there is to be a disclosure phase, the memorials process is often split into two rounds, one before disclosure and one afterwards, so that the evidence revealed through disclosure can be incorporated into the second round of memorials.

**15–006** Where such a timetable is agreed by the parties in writing it will usually be adopted by the Arbitral Tribunal.[2] On the other hand, when it is proposed by an Arbitral Tribunal, it will sometimes be rejected by the parties as being contrary to their expectations for an LCIA arbitration. There is, for example, a perception for some that the sequential delivery of witness statements and expert reports with memorials can make them too wide ranging, anticipating a case not yet submitted, whereas simultaneous exchange after the factual and legal issues have been ventilated in submissions allows the witnesses to focus on those issues. However, others consider that it can be more efficient to deal with the legal submissions and evidence together. Ultimately, it is for the parties, their legal representatives and the Arbitral Tribunal to adopt the procedures that are best suited to the circumstances of each particular case.

It is becoming increasingly common for Arbitral Tribunals to order that the submissions and supporting documents should be provided in hard copy and in electronic format that can be searched and edited by the Arbitral Tribunal. This can greatly assist the Arbitral Tribunal in its work. Similarly, the Arbitral Tribunal may also require the parties to submit agreed tables or schedules, *dramatis personae*, chronologies and/or lists of agreed matters and/or issues.

---

[2] See Articles 14.2–14.4.

These commonly adopted procedures in LCIA arbitration are similar to those adopted by parties and Tribunals in international arbitration proceedings conducted under other institutional or ad hoc rules. This is an area in which noticeable harmonisation in practice has occurred.[3]

15–007

Article 15 is longer than the 1998 edition equivalent and contains a number of changes, some of which serve primarily to update and streamline the procedure it sets out, whilst others are likely to have a greater impact. Perhaps the most significant is in new Article 15.10, which seeks to ensure that the Arbitral Tribunal proceeds to make it award "as soon as reasonably possible" and, to that end, that any deliberations take place quickly after the hearing.

**15.1 Unless the parties have agreed or jointly proposed in writing otherwise or the Arbitral Tribunal should decide differently, the written stage of the arbitration and its procedural time-table shall be as set out in this Article 15.**

If the parties have not reached agreement in writing, or made joint proposals in writing to the Arbitral Tribunal (pursuant to Article 14.2) regarding the conduct of the written stage of the proceedings, and the Arbitral Tribunal does not consider that a different process should apply, then Article 15.1 provides that the default procedure set out in Articles 15.2–15.8 applies.

15–008

**15.2 Within 28 days of receipt of the Registrar's written notification of the Arbitral Tribunal's formation, the Claimant shall deliver to the Arbitral Tribunal and all other parties either: (i) its written election to have its Request treated as its Statement of Case complying with this Article 15.2; or (ii) its written Statement of Case setting out in sufficient detail the relevant facts and legal submissions on which it relies, together with the relief claimed against all other parties, and all essential documents.**

Under the Article 15 default procedure, the Claimant has 28 days from when it is notified of the constitution of the Arbitral Tribunal to deliver one of the following:

15–009

(a) a written election informing the other parties and Arbitral Tribunal that it wishes to let its Request stand as its Statement of Case; or

(b) its written Statement of Case, setting out in detail the relevant facts and legal argumentation relied upon by the Claimant, together with an indication of the relief claimed.

Delivery of the Statement of Case (or written election), and of all other written statements, is to be made to the Arbitral Tribunal, to all other parties and to the

15–010

---

[3] Emmanuel Gaillard and John Savage (eds), *Fouchard Gaillard Goldman on International Commercial Arbitration* (Kluwer, 1999), pp.690–708.

Registrar. This last requirement, to copy the Registrar in, is not stated in Article 15 but is contained in Article 13.3.

The Statement of Case is intended to be a detailed explanation of the Claimant's case, setting out its position on both the facts and the law. It differs in this respect from the Particulars of Claim in English court proceedings, which are a concise statement of the relevant facts,[4] with the Claimant's position on the law being postponed until skeleton arguments are submitted shortly before the hearing.

15–011   The Statement of Case is usually far more detailed than the Request for Arbitration, in which only a brief summary of the background to the dispute and the claims advanced is required. An election to treat the Request for Arbitration as the Statement of Case is therefore usually only appropriate in straightforward cases, in which the background facts and legal submissions are adequately made out and proven within the confines of the Request.

Of course, if the Claimant wants to proceed as quickly as possible, it can always set out its full case in the Request for Arbitration (or, as is sometimes done, append a detailed Statement of Case as an Annex to the Request) and then elect under Article 15.2(ii) to have this stand as its Statement of Case. However, whilst this approach has successfully been adopted in simple cases, such as straightforward debt claims or some cases arising from sale of goods contracts in the commodities sector, in most complex cases Claimants prefer to wait until the Arbitral Tribunal has been appointed and the procedure is under way before setting out their case in full. As well as allowing the Claimant more time to prepare its case, this avoids front-loading the costs of the arbitration and allows the Claimant to see what the Respondent(s) has to say in its Response before setting out its full case.

15–012   It should be noted that if a written election is to be made, it should be communicated to the Arbitral Tribunal, the other parties and the Registrar within the 28 days specified, not before. Claimants have occasionally sought to make the election, by anticipation, in the Request, but the terms of Article 15 are clear: an election is to be made not to the Registrar but to the Arbitral Tribunal, once appointed.

Whichever route is taken, the Claimant must ensure that the Statement of Case provides a sufficiently detailed exposition of the facts and the law in order to meet any legal and evidential burdens the Claimant must overcome in order to succeed in its case.

15–013   Article 15.2 also requires the Claimant to set out "the relief claimed against all other parties" in its Statement of Case. For clarity, and to ensure that the Respondent(s) and Arbitral Tribunal are aware of the claims being advanced, the relief sought should be set out in a separate section of the Statement of Case (normally at the end of the submission), with each relief which the Arbitral Tribunal is asked to award (e.g. declaration, damages, injunction etc) stated in a separate paragraph or sub-paragraph.

**15.3  Within 28 days of receipt of the Claimant's Statement of Case or the Claimant's election to treat the Request as its Statement of Case, the Respondent shall deliver to the Arbitral Tribunal and all other parties**

---

[4] English Civil Procedure Rules, 16.4

**either: (i) its written election to have its Response treated as its Statement of Defence and (if applicable) Cross-claim complying with this Article 15.3; or (ii) its written Statement of Defence and (if applicable) Statement of Cross-claim setting out in sufficient detail the relevant facts and legal submissions on which it relies, together with the relief claimed against all other parties, and all essential documents.**

Article 2 of the LCIA Rules provides that the Respondent should submit a Response to the Claimant's Request and it prescribes what information the Response should contain. Although expressed in mandatory terms, the Rules envisage that a Respondent may elect not to submit a Response. Article 2.4 provides that a Respondent which does not deliver a Response is not precluded from advancing a defence or cross-claim in the arbitration at a later stage and the Respondent could wait until it has to submit its Statement of Defence before setting out its own case.[5]   **15–014**

As with the Claimant's Statement of Case, the Statement of Defence is intended to be a detailed explanation of the Respondent's defence to the claims made against it by the Claimant and, where relevant, of the cross-claims it advances.

Article 15.3 does not require the Respondent to indicate expressly in the Statement of Defence which of the Claimant's contentions are admitted, and which denied.[6] In line with common practice, Article 15.3 recognises that the Respondent may consider it more appropriate or convenient simply to state the relevant facts and legal contentions without a paragraph by paragraph response to the Claimant's Statement of Case. Nevertheless, a Statement of Defence that left the Arbitral Tribunal with doubts as to which parts of the Claimant's case were accepted by the Respondent, and which were denied, would certainly be incomplete. The Respondent should take care to ensure that it has set out its position on all elements of the Claimant's claim(s).   **15–015**

The Respondent should ensure that the claims made against it fall within the jurisdiction of the Arbitral Tribunal to determine to the dispute, and raise any objections in the Statement of Defence to the jurisdiction of the Arbitral Tribunal over the claims made, as any potential jurisdictional challenges could be deemed to have been waived after that point.[7]

Article 15.3 provides a time limit of 28 days from receipt of the Claimant's Statement of Case (or of written notice of the Claimant's election to rely on its Request) for submission of the Respondent's Statement of Defence (and Cross-claim if any). Alternatively, the Respondent may make a written election by that time that the Response should stand as the Statement of Defence and Cross-claim (if any).   **15–016**

Whichever route is taken, the Respondent must ensure that the Statement of Defence provides enough details to rebut any claim put forward by the Claimant,

---

[5] Note that if the Respondent does not deliver a Response it will still need to exercise any right to nominate an arbitrator or this may be lost.
[6] By contrast, the 1998 version of Article 15.3 stated that the "Statement of Defence [shall set] out in sufficient detail which of the facts and contentions of law in the Statement of Case or Request . . . it admits or denies . . ." (Appendix 4).
[7] See Article 23.3.

and to meet any legal and evidential burdens the Respondent must prove in order to succeed on any cross-claim it advances.

Where a cross-claim is advanced, the Statement of Defence and Cross-claim must set out "the relief claimed against all other parties". For clarity, and to ensure that the other parties and Arbitral Tribunal are aware of the cross-claims being advanced, the relief sought should be set out in a separate section (normally at the end of the submission), with each relief that the Arbitral Tribunal is asked to award (declaration, damages, injunction etc) stated in a separate paragraph or sub-paragraph.

> **15.4** Within 28 days of receipt of the Respondent's Statement of Defence and (if applicable) Statement of Cross-claim or the Respondent's election to treat the Response as its Statement of Defence and (if applicable) Cross-claim, the Claimant shall deliver to the Arbitral Tribunal and all other parties a written Statement of Reply which, where there are any cross-claims, shall also include a Statement of Defence to Cross-claim in the same manner required for a Statement of Defence, together with all essential documents.

15-017  Comments made above in respect of the Statements of Case and Defence apply equally to the Statement of Reply and Defence to Cross-claim. The Claimant should ensure that any cross-claims advanced by the Respondent are properly addressed, and that any objections to the jurisdiction of the Arbitral Tribunal over any cross-claims are duly raised in the Statement of Defence to Cross-claim.[8]

> **15.5** If the Statement of Reply contains a Statement of Defence to Cross-claim, within 28 days of its receipt the Respondent shall deliver to the Arbitral Tribunal and all other parties its written Statement of Reply to the Defence to Cross-claim, together with all essential documents.

15-018  Article 15.5 allows the Respondent a right of reply to the Statement of Defence to Cross-claim and places the Respondent on an equal footing to the Claimant (who is entitled to respond to the Statement of Defence). The Reply to Defence to Cross-claim must be delivered to the Arbitral Tribunal and the other parties within 28 days of the Statement of Defence to Cross-claim.

Consistent with English procedural traditions, in which the Claimant has the last word, Article 15 does not permit the Respondent an automatic right of response to the Claimant's Reply where there has been no cross-claim. Not permitting the Respondent an automatic right of reply may seem unfair to those from jurisdictions with different legal traditions, or when the Claimant's Reply raises new factual or legal contentions. In appropriate cases, the Arbitral Tribunal may permit the submission of additional written statements under Article 15.7.

---

[8] Any potential objection to jurisdiction that is not raised at this point could be deemed to have been waived (see Article 23.3).

Comments made above in respect of the Statement of Reply and Defence to Cross-claim apply also to the Statement of Reply to the Defence to Cross-claim.

**15.6** **The Arbitral Tribunal may provide additional directions as to any part of the written stage of the arbitration (including witness statements, submissions and evidence), particularly where there are multiple claimants, multiple respondents or any cross-claim between two or more respondents or between two or more claimants.**

Article 15.6 is a new addition to the LCIA Rules. It clarifies that the Article 15 default procedures can and should, where appropriate, be adapted by the Arbitral Tribunal to meet the requirements and circumstances of individual cases and to deal with written evidence. Its scope is thus wider than the "Written Statements" of the title of Article 15 and extends to the written evidence, in respect of which other specific default provisions are set out, for example in Article 20 (Witness(es)). **15–019**

The examples contemplated in Article 15.6 include multi-party disputes in which the parties do not fall into readily identifiable groups of Claimants with aligned interests against a group of aligned Respondents. It is not difficult to imagine that other circumstances will arise in which directions from the Arbitral Tribunal will be required. However, cases in which repeated intervention by the Arbitral Tribunal is needed may have been unsuitable for the Article 15 default procedure in the first case.

**15.7** **No party may submit any further written statement following the last of these Statements, unless otherwise ordered by the Arbitral Tribunal.**

Article 15.7 is another new addition to the LCIA Rules. It prohibits the parties from serving additional written submissions without the permission of the Arbitral Tribunal. **15–020**

This provision aims to curtail the extended exchange of written submissions by the parties; a practice that has been more common than desirable. Arbitral Tribunals which might previously have been concerned that to curtail the exchange of written statements or to reject any unsolicited submissions could jeopardise the enforceability of the award, should now be able to draw comfort from this Article, and utilise it to retain control over the proceedings.

Rejoinders and Sur-Rejoinders will sometimes be allowed by Arbitral Tribunals in cases in which an oral hearing is not held. In those cases, these final submissions give the parties opportunities to make points which might otherwise have been raised in such a hearing.

**15.8** **If the Respondent fails to submit a Statement of Defence or the Claimant a Statement of Defence to Cross-claim, or if at any time any party fails to avail itself of the opportunity to present its written**

case in the manner required under this Article 15 or otherwise by order of the Arbitral Tribunal, the Arbitral Tribunal may nevertheless proceed with the arbitration (with or without a hearing) and make one or more awards.

15–021   Article 15.8 confirms that the failure by a party to avail itself of the opportunity to deliver a Statement of Defence (or any other written statement), or other opportunity to present its case, shall not prevent the Arbitral Tribunal from proceeding with the arbitration and rendering an award on the basis of the submissions and materials before it.

An Arbitral Tribunal will usually be careful to ensure that a recalcitrant party is given notice of the required written statement and may well allow further time for it to be provided, in order to avoid a future challenge to the award on the grounds of procedural irregularity or lack of due process. The power to proceed with the arbitration, even if the relevant statement(s) is not provided, is consistent with the powers of many national arbitration laws and other institutional arbitration rules,[9] and helps to prevent a party from sabotaging the arbitration process through lack of engagement and delay.

**15.9**   **As soon as practicable following this written stage of the arbitration, the Arbitral Tribunal shall proceed in such manner as has been agreed in writing by the parties or pursuant to its authority under the Arbitration Agreement.**

**15.10**   **In any event, the Arbitral Tribunal shall seek to make its final award as soon as reasonably possible following the last submission from the parties (whether made orally or in writing), in accordance with a timetable notified to the parties and the Registrar as soon as practicable (if necessary, as revised and re-notified from time to time). When the Arbitral Tribunal (not being a sole arbitrator) establishes a time for what it contemplates shall be the last submission from the parties (whether written or oral), it shall set aside adequate time for deliberations as soon as possible after that last submission and notify the parties of the time it has set aside.**

15–022   Articles 15.9 and 15.10 place some urgency upon the Arbitral Tribunal to proceed with the arbitration following the written stage provided for in Article 15, and also (later in the proceedings) to render its final award following the last oral or written submission from the parties (which will often be made at or shortly after the final hearing).

Article 15.9 states that "As soon as practicable" following the written stage the Arbitral Tribunal should proceed with the conduct of the reference in accordance

---

[9] Article 6.8 of the ICC Rules; Article 30 of the UNCITRAL Arbitration Rules (Appendix 11); Article 25 of the UNCITRAL Model Law (Appendix 10) and s.41(4) of the English Arbitration Act 1996 (Appendix 7). Notably, the LCIA Rules do not contain a provision equivalent to s.41(3) of the 1996 Act, which permits a Tribunal to make an award dismissing a claim when the Claimant is guilty of inexcusable delay in pursuing its claim.

with the written agreement of the parties, or as it has directed pursuant to Article 14.1 of the LCIA Rules.

Article 15.10 is a new provision. It requires the Arbitral Tribunal not only to render the final award as soon as possible after the final written or oral submission from the parties, but also to notify the parties and LCIA Registrar of the timetable within which it expects to be able to do so. An Arbitral Tribunal consisting of three (or more) arbitrators is also required to set aside "adequate" time for deliberations and to notify the parties of the time it has set aside.

**15–023**

These provisions have no direct equivalents in other major institutional rules.[10] They are intended to give the parties an indication of how long they will need to wait for the award and to place some pressure upon the Arbitral Tribunal to produce the award as quickly as it reasonably can. At the very least these provisions should encourage a dialogue between the parties and the Arbitral Tribunal regarding the timing of the award and leave the parties with realistic expectations.

These welcome provisions must be seen against the background of complaints amongst users over delay in the conduct of international arbitration (and particularly in the production of awards), and it is hoped that they will assist in reducing the time taken to produce awards.[11] However, the LCIA's record has always been relatively good: around one half of arbitrations which go to a final award are concluded within 12 months.[12]

---

[10] The ICC Rules provide that the final award must be rendered within six months of the Terms of Reference, but in practice that deadline is usually extended by the ICC Court, operating through the Secretariat.

[11] See, for example, Michael McIlwrath and Roland Schroeder, "The View from an International Arbitration Customer: In Dire Need of Early Resolution" (2008) 74(1) *Arbitration*, pp.3–11.

[12] LCIA website FAQs, *http://www.lcia.org/Frequently_Asked_Questions.aspx#length* [Accessed November 14, 2014].

## Article 16—Seat(s) of Arbitration and Place(s) of Hearings

**16.1** The parties may agree in writing the seat (or legal place) of their arbitration at any time before the formation of the Arbitral Tribunal and, after such formation, with the prior written consent of the Arbitral Tribunal.

**16.2** In default of any such agreement, the seat of the arbitration shall be London (England), unless and until the Arbitral Tribunal orders, in view of the circumstances and after having given the parties a reasonable opportunity to make written comments to the Arbitral Tribunal, that another arbitral seat is more appropriate. Such default seat shall not be considered as a relevant circumstance by the LCIA Court in appointing any arbitrators under Articles 5, 9A, 9B, 9C and 11.

**16.3** The Arbitral Tribunal may hold any hearing at any convenient geographical place in consultation with the parties and hold its deliberations at any geographical place of its own choice; and if such place(s) should be elsewhere than the seat of the arbitration, the arbitration shall nonetheless be treated for all purposes as an arbitration conducted at the arbitral seat and any order or award as having been made at that seat.

**16.4** The law applicable to the Arbitration Agreement and the arbitration shall be the law applicable at the seat of the arbitration, unless and to the extent that the parties have agreed in writing on the application of other laws or rules of law and such agreement is not prohibited by the law applicable at the arbitral seat.

### Introduction

**16–001** The presence of "London" in its name has led to a perception, in some quarters, that the LCIA is not a truly international institution. It has also led to the mistaken assumption that proceedings will always be held in London and will be governed by English law.

At the same time, international parties, which have previously used ad hoc arbitration in London, but are now looking for the added value of administered proceedings under the auspices of a recognised institution, will often expect that reference to the LCIA will suffice to ensure that the proceedings do take place in London and that they will have recourse to the Commercial Court in London, if necessary. International trading houses which have conducted arbitrations in

London for many years (in some cases for more than a century) through long-established trade associations will have similar expectations.[1]

Article 16 confirms that parties are free to choose the seat of their arbitration, but it also provides that in the absence of choice London will be the default seat unless the Arbitral Tribunal should decide that another seat would be more appropriate.

16–002

The location of the seat determines what procedural law ("*lex arbitri*") will apply to the arbitration. Issues arising in connection with the commencement and conduct of the arbitration should be decided in accordance with this law.[2]

If London is chosen, the English Arbitration Act 1996 will apply.[3] The 1996 Act confirms that the "seat" means the "juridical seat" of the arbitration.[4] It goes on to provide that the seat may be "designated" by (a) the parties, (b) the arbitral institution, or (c) the Arbitral Tribunal if so authorised by the parties. This is precisely the scheme of Article 16 of the Rules.

16–003

The 2010 Choices in International Arbitration survey by the School of International Arbitration, Queen Mary University of London found that, across all arbitrations, London was by far the most popular choice of seat amongst the international corporations who took part in the research.[5] Of those who took part in the research, 30 per cent preferred London, 9 per cent Geneva, and 7 per cent Paris, Singapore and Tokyo.

The survey found that the most important influence on the choice of seat (62 per cent) was the formal legal infrastructure, e.g. the national arbitration law, the track record in enforcing agreements to arbitrate and arbitral awards, and the neutrality and impartiality of the legal system.

16–004

This set of reasons is logical: the "juridical seat" is not necessarily the same as the venue of the arbitration, i.e. the place where hearings will be held. In choosing a seat, parties need not be concerned by such matters as the quality of hotels and transport infrastructure. Article 16 confirms that hearings may take place at "any convenient geographical place" chosen by the Arbitral Tribunal. However, in practice, hearings will most often take place at the seat.[6]

---

[1] For example, the Arbitration Rules of the Refined Sugar Association (established in 1891, and having more than 100 members from 40 different countries) contain the following provisions at r.8: "For the purpose of all proceedings in arbitration, the contract shall be deemed to have been made in England, any correspondence in reference to the offer, the acceptance, the place of payment or otherwise, notwithstanding, and England shall be regarded as the place of performance. Disputes shall be settled according to the law of England wherever the domicile, residence or place of business of the parties to the contract may be or become. The seat of the Arbitration shall be England and all proceedings shall take place in England. It shall not be necessary for the award to state expressly the seat of the arbitration."

[2] The Geneva Protocol of 1923 states: "The arbitral procedure, including the constitution of the arbitral tribunal, shall be governed by the will of the parties and by the law of the country in whose territory the arbitration takes place...". However, some national laws permit parties to choose a procedural law which is different from the law of the seat (e.g. s.4(5) of the English Arbitration Act 1996 (Appendix 7)) and this is endorsed by Article 16.4 of the Rules.

[3] English Arbitration Act 1996 s.2 (Appendix 7).

[4] English Arbitration Act 1996 s.3 (Appendix 7).

[5] Available at *http://www.arbitration.qmul.ac.uk/docs/123290.pdf* [Accessed November 5, 2014].

[6] Article V(1)(d) and (e) of the New York Convention 1958 refer respectively to the law of the country in which the arbitration took place and in which the award was made as relevant to a challenge to the recognition and enforcement of an award (Appendix 9).

**16.1 The parties may agree in writing the seat (or legal place) of their arbitration at any time before the formation of the Arbitral Tribunal and, after such formation, with the prior written consent of the Arbitral Tribunal.**

16–005   The definition of "seat" in the parenthesis in Article 16.1 overcomes ambiguities and uncertainties. The 1985 version of the Rules spoke only of the "place of arbitration". In *ABB Lummus Global Ltd v Keppel Fels Ltd*,[7] a case which was heard in the Commercial Court in London after the English Arbitration Act 1996 came into force but before the 1998 Rules were introduced, Clarke J had to decide what the parties' post-contractual agreement on London as the "place" of the arbitration meant. The arbitration clause in the parties' contract had provided that disputes were to be referred to the LCIA but also that they were to be "settled in accordance with Singapore law". Clarke J decided that the word "place" in the LCIA Rules described "the legal place or seat of the arbitration" (the formulation now found in the Rules). On this basis, he went on to decide that the parties' choice of London amounted to a variation of their contract so that the "curial or procedural law was to be English", not Singapore law.

The same wording, using both "seat" and "place", is found in the LCIA's recommended clause: "The seat, or legal place, of arbitration shall be [City and/or Country]".[8] Depending on the context, however, "place" on its own could mean only the venue for hearings.

16–006   The parties' written agreement on the seat need not be made in the arbitration clause or other original arbitration agreement. The seat is one of the matters which the parties may address in the exchange of Request and Response: Articles 1.1(iv) and 2.1(iv). In the vast majority of cases, agreement on the seat will have been reached before the Arbitral Tribunal is appointed. It is one of the matters to which the LCIA Secretariat will draw the parties' attention in its first letter to them. They may reach agreement in correspondence or, after the appointment of the Arbitral Tribunal, in "written comments" invited by the Arbitral Tribunal (see Article 16.2).

The 1998 version of the Rules made no distinction between an agreement reached prior to the appointment of the Arbitral Tribunal and one made afterwards. The new wording contains the proviso that a post-appointment agreement requires the "prior written consent of the Arbitral Tribunal". This requirement is consistent with the general principles that the Arbitral Tribunal should be consulted in relation to matters which were undecided at the time of its appointment and that it should have the power to veto agreements and procedural steps which run contrary to its own expectations and responsibilities (cf. Articles 14.2 and 14.4).

**16.2 In default of any such agreement, the seat of the arbitration shall be London (England), unless and until the Arbitral Tribunal orders, in view of the circumstances and after having given the parties a**

---

[7] *ABB Lummus Global Ltd v Keppel Fels Ltd (formerly Far East Levingston Shipbuilding Ltd)* [1999] 2 Lloyd's Rep. 24.
[8] See Part III.

reasonable opportunity to make written comments to the Arbitral Tribunal, that another arbitral seat is more appropriate. Such default seat shall not be considered as a relevant circumstance by the LCIA Court in appointing any arbitrators under Articles 5, 9A, 9B, 9C and 11.

By providing for a default seat, the Rules ensure that an arbitration does not proceed in a juridical vacuum and that the participants will know to which courts they will be able to turn for support. **16–007**

More than 80 per cent of parties in LCIA arbitrations are from jurisdictions outside the UK.[9] In choosing the LCIA for the resolution of their disputes, international parties often make a deliberate choice of a London seat too. By making London the primary default seat, Article 16.2 thus reflects the assumed expectations of most parties who choose the LCIA for the resolution of their disputes.

However, London can be displaced in favour of another seat if the Arbitral Tribunal should so decide. Under the 1998 Rules, it was the LCIA Court that could make this decision, which was in line with the regime under the ICC Arbitration Rules. The new wording returns this power to the Arbitral Tribunal, which is where it had resided in the 1985 Rules.[10] **16–008**

One of the effects of this change is to make London the default seat during the initial phase of the arbitration, i.e. before the Arbitral Tribunal is appointed by the LCIA Court. Under the 1998 Rules, the LCIA Court could make a decision on the seat before appointing the arbitrator(s), which would then allow the seat to be a factor in the choice of candidates, whether by the LCIA Court, by the parties if they had not by then made their nominations, or by their nominees selecting the presiding arbitrator. The final sentence of Article 16.2 now confirms that the default seat will not be a factor which the LCIA Court will consider when appointing arbitrators.

As London will always be the default seat "until" the Arbitral Tribunal is appointed and decides that another seat is more appropriate, this declaration at the end of Article 16.2 may be seen as intending to communicate the message that the LCIA Court will not be Anglocentric in its selection of arbitrators. It also confirms that the LCIA Court will not allow the Arbitral Tribunal's choice of seat to influence its selection of a replacement arbitrator as and when such a selection may become necessary. However, the parties are free to consider the default seat a factor when making their nominations: if they wish to change the seat to another jurisdiction, they may look for candidates who could be expected to favour such a switch. **16–009**

In practice, under the 1998 Rules, the LCIA Court was rarely faced with a decision about the seat of an arbitration.[11] In many cases in which no seat was chosen in the parties' arbitration agreement, the Claimant confirmed in its Request for

---

[9] In 2013, 18.6% of parties were from the UK, according to the Registrar's Report for that year available on the LCIA's website.

[10] This is also in line with Article 18 of the UNCITRAL Arbitration Rules 2010 (Appendix 11). It diverges, though, from Article 18 of the ICC Rules 2012, which provides that the ICC Court has this power.

[11] Between 2011 and 2013, 13 applications were made under Article 16 (6 in 2011, 0 in 2012 and 7 in 2013). London was designated as the seat in almost all cases.

Arbitration that it was content to proceed with London as the seat and the Respondent confirmed likewise in its Response. This reflects the reality that in choosing the LCIA for the resolution of their disputes, international parties usually wish to have English arbitration law govern the proceedings and to have the support of the Commercial Court in London.

16–010  After the English Court of Appeal decided in *Jivraj v Hashwani*[12] that an arbitration agreement was void if it prescribed the religion or nationality of arbitrators, some law firms representing parties in LCIA arbitrations became anxious that by choosing the Rules with their nationality requirements in Article 6, parties could render their arbitration agreements void. One response to this was for parties, in their Request and Response, to agree to exclude Article 6. Another response by a party in one case was to seek to displace London as the default seat of the arbitration in favour of a jurisdiction which did not impose such restrictions on the parties' choice of criteria for the selection of arbitrators. In the event, the case settled before the LCIA Court had to make a decision on the point.

16–011  Should the House of Lords' decision in *Jivraj v Hashwani*[13] be overturned following the pending complaint to the European Commission, this route to avoiding Article 6 will no longer be available: under the new wording of Article 16.2, the Arbitral Tribunal will already have been appointed before London can be displaced as the default seat.

The Arbitral Tribunal's decision on the seat will be in the form of an "order". As such, it could appear in the first procedural order alongside decisions on other procedural matters. In this respect, the reference to "written" comments being made by the parties to the Arbitral Tribunal is a perhaps redundant survival from the 1998 wording: the parties' comments, or some of them, could perfectly well be made orally at a directions hearing, if one is held, and they could also be made in the Request and Response addressed to the Registrar.[14]

16–012  As to the factors which the Arbitral Tribunal will consider, neutrality is likely to be paramount. However, it should be noted that in cases in which one party is British, Article 6 should operate to ensure that the sole arbitrator or presiding arbitrator is of a different nationality, so that a safeguard is already in place in that regard.

**16.3 The Arbitral Tribunal may hold any hearing at any convenient geographical place in consultation with the parties and hold its deliberations at any geographical place of its own choice; and if such place(s) should be elsewhere than the seat of the arbitration, the arbitration shall nonetheless be treated for all purposes as an arbitration**

---

[12] *Jivraj v Hashwani* [2010] EWCA Civ 712.
[13] *Jivraj v Hashwani* [2011] UKSC 40.
[14] Article 16.1 of the 1998 version required the LCIA Court to give the parties "an opportunity to make written comment" (Appendix 4). As the LCIA Court does not hold hearings, written submissions would be the method by which the parties' respective arguments could be brought to its attention. The survival of this wording in new Article 16.2 is likely to reflect an intention to ensure that the Arbitral Tribunal will allow time for written submissions on the issue, but without precluding the possibility that it be addressed at an oral hearing.

deliberately chosen to arbitrate in one place disputes which have arisen under a contract governed by the law of another place".

**16–016** In another insurance case, the Court of Appeal was again faced with an absence of an express choice of law governing the arbitration agreement and held that the law with which the arbitration agreement was most closely connected (the test under English law) was, in that particular case, the law of the seat of the arbitration.[17] The governing law of the insurance policy was Brazilian law and Moore-Bick LJ recognised that there were "powerful factors in favour of an implied choice of Brazilian law as the governing law of the arbitration agreement". The assured argued in favour of Brazilian law and that the arbitration agreement was enforceable under that law only with its consent. Moore-Bick LJ held that there were two other considerations which indicated that English law should govern: (i) the choice of a London seat and (ii) the improbability that the parties had intended their arbitration agreement to be governed by a law which made it so "one-sided". Lord Neuberger MR agreed, adding "it may be that it is inevitable that the answer must depend on all the terms of the particular contract, when read in the light of the surrounding circumstances and commercial common sense."

However, in a subsequent case concerning challenges to awards in two LCIA arbitrations, brought under s.67 of the English Arbitration Act 1996, Andrew Smith J in the Commercial Court held that "the law that governs the scope of the jurisdiction of the Tribunal appointed under the LCIA rules for Arbitration" (which he suggested might be called "the law of the reference") was intended by the parties, on his analysis of the arbitration clause in its particular context, to be the substantive law of the contract, which was Indian law, and not the law of the seat, which was London.[18] The wording of Article 16 in the 1998 Rules did not mention the "law applicable to the Arbitration Agreement" (as distinct from the "law applicable to the arbitration") and it did not, therefore, assist the judge in that case.[19]

**16–017** Both of these authorities were considered by Hamblen J in the Commercial Court in applications under the English Arbitration Act 1996 in a case heard at the end of 2013.[20] The judge distilled the guidance provided by these authorities. He confirmed that the proper law of the arbitration agreement is to be determined by "undertaking a three-stage enquiry into (i) express choice, (ii) implied choice and (iii) the system of law with which the arbitration agreement has the closest and most real connection". His concluding point was:

---

[17] *Sulamérica Cia Nacional de Seguros SA & Ors v Enesa Engenharia SA & Ors* [2012] EWCA Civ 638.
[18] *Arsanovia Ltd, Burley Holdings Ltd and Unitech Ltd v Cruz City 1 Mauritius Holdings* [2012] EWHC 3702 (Comm).
[19] The new wording of the Article might not necessarily have produced a different result in *Arsanovia*: Andrew Smith J thought that it was "strongly arguable" that the parties had made an express choice of Indian law as the law of the Arbitration Agreement, noting, "express terms do not stipulate only what is absolutely and unambiguously explicit". He might well have found that the parties had "agreed in writing" on the application of Indian law to the Arbitration Agreement, even though the seat was London.
[20] *Habas Sinai Ve Tibbi Gazlar Istihsal Endustrisi AS v VSC Steel Co Ltd* [2013] EWHC 4071 (Comm).

"Where there are sufficient factors pointing the other way to negate the implied choice derived from the express choice of law in the matrix contract the arbitration agreement will be governed by the law with which it has the closest and most real connection. That is likely to be the law of the country of seat, being the place where the arbitration is to be held and which will exercise the supporting and supervisory jurisdiction necessary to ensure that the procedure is effective."

The new wording in Article 16.4 should provide certainty in those cases in which no other express choice of law to govern the Arbitration Agreement has been made in the contract in dispute: in an arbitration under the LCIA Rules, it should be the law of the seat.

**16–018**

As far as the procedural law is concerned, the parties are free to choose another procedural law to the extent permitted by their Arbitration Agreement or by the law of the seat. In England, for example, the mandatory provisions of the English Arbitration Act 1996 will apply to an arbitration with its seat in England, even if a different law is chosen to govern the procedure.[21] As noted above, s.4(5) of the Act contemplates such a choice. However, it is rarely, if ever, going to be useful to have an additional procedural law in play and it could lead to severe complications. If such an agreement is made, it is likely to be the result of a compromise and not of a considered decision.

---

[21] English Arbitration Act 1996 ss.2 and 4.

## Article 17—Language(s) of Arbitration

**17.1** The initial language of the arbitration (until the formation of the Arbitral Tribunal) shall be the language or prevailing language of the Arbitration Agreement, unless the parties have agreed in writing otherwise.

**17.2** In the event that the Arbitration Agreement is written in more than one language of equal standing, the LCIA Court may, unless the Arbitration Agreement provides that the arbitration proceedings shall be conducted from the outset in more than one language, determine which of those languages shall be the initial language of the arbitration.

**17.3** A non-participating or defaulting party shall have no cause for complaint if communications to and from the LCIA Court and Registrar are conducted in the initial language(s) of the arbitral seat.

**17.4** Following the formation of the Arbitral Tribunal, unless the parties have agreed upon the language or languages of the arbitration, the Arbitral Tribunal shall decide upon the language(s) of the arbitration after giving the parties a reasonable opportunity to make written comments and taking into account the initial language(s) of the arbitration and any other matter it may consider appropriate in the circumstances.

**17.5** If any document is expressed in a language other than the language(s) of the arbitration and no translation of such document is submitted by the party relying upon the document, the Arbitral Tribunal may order or (if the Arbitral Tribunal has not been formed) the Registrar may request that party to submit a translation of all or any part of that document in any language(s) of the arbitration or of the arbitral seat.

### Introduction

**17–001** Just as the seat of an LCIA arbitration will not necessarily be London, so the language in which the arbitration is conducted will not necessarily be English. This is one of the features of the Rules, which distinguishes them from rules with a national focus and which confirms their international intent.

To put Article 17 in context, it should be noted that whilst the English Arbitration Act 1996 contemplates the use of other languages in the proceedings,[1] the rules of

---

[1] English Arbitration Act 1996 s.34(2)(b) (Appendix 7).

other arbitral bodies based in London but serving international users do not include specific provisions about language. The LMAA Terms, for example, are silent about this.[2] The Rules provide an exception to the general assumption that English will be the language of an arbitration conducted in London or under the auspices of an institution based in London.

Whilst Article 17 does allow parties, the LCIA Court and Arbitral Tribunals to choose other languages, it should be recognised that, in practice, almost 99 per cent of LCIA arbitrations are conducted in English.

17–002

The prevalence of English and, in some regions of the world, just a handful of other languages, is one of the factors which has led Jan Paulsson, a former President of the LCIA Court, to suggest the use of the term "universal" in place of "international" arbitration. He has spoken of:

"the convergence of the way disputes are resolved, so that disputants and advocates and arbitrators of any nationality can be found everywhere, doing the same thing in the same way – with an ever-decreasing number of linguistic barriers."

He has added:

17–003

"English is dominant, Spanish is in the ascendant; Mandarin, German and Arabic are holding their own in particular contexts; French has plummeted in a few decades – but that is about it. A hundred other languages are out of the running, and if one of them is yours and you want to participate, you must retool."[3]

The cases in which a language other than English will be chosen for the conduct of the arbitration will most usually be ones in which the parties on both sides speak this language as their first language.

LCIA arbitration is sometimes chosen for the resolution of disputes between parties of the same nationality who, for whatever reasons, want to keep disputes not only out of their local courts but also out of the hands of local arbitral institutions. In recent years, the LCIA has administered, for example, an arbitration between two Spanish companies and one between two Finnish companies, both with their seats in London. In the Spanish case, the arbitration clause stipulated that the Chair of the Arbitral Tribunal must not be Spanish but must speak Spanish because the proceedings were to be conducted in that language. In the Finnish case, the clause stipulated that the proceedings were to be conducted in Finnish, which effectively meant that the sole arbitrator had to be Finnish.[4]

17–004

---

[2] Similarly, the Refined Sugar Association Arbitration Rules contain no provisions about language, but their insistence on both the seat and substantive law being English suggest that no other language would be welcome.

[3] Alexander Lecture, Chartered Institute of Arbitrators, November 29, 2012, "Universal arbitrations – what we gain, what we lose" ((2013) 79(2) *Arbitration* 185).

[4] These are both examples of cases in which the parties' own stipulations in their arbitration clause would fall foul of the equality legislation as interpreted by the Court of Appeal in its decision in *Jivraj v Hashwani* [2010] EWCA Civ 712 (subsequently overturned by the Supreme Court [2011] UKSC 40), without the operation of Article 6 of the Rules.

In recent years, London has served as the jurisdiction of choice for the resolution of disputes between parties from Russia and the CIS. It is not only the Commercial Court which has attracted Russian speaking disputants; so has the LCIA. In 2012, 6 per cent of parties in LCIA arbitrations were either Russian or Kazakh and a further 8 per cent were from Cyprus or the British Virgin Islands, where many offshore companies of Russian and CIS ownership are based. In such cases, English law will often be the governing law of the contract and that is one of the principal reasons for the choice of London as the seat of the arbitration and for English as the language of the arbitration. These international parties have often chosen LCIA arbitration precisely because they want an English lawyer, or a panel of English lawyers, to decide their dispute and they are, therefore, prepared to have the proceedings conducted in English.

**17–005** The 1998 Rules were available from the LCIA in the following languages in addition to English: Arabic, Chinese, French, German, Italian, Portuguese, Russian and Spanish. The 2014 Rules can be expected to be available in the same languages. It was noted on the LCIA's website in relation to all these versions: "In the event of any discrepancy or inconsistency between the English version of the LCIA Rules and the Rules in any other language, the English version will prevail."

Although the LCIA Secretariat is relatively small, its staff speak a number of different languages. Whilst most of the lawyers in the Secretariat are qualified as English solicitors, some have also studied and/or practised abroad. For example, in 2011 there were as many as three French lawyers, two of whom were dual-qualified, and one of whom was a Russian speaker and another a Spanish speaker. A native Russian speaker joined the Secretariat as Counsel in 2013.

**17–006** Native English speakers are a minority in the LCIA Court. Members speak a wide variety of languages and many are multilingual and qualified in more than one jurisdiction. They can be called upon to assist when problems arise in particular languages.

The LCIA's database of arbitrators includes speakers of many more languages than have ever appeared in LCIA arbitrations. Details of members of the LCIA, as contained in its annual directory, include the languages which they speak.

**17–007** An institutional arbitration involves more participants than an ad hoc arbitration. Their roles in the arbitration may be specific, administrative and temporary but nevertheless critical to the smooth running of the proceedings. What these participants communicate to the parties at particular junctures could come to be scrutinised by a court in a non English-speaking jurisdiction. This is one of the reasons why the scheme of Article 17 separates the initial pre-appointment phase, essentially in the hands of the LCIA Secretariat and LCIA Court, from the full proceedings managed by the Arbitral Tribunal. The choice of language in each of these two phases can be different. Article 17 sets out how, and by whom, decisions will be made about this.

By allowing for different languages to be used in the arbitration, and by setting a clear framework as to how these are to be chosen, Article 17 is, like other provisions of the Rules, flexible, practical and non-Anglocentric. It puts the parties in charge but helps where there might be a problem and where a party does not cooperate.

**17.1 The initial language of the arbitration (until the formation of the Arbitral Tribunal) shall be the language or prevailing language of the Arbitration Agreement, unless the parties have agreed in writing otherwise.**

In accordance with the principle of party autonomy, any agreement made between the parties in relation to the language of the arbitration will prevail. It is good practice for the language of the arbitration to be stipulated in the arbitration clause of a contract.[5] The LCIA's recommended clause has the following wording: "The language to be used in the arbitration shall be [ ]."[6]

17–008

If the parties' arbitration agreement provides that the language of the arbitration is to be a language other than English, all correspondence from the LCIA Secretariat, from the filing of the Request for Arbitration onwards, should be in that language.

Agreement on the language, as on other procedural matters, may be reached between the parties in correspondence or in the exchange of Request and Response.[7] Language is one of the specific examples of procedural matters to be addressed in the Request, which are given at Article 1.1(iv). It also appears at Article 2.1(iv), which confirms that the Respondent may respond to any statement or proposal made by the Claimant or may make any proposal itself.

17–009

If the parties' arbitration clause or other agreement is silent as to the language, it is the language (or prevailing language) in which that clause or agreement is drafted which will be used in the initial phase of the arbitration.

In practical terms, this means that a Request for Arbitration, in a dispute under a contract in Russian and English, in which the Russian version is stated to prevail, but in which the arbitration clause is silent as to the language of the arbitration, should be drafted and submitted in Russian, not English. In such a case the Response should also be drafted in Russian.

17–010

In cases in which the Claimant's representatives have understood this need to file the Request for Arbitration in a language other than English, they have usually provided a translation into English at the same time but expressly for ease of reference and guidance only.

**17.2 In the event that the Arbitration Agreement is written in more than one language of equal standing, the LCIA Court may, unless the Arbitration Agreement provides that the arbitration proceedings shall be conducted from the outset in more than one language, determine which of those languages shall be the initial language of the arbitration.**

---

[5] This will not necessarily be the prevailing language of the contract in dispute. In an LCIA arbitration filed in 2012, the dispute was between a Kazakh Claimant and a Chinese Respondent. Their contract was written in four languages: Russian, English, Chinese and Kazakh, with the Russian version prevailing. The substantive law of the contract was Kazakh. The arbitration clause stipulated a London seat and that the language of the arbitration was to be English.

[6] See the LCIA Recommended Clauses in Part III.

[7] In an LCIA arbitration filed in 2010, the parties were Russian but resident in Nice. They were all represented by law firms in Nice who agreed, on their behalf, that the arbitration should be conducted in French.

17–011   For reasons, no doubt, of speed, practicality and cost, the Rules aim for a single language to be used in the initial phase of the arbitration, unless, of course, the parties agree otherwise.

Arbitrations conducted in more than one language are extremely rare and costly. Article 17.2 allows for this possibility but provides a practical solution so that the proceedings may be put on foot with the administrative steps, and the LCIA Court's participation, being conducted in a single language. This will, in effect, be the "prevailing language" for this initial phase and any communications during this phase should be analysed by any competent court under that language.

17–012   There has been an interesting change in the 2014 Rules with the addition of the words "from the outset" in Article 17.2. The implication is that if the parties' arbitration agreement is written in two languages of equal standing, but does not specify in clear terms that they should both be used, not only in the proceedings conducted by the Arbitral Tribunal but also from the filing of the Request for Arbitration, it will be open to the LCIA Court to determine that one of these languages, say English, should be used exclusively for correspondence and other communications until the (multilingual) Arbitral Tribunal is appointed. This is a matter upon which parties may seek a decision from the LCIA Court in the Request or subsequent communications. It is also a matter upon which the LCIA Court can make a determination at the request of the LCIA Secretariat of its own initiative with a view to the smooth running of the pre-appointment phase of the arbitration. A choice of "the" initial language does not preclude the LCIA Secretariat from providing translations into the other language(s) as well, for information and/or guidance, and it has, in practice, done so in some cases.

In this situation, the LCIA Court may make its own determination as to which language will be used in this initial phase whilst leaving it to the Arbitral Tribunal to make a decision, possibly in favour of the other language, for the balance of the proceedings. In making this determination, the LCIA Court is not required to invite submissions from both parties. The determination may thus be made quickly on the date on which the Request for Arbitration is filed and before the LCIA Secretariat has written to the parties to confirm the commencement of the arbitration.

> **17.3 A non-participating or defaulting party shall have no cause for complaint if communications to and from the LCIA Court and Registrar are conducted in the initial language(s) of the arbitral seat.**

17–013   Before the arbitration procedure has been taken in hand by an Arbitral Tribunal, a Claimant's representative may find it convenient to communicate with the LCIA in a language which is not the Respondent's own language. Likewise, it may be convenient for the LCIA Registrar to continue to communicate with the parties in the same language throughout the proceedings. However, a defaulting Respondent could subsequently seek to defend enforcement proceedings under the New York Convention on the basis that it was not given "proper notice" of the appointment of the Arbitral Tribunal or of the arbitration proceedings because communications were in a language which it did not speak.[8] Article 17.3 anticipates such complaints by confirming that a non-participating or defaulting party shall "have no cause for complaint" if the language used for communications between the parties and the LCIA is the language of the arbitral seat.

Article 17.3 thus provides comfort to a Claimant, and also to the LCIA Registrar, in a case in which the administrative communications (including e.g. the Notice of Appointment of the Arbitral Tribunal) are conducted in a language, typically English, which, being the language of the seat, is convenient to everybody participating but which may be different from the language in which the Arbitration Agreement is drafted or even different from the language expressly chosen for the arbitration in that agreement. The language used by the Arbitral Tribunal for its communications and, importantly, in its procedural orders and awards, will, though, be the language chosen by the parties, if that choice has in fact been made in the Arbitration Agreement, so that, in those circumstances, the defaulting Respondent will, in practice, have received notices of the proceedings from the Arbitral Tribunal itself, if not from the LCIA Secretariat, in a language which it has expressly agreed.

Article 17.1 of the 1998 Rules carried a slightly different proviso: "a non-participating or defaulting party shall have no cause for complaint if communications to and from the Registrar and the arbitration proceedings are conducted in English". The new wording removes this bias in favour of English (though in practice it has been the language of almost 99 per cent of LCIA arbitrations).

**17.4 Following the formation of the Arbitral Tribunal, unless the parties have agreed upon the language or languages of the arbitration, the Arbitral Tribunal shall decide upon the language(s) of the arbitration after giving the parties a reasonable opportunity to make written comments and taking into account the initial language(s) of the arbitration and any other matter it may consider appropriate in the circumstances.**

If there is no agreement on it between the parties, the language of the arbitration will be one of the matters which the Arbitral Tribunal will seek to decide upon at an initial directions hearing or following an exchange of correspondence pursuant to Articles 14.1 and 14.2. Article 17.4 provides for "written comments" from the parties. It would be usual for oral submissions to be accepted at a directions hearing (or conference call), if one is held, as well.

The language so chosen need not be the language of the Arbitration Agreement or of the seat but is likely to be a language which is spoken by a majority of the key participants in the proceedings. In making its decision, the Arbitral Tribunal should have regard to the principle of fair and equitable treatment as well as to the enforceability of its awards.

17–014

---

[8] Article V(1)(b) of the New York Convention (Appendix 9).

**17.5** **If any document is expressed in a language other than the language(s) of the arbitration and no translation of such document is submitted by the party relying upon the document, the Arbitral Tribunal may order or (if the Arbitral Tribunal has not been formed) the Registrar may request that party to submit a translation of all or any part of that document in any language(s) of the arbitration or of the arbitral seat.**

**17–015** The language(s) of the arbitration, as agreed between the parties or decided by the Arbitral Tribunal, may be different from the language(s) in which pre-existing documents which come to be submitted in the arbitration may have been written. This could be any language in which transactions and/or events in dispute took place.

It is generally accepted practice that a party relying upon a document should provide a translation of it. This is reflected in Article 3(12)(d) of the IBA Rules on the Taking of Evidence in International Arbitration: "translations of Documents shall be submitted together with the originals and marked as translations with the original language identified".

However, it should be noted that Article 17.5 is permissive, not prescriptive. It is open to an Arbitral Tribunal to make alternative procedural orders in relation to the translation of documents. For example, if the language of a large number of documents is one which is spoken by both parties, the Arbitral Tribunal may decide that only certain documents or certain parts of them require translation from that language into the language of the arbitration.

Likewise, whilst the Registrar may ask for translations of documents submitted with a Request for Arbitration, the absence of translations does not render the Request invalid; nor does such a request for translations stop time running for the filing of a Response.[9]

---

[9] Article 5.1.

## Article 18—Legal Representatives

18.1 Any party may be represented in the arbitration by one or more authorised legal representatives appearing by name before the Arbitral Tribunal.

18.2 Until the Arbitral Tribunal's formation, the Registrar may request from any party: (i) written proof of the authority granted by that party to any legal representative designated in its Request or Response; and (ii) written confirmation of the names and addresses of all such party's legal representatives in the arbitration. After its formation, at any time, the Arbitral Tribunal may order any party to provide similar proof or confirmation in any form it considers appropriate.

18.3 Following the Arbitral Tribunal's formation, any intended change or addition by a party to its legal representatives shall be notified promptly in writing to all other parties, the Arbitral Tribunal and the Registrar; and any such intended change or addition shall only take effect in the arbitration subject to the approval of the Arbitral Tribunal.

18.4 The Arbitral Tribunal may withhold approval of any intended change or addition to a party's legal representatives where such change or addition could compromise the composition of the Arbitral Tribunal or the finality of any award (on the grounds of possible conflict or other like impediment). In deciding whether to grant or withhold such approval, the Arbitral Tribunal shall have regard to the circumstances, including: the general principle that a party may be represented by a legal representative chosen by that party, the stage which the arbitration has reached, the efficiency resulting from maintaining the composition of the Arbitral Tribunal (as constituted throughout the arbitration) and any likely wasted costs or loss of time resulting from such change or addition.

18.5 Each party shall ensure that all its legal representatives appearing by name before the Arbitral Tribunal have agreed to comply with the general guidelines contained in the Annex to the LCIA Rules, as a condition of such representation. In permitting any legal representative so to appear, a party shall thereby represent that the legal representative has agreed to such compliance.

18.6 In the event of a complaint by one party against another party's legal representative appearing by name before the Arbitral Tribunal (or of such complaint by the Arbitral Tribunal upon its own initiative), the Arbitral Tribunal may decide, after consulting the parties and granting that legal representative a reasonable opportunity to answer the complaint, whether or not the legal representative has violated the general guidelines. If such violation is found by the Arbitral Tribunal, the Arbitral Tribunal may order any or all of the following sanctions against the legal representative: (i) a written reprimand; (ii) a written caution as to future conduct in the arbitration; and (iii) any other measure necessary to fulfil within the arbitration the general duties required of the Arbitral Tribunal under Articles 14.4(i) and (ii).**

## Introduction

18–001　This largely new provision is primarily a response to two matters. The first is that problems have arisen in international arbitrations where parties have selected, after the appointment of the Tribunal, legal representatives from the same barristers' chambers as one of the arbitrators or with another close connection to one of the arbitrators, in some cases at a very late stage in the proceedings, giving rise to a potential and/or perceived conflict of interest. As a result, Tribunals have sought to prevent this problem from arising in the first place. The second matter is the introduction of Guidelines to address the behaviour of the parties' legal representations, in an attempt to prevent or deter inappropriate tactics being used in the conduct of the arbitration.

The new focus on the "legal" representatives of the parties, as distinct from other representatives, no doubt results from the issues noted above. Nonetheless, this sits rather uneasily with the origins and conduct of many arbitrations. Arbitration developed as an alternative to litigation in state courts. Not only could cases be decided by non-lawyers (e.g. by traders, surveyors and engineers), but the parties could dispense with the services of lawyers altogether. They could represent themselves or engage other people in their line of business to assist them.

18–002　Some arbitration rules contain bans on lawyers. For example, the Grain and Feed Trade Association (GAFTA) based in London, does not allow lawyers to represent parties at arbitration hearings, unless the parties expressly agree.[1] However, in GAFTA arbitrations, lawyers are permitted to assist in the background with drafting submissions[2] and the general practice is for parties to be represented at hearings by "trade representatives", often retired traders with experience of such disputes. The regime in arbitrations under the rules of the Federation of Oils, Seeds and Fats Associations (FOSFA) is similar.

The Arbitration Regulations of the London Metal Exchange contain the following stipulation: "Neither party shall be represented at any hearing by a legal

---

[1] Rule 16.1 of the GAFTA Arbitration Rules Form No.125.
[2] Rule 16.2 of the GAFTA Arbitration Rules Form No.125.

practitioner without the consent of the Tribunal, such consent to be requested not later than Close of Pleadings".[3]

In LCIA arbitrations, it is not unusual for parties to represent themselves, particularly in the early stages. Occasionally they will seek help from brokers, agents or consultants, and ask them to correspond with the LCIA Secretariat on their behalf. One of the advantages of LCIA arbitration has been the neutral oversight of the procedure by the institution, which allows parties to have the confidence to embark on an arbitration without necessarily resorting to lawyers should they not wish to do so.  **18–003**

Article 18 was the shortest article in the 1998 LCIA Rules.[4] It was headed "Party Representation" and simply confirmed that (i) parties in LCIA arbitrations could be represented by anybody of their choice, whether a legal practitioner or not and (ii) the Arbitral Tribunal could require proof of authority granted to the representative.

Article 18 has undergone a radical, and potentially controversial, overhaul in the 2014 version of the Rules. Now headed "Legal Representatives", it assumes that parties will appoint lawyers to represent them, and it contains detailed rules about notifying the Arbitral Tribunal and the Registrar of any such appointments and of any change to a party's legal team.  **18–004**

It also requires parties to ensure that their legal representatives have agreed to comply with Guidelines in a new Annex to the Rules, breach of which entitles the Arbitral Tribunal to order certain sanctions to be applied. These Guidelines are inspired by the IBA Guidelines on Party Representation in International Arbitration, which were published in 2013.

The new provisions in Article 18 will be seen by some as a departure from the commercial character of the LCIA Rules. The presumption that the parties will appoint lawyers to represent them, and the Guidelines which it is the parties' duty to ensure are agreed by their lawyers (with the implicit further presumption that the arbitrators will be lawyers too), contributes to a general impression, which is new in this context, that an arbitration under the LCIA Rules is essentially an enterprise for lawyers.  **18–005**

Whilst there is no express ban on non-lawyer representation, and whilst there may be good reasons for the expansion of Article 18, the presence of such detailed provisions about legal representatives could deter some commercial parties who were previously attracted by the simplicity and flexibility of the LCIA Rules in contrast to those of other arbitral institutions and to the practices in local courts.[5]

The rationale for the new provisions, their implications and the significance of the Guidelines in the new Annex are all discussed below.

---

[3] LME Arbitration Regulations, reg.8 ("Party Representatives").
[4] See the 1998 Rules reproduced at Appendix 4.
[5] The commercial intent of the founders of the LCIA is encapsulated in the words used at the inauguration of the Chamber of Arbitration, the LCIA's predecessor, in 1891, which drew a clear distinction between "the law" and the new arbitration service which it was going to offer: "This Chamber is to have all the virtues which the law lacks. It is to be expeditious where the law is slow, cheap where the law is costly, simple where the law is technical, a peacemaker instead of a stirrer-up of strife."

**18.1 Any party may be represented in the arbitration by one or more authorised legal representatives appearing by name before the Arbitral Tribunal.**

18–006  This Article is entitled "Legal Representatives" and it deals exclusively with this kind of representative. The 1998 Rules had expressly permitted the appointment of "any other representatives" as an alternative. Although such express permission is now absent, there is nothing in the 2014 Rules which actually forbids another kind of representative being appointed by a party.

Nor is there any reason why a party cannot represent itself in an LCIA arbitration should it wish to do so. Large corporations and governments, for example, sometimes keep the conduct of an arbitration in-house.

18–007  There is also no requirement for a party based outside the UK to have a representative or agent in London, although they often do, not least because of the application of English procedural law to an arbitration with its seat in London. Canadian, US, French and Swiss law firms, for example, sometimes represent parties in LCIA arbitrations with limited (sometimes no) assistance from lawyers based in the UK. They will correspond with the LCIA and the Arbitral Tribunal direct from Toronto, New York, Paris or Geneva and will travel to London, or whichever other venue might be chosen, for the hearing. In recent years, Russian, Ukrainian, Kazakh, Brazilian and Chinese law firms have also filed Requests for Arbitration at the LCIA themselves, with limited support from English lawyers, for example to settle submissions and/or to advise on English procedural law.

Read with Articles 18.2 and 18.4, it is clear that the restriction in the adjective "authorised" means no more than that the legal representative should be authorised by the relevant party.[6]

18–008  The 1998 version of this Article did not include the words "appearing by name before the Arbitral Tribunal". The "representation" covered by Article 18 implicitly covered the full length of the arbitration, i.e. including the initial phase before the Arbitral Tribunal is appointed by the LCIA Court. The new wording focuses on the post-appointment phases of the arbitration and the emphasis is on the Arbitral Tribunal's role in supervising the parties' legal representation[7] (in light of the conflict issues noted above).

The words "appearing by name" are not entirely clear. They could be taken to suggest that the names of all lawyers instructed in the arbitration should be communicated to the Arbitral Tribunal, even if they are only assisting a party in the background, e.g. by reviewing submissions drafted in-house or advising on discrete issues relating to disclosure or expert evidence. However, given the issue of conflicts that these provisions address, the better interpretation is that they are intended, instead, to ensure that only those lawyers who choose to put their names to submissions and/or to appear at hearings (causing a potential issue from a conflicts perspective) need be concerned by the provisions of Article 18.

---

[6] This addition in the 2014 Rules is otiose and could lead to confusion for new users who might gain the impression that it is necessary to have their lawyers approved by the LCIA.

[7] Similar shifts in the 2014 Rules towards the Arbitral Tribunal and its powers post-appointment have been noted elsewhere, e.g. in Article 13 ("Communications between Parties and the Arbitral Tribunal").

It should be noted that Article 1.1(i) requires contact details of the Claimant's  18–009
legal representatives (if any), and those of all other parties, to be included in the
Request for Arbitration. Likewise Article 2.1(i) requires contact details for the
Respondent's legal representatives to be set out in the Response. Against that
background, "appearing by name" may be a reference to such a notification of the
identity of a party's formal legal representative.

The IBA Guidelines on Party Representation in International Arbitration
provide that party representatives "should identify themselves to the other Party
or Parties and the Arbitral Tribunal at the earliest opportunity".[8] The LCIA's
requirement that the identities of legal representatives be included in the Request
and Response fulfils this aim.

**18.2 Until the Arbitral Tribunal's formation, the Registrar may request from any party: (i) written proof of the authority granted by that party to any legal representative designated in its Request or Response; and (ii) written confirmation of the names and addresses of all such party's legal representatives in the arbitration. After its formation, at any time, the Arbitral Tribunal may order any party to provide similar proof or confirmation in any form it considers appropriate.**

The filing of a power of attorney by a party's lawyer is a requirement in some  18–010
state courts. The provision of written confirmation of representation is also a
requirement in some arbitration rules, e.g. Rule 30 of the Procedural Rules of the
Court of Arbitration for Sport.

The ICC Arbitration Rules, which came into effect in 2012, now include a
provision, which is similar to Article 18.2 of the LCIA Rules, and likewise extends
the discretion to require proof of authority to the ICC Secretariat.

In practice, Arbitral Tribunals in LCIA arbitrations rarely require the produc-  18–011
tion of powers of attorney. They will occasionally do so when, for example, one
of the parties insists that the other prove that its representatives have authority.

Questions as to whether lawyers were authorised to represent parties can arise on
enforcement of awards in certain jurisdictions, for example, in Eastern European
countries or the Middle East. If parties from these jurisdictions have not volunteered
powers of attorney at the outset of the arbitration (for example, with the Request or
Response), Arbitral Tribunals may order them on application by one of the parties
or of their own motion and having regard to the enforceability of their award.

Arbitral Tribunals should also be conscious of the local law and practice appli-  18–012
cable at the seat of the arbitration in relation to the legal representatives entitled to
appear before them and in relation to the formalities that might need to be
completed.

It is not unknown for more than one law firm to claim to represent a party at the
outset of an arbitration, perhaps as the result of muddled instructions and/or an
excess of enthusiasm. In one such case, two law firms nominated a different

---

[8] Guideline 4 (Appendix 14).

candidate as arbitrator on behalf of the Claimant. In such circumstances, it is useful for the Registrar to require proof of authority from the party itself.

If at the commencement of the proceedings a firm of solicitors has instructed a barrister to assist, the barrister's details should be notified to the LCIA Secretariat at the same time as the solicitors' details.

> **18.3 Following the Arbitral Tribunal's formation, any intended change or addition by a party to its legal representatives shall be notified promptly in writing to all other parties, the Arbitral Tribunal and the Registrar; and any such intended change or addition shall only take effect in the arbitration subject to the approval of the Arbitral Tribunal.**

18–013 It has always been good practice to keep the LCIA informed of any changes to a legal team, e.g. when a barrister has been instructed. The Rules do not contain a ban on instructing a barrister from the same chambers as a member of the Arbitral Tribunal. However, parties in LCIA arbitrations have sometimes protested when this has happened.[9]

The 2014 Rules have introduced this new rule which expressly requires any intended change or addition, after the appointment of the Arbitral Tribunal, to be notified to the Arbitral Tribunal, whose approval must be obtained before the change or addition may take effect. The primary purpose of this new rule (as confirmed in Article 18.4 below) is to give the Arbitral Tribunal the power to avoid potential conflicts of interest.

18–014 An Arbitral Tribunal in an LCIA arbitration now has the power to take an arguably draconian step of refusing to allow a barrister or other advocate to participate as counsel. This innovation has its origins in the controversial decision of the ICSID Tribunal in *Hrvatska Elektroprivreda d.d. v Republic of Slovenia* (ICSID Case No. ARB/05/24 (2008)), in which shortly before the final evidentiary hearing a barrister was instructed to appear before a Tribunal which included an arbitrator member of the barrister's own chambers. The decision to exclude the barrister certainly concentrated the minds of the international arbitration community in London.

The ICSID Tribunal, which included the former President of the LCIA Court, Jan Paulsson, considered that the justifiability of an apprehension of partiality depended on "all relevant circumstances". In that arbitration, the circumstances included "the fact that the London Chambers system is wholly foreign to the Claimant", the Respondent's decision not to inform the Claimant or the Tribunal of the barrister's involvement until the last minute and the fact that neither party wished to challenge any of the members of the Tribunal.

18–015 The latter point was crucial to the Tribunal's decision to exclude the barrister in order to "preserve the integrity of its proceedings". In his article, "Arbitrator Integrity: The Transient and the Permanent" in the *San Diego Law Review*,[10]

---

[9] General Standard 7(b) of the 2014 IBA Guidelines on Conflicts of Interest provide that parties should disclose the identity of their legal counsel as well as any relationship they have with any member of the Tribunal, including membership of the same barristers chambers.

[10] (2009) 46(3) *San Diego Law Review* 629.

Prof. William W. Park, the current President of the LCIA Court, refers to that ICSID decision and explains that, whilst barristers see no reason why one member of the same chambers should not sit as arbitrator in a case where another serves as advocate, not all are convinced that "the integrity of proceedings remains uncompromised".[11]

Since the decision in the *Hrvatska Elektroprivreda d.d* case a number of attempts have been made to exclude counsel from proceedings, generally unsuccessfully.[12] However, the authors are aware that in the months leading up to the adoption of the 2014 LCIA Rules, the same rationale was employed to exclude a non-barrister advocate from proceeding in an UNCITRAL arbitration. It is understood that the circumstances were similar to *Hrvatska* in that the involvement of the advocate in question was not made known until a short time before the final hearing, by which time the advocate had become Chairman of an LCIA Arbitral Tribunal in which the Chairman of the UNCITRAL Arbitration was a co-arbitrator. The opposing party argued that the advocate should be excluded from the hearing in order to avoid an appearance that the Chairman in the UNCITRAL Arbitration might side with him in order to gain his favour in the LCIA Arbitration.

The safeguarding of the "integrity of the proceedings" is the stated purpose of the Arbitral Tribunal's power to exclude a "Party Representative" in Guideline 6 of the IBA Guidelines on Party Representation. That Guideline expressly provides sanctions for breach of the preceding Guideline, which says: **18–016**

"Once the Arbitral Tribunal has been constituted, a person should not accept representation of a Party in the arbitration when a relationship exists between the person and an Arbitrator that would create a conflict of interest, unless none of the parties objects after proper disclosure".[13]

As far as barristers are concerned, the critical word in that Guideline is *"would"*: it has always been the English Bar's position, endorsed by the English courts, that a barrister's membership of the same chambers as an arbitrator does not necessarily create a conflict of interest.[14] The international view is more equivocal, as illustrated by the presence of this scenario in the Orange List of the IBA Guidelines on Conflicts of Interest in International Arbitration (Appendix 13). **18–017**

Whilst a barrister may feel able to accept instructions in such a situation, it is clear from these new provisions in Article 18.3, and from the wording of Article 18.4, discussed below, that an Arbitral Tribunal, in an LCIA arbitration, now has the power effectively to exclude the barrister on the basis of the risk that his or her

---

[11] Prof. Park develops the point as follows: "In response to doubts about the ethics of their practice, some barristers suggest that outsiders just do not understand the system, characterizing the critiques as naive. Like a Paris waiter impugning a tourist's ability to speak French in order to distract him from insisting on the correct change, the critique aims to camouflage what is at stake. Often, however, outsiders do understand the mechanics of chambers. They simply evaluate the dangers differently." See also Prof. Park's similar remarks in his article, "Rectitude in International Arbitration" (2011) 27(3) Arbitration Int. 473–526, devoted to LCIA arbitrator challenge decisions.

[12] For example, see *The Rompetrol Group NV v Romania* (ICSID Case No. ARB/06/3).

[13] Guideline 5 (Appendix 14).

[14] The leading case is *Laker Airways Inc v FLS Aerospace Ltd and Stanley Jeffrey Burnton* [2000] 1 W.L.R. 113.

involvement "could" compromise the composition of the Arbitral Tribunal or the finality of an award on the grounds of "possible" conflict.

**18–018** In practice, in LCIA arbitrations, the Registrar or case handler will sometimes note that a barrister's name has appeared at the foot of submissions without any other notification of his or her involvement, or of his or her contact details, having been given by the party's solicitors (a peculiar English habit, inherited from traditional court procedure but which remains surprisingly common in arbitration). The Secretariat will then draw his or her involvement to all parties' and the Arbitral Tribunal's attention. If the barrister practises from the same chambers as a member of the Arbitral Tribunal, this should be specifically noted at the same time (but without any reference to Articles 5.3 or 10.4) at this stage. In accordance with the new provisions in Article 18, it now falls on the parties themselves to provide this information *before* the barrister is instructed or other new lawyer, counsel or advocate is involved, and it is for the Arbitral Tribunal to decide if it causes it any difficulty.

> **18.4 The Arbitral Tribunal may withhold approval of any intended change or addition to a party's legal representatives where such change or addition could compromise the composition of the Arbitral Tribunal or the finality of any award (on the grounds of possible conflict or other like impediment). In deciding whether to grant or withhold such approval, the Arbitral Tribunal shall have regard to the circumstances, including: the general principle that a party may be represented by a legal representative chosen by that party, the stage which the arbitration has reached, the efficiency resulting from maintaining the composition of the Arbitral Tribunal (as constituted throughout the arbitration) and any likely wasted costs or loss of time resulting from such change or addition.**

**18–019** The grounds on which the Arbitral Tribunal may exercise its discretion to withhold approval of a new legal representative are set out in Article 18.4. As noted above, the particular criteria mentioned here are the risks of compromising either (a) the composition of the Arbitral Tribunal or (b) the finality of any award.

The grounds on which such a risk might be considered to arise are stated to be "possible conflict or other like impediment". The possibility of conflicts which the draftsmen of the 2014 Rules had in mind was clearly lawyers' conflicts, including the possibility of the perception of such a conflict in the context of English barristers' chambers, or other relationship, as described above, where professional rules do not forbid such representation, however much it might be frowned upon elsewhere.

**18–020** When faced with a conflict created by the appointment of a new advocate or lawyer, the traditional solution has been for the arbitrator affected, not the lawyer, to tender his resignation. Indeed, this will still be an appropriate course of conduct for an arbitrator in circumstances where his or her resignation will not cause significant disruption. The new provisions shift the balance by allowing the Arbitral Tribunal to protect the integrity of the proceedings and award by withholding approval of a lawyer in such a situation, without disrupting the arbitral process. This will be seen as a welcome change by the international arbitral community.

The risk of compromising the "finality" of an award will arise, for example, if an unresolved conflict leads to an award being challenged. Under Article 32.2, the Arbitral Tribunal has a duty to "make every reasonable effort to ensure that any award is legally recognised and enforceable at the arbitral seat". Whilst the extent of this duty is debatable,[15] it will be a factor for the Arbitral Tribunal to consider.

The second sentence of Article 18.4 sets out some of the other matters which the Arbitral Tribunal should take into account when exercising its discretion. Having regard to the enforceability of a final award, it should obviously be careful to avoid a challenge based on an allegation that it has deprived a party of the opportunity to be legally represented. Likewise it should be careful to avoid taking steps which could disrupt or delay the proceedings to an extent which could imperil the enforceability of an award. For example, if a party is facing insolvency, and the adjournment of a hearing and the replacement of an arbitrator could lead to the award being issued at a time when that party is in liquidation, the exclusion of counsel might be a quicker and fairer solution than a resignation from the Arbitral Tribunal.  **18–021**

In exercising this new power, an Arbitral Tribunal will be concerned to avoid being perceived as a "stirrer up of strife".[16] Whereas an arbitrator might avoid a challenge based on an alleged conflict with a legal representative, he or she might now be challenged on the basis of a decision to withhold approval of the same legal representative. It remains to be seen if the number of challenges will be reduced and if this reform will improve efficiency.

**18.5 Each party shall ensure that all its legal representatives appearing by name before the Arbitral Tribunal have agreed to comply with the general guidelines contained in the Annex to the LCIA Rules, as a condition of such representation. In permitting any legal representative so to appear, a party shall thereby represent that the legal representative has agreed to such compliance.**

The General Guidelines for the Parties' Legal Representatives, contained in the new Annex to the LCIA Rules, have already been mentioned above, including in the context of Article 13 ("Communications between Parties and the Arbitral Tribunal").  **18–022**

Although the Guidelines themselves should largely be uncontroversial (few practitioners could quibble with their strictures against unilateral contact, the procuring of false evidence or the concealing of documents ordered to be produced), the Annex has been heralded as the most radical addition to the 2014 Rules.[17]

---

[15] See for example, Christopher Boog et al., "The Lazy Myth of the Arbitral Tribunal's Duty to Render an Enforceable Award", Kluwer Arbitration Blog, January 28, 2013.
[16] See fn.5 above.
[17] For example, Sebastian Perry and Richard Woolley,"LCIA unveils draft guidelines for counsel conduct"(2014) G.A.R.

18–023    In essence, the LCIA Guidelines are a shortened (one page) version of the IBA Guidelines on Party Representation in International Arbitration, which were published in 2013. This is a list of the LCIA Guidelines, which have corresponding IBA Guidelines:

Paragraph 1 (no derogation from laws professional codes)—IBA Guideline 3

Paragraph 3 (not knowingly make false statements)—IBA Guideline 9

Paragraph 4 (not knowingly procure false evidence)—IBA Guideline 11

Paragraph 5 (not knowingly conceal documents)—IBA Guideline 16

Paragraph 6 (no unilateral contact with arbitrators)—IBA Guideline 7

18–024    The LCIA Guidelines are described in para.1 as "general" and as intended "to promote the good and equal conduct of the parties' legal representatives appearing by name within the arbitration". There can be no objection to the promotion of good conduct, but practices in arbitration and standards of professional behaviour differ between jurisdictions, making the promotion of such conduct, let alone of "equal" conduct, difficult to achieve.

This is the dilemma which has been much debated by practitioners in recent years, and which led the IBA to issue its Guidelines in 2013. In his keynote address to the ICCA Conference in 2010, Doak Bishop had called for a "uniform, binding Code of Ethics" for lawyers practising before international arbitral tribunals. He cited Johnny Veeder, one of the draftsmen of the LCIA Rules, who, in his 2001 Goff Lecture, had posed the question, "What are the professional rules applicable to an Indian lawyer in a Hong Kong arbitration between a Bahraini claimant and a Japanese defendant represented by New York lawyers?" Veeder had remarked, "the answer is no more obvious than it would be in London, Paris, Geneva and Stockholm. There is no clear answer."

18–025    Bishop raised two hypothetical situations of his own, the first relating to document production and the second to the preparation of fact and expert witnesses.[18] In the first situation, he said that it was his understanding that the ethical rules for American and Italian lawyers might be in direct conflict.

There are six IBA Guidelines in relation to "Information Exchange and Disclosure" (12–17). The Comments say that it is common for different standards to be applied in the same arbitration and that these Guidelines are "intended to foster the taking of objectively reasonable steps to preserve, search for and produce Documents that a Party has an obligation to disclose". It is significant that these Guidelines have not been adopted in full by the LCIA. Instead, only Guideline 16, on the concealment of documents ordered to be produced, has found its way into Paragraph 5.

18–026    In making an order to produce a document, an Arbitral Tribunal could have followed a variety of procedures and could have considered a variety of ethical

---

[18] For a discussion of different national practices in relation to the preparation of witness evidence and the IBA Guidelines on this, see the commentary on Article 20.6 below.

standards and objections. The LCIA Guideline implicitly recognises this and fundamentally only expects compliance with the Arbitral Tribunal's order after it has been made. However, it should be remembered that there is a proviso in Paragraph 1: the Guidelines shall not derogate from "any mandatory laws, rules of law, professional rules or codes of conduct if and to the extent that they are shown to apply to a legal representative appearing in the arbitration".

Taking document production as an example, then, the LCIA Guidelines fall far short of the set of rules envisaged by Doak Bishop and are less expansive (some would say intrusive) than the recent IBA Guidelines. However brief and relatively uncontroversial they might be, it is their inclusion in the LCIA Rules, with the obligation on parties to ensure that their legal representatives agree to comply with them, that is seen as a revolutionary step.

There is one LCIA Guideline which is not found in the IBA Guidelines. This is Paragraph 2, which provides that a legal representative should not engage in activities "intended unfairly" to obstruct the arbitration or to jeopardise the finality of any award, "including repeated challenges to an arbitrator's appointment or to the jurisdiction or authority of the Arbitral Tribunal known to be unfounded by that legal representative". **18–027**

Any challenge known by a legal representative to be "unfounded" could be regarded as unethical, whether or not it is "repeated". Furthermore, a single but late challenge (e.g. on the eve of a hearing) is just as likely to obstruct an arbitration. Arbitrators are naturally irritated when challenges are made, and they will no doubt welcome this Guideline. However, in practice, it will be difficult for Arbitral Tribunals to make decisions about a party's intentions when it takes a step or about its knowledge as to how well founded a challenge might be.[19]

The requirement is that a party should ensure that its legal representatives, who appear by name, agree to comply with the Guidelines. Of course, it is likely that it is the party's legal representatives, not the party itself, who will be aware of the contents of the LCIA Rules and of the new Guidelines. However, English solicitors or other lawyers might instruct a barrister to deal with discrete aspects of the case, e.g. drafting parts of the submissions or cross-examining witnesses. In that situation, the barrister might not bother to familiarise himself or herself with the Rules. However, the barrister will appear by name and the solicitors should, therefore, ensure that he or she has read and agreed to the Guidelines. **18–028**

**18.6 In the event of a complaint by one party against another party's legal representative appearing by name before the Arbitral Tribunal (or of such complaint by the Arbitral Tribunal upon its own initiative), the Arbitral Tribunal may decide, after consulting the parties and granting that legal representative a reasonable opportunity to answer the complaint, whether or not the legal representative has violated the general guidelines. If such violation is found by the Arbitral**

---

[19] For an example of a case involving multiple challenges, but in which it might be difficult to determine purely tactical motives designed to obstruct the arbitration, see the abstract of the three decisions in LCIA Reference No. 3431 (2011) 27(3) ("Special Challenges" issue) Arbitration Int. 358.

## Article 19—Oral Hearings

**19.1** Any party has the right to a hearing before the Arbitral Tribunal on the parties' dispute at any appropriate stage of the arbitration (as decided by the Arbitral Tribunal), unless the parties have agreed in writing upon a documents-only arbitration. For this purpose, a hearing may consist of several part-hearings (as decided by the Arbitral Tribunal).

**19.2** The Arbitral Tribunal shall organise the conduct of any hearing in advance, in consultation with the parties. The Arbitral Tribunal shall have the fullest authority under the Arbitration Agreement to establish the conduct of a hearing, including its date, form, content, procedure, time-limits and geographical place. As to form, a hearing may take place by video or telephone conference or in person (or a combination of all three). As to content, the Arbitral Tribunal may require the parties to address a list of specific questions or issues arising from the parties' dispute.

**19.3** The Arbitral Tribunal shall give to the parties reasonable notice in writing of any hearing.

**19.4** All hearings shall be held in private, unless the parties agree otherwise in writing.

### Introduction

Article 19 sets out each party's right to require an oral hearing(s) and certain broad principles to be applied or considered in connection with hearings (whether procedural, jurisdictional or merits hearings). The detailed organisation and planning of hearings is left to the parties and the Arbitral Tribunal to decide in light of the particular circumstances of each case.

19–001

It is common in LCIA arbitrations (and other international arbitration systems) for the final hearing date to be fixed early in the arbitration, according to the availability of the Arbitral Tribunal and the parties, and for the procedural steps to be fixed so as to span the intervening period. This reflects the significant time commitment required for many final hearings and the need to plan this some considerable time in advance (particularly where there are three busy arbitrators to co-ordinate). Once a hearing has been fixed, there would often be significant time and cost consequences involved in changing it. Accordingly, Arbitral Tribunals in LCIA arbitrations generally strive to maintain hearing dates where practicable.

**19–002**  In contrast to the LCIA tradition, in ad hoc and trade association arbitrations in London, hearing dates are not generally fixed until after the exchange of submissions at the earliest. English arbitrators (and their clerks, in the case of barristers) are sometimes reluctant to put hearing dates in their diaries before they have seen the parties plead their case out in full, and they will sometimes protest to their co-arbitrators and the parties when asked about their availability for a hearing, a short time after appointment. Nonetheless, the international norm is to fix the dates for the final hearing at an early stage. In practice, fixing dates for the final hearing as early as practicable imposes discipline and tends to increase the speed of the proceedings.

Experienced international Arbitral Tribunals will often seek to keep hearing lengths as short as reasonably practicable (consistent with their duty to avoid unnecessary expense under Article 14.4(ii)), with some very complex matters being dealt with in two weeks or less. Many merits hearings in LCIA arbitrations are fixed for no longer than five days (one week). This is made possible in many cases by ensuring that legal submissions and witness/expert evidence are dealt with substantially in advance in writing, with the hearing being concerned principally with the cross-examination of witnesses/experts.

**19–003**  Most arbitrators in LCIA arbitrations avail themselves of the opportunity to levy cancellation charges for time reserved for hearings but not used as a result of late postponement or cancellation (section 2 (iii), "Schedule of Arbitration Costs"). The longer the hearing, the higher the charges. The risk of incurring such charges is an incentive for early settlement. The LCIA's standard cancellation terms for arbitrators to use, are:

> "In the event of cancellation or postponement less than 4 weeks before the start of the hearing, or at any time during the hearing, the Tribunal may charge 50% of its notional daily sitting rate, based on a [?]-hour day multiplied by the number of days reserved for the hearing; and in the event of cancellation or postponement more than 4 weeks, but less than 12 weeks, before the start of the hearing, 30% of its daily sitting rate multiplied by the number of days reserved for the hearing."

> **19.1 Any party has the right to a hearing before the Arbitral Tribunal on the parties' dispute at any appropriate stage of the arbitration (as decided by the Arbitral Tribunal), unless the parties have agreed in writing upon a documents-only arbitration. For this purpose, a hearing may consist of several part-hearings (as decided by the Arbitral Tribunal).**

**19–004**  Each party has the right to require an oral hearing(s) unless it has agreed otherwise in writing. Whilst the right to a hearing(s) under the 1998 LCIA Rules referred expressly only to hearings on the merits of the dispute, Article 19.1 does not contain any such limitation. Rather, Article 19.1 states that the right is to a hearing "at any appropriate stage of the arbitration" and therefore not necessarily at the end. The right therefore extends to procedural and jurisdictional hearings as well as hearings on the merits.

The right to require a hearing also exists whether or not the Arbitral Tribunal considers such a hearing to be necessary or desirable, although it is subject to the Arbitral Tribunal's right to decide whether it is an "appropriate stage" for the hearing in question to be held.

As for hearings on the merits, leaving to one side specialist procedures for particular sectors (for example, commodities), it is the norm in international arbitration for there to be an oral hearing, and Article 19.1 establishes the right to a hearing as the default position. Documents-only arbitrations are relatively rare under the LCIA Rules, but Article 19.1 also confirms that they are available. This short form procedure is generally considered to be appropriate in relatively low value disputes, in which a sole arbitrator has been appointed, and in which witness evidence does not have to be tested by cross-examination.

19–005

In cases in which the Respondent has not participated, Arbitral Tribunals often like to hold a hearing on the merits, ensuring that notice is given to the Respondent, thereby making it more difficult for the Respondent to complain, at the enforcement stage, that it was not given an opportunity to present its case (Article V(1)(b) of the New York Convention). It has been known for a Respondent to make its first appearance in an arbitration by attending the hearing on the merits.

It is sometimes necessary and/or appropriate to split up a hearing (over different dates and, sometimes, locations). This is expressly permitted, if the Arbitral Tribunal so decides, by Article 19.1.

19–006

It should be noted that, for the purposes of calculating cancellation charges, time stops running at the end of the first phase of a split hearing and starts again at the beginning of the second. Thus if the second phase is scheduled for three months later than the first, only the first phase should attract cancellation charges if the case settles a few days before the hearing and if the arbitrators are entitled to raise charges for such a cancellation within three months of the commencement of the hearing.

> **19.2** The Arbitral Tribunal shall organise the conduct of any hearing in advance, in consultation with the parties. The Arbitral Tribunal shall have the fullest authority under the Arbitration Agreement to establish the conduct of a hearing, including its date, form, content, procedure, time-limits and geographical place. As to form, a hearing may take place by video or telephone conference or in person (or a combination of all three). As to content, the Arbitral Tribunal may require the parties to address a list of specific questions or issues arising from the parties' dispute.

The geographical place of any meeting or hearing is not to be confused with the seat of the arbitration.[1] Whilst the seat of the arbitration will generally not change,

19–007

---

[1] The latter being the legal place at which the arbitration is deemed to take place, regardless of any physical location—see Article 16 and the commentary at 16–005 and 16–013.

the physical location of any meetings or hearings can be fixed and changed as often as the Arbitral Tribunal decides is appropriate, usually to accommodate the convenience of the Arbitral Tribunal, the parties, witnesses and/or experts.

There are venues specifically set up to conduct arbitration hearings, such as the International Dispute Resolution Centre in London. However, many arbitration hearings take place in hotel conference rooms, lawyers' offices and other ad hoc venues that can cater for the needs of the hearing, including space, break-out rooms, copying, communications and IT support, refreshments etc.

19–008    In practice, the detailed arrangements for any meetings or hearings will usually be made in consultation between the Arbitral Tribunal, the parties and the LCIA Secretariat. It is one of the functions of the LCIA Secretariat to assist with the organising of hearings if the parties ask for this service. The Secretariat has considerable experience of making practical arrangements for hearings, mainly at the IDRC in London but also at other venues in the UK and abroad (e.g. in Paris, Vienna, Budapest, at the World Bank and at major hotels in the US in the *US v Canada* softwood lumber cases). The Secretariat's hourly rates are lower than lawyers' rates, so this service can be quite cost effective. The LCIA also has good relations with transcribers and interpreters and can often assist the parties in that regard. Parties also appreciate the convenience of having their joint deposits used for paying for hearing rooms etc (Article 24.1).

However, Article 19.2 makes clear that it is ultimately for the Arbitral Tribunal to organise the conduct of the hearing, albeit in consultation with the parties. This represents an expansion of the provisions under the 1998 LCIA Rules, which only referred to the Arbitral Tribunal fixing the date, time, time-limits and place of meetings and hearings (see also Article 16.3 in this regard). Article 19.2 now also refers to the Arbitral Tribunal establishing the conduct of the hearing, including its form, content and procedures.

19–009    As for the form of the hearing, Article 19.2 states that a hearing may take place by video or teleconference as well as in person.

Arbitral Tribunals are generally more flexible as regards hearing times than national courts, with hearing days often starting earlier and/or finishing later, and sometimes including weekends, depending upon the needs of the case.

19–010    Whilst hearings in international arbitrations are normally concerned principally with the cross-examination of witnesses/experts, there is usually also a limited opportunity for parties to make oral submissions to the Arbitral Tribunal. Article 19.2 notes that the Arbitral Tribunal may take the opportunity to focus the parties' attention on specific points which the Arbitral Tribunal would like them to cover in such submissions.

There is nothing to stop an Arbitral Tribunal from simply asking questions of parties' Counsel during the course of the hearing. However, if the Arbitral Tribunal has identified before the hearing questions that it would like to be addressed, it may be more efficient for the Counsel to be notified in advance by means of a list of questions.

19–011    The list of questions from an Arbitral Tribunal can take various forms. It could simply be a general checklist of matters to be covered (either in pre-hearing written submissions or at the hearing itself) or it could be focused on a particular area which has not been adequately addressed or is causing particular difficulty for the Arbitral Tribunal. The Arbitral Tribunal will be aware that, in the case of a focused list of questions, the parties are likely to seek to ascertain from the list how the Arbitral Tribunal is thinking about the case, and that it should not appear to have closed its mind to matters still in issue at the hearing.

Meetings and, particularly, hearings can be difficult to arrange (with several busy diaries to be co-ordinated) and are a comparatively expensive part of many arbitrations. Conscious of this, parties and Arbitral Tribunals normally seek to limit the time scheduled for meetings and hearings as far as reasonably practicable, whilst maintaining safety margin (because an incomplete meeting or hearing which requires rescheduling is very inefficient). This means that there is often little time to spare and careful scheduling can be required. Simply splitting the time available between the parties will not always be appropriate. Article 19.2 therefore gives the Arbitral Tribunal significant authority and discretion to decide upon scheduling matters, subject always to its general duties to act fairly and to allow each party a reasonable opportunity to put its case and deal with that of its opponent under Article 14.4. The LCIA has chess clocks, which are sometimes used in hearings to ensure that each side's counsel uses the same amount of time in, for example, opening or closing speeches.

**19.3 The Arbitral Tribunal shall give to the parties reasonable notice in writing of any hearing.**

The obligation to give the parties reasonable notice of any hearing runs alongside the Arbitral Tribunal's duty to give each party "a reasonable opportunity of putting its case and dealing with that of its opponent", pursuant to Article 14.4(i) of the LCIA Rules,[2] which it might not be able to do if given insufficient notice of a hearing. In the case of substantive hearings, reasonable notice may be a long time, although in practice, as noted above, final hearings are often fixed early in the arbitration so that this is not an issue.

**19-012**

**19.4 All hearings shall be held in private, unless the parties agree otherwise in writing.**

The degree of confidentiality in arbitration varies between rules and laws and is often a matter of debate. Article 30 sets out the general position as to the confidentiality of awards, materials, documents and the deliberations of the Arbitral Tribunal in LCIA arbitration.

**19-013**

Article 19.4 confirms the basic position that meetings and hearings should only be attended by the Arbitral Tribunal, the parties, their representatives and others that the parties and the Arbitral Tribunal agree may be present (such as a tribunal secretary, transcript writers, witnesses etc). Occasionally, the parties may agree that

---

[2] See 14–011—14–014. See also s.33(1) of the English Arbitration Act 1996 (Appendix 7), Article 34(2)(a)(ii) of the UNCITRAL Model Law (Appendix 10) and Article V(1)(b) of the New York Convention (Appendix 9).

hearings should be open to the public, as happened, for example, in the *US v Canada* softwood lumber arbitrations.[3] Article 19.4 expressly states that any such agreement must be in writing. The Arbitral Tribunal cannot order a hearing to be in public without the written agreement of the parties.

**19–014**  The location of most arbitration meetings and hearings in law firms' offices, arbitral institutions' premises and hotel conference rooms, together with the relatively small number of persons usually present, means that it is usually a straightforward matter to ensure that only those who should be attending are present at the meeting or hearing. However, it is also common practice for a written record of attendees to be taken on a daily basis (often by circulating a sheet for those present to sign).

---

[3] See, for example, John R. Crook ed., "Contemporary Practice of the United States Relating to International Law: United States and Canada Arbitrate a Softwood Lumber Dispute in the London Court of International Arbitration" (2008) 102 Am J. Int'l 192.

## Article 20—Witness(es)

20.1 Before any hearing, the Arbitral Tribunal may order any party to give written notice of the identity of each witness that party wishes to call (including rebuttal witnesses), as well as the subject-matter of that witness's testimony, its content and its relevance to the issues in the arbitration.

20.2 Subject to any order otherwise by the Arbitral Tribunal, the testimony of a witness may be presented by a party in written form, either as a signed statement or like document.

20.3 The Arbitral Tribunal may decide the time, manner and form in which these written materials shall be exchanged between the parties and presented to the Arbitral Tribunal; and it may allow, refuse, or limit the written and oral testimony of witnesses (whether witnesses of fact or expert witnesses).

20.4 The Arbitral Tribunal and any party may request that a witness, on whose written testimony another party relies, should attend for oral questioning at a hearing before the Arbitral Tribunal. If the Arbitral Tribunal orders that other party to secure the attendance of that witness and the witness refuses or fails to attend the hearing without good cause, the Arbitral Tribunal may place such weight on the written testimony or exclude all or any part thereof altogether as it considers appropriate in the circumstances.

20.5 Subject to the mandatory provisions of any applicable law, rules of law and any order of the Arbitral Tribunal otherwise, it shall not be improper for any party or its legal representatives to interview any witness or potential witness for the purpose of presenting his or her testimony in written form or producing such person as an oral witness at any hearing.

20.6 Subject to any order by the Arbitral Tribunal otherwise, any individual intending to testify to the Arbitral Tribunal may be treated as a witness notwithstanding that the individual is a party to the arbitration or was, remains or has become an officer, employee, owner or shareholder of any party or is otherwise identified with any party.

20.7 Subject to the mandatory provisions of any applicable law, the Arbitral Tribunal shall be entitled (but not required) to administer any appropriate oath to any witness at any hearing, prior to the oral testimony of that witness.

20.8 Any witness who gives oral testimony at a hearing before the Arbitral Tribunal may be questioned by each of the parties under the control of the Arbitral Tribunal. The Arbitral Tribunal may put questions at any stage of such testimony.

## Introduction

**20–001**  The length of Article 20 may suggest that it contains detailed rules about the presentation of witness evidence. In reality, it largely does the opposite: as with other provisions in relation to the arbitral procedure, it is deliberately permissive rather than prescriptive. Article 20 confirms that the Arbitral Tribunal may receive witness evidence in a wide variety of ways and that both the Arbitral Tribunal and the parties have the right to test such evidence.

Neither common law nor civil law practitioners should assume that their own ways of presenting and treating evidence will apply in an arbitration conducted under the Rules. These are matters for discussion between the parties and with the Arbitral Tribunal.

**20–002**  It is an outstanding feature of English civil procedure that oral evidence remains of paramount importance. The need to hear witnesses is one of the reasons why English court cases can be so lengthy. A judge's view of a witness's credibility can influence the outcome of a case and judges do not hesitate to state those views in their judgments.[1]

In contrast, in France, for example, there is a preference for written as opposed to oral evidence. Rules have developed as to how written documents may be proved or authenticated and as to whose written testimony should be accepted. Factual enquiries, including interviews, may be conducted by *huissiers*, for example, who, like *notaires* who draw up wills and conveyances, are officers of the state.

**20–003**  In the English courts, a Claimant has always been expected to give oral evidence at trial in support of his or her claim. A written statement will be confirmed by this witness to be genuine and he or she will submit to cross-examination on it by the Defendant's counsel. The courts and legislature have modified the procedure over recent years but the preference for the personal attendance of the parties at court remains strong.[2]

---

[1] For example, Gloster J's view of Boris Berezovsky in his case against Roman Abramovich (*Berezovsky v Abramovich* [2012] EWHC 2463 (Comm)): "I found Mr Berezovsky an unimpressive, and inherently unreliable, witness, who regarded truth as a transitory, flexible concept, which could be moulded to suit his current purposes. At times the evidence which he gave was deliberately dishonest; sometimes he was clearly making his evidence up as he went along in response to the perceived difficulty in answering the questions in a manner consistent with his case; at other times, I gained the impression that he was not necessarily being deliberately dishonest, but had deluded himself into believing his own version of events."

[2] For example, the lengthy court battle over whether Roman Polanski, the film director, a fugitive from justice and the Claimant in a libel action, should be permitted to give evidence by video link on the grounds that it was unsafe for him to travel to England where a US arrest warrant could be served on him. The House of Lords overturned a decision of the Court of Appeal and allowed Mr Polanski to appear as a witness in this way. One of the questions was whether his written statement should be rejected as evidence if he did not give oral evidence in support of it. Baroness Hale gave a succinct summary of the law: "It remains the general procedural rule that any fact which needs to be proved by the evidence of witnesses is to be proved at trial by their oral evidence: see CPR 32.2(1)(a). But in civil proceedings this is now a matter of procedure rather than substance. The substantive rule is that all relevant evidence is admissible unless there is a rule excluding it ... Section 1(1) of the 1995 [Civil Evidence] Act provides simply that: 'In civil proceedings evidence shall not be excluded on the ground that it is hearsay'." *Polanski v Conde Nast Publications Ltd* [2005] UKHL 10.

Arbitration in England has tended to follow the basic framework of court procedure as far as the presentation and admissibility of evidence is concerned. However, "documents only" procedures have also been adopted by a number of bodies and written witness statements have become widely accepted without the accompanying need for the witness to attend the hearing in person.  **20–004**

The ICC Arbitration Rules take a different approach, more akin to court procedure in civil jurisdictions. This is evident from the title to Article 25 of the ICC Rules: "Establishing the Facts of the Case". It is for the Arbitral Tribunal to establish the facts and it may do so by "all appropriate means", including, at its option, hearing witnesses. Although in modern practice it is very common, there is no legal presumption in favour of witness evidence, whether oral or written.

The different cultural and legal approaches to the probative value of oral as against written evidence, and of the adversarial as against the investigative route to determining the facts of a case, form the background to Article 20, which seeks to include, and permit, features from both the common law and civil law systems.  **20–005**

The IBA Rules on the Taking of Evidence in International Arbitration (revised and adopted in 2010) also seek to synthesise the two systems. Articles 4 and 8 of the IBA Rules contain provisions which are similar to provisions in Article 20 of the LCIA Rules, but they go further and prescribe, for example, the contents of a witness statement.[3]

The IBA Rules are sometimes adopted, in whole or in part, in the first procedural order in LCIA arbitrations, but the practice is by no means universal. Bespoke directions in relation to witness evidence will also be made by Arbitral Tribunals working within the framework of Article 20 and with the flexibility which it permits.  **20–006**

**20.1 Before any hearing, the Arbitral Tribunal may order any party to give written notice of the identity of each witness that party wishes to call (including rebuttal witnesses), as well as the subject matter of that witness's testimony, its content and its relevance to the issues in the arbitration.**

Coming as it does immediately after Article 19, which deals with hearings, this initial provision of Article 20 is perhaps indicative of the English assumption that witness evidence will be required and that it will be given orally at the hearing.[4]  **20–007**

The purpose of Article 20.1 is to allow the Arbitral Tribunal to direct, usually following a directions hearing and in its first procedural order, that the parties give formal notice of the witnesses whom they intend to call to give oral evidence. In this way, the parties and their representatives are not taken by surprise once the hearing is under way. They and the Arbitral Tribunal are also thereby able to make reasonable estimates of the time that will be needed at the hearing for the cross-examination of witnesses.

---

[3] Article 4.5.
[4] The wording remains similar to that in the 1985 Rules (Article 11.1): "Before any hearing, the Tribunal may require any party to give notice of the identity of witnesses it wishes to call as well as the subject matter of their testimony and its relevance to the issues."

20–008    It is current practice in international arbitration for written witness statements to be submitted in advance of the hearing. In LCIA arbitrations, witness statements are generally exchanged after the parties' written statements and any disclosure phase. However, in some cases, parties agree or are directed by the Arbitral Tribunal to provide their witness statements with their submissions (i.e. in "memorials").[5]

The other side and the Arbitral Tribunal are informed of the identities of the witnesses and of the subject matter of their testimony by way of the contents of the written statements. Whether these witnesses, and others whose statements have not been provided, should attend the hearing for cross-examination is then a matter for subsequent directions.

### 20.2 Subject to any order otherwise by the Arbitral Tribunal, the testimony of a witness may be presented by a party in written form, either as a signed statement or like document.

20–009    The usual practice in relation to witness statements is confirmed in Article 20.2. Different methods of signing and verifying statements are also accommodated. It is for the Arbitral Tribunal to make directions in relation to any particular requirements. Unless and until it does so, there can be no objection to a straightforward statement (usually ending with an affirmation of its truth) or to an affidavit sworn, for example, in front of a lawyer, a notary or a consular official.[6]

If parties or their representatives wish to have clarity on the form a witness statement should take, they should communicate their enquiry to the Arbitral Tribunal (with a copy to the LCIA in the usual way) and not direct to the Registrar: the LCIA Secretariat does not maintain practice guidelines beyond the wording of the Rules.

### 20.3 The Arbitral Tribunal may decide the time, manner and form in which these written materials shall be exchanged between the parties and presented to the Arbitral Tribunal; and it may allow, refuse, or limit the written and oral testimony of witnesses (whether witnesses of fact or expert witnesses).

20–010    The tradition in ad hoc arbitration in London is for the parties' solicitors to exchange witness statements on a date ordered by the Arbitral Tribunal. As with the disclosure of documents, the Arbitral Tribunal will not usually wish to receive copies of the statements itself at this stage, preferring to wait until hearing bundles are prepared. The Rules, on the other hand, recognise that the Arbitral Tribunal may order that it receive copies of witness statements at the same time as the parties.[7] With the prevalence of email communications, this is often a question of

---

[5] This practice, which is common in other forms of arbitration (such as under the ICC, UNICTRAL and ICSID Rules) is not the default procedure under the LCIA Rules and, if desired, must therefore be agreed by the parties and/or directed by the Arbitral Tribunal. See 15–005 above.

[6] The version of this provision in the 1998 Rules included "a sworn affidavit" (Appendix 4). See new Article 20.7 below in relation to the administering of oaths by Arbitral Tribunals.

[7] This corresponds to the practice contemplated in Article 4.4 of the IBA Rules on the Taking of Evidence in International Arbitration (Appendix 12).

copying the Arbitral Tribunal into relevant emails: it is becoming more common for arbitrators not to require hard copies of evidence until the hearing bundles are submitted to them.

In order to facilitate simultaneous exchange, the parties' representatives can arrange for the Registrar to receive and then distribute the statements (e.g. by forwarding emails if they have been communicated in that way).[8]

The second limb of Article 20.3 confirms the Arbitral Tribunal's general powers in relation to witness evidence, which are, of course, subject to its duties under Article 14.4 and to the law governing the procedure. Article 8.2 of the IBA Rules permits an Arbitral Tribunal to "limit or exclude any question to, answer by or appearance of a witness if it considers such question, answer or appearance to be irrelevant, immaterial, unreasonably burdensome, duplicative or otherwise covered by a reason for objection set forth in Article 9.2". These criteria, together with those in Article 9.2 of the IBA Rules ("Admissibility and Assessment of Evidence"), give some idea of the reasons which an Arbitral Tribunal might safely invoke in order to limit or exclude witness evidence.

**20.4 The Arbitral Tribunal and any party may request that a witness, on whose written testimony another party relies, should attend for oral questioning at a hearing before the Arbitral Tribunal. If the Arbitral Tribunal orders that other party to secure the attendance of that witness and the witness refuses or fails to attend the hearing without good cause, the Arbitral Tribunal may place such weight on the written testimony or exclude all or any part thereof altogether as it considers appropriate in the circumstances.**

As mentioned above in relation to Article 20.1, the general rule in international arbitration is that written witness statements will be exchanged in advance of the hearing on the merits. These will generally stand as the witness's evidence in chief.[9]

**20-011**

It is open to each side to ask that identified witnesses from the other side attend the hearing for cross-examination ("oral questioning"). The Arbitral Tribunal will usually accede to such a request, but it has the right to refuse it, as confirmed by Article 20.3.

The importance of the opportunity to test witness evidence by cross-examination is confirmed by the second sentence of Article 20.4. The Arbitral Tribunal has complete discretion as to how it will treat the written statement of a witness who, without a good reason ("cause"), does not appear at a hearing after a party has been ordered to arrange his or her attendance. The wording is less harsh than Article 4.7 of the IBA Rules which makes exclusion of the evidence the default in these circumstances.[10]

**20-012**

---

[8] This service was specifically provided for in a Schedule to the 1981 Rules at C5. It is rarely used but is still available. It can avoid logistical and time-zone problems.

[9] Article 8.4 of the IBA Rules provides: "If the witness has submitted a Witness Statement or an Expert Report, the witness shall confirm it. The Parties may agree or the Arbitral Tribunal may order that the Witness Statement or Expert Report shall serve as that witness's direct testimony" (Appendix 12).

[10] ". . . the Arbitral Tribunal shall disregard any Witness Statement related to that Evidentiary Hearing by that witness unless, in exceptional circumstances, the Arbitral Tribunal decides otherwise."

It is good practice to give the Arbitral Tribunal and other parties as much notice as possible of any impediment to the appearance of a witness. Depending on the importance of the witness's evidence, the reasons for his or her non-attendance and other considerations, including the Arbitral Tribunal's duties under Article 14.4, it may be possible to postpone the whole hearing, have this witness heard on another day or arrange for his or her appearance to be made by video link.

**20–013** If the hearing is to be in London, and there have been delays in obtaining a visa for a witness, the Registrar may be able to assist, e.g. by writing to the relevant Consulate in support of the application and to explain the importance and urgency of the matter. Applications have been expedited following the despatch of such letters on several occasions.

As the new opening words of Article 20.4 confirm, the Arbitral Tribunal may call a witness who has not been called by one of the parties. Provision for this possibility is also made in the IBA Rules on the Taking of Evidence in International Arbitration at Article 8.5, which confirms that any witness questioned by the Arbitral Tribunal may also be questioned by the parties.[11] As noted above, civil law practitioners are more accustomed to arbitrators conducting their own factual enquiries, but the blend of common and civil law approaches in Article 20 provides flexibility to tailor the evidential aspects of the procedure to the particular case in hand.

**20.5 Subject to the mandatory provisions of any applicable law, rules of law and any order of the Arbitral Tribunal otherwise, it shall not be improper for any party or its legal representatives to interview any witness or potential witness for the purpose of presenting his or her testimony in written form or producing such person as an oral witness at any hearing.**

**20–014** Professional and procedural rules in some jurisdictions prevent lawyers from interviewing witnesses. Article 20.5 confirms that, subject to any mandatory laws or rules of law which might apply to them or any order of the Arbitral Tribunal, the parties and their lawyers are free to do this. The IBA Rules on the Taking of Evidence in International Arbitration contain very similar provisions.[12] In practice, the vast majority of witness statements are prepared by lawyers following interviews which they have conducted.

The IBA Guidelines on Party Representation in International Arbitration include the general duty for lawyers to "ensure that a Witness Statement reflects the Witness's own account of relevant facts, events and circumstances."[13] Local guidelines can be stricter and more detailed. The Bar Standards Board in England has published *Guidance on Witness Preparation*, which urges barristers to take "great care" to avoid any suggestion "that the evidence in the witness statement has been manufactured by the legal representatives".

**20–015** Article 20.5 says nothing about "witness coaching", i.e. mock cross-examination of a witness on the evidence to be given in the particular arbitration. In England,

---

[11] Appendix 12.
[12] Article 4.3 (Appendix 12).
[13] Guideline 21 (Appendix 14).

the practice was condemned in a judgment in a criminal case in 2005, in which the judge said:

"The witness should give his or her own evidence, so far as practicable uninfluenced by what anyone else has said, whether in formal discussions or informal conversations. The rule reduces, indeed hopefully avoids, any possibility that one witness may tailor his evidence in the light of what anyone else said, and equally, avoids any unfounded perception that he may have done so. These risks are inherent in witness training."[14]

However, English barristers and solicitors are permitted to give general advice and to explain, for example, the layout of the courtroom ("witness familiarisation"). Specialist trainers are sometimes employed to prepare witnesses, including expert witnesses, before hearings. They may use fictional cases to avoid infringing ethical rules.

20–016

Other jurisdictions are more tolerant of witness coaching. In the US it is generally accepted. Counsel in the US may suggest answers that witnesses may use, so long as they are not false.[15]

Lawyers from both these legal and ethical backgrounds, as well as from other diverse legal cultures, encounter each other in international arbitration. Guideline 24 of the IBA Guidelines on Party Representation confirms that party representatives may "meet or interact with Witnesses and Experts in order to discuss and prepare their prospective testimony".[16]

20–017

The Comment on this Guideline is relatively detailed. It confirms that preparation may include "practise questions and answers" but it also confirms that the contacts should not "alter the genuineness of the Witness or Expert evidence". The Guidelines thus acknowledge a practice which is widespread in international arbitration whilst at the same time setting out some safeguards.

A survey of international arbitration practitioners conducted in 2012 found that 62 per cent of Respondents considered mock cross-examination of witnesses appropriate and only a small minority (24 per cent) considered it inappropriate. Unsurprisingly, North American Respondents were its most enthusiastic supporters (81 per cent).[17]

**20.6 Subject to any order by the Arbitral Tribunal otherwise, any individual intending to testify to the Arbitral Tribunal may be treated as a witness notwithstanding that the individual is a party to the arbitration or was, remains or has become an officer, employee, owner or shareholder of any party or is otherwise identified with any party.**

---

[14] *R. v Momodou and Limani* [2005] EWCA Crim 177.
[15] I. Meredith and H. Khan, "Witness Preparation in International Arbitration – A Cross Cultural Minefield" (2011) *Mealey's International Arbitration Report*.
[16] Appendix 14.
[17] 2012 International Arbitration Survey: Current and Preferred Practices in the Arbitral Process, Queen Mary University of London and White & Case: *http://www.whitecase.com/files/Uploads/Documents/Arbitration/Queen-Mary-University-London-International-Arbitration-Survey-2012.pdf* [Accessed November 14, 2014].

20–018   As mentioned above in the introduction to the commentary to this Article, there is a general principle of English law that a Claimant is expected to give evidence in support of his or her claim and to submit to cross-examination on it. This is in direct conflict with a rule which applies in many civil law jurisdictions and which is summarised in the Latin maxim *"Nemo in propria causa testis esse debet"* ("Nobody should be a witness in his own cause").

Article 20.6 confirms the principle that the parties to the arbitration may themselves appear as witnesses. Parties should note, though, that this will not necessarily be the case: the Arbitral Tribunal is empowered to decide otherwise.[18] The permissive, rather than prescriptive, intent of Article 20 is thus maintained.

**20.7 Subject to the mandatory provisions of any applicable law, the Arbitral Tribunal shall be entitled (but not required) to administer any appropriate oath to any witness at any hearing, prior to the oral testimony of that witness.**

20–019   This is a new addition in the 2014 Rules. It confirms that arbitrators in LCIA arbitrations have the power (but not the obligation) to administer oaths before witnesses give oral testimony at hearings. This was a power conferred on arbitrators by s.38(5) of the English Arbitration Act 1996. It is little used in practice.

**20.8 Any witness who gives oral testimony at a hearing before the Arbitral Tribunal may be questioned by each of the parties under the control of the Arbitral Tribunal. The Arbitral Tribunal may put questions at any stage of such testimony.**

20–020   Cross-examination of witnesses at a hearing has become the norm in international arbitrations. A survey conducted in 2012 found that 90 per cent of the more than 700 Respondents believed that cross-examination was either always or usually an effective form of testing factual evidence.[19]

The same survey found that, according to the Respondents, witnesses were questioned primarily by legal representatives (83 per cent) rather than by the Arbitral Tribunal (17 per cent). However, reflecting the points made above in the introduction to the commentary on this Article, questioning by the Arbitral Tribunal was more common amongst civil lawyers (24 per cent) than common lawyers (10 per cent).

20–021   The second sentence of Article 20.5 confirms that the Arbitral Tribunal is permitted to be proactive and to intervene with its own questions at any time during the cross-examination. In cases in which the Respondent has not made an appearance, but in which the Arbitral Tribunal has called a hearing and has asked

---

[18] There has been a change to the 1998 Rules in this respect: the wording of Article 20.7 had required that a party "shall" be treated as a witness and gave no scope to the Arbitral Tribunal to exclude such evidence (Appendix 4).
[19] See fn.17.

that the Claimant or a senior officer of the Claimant company attend in person, it will often put questions to this witness itself and record answers in its award.

An alternative to cross-examination is witness conferencing, a concept promoted by Wolfgang Peter, former President of the LCIA's European Users' Council.[20] This is a flexible technique (more commonly used with experts) whereby witnesses presented by two or more parties are questioned together, allowing, for example, a legal representative for one party to cross-examine the opponent's witness before turning to his own side's witness for rebuttal and then re-examining the opponent's witness with the benefit of those answers. It is a technique increasingly used in LCIA arbitrations.[21]

---

[20] Wolfgang Peter, "Witness 'Conferencing'" (2002) 18(1) Arbitration Int. 47.
[21] Similarly, the "hot-tubbing" of experts, where the party-appointed experts are questioned together by the Arbitral Tribunal, is increasingly used.

# Article 21—Expert(s) to Arbitral Tribunal

**21.1** The Arbitral Tribunal, after consultation with the parties, may appoint one or more experts to report in writing to the Arbitral Tribunal and the parties on specific issues in the arbitration, as identified by the Arbitral Tribunal.

**21.2** Any such expert shall be and remain impartial and independent of the parties; and he or she shall sign a written declaration to such effect, delivered to the Arbitral Tribunal and copied to all parties.

**21.3** The Arbitral Tribunal may require any party at any time to give to such expert any relevant information or to provide access to any relevant documents, goods, samples, property, site or thing for inspection under that party's control on such terms as the Arbitral Tribunal thinks appropriate in the circumstances.

**21.4** If any party so requests or the Arbitral Tribunal considers it necessary, the Arbitral Tribunal may order the expert, after delivery of the expert's written report, to participate in a hearing at which the parties shall have a reasonable opportunity to question the expert on the report and to present witnesses in order to testify on relevant issues arising from the report.

**21.5** The fees and expenses of any expert appointed by the Arbitral Tribunal under this Article 21 may be paid out of the deposits payable by the parties under Article 24 and shall form part of the Arbitration Costs under Article 28.

### Introduction

**21–001** This Article provides the Arbitral Tribunal with the power to appoint one or more experts to assist it with the resolution of the dispute.

Commonly, where expert evidence is required, rather than the Arbitral Tribunal appointing an expert(s), the parties each engage their own (independent) expert(s) in the relevant area(s) and the Arbitral Tribunal is left to resolve any differences between the expert evidence itself.

**21–002** The Rules do not make express provision for party-appointed experts, and the absence of reference to them in Article 21 is sometimes mistakenly treated by parties unfamiliar with LCIA arbitration as a prohibition against them in favour of single, Arbitral Tribunal-appointed, experts. There is no such prohibition.

In principle, Article 20 covers both factual and expert witnesses, but the only mention of experts there is in relation to allowing, excluding or limiting them;

nothing is said about the manner or timing of their appointment or how they should carry out their assignment.

In practice, a procedural order at an early stage of the arbitration will usually include a timetable for the exchange of experts' reports and for meetings of experts.  21–003

Whilst it may appear potentially efficient for the Arbitral Tribunal to appoint a single expert to assist in dealing with an area of dispute (and a similar practice is regularly adopted by courts in some civil law jurisdictions), rather than for each party to appoint an expert, the reality of many cases is that each party would appoint its own expert in any event. Many parties in high value cases would consider that they needed expert assistance in order to maximise their chances of influencing the Arbitral Tribunal's expert or, if necessary, questioning such expert's preliminary views. This would then lead to three experts for each area rather than one or two, and the Arbitral Tribunal would still be left to resolve any differences between them. There is sometimes also concern that the Arbitral Tribunal could, in practice (although not permitted to do so), effectively delegate part of its decision-making to the expert.

Therefore, whilst similar provisions for Arbitral Tribunal-appointed experts are contained in other arbitration rules (e.g. Article 25.4 of the 2012 ICC Rules and Article 29 of the 2010 UNCITRAL Rules), this power is rarely used in practice. One instance where it was used under the 1998 LCIA Rules was for the appointment of an accountant to carry out an exercise to calculate quantum, where the methodology was uncontroversial but the work had not yet been done by either side. Another instance, again under the 1998 LCIA Rules, was for the appointment of an expert to advise the Arbitral Tribunal on the confidentiality of documents in an arbitration which was partly non-confidential.

**21.1 The Arbitral Tribunal, after consultation with the parties, may appoint one or more experts to report in writing to the Arbitral Tribunal and the parties on specific issues in the arbitration, as identified by the Arbitral Tribunal.**

Article 21.1 bestows power upon the Arbitral Tribunal to appoint its own expert(s). Under the 1998 LCIA Rules (in common with s.37(1) of the English Arbitration Act 1996), this power was expressly subject to any written agreement of the parties to the contrary. However, it was rare for parties to make a written agreement excluding this power of the Arbitral Tribunal (at the time of contract-drafting few parties go into this level of detail as to the management of future disputes). Even once the dispute has arisen, the parties are unlikely to see the need to address this question unless and until the Arbitral Tribunal indicates that it is considering appointing an expert (which, as noted above, is relatively rare in LCIA arbitrations).  21–004

In contrast to the position under the 1998 Rules, Article 21.1 now requires the Arbitral Tribunal to consult with parties prior to appointing an expert. This is consistent with the ICC and UNCITRAL Rules and was, in practice, always to be expected in any event.

The Arbitral Tribunal may appoint "one or more experts" (in theory any number) and on any "specific issues", whether legal, technical, accounting or  21–005 otherwise, subject always to its general duties under Article 14.4(ii), for example, to adopt suitable procedures and avoid unnecessary expense.

The 1998 LCIA Rules simply referred to experts reporting to the Arbitral Tribunal. Article 21.1 now makes clear that any Arbitral Tribunal-appointed expert will provide his or her report to the parties as well as to the Arbitral Tribunal. Indeed, it is crucial that they do so in order that the parties understand the evidence before the Arbitral Tribunal and can have a proper opportunity to address it.

> **21.2 Any such expert shall be and remain impartial and independent of the parties; and he or she shall sign a written declaration to such effect, delivered to the Arbitral Tribunal and copied to all parties.**

21–006  Any experts are to be and remain "impartial and independent of the parties". The additional stipulation in the 1998 LCIA Rules that this must be "throughout the arbitration proceedings" has been deleted, presumably as unnecessary. Whilst experts appointed by the parties should also generally be independent and impartial, the fact that an expert has been appointed directly by the Arbitral Tribunal means that they should not be prone to any suggestion that they are the "hired gun" of a party.

Article 21.2 now requires that experts sign a written declaration confirming their impartiality and independence. Whilst this is a new requirement, which did not exist under the 1998 LCIA Rules, in practice even under those Rules the LCIA Secretariat asked tribunal-appointed experts to sign statements of independence similar to those signed by arbitrators.

Nonetheless, an Arbitral Tribunal-appointed expert is merely an adviser to the Arbitral Tribunal (albeit most likely a very influential one), and the Arbitral Tribunal should assess the expert's evidence in a similar way to evidence presented by a party-appointed expert. The Arbitral Tribunal should not simply accept its expert's evidence without applying its own mind to the issues, as that would be an improper delegation of its role.

> **21.3 The Arbitral Tribunal may require any party at any time to give to such expert any relevant information or to provide access to any relevant documents, goods, samples, property, site or thing for inspection under that party's control on such terms as the Arbitral Tribunal thinks appropriate in the circumstances.**

21–007  Once appointed, the expert(s) will require the relevant information on which to found their expert opinion. Article 21.3 therefore provides the Arbitral Tribunal with an express power to require a party, at any time, to give the information, or provide access (under that party's control) to the information, to the expert.

> **21.4 If any party so requests or the Arbitral Tribunal considers it necessary, the Arbitral Tribunal may order the expert, after delivery of the expert's written report, to participate in a hearing at which the**

**parties shall have a reasonable opportunity to question the expert on the report and to present witnesses in order to testify on relevant issues arising from the report.**

Article 21.4 provides the Arbitral Tribunal with the power to order the expert(s) to attend a hearing at which the expert may effectively be cross-examined by the parties and/or the parties may submit their own evidence as to issues arising from the expert's report. It is noted that the Rules refer to "witnesses" being presented and not to "expert witnesses". However, in practice, the Arbitral Tribunal is likely to allow each party to appoint/present both factual and expert witnesses where appropriate.  21–008

The ability to question the expert and present evidence is an important safeguard for the parties. Under the 1998 LCIA Rules, whilst the parties could waive this right, the Arbitral Tribunal could not itself deny it to them. However, Article 21.4 now places the matter in the hands of the Arbitral Tribunal, which "may order" the expert's participation in a hearing (and so could decide not to do so). It is unlikely that, without very good reason, a party would be denied any opportunity to question an Arbitral Tribunal-appointed expert at a hearing (where it wished to do so).

Note that the Arbitral Tribunal generally has power, under Article 20.3, to "refuse or limit" the testimony of party-appointed witnesses and experts. In the context of Arbitral Tribunal-appointed experts, the Arbitral Tribunal must nonetheless allow the parties "a reasonable opportunity to question the expert on the report and to present witnesses in order to testify on relevant issues arising from the report".

**21.5 The fees and expenses of any expert appointed by the Arbitral Tribunal under this Article 21 may be paid out of the deposits payable by the parties under Article 24 and shall form part of the Arbitration Costs under Article 28.**

This Article confirms that Arbitral Tribunal-appointed experts may be paid out of the deposits paid to the LCIA by the parties (in contrast to the parties each having to pay the experts that they engage directly). The ultimate allocation of those costs as between the parties may therefore form part of the allocation by the Arbitral Tribunal of the "Arbitration Costs" (the rather confusing phrase used in the LCIA Rules to refer to the costs which are not legal or other costs directly incurred by the parties—see Article 28). The LCIA Secretariat will in practice confirm to the parties the hourly rate or fixed fee agreed with the expert. Estimates for the expert's fees will be obtained by the Secretariat, in the same way as estimates are obtained from arbitrators, in order that interim deposits may be set at the correct levels.  21–009

## Article 22—Additional Powers

22.1 The Arbitral Tribunal shall have the power, upon the application of any party or (save for sub-paragraphs (viii), (ix) and (x) below) upon its own initiative, but in either case only after giving the parties a reasonable opportunity to state their views and upon such terms (as to costs and otherwise) as the Arbitral Tribunal may decide:

(i) to allow a party to supplement, modify or amend any claim, defence, cross-claim, defence to cross-claim and reply, including a Request, Response and any other written statement, submitted by such party;

(ii) to abridge or extend (even where the period of time has expired) any period of time prescribed under the Arbitration Agreement, any other agreement of the parties or any order made by the Arbitral Tribunal;

(iii) to conduct such enquiries as may appear to the Arbitral Tribunal to be necessary or expedient, including whether and to what extent the Arbitral Tribunal should itself take the initiative in identifying relevant issues and ascertaining relevant facts and the law(s) or rules of law applicable to the Arbitration Agreement, the arbitration and the merits of the parties' dispute;

(iv) to order any party to make any documents, goods, samples, property, site or thing under its control available for inspection by the Arbitral Tribunal, any other party, any expert to such party and any expert to the Tribunal;

(v) to order any party to produce to the Arbitral Tribunal and to other parties documents or copies of documents in their possession, custody or power which the Arbitral Tribunal decides to be relevant;

(vi) to decide whether or not to apply any strict rules of evidence (or any other rules) as to the admissibility, relevance or weight of any material tendered by a party on any issue of fact or expert opinion; and to decide the time, manner and form in which such material should be exchanged between the parties and presented to the Arbitral Tribunal;

(vii) to order compliance with any legal obligation, payment of compensation for breach of any legal obligation and specific performance of any agreement (including any arbitration agreement or any contract relating to land);

(viii) to allow one or more third persons to be joined in the arbitration as a party provided any such third person and the

**22.6** Without prejudice to the generality of Articles 22.1(ix) and (x), the LCIA Court may determine, after giving the parties a reasonable opportunity to state their views, that two or more arbitrations, subject to the LCIA Rules and commenced under the same arbitration agreement between the same disputing parties, shall be consolidated to form one single arbitration subject to the LCIA Rules, provided that no arbitral tribunal has yet been formed by the LCIA Court for any of the arbitrations to be consolidated.

### Introduction—Powers of the Tribunal and LCIA Court

22–001   As with most international arbitration procedures, parties in LCIA arbitrations are free, as part of their agreement to arbitrate or at any time thereafter, to agree on how the arbitration should be conducted and on the powers that may be exercised by the Arbitral Tribunal and, to a degree, by the LCIA Court. This freedom is subject to the mandatory laws at the seat of arbitration which prevail over any party agreement in this regard. Article 19 of the UNCITRAL Model Law reflects the general consensus:

> "(1) Subject to the provisions of this Law, the parties are free to agree on the procedure to be followed by the Arbitral Tribunal in conducting the proceedings."

22–002   Section 38(1) of the English Arbitration Act 1996 similarly provides that the parties are "free to agree on the powers exercisable by the Arbitral Tribunal for the purposes of and in relation to the proceedings." Article 22 of the LCIA Rules constitutes an agreement regarding the powers exercisable by the Arbitral Tribunal.

The 2014 edition of Article 22 has seen numerous revisions, as a result of which certain powers of the Arbitral Tribunal no longer feature as express powers,[1] whilst others have been added. Significantly, in addition to providing powers for the Arbitral Tribunal, Article 22 now also provides for the exercise of certain powers by the LCIA Court, both in relation to the consolidation of separate arbitral proceedings and in relation to the extension and curtailment of time limits. These revisions could, to a limited extent at least, result in a greater involvement of the LCIA Court in the conduct of certain arbitral references.

### *Consolidation and joinder*

22–003   Of the new powers exercisable by Arbitral Tribunals and the LCIA Court, the most controversial will likely be the power under certain conditions to consolidate

---

[1] For example, the power to rectify contracts between the parties, formerly expressly set out in Article 22.1(g), is no longer contained in the express provisions of Article 22.1 of the LCIA Rules. However, under s.48(5)(c) of the English Arbitration Act 1996, in arbitral proceedings to which the Act applies, the Arbitral Tribunal will have the power to rectify a deed or other document, unless the parties otherwise agree. The revised provisions of Article 22.1 of the LCIA Rules do not amount to an agreement to exclude the provisions of s.48(5)(c) of the 1996 Act (Appendix 7).

different LCIA arbitration proceedings.[2] Arbitral Tribunals already had the power to join third parties to arbitrations under Article 22.1(h) of the 1998 Rules, a power which was itself controversial and which made the LCIA Rules distinctive. That power is retained in Article 22.1(viii), but the new powers go further.

In many cases, the consolidation of proceedings involving the same legal and factual issues and the same commercial relationships will serve the ends of justice by avoiding duplication of time and cost, and eliminating the risk of inconsistent decisions. In the context of litigation before national courts, the availability of joinder and consolidation is generally assumed and accepted on that basis.

Nevertheless, the prospect of consolidation and joinder in an arbitration context is viewed by some as offending against basic principles. It has been said that joinder and consolidation would undermine the rights of parties to arbitrate only against parties to their arbitration agreement under an agreed set of rules and to select the arbitrators of their choice; and that joinder and consolidation would contravene the rights of confidentiality and privacy, and could even increase the costs for some parties. Rather unpersuasively it has even been argued that the power to consolidate is contrary to the principle of party autonomy.[3]

22–004

The drafters of the 2014 LCIA Rules have greatly reduced the scope for controversy by limiting the circumstances in which the power to consolidate can be exercised (see below). Further, the powers of the Arbitral Tribunal to order consolidation are subject to the approval of the LCIA Court. Interestingly, however, the drafters of the new LCIA Rules did not limit the application of these provisions to Arbitration Agreements entered into after the 2014 Rules came into force, as they did, for example, with the Emergency Arbitrator procedure under Article 9B.

**22.1 The Arbitral Tribunal shall have the power, upon the application of any party or (save for sub-paragraphs (viii), (ix) and (x) below) upon its own initiative, but in either case only after giving the parties a reasonable opportunity to state their views and upon such terms (as to costs and otherwise) as the Arbitral Tribunal may decide: ...**

Article 22.1 sets out a clear statement of the powers exercisable by the Arbitral Tribunal in particular circumstances; leaving parties with the option of reaching an agreement to curtail or extend those powers either in their Arbitration Agreement or during the course of the arbitration process.

22–005

The Arbitral Tribunal is obliged to give the parties "a reasonable opportunity to state their views" before any such powers are exercised. This is consistent with the obligation of any Arbitral Tribunal to "act fairly and impartially as between all

---

[2] Under Article 22.1(iv) and (x), an Arbitral Tribunal can order consolidation with the approval of the LCIA Court, and under 22.6 the LCIA Court can order consolidation of proceedings where no Arbitral Tribunal has been appointed.

[3] See the discussion in Gary B. Born, *International Commercial Arbitration*, 2nd edn (Kluwer Law International, 2014), Ch.18 "Consolidation, Joinder and Intervention in International Arbitration", pp.2564–2613.

parties, giving each a reasonable opportunity of putting its case and dealing with that of its opponent" set out in Article 14 of the LCIA Rules.

**22–006** With the exception of the powers to effect joinder (Article 22.1(viii)) or to consolidate separate arbitration proceedings (Articles 22.1(ix) and (x)), the Arbitral Tribunal may act on its own volition, or initiative.

Finally, Article 22.1 allows the Arbitral Tribunal to make any order or relief it grants subject to such terms and conditions it considers appropriate, including in relation to the payment of costs or, for example, the provision of some form of counter-security.

The specific powers conferred on the Arbitral Tribunal by Article 22.1 are set out in the sub-paragraphs of Articles 22.1 discussed below.

> **22.1(i) to allow a party to supplement, modify or amend any claim, defence, cross-claim, defence to cross-claim and reply, including a Request, Response and any other written statement, submitted by such party;**

**22–007** During the course of the arbitration the perception of the dispute may evolve through, for example, factual discovery, admissions, or preliminary or partial determinations of the Arbitral Tribunal, to the extent that a party will consider it necessary to amend its factual and/or legal submissions. The Arbitral Tribunal will seek to hold the balance between the right of a party to present (and amend) its case during the arbitration, and the need to avoid prejudice, wasted costs and unfairness to other parties, all of which can arise if amendments occur belatedly. The Arbitral Tribunal may impose terms in an effort to hold such a proper balance between the two sides in these circumstances.

It should be noted that the reference to amendments to a Request and Response must be to those documents in their capacity as statements of case submitted to the Arbitral Tribunal if the relevant parties have chosen that they should stand as such statements pursuant to Articles 15.2 and 15.3. Neither the LCIA Court, nor the Secretariat, has any power to allow amendments to a Request or Response in isolation.

> **22.1(ii) to abridge or extend (even where the period of time has expired) any period of time prescribed under the Arbitration Agreement, any other agreement of the parties or any order made by the Arbitral Tribunal;**

**22–008** Providing a fair means for the resolution of a dispute, and giving each party a reasonable opportunity of putting its case and dealing with that of its opponent(s),[4] often requires the Arbitral Tribunal to change specific deadlines provided for under the LCIA Rules, the Arbitration Agreement or in procedural directions it

---

[4] See Article 14.4(i) above.

has given, normally by extending them. Article 22.1(ii) makes it clear that it can shorten or lengthen any such deadline or time limit.

The greater the change to the overall timetable, or prejudice to the remaining parties (for example, in leaving them less time to prepare to present their case and respond to the case put against them), the more reluctant the Arbitral Tribunal will be to change a deadline. For example, it is relatively rare for an Arbitral Tribunal to agree to a timetable revision that results in delaying a substantive or evidentiary hearing; although this does occur from time to time.

Practitioners more used to ad hoc and trade association arbitrations should note that the experience of users of LCIA arbitration is that extensions of time to procedural deadlines are generally sought less often, and that timetables set early in a reference are largely adhered to by the parties.

22–009

It is noteworthy that the Arbitral Tribunal is empowered to change a time limit in any part of the Arbitration Agreement, including in the clause or signed agreement by which the LCIA Rules were incorporated.

**Article 22.1(iii) to conduct such enquiries as may appear to the Arbitral Tribunal to be necessary or expedient, including whether and to what extent the Arbitral Tribunal should itself take the initiative in identifying relevant issues and ascertaining relevant facts and the law(s) or rules of law applicable to the Arbitration Agreement, the arbitration and the merits of the parties' dispute;**

At first sight the idea that the Arbitral Tribunal can act inquisitorially might give rise to concern for some parties, particularly those who are used to conducting proceedings in common-law jurisdictions.[5] However, these powers are only exercised after the parties have been able to state their views, and the Arbitral Tribunal is constrained by its general duties in Article 14.

22–010

The scope of this power is wide, extending to all the main elements of any dispute, including "the merits", the proceedings and the Arbitration Agreement itself. This specific power in the LCIA Rules addresses the situation where the Arbitral Tribunal considers that there are important aspects of the dispute overlooked or inadequately covered by the parties in their submissions, but which must be addressed in order to resolve that dispute fairly and efficiently.

Nevertheless, it would be unsafe for an Arbitral Tribunal to rely on facts or legal theories upon which the parties have not been invited to comment.[6]

22–011

As discussed above in relation to Article 16.4, the law governing the contract in dispute, the law of the seat of the arbitration and the law of the Arbitration Agreement can all be different. With a view to rendering an enforceable award, an Arbitral Tribunal may wish to conduct its own enquiries into relevant aspects of any of these applicable laws, in all of which the parties' legal representatives may

---

[5] For a discussion of the adversarial as against the investigative route to determining the facts of a case, and attempts to permit and synthesise both routes, see the introduction to the comments on Article 20 ("Witnesses") above.

[6] Otherwise the award may become unenforceable on the grounds of *ultra petita*.

not necessarily be qualified themselves. If it does so, it should invite the parties' submissions on any issues which its enquiries disclose as relevant.

### 22.1(iv) to order any party to make any documents, goods, samples, property, site or thing under its control available for inspection by the Arbitral Tribunal, any other party, any expert to such party and any expert to the Tribunal;

22–012 Under Article 22.1(iv) the Arbitral Tribunal may make an order requiring any party to make documents, goods, samples, property, sites or any other thing under its control available for inspection by the other parties, the Arbitral Tribunal or any experts to a party or to the Arbitral Tribunal. The power of the Arbitral Tribunal to make such orders is also reflected in Articles 6.3 and 7 of the IBA Rules on the Taking of Evidence in International Arbitration and the procedures of many other international arbitration rules.

Enforcement of such orders against an unwilling party will depend on support from the court having jurisdiction over the property or site in question. This will depend on the laws at that place which define the powers of the court in relation to arbitration proceedings, and there may be a distinction between those powers available for a domestic arbitration, and those available for an international arbitration conducted outside the relevant jurisdiction. Under Article 27 of the UNCITRAL Model Law, the Arbitral Tribunal or a party with the approval of the Arbitral Tribunal may request assistance from a competent court in taking evidence, but this again is subject to the applicable procedural laws. In the English context, s.38(4) of the English Arbitration Act 1996 contains equivalent provisions, and s.44 of the same Act allows the court to make equivalent orders in support of arbitral proceedings.

### 22.1(v) to order any party to produce to the Arbitral Tribunal and to other parties documents or copies of documents in their possession, custody or power which the Arbitral Tribunal decides to be relevant;

22–013 The power of the Arbitral Tribunal to order the production and disclosure of documents under Article 21.1(v) is wide. Once the Arbitral Tribunal has determined that a document or class of documents is relevant, then it has the power to order production. However, there are a number of underlying considerations which will affect the exercise of that power.

An applicant will have to establish relevance to the issues falling to be determined in the arbitration. Many Arbitral Tribunals require the parties to provide them with submissions in the form of a table, referred to as a "Redfern Schedule",[7] in which:

---

[7] Called a "Redfern Schedule" after Mr Alan Redfern, the arbitrator who is credited with promoting this practice.

- the first column contains an identification of the documents or categories of documents that have been requested;

- the second column contains a short description of the reasons for each request;

- the third column contains a summary of any objections by the other party to the production of the documents or categories of documents requested; and

- unless provision is also made for a reply by the requesting party, the fourth column is left blank for the decision of the Arbitral Tribunal on each request.

International arbitrators will have different approaches to the scope of disclosure each party must make. Arbitrators from civil law jurisdictions are often said to be less keen to order disclosure than their colleagues from common law jurisdictions. However, in recent years growing reliance has been placed by many international arbitrators, including in LCIA arbitration proceedings, on the provisions of the IBA Rules on the Taking of Evidence in International Arbitration. In particular, Articles 3 and 9.2 of the IBA Rules are regularly cited as containing the relevant principles governing documentary disclosure in international arbitration.  22–014

Thus, the requesting party will have to satisfy the Arbitral Tribunal that the document is not in its possession, but is within the possession, power or control of the other party; and that the document is relevant to the case, and material to the outcome. The Arbitral Tribunal will then consider the request in light of the circumstances and legitimate interests of the prospective producing party, taking account of claims to privilege from production, whether the production would place an unreasonable burden on that party and any need to safeguard confidentiality.

In general, the disclosure phase of LCIA arbitrations is less time-consuming and burdensome than in English court proceedings. It is the experience of users that extensions of time to complete disclosure exercises are sought less often than in court or in ad hoc and trade association arbitrations, and they rarely disturb the dates fixed for the final hearing.  22–015

Arbitral Tribunals will on occasion have to address these issues in the light of very large amounts of electronic data. For court proceedings there is case-law (especially in the US) and protocols have been created for dealing with electronic document discovery. The IBA Rules on the Taking of Evidence in International Commercial Arbitration defines "document" to mean "a writing of any kind, whether recorded on paper, electronic means, audio or visual recordings or any other mechanical or electronic means of storing or recording information", but apart from recognising electronic documents, these rules do not specifically deal with the issues which arise. Parties might therefore consider making specific provision in their contract dealing with the evidential issues arising where there is likely to be a substantial amount of electronic documents. Suggested "Guidelines for Disclosure of Electronically Stored Information in International Arbitration" have been published in at least one journal, and no doubt the issues will be debated further until a standard is widely adopted, as occurred with the IBA Rules.[8]

---

[8] Robert H. Smit and Tyler B. Robinson, "E-Disclosure in International Arbitration" (2008) 24(1) Arbitration Int.

**22–016**  Article 30 of the LCIA Rules provides that all documents produced by the parties in the proceedings not otherwise in the public domain shall be subject to an undertaking of confidentiality. Where the objection is to a party seeing confidential documents, then arbitrators may be asked to make an order subject to terms; for example, that certain confidential documents are seen only by named individuals and counsel who give suitable undertakings before copies are provided, and that reference to them during a hearing is regulated so that the confidence is protected.

> **22.1(vi) to decide whether or not to apply any strict rules of evidence (or any other rules) as to the admissibility, relevance or weight of any material tendered by a party on any issue of fact or expert opinion; and to decide the time, manner and form in which such material should be exchanged between the parties and presented to the Arbitral Tribunal;**

**22–017**  This provision reflects the idea that the Arbitral Tribunal is master of the procedure at an arbitration hearing, subject to any agreement between the parties and mandatory laws. A very similar provision is found in s.34(2)(f) of the English Arbitration Act 1996, although since that is not a mandatory provision the LCIA Rules will prevail in arbitrations with an English seat.

This does not mean however that an Arbitral Tribunal can necessarily admit *any* material as evidence and proceed to base its decision on such material. The Arbitral Tribunal is obliged to comply with Article 14.1 of the LCIA Rules under which it must "act fairly and impartially as between the parties, giving each a reasonable opportunity of putting its case and dealing with that of its opponents", as well as to abide by any applicable laws at the seat of arbitration.

**22–018**  So, for example, evidence of "without prejudice" negotiations is to be excluded from the record of an arbitration seated in England, as a matter of English law (as well as the laws of some other jurisdictions), on the grounds of public policy.[9] The issue was illustrated in *Finney Lock Seeds Ltd v George Mitchell (Chesterhall) Ltd*,[10] where the court considered a case where the arbitrators had been given a wide power under the applicable rules of arbitration,[11] and they had admitted as evidence without prejudice correspondence. The court reasoned:

> "Mr Twigg says that the rule is sufficient to enable the arbitrators to have regard to the without prejudice correspondence. I do not agree. I think it enables the arbitrators to have regard to oral evidence which may properly be admitted and it may enable them, in a proper case, to disregard the hearsay

---

[9] The IBA Rules on the Taking of Evidence in International Arbitration also recognises the privilege protecting without prejudice settlement negotiations (Appendix 12).
[10] [1979] 2 Lloyd's Rep. 301.
[11] The Arbitration Rules of the British Association of Grain Seed Feed and Agricultural Merchants: "The Arbitrators and Umpire shall have absolute discretion as to the conduct of all proceedings and are at liberty to act upon evidence and/or information as they may think fit and to call for such documents in the possession of the parties to the dispute as they deem necessary . . .".

rule. But I do not think the rule is so wide as to entitle them in the absence of consent to have regard to evidence of without prejudice negotiations . . .".

Apart from documents which should be excluded on sound legal grounds pertaining at the seat of arbitration, such as privileged documents, most Arbitral Tribunals tend to allow most material to be presented (provided that this is done in a timely fashion) in an effort to meet the obligation to give each party a reasonable opportunity of putting its case, and to avoid claims of serious irregularity or other such challenges to their award. However, this tendency should be carefully weighed against the obligation to avoid "unnecessary delay or expense" pursuant to Article 14.1(ii) of the LCIA Rules.

**22–019**

Some commentators have suggested that arbitral institutions should be "actively discouraging arbitrators from all legal backgrounds (common law and civil law) from the view that they should let everything in and decide later what is important or relevant".[12] So, with this power in mind, LCIA Arbitral Tribunals should consider whether to exclude unimportant or irrelevant material where needed to meet the need for timely resolution. The suggested approach is to be encouraged, even if (or perhaps because) it requires greater self-discipline of the arbitrators and a good grasp by them of the issues and associated evidence from an early stage in the proceedings.

The wording of Article 22.1(vi) serves to remind arbitrators and parties that they should not make assumptions about the manner in which evidence is presented. This is a matter which can be addressed at the first procedural hearing and/or in the first procedural directions issued by the Arbitral Tribunal.

**22–020**

At the same time, the wording could protect arbitrators who make decisions about the admissibility of evidence which might, for example, run counter to the practice in the local courts of the seat of the arbitration.

**22.1(vii) to order compliance with any legal obligation, payment of compensation for breach of any legal obligation and specific performance of any agreement (including any arbitration agreement or any contract relating to land);**

Article 22.1(vii) sets out basic remedies that may be ordered by the Arbitral Tribunal. In particular, it provides that the Arbitral Tribunal may order any party to comply with any legal obligation, to pay compensation for the breach of any such obligation, or order any party to specifically perform any agreement.

**22–021**

These provisions are new to the 2014 Rules. Whilst they may be regarded as no more than a statement of the obvious, and contain default remedies provided for in s.48 of the English Arbitration Act 1996, they are a useful confirmation of the Arbitral Tribunal's powers, particularly in relation to non-monetary relief.[13]

---

[12] "The View from an International Arbitration Customer: In Dire Need of Early Resolution" by Michael McIlwrath and Roland Schroeder (2008) 74(1) *Arbitration*.

[13] For a discussion of such relief in international arbitration, see Michael E. Schneider and Joachim Knoll (eds), *Performance as a Remedy: Non-Monetary Relief in International Arbitration* (ASA special series No.30) (Huntington, NY: Juris Publishing, 2011). Chapter 11 contains a report on a number of LCIA cases in which non-monetary relief has been granted, whether on an interim or final basis.

**22–022**  The obligation ordered to be performed can include an obligation to participate in an arbitration and not to pursue court proceedings. Arbitral Tribunals in LCIA arbitrations have been known to order parties to comply with Arbitration Agreements in this way. Of course, such anti suit injunctions do not have the force of injunctions issued by a state court, to which penal sanctions can be attached.

The inclusion of contracts relating to land overcomes an exception in s.48(5)(b) of the English Arbitration Act 1996 and may be of assistance in cases involving other national laws, where there might be doubt about an Arbitral Tribunal's power to make decisions relating to real property.

> **22.1(viii)** to allow one or more third persons to be joined in the arbitration as a party provided any such third person and the applicant party have consented to such joinder in writing following the Commencement Date or (if earlier) in the Arbitration Agreement; and thereafter to make a single final award, or separate awards, in respect of all parties so implicated in the arbitration;

**22–023**  This power (previously contained in Article 22.1(h) of the 1998 Rules) represents an early innovation of the LCIA Rules, aimed at the problems that may arise where multiple parties are interested in the outcome of a dispute. For example, this may occur in cases involving a chain of contracts (common in the shipping and commodities sectors), or multi-party contracts, or multi-contract engineering or construction projects.

### Scheme of LCIA Article 22.1(viii)

**22–024**  Article 22.1(viii) of the LCIA Rules provides that the Arbitral Tribunal has the power to join one or more third parties to the arbitration proceedings where:

- one or more parties apply for a joinder;[14]

- the third party or parties (and the applicant) have consented in writing to be joined; and

- the remaining parties have been given a reasonable opportunity to state their views.

**22–025**  Once any third party has been joined, it is a party to the arbitration proceedings. Subject to the scope of the Arbitration Agreement, it may bring claims in its own name against any other party and be the subject of counterclaims by any party. The Arbitral Tribunal can make a single award disposing of all claims in the proceedings, or separate awards for those brought by or against the joined party/ies.

---

[14] Under Article 22.1 the Arbitral Tribunal may not exercise its powers under Articles 22.1(viii)–22.1(x) of its own volition.

The purpose of Article 22.1(viii) is plainly to prevent the potential for wasted time and expense, and the risk of contradictory awards, that necessarily arises when separate arbitration or other proceedings are required to resolve disputes involving related parties, related business relationships and related questions of fact and law.

## Potential drawbacks to joinder under the LCIA Rules

Against the potential benefit of joinder under Article 22.1(viii), five principal reasons have been cited as to why joinder is undesirable:[15]   **22–026**

- the joined party is unable to nominate or participate in the selection of an arbitrator;

- the confidentiality of the parties' arbitration will be breached, or at least diminished;

- there is a risk of increased costs disproportionately falling on one party;

- the arbitration may be delayed as a consequence; and

- joinder without the consent of all parties is contrary to the principle of party autonomy.[16]

## Forced joinder?

Article 22.1(viii) allows what has been referred to as "forced joinder"[17] (i.e. the joinder of a party or parties without the consent of all of the parties at the time of joinder). However, parties who agree to LCIA arbitration without making a caveat in this regard consent in advance to the possibility of the Arbitral Tribunal exercising Article 22.1(viii) powers both for and against it. As Lew, Mistelis and Kröll have stated: the consequence of agreeing to the LCIA Rules is that "none of the parties can object when a third party wants to join with the consent of another party."[18] Nevertheless, the label "forced joinder" was adopted in the Singapore Court of Appeal case of *PT First Media TBK v Astro Nusantara International BV*,[19] as an "apt"[20] term to describe consolidation under the LCIA Rules and Swiss Rules.   **22–027**

---

[15] For example, see Gary B. Born, *International Arbitration: Law and Practice* (Kluwer Law International 2012), Ch.12 "Multiparty and Multicontract Issues in International Arbitration", para.12.01.

[16] See, for example, the UNCITRAL Report of the Working Group on Arbitration and Conciliation on the Work of its Forty-Sixth Session (A/CN.9/619, February 5–9, 2007 at paras 121–126), noting that a proposal to allow for joinder of non-parties to the arbitration agreement had been considered but rejected as being contrary to fundamental principles of consent of parties in arbitration.

[17] Gary B. Born, *International Commercial Arbitration* (2014), Ch.18 "Consolidation, Joinder and Intervention in International Arbitration", para.18.02[C][4].

[18] Julian D.M. Lew et al., *Comparative International Commercial Arbitration* (Kluwer Law International, 2003), para.16–42.

[19] [2013] SCGA 57.

[20] [2013] SCGA 57 at [176].

*An indeterminate class of potential disputants?*

22–028   Article 22.1(viii) places no restrictions on the class of persons who may be joined to the arbitrations, as long as both the applicant and proposed joiner have consented to the joinder in writing. There is no requirement that the joined party should be a party to the Arbitration Agreement under which the arbitration was commenced (although if they are not it may limit the claims that can be made by or against such party in the arbitration).

In *PT First Media TBK v Astro Nusantara International BV*,[21] the Singapore Court of Appeal considered this issue in detail, by reference to Article 24.1(b) of the 2007 SIAC Rules. The Tribunal in that case had ordered the joinder of third parties which were not parties to the original arbitration agreement. The Court of Appeal accepted the challenge to the award holding that Article 24.1(b), which permitted the joinder of "other parties", only permitted the joinder of other parties to the arbitration agreement. The Court of Appeal contrasted Article 24.1(b) of the 2007 SIAC Rules with Article 22.1(h) of the 1998 LCIA Rules,[22] concluding that:

> "... if indeed r 24.1(b) was intended to vest tribunals with such a broad power to join non-parties, we think it scarcely credulous that the language used to convey this should be so unclear. The use of a differentiating term like 'third person', *as with the 1998 LCIA Rules* and the Swiss Rules, would have been a straightforward solution".[23] [Emphasis added.]

22–029   In practice, the requirements of post-commencement of proceedings consent of one of the parties to the arbitration and of the Arbitral Tribunal itself, as well as the checks on the exercise of the Arbitral Tribunal's jurisdiction, will in the vast majority of cases offer sufficient safeguards against the potential for joinder of parties with no appropriate connection with the disputes or business transaction from which the dispute before the Arbitral Tribunal arose.

*Expressions of contrary intent*

22–030   The powers conferred under the 1998 edition of Article 22.1 of the LCIA Rules, including 22.1(h), were expressly stated to apply unless the parties agreed otherwise. This proviso has been removed from the 2014 edition of Article 22.1, but the power of the Arbitral Tribunal to join third parties could still be excluded by the parties if they agreed to do so.

*Exercise of the Arbitral Tribunal's discretion to join third parties*

22–031   Where the power of the Arbitral Tribunal to order joinder is established, the question that remains is in what circumstances the Arbitral Tribunal should exercise its discretion to do so.

---

[21] [2013] SCGA 57.
[22] Which is on near identical terms to Article 22.1(viii) of the 2014 LCIA Rules.
[23] *PT First Media TBK v Astro Nusantara International* at [180]. The Court of Appeal used the expression "forced joinder" to describe the joinder of a third party where one of the original parties to the arbitration did not consent to that joinder.

The LCIA Rules offer no guidance on this, nor do the UCNITRAL Model Law or the English Arbitration Act 1996. It is for the Arbitral Tribunal to exercise its discretion in light of the circumstances of the case. For example, joinder may be ordered where to do so would serve the policy objectives of overall savings of time and cost and/or avoiding the risk of conflicting decisions by different Arbitral Tribunals considering the same issues. These objectives are most likely to be fulfilled in cases involving the same or related questions of fact and evidence, the same or related business relationships, contracts or transactions, the same or related questions of law and where all of the disputes fall within the jurisdiction of the Arbitral Tribunal in the particular reference.

An Arbitral Tribunal should not order joinder where that is likely to cause unreasonable delay or unjustified cost to an objecting party.[24] Whilst any adverse impact of a joinder could in theory be corrected by an appropriate award of costs or interest, the later in the process the application is made the more likely it is to cause unjustified disruption and accordingly the less likely (absent good reason) it should be to succeed. Clearly an application for joinder which the Arbitral Tribunal perceives as being designed to delay or disrupt the arbitral proceedings should be rejected.   22–032

### Article 22.1(ix)–(x) and 22.6

#### *Consolidation—Introductory comment*

Articles 22.1(ix), 22.1(x) and 22.6 of the LCIA Rules empower the Arbitral Tribunal and LCIA Court to consolidate separately commenced arbitrations into a single arbitration proceeding. As the powers conferred by these sub-articles to a large extent overlap or complement each other, they are considered together with Article 22.6 *(the latter being reviewed out of sequence).*   22–033

It should be noted at the outset that Article 22.1 does not deal with concurrent proceedings. Under s.35 of the English Arbitration Act 1996, the parties may agree to confer on the Arbitral Tribunal the power to order concurrent hearings. Whilst the parties' agreement in relation to consolidation of proceedings is set out in Article 22.1, a separate agreement would be needed from them if their preference was to keep two or more arbitrations separate (with separate final awards on conclusion) but to save time and costs by having them run in parallel with a single hearing at which the evidence in all of them would be heard and tested. This may be what the parties actually want in a particular case, but their representatives will sometimes confuse concurrent proceedings with consolidation.

As noted in the introduction to the commentary on Article 22, the powers of national courts to consolidate proceedings in circumstances where to do so would save time or cost, or otherwise further the interests of justice, or the administration of justice, is a common feature of many legal systems. Further, it must be accepted that the judicious consolidation of two or more sets of proceedings involving the same legal and factual issues and the same commercial relationship will often   22–034

---

[24] Gary B. Born, *International Commercial Arbitration* (2014), Ch.18 "Consolidation, Joinder and Intervention in International Arbitration", p.2594.

serve the ends of justice by avoiding duplication of time and cost, as well as eliminating the risk of inconsistent decisions.

Until recently, many commentators and practitioners were opposed to the possibility of consolidating international arbitration proceedings, on the grounds that such consolidation was contrary to the principles of privacy, confidentiality and party autonomy, and could give rise to a number of practical difficulties.[25] Thus in England the Departmental Advisory Committee Report on the Arbitration Bill 1996 took the view that it would negate the principle of party autonomy to give the Tribunal or the court power to order consolidation, and would frustrate the agreement of the parties to have their own Tribunal for their own disputes.[26] Section 35 of the English Arbitration Act 1996 therefore only provides that parties are free to agree that arbitral proceedings may be consolidated and that they can confer such power on the Tribunal. Nor was a provision allowing for consolidation included in the 2010 UNCITRAL Arbitration Rules, following concerns over its workability.[27] Nevertheless, the attitudes in the international arbitration community towards consolidation of closely related arbitration proceedings are shifting. Since 2010 a number of leading international arbitration rules have allowed for consolidation of arbitral proceedings, including the SCC,[28] ICC,[29] HKIAC,[30] Swiss Rules[31] and the IDRC.[32] Of those institutional rules adopting consolidation provisions, the LCIA Rules are amongst the most restrictive, only allowing for consolidation without the express agreement of the disputing parties in limited circumstances.

*Exercising the power to consolidate proceedings*

22–035　Whilst each of Articles 22.1(ix), 22.1(x) and 22.6 sets out the specific circumstances in which the powers conferred by them to order consolidation of

---

[25] See the discussion in Gary B. Born, *International Commercial Arbitration* (2014), Ch.18 "Consolidation, Joinder and Intervention in International Arbitration", pp.2564–2613.

[26] See paras 180–182, Appendix 8.

[27] Report of the Working Group on Arbitration and Conciliation on the Work of its Forty-Sixth Session (A/CN.9/619, 5-9) February 2007 at paras 116–120.

[28] Article 11 of the 2010 SCC Rules allows the Board of the SCC to consolidate new claims with existing proceedings where the new claims concern the same parties and the same legal relationship, provided that the Tribunal must first be consulted.

[29] Article 10 of the 2012 ICC Rules permits consolidation by the ICC Court where the parties expressly agree; where all of the claims in the arbitrations are made under the same arbitration agreement; or where the claims in the arbitrations are made under different arbitration agreements, the arbitrations are between the same parties, the disputes in the arbitrations arise in connection with the same legal relationship, and the ICC Court finds the arbitration agreements to be compatible.

[30] Article 28 of the 2013 HKIAC Rules permits consolidation of arbitral proceedings, where the parties agree, where all the claims are made under the same arbitration agreement, or where the claims in both arbitrations involve more than one arbitration agreement, involve the same question of law or fact, and arise out of the same transactions or series of transactions, and the arbitration agreements are compatible.

[31] Article 4.1 of the Swiss Rules permits consolidation if new claims are brought involving the same parties, as well as when a new Notice of Arbitration is submitted between parties that are not identical to the parties in the pending arbitral proceedings.

[32] Article 8 of the 2014 IDRC Rules provides that for consolidation where the parties have expressly agreed, where all of the claims and counterclaims in the arbitrations are made under the same arbitration agreement; or where the claims are made under more than one arbitration agreement and the arbitrations involve the same parties, the same legal relationship and the arbitration agreements are compatible.

arbitration proceedings may be exercised, they provide no guidance as to the circumstances in which the power should be exercised.

Similarly to the power to order joinder pursuant to Article 22.1(viii) of the LCIA Rules, the policy objective of the power to effect consolidation is undoubtedly to prevent or avoid the possibility of wasted time and expense as well as the risk of conflicting decisions by different Arbitral Tribunals in relation to closely related factual and/or legal disputes. Any exercise of the power to consolidate arbitrations should therefore be chiefly concerned with the attainment of those policy objectives.

Some of the other institutional arbitration rules, particularly the 2014 edition of the IDRC Rules, provide some guidance as to the factors which might be taken into account in deciding whether separate arbitration proceedings should be consolidated, including the following:  22–036

- the views of the parties;[33]
- all relevant background circumstances;[34]
- whether one or more arbitrator is appointed/confirmed in more than one of the arbitrations;[35]
- the links between the cases and the progress already made in the pending arbitral proceedings;[36]
- the applicable law;[37]
- the progress made in any of the arbitrations;[38]
- whether the arbitrations raise common issues of law and fact; and[39]
- whether "the consolidation of the arbitrations would serve the interests of justice and efficiency".[40]

Regard should also be had to:  22–037

- the compatibility of the jurisdiction, or putative jurisdiction, of the Arbitral Tribunal in each arbitration; and
- the negative impact consolidation may have on any particular party, compared with the overall advantages that would be secured, and whether any disproportionate adverse impact on a party might be mitigated by the imposition by the Arbitral Tribunal of terms in relation to costs or otherwise, pursuant to Article 22.1, or by making a provisional order of any relief pursuant to Article 25.1(iii) of the LCIA Rules.

---

[33] Swiss Rules, SCC Rules.
[34] ICC Rules, IDRC Rules, HKIAC Rules and Swiss Rules.
[35] ICC Rules, IDRC Rules, HKIAC Rules and Swiss Rules.
[36] Swiss Rules.
[37] IDRC Rules.
[38] IDRC Rules.
[39] IDRC Rules.
[40] IDRC Rules.

## Mechanics

**22-038** The LCIA Rules are also silent as to the mechanics of consolidation and contain no suggestion regarding the procedural consequences of consolidation (such as the need to repeat any part of the arbitration, the validity and effect of any prior procedural orders and the directions that might be needed from the Arbitral Tribunal).

The power in Articles 22.1(ix) and (x) vests in the Arbitral Tribunal (after its appointment), so that no issues arise in relation to the nomination of arbitrators to the Arbitral Tribunal in those cases. The LCIA Court's power in Article 22.6 to consolidate arbitrations pre-appointment is exercisable only in relation to the same arbitration agreement between the same disputing parties, so that no issues should arise in relation to the nominations of arbitrators in those cases either.

### 22.1(ix) to order, with the approval of the LCIA Court, the consolidation of the arbitration with one or more other arbitrations into a single arbitration subject to the LCIA Rules where all the parties to the arbitrations to be consolidated so agree in writing;

**22-039** Article 22.1(ix) provides that the Arbitral Tribunal shall have the power to consolidate its arbitration with other arbitration proceedings into a single arbitral reference conducted under the LCIA Rules where:

(a) a party applies for consolidation;[41]

(b) all of the parties to the arbitrations to be consolidated have agreed to the consolidation in writing; and

(c) the LCIA Court approves the consolidation order.

**22-040** The requirement for an agreement in writing to the consolidation by all of the parties in the arbitrations to be consolidated suggests that something more is required than the agreement to refer disputes for resolution under the LCIA Rules. The Article does not go as far as stating that the agreement to the proposed consolidation must be secured following the commencement of the relevant arbitration proceedings, and there is no particular policy reason why such a requirement should be imposed. Indeed, Article 22.1(ix) would serve very little purpose if all it did was to confirm that parties to existing separate arbitral references may agree to the consolidation of the separate proceedings.

Nor is there a requirement in this Sub-Article that all of the arbitrations should have been commenced under the LCIA Rules or under the same Arbitration Agreement. Such requirements are clearly unnecessary where all of the parties expressly consent to consolidation into one arbitration under the LCIA Rules.

---

[41] Under Article 22.1, the Arbitral Tribunal may not exercise its powers under Articles 22.1(viii)–22.1(x) of its own volition.

Where the power to consolidate separate arbitration proceedings under Article 22.1(ix) is established, it is submitted that the Arbitral Tribunal and LCIA Court should have regard to the matters set out at 22–036—22–037.

**22.1(x) to order, with the approval of the LCIA Court, the consolidation of the arbitration with one or more other arbitrations subject to the LCIA Rules commenced under the same arbitration agreement or any compatible arbitration agreement(s) between the same disputing parties, provided that no arbitral tribunal has yet been formed by the LCIA Court for such other arbitration(s) or, if already formed, that such tribunal(s) is(are) composed of the same arbitrators; and**

Under Article 22.1(x), the Arbitral Tribunal may consolidate proceedings without any separate written consent from the parties where:

(a) a party applies for consolidation;[42]

(b) all of the arbitration proceedings are subject to the LCIA Rules;

(c) all of the arbitrations are commenced under:

   (i) the same Arbitration Agreement; or

   (ii) compatible Arbitration Agreements;

(d) all arbitrations involve the same disputing parties;

(e) the Arbitral Tribunal to which the application is made is the only Arbitral Tribunal that has been formed, or if other Arbitral Tribunals are formed then they are all comprised of the same arbitrators; and

(f) the LCIA Court approves the consolidation order.

**22-041**

Notwithstanding the absence of a requirement for prior consent (beyond consent to the LCIA Rules generally), the circumstances contemplated by Article 22.1(x) are narrow and hardly controversial. In particular, the restriction of consolidation to arbitrations involving the same disputing parties will avoid the concerns over loss of the confidentiality and privacy of the proceedings which might arise in the context of joinder under Article 22.1(viii).

**22-042**

The possibility of consolidating arbitrations with "compatible arbitration agreements" will not extend the scope of consolidation significantly. Any consolidation would still be limited to proceedings involving the same parties and only where the arbitrations are all under the LCIA Rules. Where the arbitrations to be consolidated were not commenced under the same Arbitration Agreement, the Arbitration Agreements must all be "compatible". Thus the consolidation of arbitration proceedings commenced under Arbitration Agreements providing for different

---

[42] Under Article 22.1, the Arbitral Tribunal may not exercise its powers under Articles 22.1(viii)–22.1(x) of its own volition.

"seats" or a different number of arbitrators should likely not be permitted. Arbitration Agreements often contain other bespoke provisions which could serve to render them incompatible with other Arbitration Agreements between the same parties.

Where the power to consolidate separate arbitration proceedings under Article 22.1(x) is established, the Arbitral Tribunal and LCIA Court will still have to exercise discretion, having regard to such matters as those discussed at 22–035—22–037 above.

> **22.6 Without prejudice to the generality of Articles 22.1(ix) and (x), the LCIA Court may determine, after giving the parties a reasonable opportunity to state their views, that two or more arbitrations, subject to the LCIA Rules and commenced under the same arbitration agreement between the same disputing parties, shall be consolidated to form one single arbitration subject to the LCIA Rules, provided that no arbitral tribunal has yet been formed by the LCIA Court for any of the arbitrations to be consolidated.**

22–043 Article 22.6 provides for the consolidation of two or more arbitration proceedings subject to the LCIA Rules directly by the LCIA Court whether or not the parties have given their express written consent, where:

- the arbitrations are commenced under the same Arbitration Agreement;
- the arbitrations are between the same disputing parties; and
- no Arbitral Tribunal has yet been appointed by the LCIA Court in any of the arbitrations to be consolidated.

22–044 Article 22.6 does not state whether the LCIA Court can exercise its power to effect the consolidation of arbitrations on its own volition. In practice, the situation in which the power might be exercised could arise where the Registrar has noted connections and similarities in two arbitrations filed one after another, perhaps by each of two parties in turn. The Registrar might then invite the parties to advise whether they would like a consolidation. Such an invitation could give rise to a request by one or both parties that the LCIA Court determine that the arbitrations be consolidated. It is hard to conceive of a situation in which the LCIA Court would proceed with a consolidation in the face of opposition from both parties.

Substantively, the power afforded to the LCIA Court under Article 22.6 adds little to the powers afforded to Arbitral Tribunals under Articles 22.1(ix) and 22.1(x). Article 22.6 does not set out the consequences of consolidation in relation to the designation of the parties as Claimants or Respondents. Common sense suggests that in simple cases the party or parties commencing proceedings first will be designated as Claimant, but this will be a matter upon which the LCIA Court will have to exercise its discretion in light of the circumstances of the dispute, if the parties do not agree.

The consolidation and the background facts and events will be recorded in the Form of Appointment recording the LCIA Court's appointment of the single Arbitral Tribunal, which will be attached to the Notice of Appointment sent to the parties.

**22.1(xi) to order the discontinuance of the arbitration if it appears to the Arbitral Tribunal that the arbitration has been abandoned by the parties or all claims and any cross-claims withdrawn by the parties, provided that, after fixing a reasonable period of time within which the parties shall be invited to agree or to object to such discontinuance, no party has stated its written objection to the Arbitral Tribunal to such discontinuance upon the expiry of such period of time.**

Article 22.1(xi) allows an Arbitral Tribunal to discontinue an arbitration where the withdrawal of all claims and cross-claims, or the simple lack of activity, indicates that the parties have lost interest in or have abandoned the proceedings. Where it appears to the Arbitral Tribunal that this is the case it must invite the parties to agree to or object to the discontinuance within a reasonable time. If no party objects within the given period, then the Arbitral Tribunal may discontinue the arbitration proceedings.

22–045

The power to discontinue proceedings may be exercised upon the application of any party or by the Arbitral Tribunal on its own volition.

If deposited funds remain on account with the LCIA, it may be appropriate for the Arbitral Tribunal to make a final award recording the LCIA Court's determination of the Arbitration Costs[43] before those are paid and any balance is distributed to the parties. On the other hand, if there is a shortfall, the parties will remain jointly and severally liable for it. The Arbitral Tribunal's order under Article 22.1(xi) will constitute confirmation that the arbitration is "concluded" for the purposes of Article 28.6 of the Rules.

**22.2 By agreeing to arbitration under the Arbitration Agreement, the parties shall be treated as having agreed not to apply to any state court or other legal authority for any order available from the Arbitral Tribunal (if formed) under Article 22.1, except with the agreement in writing of all parties.**

Article 22.2 provides that once the Arbitral Tribunal is constituted, the parties to LCIA arbitration may only apply to a national court for relief available from the Arbitral Tribunal with the written agreement of all parties.

22–046

This is in line with Article 9.12 of the LCIA Rules, which protects the parties' right to apply to state courts for interim relief prior to the constitution of the Arbitral Tribunal as well as with s.44(4) of the English Arbitration Act 1996, which allows parties to apply for assistance from the courts in non-urgent matters only with the permission of the Arbitral Tribunal or with the agreement of all parties.

---

[43] Pursuant to Articles 28.2 and 28.7.

**22.3 The Arbitral Tribunal shall decide the parties' dispute in accordance with the law(s) or rules of law chosen by the parties as applicable to the merits of their dispute. If and to the extent that the Arbitral Tribunal decides that the parties have made no such choice, the Arbitral Tribunal shall apply the law(s) or rules of law which it considers appropriate.**

22–047  Article 22.3 provides that the Arbitral Tribunal shall decide the dispute referred to it by the parties in accordance with the substantive law chosen by the parties as applicable to the merits of the dispute. The law governing the merits of the dispute may or may not be the same as the law of the seat of the arbitration and/or the law applicable to the Arbitration Agreement entered into by the parties.

Much has been written about the choice of law in international arbitration, of which the relevant chapters in Lew, Mistelis and Kröll[44] and Born[45] are two of a number of leading examples. According to Lew, Mistelis and Kröll:

> "The determination of the applicable substantive law is a critical issue in international arbitration. It has a legal, practical and psychological influence on every arbitration. Nothing is more important in any international arbitration than knowing the legal or other standards to apply to measure the rights and obligations of the parties. This is an independent exercise in the dispute resolution process for resolving the dispute itself."[46]

*Express choice of law*

22–048  In most cases involving commercial transactions, the parties will have recorded this choice of substantive law in the contract or agreement giving rise to the dispute. Even if the parties' contract does not contain a choice of law provision, it is still open to the parties to agree on the applicable law in the course of the arbitral proceedings, for example, in an exchange of correspondence between the parties, in the Request and Response or in the written statements or other submissions.

In any case in which the parties have made an express choice of applicable law, Article 22.3 requires the Arbitral Tribunal to apply that choice to the determination of the parties' dispute.

*No express choice of law*

22–049  In more cases than might be expected, commercial contracts contain no express choice of law. In other cases the dispute or claims do not involve an alleged breach of a contractual term, which might render a contractual choice of law inapplicable.

Where there is no agreement between the parties as to the choice of law, the LCIA Rules require the Arbitral Tribunal to decide which substantive law governs

---

[44] Julian D.M. Lew et al., *Comparative International Commercial Arbitration* (2003).
[45] Gary B. Born, *International Commercial Arbitration* (2014).
[46] Julian D.M. Lew et al., *Comparative International Commercial Arbitration* (2003), Ch.17 "Determination of Applicable Law", pp.411–437 at p.411.

the dispute between the parties. Under Article 22.3, the Arbitral Tribunal is not required to apply conflict of laws rules.[47] It can make a direct selection of the applicable substantive law it considers "appropriate" and apply that law to the determination of the dispute. According to Lew, Mistelis and Kröll:

"This rule recognise[s] what arbitrators do in practice. It may be considered a tailor-made choice of law process or conflict of laws rule, with a flexible connecting factor, specific for international arbitration. Arbitrators apply the substantive law or rules, or non-legal standard they consider appropriate in the particular circumstances of the case. What remains unclear, objectively, is the meaning of "appropriate" in these laws and rules."[48]

Born also reflects on the uncertainty inherent in the direct selection approach, **22–050** allowing Tribunals to select an "appropriate" substantive law without reference to conflict of law rules.[49] Nevertheless, this is the standard now applied in almost all of the important institutional arbitration rules.[50]

Whilst Arbitral Tribunals applying the second half of Article 22.3 of the LCIA Rules are not strictly required to provide detailed reasoning for their selection of a substantive law, in practice they will, in the majority of cases,[51] seek to ascertain the substantive law with the closest connection to the dispute(s) between the parties, having regard to any number of connecting factors and well-known principles of conflicts of laws, including some or all of the following:

- any applicable mandatory laws;
- the place of performance of the contract or disputed obligation(s);
- the nationality of the parties;
- the place of arbitration;
- any course of dealings between the parties;
- any trade or industry customs;

---

[47] In the past a number of institutional arbitration rules required the arbitrators to apply the conflict of laws rules they considered appropriate, although that approach might now be considered to be outmoded. However, Article 33 of the Swiss Rules states that where the parties have not made a choice of substantive law the arbitrators must apply "the rules of law with which the dispute has the closest connection".
[48] Julian D.M. Lew et al., *Comparative International Commercial Arbitration* (2003), Ch.17 "Determination of Applicable Law", para.7–72, references omitted.
[49] Gary B. Born, *International Commercial Arbitration* (2014), Ch.19 "Choice of Substantive Law in International Arbitration", pp.2614–2778 at 2645–6.
[50] Including the ICC Rules, SCC Rules, ICDR International Rules, UNCITRAL Rules, SIAC Rules and others. A different approach appears to have been adopted in Article 33 of the Swiss Rules which provides that where the parties have not made a choice of substantive law the arbitrators must apply "the rules of law with which the dispute has the closest connection".
[51] Commentaries on international arbitration practice also suggest that granting arbitrators very wide discretion to apply the law they consider appropriate could permit an arbitral tribunal to apply non-national laws or rules, such as the principles of "*lex mercatoria*". Whilst there are a number of relatively well-publicised examples of the application of such principles, these occurrences are rare and do not merit detailed comment here.

**22.5 Subject to any order of the Arbitral Tribunal under Article 22.1(ii), the LCIA Court may also abridge or extend any period of time under the Arbitration Agreement or other agreement of the parties (even where the period of time has expired).**

Article 22.5 provides that, subject to any order of the Arbitral Tribunal, the LCIA Court may also extend or shorten any time period agreed by the parties in the Arbitration Agreement or that is provided for in the LCIA Rules.

22–053

The power of the LCIA Court is subject to any order by the Arbitral Tribunal. Accordingly the power of the LCIA Court should only be exercised in relation to matters over which the Arbitral Tribunal has no authority, or which arise prior to the constitution of the Arbitral Tribunal. Such matters therefore most likely include the time limits for the delivery of the Response,[56] any time limits agreed for the nomination of arbitrators,[57] and the urgent constitution of the Arbitral Tribunal, or appointment of a Replacement Arbitrator.[58]

**22.6**

Article 22.6 is discussed at 22–043—22–044 above with Articles 22.1(ix) and (x).

---

[56] Article 2.
[57] Article 7.
[58] Respectively, Articles 9A and 9C.

## Article 23—Jurisdiction and Authority

23.1 The Arbitral Tribunal shall have the power to rule upon its own jurisdiction and authority, including any objection to the initial or continuing existence, validity, effectiveness or scope of the Arbitration Agreement.

23.2 For that purpose, an arbitration clause which forms or was intended to form part of another agreement shall be treated as an arbitration agreement independent of that other agreement. A decision by the Arbitral Tribunal that such other agreement is non-existent, invalid or ineffective shall not entail (of itself) the non-existence, invalidity or ineffectiveness of the arbitration clause.

23.3 An objection by a Respondent that the Arbitral Tribunal does not have jurisdiction shall be raised as soon as possible but not later than the time for its Statement of Defence; and a like objection by any party responding to a cross-claiming party shall be raised as soon as possible but not later than the time for its Statement of Defence to Cross-claim. An objection that the Arbitral Tribunal is exceeding the scope of its authority shall be raised promptly after the Arbitral Tribunal has indicated its intention to act upon the matter alleged to lie beyond its authority. The Arbitral Tribunal may nevertheless admit an untimely objection as to its jurisdiction or authority if it considers the delay justified in the circumstances.

23.4 The Arbitral Tribunal may decide the objection to its jurisdiction or authority in an award as to jurisdiction or authority or later in an award on the merits, as it considers appropriate in the circumstances.

23.5 By agreeing to arbitration under the Arbitration Agreement, after the formation of the Arbitral Tribunal the parties shall be treated as having agreed not to apply to any state court or other legal authority for any relief regarding the Arbitral Tribunal's jurisdiction or authority, except (i) with the prior agreement in writing of all parties to the arbitration, or (ii) the prior authorisation of the Arbitral Tribunal, or (iii) following the latter's award on the objection to its jurisdiction or authority.

## Introduction

The notion that the Arbitral Tribunal itself should have the power to determine its own jurisdiction is widely accepted internationally. It is enshrined in Article 16 of the UNCITRAL Model Law[1] and was adopted into English law by s.30 of the English Arbitration Act 1996. The language used in the English statute ("competence of tribunal to rule on its own jurisdiction") reflects the French *compétence-compétence* and German *Kompetenz-Kompetenz*.

Article 23 of the Rules confirms that decisions on jurisdiction are matters for the Arbitral Tribunal, not for the LCIA Secretariat or LCIA Court and not, in the first instance at least, for state courts. It sets out the scope of the issues which may fall to be ruled upon by the Arbitral Tribunal in exercising this power. In line with the wording of the UNCITRAL Model Law, Article 23 refers expressly to "authority" as well as jurisdiction.[2] It thus confirms that the power extends to decisions about whether the Arbitral Tribunal is entitled to award particular reliefs or remedies.

Allied to the principle that an Arbitral Tribunal should be competent to rule on its own jurisdiction is the doctrine of the separability of the Arbitration Agreement. The doctrine is likewise enshrined in Article 16 of the UNCITRAL Model Law: "... an arbitration clause which forms part of a contract shall be treated as an agreement independent of the other terms of the contract."[3] This doctrine permits an Arbitral Tribunal to rule on its own jurisdiction even if, in so doing, it should decide that the contract, in which the Arbitration Agreement is contained, is invalid or unenforceable.

The Arbitral Tribunal's ruling, whether made at an interim stage or in a final award, and however it might be characterised, may not be the end of the matter. Article 23.5 confirms that the Arbitral Tribunal's jurisdiction may ultimately be decided by state courts. However, it also sets out the conditions which must be fulfilled before an application may be made to the courts.

A review of an arbitral award containing a decision on jurisdiction may also occur when the award comes to be enforced. Under Article V(1)(a) of the New York Convention 1958, a court may refuse enforcement if it determines that the arbitration agreement is not valid.

In *Dallah Real Estate and Tourism Holding Co v The Ministry of Religious Affairs, Government of Pakistan*,[4] the UK Supreme Court considered an award made by an ICC Tribunal sitting in Paris and held that "there was no material sufficient to justify the tribunal's conclusion" that the Pakistan government was a party to the arbitration agreement. The Supreme Court noted that there was no basis to imply a concept of "deference" to the Tribunal's decision on jurisdiction into Article V of the New York Convention. The French courts, on the other hand, endorsed the Tribunal's decision. The different results have given rise to the criticism that the English Courts are less supportive of arbitration than the French

---

[1] UNCITRAL Model Law on International Commercial Arbitration 1985, as amended in 2006 (Appendix 10).
[2] See Article 16 of the UNCITRAL Model Law (Appendix 10). See also Article 23 of the 2010 UNCITRAL Arbitration Rules (Appendix 11).
[3] Article 23 of the 2010 UNCITRAL Arbitration Rules reproduces this wording (Appendix 11).
[4] [2010] UKSC 46.

Courts but commentators have also suggested that users can have confidence in a jurisdiction which takes its responsibilities under the New York Convention seriously.[5]

**23–004** Article 23 sets out when a challenge to the Arbitral Tribunal's jurisdiction or authority should be made and when the Arbitral Tribunal may make its decisions on such a challenge.

Before the Arbitral Tribunal is appointed, the LCIA Secretariat will have decided that the Arbitration Agreement is one under which it is at least conceivable that the LCIA could have jurisdiction. This is not in the nature of a prima facie review as conducted by the ICC Secretariat under the ICC Rules.[6] Rather, it is a question of checking the Arbitration Agreement cited by the Claimant in the Request for Arbitration and of drawing to the parties' attention, in the first instance, any defects or issues which could make it impossible for an Arbitral Tribunal to assume jurisdiction under the Rules.[7]

**23–005** Examples of cases which have been sifted out in this way are ones which provide for arbitration under the ICC Rules or which make no reference to any institution or any institutional rules.[8] Lawyers unfamiliar with arbitration are sometimes unaware that the LCIA is a different body from the ICC whilst lawyers unfamiliar with the long and continuing tradition of ad hoc commercial arbitration in London sometimes assume that a reference to arbitration in London must be a reference to the LCIA.

The LCIA occasionally acts as an appointing authority in ad hoc arbitrations and will also administer arbitrations under the UNCITRAL Rules if the parties so agree. Arbitration agreements providing for one or both of these services, but not for the LCIA Rules, are sometimes misunderstood by Claimants and even by lawyers acting for them. Requests for Arbitration are then filed when the proper first step might instead have been the appointment of an arbitrator and notice of that appointment to the opponent. Having considered the situation after it has been explained by the Secretariat, the parties will sometimes agree a variation to their arbitration agreement so that the arbitration may proceed under the LCIA Rules. It is the Secretariat's practice to quote the text of the Arbitration Agreement in its first letter to the parties and to draw their attention to any problems or questions which might arise in connection with it. If the Request for Arbitration has, for example, been filed in the name of a party which does not appear on the parties' agreement, the Registrar might ask for details of an assignment or change of name.

**23–006** If the Arbitration Agreement requires the parties to negotiate before the arbitration is commenced, this will be noted, and comments may be invited, but the Secretariat will not reject the Request, as it is sometimes invited to do by a Respondent, on the grounds that evidence of negotiation has not been forthcoming

---

[5] For example, Devika Khanna, "Dallah: The Supreme Court's Positively Pro-Arbitration 'No' to Enforcement" (2011) 28(2) J. Int. Arb. 127–135.
[6] Article 6(4) of the ICC Rules 2012. See also Calvin Chan, "Of Arbitral Institutions and Provisional Determinations on Jurisdiction, the Global Gold case" (2009) 25(3) Arb. Int. 403–426.
[7] For the definition of "Arbitration Agreement" under the Rules, and a discussion of the requirements, see the commentary on the Preamble above.
[8] On the other hand, a reference to the London Chamber of Commerce could be enough to bring the dispute within the LCIA's jurisdiction: see the commentary on the Preamble above.

or is unsatisfactory; this is a jurisdictional issue which should be submitted to the Arbitral Tribunal once appointed.[9]

If a pair or a group of contracts, made between the same parties and containing the same LCIA arbitration clause, has given rise to disputes under more than one of them, a Claimant will sometimes be tempted to file a single Request. The wording of the arbitration clause may be sufficiently wide to allow this[10] but the Secretariat will, in any event, note the point and may invite the parties to agree that a single Arbitral Tribunal be appointed.[11]

**23.1 The Arbitral Tribunal shall have the power to rule upon its own jurisdiction and authority, including any objection to the initial or continuing existence, validity, effectiveness or scope of the Arbitration Agreement.**

Article 23.1 contains the statement of the principle that the Arbitral Tribunal is competent, initially at least, to determine its own jurisdiction. As noted above, the wording now also includes the Arbitral Tribunal's "authority". 23–007

A wide range of objections can be considered under the provisions of Article 23, including objections as to the identities of the parties, the contract(s) in dispute, the subject matter of the dispute, and the relief that may be available.

Questions about the effect of an insolvency, and the appointment of a liquidator, can concern both the jurisdiction (e.g. whether state courts must take over the litigation) and the authority (e.g. whether proceedings must be stayed) of the Arbitral Tribunal. 23–008

A change to the 1998 Rules is the addition of "scope" in Article 23.1. The new wording confirms that the Arbitral Tribunal has the power to decide to what extent the Arbitration Agreement confers or limits jurisdiction in relation to particular kinds of disputes between the parties.

Since the House of Lords' decision in the *Fiona Trust* case,[12] the position under English law is that unless the Arbitration Agreement contains clear wording to the contrary, the assumption will be that the parties, as "rational businessmen", intended all of their disputes arising out of the same relationship to be submitted

---

[9] In *Emirates Trading Agency LLC v Prime Mineral Exports Private Ltd* [2014] EWHC 2104 (Comm), the English High Court held that a provision in a multi-tiered dispute resolution clause requiring the parties to hold settlement discussions in good faith for a time-limited period of four weeks prior to the commencement of arbitration was enforceable. Nevertheless, the question of whether any arbitration is properly commenced is a jurisdictional question for the arbitrators, not the LCIA Secretariat.

[10] Depending on the circumstances, such an approach might be appropriate as a matter of English law, under which the interpretation of "an arbitration clause should start from the assumption that the parties, as rational businessmen, are likely to have intended any dispute arising out of the relationship into which they have entered or purported to enter to be decided by the same tribunal [. . .] unless the language makes it clear that certain questions were intended to be excluded from the arbitrator's jurisdiction." See *Fiona Trust & Holding Corp v Yuri Privalov* [2007] UKHL 40 [13]. Again, this is a question for the Arbitral Tribunal, once appointed.

[11] An application under Articles 22.1 and 22.6 for consolidation might now be appropriate, see 22–033—22–044 above.

[12] *Fiona Trust & Holding Corp v Yuri Privalov* [2007] UKHL 40.

to the same Tribunal. In *Fiona Trust*, the issue was whether the arbitrator had jurisdiction to decide whether the contracts had been rescinded for bribery.

> **23.2 For that purpose, an arbitration clause which forms or was intended to form part of another agreement shall be treated as an arbitration agreement independent of that other agreement. A decision by the Arbitral Tribunal that such other agreement is non-existent, invalid or ineffective shall not entail (of itself) the non-existence, invalidity or ineffectiveness of the arbitration clause.**

23–009  As noted above, allied to the principle that a Tribunal should have the power to rule on its own jurisdiction is the doctrine of the separability of the arbitration agreement. This doctrine confers on the Arbitral Tribunal the jurisdiction to decide that the contract in which the arbitration agreement is contained is itself invalid. The doctrine is confirmed in Article 23.2 and also in the LCIA's Recommended Clause for future disputes.[13]

The language of Article 23.2 is similar to s.7 of the English Arbitration Act 1996, which is itself entitled "Separability of arbitration agreement".

23–010  An example of an English case in which the doctrine of separability was upheld is *Fiona Trust* mentioned above. The House of Lords decided that whilst the main contract (a series of charterparties) was voidable for bribery, the arbitration clause was not thereby invalidated. Lord Hoffmann explained the principle succinctly:

> "The arbitration agreement must be treated as a *"distinct agreement"* and can be void or voidable only on grounds which relate directly to the arbitration agreement. Of course there may be cases in which the ground upon which the main agreement is invalid is identical with the ground upon which the arbitration agreement is invalid. For example, if the main agreement and the arbitration agreement are contained in the same document and one of the parties claims that he never agreed to anything in the document and that his signature was forged, that will be an attack on the validity of the arbitration agreement. But the ground of attack is not that the main agreement was invalid. It is that the signature to the arbitration agreement, as a *"distinct agreement"*, was forged. Similarly, if a party alleges that someone who purported to sign as agent on his behalf had no authority whatever to conclude any agreement on his behalf, that is an attack on both the main agreement and the arbitration agreement."[14]

23–011  Lord Hoffmann held that whilst an agent acting for the owners might have been bribed to consent to the main agreement, that did not show that he had been bribed to enter into the arbitration agreement. He noted:

> "It would have been remarkable for him to enter into any charter without an arbitration agreement, whatever its other terms had been."[15]

---

[13] See the commentary on the Recommended Clauses in Part III and the discussion of separability there.
[14] [2007] UKHL 40 [17].
[15] [2007] UKHL 40 [19].

A party will not necessarily become a party to an arbitration clause by signing a contract and agreeing to be bound by a certain number of other obligations contained in it. This was the finding in another English case, *Arsanovia Ltd v Cruz City 1 Mauritius Holdings*,[16] a decision in relation to a series of three arbitrations under the LCIA Rules. The Arbitral Tribunal had held that the parties intended that the arbitration clause in a contract would apply to a particular party with respect to disputes arising out of or in connection with the limited substantive obligations which it had expressly assumed under that contract, even though the arbitration clause was not in the list of direct obligations set out on the signature page executed by that party's director.[17] The judge disagreed, finding that the wording of the signature page was not sufficient to make that particular party subject to the arbitration clause in the contract.

23-012

**23.3 An objection by a Respondent that the Arbitral Tribunal does not have jurisdiction shall be raised as soon as possible but not later than the time for its Statement of Defence; and a like objection by any party responding to a cross-claiming party shall be raised as soon as possible but not later than the time for its Statement of Defence to Cross-claim. An objection that the Arbitral Tribunal is exceeding the scope of its authority shall be raised promptly after the Arbitral Tribunal has indicated its intention to act upon the matter alleged to lie beyond its authority. The Arbitral Tribunal may nevertheless admit an untimely objection as to its jurisdiction or authority if it considers the delay justified in the circumstances.**

It is a well-established principle in litigation and arbitration worldwide that jurisdiction challenges should be raised at the outset of proceedings (*"in limine litis"*) or at the earliest opportunity if grounds become known later. This principle is clearly enunciated in article 16(2) of the UNCITRAL Model Law and in article 23.2 of the UNCITRAL Arbitration Rules, in language very similar to the language of Article 23.3 of the LCIA Rules.

23-013

Objections to an Arbitral Tribunal's jurisdiction would normally be raised in the Response. Article 2 in the new version of the Rules contains a requirement that the Response include "confirmation or denial" of the claims, "including the Claimant's invocation of the Arbitration Agreement in support of its claim".[18]

Arbitrators will generally receive copies of the Request and Response before their appointment and should, in any event, be informed of any known prospective jurisdiction challenges by the Secretariat when they are initially contacted. Pursuant to its powers under Article 14, the Arbitral Tribunal will determine (if the parties do not agree) how the jurisdiction challenge should be dealt with, whether by way of separate written submissions ("bifurcation") or simultaneously with other issues.

23-014

---

[16] [2012] EWHC 3702 (Comm) (Andrew Smith J).
[17] The wording signed by this party was: "The undersigned hereby executes this Agreement to be bound by the direct obligations imposed upon them, under Clauses…".
[18] Article 2.1(ii).

The difficulties of accommodating a jurisdiction challenge which is raised for the first time in the Statement of Defence are illustrated in the abstract of the decision of the Division of the LCIA Court on the challenge to a presiding arbitrator of an Arbitral Tribunal in LCIA Arbitration No. 5665.[19] In that case, the Claimants' lawyer complained to the Arbitral Tribunal that the Respondents had restricted their Statement of Defence to jurisdictional objections which were not sufficiently developed. They argued that they would suffer prejudice if the Respondents were to file submissions on the merits only in their final submissions, leaving them with no opportunity to respond. They asked for a new procedural timetable with jurisdiction to be dealt with as a preliminary issue. The Respondents disagreed with this proposal for bifurcation and it was subsequently abandoned after an agreement was reached on the joinder of additional parties.

23–015　The "longstop" provision for raising jurisdictional objections in the Statement of Defence serves two functions. First it recognises that valid jurisdictional defences can arise in cases in which a valid arbitration is invoked, but claims are nevertheless then made which fall outside of the scope of that Arbitration Agreement because they concern matters that are not related to that Arbitration Agreement or are outside the scope of the reference, for example because they relate to new disputes. Such challenges might only arise or become apparent after the Claimant has articulated its claims, or the Respondent its counterclaims in full. Second, it is designed to minimise disruption and to ensure, as far as possible and depending on the case, that if a jurisdiction challenge is successful, time and costs will not have been wasted.

As far as objections to its "authority" are concerned, an Arbitral Tribunal does not have such a "longstop". How much time is afforded by "promptly" will, no doubt, depend on the circumstances. It is suggested that some guidance might be found in Article 10, which gives a party 14 days from becoming aware of grounds for a challenge to an arbitrator to file a written statement of reasons with the LCIA Court.

23–016　In practice, an objection that an arbitrator has exceeded his authority will sometimes turn into a challenge to that arbitrator, which will be determined by the LCIA Court. For example, in LCIA Arbitration No. 3431, a Division of the LCIA Court considered and dismissed challenges, which included objections that the arbitrator had not acted fairly by allowing the arbitration to proceed without requisite funding being in place and also whilst the challenge was being decided.[20] Such objections should be raised first with the Arbitral Tribunal itself and will only be entertained by the LCIA Court as a challenge under Article 10 if they fall within the scope of Article 10.2(ii).

The final sentence of Article 23.3 confirms that an Arbitral Tribunal has a general discretion to entertain a late objection to its jurisdiction or authority. Article 22.1(ii) confirms the Arbitral Tribunal's general power to grant extensions of time. However, it is useful to have this confirmation here also, particularly since no specific periods of time are set out for the objections covered by Article 23, so that the applicability of Article 22.1(ii) might be brought into doubt.

---

[19] (2011) 27(3) Arbitration Int. 395–412, at p.397.
[20] (2011) 27(3) Arbitration Int. 358.

**23.4 The Arbitral Tribunal may decide the objection to its jurisdiction or authority in an award as to jurisdiction or authority or later in an award on the merits, as it considers appropriate in the circumstances.**

As noted above, it will be for the Arbitral Tribunal to decide (if the parties do not agree) whether the proceedings should be bifurcated to allow a jurisdictional challenge to be heard separately as a preliminary issue. 23–017

There will be cases in which the issue of jurisdiction, and the evidence relating to it, is so closely linked to the merits that it will not be worthwhile to have it dealt with separately. For example, an alleged failure to perform a contract might be linked to a denial that the contract, including its arbitration clause, is binding upon the parties or was ever concluded or entered into.

A decision on jurisdiction should always be made in an award, whether a partial award (confirming jurisdiction before an award on the merits is made) or a final award (determining that the Arbitral Tribunal does not have jurisdiction or that it does have jurisdiction and deciding the merits at the same time). 23–018

For reasons of speed, an Arbitral Tribunal might issue a "ruling" confirming its jurisdiction after an exchange of submissions and possibly a hearing devoted to the issue. If so, it should record that decision and its reasons in full in the final award after the merits hearing.

The way jurisdiction challenges are handled can give rise to issues in relation to deposits on account of the Arbitration Costs[21] under Article 24. Respondents might be reluctant to pay their share of the initial deposit, being concerned not to be seen to be taking any steps which might affirm the Arbitral Tribunal's jurisdiction or simply because they are confident of a finding that the Arbitral Tribunal does not have jurisdiction. Claimants might protest that the Respondents should pay for "their" challenge but the pragmatic response is to lodge the funds and then to seek a costs award in due course.

**23.5 By agreeing to arbitration under the Arbitration Agreement, after the formation of the Arbitral Tribunal the parties shall be treated as having agreed not to apply to any state court or other legal authority for any relief regarding the Arbitral Tribunal's jurisdiction or authority, except (i) with the prior agreement in writing of all parties to the arbitration, or (ii) the prior authorisation of the Arbitral Tribunal, or (iii) following the latter's award on the objection to its jurisdiction or authority.**

As noted in the introduction to the commentary on Article 23, an Arbitral Tribunal's decision on jurisdiction may be reviewed by state courts. Article 23.5 confirms that the Arbitral Tribunal should be given time to make its own determination first, unless the parties have agreed otherwise or unless it grants permission for an application direct to court. 23–019

---

[21] "Arbitration Costs" are defined in Article 28.1.

For an example of a decision of the English High Court upholding an LCIA Arbitral Tribunal's award on jurisdiction, see *Habas Sinai Ve Tibbi Gazlar Isthisal Endustri AS v Sometal SAL*[22] mentioned above in the context of the Preamble.

It is open to a party to issue a jurisdiction challenge in a state court after the filing of the Request for Arbitration but before the Arbitral Tribunal has been appointed. This is confirmed by the addition of the words "after the formation of the Arbitral Tribunal" in the 2014 version of Article 23.5 of the Rules.

---

[22] [2010] EWHC 29 (Comm).

## Article 24—Deposits

24.1 The LCIA Court may direct the parties, in such proportions and at such times as it thinks appropriate, to make one or more payments to the LCIA on account of the Arbitration Costs. Such payments deposited by the parties may be applied by the LCIA Court to pay any item of such Arbitration Costs (including the LCIA's own fees and expenses) in accordance with the LCIA Rules.

24.2 All payments made by parties on account of the Arbitration Costs shall be held by the LCIA in trust under English law in England, to be disbursed or otherwise applied by the LCIA in accordance with the LCIA Rules and invested having regard also to the interests of the LCIA. Each payment made by a party shall be credited by the LCIA with interest at the rate from time to time credited to an overnight deposit of that amount with the bank(s) engaged by the LCIA to manage deposits from time to time; and any surplus income (beyond such interest) shall accrue for the sole benefit of the LCIA. In the event that payments (with such interest) exceed the total amount of the Arbitration Costs at the conclusion of the arbitration, the excess amount shall be returned by the LCIA to the parties as the ultimate default beneficiaries of the trust.

24.3 Save for exceptional circumstances, the Arbitral Tribunal should not proceed with the arbitration without having ascertained from the Registrar that the LCIA is or will be in requisite funds as regards outstanding and future Arbitration Costs.

24.4 In the event that a party fails or refuses to make any payment on account of the Arbitration Costs as directed by the LCIA Court, the LCIA Court may direct the other party or parties to effect a substitute payment to allow the arbitration to proceed (subject to any order or award on Arbitration Costs).

24.5 In such circumstances, the party effecting the substitute payment may request the Arbitral Tribunal to make an order or award in order to recover that amount as a debt immediately due and payable to that party by the defaulting party, together with any interest.

24.6 Failure by a claiming or cross-claiming party to make promptly and in full any required payment on account of Arbitration Costs may be treated by the Arbitral Tribunal as a withdrawal from the arbitration of the claim or cross-claim respectively, thereby removing such claim or cross-claim (as the case may be) from the scope of the Arbitral

Tribunal's jurisdiction under the Arbitration Agreement, subject to any terms decided by the Arbitral Tribunal as to the reinstatement of the claim or cross-claim in the event of subsequent payment by the claiming or cross-claiming party. Such a withdrawal shall not preclude the claiming or cross-claiming party from defending as a respondent any claim or cross-claim made by another party.

**Introduction**

24–001   Article 24 empowers the LCIA Court to direct parties to make advance deposits with the LCIA in respect of costs which it is anticipated will be incurred on the parties' behalf. These deposits are separate from the £1,750 Registration Fee payable by the Claimant with the Request for Arbitration.

The deposits are held, on behalf of the parties, in separate accounts at the LCIA's bank. It should be noted that the LCIA is not itself liable to the arbitrators, experts or other providers but will discharge the parties' liabilities, on their behalf, from the funds held in these accounts, in accordance with the Rules, the Schedule of Arbitration Costs and directions made, as appropriate, by the Arbitral Tribunal and the LCIA Court.

24–002   In substantial cases, the deposits are often taken incrementally, as the arbitration progresses. This avoids the parties having to deposit a very substantial sum in respect of the anticipated total Arbitration Costs[1] at an early stage.

Interest is paid on deposits taken by the LCIA at the "overnight deposit" rate of the bank used by the LCIA to manage deposits.

24–003   If a party does not pay its share of a deposit then the other party or parties may need to make that payment instead in order to allow the arbitration to proceed. If so, then the paying party/parties may seek to recover the sums paid (and interest) from the defaulting party. If the defaulting party is claiming or cross-claiming in the arbitration, its failure to pay the deposit may be treated as a withdrawal of its claim/cross-claim (although it will still be able to defend claims or cross-claims made against it).

The subsequent determination and allocation of the costs covered by the deposits, together with the legal and other expenses incurred by the parties, are dealt with in Article 28. It should be noted that deposits cannot be included in a claim for costs. They remain the parties' own funds, albeit held in trust by the LCIA. Instead, the parties' costs submissions should address the allocation of the Arbitration Costs; it will be for the LCIA Secretariat to complete the accounting, calculating the effect of that allocation on the funds still held and on the parties' respective contributions.

24–004   Article 26.7 requires that "all Arbitration Costs have been paid in full to the LCIA in accordance with Articles 24 and 28" before the award is transmitted by the LCIA Court to the parties.[2] For an explanation as to how the Arbitral Tribunal and the LCIA Secretariat ensure that these requirements are met, see the commentary on Article 26.2 below.

---

[1] "Arbitration Costs" are defined in Article 28.1.
[2] See also s.56 of the English Arbitration Act 1996 (Appendix 7).

Any surplus funds held by the LCIA at the conclusion of the arbitration are returned to the parties.

**24.1 The LCIA Court may direct the parties, in such proportions and at such times as it thinks appropriate, to make one or more payments to the LCIA on account of the Arbitration Costs. Such payments deposited by the parties may be applied by the LCIA Court to pay any item of such Arbitration Costs (including the LCIA's own fees and expenses) in accordance with the LCIA Rules.**

In this context, the phrase "Arbitration Costs" means costs other than the legal or other expenses incurred (directly) by the parties themselves.[3] As it is anticipated that the LCIA will pay these costs on behalf of the parties, the deposits are necessary to ensure that the LCIA has the requisite funds. The "Arbitration Costs" include the fees and expenses of the Arbitral Tribunal, any expert appointed by the Arbitral Tribunal, the LCIA Secretariat and of the LCIA Court (if any). If other costs are incurred for the parties, such as the costs of hiring a hearing venue, the LCIA will also pay these out of the deposits paid by the parties.

The LCIA's charges and approach to the fees and expenses of the arbitrators are addressed in connection with Article 28.

The LCIA will normally seek an initial deposit, intended to cover the preliminary stage of the arbitration, once it has appointed the Arbitral Tribunal and has had an opportunity to consult it as to the appropriate amount. Depending on the size and complexity of the case, this initial deposit may be intended to cover all of the costs up to, but not including, the main hearing, or it may simply be a stage payment. The LCIA will then seek a further advance(s) as required as the arbitration progresses (for example, prior to a hearing when relatively substantial costs are generally incurred), thereby spreading the costs burden for the parties and more accurately tracking the costs to be incurred.[4]

The LCIA Secretariat is, of course, aware of the various stages of the arbitration, as it receives copies of the parties' correspondence with the Arbitral Tribunal (see Article 13.1) and seeks updates from the tribunals as to anticipated costs (and in practice the LCIA Court's powers under Article 24.1 are exercised by the Registrar subject to the LCIA Court's supervision.)[5]

24–005

24–006

24–007

---

[3] See the definition in Article 28.1. Article 24 of the 1998 LCIA Rules referred to "the costs of the arbitration", which was a little confusing given that parties would in common parlance also refer to the legal and other costs that they incur directly as "the costs of the arbitration" (Appendix 4). Some other minor, largely cosmetic changes have also been made to the previous Article 24, but its application in practice remains essentially the same.

[4] This procedure can be contrasted with the ICC approach, which is to take a provisional advance on costs from the Claimant(s) to cover the period up to the Terms of Reference, but then a full advance from the parties intended to cover all the remaining costs (although this can be adjusted later if the ICC considers it appropriate). The full advance for high value cases can be a very significant sum. Whilst the "ad valorem" basis provides the parties with a better indication at the outset of what the "Arbitration Costs" (in LCIA Rules parlance) will be, this is of limited value given that they are only part of the overall costs (with the costs of legal counsel usually being far greater) and are still subject to change. It is also to be hoped that the parties' legal advisers can provide any costs estimates that their clients might require in this regard.

[5] See s.5(i) of the LCIA's Schedule of Arbitration Costs (Appendix 2) and the commentary on the Schedule at the end of this Part.

The LCIA directs deposits from the parties "in such proportions and at such times as it thinks appropriate", but the Secretariat will always consult with the Arbitral Tribunal in this regard. In many arbitrations, the deposits are split between the Claimant(s) on the one side and the Respondent(s) on the other, in equal portions, but Article 24.1 allows the LCIA to seek alternative shares of deposits where it considers this more appropriate (for example, because there are three or more parties whose interests are not aligned, or where one party has only a limited role).[6] Article 24.1 (taken together with Article 24.4) also allows the LCIA to seek deposits from just one of the parties to the arbitration proceedings. Such directions are sometimes challenged by the affected party who will, for example, ask that the other party first be directed to pay a one half share, so that as soon as it fails to comply, it may then make the payment itself and apply for an award against it under Article 24.5. The Secretariat has been sympathetic to such requests for modifications of directions.

**24–008** The LCIA may submit interim invoices and seek payment direct from the parties or release the funds to itself, the arbitrators or experts as appropriate from the deposits held.[7] In practice, accounting will usually take place after awards have been issued, whether interim or final.

Any request by an arbitrator to the LCIA for an interim payment must be supported by a fee note and details of the time spent (to be charged at the agreed rates).[8] Invoices from the arbitrators and financial summaries of the payments and sums remaining on deposit are provided to the parties by the LCIA. The Secretariat scrutinises the arbitrators' fee notes and their breakdowns of time, before paying them. This is regarded as one of the LCIA's useful services. It allows the parties to control the arbitrators' costs without themselves raising queries, which might embarrass them.

It is worth noting that, in practice, "the Registrar has the authority of the LCIA Court to make the directions referred to, under the supervision of the Court",[9] both in relation to taking deposits and releasing the funds. However, any dispute regarding administration costs or the fees and expenses of the Arbitral Tribunal is to be determined by the LCIA Court.[10]

> **24.2 All payments made by parties on account of the Arbitration Costs shall be held by the LCIA in trust under English law in England, to be disbursed or otherwise applied by the LCIA in accordance with the LCIA Rules and invested having regard also to the interests of the LCIA. Each payment made by a party shall be credited by the LCIA with interest at the rate from time to time credited to an overnight deposit of that amount with the bank(s) engaged by the LCIA to**

---

[6] Under Article 36(2) of the 2012 ICC Rules, the full advance on costs is "payable in equal shares". Similarly, the parties normally pay in equal shares under the 2010 SIAC Rules "unless the Registrar directs otherwise" (Article 30.2). Article 43(1) of the 2010 UNCITRAL Rules also prescribes equal deposits from each party (Appendix 11).
[7] See s.4 of the LCIA's Schedule of Arbitration Costs (Appendix 2).
[8] See s.2(iv), 4 and 5(ii) of the LCIA's Schedule of Arbitration Costs (Appendix 2).
[9] See s.5(i) of the LCIA's Schedule of Arbitration Costs (Appendix 2).
[10] See s.5(iv) of the LCIA's Schedule of Arbitration Costs (Appendix 2).

manage deposits from time to time; and any surplus income (beyond such interest) shall accrue for the sole benefit of the LCIA. In the event that payments (with such interest) exceed the total amount of the Arbitration Costs at the conclusion of the arbitration, the excess amount shall be returned by the LCIA to the parties as the ultimate default beneficiaries of the trust.

This new provision, which reflects and confirms the long-term practice of the LCIA, clarifies the legal status of the deposits paid to the LCIA (they are held under an English law trust) and explains how interest will be earned and applied. Whilst some institutions retain any interest earned on deposits, Article 24.2 confirms that the LCIA credits the parties with interest at the "overnight deposit" rate payable by the bank(s) engaged to deal with those deposits. If the LCIA obtains a more favourable rate of return on the deposits than the "overnight deposit" rate it will take the benefit of the "surplus income". The interest paid to the parties is added to the deposits and will be applied against the Arbitration Costs, with any excess at the conclusion of the proceedings being returned to the parties. 24–009

24.3 Save for exceptional circumstances, the Arbitral Tribunal should not proceed with the arbitration without having ascertained from the Registrar that the LCIA is or will be in requisite funds as regards outstanding and future Arbitration Costs.

This provision passes some of the burden of ensuring that the arbitration is properly funded from the LCIA to the Arbitral Tribunal. The saving for "exceptional circumstances" (and ability to proceed when the LCIA is not, but "will be", in requisite funds) did not appear in the 1998 LCIA Rules, although in practice, particularly during periods of intense activity (such as hearings), the Arbitration Costs incurred can sometimes exceed for a period the sums held on deposit. In such circumstances, a further deposit will be directed in order to allow the arbitration to progress and/or any award to be issued to the parties. In any event, it is important for the Arbitral Tribunal to liaise with the Registrar[11] so that the funds held on deposit can be matched with the sums needed for the next steps to be taken (for which the LCIA needs the Arbitral Tribunal's input). 24–010

24.4 In the event that a party fails or refuses to make any payment on account of the Arbitration Costs as directed by the LCIA Court, the LCIA Court may direct the other party or parties to effect a substitute payment to allow the arbitration to proceed (subject to any order or award on Arbitration Costs).

---

[11] Under the 1998 LCIA Rules (Appendix 4), express provision was also made for the Arbitral Tribunal to liaise with any Deputy Registrar, but this is no longer express.

24–011   This Article allows the LCIA to ensure that the arbitration is properly funded even though one of the parties (usually, but not always, a Respondent) refuses to provide a deposit.[12] As with the LCIA Court's power under Article 24.1, its power under Article 24.4 has been delegated to the Registrar, under the supervision of the LCIA Court.[13]

This will sometimes occur where a Respondent does not take part in the arbitration. In such event, assuming that the Claimant pays the whole deposit itself, the Arbitral Tribunal can nonetheless continue with the proceedings and ultimately make an award. In this regard, Article 24.4 complements, and supports, Article 15.8 of the Rules, which provides that:

> "If the Respondent fails to submit a Statement of Defence . . . or if at any time any party fails to avail itself of the opportunity to present its written case in the manner required under this Article 15 or otherwise by order of the Arbitral Tribunal, the Arbitral Tribunal may nevertheless proceed with the arbitration (with or without a hearing) and make one or more awards."[14]

24–012   However, Article 24.4 is not limited to situations where one party plays no part in the arbitration. Article 24.4 also operates where a party is fully engaged in the arbitration save that it decides, for whatever reason, not to pay the deposit directed by the LCIA. This might occur, for example, where a party contests jurisdiction or after a hearing where a party perceives that it is unlikely to receive an award in its favour or where it believes that the other party has no serious intention of seeing the arbitration through to its conclusion.

Indeed, whichever party decides not to pay the sums required by the LCIA, there is no choice for a party that wishes to continue, other than to pay the shortfall itself. However, it may not have to do so immediately: the LCIA and the Arbitral Tribunal may be prepared to agree that the arbitration will proceed for the time being with the share of the deposit already paid, setting a new deadline in due course for the substitute payment.

**24.5   In such circumstances, the party effecting the substitute payment may request the Arbitral Tribunal to make an order or award in order to recover that amount as a debt immediately due and payable to that party by the defaulting party, together with any interest.**

24–013   Where a party pays a deposit in place of a non-paying party, the paying party is entitled to recover the sum paid "as a debt immediately due and payable" from the defaulting party, together with interest.[15] The paying party therefore has a cause of

---

[12] The approach under the 2012 ICC Rules (Article 36(5)) and 2010 UNCITRAL Rules (Article 43(4)) (see Appendix 11) is slightly different, providing that the other parties may pay the advance on costs in order to allow the arbitration to proceed.

[13] Section 5(i) of the LCIA's Schedule of Arbitration Costs (Appendix 2).

[14] This Article closely follows, in turn, s.41(4)(b) of the English Arbitration Act 1996 (Appendix 7).

[15] Under the 1998 LCIA Rules (Appendix 4), similar provision was made as part of Article 24.3, but without express reference to the Arbitral Tribunal having jurisdiction to make an order or award, or to the recovery of interest, and, in practice, many parties waited until after the final allocation of costs to pursue the debt.

action separate from the other claims or counterclaims in the arbitration proceedings and in relation to which the Arbitral Tribunal has jurisdiction. Accordingly, it is open to the innocent party to seek an order or a partial final award in relation to the debt and to seek to enforce that award against the non-paying party.[16]

The other potential sanction against a non-paying party that has brought a claim or counterclaim is contained in Article 24.6 (discussed below).

Whilst there is nothing preventing a non-paying Respondent from continuing to defend the claim made against it, in practice most Respondents (whether or not they have a counterclaim, so that Article 24.6 could apply) do pay their share of deposits, presumably not least because of a wish to remain in good standing in the eyes of the Arbitral Tribunal.

**24.6 Failure by a claiming or cross-claiming party to make promptly and in full any required payment on account of Arbitration Costs may be treated by the Arbitral Tribunal as a withdrawal from the arbitration of the claim or cross-claim respectively, thereby removing such claim or cross-claim (as the case may be) from the scope of the Arbitral Tribunal's jurisdiction under the Arbitration Agreement, subject to any terms decided by the Arbitral Tribunal as to the reinstatement of the claim or cross-claim in the event of subsequent payment by the claiming or cross-claiming party. Such a withdrawal shall not preclude the claiming or cross-claiming party from defending as a respondent any claim or cross-claim made by another party.**

This Article provides a strong deterrent to a Claimant or cross-claiming Respondent against failing to pay a deposit[17] directed from them (but of course has no impact upon a Respondent without a cross-claim). **24–014**

Article 24.6 does not stipulate that deposits must be paid within any particular time frame but simply requires payment to be made "promptly" and "in full". In practice, the Arbitral Tribunal and the LCIA Court will give a defaulting party reasonable notice (e.g. two or three weeks) of the consequences of its continued default and are likely to be fairly flexible in resolving the matter (for example, allowing further time), subject to the need to progress arbitrations without undue delay.[18] Note also, in this regard, the express recognition that an Arbitral Tribunal may provide terms "as to the reinstatement of the claim or cross-claim" if payment is subsequently made.

The "Special Challenges" issue of *Arbitration International*[19] contains an abstract of a challenge decision in LCIA Reference No. 7990, in which the sole arbitrator, in consultation with the LCIA Court, had decided that the claim was to **24–015**

---

[16] In some cases, the paying party will, in effect, await the accounting in relation to Arbitration Costs in the final award (deposits cannot be claimed as legal costs) thereby avoiding, for example, the expense of additional proceedings. In other cases, there might be advantages to obtaining an award and pursuing a separate enforcement action.

[17] In this context a deposit would include any "substitute payment to allow the arbitration to proceed" under Article 24.4.

[18] See, for example, Article 14.

[19] (2011) 27(3).

be treated as withdrawn after the Claimant had failed to lodge a substitute deposit, despite its being split into instalments and despite extensions. The Claimant insisted that the Respondent must pay its share but the Respondent clearly took the view that the Claimant did not have the resources and/or commitment to see the arbitration through. The abstract records that the arbitrator explained to the Claimant that the Respondent could not be directed to pay by way of substitute payment a sum which was itself due from the Claimant by way of a substitute payment in default of a payment by the Respondent. The challenge was dismissed, the Vice President of the LCIA Court having found nothing which could have given rise to justifiable doubts as to the arbitrator's impartiality or independence.

The withdrawal of a claim or cross-claim is not the same as a decision on its substance, and what might happen next depends upon the circumstances. If a sole Claimant's claim is withdrawn then the arbitration will subsequently be terminated (with an award if the Respondent requests it and the LCIA is in funds for the purpose) unless the Respondent wishes to pursue a cross-claim (and is prepared to fund the Arbitration Costs).

**24–016**  The reference to the claim/cross-claim being removed "from the scope of the Arbitral Tribunal's jurisdiction" did not appear in the 1998 LCIA Rules, and may make it more difficult for a withdrawn claim or cross-claim to be reintroduced into the arbitration unless this has been specifically provided for by terms "as to the reinstatement" of such claim or cross-claim if the payment is subsequently made. If the claim has been removed from the scope of the Arbitral Tribunal's jurisdiction without such terms as to its reinstatement, the agreement of the other parties, as well as the permission of the Arbitral Tribunal, would be required for the claim to be reintroduced.[20] If the arbitration is terminated, then the Claimant could still seek to pursue its claim (which will not have been determined) in another proceeding.

If a Respondent's cross-claim is withdrawn, the Claimant may be directed to make a substitute payment in accordance with Article 24.4. Again, it is possible for the Respondent later to seek to reintroduce its cross-claim into the arbitration[21] or to commence separate proceedings in that regard. However, as with reintroducing a claim, if the counterclaim has been removed from the scope of the Arbitral Tribunal's jurisdiction without terms for its reinstatement, the agreement of the other parties, as well as the permission of the Arbitral Tribunal, would be required for it to be reintroduced.

The provisions as to the withdrawal of claims or cross-claims for failure to make payments on account do not affect the right of a party to defend against claims or cross-claims made against it.

---

[20] Any such agreement/permission would be likely to be conditional upon the Claimant paying the required deposit and, possibly, any costs wasted as a result of the previous withdrawal.

[21] Again, any such agreement/permission would be likely to be conditional upon the Respondent paying the required deposit and, possibly, any costs wasted as a result of the previous withdrawal.

## Article 25—Interim and Conservatory Measures

25.1 The Arbitral Tribunal shall have the power upon the application of any party, after giving all other parties a reasonable opportunity to respond to such application and upon such terms as the Arbitral Tribunal considers appropriate in the circumstances:

(i) to order any respondent party to a claim or cross-claim to provide security for all or part of the amount in dispute, by way of deposit or bank guarantee or in any other manner;

(ii) to order the preservation, storage, sale or other disposal of any documents, goods, samples, property, site or thing under the control of any party and relating to the subject-matter of the arbitration; and

(iii) to order on a provisional basis, subject to a final decision in an award, any relief which the Arbitral Tribunal would have power to grant in an award, including the payment of money or the disposition of property as between any parties.

Such terms may include the provision by the applicant party of a cross-indemnity, secured in such manner as the Arbitral Tribunal considers appropriate, for any costs or losses incurred by the respondent party in complying with the Arbitral Tribunal's order. Any amount payable under such cross-indemnity and any consequential relief may be decided by the Arbitral Tribunal by one or more awards in the arbitration.

25.2 The Arbitral Tribunal shall have the power, upon the application of a party, after giving all other parties a reasonable opportunity to respond to such application, to order any claiming or cross-claiming party to provide or procure security for Legal Costs and Arbitration Costs by way of deposit or bank guarantee or in any other manner and upon such terms as the Arbitral Tribunal considers appropriate in the circumstances. Such terms may include the provision by that other party of a cross-indemnity, itself secured in such manner as the Arbitral Tribunal considers appropriate, for any costs and losses incurred by such claimant or cross-claimant in complying with the Arbitral Tribunal's order. Any amount payable under such cross-indemnity and any consequential relief may be decided by the Arbitral Tribunal by one or more awards in the arbitration. In the event that a claiming or cross-claiming party does not comply with any order to provide security, the Arbitral Tribunal may stay that party's claims or cross-claims or dismiss them by an award.

**25.3** The power of the Arbitral Tribunal under Article 25.1 shall not prejudice any party's right to apply to a state court or other legal authority for interim or conservatory measures to similar effect: (i) before the formation of the Arbitral Tribunal; and (ii) after the formation of the Arbitral Tribunal, in exceptional cases and with the Arbitral Tribunal's authorisation, until the final award. After the Commencement Date, any application and any order for such measures before the formation of the Arbitral Tribunal shall be communicated promptly in writing by the applicant party to the Registrar; after its formation, also to the Arbitral Tribunal; and in both cases also to all other parties.

**25.4** By agreeing to arbitration under the Arbitration Agreement, the parties shall be taken to have agreed not to apply to any state court or other legal authority for any order for security for Legal Costs or Arbitration Costs.

**Introduction**

25–001  The rules contained in this Article are of central importance. When choosing between courts and arbitration for the resolution of disputes, parties and their lawyers are concerned not only with how the merits of their case will be decided but also with the ancillary powers that can be exercised to assist them in obtaining the result they are looking for, whether in the enforceability of the final decision or in recovering costs spent in defending a bad claim. Likewise, in choosing between different sets of arbitration rules, parties and their lawyers will consider the powers of the Arbitral Tribunal and the extent to which the rules would require them to resort to the courts for support.

The types of measures which Article 25 permits an Arbitral Tribunal to order in the course of an LCIA arbitration can be broken down broadly as follows:

(a) conservatory measures for the purpose of securing the enforcement of the award (Articles 25.1(i) and (ii));

(b) provisional relief in advance of a final award (Article 25.1(iii)); and

(c) orders for the provision of security for the costs of defending a claim (Article 25.2).

25–002  Article 25.3 confirms that the parties' freedom to apply to state courts for the first two types of measures is not excluded. However, under Article 25.4, they shall be taken to have agreed not to apply to the courts for any order in respect of the third type (security for costs).

There is a certain amount of overlap between the first two types of measures, particularly as far as their practical effect is concerned. For example, both can deal with the disposal of property and can result in a readjustment in the financial or corporate relationship between the parties pending a final decision on the merits.

power. Again, for the purposes of an LCIA arbitration with a seat in London, Article 25.1(iii) confirms that the parties have agreed that the Arbitral Tribunal may order on a provisional basis any remedy that it would have the power to grant in a final award.

If the Arbitral Tribunal is satisfied that it has the power, under the law of the seat, to grant any relief sought under Article 25, it must still consider whether and how it should exercise its discretion to do so. The LCIA Rules do not contain any criteria for the exercise of this power by the Arbitral Tribunal. Nor does the English Arbitration Act 1996 offer guidance.

**25–007** By contrast, both Article 26(3) of the UNCITRAL Rules (2010) and Article 17A(1) of the UNCITRAL Model Law (2006) require an applicant for interim measures to satisfy the Tribunal that:

(a) "harm not adequately reparable by an award of damages is likely to result if the measure is not ordered, and such harm substantially outweighs the harm that is likely to result to the party against whom the measure is directed if the measure is granted." This is probably the most important test which the Arbitral Tribunal can be expected to apply to applications for interim or conservatory relief; and

(b) there is a reasonable possibility that the requesting party will succeed on the merits of the claim. Whether the Arbitral Tribunal should be satisfied that the claim has a reasonable possibility of succeeding (Article 17A(1)(b) of the UNCITRAL Rules), or that there is a prima facie case, can be problematic. As discussed below, the Arbitral Tribunal will be concerned not to be accused of any kind of pre-judgment.

**25–008** In practice, most Arbitral Tribunals are likely to expect an applicant seeking interim or conservatory measures to establish that it has a prima facie (or reasonable) case on jurisdiction and on the merits of its claim and that the measures sought:

(a) are required to prevent irreparable or substantial harm to the applicant;

(b) are required urgently and cannot await the final determination of the disputes; and

(c) will not dispose of the dispute or render the final determination of the dispute unnecessary.[3]

---

[3] Julian D.M. Lew "Commentary on Interim and Conservatory Measures in ICC Arbitration Cases" (2000) 11(1) *ICC International Court of Arbitration Bulletin*. Yesilirmak identifies a number of additional "positive" criteria that should be established by an applicant for provisional measures, which may be summarised as: a prima facie case on the jurisdiction of the Tribunal and on the merits; urgency or imminent danger of substantial prejudice if the measure requested is not granted; and proportionality. He has also identified a number of negative criteria which may lead to the application being denied, namely that the measure sought must not constitute final relief, if the applicant does not have "clean hands", if the measure is not capable of being performed; or the measure sought would not prevent the alleged harm; see Ali Yesilirmak, *Provisional Measures in International Commercial Arbitration* (Kluwer Law International, 2005), Ch.5 "Arbitral Provisional Measures", pp.159–236. Born states that in practice "most international arbitral tribunals require showings of (a) a risk of serious or irreparable harm to the claimant; (b) urgency; and (c) no prejudgment of the merits, whilst some tribunals also require the claimant to establish a prima facie case on the merits, a prima facie case on jurisdiction, and to establish that the balance of hardships weighs

The Arbitral Tribunal also has discretion as to the terms on which it makes any order under Article 25. These may include cross-indemnities as noted below.

**25.1 The Arbitral Tribunal shall have the power upon the application of any party, after giving all other parties a reasonable opportunity to respond to such application and upon such terms as the Arbitral Tribunal considers appropriate in the circumstances: . . .**

The introductory words in Article 25.1 confirm that the Arbitral Tribunal's powers to grant interim and conservatory measures are exercisable upon an application by any party and on the basis that the other parties have the right to oppose such an application. 25–009

The 1998 version of the Rules expressly confirmed that the parties were free to opt out of conferring on the Arbitral Tribunal the powers in relation to conservatory and interim measures, which follow. Although no longer express, this opt out should still be available in practice: there is no statement that the provisions of Article 25 are mandatory.

Surprising as it may seem to some practitioners, arbitration clauses do occasionally exclude Article 25.1. There remains a nervousness in some quarters about the ability and willingness of Arbitral Tribunals to make orders of this kind, although in practice many arbitrators have made good use of these powers. 25–010

**25.1(i) to order any respondent party to a claim or cross-claim to provide security for all or part of the amount in dispute, by way of deposit or bank guarantee or in any other manner;**

The provision of security for the amount in dispute, often referred to as "security for a claim", is intended to guarantee the payment of a final award or the availability of funds against which a final award may be enforced. In general it will only be granted where the applicant has demonstrated that it is highly likely that any award in its favour would be rendered unenforceable either due to the unavailability of funds or for some other reason.[4] 25–011

In practice, the Arbitral Tribunal's power to order security for a claim is very rarely invoked and even more rarely exercised. However, the presence of these provisions in the Rules is one of the factors that can persuade parties to agree to provide security at an early stage in an arbitration.

There is no requirement for parties to inform the LCIA Secretariat or the Arbitral Tribunal if such an agreement has been made. The Secretariat may be made aware of the existence of a bank guarantee, for example, when a successful 25–012

---

in its favour" (references omitted); see Born, *International Commercial Arbitration* (2014), Ch.17 "Provisional Relief in International Arbitration", pp.2424–2563 at p.2467.

[4] Yesilirmak, *Provisional Measures in International Commercial Arbitration* (2005), Ch.5 "Arbitral Provisional Measures", pp.159–236, at para.7.3.

party seeks its help in putting together the documentation required to trigger payment under it, such as a copy of the award certified by the Registrar.

The question of obtaining security for a claim against an impecunious or elusive Respondent may be addressed before the Request for Arbitration is filed. If security is not obtained voluntarily, a Claimant might resort to court applications, whether in its opponent's home jurisdiction or in another favourable jurisdiction where assets might be located and seized.

25–013   Article 9 of the UNCITRAL Model Law confirms that it is not incompatible with an arbitration agreement for a party to apply to court for interim measures and for a court to grant them. However, Article 25.3 of the Rules imposes a restriction: if such an application to court is made after the formation of the Arbitral Tribunal, it has to be an "exceptional case" and made with the permission of the Arbitral Tribunal.

An application to the Arbitral Tribunal for security for a claim has two disadvantages. First, it cannot be made ex parte: the Respondent will be warned that the Claimant is looking for security and will have opportunities both to resist the application and to arrange its affairs in such a way as to protect its assets. Secondly, the Arbitral Tribunal has no power to enforce its own order: a court order for the seizure of assets may still be required if the Respondent is to be compelled to lodge security. Under s.42 of the English Arbitration Act 1996, the English courts have power to make an order requiring a party to comply with a peremptory order made by the Arbitral Tribunal.

25–014   These drawbacks, and the restrictions in Article 25.3, are reasons why applications for conservatory arrests of assets are more often made in court before the arbitration is commenced or, quite often, in the interval before the LCIA Court has appointed the Arbitral Tribunal. Evidence of the filing of a Request for Arbitration can be useful to satisfy a court that proceedings on the merits have commenced in the proper forum. The LCIA Secretariat will usually acknowledge receipt of a Request within a day of its being filed. Its letter can be presented to a court in support of an application for a freezing order, for example, under s.44 of the English Arbitration Act 1996.

Following the freezing of assets, a Respondent will usually agree to provide a bank guarantee or to lodge funds in an escrow account, by way of security, in order to release the assets. If an application for security is made direct to the Arbitral Tribunal, it may make an order as to the form of security to be provided. It may order funds to be lodged in an account held by the LCIA. The Secretariat holds deposits towards the Arbitration Costs (see Article 24 above) and is well equipped to hold funds as security for a claim or as security for costs (see below).

In practice, the parties will often agree the form of security to be provided and themselves liaise with the Secretariat if its fundholding services are to be used.

> **25.1(ii) to order the preservation, storage, sale or other disposal of any documents, goods, samples, property, site or thing under the control of any party and relating to the subject-matter of the arbitration;**

In addition to the power to order security to cover the amount of a claim, an **25–015** Arbitral Tribunal has the power to order other conservatory measures for the purposes of ensuring that its final award will be enforceable.

This power has been invoked in applications for the freezing of assets, but such orders are rarely made. An Arbitral Tribunal does not have jurisdiction over third parties, e.g. banks. As noted above, they can more usefully be obtained from the courts, particularly before the Arbitral Tribunal has been formed.

More commonly, the power is used in disputes over the ownership of assets, **25–016** where it is important that those assets, if still in the hands of one of the parties, should not be transferred to third parties until the Arbitral Tribunal has finally determined the matter. Measures can include injunctions against disposing of shares and orders for the preservation of cargo or machinery in particular locations.[5]

**25.1(iii) to order on a provisional basis, subject to a final decision in an award, any relief which the Arbitral Tribunal would have power to grant in an award, including the payment of money or the disposition of property as between any parties.**

There is a degree of overlap between Articles 25.1(ii) and 25.1(iii), particularly as **25–017** far as the disposition of property is concerned. Both provisions have been used by parties to obtain orders to prevent the disposal of shares, for example. However, there is an important distinction outlined in the introduction to the comments on this Article: Article 25.1(ii) deals with conservatory measures which could assist the enforceability of the final award whilst Article 25.1(iii) allows the Arbitral Tribunal to order, on a provisional basis, all or part of the relief that it is seeking to obtain in the final award.

In exercising this power, an Arbitral Tribunal may order the same relief it might have granted in a final award by way of a temporary, *provisional*, order. Although arbitrators can sometimes give their awards confusing titles, there is a clear difference in substance between an interim order, which makes provisional determinations, and a partial (or partial final) award, which is final as to its subject matter. An interim order made pursuant to Article 25.1(iii) remains subject to final determination and should not be enforceable under the New York Convention 1958. On the other hand, an award requiring a party to make an interim payment on account, which might be supplemented in the final award but which could not be reversed, will be a partial final award by the Arbitral Tribunal. Such a partial final award should be enforceable under the New York Convention.

An example of a situation where Article 25.1(iii) may be used is in a dispute **25–018** under a sale and purchase contract, which contains terms requiring a payment to be made before any claim for damages for defects could be entertained, a "pay now, claim later" contract. Whether a contract does require payment first, and whether an Arbitral Tribunal should make a provisional order to enforce such a

---

[5] For a discussion of the nature of the Arbitral Tribunal's power ("freezing injunction"/"stopping the clock") under Article 25.1(b), as it was under the 1998 Rules, see *Barnwell Enterprises Ltd v ECP Africa FII Investments LLC* [2013] EWHC 2517 (Comm).

provision, can be difficult issues. Whilst the first is a matter of contractual interpretation, the second is a matter of discretion.[6]

In a series of arbitrations, heard together in 2008, an LCIA Arbitral Tribunal was faced with an application from the Claimant seller for an order for provisional payment of 90 per cent of the value of the contractual goods. The Arbitral Tribunal was divided but the majority decided that it would deny the application, explaining that expressing a provisional view "would create difficulties for the Tribunal in seeking to determine that issue on a final basis on different evidence". The dissenting arbitrator's view was that "as a matter of cash flow, the parties intended the Claimant to be holding 90% and the [Respondents] 10% of the price until issues of quality etc were finally determined".

25–019   Having succeeded in defeating the application under Article 25.1(c) (as it then was), the Respondents lodged a challenge to the dissenting arbitrator, the Claimant's nominee, pursuant to Articles 10.2–10.4 of the Rules. An abstract of the decision of the Division of the LCIA Court appointed to determine the challenge appears in the challenges special issue of *Arbitration International*.[7] It is of interest not only for the discussion of the possibility of prejudgment of the merits, giving rise to an appearance of bias, but also for the LCIA Court's views on the scope of Article 25.1(c).

The Respondents had cited Professor Julian Lew:

> "In dealing with a request for an interim measure, an arbitral tribunal must refrain from pre-judging the merits of the case. By way of illustration, an arbitral tribunal will generally refuse to grant such a measure, where the request essentially covers what it is asked to resolve in the substantive arbitration. The underlying principle is clear: if the request for relief is made on both an interim and permanent basis, only the latter will, in principle, be granted."[8]

25–020   The Division held that the scholarly objections to prejudging merits, as cited by the Respondents, usually related only to interim measures that preserve the status quo (e.g. Article 25.1(ii)), whereas the type of relief authorised under Article 25.1(c) (now Article 25.1(iii)) was obviously intended to do more than this. A grant of a provisional order under Article 25.1(c) required a preliminary judgement about the correctness of the applicant's position on at least some part of the merits of the case. The Division decided that the interpretation of the contract by the Claimant's nominated arbitrator could not be considered unreasonable to the point of evidence of bias or of a closed mind.

The publication of the abstract of this important decision should dissuade parties from protesting about prejudgement when an application under Article 25.1(iii) is considered. However, it also confirms the difficulties faced by an Arbitral Tribunal in such a situation. It is interesting to note in this regard that the Claimant's nominated arbitrator had suggested that any provisional order for

---

[6] The leading English case confirming that arbitrators have complete discretion as to whether or not to issue an interim award is *Exmar BV v National Iranian Tanker Co* [1992] 1 Lloyd's Rep 169, which predates s.39(2) of the English Arbitration Act 1996.

[7] (2011) 27(3) Arbitration Int. LCIA Reference No. 81007/81008/81024/81025, Decision Rendered June 16, 2008.

[8] Julian D.M. Lew, *"Commentary on Interim Measures and Conservatory Measures in ICC Arbitration Cases"* (2000) 11(1) *ICC International Court of Arbitration Bulletin*, para.30.

payment should be conditional on an undertaking by the Claimant to indemnify the Respondents for damages suffered from the issuance of the order. No specific provision for such an indemnity was contained in Article 25.1(c) of the 1998 version of the Rules.

> "Such terms may include the provision by the applicant party of a cross-indemnity, secured in such manner as the Arbitral Tribunal considers appropriate, for any costs or losses incurred by the respondent party in complying with the Arbitral Tribunal's order. Any amount payable under such cross-indemnity and any consequential relief may be decided by the Arbitral Tribunal by one or more awards in the arbitration."

25-021 The final paragraph of Article 25.1 is concerned with the terms that might be imposed by the Arbitral Tribunal as conditions for granting the relief sought. The provision of a cross-indemnity is often required when a court grants a freezing injunction or other conservatory measure that could affect a party's ordinary course of business. Likewise, the UNCITRAL Model Law recognises in Article 17E that a Tribunal should have the power to require a party applying for an interim measure to provide appropriate security in connection with it.

An order for security for a claim to be provided by way of a bank guarantee or deposit (under Article 25.1 (i)) is designed to avoid the need for freezing assets and to prevent adverse commercial consequences of this kind: it should not normally give rise to costs other than bank fees. Funds held on deposit at the LCIA will attract interest, which can cover the LCIA's own charges for this service and can go some way to compensating the paying party for not having the use of the money for the duration of the arbitration.

25-022 The 1998 version of the Rules provided for the power to order a cross-indemnity only in connection with security under Article 25.1(a) as it then was, which was peculiar (and possibly an error). The extension of the power to the other orders available under Article 25.1 is logical.

> **25.2** The Arbitral Tribunal shall have the power, upon the application of a party, after giving all other parties a reasonable opportunity to respond to such application, to order any claiming or cross-claiming party to provide or procure security for Legal Costs and Arbitration Costs by way of deposit or bank guarantee or in any other manner and upon such terms as the Arbitral Tribunal considers appropriate in the circumstances. Such terms may include the provision by that other party of a cross-indemnity, itself secured in such manner as the Arbitral Tribunal considers appropriate, for any costs and losses incurred by such claimant or cross-claimant in complying with the Arbitral Tribunal's order. Any amount payable under such cross-indemnity and any consequential relief may be decided by the Arbitral Tribunal by one or more awards in the arbitration. In the event that a claiming or cross-claiming party does not comply with any order to provide security, the Arbitral Tribunal may stay that party's claims or cross-claims or dismiss them by an award.

25–023　The power to order security for costs is another which is relatively rarely invoked or applied; according to statistics from the Registrar, 16 such applications were made in 2013 and 10 were granted. In England, the practice prior to the English Arbitration Act 1996 had been to apply to the court in all matters relating to costs, as well as for interim and conservatory measures. By s.38(3) of the 1996 Act, a Tribunal has this power to order security for costs. This is a matter for the discretion of the Tribunal. The only ground on which, under the Act, it should not base its decision is that the Claimant is based outside the UK. It is obvious that in international arbitration all nationalities should be treated equally.

In practice, there are other ways to test whether a Claimant has the ability or the will to pursue its claim. For example, it must pay its share of the initial deposit on account of the Arbitration Costs, pursuant to Article 24.1.

25–024　It should be remembered that, in accordance with Article 24.3, the Arbitral Tribunal should not entertain any applications, including any applications for security for costs, without ascertaining that the LCIA is in requisite funds. It is not unknown for an application under Article 25.2 to be decided by an Arbitral Tribunal when a deposit has been lodged only by the Respondent making the application.

Tribunals can be slow to apply the ultimate sanction of dismissing a claim. They will usually be concerned to ensure that the Claimant has received plenty of notice and has been given sufficient opportunities to lodge the security. In England, it is a power which is specifically permitted by s.41(6) of the English Arbitration Act 1996 but it should be exercised with caution in any jurisdiction.

25–025　It should be noted that the power is to award security for both "Legal Costs" (lawyers' fees and expenses) and "Arbitration Costs" (the arbitrators' fees and the LCIA's administrative charges), as defined in Article 28.1 of the Rules.[9] As far as the latter is concerned, the parties are directed to pay deposits on account and it is the applicant's current and estimated future share of those amounts for which security may be obtained. Should any balance remain to the applicant's credit on the account held by the LCIA at the conclusion of the arbitration, it should be returned by the LCIA and should therefore fall to be deducted from any claim on the security.

> **25.3** The power of the Arbitral Tribunal under Article 25.1 shall not prejudice any party's right to apply to a state court or other legal authority for interim or conservatory measures to similar effect: (i) before the formation of the Arbitral Tribunal; and (ii) after the formation of the Arbitral Tribunal, in exceptional cases and with the Arbitral Tribunal's authorisation, until the final award. After the Commencement Date, any application and any order for such

---

[9] The definitions in Article 28 and the clear wording in Article 25.4 should avoid the uncertainty and the result which afflicted the providers of security for costs in an English Commercial Court decision relating to a shipping arbitration, *Wealcan Enterprises Inc v Banque Algerienne du Commerce Exterieur SA* [2012] EWHC 4151 (Comm). "Recoverable legal costs" and "costs of defending Charterer's claims" were held to include arbitrators' fees, even though they were not specifically mentioned in the guarantee.

**measures before the formation of the Arbitral Tribunal shall be communicated promptly in writing by the applicant party to the Registrar; after its formation, also to the Arbitral Tribunal; and in both cases also to all other parties.**

The interplay between applications to the Arbitral Tribunal and to court has been discussed above. This came before the English courts in *U&M Mining Zambia Ltd v Konkola Copper Mines Plc*,[10] in which Blair J held:    **25–026**

> "By expressly stipulating that the power of the Arbitral Tribunal to order interim and conservatory measures is not to prejudice a party's right to apply to a state court before the formation of the Arbitral Tribunal, in my view Article 25.3 implicitly recognises the party's right to do so."

In *Barnwell Enterprises Ltd v ECP Africa FII Investments LLC*,[11] Hamblen J decided that he would grant interim relief "as a short term measure to preserve the status quo so as to enable the matter to be put back before the Tribunal". In the event, the Arbitral Tribunal in this LCIA arbitration (chaired by Professor Albert Jan van den Berg) decided that it did not have jurisdiction over the particular agreement in respect of which relief had been sought.[12]    **25–027**

**25.4 By agreeing to arbitration under the Arbitration Agreement, the parties shall be taken to have agreed not to apply to any state court or other legal authority for any order for security for Legal Costs or Arbitration Costs.**

As noted above, under Article 25.2, an Arbitral Tribunal has a power to award security for Legal Costs and Arbitration Costs. Article 25.4 confirms that this power is exclusive: by agreeing to arbitration under the Rules, the parties forego the right to seek security for costs through the courts.    **25–028**

---

[10] [2013] EWHC 260 (Comm).
[11] [2013] EWHC 2517 (Comm), reported in [2014] 1 Lloyd's Law Reports 171.
[12] As reported in *Global Arbitration Review*, "LCIA panel rules in East African private equity dispute" March 7, 2014.

## Article 26—Award(s)

26.1 The Arbitral Tribunal may make separate awards on different issues at different times, including interim payments on account of any claim or cross-claim (including Legal and Arbitration Costs). Such awards shall have the same status as any other award made by the Arbitral Tribunal.

26.2 The Arbitral Tribunal shall make any award in writing and, unless all parties agree in writing otherwise, shall state the reasons upon which such award is based. The award shall also state the date when the award is made and the seat of the arbitration; and it shall be signed by the Arbitral Tribunal or those of its members assenting to it.

26.3 An award may be expressed in any currency, unless the parties have agreed otherwise.

26.4 Unless the parties have agreed otherwise, the Arbitral Tribunal may order that simple or compound interest shall be paid by any party on any sum awarded at such rates as the Arbitral Tribunal decides to be appropriate (without being bound by rates of interest practised by any state court or other legal authority) in respect of any period which the Arbitral Tribunal decides to be appropriate ending not later than the date upon which the award is complied with.

26.5 Where there is more than one arbitrator and the Arbitral Tribunal fails to agree on any issue, the arbitrators shall decide that issue by a majority. Failing a majority decision on any issue, the presiding arbitrator shall decide that issue.

26.6 If any arbitrator refuses or fails to sign the award, the signatures of the majority or (failing a majority) of the presiding arbitrator shall be sufficient, provided that the reason for the omitted signature is stated in the award by the majority or by the presiding arbitrator.

26.7 The sole or presiding arbitrator shall be responsible for delivering the award to the LCIA Court, which shall transmit to the parties the award authenticated by the Registrar as an LCIA award, provided that all Arbitration Costs have been paid in full to the LCIA in accordance with Articles 24 and 28. Such transmission may be made by any electronic means, in addition to paper form (if so requested by any party). In the event of any disparity between electronic and paper forms, the paper form shall prevail.

**26.8** Every award (including reasons for such award) shall be final and binding on the parties. The parties undertake to carry out any award immediately and without any delay (subject only to Article 27); and the parties also waive irrevocably their right to any form of appeal, review or recourse to any state court or other legal authority, insofar as such waiver shall not be prohibited under any applicable law.

**26.9** In the event of any final settlement of the parties' dispute, the Arbitral Tribunal may decide to make an award recording the settlement if the parties jointly so request in writing (a "Consent Award"), provided always that such Consent Award shall contain an express statement on its face that it is an award made at the parties' joint request and with their consent. A Consent Award need not contain reasons. If the parties do not jointly request a Consent Award, on written confirmation by the parties to the LCIA Court that a final settlement has been reached, the Arbitral Tribunal shall be discharged and the arbitration proceedings concluded by the LCIA Court, subject to payment by the parties of any outstanding Arbitration Costs in accordance with Articles 24 and 28.

## Introduction

Article 26 is one of the most important provisions in the Rules. Much of the Article is concerned with obligations on and instructions to the Arbitral Tribunal in relation to the production of enforceable awards. Article 26.8 is the only provision which really bites on the parties—and it does so in a very important way, obliging them to carry out any award immediately (subject to Article 27) and waiving their right to appeal or other forms of recourse to the extent not mandatory under applicable law. In England, that means that there is no right to appeal on a question of law[1] (there is, in any event, no right to appeal on a question of fact) but the rights to challenge an award for serious irregularity[2] or substantive jurisdiction[3] remain. **26–001**

One of the attractions of institutional arbitration is that awards will quite literally bear the institution's stamp, making them more easily recognised in courts around the world. Article 26 sets out the role of the Registrar in authenticating awards and in transmitting them to the parties.

Although, on its face, this Article appears rather different to the equivalent Article under the 1998 LCIA Rules, and there have been some changes, much of the text is the same but has been reproduced in a different order within the Article. **26–002**

**26.1 The Arbitral Tribunal may make separate awards on different issues at different times, including interim payments on account of any**

---

[1] English Arbitration Act 1996 s.69 (Appendix 7).
[2] English Arbitration Act 1996 s.68 (Appendix 7).
[3] English Arbitration Act 1996 s.67 (Appendix 7).

claim or cross-claim (including Legal and Arbitration Costs). Such awards shall have the same status as any other award made by the Arbitral Tribunal.

26–003  Arbitral Tribunals may make any numbers of awards—each of which, crucially, is stated to have the same status and effect, and each of which can be enforced separately. This gives a great deal of freedom to the Arbitral Tribunal and is helpful from an administrative point of view.

Article 26.1 incorporates what was Article 26.7 under the 1998 LCIA Rules, with the addition of reference to awards on "interim payments on account" of any claim or cross-claim "including Legal and Arbitration Costs".[4]

In practice, Arbitral Tribunals make a variety of awards, including partial (e.g. on jurisdiction—see Article 23) and interim, as well as final. The LCIA leaves it to the Arbitral Tribunal to decide what title a particular award should bear.

**26.2 The Arbitral Tribunal shall make any award in writing and, unless all parties agree in writing otherwise, shall state the reasons upon which such award is based. The award shall also state the date when the award is made and the seat of the arbitration; and it shall be signed by the Arbitral Tribunal or those of its members assenting to it.**

26–004  The Arbitral Tribunal is obliged to make its award in writing (and the parties cannot derogate from this requirement of the Rules). This is an important requirement—unless there is a written award, it is very difficult indeed to enforce the Arbitral Tribunal's determination and that determination would be open to a multitude of challenges on enforcement.

The award must also contain the reasons upon which it is based (unless the parties agree in writing). Again, this avoids challenges arising in circumstances where the Arbitral Tribunal does not deliver a reasoned award.

26–005  Awards without reasons used to be issued fairly commonly in London arbitrations, but this was generally in trades in which the parties wanted a quick decision from a sole arbitrator and in the meantime might be continuing to do business with each other on a London exchange, of which the arbitrator might also be a member. Such awards have become rare in commercial arbitrations, particularly in international cases.

The award must state the date when it is made and the seat of arbitration, and is to be signed by those members of the Arbitral Tribunal who agree with its contents.

---

[4] In *"Ocean Glory"* [2014] EWHC 2521 (Comm), Eder J has described the term "interim award" as "a constant source of confusion", which "should be abandoned". The English Arbitration Act 1996 does not use the term. Following the reasoning of the Court of Appeal in *Sucafina v Rotenberg* [2012] EWCA Civ 637, an award which contains a decision about a payment on account should be called a "partial final award". "Legal Costs" are defined in Article 28.3 as the "legal or other expenses incurred by a party", as distinct from the "Arbitration Costs", defined in Article 28.1, which are the remainder of the costs, incurred by the parties and paid by the LCIA on their behalf out of the advances of costs paid to the LCIA by the parties.

The latter of these requirements helps demonstrate that the award is genuine and authentic (which is important in terms of Article IV of the New York Convention). It also helps to overcome the "dated in Paris" issue which arose in the English case of *Hiscox v Outhwaite (No. 1)*.[5] In that case, the seat was actually London, but this was not stated on the face of the award. The arbitrator, then resident in Paris, dated the award in the French manner by adding the name of the place in which he was signing. The confusion led to litigation all the way to the House of Lords, and eventually to the introduction of s.53 of the English Arbitration Act 1996, which states that an award in an arbitration with an English seat shall be treated as made there, regardless of where it was actually signed.

As noted below in relation to Article 26.7, the date on which an award is made can be critical. Conscious of the importance of the date of the award and of the obligation to ensure that the Arbitration Costs have been paid in full (Article 26.7) or, in the case of an interim award (in a continuing arbitration), that the LCIA is in funds (Article 24.3) as at that date, the Secretariat will seek to liaise closely with the Arbitral Tribunal, more particularly with the presiding arbitrator. If there is a shortfall, the parties will be directed to pay it before the award is issued by the LCIA. In such a situation, the Registrar might, for example, set a deadline of one week for the payment. If it has not been effected by then, the Arbitral Tribunal might nevertheless finalise, sign and date its award on or shortly after that deadline. The Registrar would then inform the parties that the award has been signed on that date, has been delivered to the LCIA or is expected to reach the LCIA within 24 hours, and that it will be delivered to them upon receipt of the outstanding sum. A party keen to receive the award and/or concerned about possible recourse will be anxious to put the LCIA in funds at that point. It may even pay the other side's share of the shortfall or deposit, voluntarily, as a precaution.

**26–006**

It should be noted that a final award should contain a determination of the full Arbitration Costs (see Article 28.2) but not necessarily a summary of the payments of deposits made by the parties (in accordance with Article 24) to cover these costs (which is essentially an administrative matter which can be confirmed with the Secretariat). In the scenario described above, in which a shortfall is ascertained before the award is issued by the LCIA, the Arbitral Tribunal will not know on the date on which it signs its award, who will make the final payment. Its award will contain the LCIA Court's determination of the Arbitration Costs as at the date of the award but, the final payment being a future event, it cannot state, in the award, how much of those costs one party *has* borne and will have the right to recover from the other. That accounting will be set out in the financial summary which the LCIA Secretariat will send to the parties separately.

Parties who wish to see the precise accounting set out in the award itself (to make the Article 28.2 decision more easily enforceable) should liaise with the LCIA Secretariat to ensure that the LCIA is in funds in good time before the date on which the award is signed and to request that the Arbitral Tribunal address this matter.

**26–007**

---

[5] [1992] 1 A.C. 562.

In order to aid the enforceability of an award which is not a final award (and which does not, therefore, need to contain a determination of the Arbitration Costs), an Arbitral Tribunal should likewise liaise with the LCIA Secretariat, in advance, and inform it of all of its fees and expenses up to and including the writing of that award. If the LCIA is not in funds on the date on which the award is signed, further deposits will be directed before it is released.

26–008 There will be circumstances in which an interim award is particularly urgent and in which the shortfall is small. Those might constitute "exceptional circumstances" for the purposes of the new wording of Article 24.3.

Awards are typed up by the arbitrators themselves, not by the LCIA. It is the arbitrators' responsibility to organise how and when they will be signed and how many original signed versions will be required. Again, the LCIA Secretariat will liaise with the presiding arbitrator in this regard and will be able to assist in making arrangements for the signature pages to be circulated. In cases of exceptional urgency, and where the three arbitrators are separated by great distances, separate signature pages, bearing the signature of one arbitrator each, may be issued. The time needed to collect final payments might be sufficient to allow a single page to be sent to one or two arbitrators for signature and then to London. The date of the award should be the date on which the final signature is added.

26–009 These requirements of form follow very closely the template laid out in s.52 of the English Arbitration Act 1996.

Article 26.2 is almost identical to Article 26.1 under the 1998 LCIA Rules.

### 26.3 An award may be expressed in any currency, unless the parties have agreed otherwise.

26–010 Article 26.3 allows the Arbitral Tribunal to select the currency for the award unless the parties have agreed upon a particular currency or currencies. There is no express requirement that such agreement be in writing.

### 26.4 Unless the parties have agreed otherwise, the Arbitral Tribunal may order that simple or compound interest shall be paid by any party on any sum awarded at such rates as the Arbitral Tribunal decides to be appropriate (without being bound by rates of interest practised by any state court or other legal authority) in respect of any period which the Arbitral Tribunal decides to be appropriate ending not later than the date upon which the award is complied with.

26–011 In the absence of agreement by the parties,[6] Article 26.4 allows the Arbitral Tribunal to make such order regarding the payment of interest on the sums

---

[6] As with Article 26.3, there is no express requirement that the agreement of the parties as to interest be in writing.

awarded as it, in its discretion, considers appropriate. The Arbitral Tribunal need not have regard to rates of interest practised in state courts, and may order compound interest (which is more commercially realistic) or simple interest (which was the norm in England prior to the English Arbitration Act 1996).

The LCIA does not have any particular guidelines in relation to awards of interest but its Accounts department is able to assist with providing information about historical rates. Appropriate rates will often depend on the currency of the relevant transaction. For example, a successful party based in and operating in the US might be awarded interest at a rate related to US Prime whilst a party conducting its trading in US dollars but based outside the US might be awarded interest at a rate based on LIBOR US dollar three monthly with an uplift.

An award cannot provide that interest continues to accrue after the date on which the award is complied with. This provision fits with the general principle under English law that damages that result from one and the same cause of action must be assessed and recovered once and for all, and the Claimant must sue in one action for all his loss, past, present and future, certain and contingent.[7]

26-012

Article 26.4 is similar to Article 26.6 under the 1998 LCIA Rules, save that it refers to rates of interest "practised" by courts rather than "legal rates of interest imposed" by them, and it states that the Arbitral Tribunal is not bound by rates of interest imposed by "other legal authority" as well as "by any state court".

**26.5 Where there is more than one arbitrator and the Arbitral Tribunal fails to agree on any issue, the arbitrators shall decide that issue by a majority. Failing a majority decision on any issue, the presiding arbitrator shall decide that issue.**

This provision allows the Arbitral Tribunal to decide issues (and, potentially, the entire award) by a majority. In circumstances where even a majority decision cannot be reached, the opinions and decisions of the presiding arbitrator will form the binding award.

26-013

Article 26.5 is similar to Article 26.3 under the 1998 LCIA Rules, save that it refers to "Where there is more than one arbitrator" rather than "Where there are three arbitrators" (recognising that in unusual cases there may be other numbers of arbitrators) and to the "presiding arbitrator" rather than the "chairman".

**26.6 If any arbitrator refuses or fails to sign the award, the signatures of the majority or (failing a majority) of the presiding arbitrator shall be sufficient, provided that the reason for the omitted signature is stated in the award by the majority or by the presiding arbitrator.**

---

[7] *Darley Main Colliery Co v Mitchell* (1886) 11 App Cas 127 at 133, HL, per Lord Halsbury; *Gibbs v Cruikshank* (1872–1873) LR 8 CP 454 at 460 per Bovill CJ; *Sanders v Hamilton* (1907) 96 LT 679; *Furness, Withy & Co Ltd v J&E Hall Ltd* (1909) 25 TLR 233; *Conquer v Boot* [1928] 2 KB 336.

26–014   Following on from Article 26.5, this provision allows an award to be final and binding when signed only by a majority or by the presiding arbitrator alone. The reason for the omitted signature must be stated in the award (an exception to the general position that the arbitrator's deliberations are confidential—Article 30.2).

26–015   Article 26.2 of the 1998 LCIA Rules, which confirmed the ability of the remaining arbitrators to proceed where an arbitrator failed to comply with mandatory provisions of applicable law relating to making an award, has not been repeated in these Rules.

Dissenting opinions are comparatively rare in LCIA arbitrations. However, the international character of these arbitrations and of the Arbitral Tribunals appointed to hear them means that a few party-nominated arbitrators from the home jurisdiction of a losing party will feel it incumbent on them to make detailed dissenting opinions, sometimes mirroring the majority award in recitals and length. In those circumstances, the LCIA Secretariat plays an important role in liaising also with the presiding and dissenting arbitrators and also with the LCIA Court in relation to the determination of the Arbitration Costs.

26–016   Dissenting opinions, not being awards, will not be issued under the LCIA's seal (see Article 26.7 below). The award will usually be signed by all three arbitrators with the fact of the dissent noted in the award and perhaps next to the dissenting arbitrator's signature.

> **26.7** The sole or presiding arbitrator shall be responsible for delivering the award to the LCIA Court, which shall transmit to the parties the award authenticated by the Registrar as an LCIA award, provided that all Arbitration Costs have been paid in full to the LCIA in accordance with Articles 24 and 28. Such transmission may be made by any electronic means, in addition to paper form (if so requested by any party). In the event of any disparity between electronic and paper forms, the paper form shall prevail.

26–017   Once the award has been finalised and signed by the Arbitral Tribunal, or those arbitrators who assent to it (Article 26.2), the award is delivered to the LCIA Court, in practice to the Registrar at the LCIA's offices in London. As a practical matter (although not required by the Rules), the LCIA Secretariat typically reviews the award (and indeed may have reviewed drafts of the award) in order to check it for typographical and arithmetical errors, and also that it complies with the Rules. This proofreading "plus" service is often requested by Arbitral Tribunals, particularly by sole arbitrators. At the modest hourly rates charged for Counsel at the LCIA, it is regarded as cost effective. It certainly reduces the instances of clerical errors, about which complaints are often levelled against arbitrators in ad hoc arbitrations.

The LCIA Court then ascertains whether the Arbitration Costs have been paid in accordance with Articles 24 and 28, and the Registrar will further advise the parties if that is not the case. Usually, the fact that the LCIA is in possession of a final award results in prompt payments of any outstanding costs. However, if a party is certain that it has not been successful, that party may try to delay the issue of the award by not paying its share of any outstanding costs and forcing the other party or parties to pay on its behalf so that they can get hold of the award. The uncertainty of who will make the final payment has consequences for what the Arbitral Tribunal can say, in its award, about the precise liabilities of the respective parties in relation to the Arbitration Costs, as noted above.[8]

Once the issue of costs has been addressed and outstanding costs have been fully paid, the award is then formally issued to the parties.

Prudent Arbitral Tribunals ought to work with the LCIA to ensure that the award can be dated as close to the date of its issue by the LCIA Court as possible. As explained above, in practice, the LCIA Secretariat will seek to liaise with Arbitral Tribunals for these purposes. If the Arbitral Tribunal does not liaise in advance and, for example, dates the award and then delays in sending it to the LCIA, which then experiences issues over the payment of outstanding costs, there is a real risk that, by the time the parties receive the award, a significant amount of time has elapsed since the actual date of the award. This does not have an impact on the timing of requests for correction of the award, or requests for additional awards, under Article 27 of the Rules, but may have an impact on the time available in which to bring a challenge under (for example) the English Arbitration Act 1996—s.70(3) provides that a challenge must be mounted within 28 days "of the date of the award". 26–018

There has been a curious change to the wording of these provisions in relation to the despatch of awards to the parties. In the 1998 LCIA Rules, Article 26.5 provided that the LCIA Court would transmit "certified copies" of the award to the parties. In practice, these copies were bound under an LCIA cover, the LCIA's seal (a blind stamp) was appended to that cover and a "certified copy" stamp, signed and dated by the Registrar, was added to the first page. It was usual for parties to wish to receive originals as well as certified copies, so originals were likewise bound and sealed (but not certified or in any way signed by the Registrar). Typically, each party would receive one original and one certified copy of an award and the Secretariat would seek to ensure that it received a sufficient number of originals from the Arbitral Tribunal to allow each party to receive one and the Secretariat to retain one.

The new wording has abandoned "certified copies" and now requires an award to be "authenticated by the Registrar as an LCIA award". This new provision may be designed to address a surprising 2008 decision of the Supreme Court of Austria, which suggested that there was a lacuna in the LCIA Rules in relation to the certification of awards for the purposes of recognition under the New York Convention 1958.[9] The decision was odd because the award which the Supreme Court refused to enforce was not, in fact, an award under the LCIA Arbitration Rules but instead an award in an arbitration under the UNCITRAL Arbitration Rules administered by the LCIA. The criticism that the Registrar was not given 26–019

---

[8] Article 26.1.
[9] *O Limited (Cyprus) v M Corp (formerly A, Inc) (US) and others*, Supreme Court, Austria, September 3, 2008, 3Ob35/08f, XXXIV Y.B. COM. ARB. 409 (2009) cited in *http://www.newyorkconvention1958.org/index.php?lvl=cmspage&pageid=11&provision=224* [Accessed November 14, 2014].

specific power, under Article 26.5 of the LCIA Rules, to certify copies of awards was, therefore misplaced.

It is questionable whether the revision to the Rules and any subsequent alterations in the practice adopted by the Registrar will be sufficient to constitute "due" authentication for the purposes of Article IV(1)(a) of the New York Convention. Authentication by the LCIA Registrar may be insufficient on its own.

**26–020** In contrast to the 1998 LCIA Rules, Article 26.7 now states that the award may be transmitted to the parties in electronic form as well as the hard copy (the hard copy, which must be authenticated by the Registrar as an LCIA award, taking precedence in the case of any inconsistency). In those circumstances, the award will be sent by the Registrar by email to the parties' representatives and to anybody else specifically requested and agreed by the parties.

The "transmission" of hard copies of the award will generally be made by courier service. Parties should ensure that the LCIA Secretariat has up-to-date addresses for this purpose. If they are aware that a defaulting party's address may not be reliable (e.g. that there is a risk that at that address the award may be accepted by somebody unconnected with the party), they should inform the LCIA and seek to assist it in finding a secure way to deliver the award. Parties are free to make arrangements to collect the award from the LCIA's offices at the same time that it is sent to other parties by other means.

> **26.8** Every award (including reasons for such award) shall be final and binding on the parties. The parties undertake to carry out any award immediately and without any delay (subject only to Article 27); and the parties also waive irrevocably their right to any form of appeal, review or recourse to any state court or other legal authority, insofar as such waiver shall not be prohibited under any applicable law.

**26–021** This crucial provision (which largely replicates Article 26.9 of the 1998 LCIA Rules) is three-fold, containing:

(i) the parties' agreement that awards (and the reasons for them) shall be final and binding as soon as they have been transmitted to the parties. This is an important part of the arbitration mechanism: the final and binding nature of arbitration is what helps set it apart from other forms of contract-based dispute resolution and allows awards to be enforced as provided in the New York Convention;

(ii) an undertaking on the part of the parties to carry out any award immediately and without any delay (unless a request for corrections or an additional award is made under Article 27). This provision allows the successful party to put immediate pressure on the unsuccessful party and, if payment is not forthcoming, gives the successful party a firm basis for commencing enforcement proceedings; and

(iii) a waiver of the parties' rights "to any form of appeal, review or recourse to any state court or other legal authority" insofar as such a waiver is not prohibited by applicable law.

Under English law, the effect of Article 26.8 is that the parties waive their rights to appeal under s.69 of the English Arbitration Act 1996 (on a question of English law arising out of an award). This is important, as it helps safeguard one of the potential features of arbitration valued by many parties: its finality. Without lengthy appeals, arbitration has the realistic potential to be quicker and cheaper than litigation before many national courts.

**26–022**

In *Royal & Sun Alliance Insurance v BA Systems (Operations) Ltd*,[10] the parties accepted that specific provisions in their arbitration agreement that appeals could be made on points of law displaced Article 26.9 (as it then was). The judge noted:

> "It is common ground that in arbitral proceedings governed by the LCIA rules alone the waiver in article 26 would be effective to exclude the right of appeal conferred by s 69 of the 1996 Act: see the opening words of s 69(1)".

The question of whether the parties, having chosen the LCIA Rules, were entitled to override such a fundamental provision was not an issue. The court was concerned, instead, with the question whether, in light of the parties' agreement that such appeals were allowed, leave to appeal was required first. The court decided that leave was not needed.

**26–023**

**26.9 In the event of any final settlement of the parties' dispute, the Arbitral Tribunal may decide to make an award recording the settlement if the parties jointly so request in writing (a "Consent Award"), provided always that such Consent Award shall contain an express statement on its face that it is an award made at the parties' joint request and with their consent. A Consent Award need not contain reasons. If the parties do not jointly request a Consent Award, on written confirmation by the parties to the LCIA Court that a final settlement has been reached, the Arbitral Tribunal shall be discharged and the arbitration proceedings concluded by the LCIA Court, subject to payment by the parties of any outstanding Arbitration Costs in accordance with Articles 24 and 28.**

The Arbitral Tribunal may make a "Consent Award"—an award recording the settlement by the parties of the dispute between them (which need not be reasoned, but which must contain an express statement on its face that it is an award made at the parties' joint request and with their consent).

**26–024**

Article 26.9 provides for an even simpler method of ending an arbitration following a settlement: the parties can simply write together to the LCIA Court

---

[10] [2008] EWHC 743 (Comm).

and provide notice that a settlement has been reached. The Arbitral Tribunal can then be discharged as soon as any outstanding deposits and costs are paid.

However, a consent award, being a final award, carries the benefit of enforceability under the 1958 New York Convention. As it is an award under the LCIA Rules it should contain the LCIA Court's determination of the Arbitration Costs, unless the parties have settled liability for such costs (Articles 28.1 and 28.2). Parties should ensure that the draft wording of a consent award is submitted to the LCIA Secretariat, as well as to the Arbitral Tribunal, so that the costs aspects, and any other formalities necessary to comply with the Rules, can be filled in.

# Article 27—Correction of Award(s) and Additional Award(s)

27.1 Within 28 days of receipt of any award, a party may by written notice to the Registrar (copied to all other parties) request the Arbitral Tribunal to correct in the award any error in computation, any clerical or typographical error, any ambiguity or any mistake of a similar nature. If the Arbitral Tribunal considers the request to be justified, after consulting the parties, it shall make the correction within 28 days of receipt of the request. Any correction shall take the form of a memorandum by the Arbitral Tribunal.

27.2 The Arbitral Tribunal may also correct any error (including any error in computation, any clerical or typographical error or any error of a similar nature) upon its own initiative in the form of a memorandum within 28 days of the date of the award, after consulting the parties.

27.3 Within 28 days of receipt of the final award, a party may by written notice to the Registrar (copied to all other parties), request the Arbitral Tribunal to make an additional award as to any claim or cross-claim presented in the arbitration but not decided in any award. If the Arbitral Tribunal considers the request to be justified, after consulting the parties, it shall make the additional award within 56 days of receipt of the request.

27.4 As to any claim or cross-claim presented in the arbitration but not decided in any award, the Arbitral Tribunal may also make an additional award upon its own initiative within 28 days of the date of the award, after consulting the parties.

27.5 The provisions of Article 26.2 to 26.7 shall apply to any memorandum or additional award made hereunder. A memorandum shall be treated as part of the award.

**Introduction**

27–001 Article 27 plays a key role in ensuring the integrity of the arbitration process: it provides the parties with a safety valve—the ability to ask the Arbitral Tribunal (which may otherwise be functus officio—having exhausted their jurisdiction by issuing a final award) to correct an award it has issued—and helps give the parties a means of potentially sorting out an issue(s) with the award without having to pursue a challenge through the courts.

Such errors can usually be avoided if the award is proofread before signature. **27–004** The LCIA Secretariat can assist arbitrators by offering to proofread awards but Arbitral Tribunals do not always avail themselves of this service. Sometimes they will have an administrative secretary proofread the award but the errors may have been introduced by the administrative secretary. A fresh pair of eyes is always preferable.

A party's application for corrections must be made in writing to the Registrar (not to the Arbitral Tribunal directly), copied to the other parties to the proceedings. This is a purely administrative arrangement (reflecting the fact that the proceedings before the Arbitral Tribunal may otherwise be closed) and the Registrar will pass on the application to the Arbitral Tribunal. The Registrar will co-ordinate the process and the Arbitral Tribunal's response, keeping an eye on the time limits and consulting the Arbitral Tribunal to ensure that they are met or extended as appropriate.

The Arbitral Tribunal has 28 days[3] from the date of receipt of the application in **27–005** which to make any correction(s). If it decides that the request is justified, it must consult with the parties before making the correction.[4] In practice, the consultation will usually commence with an email to the parties, inviting those who did not make the request to comment on it. No consultation is required if the Arbitral Tribunal does not consider the request to be justified.

Any correction(s) must be made in the form of a memorandum. By Article 27.5, the provisions of Articles 26.2–26.7, relating to awards, apply to any memorandum. In terms of its form, this means that the memorandum must be in writing, state the reasons upon which it is based (unless the parties agree otherwise), be dated, state the seat of arbitration and be signed by the Arbitral Tribunal (or those members assenting to it). That memorandum then effectively becomes part of the award itself. (For the sake of good order, this should also be stated on the face of the memorandum (Article 27.5).)

As noted above, s.70(2) of the English Arbitration Act 1996 requires recourse to **27–006** any available arbitral process of appeal or review, or under s.57 to correct slips or make an additional award, before a challenge to or appeal against an award can be made to the courts. However, s.70(3) of the 1996 Act, which concerns the timing for any challenge or appeal to the courts, only refers to extending the time for a challenge or appeal where there has been an "arbitral process of appeal or review". In such a case, the 28-day period for applying to challenge or appeal against an award is to run from "the date when the applicant or appellant was notified of the result of that process". Section 70(2) distinguishes between any "arbitral process of appeal or review" on the one hand and corrections to the award or additional awards on the other. Therefore, the extended time allowed by s.70(3) to make challenges and appeals following any "arbitral process of appeal or review" does not appear to apply where there have just been corrections or additional awards.

The English court authorities on s.57 suggest that, where an application has been made under s.57, time for a challenge or appeal should not start to run until the date on which the decision on that application is made, the rationale being that

---

[3] The Arbitral Tribunal has a general power to abridge or extend time periods under Article 22.1(ii), or the LCIA Court may do so under Article 22.5, even where they have already expired.

[4] This is a change from the 1998 LCIA Rules, which did not require any consultation with the parties.

this is the date that the award as amended/supplemented/confirmed is made for the purposes of s.70(3) of the English Arbitration Act 1996.[5] Note that s.70(3) refers to the "date of the award" in the context of the original award but the date when a party is "notified of the result" of an "arbitral process of appeal or review". On the basis of the reasoning that the correction or additional award leads to a new award or new date for the award as confirmed, it should perhaps be the date of the new award or decision on a correction that is relevant for the timing of a challenge or appeal rather than the date that the additional award or decision on corrections is received by the parties. However, this is not entirely clear.

27–007 As a further potential complication, an application to a Tribunal under s.57 of the English Arbitration Act 1996 may relate to part of the award which is not the subject of a challenge or appeal. In those circumstances, it appears that the time period for the challenge or appeal to the courts may remain tied to the date of the original award provided that the issues can be severed.[6]

The same issues and reasoning as applied above in relation to s.57 may therefore be applied where an application is made under Article 27.1.

In any event, the English court has power to extend the time for making a challenge or appeal.[7]

**27.2 The Arbitral Tribunal may also correct any error (including any error in computation, any clerical or typographical error or any error of a similar nature) upon its own initiative in the form of a memorandum within 28 days of the date of the award, after consulting the parties.**

27–008 Article 27.2 allows the Arbitral Tribunal itself, after consulting the parties,[8] to correct any error in the award, although the Arbitral Tribunal is allowed 28 days[9] from the date of the award (rather than 28 days from the date of receipt of the award as is the case for party corrections—so, potentially, a shorter timeframe).

**27.3 Within 28 days of receipt of the final award, a party may by written notice to the Registrar (copied to all other parties), request the Arbitral Tribunal to make an additional award as to any claim or cross-claim presented in the arbitration but not decided in any award. If the Arbitral Tribunal considers the request to be justified,**

---

[5] See *Blackdale Ltd v McLean Homes South East Ltd*, [2001] All ER (D) 55 (Nov) per HHJ Humphrey Lloyd QC and *Al Hadha Trading Co v Tradigrain SA* [2002] 2 Lloyd's Rep. 512, per HHJ Havelock-Allan QC.

[6] See *Al Hadha Trading Co v Tradigrain SA* [2002] 2 Lloyd's Rep. 512, per HHJ Havelock-Allan QC.

[7] See s.80(5) of the English Arbitration Act 1996, which refers to the relevant rules of court in this regard (Appendix 7).

[8] This is a change from the 1998 LCIA Rules, which did not require any consultation with the parties (Appendix 4).

[9] The Arbitral Tribunal has a general power to abridge or extend time periods under Article 22.1(ii), even where they have already expired.

**after consulting the parties, it shall make the additional award within 56 days of receipt of the request.**

A party has 28 days[10] from the date of receipt of the final award to ask the Arbitral Tribunal (via the Registrar) to "make an additional award as to any claim or cross-claim presented in the arbitration but not decided in any award". This provides an opportunity to deal with an omission of this kind without having to challenge the award in the courts. As with an application for corrections under Article 27.1 (discussed above), a party's request must be made in writing to the Registrar, copied to the other parties to the proceedings.  27–009

Again, if the Arbitral Tribunal considers the request to be justified, it must consult with the parties before making an additional award.[11] The Arbitral Tribunal has 56 days[12] from the date of receipt of the application to make any additional award.

By Article 27.5, the provisions of Articles 26.2–26.7, relating to awards, apply to any additional award. In terms of its form, this means that the additional award must be in writing, state the reasons upon which it is based (unless the parties agree otherwise), be dated, state the seat of arbitration and be signed by the Arbitral Tribunal (or those members assenting to it). That additional award then effectively becomes part of the original award.  27–010

The discussion above as to time limits for challenges and appeals in the court where there has been an application to the Arbitral Tribunal for corrections under Article 27.1 is also relevant in the context of additional awards. Given that, under Article 27.5, the additional award is to "be treated as part of the award", the same rationale could be applied as for corrections and time for a challenge or appeal be extended so as to run from the date the additional award is communicated to the parties.

Again, in any event, the English court has power to extend the time for making a challenge or appeal.[13]

**27.4 As to any claim or cross-claim presented in the arbitration but not decided in any award, the Arbitral Tribunal may also make an additional award upon its own initiative within 28 days of the date of the award, after consulting the parties.**

Article 27.4 allows the Arbitral Tribunal itself, after consulting the parties, to make an additional award covering a claim or cross-claim not decided in the award, although the Arbitral Tribunal is allowed 28 days[14] from the date of the  27–011

---

[10] The Arbitral Tribunal has a general power to abridge or extend time periods under Article 22.1(ii), or the LCIA Court may do so under Article 22.5, even where they have already expired.
[11] This is a change from the 1998 LCIA Rules, which did not require any consultation with the parties (Appendix 4).
[12] The Arbitral Tribunal has a general power to abridge or extend time periods under Article 22.1(ii), even where they have already expired.
[13] See s.80(5) of the English Arbitration Act 1996, which refers to the relevant rules of court in this regard (Appendix 7).
[14] The Arbitral Tribunal has a general power to abridge or extend time periods under Article 22.1(ii), or the LCIA Court may do so under Article 22.5, even where they have already expired.

award (rather than 28 days from the date of receipt of the award as is the case for an additional award requested by a party—so, potentially, a shorter timeframe).

**27.5 The provisions of Article 26.2 to 26.7 shall apply to any memorandum or additional award made hereunder. A memorandum shall be treated as part of the award.**

27–012 By Article 27.5, the provisions of Articles 26.2–26.7, relating to awards, apply to any memorandum correcting the award or any additional award. In terms of their form, this means that the memorandum or additional award must be in writing, state the reasons upon which it is based (unless the parties agree otherwise), be dated, state the seat of arbitration and be signed by the Arbitral Tribunal (or those members assenting to it). As noted above in relation to Article 27.1, it should also, for the sake of good order, recite these provisions of Article 27.5.

## Article 28—Arbitration Costs and Legal Costs

28.1 The costs of the arbitration other than the legal or other expenses incurred by the parties themselves (the "Arbitration Costs") shall be determined by the LCIA Court in accordance with the Schedule of Costs. The parties shall be jointly and severally liable to the LCIA and the Arbitral Tribunal for such Arbitration Costs.

28.2 The Arbitral Tribunal shall specify by an award the amount of the Arbitration Costs determined by the LCIA Court (in the absence of a final settlement of the parties' dispute regarding liability for such costs). The Arbitral Tribunal shall decide the proportions in which the parties shall bear such Arbitration Costs. If the Arbitral Tribunal has decided that all or any part of the Arbitration Costs shall be borne by a party other than a party which has already covered such costs by way of a payment to the LCIA under Article 24, the latter party shall have the right to recover the appropriate amount of Arbitration Costs from the former party.

28.3 The Arbitral Tribunal shall also have the power to decide by an award that all or part of the legal or other expenses incurred by a party (the "Legal Costs") be paid by another party. The Arbitral Tribunal shall decide the amount of such Legal Costs on such reasonable basis as it thinks appropriate. The Arbitral Tribunal shall not be required to apply the rates or procedures for assessing such costs practised by any state court or other legal authority.

28.4 The Arbitral Tribunal shall make its decisions on both Arbitration Costs and Legal Costs on the general principle that costs should reflect the parties' relative success and failure in the award or arbitration or under different issues, except where it appears to the Arbitral Tribunal that in the circumstances the application of such a general principle would be inappropriate under the Arbitration Agreement or otherwise. The Arbitral Tribunal may also take into account the parties' conduct in the arbitration, including any co-operation in facilitating the proceedings as to time and cost and any non-co-operation resulting in undue delay and unnecessary expense. Any decision on costs by the Arbitral Tribunal shall be made with reasons in the award containing such decision.

28.5 In the event that the parties have howsoever agreed before their dispute that one or more parties shall pay the whole or any part of the Arbitration Costs or Legal Costs whatever the result of any dispute, arbitration or award, such agreement (in order to be effective) shall be confirmed by the parties in writing after the Commencement Date.

**28.6 If the arbitration is abandoned, suspended, withdrawn or concluded, by agreement or otherwise, before the final award is made, the parties shall remain jointly and severally liable to pay to the LCIA and the Arbitral Tribunal the Arbitration Costs determined by the LCIA Court.**

**28.7 In the event that the Arbitration Costs are less than the deposits received by the LCIA under Article 24, there shall be a refund by the LCIA to the parties in such proportions as the parties may agree in writing, or failing such agreement, in the same proportions and to the same payers as the deposits were paid to the LCIA.**

### Introduction

28–001 Article 28 deals with the determination and allocation of the costs incurred by the parties in the arbitration. Those costs are divided into two categories: (1) the costs of the Arbitral Tribunal and of the LCIA's administrative services, which are paid by the LCIA on behalf of the parties (the payment of deposits to cover those costs is dealt with in Article 24); and (2) the costs incurred directly by the parties. As noted previously in relation to Article 24, the LCIA does not incur costs itself: liabilities for Arbitration Costs are incurred by the parties and are met by the LCIA on their behalf from the funds which they have entrusted to the LCIA. The LCIA's administration charges are raised by the LCIA and are incurred by the parties.

Unless the Arbitral Tribunal considers it inappropriate for a particular case, the general principle is that the allocation by the Arbitral Tribunal of both categories of costs "should reflect the parties' relative success and failure in the award or arbitration or under different issues".[1]

**28.1 The costs of the arbitration other than the legal or other expenses incurred by the parties themselves (the "Arbitration Costs") shall be determined by the LCIA Court in accordance with the Schedule of Costs. The parties shall be jointly and severally liable to the LCIA and the Arbitral Tribunal for such Arbitration Costs.[2]**

28–002 The "Arbitration Costs" referred to here are the fees and expenses of the Arbitral Tribunal and any expert appointed by it, and the fees and expenses of the LCIA itself (being the costs that the LCIA would normally pay out of the deposits it holds).[3] These costs are determined by the LCIA Court (rather than by the Arbitral Tribunal) on the basis of calculations made by the LCIA Secretariat using information gathered and provided to the LCIA Secretariat as to costs incurred and time

---

[1] The express reference in Article 28.4 to costs allocation potentially being tied to success or failure in relation to "different issues" is a new addition, which did not appear in the 1998 LCIA Rules, although this always fell within the Arbitral Tribunal's general discretion on costs allocation.

[2] The final sentence of Article 28.1 is mirrored in section 6(i) of the LCIA's Schedule of Arbitration Costs (Appendix 2).

[3] Article 28 of the 1998 LCIA Rules referred to "the costs of the arbitration", which was a little confusing given that parties would in common parlance also refer to the legal and other costs that they incur directly as "the costs of the arbitration" (Appendix 4).

spent and the Schedule(s) of Arbitration Costs applicable at the relevant time.[4] For more detailed discussion of the composition and calculation of Arbitration Costs, see the Commentary on the Schedule of Arbitration Costs (LCIA) below.

As the bulk of these costs are likely to be the fees of the Arbitral Tribunal, having the LCIA Court determine them maintains some separation between the parties and the arbitrators over what could be sensitive issues. If the Arbitral Tribunal has made errors in its billing or if the LCIA Court considers its fees and/or expenses to be excessive, these matters will be addressed by the LCIA without the parties being troubled by them. The LCIA's control of costs is one of the primary reasons why parties choose arbitration under its Rules.

In relation to the LCIA's own charges and expenses, section 1 of the Schedule of Arbitration Costs (LCIA) (effective October 1, 2014) provides for the following charges: **28–003**

(a) £1,750 Registration Fee (payable in advance with Request for Arbitration and non-refundable);

(b) £250 per hour for the Registrar/Deputy Registrar;

(c) £225 per hour for the Counsel;

(d) £175 per hour for case administrators;

(e) £150 per hour for casework accounting functions;

(f) charges calculated using hourly rates advised by members of the LCIA Court for time spent by them in deciding challenges;

(g) a sum "equivalent to 5 per cent of the fees" of the Arbitral Tribunal (excluding expenses) for the LCIA's general overhead; and

(h) expenses "incurred by the Secretariat and by members of the LCIA Court, in connection with the arbitration (such as postage, telephone, facsimile, travel etc.) and additional arbitration support services, whether provided by the Secretariat or by the members of the LCIA Court from their own resources or otherwise".

The LCIA staff working on a case will record time spent on administrative and accounting activities on that case. Details will be provided in invoices sent to the parties at various intervals during the arbitration.

Section 2(i) of the Schedule of Arbitration Costs provides that the fees of the Arbitral Tribunal: **28–004**

"... will be calculated by reference to work done by its members in connection with the arbitration and will be charged at rates appropriate to the particular circumstances of the case, including its complexity and the special qualifications of the arbitrators."

The arbitrators' fees are based on hourly rates, fixed by agreement between the LCIA and the arbitrator in question, but which are not to exceed £450 save in **28–005**

---

[4] The Schedule of Costs, which forms part of the LCIA Rules, is updated from time to time.

exceptional cases. In such exceptional cases (which are comparitively rare), higher hourly rates may be: (i) fixed by the LCIA Court on the recommendation of the Registrar, following consultations with the arbitrator(s); and (ii) agreed expressly by all parties. For many senior arbitrators, the £450 cap will be less than their normal charges and this can therefore save the parties considerable sums over the life of an arbitration as compared with appointing the same arbitrators on an ad hoc basis. In appropriate cases, where the sums involved are low, arbitrators have charged as little as £250 per hour.

The arbitrators may charge for travelling time and for time reserved for hearings but not used as a result of late postponement or cancellation (provided that the basis for such charge has been advised in writing to, and approved by, the LCIA Court).[5] If the Arbitral Tribunal is going to avail itself of this right, the parties should be given details in the notice of appointment of the Arbitral Tribunal. Such charges, which are common, are intended to compensate arbitrators who might be unable to find work to occupy time reserved but not then used for an arbitration. However, it might be questioned whether, in many cases, they are truly justified. This is particularly the case given that the cancellation periods used often extend to several months before the hearing in question and arbitrators are often busy practitioners with more than one case to attend to at any one time. Parties who are concerned about such arrangements may wish to raise the issue with the Registrar.

**28–006** The arbitrators can also recover expenses reasonably incurred in connection with the arbitration. The LCIA Secretariat is vigilant on expenses and explains to arbitrators, when necessary, that luxury hotels and first class air fares will not usually be considered reasonable.

The use of hourly rates for the fees of the arbitrator(s) and the LCIA requires detailed records to be kept (for vetting by the LCIA Court) and contrasts with the approach of some other institutions[6] in fixing the fees of the arbitrator(s) and the institutions' own charges by reference to the amount in dispute (the "ad valorem" basis). There is debate as to which system works best for the parties in practice. Advocates for the use of hourly rates suggest that this produces fees which are a fair reflection of the work which is actually carried out (and good value for many given the cap on the rate for arbitrators). Where substantial sums are at issue, calculating fees by reference to a percentage of those sums will produce a relatively high figure which might not seem justified if the dispute is straightforward and quick to resolve. Advocates for the ad valorem basis suggest that this provides an incentive for the arbitrators to be as efficient as they can, although it might be expected that this would be their approach in any event. It is also sometimes suggested that the ad valorem basis provides a disincentive to parties to inflate their claims, although again, it might be doubted whether this has much influence in practice.

**28–007** By the final sentence of Article 28.1, each of the Claimant(s) and the Respondent(s) agree to be jointly and severally liable to the Arbitral Tribunal and the LCIA for the Arbitration Costs. It follows that the LCIA (or the Arbitral Tribunal) could claim the costs, in full, against any or all of the parties. If there is a shortfall of costs before the final award is sent to the parties, the LCIA is entitled

---

[5] The LCIA's standard cancellation formula is set out at 19–003 above.
[6] Notably, the ICC, SIAC and SCC.

to seek payment from only one party if, for example, that party is the only one to have participated in the arbitration and to have paid deposits.

Article 28.1 works together with Article 24.3, which expressly allows the LCIA to seek a substitute deposit payment from one of the parties to the arbitration where the other party fails or refuses to make its own deposit payment. These provisions, coupled with Article 15.9, ensure that the arbitration can proceed even if one party does not take part and does not pay its share of the fees.

The ultimate impact of not paying the Arbitration Costs is reflected in Article 26.7 of the LCIA Rules, which states that the LCIA Court will transmit the awards to the parties "provided that all Arbitration Costs have been paid in full to the LCIA in accordance with Articles 24 and 28".[7] The procedure for dealing with final deposits and shortfalls is described above in relation to Article 26.

**28–008**

**28.2 The Arbitral Tribunal shall specify by an award the amount of the Arbitration Costs determined by the LCIA Court (in the absence of a final settlement of the parties' dispute regarding liability for such costs). The Arbitral Tribunal shall decide the proportions in which the parties shall bear such Arbitration Costs. If the Arbitral Tribunal has decided that all or any part of the Arbitration Costs shall be borne by a party other than a party which has already covered such costs by way of a payment to the LCIA under Article 24, the latter party shall have the right to recover the appropriate amount of Arbitration Costs from the former party.**

In the absence of a final settlement between the parties, prior to finalising its award, the Arbitral Tribunal will obtain from the LCIA a statement of the total Arbitration Costs as determined by the LCIA Court (with the assistance of the Registrar), which must be specified in the award. If there has been a settlement, the procedure is that the LCIA Court will make its determination of the Arbitration Costs and the Secretariat will communicate a financial summary to the parties. In that situation, provided that the parties are able to agree between them their respective liabilities for those costs, and consequently the amounts of any shortfalls and refunds, the Arbitral Tribunal may not be required to deal with the Arbitration Costs in an award.

**28–009**

Absent any agreement between the parties as to the allocation of Arbitration Costs (dealt with in Article 28.5), it is then for the Arbitral Tribunal to set out in its award the proportions in which it has determined in its discretion (subject to Article 28.4) that the parties shall bear those costs. Note that these "Arbitration Costs" are those referenced in Article 28.1, and do not include the legal or other expenses incurred directly by the parties (which are dealt with in Article 28.3). Article 28.2 obliges the Arbitral Tribunal to state the Arbitration Costs in its award and allocate them between the parties. This is therefore a duty of the Arbitral Tribunal, regardless of the submissions made by the parties. There is no such duty in relation to the "legal or other expenses" incurred directly by the parties. Statistics from the Registrar confirm that in 92 awards made in 2012 and 2013 containing decisions on costs, Arbitration Costs were to be paid in full by one party in 73 and were

---

[7] Article 26.7 is mirrored in para.6(iii) of the LCIA's Schedule of Arbitration Costs (Appendix 2).

**28–010** apportioned (though not necessarily equally) between the parties in 19; in 3 cases, whilst decisions were made on the apportionment of Arbitration Costs, no decisions were made as to the apportionment of Legal Costs.

The final sentence of Article 28.2 deals with the scenario where the Arbitral Tribunal's allocation of the Arbitration Costs does not reflect the deposits already paid by the parties. In those circumstances, the party that has paid to the LCIA by way of deposit more than its share of the Arbitration Costs (as now determined by the Arbitral Tribunal) can recover the appropriate balance of costs from the other party.

This rule is helpful because, as explained above in relation to Article 26.2, the Arbitral Tribunal will often not know when it makes its award which party will make the final payment towards the Arbitration Costs and it will therefore not be able to state, in its award, who owes how much to whom in accordance with its decision on the allocation of those costs. This is an accounting matter for the LCIA Secretariat. In that situation, in order to make a recovery on enforcement, the party entitled to the appropriate balance cannot rely on the award itself and must invoke this rule in support.

> **28.3 The Arbitral Tribunal shall also have the power to decide by an award that all or part of the legal or other expenses incurred by a party (the "Legal Costs") be paid by another party. The Arbitral Tribunal shall decide the amount of such Legal Costs on such reasonable basis as it thinks appropriate. The Arbitral Tribunal shall not be required to apply the rates or procedures for assessing such costs practised by any state court or other legal authority.**

**28–011** Article 28.3 deals with the legal or other expenses that the parties incur directly themselves (referred to as the "Legal Costs") as distinct from the Arbitration Costs incurred through the LCIA. The Legal Costs (which are usually the bulk of the costs incurred) include, but are not limited to, the fees and expenses of the parties' legal representatives, the fees and expenses of any experts instructed by the parties (as distinct from any Arbitral Tribunal-appointed expert) and any other incidental costs (such as expenses incurred in relation to attending hearings and having them transcribed, expenses of witnesses and so on).

The Arbitral Tribunal has the power, or discretion, to make an order in relation to the Legal Costs incurred, rather than the duty which exists in relation to the Arbitration Costs.[8] Arbitral Tribunals can and do decline to exercise this power.

**28–012** Absent any agreement between the parties (dealt with in Article 28.5), it is for the discretion of the Arbitral Tribunal (subject to Article 28.4) whether and, if so, how to allocate in its award the Legal Costs incurred by each of the parties and therefore for the parties to make submissions to the Arbitral Tribunal as appropriate. As with the Arbitration Costs, the Arbitral Tribunal has the discretion to order that the parties should each bear their own Legal Costs, or that one party should bear a greater proportion, or all, of the Legal Costs. According to statistics from the Registrar, in 92 awards dealing with costs and made in 2012 and 2013, Legal Costs were awarded to one party in 35 cases, were apportioned differently in 47, and each party was ordered to bear its own in seven; no decision at all was made in three.

---

[8] In some jurisdictions, for example the US, it is common for parties to bear their own legal costs.

Fixing the amount of the Legal Costs to be paid by a party is also at the discretion of the Arbitral Tribunal, provided that any determination of those costs is on a "reasonable basis". In broad terms, this means that the Arbitral Tribunal has the discretion to reduce, or disallow altogether where reasonable, any particular item claimed by the parties under the head of Legal Costs. This provision allows Arbitral Tribunals to reduce, for example, claims for legal fees, costs or expenses which it considers to be unreasonably high.

The Arbitral Tribunal's discretion to decide for itself how to benchmark the reasonableness of the Legal Costs claimed is underlined by the last sentence of Article 28.3 (which did not appear in the 1998 LCIA Rules), which expressly frees the Arbitral Tribunal from having to apply "the rates or procedures for assessing such costs practised by any state court or other legal authority".  **28–013**

The 1998 version of this rule required the Arbitral Tribunal to "fix the amount of each item comprising such costs", which reflected s.63(3)(b) of the English Arbitration Act 1996, i.e. English practice. In principle, Arbitral Tribunals were required to carry out an "assessment" (or "taxation") of costs, examining schedules of costs and considering the reasonableness of each item claimed. This is the normal practice in many London-seated arbitrations[9] but, in LCIA arbitrations under the 1998 Rules, Arbitral Tribunals unfamiliar with this peculiar English approach to costs could ignore this requirement (or interpret it differently) and fix the recoverable amounts of costs on a "broad brush" principle more usually applicable in international arbitrations.

It remains to be seen what impact the new wording will have on costs awards. One possible effect will be a decline in confidence amongst after the event insurers, for whom LCIA arbitration used to present the attraction that their liability to pay the costs of their insured's opponent should be assessed for reasonableness item by item by the Arbitral Tribunal, i.e. "adjusted" in a manner similar to the assessment of an insured loss.  **28–014**

It should be noted that if the decisions on costs are to be included in the final award, it is usual practice for the Arbitral Tribunal to invite the parties to file costs submissions and schedules simultaneously at the end of the proceedings.

**28.4 The Arbitral Tribunal shall make its decisions on both Arbitration Costs and Legal Costs on the general principle that costs should reflect the parties' relative success and failure in the award or arbitration or under different issues, except where it appears to the Arbitral Tribunal that in the circumstances the application of such a general principle would be inappropriate under the Arbitration Agreement or otherwise. The Arbitral Tribunal may also take into account the parties' conduct in the arbitration, including any co-operation in facilitating the proceedings as to time and cost and any non-co-operation resulting in undue delay and unnecessary expense. Any decision on costs by the Arbitral Tribunal shall be made with reasons in the award containing such decision.**

---

[9] See, for example, the Chartered Institute of Arbitrators' Practice Guideline 9 at para 5.4, which advises arbitrators that an assessment of costs is "essential" and that they should issue "an award setting out the items of recoverable costs and the amount referable to each item".

28–015    Article 28.4 broadly reflects the "loser pays" principle, although with some refinements. Unless there are particular circumstances which suggest that this approach is not appropriate, the Arbitral Tribunal is obliged to make its costs orders according to what it adjudges to be the relative success and failure of the parties. Therefore, in a simple case of a clear winner and loser, the general principle would mean that the successful party should recover its reasonable costs from the unsuccessful party. However, in many cases the parties will each have successes and failures in relation to different aspects of and issues in the arbitration. The concept of relative success and failure therefore caters for this more complex position, and is itself subject to the Arbitral Tribunal considering that, in light of the particular circumstances, that approach is inappropriate.

Article 28.4 may be compared with s.61(2) of the English Arbitration Act 1996, which provides that:

> "Unless the parties otherwise agree, the tribunal shall award costs on the general principle that costs should follow the event[10] except where it appears to the tribunal that in the circumstances this is not appropriate in relation to the whole or part of the costs".

28–016    Article 42(1) of the 2010 UNCITRAL Rules provides that:

> "The costs of the arbitration shall in principle be borne by the unsuccessful party or parties" but that the Tribunal "may apportion each of such costs between the parties if it determines that apportionment is reasonable, taking into account the circumstances of the case".

The ICC Rules, on the other hand, in Article 37(4), simply state that:

> "The final award shall fix the costs of the arbitration[11] and decide which of the parties shall bear them or in what proportion they shall be borne by the parties".

28–017    In many cases, determining the relative success and failure of the parties in the award is a complex exercise. That might be the case where, for example, the "winner" has succeeded on a slim majority of the multiple issues in the dispute or where the "loser" has in fact won on most of the issues, but lost on particular issues that render it the net financial "loser" because it is ordered to pay money to the "winner". In such circumstances, the Arbitral Tribunal has the ability to adopt different approaches and, for example, allocate costs on an issue by issue basis.

Article 28.4 also allows the Arbitral Tribunal the latitude to allocate costs in a way that penalises parties for unreasonable conduct during the arbitration proceedings. That unreasonable conduct might take the form of advancing unmeritorious arguments or being unnecessarily aggressive including conduct constituting a breach by Legal Representation of the principles set out in the Annex to the Rules and as otherwise contemplated by Article 18.6. It might also include the unreasonable rejection

---

[10] Stating that costs should "follow the event" suggests that there is a winner or loser and might therefore be regarded as a more blunt instrument than reflecting the parties' relative success and failure, although this might make little difference in practice, especially given the Arbitral Tribunal's overarching discretion where it does not consider this approach to be appropriate for "the whole or part of the costs".

[11] For these purposes, under the ICC Rules, the "costs of the arbitration" include the legal costs and expenses incurred by the parties.

of settlement initiatives or offers made during the proceedings (either on an open basis or on a "without prejudice, save as to costs" basis).[12]

Other options are open to the Arbitral Tribunal. As noted above, the Arbitral Tribunal has the discretion to order that the parties should each bear their own costs, or that the costs should be split equally between the parties. The Arbitral Tribunal also has the ability to apportion the Arbitration Costs differently from the "Legal Costs" incurred by the parties.  **28–018**

In practice it is common for the winning party to suffer some reduction in the Legal Costs awarded to it on the grounds of reasonableness, especially in long and / or complex cases. The approach adopted by the Arbitral Tribunal will often reflect the legal background and experience of the arbitrator. In this regard LCIA arbitration is similar to London seated arbitration under the rules of other major international arbitration institutions. Where the seat of arbitration is England and Wales, s.63(1) of the Arbitration Act 1996 allows the parties to agree what costs are recoverable. If the parties do not agree (as is generally the case), s.63(3) allows the Arbitral Tribunal to determine in its award the recoverable costs "on such basis as it thinks fit" and, unless determined otherwise by the Arbitral Tribunal, "on the basis that there shall be allowed a reasonable amount in respect of all costs reasonably incurred".[13] This provision potentially allows considerable argument as to whether the costs have been reasonably incurred and whether the amount of the costs is itself reasonable, although Arbitral Tribunals often take a commercial, pragmatic approach.[14]

**28.5 In the event that the parties have howsoever agreed before their dispute that one or more parties shall pay the whole or any part of the Arbitration Costs or Legal Costs whatever the result of any dispute, arbitration or award, such agreement (in order to be effective) shall be confirmed by the parties in writing after the Commencement Date.**

An agreement between the parties regarding payment of potential future costs might result from, for example, a situation where the Respondent has promised to indemnify the Claimant for its Legal Costs in relation to the particular issue in dispute. However, where the seat of the arbitration is England and Wales, s.60 of the Arbitration Act 1996 stipulates that:  **28–019**

"An agreement which has the effect that a party is to pay the whole or part of the costs of the arbitration[15] in any event is only valid if made after the dispute in question has arisen".

Article 28.5, which is a new provision, not found in the 1998 LCIA Rules, seeks to address any s.60 issue by requiring the parties to confirm their agreement as to

---

[12] See, in this regard, and in relation to the issue of costs awards in international commercial arbitration more generally, Jonathan Wood, "Protection Against Adverse Costs Awards in International Arbitration", JICARB (2008) 74(2) 139.
[13] Per s.63(5)(a) of the English Arbitration Act 1996 (Appendix 7). Note that s.63(3) also provides that if the Tribunal determines the recoverable costs on the basis that it thinks is fit, "it shall specify: (a) the basis on which it has acted; and (b) the items of recoverable costs and the amount referable to each".
[14] Note that s.63(5)(b) of the Arbitration Act 1996 provides that "any doubt as to whether costs were reasonably incurred or were reasonable in amount shall be resolved in favour of the paying party".
[15] In this context, the "costs of the arbitration" are defined in s.59 of the Arbitration Act 1996 to include legal or other costs of the parties (and are therefore not limited to the "Arbitration Costs" referred to in the LCIA Rules).

costs allocation again after the arbitration has commenced (and so by definition after the dispute has arisen). Section 60 is a mandatory provision of the English Arbitration Act 1996, based on public policy considerations, and cannot therefore be excluded by the parties. To the extent that Article 28.5 seeks to impose a strict obligation on the parties to confirm an agreement as to costs allocation after commencement of the arbitration its enforceability may therefore be open to question on public policy grounds.

**28.6 If the arbitration is abandoned, suspended, withdrawn or concluded, by agreement or otherwise, before the final award is made, the parties shall remain jointly and severally liable to pay to the LCIA and the Arbitral Tribunal the Arbitration Costs determined by the LCIA Court.**

28–020  Article 28.6 confirms that the parties remain jointly and severally liable for the "Arbitration Costs", even if the arbitration has been "abandoned, suspended or concluded" early. As explained above in the context of Article 28.1, the LCIA can enforce the parties' payment obligation, in full, against any party (or all of them, if it so chooses).

**28.7 In the event that the Arbitration Costs are less than the deposits received by the LCIA under Article 24, there shall be a refund by the LCIA to the parties in such proportions as the parties may agree in writing, or failing such agreement, in the same proportions and to the same payers as the deposits were paid to the LCIA.**

28–021  If the parties have paid sufficient deposits on account of the "Arbitration Costs", this Article governs the refund to the parties of the excess deposit held by the LCIA.

In practice, Article 28.7 will most often come into play following a settlement. In such event, the LCIA Court will determine the "Arbitration Costs" and the parties will be provided with a statement of those sums held by the LCIA and those that have been spent. The parties may agree in writing the proportions for the refund of any remaining amounts held by the LCIA they are each to receive (but they should liaise with the LCIA Secretariat to obtain an up to date financial summary and to check their sums, thereby avoiding making an agreement which is contrary to their expectations or impossible to implement). If not, the amounts held by the LCIA will be refunded in the same proportions as the deposits were made by the parties (which is typically in equal shares).

As explained in section 3(ii) of the LCIA's Schedule of Arbitration Costs, the payments made by the parties on account of the Arbitration Costs are held by the LCIA in trust and invested. Interest is credited to the sums held, which will be refunded to the parties if the "Arbitration Costs" are less than the sums paid by the parties by way of deposit pursuant to Article 24 (plus the interest earned).[16]

---

[16] As explained in relation to Article 24.2, the parties are credited with interest at the overnight deposit rate, with any surplus income being retained by the LCIA.

ARTICLE 29—DETERMINATIONS AND DECISIONS BY LCIA COURT

**29.1** The determinations of the LCIA Court with respect to all matters relating to the arbitration shall be conclusive and binding upon the parties and the Arbitral Tribunal, unless otherwise directed by the LCIA Court. Save for reasoned decisions on arbitral challenges under Article 10, such determinations are to be treated as administrative in nature; and the LCIA Court shall not be required to give reasons for any such determination.

**29.2** To the extent permitted by any applicable law, the parties shall be taken to have waived any right of appeal or review in respect of any determination and decision of the LCIA Court to any state court or other legal authority. If such appeal or review takes place due to mandatory provisions of any applicable law or otherwise, the LCIA Court may determine whether or not the arbitration should continue, notwithstanding such appeal or review.

**Introduction**

The LCIA Court has wide-ranging administrative powers under the LCIA Rules, including selecting and appointing arbitrators (Articles 5 and 8), deciding applications for the expedited formation of the Arbitral Tribunal and appointment of Emergency Arbitrators (Article 9), dealing with challenges to arbitrators (Article 10), determining the initial language to be used (Article 17.2), in certain circumstances determining applications for the extension or shortening of time limits (Article 22.5), consolidating proceedings (Article 22.6) and setting the "Arbitration Costs" (Articles 24 and 28).

29–001

Article 29 states that determinations of the LCIA Court are conclusive and binding (unless directed otherwise)[1] and administrative in nature (so generally no reasons are required to be given), and seeks to circumscribe the ability to challenge those decisions.

As explained below in connection with Article 29.2, for arbitrations with their seat in England and Wales, parties have the non-derogable right to apply to the English courts to remove an arbitrator on the grounds specified in s.24 of the English Arbitration Act 1996. This is not a right of appeal or review but a right to a new hearing on the issue.

29–002

Likewise, parties to English seated arbitrations have the non-derogable right to have the amount of the arbitrators' fees and expenses considered and adjusted by the English courts (s.28 of the 1996 Act). The LCIA Court's determinations of

---

[1] As noted below, the decisions of the LCIA Court in relation to the initial language of the arbitration under Article 17.2, and in relation to time limits pursuant to Article 22.5 of the Rules are expressly subject to subsequent orders of the Arbitral Tribunal.

costs under Article 28 are thus susceptible to review. The LCIA Secretariat's scrutiny of arbitrators' fees and the LCIA Court's diligence in maintaining the institution's reputation for reasonableness have meant that there have not yet been any referrals to court under s.28.[2]

> **29.1** The determinations of the LCIA Court with respect to all matters relating to the arbitration shall be conclusive and binding upon the parties and the Arbitral Tribunal, unless otherwise directed by the LCIA Court. Save for reasoned decisions on arbitral challenges under Article 10, such determinations are to be treated as administrative in nature; and the LCIA Court shall not be required to give reasons for any such determination.

29–003  Through Article 29.1, by agreeing to arbitration under the LCIA Rules, parties agree that as well as decisions of any Arbitral Tribunal being binding upon them, the determinations[3] of the LCIA Court shall also be conclusive and binding.

This helps to ensure that the administrative aspects of any arbitration run as smoothly as possible, particularly in the early stages where the LCIA Court's assistance is often required (for example, in relation to the selection and appointment of arbitrators). Without such a provision, and should a party be able to challenge all the decisions of the LCIA Court, there would be great potential for mischief.[4]

29–004  Article 29.1 also confirms that the LCIA Court's decisions are to be treated as administrative in nature, so that, other than decisions as to arbitral challenges, where reasons are to be given,[5] no reasons are required.

The LCIA Court's role is not to decide the disputes and differences of law and fact that have arisen between the parties (that is the Arbitral Tribunal's role). The LCIA Court simply seeks to ensure that the arbitration process operates properly. With no general requirement for reasons to be given, the LCIA Court can make its determinations more quickly and cheaply. No prejudice is suffered by the parties because they have no right to challenge the determinations in any event.

29–005  The exception for decisions as to challenges of arbitrators reflects the LCIA Court's practice under the 1998 LCIA Rules, which was to give reasons for those decisions even though at the time it was not required to do so.[6] Abstracts of decisions have been published in an anonymised format.[7] This provides the arbitration

---

[2] In contrast, the Grain and Feed Trade Association (GAFTA) costs regime and practices came in for criticism in *Agrimex Ltd v Tradigrain Ltd* [2003] EWHC 1656 (Comm), a case which is of interest also for judicial views on the speed with which arbitrators ought to draft awards.

[3] The reference to "determinations" is a change from the reference to "decisions" under the 1998 LCIA Rules, and is of wider scope.

[4] This is subject to minor exceptions in respect of specific functions of the LCIA Court introduced in the 2014 version of the LCIA Rules, which are intended as stop-gap powers to be exercised pending or subject to review and subsequent determinations by the Arbitral Tribunal. They include the power to set the initial language of the arbitration, pursuant to Article 17.2 and the power to abridge or extend any time limit under Article 22.6.

[5] See Article 10.6.

[6] Article 10.6 of the new LCIA Rules does now require the LCIA Court to give reasons for these particular decisions.

[7] See Geoff Nicholas and Constantine Partasides, "LCIA Court Decisions on Challenge to Arbitrators: A Proposal to Publish" (2007) 23(1) Arbitration Int. 1, in which the authors argue that

community with the benefit of the approach taken by the LCIA Court and, correspondingly, more concrete guidance as to what, in practice, has been considered a lack of arbitrator impartiality or independence.[8]

**29.2 To the extent permitted by any applicable law, the parties shall be taken to have waived any right of appeal or review in respect of any determination and decision of the LCIA Court to any state court or other legal authority. If such appeal or review takes place due to mandatory provisions of any applicable law or otherwise, the LCIA Court may determine whether or not the arbitration should continue, notwithstanding such appeal or review.**

Article 29.2 is not concerned with actions against the LCIA Court[9] but rather with actions to contest its determinations and decisions regarding the administration of the arbitration. Article 29.2 waives any right that the parties may have to appeal or review determinations and decisions of the LCIA Court before any state court or other legal authority, in so far as such waiver is permitted by any applicable law.[10]

The Article therefore expressly recognises that some laws may restrict the parties' ability to waive such rights. As a matter of English law, there are limited routes to appeal or review a decision of the LCIA Court.[11]

The most contentious decisions of the LCIA Court are likely, in practice, to be those relating to challenges to arbitrators. Under English law, parties have the non-derogable right to apply to the English courts to remove an arbitrator on the grounds specified in s.24 of the English Arbitration Act 1996.[12] An application to the court under s.24 is not an appeal from or challenge to a decision of the LCIA Court, but rather a new application to be heard afresh by the court.[13] In terms of timing though, by s.24(2), such application could not be made until after the relevant party had first exhausted any available recourse to the LCIA Court pursuant to Article 10.

29–006

29–007

---

the LCIA should publish its challenge decisions, which was followed in 2011 by the "Special Challenges" issue of *Arbitration International* 27(3). Reasoned challenge decisions are rarely given, let alone published, by other institutions. Article 11(4) of the 2012 ICC Rules provides, for example, that "The decisions of the Court as to the appointment, confirmation, challenge or replacement of an arbitrator shall be final, and the reasons for such decisions shall not be communicated". The ICC has been criticised for its refusal to amend this provision: see Yves Derains and Eric A. Schwartz, *A Guide to the ICC Rules of Arbitration*, 2nd edition (Kluwer Law International, 2005), p.140.

[8] English court decisions under s.24 of the English Arbitration Act 1996 provide another valuable source of information in this regard. See, for example, *A v B* [2011] EWHC 2345 (Comm), which concerned an LCIA arbitration and in which the LCIA Court's decision to dismiss the challenge was endorsed.

[9] In this regard note, in any event, the exclusion of liability in Article 31 of the LCIA Rules.

[10] The reference to "any applicable law" is wider than the provision previously made in Article 29.2 of the 1998 LCIA Rules, which referred only to the extent permitted by law of the seat of the arbitration (Appendix 4).

[11] As a matter of common law it might, for example, be possible to challenge a decision of the LCIA Court on the basis of fraud. That right would not be defeated by the language of Article 29.2.

[12] Grounds for removal of an arbitrator pursuant to s.24 of the English Arbitration Act 1996 concern the arbitrator's impartiality, qualifications, physical or mental capacity or refusal/failure properly to conduct the proceedings or to use all reasonable despatch.

[13] See, for example, the comments of Flaux J in *A v B* [2011] EWHC 2345 (Comm) at [18].

Article 29.2 provides that if appeals or reviews of LCIA Court determinations and decisions are possible, the LCIA Court may "determine whether or not the arbitration should continue, notwithstanding such appeal or review". The LCIA Rules therefore reserve to the LCIA Court the right to decide whether the arbitration should proceed or be suspended pending the decision in any such appeal or review.[14]

Under English law, the Tribunal is given the power to continue the arbitration pending the decision of the court on an application to remove an arbitrator under s.24 of the English Arbitration Act 1996. There could therefore be thought to be a potential conflict between the Tribunal's power under the 1996 Act and the LCIA Court's rights under the LCIA Rules. However, as already noted, the court's decision under s.24 is not an "appeal or review" of the LCIA Court's decision but rather a new hearing of the issue. In practice, it seems likely that if the LCIA Court has upheld the position of an arbitrator on a challenge it would defer to the Arbitral Tribunal as to whether or not to proceed pending the decision in an application to the court.

As noted at 29–002 above, parties also have a non-derogable right to have the amount of the Arbitration Costs considered and adjusted by the English courts if their arbitration is seated in London (s.28 of the English Arbitration Act 1996).

---

[14] Although the wording of Article 29.2 could be interpreted as empowering the LCIA Court effectively to terminate the arbitration altogether in light of an appeal against or review of one of its decisions, the better interpretation is that it is concerned with whether or not to stay the arbitration pending the outcome of the appeal or review.

ARTICLE 30—CONFIDENTIALITY

**30.1 The parties undertake as a general principle to keep confidential all awards in the arbitration, together with all materials in the arbitration created for the purpose of the arbitration and all other documents produced by another party in the proceedings not otherwise in the public domain, save and to the extent that disclosure may be required of a party by legal duty, to protect or pursue a legal right, or to enforce or challenge an award in legal proceedings before a state court or other legal authority.**

**30.2 The deliberations of the Arbitral Tribunal shall remain confidential to its members, save as required by any applicable law and to the extent that disclosure of an arbitrator's refusal to participate in the arbitration is required of the other members of the Arbitral Tribunal under Articles 10, 12, 26 and 27.**

**30.3 The LCIA does not publish any award or any part of an award without the prior written consent of all parties and the Arbitral Tribunal.**

## Introduction

Arbitration can provide greater privacy and confidentiality than litigation (which in the English and many other national courts is generally open to the public). Confidentiality is therefore often touted as one of the key advantages of arbitration, although the extent of any confidentiality and whether it is an advantage, a disadvantage or simply a feature depends upon the parties' perspectives, their agreement and the applicable law(s). 30–001

In most cases, the parties could provide in their arbitration agreements for the level of confidentiality that they desire. However, it is relatively unusual for them to do so. Whilst some parties may be content with the relevant default position, others just never address the issue.

Absent express provision by the parties, the degree of confidentiality afforded to arbitrations can differ substantially according to any arbitration rules adopted and the applicable law(s).[1] For example, under English substantive law, a duty of confidentiality in relation to arbitration proceedings under common law is implied into 30–002

---

[1] For a survey and explanation of the approach to confidentiality across a number of jurisdictions, see the International Law Association's International Commercial Arbitration Committee's Report and Recommendations on "Confidentiality in International Commercial Arbitration" by Filip de Ly, Mark Friedman and Luca Radicati di Brozolo (2012) 28(3) Arbitration Int. 355.

the arbitration agreement, although this is subject to a number of exceptions.[2] Under the laws of some other jurisdictions there is no implied obligation of confidentiality.[3] It cannot, therefore, be assumed that arbitration proceedings will necessarily be confidential without examining the agreements reached and knowing what laws apply. For example, for an arbitration with its seat in England and Wales, but where the governing law of the Arbitration Agreement is not English law, the rules (if any) on confidentiality (absent any stipulations by the parties) will depend upon that governing law and what (if any) arbitration rules have been adopted.[4]

If the LCIA Rules have been selected, Article 30 seeks to ensure that, even absent specific provision by the parties, there are obligations of confidentiality. The parties' undertaking in Article 30.1, combined with the restrictions in Article 30.2 and Article 30.3, augment the applicable law, which might not contain such wide-ranging provisions as to confidentiality.[5] If the parties do not want these confidentiality obligations, they are free to agree in writing that they do not apply. The LCIA Rules therefore simply set the default position as requiring confidentiality.

> **30.1** The parties undertake as a general principle to keep confidential all awards in the arbitration, together with all materials in the arbitration created for the purpose of the arbitration and all other documents produced by another party in the proceedings not otherwise in the public domain, save and to the extent that disclosure may be required of a party by legal duty, to protect or pursue a legal right, or to enforce or challenge an award in legal proceedings before a state court or other legal authority.

**30–003** Article 30.1 contains the parties' express agreement to keep the documents referenced confidential, subject to the specific exceptions stated.

The categories of documents subject to the confidentiality undertaking are as follows:

(a) *"all awards in the arbitration"*: This extends to any partial or interim awards, as well as final awards. This category does not include any directions or orders (or other communications) received from the Arbitral Tribunal, which arguably fall within the next category;

---

[2] This duty of confidentiality is implied as a matter of English law into the arbitration agreement between the parties (see *Oxford Shipping Co Ltd v Nippon Yusen Kaisha (The "Eastern Saga" (No.2))* [1984] 3 All E.R. 835, *Ali Shipping Corp v Shipyard Trogir* [1998] 2 All E.R. 136 and *Department of Economic Policy and Development of the City of Moscow v Bankers Trust Co* [2004] EWCA Civ 314), and is a substantive rule of arbitration (*Emmott v Michael Wilson & Partners Ltd* [2008] EWCA Civ 184, per Lawrence Collins LJ at [84] and [106]). However, this policy may give way to interests of justice (and possibly public interest) or where it is reasonably necessary for the protection of the legitimate interests of an arbitrating party (*Emmott v Michael Wilson*). Confidentiality was deliberately not dealt with in the Arbitration Act 1996 upon the basis that it was better dealt with by the courts at common law (see, for example, the Departmental Advisory Committee Report on the 1996 Act, dated November 2006).

[3] See *Esso Australia Resources Ltd v Plowman* [1995] 183 CLR 10.

[4] Note in this regard that the 2012 ICC Rules do not make any express provision for the confidentiality of the award, although, under Article 26(3), hearings take place in private.

[5] If the governing law is English, the obligations of confidentiality under Article 30 are broadly the same as those implied by the common law.

Article 27 matches in most respects the default provision in this regard in s.57(3) of the English Arbitration Act 1996:

"The tribunal may on its own initiative or on the application of a party:

(a) correct an award so as to remove any clerical mistake or error arising from an accidental slip or omission or clarify or remove any ambiguity in the award; or

(b) make an additional award in respect of any claim (including a claim for interest or costs) which was presented to the tribunal but was not dealt with in the award".

27–002 However, Article 27 does not extend to the related concept of interpretation found in Article 35(2) of the 2012 ICC Rules. In this respect the LCIA Rules favour the finality of the award.[1]

It is worth noting that this review process is an important precursor to commencing a challenge in some jurisdictions. For example, s.70(2) of the English Arbitration Act 1996 provides that "An application or appeal may not be brought if the applicant or appellant has not first exhausted: (a) any available arbitral process of appeal or review; and (b) any available recourse under section 57. . .". This has given rise to difficult questions as to the effect of such applications on the time limits for bringing a challenge or appeal (discussed further below).

> **27.1** Within 28 days of receipt of any award, a party may by written notice to the Registrar (copied to all other parties) request the Arbitral Tribunal to correct in the award any error in computation, any clerical or typographical error, any ambiguity or any mistake of a similar nature. If the Arbitral Tribunal considers the request to be justified, after consulting the parties, it shall make the correction within 28 days of receipt of the request. Any correction shall take the form of a memorandum by the Arbitral Tribunal.

27–003 A party has 28 days[2] from the date of its receipt of any award to ask the Arbitral Tribunal to correct any slips in the award (that is, any "error in computation, any clerical or typographical error, any ambiguity or any mistake of a similar nature").

Types of errors covered by Article 27 include mistakes in the spelling of names of parties, and arithmetical errors in calculating damages or interest. Whilst easily made and trivial in themselves, errors of this kind could cause difficulties on enforcement.

---

[1] The addition to the 2014 version of Article 27.1 of a reference to the correction of "any ambiguity" does not appear to extend (necessarily) to providing an explanation or additional reasons in the award.

[2] Article 27.1 of the 1998 LCIA Rules allowed 30 days for this but expressly recognised the possibility that the parties might fix a lesser period. This has not been reproduced in the current Rules. However, the Tribunal has a general power to abridge or extend time periods under Article 22.1(ii), even where they have already expired. To the extent that the Arbitral Tribunal may be deemed to have fulfilled or discharged its office, the LCIA Court might still have the power to extend the time limit under Article 22.5.

(b) all "*materials in the arbitration created for the purpose of the arbitration*": This category is very broad and, it would seem, extends to any document of any kind created for the purpose of the arbitration, regardless of whether that document was produced to the other party or the Arbitral Tribunal or not. This category would cover, for example, directions, orders and other communications received from the Arbitral Tribunal, submissions and pleadings from the parties, correspondence between the parties, transcripts of hearings and a party's own "materials" relating to the arbitration (which might include internal work product discussing the proceedings and advice from lawyers); and

(c) "*all other documents produced by another party in the proceedings not otherwise in the public domain*": This captures, in particular, documents used by a party to support its arguments or disclosed in response to requests from the other party as part of any disclosure process.

The parties' confidentiality undertaking is subject to a number of important qualifications. A party can disclose documents where "*required*": 30–004

(a) by a "*legal duty*" (which may arise, for example, where a party must disclose documents following an order from a court or other judicial or regulatory authority, or to comply with tax or accounting rules);

(b) "*to protect or pursue a legal right*" (a potentially wide ranging proviso that might even encompass matters outside the scope of the dispute referred to arbitration); or

(c) "*to enforce or challenge an award in legal proceedings before a state court or other legal authority*". In such circumstances, the court or other legal authority must logically have sight of, for example, the award in order to consider the challenge before it. If such proceedings are advanced solely to put the award in the public domain, that would arguably be a breach of the confidentiality undertaking.

**30.2 The deliberations of the Arbitral Tribunal shall remain confidential to its members, save as required by any applicable law and to the extent that disclosure of an arbitrator's refusal to participate in the arbitration is required of the other members of the Arbitral Tribunal under Articles 10, 12, 26 and 27.**

The purpose of Article 30.2 is to ensure that the Arbitral Tribunal's own deliberations remain confidential as between the individual members of the Arbitral Tribunal. This avoids the deliberations becoming the focus of attempts by the parties to obtain further information about the process which leads to the production of awards, for example, in connection with a challenge. More importantly, this ensures that the Arbitral Tribunal can discuss the merits of the case freely, and without any concern that those discussions might later become public knowledge. 30–005

The cloak of confidentiality covering the Arbitral Tribunal's deliberations can be lifted where required by applicable law and to the extent that disclosure of an arbitrator's refusal to participate in the arbitration is required of the other arbitrators. This may arise in some of the circumstances set out in:

(a) Article 10, which deals with the revocation of an arbitrator's appointment, including on grounds that the arbitrator (i) acts "in deliberate violation of the Arbitration Agreement; (ii) does not act fairly or impartially as between the parties; or (iii) does not conduct or participate in the arbitration with reasonable efficiency, diligence and industry" (Article 10.2);

(b) Article 12, which deals with the majority power to continue proceedings where an arbitrator "refuses or persistently fails to participate in the deliberations" (Article 12.1);

(c) Article 26, which deals with the award, including issues relating to the failure of an arbitrator to sign the award (Article 26.6); and

(d) Article 27, which concerns the correction of awards and additional awards, to which Articles 26.2 to 26.7 again apply.

### 30.3 The LCIA does not publish any award or any part of an award without the prior written consent of all parties and the Arbitral Tribunal.

**30–006** Unlike some arbitral institutions (the ICC being a notable example), the LCIA Court does not publish any awards issued by Arbitral Tribunals constituted under the LCIA Rules (even in an anonymised format).

That notwithstanding, Article 30.3 allows an award to be published in whole or in part with the prior written consent of the parties and the Arbitral Tribunal. It is worth noting, however, that an award may become public during court proceedings to enforce the award.

In the softwood lumber disputes between the US and Canada, the parties themselves published non-confidential versions of the awards specifically prepared for this purpose by the Arbitral Tribunals.

## Article 31—Limitation of Liability

**31.1 None of the LCIA (including its officers, members and employees), the LCIA Court (including its President, Vice-Presidents, Honourary Vice-Presidents and members), the Registrar (including any deputy Registrar), any arbitrator, any Emergency Arbitrator and any expert to the Arbitral Tribunal shall be liable to any party howsoever for any act or omission in connection with any arbitration, save: (i) where the act or omission is shown by that party to constitute conscious and deliberate wrongdoing committed by the body or person alleged to be liable to that party; or (ii) to the extent that any part of this provision is shown to be prohibited by any applicable law.**

**31.2 After the award has been made and all possibilities of any memorandum or additional award under Article 27 have lapsed or been exhausted, neither the LCIA (including its officers, members and employees), the LCIA Court (including its President, Vice-Presidents, Honourary Vice-Presidents and members), the Registrar (including any deputy Registrar), any arbitrator, any Emergency Arbitrator or any expert to the Arbitral Tribunal shall be under any legal obligation to make any statement to any person about any matter concerning the arbitration; nor shall any party seek to make any of these bodies or persons a witness in any legal or other proceedings arising out of the arbitration.**

**Introduction**

Article 31 has two limbs:  31–001

(a) it seeks to limit the liability of the LCIA and those that the LCIA appoints for the parties (the arbitrators and any expert they in turn appoint) to situations involving "conscious and deliberate wrongdoing" (although it expressly recognises that mandatory provisions of applicable law may require there to be greater liability); and

(b) it provides that, once the arbitration is over, the same persons shall not have any legal obligation to make any statement concerning the arbitration and prohibits the parties from seeking to make any such person a witness in proceedings arising out of the arbitration (such as proceedings to set aside or to enforce the award).

These are important protections given the otherwise significant prospect of litigation being brought by a disappointed party.

**31.1** None of the LCIA (including its officers, members and employees), the LCIA Court (including its President, Vice-Presidents, Honourary Vice-Presidents and members), the Registrar (including any deputy Registrar), any arbitrator, any Emergency Arbitrator and any expert to the Arbitral Tribunal shall be liable to any party howsoever for any act or omission in connection with any arbitration, save: (i) where the act or omission is shown by that party to constitute conscious and deliberate wrongdoing committed by the body or person alleged to be liable to that party; or (ii) to the extent that any part of this provision is shown to be prohibited by any applicable law.

**31–002** Article 31.1 seeks to protect the organs and representatives of the LCIA, as well as the Arbitral Tribunal and any expert appointed by the Arbitral Tribunal (but not by the parties), from liability for acts and omissions in connection with an LCIA arbitration, except in cases of "conscious and deliberate wrongdoing"[1] and/or to the extent that applicable law will not allow liability to be limited. The limitation of liability in Article 31.1 reflects and builds upon the English Arbitration Act 1996, which provides, in ss.29 and 74 (both mandatory provisions), that:

> "29(1) An arbitrator is not liable for anything done or omitted in the discharge or purported discharge of his functions as arbitrator unless the act or omission is shown to have been in bad faith.[2]
>
> [...]
>
> 74(1) An arbitral or other institution or person designated or requested by the parties to appoint or nominate an arbitrator is not liable for anything done or omitted in the discharge or purported discharge of that function unless the act or omission is shown to have been in bad faith.
>
> (2) An arbitral or other institution or person by whom an arbitrator is appointed or nominated is not liable, by reason of having appointed or nominated him, for anything done or omitted by the arbitrator (or his employees or agents) in the discharge or purported discharge of his functions as arbitrator."[3]

---

[1] Article 31.1 may not protect an arbitrator from a claim of corruption along the lines alleged against the arbitrators in *Gulf Petro Trading Company, Inc. (US) and others v Nigerian National Petroleum Corporation (Nigeria), Bola Ajibola (Nigeria) and others*, United States District Court, Eastern District of Texas, Beaumont Division, March 15, 2006.

[2] This protection does not affect any liability incurred by an arbitrator as a result of a resignation (pursuant to s.29(3) of the English Arbitration Act 1996 (Appendix 7))—that liability can be agreed with the parties or determined by the court (pursuant to s.25). See the commentary in R. Merkin and L. Flannery, *Arbitration Act 1996*, 5th edn (London: Informa Law, 2014), pp.100–101.

[3] Note that s.29(1) of the 1996 Act applies to employees and agents of arbitrators (pursuant to s.29(2)) and ss.74(1) and 74(2) of the 1996 Act "apply to an employee or agent of an arbitral or other institution or person as they apply to the institution or person himself" (pursuant to s.74(3)).

Article 31.1 is likely to be of greater relevance for arbitrators seated in jurisdictions where there is more limited statutory or other immunity for arbitrators and institutions than in England and Wales.[4]

Article 31.1 is similar in scope and approach to Article 40 of the 2012 ICC Rules, although the latter does not contain the express exception for "conscious and deliberate wrongdoing". Article 40 provides that:

> "The arbitrators, any person appointed by the Arbitral Tribunal, the emergency arbitrator, the court and its members, the ICC and its employees, and the ICC National Committees and Groups and their employees and representatives shall not be liable to any person for any act or omission in connection with the arbitration, except to the extent such limitation of liability is prohibited by applicable law."

Whilst the old UNCITRAL Rules (1976 version) did not contain any equivalent provision to Article 31.1 of the LCIA Rules, the 2010 UNCITRAL Rules do have a very similar provision at Article 16:

**31-003**

> "Save for intentional wrongdoing, the parties waive, to the fullest extent permitted under the applicable law, any claim against the arbitrators, the appointing authority and any person appointed by the Arbitral Tribunal based on any act or omission in connection with the arbitration."

**31.2 After the award has been made and all possibilities of any memorandum or additional award under Article 27 have lapsed or been exhausted, neither the LCIA (including its officers, members and employees), the LCIA Court (including its President, Vice-Presidents, Honourary Vice-Presidents and members), the Registrar (including any deputy Registrar), any arbitrator, any Emergency Arbitrator or any expert to the Arbitral Tribunal shall be under any legal obligation to make any statement to any person about any matter concerning the arbitration; nor shall any party seek to make any of these bodies or persons a witness in any legal or other proceedings arising out of the arbitration.**

Article 31.2 again protects the same entities as under Article 31.1, this time from having to make a statement concerning the arbitration or being asked to be a witness in any proceedings arising out of the arbitration, once their role has finished (because an award has been made and the parties' rights to corrections and/or additional awards have ended).

**31-004**

As a matter of practice, the Registrar does provide statements about arbitrations when these are sought for the purposes of the enforcement of awards in particular jurisdictions. Such statements could comprise a summary of the LCIA

---

[4] The UNCITRAL Model Law does not contain any provisions relating to the immunity from liability of arbitrators or arbitral institutions.

proceedings, together with confirmation that the award sought to be enforced was made in those proceedings. Sometimes the Registrar will be asked to state that the award is final and that no recourse is possible. This is a matter of law, upon which the Registrar has no authority to give an opinion. The Registrar's response may be confined to a recital of the provisions of Article 26.8.

## Article 32—General Rules

**32.1** A party who knows that any provision of the Arbitration Agreement has not been complied with and yet proceeds with the arbitration without promptly stating its objection as to such non-compliance to the Registrar (before the formation of the Arbitral Tribunal) or the Arbitral Tribunal (after its formation), shall be treated as having irrevocably waived its right to object for all purposes.

**32.2** For all matters not expressly provided in the Arbitration Agreement, the LCIA Court, the LCIA, the Registrar, the Arbitral Tribunal and each of the parties shall act at all times in good faith, respecting the spirit of the Arbitration Agreement, and shall make every reasonable effort to ensure that any award is legally recognised and enforceable at the arbitral seat.

**32.3** If and to the extent that any part of the Arbitration Agreement is decided by the Arbitral Tribunal, the Emergency Arbitrator, or any court or other legal authority of competent jurisdiction to be invalid, ineffective or unenforceable, such decision shall not, of itself, adversely affect any order or award by the Arbitral Tribunal or the Emergency Arbitrator or any other part of the Arbitration Agreement which shall remain in full force and effect, unless prohibited by any applicable law.

### Introduction

This final Article of the LCIA Rules has three separate but linked objectives: 32–001

(a) to ensure that objections to the arbitration proceedings are raised promptly, so that they can be addressed or effectively be eliminated by waiver, thereby protecting the ultimate award;

(b) recognising that the Arbitration Agreement (including the Rules incorporated therein) will not cover every eventuality, to ensure that its spirit is followed and any award will be enforceable, at least at the seat of arbitration; and

(c) to ensure that, unless prohibited by applicable law, any order or award and the rest of the Arbitration Agreement is not compromised by a severable defect in the Arbitration Agreement.

**32.1 A party who knows that any provision of the Arbitration Agreement has not been complied with and yet proceeds with the arbitration without promptly stating its objection as to such non-compliance to the Registrar (before the formation of the Arbitral Tribunal) or the Arbitral Tribunal (after its formation), shall be treated as having irrevocably waived its right to object for all purposes.**

32–002 In order to lose its right to object, a party must:

(a) have actual knowledge that a provision of the "Arbitration Agreement" (defined in the Preamble to the Rules as including the Rules themselves, which are assumed to have been incorporated by reference into the parties' contract), has not been complied with; and

(b) proceed with the arbitration without promptly raising its objection to that non-compliance with the Registrar or, if formed, the Arbitral Tribunal.

The practical effect of this is that a party becoming aware of a non-compliance must decide whether to raise an objection, or to let the matter go. It is implicit that the party cannot reserve its rights to raise an objection at a later stage. This means that the Registrar or Arbitral Tribunal is given the opportunity to deal with any issues at an early stage and the scope for later challenges to awards on the basis of such non-compliance is minimised.

32–003 Article 32.1 ties in closely with s.73 (a mandatory section) of the English Arbitration Act 1996, which provides that:

"(1) If a party to arbitral proceedings takes part, or continues to take part, in the proceedings without making, either forthwith or within such time as is allowed by the arbitration agreement or the tribunal or by any provision of this Part, any objection:

(a) that the tribunal lacks substantive jurisdiction,

(b) that the proceedings have been improperly conducted,

(c) that there has been a failure to comply with the arbitration agreement or with any provision of this Part, or

(d) that there has been any other irregularity affecting the tribunal or the proceedings,

he may not raise that objection later, before the tribunal or the court, unless he shows that, at the time he took part or continued to take part in the proceedings, he did not know and could not with reasonable diligence have discovered the grounds for the objection.

(2) Where the arbitral tribunal rules that it has substantive jurisdiction and a party to arbitral proceedings who could have questioned that ruling:

(a) by any available arbitral process of appeal or review, or

(b) by challenging the award,

does not do so, or does not do so within the time allowed by the arbitration agreement or any provision of this Part, he may not object later to the tribunal's substantive jurisdiction on any ground which was the subject of that ruling."

Section 73 of the English Arbitration Act 1996 is derived from the UNCITRAL Model Law, which provides (in Article 4):  **32–004**

"A party who knows that any provision of this Law from which the parties may derogate[1] or any requirement under the arbitration agreement has not been complied with and yet proceeds with the arbitration without stating his objection to such non-compliance without undue delay or, if a time-limited is provided therefor, within such period of time, shall be deemed to have waived his right to object."

Like Article 32.1 of the LCIA Rules, Article 4 of the UNCITRAL Model Law requires there to be actual knowledge of non-compliance. The English Arbitration Act 1996 instead has a lower threshold: there the party making the objection must show that it could not, with "reasonable diligence", have discovered the non-compliance.  **32–005**

Article 39 of the 2012 ICC Rules is in similar terms to the UNCITRAL Model Law and Article 32.1 of the LCIA Rules, stating:

"A party which proceeds with the arbitration without raising its objection to a failure to comply with any provision of the Rules, or of any other rules applicable to the proceedings, any direction given by the arbitral tribunal, or any requirement under the arbitration agreement relating to the constitution of the arbitral tribunal or the conduct of the proceedings, shall be deemed to have waived its right to object."

Article 32 of the 2010 UNCITRAL Rules also takes a similar approach:  **32–006**

"A failure by any party to object promptly to any non-compliance with these Rules or with any requirement of the arbitration agreement shall be deemed to be a waiver of the right of such party to make such an objection, unless such party can show that, under the circumstances, its failure to object was justified."

**32.2 For all matters not expressly provided in the Arbitration Agreement, the LCIA Court, the LCIA, the Registrar, the Arbitral Tribunal and each of the parties shall act at all times in good faith, respecting the spirit of the Arbitration Agreement, and shall make every reasonable effort to ensure that any award is legally recognised and enforceable at the arbitral seat.**

Where matters are not expressly provided in the Arbitration Agreement, the LCIA Court, the Arbitral Tribunal, the LCIA, the Registrar and the parties now[2] have an  **32–007**

---

[1] The wording of the UNCITRAL Model Law indicates here that a party cannot lose its right to object in relation to non-compliance with mandatory provisions of the Model Law (Appendix 10).
[2] There was no such obligation in the 1998 LCIA Rules (Appendix 4).

obligation to act in good faith, although note that the limitation of liability contained in Article 31.1 means that, save for the parties, they will not generally be liable in the absence of "conscious and deliberate wrongdoing".

The LCIA Court, the Arbitral Tribunal, the LCIA, the Registrar and the parties must also, in dealing with the matter not provided for, respect the "spirit of the Arbitration Agreement". This presumably means that they should seek to extrapolate from the Arbitration Agreement as far as they can, and deal with the matter in the way that it is presumed the parties would have intended when making the Arbitration Agreement if they had considered the matter then.

32–008   Parties to arbitrations in England might also be assisted by s.1 of the English Arbitration Act 1996, which states:

> "The provisions of this Part are founded on the following principles, and shall be construed accordingly:
>
> (a) the object of arbitration is to obtain the fair resolution of disputes by an impartial tribunal without unnecessary delay or expense;
>
> (b) the parties should be free to agree how their disputes are resolved, subject only to such safeguards as are necessary in the public interest . . .".

32–009   Article 41 of the 2012 ICC Rules is in similar terms to Article 32.2 of the LCIA Rules and again lacks any explanation as to what the "spirit" of the ICC Rules is:

> "In all matters not expressly provided for in the Rules, the Court and the arbitral tribunal shall act in the spirit of the Rules and shall make every effort to make sure that the award is enforceable at law."

32–010   As well as acting in good faith and in the spirit of the Arbitration Agreement, the LCIA Court, the Arbitral Tribunal, the LCIA, the Registrar and the parties must also "make every reasonable effort to ensure that any award is legally recognised and enforceable at the arbitral seat".[3] A party who expects to enforce an award in another jurisdiction should ensure that any particular formalities or requirements for awards are brought to the attention of the Arbitral Tribunal: the Arbitral Tribunal has no duty to carry out its own investigations and nor does the LCIA.

> **32.3 If and to the extent that any part of the Arbitration Agreement is decided by the Arbitral Tribunal, the Emergency Arbitrator, or any court or other legal authority of competent jurisdiction to be invalid, ineffective or unenforceable, such decision shall not, of itself, adversely affect any order or award by the Arbitral Tribunal or the Emergency Arbitrator or any other part of the Arbitration Agreement**

---

[3] The 1998 LCIA Rules did not expressly limit the obligation to make every reasonable effort to ensure that an award is legally enforceable, to the seat of arbitration, although the extent to which reasonable efforts would have extended to looking at other jurisdictions where enforcement might be sought was open to debate (Appendix 4).

**which shall remain in full force and effect, unless prohibited by any applicable law.**

This is a new provision, which did not appear in Article 32 of the 1998 LCIA Rules. It seeks to ensure that, unless prohibited by applicable law, any order or award or the rest of the Arbitration Agreement is not compromised by a severable defect in the Arbitration Agreement.

**32–011**

# ANNEX TO THE LCIA RULES

GENERAL GUIDELINES FOR THE PARTIES' LEGAL REPRESENTATIVES

(ARTICLES 18.5 AND 18.6 OF THE LCIA RULES)

*Paragraph 1*: These general guidelines are intended to promote the good and equal conduct of the parties' legal representatives appearing by name within the arbitration. Nothing in these guidelines is intended to derogate from the Arbitration Agreement or to undermine any legal representative's primary duty of loyalty to the party represented in the arbitration or the obligation to present that party's case effectively to the Arbitral Tribunal. Nor shall these guidelines derogate from any mandatory laws, rules of law, professional rules or codes of conduct if and to the extent that any are shown to apply to a legal representative appearing in the arbitration.

*Paragraph 2:* A legal representative should not engage in activities intended unfairly to obstruct the arbitration or to jeopardise the finality of any award, including repeated challenges to an arbitrator's appointment or to the jurisdiction or authority of the Arbitral Tribunal known to be unfounded by that legal representative.

*Paragraph 3*: A legal representative should not knowingly make any false statement to the Arbitral Tribunal or the LCIA Court.

*Paragraph 4*: A legal representative should not knowingly procure or assist in the preparation of or rely upon any false evidence presented to the Arbitral Tribunal or the LCIA Court.

*Paragraph 5*: A legal representative should not knowingly conceal or assist in the concealment of any document (or any part thereof) which is ordered to be produced by the Arbitral Tribunal.

*Paragraph 6*: During the arbitration proceedings, a legal representative should not deliberately initiate or attempt to initiate with any member of the Arbitral Tribunal or with any member of the LCIA Court making any determination or decision in regard to the arbitration (but not including the Registrar) any unilateral contact relating to the arbitration or the parties' dispute, which has not been disclosed in writing prior to or shortly after the time of such contact to all other parties, all members of the Arbitral Tribunal (if comprised of more than one arbitrator) and the Registrar in accordance with Article 13.4.

*Paragraph 7*: **In accordance with Articles 18.5 and 18.6, the Arbitral Tribunal may decide whether a legal representative has violated these general guidelines and, if so, how to exercise its discretion to impose any or all of the sanctions listed in Article 18.6.**

## Introduction

### Background

The General Guidelines for the Parties' Legal Representatives set out in the Annex to the LCIA Rules (the "LCIA Annex") provide a contractually binding (on the parties) set of ethical principles governing the conduct of legal representatives appearing in LCIA arbitration proceedings. Article 18.5 provides that each party is to ensure that all its legal representatives "appearing by name" have agreed to comply with the Guidelines.  **33–001**

As noted in the commentary on Article 18.5, the LCIA Annex addresses concerns that the lack of generally applicable professional or ethical rules to govern the conduct of the parties' legal representatives in international arbitration proceedings could lead to an uneven playing field for parties from different jurisdictions. Such concerns predate the introduction of the 2014 LCIA Rules by at least 40 years.[1] The perceived problems arise from the fact that lawyers from different jurisdictions, who are educated in different legal-ethical cultures and ultimately bound by different rules of professional conduct, appear before the same Tribunal.

Indeed, it is commonly the case that one lawyer's professional duty of loyalty to the client is another lawyer's breach of ethical standards.[2] The difficulty may be compounded where the Tribunal itself is comprised of arbitrators from altogether different legal backgrounds. In the absence of agreement, the question which arises in cases of conflict between applicable rules, and which often remains unanswered, is which ethical norms should apply.[3]  **33–002**

In recent years, increasing concerns have also been expressed about the apparent phenomenon of parties and their representatives in international arbitration proceedings intentionally engaging in conduct of questionable ethical probity with a view to delaying and/or disrupting the proceedings.[4]

---

[1] See Tom Cummins, "The IBA Guidelines on Party Representation in International Arbitration – Levelling the Playing Field?" (2014) 30(3) Arbitration Int. 429–456 at 429 under (b) "Forerunners to the IBA's Initiative".

[2] Differences between the approaches to documentary disclosure and witness preparation are commonly cited areas in which ethical norms from different jurisdictions are in conflict. Other matters in relation to which different approaches are taken in different jurisdictions include rules regarding professional conflicts of interest, the permissibility of communications with party-appointed arbitrators and the counsel's duty of candour to the Tribunal. See, for example, William W. Park, "A Fair Fight: Professional Guidelines in International Arbitration" (2014) 30(3) Arbitration Int. 409–428 at 436.

[3] Jeffrey Waincymer, "Regulatory Developments in the Control of Counsel in International Arbitration – The IBA Guidelines on Party Representation in International Arbitration and the New LCIA Rules and Annex, Arbitration International" (2014) 30(3) Arbitration Int. 513.

[4] With numerous conferences and learned articles dealing with the ethical conduct of legal representatives in international arbitration and the perceived prevalence of so-called "Guerrilla Tactics" in international arbitration. A few examples include: "Guerrilla Tactics in International Arbitration

**33-003**  Within the debate over the existence and scope of ethical duties of legal representatives in international arbitration,[5] increasingly powerful calls were made for the codification of ethical standards commonly accepted amongst arbitration practitioners.[6] These led first to the adoption of the voluntary "soft-law" provisions of the 2013 IBA Guidelines on Party Representation in International Arbitration (the "IBA Guidelines"). Now, with the adoption of the 2014 LCIA Rules, we have the first contractually binding code of conduct for legal representatives policed by an international arbitration institution.

The IBA Guidelines were published following nearly five years of consultation by the IBA's Taskforce on Counsel Conduct in International Arbitration. They contain a set of interpretive "Comments on the Guidelines" (the "Comments"). In light of their shared background and the common aims of the IBA Guidelines and the LCIA Annex, the Comments might well be regarded as relevant to the construction of the relevant paragraphs of the LCIA Annex as well.

*Overview*

**33-004**  The LCIA Annex can be divided into three broad sections: an introductory provision stating the general purpose and scope of the LCIA Annex (para.1), rules of

---

& Litigation", TDM 2 (2010) (a series of articles); Stephan Wilske, "Arbitration Guerrillas at the Gate: Preserving the Civility of Arbitral Proceedings when the Going Gets (Extremely) Tough", in Klausegger et al. (eds), *Austrian Yearbook on International Arbitration 2011* (Manz'sche Verlags, 2011); G. Horvath, "Guerrilla Tactics in Arbitration, an Ethical Battle: Is there Need for a Universal Code of Ethics?", *Austrian Yearbook on International Arbitration 2011* (2011) p.297; R. Doak Bishop and Margrete Stevens, "Advocacy and Ethics in International Arbitration: The Compelling Need for a Code of Ethics in International Arbitration: Transparency, Integrity and Legitimacy", in A.J. van den Berg (ed.), *Arbitration Advocacy in Changing Times* (ICCA Congress series) (Kluwer Law International, 2011), pp.391, 393; G. Horvath and S. Wilske (eds), *Guerrilla Tactics in International Arbitration* (Kluwer Law International, 2013); and Catherine A. Rogers, "Guerilla Tactics and Ethical Regulation", Penn State Law Research Paper No. 23-2013 (2013).

[5] The debate has been comprehensively reviewed and analysed in three articles appearing in the volume of the LCIA's journal *Arbitration International* published alongside the entry into force of the 2014 LCIA Rules; see William W. Park, "A Fair Fight: Professional Guidelines in International Arbitration" (2014) 30(3) Arbitration Int. 409; Tom Cummins, "The IBA Guidelines on Party Representation in International Arbitration – Levelling the Playing Field?" (2014) 30(3) Arbitration Int. 429; and Jeffrey Waincymer, "Regulatory Developments in the Control of Counsel in International Arbitration – The IBA Guidelines on Party Representation in International Arbitration and the New LCIA Rules and Annex, Arbitration International" (2014) 30(3) Arbitration Int. 513.

[6] For example. Cyrus Benson, "Can Professional Ethics Wait? The Need for Transparency in International Arbitration" (2009) 3 D.R.I.; R. Doak Bishop and Margrete Stevens, "Advocacy and Ethics in International Arbitration: The Compelling Need for a Code of Ethics in International Arbitration: Transparency, Integrity and Legitimacy", in A.J. van den Berg (ed.), *Arbitration Advocacy in Changing Times* (ICCA Congress series) (Kluwer Law International, 2011), pp.391, 393. Dissent by equally respected and powerful practitioners and commentators, led principally by the then President of the Swiss Arbitration Association, Michael E. Schneider (see Michael E. Schneider "President's Message: Yet another Opportunity to Waste Time and Money on Procedural Skirmishes: The IBA Guidelines on Party Representation" (2013) 31(3) ASA Bull. 497), and the ASA position paper, "IBA Guidelines On Party Representation In International Arbitration Comments And Recommendations By The Board Of The Swiss Arbitration Association (Asa)" (April 4, 2014) *http://www.arbitration-ch.org/pages/en/asa/news-&-projects/details/972.ethics-and-party-representation-asa-contributes-to-the-debate.html* [Accessed November 14, 2014], continue to attract a great deal of sympathy from many experienced practitioners, but have failed to win the argument.

ethics (paras 2–6), and sanctions (para.7).[7] The ethical rules adopted prohibit intentionally obstructive practices (para.2), dishonest practices (paras 3–5) and unilateral communications between legal representatives and the Arbitral Tribunal or LCIA Court in relation to the arbitration (para.6).

A number of ethical questions were not specifically addressed by the IBA Guidelines.[8] The same is all the more true with regard to the LCIA Annex, which adopts a less detailed approach, leaning towards a statement of general principles rather than specific rules. Clearly the LCIA Annex does not (and could not sensibly have) set out to address every aspect of the conduct of legal representatives within the confines of its seven paragraphs.[9]

The commentary on Article 18.5 contains a list of the LCIA Guidelines which have corresponding IBA Guidelines.

*Utility*

Time will tell whether the innovative adoption of a binding set of ethical rules will serve, as intended, as a general deterrent and an aid to Arbitral Tribunals seeking to conduct fair and impartial proceedings, avoiding unnecessary delay and expense in accordance with the overriding duty pursuant to Article 14.4 of the LCIA Rules, or whether "presented as the solution to what in reality appears only as a marginal problem, [it] risk[s] becoming a major source of procedural motions and disruption"[10] in the hands of cynical parties, intent on disrupting the arbitral process in order to delay an unfavorable outcome. The inclusion of the General Guidelines in the Annex, which can be amended separately from the Rules[11] affords the LCIA an opportunity to adopt any changes that may appear necessary a practice develops.

**33–005**

***Paragraph 1*: These general guidelines are intended to promote the good and equal conduct of the parties' legal representatives appearing by name within the arbitration. Nothing in these guidelines is intended to derogate from the Arbitration Agreement or to undermine any legal representative's primary duty of loyalty to the party represented in the arbitration or the obligation to present that party's case effectively to the Arbitral Tribunal. Nor shall these guidelines derogate from any mandatory laws, rules of law,**

---

[7] This must be read together with Article 18.6 of the LCIA Rules, which set out the sanctions which the Arbitral Tribunal may impose on legal representatives who fail to comply with the standards set out in the General Guidelines.

[8] See, for example, Tom Cummins, "The IBA Guidelines on Party Representation in International Arbitration – Levelling the Playing Field?" (2014) 30(3) Arbitration Int. 453: omitted matters he mentions include courtesy and respect, identification of adverse authority, improperly obtained evidence and the status of settlement negotiations.

[9] By contrast, the *English Bar Standards Board Handbook* concerning the conduct of English Barristers is more than 250 pages long.

[10] Michael E. Schneider, "President's Message: Yet another Opportunity to Waste Time and Money on Procedural Skirmishes: The IBA Guidelines on Party Representation" (2013) 31(3) ASA Bull. 497. In a subsequent President's Message, Elliott Geisinger, ASA's new President raised the prospect of developing a process for distilling the *"truly international"* core ethical norms common to all arbitral institutions and, significantly, for enforcing them. *http://www.arbitration-ch.org/pages/en/asa/news-&-projects/presidents-message/index.htm* [Accessed November 14, 2014].

[11] See the Preamble and commentary at P–011.

professional rules or codes of conduct if and to the extent that any are shown to apply to a legal representative appearing in the arbitration.

33–006 Paragraph 1 of the Annex states the general intention of the Guidelines as well as the scope of their application both personally and substantively.

### Intent of the LCIA Annex

33–007 Whilst the general intent of the Annex is stated to be the promotion of "good and equal conduct of the parties' legal representatives", there is no statement of what "good" or "equal" conduct means.

What amounts to "good" conduct or, conversely, bad conduct, is invariably so highly contextual as to place both within the class of elephants and pornography: difficult to define, but one knows it when one sees it.[12]

33–008 The reference to the promotion of "equal conduct" must, in the context of the LCIA Annex, be read to refer to the promotion of equivalent standards of ethical conduct applying to the representatives of all parties in any particular arbitration.

Professor Park equates this proviso with the passage in the Preamble to the IBA Guidelines, stating that they "are inspired by the principle that party representatives should act with integrity and honesty and should not engage in activities designed to produce unnecessary delay or expense, including tactics aimed at obstructing the arbitration proceedings."[13]

### Personal application

33–009 Paragraph 1 limits the application of the LCIA Annex to the "legal representatives appearing by name within the arbitration". As noted above, Article 18.1 of the LCIA Rules provides that parties may be represented by one or more legal representatives appearing in the proceedings by name. Article 18.5 requires parties to ensure that any such representatives have agreed to comply with the LCIA Annex as a condition to such representation.

The reference to legal representatives "appearing by name" indicates the personal nature of the obligation assumed by each legal representative involved in and responsible for the representation of a party in an LCIA arbitration. Such legal representatives cannot hide behind the name of a law firm or attribute any personal ethical lapses to such firm.

33–010 There is nothing in the LCIA Rules that would prevent a party from appointing an authorised representative (appearing by name) who is not legally qualified in any jurisdiction.[14] Whilst the text of Paragraph 1 only refers expressly to legal representatives, it is submitted that it would be a peculiar result if such non-legal representatives were not also to be bound by the terms of the LCIA Annex.[15] As a

---

[12] William W. Park, "Arbitration's Discontents: Of Elephants and Pornography" (2001) 17(3) Arbitration Int. 263.
[13] William W. Park, "A Fair Fight: Professional Guidelines in International Arbitration" (2014) 30(3) Arbitration Int. 409–428 at 421.
[14] This was expressly provided for in the 1998 edition of the LCIA Rules (Appendix 4).
[15] The potential for ethical imbalance is perhaps even more strongly pronounced in cases in which one

practical matter, where this may be an issue, Arbitral Tribunals may seek to confirm the position with the parties.

In any event, in the context of arbitration proceedings seated in England at least, s.40 of the English Arbitration Act 1996 requires the parties to "do all things necessary for the proper and expeditious conduct of the arbitral proceedings", whilst Article 14.5 of the LCIA Rules provides "at all times the parties shall do everything necessary in good faith for the fair, efficient and expeditious conduct of the arbitration, including the Arbitral Tribunal's discharge of its general duties". These provisions undoubtedly require parties to instruct their representatives to conduct themselves ethically, avoiding any conduct that might frustrate the arbitral process.

*Substantive limits*

Similar to the scope of the IBA Guidelines, the LCIA Annex is not intended to deviate from, diminish or circumvent any obligation owed by any party or representative in the proceedings pursuant to the Arbitration Agreement, any mandatory rules or any professional codes of conduct applicable to a legal representative appearing in the arbitration.

**33–011**

*Paragraph 2:* **A legal representative should not engage in activities intended unfairly to obstruct the arbitration or to jeopardise the finality of any award, including repeated challenges to an arbitrator's appointment or to the jurisdiction or authority of the Arbitral Tribunal known to be unfounded by that legal representative.**

Paragraph 2 requires legal representatives not intentionally and unfairly to hinder or impede the arbitration or endanger the finality of the ultimate award. Specific reference is made in this regard to "repeated challenges" as a practical example of where such tactics may have been employed in the past.

**33–012**

Notably, Paragraph 2 only prohibits conduct that is intended to be unfair. Thus, for example, repeated challenges that are honestly believed by the representatives advancing them to be well founded will not be caught by the prohibition. This limitation of the scope of the rule is presumably aimed at preserving the ability of representatives to take proper advantage of the procedures available under the LCIA Rules, as well as to make objections to any aspect of procedure adopted by the Arbitral Tribunal, where they genuinely consider it fair to do so. However, this subjective element may dramatically narrow its application in practice. Further, as Waincymer[16] points out, the "intent" component of the ethical rule also raises questions as to the standard of proof that a complainant should be required to meet in order to substantiate allegations of dishonesty by representatives.

---

party chooses to be represented by a lay person, who may not be bound by any code of professional conduct; whilst the other is represented by a qualified lawyer subject to the disciplinary powers of a professional body as well as by national laws and regulations.

[16] Jeffrey Waincymer, "Regulatory Developments in the Control of Counsel in International Arbitration – The IBA Guidelines on Party Representation in International Arbitration and the New LCIA Rules and Annex" (2014) 30(3) Arbitration Int.

***Paragraph 3*: A legal representative should not knowingly make any false statement to the Arbitral Tribunal or the LCIA Court.**

33–013  Paragraph 3 prohibits legal representatives from lying to the Arbitral Tribunal or the LCIA Court. The language of the paragraph is limited to false statements, but may extend, for example, to making submissions based on authority known to be false.[17]

As with Paragraph 2, contravention of this rule necessarily includes a (subjective) component of intent that might be difficult to prove.

***Paragraph 4*: A legal representative should not knowingly procure or assist in the preparation of or rely upon any false evidence presented to the Arbitral Tribunal or the LCIA Court.**

33–014  Paragraph 4 requires legal representatives to refrain from procuring or assisting in the preparation of false evidence, or from relying on any false evidence.

In as far as it goes, this provision is rather straightforward, but again the requirement of subjective knowledge and intent plays a central role. Further, the LCIA Annex is silent as to whether a legal representative is required to enquire about the authenticity of any evidence presented by a client and, if so, how far should such enquiries go.

This guideline is consistent with other guidelines (e.g. IBA and the English Bar Standards Board) on the preparation of witness evidence.[18]

***Paragraph 5*: A legal representative should not knowingly conceal or assist in the concealment of any document (or any part thereof) which is ordered to be produced by the Arbitral Tribunal.**

33–015  Paragraph 5 addresses the conduct of legal representatives in the context of documentary disclosure. It prohibits the legal representatives from knowingly contravening a document production order of the Arbitral Tribunal. The prohibition against hiding evidence that is required to be produced may appear to be no more than the flip side of the rule in Paragraph 4, which prohibits the knowing creation or reliance on false evidence. On the other hand, in some jurisdictions, in which a lawyer's duty to the client overrides any duty owed to a Tribunal, such a duty might be far less obvious.[19]

Like the preceding paragraphs, Paragraph 5 contains an element of intentional, knowing, misconduct.

---

[17] William W. Park, "A Fair Fight: Professional Guidelines in International Arbitration" (2014) 30(3) Arbitration Int. 409–428 at 421: "There are also warnings against . . . reliance on authority known to be unfounded" although the word "unfounded", only appears in the Annex in Paragraph 2 in the context of challenges to the Arbitral Tribunal.
[18] See the commentary on Article 20.5.
[19] See the commentary on Article 20.5.

As noted in the commentary on Article 18.5, the generality and succinctness of para.5 stands in stark contrast to IBA Guidelines 12–17, which provide specific guidance concerning the conduct of party representatives in ensuring that the party s/he represents understands and complies with its duties to preserve and disclose documents.

*Paragraph 6*: **During the arbitration proceedings, a legal representative should not deliberately initiate or attempt to initiate with any member of the Arbitral Tribunal or with any member of the LCIA Court making any determination or decision in regard to the arbitration (but not including the Registrar) any unilateral contact relating to the arbitration or the parties' dispute, which has not been disclosed in writing prior to or shortly after the time of such contact to all other parties, all members of the Arbitral Tribunal (if comprised of more than one arbitrator) and the Registrar in accordance with Article 13.4.**

Paragraph 6 mirrors Article 13.4 of the LCIA Rules extending to legal representatives the prohibitions applicable under that article to parties. The LCIA Annex only concerns ex parte communications following the commencement of the arbitration. Pre-selection/Arbitral Tribunal formation communications with a potential nominee or nominated arbitrator are not addressed in the LCIA Annex but are dealt with under Article 13.5 of the LCIA Rules. **33–016**

*Paragraph 7*: **In accordance with Articles 18.5 and 18.6, the Arbitral Tribunal may decide whether a legal representative has violated these general guidelines and, if so, how to exercise its discretion to impose any or all of the sanctions listed in Article 18.6.**

Paragraph 7 states that an Arbitral Tribunal that is persuaded that a legal representative has violated the provisions of the LCIA Annex may impose sanctions on that representative in accordance with Articles 18.5 and 18.6 of the LCIA Rules. **33–017**

Article 18.5 does not contain a reference to sanctions, but sets out the contractual basis for the application of the LCIA Annex to legal representatives appearing in LCIA arbitration.

Article 18.6 provides that where a named legal representative of a party "has engaged in serious or persisting violation of the general guidelines" it might impose one of three sanctions: **33–018**

(a) a written reprimand;

(b) a written caution as to future conduct; and

(c) "any other measure necessary to fulfil within the arbitration the general duties required of the Arbitral Tribunal under Articles 14.4(i) and (ii)".

**33–019**  The first and second sanctions might appear unlikely to deter a legal representative who has seriously or persistently breached (with intent) the provisions of the Annex from engaging in further similar conduct.

The third option, involving any other measure necessary to fulfil the duties of the Arbitral Tribunal under Articles 14.4(i) and (ii) (to act fairly and impartially avoiding unnecessary delay and expense) is potentially wide ranging but rather unclear. Whilst the instructing parties may face cost sanctions and/or adverse inferences as a result of the actions taken by their legal representatives (which may in practice be an effective deterrent in most cases), the sanctions in Article 18.6 are aimed at the legal representatives themselves (not, at least directly, the parties instructing them).

**33–020**  One 'Big Question' is whether an Arbitral Tribunal, faced with serious or persistent violations of the LCIA Annex, has the power to exclude the named representative from the proceedings.[20] On the one hand, the proviso "any other measure" in Article 18.6 contemplates a power to adopt an unlimited array of measures that achieves the stated purpose. Waincymer states in relation to the similarly worded IBA Guideline 26(d):

> "The final remedy is general, neither expressly allowing for nor excluding the power of a tribunal to exclude the offending counsel, which will be the most contentious option. As suggested at the outset, the better view is that such power potentially exists in extreme circumstances, although there may be many cases where this would be inadvisable, such as improper conduct of a Government Attorney-General in an investment dispute. On the other hand, one would expect a reasonable consensus that counsel that attempts a bribe or physically assaults an arbitrator and continues to threaten to do so, could be excluded without concerns for enforcement, as long as a reasonable opportunity for a replacement was afforded."[21]

**33–021**  On the other hand, the possibility of granting the Arbitral Tribunal the express power to exclude legal representatives as a sanction for misconduct was mooted in early drafts of the 2014 LCIA Rules, but the power was ultimately not included. Professor Park notes:

> "Even without effective penalties, however, guidelines still promote equality of arms, to the extent of communicating useful information to lawyers from diverse backgrounds. Markers tell both sides what is expected. Although not perfect, the current initiative toward guidelines for party representatives constitutes a first attempt to address the need for a relatively level playing field."[22]

---

[20] See Alan Scott Rau, "Arbitrators Without Powers? Disqualifying Counsel in Arbitral Proceedings" (2014) 30(3) Arbitration Int. 457 for a general discussion not directly dealing with the final version of the text of Paragraph 7 of the Annex.

[21] Jeffrey Waincymer, "Regulatory Developments in the Control of Counsel in International Arbitration – The IBA Guidelines on Party Representation in International Arbitration and the New LCIA Rules and Annex, Arbitration International" (2014) 30(3) Arbitration Int. 544.

[22] William W. Park, "A Fair Fight: Professional Guidelines in International Arbitration" (2014) 30(3) Arbitration Int. 409–428 at 422.

# SCHEDULE OF ARBITRATION COSTS (LCIA)

*effective 1 October 2014*

For arbitrations conducted under the LCIA arbitration rules (the Rules).

This schedule of arbitration costs (the Schedule), as amended from time to time by the LCIA, forms part of the Rules, and will apply in all current and future arbitrations as from its effective date.

*1. Administrative charges*

1(i) Registration Fee (payable in advance with the Request for Arbitration: non-refundable). *£1,750*

1(ii) Time spent* by the Secretariat of the LCIA in the administration of the arbitration.**

Registrar / Deputy Registrar *£250 per hour*

Counsel *£225 per hour*

Case administrators *£175 per hour*

Casework accounting functions *£150 per hour*

1(iii) Time spent by members of the LCIA Court in carrying out their functions in deciding any challenge brought under the Rules.**

*at hourly rates advised by members of the LCIA Court*

1(iv) A sum equivalent to 5% of the fees of the Tribunal (excluding expenses) in respect of the LCIA's general overhead.**

1(v) Expenses incurred by the Secretariat and by members of the LCIA Court, in connection with the arbitration (such as postage, telephone, facsimile, travel etc.), and additional arbitration support services, whether provided by the Secretariat or by the members of the LCIA Court from their own resources or otherwise.**

1(vi) The LCIA's charges will be invoiced in sterling, but may be paid in other convertible currencies, at rates prevailing at the time of payment.

1(vii) Charges may be subject to Value Added Tax at the prevailing rate.

*2. Fees and expenses of the Tribunal*

2(i) The Tribunal's fees will be calculated by reference to work done by its members in connection with the arbitration and will be charged at rates appropriate to the particular circumstances of the case, including its complexity and the special qualifications of the arbitrators. The Tribunal shall agree in writing upon fee rates conforming to the Schedule prior to its appointment by the LCIA Court. The rates will be advised by the Registrar to the parties at the time of the appointment of the Tribunal, but may be reviewed if the duration or a change in the circumstances of the arbitration requires.

Fees shall be at hourly rates *not exceeding £450*.

However, in exceptional cases, the rate may be higher, provided that, in such cases, (i) the fees of the Tribunal shall be fixed by the LCIA Court on the recommendation of the Registrar, following consultations with the arbitrator(s), and (ii) the fees shall be agreed expressly by all parties.

2(ii)  The Tribunal's fees may include a charge for time spent travelling.

2(iii) The Tribunal's fees may also include a charge for time reserved but not used as a result of late postponement or cancellation of hearings, provided that the basis for such charge shall be advised in writing to, and approved by, the LCIA Court and that the parties have been informed in advance.

2(iv) The Tribunal may also recover such expenses as are reasonably incurred in connection with the arbitration, and as are reasonable in amount, provided that claims for expenses should be supported by invoices or receipts.

2(v) The Tribunal's fees shall be invoiced in the currency of account between the Tribunal and the parties.

2(vi) In the event of the revocation of the appointment of any arbitrator, pursuant to the provisions of Article 10 of the Rules, the LCIA Court shall, in accordance with Article 10.7, determine the amount of fees and expenses (if any) to be paid for the former arbitrator's services as it may consider appropriate in all the circumstances.

2(vii) Charges may be subject to Value Added Tax at the prevailing rate.

*3. Deposits*

3(i) The LCIA Court may direct the parties, in such proportions and at such times as it thinks appropriate, to make one or more payments to the LCIA on account of the costs of the arbitration, other than the legal or other expenses incurred by the parties themselves (the Arbitration Costs). Such payments deposited by the parties may be applied by the LCIA Court to pay any item of such Arbitration Costs (including the LCIA's own fees and expenses) in accordance with the LCIA Rules.

3(ii) All payments made by parties on account of the Arbitration Costs shall be held by the LCIA in trust under English law in England, to be disbursed or otherwise applied by the LCIA in accordance with the LCIA Rules and invested having regard also to the interests of the LCIA. Each payment made by a party shall be credited by the LCIA with interest at the rate from time to time credited to an overnight deposit of that amount with the bank(s) engaged by the LCIA to manage deposits from time to time; and any surplus income (beyond such interest) shall accrue for the sole benefit of the LCIA. In the event that payments (with such interest) exceed the total amount of the Arbitration Costs at the conclusion of the arbitration, the excess amount shall be returned by the LCIA to the parties as the ultimate default beneficiaries of the trust.

3(iii) Save for exceptional circumstances, the Arbitral Tribunal should not proceed with the arbitration without having ascertained from the Registrar that the LCIA is or will be in requisite funds as regards outstanding and future Arbitration Costs.

3(iv) In the event that a party fails or refuses to make any payment on account of the Arbitration Costs as directed by the LCIA Court, the LCIA Court may direct the other party or parties to effect a substitute payment to allow the arbitration to proceed (subject to any order or award on Arbitration Costs).

3(v) In such circumstances, the party effecting the substitute payment may request the Arbitral Tribunal to make an order or award in order to recover that amount as a debt immediately due and payable to that party by the defaulting party, together with any interest.

## 4. Interim payments

When interim payments are required to cover any part of the Arbitration Costs, including the LCIA's administrative charges; the fees or expenses of members of the LCIA Court, the Tribunal's fees or expenses, including the fees or expenses of any expert appointed by the Tribunal, the fees or expenses of any Secretary to the Tribunal; or charges for hearing rooms and other support services, such payments may be made against the invoices for any of the above from funds held on deposit. If no or insufficient funds are held at the time the interim payment is required, the invoices for any of the above may be submitted for payment direct by the parties.

## 5. Registrar's authority

5(i) For the purposes of sections 3(i) and 3(iv) above, and of Articles 24.1 and 24.4 of the Rules, the Registrar has the authority of the LCIA Court to make the directions referred to, under the supervision of the Court.

5(ii) For the purposes of section 4 above, and of Article 24.1 of the Rules, the Registrar has the authority of the LCIA Court to approve the payments referred to.

5(iii) Any request by an arbitrator for payment on account of his fees shall be supported by a fee note, which shall include, or be accompanied by, a detailed breakdown of the time spent at the rates that have been advised to the parties by the LCIA, and the fee note will be forwarded to the parties prior to settlement of the account.

5(iv) Any dispute regarding the LCIA's administrative charges, or the fees and expenses of the Tribunal shall be determined by the LCIA Court.

## 6. Arbitration costs

6(i) The parties shall be jointly and severally liable to the Tribunal and the LCIA for the costs of the arbitration (other than the legal or other costs incurred by the parties themselves).

6(ii) Any bank charges incurred on any transfer of funds by the parties to the LCIA shall be borne exclusively by the party or parties transferring the funds.

6(iii) In accordance with Article 26.7 of the Rules, the Tribunal's Award(s) shall be transmitted to the parties by the LCIA Court provided that the costs of the arbitration have been paid to the LCIA in accordance with Article 28 of the Rules.

## 7. Emergency Arbitrator

7(i) Application fee (payable with the application for the appointment of an Emergency Arbitrator under Article 9B of the Rules: non-refundable).

£8,000

7(ii) Emergency Arbitrator's fee, to cover time charges and expenses (payable with the application for the appointment of an Emergency Arbitrator: non-refundable if the LCIA Court appoints an Emergency Arbitrator).

£20,000

7(iii) The Emergency Arbitrator's fee may be increased by the LCIA Court on the recommendation of the Registrar at any time during the emergency proceedings if the particular circumstances of the case are deemed to warrant a higher fee.

7(iv) In the event of a challenge by any party to the Emergency Arbitrator, the party that applied for the appointment of the Emergency Arbitrator shall pay forthwith to the LCIA such further sum as may be directed by the LCIA Court in respect of the fees and expenses of the individual or division appointed to decide the challenge.

7(v) If the LCIA refuses an application for the appointment of an Emergency Arbitrator, the Emergency Arbitrator's fee shall be treated as a deposit lodged by the applicant party on account of the Arbitration Costs in accordance with Article 24 of the Rules and the Schedule.

\* Minimum unit of time in all cases: 15 minutes.

\*\* Items 1(ii), 1(iii), 1(iv) and 1(v) above, are payable on interim invoice; with the award, or as directed by the LCIA Court under Article 24.1 of the Rules.

## Introduction

The Schedule of Arbitration Costs forms part of the Rules, as confirmed in the Preamble. The printed version is a separate leaflet loosely inserted in the Rules booklet. It can also be found on the LCIA's website under the "Arbitration" tab. It is updated, from time to time, when the LCIA's administrative charges and/or the arbitrators' maximum hourly rates are changed.

The Schedule is largely concerned with the calculation of the Arbitration Costs (as defined in Article 28) and the mechanics of billing and payment. It should be read alongside Article 28 and also Article 24 ("Deposits"). Much of the text of Article 24 is reproduced in s.3 of the Schedule.

An important addition to the new edition of the Schedule is s.7 ("Emergency Arbitrator"), which sets out the fees payable on an application under Article 9B.

34–001

34–002

### *effective 1 October 2014*

**For arbitrations conducted under the LCIA arbitration rules (the Rules).**

**This schedule of arbitration costs (the Schedule), as amended from time to time by the LCIA, forms part of the Rules, and will apply in all current and future arbitrations as from its effective date.**

The Schedule came into force on the same date as the 2014 Rules: October 1, 2014. It is stated to apply not only in arbitrations commenced on or after that date but also in arbitrations already being administered under the Rules as at that date. The new Schedule is thus one part of the 2014 Rules which will apply to arbitrations commenced before October 1, 2014. It is identical to the previous version, dated January 1, 2014, save for the Emergency Arbitrator provisions in s.7.

The Preamble to the Schedule confirms that it is for arbitrations under the LCIA Rules. There are separate Schedules for ad hoc arbitrations and for arbitrations in which the LCIA has been agreed or designated (e.g. by a state court or by the Permanent Court of Arbitration) as an appointing authority.

34–003

## 1. Administrative charges

### 1(i) Registration Fee (payable in advance with the Request for Arbitration: non-refundable). *£1,750*

34–004 Payment of the registration fee is an essential component of the commencement of an arbitration under the Rules. Article 1.1(vi) provides that a Claimant must confirm, when filing its Request for Arbitration, that the fee "has been or is being paid to the LCIA". Failure to pay will result in the arbitration being treated as "not having been commenced under the Arbitration Agreement".

The registration fee is non-refundable and is payable in the same amount, regardless of the size and complexity of the arbitration and of the amount of time spent by the LCIA Secretariat in dealing with the Request when it is filed. Time-based administrative charges will also be incurred (see below) and the Secretariat's clock will start running the moment the Request is filed. However, those administrative charges will be invoiced only after the Arbitral Tribunal has been appointed or after the arbitration has been terminated if earlier (see Article 28.6); save in the case of an application for the appointment of an Emergency Arbitrator (Article 9B), the registration fee is the only advance payment that has to be made by the Claimant.

34–005 When the LCIA Secretariat comes to prepare the financial summary at the close of the arbitration, the registration fee will be counted as a payment made by the Claimant. It will form part of the Arbitration Costs. Parties should be alert to this when agreeing terms as to the apportionment of costs and the distribution of funds held by the LCIA on the settlement of an arbitration. They should ask the Secretariat for a financial summary at that time and should check whether their proposed terms can be implemented as drawn or whether some modifications might be necessary to take account of this initial payment of the registration fee and any other issues.[1] The registration fee is not itself a deposit.[2]

The fee may be paid by bank transfer (as to which the LCIA's Accounts Department will provide details) or by cheque lodged with the Request. If an online filing is made, it may be paid by credit card. It should be noted that VAT may be payable by some Claimants: the LCIA Secretariat can advise.

### (ii) Time spent* by the Secretariat of the LCIA in the administration of the arbitration.**

**Registrar / Deputy Registrar** *£250 per hour*

**Counsel** *£225 per hour*

**Case administrators** *£175 per hour*

**Casework accounting functions** *£150 per hour*

34–006 The LCIA Secretariat charges for the time it spends on administrative tasks in connection with the arbitration. These tasks are described in the commentary on

---

[1] Article 28.2 deals with costs on a settlement.
[2] Article 24.1.

Article 3.2. They begin with the receipt and acknowledgement of the Request for Arbitration.

A footnote to the Schedule notes that the minimum unit of time is 15 minutes. The mere reading of inter-parties' correspondence copied to the LCIA, but which does not require action by the Secretariat, does not generally result in separate charges.

Itemised invoices, containing details of how time charged has been spent, will be provided at regular intervals during the arbitration, and when it has completed. As confirmed in the second footnote to the Schedule, these invoices are payable on receipt. In practice, they will usually be paid from deposits. If the funds held are inadequate, further deposits will be directed, hence the reference to Article 24.1 in the footnote. The procedure for dealing with final deposits and shortfalls is described in the commentary on Article 26.2. 34–007

Bearing in mind that the Registrar, Deputy Registrar and Counsel are usually qualified lawyers, their hourly rates are modest. The Registrar and Deputy Registrar will, from time to time, be involved in sensitive and delicate tasks, such as raising enquiries about potential conflicts with a party's nominee or ensuring the confidentiality of an arbitration which has aroused press interest. It is perhaps in recognition of such additional responsibilities that the hourly rate of the Registrar and Deputy Registrar has been set at a slightly higher level than that of Counsel.

The case administrators deal with administrative and financial aspects of an arbitration after the formation of the Arbitral Tribunal. They liaise with the arbitrators and/or with the arbitrators' clerks about their fees and billing and draw up financial summaries. They prepare the dossiers that are submitted to the LCIA Court for the determination of the Arbitration Costs.[3] They liaise closely with the Counsel in the Secretariat who is responsible for the case. 34–008

The LCIA also charges hourly rates for its accounting staff in arbitrations under its own Rules, as well as in relation to fundholding services provided to parties in other arbitrations. It does so on the same basis of a 15 minutes minimum unit. The rate is £150 per hour.

An effect of these time-based charges, as opposed to an "ad valorem" system, is that if a case settles early, say shortly after the appointment of a sole arbitrator, the charges can appear to be relatively high, likely several thousand pounds, whilst the arbitrator's fees may be relatively low, perhaps only a few hundred pounds. This is because the administrative tasks are very much "front loaded" with many of them required at the beginning of the arbitration, dealing with the Request and Response and the appointment of the Arbitral Tribunal. If a case settles later in the proceedings, the Secretariat's time based charges will comprise a far smaller percentage of the total Arbitration Costs and they may be exceeded by the 5 per cent on the arbitrators' fees (see below). 34–009

**(iii) Time spent by members of the LCIA Court in carrying out their functions in deciding any challenge brought under the Rules.\*\***

---

[3] Article 28.1.

*at hourly rates advised by members of the LCIA Court*

**34–010** Members of the LCIA Court will not generally charge for their time in making decisions in connection with particular arbitrations. The exception arises when they are appointed to a Division to determine a challenge to an arbitrator under Article 10.

Their hourly rates will be at or below the maximum for arbitrators (see s.2(i) below).

**34–011** The Division's fees will form part of the "costs of the challenge", which are discussed in relation to Article 10.7.

> **(iv) A sum equivalent to 5% of the fees of the Tribunal (excluding expenses) in respect of the LCIA's general overhead.**

**34–012** A charge based on a percentage of the arbitrators' fees may seem to be a peculiar way of paying for the Secretariat's general overhead, but there is logic to it. The longer and more complex an arbitration is, the more time it will take up, not only for the arbitrators but also for the members of the Secretariat who follow the proceedings through the correspondence which is copied to the LCIA. Collecting an additional sum equivalent to 5 per cent of the arbitrators' fees is a way of ensuring that the LCIA is remunerated for its general administrative service (keeping alert to procedural incidents and costs implications) approximately in proportion to the demands of the case.

> **(v) Expenses incurred by the Secretariat and by members of the LCIA Court, in connection with the arbitration (such as postage, telephone, facsimile, travel etc.), and additional arbitration support services, whether provided by the Secretariat or by the members of the LCIA Court from their own resources or otherwise**

**34–013** In addition to the LCIA's time-based charges and the 5 per cent charge, the Secretariat may charge for its disbursements, such as couriers. The LCIA's first invoice in an arbitration is likely to include such expenses because its first letter to the parties, upon receipt of the Request for Arbitration, will usually be sent by courier. The costs of printing and sending a Division's decision may likewise be charged as disbursements by the members of the LCIA Court who have incurred them.[4]

> **(vi) The LCIA's charges will be invoiced in sterling, but may be paid in other convertible currencies, at rates prevailing at the time of payment.**

---

[4] It should be noted that a decision on a challenge is not bound and authenticated by the LCIA in the same way as an award, and may be sent to the parties direct by the Division.

Whilst arbitrators may charge their fees in other currencies, the LCIA's administrative charges will be invoiced in sterling. However, the LCIA also has bank accounts which hold Euros, US Dollars and other currencies, and is able to accept payment in those currencies.   34–014

**(vii) Charges may be subject to Value Added Tax at the prevailing rate.**

The LCIA is obliged to add VAT to its charges to parties who are not entitled to an exemption. Companies registered for VAT in the EU should provide their VAT number in order to avoid having VAT added to their bills.   34–015

*2. Fees and expenses of the Tribunal*

**2(i) The Tribunal's fees will be calculated by reference to work done by its members in connection with the arbitration and will be charged at rates appropriate to the particular circumstances of the case, including its complexity and the special qualifications of the arbitrators. The Tribunal shall agree in writing upon fee rates conforming to the Schedule prior to its appointment by the LCIA Court. The rates will be advised by the Registrar to the parties at the time of the appointment of the Tribunal, but may be reviewed if the duration or a change in the circumstances of the arbitration requires. Fees shall be at hourly rates *not exceeding £450*.**

Arbitrators charge their fees at hourly rates, which are agreed in each arbitration in each consultation with the LCIA Secretariat and in line with guidance from the LCIA Court.   34–016

Rates may be reviewed if the duration or a change of circumstances justifies this. The typical situation in which the LCIA Court might allow an increase in the hourly rates during the course of an arbitration would be in the last few months before a long hearing, which was supposed to have taken place a year earlier (when the rate was lower) but had been adjourned. Another situation might be where an arbitration has been complicated by the joinder of additional parties.

As discussed in the commentary to Article 5.4, the current maximum rate of £450 is lower than many arbitrators would normally charge. The LCIA has a reputation for keeping the hourly rates capped at moderate levels and also for monitoring the arbitrators' fees during the course of the arbitration and for scrutinising their invoices.   34–017

**However, in exceptional cases, the rate may be higher, provided that, in such cases, (i) the fees of the Tribunal shall be fixed by the LCIA Court on the recommendation of the Registrar, following consultations with the arbitrator(s), and (ii) the fees shall be agreed expressly by all parties.**

34–018  It is only in exceptional cases that the maximum hourly rate (currently £450) can be exceeded. This has occurred, for example, in cases in which the parties have jointly agreed upon the appointment of a particular sole arbitrator in a complex, high value and urgent dispute. The arbitrator's own explanations and those of the parties for agreeing fee rates at such a level should be provided to the Registrar in writing and will be forwarded to the LCIA Court with a recommendation.

### (ii) The Tribunal's fees may include a charge for time spent travelling.

34–019  International arbitration will frequently require international travel by arbitrators. Time spent travelling may be charged to the parties but the usual rule is that it should be limited to eight hours in the day.

### (iii) The Tribunal's fees may also include a charge for time reserved but not used as a result of late postponement or cancellation of hearings, provided that the basis for such charge shall be advised in writing to, and approved by, the LCIA Court and that the parties have been informed in advance.

34–020  The Arbitral Tribunal may raise cancellation charges for hearing time booked but not used. The wording of the LCIA's standard cancellation terms is set out in the commentary on Article 19 ("Hearings").

### (iv) The Tribunal may also recover such expenses as are reasonably incurred in connection with the arbitration, and as are reasonable in amount, provided that claims for expenses should be supported by invoices or receipts.

34–021  As noted in relation to Article 28.1, the LCIA Secretariat is vigilant on expenses. It will, for example, query bookings at luxury hotels and whether a visit to London for a hearing might also have been used for another business purpose. Supporting invoices or receipts should accompany arbitrators' fee notes, which are scrutinised by the case administrators.

### (v) The Tribunal's fees shall be invoiced in the currency of account between the Tribunal and the parties.

34–022  Arbitrators' fees will generally be invoiced in sterling but can also be invoiced in another currency which might be one used by both parties in the ordinary course of business, e.g. US Dollars.

(vi) In the event of the revocation of the appointment of any arbitrator, pursuant to the provisions of Article 10 of the Rules, the LCIA Court shall, in accordance with Article 10.7, determine the amount of fees and expenses (if any) to be paid for the former arbitrator's services as it may consider appropriate in all the circumstances.

Depending on the circumstances of the revocation of an arbitrator's appointment, it may or may not be appropriate for the arbitrator to be paid fees and expenses. This is discussed, with an example, in the commentary on Article 10.7.

(vii) Charges may be subject to Value Added Tax at the prevailing rate.

Arbitrators may be obliged to add VAT to their fees. Their invoices are addressed to the parties, not the LCIA, though they will generally be paid from the deposits held by the LCIA. Whether VAT should be charged will depend on where the arbitrator is resident and his or her tax status, and the location of the parties.

## 3. Deposits

3(i) The LCIA Court may direct the parties, in such proportions and at such times as it thinks appropriate, to make one or more payments to the LCIA on account of the costs of the arbitration, other than the legal or other expenses incurred by the parties themselves (the Arbitration Costs). Such payments deposited by the parties may be applied by the LCIA Court to pay any item of such Arbitration Costs (including the LCIA's own fees and expenses) in accordance with the LCIA Rules.

3(ii) All payments made by parties on account of the Arbitration Costs shall be held by the LCIA in trust under English law in England, to be disbursed or otherwise applied by the LCIA in accordance with the LCIA Rules and invested having regard also to the interests of the LCIA. Each payment made by a party shall be credited by the LCIA with interest at the rate from time to time credited to an overnight deposit of that amount with the bank(s) engaged by the LCIA to manage deposits from time to time; and any surplus income (beyond such interest) shall accrue for the sole benefit of the LCIA. In the event that payments (with such interest) exceed the total amount of the Arbitration Costs at the conclusion of the arbitration, the excess amount shall be returned by the LCIA to the parties as the ultimate default beneficiaries of the trust.

3(iii) Save for exceptional circumstances, the Arbitral Tribunal should not proceed with the arbitration without having ascertained from the Registrar that the LCIA is or will be in requisite funds as regards outstanding and future Arbitration Costs.

3(iv) **In the event that a party fails or refuses to make any payment on account of the Arbitration Costs as directed by the LCIA Court, the LCIA Court may direct the other party or parties to effect a substitute payment to allow the arbitration to proceed (subject to any order or award on Arbitration Costs).**

3(v) **In such circumstances, the party effecting the substitute payment may request the Arbitral Tribunal to make an order or award in order to recover that amount as a debt immediately due and payable to that party by the defaulting party, together with any interest.**

34–025 The text of s.3 is almost identical to that of Article 24. The differences are the addition of the definition of "Arbitration Costs" in s.3(i) (from Article 28) and the absence of the provisions relating to the Arbitral Tribunal's powers in the event of non-payment (Article 24.6).

### 4. Interim payments

**When interim payments are required to cover any part of the Arbitration Costs, including the LCIA's administrative charges; the fees or expenses of members of the LCIA Court, the Tribunal's fees or expenses, including the fees or expenses of any expert appointed by the Tribunal, the fees or expenses of any Secretary to the Tribunal; or charges for hearing rooms and other support services, such payments may be made against the invoices for any of the above from funds held on deposit. If no or insufficient funds are held at the time the interim payment is required, the invoices for any of the above may be submitted for payment direct by the parties.**

34–026 During the course of an arbitration, the assigned case administrator in the LCIA Secretariat will liaise with the Arbitral Tribunal in order to keep up to date with fees and expenses incurred. At appropriate junctures, arbitrators' and other service providers' invoices will be paid from the deposits held. This may occur, for example, after an interlocutory hearing and the issue of a procedural order or after the passage of six months since the last financial update. The invoices will be forwarded to the parties by the case administrator who will usually raise and pay an invoice for the LCIA's administrative charges (including 5 per cent on the arbitrators' fees) at the same time.

The Schedule has a reference to "the fees or expenses of any Secretary to the Tribunal". This is the only mention of administrative secretaries in the Rules. As confirmed on the LCIA's website,[5] the LCIA has no objection, in principle, to the appointment of a Secretary or Clerk to the Arbitral Tribunal, provided that the parties agree, and subject to the usual conflicts checks. However, as also confirmed on its website, the LCIA Secretariat is well placed to provide many of the administrative services which may be delegated to a Secretary, such as booking hearing rooms, keeping an eye on procedural timetables, sending reminders to the Arbitral

---

[5] Under FAQs (*http://www.lcia.org*) [Accessed December 4, 2014].

Tribunal and parties' representatives, and proofreading awards. The hourly rates of members of the LCIA Secretariat are relatively modest and may be lower than the hourly rate of a lawyer who might be appointed as a Secretary. In practice, administrative secretaries are only appointed in a minority of LCIA arbitrations.

**34–027** The LCIA website states: "The duties of the administrative secretary should neither conflict with those for which the parties are paying the LCIA Secretariat, nor constitute any delegation of the Tribunal's authority". This is the message which is communicated by the LCIA Secretariat to the Arbitral Tribunal and to the parties when the appointment of an administrative secretary is proposed. The Registrar or LCIA Counsel will also inform the Arbitral Tribunal and the administrative secretary that his or her activities should be confined to such matters as "organising papers for the Tribunal, highlighting relevant legal authorities, maintaining factual chronologies, keeping the Tribunal's time sheets and so forth."[6]

The ICC has a "Note on the Appointment, Duties and Remuneration of Administrative Secretaries"[7] which contains a fuller exposition of the lines to be drawn between the arbitrators' duties and the tasks which can be delegated to administrative secretaries.[8] Those lines are essentially the same in arbitrations under the LCIA Rules.

**34–028** In ICC arbitrations, the administrative secretary is remunerated from the funds available for the fees of all arbitrators; no additional fees should be charged. In LCIA arbitrations, in which the arbitrators' fees are calculated on the basis of hourly rates, the administrative secretary may raise fees on the same, hourly rate, basis. However, it is usually expected that the administrative secretary's rate will be much lower (perhaps half) the arbitrators' rates and possibly nil, particularly if the lawyer undertaking this role is doing so primarily for educational purposes and for the experience it affords to the secretary.

The administrative secretary's fee notes and expenses claims will be scrutinised by the LCIA Secretariat in the same way as arbitrators' invoices. Full narratives of time spent are expected. Should any of the activities billed consist of duplication of the arbitrators' work, learning time, or tasks which should not properly be delegated to an administrative secretary (e.g. drafting parts of a final award), queries will be raised with the secretary and with the presiding arbitrator.

**34–029** If the deposits are insufficient to cover the various fees and charges listed in s.4, the Secretariat may raise invoices to cover any shortfall, in addition to directing the lodging of further deposits.

---

[6] LCIA website, FAQs.
[7] http://www.iccwbo.org/Products-and-Services/Arbitration-and-ADR/Flash-news/Introduction-of-revised-Note-on-the-Appointment,-Duties-and-Remuneration-of-Administrative-Secretaries/ [Accessed November 9, 2014].
[8] "Under no circumstances may the Arbitral Tribunal delegate decision-making functions to an Administrative Secretary. Nor should the Arbitral Tribunal rely on the Administrative Secretary to perform any essential duties of an arbitrator. The Administrative Secretary may not act, or be required to act, in such a manner as to prevent or discourage direct communications amongst the arbitrators, between the Arbitral Tribunal and the parties, or between the Arbitral Tribunal and the Secretariat. A request by an Arbitral Tribunal to an Administrative Secretary to prepare written notes or memoranda shall in no circumstances release the Arbitral Tribunal from its duty personally to review the file and/or to draft any decision of the Arbitral Tribunal. When in doubt about which tasks may be performed by an Administrative Secretary, the Arbitral Tribunal or the Administrative Secretary should contact the Secretariat."

### 5. Registrar's authority

**5(i) For the purposes of sections 3(i) and 3(iv) above, and of Articles 24.1 and 24.4 of the Rules, the Registrar has the authority of the LCIA Court to make the directions referred to, under the supervision of the Court.**

34–030   The role and functions of the Registrar are described in the commentary on Article 3.2. Section 5(i) of the Schedule confirms that the Registrar has authority to direct the payment of deposits and substitute payments.

**(ii) For the purposes of section 4 above, and of Article 24.1 of the Rules, the Registrar has the authority of the LCIA Court to approve the payments referred to.**

34–031   Article 24.1 permits the LCIA Court to apply deposits to pay any item of Arbitration Costs, i.e. arbitrators' fees, the LCIA's administrative charges, the fees of an expert appointed by the Arbitral Tribunal and other such fees and expenses, as listed in s.4 ("Interim payments"). Section 5(ii) confirms that the Registrar has authority to approve such payments, i.e. to arrange for them to be made without recourse to the LCIA Court. It is only at the close of the arbitration, or if there is a particular reason to do so earlier (e.g. in an award on a discrete issue which also decides liability for the costs of deciding that issue), that the LCIA Court will be asked to determine the Arbitration Costs.[9]

**(iii) Any request by an arbitrator for payment on account of his fees shall be supported by a fee note, which shall include, or be accompanied by, a detailed breakdown of the time spent at the rates that have been advised to the parties by the LCIA, and the fee note will be forwarded to the parties prior to settlement of the account.**

34–032   This sub-section and the following one do not strictly fit under the heading "Registrar's Authority". Section 5(iii) is concerned with the interim fee notes and supporting information which arbitrators are obliged to provide to the LCIA before any payments on account can be made and which will be forwarded to the parties, usually with a financial summary and an invoice for any outstanding administrative charges of the LCIA, as outlined in the commentary on s.4 above.

**(iv) Any dispute regarding the LCIA's administrative charges, or the fees and expenses of the Tribunal shall be determined by the LCIA Court.**

34–033   If a party has a complaint about the LCIA's administrative charges or the arbitrators' fees, it should be addressed, in the first instance, to the Registrar. Should the

---

[9] Article 28.1.

party remain dissatisfied and refuse to pay any items billed, the dispute will be referred to the LCIA Court, usually to the President or a Vice President, who will make a decision on the matter.

In arbitrations seated in England, parties have the right to apply to the court under s.28 of the Arbitration Act 1996 for "an order that the amount of the arbitrators' fees and expenses shall be considered and adjusted by such means and upon such terms as it may direct". This is a mandatory provision of the 1996 Act, which s.5(iv) of the Schedule cannot substitute. However, a reference to the LCIA Court for determination of a dispute about Arbitration Costs will be quicker and less expensive than an application to court. Unlike the Grain and Feed Trade Association in *Agrimex Ltd v Tradigrain Ltd*,[10] the LCIA has not faced an application under s.28 or a judicial finding that fees were "excessive".

### 6. Arbitration costs

**6(i) The parties shall be jointly and severally liable to the Tribunal and the LCIA for the costs of the arbitration (other than the legal or other costs incurred by the parties themselves).**

Section 6 deals with the liability of the parties for the Arbitration Costs, as defined in this opening sub-section and in Article 28.1. As between the parties, the Arbitral Tribunal may ultimately decide that one should bear all of the costs and the other none or, for example, that the proportions for which they should each be liable should depend on their relative success on different issues.[11] However, as between the parties and the LCIA, the parties are jointly and severally liable for the Arbitration Costs.

34–034

**(ii) Any bank charges incurred on any transfer of funds by the parties to the LCIA shall be borne exclusively by the party or parties transferring the funds.**

The case administrator assigned to the arbitration will keep accurate records of the amounts paid by each party, which will be set out in the financial summaries sent to the parties when invoices are paid, as outlined in relation to s.4. These amounts will be net of any bank charges incurred when the funds are lodged.

34–035

**(iii) In accordance with Article 26.7 of the Rules, the Tribunal's Award(s) shall be transmitted to the parties by the LCIA Court provided that the costs of the arbitration have been paid to the LCIA in accordance with Article 28 of the Rules.**

---

[10] [2003] EWHC 1656; [2003] 2 Lloyd's Rep 537.
[11] Article 28.2.

34-036    If the deposits lodged by the parties are insufficient to cover the Arbitral Tribunal's fees and expenses, and the LCIA's administrative charges up to and including the issue of the award, the Registrar will call for an additional payment. The process is described in the commentary on Articles 26.2 and 26.7.

### 7. Emergency Arbitrator

7(i)   Application fee (payable with the application for the appointment of an Emergency Arbitrator under Article 9B of the Rules: non-refundable).

*£8,000*

7(ii)  Emergency Arbitrator's fee, to cover time charges and expenses (payable with the application for the appointment of an Emergency Arbitrator: non-refundable if the LCIA Court appoints an Emergency Arbitrator).

*£20,000*

34-037    The Emergency Arbitrator provisions are new in this version of the Schedule. According to Article 9.5, the Schedule of Costs prescribes the amount of a "Special Fee", which is payable with an application under Article 9B for the appointment of an Emergency Arbitrator. The October 2014 Schedule does not, in fact, use the term "Special Fee", which may cause some confusion.[12] Instead, the Schedule sets out two amounts which are payable with the application: (i) an application fee of £8,000 and (ii) the Emergency Arbitrator's fee of £20,000.

These fees are similar in amount, and in the manner in which they are split, to the ICC's fees on an application under its Emergency Arbitrator Rules.[13] At first glance it is surprising that the fees should be so high: in terms of hourly rates, they represent 32 hours of the Registrar's time at £250 per hour and 44 hours of the Emergency Arbitrator's at £450 per hour, almost an entire working week by both. Fees of that magnitude may suggest that the role of the Emergency Arbitrator may extend beyond the initial or most pressing "emergency", or that the procedure he or she adopts could involve more than one hearing over a period of some days, or might even involve policing compliance with the initial order or award until the appointment of the Arbitral Tribunal. In any event, the period up until the constitution of the Arbitral Tribunal is one which will likely occupy the Secretariat and the appointed Emergency Arbitrator for at least a number of days, possibly weeks, as also reflected in the three days allowed for the appointment[14] and 14 days for the Emergency Arbitrator's decision.[15]

It is also surprising that the Emergency Arbitrator's fees are non-refundable, at least in part if the parties come to an agreement on the relief sought or the emer-

---

[12] The discrepancy may have been a simple drafting error which might be rectified in later versions of the Schedule.
[13] Appendix V, Article 7(1) of the ICC Arbitration Rules 2012. The total fees are currently US$40,000.
[14] Article 9.6.
[15] Article 9.8.

gency dissipates after the Emergency Arbitrator is appointed. In contrast, the ICC allows for a reimbursement to the applicant, should the Emergency Arbitrator proceedings not take place, or be terminated prior to the making of an Order.[16] It is not unusual for emergencies (e.g. the preservation of assets, an inspection of equipment or defective goods) to be resolved between parties, particularly after the commencement of proceedings instigated for the purpose of doing so. The LCIA's regime does, though, make a concession if the Emergency Arbitrator is not appointed; his fee is to be treated as a deposit (s.7(v)), which could ultimately be returned to the paying party, at least in part, if the arbitration did not proceed.

> (iii) **The Emergency Arbitrator's fee may be increased by the LCIA Court on the recommendation of the Registrar at any time during the emergency proceedings if the particular circumstances of the case are deemed to warrant a higher fee.**

The LCIA Court can increase the Emergency Arbitrator's fee, but there is no provision for it to be decreased. The fee is a lump sum and not expressly calculated according to hourly rates. It is to be presumed, however, that an increase might be requested by the appointed arbitrator if the proceedings are more time-consuming than expected. It would not be unreasonable to expect that the fee would be reduced if the Emergency Arbitrator procedure took less time.  34–038

> (iv) **In the event of a challenge by any party to the Emergency Arbitrator, the party that applied for the appointment of the Emergency Arbitrator shall pay forthwith to the LCIA such further sum as may be directed by the LCIA Court in respect of the fees and expenses of the individual or division appointed to decide the challenge.**

A potential additional expense of the Emergency Arbitrator procedure, not one encountered with urgent applications to court, is the cost of dealing with any challenge to the arbitrator. The LCIA Court may direct a "further sum" to be paid for the fees of the President, Vice President or Division who will determine a challenge. It is not clear whether this is likewise a lump sum payable in advance, a deposit for fees to be incurred at hourly rates, or a payment for such fees already incurred when the direction is made.  34–039

> (v) **If the LCIA refuses an application for the appointment of an Emergency Arbitrator, the Emergency Arbitrator's fee shall be treated as a deposit lodged by the applicant party on account of the Arbitration Costs in accordance with Article 24 of the Rules and the Schedule.**

---

[16] Article 7(5) of the Emergency Arbitrator Rules.

**34–040** As noted above, whilst the Emergency Arbitrator's fee is non-refundable, it may, if no such arbitrator is appointed, be treated as a deposit lodged by the applicant as its share of the advance on the Arbitral Tribunal's fees and the LCIA's administrative charges. The trigger for the forfeit of the fee is the appointment of the Emergency Arbitrator: a resolution of the emergency can be agreed by the parties within hours of the appointment and the arbitrator may not have done any work on the case but the fee will not in those circumstances be treated as a deposit. Nevertheless, depending on the circumstances, it can be expected that an Emergency Arbitrator might forgo his fee, or part of it, and that the LCIA Court might be flexible about the operation of these provisions.

# PART III—COMMENTARY ON THE LCIA RECOMMENDED CLAUSES

# COMMENTARY ON THE LCIA RECOMMENDED CLAUSES

*Future disputes*

Any dispute arising out of or in connection with this contract, including any question regarding its existence, validity or termination, shall be referred to and finally resolved by arbitration under the LCIA Rules, which Rules are deemed to be incorporated by reference into this clause.

The number of arbitrators shall be [one/three].

The seat, or legal place, of arbitration shall be [City and/or Country].

The language to be used in the arbitral proceedings shall be [ ].

The governing law of the contract shall be the substantive law of [ ].

*Existing disputes*

A dispute having arisen between the parties concerning [ ], the parties hereby agree that the dispute shall be referred to and finally resolved by arbitration under the LCIA Rules.

The number of arbitrators shall be [one/three].

The seat, or legal place, of arbitration shall be [City and/or Country].

The language to be used in the arbitral proceedings shall be [ ].

The governing law of the contract [is/shall be] the substantive law of [ ].

### Introduction

The clauses reviewed in this Part are recommended by the LCIA to parties wishing to resolve disputes under the LCIA Rules. They can be found both on its website and on the final two pages of the institution's booklet containing the 2014 Rules. There have been no changes to the recommended clauses to coincide with the publication of the new 2014 Rules: their brevity and simplicity have stood the test of time. 　III–001

There are two types of clauses. The first is for incorporation in a contract as a dispute resolution clause. The second is the main body of an agreement to refer existing disputes to arbitration under the LCIA Rules.

Both clauses are extremely short, essentially because the issues which they address, and other issues which they do not, are more fully covered in the Rules. They fulfil the requirements for an "agreement" specified in the Preamble. 　III–002

It would be sufficient for parties wishing to refer future disputes to LCIA arbitration to be as concise as stating "LCIA Arbitration, London".[1] However, the wording of each of the recommended clauses deals with a few points and options to which the parties should turn their attention before signing their agreements.

III–003   An extensive wealth of literature exists on the topic of how to draft international arbitration agreements, and on the consequences of failing to do so correctly,[2] and there is certainly no need for another exposition of this matter here. The commentary on the Preamble (where "Arbitration Agreement" first appears in he Rules) contains a discussion of the meaning and nature of such agreements. This Part is concerned with the consequences of making an Arbitration Agreement, the matters to consider when doing so, the particular wording of the recommended clauses and with modifications which might be made to them, e.g. for the nomination of arbitrators. More general discussions of such issues as jurisdiction and separability, which are critical to the drafting and the effect of arbitration clauses, will be found in the commentary on Article 23.

*Consequences of entering into an arbitration agreement*

III–004   Entering into an arbitration agreement relating to an international transaction has a number of consequences.

First, the parties accept an enforceable obligation to refer disputes covered by the agreement to arbitration instead of to national courts. Under Article II of the New York Convention, the courts of a member state must stay proceedings that are commenced in respect of which there exists:

"an agreement in writing under which the parties undertake to submit to arbitration all or any differences which have arisen or which may arise between them in respect of a defined legal relationship, whether contractual or not, concerning a subject matter capable of settlement by arbitration".[3]

---

[1] See *Manistaumunaigaz Oil Production Association v United World Trade Inc* [1995] Lloyd's Rep. 619, in which a similar clause was upheld as a valid ICC arbitration agreement.

[2] For example: R. Doak Bishop, *A Practical Guide for Drafting International Arbitration Clauses*, http://www.kslaw.com/library/pdf/bishop9.pdf [Accessed October 26, 2014]; Bond, "How to Draft an Arbitration Clause" (1989) 6(2) J. Int. Arb. 65; Gary B. Born, *International Arbitration and Forum Selection Agreements: Drafting and Enforcing*, 4th edn (Kluwer Law International, 2013); Paul D. Friedland, *Arbitration Clauses for International Contracts* (Huntington, NY: JurisNet, 2007); P. Gélinas, "Arbitration Clauses: Achieving Effectiveness", in A.J. van den Berg (ed.), *Improving the Efficiency of Arbitration Agreements and Awards: 40 Years of Application of the New York Convention* (ICCA Congress series) (Kluwer Law International, 1999), p.47; Julian D.M. Lew, "Arbitration Agreements: Form and Character", in P. Sarčević (ed.), *Essays on International Commercial Arbitration* (London: Graham & Trotman, 1989), p.55; Julian D.M. Lew et al., *Comparative International Commercial Arbitration* (The Hague: Kluwer Law International, 2003), Ch.8; William W. Park, *International Forum Selection* (Kluwer Law International, 1995), Ch.4; Paulsson et al., *The Freshfields Guide to Arbitration and ADR*, 2nd edn (Kluwer Law International, 1999); Alan Redfern et al., *Law and Practice of International Commercial Arbitration*, 4th edn (London: Sweet & Maxwell, 2004), Ch.3; B.G. Davis, "Pathological Clauses: Frédéric Eisemann's Still Vital Criteria" (1991) 7(4) Arbitration Int. 365.

[3] Article II(1) of the New York Convention (Appendix 9).

The courts must refer the parties to arbitration.[4] This Convention requirement is recognised in practice in Article 8 of the UNCITRAL Model Law and various national laws around the world.[5]

Secondly, any unilateral attempt to bring substantive proceedings[6] in national courts amounts to a breach of the arbitration agreement or clause, in respect of which an award of damages or an injunction may be available.[7]

III–005

The third consequence is that an award rendered by a Tribunal constituted pursuant to a valid arbitration agreement is internationally enforceable under the terms of the New York Convention and other applicable conventions.[8]

The fourth main effect of an arbitration agreement is that it "establishes the jurisdiction and authority of the Tribunal over that of the courts . . . [and] is the basic source of the power of the arbitrators."[9] The flip side of this enabling function is that the arbitration agreement also sets the outer limits of the Tribunal's authority and jurisdiction.[10]

III–006

Thus a properly drafted arbitration agreement is crucial to the arbitral process. By contrast, a carelessly drafted arbitration agreement could result in the parties wasting time and costs litigating over the validity and effect of the arbitration agreement and the jurisdiction of the Tribunal before they can address the merits of the dispute. They may ultimately find that they have forfeited their right to arbitrate any disputes,[11] and that all or certain matters must be litigated in potentially inhospitable national courts. Worse still, parties who fail to conclude a valid arbitration agreement under the relevant laws risk finding that, having arbitrated a dispute, the award rendered by the Tribunal is unenforceable.[12]

Although it is by no means mandatory to do so,[13] by adopting the LCIA recommended arbitration clause, parties can avoid major potential pitfalls and the risk associated with re-inventing this important arbitral wheel.

III–007

---

[4] Article II(3) of the New York Convention (Appendix 9).
[5] For example, Belgian Judicial Code Article 1681; English Arbitration Act 1996 s.9; Indian Arbitration and Conciliation Act 1996 s.45; Russian Federation Law 5338-1 of 1993 Article 8(1).
[6] In contrast to ancillary court proceedings, for example, for the preservation of assets, anti-suit injunctions or other interim relief.
[7] See, for example, *Mantovani v Carapelli SpA* [1978] 2 Lloyd's Rep. 63; *A v B* (No.2) [2007] 1 All E.R. (Comm) 633, stating that damages for breach of an arbitration agreement will normally permit the innocent party to recover all of the legal costs it expended on an indemnity basis; *The Angelic Grace* [1995] 1 Lloyd's Rep. 87; *Donohue v Armco* [2000] EWCA Civ 94.
[8] Such as the 1961 European Convention; the 1965 Washington Convention; the 1972 Moscow Convention; the 1975 Inter-American Convention on International Commercial Arbitration (Panama Convention); and the 1987 Arab Convention on Commercial Arbitration (Amman Convention).
[9] Lew et al., *Comparative International Commercial Arbitration* (2003), p.100 at 6–2.
[10] See Article 23.1.
[11] See Article 16 of the UNCITRAL Model Law (Appendix 10), ss.30–32 and 67 of the English Arbitration Act 1996 (Appendix 7), and see *Dallah Real Estate & Tourism Holding Co v Ministry of Religious Affairs, Government of Pakistan* [2010] UKSC 46, emphasising the supervisory role of the courts of the seat as well as enforcement courts.
[12] Article V(1)(a) of the New York Convention (Appendix 9).
[13] It would be sufficient for parties wishing to refer future disputes to LCIA arbitration to be as concise as stating "LCIA Arbitration, London"; see *Manistaumunaigaz Oil Production Association v United World Trade Inc* [1995] 1 Lloyd's Rep. 617, in which a similar clause was upheld as a valid ICC arbitration agreement.

## Initial considerations

III–008  Nevertheless, even where the parties agree to adopt an LCIA recommended clause, the process may still become unhinged if due attention is not afforded to a few additional significant issues. Parties should always consider at least two important questions concerning their contractual counterparts.

The first question is whether the counterpart(s) has the legal capacity to enter into an arbitration agreement. Questions of legal capacity are governed by the personal law of the entity in question, and should not be assumed.[14]

III–009  The second question is whether all of the potentially necessary parties are bound by the arbitration agreement. As a general rule, a Tribunal will only have jurisdiction over the parties to the arbitration agreement. Joining third parties or consolidating parallel proceedings are theoretically possible under the LCIA Rules but only in limited circumstances.[15]

Finally, parties should bear in mind that not all disputes can lawfully be determined in arbitration. The extent to which a national law permits or prohibits the reference of particular types of disputes to arbitration may differ from jurisdiction to jurisdiction. "Classic" examples of disputes that are not arbitrable include criminal law disputes, inheritance law, and matters pertaining to the content of public registers. An arbitration agreement concerning matters not "capable of settlement by arbitration" might not be recognised and enforced by national courts,[16] with the consequence that parties could end up litigating before the national courts. Equally, an enforcement court might decline to enforce an arbitral award concerning a subject matter that is "not capable of settlement by arbitration under the law of that country."[17]

## Future disputes

**Any dispute arising out of or in connection with this contract, including any question regarding its existence, validity or termination, shall be referred to and finally resolved by arbitration under the LCIA Rules, which Rules are deemed to be incorporated by reference into this clause.**

**The number of arbitrators shall be [one/three].**

**The seat, or legal place, of arbitration shall be [City and/or Country].**

**The language to be used in the arbitral proceedings shall be [ ].**

**The governing law of the contract shall be the substantive law of [ ].**

III–010  The first paragraph of the recommended clause for "future disputes" has four important functions.

---

[14] For example, in some countries corporations are prohibited from entering into international arbitration agreements or proceedings without special corporate or other authorisations. Governments and government entities might also require specific approval.
[15] See Article 22(viii).
[16] Article II.1 of the New York Convention (Appendix 9).
[17] Article V(2)(a) of the New York Convention (Appendix 9).

First, it defines the scope of the arbitral reference in the widest terms possible. The expression "Any dispute arising out of or in connection with this contract . . ." has long been regarded by scholars[18] and judges[19] alike as conferring on the Tribunal the widest jurisdiction over all claims between the parties whether arising in contract, tort, trust, restitution, under statute or other causes of action, as long as the dispute factually or legally relates to the legal relationship in question. It is the formulation adopted for recommended clauses by many international arbitration institutions of repute.[20]

Until relatively recently, English lawyers would have contrasted this form of words with another common clause conferring jurisdiction over any disputes arising "under this contract" and other forms of wording. However, the Court of Appeal and concurring House of Lords decisions respectively in *Fiona Trust & Holding Corporation v Uri Privalov*[21] and *Premium Nafta Products Limited (20th Defendant) and others (Respondents) v Fili Shipping Company Limited (14th Claimant) and others (Appellants)*,[22] brought English law into line with many other jurisdictions, holding that the commercial purpose of the arbitration offers far better insight into the parties' intentions than "linguistic nuances".[23] As a matter of English law, the starting point is now that an arbitration clause should be construed in accordance with a presumption that businessmen would have intended all future disputes to be resolved by the same Tribunal: III–011

> "unless the language makes it clear that certain questions were intended to be excluded from the arbitrator's jurisdiction. As Longmore LJ remarked, at para 17 [of *Fiona Trust*]: 'if any businessman did want to exclude disputes about the validity of a contract, it would be comparatively easy to say so.'"[24]

The practical consequence of this approach is that parties who want to exclude any matter from the jurisdiction of the arbitrators (for example, because they consider that an expert determination is more appropriate in respect of a certain class of dispute) should do so expressly and in clear terms. Contracts sometimes contain inconsistencies with regard to the allocation of jurisdiction between experts, arbitrators and the courts, potentially rendering one part of their choice ineffective.[25] III–012

The second function of the first paragraph of the clause is to place the doctrine of the autonomy or separability of the arbitration clause on a contractual footing. This is achieved by expressly referring to the arbitrators "any question regarding

---

[18] Redfern et al., *Law and Practice of International Commercial Arbitration* (2004), para.3–38; Lew et al., *Comparative International Commercial Arbitration* (2003), pp.151–152, para.7–63.

[19] *JJ Ryan & Sons Inc v Rhone Poulenc Textile SA*, 863 F.2d 315, 321 (4th Cir. 1988); *Ethiopian Oilseeds Pulses Export Corp v Rio Del Mar Foods Inc* [1990] 1 Lloyd's Rep. 86; *Kaverit Steel & Crane Ltd v Kone Corp* (1992) 87 D.L.R. (4th) 129 (Court of Appeal of Alberta); *Francis Travel Marketing Pty Ltd v Virgin Atlantic Airways Ltd* (1996) 39 N.S.W.L.R. 160.

[20] For example, the Arbitration Institute of the Stockholm Chamber of Commerce (SCC) Model Arbitration Clause; Standard ICC Arbitration Clause; Singapore International Arbitration Centre Model Arbitration Clause.

[21] [2007] EWCA Civ 20.

[22] [2007] UKHL 40, on appeal from *Fiona Trust* [2007] EWCA Civ 20.

[23] [2007] UKHL 40, on appeal from *Fiona Trust* at [12], per Lord Hoffmann.

[24] [2007] UKHL 40, on appeal from *Fiona Trust* at [13], per Lord Hoffmann.

[25] Bishop, *A Practical Guide for Drafting International Arbitration Clauses*, pp.71–72; B.G. Davis, "Pathological Clauses: Frédéric Eisemann's Still Vital Criteria" (1991) 7(4) Arbitration Int. 365.

[the] existence, validity or termination" of the underlying commercial contract. Thus, even in jurisdictions where arbitration clauses or agreements are not, as a matter of law, considered separate from the underlying commercial contract, it may still be argued that as a matter of contract the LCIA arbitration clauses are distinct agreements and that the arbitrators do have the power to determine all jurisdictional questions, including disputes relating to the initial validity of the underlying commercial contract.[26]

III–013 The third function of this paragraph is the indication that disputes referred to arbitration under this clause are to be "... finally resolved by arbitration under the LCIA Rules ...", i.e. without further review or recourse to any other tribunal or court.[27] The finality of an LCIA award is further confirmed in Article 26.8 of the Rules, where rights of appeal to or review by national courts are expressly waived to the extent that such waiver is permissible. One effect of these provisions on arbitration proceedings with an English seat, is that the limited right to appeal on points of English law under s.69 of the English Arbitration Act 1996 is excluded.

Finally and significantly, the function of the last proviso of the first paragraph of the recommended clause, "... which Rules are deemed to be incorporated by reference into this clause", is to incorporate the entire text of the LCIA Rules into the text of the parties' arbitration clause.[28] By adopting this clause the parties have thus agreed not only to the appointment of arbitrators by the LCIA, but also to the procedural framework set out in the Rules as well as the various elections they contain, for example in relation to the powers of Arbitral Tribunals and the powers of national courts. The express incorporation of institutional rules into an arbitration clause is now a common feature in the arbitration clauses recommended by international arbitration institutions.[29]

III–014 Two important practical implications should be borne in mind. First, although the LCIA recommended clause may appear short to those accustomed to seeing long-form arbitration clauses, it does in fact provide a comprehensive arbitral procedure. Secondly, textual additions or modifications to the recommended clause could result in unintended conflicts between the clause and the Rules, and should therefore only be undertaken with caution. On the other hand, any desired modification of the Rules should be made in clear, express, terms.

Parties who are content to follow the scheme of the LCIA Rules without modification are still expected under the terms of the recommended clause to make a number of important choices, discussed below.

---

[26] This argument can also be made based on upon the incorporation of the LCIA Rules (and in particular Article 23) into the contract; see below.

[27] But see *Shell Egypt West Manzala GmbH v Dana Gas Egypt Ltd* (formerly Centurion Petroleum Corp) [2010] 2 All E.R. (Comm) 442, in which the phrase "final, conclusive and binding" in an UNCITRAL arbitration clause was held not to exclude the statutory right under s.69 of the English Arbitration Act 1996 to appeal an award on questions of English law.

[28] The circle is completed by the wording of the Preamble, under which the parties are taken to have agreed that "such LCIA Rules form part of their agreement (collectively, the "Arbitration Agreement")".

[29] International Centre for Dispute Resolution (Division of the AAA); The Arbitration Institute of the Stockholm Chamber of Commerce; International Arbitral Centre of the Austrian Federal Economic Chamber; International Chamber of Commerce; Singapore International Arbitration Centre; Swiss Chambers of Commerce; World Intellectual Property Organization and others.

### (a) One or three arbitrators

**The number of arbitrators shall be [one/three].**

The primary procedure under the Rules is that the LCIA Court will select the Arbitral Tribunal. If no number is specified by the parties, it will usually appoint a sole arbitrator: Article 5.8. The recommended clause gives the parties an opportunity to choose whether they would like a sole arbitrator or a panel of three.

A panel of three arbitrators will probably take longer to determine the dispute and undoubtedly cost significantly more than a sole arbitrator. Nevertheless, in particularly complex or high value cases, these drawbacks might well be counterbalanced by the quality-control advantages afforded by a three-member Tribunal, and perhaps by the varied expertise and backgrounds which such a Tribunal can bring to bear on a dispute. Provided they are all competent in their own right, few would argue with the notion that "three minds are better than one". Even the most seasoned arbitrator is likely to benefit in some cases from collaborating with colleagues.

The default position under the LCIA Rules is that all the arbitrators are selected and appointed by the LCIA Court. If the parties wish to nominate arbitrators themselves (which they commonly do if they opt for a three-member Arbitral Tribunal), they must agree to this, either in their Arbitration Agreement or subsequently.

A fairly standard addition to the LCIA recommended clause in a contract between two parties is therefore "and each party shall nominate an arbitrator". When read in conjunction with Articles 1 and 2, this addition allows the Claimant to nominate an arbitrator in the Request for Arbitration and the Respondent to nominate an arbitrator in the Response. On this basis, the presiding arbitrator would still be selected and appointed by the LCIA Court. A common alternative to this default nomination is for the two party-nominated arbitrators to be given the power to nominate the presiding arbitrator, for example, "The two party-nominated arbitrators shall jointly nominate the presiding arbitrator within [14] days of the last of their nominations."[30]

In multi-party contracts the parties should also consider whether they wish to include a provision in the Arbitration Agreement that, in the event of a dispute, certain companies represent one side and others represent another side (as Claimant and Respondent respectively) for the purposes of the formation of the Arbitral Tribunal. Unless such an agreement is concluded, the parties in a multi-party arbitration will lose the opportunity to nominate an arbitrator.[31] Some arbitration clauses provide for two categories of dispute, the first (say up to US$100k) to be heard by a sole arbitrator and the second by a panel of three. However, where the speed of the reference is likely to be of paramount importance, a sole arbitrator might be more appropriate even in high value matters. Again, the default position under the LCIA Rules is for the selection and appointment of a sole arbitrator to

---

[30] The timing for the joint nomination is often made to run from the second nomination rather than the appointment of the party-nominated arbitrators because LCIA practice is to appoint all three arbitrators together.

[31] See Article 8.

be made by the LCIA Court. The parties can nevertheless agree a list procedure or other method by which they might participate in the selection.

### (b) The seat of the arbitration

**The seat, or legal place, of arbitration shall be [City and/or Country].**

III–018　The choice of the seat of the arbitration will (in the absence of a different express selection) determine the procedural law of the arbitration.[32] This can have a profound impact on the conduct of the arbitration. Moreover, parties should also bear in mind that the choice of seat will, under English law, also provide an indication as to the law governing the Arbitration Agreement,[33] which is also the default position under Article 16.4 of the LCIA Rules. Further, both English[34] and US courts have in recent years held that the choice of an arbitral seat will be treated as an exclusive choice of forum for remedies seeking to challenge or attack an award.

Thus the choice of seat can, for example, impact on the following aspects of the arbitration:

- the validity of the Arbitration Agreement;
- the arbitrability of the dispute;
- the constitution of the Arbitral Tribunal and challenges to arbitrators;
- the procedural and substantive powers of the Arbitral Tribunal—including whether it can exercise the power to rule on its own jurisdiction, or order interim measures;
- the detailed requirements of procedural justice;
- procedures applicable in the absence of party agreement;
- the limits of the parties' autonomy to agree on matters relating to the conduct of the arbitration; and
- the availability of court assistance in support of the arbitration.

III–019　The freedom to designate an arbitral seat unrelated to the physical place of the arbitration or any other aspect of the underlying business relationship is today accepted as one important manifestation of the principle of party autonomy.[35] The proviso in the LCIA's recommended clause allowing the parties to agree on the legal place of the arbitration is one manifestation of that right. Nevertheless, the procedural conduct of any arbitration will in certain fundamental respects ultimately always be prescribed by the mandatory laws of the physical place of the

---

[32] Often also referred to as the "curial law" or the "*lex arbitri*".
[33] *C v D* [2007] EWCA Civ 1282.
[34] *C v D* [2007] EWCA Civ 1282.
[35] The utility of making such a choice has been doubted, see Redfern et al., *Law and Practice of International Commercial Arbitration* (2004), para.2–20.

arbitration.[36] For that reason the wisdom of divorcing the legal place of the arbitration from the physical place has been doubted by some leading commentators.[37] Further, in one case at least such a separation led to a surprising result when the court of the designated seat refused to accept the parties' choice and declined to exercise supervisory jurisdiction over the proceedings, because the proceedings had no real connection with the designated seat.[38] Further, considering that the New York Convention requires adherence to the procedural arbitration law of the place where the proceedings were held,[39] in most cases it is preferable for the seat of the arbitration also to be the actual place where the arbitration (or at least the final hearing) is held.

Nevertheless, the choice of venue for hearings need not be specified in the arbitration clause: this is a matter which can be addressed with the Arbitral Tribunal (for example, at the first procedural hearing). Under the terms of Article 9.2, the Arbitral Tribunal has the "fullest authority" to establish the "geographical place" of the hearing.

Failing expressly to designate a seat for the arbitration will trigger the default provisions of the applicable Rules of Arbitration and/or of the relevant national laws.[40] Either way the parties could miss an opportunity to influence the conduct of any subsequent arbitration proceedings and potentially the enforceability of any award.  III–020

Under the LCIA Rules, failing designation by the parties, London, England shall be the seat, unless the Arbitral Tribunal considers that in all of the circumstances a different seat is more appropriate.


### (c) Language

**The language to be used in the arbitral proceedings shall be [ ].**

In most cases, choosing the language of the arbitration will be straightforward. The parties will have transacted in a particular language, and the contract will have been written in the same language. In most cases the choice of language for the arbitration will follow this course of conduct.  III–021

Complexities can arise when transacting with sovereign states or state entities, which are required as a matter of policy to transact in their own national language, or where the commercial bargaining power of parties is evenly matched. These situations often give rise to dual language contracts and arbitrations. However, the added delay and cost resulting from the need to provide for the translation of all documents (or even all key documents) as well as for the simultaneous translation of any oral proceedings, is significant, and dual language arbitrations should therefore be avoided where possible.

---

[36] Article V(1)(e) of the New York Convention (Appendix 9).
[37] Redfern et al., *Law and Practice of International Commercial Arbitration* (2004), paras 3.63–3.66.
[38] *The Titan Corporation v Alcatel CIT SA*, in A.J. van den Berg (ed.), *Yearbook Commercial Arbitration* (Kluwer Law International, 2005), Vol.30, pp.139–143.
[39] Articles V(1)(d) and (e).
[40] For example, UNCITRAL Model Law Article 20(1) (Appendix 10).

III–022   As a general rule of thumb, obscure languages should also be avoided where possible, so as not to limit the pool of qualified arbitrators. Recognising the difficulties that may arise in dual language arbitrations, the LCIA Rules permit the LCIA Court to decide which language shall be the "initial language of the arbitration". Failure to make any choice will render the matter for determination by the Arbitral Tribunal.

### (d) Choice of substantive law

**The governing law of the contract shall be the substantive law of [ ].**

III–023   Choice of law clauses are not peculiar to contracts containing arbitration clauses and similar considerations apply to both, although one clear distinction relates to the consequence of failing to make a choice. Whereas national courts are generally bound by complex and highly technical conflicts of laws rules in such circumstances, an LCIA Arbitral Tribunal has a wide discretion and is required only to decide the dispute in accordance with "the law(s) or rules of law which it considers appropriate".

The reference in the recommended clause to "the *substantive* law of [ ]" (emphasis added) is intended to avoid any scope for argument that any choice made by the parties should include the conflicts of laws rules of the selected country.

III–024   A separate issue for consideration is whether to provide expressly for the law governing the Arbitration Agreement itself. Whilst, in many cases, the law governing the Arbitration Agreement will be the same as that governing the underlying agreement, this is not necessarily the case. Where there may be any doubt in this regard, parties may wish to make express stipulation as to the governing law of the Arbitration Agreement. In the absence of such a stipulation, Article 16.4 provides that the law applicable to the Arbitration Agreement shall be the law of the seat.

*Existing disputes*

**A dispute having arisen between the parties concerning [ ], the parties hereby agree that the dispute shall be referred to and finally resolved by arbitration under the LCIA Rules.**

**The number of arbitrators shall be [one/three].**

**The seat, or legal place, of arbitration shall be [City and/or Country].**

**The language to be used in the arbitral proceedings shall be [ ].**

**The governing law of the contract [is/shall be] the substantive law of [ ].**

III–025   Most of the comments made in relation to the future disputes clause apply also to the existing disputes clause and need not be repeated.

The most important aspect of this clause will be the parties' negotiated description of the matter(s) in relation to which the dispute has arisen and over which the Arbitral Tribunal must exercise jurisdiction. Any claims not relating to the agreed subject matter will be excluded from the reference to arbitration, so careful drafting of the Arbitration Agreement is all the more important.

Another practical question parties may wish to consider is whether, in addition to the existing disputes that have already been identified, further disputes could still arise out of the same subject matter. If that possibility exists, the parties may choose to adopt elements of the future disputes clause into the Arbitration Agreement as well, in order to mitigate the risk of parallel proceedings in national courts and the prospect of conflicting decisions. **III–026**

One notable difference between the "future disputes" and "existing disputes" recommended clauses is that the latter does not expressly incorporate by reference the LCIA Rules into the Arbitration Agreement. The reason for this is unclear but, in any event, the Preamble provides for "reverse" incorporation of the Rules into the Arbitration Agreement.

The recommended clause contains the bare bones of what could usefully be agreed in relation to the referral of an existing dispute to LCIA arbitration. Knowing the nature and potential size of the dispute, the parties might be in a position to agree some aspects of the procedure and timetable at this stage. For example, as confirmed in the FAQs on the LCIA's website, the Secretariat is able to provide recommended wording for fast track arbitrations.

# PART IV—DIFC-LCIA ARBITRATION CENTRE

by Robert Karrar-Lewsley

# DIFC-LCIA ARBITRATION CENTRE

## Introduction

The DIFC-LCIA Arbitration Centre opened in February 2008 and has quickly become a key part of the arbitration infrastructure in the Gulf region. It is the first overseas branch of the LCIA and is a result of a joint venture between the LCIA and the Dubai International Financial Centre (DIFC), a separate legal jurisdiction in the centre of Dubai. It combines the benefits of using the LCIA with the regional convenience of being located in one the Middle East's most important trade hubs. The centre epitomises the innovative approach to arbitration that the UAE has adopted in recent years, and which is being emulated throughout the Gulf.

IV–001

This Part will put the centre in context by describing the recent increase in demand for arbitration in the Middle East, the modernisation of many of the region's arbitration laws, and the differences between the separate arbitral regimes found in Dubai and the DIFC. It will then review the DIFC-LCIA Rules and comment on the centre's likely future.

Note that, at the time of writing, the DIFC-LCIA has not yet issued new rules in light of the release of the 2014 LCIA Rules. However, it is expected that the DIFC-LCIA will do so very shortly and that its new rules will follow the 2014 LCIA Rules closely.

## Background

### 1) The demand for arbitration and a modern arbitral framework

The Middle East has always been an important region for trade due to its location between Europe, Asia and Africa. Multinational companies increasingly use the GCC as a base for regional operations,[1] and the additional commercial activity has brought with it more disputes. In recent years the number of disputes has sharply increased due to the impact of the global economic crisis. This has focused attention on the perceived inadequacies of local courts, which are often seen as slow, inefficient and unsophisticated. Demand has inevitably grown for an alternative dispute resolution system which is more robust and appealing to the international business community.

IV–002

Arbitration has successfully been used to satisfy this need. In the past 10 years there has been a proliferation of arbitral institutions in the region and many local arbitration laws have been modernised. This recent trend began with the UAE. In

---

[1] "GCC Trade and Investment Flows", The Economist Intelligence Unit (2011) 6. http://www.graphics.eiu.com/upload/eb/GCC_Trade_and_Investment_Flows_Falcon%20South_Web_22_MARCH_2011.pdf [Accessed September 3, 2014].

2004, it created the DIFC, a separate English-language common law jurisdiction in the heart of the civil law Gulf. The DIFC launched with its own arbitration law (Law No.8 of 2004), a law based on the UNCITRAL Model Law and widely seen as a significant improvement on the pre-existing UAE federal law on arbitration.

IV–003   In 2006, the UAE acceded to the New York Convention and in 2007 it modernised the rules of the Dubai International Arbitration Centre (DIAC), which has since become the most used arbitration centre in the Middle East. The next year, the DIFC-LCIA was launched, and a new arbitration law for the DIFC (Law No.1 of 2008) made the DIFC available as a seat for international arbitration (as under the 2004 Law its use was restricted to DIFC companies).

Other countries have similarly modernised their arbitration framework. Qatar set up the Qatar Financial Centre (QFC) in 2005 with arbitral rules based on the Model Law.[2] The QFC is similar in concept to the DIFC, but is not a physical area and so has the unusual distinction of being a seat which is entirely abstract. In 2006, Qatar set up the Qatar International Centre for Commercial Arbitration, an arbitral institution which in 2012 adopted a modern set of rules based on the UNCITRAL Rules.

IV–004   Bahrain has always been one of the more advanced counties in the region when it comes to arbitration. In 2009, it followed Dubai's lead by partnering with a Western institution, in this case the American Arbitration Association, to create the BCDR-AAA ("BCDR" stands for Bahrain Centre for Dispute Resolution). Bahrain also revised its arbitration law to create an innovative "arbitration freezone", which makes it possible for international parties to seat an arbitration in Bahrain but to agree that a national court other than that of Bahrain will have the power to annul the award.[3] The latest Gulf state to modernise its arbitration law is Saudi Arabia, which in 2012 promulgated a new law based on the Model Law.

All the various national systems have their merits, but in creating the DIFC the UAE has established a jurisdiction for international arbitration that is capable of being compared to the traditional seats in Europe and America, both in terms of its legal framework and its facilities.

IV–005   The status of international arbitration in the Middle East has, therefore, never been so high. This is particularly remarkable because for a long time international arbitration was not viewed in a positive light. Although arbitration and other methods of alternative dispute resolution have a long history in the Middle East, the reputation of international arbitration in its modern conception suffered following a series of well-known awards in the middle of the 20th century that not only held against local interests in favour of Western companies, but were seen as dismissive (and at times insulting) towards local laws and customs.[4] In a region that was attempting to recover from the oppression of colonialism, there was little enthusiasm for a system that seemed weighted in favour of Western interests.

Time has passed, and many of the Gulf states are now in fierce competition with each other to be seen as the natural home for international commerce and, by

---

[2] Qatar Financial Centre Regulation No.8 of 2005.
[3] Bahraini Decree No.30 of 2009.
[4] For example, in the matter of an arbitration between Petroleum Development (Trucial Coast) Ltd and the Sheikh of Abu Dhabi ([1952] ICLQ 247).

extension, international commercial arbitration. This has not only led to the new arbitral regimes and institutions described above, but also to an associated increase in events concerning arbitration. Seminars and training courses are frequently held, with regular events being organised by the Chartered Institute of Arbitrators, the ICC and others. This has further served to raise the profile of arbitration in the region and fostered a more substantial arbitration culture.

## 2) *Arbitration in Dubai and the UAE*

Dubai is one of seven Emirates that make up the United Arab Emirates. The country was formed in 1971 as a federation, and it is located on the southeast of the Arabian Peninsula. Each Emirate is governed by its own ruling monarch, but there is an overriding federal government headed by a national president. By convention, the National President is the Ruler of Abu Dhabi (the largest and richest of the Emirates), with the Ruler of Dubai acting as Prime Minister.  **IV–006**

The UAE has always been an active trading hub, but in recent years the level of investment has grown hugely. Dubai has become one of the most developed cities in the world, and boasts many unique structures, such as the world's tallest building and largest shopping mall. It has benefited from being a stable, modern and relatively open society in a region that tends to lack these attributes.

### *Arbitration in Dubai*

Dubai does not have its own arbitration law, but is covered by the federal law on arbitration which currently consists of a handful of provisions in the UAE Civil Procedure Law of 1992. Although hundreds of arbitrations are successfully carried out each year under this law, it is widely seen as dated and inadequate. A new law, largely based on the Model Law, has been drafted and circulated, but it is unclear when this will be enacted and what its final form will be.  **IV–007**

The existing law has the following key features:

(a) Arbitral agreements must be in writing.

(b) Parties are free to choose their arbitrators (provided there is an odd number). In the event a party does not appoint an arbitrator the local UAE court has the power to appoint the arbitrator.

(c) Parties are free to choose their representatives.

(d) The local court has a number of powers that it can exercise in support of the arbitration. For example, it has the power to dismiss an arbitrator if the arbitrator has performed his duties negligently. It may also order that a party disclose documents, or that a witness be punished for not giving evidence.

Although the Tribunal has procedural freedom, there are some parochial rules found in the law. For example:  **IV–008**

(a) If a document is contested as forged the arbitrator shall suspend work until the criminal investigation has been completed. This can lead to cynical police complaints by parties wishing to frustrate the arbitral process.

(b) The arbitration must be completed within six months of the date of the first arbitration session, unless the parties agree otherwise. This can be overlooked by inexperienced parties and tribunals.

(c) Any testimony from a witness must be sworn on oath, and it must be the arbitrator who administers the oath.

(d) If the award is signed outside of the UAE then it is to be considered a foreign award, irrespective of the fact that the seat of the arbitration is the UAE.

(e) Case law has also developed a number of other procedural rules regarding how awards are to be rendered, including that they must be signed on each page and attach the Terms of Reference.

*Enforcement of awards*

IV–009   The law makes clear that it is not open to the parties to contest the merits of an award. Only procedural deficiencies can be used to annul it. These include the fact that the arbitral agreement was flawed or non-existent; that the arbitrator went beyond the limits of the reference; or that the arbitrator's appointment was not in accordance with the law. The provisions also allow annulment where there has been an invalidity in the ruling or in the procedures which influence the ruling[5] of the UAE Civil Procedure Code, Federal Law No.(11) of 1992. Unfortunately, the law is not clear as to what these deficiencies may be and so local judges have a broad discretion.

In relation to foreign awards the enforcement procedure has changed significantly since the UAE's ratification of the New York Convention in 2006. The old provisions made it extremely difficult to enforce foreign awards, but in recent years the courts have been applying the criteria stipulated under the New York Convention and a number of foreign awards have been enforced. In 2010 the Fujairah courts produced the first reported judgment of a foreign award being enforced in the UAE under the New York Convention, though the ratification proceedings were not contested. Later in the year, in the case of *Maxtel International FZE v Airmec Dubai LLC*,[6] the Dubai Court of First Instance ordered the enforcement of a foreign award under the New York Convention, this time after a contested hearing. The judgment has since been upheld in the Court of Appeal and Court of Cassation. The judgment is of particular interest because it involved a DIFC-LCIA award, albeit one issued pursuant to an arbitration seated in London rather than Dubai.

---

[5] Article 216(1)(c)
[6] Cassation Appeal No. 132 of 2012.

*Challenges*

Perhaps the most significant issue with using the UAE as a seat is that the UAE courts can be highly unpredictable. There are four separate civil court systems in the UAE (those of Dubai, Ras Al Khaimah, Abu Dhabi and the federal courts based in Abu Dhabi which are used by the other four Emirates (and also by Abu Dhabi for some matters). These courts diverge on some issues and can render conflicting judgments. There is no system of binding precedent, which leaves judges with wide discretion. The situation is complicated by the fact that the judges in these courts (especially first instance courts) are often seconded from other Arab countries, such as Egypt and Sudan, and can be unfamiliar with UAE law. The absence of regular court reporting makes it difficult to access accurate legal reports, and judgments are usually brief with only a minimum of legal reasoning.

An example of the local courts' inconsistency is that although the Dubai Court of First Instance enforced a foreign award under the New York Convention in the *Maxtel* case (London seat), this did not stop the same court later refusing the enforcement of a Paris award on the basis that the award-debtor had no domicile or place of residence in the UAE, even though this is not a requirement under the New York Convention.[7]

The court process is also lengthy, with the majority of cases being appealed to the Court of Appeal and then to the Court of Cassation, often on spurious grounds. Since legal costs are not awarded by the courts there is no cost sanction for cynically drawing the process out. It can often take two or three years before a final judgment is rendered and the enforcement process can begin.

The UAE legal system is largely based on the Egyptian system, which is a model for many Middle Eastern countries. The issues raised above are therefore commonly found in other Arab countries.

Despite the above, it should nevertheless be acknowledged that in recent years the UAE courts have begun to show a more supportive attitude towards arbitration, most notably by enforcing foreign awards under the New York Convention.

## 3) The DIFC

The Dubai International Financial Centre (DIFC) is an autonomous jurisdiction in the centre of Dubai's commercial district. It was established in 2004 and is exempt from all civil and commercial federal laws. Although the UAE is an Arabic-language civil law jurisdiction (like almost all countries in the region), the DIFC is English-language and has a common law system.

The DIFC legal regime is closely modelled on the English legal system, but has been adapted to incorporate international best practice and local requirements. For example, its arbitration law is not based on the English Arbitration Act 1996 but on the UNCITRAL Model Law. The DIFC is bound by all the international treaties that the UAE has ratified, including the New York Convention (which the UAE acceded to in 2006 without any reservations).

---

[7] Dubai Court of Cassation Judgment No. 156 of 2013.

**IV–013** The DIFC has its own courts, consisting of the Court of First Instance and the Court of Appeal. The courts have been modelled on the commercial courts of England, and its rules are essentially an adapted version of the English Civil Procedure Rules. The DIFC court judges have been selected from the judiciary of other common law jurisdictions (England, Singapore, New Zealand, Malaysia) with some Emiratis. Many of these judges are well-known international arbitrators, including the current Chief Justice Michael Hwang. The DIFC courts already have a strong reputation for being pro-arbitration.

Arbitration in the DIFC is markedly different to that in the UAE, and has a number of key advantages for international business:

(a) The DIFC arbitration law is heavily based in the Model Law, and as such is modern, comprehensive and familiar. There are no obscure provisions which will cause problems or create inefficiency.

(b) The DIFC courts are familiar and supportive of arbitration and can be relied on to give efficient assistance, including interim measures.

(c) The DIFC and its courts are English language, and the courts are more accessible than the local courts.

**IV–014** The only cause for concern regarding the DIFC is that it is largely untested as an arbitral seat. There have only been a handful of DIFC court judgments relating to arbitration, and although on the whole they are supportive it will take time for a substantial body of case law to develop. It also remains unclear how DIFC awards will be received in other countries, although as UAE awards they should be enforced under the New York Convention and other regional treaties that the UAE is bound by.

As regards the enforcement of DIFC awards in the UAE, it is usually advisable to have the award ratified by the DIFC courts and then recognised by the Dubai courts (which will then arrange enforcement in the other Emirates). This was done in 2012 in the case of *Property Concepts FZE v Lootah Network Real Estate & Commercial Brokerage*,[8] which involved a DIFC-LCIA award ratified by the DIFC courts, and then enforced by the Dubai courts under a protocol of enforcement then existing between the Dubai and DIFC courts (and since made into law through an amendment to Dubai Law No.12 of 2004 in October 2011).

*Dispute Resolution Authority*

**IV–015** In May 2014 the creation of the DIFC "Dispute Resolution Authority" was announced, to be led by the current DIFC courts' Chief Justice, Michael Hwang SC. This is to consist of the DIFC courts and a new "Arbitration Institute". The Arbitration Institute will be responsible for promoting arbitration in the DIFC, hosting conferences and lectures, issuing guidance and co-operating with other arbitral institutions and bodies. It is not expected that the Arbitration Institute will administer arbitrations. As regards the DIFC-LCIA, it is assumed that the centre will either eventually form part of the new Dispute Resolution Authority, or at least work closely with it, but this remains to be seen.

---

[8] ARB 001/2010, Order of October 19, 2010.

*Judgments into DIFC-LCIA awards?*

The DIFC remains an innovative and evolving jurisdiction, and this has recently been illustrated by an ambitious draft Practice Direction (amending Practice Direction No.2 of 2012 DIFC Court's Jurisdiction) circulated for public consultation in July 2014. If issued, the Practice Direction would, under certain conditions, enable DIFC court judgments to be converted into DIFC-LCIA arbitral awards.

IV–016

Essentially, parties would agree in writing that any dispute arising from the DIFC courts' judgment will be settled by DIFC-LCIA arbitration. This would mean that parties either comply with the DIFC court judgment, or else the matter will be referred to DIFC-LCIA arbitration, resulting in an arbitral award that incorporates the DIFC court judgment and allows for wider enforcement under the New York Convention.

A discussion of whether such a system is viable is beyond the scope of this work, but the initiative reflects the fact that the DIFC is attempting to be a thought-leader in arbitration, rather than simply adopting the latest developments from the West.

IV–017

### The DIFC-LCIA and its Rules

*The DIFC-LCIA and the DIFC*

The DIFC-LCIA is located in the DIFC, but is wholly independent of the DIFC. It can administer arbitrations wherever they are seated. Because parties often choose an arbitral institution located in or close to the seat of arbitration, there has been a perception that the use of the DIFC-LCIA is tied to using the DIFC as a seat. This is not the case, although under Article 16.1 of the DIFC-LCIA Arbitration Rules the DIFC will be the seat if the contract is silent on the issue.

IV–018

The independence of the DIFC-LCIA from the DIFC was explicitly acknowledged in the first DIFC court judgment regarding arbitration in the DIFC. In the case of *Dhir v Waterfront Property Investment Ltd*,[9] Michael Hwang DCJ stated there is "no inexorable or symbiotic link between the DIFC-LCIA Arbitration Centre and the DIFC".[10] He held that although there was a DIFC-LCIA arbitration clause in the agreement, this did not mean that there was a significant connection between the agreement and the DIFC "because the DIFC-LCIA Arbitration Centre can administer an arbitration with a seat outside of the DIFC".[11] The independence of the DIFC-LCIA from the DIFC is important for practitioners to appreciate so that they do not unduly limit the options available.

The DIFC-LCIA does support the DIFC in relation to its Financial Markets Tribunal. This Tribunal is overseen by the Dubai Financial Services Authority (DFSA) and deals with alleged breaches of laws, rules or legislation administered by the DFSA. The President of the Financial Markets Tribunal has appointed the

IV–019

---

[9] CFI 011/2009 [2006–09] DIFC CLR 12.
[10] CFI 011/2009 [2006–09] DIFC CLR 12 [91].
[11] CFI 011/2009 [2006–09] DIFC CLR 12 [85].

DIFC-LCIA to provide the services of the Financial Market Tribunal Registrar, and the DIFC-LCIA has to date assisted with two cases.

### The DIFC-LCIA Rules

IV–020 At the time of writing the DIFC-LCIA has not yet issued revised rules in light of the release of the 2014 LCIA Rules, and the comments made therefore reflect the 2008 DIFC-LCIA Rules. However, it is expected that new DIFC-LCIA Rules will be issued shortly and that they will follow the 2014 LCIA Rules closely, as the existing rules closely followed the 1998 LCIA Rules, even to the extent of keeping the same article numbers and references to obsolete technology (e.g. telex in Article 4.1). The only difference is that the Registrar is now "the DIFC-LCIA Registrar" and the default seat is the DIFC rather than London.

An important aspect of the 2008 DIFC-LCIA Rules is that the LCIA Court retains its role as the appointing authority. This ensures the quality of tribunals and allows users access to the LCIA database of experienced arbitrators. The DIFC-LCIA is also developing a database of local arbitrators which the LCIA Court can draw upon. Although the LCIA Court retains this function, the parties do not directly correspond with the court. Under Article 3.3 of the 2008 DIFC-LCIA Rules, all communications with the LCIA Court must be addressed to the Registrar of the DIFC-LCIA.

IV–021 There would have been a temptation when developing the DIFC-LCIA to update the 1998 LCIA Rules. This however would have undermined a key selling point of the DIFC-LCIA, which is that by adopting the 1998 LCIA Rules unchanged it can claim to have a robust and tested set of rules despite being a new institution. This has given users confidence and has resulted in the DIFC-LCIA being warmly received in the region.

However, now that the LCIA has issued new rules, the DIFC-LCIA is expected to follow suit.

### The use of the DIFC-LCIA so far

IV–022 The DIFC-LCIA does not publish official statistics regarding its use, but it has provided the following information based on the work undertaken by the centre so far:

(a) Number of registered cases:

2008: 0

2009: 11

2010: 2

2011: 3

2012: 12

2013: 3

2014: 11 (as of September 1, 2014)

There was a sharp increase in cases in 2009, which is when the global financial crisis severely affected the UAE economy. It is likely that many of these referrals were the result of parties choosing the DIFC-LCIA after the dispute had arisen.

A steady caseload is now building due to the natural lag between parties writing DIFC-LCIA clauses into their contracts and disputes arising from them.

(b) As of September 1, 2014 the centre has 11 active cases, the others having settled or been concluded with an arbitral award.

(c) About 62 per cent of cases have the DIFC as their seat, with 33 per cent Dubai (excluding DIFC) and 5 per cent London or elsewhere. Using the DIFC-LCIA with the DIFC as a seat is therefore a popular combination, although note that the DIFC is the default seat under Article 16.1 of the DIFC-LCIA Arbitration Rules.

(d) About 71 per cent of cases are international (at least one party is non-UAE).

(e) The cases relate to disputes regarding, amongst other things, construction, shareholder agreements, oil and gas, renewable energy, shipping, telecommunications, financial services and general commercial matters. Unlike the DIAC, there are few cases relating to real estate.

(f) The size of disputes varies, with the largest being a construction case valued at AED 1.2 billion.

(g) About three quarters of appointments arise from selections made by the LCIA Court, the rest being party-nominated.

(h) In terms of the nationality of arbitrators, about 71 per cent are British, 9 per cent American, 5 per cent European, and 15 per cent from the Middle East or elsewhere.

(i) Most cases have taken about 12–14 months to complete (either by way of settlement or final award).

(j) Although the DIFC-LCIA is capable of conducting arbitrations in Arabic, so far all arbitrations have been in English.

At least two DIFC-LCIA awards have been successfully enforced. In *Maxtel International FZE v Airmec Dubai LLC*,[12] the Dubai Court of Cassation enforced a DIFC-LCIA award, the seat being London; and in *Property Concepts FZE v Lootah Network Real Estate & Commercial Brokerage*, a London-seated DIFC-LCIA award was ratified by the DIFC courts and then enforced by the Dubai courts. There have not been any reports of a DIFC-LCIA award being refused enforcement.

The institution is still in its infancy so caution should be taken before drawing conclusions from the above statistics. However, what seems clear is that the

---

[12] Cassation Appeal No. 132 of 2012.

DIFC-LCIA is being used in relation to a range of international cases, including some that are sizeable, and they are being dealt with efficiently. Considering its youth, this is a remarkable achievement.

## The DIFC-LCIA compared to other regional institutions

IV–024    The Middle East has a number of arbitral institutions, but the DIFC-LCIA is significantly different in two material respects. The first is in relation to the involvement of third parties. The 2008 DIFC-LCIA Rules retain Article 22.1(h) of the 1998 LCIA Rules, which allows a third party to be joined to the arbitration despite not being a signatory to the Arbitration Agreement, provided one of the parties applies for this and the third party and the Tribunal consent. None of the other arbitral centres (or regional arbitration laws) contain such a rule. Although some parties may be concerned that a third party may be joined without their consent, for most parties the prospect of being able to avoid multiple proceedings because all the relevant parties are not signed to the same agreement will be attractive.

The other key difference is that tribunal fees in DIFC-LCIA arbitration are charged on an hourly basis, whereas most other institutions in the area quantify fees as a proportion of the amount in dispute. The only similar institution in this respect is the BCDR-AAA in Bahrain, which opened in 2009. Assessing fees on a time-spent basis is a more transparent method than assessing them by reference to the value in dispute (which may have no connection to the complexity or nature of the issues involved). Whilst some may consider that the use of hourly rates mean potential users have less certainty regarding what the likely tribunal costs will be, it should be remembered that there is always some uncertainty regarding the level of fees because even when fees are based on the amount in dispute these can be increased later if the dispute turns out to be more complicated than originally thought.

IV–025    As regards the cost schedule for the DIFC-LCIA, it is laid out in the same manner as that for the LCIA. Amounts are detailed in Emirati dirhams (AED), and depending on the exchange rates the fees are broadly similar to the LCIA equivalent.

The DIFC-LCIA also offers mediation services and has the same mediation rules as the LCIA. Formal mediation is not common in the Middle East and is often overlooked as a method of dispute resolution, but in recent years its profile has risen. The fact that the DIFC-LCIA Mediation Rules are based on the tested rules of the LCIA mean that it is well placed to attract those seeking mediation services.

Finally, although not explicitly stated in its rules or on its website, the DIFC-LCIA is able to act as an appointing authority for expert determinations.

## The future of the DIFC-LCIA

IV–026    There is every reason to believe that the DIFC-LCIA will continue to go from strength to strength. Since the essence of the institution is that it is (for all intents and purposes) the LCIA but based in the DIFC, it is likely to follow any changes that the LCIA makes to its rules, and indeed a new set of DIFC-LCIA Rules is expected shortly so that the institution remains in step with the 2014 LCIA Rules.

At present, the DIFC-LCIA does not have a mechanism for appointing an Emergency Arbitrator, as has been incorporated into recent updates of the ICC, SIAC and LCIA Rules, and which will likely be brought in with the forthcoming revised DIFC-LCIA Rules. Such a development will doubtless be welcome, but it is unlikely to be used extensively. Emergency Arbitrators are not a feature of other institutions in the region and there would be concerns as to whether the local courts would be supportive of the concept and the orders made by an Emergency Arbitrator. The DIFC-LCIA does however have a procedure for the expedited formation of the Arbitral Tribunal (Article 9 of the DIFC-LCIA Arbitration Rules), which allows the usual timescales to be reduced. Since the Tribunal constituted under this expedited procedure is the final tribunal and not a temporary one, there are unlikely to be any issues when it comes to enforcement.

Looking into the long-term future, it is conceivable that as the DIFC-LCIA grows and becomes more popular, it will have less need to rely on the reputation of the LCIA and will take on an independent identity. Even if it never (and never wishes) to become fully independent of the LCIA, a more independent DIFC-LCIA would allow for the possibility of the two institutions trying different approaches to the same problems in their rules, and learning from each other. This could lead to the LCIA Rules evolving faster than other institutional rules, enabling the LCIA to stay ahead in the increasingly competitive arbitration market. **IV–027**

## Conclusion

Although the LCIA has always been available, its remoteness has limited its use in the Middle East. The DIFC-LCIA has brought the LCIA to the Gulf and to the wide range of international businesses which do business there and the surrounding region. The centre's rules and costs structure are the same as the pre–2014 LCIA Rules, which gives users confidence, and are significantly different from those of other regional institutions, which makes it stand out. It is expected that the DIFC-LCIA will shortly issue new rules, modelled closely on the 2014 LCIA Rules (including provisions for Emergency Arbitrators). **IV–028**

The DIFC-LCIA is a young institution and it will take time both for parties to agree to arbitration under its rules and for such disputes to arise. Even so, a number of arbitrations have already been administered by the DIFC-LCIA, including two awards that have been enforced in Dubai. This has shown that DIFC-LCIA arbitration is an effective and viable choice for clients in the region.

It is expected that the DIFC-LCIA will continue to expand its caseload in future years and become a permanent and valuable feature in the arbitration landscape of the Middle East.

# PART V—LCIA INDIA

by Ciccu Mukhopadhaya, Senior Counsel

# LCIA INDIA

## Introduction

LCIA India was established in April 2009, but only became operational in April 2010 when the LCIA India Arbitration Rules and the LCIA India Mediation Rules were launched. It has its headquarters in New Delhi. It is the first international institution to establish a separate entity to provide arbitration services in India. In order to do so, LCIA India has drafted a new set of rules (largely the same as the LCIA (London) Rules), including a fee structure aimed at the Indian market.

This Part will provide a short review of the background to the Indian arbitration market and the Indian legal framework for arbitration, a brief insight into Indian arbitration practice (particularly in relation to the appointment of arbitrators and the conduct of proceedings) and, finally, what LCIA India offers in that context.

V–001

## Background—The Indian arbitration market

India, being a large country with a huge population and robust commercial trade, both domestic and international, has a very substantial arbitration market which has been steadily growing. The arbitration market comprises a very large number of purely domestic arbitrations as well as a fair number of international arbitrations seated in India. The latter has increased exponentially with the liberalisation of the economic regime and foreign direct investments playing an important role in the economy of the country.

V–002

Most ad hoc arbitration proceedings conducted in India, be it before a sole arbitrator or a three-member tribunal, are scheduled in a manner that is prone to delays.

Most commonly, arbitrators are retired judges of the High Court or Supreme Court of India. Seldom does an Indian tribunal conduct arbitrations such that the first procedural order covers all the steps required up to and including the hearing of a particular case. In Indian arbitrations, the first procedural order would usually provide only for the exchange of pleadings, whereafter further sittings of the Tribunal take place and dates for further proceedings are fixed. Evidence hearings are usually prolonged, with several sittings—often with months in between hearings. Final hearings can also be long affairs, and seldom is the equal time principle followed.

V–003

The above position prevails even in international arbitrations seated in India, unless the Tribunal comprises one or more international arbitrators.

By and large, the conduct of arbitration in this manner is unsatisfactory, and many parties and experienced arbitration lawyers would prefer that arbitrations

V–004

were conducted more in line with general international practice under institutional rules such as those of the LCIA or ICC.

Indeed, arbitration practitioners in India have for many years felt the need for an efficient and good institution rendering arbitration services in the country. The Indian Council of Arbitration, established in 1965, has had limited success for a variety of reasons. The International Centre for Alternative Dispute Resolution (ICADR) (1995), a more recent institution, has also only had a small impact. The majority of Indian arbitrations continue to be ad hoc arbitrations governed not by any set of international or institutional rules but simply based on procedures framed by arbitrators under the (Indian) Arbitration & Conciliation Act 1996 (the (Indian) 1996 Act).

V–005  Seeing the potential for institutional arbitrations in India, and given that the London Court of International Arbitration has, over the years, acquired a reputation amongst Indian arbitration practitioners for its user-friendly rules and efficient administration of arbitration, it is hoped by many that LCIA India will bring international best practices to the conduct of arbitrations in India.

## Legal framework for arbitration in India: the (Indian) 1996 Act

V–006  In January 1996, the Indian legislature brought in the (Indian) Arbitration & Conciliation Ordinance 1996, which was later adopted as an Act by the Parliament. It consolidates into one enactment what had prior thereto been covered by three different laws: the Arbitration Act 1940, the Arbitration (Protocol and Convention) Act 1937, and the Foreign Awards (Recognition and Enforcement) Act 1961.

Largely based on the UNCITRAL Model Law, the (Indian) 1996 Act is divided into three Parts: Part I deals with domestic arbitrations and international arbitrations seated in India; Part II provides for enforcement of foreign arbitral awards and for enforcement of arbitration agreements where the arbitration is seated outside India (this covers both Geneva Protocol awards as well as New York Convention awards); and Part III provides for conciliation, an alternative dispute resolution method for which, prior to the (Indian) 1996 Act, there was no legislation in force in India.

### *Judicial intervention*

V–007  From the time it came into force, a series of decisions of the Supreme Court of India have interpreted various provisions of the (Indian) 1996 Act. Some of those decisions were arbitration friendly but most, unfortunately, were contrary to the spirit and substance of the (Indian) 1996 Act. However, the more recent trend is promising. Further, there is a move to amend the (Indian) 1996 Act.

### *Court jurisdiction in relation to arbitration proceedings*

V–008  With the intent to minimise courts' interference in arbitration, Part I of the (Indian) 1996 Act includes in s.5 a restriction on the courts' jurisdiction (whilst not ousting it completely) where there is an arbitration agreement. The courts' jurisdiction is thereby restricted to matters for which the (Indian) 1996 Act itself expressly contemplates the courts' action.

Notwithstanding the said provision, the courts have continued to interfere and entertain proceedings when no such interference was intended by the (Indian) 1996 Act.

## *Enforcement of arbitration agreements*

If an action was brought in a court by a party despite having agreed to arbitrate disputes covered by such action, upon the defendant making an application for reference of the disputes to arbitration, in accordance with s.8 of the (Indian) 1996 Act, it is mandatory for the court to refer the disputes to arbitration. Initially, the view taken by the Supreme Court in this context was that once there was an arbitration agreement and the same was relied on by a Defendant, the court had no jurisdiction to proceed with the suit.[1]

V–009

Subsequently, however, in light of the judgment of seven judges of the Supreme Court in *SBP v Patel Engineering Ltd*,[2] notwithstanding a party relying on an arbitration agreement in such proceedings, if the Plaintiff contests the existence or validity of the Arbitration Agreement, it is now incumbent upon the court to decide finally on matters relating to the existence or validity of the Arbitration Agreement before referring the parties to the arbitration. Although s.8(3) of the (Indian) 1996 Act provides that, notwithstanding such a suit, an arbitration can proceed on the same subject matter, and notwithstanding s.16 of the (Indian) 1996 Act providing for the Arbitral Tribunal to determine its own jurisdiction (the *compétence-compétence* principle) as a result of the *SBP* case, such provisions have been largely diluted. Fortunately, in a more recent judgment,[3] the Supreme Court has, in explaining *SBP*, limited the courts' mandatory decision-making process to certain matters, leaving other jurisdictional issues to be decided by the arbitrators, or the court at least has a discretion to leave the decision of such matters to the Arbitral Tribunal.

## *Default appointment of arbitrators*

Where the Arbitration Agreement does not itself provide for a specific appointing authority, or for appointment of a sole or presiding arbitrator (or where a party fails to appoint an arbitrator), s.11 of the (Indian) 1996 Act provides for the Chief Justice of the concerned High Court or his designate in the case of a domestic arbitration, and the Chief Justice of India or his designate in the case of an international arbitration seated in India, to appoint such an arbitrator on the application of a party.

V–010

The Supreme Court initially held that the power of the Chief Justice or his designate was an administrative power and, in view of s.16 of the (Indian) 1996 Act, the court was not required to go into the existence or validity of an arbitration

---

[1] *HPCL v Pink City Midway Petroleum* 2003 (6) SCC 503.
[2] (2005) 8 SCC 618.
[3] *National Insurance Co Ltd v Boghara Polyfab Pvt Ltd* (2009) 1 SCC 267; *Arasmeta Captive Power Co v Lafarge India Pvt Ltd* (2014) 4 Arb LR 439.

agreement before making an appointment of an arbitrator.[4] However, once again, in *SBP* (above), seven judges of the Supreme Court overruled *Konkan Railways* to hold that the power under s.11 of the (Indian) 1996 Act was a judicial power and, if a party raised an objection as to the existence and validity of an arbitration (or even if a party raised an objection that the claim for arbitration was hopelessly time barred), the court had to decide such matters finally before appointing an arbitrator.

V–011   As a result, the appointment process itself sometimes can be quite prolonged and much of the purpose of the expeditious resolution of disputes can be destroyed.

An important development in relation to international commercial arbitrations seated in India is that, in *Reliance Industries Ltd v UOI*,[5] the court held that the presiding arbitrator should have a neutral nationality.

*Interim relief*

V–012   One of the most frequently used provisions of the (Indian) 1966 Act is s.9, which provides for interim measures of protection prior to arbitration, during arbitration and after an award but prior to its enforcement. Whilst s.9 is in Part I, and therefore was intended to be limited in its application to purely Indian-seated arbitrations, in *Bhatia International v Bulk Trading SA*,[6] the Supreme Court held that Part I applied also to arbitrations seated outside India and that s.9 was therefore available as a remedy in cases of foreign-seated arbitrations. Whilst by itself the judgment (although wrong) may not have been all that deleterious in its consequences, the natural fallout of holding Part I as being applicable to foreign arbitrations was so.

Subsequently, in *Venture Global Engineering v Satyam Computers Services Ltd*,[7] the Supreme Court held, following *Bhatia International*, that even a foreign award could be subject to a setting aside action within India. Both *Bhatia International* and *Venture Global* were later referred to a larger bench of five judges which did overrule them,[8] but only prospectively, i.e. the overruling being applicable to arbitration agreements entered into after September 6, 2012.

V–013   Since *Bhatia International* held that Part I could be impliedly or expressly excluded, in some decisions the Indian Supreme Court has rightly held that the choice of foreign seat of arbitration would effectively amount to an implied exclusion of Part I, particularly if the curial law and/or proper law of the Arbitration Agreement was a foreign law.[9] More recently, the Bombay High Court has, after detailed analysis, reached the same conclusion.[10]

---

[4] *Konkan Railways Corp Ltd v Rani Construction Pvt Ltd* (2002) 2 SCC 388.
[5] Decided on March 31, 2014 in Arbitration Petition No.27 of 2013.
[6] (2002) 4 SCC 105.
[7] (2008) 4 SCC 190.
[8] *Bharat Aluminium Co v Kaiser Aluminum Technical Services Inc* (2012) 9 SCC 552 ("*Balco*").
[9] *Dozco India Pvt Ltd v Doosan Infracore Co Ltd* (2011) 6 SCC 179; *Videocon Industries Ltd v UOI* (2011) 6 SCC 161.
[10] *HSBC PI Holdings (Mauritius) Ltd v Avitel Post Studioz Ltd* (Manu/MH /0050/2014); an appeal was subsequently filed by Avitel Post Studioz (Manu/MH/1147/2014) which was dismissed by a Division Bench of the Bombay High Court. A Special Leave Petition filed in the Supreme Court is presently pending; see also *Reliance Industries Ltd v UOI* (2014) 7 SCC 603—the court overturned the decision of the Delhi High Court and confirmed that in circumstances where an arbitration is seated outside India, and the parties have expressly chosen a foreign law to govern the arbitration

An interesting question arises in the context of *Bhatia International, Venture Global and Balco*. The effect of *Balco* is that when the seat of arbitration is outside India, Part I of the (Indian) 1996 Act does not apply and hence the Indian courts have no jurisdiction to entertain petitions to set aside foreign awards. It is equally well settled under Indian law that courts cannot confer jurisdiction when there is none.[11] In essence, *Bhatia International, Venture Global* and *Balco* have the effect of creating jurisdiction in the Indian courts to entertain a petition for interim relief under s.9, or for setting aside a foreign award under s.34 of Part I. Applying the law that the courts cannot confer jurisdiction when there is none, notwithstanding these decisions, it would be open for a party to urge that, because the court lacks jurisdiction as Part I does not apply, the prospective overruling in the *Balco* case would be of little meaning and the court is bound to dismiss such a petition as being without jurisdiction, even where the Arbitration Agreement was entered into prior to September 6, 2012.

### Challenges to awards under the (Indian) 1996 Act

Whilst s.34 of the (Indian) 1996 Act provides for limited challenges to an award, more or less on the lines of the New York Convention objections to enforcement of a foreign award, in practice, in view of the decision of the Supreme Court in *ONGC v Saw Pipes Ltd*,[12] challenges on the ground of public policy had become literally challenges on the merits of the award, particularly so as a result of the Supreme Court's judgment in *Phulchand Exports Ltd v OOO Patriot*.[13]

V–014

However, fairly quickly the court expressly overruled *Phulchand*[14] and held that the term "public policy" in s.48 of the (Indian) 1996 Act should be given a narrow meaning, applying the test laid down in the earlier judgment of the court in *Renusagar Power Co v General Electric Co*.[15]

### Separability

Recently, in *Enercon (India) Ltd v Enercon GmBH*,[16] the Supreme Court upheld the concept of the separability of the arbitration clause from the underlying contract. The Supreme Court held that s.16 of the (Indian) 1996 Act recognised that the substantive agreement and the Arbitration Agreement formed two separate contracts, and the legitimacy and validity of the latter could not be affected even if one claims that the former is void or voidable or unconcluded.

V–015

In yet another pro-arbitration decision emanating from the Supreme Court, in the case of *World Sport Group (Mauritius) Ltd v MSM Satellite (Singapore) Pte Ltd*,[17] the court referred to arbitration a dispute involving allegations of fraud. In

---

agreement, notwithstanding the choice of Indian substantive law, the Indian courts do not have jurisdiction to set aside the arbitral award.

[11] *Kiran Singh v Chaman Paswan* – AIR1954SC340 = [1955]1SCR117.
[12] (2003) 5 SCC 705.
[13] (2011) 10 SCC 300.
[14] *Shri Lal Mahal Ltd v Progetto Grano Spa* (2014) 2 SCC 433.
[15] (1994) Supp (1) SCC 644.
[16] (2014) 5 SCC 1.
[17] 2014 (1) ARBLR 197.

V-016 doing so, the court restrictively read its previous decision in *N. Radhakrishnan v Maestro Engineering*[18] where it was held that issues of fraud fell more properly to be determined by courts. The court held that the interpretation given in *Radhakrishnan* applied only to domestic arbitration. This recent decision further reduces the risk of interference by courts in foreign-seated arbitrations.

Subsequently, in *Swiss Timing Ltd v Organising Committee 2010 Olympic Games, Delhi*,[19] a single judge of the Supreme Court, whilst deciding a Section 11 Petition, held that the decision in *Radhakrishnan* had been decided "*per incuriam*" on the point of the arbitrability of fraud and that, even in the context of Indian-seated arbitrations, allegations of fraud are capable of being dealt with by arbitral tribunals. However, in a very recent decision, it has been held that decisions under s.11 of the (Indian) 1996 Act have no precedential value.[20] Hence *Swiss Timing* may be of no real positive impact.

## LCIA India

V-017 As noted, LCIA India was established in April 2009 and the LCIA India Arbitration Rules and the LCIA India Mediation Rules were launched in April 2010. Headquartered in New Delhi, LCIA India is the first, and still the only, international arbitration institution to establish a separate entity to provide arbitration services in India.

LCIA India does not have a separate supervising body or court. The LCIA Court in London acts as the substantive court for LCIA India as it does for the two other LCIA subsidiaries, i.e. DIFC-LCIA Arbitration Centre (Dubai) and LCIA-MIAC Arbitration Centre (Mauritius).

V-018 LCIA India is fairly young. To date, the number of cases it has actually had the occasion to administer has not reached a double digit figure, but one would expect them to gather momentum over the next three to four years. Obviously, given that the LCIA India Rules were launched only in April 2010, contracts prior thereto could not have incorporated the LCIA India Rules in their arbitration agreements. Contracts thereafter would have little chance to go into dispute within such a short time. However, the first contractually incorporated LCIA India Rules arbitration kicked off recently. All the other cases to date had been ad hoc arbitrations converted by consent of the parties into an institutional one under the LCIA India Rules.

## LCIA India Rules

V-019 Rather than simply adopting the 1998 English version of the LCIA Rules, LCIA India drafted a new set of rules—the 2010 LCIA India Rules—including a fee structure, aimed at the Indian market.

---

[18] (2010) 1 SCC 72.
[19] (2014) 6 SCC 677.
[20] Judgment dated September 10, 2014 passed by the Supreme Court in *State of West Bengal v Associated Contractors* at [17].

The 2010 LCIA India Rules are largely based on the 1998 LCIA Rules, but have a number innovations introduced in order to streamline the conduct of proceedings, in particular bearing in mind the provisions of the (Indian) 1996 Act and the general practice of arbitration in India.

The 2014 LCIA Rules have come into force and LCIA India is also in the process of adopting a revised set of arbitration rules. Just as the 2010 LCIA India Rules closely mirrored the 1998 LCIA Arbitration Rules, the new LCIA India Rules are expected, when adopted, closely to follow the 2014 LCIA Rules, with some minor, India-specific modifications, albeit fewer than in the 2010 Rules.

V–020

Many of the differences between the 2010 India Rules and the 1998 LCIA Rules have already been eliminated following the introduction of the 2014 LCIA Rules. Thus:

- The LCIA India Rules include an express requirement that all prospective arbitrators confirm their ability to devote sufficient time to ensure the expeditious conduct of the arbitration (Article 5.3(b)). The 2014 LCIA Rules now contain a similar provision (Article 5.4).

- Article 28.4(b) was a provision newly introduced by the 2010 LCIA India Rules, which provides that the Tribunal may take into account the conduct and co-operation, or non-co-operation, of the parties during the arbitration when determining the allocation of costs. This principle is now contained in Articles 18.4, 28.4 and the Annexure of the 2014 LCIA Rules.

- Articles 5.6 and 5.7 of the 2010 LCIA India Rules provide that the appointment of presiding arbitrators is to be done solely by the LCIA Court. Article 5.6 of the 1998 LCIA Rules only forbade the appointment of a presiding arbitrator who was nominated by one party alone. The 2014 LCIA Rules do not contain a similar provision and it remains to be seen whether the prohibition will be maintained in the revised edition of the LCIA India Rules in due course. This might be so in light of the (perhaps historical) propensity of the Indian courts to entertain challenges to arbitrators and awards that might have been rejected in other jurisdictions.

- The LCIA India Rules, although directed at parties doing business in and through India, are essentially an international set of rules, which are suitable for operation under any system of law, and can be used in any seat or venue throughout the world. Unlike the 1998 LCIA Rules, which provide for London as a default seat (in the absence of parties agreement to the contrary), the LCIA India Rules do not provide for a default seat. In the absence of parties' agreement of a seat, the seat would be determined by the LCIA Court, taking into account, inter alia, the parties' proposals. The 2014 LCIA Rules still maintain London as the default seat of arbitration, subject to any order by the Arbitral Tribunal once appointed. Thus the LCIA Court has no involvement in the selection of the seat of the arbitration in the case of arbitrations commenced under the 2014 LCIA Rules. It remains to be seen whether these provisions will be kept in the expected revision of the LCIA India Rules. London is clearly not an appropriate default seat for

LCIA India arbitration proceedings, but LCIA India might still consider that the LCIA Court should remain responsible for designating a seat in cases where the parties have not designated a seat, pending a final determination by the Tribunal.

**Notes for Arbitrators**

V–021    LCIA India has also produced a set of "Notes for Arbitrators" to provide guidance to arbitrators conducting arbitrations under the LCIA India Rules, on a wide range of issues relating to the conduct of arbitral proceedings, including independence, impartiality, confidentiality and the management of time and costs.

The notes, which were presumably drafted as an introduction to LCIA procedures for arbitrators in a jurisdiction with a long and rich tradition of national arbitration, provide an interesting and instructive read for any arbitrator embarking on his or her first LCIA arbitration, whether under the LCIA India Rules or otherwise.

# PART VI—LCIA-MIAC ARBITRATION CENTRE

by Duncan Bagshaw

# LCIA-MIAC ARBITRATION CENTRE

**Mauritius**

The Republic of Mauritius is an independent island nation in the Indian Ocean, off the coast of Madagascar. Originally uninhabited, for most of the 18th to 20th centuries it was a colonial trading post, first of the French and then of the British empires, supplying sugar to Africa and Europe. **VI–001**

In 1962, Mauritius gained independence from the UK, and in 1992 it became a republic. Since then, its economy has diversified, first into tourism and light manufacturing, and then into financial, corporate and other services.

In recent years, Mauritius has established itself as a centre for international business and finance. It is a popular location for the incorporation of international companies and other structures which serve as investment vehicles. This popularity has been achieved through a combination of low taxation rates for international business, a strong network of Double Taxation Agreement treaties and a system of regulation which is simultaneously attractive to foreign investors and reassuring to foreign governments for its transparency and the quality of its regulatory regime. **VI–002**

Against this background, the Government of Mauritius decided that a strong system of international dispute resolution would complement its financial services and international business sectors, by allowing overseas investors and businesses to resolve disputes concerning their assets and activities in the same jurisdiction as they had chosen as the legal and regulatory base for the projects.

The Government also recognised that Mauritius had the potential to become a centre for the resolution of disputes between parties with no connection to Mauritius, but who might choose it as a neutral, convenient and reliable venue. **VI–003**

There are good reasons for this confidence in the potential of Mauritius to become a major centre for international dispute resolution. Mauritius is generally considered to be amongst the most politically and economically stable jurisdictions in Africa.[1] Mauritius also has the unique quality of being an African country, both geographically and politically,[2] but with a cultural diversity which means that it is also regarded as neutral by Asian parties. The population comprises people of South Asian, African, European, Chinese and South-East Asian heritage. Mauritius' first language for legal matters and official business is English, but both English and French are spoken by almost all of the population, who

---

[1] Mauritius has been ranked first for several consecutive years in the Mo Ibrahim Index of African Governance (*http://www.moibrahimfoundation.org/country/mauritius/*) [Accessed November 1, 2014] and is ranked first in Africa in the World Bank's 2014 Doing Business report *(http://www.doingbusiness.org/rankings)* [Accessed November 5, 2014].

[2] Mauritius is a member of the African Union, the Southern African Development Community and the Common Market for East and Southern Africa.

communicate on a day-to-day basis in a French-based Creole. Legislation is drafted in English and the court system follows procedures which are closer to those of the English courts than the courts of France, but the substantive laws are based, for the most part, on French civil law, which was retained after Britain took control of the island from France. Recent legislation, especially in company and commercial matters, has tended to be based upon English statutes.

VI–004   The cultural diversity of Mauritius is reflected in the day-to-day operations of Mauritian businesses. Visitors to any Mauritian hotel may be struck by the mixture of French and English-speaking tourists, both equally at ease with the staff who speak to them fluently in their own language. Mauritian international lawyers and finance professionals must switch between English and French as they consider first the *Code de Procédure Civile* in French and then the Rules of the Supreme Court in English, or as they take telephone calls from clients in Mumbai or Cape Town in English and from Yaoundé or Paris in French.

The island is developing rapidly. The bustling capital city, Port Louis, and the modern commercial centre known as Cyber City, home to major international banks and professional services firms, are very far from the images of beaches and palm trees for which Mauritius is well known.

**The arbitration environment in Africa**

VI–005   International arbitration is not new to Africa, but it is fair to say that no arbitral institution based on the continent has yet established itself as a major international centre. South Africa probably hosts the highest number of domestic arbitrations in Africa, but it has been hampered by a failure to update its legislation,[3] and by suggestions that it may have an unfriendly attitude towards arbitration.[4] Nigeria has a busy domestic arbitration scene, but no international centre has yet established itself there as a realistic choice for parties looking for a neutral, reliable venue in Africa. Cairo's Regional Centre for International Commercial Arbitration is long established and has a high volume of cases, but its focus has been upon domestic matters and some cases arising out of other Middle East and North African states.[5]

For some time, therefore, there has been an appetite for a venue in sub-Saharan Africa where commercial and investment disputes touching upon African issues and business can be resolved. This reflects the increased level of investment into African countries and trade with African states and companies. Investment inflows to sub-Saharan Africa increased by 25 per cent to US$36.9 billion in 2011. The GDP;PPP[6] of sub-Saharan Africa increased from US$1,200 billion in 2004 to

---

[3] The Arbitration Act 1965.
[4] For example, Rukia Baruti, "Is Africa Finally Confronting its Challenges on Investment Treaty Arbitration?" in Kluwer Arbitration Blog, November 4, 2011.
[5] In the first quarter of 2013, all of the parties to cases filed at the CRCICA were Egyptian except for one party from each of Saudi Arabia, Russia, Germany, Ukraine and the British Virgin Islands. See the Cairo Regional Centre for International Arbitration Annual Report, 2012–2013, p.10. Source: *http://www.crcica.org.eg* [Accessed December 4, 2014].
[6] GDP;PPP is gross domestic product converted to international dollars using purchasing power parity rates.

US$2,200 billion in 2011.[7] The opportunity for an African centre to emerge can also be attributed to the decreasing extent to which African business is done with European and American governments and companies, who might be more likely to insist upon arbitration being administered in a traditional venue for international arbitration such as London or Geneva. The share of trade done with African nations by European businesses declined from 51 per cent to 30 per cent in the 10 years to 2009, and the share done by Asian countries doubled.[8] This trend has continued and, according to Standard Bank, China's investment into Africa is anticipated to reach US$50 billion by 2015 (an increase of 70 per cent since 2009).

There is also a less quantifiable factor at work. International arbitration, particularly investment arbitration, has at times been accused of being a small club, dominated by European lawyers. As Salim Moollan[9] put it at the ICCA Congress in Miami in 2014: VI–006

"There exists a hiatus today between a formal discourse – frequently repeated at international conferences – emphasising the 'inclusiveness' of international arbitration, and a perception of our field in the developing world as predominantly Euro- or Americano-centric.

This gives rise to a risk of arbitration being perceived as a 'foreign' process imposed from abroad, as an unwanted but inevitable corollary of trade and investment flows.

The conceptual premise of the Mauritian project is that the answer to this is to make sure that the developing world has its say in the process and in its development, and for international arbitration progressively to become part and parcel of the legal culture of developing countries.

The aim is accordingly to create a platform run for the benefit of the region as a whole to build capacity in the field of international dispute resolution, so that (within a generation) Africa can draw on the expertise of specialist African arbitrators and lawyers."

Whilst international arbitration has developed significantly in Asia in recent years, the same cannot be said for the African continent. One way to address these concerns is to develop the infrastructure, expertise and facilities for international arbitration in Africa, and to use African arbitrators and lawyers where appropriate. By becoming an attractive seat of arbitration and a centre for international dispute resolution, Mauritius can lead the way in this process for other African nations. VI–007

### The development of the Mauritius infrastructure

Against this background, the Government of Mauritius concluded that Mauritius could become a successful and credible African venue for international dispute resolution. Its project to achieve this has involved two key areas of development. VI–008

---

[7] Africa Development Indicators 2012/13, The World Bank.
[8] Source: McKinsey.
[9] Chairman of the UNCITRAL Working Group on Arbitration; Barrister, Essex Court Chambers and Chambers of Sir Hamid Moollan QC.

First, the legal framework for international arbitration had to be brought up to date and made sufficiently attractive to overseas parties to justify their adoption of a Mauritian seat for arbitration of their cross-border disputes. Secondly, the physical and administrative infrastructure was needed to demonstrate that substantial disputes could be administered from and resolved in Mauritius.

Mauritius became a signatory to the New York Convention in 1996. The former system of arbitration law was found in the *Code de Procédure Civile* and governed both domestic and international disputes. In 2008 legislation was passed which separated the regimes under Mauritian law for domestic and international matters. International arbitration matters seated in Mauritius have, since 2009, been governed exclusively by the International Arbitration Act 2008 (the 2008 Act), which came into force on January 1, 2009. The 2008 Act was enacted with the expressed intention to "promote the use of Mauritius as a jurisdiction of choice in the field of international arbitration. . .".[10] It applies to all international arbitrations seated in Mauritius and, in part, to all other international arbitrations.

**VI–009** The 2008 Act is based upon the UNCITRAL Model Law. It follows the Model Law's approach to the standard to be applied to challenges to arbitral awards. But it also includes particular innovations which set Mauritius apart from other Model Law jurisdictions. The UNCITRAL Model Law envisages that countries which adopt Model Law-based legislation will designate a court or other authority[11] to perform certain functions, namely the power to resolve disputes and to break deadlocks over the appointment and replacement of arbitrators, disputes over arbitrators' fees and challenges to arbitrators. These matters would require court intervention in most jurisdictions, but in Mauritius the power to resolve such issues is reserved to the Permanent Court of Arbitration (PCA), based in The Hague, with no review of the PCA's decision by the courts of Mauritius. The Supreme Court's role in the issues that have been considered by the PCA is limited to considering them if they arise upon a challenge to an award, or upon enforcement. For example, the Supreme Court may be asked to set aside an award on the grounds that an arbitrator did not possess mandatory characteristics agreed upon by the parties in the arbitration agreement, whereas the PCA has previously declined to uphold a challenge to an arbitrator on the same grounds.

In order to carry out its statutory functions under the 2008 Act effectively, the PCA opened its first overseas office in Mauritius in September 2010, with the support of the Government of Mauritius. The PCA office in Mauritius is home to the PCA Representative in Mauritius. In addition to acting as an administrative office for the PCA's statutory role under the 2008 Act, it also works to build capacity and to promote good practice in international dispute resolution procedures in the region.

**VI–010** The 2008 Act takes advantage of the structure of the court system in Mauritius to provide a shortened, superior system of court adjudication and appeals in international arbitration matters. The first instance court in such cases is the highest court in Mauritius; a panel of three Supreme Court judges. Decisions of the Supreme Court can be appealed to the Judicial Committee of the Privy Council of

---

[10] Subtitle of the International Arbitration Act 2008.
[11] UNCITRAL Model Law Article 6 (Appendix 10).

England and Wales. Such appeals are brought before the Privy Council as of right, so that the process should be swifter than most appeals to the Privy Council.

A particular feature of the 2008 Act is in its application of the so-called "negative effect" of *compétence-compétence*. Section 5 of the 2008 Act, which applies to all international arbitrations, requires the court to stay proceedings and refer the matter to arbitration where a party asserts that the dispute is subject to an arbitration agreement, unless a party shows on a prima facie assessment that there is a "very strong probability" that the Arbitration Agreement is void, inoperative or incapable of being performed. This provision is similar to that in the French legislation,[12] except that, in Mauritius, the court's approach is the same whether or not the Arbitral Tribunal has been constituted.

The court's power to grant and enforce interim measures, such as injunctive relief, also extends to allow orders to be made to support arbitration proceedings which are not seated in Mauritius. The 2008 Act, like the UNICTRAL Model Law, limits the exercise of this power so as to require applications to be made to the Arbitral Tribunal if they could for the time being act effectively. The 2008 Act also expressly allows enforcement of interim relief granted by an arbitral tribunal. It remains to be seen whether and in what circumstances relief granted by an emergency tribunal such as might be formed under Article 9B of the LCIA Arbitration Rules (2014 version) would be enforced under this provision but the spirit of the act, designed to promote international arbitration and to make Mauritius attractive as a venue, suggests that it would. **VI–011**

In June 2013, amendments to the 2008 Act came into force, so as to respond to commentary and judicial treatment of the 2008 Act by clarifying the legislation and taking steps to further advance the stated aim of making Mauritius an attractive seat. The wording of the 2008 Act has been amended to emphasise that an "international arbitration" as defined by the 2008 Act may be seated in Mauritius or outside Mauritius. The difference is that only arbitrations seated in Mauritius are subject to the full provisions of the 2008 Act. The provisions which permit arbitration clauses (with a mandatory Mauritian seat) to be included in the company constitutions of Mauritian Global Business Licence Companies have been clarified to make it clear that the parties have a free choice of seat in relation to arbitration clauses in any other instrument, such as a shareholder's agreement. The reciprocity reservation has been removed from the adoption of the New York Convention in Mauritius, and the amending legislation has confirmed the equal status of the French and English languages in international arbitration matters before the court. This allows arbitral awards written in French or English to be enforced in Mauritius without being translated.

The 2013 amendments also introduced an express power[13] for the court to keep any court proceedings under the 2008 Act (or for enforcement) private, thereby respecting the confidentiality of the proceedings in appropriate cases. The court may do so where the parties agree, or where the court considers that publicity would prejudice the interests of justice, taking into account the specific features of international arbitration, including any expectation of confidentiality which the **VI–012**

---

[12] *Code de Procédure Civile* Article 1448.
[13] 2008 Act s.42(1A) and 42(1B).

parties may have had when concluding their arbitration agreement or any need to protect confidential information.[14]

Other aspects of the legal framework are also subject to continuing development by the Government of Mauritius. Modern rules of court have been introduced to govern court procedures related to international arbitration matters, and work is being done with the six designated Judges of the Supreme Court, who will hear such matters, to put these new rules into effective operation.

VI–013   Since it is already operating as an international business centre, Mauritius is reasonably well equipped with the support services that the users of a venue for international arbitration will require. The hotel and conference facilities are of a high standard and offer fast data connections and sophisticated business support services. Hotel rooms or serviced offices can be rented for short periods to be used as a base before and during longer hearings. Translation and transcription services are readily available. Translators are available locally between French and English and most languages used for business in the region, notably Portuguese, Chinese and the languages of the Indian sub-continent.

In 2010, the Government of Mauritius announced[15] that it planned in due course to support the development of a dedicated hearing centre in Mauritius. The development of that hearing centre is well under way at the time of writing, and it is expected to be operational in 2015. The new centre will offer state of the art facilities to rival those in the other major centres of the world. Parties entering into contracts now can therefore expect that the hearing centre will be available to host arbitration hearings arising from such contracts in future years.

## The LCIA-MIAC Arbitration Centre and the LCIA-MIAC Arbitration Rules

VI–014   The LCIA entered into this environment already well known for promoting the establishment of regional centres for the practice of LCIA-style international arbitration in alternative venues to the LCIA's main offices in London. The first such project was LCIA's collaboration with the Dubai International Financial Centre in 2008 to launch the DIFA-LCIA Arbitration Centre. In 2009, LCIA India was established as the first independent overseas office of the LCIA.

In 2011, the LCIA and the Government of Mauritius agreed to establish "the LCIA-MIAC Arbitration Centre" in Mauritius, known as LCIA-MIAC. LCIA-MIAC is an independent institution, with its own arbitration rules and mediation rules. It has its own Secretariat to carry out the administration of procedures, which is headed by the Registrar.

VI–015   LCIA-MIAC's Arbitration Rules and Mediation Rules are based on the LCIA's Rules, with only small changes to reflect some differences in the law of Mauritius (see below). The Rules are shortly to be updated to reflect the changes to the LCIA Arbitration Rules which came into operation on October 1, 2014. The updated LCIA-MIAC Rules will include provisions providing for Emergency Arbitrators.

[14] 2008 Act s.42(1B)(a)(ii).
[15] Speech of the Prime Minister of Mauritius at the Opening of the Mauritius International Arbitration Conference 2010.

Like the equivalent provision in the 2014 LCIA Rules, this will only apply prospectively where the Arbitration Agreement is entered into after the updated rules come into force, or where the parties have so agreed.[16] It is intended that the updated LCIA-MIAC Rules will also include an Appendix, like that in the LCIA Rules, setting out guidelines for parties' legal representatives.

LCIA-MIAC uses systems for the management of its procedures and handling of funds which are similar to those of the LCIA. The LCIA provides support and guidance in relation to the overall direction and good operation of LCIA-MIAC, and lends support to operational aspects of the functioning of LCIA-MIAC, for example, Information Technology resources.

VI–016 The LCIA Court has the same supervisory role in matters administered by LCIA-MIAC as under the LCIA Rules. Therefore, under the LCIA-MIAC Rules, it is the LCIA Court which appoints arbitrators. An agreement between the parties that they will appoint arbitrators themselves is treated as an agreement to nominate only.[17] The parties can agree to nominate an individual or individuals but the LCIA Court will formally appoint the nominated person(s) only after carrying out the checks on qualifications and conflicts which it would do for LCIA matters. The LCIA Court also acts as the authority which resolves disputes over the suitability and qualifications of proposed arbitrators, and adjudicates upon challenges to arbitrators in the first instance. The LCIA Court has a supervisory role over the costs of the arbitration (other than the parties' own lawyers' fees) by reviewing the costs charged by LCIA-MIAC and the arbitrators to ensure that they are reasonable and comply with the costs schedule or any other agreement.

Arbitrations and other procedures administered by LCIA-MIAC will take a similar course to those administered by the LCIA, with LCIA-MIAC's Secretariat taking the place of the LCIA's Secretariat in administrative matters. As one would expect, the Rules allow the greatest flexibility to the Tribunal and the parties to tailor the structure of the arbitration and the procedures to the case in hand.

VI–017 Like the LCIA, LCIA-MIAC allows a high level of flexibility as to the identity of the arbitrator(s). There is no limited panel from which arbitrators must be drawn. The parties may nominate an arbitrator who is not known to LCIA-MIAC, provided that the LCIA Court is satisfied that it is appropriate to appoint the nominee, as mentioned above. If LCIA-MIAC is asked to nominate an arbitrator then it will do so having regard to any agreed parameters and drawing upon both the knowledge and experience of the LCIA, and LCIA-MIAC's own regional expertise to identify the most appropriate arbitrator.

The Secretariat of LCIA-MIAC will operate most commonly in English and French, but the language of the proceedings is a matter on which the parties have the freedom to agree, or alternatively on which the arbitrators may decide. The LCIA-MIAC Arbitration Rules have been translated into Chinese and French, and a Portuguese translation is planned.

---

[16] Article 9B.14.
[17] Article 7.1.

VI–018   Hearings may take place in any location chosen by the parties or decided by the Tribunal, and may be in person, by telephone or video-link depending on the nature of the hearing and the requirements of the case.

The LCIA-MIAC Rules have since 2012 included, in the duties of the arbitrators set out in the Rules, the duty to act expeditiously. This duty was introduced into the LCIA Rules in the 2014 Rules, and accordingly will remain in the updated LCIA-MIAC Rules.[18] The word "expeditious" was included on the grounds that it sends an explicit message to the arbitrators and parties that, whilst speed is not a goal to be achieved at the expense of fairness, it is nevertheless a major concern for most parties to international arbitrations and this should inform the approach and procedures selected by the Tribunal.

VI–019   Similarly, the arbitrator's duty to disclose potential conflicts of interest, as formulated in the new LCIA Rules, matches that which was already provided for in the LCIA-MIAC Rules, namely that arbitrator should disclose any circumstance currently known to the candidate likely to give rise in the mind of any party to any justifiable[19] doubts as to his or her impartiality or independence. This duty therefore remains in the LCIA-MIAC Rules.

The LCIA-MIAC Rules provide that, where the Arbitration Agreement does not expressly determine the seat or legal place of the arbitration, the seat will be Mauritius unless the LCIA Court determines otherwise.[20] This presumption is consistent with the parties' choice of LCIA-MIAC as the institution administering the dispute, and suggests confidence on the part of the LCIA Court in the Mauritian legislation on international arbitration. LCIA-MIAC can also administer arbitrations which are not seated in Mauritius, and hearings can take place wherever is convenient.[21] The 2008 Act makes it clear[22] that the seat of arbitration may be different from the place where hearings and other meetings take place. In most other jurisdictions there is also no requirement for the administration of the arbitration, or the hearings, to take place in the country of the seat and most institutional rules make this clear.[23]

VI–020   The LCIA-MIAC Rules have since 2012 provided that, unless the parties have agreed in writing on the application of other laws, the law applicable to the Arbitration Agreement and to the arbitration shall be the law applicable at the seat of the arbitration. This provision therefore will remain in the LCIA-MIAC Rules since they were updated to reflect the 2014 LCIA Rules.

The procedure for the replacement of an arbitrator who has been removed has been varied slightly from that in the LCIA Rules, so that an arbitrator who resigns, or is removed due to his inability or unfitness to act or following a party challenge, shall be replaced following the procedure by which he was appointed.[24] This difference from the LCIA Rules follows the approach set out in the 2008 Act and therefore it seems likely that this difference will be retained in the updated

---

[18] Article 14.4(ii).
[19] Article 5.3 of the 1998 LCIA Rules used the expression "justified".
[20] Article 16.1.
[21] Article 16.2.
[22] 2008 Act s.10.
[23] As do the UNCITRAL Rules; see Article 18.2.
[24] Article 11.3.

LCIA-MIAC Rules.[25] Under the LCIA Rules, the procedure followed for replacement of arbitrators is determined by the LCIA Court. Practitioners should be alert to this slight departure from the LCIA Rules.

**The future**

Feedback received by LCIA-MIAC from lawyers and professional advisors demonstrates that dispute resolution clauses which feature LCIA-MIAC as the institution administering arbitration or other ADR procedures are regularly being written in to contracts and other instruments. LCIA-MIAC arbitration clauses are most commonly being included in contracts involving companies incorporated in Mauritius by foreign investors, and in contracts made between foreign investors and African parties. VI–021

LCIA-MIAC has now received referrals to administer its first international cases, and expects to see a growing caseload as disputes arise out of the contracts incorporating clauses providing for LCIA-MIAC arbitration.

The programme of conferences and events in Mauritius and overseas organised by LCIA-MIAC continues to raise the profile of Mauritius as a leading centre for international arbitration. The Biennial Mauritius International Arbitration Conference has been held successfully in 2010, 2012 and 2014. Of particular note is the decision of the International Council for Commercial Arbitration (ICCA) to hold the 23rd ICCA Congress in Mauritius in 2016. This will be the first ICCA Congress to be held in an African country. VI–022

Whilst no arbitral institution can hope to establish itself overnight, the prospects for Mauritius to become a credible and popular centre are good, taking into account Mauritius' neutrality and reliability, the care and determination which has gone into establishing the legal system, the developing infrastructure for arbitration business and the LCIA-MIAC Arbitration Centre. Provided this hard work continues, there is every reason to think that LCIA-MIAC may take its place amongst the major centres of the world in the not too distant future.

---

[25] 2008 Act s.16(1).

# APPENDICES

# Appendix 1

# LCIA ARBITRATION RULES 2014

**Preamble**

Where any agreement, submission or reference howsoever made or evidenced in writing (whether signed or not) provides in whatsoever manner for arbitration under the rules of or by the LCIA, the London Court of International Arbitration, the London Court of Arbitration or the London Court, the parties thereto shall be taken to have agreed in writing that any arbitration between them shall be conducted in accordance with the LCIA Rules or such amended rules as the LCIA may have adopted hereafter to take effect before the commencement of the arbitration and that such LCIA Rules form part of their agreement (collectively, the "Arbitration Agreement"). These LCIA Rules comprise this Preamble, the Articles and the Index, together with the Annex to the LCIA Rules and the Schedule of Costs as both from time to time may be separately amended by the LCIA (the "LCIA Rules").

**Article 1  Request for Arbitration**

1.1  Any party wishing to commence an arbitration under the LCIA Rules (the "Claimant") shall deliver to the Registrar of the LCIA Court (the "Registrar") a written request for arbitration (the "Request"), containing or accompanied by:

- (i) the full name and all contact details (including postal address, e-mail address, telephone and facsimile numbers) of the Claimant for the purpose of receiving delivery of all documentation in the arbitration; and the same particulars of the Claimant's legal representatives (if any) and of all other parties to the arbitration;
- (ii) the full terms of the Arbitration Agreement (excepting the LCIA Rules) invoked by the Claimant to support its claim, together with a copy of any contractual or other documentation in which those terms are contained and to which the Claimant's claim relates;
- (iii) a statement briefly summarising the nature and circumstances of the dispute, its estimated monetary amount or value, the transaction(s) at issue and the claim advanced by the Claimant against any other party to the arbitration (each such other party being here separately described as a "Respondent");

(iv) a statement of any procedural matters for the arbitration (such as the arbitral seat, the language(s) of the arbitration, the number of arbitrators, their qualifications and identities) upon which the parties have already agreed in writing or in respect of which the Claimant makes any proposal under the Arbitration Agreement;

(v) if the Arbitration Agreement (or any other written agreement) howsoever calls for any form of party nomination of arbitrators, the full name, postal address, e-mail address, telephone and facsimile numbers of the Claimant's nominee;

(vi) confirmation that the registration fee prescribed in the Schedule of Costs has been or is being paid to the LCIA, without which actual receipt of such payment the Request shall be treated by the Registrar as not having been delivered and the arbitration as not having been commenced under the Arbitration Agreement; and

(vii) confirmation that copies of the Request (including all accompanying documents) have been or are being delivered to all other parties to the arbitration by one or more means to be identified specifically in such confirmation, to be supported then or as soon as possible thereafter by documentary proof satisfactory to the LCIA Court of actual delivery (including the date of delivery) or, if actual delivery is demonstrated to be impossible to the LCIA Court's satisfaction, sufficient information as to any other effective form of notification.

1.2 The Request (including all accompanying documents) may be submitted to the Registrar in electronic form (as e-mail attachments) or in paper form or in both forms. If submitted in paper form, the Request shall be submitted in two copies where a sole arbitrator is to be appointed, or, if the parties have agreed or the Claimant proposes that three arbitrators are to be appointed, in four copies.

1.3 The Claimant may use, but is not required to do so, the standard electronic form available on-line from the LCIA's website for LCIA Requests.

1.4 The date of receipt by the Registrar of the Request shall be treated as the date upon which the arbitration has commenced for all purposes (the "Commencement Date"), subject to the LCIA's actual receipt of the registration fee.

1.5 There may be one or more Claimants (whether or not jointly represented); and in such event, where appropriate, the term "Claimant" shall be so interpreted under the Arbitration Agreement.

**Article 2 Response**

2.1 Within 28 days of the Commencement Date, or such lesser or greater period to be determined by the LCIA Court upon application by any party or upon its own initiative (pursuant to Article 22.5), the Respondent shall deliver to the

Registrar a written response to the Request (the "Response"), containing or accompanied by:

(i) the Respondent's full name and all contact details (including postal address, e-mail address, telephone and facsimile numbers) for the purpose of receiving delivery of all documentation in the arbitration and the same particulars of its legal representatives (if any);

(ii) confirmation or denial of all or part of the claim advanced by the Claimant in the Request, including the Claimant's invocation of the Arbitration Agreement in support of its claim;

(iii) if not full confirmation, a statement briefly summarising the nature and circumstances of the dispute, its estimated monetary amount or value, the transaction(s) at issue and the defence advanced by the Respondent, and also indicating whether any cross-claim will be advanced by the Respondent against any other party to the arbitration (such cross-claim to include any counterclaim against any Claimant and any other cross-claim against any Respondent);

(iv) a response to any procedural statement for the arbitration contained in the Request under Article 1.1(iv), including the Respondent's own statement relating to the arbitral seat, the language(s) of the arbitration, the number of arbitrators, their qualifications and identities and any other procedural matter upon which the parties have already agreed in writing or in respect of which the Respondent makes any proposal under the Arbitration Agreement;

(v) if the Arbitration Agreement (or any other written agreement) howsoever calls for party nomination of arbitrators, the full name, postal address, e-mail address, telephone and facsimile numbers of the Respondent's nominee; and

(vi) confirmation that copies of the Response (including all accompanying documents) have been or are being delivered to all other parties to the arbitration by one or more means of delivery to be identified specifically in such confirmation, to be supported then or as soon as possible thereafter by documentary proof satisfactory to the LCIA Court of actual delivery (including the date of delivery) or, if actual delivery is demonstrated to be impossible to the LCIA Court's satisfaction, sufficient information as to any other effective form of notification.

2.2 The Response (including all accompanying documents) may be submitted to the Registrar in electronic form (as e-mail attachments) or in paper form or in both forms. If submitted in paper form, the Response shall be submitted in two copies where a sole arbitrator is to be appointed, or, if the parties have agreed or the Respondent proposes that three arbitrators are to be appointed, in four copies.

2.3 The Respondent may use, but is not required to do so, the standard electronic form available on-line from the LCIA's website for LCIA Responses.

2.4 Failure to deliver a Response within time shall constitute an irrevocable waiver of that party's opportunity to nominate or propose any arbitral candidate. Failure to deliver any or any part of a Response within time or at all shall not (by itself) preclude the Respondent from denying any claim or from advancing any defence or cross-claim in the arbitration.

2.5 There may be one or more Respondents (whether or not jointly represented); and in such event, where appropriate, the term "Respondent" shall be so interpreted under the Arbitration Agreement.

### Article 3 LCIA Court and Registrar

3.1 The functions of the LCIA Court under the Arbitration Agreement shall be performed in its name by the President of the LCIA Court (or any of its Vice-Presidents, Honorary Vice-Presidents or former Vice-Presidents) or by a division of three or more members of the LCIA Court appointed by its President or any Vice-President (the "LCIA Court").

3.2 The functions of the Registrar under the Arbitration Agreement shall be performed under the supervision of the LCIA Court by the Registrar or any deputy Registrar.

3.3 All communications in the arbitration to the LCIA Court from any party, arbitrator or expert to the Arbitral Tribunal shall be addressed to the Registrar.

### Article 4 Written Communications and Periods of Time

4.1 Any written communication by the LCIA Court, the Registrar or any party may be delivered personally or by registered postal or courier service or (subject to Article 4.3) by facsimile, e-mail or any other electronic means of telecommunication that provides a record of its transmission, or in any other manner ordered by the Arbitral Tribunal.

4.2 Unless otherwise ordered by the Arbitral Tribunal, if an address has been agreed or designated by a party for the purpose of receiving any communication in regard to the Arbitration Agreement or (in the absence of such agreement or designation) has been regularly used in the parties' previous dealings, any written communication (including the Request and Response) may be delivered to such party at that address, and if so delivered, shall be treated as having been received by such party.

4.3 Delivery by electronic means (including e-mail and facsimile) may only be effected to an address agreed or designated by the receiving party for that purpose or ordered by the Arbitral Tribunal.

4.4 For the purpose of determining the commencement of any time-limit, a written communication shall be treated as having been received by a party on the day it is delivered or, in the case of electronic means, transmitted in accordance with Articles 4.1 to 4.3 (such time to be determined by reference to the recipient's time-zone).

4.5 For the purpose of determining compliance with a time-limit, a written communication shall be treated as having been sent by a party if made or transmitted in accordance with Articles 4.1 to 4.3 prior to or on the date of the expiration of the time-limit.

4.6 For the purpose of calculating a period of time, such period shall begin to run on the day following the day when a written communication is received by the addressee. If the last day of such period is an official holiday or non-business day at the place of that addressee (or the place of the party against whom the calculation of time applies), the period shall be extended until the first business day which follows that last day. Official holidays and non-business days occurring during the running of the period of time shall be included in calculating that period.

**Article 5  Formation of Arbitral Tribunal**

5.1 The formation of the Arbitral Tribunal by the LCIA Court shall not be impeded by any controversy between the parties relating to the sufficiency of the Request or the Response. The LCIA Court may also proceed with the arbitration notwithstanding that the Request is incomplete or the Response is missing, late or incomplete.

5.2 The expression the "Arbitral Tribunal" includes a sole arbitrator or all the arbitrators where more than one.

5.3 All arbitrators shall be and remain at all times impartial and independent of the parties; and none shall act in the arbitration as advocate for or representative of any party. No arbitrator shall advise any party on the parties' dispute or the outcome of the arbitration.

5.4 Before appointment by the LCIA Court, each arbitral candidate shall furnish to the Registrar (upon the latter's request) a brief written summary of his or her qualifications and professional positions (past and present); the candidate shall also agree in writing fee-rates conforming to the Schedule of Costs; the candidate shall sign a written declaration stating: (i) whether there are any circumstances currently known to the candidate which are likely to give rise in the mind of any party to any justifiable doubts as to his or her impartiality or independence and, if so, specifying in full such circumstances in the declaration; and (ii) whether the candidate is ready, willing and able to devote sufficient time, diligence and industry to ensure the expeditious and efficient conduct of the arbitration. The candidate shall furnish promptly such agreement and declaration to the Registrar.

5.5 If appointed, each arbitral candidate shall thereby assume a continuing duty as an arbitrator, until the arbitration is finally concluded, forthwith to disclose in writing any circumstances becoming known to that arbitrator after the date of his or her written declaration (under Article 5.4) which are likely to give rise in the mind of any party to any justifiable doubts as to his or her impartiality or independence, to be delivered to the LCIA Court, any other members of the Arbitral Tribunal and all parties in the arbitration.

5.6 The LCIA Court shall appoint the Arbitral Tribunal promptly after receipt by the Registrar of the Response or, if no Response is received, after 35 days from the Commencement Date (or such other lesser or greater period to be determined by the LCIA Court pursuant to Article 22.5).

5.7 No party or third person may appoint any arbitrator under the Arbitration Agreement: the LCIA Court alone is empowered to appoint arbitrators (albeit taking into account any written agreement or joint nomination by the parties).

5.8 A sole arbitrator shall be appointed unless the parties have agreed in writing otherwise or if the LCIA Court determines that in the circumstances a three-member tribunal is appropriate (or, exceptionally, more than three).

5.9 The LCIA Court shall appoint arbitrators with due regard for any particular method or criteria of selection agreed in writing by the parties. The LCIA Court shall also take into account the transaction(s) at issue, the nature and circumstances of the dispute, its monetary amount or value, the location and languages of the parties, the number of parties and all other factors which it may consider relevant in the circumstances.

5.10 The President of the LCIA Court shall only be eligible to be appointed as an arbitrator if the parties agree in writing to nominate him or her as the sole or presiding arbitrator; and the Vice Presidents of the LCIA Court and the Chairman of the LCIA Board of Directors (the latter being ex officio a member of the LCIA Court) shall only be eligible to be appointed as arbitrators if nominated in writing by a party or parties – provided that no such nominee shall have taken or shall take thereafter any part in any function of the LCIA Court or LCIA relating to such arbitration.

**Article 6 Nationality of Arbitrators**

6.1 Where the parties are of different nationalities, a sole arbitrator or the presiding arbitrator shall not have the same nationality as any party unless the parties who are not of the same nationality as the arbitral candidate all agree in writing otherwise.

6.2 The nationality of a party shall be understood to include those of its controlling shareholders or interests.

6.3 A person who is a citizen of two or more States shall be treated as a national of each State; citizens of the European Union shall be treated as nationals of its different Member States and shall not be treated as having the same nationality; a citizen of a State's overseas territory shall be treated as a national of that territory and not of that State; and a legal person incorporated in a State's overseas territory shall be treated as such and not (by such fact alone) as a national of or a legal person incorporated in that State.

**Article 7 Party and Other Nominations**

7.1 If the parties have agreed howsoever that any arbitrator is to be appointed by one or more of them or by any third person (other than the LCIA Court), that agreement shall be treated under the Arbitration Agreement as an agreement to nominate an arbitrator for all purposes. Such nominee may only be appointed by the LCIA Court as arbitrator subject to that nominee's compliance with Articles 5.3 to 5.5; and the LCIA Court shall refuse to appoint any nominee if it determines that the nominee is not so compliant or is otherwise unsuitable.

7.2 Where the parties have howsoever agreed that the Claimant or the Respondent or any third person (other than the LCIA Court) is to nominate an arbitrator and such nomination is not made within time or at all (in the Request, Response or otherwise), the LCIA Court may appoint an arbitrator notwithstanding any absent or late nomination.

7.3 In the absence of written agreement between the Parties, no party may unilaterally nominate a sole arbitrator or presiding arbitrator.

### Article 8  Three or More Parties

8.1 Where the Arbitration Agreement entitles each party howsoever to nominate an arbitrator, the parties to the dispute number more than two and such parties have not all agreed in writing that the disputant parties represent collectively two separate "sides" for the formation of the Arbitral Tribunal (as Claimants on one side and Respondents on the other side, each side nominating a single arbitrator), the LCIA Court shall appoint the Arbitral Tribunal without regard to any party's entitlement or nomination.

8.2 In such circumstances, the Arbitration Agreement shall be treated for all purposes as a written agreement by the parties for the nomination and appointment of the Arbitral Tribunal by the LCIA Court alone.

### Article 9A  Expedited Formation of Arbitral Tribunal

9.1 In the case of exceptional urgency, any party may apply to the LCIA Court for the expedited formation of the Arbitral Tribunal under Article 5.

9.2 Such an application shall be made to the Registrar in writing (preferably by electronic means), together with a copy of the Request (if made by a Claimant) or a copy of the Response (if made by a Respondent), delivered or notified to all other parties to the arbitration. The application shall set out the specific grounds for exceptional urgency requiring the expedited formation of the Arbitral Tribunal.

9.3 The LCIA Court shall determine the application as expeditiously as possible in the circumstances. If the application is granted, for the purpose of forming the Arbitral Tribunal the LCIA Court may abridge any period of time under the Arbitration Agreement or other agreement of the parties (pursuant to Article 22.5).

### Article 9B  Emergency Arbitrator

9.4 Subject always to Article 9.14 below, in the case of emergency at any time prior to the formation or expedited formation of the Arbitral Tribunal (under

Articles 5 or 9A), any party may apply to the LCIA Court for the immediate appointment of a temporary sole arbitrator to conduct emergency proceedings pending the formation or expedited formation of the Arbitral Tribunal (the "Emergency Arbitrator").

9.5 Such an application shall be made to the Registrar in writing (preferably by electronic means), together with a copy of the Request (if made by a Claimant) or a copy of the Response (if made by a Respondent), delivered or notified to all other parties to the arbitration. The application shall set out, together with all relevant documentation: (i) the specific grounds for requiring, as an emergency, the appointment of an Emergency Arbitrator; and (ii) the specific claim, with reasons, for emergency relief. The application shall be accompanied by the applicant's written confirmation that the applicant has paid or is paying to the LCIA the Special Fee under Article 9B, without which actual receipt of such payment the application shall be dismissed by the LCIA Court. The Special Fee shall be subject to the terms of the Schedule of Costs. Its amount is prescribed in the Schedule, covering the fees and expenses of the Emergency Arbitrator and the administrative fees and expenses of the LCIA, with additional charges (if any) of the LCIA Court. After the appointment of the Emergency Arbitrator, the amount of the Special Fee payable by the applicant may be increased by the LCIA Court in accordance with the Schedule. Article 24 shall not apply to any Special Fee paid to the LCIA.

9.6 The LCIA Court shall determine the application as soon as possible in the circumstances. If the application is granted, an Emergency Arbitrator shall be appointed by the LCIA Court within three days of the Registrar's receipt of the application (or as soon as possible thereafter). Articles 5.1, 5.7, 5.9, 5.10, 6, 9C, 10 and 16.2 (last sentence) shall apply to such appointment. The Emergency Arbitrator shall comply with the requirements of Articles 5.3, 5.4 and (until the emergency proceedings are finally concluded) Article 5.5.

9.7 The Emergency Arbitrator may conduct the emergency proceedings in any manner determined by the Emergency Arbitrator to be appropriate in the circumstances, taking account of the nature of such emergency proceedings, the need to afford to each party, if possible, an opportunity to be consulted on the claim for emergency relief (whether or not it avails itself of such opportunity), the claim and reasons for emergency relief and the parties' further submissions (if any). The Emergency Arbitrator is not required to hold any hearing with the parties (whether in person, by telephone or otherwise) and may decide the claim for emergency relief on available documentation. In the event of a hearing, Articles 16.3, 19.2, 19.3 and 19.4 shall apply.

9.8 The Emergency Arbitrator shall decide the claim for emergency relief as soon as possible, but no later than 14 days following the Emergency Arbitrator's appointment. This deadline may only be extended by the LCIA Court in exceptional circumstances (pursuant to Article 22.5) or by the written agreement of all parties to the emergency proceedings. The Emergency Arbitrator may make any order or award which the Arbitral Tribunal could make under the Arbitration Agreement (excepting Arbitration and Legal Costs under Articles 28.2 and 28.3); and, in addition, make any order adjourning the consideration of all or any part of the claim for emergency relief to the proceedings conducted by the Arbitral Tribunal (when formed).

9.9 An order of the Emergency Arbitrator shall be made in writing, with reasons. An award of the Emergency Arbitrator shall comply with Article 26.2 and, when made, take effect as an award under Article 26.8 (subject to Article 9.11). The Emergency Arbitrator shall be responsible for delivering any order or award to the Registrar, who shall transmit the same promptly to the parties by electronic means, in addition to paper form (if so requested by any party). In the event of any disparity between electronic and paper forms, the electronic form shall prevail.

9.10 The Special Fee paid shall form a part of the Arbitration Costs under Article 28.2 determined by the LCIA Court (as to the amount of Arbitration Costs) and decided by the Arbitral Tribunal (as to the proportions in which the parties shall bear Arbitration Costs). Any legal or other expenses incurred by any party during the emergency proceedings shall form a part of the Legal Costs under Article 28.3 decided by the Arbitral Tribunal (as to amount and as to payment between the parties of Legal Costs).

9.11 Any order or award of the Emergency Arbitrator (apart from any order adjourning to the Arbitral Tribunal, when formed, any part of the claim for emergency relief) may be confirmed, varied, discharged or revoked, in whole or in part, by order or award made by the Arbitral Tribunal upon application by any party or upon its own initiative.

9.12 Article 9B shall not prejudice any party's right to apply to a state court or other legal authority for any interim or conservatory measures before the formation of the Arbitration Tribunal; and it shall not be treated as an alternative to or substitute for the exercise of such right. During the emergency proceedings, any application to and any order by such court or authority shall be communicated promptly in writing to the Emergency Arbitrator, the Registrar and all other parties.

9.13 Articles 3.3, 13.1–13.4, 14.4, 14.5, 16, 17, 18, 22.3, 22.4, 23, 28, 29, 30, 31 and 32 and the Annex shall apply to emergency proceedings. In addition to the provisions expressly set out there and in Article 9B above, the Emergency Arbitrator and the parties to the emergency proceedings shall also be guided by other provisions of the Arbitration Agreement, whilst recognising that several such provisions may not be fully applicable or appropriate to emergency proceedings. Wherever relevant, the LCIA Court may abridge under any such provisions any period of time (pursuant to Article 22.5).

9.14 Article 9B shall not apply if either: (i) the parties have concluded their arbitration agreement before 1 October 2014 and the parties have not agreed in writing to 'opt in' to Article 9B; or (ii) the parties have agreed in writing at any time to 'opt out' of Article 9B.

**Article 9C Expedited Appointment of Replacement Arbitrator**

9.15 Any party may apply to the LCIA Court for the expedited appointment of a replacement arbitrator under Article 11.

9.16 Such an application shall be made in writing to the Registrar (preferably by electronic means), delivered (or notified) to all other parties to the arbitration; and it shall set out the specific grounds requiring the expedited appointment of the replacement arbitrator.

9.17 The LCIA Court shall determine the application as expeditiously as possible in the circumstances. If the application is granted, for the purpose of expediting the appointment of the replacement arbitrator the LCIA Court may abridge any period of time in the Arbitration Agreement or any other agreement of the parties (pursuant to Article 22.5).

**Article 10  Revocation and Challenges**

10.1 The LCIA Court may revoke any arbitrator's appointment upon its own initiative, at the written request of all other members of the Arbitral Tribunal or upon a written challenge by any party if: (i) that arbitrator gives written notice to the LCIA Court of his or her intent to resign as arbitrator, to be copied to all parties and all other members of the Arbitral Tribunal (if any); (ii) that arbitrator falls seriously ill, refuses or becomes unable or unfit to act; or (iii) circumstances exist that give rise to justifiable doubts as to that arbitrator's impartiality or independence.

10.2 The LCIA Court may determine that an arbitrator is unfit to act under Article 10.1 if that arbitrator: (i) acts in deliberate violation of the Arbitration Agreement; (ii) does not act fairly or impartially as between the parties; or (iii) does not conduct or participate in the arbitration with reasonable efficiency, diligence and industry.

10.3 A party challenging an arbitrator under Article 10.1 shall, within 14 days of the formation of the Arbitral Tribunal or (if later) within 14 days of becoming aware of any grounds described in Article 10.1 or 10.2, deliver a written statement of the reasons for its challenge to the LCIA Court, the Arbitral Tribunal and all other parties. A party may challenge an arbitrator whom it has nominated, or in whose appointment it has participated, only for reasons of which it becomes aware after the appointment has been made by the LCIA Court.

10.4 The LCIA Court shall provide to those other parties and the challenged arbitrator a reasonable opportunity to comment on the challenging party's written statement. The LCIA Court may require at any time further information and materials from the challenging party, the challenged arbitrator, other parties and other members of the Arbitral Tribunal (if any).

10.5 If all other parties agree in writing to the challenge within 14 days of receipt of the written statement, the LCIA Court shall revoke that arbitrator's appointment (without reasons).

10.6 Unless the parties so agree or the challenged arbitrator resigns in writing within 14 days of receipt of the written statement, the LCIA Court shall decide the challenge and, if upheld, shall revoke that arbitrator's appointment. The LCIA Court's decision shall be made in writing, with reasons; and a copy shall be transmitted by the Registrar to the parties, the challenged arbitrator and other members of the Arbitral Tribunal (if any). A challenged arbitrator who resigns in writing prior to the LCIA Court's decision shall not be considered as having admitted any part of the written statement.

10.7 The LCIA Court shall determine the amount of fees and expenses (if any) to be paid for the former arbitrator's services, as it may consider appropriate in the circumstances. The LCIA Court may also determine whether, in what amount and to whom any party should pay forthwith the costs of the challenge; and the LCIA Court may also refer all or any part of such costs to the later decision of the Arbitral Tribunal and/or the LCIA Court under Article 28.

**Article 11  Nomination and Replacement**

11.1 In the event that the LCIA Court determines that justifiable doubts exist as to any arbitral candidate's suitability, independence or impartiality, or if a nominee declines appointment as arbitrator, or if an arbitrator is to be replaced for any reason, the LCIA Court may determine whether or not to follow the original nominating process for such arbitral appointment.

11.2 The LCIA Court may determine that any opportunity given to a party to make any re-nomination (under the Arbitration Agreement or otherwise) shall be waived if not exercised within 14 days (or such lesser or greater time as the LCIA Court may determine), after which the LCIA Court shall appoint the replacement arbitrator without such re-nomination.

**Article 12  Majority Power to Continue Deliberations**

12.1 In exceptional circumstances, where an arbitrator without good cause refuses or persistently fails to participate in the deliberations of an Arbitral Tribunal, the remaining arbitrators jointly may decide (after their written notice of such refusal or failure to the LCIA Court, the parties and the absent arbitrator) to continue the arbitration (including the making of any award) notwithstanding the absence of that other arbitrator, subject to the written approval of the LCIA Court.

12.2 In deciding whether to continue the arbitration, the remaining arbitrators shall take into account the stage of the arbitration, any explanation made by or on behalf of the absent arbitrator for his or her refusal or non-participation, the likely effect upon the legal recognition or enforceability of any award at the seat of the arbitration and such other matters as they consider appropriate in the circumstances. The reasons for such decision shall be stated in any award made by the remaining arbitrators without the participation of the absent arbitrator.

12.3 In the event that the remaining arbitrators decide at any time thereafter not to continue the arbitration without the participation of the absent arbitrator, the remaining arbitrators shall notify in writing the parties and the LCIA Court of such decision; and, in that event, the remaining arbitrators or any party may refer the matter to the LCIA Court for the revocation of the absent arbitrator's appointment and the appointment of a replacement arbitrator under Articles 10 and 11.

## Article 13  Communications between Parties and Arbitral Tribunal

13.1   Following the formation of the Arbitral Tribunal, all communications shall take place directly between the Arbitral Tribunal and the parties (to be copied to the Registrar), unless the Arbitral Tribunal decides that communications should continue to be made through the Registrar.

13.2   Where the Registrar sends any written communication to one party on behalf of the Arbitral Tribunal or the LCIA Court, he or she shall send a copy to each of the other parties.

13.3   Where any party delivers to the Arbitral Tribunal any communication (including statements and documents under Article 15), whether by electronic means or otherwise, it shall deliver a copy to each arbitrator, all other parties and the Registrar; and it shall confirm to the Arbitral Tribunal in writing that it has done or is doing so.

13.4   During the arbitration from the Arbitral Tribunal's formation onwards, no party shall deliberately initiate or attempt to initiate any unilateral contact relating to the arbitration or the parties' dispute with any member of the Arbitral Tribunal or any member of the LCIA Court exercising any function in regard to the arbitration (but not including the Registrar), which has not been disclosed in writing prior to or shortly after the time of such contact to all other parties, all members of the Arbitral Tribunal (if comprised of more than one arbitrator) and the Registrar.

13.5   Prior to the Arbitral Tribunal's formation, unless the parties agree otherwise in writing, any arbitrator, candidate or nominee who is required to participate in the selection of a presiding arbitrator may consult any party in order to obtain the views of that party as to the suitability of any candidate or nominee as presiding arbitrator, provided that such arbitrator, candidate or nominee informs the Registrar of such consultation.

## Article 14  Conduct of Proceedings

14.1   The parties and the Arbitral Tribunal are encouraged to make contact (whether by a hearing in person, telephone conference-call, video conference or exchange of correspondence) as soon as practicable but no later than 21 days from receipt of the Registrar's written notification of the formation of the Arbitral Tribunal.

14.2   The parties may agree on joint proposals for the conduct of their arbitration for consideration by the Arbitral Tribunal. They are encouraged to do so in consultation with the Arbitral Tribunal and consistent with the Arbitral Tribunal's general duties under the Arbitration Agreement.

14.3   Such agreed proposals shall be made by the parties in writing or recorded in writing by the Arbitral Tribunal at the parties' request and with their authority.

14.4   Under the Arbitration Agreement, the Arbitral Tribunal's general duties at all times during the arbitration shall include:

(i) a duty to act fairly and impartially as between all parties, giving each a reasonable opportunity of putting its case and dealing with that of its opponent(s); and

(ii) a duty to adopt procedures suitable to the circumstances of the arbitration, avoiding unnecessary delay and expense, so as to provide a fair, efficient and expeditious means for the final resolution of the parties' dispute.

14.5 The Arbitral Tribunal shall have the widest discretion to discharge these general duties, subject to such mandatory law(s) or rules of law as the Arbitral Tribunal may decide to be applicable; and at all times the parties shall do everything necessary in good faith for the fair, efficient and expeditious conduct of the arbitration, including the Arbitral Tribunal's discharge of its general duties.

14.6 In the case of an Arbitral Tribunal other than a sole arbitrator, the presiding arbitrator, with the prior agreement of its other members and all parties, may make procedural orders alone.

**Article 15 Written Statements**

15.1 Unless the parties have agreed or jointly proposed in writing otherwise or the Arbitral Tribunal should decide differently, the written stage of the arbitration and its procedural time-table shall be as set out in this Article 15.

15.2 Within 28 days of receipt of the Registrar's written notification of the Arbitral Tribunal's formation, the Claimant shall deliver to the Arbitral Tribunal and all other parties either: (i) its written election to have its Request treated as its Statement of Case complying with this Article 15.2; or (ii) its written Statement of Case setting out in sufficient detail the relevant facts and legal submissions on which it relies, together with the relief claimed against all other parties, and all essential documents.

15.3 Within 28 days of receipt of the Claimant's Statement of Case or the Claimant's election to treat the Request as its Statement of Case, the Respondent shall deliver to the Arbitral Tribunal and all other parties either: (i) its written election to have its Response treated as its Statement of Defence and (if applicable) Cross-claim complying with this Article 15.3; or (ii) its written Statement of Defence and (if applicable) Statement of Cross-claim setting out in sufficient detail the relevant facts and legal submissions on which it relies, together with the relief claimed against all other parties, and all essential documents.

15.4 Within 28 days of receipt of the Respondent's Statement of Defence and (if applicable) Statement of Cross-claim or the Respondent's election to treat the Response as its Statement of Defence and (if applicable) Cross-claim, the Claimant shall deliver to the Arbitral Tribunal and all other parties a written Statement of Reply which, where there are any cross-claims, shall also include a Statement of Defence to Cross-claim in the same manner required for a Statement of Defence, together with all essential documents.

15.5 If the Statement of Reply contains a Statement of Defence to Cross-claim, within 28 days of its receipt the Respondent shall deliver to the Arbitral Tribunal and all other parties its written Statement of Reply to the Defence to Cross-claim, together with all essential documents.

15.6 The Arbitral Tribunal may provide additional directions as to any part of the written stage of the arbitration (including witness statements, submissions and evidence), particularly where there are multiple claimants, multiple respondents or any cross-claim between two or more respondents or between two or more claimants.

15.7 No party may submit any further written statement following the last of these Statements, unless otherwise ordered by the Arbitral Tribunal.

15.8 If the Respondent fails to submit a Statement of Defence or the Claimant a Statement of Defence to Cross-claim, or if at any time any party fails to avail itself of the opportunity to present its written case in the manner required under this Article 15 or otherwise by order of the Arbitral Tribunal, the Arbitral Tribunal may nevertheless proceed with the arbitration (with or without a hearing) and make one or more awards.

15.9 As soon as practicable following this written stage of the arbitration, the Arbitral Tribunal shall proceed in such manner as has been agreed in writing by the parties or pursuant to its authority under the Arbitration Agreement.

15.10 In any event, the Arbitral Tribunal shall seek to make its final award as soon as reasonably possible following the last submission from the parties (whether made orally or in writing), in accordance with a timetable notified to the parties and the Registrar as soon as practicable (if necessary, as revised and re-notified from time to time). When the Arbitral Tribunal (not being a sole arbitrator) establishes a time for what it contemplates shall be the last submission from the parties (whether written or oral), it shall set aside adequate time for deliberations as soon as possible after that last submission and notify the parties of the time it has set aside.

**Article 16 Seat(s) of Arbitration and Place(s) of Hearing**

16.1 The parties may agree in writing the seat (or legal place) of their arbitration at any time before the formation of the Arbitral Tribunal and, after such formation, with the prior written consent of the Arbitral Tribunal.

16.2 In default of any such agreement, the seat of the arbitration shall be London (England), unless and until the Arbitral Tribunal orders, in view of the circumstances and after having given the parties a reasonable opportunity to make written comments to the Arbitral Tribunal, that another arbitral seat is more appropriate. Such default seat shall not be considered as a relevant circumstance by the LCIA Court in appointing any arbitrators under Articles 5, 9A, 9B, 9C and 11.

16.3 The Arbitral Tribunal may hold any hearing at any convenient geographical place in consultation with the parties and hold its deliberations at any geographical place of its own choice; and if such place(s) should be elsewhere than the seat of the arbitration, the arbitration shall nonetheless be treated for all purposes as an arbitration conducted at the arbitral seat and any order or award as having been made at that seat.

16.4 The law applicable to the Arbitration Agreement and the arbitration shall be the law applicable at the seat of the arbitration, unless and to the extent that the parties have agreed in writing on the application of other laws or rules of law and such agreement is not prohibited by the law applicable at the arbitral seat.

### Article 17 Language(s) of Arbitration

17.1 The initial language of the arbitration (until the formation of the Arbitral Tribunal) shall be the language or prevailing language of the Arbitration Agreement, unless the parties have agreed in writing otherwise.

17.2 In the event that the Arbitration Agreement is written in more than one language of equal standing, the LCIA Court may, unless the Arbitration Agreement provides that the arbitration proceedings shall be conducted from the outset in more than one language, determine which of those languages shall be the initial language of the arbitration.

17.3 A non-participating or defaulting party shall have no cause for complaint if communications to and from the LCIA Court and Registrar are conducted in the initial language(s) of the arbitration or of the arbitral seat.

17.4 Following the formation of the Arbitral Tribunal, unless the parties have agreed upon the language or languages of the arbitration, the Arbitral Tribunal shall decide upon the language(s) of the arbitration after giving the parties a reasonable opportunity to make written comments and taking into account the initial language(s) of the arbitration and any other matter it may consider appropriate in the circumstances.

17.5 If any document is expressed in a language other than the language(s) of the arbitration and no translation of such document is submitted by the party relying upon the document, the Arbitral Tribunal may order or (if the Arbitral Tribunal has not been formed) the Registrar may request that party to submit a translation of all or any part of that document in any language(s) of the arbitration or of the arbitral seat.

### Article 18 Legal Representatives

18.1 Any party may be represented in the arbitration by one or more authorised legal representatives appearing by name before the Arbitral Tribunal.

18.2 Until the Arbitral Tribunal's formation, the Registrar may request from any party: (i) written proof of the authority granted by that party to any legal representative designated in its Request or Response; and (ii) written confirmation of the names and addresses of all such party's legal representatives in the arbitration.

After its formation, at any time, the Arbitral Tribunal may order any party to provide similar proof or confirmation in any form it considers appropriate.

18.3 Following the Arbitral Tribunal's formation, any intended change or addition by a party to its legal representatives shall be notified promptly in writing to all other parties, the Arbitral Tribunal and the Registrar; and any such intended change or addition shall only take effect in the arbitration subject to the approval of the Arbitral Tribunal.

18.4 The Arbitral Tribunal may withhold approval of any intended change or addition to a party's legal representatives where such change or addition could compromise the composition of the Arbitral Tribunal or the finality of any award (on the grounds of possible conflict or other like impediment). In deciding whether to grant or withhold such approval, the Arbitral Tribunal shall have regard to the circumstances, including: the general principle that a party may be represented by a legal representative chosen by that party, the stage which the arbitration has reached, the efficiency resulting from maintaining the composition of the Arbitral Tribunal (as constituted throughout the arbitration) and any likely wasted costs or loss of time resulting from such change or addition.

18.5 Each party shall ensure that all its legal representatives appearing by name before the Arbitral Tribunal have agreed to comply with the general guidelines contained in the Annex to the LCIA Rules, as a condition of such representation. In permitting any legal representative so to appear, a party shall thereby represent that the legal representative has agreed to such compliance.

18.6 In the event of a complaint by one party against another party's legal representative appearing by name before the Arbitral Tribunal (or of such complaint by the Arbitral Tribunal upon its own initiative), the Arbitral Tribunal may decide, after consulting the parties and granting that legal representative a reasonable opportunity to answer the complaint, whether or not the legal representative has violated the general guidelines. If such violation is found by the Arbitral Tribunal, the Arbitral Tribunal may order any or all of the following sanctions against the legal representative: (i) a written reprimand; (ii) a written caution as to future conduct in the arbitration; and (iii) any other measure necessary to fulfil within the arbitration the general duties required of the Arbitral Tribunal under Articles 14.4(i) and (ii).

**Article 19  Oral Hearing(s)**

19.1 Any party has the right to a hearing before the Arbitral Tribunal on the parties' dispute at any appropriate stage of the arbitration (as decided by the Arbitral Tribunal), unless the parties have agreed in writing upon a documents-only arbitration. For this purpose, a hearing may consist of several part-hearings (as decided by the Arbitral Tribunal).

19.2 The Arbitral Tribunal shall organise the conduct of any hearing in advance, in consultation with the parties. The Arbitral Tribunal shall have the fullest authority under the Arbitration Agreement to establish the conduct of a hearing, including its date, form, content, procedure, time-limits and geographical place. As to form, a hearing may take place by video or telephone conference or in person (or a combination of all three). As to content, the Arbitral Tribunal may require the parties to address a list of specific questions or issues arising from the parties' dispute.

19.3 The Arbitral Tribunal shall give to the parties reasonable notice in writing of any hearing.

19.4 All hearings shall be held in private, unless the parties agree otherwise in writing.

**Article 20 Witness(es)**

20.1 Before any hearing, the Arbitral Tribunal may order any party to give written notice of the identity of each witness that party wishes to call (including rebuttal witnesses), as well as the subject-matter of that witness's testimony, its content and its relevance to the issues in the arbitration.

20.2 Subject to any order otherwise by the Arbitral Tribunal, the testimony of a witness may be presented by a party in written form, either as a signed statement or like document.

20.3 The Arbitral Tribunal may decide the time, manner and form in which these written materials shall be exchanged between the parties and presented to the Arbitral Tribunal; and it may allow, refuse or limit the written and oral testimony of witnesses (whether witnesses of fact or expert witnesses).

20.4 The Arbitral Tribunal and any party may request that a witness, on whose written testimony another party relies, should attend for oral questioning at a hearing before the Arbitral Tribunal. If the Arbitral Tribunal orders that other party to secure the attendance of that witness and the witness refuses or fails to attend the hearing without good cause, the Arbitral Tribunal may place such weight on the written testimony or exclude all or any part thereof altogether as it considers appropriate in the circumstances.

20.5 Subject to the mandatory provisions of any applicable law, rules of law and any order of the Arbitral Tribunal otherwise, it shall not be improper for any party or its legal representatives to interview any potential witness for the purpose of presenting his or her testimony in written form to the Arbitral Tribunal or producing such person as an oral witness at any hearing.

20.6 Subject to any order by the Arbitral Tribunal otherwise, any individual intending to testify to the Arbitral Tribunal may be treated as a witness notwithstanding that the individual is a party to the arbitration or was, remains or has become an officer, employee, owner or shareholder of any party or is otherwise identified with any party.

20.7 Subject to the mandatory provisions of any applicable law, the Arbitral Tribunal shall be entitled (but not required) to administer any appropriate oath to any witness at any hearing, prior to the oral testimony of that witness.

20.8 Any witness who gives oral testimony at a hearing before the Arbitral Tribunal may be questioned by each of the parties under the control of the Arbitral Tribunal. The Arbitral Tribunal may put questions at any stage of such testimony.

**Article 21 Expert(s) to Arbitral Tribunal**

21.1 The Arbitral Tribunal, after consultation with the parties, may appoint one or more experts to report in writing to the Arbitral Tribunal and the parties on specific issues in the arbitration, as identified by the Arbitral Tribunal.

21.2 Any such expert shall be and remain impartial and independent of the parties; and he or she shall sign a written declaration to such effect, delivered to the Arbitral Tribunal and copied to all parties.

21.3 The Arbitral Tribunal may require any party at any time to give to such expert any relevant information or to provide access to any relevant documents, goods, samples, property, site or thing for inspection under that party's control on such terms as the Arbitral Tribunal thinks appropriate in the circumstances.

21.4 If any party so requests or the Arbitral Tribunal considers it necessary, the Arbitral Tribunal may order the expert, after delivery of the expert's written report, to participate in a hearing at which the parties shall have a reasonable opportunity to question the expert on the report and to present witnesses in order to testify on relevant issues arising from the report.

21.5 The fees and expenses of any expert appointed by the Arbitral Tribunal under this Article 21 may be paid out of the deposits payable by the parties under Article 24 and shall form part of the Arbitration Costs under Article 28.

**Article 22 Additional Powers**

22.1 The Arbitral Tribunal shall have the power, upon the application of any party or (save for sub-paragraphs (viii), (ix) and (x) below) upon its own initiative, but in either case only after giving the parties a reasonable opportunity to state their views and upon such terms (as to costs and otherwise) as the Arbitral Tribunal may decide:

(i) to allow a party to supplement, modify or amend any claim, defence, cross-claim, defence to cross-claim and reply, including a Request, Response and any other written statement, submitted by such party;

(ii) to abridge or extend (even where the period of time has expired) any period of time prescribed under the Arbitration Agreement, any other agreement of the parties or any order made by the Arbitral Tribunal;

(iii) to conduct such enquiries as may appear to the Arbitral Tribunal to be necessary or expedient, including whether and to what extent the Arbitral Tribunal should itself take the initiative in identifying relevant issues and ascertaining relevant facts and the law(s) or rules of law applicable to the Arbitration Agreement, the arbitration and the merits of the parties' dispute;

(iv) to order any party to make any documents, goods, samples, property, site or thing under its control available for inspection by the Arbitral Tribunal, any other party, any expert to such party and any expert to the Tribunal;

(v) to order any party to produce to the Arbitral Tribunal and to other parties documents or copies of documents in their possession, custody or power which the Arbitral Tribunal decides to be relevant;

(vi) to decide whether or not to apply any strict rules of evidence (or any other rules) as to the admissibility, relevance or weight of any material tendered by a party on any issue of fact or expert opinion; and to decide the time, manner and form in which such material should be exchanged between the parties and presented to the Arbitral Tribunal;

(vii) to order compliance with any legal obligation, payment of compensation for breach of any legal obligation and specific performance of any agreement (including any arbitration agreement or any contract relating to land);

(viii) to allow one or more third persons to be joined in the arbitration as a party provided any such third person and the applicant party have consented to such joinder in writing following the Commencement Date or (if earlier) in the Arbitration Agreement; and thereafter to make a single final award, or separate awards, in respect of all parties so implicated in the arbitration;

(ix) to order, with the approval of the LCIA Court, the consolidation of the arbitration with one or more other arbitrations into a single arbitration subject to the LCIA Rules where all the parties to the arbitrations to be consolidated so agree in writing;

(x) to order, with the approval of the LCIA Court, the consolidation of the arbitration with one or more other arbitrations subject to the LCIA Rules commenced under the same arbitration agreement or any compatible arbitration agreement(s) between the same disputing parties, provided that no arbitral tribunal has yet been formed by the LCIA Court for such other arbitration(s) or, if already formed, that such tribunal(s) is(are) composed of the same arbitrators; and

(xi) to order the discontinuance of the arbitration if it appears to the Arbitral Tribunal that the arbitration has been abandoned by the parties or all claims and any cross-claims withdrawn by the parties, provided that, after fixing a reasonable period of time within which the parties shall be invited to agree or to object to such discontinuance, no party has stated its written objection to the Arbitral Tribunal to such discontinuance upon the expiry of such period of time.

22.2 By agreeing to arbitration under the Arbitration Agreement, the parties shall be treated as having agreed not to apply to any state court or other legal authority for any order available from the Arbitral Tribunal (if formed) under Article 22.1, except with the agreement in writing of all parties.

22.3 The Arbitral Tribunal shall decide the parties' dispute in accordance with the law(s) or rules of law chosen by the parties as applicable to the merits of their dispute. If and to the extent that the Arbitral Tribunal decides that the parties have made no such choice, the Arbitral Tribunal shall apply the law(s) or rules of law which it considers appropriate.

22.4 The Arbitral Tribunal shall only apply to the merits of the dispute principles deriving from "ex aequo et bono", "amiable composition" or "honourable engagement" where the parties have so agreed in writing.

22.5 Subject to any order of the Arbitral Tribunal under Article 22.1(ii), the LCIA Court may also abridge or extend any period of time under the Arbitration Agreement or other agreement of the parties (even where the period of time has expired).

22.6 Without prejudice to the generality of Articles 22.1(ix) and (x), the LCIA Court may determine, after giving the parties a reasonable opportunity to state their views, that two or more arbitrations, subject to the LCIA Rules and commenced under the same arbitration agreement between the same disputing parties, shall be consolidated to form one single arbitration subject to the LCIA Rules, provided that no arbitral tribunal has yet been formed by the LCIA Court for any of the arbitrations to be consolidated.

**Article 23 Jurisdiction and Authority**

23.1 The Arbitral Tribunal shall have the power to rule upon its own jurisdiction and authority, including any objection to the initial or continuing existence, validity, effectiveness or scope of the Arbitration Agreement.

23.2 For that purpose, an arbitration clause which forms or was intended to form part of another agreement shall be treated as an arbitration agreement independent of that other agreement. A decision by the Arbitral Tribunal that such other agreement is non-existent, invalid or ineffective shall not entail (of itself) the non-existence, invalidity or ineffectiveness of the arbitration clause.

23.3 An objection by a Respondent that the Arbitral Tribunal does not have jurisdiction shall be raised as soon as possible but not later than the time for its Statement of Defence; and a like objection by any party responding to a cross-claiming party shall be raised as soon as possible but not later than the time for its Statement of Defence to Cross-claim. An objection that the Arbitral Tribunal is exceeding the scope of its authority shall be raised promptly after the Arbitral Tribunal has indicated its intention to act upon the matter alleged to lie beyond its authority. The Arbitral Tribunal may nevertheless admit an untimely objection as to its jurisdiction or authority if it considers the delay justified in the circumstances.

23.4 The Arbitral Tribunal may decide the objection to its jurisdiction or authority in an award as to jurisdiction or authority or later in an award on the merits, as it considers appropriate in the circumstances.

23.5 By agreeing to arbitration under the Arbitration Agreement, after the formation of the Arbitral Tribunal the parties shall be treated as having agreed not to apply to any state court or other legal authority for any relief regarding the Arbitral Tribunal's jurisdiction or authority, except (i) with the prior agreement in writing of all parties to the arbitration, or (ii) the prior authorisation of the Arbitral Tribunal, or (iii) following the latter's award on the objection to its jurisdiction or authority.

**Article 24  Deposits**

24.1 The LCIA Court may direct the parties, in such proportions and at such times as it thinks appropriate, to make one or more payments to the LCIA on account of the Arbitration Costs. Such payments deposited by the parties may be applied by the LCIA Court to pay any item of such Arbitration Costs (including the LCIA's own fees and expenses) in accordance with the LCIA Rules.

24.2 All payments made by parties on account of the Arbitration Costs shall be held by the LCIA in trust under English law in England, to be disbursed or otherwise applied by the LCIA in accordance with the LCIA Rules and invested having regard also to the interests of the LCIA. Each payment made by a party shall be credited by the LCIA with interest at the rate from time to time credited to an overnight deposit of that amount with the bank(s) engaged by the LCIA to manage deposits from time to time; and any surplus income (beyond such interest) shall accrue for the sole benefit of the LCIA. In the event that payments (with such interest) exceed the total amount of the Arbitration Costs at the conclusion of the arbitration, the excess amount shall be returned by the LCIA to the parties as the ultimate default beneficiaries of the trust.

24.3 Save for exceptional circumstances, the Arbitral Tribunal should not proceed with the arbitration without having ascertained from the Registrar that the LCIA is or will be in requisite funds as regards outstanding and future Arbitration Costs.

24.4 In the event that a party fails or refuses to make any payment on account of the Arbitration Costs as directed by the LCIA Court, the LCIA Court may direct the other party or parties to effect a substitute payment to allow the arbitration to proceed (subject to any order or award on Arbitration Costs).

24.5 In such circumstances, the party effecting the substitute payment may request the Arbitral Tribunal to make an order or award in order to recover that amount as a debt immediately due and payable to that party by the defaulting party, together with any interest.

24.6 Failure by a claiming or cross-claiming party to make promptly and in full any required payment on account of Arbitration Costs may be treated by the Arbitral Tribunal as a withdrawal from the arbitration of the claim or cross-claim respectively, thereby removing such claim or cross-claim (as the case may be) from the scope of the Arbitral Tribunal's jurisdiction under the Arbitration Agreement, subject to any terms decided by the Arbitral Tribunal as to the reinstatement of the claim or cross-claim in the event of subsequent payment by the claiming or cross-claiming party. Such a withdrawal shall not preclude the claiming or cross-claiming party from defending as a respondent any claim or cross-claim made by another party.

## Article 25  Interim and Conservatory Measures

25.1   The Arbitral Tribunal shall have the power upon the application of any party, after giving all other parties a reasonable opportunity to respond to such application and upon such terms as the Arbitral Tribunal considers appropriate in the circumstances:

(i) to order any respondent party to a claim or cross-claim to provide security for all or part of the amount in dispute, by way of deposit or bank guarantee or in any other manner;

(ii) to order the preservation, storage, sale or other disposal of any documents, goods, samples, property, site or thing under the control of any party and relating to the subject-matter of the arbitration; and

(iii) to order on a provisional basis, subject to a final decision in an award, any relief which the Arbitral Tribunal would have power to grant in an award, including the payment of money or the disposition of property as between any parties.

Such terms may include the provision by the applicant party of a cross-indemnity, secured in such manner as the Arbitral Tribunal considers appropriate, for any costs or losses incurred by the respondent party in complying with the Arbitral Tribunal's order. Any amount payable under such cross-indemnity and any consequential relief may be decided by the Arbitral Tribunal by one or more awards in the arbitration.

25.2   The Arbitral Tribunal shall have the power upon the application of a party, after giving all other parties a reasonable opportunity to respond to such application, to order any claiming or cross-claiming party to provide or procure security for Legal Costs and Arbitration Costs by way of deposit or bank guarantee or in any other manner and upon such terms as the Arbitral Tribunal considers appropriate in the circumstances. Such terms may include the provision by that other party of a cross-indemnity, itself secured in such manner as the Arbitral Tribunal considers appropriate, for any costs and losses incurred by such claimant or cross-claimant in complying with the Arbitral Tribunal's order. Any amount payable under such cross-indemnity and any consequential relief may be decided by the Arbitral Tribunal by one or more awards in the arbitration. In the event that a claiming or cross-claiming party does not comply with any order to provide security, the Arbitral Tribunal may stay that party's claims or cross-claims or dismiss them by an award.

25.3   The power of the Arbitral Tribunal under Article 25.1 shall not prejudice any party's right to apply to a state court or other legal authority for interim or conservatory measures to similar effect: (i) before the formation of the Arbitral

Tribunal; and (ii) after the formation of the Arbitral Tribunal, in exceptional cases and with the Arbitral Tribunal's authorisation, until the final award. After the Commencement Date, any application and any order for such measures before the formation of the Arbitral Tribunal shall be communicated promptly in writing by the applicant party to the Registrar; after its formation, also to the Arbitral Tribunal; and in both cases also to all other parties.

25.4 By agreeing to arbitration under the Arbitration Agreement, the parties shall be taken to have agreed not to apply to any state court or other legal authority for any order for security for Legal Costs or Arbitration Costs.

**Article 26 Award(s)**

26.1 The Arbitral Tribunal may make separate awards on different issues at different times, including interim payments on account of any claim or cross-claim (including Legal and Arbitration Costs). Such awards shall have the same status as any other award made by the Arbitral Tribunal.

26.2 The Arbitral Tribunal shall make any award in writing and, unless all parties agree in writing otherwise, shall state the reasons upon which such award is based. The award shall also state the date when the award is made and the seat of the arbitration; and it shall be signed by the Arbitral Tribunal or those of its members assenting to it.

26.3 An award may be expressed in any currency, unless the parties have agreed otherwise.

26.4 Unless the parties have agreed otherwise, the Arbitral Tribunal may order that simple or compound interest shall be paid by any party on any sum awarded at such rates as the Arbitral Tribunal decides to be appropriate (without being bound by rates of interest practised by any state court or other legal authority) in respect of any period which the Arbitral Tribunal decides to be appropriate ending not later than the date upon which the award is complied with.

26.5 Where there is more than one arbitrator and the Arbitral Tribunal fails to agree on any issue, the arbitrators shall decide that issue by a majority. Failing a majority decision on any issue, the presiding arbitrator shall decide that issue.

26.6 If any arbitrator refuses or fails to sign the award, the signatures of the majority or (failing a majority) of the presiding arbitrator shall be sufficient, provided that the reason for the omitted signature is stated in the award by the majority or by the presiding arbitrator.

26.7 The sole or presiding arbitrator shall be responsible for delivering the award to the LCIA Court, which shall transmit to the parties the award authenticated by the Registrar as an LCIA award, provided that all Arbitration Costs have been paid in full to the LCIA in accordance with Articles 24 and 28. Such transmission may be made by any electronic means, in addition to paper form (if so requested by any party). In the event of any disparity between electronic and paper forms, the paper form shall prevail.

26.8 Every award (including reasons for such award) shall be final and binding on the parties. The parties undertake to carry out any award immediately and without any delay (subject only to Article 27); and the parties also waive irrevocably their right to any form of appeal, review or recourse to any state court or other legal authority, insofar as such waiver shall not be prohibited under any applicable law.

26.9 In the event of any final settlement of the parties' dispute, the Arbitral Tribunal may decide to make an award recording the settlement if the parties jointly so request in writing (a "Consent Award"), provided always that such Consent Award shall contain an express statement on its face that it is an award made at the parties' joint request and with their consent. A Consent Award need not contain reasons. If the parties do not jointly request a Consent Award, on written confirmation by the parties to the LCIA Court that a final settlement has been reached, the Arbitral Tribunal shall be discharged and the arbitration proceedings concluded by the LCIA Court, subject to payment by the parties of any outstanding Arbitration Costs in accordance with Articles 24 and 28.

**Article 27  Correction of Award(s) and Additional Award(s)**

27.1 Within 28 days of receipt of any award, a party may by written notice to the Registrar (copied to all other parties) request the Arbitral Tribunal to correct in the award any error in computation, any clerical or typographical error, any ambiguity or any mistake of a similar nature. If the Arbitral Tribunal considers the request to be justified, after consulting the parties, it shall make the correction within 28 days of receipt of the request. Any correction shall take the form of a memorandum by the Arbitral Tribunal.

27.2 The Arbitral Tribunal may also correct any error (including any error in computation, any clerical or typographical error or any error of a similar nature) upon its own initiative in the form of a memorandum within 28 days of the date of the award, after consulting the parties.

27.3 Within 28 days of receipt of the final award, a party may by written notice to the Registrar (copied to all other parties), request the Arbitral Tribunal to make an additional award as to any claim or cross-claim presented in the arbitration but not decided in any award. If the Arbitral Tribunal considers the request to be justified, after consulting the parties, it shall make the additional award within 56 days of receipt of the request.

27.4 As to any claim or cross-claim presented in the arbitration but not decided in any award, the Arbitral Tribunal may also make an additional award upon its own initiative within 28 days of the date of the award, after consulting the parties.

27.5 The provisions of Article 26.2 to 26.7 shall apply to any memorandum or additional award made hereunder. A memorandum shall be treated as part of the award.

**Article 28  Arbitration Costs and Legal Costs**

28.1 The costs of the arbitration other than the legal or other expenses incurred by the parties themselves (the "Arbitration Costs") shall be determined by the LCIA

Court in accordance with the Schedule of Costs. The parties shall be jointly and severally liable to the LCIA and the Arbitral Tribunal for such Arbitration Costs.

28.2 The Arbitral Tribunal shall specify by an award the amount of the Arbitration Costs determined by the LCIA Court (in the absence of a final settlement of the parties' dispute regarding liability for such costs). The Arbitral Tribunal shall decide the proportions in which the parties shall bear such Arbitration Costs. If the Arbitral Tribunal has decided that all or any part of the Arbitration Costs shall be borne by a party other than a party which has already covered such costs by way of a payment to the LCIA under Article 24, the latter party shall have the right to recover the appropriate amount of Arbitration Costs from the former party.

28.3 The Arbitral Tribunal shall also have the power to decide by an award that all or part of the legal or other expenses incurred by a party (the "Legal Costs") be paid by another party. The Arbitral Tribunal shall decide the amount of such Legal Costs on such reasonable basis as it thinks appropriate. The Arbitral Tribunal shall not be required to apply the rates or procedures for assessing such costs practised by any state court or other legal authority.

28.4 The Arbitral Tribunal shall make its decisions on both Arbitration Costs and Legal Costs on the general principle that costs should reflect the parties' relative success and failure in the award or arbitration or under different issues, except where it appears to the Arbitral Tribunal that in the circumstances the application of such a general principle would be inappropriate under the Arbitration Agreement or otherwise. The Arbitral Tribunal may also take into account the parties' conduct in the arbitration, including any co-operation in facilitating the proceedings as to time and cost and any non-co-operation resulting in undue delay and unnecessary expense. Any decision on costs by the Arbitral Tribunal shall be made with reasons in the award containing such decision.

28.5 In the event that the parties have howsoever agreed before their dispute that one or more parties shall pay the whole or any part of the Arbitration Costs or Legal Costs whatever the result of any dispute, arbitration or award, such agreement (in order to be effective) shall be confirmed by the parties in writing after the Commencement Date.

28.6 If the arbitration is abandoned, suspended, withdrawn or concluded, by agreement or otherwise, before the final award is made, the parties shall remain jointly and severally liable to pay to the LCIA and the Arbitral Tribunal the Arbitration Costs determined by the LCIA Court.

28.7 In the event that the Arbitration Costs are less than the deposits received by the LCIA under Article 24, there shall be a refund by the LCIA to the parties in such proportions as the parties may agree in writing, or failing such agreement, in the same proportions and to the same payers as the deposits were paid to the LCIA.

**Article 29 Determinations and Decisions by LCIA Court**

29.1 The determinations of the LCIA Court with respect to all matters relating to the arbitration shall be conclusive and binding upon the parties and the Arbitral

Tribunal, unless otherwise directed by the LCIA Court. Save for reasoned decisions on arbitral challenges under Article 10, such determinations are to be treated as administrative in nature; and the LCIA Court shall not be required to give reasons for any such determination.

29.2   To the extent permitted by any applicable law, the parties shall be taken to have waived any right of appeal or review in respect of any determination and decision of the LCIA Court to any state court or other legal authority. If such appeal or review takes place due to mandatory provisions of any applicable law or otherwise, the LCIA Court may determine whether or not the arbitration should continue, notwithstanding such appeal or review.

**Article 30  Confidentiality**

30.1   The parties undertake as a general principle to keep confidential all awards in the arbitration, together with all materials in the arbitration created for the purpose of the arbitration and all other documents produced by another party in the proceedings not otherwise in the public domain, save and to the extent that disclosure may be required of a party by legal duty, to protect or pursue a legal right, or to enforce or challenge an award in legal proceedings before a state court or other legal authority.

30.2   The deliberations of the Arbitral Tribunal shall remain confidential to its members, save as required by any applicable law and to the extent that disclosure of an arbitrator's refusal to participate in the arbitration is required of the other members of the Arbitral Tribunal under Articles 10, 12, 26 and 27.

30.3   The LCIA does not publish any award or any part of an award without the prior written consent of all parties and the Arbitral Tribunal.

**Article 31  Limitation of Liability**

31.1   None of the LCIA (including its officers, members and employees), the LCIA Court (including its President, Vice-Presidents, Honourary Vice-Presidents and members), the Registrar (including any deputy Registrar), any arbitrator, any Emergency Arbitrator and any expert to the Arbitral Tribunal shall be liable to any party howsoever for any act or omission in connection with any arbitration, save: (i) where the act or omission is shown by that party to constitute conscious and deliberate wrongdoing committed by the body or person alleged to be liable to that party; or (ii) to the extent that any part of this provision is shown to be prohibited by any applicable law.

31.2   After the award has been made and all possibilities of any memorandum or additional award under Article 27 have lapsed or been exhausted, neither the LCIA (including its officers, members and employees), the LCIA Court (including its President, Vice-Presidents, Honourary Vice-Presidents and members), the Registrar (including any deputy Registrar), any arbitrator, any Emergency Arbitrator or any expert to the Arbitral Tribunal shall be under any legal obligation to make any statement to any person about any matter concerning the arbitration; nor shall any party seek to make any of these bodies or persons a witness in any legal or other proceedings arising out of the arbitration.

**Article 32 General Rules**

32.1 A party who knows that any provision of the Arbitration Agreement has not been complied with and yet proceeds with the arbitration without promptly stating its objection as to such non-compliance to the Registrar (before the formation of the Arbitral Tribunal) or the Arbitral Tribunal (after its formation), shall be treated as having irrevocably waived its right to object for all purposes.

32.2 For all matters not expressly provided in the Arbitration Agreement, the LCIA Court, the LCIA, the Registrar, the Arbitral Tribunal and each of the parties shall act at all times in good faith, respecting the spirit of the Arbitration Agreement, and shall make every reasonable effort to ensure that any award is legally recognised and enforceable at the arbitral seat.

32.3 If and to the extent that any part of the Arbitration Agreement is decided by the Arbitral Tribunal, the Emergency Arbitrator, or any court or other legal authority of competent jurisdiction to be invalid, ineffective or unenforceable, such decision shall not, of itself, adversely affect any order or award by the Arbitral Tribunal or the Emergency Arbitrator or any other part of the Arbitration Agreement which shall remain in full force and effect, unless prohibited by any applicable law.

**Index (in alphabetical order)**

| | |
|---|---|
| *Arbitral Tribunal:* | *see Article 5.2;* |
| *Arbitration Agreement:* | *see Preamble;* |
| *Arbitration Costs:* | *see Article 28.1;* |
| *Claimant:* | *see Articles 1.1 & 1.5;* |
| *Commencement Date:* | *see Article 1.4;* |
| *Consent Award:* | *see Article 26.9;* |
| *Cross-claim:* | *see Article 2.1(iii);* |
| *Emergency Arbitrator:* | *see Articles 5.2 & 9.4;* |
| *LCIA Court:* | *see Article 3.1;* |
| *LCIA Rules:* | *See Preamble;* |
| *Legal Costs:* | *see Article 28.3;* |
| *Legal Representatives:* | *see Articles 1.1(i); 2.1(i), 18.1, 18.3 & 18.4;* |
| *Registrar:* | *see Articles 1.1 & 3.2;* |

| | |
|---|---|
| *Request:* | see Article 1.1; |
| *Respondent:* | see Articles 1.1(iii) & 2.5; |
| *Response:* | see Article 2.1; |
| *Special Fee:* | see Article 9.5; |
| *Statement of Case* | see Article 15.2; |
| *Statement of Defence* | see Article 15.3; |
| *Statement of Cross-claim* | see Article 15.3; |
| *Statement of Defence to Cross-claim* | see Article 15.4; and |
| *Statement of Reply* | see Article 15.4. |

*(N.B. This Index comprises both defined and other undefined terms. All references to any person or party include both masculine and feminine).*

## ANNEX TO THE LCIA RULES

*General Guidelines for the Parties' Legal Representatives*
*(Articles 18.5 and 18.6 of the LCIA Rules)*

*Paragraph 1*: These general guidelines are intended to promote the good and equal conduct of the parties' legal representatives appearing by name within the arbitration. Nothing in these guidelines is intended to derogate from the Arbitration Agreement or to undermine any legal representative's primary duty of loyalty to the party represented in the arbitration or the obligation to present that party's case effectively to the Arbitral Tribunal. Nor shall these guidelines derogate from any mandatory laws, rules of law, professional rules or codes of conduct if and to the extent that any are shown to apply to a legal representative appearing in the arbitration.

*Paragraph 2*: A legal representative should not engage in activities intended unfairly to obstruct the arbitration or to jeopardise the finality of any award, including repeated challenges to an arbitrator's appointment or to the jurisdiction or authority of the Arbitral Tribunal known to be unfounded by that legal representative.

*Paragraph 3*: A legal representative should not knowingly make any false statement to the Arbitral Tribunal or the LCIA Court.

*Paragraph 4*: A legal representative should not knowingly procure or assist in the preparation of or rely upon any false evidence presented to the Arbitral Tribunal or the LCIA Court.

*Paragraph 5*: A legal representative should not knowingly conceal or assist in the concealment of any document (or any part thereof) which is ordered to be produced by the Arbitral Tribunal.

*Paragraph 6*: During the arbitration proceedings, a legal representative should not deliberately initiate or attempt to initiate with any member of the Arbitral Tribunal or with any member of the LCIA Court making any determination or decision in regard to the arbitration (but not including the Registrar) any unilateral contact relating to the arbitration or the parties' dispute, which has not been disclosed in writing prior to or shortly after the time of such contact to all other parties, all members of the Arbitral Tribunal (if comprised of more than one arbitrator) and the Registrar in accordance with Article 13.4.

*Paragraph 7*: In accordance with Articles 18.5 and 18.6, the Arbitral Tribunal may decide whether a legal representative has violated these general guidelines and, if so, how to exercise its discretion to impose any or all of the sanctions listed in Article 18.6.

## APPENDIX 2

## SCHEDULE OF ARBITRATION COSTS (LCIA)
*effective 1 October 2014*

For arbitrations conducted under the LCIA arbitration rules (the Rules).

This schedule of arbitration costs (the Schedule), as amended from time to time by the LCIA, forms part of the Rules, and will apply in all current and future arbitrations as from its effective date.

### 1. Administrative charges

1(i)  Registration Fee (payable in advance with the Request for Arbitration: non- refundable). **£1,750**

1(ii)  Time spent* by the Secretariat of the LCIA in the administration of the arbitration.**

| | |
|---|---|
| Registrar / Deputy Registrar | **£250 per hour** |
| Counsel | **£225 per hour** |
| Case administrators | **£175 per hour** |
| Casework accounting functions | **£150 per hour** |

1(iii)  Time spent by members of the LCIA Court in carrying out their functions in deciding any challenge brought under the Rules.**

**at hourly rates advised by members of the LCIA Court**

1(iv)  A sum equivalent to 5% of the fees of the Tribunal (excluding expenses) in respect of the LCIA's general overhead.**

1(v)  Expenses incurred by the Secretariat and by members of the LCIA Court, in connection with the arbitration (such as postage, telephone, facsimile, travel etc.), and additional arbitration support services, whether provided by the Secretariat or by the members of the LCIA Court from their own resources or otherwise.**

1(vi)  The LCIA's charges will be invoiced in sterling, but may be paid in other convertible currencies, at rates prevailing at the time of payment.

1(vii)  Charges may be subject to Value Added Tax at the prevailing rate.

## 2. Fees and expenses of the Tribunal

2(i) The Tribunal's fees will be calculated by reference to work done by its members in connection with the arbitration and will be charged at rates appropriate to the particular circumstances of the case, including its complexity and the special qualifications of the arbitrators. The Tribunal shall agree in writing upon fee rates conforming to the Schedule prior to its appointment by the LCIA Court. The rates will be advised by the Registrar to the parties at the time of the appointment of the Tribunal, but may be reviewed if the duration or a change in the circumstances of the arbitration requires.

Fees shall be at hourly rates **not exceeding £450**.

However, in exceptional cases, the rate may be higher, provided that, in such cases, (i) the fees of the Tribunal shall be fixed by the LCIA Court on the recommendation of the Registrar, following consultations with the arbitrator(s), and (ii) the fees shall be agreed expressly by all parties.

2(ii) The Tribunal's fees may include a charge for time spent travelling.

2(iii) The Tribunal's fees may also include a charge for time reserved but not used as a result of late postponement or cancellation of hearings, provided that the basis for such charge shall be advised in writing to, and approved by, the LCIA Court and that the parties have been informed in advance.

2(iv) The Tribunal may also recover such expenses as are reasonably incurred in connection with the arbitration, and as are reasonable in amount, provided that claims for expenses should be supported by invoices or receipts.

2(v) The Tribunal's fees shall be invoiced in the currency of account between the Tribunal and the parties.

2(vi) In the event of the revocation of the appointment of any arbitrator, pursuant to the provisions of Article 10 of the Rules, the LCIA Court shall, in accordance with Article 10.7, determine the amount of fees and expenses (if any) to be paid for the former arbitrator's services as it may consider appropriate in all the circumstances.

2(vii) Charges may be subject to Value Added Tax at the prevailing rate.

## 3. Deposits

3(i) The LCIA Court may direct the parties, in such proportions and at such times as it thinks appropriate, to make one or more payments to the LCIA on account of the costs of the arbitration, other than the legal or other expenses incurred by the parties themselves (the Arbitration Costs). Such payments deposited by the parties may be applied by the LCIA Court to pay any item of such Arbitration Costs (including the LCIA's own fees and expenses) in accordance with the LCIA Rules.

3(ii) All payments made by parties on account of the Arbitration Costs shall be held by the LCIA in trust under English law in England, to be disbursed or otherwise applied by the LCIA in accordance with the LCIA Rules and invested having regard also to the interests of the LCIA. Each payment made by a party shall be credited by the LCIA with interest at the rate from time to time credited to an overnight deposit of that amount with the bank(s) engaged by the LCIA to manage deposits from time to time; and any surplus income (beyond such interest) shall accrue for the sole benefit of the LCIA. In the event that payments (with such interest) exceed the total amount of the Arbitration Costs at the conclusion of the arbitration, the excess amount shall be returned by the LCIA to the parties as the ultimate default beneficiaries of the trust.

3(iii) Save for exceptional circumstances, the Arbitral Tribunal should not proceed with the arbitration without having ascertained from the Registrar that the LCIA is or will be in requisite funds as regards outstanding and future Arbitration Costs.

3(iv) In the event that a party fails or refuses to make any payment on account of the Arbitration Costs as directed by the LCIA Court, the LCIA Court may direct the other party or parties to effect a substitute payment to allow the arbitration to proceed (subject to any order or award on Arbitration Costs).

3(v) In such circumstances, the party effecting the substitute payment may request the Arbitral Tribunal to make an order or award in order to recover that amount as a debt immediately due and payable to that party by the defaulting party, together with any interest.

**4. Interim payments**

When interim payments are required to cover any part of the Arbitration Costs, including the LCIA's administrative charges; the fees or expenses of members of the LCIA Court, the Tribunal's fees or expenses, including the fees or expenses of any expert appointed by the Tribunal, the fees or expenses of any Secretary to the Tribunal; or charges for hearing rooms and other support services, such payments may be made against the invoices for any of the above from funds held on deposit. If no or insufficient funds are held at the time the interim payment is required, the invoices for any of the above may be submitted for payment direct by the parties.

## 5. Registrar's authority

5(i) For the purposes of sections 3(i) and 3(iv) above, and of Articles 24.1 and 24.4 of the Rules, the Registrar has the authority of the LCIA Court to make the directions referred to, under the supervision of the Court.

5(ii) For the purposes of section 4 above, and of Article 24.1 of the Rules, the Registrar has the authority of the LCIA Court to approve the payments referred to.

5(iii) Any request by an arbitrator for payment on account of his fees shall be supported by a fee note, which shall include, or be accompanied by, a detailed breakdown of the time spent at the rates that have been advised to the parties by the LCIA, and the fee note will be forwarded to the parties prior to settlement of the account.

5(iv) Any dispute regarding the LCIA's administrative charges, or the fees and expenses of the Tribunal shall be determined by the LCIA Court.

## 6. Arbitration costs

6(i) The parties shall be jointly and severally liable to the Tribunal and the LCIA for the costs of the arbitration (other than the legal or other costs incurred by the parties themselves).

6(ii) Any bank charges incurred on any transfer of funds by the parties to the LCIA shall be borne exclusively by the party or parties transferring the funds.

6(iii) In accordance with Article 26.7 of the Rules, the Tribunal's Award(s) shall be transmitted to the parties by the LCIA Court provided that the costs of the arbitration have been paid to the LCIA in accordance with Article 28 of the Rules.

## 7. Emergency Arbitrator

7(i) Application fee (payable with the application for the appointment of an Emergency Arbitrator under Article 9B of the Rules: non-refundable).

**£8,000**

7(ii) Emergency Arbitrator's fee, to cover time charges and expenses (payable with the application for the appointment of an Emergency Arbitrator: non-refundable if the LCIA Court appoints an Emergency Arbitrator).

**£20,000**

7(iii)  The Emergency Arbitrator's fee may be increased by the LCIA Court on the recommendation of the Registrar at any time during the emergency proceedings if the particular circumstances of the case are deemed to warrant a higher fee.

7(iv)  In the event of a challenge by any party to the Emergency Arbitrator, the party that applied for the appointment of the Emergency Arbitrator shall pay forthwith to the LCIA such further sum as may be directed by the LCIA Court in respect of the fees and expenses of the individual or division appointed to decide the challenge.

7(v)  If the LCIA refuses an application for the appointment of an Emergency Arbitrator, the Emergency Arbitrator's fee shall be treated as a deposit lodged by the applicant party on account of the Arbitration Costs in accordance with Article 24 of the Rules and the Schedule.

---

\* Minimum unit of time in all cases: 15 minutes.
\*\* Items 1(ii), 1(iii), 1(iv) and 1(v) above, are payable on interim invoice; with the award, or as directed by the LCIA Court under Article 24.1 of the Rules.

APPENDIX 3

# CONSTITUTION OF THE LCIA ARBITRATION COURT

Adopted 1990, amended 1998, 2002, 2008, 2009, 2010 and 2011

A. COMPOSITION

1. The Arbitration Court ("the Court") shall, subject to Articles A.4 and B.3, consist of up to thirty five members appointed by the Board of Directors of the LCIA ("the Board") on the recommendation of the Court, of whom up to six shall be from the United Kingdom and the remainder from other countries.

2. The members of the Court shall serve for a five-year term. Save in exceptional circumstances, they shall not be re-appointed to consecutive terms.

3. The Court shall make recommendations to the Board to fill appointments arising from retirements or casual vacancies and on other issues relating to the composition of the Court from time to time as appropriate.

4. Any member appointed on the nomination of any body other than the Court, entitled so to nominate by virtue of an agreement reached between the LCIA and that body, may be appointed in addition to the number of members prescribed by Article A.1.

B. OFFICERS OF THE COURT

1. The Officers of the Court shall consist of:

   (a) a President appointed by the Board on the recommendation of the Court, to serve for a period of up to three years, and to be eligible for reappointment; and

   (b) up to seven Vice-Presidents appointed by the Court, to serve until the expiry of their terms as members of the Court. Due regard shall be given to a balanced international representation.

2. At the request of the President or, if not available, of the Registrar or a deputy Registrar, any Vice-President shall be entitled to exercise any of the functions and powers of the President.

3. Former Presidents will be invited by the Court to attend and to vote at Court meetings as Honorary Vice Presidents, for as long as they wish, and are not

deemed to be ordinary members for the purposes of the number of members prescribed by Article A.1, though they shall be eligible for appointment for the purposes of Article D.3

## C. REGISTRARS AND DEPUTY REGISTRARS

**1.** There shall be a Registrar and may be a deputy Registrar or deputy Registrars appointed by the Board.

**2.** There may be additional Registrars and/or deputy Registrars appointed by the Board, or by the board of directors of any branch or subsidiary of the LCIA, or jointly by the Board and the board of directors of any company in a joint venture with the LCIA, to fulfil such roles pursuant to such rules and/or procedures as the Court and the Board, or the Court and the board of directors of any branch or subsidiary of the LCIA, or the Court and the Board and the board of directors of any company in a joint venture with the LCIA, may publish from time to time.

## D. FUNCTIONS OF THE COURT

**1.** The Court shall have power to do anything which it may consider appropriate for the proper performance of its functions, and in particular:

(a) to act as appointing authority under the LCIA Rules, any rules or procedures published pursuant to Article C.2, the UNCITRAL Rules, and in any other case where an agreement provides for appointments by the LCIA;

(b) to perform the functions conferred on it by any applicable rules of arbitration, mediation or conciliation, whether the LCIA Rules, any rules or procedures published pursuant to Article C.2, the UNCITRAL Rules, or any other arbitration, mediation or conciliation rules;

(c) to keep the LCIA Rules, and any rules or procedures published pursuant to Article C.2, and their associated schedules of costs, under review;

(d) to make recommendations to the Board as appropriate concerning the introduction of new general or specialist rules; and

(e) to promote the objectives of the LCIA and of international commercial arbitration generally.

**2.** All appointments of arbitrators and mediators shall be made in the name of the Court by the President or by a Vice President.

**3.** All other functions of the Court under Articles D.1(a) and D.1(b) shall be performed in the name of the Court:

(a) by the President or a Vice-President; or

(b) by an Honorary Vice-President, or a former Vice-President of the Court, appointed by the President or a Vice-President; or

**(c)** by 3 or 5-member divisions of the Court appointed by the President or a Vice-President, and chaired by the President, a Vice-President, an Honorary Vice-President, or a former Vice-President of the Court; or

**(d)** in the case of administrative functions by a Registrar or deputy Registrar pursuant to Article G(i).

**4.** For the purpose of performing specific tasks in relation to the functions of the Court under Articles D.1(c) to D.1(e), the President may set up ad hoc sub-committees of the Court chaired by any member appointed by the President, which shall report back to the Court.

**5.** In the performance of its functions under this Constitution, the Court, its Officers, its members and its former Vice-Presidents shall at all times act independently of the Board.

**6.** No member or former member of the Court who has a connection with an arbitration in relation to which the LCIA exercises any functions of any kind may participate in or influence any decision of the Court relating to such arbitration.

E. MEETINGS OF THE COURT

**1.** The Court shall meet as often as required and at least once a year.

**2.** Meetings shall be chaired by the President or a Vice-President. A quorum shall be seven. The Chairman of the meeting shall have a casting vote.

F. APPOINTMENT OF COURT MEMBERS AS ARBITRATORS

**1.** All members of the Court shall be eligible for appointment as arbitrators. However:

**(a)** the President shall only be eligible to serve as an arbitrator if the parties agree to nominate him as sole arbitrator or as Chairman; and

**(b)** the Vice-Presidents shall only be eligible to serve as arbitrators if nominated by a party or the parties.

**2.** The President or Vice Presidents so nominated shall take no part in the appointment of an arbitral tribunal to which they have been nominated, or in any other function of the Court relating to such arbitration.

G. FUNCTIONS OF THE REGISTRARS AND DEPUTY REGISTRARS

The Registrars and the deputy Registrars shall:

**(i)** carry out in the name of the Court such day to day operations of the Court and administrative functions under any applicable arbitration, mediation or conciliation rules or procedures as may be authorised by the President from time to time; and

**(ii)** service the Court and any division or sub-committee set up under Article D.3.

## H. AMENDMENTS

The provisions of this Constitution may only be amended with the mutual consent of the Court and the Board.

# Appendix 4

# LCIA ARBITRATION RULES 1998

Where any agreement, submission or reference provides in writing and in whatsoever manner for arbitration under the rules of the LCIA or by the Court of the LCIA ("the LCIA Court"), the parties shall be taken to have agreed in writing that the arbitration shall be conducted in accordance with the following rules ("the Rules") or such amended rules as the LCIA may have adopted hereafter to take effect before the commencement of the arbitration. The Rules include the Schedule of Costs in effect at the commencement of the arbitration, as separately amended from time to time by the LCIA Court.

**Article 1  The Request for Arbitration**

1.1 Any party wishing to commence an arbitration under these Rules ("the Claimant") shall send to the Registrar of the LCIA Court ("the Registrar") a written request for arbitration ("the Request"), containing or accompanied by:

- (a) the names, addresses, telephone, facsimile, telex and e-mail numbers (if known) of the parties to the arbitration and of their legal representatives;
- (b) a copy of the written arbitration clause or separate written arbitration agreement invoked by the Claimant ("the Arbitration Agreement"), together with a copy of the contractual documentation in which the arbitration clause is contained or in respect of which the arbitration arises;
- (c) a brief statement describing the nature and circumstances of the dispute, and specifying the claims advanced by the Claimant against another party to the arbitration ("the Respondent");
- (d) a statement of any matters (such as the seat or language(s) of the arbitration, or the number of arbitrators, or their qualifications or identities) on which the parties have already agreed in writing for the arbitration or in respect of which the Claimant wishes to make a proposal;
- (e) if the Arbitration Agreement calls for party nomination of arbitrators, the name, address, telephone, facsimile, telex and e-mail numbers (if known) of the Claimant's nominee;

(f) the fee prescribed in the Schedule of Costs (without which the Request shall be treated as not having been received by the Registrar and the arbitration as not having been commenced);

(g) confirmation to the Registrar that copies of the Request (including all accompanying documents) have been or are being served simultaneously on all other parties to the arbitration by one or more means of service to be identified in such confirmation.

1.2 The date of receipt by the Registrar of the Request shall be treated as the date on which the arbitration has commenced for all purposes. The Request (including all accompanying documents) should be submitted to the Registrar in two copies where a sole arbitrator should be appointed, or, if the parties have agreed or the Claimant considers that three arbitrators should be appointed, in four copies.

**Article 2  The Response**

2.1 Within 30 days of service of the Request on the Respondent, (or such lesser period fixed by the LCIA Court), the Respondent shall send to the Registrar a written response to the Request ("the Response"), containing or accompanied by:

(a) confirmation or denial of all or part of the claims advanced by the Claimant in the Request;

(b) a brief statement describing the nature and circumstances of any counter-claims advanced by the Respondent against the Claimant;

(c) comment in response to any statements contained in the Request, as called for under Article 1.1(d), on matters relating to the conduct of the arbitration;

(d) if the Arbitration Agreement calls for party nomination of arbitrators, the name, address, telephone, facsimile, telex and e-mail numbers (if known) of the Respondent's nominee; and

(e) confirmation to the Registrar that copies of the Response (including all accompanying documents) have been or are being served simultaneously on all other parties to the arbitration by one or more means of service to be identified in such confirmation.

2.2 The Response (including all accompanying documents) should be submitted to the Registrar in two copies, or if the parties have agreed or the Respondent considers that three arbitrators should be appointed, in four copies.

2.3 Failure to send a Response shall not preclude the Respondent from denying any claim or from advancing a counterclaim in the arbitration. However, if the Arbitration Agreement calls for party nomination of arbitrators, failure to send a Response or to nominate an arbitrator within time or at all shall constitute an irrevocable waiver of that party's opportunity to nominate an arbitrator.

## Article 3 The LCIA Court and Registrar

3.1 The functions of the LCIA Court under these Rules shall be performed in its name by the President or a Vice President of the LCIA Court or by a division of three or five members of the LCIA Court appointed by the President or a Vice President of the LCIA Court, as determined by the President.

3.2 The functions of the Registrar under these Rules shall be performed by the Registrar or any deputy Registrar of the LCIA Court under the supervision of the LCIA Court.

3.3 All communications from any party or arbitrator to the LCIA Court shall be addressed to the Registrar.

## Article 4 Notices and Periods of Time

4.1 Any notice or other communication that may be or is required to be given by a party under these Rules shall be in writing and shall be delivered by registered postal or courier service or transmitted by facsimile, telex, e-mail or any other means of telecommunication that provide a record of its transmission.

4.2 A party's last-known residence or place of business during the arbitration shall be a valid address for the purpose of any notice or other communication in the absence of any notification of a change to such address by that party to the other parties, the Arbitral Tribunal and the Registrar.

4.3 For the purpose of determining the date of commencement of a time limit, a notice or other communication shall be treated as having been received on the day it is delivered or, in the case of telecommunications, transmitted in accordance with Articles 4.1 and 4.2.

4.4 For the purpose of determining compliance with a time limit, a notice or other communication shall be treated as having been sent, made or transmitted if it is dispatched in accordance with Articles 4.1 and 4.2 prior to or on the date of the expiration of the time-limit.

4.5 Notwithstanding the above, any notice or communication by one party may be addressed to another party in the manner agreed in writing between them or, failing such agreement, according to the practice followed in the course of their previous dealings or in whatever manner ordered by the Arbitral Tribunal.

4.6 For the purpose of calculating a period of time under these Rules, such period shall begin to run on the day following the day when a notice or other communication is received. If the last day of such period is an official holiday or a non-business day at the residence or place of business of the addressee, the period is extended until the first business day which follows. Official holidays or non-business days occurring during the running of the period of time are included in calculating that period.

4.7 The Arbitral Tribunal may at any time extend (even where the period of time has expired) or abridge any period of time prescribed under these Rules or under the Arbitration Agreement for the conduct of the arbitration, including any notice or communication to be served by one party on any other party.

**Article 5  Formation of the Arbitral Tribunal**

5.1 The expression "the Arbitral Tribunal" in these Rules includes a sole arbitrator or all the arbitrators where more than one. All references to an arbitrator shall include the masculine and feminine. (References to the President, Vice President and members of the LCIA Court, the Registrar or deputy Registrar, expert, witness, party and legal representative shall be similarly understood).

5.2 All arbitrators conducting an arbitration under these Rules shall be and remain at all times impartial and independent of the parties; and none shall act in the arbitration as advocates for any party. No arbitrator, whether before or after appointment, shall advise any party on the merits or outcome of the dispute.

5.3 Before appointment by the LCIA Court, each arbitrator shall furnish to the Registrar a written résumé of his past and present professional positions; he shall agree in writing upon fee rates conforming to the Schedule of Costs; and he shall sign a declaration to the effect that there are no circumstances known to him likely to give rise to any justified doubts as to his impartiality or independence, other than any circumstances disclosed by him in the declaration. Each arbitrator shall thereby also assume a continuing duty forthwith to disclose any such circumstances to the LCIA Court, to any other members of the Arbitral Tribunal and to all the parties if such circumstances should arise after the date of such declaration and before the arbitration is concluded.

5.4 The LCIA Court shall appoint the Arbitral Tribunal as soon as practicable after receipt by the Registrar of the Response or after the expiry of 30 days following service of the Request upon the Respondent if no Response is received by the Registrar (or such lesser period fixed by the LCIA Court). The LCIA Court may proceed with the formation of the Arbitral Tribunal notwithstanding that the Request is incomplete or the Response is missing, late or incomplete. A sole arbitrator shall be appointed unless the parties have agreed in writing otherwise, or unless the LCIA Court determines that in view of all the circumstances of the case a three-member tribunal is appropriate.

5.5 The LCIA Court alone is empowered to appoint arbitrators. The LCIA Court will appoint arbitrators with due regard for any particular method or criteria of selection agreed in writing by the parties. In selecting arbitrators consideration will be given to the nature of the transaction, the nature and circumstances of the dispute, the nationality, location and languages of the parties and (if more than two) the number of parties.

5.6 In the case of a three-member Arbitral Tribunal, the chairman (who will not be a party-nominated arbitrator) shall be appointed by the LCIA Court.

## Article 6  Nationality of Arbitrators

6.1 Where the parties are of different nationalities, a sole arbitrator or chairman of the Arbitral Tribunal shall not have the same nationality as any party unless the parties who are not of the same nationality as the proposed appointee all agree in writing otherwise.

6.2 The nationality of parties shall be understood to include that of controlling shareholders or interests.

6.3 For the purpose of this Article, a person who is a citizen of two or more states shall be treated as a national of each state; and citizens of the European Union shall be treated as nationals of its different Member States and shall not be treated as having the same nationality.

## Article 7  Party and Other Nominations

7.1 If the parties have agreed that any arbitrator is to be appointed by one or more of them or by any third person, that agreement shall be treated as an agreement to nominate an arbitrator for all purposes. Such nominee may only be appointed by the LCIA Court as arbitrator subject to his prior compliance with Article 5.3. The LCIA Court may refuse to appoint any such nominee if it determines that he is not suitable or independent or impartial.

7.2 Where the parties have howsoever agreed that the Respondent or any third person is to nominate an arbitrator and such nomination is not made within time or at all, the LCIA Court may appoint an arbitrator notwithstanding the absence of the nomination and without regard to any late nomination. Likewise, if the Request for Arbitration does not contain a nomination by the Claimant where the parties have howsoever agreed that the Claimant or a third person is to nominate an arbitrator, the LCIA Court may appoint an arbitrator notwithstanding the absence of the nomination and without regard to any late nomination.

## Article 8  Three or More Parties

8.1 Where the Arbitration Agreement entitles each party howsoever to nominate an arbitrator, the parties to the dispute number more than two and such parties have not all agreed in writing that the disputant parties represent two separate sides for the formation of the Arbitral Tribunal as Claimant and Respondent respectively, the LCIA Court shall appoint the Arbitral Tribunal without regard to any party's nomination.

8.2 In such circumstances, the Arbitration Agreement shall be treated for all purposes as a written agreement by the parties for the appointment of the Arbitral Tribunal by the LCIA Court.

## Article 9  Expedited Formation

9.1 In exceptional urgency, on or after the commencement of the arbitration, any party may apply to the LCIA Court for the expedited formation of the Arbitral

Tribunal, including the appointment of any replacement arbitrator under Articles 10 and 11 of these Rules.

9.2   Such an application shall be made in writing to the LCIA Court, copied to all other parties to the arbitration; and it shall set out the specific grounds for exceptional urgency in the formation of the Arbitral Tribunal.

9.3   The LCIA Court may, in its complete discretion, abridge or curtail any time-limit under these Rules for the formation of the Arbitral Tribunal, including service of the Response and of any matters or documents adjudged to be missing from the Request. The LCIA Court shall not be entitled to abridge or curtail any other time-limit.

**Article 10   Revocation of Arbitrator's Appointment**

10.1   If either (a) any arbitrator gives written notice of his desire to resign as arbitrator to the LCIA Court, to be copied to the parties and the other arbitrators (if any) or (b) any arbitrator dies, falls seriously ill, refuses, or becomes unable or unfit to act, either upon challenge by a party or at the request of the remaining arbitrators, the LCIA Court may revoke that arbitrator's appointment and appoint another arbitrator. The LCIA Court shall decide upon the amount of fees and expenses to be paid for the former arbitrator's services (if any) as it may consider appropriate in all the circumstances.

10.2   If any arbitrator acts in deliberate violation of the Arbitration Agreement (including these Rules) or does not act fairly and impartially as between the parties or does not conduct or participate in the arbitration proceedings with reasonable diligence, avoiding unnecessary delay or expense, that arbitrator may be considered unfit in the opinion of the LCIA Court.

10.3   An arbitrator may also be challenged by any party if circumstances exist that give rise to justifiable doubts as to his impartiality or independence. A party may challenge an arbitrator it has nominated, or in whose appointment it has participated, only for reasons of which it becomes aware after the appointment has been made.

10.4   A party who intends to challenge an arbitrator shall, within 15 days of the formation of the Arbitral Tribunal or (if later) after becoming aware of any circumstances referred to in Article 10.1, 10.2 or 10.3, send a written statement of the reasons for its challenge to the LCIA Court, the Arbitral Tribunal and all other parties. Unless the challenged arbitrator withdraws or all other parties agree to the challenge within 15 days of receipt of the written statement, the LCIA Court shall decide on the challenge.

**Article 11   Nomination and Replacement of Arbitrators**

11.1   In the event that the LCIA Court determines that any nominee is not suitable or independent or impartial or if an appointed arbitrator is to be replaced for any reason, the LCIA Court shall have a complete discretion to decide whether or not to follow the original nominating process.

11.2 If the LCIA Court should so decide, any opportunity given to a party to make a re-nomination shall be waived if not exercised within 15 days (or such lesser time as the LCIA Court may fix), after which the LCIA Court shall appoint the replacement arbitrator.

## Article 12 Majority Power to Continue Proceedings

12.1 If any arbitrator on a three-member Arbitral Tribunal refuses or persistently fails to participate in its deliberations, the two other arbitrators shall have the power, upon their written notice of such refusal or failure to the LCIA Court, the parties and the third arbitrator, to continue the arbitration (including the making of any decision, ruling or award), notwithstanding the absence of the third arbitrator.

12.2 In determining whether to continue the arbitration, the two other arbitrators shall take into account the stage of the arbitration, any explanation made by the third arbitrator for his non-participation and such other matters as they consider appropriate in the circumstances of the case. The reasons for such determination shall be stated in any award, order or other decision made by the two arbitrators without the participation of the third arbitrator.

12.3 In the event that the two other arbitrators determine at any time not to continue the arbitration without the participation of the third arbitrator missing from their deliberations, the two arbitrators shall notify in writing the parties and the LCIA Court of such determination; and in that event, the two arbitrators or any party may refer the matter to the LCIA Court for the revocation of that third arbitrator's appointment and his replacement under Article 10.

## Article 13 Communications between Parties and the Arbitral Tribunal

13.1 Until the Arbitral Tribunal is formed, all communications between parties and arbitrators shall be made through the Registrar.

13.2 Thereafter, unless and until the Arbitral Tribunal directs that communications shall take place directly between the Arbitral Tribunal and the parties (with simultaneous copies to the Registrar), all written communications between the parties and the Arbitral Tribunal shall continue to be made through the Registrar.

13.3 Where the Registrar sends any written communication to one party on behalf of the Arbitral Tribunal, he shall send a copy to each of the other parties. Where any party sends to the Registrar any communication (including Written Statements and Documents under Article 15), it shall include a copy for each arbitrator; and it shall also send copies direct to all other parties and confirm to the Registrar in writing that it has done or is doing so.

## Article 14 Conduct of the Proceedings

14.1 The parties may agree on the conduct of their arbitral proceedings and they are encouraged to do so, consistent with the Arbitral Tribunal's general duties at all times:

(i) to act fairly and impartially as between all parties, giving each a reasonable opportunity of putting its case and dealing with that of its opponent; and

(ii) to adopt procedures suitable to the circumstances of the arbitration, avoiding unnecessary delay or expense, so as to provide a fair and efficient means for the final resolution of the parties' dispute.

Such agreements shall be made by the parties in writing or recorded in writing by the Arbitral Tribunal at the request of and with the authority of the parties

14.2 Unless otherwise agreed by the parties under Article 14.1, the Arbitral Tribunal shall have the widest discretion to discharge its duties allowed under such law(s) or rules of law as the Arbitral Tribunal may determine to be applicable; and at all times the parties shall do everything necessary for the fair, efficient and expeditious conduct of the arbitration.

14.3 In the case of a three-member Arbitral Tribunal the chairman may, with the prior consent of the other two arbitrators, make procedural rulings alone.

**Article 15 Submission of Written Statements and Documents**

15.1 Unless the parties have agreed otherwise under Article 14.1 or the Arbitral Tribunal should determine differently, the written stage of the proceedings shall be as set out below.

15.2 Within 30 days of receipt of written notification from the Registrar of the formation of the Arbitral Tribunal, the Claimant shall send to the Registrar a Statement of Case setting out in sufficient detail the facts and any contentions of law on which it relies, together with the relief claimed against all other parties, save and insofar as such matters have not been set out in its Request.

15.3 Within 30 days of receipt of the Statement of Case or written notice from the Claimant that it elects to treat the Request as its Statement of Case, the Respondent shall send to the Registrar a Statement of Defence setting out in sufficient detail which of the facts and contentions of law in the Statement of Case or Request (as the case may be) it admits or denies, on what grounds and on what other facts and contentions of law it relies. Any counterclaims shall be submitted with the Statement of Defence in the same manner as claims are to be set out in the Statement of Case.

15.4 Within 30 days of receipt of the Statement of Defence, the Claimant shall send to the Registrar a Statement of Reply which, where there are any counterclaims, shall include a Defence to Counterclaim in the same manner as a defence is to be set out in the Statement of Defence.

15.5 If the Statement of Reply contains a Defence to Counterclaim, within 30 days of its receipt the Respondent shall send to the Registrar a Statement of Reply to Counterclaim.

15.6 All Statements referred to in this Article shall be accompanied by copies (or, if they are especially voluminous, lists) of all essential documents on which the party concerned relies and which have not previously been submitted by any party, and (where appropriate) by any relevant samples and exhibits.

15.7 As soon as practicable following receipt of the Statements specified in this Article, the Arbitral Tribunal shall proceed in such manner as has been agreed in writing by the parties or pursuant to its authority under these Rules.

15.8 If the Respondent fails to submit a Statement of Defence or the Claimant a Statement of Defence to Counterclaim, or if at any point any party fails to avail itself of the opportunity to present its case in the manner determined by Article 15.2 to 15.6 or directed by the Arbitral Tribunal, the Arbitral Tribunal may nevertheless proceed with the arbitration and make an award.

**Article 16 Seat of Arbitration and Place of Hearings**

16.1 The parties may agree in writing the seat (or legal place) of their arbitration. Failing such a choice, the seat of arbitration shall be London, unless and until the LCIA Court determines in view of all the circumstances, and after having given the parties an opportunity to make written comment, that another seat is more appropriate.

16.2 The Arbitral Tribunal may hold hearings, meetings and deliberations at any convenient geographical place in its discretion; and if elsewhere than the seat of the arbitration, the arbitration shall be treated as an arbitration conducted at the seat of the arbitration and any award as an award made at the seat of the arbitration for all purposes.

16.3 The law applicable to the arbitration (if any) shall be the arbitration law of the seat of arbitration, unless and to the extent that the parties have expressly agreed in writing on the application of another arbitration law and such agreement is not prohibited by the law of the arbitral seat.

**Article 17 Language of Arbitration**

17.1 The initial language of the arbitration shall be the language of the Arbitration Agreement, unless the parties have agreed in writing otherwise and providing always that a non-participating or defaulting party shall have no cause for complaint if communications to and from the Registrar and the arbitration proceedings are conducted in English.

17.2 In the event that the Arbitration Agreement is written in more than one language, the LCIA Court may, unless the Arbitration Agreement provides that the arbitration proceedings shall be conducted in more than one language, decide which of those languages shall be the initial language of the arbitration.

17.3 Upon the formation of the Arbitral Tribunal and unless the parties have agreed upon the language or languages of the arbitration, the Arbitration Tribunal shall decide upon the language(s) of the arbitration, after giving the parties an opportunity to make written comment and taking into account the initial language of the arbitration and any other matter it may consider appropriate in all the circumstances of the case.

17.4 If any document is expressed in a language other than the language(s) of the arbitration and no translation of such document is submitted by the party relying upon the document, the Arbitral Tribunal or (if the Arbitral Tribunal has not been formed) the LCIA Court may order that party to submit a translation in a form to be determined by the Arbitral Tribunal or the LCIA Court, as the case may be.

**Article 18  Party Representation**

18.1 Any party may be represented by legal practitioners or any other representatives.

18.2 At any time the Arbitral Tribunal may require from any party proof of authority granted to its representative(s) in such form as the Arbitral Tribunal may determine.

**Article 19  Hearings**

19.1 Any party which expresses a desire to that effect has the right to be heard orally before the Arbitral Tribunal on the merits of the dispute, unless the parties have agreed in writing on documents-only arbitration.

19.2 The Arbitral Tribunal shall fix the date, time and physical place of any meetings and hearings in the arbitration, and shall give the parties reasonable notice thereof.

19.3 The Arbitral Tribunal may in advance of any hearing submit to the parties a list of questions which it wishes them to answer with special attention.

19.4 All meetings and hearings shall be in private unless the parties agree otherwise in writing or the Arbitral Tribunal directs otherwise.

19.5 The Arbitral Tribunal shall have the fullest authority to establish time-limits for meetings and hearings, or for any parts thereof.

**Article 20  Witnesses**

20.1 Before any hearing, the Arbitral Tribunal may require any party to give notice of the identity of each witness that party wishes to call (including rebuttal witnesses), as well as the subject matter of that witness's testimony, its content and its relevance to the issues in the arbitration.

20.2 The Arbitral Tribunal may also determine the time, manner and form in which such materials should be exchanged between the parties and presented to the Arbitral Tribunal; and it has a discretion to allow, refuse, or limit the appearance of witnesses (whether witness of fact or expert witness).

20.3 Subject to any order otherwise by the Arbitral Tribunal, the testimony of a witness may be presented by a party in written form, either as a signed statement or as a sworn affidavit.

20.4  Subject to Article 14.1 and 14.2, any party may request that a witness, on whose testimony another party seeks to rely, should attend for oral questioning at a hearing before the Arbitral Tribunal. If the Arbitral Tribunal orders that other party to produce the witness and the witness fails to attend the oral hearing without good cause, the Arbitral Tribunal may place such weight on the written testimony (or exclude the same altogether) as it considers appropriate in the circumstances of the case.

20.5  Any witness who gives oral evidence at a hearing before the Arbitral Tribunal may be questioned by each of the parties under the control of the Arbitral Tribunal. The Arbitral Tribunal may put questions at any stage of his evidence.

20.6  Subject to the mandatory provisions of any applicable law, it shall not be improper for any party or its legal representatives to interview any witness or potential witness for the purpose of presenting his testimony in written form or producing him as an oral witness.

20.7  Any individual intending to testify to the Arbitral Tribunal on any issue of fact or expertise shall be treated as a witness under these Rules notwithstanding that the individual is a party to the arbitration or was or is an officer, employee or shareholder of any party.

### Article 21 Experts to the Arbitral Tribunal

21.1  Unless otherwise agreed by the parties in writing, the Arbitral Tribunal:

(a) may appoint one or more experts to report to the Arbitral Tribunal on specific issues, who shall be and remain impartial and independent of the parties throughout the arbitration proceedings; and

(b) may require a party to give any such expert any relevant information or to provide access to any relevant documents, goods, samples, property or site for inspection by the expert.

21.2  Unless otherwise agreed by the parties in writing, if a party so requests or if the Arbitral Tribunal considers it necessary, the expert shall, after delivery of his written or oral report to the Arbitral Tribunal and the parties, participate in one or more hearings at which the parties shall have the opportunity to question the expert on his report and to present expert witnesses in order to testify on the points at issue.

21.3  The fees and expenses of any expert appointed by the Arbitral Tribunal under this Article shall be paid out of the deposits payable by the parties under Article 24 and shall form part of the costs of the arbitration.

### Article 22 Additional Powers of the Arbitral Tribunal

22.1  Unless the parties at any time agree otherwise in writing, the Arbitral Tribunal shall have the power, on the application of any party or of its own motion, but in either case only after giving the parties a reasonable opportunity to state their views:

(a) to allow any party, upon such terms (as to costs and otherwise) as it shall determine, to amend any claim, counterclaim, defence and reply;

(b) to extend or abbreviate any time-limit provided by the Arbitration Agreement or these Rules for the conduct of the arbitration or by the Arbitral Tribunal's own orders;

(c) to conduct such enquiries as may appear to the Arbitral Tribunal to be necessary or expedient, including whether and to what extent the Arbitral Tribunal should itself take the initiative in identifying the issues and ascertaining the relevant facts and the law(s) or rules of law applicable to the arbitration, the merits of the parties' dispute and the Arbitration Agreement;

(d) to order any party to make any property, site or thing under its control and relating to the subject matter of the arbitration available for inspection by the Arbitral Tribunal, any other party, its expert or any expert to the Arbitral Tribunal;

(e) to order any party to produce to the Arbitral Tribunal, and to the other parties for inspection, and to supply copies of, any documents or classes of documents in their possession, custody or power which the Arbitral Tribunal determines to be relevant;

(f) to decide whether or not to apply any strict rules of evidence (or any other rules) as to the admissibility, relevance or weight of any material tendered by a party on any matter of fact or expert opinion; and to determine the time, manner and form in which such material should be exchanged between the parties and presented to the Arbitral Tribunal;

(g) to order the correction of any contract between the parties or the Arbitration Agreement, but only to the extent required to rectify any mistake which the Arbitral Tribunal determines to be common to the parties and then only if and to the extent to which the law(s) or rules of law applicable to the contract or Arbitration Agreement permit such correction; and

(h) to allow, only upon the application of a party, one or more third persons to be joined in the arbitration as a party provided any such third person and the applicant party have consented thereto in writing, and thereafter to make a single final award, or separate awards, in respect of all parties so implicated in the arbitration.

22.2 By agreeing to arbitration under these Rules, the parties shall be treated as having agreed not to apply to any state court or other judicial authority for any order available from the Arbitral Tribunal under Article 22.1, except with the agreement in writing of all parties.

22.3 The Arbitral Tribunal shall decide the parties' dispute in accordance with the law(s) or rules of law chosen by the parties as applicable to the merits of their dispute. If and to the extent that the Arbitral Tribunal determines that the parties have made no such choice, the Arbitral Tribunal shall apply the law(s) or rules of law which it considers appropriate.

22.4 The Arbitral Tribunal shall only apply to the merits of the dispute principles deriving from "ex aequo et bono", "amiable composition" or "honourable engagement" where the parties have so agreed expressly in writing.

**Article 23  Jurisdiction of the Arbitral Tribunal**

23.1 The Arbitral Tribunal shall have the power to rule on its own jurisdiction, including any objection to the initial or continuing existence, validity or effectiveness of the Arbitration Agreement. For that purpose, an arbitration clause which forms or was intended to form part of another agreement shall be treated as an arbitration agreement independent of that other agreement. A decision by the Arbitral Tribunal that such other agreement is non-existent, invalid or ineffective shall not entail ipso jure the non-existence, invalidity or ineffectiveness of the arbitration clause.

23.2 A plea by a Respondent that the Arbitral Tribunal does not have jurisdiction shall be treated as having been irrevocably waived unless it is raised not later than the Statement of Defence; and a like plea by a Respondent to Counterclaim shall be similarly treated unless it is raised no later than the Statement of Defence to Counterclaim. A plea that the Arbitral Tribunal is exceeding the scope of its authority shall be raised promptly after the Arbitral Tribunal has indicated its intention to decide on the matter alleged by any party to be beyond the scope of its authority, failing which such plea shall also be treated as having been waived irrevocably. In any case, the Arbitral Tribunal may nevertheless admit an untimely plea if it considers the delay justified in the particular circumstances.

23.3 The Arbitral Tribunal may determine the plea to its jurisdiction or authority in an award as to jurisdiction or later in an award on the merits, as it considers appropriate in the circumstances.

23.4 By agreeing to arbitration under these Rules, the parties shall be treated as having agreed not to apply to any state court or other judicial authority for any relief regarding the Arbitral Tribunal's jurisdiction or authority, except with the agreement in writing of all parties to the arbitration or the prior authorisation of the Arbitral Tribunal or following the latter's award ruling on the objection to its jurisdiction or authority.

**Article 24  Deposits**

24.1 The LCIA Court may direct the parties, in such proportions as it thinks appropriate, to make one or several interim or final payments on account of the costs of the arbitration. Such deposits shall be made to and held by the LCIA and from time to time may be released by the LCIA Court to the arbitrator(s), any expert appointed by the Arbitral Tribunal and the LCIA itself as the arbitration progresses.

24.2 The Arbitral Tribunal shall not proceed with the arbitration without ascertaining at all times from the Registrar or any deputy Registrar that the LCIA is in requisite funds.

24.3 In the event that a party fails or refuses to provide any deposit as directed by the LCIA Court, the LCIA Court may direct the other party or parties to effect a substitute payment to allow the arbitration to proceed (subject to any award on costs). In such circumstances, the party paying the substitute payment shall be entitled to recover that amount as a debt immediately due from the defaulting party.

24.4 Failure by a claimant or counterclaiming party to provide promptly and in full the required deposit may be treated by the LCIA Court and the Arbitral Tribunal as a withdrawal of the claim or counterclaim respectively.

**Article 25 Interim and Conservatory Measures**

25.1 The Arbitral Tribunal shall have the power, unless otherwise agreed by the parties in writing, on the application of any party:

(a) to order any respondent party to a claim or counterclaim to provide security for all or part of the amount in dispute, by way of deposit or bank guarantee or in any other manner and upon such terms as the Arbitral Tribunal considers appropriate. Such terms may include the provision by the claiming or counterclaiming party of a cross-indemnity, itself secured in such manner as the Arbitral Tribunal considers appropriate, for any costs or losses incurred by such respondent in providing security. The amount of any costs and losses payable under such cross-indemnity may be determined by the Arbitral Tribunal in one or more awards;

(b) to order the preservation, storage, sale or other disposal of any property or thing under the control of any party and relating to the subject matter of the arbitration; and

(c) to order on a provisional basis, subject to final determination in an award, any relief which the Arbitral Tribunal would have power to grant in an award, including a provisional order for the payment of money or the disposition of property as between any parties.

25.2 The Arbitral Tribunal shall have the power, upon the application of a party, to order any claiming or counterclaiming party to provide security for the legal or other costs of any other party by way of deposit or bank guarantee or in any other manner and upon such terms as the Arbitral Tribunal considers appropriate. Such terms may include the provision by that other party of a cross-indemnity, itself secured in such manner as the Arbitral Tribunal considers appropriate, for any costs and losses incurred by such claimant or counterclaimant in providing security. The amount of any costs and losses payable under such cross-indemnity may be determined by the Arbitral Tribunal in one or more awards. In the event that a claiming or counterclaiming party does not comply with any order to provide security, the Arbitral Tribunal may stay that party's claims or counterclaims or dismiss them in an award.

25.3 The power of the Arbitral Tribunal under Article 25.1 shall not prejudice howsoever any party's right to apply to any state court or other judicial authority for interim or conservatory measures before the formation of the Arbitral Tribunal and, in exceptional cases, thereafter. Any application and any order for such measures after the formation of the Arbitral Tribunal shall be promptly communicated by the applicant to the Arbitral Tribunal and all other parties. However, by agreeing to arbitration under these Rules, the parties shall be taken to have agreed not to apply to any state court or other judicial authority for any order for security for its legal or other costs available from the Arbitral Tribunal under Article 25.2.

**Article 26 The Award**

26.1 The Arbitral Tribunal shall make its award in writing and, unless all parties agree in writing otherwise, shall state the reasons upon which its award is based. The award shall also state the date when the award is made and the seat of the arbitration; and it shall be signed by the Arbitral Tribunal or those of its members assenting to it.

26.2 If any arbitrator fails to comply with the mandatory provisions of any applicable law relating to the making of the award, having been given a reasonable opportunity to do so, the remaining arbitrators may proceed in his absence and state in their award the circumstances of the other arbitrator's failure to participate in the making of the award.

26.3 Where there are three arbitrators and the Arbitral Tribunal fails to agree on any issue, the arbitrators shall decide that issue by a majority. Failing a majority decision on any issue, the chairman of the Arbitral Tribunal shall decide that issue.

26.4 If any arbitrator refuses or fails to sign the award, the signatures of the majority or (failing a majority) of the chairman shall be sufficient, provided that the reason for the omitted signature is stated in the award by the majority or chairman.

26.5 The sole arbitrator or chairman shall be responsible for delivering the award to the LCIA Court, which shall transmit certified copies to the parties provided that the costs of arbitration have been paid to the LCIA in accordance with Article 28.

26.6 An award may be expressed in any currency. The Arbitral Tribunal may order that simple or compound interest shall be paid by any party on any sum awarded at such rates as the Arbitral Tribunal determines to be appropriate, without being bound by legal rates of interest imposed by any state court, in respect of any period which the Arbitral Tribunal determines to be appropriate ending not later than the date upon which the award is complied with.

26.7 The Arbitral Tribunal may make separate awards on different issues at different times. Such awards shall have the same status and effect as any other award made by the Arbitral Tribunal.

26.8 In the event of a settlement of the parties' dispute, the Arbitral Tribunal may render an award recording the settlement if the parties so request in writing (a "Consent Award"), provided always that such award contains an express statement that it is an award made by the parties' consent. A Consent Award need not contain reasons. If the parties do not require a consent award, then on written confirmation by the parties to the LCIA Court that a settlement has been reached, the Arbitral Tribunal shall be discharged and the arbitration proceedings concluded, subject to payment by the parties of any outstanding costs of the arbitration under Article 28.

26.9 All awards shall be final and binding on the parties. By agreeing to arbitration under these Rules, the parties undertake to carry out any award immediately and without any delay (subject only to Article 27); and the parties also waive irrevocably their right to any form of appeal, review or recourse to any state court or other judicial authority, insofar as such waiver may be validly made.

**Article 27 Correction of Awards and Additional Awards**

27.1 Within 30 days of receipt of any award, or such lesser period as may be agreed in writing by the parties, a party may by written notice to the Registrar (copied to all other parties) request the Arbitral Tribunal to correct in the award any errors in computation, clerical or typographical errors or any errors of a similar nature. If the Arbitral Tribunal considers the request to be justified, it shall make the corrections within 30 days of receipt of the request. Any correction shall take the form of separate memorandum dated and signed by the Arbitral Tribunal or (if three arbitrators) those of its members assenting to it; and such memorandum shall become part of the award for all purposes.

27.2 The Arbitral Tribunal may likewise correct any error of the nature described in Article 27.1 on its own initiative within 30 days of the date of the award, to the same effect.

27.3 Within 30 days of receipt of the final award, a party may by written notice to the Registrar (copied to all other parties), request the Arbitral Tribunal to make an additional award as to claims or counterclaims presented in the arbitration but not determined in any award. If the Arbitral Tribunal considers the request to be justified, it shall make the additional award within 60 days of receipt of the request. The provisions of Article 26 shall apply to any additional award.

**Article 28 Arbitration and Legal Costs**

28.1 The costs of the arbitration (other than the legal or other costs incurred by the parties themselves) shall be determined by the LCIA Court in accordance with the Schedule of Costs. The parties shall be jointly and severally liable to the Arbitral Tribunal and the LCIA for such arbitration costs.

28.2 The Arbitral Tribunal shall specify in the award the total amount of the costs of the arbitration as determined by the LCIA Court. Unless the parties agree otherwise in writing, the Arbitral Tribunal shall determine the proportions in which the parties shall bear all or part of such arbitration costs. If the Arbitral Tribunal has determined that all or any part of the arbitration costs shall be borne by a party other than a party which has already paid them to the LCIA, the latter party shall have the right to recover the appropriate amount from the former party.

28.3 The Arbitral Tribunal shall also have the power to order in its award that all or part of the legal or other costs incurred by a party be paid by another party, unless the parties agree otherwise in writing. The Arbitral Tribunal shall determine and fix the amount of each item comprising such costs on such reasonable basis as it thinks fit.

28.4 Unless the parties otherwise agree in writing, the Arbitral Tribunal shall make its orders on both arbitration and legal costs on the general principle that costs should reflect the parties' relative success and failure in the award or arbitration, except where it appears to the Arbitral Tribunal that in the particular circumstances this general approach is inappropriate. Any order for costs shall be made with reasons in the award containing such order.

28.5 If the arbitration is abandoned, suspended or concluded, by agreement or otherwise, before the final award is made, the parties shall remain jointly and severally liable to pay to the LCIA and the Arbitral Tribunal the costs of the arbitration as determined by the LCIA Court in accordance with the Schedule of Costs. In the event that such arbitration costs are less than the deposits made by the parties, there shall be a refund by the LCIA in such proportion as the parties may agree in writing, or failing such agreement, in the same proportions as the deposits were made by the parties to the LCIA.

**Article 29 Decisions by the LCIA Court**

29.1 The decisions of the LCIA Court with respect to all matters relating to the arbitration shall be conclusive and binding upon the parties and the Arbitral Tribunal. Such decisions are to be treated as administrative in nature and the LCIA Court shall not be required to give any reasons.

29.2 To the extent permitted by the law of the seat of the arbitration, the parties shall be taken to have waived any right of appeal or review in respect of any such decisions of the LCIA Court to any state court or other judicial authority. If such appeals or review remain possible due to mandatory provisions of any applicable law, the LCIA Court shall, subject to the provisions of that applicable law, decide whether the arbitral proceedings are to continue, notwithstanding an appeal or review.

**Article 30 Confidentiality**

30.1 Unless the parties expressly agree in writing to the contrary, the parties undertake as a general principle to keep confidential all awards in their arbitration, together with all materials in the proceedings created for the purpose of the arbitration and all other documents produced by another party in the proceedings not otherwise in the public domain – save and to the extent that disclosure may be required of a party by legal duty, to protect or pursue a legal right or to enforce or challenge an award in bona fide legal proceedings before a state court or other judicial authority.

30.2 The deliberations of the Arbitral Tribunal are likewise confidential to its members, save and to the extent that disclosure of an arbitrator's refusal to participate in the arbitration is required of the other members of the Arbitral Tribunal under Articles 10, 12 and 26.

30.3 The LCIA Court does not publish any award or any part of an award without the prior written consent of all parties and the Arbitral Tribunal.

**Article 31 Exclusion of Liability**

31.1 None of the LCIA, the LCIA Court (including its President, Vice Presidents and individual members), the Registrar, any deputy Registrar, any arbitrator and any expert to the Arbitral Tribunal shall be liable to any party howsoever for any act or omission in connection with any arbitration conducted by reference to these Rules, save where the act or omission is shown by that party to constitute conscious and deliberate wrongdoing committed by the body or person alleged to be liable to that party.

31.2 After the award has been made and the possibilities of correction and additional awards referred to in Article 27 have lapsed or been exhausted, neither the LCIA, the LCIA Court (including its President, Vice Presidents and individual members), the Registrar, any deputy Registrar, any arbitrator or expert to the Arbitral Tribunal shall be under any legal obligation to make any statement to any person about any matter concerning the arbitration, nor shall any party seek to make any of these persons a witness in any legal or other proceedings arising out of the arbitration.

**Article 32 General Rules**

32.1 A party who knows that any provision of the Arbitration Agreement (including these Rules) has not been complied with and yet proceeds with the arbitration without promptly stating its objection to such non-compliance, shall be treated as having irrevocably waived its right to object.

32.2 In all matters not expressly provided for in these Rules, the LCIA Court, the Arbitral Tribunal and the parties shall act in the spirit of these Rules and shall make every reasonable effort to ensure that an award is legally enforceable.

# APPENDIX 5

# LCIA MEDIATION RULES

*Effective 1 July 2012*

Where any agreement provides for mediation of existing or future disputes under the rules of the LCIA, the parties shall be taken to have agreed that the mediation shall be conducted in accordance with the following rules (the "Rules") or such amended rules as the LCIA may have adopted hereafter to take effect before the commencement of the mediation. The Rules include the Schedule of Mediation Costs (the "Schedule") in effect at the commencement of the mediation, as separately amended from time to time by the LCIA Court.

### Article 1  Commencing Mediation – prior existing agreements to mediate

1.1  Where there is a prior existing agreement to mediate under the Rules (a "Prior Agreement"), any party or parties wishing to commence a mediation shall send to the Registrar of the LCIA Court ("the Registrar") a written request for mediation (the "Request for Mediation"), which shall briefly state the nature of the dispute and the value of the claim, and should include, or be accompanied by a copy of the Prior Agreement, the names, addresses, telephone, facsimile, telex numbers and e-mail addresses (if known) of the parties to the mediation, and of their legal representatives (if known) and of the mediator proposed (if any) by the party or parties requesting mediation.

1.2  If the Request for Mediation is not made jointly by all parties to the Prior Agreement, the party requesting mediation shall, at the same time, send a copy of the Request for Mediation to the other party or parties.

1.3  The Request for Mediation shall be accompanied by the registration fee prescribed in the Schedule, without which the Request for Mediation shall not be registered.

1.4  Where there is a Prior Agreement, the date of commencement of the mediation shall be the date of receipt by the Registrar of the Request for Mediation and the registration fee.

1.5  The LCIA Court shall appoint a mediator as soon as practicable after the commencement of the mediation, with due regard for any nomination, or method or criteria of selection agreed in writing by the parties, and subject always to Article 8 of the Rules.

## Article 2  Commencing Mediation – no prior agreement

2.1   Where there is no Prior Agreement, any party or parties wishing to commence a mediation under the Rules shall send to the Registrar a Request for Mediation, which shall briefly state the nature of the dispute and the value of the claim, and should include, or be accompanied by, the names, addresses, telephone, facsimile, telex numbers and e-mail addresses (if known) of the parties to the mediation, and of their legal representatives (if known) and of the mediator proposed (if any) by the party or parties requesting mediation.

2.2   The Request for Mediation shall be accompanied by the registration fee prescribed in the Schedule, without which the Request for Mediation shall not be registered.

2.3   If the Request for Mediation is not made jointly by all parties to the dispute,

   a)   the party wishing to commence the mediation shall, at the same time, send a copy of the Request for Mediation to the other party or parties; and

   b)   the other party or parties shall, within 14 days of receiving the Request for Mediation, advise the Registrar in writing whether or not they agree to the mediation of the dispute.

2.4   In the event that the other party or parties either declines mediation, or fails to agree to mediation within the 14 days referred to at Article 2.3(b), there shall be no mediation under the Rules and the Registrar shall so advise the parties, in writing.

2.5   Where there is no Prior Agreement, the date of commencement of the mediation shall, subject to payment of the registration fee in accordance with Article 2.2, be the date that agreement to mediate is reached in accordance with Article 2.3(b).

2.6   The LCIA Court shall appoint a mediator as soon as practicable after the commencement of the mediation, with due regard for any nomination, or method or criteria of selection agreed in writing by the parties, and subject always to Article 8 of the Rules.

## Article 3  Appointment of Mediator

3.1   Before appointment by the LCIA Court, pursuant to Article 1.5 or Article 2.6, the mediator shall furnish the Registrar with a written résumé of his or her past and present professional positions; and he or she shall sign a declaration to the effect that there are no circumstances known to him or her likely to give rise to any justifiable doubts as to his or her impartiality or independence, other than any circumstances disclosed by him or her in the declaration. A copy of the mediator's résumé and declaration shall be provided to the parties.

3.2   Where the mediator has made a disclosure, pursuant to Article 3.1, or where a party independently knows of circumstances likely to give rise to justifiable doubts as to his or her impartiality or independence, a party shall be at liberty to object to his or her appointment; in which case the LCIA Court shall appoint another mediator.

### Article 4  Statements by the Parties

4.1  The parties are free to agree how, and in what form, they will inform the mediator of their respective cases, provided that, unless they have agreed otherwise, each party shall submit to the mediator, no later than 7 days before the date agreed between the mediator and the parties for the first scheduled mediation session, a brief written statement summarising its case; the background to the dispute; and the issues to be resolved.

4.2  Each written statement should be accompanied by copies of any documents to which it refers.

4.3  Each party shall, at the same time, submit a copy of the written statement and supporting documents to the other party or parties.

### Article 5  Conduct of the Mediation

5.1  The mediator may conduct the mediation in such manner as he or she sees fit, having in mind at all times the circumstances of the case and the wishes of the parties.

5.2  The mediator may communicate with the parties orally or in writing, together, or individually, and may convene a meeting or meetings at a venue to be determined by the mediator after consultation with the parties.

5.3  Nothing which is communicated to the mediator in private during the course of the mediation shall be repeated to the other party or parties, without the express consent of the party making the communication.

5.4  Each party shall notify the other party and the mediator of the number and identity of those persons who will attend any meeting convened by the mediator.

5.5  Each party shall identify a representative of that party who is authorised to settle the dispute on behalf of that party, and shall confirm that authority in writing.

5.6  Unless otherwise agreed by the parties, the mediator will decide the language(s) in which the mediation will be conducted.

### Article 6  Conclusion of the Mediation

The mediation will be at an end when, either

(a)  a settlement agreement is signed by the parties; or

(b)  the parties advise the mediator that it is their view that a settlement cannot be reached and that it is their wish to terminate the mediation; or

(c) the mediator advises the parties that, in his or her judgement, the mediation process will not resolve the issues in dispute; or

(d) the time limit for mediation provided in a Prior Agreement has expired and the parties have not agreed to extend that time limit.

## Article 7  Settlement Agreement

7.1   If terms are agreed in settlement of the dispute, the parties, with the assistance of the mediator if the parties so request, shall draw up and sign a settlement agreement, setting out such terms.

7.2   By signing the settlement agreement, the parties agree to be bound by its terms.

## Article 8  Costs

8.1   The costs of the mediation shall include the Mediator's Fees and Expenses, Time Reserved but not Used (if any), and the Administrative Charges of the LCIA, as set out in the Schedule (the "Costs").

8.2   As soon as practicable after commencement of the mediation, the LCIA will request the parties to file a deposit to be held on account of the Mediator's Fees and Expenses and the Administration Fees and Expenses (the "Deposit"). The Deposit shall be paid by the parties in equal shares or in such other proportions as they have agreed in writing.

8.3   In the event that a party fails to pay its share of the Deposit, another party may make a substitute payment to allow the mediation to proceed.

8.4   A mediator shall not be appointed and the mediation shall not proceed unless and until the Deposit has been paid in full.

8.5   In the event a mediator is not appointed; the mediation does not proceed, and the mediation was commenced pursuant to Article 1.4 or Article 2.5 of the Rules, the LCIA's Administration Fees and Expenses shall be invoiced for immediate payment by the parties in equal shares, or in such other proportions as the parties have agreed in writing.

8.6   In the event a mediator is not appointed, and the mediation does not proceed, by operation of Article 2.4 of the Rules, the LCIA's Administration Fees and Expenses shall be invoiced for immediate payment by the party or parties which requested mediation.

8.7   In the event a mediator is appointed, and the mediation does proceed:

(i)  at the conclusion of the mediation, the LCIA Court shall determine the Costs;

(ii) if the Deposit exceeds the Costs, the excess will be reimbursed to the parties in the proportions in which they have contributed to the Costs, or in such other proportions as the parties have agreed in writing; and

(iii) if the Costs exceed the Deposit, the shortfall will be invoiced for immediate payment by the parties in such proportions as the parties may have agreed in writing, or, absent such agreement, in such proportions as the LCIA Court may determine.

8.8 Any other costs incurred by the parties, whether in regard to legal fees, experts' fees or expenses of any other nature will not be part of the Costs for the purposes of the Rules.

### Article 9 Judicial or Arbitral Proceedings

Unless they have agreed otherwise, and notwithstanding the mediation, the parties may initiate or continue any arbitration or judicial proceedings in respect of the dispute which is the subject of the mediation.

### Article 10 Confidentiality and Privacy

10.1 All mediation sessions shall be private, and shall be attended only by the mediator, the parties and those individuals identified pursuant to Article 5.4.

10.2 The mediation process and all negotiations, and statements and documents prepared for the purposes of the mediation, shall be confidential and covered by "without prejudice" or negotiation privilege.

10.3 The mediation shall be confidential. Unless agreed among the parties, or required by law, neither the mediator nor the parties may disclose to any person any information regarding the mediation or any settlement terms, or the outcome of the mediation.

10.4 All documents or other information produced for or arising in relation to the mediation will be privileged and will not be admissible in evidence or otherwise discoverable in any litigation or arbitration, except for any documents or other information which would in any event be admissible or discoverable in any such litigation or arbitration.

10.5 There shall be no formal record or transcript of the mediation.

10.6 The parties shall not rely upon, or introduce as evidence in any arbitral or judicial proceedings, any admissions, proposals or views expressed by the parties or by the mediator during the course of the mediation.

### Article 11 Limitation of Liability

11.1 None of the LCIA (including its officers and employees), the LCIA Court (including its President, Vice-Presidents and individual members), the Registrar, any deputy Registrar, and any mediator shall be liable to any party howsoever for any act or omission in connection with any mediation conducted by reference to the Rules, save (i) where the act or omission is shown by that party to constitute conscious and deliberate wrongdoing committed by the body or person alleged to be liable to that party and (ii) the extent to which any part of this provision is prohibited by any applicable law.

11.2   None of the LCIA (including its officers and employees), the LCIA Court (including its President, Vice-Presidents and individual members), the Registrar, any deputy Registrar, or the Mediator shall be under any legal obligation to make any statement to any person about any matter concerning the mediation, nor shall any party seek to make any of these persons a witness in any legal or other proceedings arising out of the mediation.

# APPENDIX 6

# RECOMMENDED CLAUSES

**Future Disputes**

For contracting parties who wish to have future disputes referred to mediation and/or arbitration under the auspices of the LCIA, the following clauses are recommended. Words/blanks in square brackets should be deleted/completed as appropriate.

**Mediation only**

"In the event of a dispute arising out of or relating to this contract, including any question regarding its existence, validity or termination, the parties shall seek settlement of that dispute by mediation in accordance with the LCIA Mediation Rules, which Rules are deemed to be incorporated by reference into this clause."

**Arbitration only**

"Any dispute arising out of or in connection with this contract, including any question regarding its existence, validity or termination, shall be referred to and finally resolved by arbitration under the Rules of the LCIA, which Rules are deemed to be incorporated by reference into this clause.
 The number of arbitrators shall be [one/three].
 The seat, or legal place, of arbitration shall be [City and/or Country].
 The language to be used in the arbitration shall be [............].
 The governing law of the contract shall be the substantive law of [............]."

**Mediation and Arbitration**

"In the event of a dispute arising out of or relating to this contract, including any question regarding its existence, validity or termination, the parties shall first seek settlement of that dispute by mediation in accordance with the LCIA Mediation Rules, which Rules are deemed to be incorporated by reference into this clause.
 If the dispute is not settled by mediation within [............] days of the commencement of the mediation, or such further period as the parties shall agree in writing, the dispute shall be referred to and finally resolved by arbitration under the LCIA Rules, which Rules are deemed to be incorporated by reference into this clause.

The language to be used in the mediation and in the arbitration shall be [............].

The governing law of the contract shall be the substantive law of [............].

In any arbitration commenced pursuant to this clause,

(i) the number of arbitrators shall be [one/three]; and

(ii) the seat, or legal place, of arbitration shall be [City and/or Country]."

**Existing Disputes**

If a dispute has already arisen, but there is no agreement between the parties to mediate and/or to arbitrate, the parties may enter into an agreement for those purposes. In such cases, please contact the LCIA Secretariat if recommended wording is required.

**Modifications to Recommended Clauses**

The LCIA Secretariat will be pleased to discuss any modifications to these standard clauses. For example, to provide for party nomination of arbitrators or for expedited procedures.

**Expert Determination, Adjudication and other forms of ADR**

Recommended clauses and procedures for Expert Determination for Adjudication and other forms of ADR, to be administered by the LCIA, or in which the LCIA is to act as appointing authority, are available on request from the LCIA Secretariat.

# Appendix 7

# ARBITRATION ACT 1996

## 1996 CHAPTER 23

### Part I

ARBITRATION PURSUANT TO AN ARBITRATION AGREEMENT

*Introductory*

**1** **General principles**

The provisions of this Part are founded on the following principles, and shall be construed accordingly—
    (a) the object of arbitration is to obtain the fair resolution of disputes by an impartial tribunal without unnecessary delay or expense;
    (b) the parties should be free to agree how their disputes are resolved, subject only to such safeguards as are necessary in the public interest;
    (c) in matters governed by this Part the court should not intervene except as provided by this Part.

**2** **Scope of application of provisions**

(1) The provisions of this Part apply where the seat of the arbitration is in England and Wales or Northern Ireland.

(2) The following sections apply even if the seat of the arbitration is outside England and Wales or Northern Ireland or no seat has been designated or determined—
    (a) sections 9 to 11 (stay of legal proceedings, &c.), and
    (b) section 66 (enforcement of arbitral awards).

(3) The powers conferred by the following sections apply even if the seat of the arbitration is outside England and Wales or Northern Ireland or no seat has been designated or determined—
    (a) section 43 (securing the attendance of witnesses), and
    (b) section 44 (court powers exercisable in support of arbitral proceedings);

but the court may refuse to exercise any such power if, in the opinion of the court, the fact that the seat of the arbitration is outside England and Wales or Northern Ireland, or that when designated or determined the seat is likely to be outside England and Wales or Northern Ireland, makes it inappropriate to do so.

(4) The court may exercise a power conferred by any provision of this Part not mentioned in subsection (2) or (3) for the purpose of supporting the arbitral process where—
   (a) no seat of the arbitration has been designated or determined, and
   (b) by reason of a connection with England and Wales or Northern Ireland the court is satisfied that it is appropriate to do so.

(5) Section 7 (separability of arbitration agreement) and section 8 (death of a party) apply where the law applicable to the arbitration agreement is the law of England and Wales or Northern Ireland even if the seat of the arbitration is outside England and Wales or Northern Ireland or has not been designated or determined.

## 3   The seat of the arbitration

In this Part "the seat of the arbitration" means the juridical seat of the arbitration designated—
   (a) by the parties to the arbitration agreement, or
   (b) by any arbitral or other institution or person vested by the parties with powers in that regard, or
   (c) by the arbitral tribunal if so authorised by the parties,

or determined, in the absence of any such designation, having regard to the parties' agreement and all the relevant circumstances.

## 4   Mandatory and non-mandatory provisions

(1) The mandatory provisions of this Part are listed in Schedule 1 and have effect notwithstanding any agreement to the contrary.

(2) The other provisions of this Part (the "non-mandatory provisions") allow the parties to make their own arrangements by agreement but provide rules which apply in the absence of such agreement.

(3) The parties may make such arrangements by agreeing to the application of institutional rules or providing any other means by which a matter may be decided.

(4) It is immaterial whether or not the law applicable to the parties' agreement is the law of England and Wales or, as the case may be, Northern Ireland.

(5) The choice of a law other than the law of England and Wales or Northern Ireland as the applicable law in respect of a matter provided for by a non-mandatory provision of this Part is equivalent to an agreement making provision about that matter.

For this purpose an applicable law determined in accordance with the parties' agreement, or which is objectively determined in the absence of any express or implied choice, shall be treated as chosen by the parties.

## 5 Agreements to be in writing

(1) The provisions of this Part apply only where the arbitration agreement is in writing, and any other agreement between the parties as to any matter is effective for the purposes of this Part only if in writing.

The expressions "agreement", "agree" and "agreed" shall be construed accordingly.

(2) There is an agreement in writing—
  (a) if the agreement is made in writing (whether or not it is signed by the parties),
  (b) if the agreement is made by exchange of communications in writing, or
  (c) if the agreement is evidenced in writing.

(3) Where parties agree otherwise than in writing by reference to terms which are in writing, they make an agreement in writing.

(4) An agreement is evidenced in writing if an agreement made otherwise than in writing is recorded by one of the parties, or by a third party, with the authority of the parties to the agreement.

(5) An exchange of written submissions in arbitral or legal proceedings in which the existence of an agreement otherwise than in writing is alleged by one party against another party and not denied by the other party in his response constitutes as between those parties an agreement in writing to the effect alleged.

(6) References in this Part to anything being written or in writing include its being recorded by any means.

*The arbitration agreement*

## 6 Definition of arbitration agreement

(1) In this Part an "arbitration agreement" means an agreement to submit to arbitration present or future disputes (whether they are contractual or not).

(2) The reference in an agreement to a written form of arbitration clause or to a document containing an arbitration clause constitutes an arbitration agreement if the reference is such as to make that clause part of the agreement.

## 7 Separability of arbitration agreement

Unless otherwise agreed by the parties, an arbitration agreement which forms or was intended to form part of another agreement (whether or not in writing) shall not be regarded as invalid, non-existent or ineffective because that other agreement is invalid, or did not come into existence or has become ineffective, and it shall for that purpose be treated as a distinct agreement.

## 8 Whether agreement discharged by death of a party

(1) Unless otherwise agreed by the parties, an arbitration agreement is not discharged by the death of a party and may be enforced by or against the personal representatives of that party.

(2) Subsection (1) does not affect the operation of any enactment or rule of law by virtue of which a substantive right or obligation is extinguished by death.

*Stay of legal proceedings*

## 9 Stay of legal proceedings

(1) A party to an arbitration agreement against whom legal proceedings are brought (whether by way of claim or counterclaim) in respect of a matter which under the agreement is to be referred to arbitration may (upon notice to the other parties to the proceedings) apply to the court in which the proceedings have been brought to stay the proceedings so far as they concern that matter.

(2) An application may be made notwithstanding that the matter is to be referred to arbitration only after the exhaustion of other dispute resolution procedures.

(3) An application may not be made by a person before taking the appropriate procedural step (if any) to acknowledge the legal proceedings against him or after he has taken any step in those proceedings to answer the substantive claim.

(4) On an application under this section the court shall grant a stay unless satisfied that the arbitration agreement is null and void, inoperative, or incapable of being performed.

(5) If the court refuses to stay the legal proceedings, any provision that an award is a condition precedent to the bringing of legal proceedings in respect of any matter is of no effect in relation to those proceedings.

## 10 Reference of interpleader issue to arbitration

(1) Where in legal proceedings relief by way of interpleader is granted and any issue between the claimants is one in respect of which there is an arbitration agreement between them, the court granting the relief shall direct that the issue be determined in accordance with the agreement unless the circumstances are such that proceedings brought by a claimant in respect of the matter would not be stayed.

(2) Where subsection (1) applies but the court does not direct that the issue be determined in accordance with the arbitration agreement, any provision that an award is a condition precedent to the bringing of legal proceedings in respect of any matter shall not affect the determination of that issue by the court.

## 11 Retention of security where Admiralty proceedings stayed

(1) Where Admiralty proceedings are stayed on the ground that the dispute in question should be submitted to arbitration, the court granting the stay may, if in those proceedings property has been arrested or bail or other security has been given to prevent or obtain release from arrest—
  (a) order that the property arrested be retained as security for the satisfaction of any award given in the arbitration in respect of that dispute, or
  (b) order that the stay of those proceedings be conditional on the provision of equivalent security for the satisfaction of any such award.

(2) Subject to any provision made by rules of court and to any necessary modifications, the same law and practice shall apply in relation to property retained in pursuance of an order as would apply if it were held for the purposes of proceedings in the court making the order.

*Commencement of arbitral proceedings*

## 12 Power of court to extend time for beginning arbitral proceedings, &c

(1) Where an arbitration agreement to refer future disputes to arbitration provides that a claim shall be barred, or the claimant's right extinguished, unless the claimant takes within a time fixed by the agreement some step—
  (a) to begin arbitral proceedings, or
  (b) to begin other dispute resolution procedures which must be exhausted before arbitral proceedings can be begun,

the court may by order extend the time for taking that step.

(2) Any party to the arbitration agreement may apply for such an order (upon notice to the other parties), but only after a claim has arisen and after exhausting any available arbitral process for obtaining an extension of time.

(3) The court shall make an order only if satisfied—
  (a) that the circumstances are such as were outside the reasonable contemplation of the parties when they agreed the provision in question, and that it would be just to extend the time, or
  (b) that the conduct of one party makes it unjust to hold the other party to the strict terms of the provision in question.

(4) The court may extend the time for such period and on such terms as it thinks fit, and may do so whether or not the time previously fixed (by agreement or by a previous order) has expired.

(5) An order under this section does not affect the operation of the Limitation Acts (see section 13).

(6) The leave of the court is required for any appeal from a decision of the court under this section.

## 13 Application of Limitation Acts

(1) The Limitation Acts apply to arbitral proceedings as they apply to legal proceedings.

(2) The court may order that in computing the time prescribed by the Limitation Acts for the commencement of proceedings (including arbitral proceedings) in respect of a dispute which was the subject matter—
  (a) of an award which the court orders to be set aside or declares to be of no effect, or
  (b) of the affected part of an award which the court orders to be set aside in part, or declares to be in part of no effect,

the period between the commencement of the arbitration and the date of the order referred to in paragraph (a) or (b) shall be excluded.

(3) In determining for the purposes of the Limitation Acts when a cause of action accrued, any provision that an award is a condition precedent to the bringing of legal proceedings in respect of a matter to which an arbitration agreement applies shall be disregarded.

(4) In this Part "the Limitation Acts" means—
  (a) in England and Wales, the Limitation Act 1980, the Foreign Limitation Periods Act 1984 and any other enactment (whenever passed) relating to the limitation of actions;

(b) in Northern Ireland, the Limitation (Northern Ireland) Order 1989, the Foreign Limitation Periods (Northern Ireland) Order 1985 and any other enactment (whenever passed) relating to the limitation of actions.

## 14 Commencement of arbitral proceedings

(1) The parties are free to agree when arbitral proceedings are to be regarded as commenced for the purposes of this Part and for the purposes of the Limitation Acts.

(2) If there is no such agreement the following provisions apply.

(3) Where the arbitrator is named or designated in the arbitration agreement, arbitral proceedings are commenced in respect of a matter when one party serves on the other party or parties a notice in writing requiring him or them to submit that matter to the person so named or designated.

(4) Where the arbitrator or arbitrators are to be appointed by the parties, arbitral proceedings are commenced in respect of a matter when one party serves on the other party or parties notice in writing requiring him or them to appoint an arbitrator or to agree to the appointment of an arbitrator in respect of that matter.

(5) Where the arbitrator or arbitrators are to be appointed by a person other than a party to the proceedings, arbitral proceedings are commenced in respect of a matter when one party gives notice in writing to that person requesting him to make the appointment in respect of that matter.

*The arbitral tribunal*

## 15 The arbitral tribunal

(1) The parties are free to agree on the number of arbitrators to form the tribunal and whether there is to be a chairman or umpire.

(2) Unless otherwise agreed by the parties, an agreement that the number of arbitrators shall be two or any other even number shall be understood as requiring the appointment of an additional arbitrator as chairman of the tribunal.

(3) If there is no agreement as to the number of arbitrators, the tribunal shall consist of a sole arbitrator.

## 16 Procedure for appointment of arbitrators

(1) The parties are free to agree on the procedure for appointing the arbitrator or arbitrators, including the procedure for appointing any chairman or umpire.

(2) If or to the extent that there is no such agreement, the following provisions apply.

(3) If the tribunal is to consist of a sole arbitrator, the parties shall jointly appoint the arbitrator not later than 28 days after service of a request in writing by either party to do so.

(4) If the tribunal is to consist of two arbitrators, each party shall appoint one arbitrator not later than 14 days after service of a request in writing by either party to do so.

(5) If the tribunal is to consist of three arbitrators—
    (a) each party shall appoint one arbitrator not later than 14 days after service of a request in writing by either party to do so, and
    (b) the two so appointed shall forthwith appoint a third arbitrator as the chairman of the tribunal.

(6) If the tribunal is to consist of two arbitrators and an umpire—
    (a) each party shall appoint one arbitrator not later than 14 days after service of a request in writing by either party to do so, and
    (b) the two so appointed may appoint an umpire at any time after they themselves are appointed and shall do so before any substantive hearing or forthwith if they cannot agree on a matter relating to the arbitration.

(7) In any other case (in particular, if there are more than two parties) section 18 applies as in the case of a failure of the agreed appointment procedure.

## 17 Power in case of default to appoint sole arbitrator

(1) Unless the parties otherwise agree, where each of two parties to an arbitration agreement is to appoint an arbitrator and one party ("the party in default") refuses to do so, or fails to do so within the time specified, the other party, having duly appointed his arbitrator, may give notice in writing to the party in default that he proposes to appoint his arbitrator to act as sole arbitrator.

(2) If the party in default does not within 7 clear days of that notice being given—
    (a) make the required appointment, and
    (b) notify the other party that he has done so,

the other party may appoint his arbitrator as sole arbitrator whose award shall be binding on both parties as if he had been so appointed by agreement.

(3) Where a sole arbitrator has been appointed under subsection (2), the party in default may (upon notice to the appointing party) apply to the court which may set aside the appointment.

(4) The leave of the court is required for any appeal from a decision of the court under this section.

## 18   Failure of appointment procedure

(1) The parties are free to agree what is to happen in the event of a failure of the procedure for the appointment of the arbitral tribunal.

There is no failure if an appointment is duly made under section 17 (power in case of default to appoint sole arbitrator), unless that appointment is set aside.

(2) If or to the extent that there is no such agreement any party to the arbitration agreement may (upon notice to the other parties) apply to the court to exercise its powers under this section.

(3) Those powers are—
  (a) to give directions as to the making of any necessary appointments;
  (b) to direct that the tribunal shall be constituted by such appointments (or any one or more of them) as have been made;
  (c) to revoke any appointments already made;
  (d) to make any necessary appointments itself.

(4) An appointment made by the court under this section has effect as if made with the agreement of the parties.

(5) The leave of the court is required for any appeal from a decision of the court under this section.

## 19   Court to have regard to agreed qualifications

In deciding whether to exercise, and in considering how to exercise, any of its powers under section 16 (procedure for appointment of arbitrators) or section 18 (failure of appointment procedure), the court shall have due regard to any agreement of the parties as to the qualifications required of the arbitrators.

## 20   Chairman

(1) Where the parties have agreed that there is to be a chairman, they are free to agree what the functions of the chairman are to be in relation to the making of decisions, orders and awards.

(2) If or to the extent that there is no such agreement, the following provisions apply.

(3) Decisions, orders and awards shall be made by all or a majority of the arbitrators (including the chairman).

(4) The view of the chairman shall prevail in relation to a decision, order or award in respect of which there is neither unanimity nor a majority under subsection (3).

**21    Umpire**

(1) Where the parties have agreed that there is to be an umpire, they are free to agree what the functions of the umpire are to be, and in particular—
   (a) whether he is to attend the proceedings, and
   (b) when he is to replace the other arbitrators as the tribunal with power to make decisions, orders and awards.

(2) If or to the extent that there is no such agreement, the following provisions apply.

(3) The umpire shall attend the proceedings and be supplied with the same documents and other materials as are supplied to the other arbitrators.

(4) Decisions, orders and awards shall be made by the other arbitrators unless and until they cannot agree on a matter relating to the arbitration.

In that event they shall forthwith give notice in writing to the parties and the umpire, whereupon the umpire shall replace them as the tribunal with power to make decisions, orders and awards as if he were sole arbitrator.

(5) If the arbitrators cannot agree but fail to give notice of that fact, or if any of them fails to join in the giving of notice, any party to the arbitral proceedings may (upon notice to the other parties and to the tribunal) apply to the court which may order that the umpire shall replace the other arbitrators as the tribunal with power to make decisions, orders and awards as if he were sole arbitrator.

(6) The leave of the court is required for any appeal from a decision of the court under this section.

**22    Decision-making where no chairman or umpire**

(1) Where the parties agree that there shall be two or more arbitrators with no chairman or umpire, the parties are free to agree how the tribunal is to make decisions, orders and awards.

(2) If there is no such agreement, decisions, orders and awards shall be made by all or a majority of the arbitrators.

## 23 Revocation of arbitrator's authority

(1) The parties are free to agree in what circumstances the authority of an arbitrator may be revoked.

(2) If or to the extent that there is no such agreement the following provisions apply.

(3) The authority of an arbitrator may not be revoked except—
  (a) by the parties acting jointly, or
  (b) by an arbitral or other institution or person vested by the parties with powers in that regard.

(4) Revocation of the authority of an arbitrator by the parties acting jointly must be agreed in writing unless the parties also agree (whether or not in writing) to terminate the arbitration agreement.

(5) Nothing in this section affects the power of the court—
  (a) to revoke an appointment under section 18 (powers exercisable in case of failure of appointment procedure), or
  (b) to remove an arbitrator on the grounds specified in section 24.

## 24 Power of court to remove arbitrator

(1) A party to arbitral proceedings may (upon notice to the other parties, to the arbitrator concerned and to any other arbitrator) apply to the court to remove an arbitrator on any of the following grounds—
  (a) that circumstances exist that give rise to justifiable doubts as to his impartiality;
  (b) that he does not possess the qualifications required by the arbitration agreement;
  (c) that he is physically or mentally incapable of conducting the proceedings or there are justifiable doubts as to his capacity to do so;
  (d) that he has refused or failed—
    (i) properly to conduct the proceedings, or
    (ii) to use all reasonable despatch in conducting the proceedings or making an award,
  and that substantial injustice has been or will be caused to the applicant.

(2) If there is an arbitral or other institution or person vested by the parties with power to remove an arbitrator, the court shall not exercise its power of removal unless satisfied that the applicant has first exhausted any available recourse to that institution or person.

(3) The arbitral tribunal may continue the arbitral proceedings and make an award while an application to the court under this section is pending.

(4) Where the court removes an arbitrator, it may make such order as it thinks fit with respect to his entitlement (if any) to fees or expenses, or the repayment of any fees or expenses already paid.

(5) The arbitrator concerned is entitled to appear and be heard by the court before it makes any order under this section.

(6) The leave of the court is required for any appeal from a decision of the court under this section.

## 25 Resignation of arbitrator

(1) The parties are free to agree with an arbitrator as to the consequences of his resignation as regards—
    (a) his entitlement (if any) to fees or expenses, and
    (b) any liability thereby incurred by him.

(2) If or to the extent that there is no such agreement the following provisions apply.

(3) An arbitrator who resigns his appointment may (upon notice to the parties) apply to the court—
    (a) to grant him relief from any liability thereby incurred by him, and
    (b) to make such order as it thinks fit with respect to his entitlement (if any) to fees or expenses or the repayment of any fees or expenses already paid.

(4) If the court is satisfied that in all the circumstances it was reasonable for the arbitrator to resign, it may grant such relief as is mentioned in subsection (3)(a) on such terms as it thinks fit.

(5) The leave of the court is required for any appeal from a decision of the court under this section.

## 26 Death of arbitrator or person appointing him

(1) The authority of an arbitrator is personal and ceases on his death.

(2) Unless otherwise agreed by the parties, the death of the person by whom an arbitrator was appointed does not revoke the arbitrator's authority.

## 27 Filling of vacancy, &c

(1) Where an arbitrator ceases to hold office, the parties are free to agree—
    (a) whether and if so how the vacancy is to be filled,
    (b) whether and if so to what extent the previous proceedings should stand, and

(c) what effect (if any) his ceasing to hold office has on any appointment made by him (alone or jointly).

(2) If or to the extent that there is no such agreement, the following provisions apply.

(3) The provisions of sections 16 (procedure for appointment of arbitrators) and 18 (failure of appointment procedure) apply in relation to the filling of the vacancy as in relation to an original appointment.

(4) The tribunal (when reconstituted) shall determine whether and if so to what extent the previous proceedings should stand.

This does not affect any right of a party to challenge those proceedings on any ground which had arisen before the arbitrator ceased to hold office.

(5) His ceasing to hold office does not affect any appointment by him (alone or jointly) of another arbitrator, in particular any appointment of a chairman or umpire.

## 28 Joint and several liability of parties to arbitrators for fees and expenses

(1) The parties are jointly and severally liable to pay to the arbitrators such reasonable fees and expenses (if any) as are appropriate in the circumstances.

(2) Any party may apply to the court (upon notice to the other parties and to the arbitrators) which may order that the amount of the arbitrators' fees and expenses shall be considered and adjusted by such means and upon such terms as it may direct.

(3) If the application is made after any amount has been paid to the arbitrators by way of fees or expenses, the court may order the repayment of such amount (if any) as is shown to be excessive, but shall not do so unless it is shown that it is reasonable in the circumstances to order repayment.

(4) The above provisions have effect subject to any order of the court under section 24(4) or 25(3)(b) (order as to entitlement to fees or expenses in case of removal or resignation of arbitrator).

(5) Nothing in this section affects any liability of a party to any other party to pay all or any of the costs of the arbitration (see sections 59 to 65) or any contractual right of an arbitrator to payment of his fees and expenses.

(6) In this section references to arbitrators include an arbitrator who has ceased to act and an umpire who has not replaced the other arbitrators.

## 29 Immunity of arbitrator

(1) An arbitrator is not liable for anything done or omitted in the discharge or purported discharge of his functions as arbitrator unless the act or omission is shown to have been in bad faith.

(2) Subsection (1) applies to an employee or agent of an arbitrator as it applies to the arbitrator himself.

(3) This section does not affect any liability incurred by an arbitrator by reason of his resigning (but see section 25).

*Jurisdiction of the arbitral tribunal*

## 30 Competence of tribunal to rule on its own jurisdiction

(1) Unless otherwise agreed by the parties, the arbitral tribunal may rule on its own substantive jurisdiction, that is, as to—
  (a) whether there is a valid arbitration agreement,
  (b) whether the tribunal is properly constituted, and
  (c) what matters have been submitted to arbitration in accordance with the arbitration agreement.

(2) Any such ruling may be challenged by any available arbitral process of appeal or review or in accordance with the provisions of this Part.

## 31 Objection to substantive jurisdiction of tribunal

(1) An objection that the arbitral tribunal lacks substantive jurisdiction at the outset of the proceedings must be raised by a party not later than the time he takes the first step in the proceedings to contest the merits of any matter in relation to which he challenges the tribunal's jurisdiction.

A party is not precluded from raising such an objection by the fact that he has appointed or participated in the appointment of an arbitrator.

(2) Any objection during the course of the arbitral proceedings that the arbitral tribunal is exceeding its substantive jurisdiction must be made as soon as possible after the matter alleged to be beyond its jurisdiction is raised.

(3) The arbitral tribunal may admit an objection later than the time specified in subsection (1) or (2) if it considers the delay justified.

(4) Where an objection is duly taken to the tribunal's substantive jurisdiction and the tribunal has power to rule on its own jurisdiction, it may—
  (a) rule on the matter in an award as to jurisdiction, or
  (b) deal with the objection in its award on the merits.

If the parties agree which of these courses the tribunal should take, the tribunal shall proceed accordingly.

(5) The tribunal may in any case, and shall if the parties so agree, stay proceedings whilst an application is made to the court under section 32 (determination of preliminary point of jurisdiction).

## 32 Determination of preliminary point of jurisdiction

(1) The court may, on the application of a party to arbitral proceedings (upon notice to the other parties), determine any question as to the substantive jurisdiction of the tribunal.

A party may lose the right to object (see section 73).

(2) An application under this section shall not be considered unless—
   (a) it is made with the agreement in writing of all the other parties to the proceedings, or
   (b) it is made with the permission of the tribunal and the court is satisfied—
      (i) that the determination of the question is likely to produce substantial savings in costs,
      (ii) that the application was made without delay, and
      (iii) that there is good reason why the matter should be decided by the court.

(3) An application under this section, unless made with the agreement of all the other parties to the proceedings, shall state the grounds on which it is said that the matter should be decided by the court.

(4) Unless otherwise agreed by the parties, the arbitral tribunal may continue the arbitral proceedings and make an award while an application to the court under this section is pending.

(5) Unless the court gives leave, no appeal lies from a decision of the court whether the conditions specified in subsection (2) are met.

(6) The decision of the court on the question of jurisdiction shall be treated as a judgment of the court for the purposes of an appeal.

But no appeal lies without the leave of the court which shall not be given unless the court considers that the question involves a point of law which is one of general importance or is one which for some other special reason should be considered by the Court of Appeal.

*The arbitral proceedings*

## 33 General duty of the tribunal

(1) The tribunal shall—

(a) act fairly and impartially as between the parties, giving each party a reasonable opportunity of putting his case and dealing with that of his opponent, and
(b) adopt procedures suitable to the circumstances of the particular case, avoiding unnecessary delay or expense, so as to provide a fair means for the resolution of the matters falling to be determined.

(2) The tribunal shall comply with that general duty in conducting the arbitral proceedings, in its decisions on matters of procedure and evidence and in the exercise of all other powers conferred on it.

**34    Procedural and evidential matters**

(1) It shall be for the tribunal to decide all procedural and evidential matters, subject to the right of the parties to agree any matter.

(2) Procedural and evidential matters include—
   (a) when and where any part of the proceedings is to be held;
   (b) the language or languages to be used in the proceedings and whether translations of any relevant documents are to be supplied;
   (c) whether any and if so what form of written statements of claim and defence are to be used, when these should be supplied and the extent to which such statements can be later amended;
   (d) whether any and if so which documents or classes of documents should be disclosed between and produced by the parties and at what stage;
   (e) whether any and if so what questions should be put to and answered by the respective parties and when and in what form this should be done;
   (f) whether to apply strict rules of evidence (or any other rules) as to the admissibility, relevance or weight of any material (oral, written or other) sought to be tendered on any matters of fact or opinion, and the time, manner and form in which such material should be exchanged and presented;
   (g) whether and to what extent the tribunal should itself take the initiative in ascertaining the facts and the law;
   (h) whether and to what extent there should be oral or written evidence or submissions.

(3) The tribunal may fix the time within which any directions given by it are to be complied with, and may if it thinks fit extend the time so fixed (whether or not it has expired).

**35    Consolidation of proceedings and concurrent hearings**

(1) The parties are free to agree—

(a) that the arbitral proceedings shall be consolidated with other arbitral proceedings, or
(b) that concurrent hearings shall be held, on such terms as may be agreed.

(2) Unless the parties agree to confer such power on the tribunal, the tribunal has no power to order consolidation of proceedings or concurrent hearings.

## 36 Legal or other representation

Unless otherwise agreed by the parties, a party to arbitral proceedings may be represented in the proceedings by a lawyer or other person chosen by him.

## 37 Power to appoint experts, legal advisers or assessors

(1) Unless otherwise agreed by the parties—
   (a) the tribunal may—
       (i) appoint experts or legal advisers to report to it and the parties, or
       (ii) appoint assessors to assist it on technical matters,

   and may allow any such expert, legal adviser or assessor to attend the proceedings; and

   (b) the parties shall be given a reasonable opportunity to comment on any information, opinion or advice offered by any such person.

(2) The fees and expenses of an expert, legal adviser or assessor appointed by the tribunal for which the arbitrators are liable are expenses of the arbitrators for the purposes of this Part.

## 38 General powers exercisable by the tribunal

(1) The parties are free to agree on the powers exercisable by the arbitral tribunal for the purposes of and in relation to the proceedings.

(2) Unless otherwise agreed by the parties the tribunal has the following powers.

(3) The tribunal may order a claimant to provide security for the costs of the arbitration. This power shall not be exercised on the ground that the claimant is—
   (a) an individual ordinarily resident outside the United Kingdom, or
   (b) a corporation or association incorporated or formed under the law of a country outside the United Kingdom, or whose central management and control is exercised outside the United Kingdom.

(4) The tribunal may give directions in relation to any property which is the subject of the proceedings or as to which any question arises in the proceedings, and which is owned by or is in the possession of a party to the proceedings—
    (a) for the inspection, photographing, preservation, custody or detention of the property by the tribunal, an expert or a party, or
    (b) ordering that samples be taken from, or any observation be made of or experiment conducted upon, the property.

(5) The tribunal may direct that a party or witness shall be examined on oath or affirmation, and may for that purpose administer any necessary oath or take any necessary affirmation.

(6) The tribunal may give directions to a party for the preservation for the purposes of the proceedings of any evidence in his custody or control.

## 39 Power to make provisional awards

(1) The parties are free to agree that the tribunal shall have power to order on a provisional basis any relief which it would have power to grant in a final award.

(2) This includes, for instance, making—
    (a) a provisional order for the payment of money or the disposition of property as between the parties, or
    (b) an order to make an interim payment on account of the costs of the arbitration.

(3) Any such order shall be subject to the tribunal's final adjudication; and the tribunal's final award, on the merits or as to costs, shall take account of any such order.

(4) Unless the parties agree to confer such power on the tribunal, the tribunal has no such power.

This does not affect its powers under section 47 (awards on different issues, &c.).

## 40 General duty of parties

(1) The parties shall do all things necessary for the proper and expeditious conduct of the arbitral proceedings.

(2) This includes—
    (a) complying without delay with any determination of the tribunal as to procedural or evidential matters, or with any order or directions of the tribunal, and

(b) where appropriate, taking without delay any necessary steps to obtain a decision of the court on a preliminary question of jurisdiction or law (see sections 32 and 45).

## 41 Powers of tribunal in case of party's default

(1) The parties are free to agree on the powers of the tribunal in case of a party's failure to do something necessary for the proper and expeditious conduct of the arbitration.

(2) Unless otherwise agreed by the parties, the following provisions apply.

(3) If the tribunal is satisfied that there has been inordinate and inexcusable delay on the part of the claimant in pursuing his claim and that the delay—
   (a) gives rise, or is likely to give rise, to a substantial risk that it is not possible to have a fair resolution of the issues in that claim, or
   (b) has caused, or is likely to cause, serious prejudice to the respondent,

the tribunal may make an award dismissing the claim.

(4) If without showing sufficient cause a party—
   (a) fails to attend or be represented at an oral hearing of which due notice was given, or
   (b) where matters are to be dealt with in writing, fails after due notice to submit written evidence or make written submissions,

the tribunal may continue the proceedings in the absence of that party or, as the case may be, without any written evidence or submissions on his behalf, and may make an award on the basis of the evidence before it.

(5) If without showing sufficient cause a party fails to comply with any order or directions of the tribunal, the tribunal may make a peremptory order to the same effect, prescribing such time for compliance with it as the tribunal considers appropriate.

(6) If a claimant fails to comply with a peremptory order of the tribunal to provide security for costs, the tribunal may make an award dismissing his claim.

(7) If a party fails to comply with any other kind of peremptory order, then, without prejudice to section 42 (enforcement by court of tribunal's peremptory orders), the tribunal may do any of the following—
   (a) direct that the party in default shall not be entitled to rely upon any allegation or material which was the subject matter of the order;

(b) draw such adverse inferences from the act of non-compliance as the circumstances justify;

(c) proceed to an award on the basis of such materials as have been properly provided to it;

(d) make such order as it thinks fit as to the payment of costs of the arbitration incurred in consequence of the non-compliance.

*Powers of court in relation to arbitral proceedings*

## 42 Enforcement of peremptory orders of tribunal

(1) Unless otherwise agreed by the parties, the court may make an order requiring a party to comply with a peremptory order made by the tribunal.

(2) An application for an order under this section may be made—
   (a) by the tribunal (upon notice to the parties),
   (b) by a party to the arbitral proceedings with the permission of the tribunal (and upon notice to the other parties), or
   (c) where the parties have agreed that the powers of the court under this section shall be available.

(3) The court shall not act unless it is satisfied that the applicant has exhausted any available arbitral process in respect of failure to comply with the tribunal's order.

(4) No order shall be made under this section unless the court is satisfied that the person to whom the tribunal's order was directed has failed to comply with it within the time prescribed in the order or, if no time was prescribed, within a reasonable time.

(5) The leave of the court is required for any appeal from a decision of the court under this section.

## 43 Securing the attendance of witnesses

(1) A party to arbitral proceedings may use the same court procedures as are available in relation to legal proceedings to secure the attendance before the tribunal of a witness in order to give oral testimony or to produce documents or other material evidence.

(2) This may only be done with the permission of the tribunal or the agreement of the other parties.

(3) The court procedures may only be used if—
   (a) the witness is in the United Kingdom, and
   (b) the arbitral proceedings are being conducted in England and Wales or, as the case may be, Northern Ireland.

(4) A person shall not be compelled by virtue of this section to produce any document or other material evidence which he could not be compelled to produce in legal proceedings.

## 44 Court powers exercisable in support of arbitral proceedings

(1) Unless otherwise agreed by the parties, the court has for the purposes of and in relation to arbitral proceedings the same power of making orders about the matters listed below as it has for the purposes of and in relation to legal proceedings.

(2) Those matters are—
   (a) the taking of the evidence of witnesses;
   (b) the preservation of evidence;
   (c) making orders relating to property which is the subject of the proceedings or as to which any question arises in the proceedings—
       (i) for the inspection, photographing, preservation, custody or detention of the property, or
       (ii) ordering that samples be taken from, or any observation be made of or experiment conducted upon, the property;

   and for that purpose authorising any person to enter any premises in the possession or control of a party to the arbitration;
   (d) the sale of any goods the subject of the proceedings;
   (e) the granting of an interim injunction or the appointment of a receiver.

(3) If the case is one of urgency, the court may, on the application of a party or proposed party to the arbitral proceedings, make such orders as it thinks necessary for the purpose of preserving evidence or assets.

(4) If the case is not one of urgency, the court shall act only on the application of a party to the arbitral proceedings (upon notice to the other parties and to the tribunal) made with the permission of the tribunal or the agreement in writing of the other parties.

(5) In any case the court shall act only if or to the extent that the arbitral tribunal, and any arbitral or other institution or person vested by the parties with power in that regard, has no power or is unable for the time being to act effectively.

(6) If the court so orders, an order made by it under this section shall cease to have effect in whole or in part on the order of the tribunal or of any such arbitral or other institution or person having power to act in relation to the subject-matter of the order.

(7) The leave of the court is required for any appeal from a decision of the court under this section.

**45  Determination of preliminary point of law**

(1) Unless otherwise agreed by the parties, the court may on the application of a party to arbitral proceedings (upon notice to the other parties) determine any question of law arising in the course of the proceedings which the court is satisfied substantially affects the rights of one or more of the parties.

An agreement to dispense with reasons for the tribunal's award shall be considered an agreement to exclude the court's jurisdiction under this section.

(2) An application under this section shall not be considered unless—
   (a) it is made with the agreement of all the other parties to the proceedings, or
   (b) it is made with the permission of the tribunal and the court is satisfied—
       (i) that the determination of the question is likely to produce substantial savings in costs, and
       (ii) that the application was made without delay.

(3) The application shall identify the question of law to be determined and, unless made with the agreement of all the other parties to the proceedings, shall state the grounds on which it is said that the question should be decided by the court.

(4) Unless otherwise agreed by the parties, the arbitral tribunal may continue the arbitral proceedings and make an award while an application to the court under this section is pending.

(5) Unless the court gives leave, no appeal lies from a decision of the court whether the conditions specified in subsection (2) are met.

(6) The decision of the court on the question of law shall be treated as a judgment of the court for the purposes of an appeal.

But no appeal lies without the leave of the court which shall not be given unless the court considers that the question is one of general importance, or is one which for some other special reason should be considered by the Court of Appeal.

*The award*

**46  Rules applicable to substance of dispute**

(1)   The arbitral tribunal shall decide the dispute—
   (a) in accordance with the law chosen by the parties as applicable to the substance of the dispute, or
   (b) if the parties so agree, in accordance with such other considerations as are agreed by them or determined by the tribunal.

(2) For this purpose the choice of the laws of a country shall be understood to refer to the substantive laws of that country and not its conflict of laws rules.

(3) If or to the extent that there is no such choice or agreement, the tribunal shall apply the law determined by the conflict of laws rules which it considers applicable.

## 47  Awards on different issues, &c

(1) Unless otherwise agreed by the parties, the tribunal may make more than one award at different times on different aspects of the matters to be determined.

(2) The tribunal may, in particular, make an award relating—
    (a) to an issue affecting the whole claim, or
    (b) to a part only of the claims or cross-claims submitted to it for decision.

(3) If the tribunal does so, it shall specify in its award the issue, or the claim or part of a claim, which is the subject matter of the award.

## 48  Remedies

(1) The parties are free to agree on the powers exercisable by the arbitral tribunal as regards remedies.

(2) Unless otherwise agreed by the parties, the tribunal has the following powers.

(3) The tribunal may make a declaration as to any matter to be determined in the proceedings.

(4) The tribunal may order the payment of a sum of money, in any currency.

(5) The tribunal has the same powers as the court—
    (a) to order a party to do or refrain from doing anything;
    (b) to order specific performance of a contract (other than a contract relating to land);
    (c) to order the rectification, setting aside or cancellation of a deed or other document.

## 49  Interest

(1) The parties are free to agree on the powers of the tribunal as regards the award of interest.

(2) Unless otherwise agreed by the parties the following provisions apply.

(3) The tribunal may award simple or compound interest from such dates, at such rates and with such rests as it considers meets the justice of the case—
  (a) on the whole or part of any amount awarded by the tribunal, in respect of any period up to the date of the award;
  (b) on the whole or part of any amount claimed in the arbitration and outstanding at the commencement of the arbitral proceedings but paid before the award was made, in respect of any period up to the date of payment.

(4) The tribunal may award simple or compound interest from the date of the award (or any later date) until payment, at such rates and with such rests as it considers meets the justice of the case, on the outstanding amount of any award (including any award of interest under subsection (3) and any award as to costs).

(5) References in this section to an amount awarded by the tribunal include an amount payable in consequence of a declaratory award by the tribunal.

(6) The above provisions do not affect any other power of the tribunal to award interest.

## 50 Extension of time for making award

(1) Where the time for making an award is limited by or in pursuance of the arbitration agreement, then, unless otherwise agreed by the parties, the court may in accordance with the following provisions by order extend that time.

(2) An application for an order under this section may be made—
  (a) by the tribunal (upon notice to the parties), or
  (b) by any party to the proceedings (upon notice to the tribunal and the other parties),

but only after exhausting any available arbitral process for obtaining an extension of time.

(3) The court shall only make an order if satisfied that a substantial injustice would otherwise be done.

(4) The court may extend the time for such period and on such terms as it thinks fit, and may do so whether or not the time previously fixed (by or under the agreement or by a previous order) has expired.

(5) The leave of the court is required for any appeal from a decision of the court under this section.

## 51 Settlement

(1) If during arbitral proceedings the parties settle the dispute, the following provisions apply unless otherwise agreed by the parties.

(2) The tribunal shall terminate the substantive proceedings and, if so requested by the parties and not objected to by the tribunal, shall record the settlement in the form of an agreed award.

(3) An agreed award shall state that it is an award of the tribunal and shall have the same status and effect as any other award on the merits of the case.

(4) The following provisions of this Part relating to awards (sections 52 to 58) apply to an agreed award.

(5) Unless the parties have also settled the matter of the payment of the costs of the arbitration, the provisions of this Part relating to costs (sections 59 to 65) continue to apply.

## 52  Form of award

(1) The parties are free to agree on the form of an award.

(2) If or to the extent that there is no such agreement, the following provisions apply.

(3) The award shall be in writing signed by all the arbitrators or all those assenting to the award.

(4) The award shall contain the reasons for the award unless it is an agreed award or the parties have agreed to dispense with reasons.

(5) The award shall state the seat of the arbitration and the date when the award is made.

## 53  Place where award treated as made

Unless otherwise agreed by the parties, where the seat of the arbitration is in England and Wales or Northern Ireland, any award in the proceedings shall be treated as made there, regardless of where it was signed, despatched or delivered to any of the parties.

## 54  Date of award

(1) Unless otherwise agreed by the parties, the tribunal may decide what is to be taken to be the date on which the award was made.

(2) In the absence of any such decision, the date of the award shall be taken to be the date on which it is signed by the arbitrator or, where more than one arbitrator signs the award, by the last of them.

## 55  Notification of award

(1) The parties are free to agree on the requirements as to notification of the award to the parties.

(2) If there is no such agreement, the award shall be notified to the parties by service on them of copies of the award, which shall be done without delay after the award is made.

(3) Nothing in this section affects section 56 (power to withhold award in case of non- payment).

## 56  Power to withhold award in case of non-payment

(1) The tribunal may refuse to deliver an award to the parties except upon full payment of the fees and expenses of the arbitrators.

(2) If the tribunal refuses on that ground to deliver an award, a party to the arbitral proceedings may (upon notice to the other parties and the tribunal) apply to the court, which may order that—
   (a) the tribunal shall deliver the award on the payment into court by the applicant of the fees and expenses demanded, or such lesser amount as the court may specify,
   (b) the amount of the fees and expenses properly payable shall be determined by such means and upon such terms as the court may direct, and
   (c) out of the money paid into court there shall be paid out such fees and expenses as may be found to be properly payable and the balance of the money (if any) shall be paid out to the applicant.

(3) For this purpose the amount of fees and expenses properly payable is the amount the applicant is liable to pay under section 28 or any agreement relating to the payment of the arbitrators.

(4) No application to the court may be made where there is any available arbitral process for appeal or review of the amount of the fees or expenses demanded.

(5) References in this section to arbitrators include an arbitrator who has ceased to act and an umpire who has not replaced the other arbitrators.

(6) The above provisions of this section also apply in relation to any arbitral or other institution or person vested by the parties with powers in relation to the delivery of the tribunal's award.

As they so apply, the references to the fees and expenses of the arbitrators shall be construed as including the fees and expenses of that institution or person.

(7) The leave of the court is required for any appeal from a decision of the court under this section.

(8) Nothing in this section shall be construed as excluding an application under section 28 where payment has been made to the arbitrators in order to obtain the award.

## 57 Correction of award or additional award

(1) The parties are free to agree on the powers of the tribunal to correct an award or make an additional award.

(2) If or to the extent there is no such agreement, the following provisions apply.

(3) The tribunal may on its own initiative or on the application of a party—
   (a) correct an award so as to remove any clerical mistake or error arising from an accidental slip or omission or clarify or remove any ambiguity in the award, or
   (b) make an additional award in respect of any claim (including a claim for interest or costs) which was presented to the tribunal but was not dealt with in the award.

These powers shall not be exercised without first affording the other parties a reasonable opportunity to make representations to the tribunal.

(4) Any application for the exercise of those powers must be made within 28 days of the date of the award or such longer period as the parties may agree.

(5) Any correction of an award shall be made within 28 days of the date the application was received by the tribunal or, where the correction is made by the tribunal on its own initiative, within 28 days of the date of the award or, in either case, such longer period as the parties may agree.

(6) Any additional award shall be made within 56 days of the date of the original award or such longer period as the parties may agree.

(7) Any correction of an award shall form part of the award.

## 58 Effect of award

(1) Unless otherwise agreed by the parties, an award made by the tribunal pursuant to an arbitration agreement is final and binding both on the parties and on any persons claiming through or under them.

(2) This does not affect the right of a person to challenge the award by any available arbitral process of appeal or review or in accordance with the provisions of this Part.

*Costs of the arbitration*

## 59 Costs of the arbitration

(1) References in this Part to the costs of the arbitration are to—

(a) the arbitrators' fees and expenses,
(b) the fees and expenses of any arbitral institution concerned, and
(c) the legal or other costs of the parties.

(2) Any such reference includes the costs of or incidental to any proceedings to determine the amount of the recoverable costs of the arbitration (see section 63).

## 60  Agreement to pay costs in any event

An agreement which has the effect that a party is to pay the whole or part of the costs of the arbitration in any event is only valid if made after the dispute in question has arisen.

## 61  Award of costs

(1) The tribunal may make an award allocating the costs of the arbitration as between the parties, subject to any agreement of the parties.

(2) Unless the parties otherwise agree, the tribunal shall award costs on the general principle that costs should follow the event except where it appears to the tribunal that in the circumstances this is not appropriate in relation to the whole or part of the costs.

## 62  Effect of agreement or award about costs

Unless the parties otherwise agree, any obligation under an agreement between them as to how the costs of the arbitration are to be borne, or under an award allocating the costs of the arbitration, extends only to such costs as are recoverable.

## 63  The recoverable costs of the arbitration

(1) The parties are free to agree what costs of the arbitration are recoverable.

(2) If or to the extent there is no such agreement, the following provisions apply.

(3) The tribunal may determine by award the recoverable costs of the arbitration on such basis as it thinks fit.

If it does so, it shall specify—
(a) the basis on which it has acted, and
(b) the items of recoverable costs and the amount referable to each.

(4) If the tribunal does not determine the recoverable costs of the arbitration, any party to the arbitral proceedings may apply to the court (upon notice to the other parties) which may—
   (a) determine the recoverable costs of the arbitration on such basis as it thinks fit, or
   (b) order that they shall be determined by such means and upon such terms as it may specify.

(5) Unless the tribunal or the court determines otherwise—
   (a) the recoverable costs of the arbitration shall be determined on the basis that there shall be allowed a reasonable amount in respect of all costs reasonably incurred, and
   (b) any doubt as to whether costs were reasonably incurred or were reasonable in amount shall be resolved in favour of the paying party.

(6) The above provisions have effect subject to section 64 (recoverable fees and expenses of arbitrators).

(7) Nothing in this section affects any right of the arbitrators, any expert, legal adviser or assessor appointed by the tribunal, or any arbitral institution, to payment of their fees and expenses.

## 64 Recoverable fees and expenses of arbitrators

(1) Unless otherwise agreed by the parties, the recoverable costs of the arbitration shall include in respect of the fees and expenses of the arbitrators only such reasonable fees and expenses as are appropriate in the circumstances.

(2) If there is any question as to what reasonable fees and expenses are appropriate in the circumstances, and the matter is not already before the court on an application under section 63(4), the court may on the application of any party (upon notice to the other parties)—
   (a) determine the matter, or
   (b) order that it be determined by such means and upon such terms as the court may specify.

(3) Subsection (1) has effect subject to any order of the court under section 24(4) or 25(3) (b) (order as to entitlement to fees or expenses in case of removal or resignation of arbitrator).

(4) Nothing in this section affects any right of the arbitrator to payment of his fees and expenses.

## 65 Power to limit recoverable costs

(1) Unless otherwise agreed by the parties, the tribunal may direct that the recoverable costs of the arbitration, or of any part of the arbitral proceedings, shall be limited to a specified amount.

(2) Any direction may be made or varied at any stage, but this must be done sufficiently in advance of the incurring of costs to which it relates, or the taking of any steps in the proceedings which may be affected by it, for the limit to be taken into account.

*Powers of the court in relation to award*

**66  Enforcement of the award**

(1) An award made by the tribunal pursuant to an arbitration agreement may, by leave of the court, be enforced in the same manner as a judgment or order of the court to the same effect.

(2) Where leave is so given, judgment may be entered in terms of the award.

(3) Leave to enforce an award shall not be given where, or to the extent that, the person against whom it is sought to be enforced shows that the tribunal lacked substantive jurisdiction to make the award.

The right to raise such an objection may have been lost (see section 73).

(4) Nothing in this section affects the recognition or enforcement of an award under any other enactment or rule of law, in particular under Part II of the Arbitration Act 1950 (enforcement of awards under Geneva Convention) or the provisions of Part III of this Act relating to the recognition and enforcement of awards under the New York Convention or by an action on the award.

**67  Challenging the award: substantive jurisdiction**

(1) A party to arbitral proceedings may (upon notice to the other parties and to the tribunal) apply to the court—
 (a) challenging any award of the arbitral tribunal as to its substantive jurisdiction; or
 (b) for an order declaring an award made by the tribunal on the merits to be of no effect, in whole or in part, because the tribunal did not have substantive jurisdiction.

A party may lose the right to object (see section 73) and the right to apply is subject to the restrictions in section 70(2) and (3).

(2) The arbitral tribunal may continue the arbitral proceedings and make a further award while an application to the court under this section is pending in relation to an award as to jurisdiction.

(3) On an application under this section challenging an award of the arbitral tribunal as to its substantive jurisdiction, the court may by order—

(a) confirm the award,
(b) vary the award, or
(c) set aside the award in whole or in part.

(4) The leave of the court is required for any appeal from a decision of the court under this section.

## 68 Challenging the award: serious irregularity

(1) A party to arbitral proceedings may (upon notice to the other parties and to the tribunal) apply to the court challenging an award in the proceedings on the ground of serious irregularity affecting the tribunal, the proceedings or the award.

A party may lose the right to object (see section 73) and the right to apply is subject to the restrictions in section 70(2) and (3).

(2) Serious irregularity means an irregularity of one or more of the following kinds which the court considers has caused or will cause substantial injustice to the applicant—
   (a) failure by the tribunal to comply with section 33 (general duty of tribunal);
   (b) the tribunal exceeding its powers (otherwise than by exceeding its substantive jurisdiction: see section 67);
   (c) failure by the tribunal to conduct the proceedings in accordance with the procedure agreed by the parties;
   (d) failure by the tribunal to deal with all the issues that were put to it;
   (e) any arbitral or other institution or person vested by the parties with powers in relation to the proceedings or the award exceeding its powers;
   (f) uncertainty or ambiguity as to the effect of the award;
   (g) the award being obtained by fraud or the award or the way in which it was procured being contrary to public policy;
   (h) failure to comply with the requirements as to the form of the award; or
   (i) any irregularity in the conduct of the proceedings or in the award which is admitted by the tribunal or by any arbitral or other institution or person vested by the parties with powers in relation to the proceedings or the award.

(3) If there is shown to be serious irregularity affecting the tribunal, the proceedings or the award, the court may—
   (a) remit the award to the tribunal, in whole or in part, for reconsideration,
   (b) set the award aside in whole or in part, or
   (c) declare the award to be of no effect, in whole or in part.

The court shall not exercise its power to set aside or to declare an award to be of no effect, in whole or in part, unless it is satisfied that it would be inappropriate to remit the matters in question to the tribunal for reconsideration.

(4) The leave of the court is required for any appeal from a decision of the court under this section.

## 69 Appeal on point of law

(1) Unless otherwise agreed by the parties, a party to arbitral proceedings may (upon notice to the other parties and to the tribunal) appeal to the court on a question of law arising out of an award made in the proceedings.

An agreement to dispense with reasons for the tribunal's award shall be considered an agreement to exclude the court's jurisdiction under this section.

(2) An appeal shall not be brought under this section except—
    (a) with the agreement of all the other parties to the proceedings, or
    (b) with the leave of the court.

The right to appeal is also subject to the restrictions in section 70(2) and (3).

(3) Leave to appeal shall be given only if the court is satisfied—
    (a) that the determination of the question will substantially affect the rights of one or more of the parties,
    (b) that the question is one which the tribunal was asked to determine,
    (c) that, on the basis of the findings of fact in the award—
        (i) the decision of the tribunal on the question is obviously wrong, or
        (ii) the question is one of general public importance and the decision of the tribunal is at least open to serious doubt, and
    (d) that, despite the agreement of the parties to resolve the matter by arbitration, it is just and proper in all the circumstances for the court to determine the question.

(4) An application for leave to appeal under this section shall identify the question of law to be determined and state the grounds on which it is alleged that leave to appeal should be granted.

(5) The court shall determine an application for leave to appeal under this section without a hearing unless it appears to the court that a hearing is required.

(6) The leave of the court is required for any appeal from a decision of the court under this section to grant or refuse leave to appeal.

(7) On an appeal under this section the court may by order—
   (a) confirm the award,
   (b) vary the award,
   (c) remit the award to the tribunal, in whole or in part, for reconsideration in the light of the court's determination, or
   (d) set aside the award in whole or in part.

The court shall not exercise its power to set aside an award, in whole or in part, unless it is satisfied that it would be inappropriate to remit the matters in question to the tribunal for reconsideration.

(8) The decision of the court on an appeal under this section shall be treated as a judgment of the court for the purposes of a further appeal.

But no such appeal lies without the leave of the court which shall not be given unless the court considers that the question is one of general importance or is one which for some other special reason should be considered by the Court of Appeal.

## 70 Challenge or appeal: supplementary provisions

(1) The following provisions apply to an application or appeal under section 67, 68 or 69.

(2) An application or appeal may not be brought if the applicant or appellant has not first exhausted—
   (a) any available arbitral process of appeal or review, and
   (b) any available recourse under section 57 (correction of award or additional award).

(3) Any application or appeal must be brought within 28 days of the date of the award or, if there has been any arbitral process of appeal or review, of the date when the applicant or appellant was notified of the result of that process.

(4) If on an application or appeal it appears to the court that the award—
   (a) does not contain the tribunal's reasons, or
   (b) does not set out the tribunal's reasons in sufficient detail to enable the court properly to consider the application or appeal,

the court may order the tribunal to state the reasons for its award in sufficient detail for that purpose.

(5) Where the court makes an order under subsection (4), it may make such further order as it thinks fit with respect to any additional costs of the arbitration resulting from its order.

(6) The court may order the applicant or appellant to provide security for the costs of the application or appeal, and may direct that the application or appeal be dismissed if the order is not complied with.

The power to order security for costs shall not be exercised on the ground that the applicant or appellant is—
   (a) an individual ordinarily resident outside the United Kingdom, or
   (b) a corporation or association incorporated or formed under the law of a country outside the United Kingdom, or whose central management and control is exercised outside the United Kingdom.

(7) The court may order that any money payable under the award shall be brought into court or otherwise secured pending the determination of the application or appeal, and may direct that the application or appeal be dismissed if the order is not complied with.

(8) The court may grant leave to appeal subject to conditions to the same or similar effect as an order under subsection (6) or (7).

This does not affect the general discretion of the court to grant leave subject to conditions.

## 71   Challenge or appeal: effect of order of court

(1) The following provisions have effect where the court makes an order under section 67, 68 or 69 with respect to an award.

(2) Where the award is varied, the variation has effect as part of the tribunal's award.

(3) Where the award is remitted to the tribunal, in whole or in part, for reconsideration, the tribunal shall make a fresh award in respect of the matters remitted within three months of the date of the order for remission or such longer or shorter period as the court may direct.

(4) Where the award is set aside or declared to be of no effect, in whole or in part, the court may also order that any provision that an award is a condition precedent to the bringing of legal proceedings in respect of a matter to which the arbitration agreement applies, is of no effect as regards the subject matter of the award or, as the case may be, the relevant part of the award.

*Miscellaneous*

## 72   Saving for rights of person who takes no part in proceedings

(1) A person alleged to be a party to arbitral proceedings but who takes no part in the proceedings may question—

(a) whether there is a valid arbitration agreement,
(b) whether the tribunal is properly constituted, or
(c) what matters have been submitted to arbitration in accordance with the arbitration agreement,

by proceedings in the court for a declaration or injunction or other appropriate relief.

(2) He also has the same right as a party to the arbitral proceedings to challenge an award—
(a) by an application under section 67 on the ground of lack of substantive jurisdiction in relation to him, or
(b) by an application under section 68 on the ground of serious irregularity (within the meaning of that section) affecting him;

and section 70(2) (duty to exhaust arbitral procedures) does not apply in his case.

## 73 Loss of right to object

(1) If a party to arbitral proceedings takes part, or continues to take part, in the proceedings without making, either forthwith or within such time as is allowed by the arbitration agreement or the tribunal or by any provision of this Part, any objection—
(a) that the tribunal lacks substantive jurisdiction,
(b) that the proceedings have been improperly conducted,
(c) that there has been a failure to comply with the arbitration agreement or with any provision of this Part, or
(d) that there has been any other irregularity affecting the tribunal or the proceedings,

he may not raise that objection later, before the tribunal or the court, unless he shows that, at the time he took part or continued to take part in the proceedings, he did not know and could not with reasonable diligence have discovered the grounds for the objection.

(2) Where the arbitral tribunal rules that it has substantive jurisdiction and a party to arbitral proceedings who could have questioned that ruling—
(a) by any available arbitral process of appeal or review, or
(b) by challenging the award,

does not do so, or does not do so within the time allowed by the arbitration agreement or any provision of this Part, he may not object later to the tribunal's substantive jurisdiction on any ground which was the subject of that ruling.

## 74 Immunity of arbitral institutions, &c

(1) An arbitral or other institution or person designated or requested by the parties to appoint or nominate an arbitrator is not liable for anything

done or omitted in the discharge or purported discharge of that function unless the act or omission is shown to have been in bad faith.

(2) An arbitral or other institution or person by whom an arbitrator is appointed or nominated is not liable, by reason of having appointed or nominated him, for anything done or omitted by the arbitrator (or his employees or agents) in the discharge or purported discharge of his functions as arbitrator.

(3) The above provisions apply to an employee or agent of an arbitral or other institution or person as they apply to the institution or person himself.

## 75 Charge to secure payment of solicitors' costs

The powers of the court to make declarations and orders under section 73 of the Solicitors Act 1974 or Article 71H of the Solicitors (Northern Ireland) Order 1976 (power to charge property recovered in the proceedings with the payment of solicitors' costs) may be exercised in relation to arbitral proceedings as if those proceedings were proceedings in the court.

*Supplementary*

## 76 Service of notices, &c

(1) The parties are free to agree on the manner of service of any notice or other document required or authorised to be given or served in pursuance of the arbitration agreement or for the purposes of the arbitral proceedings.

(2) If or to the extent that there is no such agreement the following provisions apply.

(3) A notice or other document may be served on a person by any effective means.

(4) If a notice or other document is addressed, pre-paid and delivered by post—
  (a) to the addressee's last known principal residence or, if he is or has been carrying on a trade, profession or business, his last known principal business address, or
  (b) where the addressee is a body corporate, to the body's registered or principal office,

it shall be treated as effectively served.

(5) This section does not apply to the service of documents for the purposes of legal proceedings, for which provision is made by rules of court.

(6) References in this Part to a notice or other document include any form of communication in writing and references to giving or serving a notice or other document shall be construed accordingly.

**77  Powers of court in relation to service of documents**

(1) This section applies where service of a document on a person in the manner agreed by the parties, or in accordance with provisions of section 76 having effect in default of agreement, is not reasonably practicable.

(2) Unless otherwise agreed by the parties, the court may make such order as it thinks fit—
   (a) for service in such manner as the court may direct, or
   (b) dispensing with service of the document.

(3) Any party to the arbitration agreement may apply for an order, but only after exhausting any available arbitral process for resolving the matter.

(4) The leave of the court is required for any appeal from a decision of the court under this section.

**78  Reckoning periods of time**

(1) The parties are free to agree on the method of reckoning periods of time for the purposes of any provision agreed by them or any provision of this Part having effect in default of such agreement.

(2) If or to the extent there is no such agreement, periods of time shall be reckoned in accordance with the following provisions.

(3) Where the act is required to be done within a specified period after or from a specified date, the period begins immediately after that date.

(4) Where the act is required to be done a specified number of clear days after a specified date, at least that number of days must intervene between the day on which the act is done and that date.

(5) Where the period is a period of seven days or less which would include a Saturday, Sunday or a public holiday in the place where anything which has to be done within the period falls to be done, that day shall be excluded.

In relation to England and Wales or Northern Ireland, a "public holiday" means Christmas Day, Good Friday or a day which under the Banking and Financial Dealings Act 1971 is a bank holiday.

**79  Power of court to extend time limits relating to arbitral proceedings**

(1) Unless the parties otherwise agree, the court may by order extend any time limit agreed by them in relation to any matter relating to the

arbitral proceedings or specified in any provision of this Part having effect in default of such agreement.

This section does not apply to a time limit to which section 12 applies (power of court to extend time for beginning arbitral proceedings, &c.).

(2) An application for an order may be made—
  (a) by any party to the arbitral proceedings (upon notice to the other parties and to the tribunal), or
  (b) by the arbitral tribunal (upon notice to the parties).

(3) The court shall not exercise its power to extend a time limit unless it is satisfied—
  (a) that any available recourse to the tribunal, or to any arbitral or other institution or person vested by the parties with power in that regard, has first been exhausted, and
  (b) that a substantial injustice would otherwise be done.

(4) The court's power under this section may be exercised whether or not the time has already expired.

(5) An order under this section may be made on such terms as the court thinks fit.

(6) The leave of the court is required for any appeal from a decision of the court under this section.

**80  Notice and other requirements in connection with legal proceedings**

(1) References in this Part to an application, appeal or other step in relation to legal proceedings being taken "upon notice" to the other parties to the arbitral proceedings, or to the tribunal, are to such notice of the originating process as is required by rules of court and do not impose any separate requirement.

(2) Rules of court shall be made—
  (a) requiring such notice to be given as indicated by any provision of this Part, and
  (b) as to the manner, form and content of any such notice.

(3) Subject to any provision made by rules of court, a requirement to give notice to the tribunal of legal proceedings shall be construed—
  (a) if there is more than one arbitrator, as a requirement to give notice to each of them; and
  (b) if the tribunal is not fully constituted, as a requirement to give notice to any arbitrator who has been appointed.

(4) References in this Part to making an application or appeal to the court within a specified period are to the issue within that period of the appropriate originating process in accordance with rules of court.

(5) Where any provision of this Part requires an application or appeal to be made to the court within a specified time, the rules of court relating to the reckoning of periods, the extending or abridging of periods, and the consequences of not taking a step within the period prescribed by the rules, apply in relation to that requirement.

(6) Provision may be made by rules of court amending the provisions of this Part—
- (a) with respect to the time within which any application or appeal to the court must be made,
- (b) so as to keep any provision made by this Part in relation to arbitral proceedings in step with the corresponding provision of rules of court applying in relation to proceedings in the court, or
- (c) so as to keep any provision made by this Part in relation to legal proceedings in step with the corresponding provision of rules of court applying generally in relation to proceedings in the court.

(7) Nothing in this section affects the generality of the power to make rules of court.

## 81 Saving for certain matters governed by common law

(1) Nothing in this Part shall be construed as excluding the operation of any rule of law consistent with the provisions of this Part, in particular, any rule of law as to—
- (a) matters which are not capable of settlement by arbitration;
- (b) the effect of an oral arbitration agreement; or
- (c) the refusal of recognition or enforcement of an arbitral award on grounds of public policy.

(2) Nothing in this Act shall be construed as reviving any jurisdiction of the court to set aside or remit an award on the ground of errors of fact or law on the face of the award.

## 82 Minor definitions

(1) In this Part—

"arbitrator", unless the context otherwise requires, includes an umpire;

"available arbitral process", in relation to any matter, includes any process of appeal to or review by an arbitral or other institution or person vested by the parties with powers in relation to that matter;

"claimant", unless the context otherwise requires, includes a counterclaimant, and related expressions shall be construed accordingly;

"dispute" includes any difference;

"enactment" includes an enactment contained in Northern Ireland legislation;

"legal proceedings" means civil proceedings in the High Court or a county court;

"peremptory order" means an order made under section 41(5) or made in exercise of any corresponding power conferred by the parties;

"premises" includes land, buildings, moveable structures, vehicles, vessels, aircraft and hovercraft;

"question of law" means—
  (a) for a court in England and Wales, a question of the law of England and Wales, and
  (b) for a court in Northern Ireland, a question of the law of Northern Ireland;

"substantive jurisdiction", in relation to an arbitral tribunal, refers to the matters specified in section 30(1)(a) to (c), and references to the tribunal exceeding its substantive jurisdiction shall be construed accordingly.

(2) References in this Part to a party to an arbitration agreement include any person claiming under or through a party to the agreement.

## 83 Index of defined expressions: Part I

In this Part the expressions listed below are defined or otherwise explained by the provisions indicated—

| | |
|---|---|
| agreement, agree and agreed | section 5(1) |
| agreement in writing | section 5(2) to (5) |
| arbitration agreement | sections 6 and 5(1) |
| arbitrator | section 82(1) |
| available arbitral process | section 82(1) |
| claimant | section 82(1) |
| commencement (in relation to arbitral proceedings) | section 14 |
| costs of the arbitration | section 59 |
| the court | section 105 |
| dispute | section 82(1) |
| enactment | section 82(1) |
| legal proceedings | section 82(1) |
| Limitation Acts | section 13(4) |
| notice (or other document) | section 76(6) |
| party— | |

| | |
|---|---|
| —in relation to an arbitration agreement | section 82(2) |
| —where section 106(2) or (3) applies | section 106(4) |
| peremptory order | section 82(1) (and see section 41(5)) |
| premises | section 82(1) |
| question of law | section 82(1) |
| recoverable costs | sections 63 and 64 |
| seat of the arbitration | section 3 |
| serve and service (of notice or other document) | section 76(6) |
| substantive jurisdiction (in relation to an arbitral tribunal) | section 82(1) (and see section 30(1)(a) to (c)) |
| upon notice (to the parties or the tribunal) | section 80 |
| written and in writing | section 5(6) |

## 84  Transitional provisions

(1) The provisions of this Part do not apply to arbitral proceedings commenced before the date on which this Part comes into force.

(2) They apply to arbitral proceedings commenced on or after that date under an arbitration agreement whenever made.

(3) The above provisions have effect subject to any transitional provision made by an order under section 109(2) (power to include transitional provisions in commencement order).

## Part II

OTHER PROVISIONS RELATING TO ARBITRATION

*Domestic arbitration agreements*

## 85  Modification of Part I in relation to domestic arbitration agreement

(1) In the case of a domestic arbitration agreement the provisions of Part I are modified in accordance with the following sections.

(2) For this purpose a "domestic arbitration agreement" means an arbitration agreement to which none of the parties is—
    (a) an individual who is a national of, or habitually resident in, a state other than the United Kingdom, or

(b) a body corporate which is incorporated in, or whose central control and management is exercised in, a state other than the United Kingdom,

and under which the seat of the arbitration (if the seat has been designated or determined) is in the United Kingdom.

(3) In subsection (2) "arbitration agreement" and "seat of the arbitration" have the same meaning as in Part I (see sections 3, 5(1) and 6).

## 86 Staying of legal proceedings

(1) In section 9 (stay of legal proceedings), subsection (4) (stay unless the arbitration agreement is null and void, inoperative, or incapable of being performed) does not apply to a domestic arbitration agreement.

(2) On an application under that section in relation to a domestic arbitration agreement the court shall grant a stay unless satisfied—
- (a) that the arbitration agreement is null and void, inoperative, or incapable of being performed, or
- (b) that there are other sufficient grounds for not requiring the parties to abide by the arbitration agreement.

(3) The court may treat as a sufficient ground under subsection (2)(b) the fact that the applicant is or was at any material time not ready and willing to do all things necessary for the proper conduct of the arbitration or of any other dispute resolution procedures required to be exhausted before resorting to arbitration.

(4) For the purposes of this section the question whether an arbitration agreement is a domestic arbitration agreement shall be determined by reference to the facts at the time the legal proceedings are commenced.

## 87 Effectiveness of agreement to exclude court's jurisdiction

(1) In the case of a domestic arbitration agreement any agreement to exclude the jurisdiction of the court under—
- (a) section 45 (determination of preliminary point of law), or
- (b) section 69 (challenging the award: appeal on point of law),

is not effective unless entered into after the commencement of the arbitral proceedings in which the question arises or the award is made.

(2) For this purpose the commencement of the arbitral proceedings has the same meaning as in Part I (see section 14).

(3) For the purposes of this section the question whether an arbitration agreement is a domestic arbitration agreement shall be determined by reference to the facts at the time the agreement is entered into.

## 88 Power to repeal or amend sections 85 to 87

(1) The Secretary of State may by order repeal or amend the provisions of sections 85 to 87.

(2) An order under this section may contain such supplementary, incidental and transitional provisions as appear to the Secretary of State to be appropriate.

(3) An order under this section shall be made by statutory instrument and no such order shall be made unless a draft of it has been laid before and approved by a resolution of each House of Parliament.

*Consumer arbitration agreements*

## 89 Application of unfair terms regulations to consumer arbitration agreements

(1) The following sections extend the application of the Unfair Terms in Consumer Contracts Regulations 1994 in relation to a term which constitutes an arbitration agreement.

For this purpose "arbitration agreement" means an agreement to submit to arbitration present or future disputes or differences (whether or not contractual).

(2) In those sections "the Regulations" means those regulations and includes any regulations amending or replacing those regulations.

(3) Those sections apply whatever the law applicable to the arbitration agreement.

## 90 Regulations apply where consumer is a legal person

The Regulations apply where the consumer is a legal person as they apply where the consumer is a natural person.

## 91 Arbitration agreement unfair where modest amount sought

(1) A term which constitutes an arbitration agreement is unfair for the purposes of the Regulations so far as it relates to a claim for a pecuniary remedy which does not exceed the amount specified by order for the purposes of this section.

(2) Orders under this section may make different provision for different cases and for different purposes.

(3) The power to make orders under this section is exercisable—
    (a) for England and Wales, by the Secretary of State with the concurrence of the Lord Chancellor,

(b) for Scotland, by the Secretary of State with the concurrence of the Lord Advocate, and

(c) for Northern Ireland, by the Department of Economic Development for Northern Ireland with the concurrence of the Lord Chancellor.

(4) Any such order for England and Wales or Scotland shall be made by statutory instrument which shall be subject to annulment in pursuance of a resolution of either House of Parliament.

(5) Any such order for Northern Ireland shall be a statutory rule for the purposes of the Statutory Rules (Northern Ireland) Order 1979 and shall be subject to negative resolution, within the meaning of section 41(6) of the Interpretation Act (Northern Ireland) 1954.

*Small claims arbitration in the county court*

## 92 Exclusion of Part I in relation to small claims arbitration in the county court

Nothing in Part I of this Act applies to arbitration under section 64 of the County Courts Act 1984.

*Appointment of judges as arbitrators*

## 93 Appointment of judges as arbitrators

(1) A judge of the Commercial Court or an official referee may, if in all the circumstances he thinks fit, accept appointment as a sole arbitrator or as umpire by or by virtue of an arbitration agreement.

(2) A judge of the Commercial Court shall not do so unless the Lord Chief Justice has informed him that, having regard to the state of business in the High Court and the Crown Court, he can be made available.

(3) An official referee shall not do so unless the Lord Chief Justice has informed him that, having regard to the state of official referees' business, he can be made available.

(4) The fees payable for the services of a judge of the Commercial Court or official referee as arbitrator or umpire shall be taken in the High Court.

(5) In this section—

"arbitration agreement" has the same meaning as in Part I; and

"official referee" means a person nominated under section 68(1)(a) of the Supreme Court Act 1981 to deal with official referees' business.

(6) The provisions of Part I of this Act apply to arbitration before a person appointed under this section with the modifications specified in Schedule 2.

*Statutory arbitrations*

**94    Application of Part I to statutory arbitrations**

(1) The provisions of Part I apply to every arbitration under an enactment (a "statutory arbitration"), whether the enactment was passed or made before or after the commencement of this Act, subject to the adaptations and exclusions specified in sections 95 to 98.

(2) The provisions of Part I do not apply to a statutory arbitration if or to the extent that their application—
   (a) is inconsistent with the provisions of the enactment concerned, with any rules or procedure authorised or recognised by it, or
   (b) is excluded by any other enactment.

(3) In this section and the following provisions of this Part "enactment"—
   (a) in England and Wales, includes an enactment contained in subordinate legislation within the meaning of the Interpretation Act 1978;
   (b) in Northern Ireland, means a statutory provision within the meaning of section 1(f) of the Interpretation Act (Northern Ireland) 1954.

**95    General adaptation of provisions in relation to statutory arbitrations**

(1) The provisions of Part I apply to a statutory arbitration—
   (a) as if the arbitration were pursuant to an arbitration agreement and as if the enactment were that agreement, and
   (b) as if the persons by and against whom a claim subject to arbitration in pursuance of the enactment may be or has been made were parties to that agreement.

(2) Every statutory arbitration shall be taken to have its seat in England and Wales or, as the case may be, in Northern Ireland.

**96    Specific adaptations of provisions in relation to statutory arbitrations**

(1) The following provisions of Part I apply to a statutory arbitration with the following adaptations.

(2) In section 30(1) (competence of tribunal to rule on its own jurisdiction), the reference in paragraph (a) to whether there is a valid arbitration

agreement shall be construed as a reference to whether the enactment applies to the dispute or difference in question.

(3) Section 35 (consolidation of proceedings and concurrent hearings) applies only so as to authorise the consolidation of proceedings, or concurrent hearings in proceedings, under the same enactment.

(4) Section 46 (rules applicable to substance of dispute) applies with the omission of subsection (1)(b) (determination in accordance with considerations agreed by parties).

**97  Provisions excluded from applying to statutory arbitrations**

The following provisions of Part I do not apply in relation to a statutory arbitration—
- (a) section 8 (whether agreement discharged by death of a party);
- (b) section 12 (power of court to extend agreed time limits);
- (c) sections 9(5), 10(2) and 71(4) (restrictions on effect of provision that award condition precedent to right to bring legal proceedings).

**98  Power to make further provision by regulations**

(1) The Secretary of State may make provision by regulations for adapting or excluding any provision of Part I in relation to statutory arbitrations in general or statutory arbitrations of any particular description.

(2) The power is exercisable whether the enactment concerned is passed or made before or after the commencement of this Act.

(3) Regulations under this section shall be made by statutory instrument which shall be subject to annulment in pursuance of a resolution of either House of Parliament.

## Part III

RECOGNITION AND ENFORCEMENT OF CERTAIN FOREIGN AWARDS

*Enforcement of Geneva Convention awards*

**99  Continuation of Part II of the Arbitration Act 1950**

Part II of the Arbitration Act 1950 (enforcement of certain foreign awards) continues to apply in relation to foreign awards within the meaning of that Part which are not also New York Convention awards.

*Recognition and enforcement of New York Convention awards*

**100 New York Convention awards**

(1) In this Part a "New York Convention award" means an award made, in pursuance of an arbitration agreement, in the territory of a state (other than the United Kingdom) which is a party to the New York Convention.

(2) For the purposes of subsection (1) and of the provisions of this Part relating to such awards—
   (a) "arbitration agreement" means an arbitration agreement in writing, and
   (b) an award shall be treated as made at the seat of the arbitration, regardless of where it was signed, despatched or delivered to any of the parties.

   In this subsection "agreement in writing" and "seat of the arbitration" have the same meaning as in Part I.

(3) If Her Majesty by Order in Council declares that a state specified in the Order is a party to the New York Convention, or is a party in respect of any territory so specified, the Order shall, while in force, be conclusive evidence of that fact.

(4) In this section "the New York Convention" means the Convention on the Recognition and Enforcement of Foreign Arbitral Awards adopted by the United Nations Conference on International Commercial Arbitration on 10th June 1958.

**101 Recognition and enforcement of awards**

(1) A New York Convention award shall be recognised as binding on the persons as between whom it was made, and may accordingly be relied on by those persons by way of defence, set-off or otherwise in any legal proceedings in England and Wales or Northern Ireland.

(2) A New York Convention award may, by leave of the court, be enforced in the same manner as a judgment or order of the court to the same effect.

   As to the meaning of "the court" see section 105.

(3) Where leave is so given, judgment may be entered in terms of the award.

**102 Evidence to be produced by party seeking recognition or enforcement**

(1) A party seeking the recognition or enforcement of a New York Convention award must produce—

(a) the duly authenticated original award or a duly certified copy of it, and
(b) the original arbitration agreement or a duly certified copy of it.

(2) If the award or agreement is in a foreign language, the party must also produce a translation of it certified by an official or sworn translator or by a diplomatic or consular agent.

**103 Refusal of recognition or enforcement**

(1) Recognition or enforcement of a New York Convention award shall not be refused except in the following cases.

(2) Recognition or enforcement of the award may be refused if the person against whom it is invoked proves—
(a) that a party to the arbitration agreement was (under the law applicable to him) under some incapacity;
(b) that the arbitration agreement was not valid under the law to which the parties subjected it or, failing any indication thereon, under the law of the country where the award was made;
(c) that he was not given proper notice of the appointment of the arbitrator or of the arbitration proceedings or was otherwise unable to present his case;
(d) that the award deals with a difference not contemplated by or not falling within the terms of the submission to arbitration or contains decisions on matters beyond the scope of the submission to arbitration (but see subsection (4));
(e) that the composition of the arbitral tribunal or the arbitral procedure was not in accordance with the agreement of the parties or, failing such agreement, with the law of the country in which the arbitration took place;
(f) that the award has not yet become binding on the parties, or has been set aside or suspended by a competent authority of the country in which, or under the law of which, it was made.

(3) Recognition or enforcement of the award may also be refused if the award is in respect of a matter which is not capable of settlement by arbitration, or if it would be contrary to public policy to recognise or enforce the award.

(4) An award which contains decisions on matters not submitted to arbitration may be recognised or enforced to the extent that it contains decisions on matters submitted to arbitration which can be separated from those on matters not so submitted.

(5) Where an application for the setting aside or suspension of the award has been made to such a competent authority as is mentioned in

subsection (2)(f), the court before which the award is sought to be relied upon may, if it considers it proper, adjourn the decision on the recognition or enforcement of the award.

It may also on the application of the party claiming recognition or enforcement of the award order the other party to give suitable security.

**104    Saving for other bases of recognition or enforcement**

Nothing in the preceding provisions of this Part affects any right to rely upon or enforce a New York Convention award at common law or under section 66.

## Part IV

GENERAL PROVISIONS

**105    Meaning of "the court": jurisdiction of High Court and county court**

(1) In this Act "the court" means the High Court or a county court, subject to the following provisions.

(2) The Lord Chancellor may by order make provision—
   (a) allocating proceedings under this Act to the High Court or to county courts; or
   (b) specifying proceedings under this Act which may be commenced or taken only in the High Court or in a county court.

(3) The Lord Chancellor may by order make provision requiring proceedings of any specified description under this Act in relation to which a county court has jurisdiction to be commenced or taken in one or more specified county courts.

Any jurisdiction so exercisable by a specified county court is exercisable throughout England and Wales or, as the case may be, Northern Ireland.

(4) An order under this section—
   (a) may differentiate between categories of proceedings by reference to such criteria as the Lord Chancellor sees fit to specify, and
   (b) may make such incidental or transitional provision as the Lord Chancellor considers necessary or expedient.

(5) An order under this section for England and Wales shall be made by statutory instrument which shall be subject to annulment in pursuance of a resolution of either House of Parliament.

(6) An order under this section for Northern Ireland shall be a statutory rule for the purposes of the Statutory Rules (Northern Ireland) Order 1979 which shall be subject to annulment in pursuance of a resolution of either House of Parliament in like manner as a statutory instrument and section 5 of the Statutory Instruments Act 1946 shall apply accordingly.

## 106 Crown application

(1) Part I of this Act applies to any arbitration agreement to which Her Majesty, either in right of the Crown or of the Duchy of Lancaster or otherwise, or the Duke of Cornwall, is a party.

(2) Where Her Majesty is party to an arbitration agreement otherwise than in right of the Crown, Her Majesty shall be represented for the purposes of any arbitral proceedings—
   (a) where the agreement was entered into by Her Majesty in right of the Duchy of Lancaster, by the Chancellor of the Duchy or such person as he may appoint, and
   (b) in any other case, by such person as Her Majesty may appoint in writing under the Royal Sign Manual.

(3) Where the Duke of Cornwall is party to an arbitration agreement, he shall be represented for the purposes of any arbitral proceedings by such person as he may appoint.

(4) References in Part I to a party or the parties to the arbitration agreement or to arbitral proceedings shall be construed, where subsection (2) or (3) applies, as references to the person representing Her Majesty or the Duke of Cornwall.

## 107 Consequential amendments and repeals

(1) The enactments specified in Schedule 3 are amended in accordance with that Schedule, the amendments being consequential on the provisions of this Act.

(2) The enactments specified in Schedule 4 are repealed to the extent specified.

## 108 Extent

(1) The provisions of this Act extend to England and Wales and, except as mentioned below, to Northern Ireland.

(2) The following provisions of Part II do not extend to Northern Ireland—
   section 92 (exclusion of Part I in relation to small claims arbitration in the county court), and
   section 93 and Schedule 2 (appointment of judges as arbitrators).

(3) Sections 89, 90 and 91 (consumer arbitration agreements) extend to Scotland and the provisions of Schedules 3 and 4 (consequential amendments and repeals) extend to Scotland so far as they relate to enactments which so extend, subject as follows.

(4) The repeal of the Arbitration Act 1975 extends only to England and Wales and Northern Ireland.

## 109 Commencement

(1) The provisions of this Act come into force on such day as the Secretary of State may appoint by order made by statutory instrument, and different days may be appointed for different purposes.

(2) An order under subsection (1) may contain such transitional provisions as appear to the Secretary of State to be appropriate.

## 110 Short title

This Act may be cited as the Arbitration Act 1996.

## Schedules

### SCHEDULE 1 — Section 4(1).

#### Mandatory provisions of Part I

sections 9 to 11 (stay of legal proceedings);
section 12 (power of court to extend agreed time limits);
section 13 (application of Limitation Acts);
section 24 (power of court to remove arbitrator);
section 26(1) (effect of death of arbitrator);
section 28 (liability of parties for fees and expenses of arbitrators);
section 29 (immunity of arbitrator);
section 31 (objection to substantive jurisdiction of tribunal);
section 32 (determination of preliminary point of jurisdiction);
section 33 (general duty of tribunal);
section 37(2) (items to be treated as expenses of arbitrators);
section 40 (general duty of parties);
section 43 (securing the attendance of witnesses);
section 56 (power to withhold award in case of non-payment);
section 60 (effectiveness of agreement for payment of costs in any event);
section 66 (enforcement of award);
sections 67 and 68 (challenging the award: substantive jurisdiction and serious irregularity), and sections 70 and 71 (supplementary provisions; effect of order of court) so far as relating to those sections;
section 72 (saving for rights of person who takes no part in proceedings);
section 73 (loss of right to object);
section 74 (immunity of arbitral institutions, &c.);
section 75 (charge to secure payment of solicitors' costs).

### SCHEDULE 2 — Section 93(6).

#### Modifications of Part I in relation to judge-arbitrators

*Introductory*

1  In this Schedule "judge-arbitrator" means a judge of the Commercial Court or official referee appointed as arbitrator or umpire under section 93.

*General*

2  (1) Subject to the following provisions of this Schedule, references in Part I to the court shall be construed in relation to a judge-arbitrator, or in relation to the appointment of a judge-arbitrator, as references to the Court of Appeal.

(2) The references in sections 32(6), 45(6) and 69(8) to the Court of Appeal shall in such a case be construed as references to the House of Lords.

*Arbitrator's fees*

3   (1) The power of the court in section 28(2) to order consideration and adjustment of the liability of a party for the fees of an arbitrator may be exercised by a judge-arbitrator.

(2) Any such exercise of the power is subject to the powers of the Court of Appeal under sections 24(4) and 25(3)(b) (directions as to entitlement to fees or expenses in case of removal or resignation).

*Exercise of court powers in support of arbitration*

4   (1) Where the arbitral tribunal consists of or includes a judge-arbitrator the powers of the court under sections 42 to 44 (enforcement of peremptory orders, summoning witnesses, and other court powers) are exercisable by the High Court and also by the judge-arbitrator himself.

(2) Anything done by a judge-arbitrator in the exercise of those powers shall be regarded as done by him in his capacity as judge of the High Court and have effect as if done by that court.

Nothing in this sub-paragraph prejudices any power vested in him as arbitrator or umpire.

*Extension of time for making award*

5   (1) The power conferred by section 50 (extension of time for making award) is exercisable by the judge-arbitrator himself.

(2) Any appeal from a decision of a judge-arbitrator under that section lies to the Court of Appeal with the leave of that court.

*Withholding award in case of non-payment*

6   (1) The provisions of paragraph 7 apply in place of the provisions of section 56 (power to withhold award in the case of non-payment) in relation to the withholding of an award for non-payment of the fees and expenses of a judge-arbitrator.

(2) This does not affect the application of section 56 in relation to the delivery of such an award by an arbitral or other institution or person vested by the parties with powers in relation to the delivery of the award.

7   (1) A judge-arbitrator may refuse to deliver an award except upon payment of the fees and expenses mentioned in section 56(1).

(2) The judge-arbitrator may, on an application by a party to the arbitral proceedings, order that if he pays into the High Court the fees

and expenses demanded, or such lesser amount as the judge-arbitrator may specify—
  (a) the award shall be delivered,
  (b) the amount of the fees and expenses properly payable shall be determined by such means and upon such terms as he may direct, and
  (c) out of the money paid into court there shall be paid out such fees and expenses as may be found to be properly payable and the balance of the money (if any) shall be paid out to the applicant.

(3) For this purpose the amount of fees and expenses properly payable is the amount the applicant is liable to pay under section 28 or any agreement relating to the payment of the arbitrator.

(4) No application to the judge-arbitrator under this paragraph may be made where there is any available arbitral process for appeal or review of the amount of the fees or expenses demanded.

(5) Any appeal from a decision of a judge-arbitrator under this paragraph lies to the Court of Appeal with the leave of that court.

(6) Where a party to arbitral proceedings appeals under sub-paragraph (5), an arbitrator is entitled to appear and be heard.

*Correction of award or additional award*

8    Subsections (4) to (6) of section 57 (correction of award or additional award: time limit for application or exercise of power) do not apply to a judge-arbitrator.

*Costs*

9    Where the arbitral tribunal consists of or includes a judge-arbitrator the powers of the court under section 63(4) (determination of recoverable costs) shall be exercised by the High Court.

10   (1) The power of the court under section 64 to determine an arbitrator's reasonable fees and expenses may be exercised by a judge-arbitrator.

(2) Any such exercise of the power is subject to the powers of the Court of Appeal under sections 24(4) and 25(3)(b) (directions as to entitlement to fees or expenses in case of removal or resignation).

*Enforcement of award*

11   The leave of the court required by section 66 (enforcement of award) may in the case of an award of a judge-arbitrator be given by the judge-arbitrator himself.

*Solicitors' costs*

12    The powers of the court to make declarations and orders under the provisions applied by section 75 (power to charge property recovered in arbitral proceedings with the payment of solicitors' costs) may be exercised by the judge-arbitrator.

*Powers of court in relation to service of documents*

13    (1) The power of the court under section 77(2) (powers of court in relation to service of documents) is exercisable by the judge-arbitrator.

(2) Any appeal from a decision of a judge-arbitrator under that section lies to the Court of Appeal with the leave of that court.

*Powers of court to extend time limits relating to arbitral proceedings*

14    (1) The power conferred by section 79 (power of court to extend time limits relating to arbitral proceedings) is exercisable by the judge-arbitrator himself.

(2) Any appeal from a decision of a judge-arbitrator under that section lies to the Court of Appeal with the leave of that court.

SCHEDULE 3    Section 107(1).

CONSEQUENTIAL AMENDMENTS

*Merchant Shipping Act 1894 (c. 60)*

1    In section 496 of the Merchant Shipping Act 1894 (provisions as to deposits by owners of goods), after subsection (4) insert—

"(5) In subsection (3) the expression "legal proceedings" includes arbitral proceedings and as respects England and Wales and Northern Ireland the provisions of section 14 of the Arbitration Act 1996 apply to determine when such proceedings are commenced.".

*Stannaries Court (Abolition) Act 1896 (c. 45)*

2    In section 4(1) of the Stannaries Court (Abolition) Act 1896 (references of certain disputes to arbitration), for the words from "tried before" to "any such reference" substitute "referred to arbitration before himself or before an arbitrator agreed on by the parties or an officer of the court".

*Tithe Act 1936 (c. 43)*

3    In section 39(1) of the Tithe Act 1936 (proceedings of Tithe Redemption Commission)—

(a) for "the Arbitration Acts 1889 to 1934" substitute "Part I of the Arbitration Act 1996";
(b) for paragraph (e) substitute—
"(e) the making of an application to the court to determine a preliminary point of law and the bringing of an appeal to the court on a point of law;";
(c) for "the said Acts" substitute "Part I of the Arbitration Act 1996".

*Education Act 1944 (c. 31)*

4   In section 75(2) of the Education Act 1944 (proceedings of Independent School Tribunals) for "the Arbitration Acts 1889 to 1934" substitute "Part I of the Arbitration Act 1996".

*Commonwealth Telegraphs Act 1949 (c. 39)*

5   In section 8(2) of the Commonwealth Telegraphs Act 1949 (proceedings of referees under the Act) for "the Arbitration Acts 1889 to 1934, or the Arbitration Act (Northern Ireland) 1937," substitute "Part I of the Arbitration Act 1996".

*Lands Tribunal Act 1949 (c. 42)*

6   In section 3 of the Lands Tribunal Act 1949 (proceedings before the Lands Tribunal)—
(a) in subsection (6)(c) (procedural rules: power to apply Arbitration Acts), and
(b) in subsection (8) (exclusion of Arbitration Acts except as applied by rules),
for "the Arbitration Acts 1889 to 1934" substitute "Part I of the Arbitration Act 1996".

*Wireless Telegraphy Act 1949 (c. 54)*

7   In the Wireless Telegraphy Act 1949, Schedule 2 (procedure of appeals tribunal), in paragraph 3(1)—
(a) for the words "the Arbitration Acts 1889 to 1934" substitute "Part I of the Arbitration Act 1996";
(b) after the word "Wales" insert "or Northern Ireland"; and
(c) for "the said Acts" substitute "Part I of that Act".

*Patents Act 1949 (c. 87)*

8   In section 67 of the Patents Act 1949 (proceedings as to infringement of pre-1978 patents referred to comptroller), for "The Arbitration Acts 1889 to 1934" substitute "Part I of the Arbitration Act 1996".

*National Health Service (Amendment) Act 1949 (c. 93)*

9    In section 7(8) of the National Health Service (Amendment) Act 1949 (arbitration in relation to hardship arising from the National Health Service Act 1946 or the Act), for "the Arbitration Acts 1889 to 1934" substitute "Part I of the Arbitration Act 1996" and for "the said Acts" substitute "Part I of that Act".

*Arbitration Act 1950 (c. 27)*

10   In section 36(1) of the Arbitration Act 1950 (effect of foreign awards enforceable under Part II of that Act) for "section 26 of this Act" substitute "section 66 of the Arbitration Act 1996".

*Interpretation Act (Northern Ireland) 1954 (c. 33 (N.I.))*

11   In section 46(2) of the Interpretation Act (Northern Ireland) 1954 (miscellaneous definitions), for the definition of "arbitrator" substitute—

> " "arbitrator" has the same meaning as in Part I of the Arbitration Act 1996;".

*Agricultural Marketing Act 1958 (c. 47)*

12   In section 12(1) of the Agricultural Marketing Act 1958 (application of provisions of Arbitration Act 1950)—
   (a) for the words from the beginning to "shall apply" substitute "Sections 45 and 69 of the Arbitration Act 1996 (which relate to the determination by the court of questions of law) and section 66 of that Act (enforcement of awards) apply"; and
   (b) for "an arbitration" substitute "arbitral proceedings".

*Carriage by Air Act 1961 (c. 27)*

13   (1) The Carriage by Air Act 1961 is amended as follows.

   (2) In section 5(3) (time for bringing proceedings)—
   (a) for "an arbitration" in the first place where it occurs substitute "arbitral proceedings"; and
   (b) for the words from "and subsections (3) and (4)" to the end substitute "and the provisions of section 14 of the Arbitration Act 1996 apply to determine when such proceedings are commenced.".

   (3) In section 11(c) (application of section 5 to Scotland)—
   (a) for "subsections (3) and (4)" substitute "the provisions of section 14 of the Arbitration Act 1996"; and
   (b) for "an arbitration" substitute "arbitral proceedings".

*Factories Act 1961 (c. 34)*

14   In the Factories Act 1961, for section 171 (application of Arbitration Act 1950), substitute—

"171    **Application of the Arbitration Act 1996**

Part I of the Arbitration Act 1996 does not apply to proceedings under this Act except in so far as it may be applied by regulations made under this Act.".

*Clergy Pensions Measure 1961 (No. 3)*

15    In the Clergy Pensions Measure 1961, section 38(4) (determination of questions), for the words "The Arbitration Act 1950" substitute "Part I of the Arbitration Act 1996".

*Transport Act 1962 (c. 46)*

16    (1) The Transport Act 1962 is amended as follows.

(2) In section 74(6)(f) (proceedings before referees in pension disputes), for the words "the Arbitration Act 1950" substitute "Part I of the Arbitration Act 1996".

(3) In section 81(7) (proceedings before referees in compensation disputes), for the words "the Arbitration Act 1950" substitute "Part I of the Arbitration Act 1996".

(4) In Schedule 7, Part IV (pensions), in paragraph 17(5) for the words "the Arbitration Act 1950" substitute "Part I of the Arbitration Act 1996".

*Corn Rents Act 1963 (c. 14)*

17    In the Corn Rents Act 1963, section 1(5) (schemes for apportioning corn rents, &c.), for the words "the Arbitration Act 1950" substitute "Part I of the Arbitration Act 1996".

*Plant Varieties and Seeds Act 1964 (c. 14)*

18    In section 10(6) of the Plant Varieties and Seeds Act 1964 (meaning of "arbitration agreement"), for "the meaning given by section 32 of the Arbitration Act 1950" substitute "the same meaning as in Part I of the Arbitration Act 1996".

*Lands Tribunal and Compensation Act (Northern Ireland) 1964 (c. 29 (N.I.))*

19    In section 9 of the Lands Tribunal and Compensation Act (Northern Ireland) 1964 (proceedings of Lands Tribunal), in subsection (3) (where Tribunal acts as arbitrator) for "the Arbitration Act (Northern Ireland) 1937" substitute "Part I of the Arbitration Act 1996".

*Industrial and Provident Societies Act 1965 (c. 12)*

20    (1) Section 60 of the Industrial and Provident Societies Act 1965 is amended as follows.

(2) In subsection (8) (procedure for hearing disputes between society and member, &c.)—
   (a) in paragraph (a) for "the Arbitration Act 1950" substitute "Part I of the Arbitration Act 1996"; and
   (b) in paragraph (b) omit "by virtue of section 12 of the said Act of 1950".

(3) For subsection (9) substitute—

"(9) The court or registrar to whom any dispute is referred under subsections (2) to (7) may at the request of either party state a case on any question of law arising in the dispute for the opinion of the High Court or, as the case may be, the Court of Session.".

*Carriage of Goods by Road Act 1965 (c. 37)*

21   In section 7(2) of the Carriage of Goods by Road Act 1965 (arbitrations: time at which deemed to commence), for paragraphs (a) and (b) substitute—

"(a) as respects England and Wales and Northern Ireland, the provisions of section 14(3) to (5) of the Arbitration Act 1996 (which determine the time at which an arbitration is commenced) apply;".

*Factories Act (Northern Ireland) 1965 (c. 20 (N.I.))*

22   In section 171 of the Factories Act (Northern Ireland) 1965 (application of Arbitration Act), for "The Arbitration Act (Northern Ireland) 1937" substitute "Part I of the Arbitration Act 1996".

*Commonwealth Secretariat Act 1966 (c. 10)*

23   In section 1(3) of the Commonwealth Secretariat Act 1966 (contracts with Commonwealth Secretariat to be deemed to contain provision for arbitration), for "the Arbitration Act 1950 and the Arbitration Act (Northern Ireland) 1937" substitute "Part I of the Arbitration Act 1996".

*Arbitration (International Investment Disputes) Act 1966 (c. 41)*

24   In the Arbitration (International Investment Disputes) Act 1966, for section 3 (application of Arbitration Act 1950 and other enactments) substitute—

"3   **Application of provisions of Arbitration Act 1996**

(1) The Lord Chancellor may by order direct that any of the provisions contained in sections 36 and 38 to 44 of the Arbitration Act 1996 (provisions concerning the conduct of arbitral proceedings, &c.) shall apply to such proceedings pursuant to the Convention as are specified in the order with or without any modifications or exceptions specified in the order.

(2) Subject to subsection (1), the Arbitration Act 1996 shall not apply to proceedings pursuant to the Convention, but this subsection shall not be taken as affecting section 9 of that Act (stay of legal proceedings in respect of matter subject to arbitration).

(3) An order made under this section—
   (a) may be varied or revoked by a subsequent order so made, and
   (b) shall be contained in a statutory instrument.".

*Poultry Improvement Act (Northern Ireland) 1968 (c. 12 (N.I.))*

25   In paragraph 10(4) of the Schedule to the Poultry Improvement Act (Northern Ireland) 1968 (reference of disputes), for "The Arbitration Act (Northern Ireland) 1937" substitute "Part I of the Arbitration Act 1996".

*Industrial and Provident Societies Act (Northern Ireland) 1969 (c. 24 (N.I.))*

26   (1) Section 69 of the Industrial and Provident Societies Act (Northern Ireland) 1969 (decision of disputes) is amended as follows.

(2) In subsection (7) (decision of disputes)—
   (a) in the opening words, omit the words from "and without prejudice" to "1937";
   (b) at the beginning of paragraph (a) insert "without prejudice to any powers exercisable by virtue of Part I of the Arbitration Act 1996,"; and
   (c) in paragraph (b) omit "the registrar or" and "registrar or" and for the words from "as might have been granted by the High Court" to the end substitute "as might be granted by the registrar".

(3) For subsection (8) substitute—

"(8) The court or registrar to whom any dispute is referred under subsections (2) to (6) may at the request of either party state a case on any question of law arising in the dispute for the opinion of the High Court.".

*Health and Personal Social Services (Northern Ireland) Order 1972 (N.I.14)*

27   In Article 105(6) of the Health and Personal Social Services (Northern Ireland) Order 1972 (arbitrations under the Order), for "the Arbitration Act (Northern Ireland) 1937" substitute "Part I of the Arbitration Act 1996".

*Consumer Credit Act 1974 (c. 39)*

28   (1) Section 146 of the Consumer Credit Act 1974 is amended as follows.

(2) In subsection (2) (solicitor engaged in contentious business), for "section 86(1) of the Solicitors Act 1957" substitute "section 87(1) of the Solicitors Act 1974".

(3) In subsection (4) (solicitor in Northern Ireland engaged in contentious business), for the words from "business done" to "Administration of Estates (Northern Ireland) Order 1979" substitute "contentious business (as defined in Article 3(2) of the Solicitors (Northern Ireland) Order 1976.".

*Friendly Societies Act 1974 (c. 46)*

29 (1) The Friendly Societies Act 1974 is amended as follows.

(2) For section 78(1) (statement of case) substitute—

"(1) Any arbitrator, arbiter or umpire to whom a dispute falling within section 76 above is referred under the rules of a registered society or branch may at the request of either party state a case on any question of law arising in the dispute for the opinion of the High Court or, as the case may be, the Court of Session.".

(3) In section 83(3) (procedure on objections to amalgamations &c. of friendly societies), for "the Arbitration Act 1950 or, in Northern Ireland, the Arbitration Act (Northern Ireland) 1937" substitute "Part I of the Arbitration Act 1996".

*Industry Act 1975 (c. 68)*

30 In Schedule 3 to the Industry Act (arbitration of disputes relating to vesting and compensation orders), in paragraph 14 (application of certain provisions of Arbitration Acts)—

(a) for "the Arbitration Act 1950 or, in Northern Ireland, the Arbitration Act (Northern Ireland) 1937" substitute "Part I of the Arbitration Act 1996", and

(b) for "that Act" substitute "that Part".

*Industrial Relations (Northern Ireland) Order 1976 (N.I.16)*

31 In Article 59(9) of the Industrial Relations (Northern Ireland) Order 1976 (proceedings of industrial tribunal), for "The Arbitration Act (Northern Ireland) 1937" substitute "Part I of the Arbitration Act 1996".

*Aircraft and Shipbuilding Industries Act 1977 (c. 3)*

32 In Schedule 7 to the Aircraft and Shipbuilding Industries Act 1977 (procedure of Arbitration Tribunal), in paragraph 2—

(a) for "the Arbitration Act 1950 or, in Northern Ireland, the Arbitration Act (Northern Ireland) 1937" substitute "Part I of the Arbitration Act 1996", and

(b) for "that Act" substitute "that Part".

*Patents Act 1977 (c. 37)*

33   In section 130 of the Patents Act 1977 (interpretation), in subsection (8) (exclusion of Arbitration Act) for "The Arbitration Act 1950" substitute "Part I of the Arbitration Act 1996".

*Judicature (Northern Ireland) Act 1978 (c. 23)*

34   (1) The Judicature (Northern Ireland) Act 1978 is amended as follows.

(2) In section 35(2) (restrictions on appeals to the Court of Appeal), after paragraph (f) insert—

"(fa) except as provided by Part I of the Arbitration Act 1996, from any decision of the High Court under that Part;".

(3) In section 55(2) (rules of court) after paragraph (c) insert—

"(cc) providing for any prescribed part of the jurisdiction of the High Court in relation to the trial of any action involving matters of account to be exercised in the prescribed manner by a person agreed by the parties and for the remuneration of any such person;".

*Health and Safety at Work (Northern Ireland) Order 1978 (N.I.9)*

35   In Schedule 4 to the Health and Safety at Work (Northern Ireland) Order 1978 (licensing provisions), in paragraph 3, for "The Arbitration Act (Northern Ireland) 1937" substitute "Part I of the Arbitration Act 1996".

*County Courts (Northern Ireland) Order 1980 (N.I.3)*

36   (1) The County Courts (Northern Ireland) Order 1980 is amended as follows.

(2) In Article 30 (civil jurisdiction exercisable by district judge)—

(a)   for paragraph (2) substitute—

"(2) Any order, decision or determination made by a district judge under this Article (other than one made in dealing with a claim by way of arbitration under paragraph (3)) shall be embodied in a decree which for all purposes (including the right of appeal under Part VI) shall have the like effect as a decree pronounced by a county court judge.";

(b)   for paragraphs (4) and (5) substitute—

"(4) Where in any action to which paragraph (1) applies the claim is dealt with by way of arbitration under paragraph (3)—

(a)   any award made by the district judge in dealing with the claim shall be embodied in a decree which for all purposes (except the right of appeal under Part VI) shall have the like effect as a decree pronounced by a county court judge;

(b) the district judge may, and shall if so required by the High Court, state for the determination of the High Court any question of law arising out of an award so made;

(c) except as provided by sub-paragraph (b), any award so made shall be final; and

(d) except as otherwise provided by county court rules, no costs shall be awarded in connection with the action.

(5) Subject to paragraph (4), county court rules may—

(a) apply any of the provisions of Part I of the Arbitration Act 1996 to arbitrations under paragraph (3) with such modifications as may be prescribed;

(b) prescribe the rules of evidence to be followed on any arbitration under paragraph (3) and, in particular, make provision with respect to the manner of taking and questioning evidence.

(5A) Except as provided by virtue of paragraph (5)(a), Part I of the Arbitration Act 1996 shall not apply to an arbitration under paragraph (3).".

(3) After Article 61 insert—

*"Appeals from decisions under Part I of Arbitration Act 1996*

61A (1) Article 61 does not apply to a decision of a county court judge made in the exercise of the jurisdiction conferred by Part I of the Arbitration Act 1996.

(2) Any party dissatisfied with a decision of the county court made in the exercise of the jurisdiction conferred by any of the following provisions of Part I of the Arbitration Act 1996, namely—

(a) section 32 (question as to substantive jurisdiction of arbitral tribunal);

(b) section 45 (question of law arising in course of arbitral proceedings);

(c) section 67 (challenging award of arbitral tribunal: substantive jurisdiction);

(d) section 68 (challenging award of arbitral tribunal: serious irregularity);

(e) section 69 (appeal on point of law),

may, subject to the provisions of that Part, appeal from that decision to the Court of Appeal.

> (3) Any party dissatisfied with any decision of a county court made in the exercise of the jurisdiction conferred by any other provision of Part I of the Arbitration Act 1996 may, subject to the provisions of that Part, appeal from that decision to the High Court.
>
> (4) The decision of the Court of Appeal on an appeal under paragraph (2) shall be final.".

*Supreme Court Act 1981 (c. 54)*

37 (1) The Supreme Court Act 1981 is amended as follows.

    (2) In section 18(1) (restrictions on appeals to the Court of Appeal), for paragraph (g) substitute—

> "(g) except as provided by Part I of the Arbitration Act 1996, from any decision of the High Court under that Part;".

(3) In section 151 (interpretation, &c.), in the definition of "arbitration agreement", for "the Arbitration Act 1950 by virtue of section 32 of that Act;" substitute "Part I of the Arbitration Act 1996;".

*Merchant Shipping (Liner Conferences) Act 1982 (c. 37)*

38 In section 7(5) of the Merchant Shipping (Liner Conferences) Act 1982 (stay of legal proceedings), for the words from "section 4(1)" to the end substitute "section 9 of the Arbitration Act 1996 (which also provides for the staying of legal proceedings).".

*Agricultural Marketing (Northern Ireland) Order 1982 (N.I.12)*

39 In Article 14 of the Agricultural Marketing (Northern Ireland) Order 1982 (application of provisions of Arbitration Act (Northern Ireland) 1937)—
    (a) for the words from the beginning to "shall apply" substitute "Section 45 and 69 of the Arbitration Act 1996 (which relate to the determination by the court of questions of law) and section 66 of that Act (enforcement of awards)" apply; and
    (b) for "an arbitration" substitute "arbitral proceedings".

*Mental Health Act 1983 (c. 20)*

40 In section 78 of the Mental Health Act 1983 (procedure of Mental Health Review Tribunals), in subsection (9) for "The Arbitration Act 1950" substitute "Part I of the Arbitration Act 1996".

*Registered Homes Act 1984 (c. 23)*

41 In section 43 of the Registered Homes Act 1984 (procedure of Registered Homes Tribunals), in subsection (3) for "The Arbitration Act 1950" substitute "Part I of the Arbitration Act 1996".

*Housing Act 1985 (c. 68)*

42   In section 47(3) of the Housing Act 1985 (agreement as to determination of matters relating to service charges) for "section 32 of the Arbitration Act 1950" substitute "Part I of the Arbitration Act 1996".

*Landlord and Tenant Act 1985 (c. 70)*

43   In section 19(3) of the Landlord and Tenant Act 1985 (agreement as to determination of matters relating to service charges), for "section 32 of the Arbitration Act 1950" substitute "Part I of the Arbitration Act 1996".

*Credit Unions (Northern Ireland) Order 1985 (N.I.12)*

44   (1) Article 72 of the Credit Unions (Northern Ireland) Order 1985 (decision of disputes) is amended as follows.

   (2) In paragraph (7)—
      (a) in the opening words, omit the words from "and without prejudice" to "1937";
      (b) at the beginning of sub-paragraph (a) insert "without prejudice to any powers exercisable by virtue of Part I of the Arbitration Act 1996,"; and
      (c) in sub-paragraph (b) omit "the registrar or" and "registrar or" and for the words from "as might have been granted by the High Court" to the end substitute "as might be granted by the registrar".

   (3) For paragraph (8) substitute—

   "(8) The court or registrar to whom any dispute is referred under paragraphs (2) to (6) may at the request of either party state a case on any question of law arising in the dispute for the opinion of the High Court.".

*Agricultural Holdings Act 1986 (c. 5)*

45   In section 84(1) of the Agricultural Holdings Act 1986 (provisions relating to arbitration), for "the Arbitration Act 1950" substitute "Part I of the Arbitration Act 1996".

*Insolvency Act 1986 (c. 45)*

46   In the Insolvency Act 1986, after section 349 insert—

**"349A   Arbitration agreements to which bankrupt is party**

   (1) This section applies where a bankrupt had become party to a contract containing an arbitration agreement before the commencement of his bankruptcy.

(2) If the trustee in bankruptcy adopts the contract, the arbitration agreement is enforceable by or against the trustee in relation to matters arising from or connected with the contract.

(3) If the trustee in bankruptcy does not adopt the contract and a matter to which the arbitration agreement applies requires to be determined in connection with or for the purposes of the bankruptcy proceedings—
>  (a) the trustee with the consent of the creditors' committee, or
>  (b) any other party to the agreement,

may apply to the court which may, if it thinks fit in all the circumstances of the case, order that the matter be referred to arbitration in accordance with the arbitration agreement.

(4) In this section—
> "arbitration agreement" has the same meaning as in Part I of the Arbitration Act 1996; and
> "the court" means the court which has jurisdiction in the bankruptcy proceedings.".

*Building Societies Act 1986 (c. 53)*

47  In Part II of Schedule 14 to the Building Societies Act 1986 (settlement of disputes: arbitration), in paragraph 5(6) for "the Arbitration Act 1950 and the Arbitration Act 1979 or, in Northern Ireland, the Arbitration Act (Northern Ireland) 1937" substitute "Part I of the Arbitration Act 1996".

*Mental Health (Northern Ireland) Order 1986 (N.I.4)*

48  In Article 83 of the Mental Health (Northern Ireland) Order 1986 (procedure of Mental Health Review Tribunal), in paragraph (8) for "The Arbitration Act (Northern Ireland) 1937" substitute "Part I of the Arbitration Act 1996".

*Multilateral Investment Guarantee Agency Act 1988 (c. 8)*

49  For section 6 of the Multilateral Investment Guarantee Agency Act 1988 (application of Arbitration Act) substitute—

> "6  **Application of Arbitration Act**
>
> (1) The Lord Chancellor may by order made by statutory instrument direct that any of the provisions of sections 36 and 38 to 44 of the Arbitration Act 1996 (provisions in relation to the conduct of the arbitral proceedings, &c.) apply, with such modifications or exceptions as are specified in the order, to such arbitration proceedings pursuant to Annex II to the Convention as are specified in the order.

(2) Except as provided by an order under subsection (1) above, no provision of Part I of the Arbitration Act 1996 other than section 9 (stay of legal proceedings) applies to any such proceedings.".

*Copyright, Designs and Patents Act 1988 (c. 48)*

50  In section 150 of the Copyright, Designs and Patents Act 1988 (Lord Chancellor's power to make rules for Copyright Tribunal), for subsection (2) substitute—

"(2) The rules may apply in relation to the Tribunal, as respects proceedings in England and Wales or Northern Ireland, any of the provisions of Part I of the Arbitration Act 1996.".

*Fair Employment (Northern Ireland) Act 1989 (c. 32)*

51  In the Fair Employment (Northern Ireland) Act 1989, section 5(7) (procedure of Fair Employment Tribunal), for "The Arbitration Act (Northern Ireland) 1937" substitute "Part I of the Arbitration Act 1996".

*Limitation (Northern Ireland) Order 1989 (N.I.11)*

52  In Article 2(2) of the Limitation (Northern Ireland) Order 1989 (interpretation), in the definition of "arbitration agreement", for "the Arbitration Act (Northern Ireland) 1937" substitute "Part I of the Arbitration Act 1996".

*Insolvency (Northern Ireland) Order 1989 (N.I.19)*

53  In the Insolvency (Northern Ireland) Order 1989, after Article 320 insert—

*"Arbitration agreements to which bankrupt is party.*

320A(1) This Article applies where a bankrupt had become party to a contract containing an arbitration agreement before the commencement of his bankruptcy.

(2) If the trustee in bankruptcy adopts the contract, the arbitration agreement is enforceable by or against the trustee in relation to matters arising from or connected with the contract.

(3) If the trustee in bankruptcy does not adopt the contract and a matter to which the arbitration agreement applies requires to be determined in connection with or for the purposes of the bankruptcy proceedings—
    (a) the trustee with the consent of the creditors' committee, or
    (b) any other party to the agreement,
may apply to the court which may, if it thinks fit in all the circumstances of the case, order that the matter be referred to arbitration in accordance with the arbitration agreement.

(4) In this Article—
"arbitration agreement" has the same meaning as in Part I of the Arbitration Act 1996; and
"the court" means the court which has jurisdiction in the bankruptcy proceedings.".

*Social Security Administration Act 1992 (c. 5)*

54   In section 59 of the Social Security Administration Act 1992 (procedure for inquiries, &c.), in subsection (7), for "The Arbitration Act 1950" substitute "Part I of the Arbitration Act 1996".

*Social Security Administration (Northern Ireland) Act 1992 (c. 8)*

55   In section 57 of the Social Security Administration (Northern Ireland) Act 1992 (procedure for inquiries, &c.), in subsection (6) for "the Arbitration Act (Northern Ireland) 1937" substitute "Part I of the Arbitration Act 1996".

*Trade Union and Labour Relations (Consolidation) Act 1992 (c. 52)*

56   In sections 212(5) and 263(6) of the Trade Union and Labour Relations (Consolidation) Act 1992 (application of Arbitration Act) for "the Arbitration Act 1950" substitute "Part I of the Arbitration Act 1996".

*Industrial Relations (Northern Ireland) Order 1992 (N.I.5)*

57   In Articles 84(9) and 92(5) of the Industrial Relations (Northern Ireland) Order 1992 (application of Arbitration Act) for "The Arbitration Act (Northern Ireland) 1937" substitute "Part I of the Arbitration Act 1996".

*Registered Homes (Northern Ireland) Order 1992 (N.I.20)*

58   In Article 33(3) of the Registered Homes (Northern Ireland) Order 1992 (procedure of Registered Homes Tribunal) for "The Arbitration Act (Northern Ireland) 1937" substitute "Part I of the Arbitration Act 1996".

*Education Act 1993 (c. 35)*

59   In section 180(4) of the Education Act 1993 (procedure of Special Educational Needs Tribunal), for "The Arbitration Act 1950" substitute "Part I of the Arbitration Act 1996".

*Roads (Northern Ireland) Order 1993 (N.I.15)*

60   (1) The Roads (Northern Ireland) Order 1993 is amended as follows.

(2) In Article 131 (application of Arbitration Act) for "the Arbitration Act (Northern Ireland) 1937" substitute "Part I of the Arbitration Act 1996".

(3) In Schedule 4 (disputes), in paragraph 3(2) for "the Arbitration Act (Northern Ireland) 1937" substitute "Part I of the Arbitration Act 1996".

*Merchant Shipping Act 1995 (c. 21)*

61  In Part II of Schedule 6 to the Merchant Shipping Act 1995 (provisions having effect in connection with Convention Relating to the Carriage of Passengers and Their Luggage by Sea), for paragraph 7 substitute—

"7  Article 16 shall apply to arbitral proceedings as it applies to an action; and, as respects England and Wales and Northern Ireland, the provisions of section 14 of the Arbitration Act 1996 apply to determine for the purposes of that Article when an arbitration is commenced.".

*Industrial Tribunals Act 1996 (c. 17)*

62  In section 6(2) of the Industrial Tribunals Act 1996 (procedure of industrial tribunals), for "The Arbitration Act 1950" substitute "Part I of the Arbitration Act 1996".

SCHEDULE 4                        Section 107(2).

REPEALS

| Chapter | Short title | Extent of repeal |
| --- | --- | --- |
| 1892 c. 43. | Military Lands Act 1892. | In section 21(b), the words "under the Arbitration Act 1889". |
| 1922 c. 51. | Allotments Act 1922. | In section 21(3), the words "under the Arbitration Act 1889". |
| 1937 c. 8 (N.I.). | Arbitration Act (Northern Ireland) 1937. | The whole Act. |
| 1949 c. 54. | Wireless Telegraphy Act 1949. | In Schedule 2, paragraph 3(3). |
| 1949 c. 97. | National Parks and Access to the Countryside Act 1949. | In section 18(4), the words from "Without prejudice" to "England or Wales". |
| 1950 c. 27. | Arbitration Act 1950. | Part I. Section 42(3). |
| 1958 c. 47. | Agricultural Marketing Act 1958. | Section 53(8). |
| 1962 c. 46. | Transport Act 1962. | In Schedule 11, Part II, paragraph 7. |
| 1964 c. 14. | Plant Varieties and Seeds Act 1964. | In section 10(4) the words from "or in section 9" to "three arbitrators)". Section 39(3)(b)(i). |

| | | |
|---|---|---|
| 1964 c. 29 (N.I.). | Lands Tribunal and Compensation Act (Northern Ireland) 1964. | In section 9(3) the words from "so, however, that" to the end. |
| 1965 c. 12. | Industrial and Provident Societies Act 1965. | In section 60(8)(b), the words "by virtue of section 12 of the said Act of 1950". |
| 1965 c. 37. | Carriage of Goods by Road Act 1965. | Section 7(2)(b). |
| 1965 c. 13 (N.I.). | New Towns Act (Northern Ireland) 1965. | In section 27(2), the words from "under and in accordance with" to the end. |
| 1969 c. 24 (N.I.). | Industrial and Provident Societies Act (Northern Ireland) 1969. | In section 69(7)—<br>(a) in the opening words, the words from "and without prejudice" to "1937";<br>(b) in paragraph (b), the words "the registrar or" and "registrar or". |
| 1970 c. 31. | Administration of Justice Act 1970. | Section 4.<br><br>Schedule 3. |
| 1973 c. 41. | Fair Trading Act 1973. | Section 33(2)(d). |
| 1973 N.I. 1. | Drainage (Northern Ireland) Order 1973. | In Article 15(4), the words from "under and in accordance" to the end.<br><br>Article 40(4).<br><br>In Schedule 7, in paragraph 9(2), the words from "under and in accordance" to the end. |
| 1974 c. 47. | Solicitors Act 1974. | In section 87(1), in the definition of "contentious business", the words "appointed under the Arbitration Act 1950". |
| 1975 c. 3. | Arbitration Act 1975. | The whole Act. |
| 1975 c. 74. | Petroleum and Submarine Pipe-Lines Act 1975. | In Part II of Schedule 2—<br>(a) in model clause 40(2), the words "in accordance with the Arbitration Act 1950"; |

|  |  |  |
|---|---|---|
|  |  | (b) in model clause 40(2B), the words "in accordance with the Arbitration Act (Northern Ireland) 1937". |
|  |  | In Part II of Schedule 3, in model clause 38(2), the words "in accordance with the Arbitration Act 1950". |
| 1976 N.I. 12. | Solicitors (Northern Ireland) Order 1976. | In Article 3(2), in the entry "contentious business", the words "appointed under the Arbitration Act (Northern Ireland) 1937". |
|  |  | Article 71H(3). |
| 1977 c. 37. | Patents Act 1977. | In section 52(4) the words "section 21 of the Arbitration Act 1950 or, as the case may be, section 22 of the Arbitration Act (Northern Ireland) 1937 (statement of cases by arbitrators); but". |
|  |  | Section 131(e). |
| 1977 c. 38. | Administration of Justice Act 1977. | Section 17(2). |
| 1978 c. 23. | Judicature (Northern Ireland) Act 1978. | In section 35(2), paragraph (g)(v). |
|  |  | In Schedule 5, the amendment to the Arbitration Act 1950. |
| 1979 c. 42. | Arbitration Act 1979. | The whole Act. |
| 1980 c. 58. | Limitation Act 1980. | Section 34. |
| 1980 N.I. 3. | County Courts (Northern Ireland) Order 1980. | Article 31(3). |
| 1981 c. 54. | Supreme Court Act 1981. | Section 148. |
| 1982 c. 27. | Civil Jurisdiction and Judgments Act 1982. | Section 25(3)(c) and (5). |
|  |  | In section 26— (a) in subsection (1), the words "to arbitration or"; |

| | | |
|---|---|---|
| | | (b) in subsection (1)(a)(i), the words "arbitration or"; |
| | | (c) in subsection (2), the words "arbitration or". |
| 1982 c. 53. | Administration of Justice Act 1982. | Section 15(6). |
| | | In Schedule 1, Part IV. |
| 1984 c. 5. | Merchant Shipping Act 1984. | Section 4(8). |
| 1984 c. 12. | Telecommunications Act 1984. | Schedule 2, paragraph 13(8). |
| 1984 c. 16. | Foreign Limitation Periods Act 1984. | Section 5. |
| 1984 c. 28. | County Courts Act 1984. | In Schedule 2, paragraph 70. |
| 1985 c. 61. | Administration of Justice Act 1985. | Section 58. |
| | | In Schedule 9, paragraph 15. |
| 1985 c. 68. | Housing Act 1985. | In Schedule 18, in paragraph 6(2) the words from "and the Arbitration Act 1950" to the end. |
| 1985 N.I. 12. | Credit Unions (Northern Ireland) Order 1985. | In Article 72(7)— (a) in the opening words, the words from "and without prejudice" to "1937"; (b) in sub-paragraph (b), the words "the registrar or" and "registrar or". |
| 1986 c. 45. | Insolvency Act 1986. | In Schedule 14, the entry relating to the Arbitration Act 1950. |
| 1988 c. 8. | Multilateral Investment Guarantee Agency Act 1988. | Section 8(3). |
| 1988 c. 21. | Consumer Arbitration Agreements Act 1988. | The whole Act. |
| 1989 N.I. 11. | Limitation (Northern Ireland) Order 1989. | Article 72. |
| | | In Schedule 3, paragraph 1. |
| 1989 N.I. 19. | Insolvency (Northern Ireland) Order 1989. | In Part II of Schedule 9, paragraph 66. |

| | | |
|---|---|---|
| 1990 c. 41. | Courts and Legal Services Act 1990. | Sections 99 and 101 to 103. |
| 1991 N.I. 7. | Food Safety (Northern Ireland) Order 1991. | In Articles 8(8) and 11(10), the words from "and the provisions" to the end. |
| 1992 c. 40. | Friendly Societies Act 1992. | In Schedule 16, paragraph 30(1). |
| 1995 c. 8. | Agricultural Tenancies Act 1995. | Section 28(4). |
| 1995 c. 21. | Merchant Shipping Act 1995. | Section 96(10). |
| | | Section 264(9). |
| 1995 c. 42. | Private International Law (Miscellaneous Provisions) Act 1995. | Section 3. |

APPENDIX 8

# THE DAC REPORTS ON THE ARBITRATION BILL 1996

**Chapter 1**
**INTRODUCTION**

1. In its Report of June 1989, the Departmental Advisory Committee on Arbitration Law (the DAC), under the chairmanship of Lord Justice Mustill (now Lord Mustill) recommended against England, Wales and Northern Ireland adopting the UNCITRAL Model Law on International Commercial Arbitration. Instead, the DAC recommended that there should be a new and improved Arbitration Act for England, Wales and Northern Ireland, with the following features (Paragraph 108):

   *1. "It should comprise a statement in statutory form of the more important principles of the English law of arbitration, statutory and (to the extent practicable) common law.*

   *2. It should be limited to those principles whose existence and effect are uncontroversial.*

   *3. It should be set out in a logical order, and expressed in language which is sufficiently clear and free from technicalities to be readily comprehensible to the layman.*

   *4. It should in general apply to domestic and international arbitrations alike, although there may have to be exceptions to take account of treaty obligations.*

   *5. It should not be limited to the subject-matter of the Model Law.*

   *6. It should embody such of our proposals for legislation as have by then been enacted: see paragraph 100 [of the 1989 Report].*

   *7. Consideration should be given to ensuring that any such new statue should, so far as possible, have the same structure and language as the Model Law, so as to enhance its accessibility to those who are familiar with the Model Law."*

2. In an Interim Report in April 1995, the DAC state as follows:

   *"The original interpretation of [paragraph 108 of the 1989 Report] led to the draft Bill which was circulated in February 1994. Although*

*undoubtedly a highly skilful piece of work, it now appears that this draft Bill did not carry into effect what most users in fact wanted. In the light of the responses, the view of the DAC is that a new Bill should still be grounded on the objectives set out in [paragraph 108 of the 1989 Report], but that, reinterpreted, what is called for is much more along the lines of a restatement of the law, in clear and 'user-friendly' language, following, as far as possible, the structure and spirit of the Model Law, rather than simply a classic exercise in consolidation."*

3. The DAC's proposals in the Interim Report led to a new draft Bill which was circulated for public consultation in July 1995. This draft was very much the product of a fresh start. Indeed, it will be noted that whereas the February 1994 draft had the following long-title:

   *"To consolidate, with amendments, the Arbitration Act 1950, the Arbitration Act 1975, the Arbitration Act 1979 and related enactments"*

   this was altered for the July 1995 draft, and now begins:

   *"An Act to restate and improve the law relating to arbitration pursuant to an arbitration agreement . . ."*

4. The DAC remained of the view, for the reasons given in the Mustill Report, that the solution was not the wholesale adoption of the Model Law. However, at every stage in preparing a new draft Bill, very close regard was paid to the Model Law, and it will be seen that both the structure and the content of the July draft Bill, and the final draft, owe much to this model.

5. The task of the Committee has been made far easier by the extraordinary quantity and quality of responses we received both to the draft Bill published in February 1994 and to the draft Bill which was published in July 1995. A large number of people put substantial time and effort into responding to both drafts and putting forward suggestions, and we are very grateful to all of them. Indeed, both these consultation exercises have proved invaluable: the former showed that a new approach was required, while the latter showed that our April 1995 proposals seemed to be on the right track. Both sets of responses also contained carefully considered suggestions, many of which have been incorporated in the Bill. It should be emphasized that those suggestions which have not been adopted were only put on one side after lengthy consideration.

6. Among those who responded were a large number of institutions who offer arbitration services (such as the ICC) or who provide rules and administration for arbitrations concerning their members (such as the commodity associations). Both domestically and internationally institutions such as these play a very significant role in the field of arbitration. It seemed to us that the Bill should specifically recognize this, and that it should safeguard their spheres of operation. Consequently, there are many references to such institutions in

the Bill, and, indeed, Clause 74 gives them what we believe to be a necessary degree of immunity from suit.

7. Given the extremely favourable response, the July 1995 draft was taken forward, with certain modifications, to form the basis of the final draft, which is explained in this Report.

8. As well as containing a guide to the provisions of the final draft, this Report also contains supplementary recommendations (in Chapter 6) on certain matters that have come to light since publication of the final draft, and since its second reading in the House of Lords.

## Chapter 2
## PART I OF THE BILL

9. The title to this Part is *Arbitration Pursuant to an Arbitration Agreement*. It is in this Part that we have attempted to restate within a logical structure the basic principles of our law of arbitration, as it relates to arbitration under an agreement to adopt this form of dispute resolution. The Bill does not purport to provide an exhaustive code on the subject of arbitration. It would simply not be practical to attempt to codify the huge body of case law that has built up over the centuries, and there would be a risk of fossilizing the common law (which has the great advantage of being able to adapt to changing circumstances) had we attempted to do so. Rather, we have sought to include what we consider to be the more important common law principles, whilst preserving all others, in so far as they are consistent with the provisions of the Bill (see Clause 81).

10. A small number of key areas, however, have not been included, precisely because they are unsettled, and because they are better left to the common law to evolve. One such example concerns privacy and confidentiality in arbitrations, which deserves special mention here.

11. Privacy and confidentiality have long been assumed as general principles in English commercial arbitration, subject to important exceptions. It is only recently that the English courts have been required to examine both the legal basis for such principles and the breadth of certain of these exceptions, without seriously questioning the existence of the general principles themselves (see eg *The Eastern Saga* [1988] 2 Lloyd's Rep 373, 379 (Leggatt LJ); *Dolling-Baker v Merrett* [1990] 1 WLF 1205, 1213 (Parker LJ); *Hassneh v Mew* [1993] 2 Lloyd's Rep 243 (Colman J); *Hyundai Engineering v Active* (unreported, 9 March 1994, Phillips J); *Ins Company v Lloyd's Syndicate* [1995] 2 Lloyd's Rep. 272 (Colman J); *London & Leeds Estates Limited v Parisbas Limited* (no 2) (1995) E.G. 134 (Mance J)).

12. In practice, there is also no doubt whatever that users of commercial arbitration in England place much importance on privacy and confidentiality as essential features of English arbitration (eg see survey of users amongst the "Fortune 500" US corporations conducted for the LCIA by the London Business School in 1992). Indeed, as Sir Patrick Neill QC stated in his 1995 "Bernstein" Lecture, it would be difficult to conceive of any greater threat to the success of English arbitration that the removal of the general principles of confidentiality and privacy.

13. Last year's decision of the High Court of Australia in *Esso/BHP v Plowman* (see [1995] 11 *Arbitration International* 234) reinforced many people's interest in seeking to codify the relevant English legal principles in the draft Arbitration Bill. The implied term as the contractual basis for such principles was not in doubt under English law, and the English Courts were upholding these principles in strong and unequivocal terms. However, the Australian decision was to the effect that, as a matter of Australian law, this contractual approach was unsustainable as regards confidentiality. This has troubled users of commercial arbitration far outside Australia. The first response has been for arbitral institutions to amend their arbitration rules to provide expressly for confidentiality and privacy. The new WIPO Rules have sought to achieve this and we understand that both the ICC and the LCIA are currently amending their respective rules to similar effect.

14. In England, the second response was to consider placing these general principles on a firm statutory basis in the Arbitration Bill. This task was initially undertaken by the DAC mid–1995, and perhaps surprisingly, it soon proved controversial and difficult.

15. Whilst none could reasonably dispute the desirability of placing these general principles beyond all doubt on a firm statutory basis, applicable to all English arbitrations within the scope of the Bill (irrespective of the substantive law applicable to the arbitration agreement), grave difficulties arose over the myriad exceptions to these principles – which are necessarily required for such a statutory provision. There is of course no statutory guidance to confidentiality in the UNCITRAL Model Law whatever; and indeed, in a different context, Lord Mustill has recently warned against an attempt to give in the abstract an accurate exposition of confidentiality at large (see *In Re D (Adoption Reports: Confidentiality)* [1995] 3 WLR 483, 496D: *"To give an accurate exposition of confidentiality at large would require a much more wide-ranging survey of the law and practice than has been necessary for a decision on the narrow issue raised by the appeal, and cannot in my opinion safely be attempted in the abstract"*)

16. For English arbitration, the exceptions to confidentiality are manifestly legion and unsettled in part; and equally, there are important exceptions to privacy (eg in *The Lena Goldfields Case* (1930), the arbitration tribunal in

London opened the hearing to the press (but not the public) in order to defend the proceedings against malicious charges made by one of the parties, the USSR). As to the former, the award may become public in legal proceedings under the Arbitration Acts 1950–1979 or abroad under the 1958 New York Convention; the conduct of the arbitration may also become public if subjected to judicial scrutiny within or without England; and most importantly, several non-parties have legitimate interests in being informed as to the content of a pending arbitration, even short of an award: eg parent company, insurer, P+I Club, guarantor, partner, beneficiary, licensor and licensee, debenture-holder, creditors' committee etc., and of course even the arbitral institution itself (such as the ICC Court members approving the draft award). Whilst non-parties to the arbitration agreement and proceedings, none of these are officious strangers to the arbitration. Further, any provisions as to privacy and confidentiality would have to deal with the duty of a company to make disclosure of, eg, arbitration proceedings and actual or potential awards which have an effect on the company's financial position. The further Australian decision in **Commonwealth of Australia v Cockatoo Dockyard Pty Ltd** (1995) 36 NSWLR 662 suggests that the public interest may also demand transparency as an exception to confidentiality: *"Can it be seriously suggested that [the parties'] private agreement can, endorsed by a procedural direction of an arbitrator, exclude from the public domain matters of legitimate concern . . ."* per Kirby J. This decision raises fresh complications, particularly for statutory corporations. We are of the view that it would be extremely harmful to English arbitration is any statutory statement of general principles in this area impeded the commercial good-sense of current practices in English arbitration.

17. Given these exceptions and qualifications, the formulation of any statutory principles would be likely to create new impediments to the practice of English arbitration and, in particular, to add to English litigation on the issue. Far from solving a difficulty, the DAC was firmly of the view that it would create new ones. Indeed, even if acceptable statutory guidelines could be formulated, there would remain the difficulty of fixing and enforcing sanctions for non-compliance. The position is not wholly satisfactory. However, none doubt at English law the existence of the general principles of confidentiality and privacy (though there is not unanimity as to their desirability). Where desirable, institutional rules can stipulate for these general principles, even where the arbitration agreement is not governed by English law. As to English law itself, whilst the breadth and existence of certain exceptions remains disputed, these can be resolved by the English courts on a pragmatic case-by- case basis. In due course, if the whole matter were ever to become judicially resolved, it would remain possible to add a statutory provision by way of amendment to the Bill. We would, however, draw attention to our supplementary recommendations on this topic in Chapter 6 below.

## Clause 1 General Principles.

18. The DAC was persuaded by the significant number of submissions which called for an introductory clause setting out basic principles. This Clause sets out three general principles. The first of these reflects what we believe to be the object of arbitration. We have not sought to define arbitration, since this poses difficulties that we discussed in our April 1995 Interim Report, and in the end we were not persuaded that an attempted definition would serve any useful purpose. We do, however, see value in setting out the object of arbitration. Fairness, impartiality and the avoidance of unnecessary delay or expense are all aspects of justice ie all requirements of a dispute resolution system based on obtaining a binding decision from a third party on the matters at issue. To our minds it is useful to stipulate that all the provisions of the Bill must be read with this object of arbitration in mind.

19. The second principle is that of party autonomy. This reflects the basis of the Model Law and indeed much of our own present law. An arbitration under an arbitration agreement is a consensual process. The parties have agreed to resolve their disputes by their own consequences. Firstly, the parties should be held to their agreement and secondly, it should in the first instance be for the parties to decide how their arbitration should be conducted. In some cases, of course, the public interest will make inroads on complete party autonomy, in much the same way as there are limitations on freedom of contract. Some matters are simply not susceptible of this form of dispute resolution (eg certain cases concerning status or many family matters) while other considerations (such as consumer protection) may require the imposition of different rights and obligations. Again, as appears from the mandatory provisions of the Bill, there are some rules that cannot be overridden by parties who have agreed to use arbitration. In general the mandatory provisions are there in order to support and assist the arbitral process and the stated object of arbitration.

20. So far as the third principle is concerned this reflects Article 5 of the Model Law. This Article provides as follows:-

    *"In matters governed by this Law, no court shall intervene except where so provided in this Law."*

21. As was pointed out in the Mustill Report (pp50–52) there would be difficulties in importing this Article as it stands. However, there is no doubt that our law has been subject to international criticism that the Courts intervene more than they should in the arbitral process, thereby ending to frustrate the choice the parties have made to use arbitration rather than litigation as the means for resolving their disputes.

22. Nowadays the Courts are much less inclined to intervene in the arbitral process than used to be the case. The limitation on the right of appeal to the Courts from awards brought into effect by the Arbitration Act 1979, and

changing attitudes generally, have meant that the Courts nowadays generally only intervene in order to support rather than displace the arbitral process. We are very much in favour of this modern approach and it seems to us that it should be enshrined as a principle in the Bill.

**Clause 2 Scope of Application of Provisions.**

23. International arbitrations can give rise to complex problems in the conflict of laws. A possible solution to some of these problems would have been to provide that all arbitrations conducted in England and Wales or in Northern Ireland should be subject to the provisions of the Bill, regardless of the parties' express or implied choice of some other system of law. We have not adopted this solution, which appears to us contrary to the basic principle that the parties should be free to agree how their disputes should be resolved. There appear to us to be no reasons of public policy to prevent the parties conducting an arbitration here under an agreement governed by the foreign law or in accordance with a foreign procedural law. Clause 4(5) also follows the same basic principle. Of course, cases may well arise where considerations of our own concepts of public policy would lead to the refusal of the Court here to enforce an arbitration award. This, however, is covered by Clause 66(3).

24. The rules of the conflict of laws as they apply to arbitration are complex, and to some extent still in a state of development by the courts. It therefore seems to us inappropriate to attempt to codify the relevant principles, beyond the simple statements set out in clause 2(1). Thus, as clause 2(2) provides, matters referable to the arbitration agreement are governed by the law of England and Wales or of Northern Ireland, as the case may be, where that is the law applicable to the arbitration agreement, and matters of procedure are governed by that law where the seat of the arbitration is in England and Wales or in Northern Ireland: "seat" is defined in Clause 3. Beyond that we have not attempted to state the relevant rules of the conflict of laws, nor to embark on the issues of characterisation by which they are invoked.

25. Sub-section (3) concerns the powers of the court to support the arbitration by staying proceedings brought in breach of an agreement to arbitrate, by compelling the attendance of witnesses, by granting those forms of interim relief which are set out in Clause 44, and by enforcing the award at common law by summary procedure. Such powers should obviously be available regardless of whether the seat of the arbitration is in England and Wales or Northern Ireland, and regardless of what law is applicable to the arbitration agreement for the arbitral proceedings. Since we have used the expression *"whatever the law applicable . . ."*, it follows that Clause 2(3) is in no way restricted by Clause 2(1). It will be noted that in extending the power of the court to grant interim relief in support of arbitrations to arbitrations having a foreign seat we have given effect to our recommendation that section 25 of the Civil Jurisdiction and Judgments Act 1982 should be extended to

arbitration proceedings. It should be appreciated that Rules of Court will have to be amended to give proper effect to the extension of the Court's jurisdiction in Clause 2(3) (ie so as to allow service out of the jurisdiction in cases where it is necessary). Sub-section (4) enables the court to refuse to exercise its power in such cases, where the fact that the arbitration has a foreign seat makes it inappropriate to exercise that power.

**Clause 3 The seat of the arbitration.**

26. The definition of *"seat of arbitration"* is required by Clause 2, and as part of the definition of *"domestic arbitration"* in Clause 85. The concept of the "seat" as the juridical seat of the arbitration is known to English law but may be unfamiliar to some users of arbitration. Usually it will be the place where the arbitration is actually conducted: but this is not necessarily so, particularly if different parts of the proceedings are held in different countries.

27. In accordance with the principle of party autonomy, Clause 3 provides that the seat may be designated by the parties themselves or in some other manner authorised by them. Failing that it must be determined objectively having regard to the parties' agreement and all other relevant circumstances. English law does not at present recognise the concept of an arbitration which has no seat, and we do not recommend that it should do so. The powers of the court where the seat is in England and Wales or in Northern Ireland are limited to those necessary to carry into effect the principles enshrined in clause 1. Where the seat is elsewhere, the court's powers are further limited by Clause 2(4). The process of consultation identified no need for an arbitration which was "delocalised" to a greater extent than this.

**Clause 4 Mandatory and Non-mandatory Provisions.**

28. This provision is designed to make clear that the Bill has certain provisions that cannot be overridden by the parties; and for ease of reference these are listed in Schedule 1 to the Bill. The Clause also makes clear that the other provisions of this Part can be changed or substituted by the parties, and exist as 'fall-back' rules that will apply if the parties do not make any such change or substitution, or do not provide for the particular matter in question. In this way, in the absence of any other contrary agreement, gaps in an arbitration agreement will be filled.

29. Sub-section (5). Although we believe that the choice of a foreign law would anyway have the effect set out in this provision, it seemed for the sake of clarity to be useful to state this expressly, so as to remind all concerned that a choice of a foreign law does amount to an agreement of the parties to which due regard should be paid.

30. It should be made clear that the phrase *"mandatory"* is not used in either of the two senses that it is used, for example, in Articles 3 and 7 of the Rome

Convention (see Goode *Commercial Law*, 2nd Ed, at 1118): the mandatory provisions of Part 1 of the Bill are only mandatory in so far as the provisions of Part 1 apply (ie by virtue of Clause 2). The mandatory provisions would have no application if Part 1 does not apply.

**Clause 5 Agreements to be in writing.**

**(a) Arbitration Agreements.**

31. Article 7 of the Model Law requires the arbitration agreement to be in writing. We have not followed the precise wording of this Article, for the reasons given in the Mustill Report (p52), though we have incorporated much of that Article in the Bill.

32. The requirement for the arbitration agreement to be in writing is the position at present under Section 32 of the Arbitration Act 1950 and Section 7 of the Arbitration Act 1975. If an arbitration agreement is not in writing then it is not completely ineffective, since the common law recognizes such agreements and is saved by Clause 81 (2)(a).

33. We remain of the view expressed in the Consultative Paper issued with the draft Clauses published in July 1995, that there should be a requirement for writing. An arbitration agreement has the important effect of contracting out of the right to go to the court ie it deprives the parties of that basic right. To our minds an agreement of such importance should be in some written form. Furthermore the need for such form should help to reduce disputed as to whether or not an arbitration agreement was made and as to its terms.

34. We have, however, provided a very wide meaning to the words "*in writing*." Indeed this meaning is wider than that found in the Model Law, but in our view, is consonant with Article II.2 of the English text of the New York Convention. The non-exhaustive definition in the English text ("*shall include*") may differ in this respect from the French and Spanish texts, but the English text is equally authentic under Article XVI of the New York Convention itself, and also accords with the Russian authentic text ("[Russian Text]*"); see also the 1989 Report of the Swiss Institute of Comparative Law on Jurisdictional Problems in International Commercial Arbitration (by Adam Samuel), at pages 81 to 85. It seems to us that English Law as it stands more than justifies this wide meaning; see, for example, ***Zambia Steel v James Clark*** [1986] 2 Lloyd's Rep. 225. In view of rapidly evolving methods of recording we have made clear that "*writing*" includes recording by any means.

**(b) Other agreements.**

35. These we have also made subject to a 'writing' requirement. Had we not done so, we could envisage disputes over whether, for example, something the

parties had agreed to during the conduct of the arbitration amounted to a variation of the arbitration agreement and required writing, or could be characterized as something else. By introducing some formality with respect to all agreements, the possibility of subsequent disputes (eg at the enforcement stage) is greatly diminished. Indeed it seemed to us that with the extremely broad definition we have given to writing, the advantages of requiring some record of what was agreed with regard to any aspect of an arbitration outweighed the disadvantages of requiring a specific form for an effective agreement.

**(c) Further points.**

36. Sub-section 5(3). This is designed to cover, amongst other things, extremely common situations such as salvage operations, where parties make an oral agreement which incorporates by reference the terms of a written form of agreement (eg Lloyd's Open Form), which contains an arbitration clause. Whilst greatly extending the definition of "writing", the DAC is of the view that given the frequency and importance of such activity, it was essential that it be provided for in the Bill. The reference could be to a written agreement containing an arbitration clause, or to a set of written arbitration rules, or to an individual written arbitration agreement. This provision would also cover agreement by conduct. For example, party A may agree to buy from party B a quantity of goods on certain terms and conditions (which include an arbitration clause) which are set out in writing and sent to party B, with a request that he sign and return the order form. If, which is by no means uncommon, party B fails to sign the order form, or send any document in response to the order, but manufactures and delivers the goods in accordance with the contract to party A, who pays for them in accordance with the contract, this could constitute an agreement "*otherwise than in writing by reference to terms which are in writing.*", and could therefore include an effective arbitration agreement. The provision therefore seeks to meet the criticisms that have been made of Article 7(2) of the Model Law in this regard (see eg the Sixth Goff Lecture, delivered by Neil Kaplan QC in Hong Kong in November 1995, (1996) 12 *Arb. Int.* 35). A written agreement made by reference to separate written terms would, of course, be caught by Clause 5(2).

37. Sub-section 5(4). There has been some concern that a writing requirement with respect to every agreement might unduly constrain the parties' freedom and flexibility with respect to, for example, minor matters of procedure during a hearing. This sub-section seeks to avoid this. An agreement will be evidenced in writing if recorded by, amongst others, a third party with the authority of the parties to the agreement. Given that this third party could of course be the tribunal, the parties are free during a hearing to make whatever arrangements or changes to the agreed procedure they wish, as long as these are recorded by the tribunal. The DAC is of the view that this presents no serious hindrance to the parties' flexibility, and has the merit of reducing the risk of disputes later on as to what exactly was agreed. Clearly, this

sub-section also has a wider effect, allowing for the recording of an oral agreement at any stage.

38. Sub-section 5(5). This provision is based on Article 7(2) of the Model Law, but with certain important changes. The DAC has been careful to emphasize that for there to be an effective arbitration agreement for the purposes of the Part, it is not enough for one party to allege in a written submission that there is an arbitration agreement, in circumstances where the other party simply fails to respond at all. If this were enough, an unfair obligation would be placed on any party (including a stranger to the proceedings in question) to take the active step of serving a written submission in order to deny this allegation. Therefore, in order to satisfy this sub-section, there must be a failure to deny an allegation by a party who has submitted a response submission.

39. It has been suggested that the term "written submissions" is too narrow, and that this should be replaced by "documents". The DAC does not agree with this, given that this would include the most informal of letters. It may well be unjust, for example, for one party to be able to point to one sentence in one letter in a long exchange with another party, in which there is an allegation that there exists an arbitration clause, and where this has not been denied.

40. Reference should also be made to sub-section 23(4). Whilst any agreement as to an arbitration must be in writing, the DAC is of the view that it is impracticable to impose a writing requirement on an agreement to terminate an arbitration. Parties may well simply walk away from proceedings, or allow the proceedings to lapse, and it could be extremely unfair if one party were allowed to rely upon an absence of writing at some future stage. Where a Claimant allows an arbitration to lapse, Clause 41(3) may be utilised.

## The Arbitration Agreement

### Clause 6 Definition of Arbitration Agreement

41. The first sub-section reflects Article 7(1) of the Model Law and provides a more informative definition than that in Section 32 of the 1950 Act. We have used the word "disputes" but this is defined in Clause 82 as including "differences" since there is some authority for the proposition that the latter term is wider than the former; see *Sykes v Fine Fare Ltd* [1967] 1 Lloyd's Rep. 53.

42. The second sub-section reflects Article 7(2) of the Model Law. In English law there is at present some conflicting authority on the question as to what is required for the effective incorporation of an arbitration clause by reference. Some of those responding to the July 1995 draft Clauses made critical comments of the views of Sir John Megaw in *Aughton v M F Kent Services* [1991] 57 BLR 1 (a construction contract case) and suggested that we should take the opportunity of making clear that the law was as stated in the charter party cases and as summarized by Ralph Gibson LJ in *Aughton*. (Similar

disquiet has been expressed about decisions following *Aughton*, such as *Ben Barrett v Henry Boot Management Ltd* [1995] Constr. Ind. Law Letter 1026). It seemed to us, however, that although we are of the view that the approach of Ralph Gibson LJ should prevail in all cases, this was really a matter for the Court to decide. The wording we have used certainly leaves room for the adoption of the charter party rules in all cases, since it refers to references to a document containing an arbitration clause as well as a reference to the arbitration itself. Thus the wording is not confined to cases where there is specific reference to the arbitration clause, which Sir John Megaw (but not Ralph Gibson LJ) considered was a requirement for effective incorporation by reference.

**Clause 7 Separability of Arbitration Agreement**

43. This Clause sets out the principle of separability which is already part of English law (see Harbour Assurance v Kansa [1993] QB 701), which is also to be found in Article 16(1) of the Model Law, and which is regarded internationally as highly desirable. However, it seems to us that the doctrine of separability is quite distinct from the question of the degree to which the tribunal is entitled to rule on its own jurisdiction, so that, unlike the Model Law, we have dealt with the latter elsewhere in the Bill (Clause 30).

44. In the draft Clauses published in July 1995 we inserted a provision to make clear that the doctrine of separability did not affect the question whether an assignment of rights under the substantive agreement carried with it the right or obligation to submit to arbitration in accordance with the arbitration agreement. This is now omitted as being unnecessary, since we have re- drafted sub-section (1) in order to follow the relevant part of Article 16 of the Model Law more closely, and to make clear that the doctrine of separability is confined to the effect of invalidity etc of the main contract on the arbitration agreement, rather than being, as it was in the July 1995 draft, a free- standing principle. Similarly, in being so restricted, this Clause is not intended to have any impact on the incorporation of an arbitration clause from one document or contract into another (which is addressed in Clause 6(2)).

45. A number of those responding to our drafts expressed the wish for the Bill to lay down rules relating to assignment, eg that the assignment of rights under the substantive agreement should be subject to any right or obligation to submit to arbitration in accordance with the arbitration agreement unless either of these agreements provided otherwise. Indeed we included such a provision in the illustrative draft published in April 1995. However, on further consideration, we concluded that it would not be appropriate to seek to lay down any such rules.

46. There were two principal reasons for reaching this view.

    i. In the first place, under English law the assignability of a contractual right is governed by the proper law of that right, while the effectiveness of the assignment is governed by the proper law of the assignment. However, where the law governing the substantive agreement (or the arbitration agreement) is not English law, different rules may well apply and there is an added problem in that those rules (under the foreign law in question) may be categorized as either substantive or procedural in nature. The Bill would therefore have to address such problems whilst simultaneously not interfering with substantive rights and obligations. We were not persuaded that it would be either practicable or of any real use to attempt to devise general rules which would deal satisfactorily with this matter.

ii. In the second place, English law distinguishes between legal and equitable assignments, so that any rules we devised would have to take this into account. In our view, an attempt to devise rules relating to assignments where no foreign law elements are involved is more the subject of reform of the law of assignment generally than of a Bill relating exclusively to arbitration.

47. Finally, it should be noted that the substantive agreement of which the arbitration agreement forms part need not itself be in writing for the Bill to apply, provided of course that the arbitration agreement itself is in writing. This should be clarified as we suggest in our supplementary recommendations in Chapter 6 below.

**Clause 8 Whether Agreement discharged by Death of a Party.**

48. This Clause sets out the present statutory position. The common law was that an arbitration agreement was discharged by the death of a party. That rule was altered by the Arbitration Act 1934 as re-enacted by Section 2 of the Arbitration Act 1950. We have avoided using the technical expression 'right of action' which is to be found in Section 2(3) of the 1950 Act and which could perhaps give rise to problems for the reasons given in the consultative paper published with the draft Clauses in July 1995. In line with party autonomy, we have provided that the parties can agree that death shall have the effect of discharging the arbitration agreement.

49. This Clause deals only with the arbitration agreement. The effect of the death of a party on the appointment of an arbitrator (also to be found in Section 2 of the 1950 Act) is now dealt with in that part of the Bill concerned with the arbitral tribunal (see Clause 26(2)).

### Stay of Legal Proceedings

**Clause 9 Stay of Legal Proceedings.**

50. We have proposed a number of changes to the present statutory position (section 4(1) of the 1950 Act and section 1 of the 1975 Act), having in mind Article 8 of the Model Law, our treaty obligations, and other considerations.

51. We have made it clear that a stay can be sought of a counterclaim as well as a claim. The existing legislation could be said not to cover counterclaims, since it required the party seeking a stay first to enter an "*appearance*", which a defendant to counterclaim could not do. Indeed, "*appearance*" is no longer the appropriate expression in the High Court in any event, and never was the appropriate expression in the county court. We have also made clear that an application can be made to stay part of legal proceedings, where other parts are not subject to an agreement to arbitrate.

52. Further, the Clause provides that an application is only to be made by a party against whom legal proceedings are brought (as opposed to any other party).

53. We have provided that an application may be made for a stay even where the matter cannot be referred to arbitration immediately, because the parties have agreed first to use other dispute resolution procedures. This reflects *dicta* of Lord Mustill ***Channel Tunnel v Balfour Beatty*** [1993] AC 334.

54. In this Clause we have made a stay mandatory unless the Court is satisfied that the arbitration agreement is null and void, inoperative, or incapable of being performed. This is the language of the Model Law and of course of the New York Convention on the Recognition and Enforcement of Foreign Arbitral Awards, presently to be found in the Arbitration Act 1975.

55. The Arbitration Act 1975 contained a further ground for refusing a stay, namely where the Court was satisfied that "*there was not in fact any dispute between the parties with regard to the matter agreed to be referred.*" These words do not appear in the New York Convention and in our view are confusing and unnecessary, for the reasons given in ***Hayter v Nelson*** [1990] 2 Lloyd's Rep. 265.

56. In Part II of the Bill these provisions are altered in cases of "*domestic arbitration agreements*" as there defined.

57. We have included a provision (sub-section (5)) that where the Court refuses to stay the legal proceedings, any term making an award a condition precedent to the bringing of legal proceedings (known as Scott v Avery clause) will cease to have effect. This avoids a situation where the arbitration clause is unworkable, yet no legal proceedings can be successfully brought. Whilst one respondent suggested that this may go too far, it appears to be a matter of basic justice that a situation in which a party can neither arbitrate nor litigate must be avoided.

**Clause 10 Reference of Interpleader Issue to Arbitration.**

58. This Clause is based on Section 5 of the 1950 Act. We have however taken the opportunity of making a stay mandatory so as to comply with the New York Convention, as well as trying to express the provision in simpler, clearer

terms. The Clause is required because 'interpleader' arises where one party claiming no right himself in the subject matter, is facing conflicting claims from other parties and does not know to which of them he should account. English law allows such a party to bring those in contention before the Court which may order the latter to fight out the question between themselves. If they have agreed to arbitrate the matter then Clause 9 would not itself operate, since the party seeking interpleader relief would not be making a claim which he had agreed to arbitrate.

59. We have not defined "*interpleader*", although some suggested that we should, given that this is a legal term of art, which goes far beyond arbitration contexts.

**Clause 11 Retention of Security where Admiralty Proceedings stayed.**

60. This Clause is not intended to do more than re-enact the present statutory position as found in Section 26 of the Civil Jurisdiction and Judgments Act 1982.

61. Clauses 9 to 11 are, of course, mandatory.

### Commencement of Arbitral Proceedings

**Clause 12 Power of Court to extend Time for beginning Arbitral Proceedings etc.**

62. We have proposed a number of changes to the existing law.

63. The major change concerns the test that the Court must apply before extending the time.

64. The power of the Court to extend a contractual time limit which would otherwise bar the claim first appeared in our law in Section 16(6) of the Arbitration Act 1934, which was re-enacted in Section 27 of the Arbitration Act 1950.

65. From paragraph 33 of the Report of the MacKinnon Committee presented to Parliament in March 1927 it can be seen that the reason for suggesting that the Court should have power to extend the time was that the vast majority of submissions to arbitration are contained in printed forms of contract, which cannot be carefully examined in the transaction of business and alteration of which it would be difficult for most people to secure. The Committee concluded that it might be sound policy to create a power to modify unconscionable provisions as regards common forms of submission in printed forms. It is also clear from Paragraph 34 of the Report that the Committee had in mind cases where the time limit was very short ie measured in days. The Committee suggested that the test should be whether the time limit created an 'unreasonable hardship.'

66. As can be seen from the Notes on Clauses to the 1934 Act, it was later felt that since the justification for giving the power was presumably either ignorance of the existence of the provision in the contract, or the acceptance of the provision through undue pressure by the other party, which could be the case whether or not the contract was in a common form, the power should not be limited to such forms.

67. Section 27 of the 1950 Act, with its test of undue hardship, seems to many to have been interpreted by the Courts in a way hardly envisaged by those who suggested the power in the first place. Indeed that interpretation seems to have changed over the years: see the discussion in Mustill and Boyd "*Commercial Arbitration*", 2nd Ed., pp 201–215. Some responses indicated dissatisfaction with the way the Courts were using Clause 27 to interfere with the bargain that the parties had made. The present legal position would seem to owe much to a time, now some 20 years ago, when the Courts were flirting with the idea that they enjoyed some general power of supervisory jurisdiction over arbitrations.

68. The justification for time limits is that they enable commercial concerns (and indeed others) to draw a line beneath transactions at a much earlier stage than ordinary limitation provisions would allow. It should be mentioned, however, that other responses suggested that the position presently reached by the Courts should be maintained.

69. The present Committee re-examined Section 27 in the light of the underlying philosophy of the Bill, namely that of party autonomy. This underlying philosophy seems to have been generally welcomed in this country and abroad and of course it fits with the general international understanding of arbitration. Party autonomy means, among other things, that any power given to the Court to override the bargain that the parties have made must be fully justified. The idea that the Court has some general supervisory jurisdiction over arbitrations has been abandoned.

70. It seemed to us in today's climate that there were three cases where the power could be justified in the context of agreed time limits to bring a claim. These are, firstly, where the circumstances are such as were outside the reasonable contemplation of the parties when they agreed the provision in question and that it would be fair to extend the time, secondly, where the conduct of one party made it unjust to hold the other to the time limit, and thirdly, where the respective bargaining position of the parties was such that it would again be unfair to hold one of them to the time limit.

71. The third of these cases seems to us to reflect the thinking of the MacKinnon Committee, while the other two have developed through the Courts' interpretation of Section 27. However this third category is really an aspect of what nowadays would be called 'consumer protection'. This part of the Bill is not concerned with consumer protection, for which provision is made elsewhere and in respect of which there is a growing body of European law.

72. In these circumstances it seemed to us to be appropriate to set out in this part of the Bill the first and second of the cases we have described. Apart from anything else, this will give the Courts the opportunity to reconsider how to proceed in the light of the philosophy underlying the Bill as a whole, namely that of party autonomy. As the MacKinnon Committee itself intimated, great care must be taken before interfering with the bargain that the parties have made.

73. It was suggested to the DAC that the principal matter to be taken into account by the court should be the length of the contractual period in question. The DAC is of the view that this is only one of several relevant matters, another factor being, for example, the contemplation of the parties. For this reason, the DAC concluded that a simple test of *"substantial injustice"*, without more, would not suffice.

74. There are some other changes.

   i. Firstly, Clause 12(1)(b) contains a reference to other dispute resolution procedures. We understand that there is an increasing use of provisions which call for mediation and other alternative dispute resolution procedures to precede recourse to arbitration, so that we thought it proper to add this to the other step covered by the Clause, namely to begin arbitral proceedings. We do not intend to widen the scope of the Clause beyond this, so that unless the step in question is one of the two kinds described, the Clause will not operate. Thus this represents only a small but we think logical extension to the present law.

   ii. Secondly, it is made a pre-condition that the party concerned first exhausts any available arbitral process for obtaining an extension of time. In the view of the Committee it would be a rare case indeed where the Court extended the time in circumstances where there was such a process which had not resulted in an extension, for it would in the ordinary case be difficult if not impossible to persuade the Court that it would be just to extend the time or unjust not to do so, where by an arbitral process to which *ex hypothesi* the applying party had agreed, the opposite conclusion had been reached.

   iii. Thirdly, we have made any appeal from a decision of the Court under this Clause subject to the leave of that Court. It seems to us that there should be this limitation, and that in the absence of some important question of principle, leave should not generally be granted. We take the same view in respect of the other cases in the Bill where we propose that an appeal requires the leave of the Court.

   iv. Fourthly, whereas the existing statutory provision refers to terms of an agreement that provide that claims shall be *"barred"*, this has been extended to read *"barred, or the claimant's right extinguished"*.

75. For obvious reasons, this Clause is mandatory.

## Clauses 13 and 14 Application of Limitation Acts and Commencement of Arbitral Proceedings.

76. The first of these provisions is designed to restate the present law. The reference to the Foreign Limitation Periods Act 1984 avoids (subject to the provisions of that Act) the imposition of an English limitation period where an applicable foreign law imposes a different period. The second provision reflects to a degree Article 21 of the Model Law, but sets out the various cases, including one not presently covered by the law. It will be noted that we have used the word "*matter*" rather than the word "*disputes.*" This is to reflect the fact that a dispute is not the same as a claim; cf Mustill and Boyd op.cit. at p29 and Commission for the New Towns v Crudens (1995) CILL 1035. The neutral word "matter" will cover both, so that an arbitration clause which refers to claims will be covered as well as one which refers to disputes.

77. Clause 13 is a mandatory provision.

### The Arbitral Tribunal

**Clause 15 The Arbitral Tribunal**

78. Article 10(1) of the Model Law provides that the parties are free to determine the number of arbitrators. We have included a like provision.

79. Article 10(2) of the Model Law stipulates that failing such determination, the number of arbitrators shall be three. This we have not adopted, preferring the existing English rule that in the absence of agreement the default number shall be one. The employment of three arbitrators is likely to be three times the cost of employing one, and it seems right that this extra burden should be available if the parties so choose, but not imposed on them. The provision for a sole arbitrator also accords both with common practice in this country, and the balance of responses the DAC received. The Model Law default does not, of course, cater for the situation where there are more than two parties to the arbitration.

**Clause 16 Procedure for the Appointment of Arbitrators**

80. Again we have had the Model Law (Article 11) very much in mind in drafting these provisions, though we have attempted to cater for more cases and also for the fact that under our law, there can be either an umpire or chairman. We should note that this has caused some confusion abroad, particularly in the United States, where what we would describe as a 'chairman' is called an 'umpire.' In Clauses 20 and 21 we set out the differences between these two which (in the absence of agreement between the parties) is the present position under English law.

81. The time limits we have imposed for appointments we consider to be fair and reasonable. They can be extended by the Court under Clause 79, but the

power of the Court in this regard is limited as set out in that Clause. In the ordinary case we would not expect the Court to allow a departure from the Clause 16 time limits.

82. It might be noted that periods of 28 days, rather than 30 days (as in the Model Law) have been used throughout the Bill, in order to reduce the likelihood of a deadline expiring on a weekend.

**Clause 17 Power in case of default to appoint sole arbitrator**

83. This Clause is intended to replace the present rules concerning the appointment of a sole arbitrator where the other party is in default (section 7(b) of the 1950 Act). It only applies to a two party case. We have stipulated that the party in default must not only appoint his arbitrator within the specified period but also inform the other party that he has done so. This in our view is a significant improvement on the present law, where the defaulting party was under no obligation to say that he had made an appointment. This was calculated to cause unnecessary delay, confusion and expense.

84. Some of those responding objected to this Clause. The DAC, however, remains of the view that this provision is an example of the Court supporting the arbitral process, and reducing the opportunities available for a recalcitrant party. The DAC is advised that section 7(b) of the 1950 Act is used a great deal, and that its very existence constitutes a deterrent to those contemplating dilatory tactics. The alternative would be to simply provide for recourse to Court. This would be overly burdensome in most cases, and is available, in any event, under the provisions of the Bill.

85. It has been suggested that the Bill should set out grounds upon which the court should exercise its discretion in Clause 17(3). The DAC is of the view, however, that this is best left for the Courts to develop, given the specific circumstances of each case, and in the light of the overall philosophy of the Bill.

86. One respondent queried the use of the "refuses" in Clause 17(1). The advantage of this is that if a party does actually refuse to appoint an arbitrator, rather than simply failing to do so, the non-defaulting party need not wait for the expiration of the relevant time period within which the defaulting party may make such an appointment, but could use the mechanism in Clause 17 straight away.

**Clause 18 Failure of Appointment Procedure**

87. Again we have had the Model Law in mind with drafting this provision. The starting point is any agreement the parties may have made to deal with a failure of the appointment procedure. In the absence of any such agreement, the Court is given the power to make appointments. This is a classic case of the Court supporting and helping to carry through the arbitration process.

88. It will be noted that we have given the Court power to revoke any appointments already made. This is to cover the case where unless the Court took this step it might be suggested thereafter that the parties had not been fairly treated, since one had his own choice arbitrator while the other had an arbitrator imposed on him by the Court in circumstances that were no fault of his own. This situation in fact arose in France in the ***Dutco*** case, where an award was invalidated for this reason.

89. The Model Law stipulates that there shall be no appeal from a decision of the Court. We have no gone as far as this, since there may well be questions of important general principle which would benefit from the authoritative appellate guidance.

### Clause 19 Court to have regard to Agreed Qualifications

90. This comes from Article 11(5) of the Model Law, which itself seeks to preserve as much of the parties' agreement as possible.

### Clauses 20 and 21 Chairman and Umpire

91. The parties are, of course, free to make what arrangements they like about the functions and powers of Chairman or Umpires. We have set out what we believe to be the position under English law in the absence of any such agreement. As we understand the current position, in the absence of an agreement between the parties, an umpire can neither take part nor attend an arbitration until the arbitrators have disagreed.

92. A cause of delay and expense often exists under our umpire system where the umpire does not attend the proceedings and it is only at an advanced stage (when the arbitrators disagree) that he takes over, for much that has gone on may have to be repeated before him. Equally, the time and expense of an umpire may be wasted if he attends but the arbitrators are able to agree on everything. We have decided that it would be preferable to stipulate that (in the absence of agreement between the parties) the umpire should attend the proceedings (as opposed to taking part in the proceedings) and be supplied with the same documents and materials as the other arbitrators. We hope, however, that common sense will prevail and that the parties will make specific agreement over this question, tailored to the circumstances of the particular case.

93. Sub-section 21(4) caused some concern amongst a few respondents, but this sub-section simply reflects what is understood to be the current position.

94. We should record that we considered whether the peculiarly English concept of an umpire should be swept away in favour of the more generally used chaired tribunal. As we have pointed out above, in the United States what we would describe as a chairman is called an umpire. In the end we decided not

to recommend this, and to continue to provide default provisions for those who wanted to continue to use this form of arbitral tribunal.

**Clause 22 Decision-making where no Chairman or Umpire.**

95. We decided to include this situation for the sake of completeness, though the default provision can only work if there is unanimity or a majority. If there is neither, then it would appear that the arbitration agreement cannot operate, unless the parties can agree, or have agreed, what is to happen.

**Clause 23 Revocation of arbitrator's authority.**

96. Statutory provisions making it impossible unilaterally to revoke the authority of an arbitrator have existed since 1833. The present Clause is designed to reflect the current position, save that we have imposed a writing requirement and thought it helpful to make express reference to arbitral institutions etc. These of course only have such powers as the parties have agreed they shall have, so that strictly this provision is not necessary, but we consider that an express reference makes for clarity.

97. Some of those responding suggested that the parties' right to agree to revoke an arbitral appointment should be limited (eg that Court approval should be required in every case). The DAC has not adopted these suggestions since any tribunal is properly regarded as the parties' tribunal and to do so would derogate from the principle of party autonomy.

98. It will be seen that various terms are used in the Bill with respect to the termination of arbitral appointment, such as *"removal"* and *"revocation of authority"*. Different terms have been adopted simply as a matter of correct English usage. The difference in terms is not intended to be of any legal significance.

99. Sub-section 23(4). Whilst any agreement as to an arbitration must be in writing, as defined earlier, the DAC is of the view that it is impracticable to impose a writing requirement on an agreement to terminate an arbitration. Parties may well simply walk away from proceedings, or allow the proceedings to lapse, and it could be extremely unfair if one party were allowed to rely upon an absence of writing at some future stage. Where a Claimant allows to arbitration to lapse, Clause 41(3) may be utilised.

**Clause 24 Power of Court to Remove Arbitrator**

100. We have set out the cases where the Court can remove an arbitrator.

101. The Model Law (Article 12) specifies justifiable doubts as to the independence (as well as impartiality) of an arbitrator as grounds for his removal. We have considered this carefully, but despite efforts to do so, no-one has persuaded us

that, in consensual arbitrations, this is either required or desirable. It seems to us that lack of independence, unless it gives rise to justifiable doubts about the impartiality of the arbitrator, is of no significance. The latter is, of course, the first of our grounds for removal. If lack of independence were to be included, then this could only be justified if it covered cases where the lack on independence did **not** give rise to justifiable doubts about impartiality, for otherwise there would be no point including lack of independence as a separate ground.

102. We can see no good reason for including 'non-partiality' lack of independence as a ground for removal and good reasons for not doing so. We do not follow what is meant to be covered by a lack on independence which does not lead to the appearance of partiality. Furthermore, the inclusion on independence would give rise to endless arguments, as it has, for example, in Sweden and the United States, where almost any connection (however remote) has been put forward to challenge the 'independence' of an arbitrator. For example, it is often the case that one member of a barristers' Chambers appears as counsel before an arbitrator who comes from the same Chambers. Is that to be regarded, without more, as a lack of independence justifying the removal of the arbitrator? We are quite certain that his would not be the case in English law. Indeed the Chairman has so decided in a case in Chambers in the Commercial Court. We would also draw attention to the article "Barristers' Independence and Disclosure" by Kendall in (1992) 8 Arb. Int. 287. We would further note in passing that even the oath taken by those appointed to the International Court of Justice; and indeed to our own High Court, refers only to impartiality.

103. Further, there may well be situations in which parties desire their arbitrators to have familiarity with a specific field, rather than being entirely independent.

104. We should emphasize that we intend to lose nothing of significance by omitting reference to independence. Lack of this quality may well give rise to justifiable doubts about impartiality, which is covered, but if it does not, then we cannot at present see anything of significance that we have omitted by not using this term.

105. We have included, as grounds for removal, the refusal or failure of an arbitrator properly to conduct the proceedings, as well as failing to use all reasonable despatch in conducting the proceedings or making an award, where the result has caused or will cause substantial injustice to the applicant. We trust that the Courts will not allow the first of these matters to be abused by those intent on disrupting the arbitral process. To this end we have included a provision allowing the tribunal to continue while an application is made. There is also Clause 73 which effectively requires a party to 'put up or shut up' if a challenge is to be made.

106. We have every confidence that the Courts will carry through the intent of this part of the Bill, which is that it should only be available where the

conduct of the arbitrator is such as to go so beyond anything that could reasonably be defended that substantial injustice has resulted or will result. The provision is not intended to allow the Court to substitute its own view as to how the arbitral proceedings should be conducted. Thus the choice by an arbitrator of a particular procedure, unless it breaches the duty laid on arbitrators by Clause 33, should on no view justify the removal of an arbitrator, even if the Court would not itself have adopted that procedure. In short, this ground only exists to cover what we hope will be the very rare case where an arbitrator so conducts the proceedings that it can fairly be said that instead of carrying through the object of arbitration as stated in the Bill, he is in effect frustrating that object. Only if the Court confines itself in this way can this power of removal be justified as a measure supporting rather than subverting the arbitral process.

107. We have also made the exhaustion of any arbitral process for challenging an arbitrator a pre-condition to the right to apply to the Court. Again it will be a very rare case indeed where the Court will remove an arbitrator notwithstanding that the process has reached a different conclusion.

108. If an arbitrator is removed by the Court, we have given the Court power to make orders in respect of his remuneration. We would expect this power to be exercised where the behaviour of the arbitrator is inexcusable to the extent that this should be marked by depriving him of all or some of his fees and expenses. This sub-section is also the subject of a supplementary recommendation in Chapter 6 below.

109. As a matter of justice, we have stipulated that an arbitrator is entitled to be heard on any application for his removal.

110. This is a mandatory provision. It seems to us that an agreement to contract out of the cases we specify would really be tantamount to an agreement to a dispute resolution procedure that is contrary to the basic principles set out in Clause 1.

**Clause 25 Resignation of Arbitrator**

111. In theory it could be said that an arbitrator cannot unilaterally resign if this conflicts with the express or implied terms of his engagement. However, as a matter of practical politics an arbitrator who refuses to go on cannot be made to do so, though of course he may incur a liability for breach of his agreement to act.

112. In this Clause we have given an arbitrator who resigns the right to go to the Court to seek relief from any liability incurred through resigning and to make orders relating to his remuneration and expenses, unless the consequences of resignation have been agreed with the parties (eg by virtue of having adopted institutional rules).

113. We have chosen the words of sub-section (1) with care so that the agreement referred to is confined to an agreement as to the consequences of resignation. A simple agreement not to resign (or only to resign in certain circumstances) with no agreement as to what will happen if this promise is broken is not within the sub-section. This has to be so since otherwise (by virtue of sub-section (2)), sub-sections (3) and (4) would never or hardly ever operate, for the arbitrator will not be under any liability or at risk as to his fees or expenses unless he is in breach by resigning.

114. In the July draft we suggested a provision which would have entitled the Court to grant relief in all circumstances including those where the arbitrator had made an agreement as to the consequences of his resignation. However, as the result of a response that we received we have concluded that where the parties have agreed with an arbitrator on the consequences it would be wrong to give the Court a power to adjust the position.

115. The reason we propose this is that circumstances may well arise in which it would be just to grant such relief to a resigning arbitrator. For example the arbitrator may (reasonably) not be prepared to adopt a procedure agreed by the parties (ie under Clause 34) during the course of an arbitration, taking the view that his duty under Clause 33 conflicts with their suggestions (the relationship between the duty of arbitrators in Clause 33 and the freedom of the parties in Clause 34, is discussed in more detail below). Again, an arbitration may drag on for far longer than could reasonably have been expected when the appointment was accepted, resulting in an unfair burden on the arbitrator. In circumstances where the Court was persuaded that it was reasonable for the arbitrator to resign, it seems only right that the Court should be able to grant appropriate relief.

**Clause 26 Death of Arbitrator or Person appointing him.**

116. The Clause complements Clause 8 and is included for the same reason. Clause 26(1) is mandatory – it is difficult to see how parties could agree otherwise.

**Clause 27 Filling of Vacancy etc.**

117. This Clause reflects Article 15 of the Model Law, but also deals with certain other important ancillary matters. It should be noted that we do not propose to re-enact the power given to the Court under Section 25 of the Arbitration Act 1950 to fill a vacancy created by its removal of an arbitrator. It seems to us that (in the absence of agreement between the parties) it is preferable for the original appointment procedure to be used, for otherwise (as in the ***Dutco*** case mentioned above) it might be argued that the parties were not being treated equally.

118. We have given the tribunal the right (when reconstituted) to determine to what extend the previous proceedings should stand, though we have also

made clear that this does not affect any right a party may have to challenge what has happened.

119. Further, we have provided in Clause 27(5) that the fact of an arbitrator ceasing to hold office will not affect any appointment made by him (whether alone or jointly) of another arbitrator, unless the parties have otherwise agreed pursuant to Clause 27(1)(c).

120. Arbitration proceedings necessarily involve the incurring of expenditure. The arbitrators have to be paid, and the parties incur expense in presenting their cases to the tribunal. The issue of costs involves at least three quite discrete elements.

   i. As a matter of general contract law, arbitrators, experts, institutions and any other payees whatsoever are entitled to be paid what has been agreed with them by any of the parties. Therefore, for example, if a party appoints an arbitrator for an agreed fee, as a matter of general contract law (rather than anything in this Bill), that arbitrator is entitled to that fee.

   ii. It is generally accepted that all parties are jointly and severally liable for the fees of an arbitrator. This is an issue as to the entitlement of arbitrators, and as such is quite distinct from the third element.

   iii. As in court litigation, when one party is successful, that party should normally recover at least a proportion of his costs. This issue, being where the burden of costs should lie, is an issue as between the parties.

121. The Bill contains provisions as to costs and fees in two separate parts: the joint and several liability owed by the parties to the arbitrators (the second element) is addressed in this clause, whilst the third element (ie the responsibility for costs as between the parties) is addressed in Clauses 59–65. The first element, being a matter of general contract law, is not specifically addressed by either set of provisions, but is preserved in both. It is extremely important to distinguish between these provisions.

122. Clause 28 is concerned with the rights of the arbitrators in respect of fees and expenses. As sub-section (5) makes clear, and as explained above, this provision is not concerned with which of the parties should (as between themselves) bear these costs as the result of the arbitration, which I dealt with later in the bill, nor with any contractual right an arbitrator may have in respect of fees and expenses.

123. As we understand the present law, the parties are jointly and severally liable to the arbitrator for his fees and expenses. The present position seems to be that if these are agreed by one party, the other party becomes liable, even if he played no part in making that agreement; and circumstances may arise in which that party is unable to obtain a reduction of the amount by taxation. It

seems to us that whilst arbitrators should be protected by this joint and several liability of the parties, a potentially unfair result must be avoided: a party who never agreed to the appointment by another party of an exceptionally expensive arbitrator should not be held jointly and severally liable for that arbitrator's exceptional fees. To this end, we have stipulated, in Clause 28(1), that a party's joint and several liability to an arbitrator only extends to *"reasonable fees."* Of course, if a party has agreed to an exceptional fee with an arbitrator, that party may still be pursued by that arbitrator, under general contract law, which is preserved in Clause 28(5).

124. We have proposed a mechanism to allow a party to go to the Court if any question arises as to the reasonableness of the arbitrator's charges. The Court is empowered to adjust fees and expenses even after they have been paid, since circumstances may well arise in which a question about the level of fees and expenses only arises after payment has been made. For example, a large advance payment may be made at a time when it is considered that the arbitration will take a long time, but this does not turn out to be the case. However, the Court must be satisfied that it is reasonable in the circumstances to order repayment. Thus an applicant who delays in making an application is likely to receive short shrift from the Court, nor is the Court likely to order repayment where the arbitrator has in good faith acted in such a way that it would be unjust to order repayment. It seems to us that it is necessary to set out expressly in the Bill that the power of the Court extends to dealing with fees and expenses already paid, since otherwise there could be an argument that this power is confined to fees and expenses yet to be paid.

125. These provisions are extended by sub-section (6) to include an arbitrator who has ceased to act and an umpire who has not replaced the other arbitrators. An arbitrator may cease to act through the operation of Clauses 23 to 26, or if an umpire takes over following a disagreement.

126. The liability in Clause 28(1) is to *"the parties."* It seems to us to follow that a person who has not participated at all, and in respect of whom it is determined that the arbitral tribunal has no jurisdiction, would not be a "party" for the purposes of this clause (cf Clause 72). More difficult questions may well arise in respect of persons who have participated, for there the doctrine of *Kompetenz-Komptenez* (Clauses 30 and 31) may have to be weighed against the proposition that a party can hardly be under any liability in respect of the fees and expenses of the tribunal which he has successfully established should not have been acting at all on the merits of the dispute.

127. It is to be noted that arbitrators' fees and expenses include, by virtue of Clause 37(2), the fees and expenses of tribunal appointed experts etc.

128. It seems that the present joint and several liability of the parties to an arbitrator for his fees may rest on some implied contract said to exist between

them. Be this as it may, such an implied contract (in so far as it related to fees and expenses) would not survive by virtue of Clause 81 of this Bill, because this only saves rules of law which are consistent with Part I. Any implied contract imposing a liability for more than reasonable fees and expenses would clearly be inconsistent with Clause 28(1). Furthermore, since Clause 28(1) gives a statutory right there remains no good reason for any implied contractual right. As stated above, any specific contract would, however, of course be preserved by Clause 28(5).

129. Contrary to some suggestions made to us, it seems to us that rights of contribution between the parties in relation to their statutory liability under Clause 28(1) can best be left to the ordinary rules which relate to joint and several liability generally.

130. Clause 28 is made mandatory, since otherwise the parties could by agreement between themselves deprive the arbitrators of what seems to us to be a very necessary protection.

**Clause 29 Immunity of Arbitrators.**

131. Although the general view seems to be that arbitrators have some immunity under the present law, this is not entirely free from doubt. We were firmly of the view that arbitrators should have a degree of immunity, and most (though not all) the responses we received expressed the same view.

132. The reasons for providing immunity are the same as those that apply to Judges in our Courts. Arbitration and litigation share this in common, that both provide a means of dispute resolution which depends upon a binding decision by an impartial third party. It is generally considered that an immunity is necessary to enable that third party properly to perform an impartial decision making function. Furthermore, we feel strongly that unless a degree of immunity is afforded, the finality of the arbitral process could well be undermined. The prospect of a losing party attempting to re-arbitrate the issues on the basis that a competent arbitrator would have decided them in favour of that party is one that we would view with dismay. The Bill provides in our view adequate safeguards to deal with cases where the arbitral process has gone wrong.

133. This is a mandatory provision. Given the need and reason for immunity, it seems to us to follow that as a matter of public policy, this should be so.

134. The immunity does not, of course, extend to cases where it is shown that the arbitrator has acted in bad faith. Our law is well acquainted with this expression and although we considered other terms, we concluded that there were unlikely to be any difficulties in practice in using this test: see, for example, ***Melton Medes Ltd v Securities and Investment Board*** [1995] 3 All ER.

135. Sub-section 29(3). There was a concern that if a provision such as this was not included, Clause 25, when read together with Clause 29, could be said to preclude a claim against an arbitrator for resigning in breach of contract and similarly a defence (based on resignation) to a claim by an arbitrator for his fees, unless "*bad faith*" is proved.

136. Since the publication of the final draft in the Bill, we have concluded that the Court should be given power to remove or modify the immunity as it sees fit when it removes an arbitrator. We consider this further in Chapter 6 below.

### Jurisdiction of the Arbitral Tribunal

**Clause 30 Competence of tribunal to rule on its own Jurisdiction.**

137. This Clause states what is called the doctrine of "*Kompetenz-Kompetenz.*" This is an internationally recognized doctrine, which is also recognized by our own law (eg ***Christopher Brown v Genossenschaft Osterreichlischer Waldbesitzer*** [1954] 1 QB 8), though this has not always been the case.

138. The great advantage of this doctrine is that is avoids delays and difficulties when a question is raised as to the jurisdiction of the tribunal. Clearly the tribunal cannot be the final arbiter of a question of jurisdiction, for this would provide a classic case of pulling oneself up by one's own bootstraps, but to deprive a tribunal of power (subject of Court review) to rule on jurisdiction would mean that a recalcitrant party could delay valid arbitration proceedings indefinitely by making spurious challenges to its jurisdiction.

139. The Clause and the following Clause are based on Article 16 of the Model Law, but unlike that model we have not made this provision mandatory so that the parties, if they wish, can agree that the tribunal shall not have this power. We have also spelt out what we mean by 'substantive jurisdiction.'

**Clause 31 Objection to Substantive Jurisdiction of Tribunal.**

140. In this Clause we set out how to challenge to the jurisdiction can be made, and the circumstances in which it must be made (following Article 16 of the Model Law). This reflects much of the Model Law but we have, for example, refrained from using expressions like 'submission of the statement of defence' since this might give the impression, which we are anxious to dispel, that every arbitration requires some formal pleading or the like.

141. The Clause, in effect, sets out three ways in which the matter may proceed.

   i. The first is that the tribunal may make an award on the question of jurisdiction. If it does so then that award may be challenged by a party under Clause 67.

ii. The second way is for the tribunal to deal with question of jurisdiction in its award on the merits. Again on the jurisdiction aspect the award may be challenged under Clause 67.

We have provided these two methods because, depending on the circumstances, the one or the other may be the better course to take, bearing in mind the duty (in Clause 33) to adopt procedures suitable to the circumstances of the particular case, avoiding unnecessary delay or expense.

iii. The third way of proceeding is for an application to be made to the Court before any award (pursuant to Clause 32). Again this third course is designed to achieve the same objective (albeit in limited circumstances). For example, cases arise where a party starts an arbitration but the other party, without taking part, raises an objection to the jurisdiction of the tribunal. In such circumstances, it might very well be cheaper and quicker for the party wishing to arbitrate to go directly to the Court to seek a favourable ruling on jurisdiction rather than seeking an award from the tribunal. Such an approach would be very much the exception and, to this end, Clause 32 is narrowly drawn. In this connection it must be remembered that a party who chooses not to take any part in an arbitration cannot in justice be required to take any positive steps to challenge the jurisdiction, for to do otherwise would be to assume against the party (before the point has been decided) that the tribunal has jurisdiction. We return to this topic when considering Clause 72.

142. Article 16(3) of the Model Law provides that the arbitral tribunal may rule on a plea as to jurisdiction either as a preliminary question or in an award on the merits. The DAC is of the view that it is unnecessary to introduce a new concept of a "preliminary ruling," which is somehow different from an award. Clause 31(4) therefore only refers to awards. This has the advantage that awards on jurisdiction will have the benefit of those provisions on awards generally (eg costs, lien, reasons, additional rewards, etc.), and, if appropriate, may be enforced in the same way as any other award.

143. A challenge to jurisdiction may well involve questions of fact as well as questions of law. Since the arbitral tribunal cannot rule finally on its own jurisdiction, it follows that both its findings of fact and its holdings of law may be challenged. The regime for challenging such awards is set out in Clause 67.

144. Clause 31(1) replaces the requirement set out in Article 16(2) of the Model Law (that a challenge to the overall jurisdiction of the tribunal must be raised no later than the submission of a statement of defence) with a requirement that such an objection be raised no later than the time a party takes the first step in the proceedings to contest the merits or any matter in relation to which he challenges the tribunal's jurisdiction. This allows for alternative procedures where there is no "statement of defence" as such.

145. Clause 31 is a mandatory provision. Under Clause 30, of course, the parties can agree that the tribunal shall not have power to rule on its own jurisdiction, but while this means (as sub-section (4) points out) that the tribunal cannot then make an award on jurisdiction, the compulsory nature of Clause 31 means that the objection must be raised as there stipulated. It seems to us that this is highly desirable by way of support for the object of arbitration as set out in Clause 1.

146. It has been suggested to the DAC that there should be a mechanism whereby an objecting party, or even a non-objecting party, could require the tribunal forthwith to make an award as to jurisdiction, rather than merely incorporating a ruling in an award on the merits. The DAC disagrees with this. Unless the parties agree otherwise, the choice as to which course to take will be left with the tribunal, who will decide what is to be done consistent with their duty under Clause 33 (see below). Indeed, in some cases in may be simply impracticable to rule on jurisdiction, before determining merits. If, however, the parties agree which course is to be taken, and if, of course, their agreement is effective (ie it does not require the tribunal to breach its mandatory duty under Clause 33) then the provision under discussion requires the tribunal to take the course chosen by the parties.

**Clause 32 Determination of preliminary point of Jurisdiction.**

147. In this Clause we have set out the procedure for the third of the possible ways of dealing with a challenge to the jurisdiction. As stated above, this Clause provides for exceptional cases only: it is not intended to detract from the basic rule as set out in Clause 30. Hence the restrictions in Clause 32(2), and the procedure in Clause 32(3). It will be noted that we have required either the agreement of the parties, or that the Court is satisfied that this is, in effect, the proper course to take. It is anticipated that the Courts will take care to prevent this exceptional provision from becoming the normal route for challenging jurisdiction. Since this Clause concerns a power exercisable by the Court in relation to the jurisdiction of the tribunal, it is in our view important enough to be made mandatory.

148. Under this Clause the tribunal may continue the arbitral proceedings and make an award whilst the application to the Court is pending. Thus a recalcitrant party will not be able to mount spurious challenges as a means of delaying the arbitral process. Under sub-section (5) of the preceding Clause the tribunal can, of course (and must if the parties agree) stay the arbitral proceedings whilst an application is made. Which course the tribunal takes (where it has power to choose) will of course depend once again on what it sees its Clause 33 duty to be.

149. The right of appeal from Court rulings is limited in the way set out in the Clause.

## The Arbitral Proceedings

### Clause 33 General Duty of the Tribunal.

150. This is one of the central proposals in our Bill (grounded on Article 18 of the Model Law). It is a mandatory provision, since, as is explained below, we fail to see how a proceeding which departed from the stipulated duties could properly be described as an arbitration. We endeavour to set out, in the simplest, clearest terms we have been able to devise, how the tribunal should approach and deal with its task, which is to do full justice to the parties. In the following Clauses we set out in detail the powers available to the tribunal for this purpose.

151. It has been suggested that the generality of Clause 33 may be problematic: that it may be an invitation to recalcitrant parties to launch challenges, or that vagueness will give rise to arguments. The advantage of arbitration is that it offers a dispute resolution system which can be tailored to the particular dispute to an extent which litigation finds it difficult to do. Thus depending on the nature of the dispute, there will be numerous ways in which the arbitration can be conducted. It is quite impossible to list all the possible variants and to set out what may or may not be done. Indeed any attempt to do so would defeat one of the main purposes of the Bill, which is to encourage arbitral tribunals not slavishly to follow court or other set procedures. It follows that the only limits can be those set out in the present clause. It is to be hoped that the Courts will take a dim view of those who try to attack awards because of suggested breaches of this clause which have no real substance. At the same time, it can hardly be suggested that awards should not be open to attack when the tribunal has not acted in accordance with the principles stated.

152. It has further been suggested that this part of the Bill will cause the demise of the amateur arbitrator. If by this is meant the demise of people who purport to act as arbitrators but who are either unable or unwilling (or both) to conduct the proceedings in accordance with what most would regard as self-evident rules of justice, then we indeed hope that this will be one of the results. But since these rules of justice are generally accepted in our democratic society, and are not merely theoretical considerations that concern lawyers alone, we can see no reason why the Bill should discourage anyone who is ready, willing and able to apply them. Indeed we consider that the Bill will encourage and support all such people.

153. Sometimes the parties to an arbitration employ lawyers who seek, in effect, to bully a non-legal arbitrator into taking a course of action which is against his better instincts, by seeking to blind him with legal 'science' to get their way. Again, in some circles it is thought that somehow the procedures in an arbitration should be modelled on Court procedures, and that to adopt other methods would be 'misconduct' (an expression that the Bill does not use) on the part of the arbitrator. This part of the bill is designed to prevent such

bullying and to explode the theory that an arbitration has always to follow Court procedures. If an arbitrator is satisfied that the way he wants to proceed fulfils his duty under this Clause and that the powers he wants to exercise are available to him under the following Clauses, then he should have the courage of his own convictions and proceed accordingly, unless the parties are agreed that he should adopt some other course.

**The relationship between Clauses 1(b), 33 and 34(1).**

154. It has been suggested to us that there could be a conflict between:

    i.  the mandatory duty cast on arbitrators by Clause 33 and

    ii. the principle of party autonomy in Clause 1(b) and the proviso in Clause 34(1)).

    As we explain below, the DAC does not consider that there is any inconsistency between these two principles.

155. Under the principle of party autonomy, the parties are free to agree upon anything to do with the arbitration, subject only to such safeguards as are necessary in the public interest (Clause 1(b)). The mandatory provisions set out those matters which have effect notwithstanding any agreement to the contrary: see Clause 4. It seems to us that the public interest dictates that Clause 33 must be mandatory ie that the parties cannot effectively agree to dispense with the duty laid on arbitrators under Clause 33. In other words, they cannot effectively agree that the arbitrators can act unfairly, or that the arbitrators can be partial, or that the arbitrators can decide that the parties (or one of them) should not have a reasonable opportunity of putting his case or answering that of his opponent, or indeed that the arbitrators can adopt procedures that are unsuitable for the particular circumstances of the case or are unnecessarily slow or expensive, so that the means for resolving the matters to be determined is unfair. It is, of course, extremely unlikely in the nature of things that the parties would wish deliberately to make such bizarre agreements, but were this to happen, then it seems to us that such agreements should be ineffective for the purposes of this Bill, ie not binding on the parties or the tribunal.

156. However, a situation could well arise in practice in cases where the parties are agreed on a method of proceeding which they consider complies with the first of the general principles set out in Clause 1 (and which therefore the tribunal could adopt consistently with its duty under Clause 33) but the tribunal takes a different view, or where they are agreed in their opposition to a method of proceeding which the tribunal considers should be adopted in order to perform its Clause 33 duty.

157. In our view it is neither desirable nor practicable to stipulate that the tribunal can override the agreement of the parties. It is not desirable, because the type

of arbitration we are discussing is a consensual process which depends on the agreement of the parties who are surely entitled (if they agree) to have the final say on how they wish their dispute to be resolved. It is not practicable, since there is no way in which the parties can be forced to adopt a method of proceedings if they are agreed that this is not the way they wish to proceed. The latter is the case even if it could be established that their agreement was ineffective since it undermined or prevented performance of the duty made mandatory by Clause 33.

158. A party would be unable to enforce an ineffective agreement against the other parties, nor would such an agreement bind the tribunal, but the problem under discussion only exists while the parties are *in fact* as one, whether or not their agreement is legally effective.

159. In circumstances such as these, the tribunal (assuming it has failed to persuade the parties to take a different course) has the choice of adopting the course preferred by the parties or of resigning. Indeed, resignation would be the only course if the parties were in agreement in rejecting the method preferred by the tribunal, and no other way of proceeding was agreed by them or considered suitable by the tribunal.

160. We have stipulated elsewhere in the Bill that the immunity we propose for the arbitrators does not extend to any liability they may be under for resigning (Clause 29) though under Clause 25 they may seek relief in respect of such liability from the Court. The reason for the limitation on immunity is that cases may arise where the resignation of the arbitrator is wholly indefensible and has caused great delay and loss. In our view Clause 25 would suffice to protect arbitrators who resigned because they reasonably believed that the agreement of the parties prevented them from properly performing their Clause 33 duty. Furthermore, arbitrators could always stipulate for the right to resign in such circumstances as a term of their appointment.

161. If, on the other hand, the tribunal adopted a method of proceeding agreed by the parties, it seems to us that none of the parties could afterwards validly complain that the tribunal has failed in its Clause 33 duty, since the tribunal would only have done what the parties had asked it to do. Again, the fact that as between the parties such an agreement may have been ineffective as undermining or preventing performance of the Clause 33 duties seems to use to be wholly irrelevant. It could of course be said that the tribunal had breached its Clause 33 duty, but this would have no practical consequences since the parties themselves would have brought about this state of affairs, and would therefore be unable to seek any relief in respect of it.

162. Some people have expressed concern that there is a danger that lawyers will agree between themselves a method of proceeding which the tribunal consider to be unnecessarily long or expensive. However, if a tribunal considered, for example, that lawyers were trying either deliberately to

'churn' the case for their own private advantage or were simply but misguidedly seeking to adopt unnecessary procedures etc., the obvious solution would be to ask them to confirm that their respective clients had been made aware of the views of the tribunal but were nevertheless in agreement that the course proposed by their lawyers should be adopted. At the end of the day, however, the fact remains that the only sanction the arbitrators have is to resign.

163. In summary, therefore, we consider that the duty of the arbitrators under Clause 33 and the right of the parties to agree how the arbitration should be conducted do fit together. Under Clause 33 the tribunal have the specified duties. Under Clause 34 therefore, the tribunal must decide all procedural and evidential matters, subject to the right of the parties to agree on any matter. If the parties reach an agreement on how to proceed which clashes with the duty of the tribunal or which the tribunal reasonably considers does so, then the arbitrators can either resign and have the protection of Clause 25, or can adopt what the parties want and will not afterwards be liable to the parties for doing so.

**Further points.**

164. In this Clause we have provided that the tribunal shall give each party a *"reasonable opportunity"* of putting his case and dealing with that of his opponent. Article 18 of the Model Law uses the expression *"full opportunity."*

165. We prefer the word *"reasonable"* because it removes any suggestion that a party is entitled to take as long as he likes, however objectively unreasonable this may be. We are sure that this was not intended by those who framed the Model Law, for it would entail that a party is entitled to an unreasonable time, which justice can hardly require. Indeed the contrary is the case, for an unreasonable time would *ex hypothesi* mean unnecessary delay and expense, things which produce injustice and which accordingly would offend the first principle of Clause 1, as well as Clauses 33 and 40.

**Clause 34 Procedural and evidential Matters.**

166. We trust that the matters we have listed in this Clause (which are partly drawn from Article 19, 20, 33, 34 and 24 of the Model Law) are largely self-evident. We have produced a non-exhaustive check-list because we think it will be helpful both arbitrating parties and to their arbitrators. We cannot emphasize too strongly that one of the strengths of the arbitral process is that it is able much more easily than any Court system to adapt its procedures to suit the particular case. Hence we have spelt this out as a duty under the preceding Clause. The list of powers helps the tribunal (and indeed the parties) to choose how best to proceed, untrammeled by technical or formalistic rules.

167. Some of those responding suggested that we should include a special code to deal with the arbitration of small claims. We have not adopted this suggestion for the very reason we have just stated. Any such code would have to have detailed rules, arbitrary monetary or other limits and other complicated provisions. In our view, proper adherence to the duties in Clause 33 will achieve the same result. A small claim will simply not need all the expensive procedural and other paraphernalia which might be required for the resolution of some huge and complicated international dispute.

168. Furthermore, we consider that associations and institutions concerned with specific areas of trade etc. can play a very significant part in formulating rules and procedures for arbitrating disputes concerning their members. Such bodies have the detailed knowledge and experience required to enable them properly to address this task, in relation both to small claims and otherwise. We feel strongly that it would be wrong for a Bill of the present kind to seek to lay down a rigid structure for any kind of case; and that different methods must be developed to suit different circumstances, by arbitral tribunals as well as those who have the necessary practical knowledge of those circumstances. Finally, of course, the Bill in no way impinges upon small claims procedures developed for use through the court system.

169. Sub-section (a). Whilst Article 20(1) of the Model Law states that, in the absence of the agreement of the parties, *"the place of arbitration shall be determined by the arbitral tribunal having regard to the circumstances of the case, including the convenience of the parties,"* sub-section 34(2)(a) does not state that the tribunal should have the convenience of the parties in mind, given that this is a consideration that is really subsumed under the general duty of the Tribunal in Clause 33, and, further, because the DAC was of the view that like considerations apply to other parts of Clause 34, such as sub-section (b), even though the Model Law does not appear to reflect this. Unlike the Model Law, sub-section (a) also refers to *"when,"* as well as *"where."*

170. Sub-section (f) makes it clear that arbitrators are not necessarily bound by the technical rules of evidence. In his 1993 Freshfields Lecture ((1994) Arbitration International Vol 10, p.1), Lord Steyn questioned why the technical rules of evidence should apply to arbitration, even if (as he doubted) there was authority for this. This provision clarifies the position. It is to be noted that Clause 34(2)(f) helps to put an end to any arguments that it is a question of law whether there is material to support a finding of fact.

171. Sub-section (g). Some anxiety was expressed at the power to act inquisitorially, to be found in sub-section (g), on grounds that arbitrators are unused to such powers and might, albeit in good faith, abuse them.

172. We do not share this view. Once again it seems to us that provided the tribunal in exercising its powers follows its simple duty as set out in Clause 33 (and sub-section (2) of this Clause tells the tribunal that this is what they

must do) then in suitable cases an inquisitorial approach to all or some of the matters involved may well be the best way of proceeding. Clause 33, however, remains a control, such that, for example, if an arbitrator takes the initiative in procuring evidence, he must give all parties a reasonable opportunity of commenting on it.

173. A number of arbitrators who responded to our July 1995 draft suggested that the tribunal should be entitled to have the last word ie should be given the power to override the agreement of the parties to follow a different course. The interrelationship of the tribunal's duties and party autonomy has already been discussed above. As is clear from that discussion, we disagree with this view for the following reasons:

   i. To give the tribunal such a power would be contrary to Article 19 of the Model Law. It would also be contrary to the present position under English law.

   ii. To allow the tribunal to override the agreement of the parties would to our minds constitute an indefensible inroad into the principle of party autonomy, upon which the Bill is based.

   iii. It is difficult to see how such a power could be backed by any effective sanction. If the parties agree not to adopt the course ordered by the tribunal, there is nothing the tribunal can do except resign.

   iv. It seems to us that the problem is more apparent than real. In most cases the parties rely on the tribunal to decide how to conduct the case and do not sit down and agree between themselves how it is to be done. In order to reflect what actually happens in practice we have accordingly reversed the way many of the other Clauses begin and stated that it is for the tribunal to decide all procedural and evidential matters, subject to the right of the parties to agree any matter. In our view, however, since arbitration is the parties' own chosen method of dispute resolution, we cannot see why they should be deprived of the right to decide what form the arbitration should take.

174. As we have made clear above, it is of course open to those who frame rules for arbitration which the parties incorporate into their agreement, to stipulate that the tribunal is to have the last word, and likewise arbitrators can stipulate this as a term of their agreement to act, though once again there would be no means, apart from the persuasion or the threat of resignation, of enforcing such a stipulation if the parties later jointly took a different view.

175. It has been suggested that there could be a conflict between the proviso in Clause 34(1) and Clause 40. This is said to arise, for example, where the parties have agreed a procedural or evidential matter which they are entitled to do under Clause 34(1), but the tribunal are intent on taking a different course. Does the parties' agreement override their duty under Clause 40?

The DAC considers that no such conflict exists:

i. The parties are free to agree on all procedural and evidential matters, pursuant to Clause 34(1).

ii. However, any such agreement will only be effective, if it is consistent with Clause 33, being a mandatory provision.

iii. Any such agreement made pursuant to Clause 34(1), and consistent with Clause 33, will define the scope of Clause 40 – ie the parties will have agreed on how the arbitration is to be conducted, or, in the words of Clause 40, what is to constitute the "*proper and expeditious conduct of the arbitral proceedings.*" The determinations of the tribunal should follow that agreement (which would not be the case if such an agreement was inconsistent with Clause 33) and *ex hypothesi* the parties should be obliged to comply.

iv. If there are matters on which the parties have not agreed, then the tribunal will fill the gap under Clause 34(1) and Clause 40(1) will again operate without conflict.

176. It has also been suggested that the Bill should include a provision that the arbitrator should encourage the parties to use other forms of ADR when this was considered appropriate. This suggestion has not been adopted, since the Bill is concerned with arbitration where the parties have chosen this rather than any other form of dispute resolution.

**Clause 35 Consolidation of Proceedings and Concurrent Hearings.**

177. This Clause makes clear that the parties may agree to consolidate their arbitration with other arbitral proceedings or to hold concurrent hearings.

178. During the consultation exercises, the DAC received submissions calling for a provision that would empower either a tribunal or the Court (or indeed both) to order consolidation or concurrent hearings. These were considered extremely carefully by the committee.

179. The problem arises in cases where a number of parties are involved. For example, in a construction project a main contractor may make a number of sub-contracts each of which contains an arbitration clause. A dispute arises in which a claim is made against one sub-contractor who seeks to blame another. In Court, of course, there is power to order consolidation or concurrent hearings, as well as procedures for allowing additional parties to be joined. In arbitrations, however, this power does not exist. The reason it does not exist is that this form of dispute resolution depends on the agreement of the contracting parties that their disputes will be arbitrated by a private tribunal, not litigated in the public courts. It follows that unless the parties otherwise agree, only their own disputes arising out of their own agreement can be referred to that agreed tribunal.

180. In our view it would amount to a negation of the principle of party autonomy to give the tribunal or the Court power to order consolidation or concurrent hearings. Indeed it would to our minds go far towards frustrating the agreement of the parties to have their own tribunal for their own disputes. Further difficulties could well arise, such as the disclosure of documents from one arbitration to another. Accordingly we would be opposed to giving the tribunal or the Court this power. However, if the parties agree to invest the tribunal with such a power, then we would have no objection.

181. Having said this, the DAC appreciates the common sense behind the suggestion. We are persuaded, however, that the problem is best solved by obtaining the agreement of the parties. Thus those who are in charge of drafting standard forms of contract, or who offer terms for arbitration services which the parties can incorporate into their agreements, (especially those institutions and associations which are concerned with situations in which there are likely to be numerous contracts and sub-contracts) could include suitable clauses permitting the tribunal to consolidate or order concurrent hearings in appropriate cases. For example, the London Maritime Arbitrators Association Rules have within them a provision along these lines. In order to encourage this, we have made clear in this Clause that with the agreement of the parties, there is nothing wrong with adopting such procedures.

182. It will be noted that whereas Clause 39 uses the expression "*[t]he parties are free to agree that the tribunal shall have power to order . . .,*" Clause 35 simply states that "*[t]he parties are free to agree. . . .*" This difference is easily explained. In both cases the parties are free to endow the tribunal with the power in question. This is implicit in Clause 35(1) by virtue of Clause 35(2). Under Clause 35(1), the parties may agree between themselves to consolidate two arbitrations, or to have concurrent hearings, before a tribunal has been appointed. This could, of course, have a bearing on how the tribunal is to be appointed in such a situation. Indeed the parties may agree on institutional rules that provide for this. However, an equivalent arrangement is difficult to imagine in the context of Clause 39. Overall, the difference in wording is not intended to impede the parties' freedom to agree what they like, when they like, in either case.

**Clause 36 Legal or other Representation.**

183. It seems to us that this reflects a basic right, though of course the parties are free to dispense with it if they wish.

184. In the draft produced in July we used the phrase "*a lawyer or other person of his choice.*" We have changed this, because we felt that it might give the impression that a party could stubbornly insist on a particular lawyer or other person, in circumstances where that individual could not attend for a long time, thus giving a recalcitrant party a good means of delaying the arbitral process. This should not happen. "*A lawyer or other person chosen*

*by him"* does not give this impression: if a party's first choice is not available, his second choice will still be a *"a lawyer or other person chosen by him."* The right to be represented exists but must not be abused. Furthermore the right must be read with the first principle of Clause 1, as well as Clauses 33 and 40. If this is done then we trust that attempts to abuse the right will fail.

185. It has been suggested to the DAC that there should be some provision requiring a party to give advance notice to all the other parties if he intends to be represented at a hearing. Whilst in some ways an attractive proposal, this would be difficult to stipulate as a statutory provision, given that it may be impossible in some circumstances, or simply unnecessary in others. Further, different sanctions may be appropriate depending on the particular case. It is clearly desirable that, as a general rule, such notice be given. If it is not, one sanction may be for the tribunal to adjourn a hearing at the defaulting party's cost. In the end, however, this must be a matter for the tribunal's discretion in each particular case.

186. It has been suggested that this Clause provides an opportunity of extending by statue the privilege enjoyed by legal advisors to non-legal advisors or representatives. We have not adopted this suggestion. It seems to us that it would be necessary to define with great precision which non-legal advisers or representatives are to be included (eg what relationship they must have to the arbitration and its conduct), and the precise classes of privilege which should be extended to them. Further, any such provision would necessarily have an impact on the position beyond arbitration. In short, it seems to us that this question cannot be confined to arbitrations and raises matters of general principle far beyond those of our remit.

**Clause 37 Power to appoint experts, legal advisers or assessors.**

187. This to our minds would be a useful power in certain cases. We trust that the provisions we suggest are self-evident. Of course, the power can only be exercised if in the circumstances of the particular case its exercise falls within the scope of the duty of the tribunal set out in Clause 33.

188. Sub-section (2) is made mandatory, to avoid the risk of the parties agreeing otherwise and thus disabling the tribunal from recovering from the parties expenses properly incurred.

**Clause 38 General Powers Exercisable by the Tribunal.**

189. These provisions represent a significant re-drawing of the relationship between arbitration and the Court. Wherever a power could properly be exercised by a tribunal rather than the Court, provision has been made for this, thereby reducing the need to incur the expense and inconvenience of making applications to Court during arbitral proceedings.

190. The first of the powers in this Clause is one which enables the tribunal to order security for costs. The power presently given to the Court to order security for costs in arbitrations is removed in its entirety.

191. This is a major change from the present position where only the Court can order security for costs. The theory which lay behind the present law is that it is the duty of an arbitral tribunal to decide the substantive merits of the dispute referred to it and that it would not be performing this duty if it stayed or struck out the proceedings pending the provision of security: see for example, **Re Unione Stearinerie Lanza and Weiner** [1917] 2 KB 558.

192. We do not subscribe to this theory, which Parliament has already abandoned in the context of striking out a claim for want of prosecution. In our view, when the parties agree to arbitrate, they are agreeing that their dispute will be resolved by this means. To our minds (in the absence of express stipulations to the contrary) this does not mean that the dispute is necessarily to be decided on its substantive merits. It is in truth an agreement that it will be resolved by the application on the agreed arbitral process. If one party then fails to comply with that process, then it seems to us that it is entirely within what the parties have agreed that the tribunal can resolve the dispute on this ground.

193. Apart from this, the proposition that the Court should involve itself in such matters as deciding whether a claimant in an arbitration should provide security for costs has received universal condemnation in the context of international arbitrations. It is no exaggeration to say that the recent decision of the House of Lords in **S.A. Coppee Lavalin NV v Ken-Ren Chemicals and Fertilisers** [1994] 2 WLR 631 was greeted with dismay by those in the international arbitration community who have at heart the desire to promote our country as a world centre for arbitration. We share those concerns.

194. It has been suggested to the DAC that the court should retain a power to order security for costs that may be incurred up to the appointment of the tribunal. We have not been persuaded, however, that this is really necessary.

195. It has been pointed out that in some cases an application for security before an arbitral tribunal might involve disclosing to that tribunal the fact that an offer of settlement had been or was about to be made. Under the court system, such disclosure can be made to a court other than that which will try the merits of the case.

196. We are not disturbed by this. It seems to us that a tribunal, properly performing its duty under Clause 33, could and should not be influenced by such matters, if the case proceeds to a hearing on the merits, nor do we accept that the disclosure of such information could somehow disqualify the tribunal from acting.

197. Clause 38(3) has been the subject of significant criticism since the Bill was introduced. In the light of this, we have concluded that it must be redrawn. Chapter 6, to which reference should be made, contains a full discussion of the problems with this provision as currently drafted, and our recommendations for its amendment.

198. Whilst the sanction in court for a failure to provide security for costs is normally a stay of the action, this is inappropriate in arbitration: if an arbitrator stayed proceedings, the arbitration would come to a halt without there necessarily being an award which could be challenged (eg if a party seeks to continue the proceedings). We have therefore included a specific sanction with respect to a failure to provide security for costs, which is to be found in Clause 41(6). This provision also follows the practice of the English Commercial Court, which changed from the old practice of ordering a stay of proceedings if security was not provided. The disadvantage of the latter course was that it left the proceedings dormant but alive, so that years later they could be revived by the provision of security.

199. Clause 38 provides the tribunal with other powers in relation to the arbitration proceedings. We trust these are self-explanatory.

**Clause 39 Power to make Provisional Awards.**

200. In the July 1995 draft Clauses, this power did not require the agreement of the parties. As a result of responses, we have concluded on further consideration that this is necessary.

201. In *The Kostas Melas* [1981] 1 Lloyd's Rep.18 at 26, Goff J, as he then was, made clear that it was no part of an arbitrator's function to make temporary or provisional financial arrangements between the parties. Furthermore, as can be demonstrated by the abundance of court cases dealing with this subject (in the context of applications for summary judgment, interim payments, *Mareva* injunctions and the like) enormous care has to be taken to avoid turning what can be a useful judicial tool into an instrument of injustice. We should add that we received responses from a number of practising arbitrators to the effect that they would be unhappy with such powers, and saw no need for them. We should note in passing that the July 1995 draft would arguably (and inadvertently) have allowed arbitrators to order *ex parte Mareva* or even *Anton Piller* relief. These draconian powers are best left to be applied by the Courts, and the provisions of the Bill with respect to such powers have been adjusted accordingly.

202. There is a sharp distinction to be drawn between making provisional or temporary arrangements, which are subject to reversal when the underlying merits are finally decided by the tribunal; and dealing severally with different issues or questions at different times and in different awards, which we

cover in Clause 47. It is for this reason that in this provision we draw attention to that Clause.

203. These considerations have led us firmly to conclude that it would only be desirable to give arbitral tribunals power to make such provisional orders where the parties have so agreed. Such agreements, of course, will have to be drafted with some care for the reasons we have stated. Subject to the safeguards of the parties' agreement and the arbitrators' duties (Clause 33), we envisage that this enlargement of the traditional jurisdiction of arbitrators could serve a very useful purpose, for example in trades and industries where cash flow is of particular importance.

**Clause 40 General Duty of the Parties.**

204. This is a mandatory provision, since it would seem that an ability to contract out of it would be a negation of the arbitral process.

205. We were asked what the sanction would be for non-compliance. The answer lies in other Clauses of the Bill. These not only give the tribunal powers in relation to recalcitrant parties (eg Clause 41), but stipulate time limits for taking certain steps (eg applications to the Court etc) and (in Clause 73) making clear that undue delay will result in the loss of rights.

**Clause 41 Powers of Tribunal in Case of Party's Default**

206. The first part of the Clause sets out the present law (section 13A of the 1950 Act, which was inserted by section 102 of the Courts and Legal Services Act 1990) giving the arbitral tribunal power to strike out for want of prosecution.

207. The second part makes clear that in the circumstances stipulated, a tribunal may proceed *ex parte*, though we have forborne from using this expression (or indeed any other legal Latin words or phrases) in the Bill. The Clause has its roots in Article 25 of the Model Law.

208. It is a basic rule of justice that a court or tribunal should give all parties an opportunity to put their case and answer that of their opponents. That is why this appears in Clause 33 of the Bill. Equally, however, and for reasons already mentioned, that opportunity should, again for reasons of justice, be limited to a reasonable one. If for no good reason such an opportunity is not taken by a party then to our minds it is only fair to the other party that the tribunal should be able to proceed as we have set out in this Clause.

209. The last part of the Clause sets out a system of peremptory orders. It will be noted that a peremptory order must be "*to the same effect*" as the preceding order which was disobeyed (sub-section (5)). It could be quite unfair for an

arbitrator to be able to make any type of peremptory order, on any matter, regardless of its connection with the default in question.

210. For the reasons mentioned earlier, sub-section (6) provides that where a party fails to comply with a peremptory order to provide security for costs, the tribunal may make an award dismissing the claim, thereby following the practice of the English Commercial Court, and avoiding the danger that the proceedings are halted indefinitely, without there being anything to challenge before the Court.

211. So far as failure to comply with other peremptory orders is concerned, we have provided a range of remedies. They do not include a power simply to make an award against the defaulting party. The reason for this is that (unlike a failure to comply with a peremptory order to provide security) it seems to us that this is too draconian a remedy, and that the alternatives we have provided very much better fit the justice of the matter.

### Powers of Court in relation to Arbitral Proceedings

### Clause 42 Enforcement of peremptory Orders of Tribunal.

212. Although in Clause 41 we have provided the tribunal with powers in relation

### Clause 43 Securing the attendance of witnesses.

213. This Clause (which corresponds to Article 27 of the Model Law, and is derived from section 12(4) and (5) of the 1950 Act) is also designed to provide Court support for the arbitral process. It will be noted, in particular, that the agreement of the parties or the permission of the tribunal is required. The reason for this is to make sure that this procedure is not used to override any procedural method adopted by the tribunal, or agreed by the parties, for the arbitration. Thus, for example, if the tribunal has decided that there shall be no oral evidence, then (unless all parties agree otherwise) this procedure cannot be used to get round the decision.

### Clause 44 Court Powers exercisable in support of arbitral Proceedings.

214. This provision corresponds in part to Article 9 of the Model Law. As part of the redefinition of the relationship between arbitration and the Court, which was mentioned above, the powers we have given the Court are intended to be used when the tribunal cannot act or act effectively, as sub-section (5) makes clear. It is under this Clause that the Court has power to order *Mareva* or *Anton Piller* relief (ie urgent protective measures to preserve assets or evidence) so as to help the arbitral process to operate effectively. Equally, there may be instances where a party seeks an order that will have an effect on a third party, which only the Court could grant. For the same reason the Court is given the other powers listed.

215. In order to prevent any suggestion that the Court might be used to interfere with or usurp the arbitral process, or indeed any attempt to do so, we have stipulated that except in cases of urgency with regard to the preservation of assets or evidence, the Court can only act with the agreement of the parties or the permission of the tribunal. We have excepted cases of urgency, since these often arise before the tribunal has been properly constituted or when in the nature of things it cannot act quickly or effectively enough.

216. Furthermore, under sub-section (6) the Court, after making an order, can in effect hand over to the tribunal the task of deciding whether or not that order should cease to have effect. This is a novel provision, but follows from the philosophy behind these provisions: if a given power could possibly be exercised by a tribunal, then it should be, and parties should not be allowed to make unilateral applications to the Court. If, however, a given power could be exercised by the tribunal, but not as effectively, in circumstances where, for example, speed is necessary, then the Court should be able to step in.

**Clause 45 Determination of Preliminary Point of Law.**

217. This Clause preserves what used to be the old Consultative Case procedure, though its availability is limited as we have set out, in order not to interfere with the arbitral process. The Clause is based on section 2 of the 1979 Act, with certain important changes.

218. It seems to us that with the limitations we have provided, this procedure can have its uses. For example, an important point of law may arise which is of great general interest and potentially the subject of a large number of arbitrations. This not infrequently happens when some major event occurs, as, for example, the closure of the Suez Canal or the United States embargo on the export of soya beans. It may well be considered by those concerned that in such special circumstances it would be cheaper and better for all to obtain a definitive answer from the Court at an early stage.

219. However, under sub-section (1), unless the parties agree, the Court must now be satisfied that determination of the given question of law will substantially affect the rights of one or more of the parties. This last point is a departure from the 1979 Act, section 1 of which makes this precondition in relation to an appeal in respect of questions of law arising out of the award, but section 2 of which does not impose it in relation to the determination of a preliminary point of law.

220. Further, unless the parties agree, the Court will now have to be satisfied of the matters set out in the sub-section (2) before considering an application, so that the procedure can only be used (even with the permission of the tribunal) in cases where its adoption will produce a substantial saving in costs to the parties or one of them. The condition in section 2(2) of the 1979 Act, which requires that the question of law be one in respect of which leave

to appeal would be likely to be given under section 1(3)(b) of that Act, is not repeated.

221. It has been suggested to the DAC that the right to refer to the Court under this Clause be removed from all non-domestic arbitrations, unless the parties otherwise agree. For the reasons given above as to the value of this provision, and for the reasons given below with respect to preserving the right of appeal in Clause 69, we were not persuaded by this.

## The Award

### Clause 46 Rules applicable to Substance of Dispute.

222. This Clause reflects much, though not all, of Article 28 of the Model Law. We have not for example, directed the tribunal to *"take into account the usages of the trade applicable to the transaction."* If the applicable law allows this to be done, then the provision is not necessary; while if it does not, then it could be said that such a direction overrides that law, which to our minds would be incorrect.

223. Sub-section (1)(b) recognizes that the parties may agree that their dispute is not to be decided in accordance with a recognized system of law but under what in this country are often called *"equity clauses,"* or arbitration *"ex aequo et bono,"* or *"amiable composition"* ie general considerations of justice and fairness etc.. It will be noted that we have avoided using this description in the Bill, just as we have avoided using the Latin and French expressions found in the Model Law. There appears to be no good reason to prevent parties from agreeing to equity clauses. However, it is to be noted that in agreeing that a dispute shall be resolved in this way, the parties are in effect excluding any right to appeal to the Court (there being no *"question of law"* to appeal).

224. Sub-section (2) does, in effect, adopt the rule found in Article 28 of the Model Law, thereby avoiding the problems of *renvoi*.

225. Sub-section (3) caters for the situation where there is no choice or agreement. This again is the language of the Model Law. In such circumstances the tribunal must decide what conflicts of law rules are applicable, and use those rules in order to determine the applicable law. It cannot simply make up rules for this purpose. It has been suggested to the DAC that more guidance be given as to the choice of a proper law, but it appears to us that flexibility is desirable, that it is not our remit to lay down principles in this highly complex area, and that to do so would necessitate a departure from the Model Law wording.

### Clause 47 Awards of Different Issues etc.

226. We regard this as a very important provision. Some disputes are very complex, raising a large number of complicated issues which, if they are all

addressed and dealt with at one hearing, would necessarily take a very long time and be very expensive. Disputes concerning large scale construction contracts are a good example, though there are many other cases.

227. In recent years both the Commercial Court and the Official Referees Court in England (which deal with large cases) have adopted a different approach. The Judge plays much more of a managerial role, suggesting and indeed directing ways in which time and money can be saved. One of the ways is to select issues for early determination, not necessarily on the basis that they will be legally determinative, in the sense that a decision is likely to help the parties to resolve their other differences themselves without the need to spend time and money on using lawyers to fight them out. This has a further advantage. Cases fought to the bitter end often result in a permanent loss of goodwill between the warring factions, thus impeding or preventing future profitable relationships between them. The result is often in truth a loss to all the parties, whether or not they were the 'winners' in the litigation.

228. In Court therefore, the old idea that a party is entitled to a full trial of everything at once has now largely disappeared: see, for example, the decision of the **House of Lords in Ashmore v Corporation of Lloyd's** [1992] 2 Lloyd's Rep 1. Furthermore, this method of approach is reflected in the views expressed by Lord Woolf in his current consideration of how to improve our system of civil justice. The same reasoning, of course, applies to arbitrations.

229. As we have said earlier, arbitration enjoys an advantage over litigation, since the arbitral tribunal is appointed to deal with the particular dispute that has arisen, and is thus in a better position to tailor the procedure to suit the particular circumstances of that dispute. Furthermore, an arbitral tribunal is often able, for the same reason, to move much quicker than the Court.

230. For these reasons, we have tried to make clear in this Clause that the tribunal is empowered to proceed in this way. This is an aspect of the duty cast upon the tribunal to adopt procedures suitable to the circumstances of the particular case, which is set out in Clause 33(1)(a). We would encourage arbitrators to adopt this approach in any case where it appears that time and money will be saved by doing so, and where such an approach would not be at the expense of any of the other requirements of justice.

231. In this connection we would draw attention to the decision of Goff J (now Lord Goff) in **The Kostas Melas op. cit.**. As we observed when considering Clause 39, the function of arbitrators is not to make temporary financial adjustments between the parties pending the resolution of the dispute, unless this is what they have agreed the arbitrators can do. As this case shows, there is a clear distinction between such arrangements and the right to make a permanent binding decision after considering the arguments, even though

the later resolution of other issues (if this becomes necessary) may overall produce a different result.

232. We should emphasize that in this Clause we are not intending to give arbitral tribunals greater or different powers from those they presently have, but to emphasize how their powers should, in suitable cases, be exercised.

233. It might also be noted that we have been careful to avoid use of the term "*interim award*," which has become a confusing term, and in its most common use, arguably a misnomer.

**Clause 48 Remedies.**

234. We trust that the matters in this Clause are self-evident. We have excluded specific performance of land contracts, so as not to change the law in this regard, but clarified the power of arbitrators to award injunctive relief. Given that the parties are free to agree on the remedies that a tribunal may order, there is nothing to restrict such remedies to those available at Court.

**Clause 49 Interest.**

235. The responses we received demonstrated to us that there was a general desire to give arbitral tribunals a general power to award compound interest.

236. There is no doubt that the absence of such a power adds to the delays (and thus the expense) of arbitrations and causes injustice, for it is often in a party's interest to delay the proceedings and the honouring of an award, since the interest eventually payable is less than can be made by holding on to funds which should be paid over to the other party, who of course is losing out by a like amount.

237. Some of those responding were fearful that arbitrators would abuse this power, and may, for example, award compound interest on a punitive rather than compensatory basis. We do not share those fears. To our minds any competent arbitrator seeking to fulfil the duties laid on him by the Bill will have no more difficulty in making decisions about compound interest than he will in deciding in any other context what fairness and justice require. Anyone who has such difficulties demonstrates, in our view, that he is really not fit to act as an arbitrator. In such a case, the award and the arbitrator will be susceptible of challenge.

238. Clause 84 and 111 allow for transitional measures. In the context of this Clause, we understand that these may prove necessary in relation to the enforcement of awards through the county courts, who we are told are not presently equipped to calculate compound interest payable from the date of the award.

## Clause 50 Extension of Time for making Award.

239. This Clause re-enacts the existing law, though with two qualifications:

    i. arbitral procedures for obtaining an extension must be exhausted before recourse to the Court; and

    ii. the Court must be satisfied that substantial injustice would be done if the time were not extended.

    It seems to us that these qualifications are needed to ensure that the Court's power is supportive rather than disruptive of the arbitral process. For the same reason, it seems to us that it would be a rare case indeed where the Court extended the time notwithstanding that this had not been done through an available arbitral process.

## Clause 51 Settlement.

240. This Clause reflects Article 30 of the Model Law. It enables an agreed settlement of the dispute to be given the status of an arbitral award, which could then be enforced as such.

241. Concern has been expressed that this provision (taken from Article 30 of the Model Law) might be used by the parties either to obtain an award in respect of matters which are simply not arbitrable (eg matters which under our law cannot be settled by agreement between the parties), or to mislead third parties (eg the tax authorities). It was suggested that any agreed award should have to state on its face that it is such.

242. Dealing first with deception, in our view there is no material difference between Clause 51 and our present law: *cf* p.59 of the Mustill Report. As that Report observes, Article 30 and our present law recognize the right of the tribunal to refuse to make an award on agreed terms if it contains an objectionable feature, eg is structured to mislead third parties. Clause 51 preserves that right. Thus unless the tribunal is itself prepared to be a party to an attempted deception, we consider the risk that misleading awards will be made to be very small. If the tribunal is prepared to conspire with the parties, then nothing we could put in Clause 51 is likely to deter it. Furthermore, the whole of Clause 51 is based upon the assumption that there is a dispute between the parties which has been referred to arbitration and then settled. Nothing in the Clause would assist parties to mislead others where there was no genuine dispute or genuine reference or genuine settlement. The Clause would simply not apply to such a situation.

243. So far as arbitrability is concerned, this is a question that goes beyond agreed awards. We discuss this question when considering Clause 66 (see also the supplementary recommendations in Chapter 6 below).

244. We are not persuaded that we should require that any agreed award should state that it is such. Both under this Clause and Clause 52 the parties are free to agree on the form the award should take. In our view this is not only the position under the Model Law but also the position under our present law. A requirement that an agreed award should state that it is such would have to be made a mandatory provision to be effective. We are not aware of any problems arising under our present law and are reluctant to impose this formal requirement. Moreover, it would of course be open to the tribunal to record the agreement in the award if they thought it was appropriate to do so. However, at the enforcement stage we agree that the Court should be informed if the award is an agreed award, if this is not apparent from the award itself. We return to this point when considering Clause 66 below (see also Chapter 6).

**Clause 52 Form of Award.**

245. This Clause follows closely Article 31 of the Model Law. There are, however, two matters worthy of particular note.

246. In the first place, as in the Model Law, we have required the tribunal to give reasons, unless the award is an agreed award or the parties have agreed that reasons need not be given.

247. To our minds, it is a basic rule of justice that those charged with making a binding decision affecting the rights and obligation of others should (unless those others agree) explain the reasons for making that decision. This was also the view of the majority of those who commented on this.

248. It was suggested that having to give reasons would be likely to add to the cost of arbitrations and encourage applications for leave to appeal to the Court.

249. We do not agree. The need for reasons is that which we have explained above and has nothing to do with the question whether or not a Court should hear an appeal from an award. Further, we have introduced stricter conditions for the bringing of appeals in any event. As to cost, it is always open to the parties to agree to dispense with reasons if they wish to do so, though in the case of domestic arbitrations this can only be done after the dispute has arisen: see Clause 69(1) and 87.

250. The second noteworthy point is that we have used the word "*seat*" instead of the Model Law phrase "*place of arbitration.*" We consider that the Model Law uses this phrase to mean the seat (there being no obvious legal reason to stipulate the geographical place where the award was made), and since we have used this word earlier in the Bill (see Clauses 2 and 3) it would in our view only cause confusion not to use it here. Of course the seat is only of importance in international arbitrations or where the question arises as to the

enforcement of an award abroad. Therefore, in a purely domestic arbitration, if an arbitrator were to fail to state the "*seat*," or to state this incorrectly, it is extremely unlikely that the award could be challenged under Clause 68(2)(h), given that such a failure would be unlikely to result in "*substantial injustice.*"

251. Sub-section (3) provides that the award shall be in writing and signed by all the arbitrators or, alternatively, by all those assenting to the award. An earlier draft of this sub-section had only stipulated that all arbitrators assenting to an award sign it. It was pointed out to the DAC, however, that (for whatever reason) some dissenting arbitrators may not wish to be identified as such, and that the provision should therefore be amended to provide for this.

252. It has been suggested to the DAC that there should be a provision allowing for somebody to sign on behalf of an arbitrator. This could invoke complicated principles of agency, and, overall, is better left to be resolved in each particular case.

**Clause 53 Place Where Award is Treated as Made.**

253. This Clause is designed to avoid disputes over where an award is made and (in cases where Part I of the Bill applies to the arbitration in question) it reverses the decision (although not the result) of the House of Lords in *Hiscox v Outhwaite* [1992] 1 AC 562.

**Clause 54 Date of Award.**

254. We trust this provision is self-explanatory.

**Clause 55 Notification of Award.**

255. This provision we also trust is self-explanatory. The obligation on the tribunal to notify the parties by service on them of copies of the award is important, given that certain time limits in the Bill for, eg challenging the award, run from the date of the award (which, under Clause 54, in the absence of any other agreement, is the date upon which it is signed). Time periods, of course, can be extended: see Clause 79. We have required the award to be notified to the "parties" so as to prevent one party from obtaining the award and sitting on it without informing the other party until the expiry of time limits for appeal etc., which we are aware has happened in practice.

256. Clause 55(3) provides that nothing in this section affects the power to withhold an award in the case of non-payment. However, it should be noted that the duty to notify all parties would of course revive once the tribunal's "lien" has been satisfied.

## Clause 56 Power to withhold Award in case of non-payment.

257. These provisions enable a party to seek the assistance of the Court if he considers that the arbitrators are asking too much for the release of their award, though it is important to note from sub-section (4) that there is no recourse if there is already arbitral machinery for an appeal or review of the fees or expenses demanded.

258. Sub-section (8) makes clear that this Clause does not affect the right to challenge fees and expenses under Clause 28 ie that paying them to get the award does not lose this right. The reason for this provision is that it may be important for a party to obtain the award quickly, rather than going to the Court for an order about fees and expenses before betting the award.

259. Unlike section 19 of the 1950 Act, this provision gives the Court a discretion to specify that a lesser amount than that claimed by the arbitrators be paid into Court, in order to have the award released. If this were not so, an arbitrator could demand an extortionate amount, in effect preventing a party from taking advantage of the mechanism provided for here.

260. For obvious reasons, this provision is mandatory.

## Clause 57 Correction of Award or Additional Award.

261. This Clause reflects Article 33 of the Model Law. In our view this is a useful provision, since it enables the arbitral process to correct itself, rather than requiring applications to the Court. In order to avoid delay, we have stipulated time limits for seeking corrections etc.

## Clause 58 Effect of Award.

262. This provision in effect simply restates the existing law.

263. It has been suggested that what is described as the other side of sub-section (1) should be spelt out in the Bill ie that whatever the parties may or may not agree, the award is of no substantive or evidential effect against any one who is neither a party nor claiming through or under a party.

264. Such a provision would, of course, have to be mandatory. It would have to confine itself to cases exclusively concerned with the laws of this country, for otherwise it could impinge on other applicable laws which have a different rule. Even where the situation was wholly domestic, it would also have to deal with all those cases (eg insurers) who are not parties to the arbitration but whose rights and obligations may well be affected by awards (agreed or otherwise) in one way or another. In our view it would be very difficult to construct an acceptable provision and we are not persuaded that it is needed.

## Costs of the Arbitration

**Clause 59 Costs of the Arbitration.**

**Clause 60 Agreement to pay costs in any event.**

**Clause 61 Award of Costs.**

**Clause 62 Effect of Agreement or Award about costs.**

**Clause 63 The recoverable costs of the arbitration.**

**Clause 64 Recoverable fees and expenses of arbitrators.**

**Clause 65 Power to limit recoverable costs.**

265. In these Clauses we have attempted to provide a code dealing with how the costs or an arbitration should be attributed between the parties. The question of the right of the arbitrators to fees and expenses is dealt with earlier in that part of the Bill concerned with the arbitral tribunal: see Clause 28.

266. Clause 59 defines costs.

267. Clause 60 is a mandatory provision preventing effective agreements to pay the whole or part of the costs in any event unless made after the dispute has arisen. The Clause is based on section 18(3) of the Arbitration Act 1950. The Committee are of the view that public policy continues to dictate that such a provision should remain.

268. Clause 62 empowers the arbitrators to make an award in relation to costs. Sub-section (2) sets out the general principle to be applied, which is the same principle that is applicable in Court.

269. It has been suggested that arbitral tribunals should not be fettered in this way, but to our minds it is helpful to state the principle, especially for those who may not be lawyers and who otherwise might not know how to proceed. Furthermore, it seems to us that there is no reason why the general principle should not apply to arbitrations: it certainly does under the present law. The parties are, of course, free to agree on other principles, subject to Clause 60.

270. Clauses 63 and 64 are we hope more or less self-explanatory. Clearly there has to be a special regime for the fees and expenses of the arbitrators, for otherwise they would be left with the power to decide for themselves whether or not they had overcharged!

271. Clause 64(4) preserves any contractual right an arbitrator may have to payment of his fees and expenses. If a party has agreed these, then it would

in our view be wrong to allow the Court to adjust the amount ie to rewrite that agreement.

272. Clause 65 contains a new proposal. It gives the tribunal power to limit in advance the amount of recoverable costs. We consider that such a power, properly used, could prove to be extremely valuable as an aid to reducing unnecessary expenditure. It also represents a facet of the duty of the tribunal as set out in Clause 33. The Clause enables the tribunal to put a ceiling on the costs, so that while a party can continue to spend as much as it likes on an arbitration it will not be able to recover more than the ceiling limit from the other party. This will have the added virtue of discouraging those who wish to use their financial muscle to intimidate their opponents into giving up through fear that by going on they might be subject to a costs order which they could not sustain.

### Powers of the Court in relation to Award

### Clause 66 Enforcement of the Award.

273. This reflects Article 35 of the Model Law. Enforcement through the Court provides the classic case of using the Court to support the arbitral process. Sub-section (3)(a) is intended to state the present law: see Mustill & Boyd, *Commercial Arbitration*, 2nd Ed., at p. 546. Sub-section (3)(b) is intended to cover cases where public policy would not recognize the validity of an award, for example awards purporting to decide matters which our law does not accept can be resolved by this means. For obvious reasons, this provision is mandatory.

274. Reference should be made to Chapter 6, where certain supplementary recommendations are made with respect to this Clause.

### Clause 67 Challenging the Award: Substantive Jurisdiction.

275. Jurisdiction has already been considered in the context of that part of the Bill dealing with the jurisdiction of the arbitral tribunal: see Clauses 30 to 32.

276. Clause 31 allows the tribunal (where it has power to rule on its own jurisdiction) to make a 'jurisdiction' award, either on its own, or as part of its award on the merits. Clause 67 provides the mechanism for challenging the jurisdiction rulings in such awards, and is a mandatory provision. It also provides a mechanism for challenges to the jurisdiction by someone who has taken no part in the arbitral proceedings. We deal with such persons below, when considering Clause 72.

277. To avoid the possibility of challenges to the jurisdiction causing unnecessary delay, the rights given by this Clause are subject to qualifications, which explains the reference in sub-section (1) to three other sections. In

addition, sub-section (2) means that a challenge to jurisdiction does not stop the tribunal from proceeding with other aspects of the arbitration while the application is pending.

**Clause 68 Challenging the Award: Serious Irregularity.**

278. We have drawn a distinction in the Bill between challenges in respect of substantive jurisdiction (ie those matters listed in Clause 30) and challenges in respect of what we have called *"serious irregularity."* We appreciate that cases may arise in which it might be difficult to decide into which category a particular set of circumstances should be placed, but since the time limits etc. for both Clause 67 and 68 are the same, this should cause no procedural difficulties. We are firmly of the view, however, that it is useful to have two categories.

279. The reason for this is that where jurisdiction is concerned, there can be no question of applying a test of *"substantial injustice"* or the like. An award of a tribunal purporting to decide the rights or obligations of a person who has not given that tribunal jurisdiction so to act simply cannot stand, though of course, if the party concerned has taken part in the arbitration, there is nothing wrong in requiring him to act without delay in challenging the award.

280. Irregularities stand on a different footing. Here we consider that it is appropriate, indeed essential, that these have to pass the test of causing *"substantial injustice"* before the Court can act. The Court does not have a general supervisory jurisdiction over arbitrations. We have listed the specific cases where a challenge can be made under this Clause. The test of *"substantial injustice"* is intended to be applied by way of support for the arbitral process, not by way of interference with that process. Thus it is only in those cases where it can be said that what has happened is so far removed from what could reasonably be expected of the arbitral process that we would expect the Court to take action. The test is not what would have happened had the matter been litigated. To apply such a test would be to ignore the fact that the parties have agreed to arbitrate, not litigate. Having chosen arbitration, the parties cannot validly complain of substantial injustice unless what has happened simply cannot on any view be defended as an acceptable consequence of that choice. In short, Clause 68 is really designed as a long stop, only available in extreme cases where the tribunal has gone so wrong in its conduct of the arbitration that justice calls out for it to be corrected.

281. By way of example, there have been cases under our present law where the Court has remitted awards to an arbitral tribunal because the lawyers acting for one party failed (or decided not to) put a particular point to the tribunal: see, for example, ***Indian Oil Corporation v Coastal (Bermuda) Ltd*** [1990] 2 Lloyd's Rep 407; ***King v Thomas McKenna*** [1991] 2 Q.B. 480; ***Breakbulk Marine v Dateline,*** 19 March 1992, unreported (jurisdiction recognised but not exercised).

282. The responses we received were critical of such decisions, on the grounds that they really did amount to an interference in the arbitral process agreed by the parties. We agree. The Clause we propose is designed not to permit such interference, by setting out a closed list of irregularities (which it will not be open to the Court to extend), and instead reflecting the internationally accepted view that the Court should be able to correct serious failure to comply with the 'due process' of arbitral proceedings: *cf* Article 34 of the Model Law.

283. This Clause is, of course, mandatory.

**Clause 69 Appeal on Point of Law**

284. We received a number of responses calling for the abolition of any right of appeal on the substantive issues in the arbitration. These were based on the proposition that by agreeing to arbitrate their dispute, the parties were agreeing to abide by the decision of their chosen tribunal, not by the decision of the Court, so that whether or not a Court would reach the same conclusion was simply irrelevant. To substitute the decision of the Court on the substantive issues would be wholly to subvert the agreement the parties had made.

285. This proposition is accepted in many countries. We have considered it carefully, but we are not persuaded that we should recommend that the right of appeal should be abolished. It seems to us, that with the safeguards we propose, a limited right of appeal is consistent with the fact that the parties have chosen to arbitrate rather than litigate. For example, many arbitration agreements contain an express choice of the law to govern the rights and obligations arising out of the bargain made subject to that agreement. It can be said with force that in such circumstances, the parties have agreed that that law will be properly applied by the arbitral tribunal, with the consequences that if the tribunal fail to do this, it is not reaching the result contemplated by the arbitration agreement.

286. In these circumstances what we propose is a right to apply to the Court to decide a point of law arising out of an award. This right is limited, however, in several ways.

   i. The point of law must substantially affect the rights of one or more of the parties. This limitation exists, of course, in our present law.

   ii. The point of law must be one that was raised before the tribunal. The responses showed that in some cases applications for leave to appeal have been made and granted on the basis that an examination of the reasons for the award shows an error on a point of law that was not raised or debated in the arbitration. This method of proceeding has echoes of the old and long discarded common law rules relating to error of law on the face of the award, and is in our view a retrograde step. In our view the right to appeal should be limited as we suggest.

iii. There have been attempts, both before and after the enactment of the Arbitration Act 1979, to dress up questions of fact as questions of law and by that means to seek an appeal on the tribunal's decision on the facts. Generally these attempts have been resisted by the Courts, but to make the position clear, we propose to state expressly that consideration by the Court of the suggested question of law is made on the basis of the findings of fact in the award.

iv. We have attempted to express in this Clause the limits put on the right to appeal by the House of Lords in Pioneer Shipping Ltd v BTP Tioxide Ltd (The Nema) [1982] AC 724.

287. With respect to the last point, we think it is very important to do this. Many of those abroad who do not have ready access to our case law were unaware that the Arbitration Act 1979 had been construed by the House of Lords in a way that very much limited the right of appeal, and which was not evident from the words of the Act themselves.

288. The test we propose is whether, in the ordinary case, the Court is satisfied that the decision of the tribunal is obviously wrong. The right of appeal is only available for such cases, for the reasons discussed above. Where the matter is one of general public importance, the test is less onerous, but the decision must still be open to serious doubt.

289. We propose a further test, namely whether, despite the agreement of the parties to resolve the matter by arbitration, it is just and proper in all the circumstances for the Court to determine the question.

290. We have been asked why we suggest this addition. The reason is that we think it desirable that this factor should be specifically addressed by the Court when it is considering an application. It seems to us to be the basis on which the House of Lords acted as it did in *The Nema* op.cit.. The Court should be satisfied that justice dictates that there should be an appeal; and in considering what justice requires, the fact that the parties have agreed to arbitrate rather than litigate is an important and powerful factor.

291. It will be noted that we have included a provision that the Court should determine an application without a hearing unless it appears to the Court that a hearing is required. This again reflects what was said in *The Nema* op.cit. about the tendency for applications for leave being turned into long and expensive court hearings. In our view, the tests for leave (ie obviously wrong or open to serious doubt) are such that in most cases the Court will be able to decide whether to allow or reject the application on written material alone.

292. Finally, a question has been raised as to whether an agreement in advance of the proceedings (ie contained in an arbitration clause or in the underlying contract) would satisfy Clause 69(2)(a). The Clause is intended to encompass such agreements, and in our view it plainly does so since the word agreement is not qualified. However, such an agreement will not automatically allow an appeal unless it complies with the other conditions set out in Clause 69 and 70.

**Clause 70 Challenge or Appeal: supplementary Provisions.**

**Clause 71 Challenge or Appeal: effect of Order of the Court.**

293. These provisions contain time-limits and other matters in relation to challenges to the award and applications and appeals. Some of these provisions are mandatory.

294. The time limit in Clause 70(3) runs from the date of the award, or, where applicable, the date when a party was notified of the result of the arbitral process of appeal or review. It has been suggested that difficulties might arise if an award is held back by the arbitrators, pending payment by the parties (ie under Clause 56). It is possible that the time limit in Clause 70(3) will have expired by the time an award is released. However, the DAC is of the view that the date of an award is the only incontrovertible date from which the time period should run. Any other starting point would result in great uncertainty (eg as to the exact point at which an award is "released" or "delivered"). Further, any difficulties arising from specific circumstances can be easily remedied by way of an extension of time under Clause 79.

**Miscellaneous**

**Clause 72 Savings for Rights of Person who takes no part in Proceedings.**

295. To our minds this is a vital position. A person who dispute that an arbitral tribunal has jurisdiction cannot be required to take part in the arbitration proceedings or to take positive steps to defend his position, for any such requirement would beg the question whether or not his objection has any substance and thus be likely to lead to gross injustice. Such a person must be entitled, if he wishes, simply to ignore the arbitral process, though of course (if his objection is not well-founded) he runs the risk of an enforceable award being made against him. Those who do decide to take part in the arbitral proceedings in order to challenge the jurisdiction are, of course, in a different category, for then, having made that choice, such people can fairly and properly be required to abide by the time limits etc. that we have proposed.

296. This is a mandatory position.

## Clause 73 Loss of Right to Object.

297. Recalcitrant parties or those who have had an award made against them often seek to delay proceedings or to avoid honouring the award by raising points on jurisdiction etc. which they have been saving up for this purpose or which they could and should have discovered and raised at an earlier stage. Article 4 of the Model Law contains some provisions designed to combat this sort of behaviour (which does the efficiency of arbitration as a form of dispute resolution no good) and we have attempted to address the same point in this Clause. In particular, unlike the Model Law, we have required a party to arbitration proceedings who has taken part or continued to take part without raising the objection in due time, to show that at that stage he neither knew nor could with reasonable diligence have discovered the grounds for his objection (the latter being an important modification to the Model Law, without which one would have to demonstrate actual knowledge, which may be virtually impossible to do). It seems to us that this is preferable to requiring the innocent party to prove the opposite, which for obvious reasons it might be difficult or impossible to do.

298. For the reasons explained when considering Clause 72, the provision under discussion cannot, of course, be applied to a party who has chosen to play no part at all in the arbitral proceedings.

## Clause 74 Immunity of arbitral Institutions etc.

299. In this mandatory provision we have provided institutions and individuals who appoint arbitrators with a degree of immunity.

300. The reason for this proposal is that without such an immunity, there is in our view a real risk that attempts will be made to hold institutions or individuals responsible for the consequences of their exercise of the power they may be given to appoint or nominate arbitrators, or for what their appointed or nominated arbitrators then do or fail to do. This would provide a means of reopening matters that were referred to arbitration, something that might be encouraged if arbitrators were given immunity (as we have also proposed in Clause 29) but nothing was said about such institutions or individuals.

301. There is an additional point of great importance. Many organisations that provide arbitration services, including Trade Associations as well as bodies whose sole function it is to provide arbitration services, do not in the nature of things have deep pockets. Indeed much of the work is done by volunteers simply in order to promote and help this form of dispute resolution. Such organisations could find it difficult if not impossible to finance the cost of defending legal proceedings or even the cost of insurance against such cost. In our view the benefits which these organisations (and indeed individuals) have on arbitration generally fully justify giving them a measure of protection so that their good work can continue.

**Clause 75 Charge to secure payment of Solicitors' costs.**

302. This is a technical provision designed to maintain the present position.

### Supplementary

**Clause 76 Service of Notices etc.**

303. The subject matter of this Clause was touched on in the MacKinnon Report which led to the Arbitration Act 1934, but at that time no action was taken.

304. In this Clause we have attempted to do three things.

   i. We have stipulated that the parties can agree on how service of notices and other documents can be done.

   ii. We have made clear that in the absence of agreement, service by *any* effective means will suffice.

   iii. We have provided in sub-section (4) an option which can best be described as a 'fail-safe' method, which a party may employ if he wishes, for example if he is not sure that other methods will be effective. We should emphasize that this fail-safe method is not a compulsory or preferred method for service, but merely a means which, if employed, will be treated as effective.

305. These provisions do not apply in respect of service in Court proceedings, for the obvious reason that such service must comply with the rules of the Court concerned.

**Clause 77 Powers of Court in relation to service of documents.**

306. In this Clause we have given the Court powers to support the arbitral process so that it is not delayed or frustrated through difficulties over service. In the nature of human affairs, it is sadly the case that potential respondents to arbitration proceedings quite often go to considerable lengths to avoid service and thus to achieve this state of affairs, by making normal methods difficult or even impossible to use effectively. This Clause should, in appropriate cases, help to deal with such cases.

**Clause 78 Reckoning Periods of Time.**

307. In our view it would be of great assistance to set out a code to deal with the reckoning of time, thus avoiding the need to refer to other sources. Hence this provision.

**Clause 79 Power of Court to extend time limits relating to arbitral Proceedings.**

308. Here we propose that the Court should have a general right to extend time limits, except time limits for starting an arbitration, which is dealt with specifically in Clause 12. We propose that the wording of the Clause be clarified as set out in Chapter 6 below.

309. This power is limited in the ways set out in this Clause. In particular, no extension will be granted unless a substantial injustice would otherwise be done and any arbitral process for obtaining an extension must first be exhausted. As we have said in other contexts, it would be a rare case indeed where we would expect the Court to grant an extension where such has not been obtained through that process. With these limitations we take the view that this provision can properly be described as supporting the arbitral process.

**Clause 80 Notice and other Requirements in connection with legal Proceedings.**

310. Legal proceedings must of course be subject to the rules of the Court concerned. We have made clear, therefore, that where the Bill provides for notice of legal proceedings to be given to others, this is a reference to such rules as the Court concerned may make; and is not a separate requirement over and above those rules.

**Clause 81 Saving for certain Matters governed by Common Law.**

311. As we have stated earlier, and as was stated in the Mustill Report, it would be neither practicable nor desirable to attempt to codify the whole of our arbitration law. Hence sub-sections (1) and (2) of this Clause.

312. It was suggested to us that a provision preserving the common law would enable arguments to be raised and accepted which were contrary to the spirit and intent of the Bill. We do not think that this will happen, in view of the opening words of the Clause and indeed the statements of principle in Clause 1. Equally, it seems to us to be necessary to make clear that the common law (so far as it is consistent with the Bill) will continue to make its great contribution to our arbitration law, a contribution that has done much to create and preserve the world wide popularity of arbitration in our country.

313. Sub-section (3) is technically necessary to make clear that the repeal of the existing statues does not have the effect of reviving the common law rules relating to errors on the face of the award.

**Clause 82 Minor Definitions.**

**Clause 83 Index of defined Expressions: Part 1.**

314. The first of these Clauses provides the definition of words and phrases which are often repeated in the body of the Bill, so that repetition of the meaning is avoided, as well as providing a ready means of discovering the meaning of certain important words and phrases. The second of these Clauses is also designed to help the reader by identifying the place where other important words and phrases are defined or explained.

**Clause 84 Transitional Provisions.**

315. This Clause sets out the general proposition, namely that the Bill will apply to arbitral proceedings commenced after the legislation comes into force, whenever the arbitration agreement is made. There are respectable precedents for this, since the Arbitration Acts 1889, and 1934 contained a like provision. The 1950 Act, of course, was not a precedent, since this was a consolidating measure. We consider this to be a useful provision, since some arbitration agreements have a very long life indeed (for example, rent review arbitration agreements under lease) and it would be most unsatisfactory if the existing law and the proposed legislation were to run in parallel (if that is the right expression) indefinitely into the future.

316. Reference should also be made to Clause 111.

**Chapter 3**
**PART II OF THE BILL**

**OTHER PROVISIONS RELATING TO ARBITRATION**
**Domestic Arbitration Agreements**

**Clause 85 Modification of Part I in relation to Domestic Arbitration Agreements.**

**Clause 86 Staying of Legal Proceedings.**

**Clause 87 Effectiveness of Agreement to exclude Court's Jurisdiction.**

**Clause 88 Power to repeal or amend ss.85 to 87.**

317. Under our present law, a distinction is drawn between domestic and other arbitrations for two main purposes.

318. In the first place, the rules for obtaining a stay of legal proceedings differ. The reason for this is that under international Conventions, a stay in favour of an arbitration is mandatory except in certain specified circumstances. The current Convention is the New York Convention and the rules under that Convention we have now set out in Clause 9. With an exception that we have already discussed above, Clause 9 simply re-enacts the Arbitration Act 1975 so far as it concerns this matter.

319. Section 1 of the Arbitration Act 1975 does not apply to domestic arbitrations as there defined. These continue to be governed by Section 4(1) of the Arbitration Act 1950, which makes the grant of a stay discretionary.

320. It is our view that consideration should be given to abolishing this distinction and applying the New York Convention rules to all cases. It seems to us that these rules fit much more happily with the concept of party autonomy than our domestic rules, which were framed at a time when attitudes to arbitration were very different and the Courts were anxious to avoid what they described as usurpation of their process.

321. For example, there are cases justifying the refusal of a stay in cases where the Court considers that the party seeking to arbitrate has no defence to the claim and is merely seeking to delay the day of judgment. This has been explained on the basis that since there is no defence to the claim, there is no dispute that can be arbitrated. The difficulty with this argument is that it logically follows that only disputable matters can be arbitrated, or, in other words, that the arbitrators have no jurisdiction to deal with cases where there is no real defence. This in turn means that a claimant cannot refer a claim to arbitration where there is no real defence, since ex hypothesi the arbitrators would have no jurisdiction. In short, this argument leads to consequences that in our view have only to be stated to be rejected. As to delaying tactics, it has been our intention throughout the Bill to provide the means whereby an agreement to arbitrate can produce (in suitable cases) a very quick answer indeed. Indeed, if in truth there is no defence to a claim, then it should not take more than a very short time for an arbitral tribunal to deal with the matter and produce an award.

322. For these reasons, which are those discussed in Nelson v Hayter [1990] 2 Lloyd's Rep. 265, we consider that this ground for preserving the distinction between domestic and other arbitrations so far as stays are concerned is highly unconvincing.

323. The domestic rules have also been used to refuse stays where the disputes are likely to involve other parties, who could not be brought into the arbitration, since the agreement to arbitrate only binds those who were party to it. Here the justification for refusing to stay legal proceedings is that it would be much better for all the concerned parties to be brought into one proceeding, so that the whole matters can be sorted out between them all.

324. This reasoning of course is in one sense supported by common sense and justice, for in certain cases it would be better and fairer for all the disputes between all the parties involved to be dealt with by one tribunal, thereby avoiding delay and the possibility of inconsistent findings by different tribunals. However, as we observed in the context of considering whether there should be a power (without the agreement of the parties) to order consolidation or concurrent hearings in arbitrations (Clause 35), to refuse a stay because other parties are involved involves tearing up the arbitration agreement that the applicant for a stay has made. In other words, with the benefit of hindsight, the Court adjusts the rights and obligations of contracting parties.

325. We fully accept that for reasons of consumer protection, this on occasion can and should be done, but we are not persuaded that it should be a general rule in the context of stays of domestic arbitrations, for it sits uneasily with the principle of party autonomy and amounts to interference with rather than support for the arbitral process.

326. We should also note that the distinction drawn between domestic and other arbitrations produces odd results. An arbitration agreement between two English people is a domestic arbitration agreement, while an agreement between an English person and someone of a different nationality is not, even if that person has spent all his time in England. Furthermore, we are aware that it could be said that the distinction discriminates against European Community nationals who are not English, and is thus contrary to European law.

327. Notwithstanding the foregoing, we do not propose in this Bill to abolish the distinction. Some defend it and we have not had an opportunity to make all the soundings we would like on this subject. What we have done is to put the domestic arbitration rules in a separate part of the Bill, and provided in Clause 88 for a power of repeal through the mechanism of a positive joint resolution of each House of Parliament.

328. What we have felt able to do is to redraft the domestic rules on stays and to make two changes. Firstly we have removed the discretion and instead set out words which are wide enough to encompass the circumstances which the cases have developed as grounds for refusing a stay. Secondly and more importantly, we have reversed the existing burden of proof (and incidentally got rid of a double or perhaps treble negative in the previous legislation). It seemed to us that it was for the party seeking to litigate something which he had previously agreed to arbitrate to persuade the Court that he should be allowed to go back on his agreement.

329. The second purpose served by making a distinction between domestic and other arbitrations is to prevent the parties in a domestic case from effectively agreeing to exclude the jurisdiction of the Court to deal with preliminary

points of law or with an appeal from an award on a point of law, until after the commencement of the arbitral proceedings. This necessarily means that until the arbitration starts such parties cannot make an effective agreement to dispense with reasons, for that is treated as an agreement to exclude the jurisdiction of the Court – see, now, Clause 69(1).

330. Again we are not persuaded of the value or the validity of this, but we have preserved the existing law for the same reason as we have preserved the present position on stays. Our own view is that this distinction should disappear.

331. It should be noted that we have not preserved the 'special categories' dealt with in Section 4 of the Arbitration Act 1979. These were intended as a temporary measure, and the weight of the responses received persuaded us that they should now go.

### Consumer Arbitration Agreements

**Clauses 89 to 93**

332. In these Clauses we have consolidated the provisions of the Consumer Arbitration Agreements Act 1988. We have suggested this in order to bring within the Bill all the current major enactments on arbitration, so as to provide as complete a code as possible.

333. We did not regard it as part of our remit to redraft this legislation, so we have not sought responses on it. However, we are aware that problems have arisen in construing this Act. For example, it has been suggested that what now appears as Clause 89 makes it far from clear whether a building contract made by a consumer falls outside the Act if the consumer has sought a number of quotes for the work.

334. We are also aware of a more fundamental problem. This country has recently implemented Council Direction 93/13 through the Unfair Terms in Consumer Contracts Regulations 1994 (SI 1994/3159). These Regulations came into force on 1st July 1995. Thus at the moment a situation exists where there are two parallel regimes for protecting consumer interests in the context of arbitration agreements.

335. To our minds this is an unsatisfactory state of affairs, likely to cause confusion and difficulties. Although we have not attempted to trespass into the field of consumer protection, it does seem to us that it would be unfortunate if the opportunity were not taken to clarify the position. On the face of it, the solution would seem to be to maintain the suggested repeal of the 1988 Act and to omit Clauses 89 to 92 of the Bill. If this were to be done, then we would welcome at least a cross-reference in the Bill to the Regulations, so that anyone reading the Bill will be made aware of them. As we understand

it, the Regulations would not affect our international obligations regarding arbitrations (for example, the New York Convention) though doubtless those charged with the question of consumer protection will consider this aspect of the matter.

336. We would, however, emphasize that the arbitration community is extremely anxious that the Bill should not be delayed. The fact is that this country has been very slow to modernise its arbitration law and this has done us no good in our endeavour to retain our pre-eminence in the field of international arbitration, a service which brings this country very substantial amounts indeed by way of invisible earnings.

337. It is for these reasons that we have included in Clause 88 a power to amend or repeal Clauses 89 to 93. If the situation cannot be clarified or settled without delaying the progress of the Bill, then this mechanism could allow the Bill to go forward with the Consumer Arbitration Agreements Act in it, and the matter dealt with later.

### Small Claims Arbitration in the County Court

**Clause 94 Exclusion of Part I in relation to small claims in the County Court.**

338. There is an entirely separate regime for the arbitration of small claims in the County Court. The Bill is not intended to affect this.

339. As we observed earlier in the Report, we considered the suggestion that we should incorporate in the Bill another system for the arbitration of small claims, but for the reasons given, we have not adopted this suggestion and do not recommend it.

### Appointment of Judges as Arbitrators

**Clause 95 Appointment of Judges as Arbitrators.**

340. In this Clause we have set out the existing provisions for the appointment of Commercial Judges and Official Referees as arbitrators.

341. We are firmly of the view that the provision should be made for any Judge to be appointed as an arbitrator, rather than limiting the power to the two kinds of Judge presently included. It was not, however, possible to obtain agreement to this proposal from the concerned departments in time to put it in the Bill.

342. We appreciate that in view of the court commitments of Judges generally, it is not possible to allow Judges to act as arbitrators whenever they are asked and are willing to do so. Hence the present requirement now set out in sub-sections (2) and (3). We would suggest that the same or a similar provision is used for all other Judges.

343. We are told that the problem is particularly acute in the field of patents and the like, where the parties are anxious to arbitrate but where the only acceptable arbitrators are Judges.

### Statutory Arbitrations

**Clauses 96 to 101**

344. These provisions adapt Part 1 to statutory arbitrations. This exercise is not within our remit and we have played no part in it.

## Chapter 4
## PART III OF THE BILL

**Clauses 102 to 107**

345. The purpose of Part III is to re-enact the substance of the provisions relating to the recognition and enforcement of foreign arbitral awards contained in Part II of the Arbitration Act 1950 and the Arbitration Act 1975, which gave effect to the UK's treaty obligations under the Geneva and New York Conventions respectively.

346. The Geneva Convention only remains in force as between state parties to that Convention which have not subsequently become parties to the New York Convention. So far as the UK is concerned, it is believed that only a few states (eg Malta) remain in that category. Accordingly, in the interest of brevity, Clause 102 states simply that Part II of the Arbitration Act 1950 continues to apply to Geneva Convention awards which are not also New York Convention awards rather than restating or reframing the non-user friendly language of Part II of the Act.

347. The New York Convention on the Recognition and Enforcement of Foreign Arbitral Awards adopted by the UN Conference on International Arbitration on 10 June 1958 is not only the cornerstone of international dispute resolution; it is an essential ingredient more generally of world trade. If it did not exist, or even if it were not to have been widely adopted by the world's trading nations, contracting parties from different legal cultures might be reduced to resolving their disputes in the courts of a country which would be alien to either one or both of them (because of doubts as to the enforceability across national boundaries of arbitration awards made in a neutral country). Clauses 102 to 107 of the Bill restate the current implementing legislation (contained in the 1975 Act) in concise and simple language.

348. As we have indicated earlier in Chapter 2, we take the view that the definition of "in writing" is consonant with Article II.2 of the New York Convention. For clarity therefore, we consider that the Bill can be improved

by including an express cross-reference to this definition in Clause 103(2). This would have the added advantage of ensuring that the enforcement of foreign awards under Clause 66 and enforcement under the New York Convention are in this respect in line with each other.

## Chapter 5
## PART IV OF THE BILL

355. We have drawn attention to Clause 111 under Clause 84. The other Clauses in this Part we trust are self-evident, and were not within the remit of the DAC, although we do welcome the inclusion of Northern Ireland.

## Chapter 6
## SUPPLEMENTARY RECOMMENDATIONS

356. The foregoing discussion is based on the text of the Bill as it was introduced in December 1995. Since that date we have had the advantage of considering the speeches made in the House of Lords on the Second Reading and some comments and suggestions from others, as well as looking once again at the text of the Bill in the course of preparing this Report. In consequence, we make the following recommendations.

**Clause 2 Scope of Application.**

357. A number of foreign readers have expressed the view that Clause 2(2)(a) does not sufficiently make clear that the applicable law referred to is the law applicable to the arbitration agreement, rather than the law applicable to the substantive agreement (which would have far reaching and wholly unintended consequences). For the sake of clarity, we would suggest an amendment along the following lines:

"... where the applicable law to that agreement is the law of England and Wales or Northern Ireland; and. . ."

**Clause 7 Separability of Arbitration Agreement.**

358. In view of the definition of "agreement" in Clause 5, we suggest that the words "(whether or not in writing)" be inserted after the words "another agreement" in Clause 7, since otherwise it could be said that this Clause is only effective in relation to such other agreements as are in writing. This is not the intention.

# APPENDIX 8 - THE DAC REPORTS ON THE ARBITRATION BILL 1996

**Clause 14(5) Commencement of Arbitral Proceedings.**

359. It has been suggested that the words "gives notice" should be replaced by "serves," in conformity with Clauses 14(3) and 14(4). This is a matter for Parliamentary Counsel to consider.

**Clause 16(6)(b) and Clause 21(4)**

360. The word "*any*" follows a negative and so could be read as meaning "*all.*" This is not the intention. We therefore suggest that the words "*one or more matters*" follow the word "*any*" in these provisions.

**Clause 24(4) Power of Court to Remove Arbitrator.**

361. We have explained in Chapter 1 above the reasoning behind Clause 29(3). Upon further reflection, it appears to us that Clause 24(4) needs to be altered for the same reason. As currently drafted, if an arbitrator resigns and is sued for his fees, he is not protected from such a breach of contract action by the immunity in Clause 29. Rather, he can apply to the Court for protection under Clause 25(3), and the Court may see fit to grant this, if appropriate. However, if an arbitrator does not resign, but is removed by the Court under Clause 24, it would appear that he will have the benefit of the immunity in Clause 29, come what may. In such circumstances, the parties could not sue him for breach of contract, unless they could demonstrate "bad faith." This is anomalous. The DAC therefore recommends that Clause 24(4) be amended to provide that as well as making such order as it thinks fit with respect to an arbitrator's entitlement to fees, where the Court removes an arbitrator, it also be given a discretion to make such order as it thinks fit with respect to an arbitrator's immunity under Clause 29. Such wide words would enable the Court, for example, to remove the immunity but impose a ceiling on the amount of any liability.

362. Arbitrators may also be removed by agreement of the parties. However, the DAC does not consider that a similar provision be made with respect to this, given that it would be contrary to the whole basis of Clause 29 for parties to be able to agree on the removal of an arbitrator's immunity.

**Clause 25(2) Resignation of Arbitrator.**

363. There is a rogue "in writing" in this sub-section, which should be deleted by virtue of Clause 5(1).

**Clause 38(3) Security for Costs.**

364. In the draft Clauses published in July 1995, the power to order security for costs was expressed in very general terms. This elicited a number of responses which expressed concern that there were no principles or

guidelines for the exercise of this power. It is certainly the case that the power to order security for costs, unless exercised with great care, can all too easily work injustice rather than justice.

365. The rules and principles applied by the Courts with respect to security for costs have been carefully worked out over many years, and are contained in a large amount of case law that has developed alongside Order 23 of the Rules of the Supreme Court. Given the concerns referred to above, the DAC considered whether to set out these rules and principles in the Bill. In the end we decided that this would be simply impracticable: a codification of all the relevant case law would be extremely difficult, would result in very lengthy and complicated provisions, and may well have an unintended impact on how this area is approached by the Courts.

366. Clause 38(3) of the current draft of the Bill reflects what we initially concluded was the only solution to this difficulty: it provides that arbitrators are to have power to order a party to provide security for costs *"wherever the court would have power . . ."* and that this power is to be exercised: *"on the same principles as the court."* In the light of many comments received since the Bill was introduced (including a significant number of criticisms of this sub-section from foreign arbitration specialists and institutions), we have had to reconsider this area, and, after much careful thought, we have concluded that Clause 38(3) requires amendment for the following reasons:

   i. As drafted, this sub-section is very far from being "user-friendly." Without referring to the Rules of the Supreme Court, and the case law referred to in the relevant part of the White Book, it would be impossible for any domestic or foreign user to determine what the nature and scope of the power conferred here is. Lay arbitrators may have difficulty locating or even, perhaps, understanding the relevant law (any error of law, of course, being a potential ground for appeal). In the case of a foreign arbitration that has its seat in this country for the sole reason that this is a neutral forum, it would be extremely undesirable for parties to have to instruct English lawyers in order to make sense of this provision. This alone could constitute a powerful disincentive to selecting this country as an arbitral seat. Indeed, throughout the Bill, we have been very careful to avoid any such express cross-references to other legal sources.

   ii. One of the grounds on which an order for security for costs may be made in Court is that the plaintiff is ordinarily resident out of the jurisdiction: see Order 23, Rule 1(1)(a) of the Rules of the Supreme Court. On further consideration of the matter, we have concluded that it would be very damaging to this country's position as the leading centre for international arbitrations to make this ground available to arbitral tribunals. It would reasonably appear to those abroad who are minded to arbitrate their claims here that foreigners were being singled out for special and undeserved treatment. (Of course if the parties agree to invest their tribunal with power to order security for costs on this ground, they are free to do so.)

iii. On reflection, the concerns expressed above as to the potential scope of the power conferred by Clause 38(3) and the possibilities of injustice may be overstated. The other provisions of the Bill confer very far-reaching powers on arbitrators, and it has been made clear throughout that this is tempered, for example, by the mandatory duty in Clause 33. The same would be true of the power to order security for costs: in exercising the power, the tribunal would have to comply with Clause 33, and any serious irregularity could form the basis of a challenge. In agreeing to arbitration, parties in effect agree that their disputes could be decided differently from a Court, although in accordance with principles of justice. The fact that arbitrators may decide an issue as to security for costs differently from a judge appears to be no more than an aspect of this. It is true that if this power is improperly exercised, a claim could, for example, be stifled without justification. It is equally true, however, that the Bill contains mechanisms for parties to challenge any such injustice or improper conduct, and sufficient warnings to arbitrators as to their mandatory duties.

367. We remain of the view that the power to order security for costs is an important one, and should be given to arbitrators, and also that some basic restrictions should be set out in this Clause, in the light of the points made above. To this end, we recommend that Clause 38(3) be deleted, and replaced with a new provision along the following lines:

*"(3) The tribunal may order a claimant to provide security for the costs of the arbitration.*

*Such power shall not be exercised on the grounds only that such party is-*

*(a) an individual ordinarily resident in a state other than the United Kingdom,*
*(b) a body corporate which was incorporated in or has its central management and control exercised in a state other than the United Kingdom."*

368. Such a provision would allow arbitrators a flexibility in exercising this power, within the confines of their strict duty in Clause 33. The risk of an order on the sole ground that a party is from abroad, would be removed. Similarly, there would be no need for an arbitrator, whether domestic or foreign, to discern the English or Northern Irish law in this area, or, indeed, to instruct local lawyers in this respect. An arbitrator may well exercise this power differently from a Court (as with many other powers conferred by the Bill), but any misuse could be corrected under the other provisions of the Bill.

369. It is of course the case that orders for security are not to be made automatically, but only when the justice of the case so requires. We appreciate that cases are likely to arise when deciding what is just may be very difficult. For example, a claimant may contend that he might be prevented from continuing if he has to put up security, whilst at the same time a respondent is contending that unless security is provided, he is likely to be ruined. However, to our minds, this is merely an example of the balancing of factors in order to achieve the most just result possible which is part of the essential function of arbitrators.

370. The power to award security for costs under the proposed provision could be exercised against counter-claimants as well as claimants. This we have covered in the definition Clause (see Clause 82(1)).

**Clause 66 Enforcement of Award.**

371. In the present Bill, we have provided that leave by a Court to enforce an award may not be given if the award was so defective in form or substance that it is incapable of enforcement, if its enforcement would be contrary to public policy or if the tribunal lacked substantive jurisdiction.

372. These are what are described as 'passive' defences to the enforcement of an award. The 'positive' steps that may be taken are those we have set out in Clause 67 to 69, together with the rights preserved in Clause 72 for someone who has taken no part in the arbitral proceedings.

373. In our view the way we have drafted Clause 66 sufficed to cover all the cases where enforcement should be refused. However, since the Bill was published it has been suggested to us that it would be advisable to spell out in more detail two particular cases, namely those where the arbitral tribunal has purported to decide matters which are simply not capable of resolution by arbitration, whatever the parties might have agreed (eg custody of a child) and those where the tribunal has made an award which (if enforced) would improperly affect the rights and obligations of those who were not parties to the arbitration agreement.

374. On the present wording, even if it could be said that either or both these cases fell outside the three categories where leave to enforce shall not be given, it does not follow that the Clause somehow sanctions enforcement in those cases. The reason for this is that the Clause does not require the Court to order enforcement, but only gives it a discretion to do so. That discretion is only fettered in a negative way ie by setting out certain cases where enforcement shall not be ordered. To our minds there is nothing to prevent a Court from refusing to enforce an award in other appropriate cases. Unlike, for example, Clause 68, there is no closed list of cases where leave to enforce an award may be refused. However, on reflection we consider that it would be preferable to set out the two cases as further instances where the

discretion of the Court is negatively fettered, and we would suggest that a further category is added to sub-section (3) along the following lines:-

*"it purports to decide matters which are not capable of resolution by arbitration or grants relief which (if enforced as a judgment or order of the court) would improperly affect the rights of persons other than the parties to the arbitration agreement."*

375. Such a provision would best appear before the catch all case of public policy. It will be noted that this wording takes advantage of the definition of parties to an arbitration agreement to be found in Clause 82(2). Furthermore, to put the matter beyond any doubt, we would suggest that it is made clear that sub-section (3) is not a closed list, by inserting suitable words.

376. It is vital to include some such word as *"improperly"* since there is no doubt that there are many cases where third party rights and obligations are perfectly properly affected, such as guarantors or insurers who have agreed to pay the amount of an award to which they are not a party. Furthermore, it must always be borne in mind that the parties' rights and obligations may well be governed by a law other than our own, under which, for example, matters are arbitrable which would not be the case under our own law. In such cases it would not automatically follow that the Court would refuse to enforce the award, unless of course public policy dictated that course.

377. Apart from the enforcement procedure set out in this clause, under our law it is possible to bring an action on an award, in much the same way as an action is brought on an agreement. This method is expressly saved in Clause 81(2)(b). There is also an oblique reference to this Clause 66(5) in the reference of *"rule of law."* On reflection, it seems to us that it would make for greater clarity to add the words *"or by an action on the award"* at the end of this sub-section.

378. There is one further point. It seems to us that there is much to be said for a suggestion that the Court must be informed on an application for enforcement if the award is an agree award (see Clause 51) if this is not apparent from the award itself, and that any enforcement order or judgment of the Court should also state that it is made in respect of an agreed award, thus putting everyone concerned on notice of that fact and avoiding the risk that third parties might be misled into believing that the award was one made at arm's length. We suggest that these requirements be added to Clause 66.

**Clause 69 Appeal of Point of Law.**

379. It has been pointed out that Clause 69(8) sets out the two pre-conditions to an appeal to the Court of Appeal as alternatives, whereas they should be cumulative (as with the similar pre-conditions in section 1(7) of the 1979 Act). We recommend that the Clause be amended accordingly.

**Clause 70 Challenge or Appeal: supplementary provisions.**

380. We note that the power to order security or bring the money payable under the award into court only extends at present to applications under Clauses 67 or 68. This should be extended so that the Court can impose these requirements as a condition of granting leave to appeal under Clause 69. This is a tool of great value, since it helps to avoid the risk that while the appeal is pending, the ability of the losing party to honour the award may (by design or otherwise) be diminished.

**Clause 74 Immunity of Arbitral Institutions etc.**

381. On reflection we consider that the wording of Clause 74(2) should be tightened so as to make clear that the institution or person concerned is not liable without more for anything done or omitted to be done by the arbitrator. Thus we suggest that the words "*by reason only of*" should be substituted for the word "*for*" in this sub-section.

**Clause 79 Powers of Court to Extend Time Limits Relating to Arbitral Proceedings.**

382. It has been pointed out to us that Clause 79(1) as presently drafted could be said to be inapplicable to, for example, Clause 70(3) where the time stipulated is not one having effect in default of agreement between the parties. We agree with this comment and suggest that Clause 79(1) be amended along the following lines:

*". . . the court may by order extend any time limit agreed by them in relation to any matter relating to the arbitral proceedings or applicable by virtue of any provision of this Part."*

**Clause 81 Saving for Certain Matters Governed by Common Law.**

383. We suggest that two additions should be made to the specific cases mentioned in sub-section (2).

384. The first of these relates to confidentiality. For reasons we have explained, we have not included specific provisions dealing with this matter. However, it seems to us that it would be valuable to highlight the fact that our law does deal with it. Thus we suggest a further category which could perhaps be in the following words:-

*"confidentiality and privacy in relation to arbitrations."*

385. The second addition we propose relates to arbitrability, which we have discussed in the context of Clause 66. Again there is a lot of important law on this topic. We suggest a further category which could perhaps be in the following words:-

*"whether a matter is capable of resolution by arbitration."*

386. The title to this Clause is *"Saving for certain matters governed by common law."* We would prefer the expression *"other rules of law"* to the words "common law" as this would include legislation and be clearer to non-lawyers and those from abroad.

**Clause 82 Minor Definitions.**

387. The definition of "question of law" started life as part of the Clause dealing with appeals to the Court; now Clause 69. The objective was to make clear that there was no question of an appeal in respect of a matter of foreign law. Our law treats questions of foreign law as questions of fact. Furthermore, we can see no good reason for allowing an appeal on foreign law, since *ex hypothesi* the Court cannot give a definitive or authoritative ruling on such matters. The Courts have refused to grant leave to appeal on questions of foreign law, but attempts are still made and it would be desirable to put the matter beyond doubt.

388. The definition was moved to this Clause. It had, of course, to accommodate the fact that the Bill is expressed to apply to Northern Ireland as well as England and Wales. However the present definition, while it does this, also seems to indicate that where the seat of the arbitration is in neither of these places, the meaning of 'question of law' is not confined to questions of (respectively) English law or the law of Northern Ireland. We would suggest that the definition be amended, so that 'question of law' means a question of law of England and Wales where the application for leave to appeal is made to a Court in England and Wales, and a question of the law of Northern Ireland, where an application for leave to appeal is made to a Court in Northern Ireland.

**Clause 85 Domestic Arbitration Agreements.**

389. It has been pointed out to us that the way "domestic arbitration agreements" is defined (which is taken from the existing legislation) means that agreements made by sovereign states which incorporate an arbitration clause fall into this category. We are sure that this was not the intention, so that if the distinction between domestic and non-domestic arbitrations is to remain, the opportunity should be taken to correct this anomaly.

390. For the reasons set out in our discussion of this Clause in Chapter 1, we recommend that this provision be extended to judges generally.

**Clauses 96–100 Statutory Arbitrations.**

391. Although the application of Part 1 to statutory arbitrations is not part of our remit, we note that during the Second Reading Lord Lester suggested that it might be a requirement of European law in cases of compulsory arbitration

that the arbitrators should be independent as well as impartial. We can offer no view on this point, but if it is felt appropriate to include any such requirements in the context of statutory arbitrations, great care should be taken to make clear that this requirement has no application to private or other consensual arbitrations, so as to avoid any risk of this concept being imported into other cases. This, for the reasons already given, would in our view be most damaging. We understand that Lord Lester shares our view that a requirement of independence for private or other consensual arbitrations is neither necessary nor desirable.

**Clause 103 New York Convention Awards.**

392. For the reasons set out in our discussion in Chapter 3, this Clause should be amended so as to cross-refer to the definition of writing to be found in Part I of the Bill, and should also incorporate the recommendation that an award should be treated as made at the seat of the arbitration, regardless of where it was signed, despatched or delivered to any of the parties.

**Clause 107 Saving for Other Bases of Recognition or Enforcement.**

393. It has been pointed out that, as drafted, this Clause may not save enforcement under Part II of the 1950 Act. This is a matter for Parliamentary Counsel to consider.

## Chapter 7
## CONCLUSIONS

394. The Arbitration Bill and this Report are the result of a long and wide-ranging process of consultation with interested parties, probably the most comprehensive for any Bill of this kind. Our recommendations are based on the many responses that we have received as well as our own researches and discussions. In a number of cases, of course, we have had to make decisions on matters where more than one point of view has been expressed. What we should emphasize, however, is that all were agreed that it is high time we had new legislation, to the extent that many people have stated to us that for this reason they were not disposed to delay progress by stubbornly insisting on their point of view on particular points; and have demonstrated that this is the case by being ready and willing to reach compromise solutions. We are convinced (as all are) that further delay will do grave and probably irretrievable damage to the cause of arbitration in this country, thus damaging our valuable international reputation as well as the promotion here of this form of dispute resolution.

395. We have attempted to produce a draft which can be read, understood and applied by everyone, not just lawyers learned in this branch of our law. Thus our aim has been to make the text 'user-friendly' and the rules it contains

clear and readily comprehensible, so that arbitration is available to all who wish to use it. This has not been an easy task, since in the nature of things this form of dispute resolution raises highly complex and sophisticated matters. We have attempted it, however, in the hope that our efforts will not only encourage and promote arbitration, but also help to achieve what we believe to be the true object of this form of dispute resolution, namely (in the words of Clause 1 of the Bill itself) to obtain the fair resolution of disputes by an impartial tribunal without unnecessary delay or expense.

# APPENDIX 9

# NEW YORK CONVENTION 1958

CONVENTION ON THE RECOGNITION AND ENFORCEMENT OF FOREIGN ARBITRAL AWARDS DONE AT NEW YORK, 10 JUNE 1958; ENTERED INTO FORCE, 7 JUNE 1959 UNITED NATIONS, TREATY SERIES, VOL. 330, P. 38, NO. 4739 (1959)

*Article I*
1. This Convention shall apply to the recognition and enforcement of arbitral awards made in the territory of a State other than the State where the recognition and enforcement of such awards are sought, and arising out of differences between persons, whether physical or legal. It shall also apply to arbitral awards not considered as domestic awards in the State where their recognition and enforcement are sought.
2. The term "arbitral awards" shall include not only awards made by arbitrators appointed for each case but also those made by permanent arbitral bodies to which the parties have submitted.
3. When signing, ratifying or acceding to this Convention, or notifying extension under article X hereof, any State may on the basis of reciprocity declare that it will apply the Convention to the recognition and enforcement of awards made only in the territory of another Contracting State. It may also declare that it will apply the Convention only to differences arising out of legal relationships, whether contractual or not, which are considered as commercial under the national law of the State making such declaration.

*Article II*
1. Each Contracting State shall recognize an agreement in writing under which the parties undertake to submit to arbitration all or any differences which have arisen or which may arise between them in respect of a defined legal relationship, whether contractual or not, concerning a subject matter capable of settlement by arbitration.
2. The term "agreement in writing" shall include an arbitral clause in a contract or an arbitration agreement, signed by the parties or contained in an exchange of letters or telegrams.
3. The court of a Contracting State, when seized of an action in a matter in respect of which the parties have made an agreement within the meaning of this article, shall, at the request of one of the parties, refer the parties to arbitration,

unless it finds that the said agreement is null and void, inoperative or incapable of being performed.

*Article III*

Each Contracting State shall recognize arbitral awards as binding and enforce them in accordance with the rules of procedure of the territory where the award is relied upon, under the conditions laid down in the following articles. There shall not be imposed substantially more onerous conditions or higher fees or charges on the recognition or enforcement of arbitral awards to which this Convention applies than are imposed on the recognition or enforcement of domestic arbitral awards.

*Article IV*

1. To obtain the recognition and enforcement mentioned in the preceding article, the party applying for recognition and enforcement shall, at the time of the application, supply:

   (a) The duly authenticated original award or a duly certified copy thereof;

   (b) The original agreement referred to in article II or a duly certified copy thereof.

2. If the said award or agreement is not made in an official language of the country in which the award is relied upon, the party applying for recognition and enforcement of the award shall produce a translation of these documents into such language. The translation shall be certified by an official or sworn translator or by a diplomatic or consular agent.

*Article V*

1. Recognition and enforcement of the award may be refused, at the request of the party against whom it is invoked, only if that party furnishes to the competent authority where the recognition and enforcement is sought, proof that:

   (a) The parties to the agreement referred to in article II were, under the law applicable to them, under some incapacity, or the said agreement is not valid under the law to which the parties have subjected it or, failing any indication thereon, under the law of the country where the award was made; or

   (b) The party against whom the award is invoked was not given proper notice of the appointment of the arbitrator or of the arbitration proceedings or was otherwise unable to present his case; or

   (c) The award deals with a difference not contemplated by or not falling within the terms of the submission to arbitration, or it contains decisions on matters beyond the scope of the submission to arbitration, provided that, if the decisions on matters submitted to arbitration can be separated from those not so submitted, that part of the award which contains decisions on matters submitted to arbitration may be recognized and enforced; or

(d) The composition of the arbitral authority or the arbitral procedure was not in accordance with the agreement of the parties, or, failing such agreement, was not in accordance with the law of the country where the arbitration took place; or

(e) The award has not yet become binding on the parties, or has been set aside or suspended by a competent authority of the country in which, or under the law of which, that award was made.

2. Recognition and enforcement of an arbitral award may also be refused if the competent authority in the country where recognition and enforcement is sought finds that:

(a) The subject matter of the difference is not capable of settlement by arbitration under the law of that country; or

(b) The recognition or enforcement of the award would be contrary to the public policy of that country.

*Article VI*
If an application for the setting aside or suspension of the award has been made to a competent authority referred to in article V(1)(e), the authority before which the award is sought to be relied upon may, if it considers it proper, adjourn the decision on the enforcement of the award and may also, on the application of the party claiming enforcement of the award, order the other party to give suitable security.

*Article VII*
1. The provisions of the present Convention shall not affect the validity of multilateral or bilateral agreements concerning the recognition and enforcement of arbitral awards entered into by the Contracting States nor deprive any interested party of any right he may have to avail himself of an arbitral award in the manner and to the extent allowed by the law or the treaties of the country where such award is sought to be relied upon.
2. The Geneva Protocol on Arbitration Clauses of 1923 and the Geneva Convention on the Execution of Foreign Arbitral Awards of 1927 shall cease to have effect between Contracting States on their becoming bound and to the extent that they become bound, by this Convention.

*Article VIII*
1. This Convention shall be open until 31 December 1958 for signature on behalf of any Member of the United Nations and also on behalf of any other State which is or hereafter becomes a member of any specialized agency of the United Nations, or which is or hereafter becomes a party to the Statute of the International Court of Justice, or any other State to which an invitation has been addressed by the General Assembly of the United Nations.
2. This Convention shall be ratified and the instruments of ratification shall be deposited with the Secretary-General of the United Nations.

*Article IX*
1. This Convention shall be open for accession to all States referred to in article VIII.
2. Accession shall be effected by the deposit of an instrument of accession with the Secretary-General of the United Nations.

*Article X*
1. Any State may, at the time of signature, ratification or accession, declare that this Convention shall extend to all or any of the territories for the international relations of which it is responsible. Such a declaration shall take effect when the Convention enters into force for the State concerned.
2. At any time thereafter any such extension shall be made by notification addressed to the Secretary-General of the United Nations and shall take effect as from the ninetieth day after the day of receipt by the Secretary-General of the United Nations of this notification, or as from the date of entry into force of the Convention for the State concerned, whichever is the later.
3. With respect to those territories to which this Convention is not extended at the time of signature, ratification or accession, each State concerned shall consider the possibility of taking the necessary steps in order to extend the application of this Convention to such territories, subject, where necessary for constitutional reasons, to the consent of the Governments of such territories.

*Article XI*
In the case of a federal or non-unitary State, the following provisions shall apply:

(a) With respect to those articles of this Convention that come within the legislative jurisdiction of the federal authority, the obligations of the federal Government shall to this extent be the same as those of Contracting States which are not federal States;

(b) With respect to those articles of this Convention that come within the legislative jurisdiction of constituent states or provinces which are not, under the constitutional system of the federation, bound to take legislative action, the federal Government shall bring such articles with a favourable recommendation to the notice of the appropriate authorities of constituent states or provinces at the earliest possible moment;

(c) A federal State Party to this Convention shall, at the request of any other Contracting State transmitted through the Secretary-General of the United Nations, supply a statement of the law and practice of the federation and its constituent units in regard to any particular provision of this Convention, showing the extent to which effect has been given to that provision by legislative or other action.

*Article XII*
1. This Convention shall come into force on the ninetieth day following the date of deposit of the third instrument of ratification or accession.

2. For each State ratifying or acceding to this Convention after the deposit of the third instrument of ratification or accession, this Convention shall enter into force on the ninetieth day after deposit by such State of its instrument of ratification or accession.

*Article XIII*
1. Any Contracting State may denounce this Convention by a written notification to the Secretary-General of the United Nations. Denunciation shall take effect one year after the date of receipt of the notification by the Secretary-General.
2. Any State which has made a declaration or notification under article X may, at any time thereafter, by notification to the Secretary-General of the United Nations, declare that this Convention shall cease to extend to the territory concerned one year after the date of the receipt of the notification by the Secretary-General.
3. This Convention shall continue to be applicable to arbitral awards in respect of which recognition or enforcement proceedings have been instituted before the denunciation takes effect.

*Article XIV*
A Contracting State shall not be entitled to avail itself of the present Convention against other Contracting States except to the extent that it is itself bound to apply the Convention.

*Article XV*
The Secretary-General of the United Nations shall notify the States contemplated in article VIII of the following:

(a) Signatures and ratifications in accordance with article VIII;

(b) Accessions in accordance with article IX;

(c) Declarations and notifications under articles I, X and XI;

(d) The date upon which this Convention enters into force in accordance with article XII;

(e) Denunciations and notifications in accordance with article XIII.

*Article XVI*
1. This Convention, of which the Chinese, English, French, Russian and Spanish texts shall be equally authentic, shall be deposited in the archives of the United Nations.
2. The Secretary-General of the United Nations shall transmit a certified copy of this Convention to the States contemplated in article VIII.

APPENDIX 10

# UNCITRAL MODEL LAW ON INTERNATIONAL COMMERCIAL ARBITRATION 1985

**With amendments as adopted in 2006**

**Resolutions adopted by the General Assembly**

*40/72. Model Law on International Commercial Arbitration of the United Nations Commission on International Trade Law*

*The General Assembly,*

*Recognizing* the value of arbitration as a method of settling disputes arising in international commercial relations,

*Convinced* that the establishment of a model law on arbitration that is acceptable to States with different legal, social and economic systems contributes to the development of harmonious international economic relations,

*Noting* that the Model Law on International Commercial Arbitration[1] was adopted by the United Nations Commission on International Trade Law at its eighteenth session, after due deliberation and extensive consultation with arbitral institutions and individual experts on international commercial arbitration,

*Convinced* that the Model Law, together with the Convention on the Recognition and Enforcement of Foreign Arbitral Awards[2] and the Arbitration Rules of the United Nations Commission on International Trade Law[3] recommended by the General Assembly in its resolution 31/98 of 15 December 1976, significantly contributes to the establishment of a unified legal framework for the fair and efficient settlement of disputes arising in international commercial relations,

1. *Requests* the Secretary-General to transmit the text of the Model Law on International Commercial Arbitration of the United Nations Commission on International Trade Law, together with the *travaux préparatoires* from the eighteenth session of the Commission, to Governments and to arbitral institutions and other interested bodies, such as chambers of commerce;

2. *Recommends* that all States give due consideration to the Model Law on International Commercial Arbitration, in view of the desirability of uniformity of

---

[1] *Official Records of the General Assembly, Fortieth Session, Supplement No. 17* (A/40/17), annex I.
[2] United Nations, *Treaty Series*, vol. 330, No. 4739, p. 38.
[3] United Nations publication, Sales No. E.77.V.6.

the law of arbitral procedures and the specific needs of international commercial arbitration practice.

*112th plenary meeting*
*11 December 1985*

[*on the report of the Sixth Committee (A/61/453)*]

61/33. Revised articles of the Model Law on International Commercial Arbitration of the United Nations Commission on International Trade Law, and the recommendation regarding the interpretation of article II, paragraph 2, and article VII, paragraph 1, of the Convention on the Recognition and Enforcement of Foreign Arbitral Awards, done at New York, 10 June 1958

*The General Assembly,*

*Recognizing* the value of arbitration as a method of settling disputes arising in the context of international commercial relations,

*Recalling* its resolution 40/72 of 11 December 1985 regarding the Model Law on International Commercial Arbitration,[1]

*Recognizing* the need for provisions in the Model Law to conform to current practices in international trade and modern means of contracting with regard to the form of the arbitration agreement and the granting of interim measures,

*Believing* that revised articles of the Model Law on the form of the arbitration agreement and interim measures reflecting those current practices will significantly enhance the operation of the Model Law,

*Noting* that the preparation of the revised articles of the Model Law on the form of the arbitration agreement and interim measures was the subject of due deliberation and extensive consultations with Governments and interested circles and would contribute significantly to the establishment of a harmonized legal framework for a fair and efficient settlement of international commercial disputes,

*Believing* that, in connection with the modernization of articles of the Model Law, the promotion of a uniform interpretation and application of the Convention on the Recognition and Enforcement of Foreign Arbitral Awards, done at New York, 10 June 1958,[2] is particularly timely,

1. *Expresses its appreciation* to the United Nations Commission on International Trade Law for formulating and adopting the revised articles of its Model Law on International Commercial Arbitration on the form of the arbitration agreement and interim measures, the text of which is contained in annex I to the report of the United Nations Commission on International Trade Law on the work of its thirty-ninth

---

[1] *Official Records of the General Assembly, Fortieth Session, Supplement No. 17* (A/40/17), annex I.
[2] United Nations, *Treaty Series*, vol. 330, No. 4739.

session,[3] and recommends that all States give favourable consideration to the enactment of the revised articles of the Model Law, or the revised Model Law on International Commercial Arbitration of the United Nations Commission on International Trade Law, when they enact or revise their laws, in view of the desirability of uniformity of the law of arbitral procedures and the specific needs of international commercial arbitration practice;

2. *Also expresses its appreciation* to the United Nations Commission on International Trade Law for formulating and adopting the recommendation regarding the interpretation of article II, paragraph 2, and article VII, paragraph 1, of the Convention on the Recognition and Enforcement of Foreign Arbitral Awards, done at New York, 10 June 1958,[2] the text of which is contained in annex II to the report of the United Nations Commission on International Trade Law on the work of its thirty-ninth session;[3]

3. *Requests* the Secretary-General to make all efforts to ensure that the revised articles of the Model Law and the recommendation become generally known and available.

*64th plenary meeting*
*4 December 2006*

---

[3] *Official Records of the General Assembly, Sixty-first Session, Supplement No. 17* (A/61/17).

## New York Convention Member States

### (accurate as at November 18, 2014)

| State | Notes | Signature | Ratification, Accession(*), Approval(†), Acceptance(‡) or Succession(§) | Entry into force |
|---|---|---|---|---|
| Afghanistan | (a), (c) | | 30/11/2004(*) | 28/02/2005 |
| Albania | | | 27/06/2001(*) | 25/09/2001 |
| Algeria | (a), (c) | | 07/02/1989(*) | 08/05/1989 |
| Antigua and Barbuda | (a), (c) | | 02/02/1989(*) | 03/05/1989 |
| Argentina | (a), (c) | 26/08/1958 | 14/03/1989 | 12/06/1989 |
| Armenia | (a), (c) | | 29/12/1997(*) | 29/03/1998 |
| Australia | | | 26/03/1975(*) | 24/06/1975 |
| Austria | | | 02/05/1961(*) | 31/07/1961 |
| Azerbaijan | | | 29/02/2000(*) | 29/05/2000 |
| Bahamas | | | 20/12/2006(*) | 20/03/2007 |
| Bahrain | (a), (c) | | 06/04/1988(*) | 05/07/1988 |
| Bangladesh | | | 06/05/1992(*) | 04/08/1992 |
| Barbados | (a), (c) | | 16/03/1993(*) | 14/06/1993 |
| Belarus | (b) | 29/12/1958 | 15/11/1960 | 13/02/1961 |
| Belgium | (a) | 10/06/1958 | 18/08/1975 | 16/11/1975 |
| Benin | | | 16/05/1974(*) | 14/08/1974 |
| Bhutan | (a), (c) | | 25/09/2014(*) | 24/12/2014 |
| Bolivia (Plurinational State of) | | | 28/04/1995(*) | 27/07/1995 |
| Bosnia and Herzegovina | (a), (c), (i) | | 01/09/1993(§) | 06/03/1992 |
| Botswana | (a), (c) | | 20/12/1971(*) | 19/03/1972 |
| Brazil | | | 07/06/2002(*) | 05/09/2002 |
| Brunei Darussalam | (a) | | 25/07/1996(*) | 23/10/1996 |
| Bulgaria | (a), (b) | 17/12/1958 | 10/10/1961 | 08/01/1962 |
| Burkina Faso | | | 23/03/1987(*) | 21/06/1987 |
| Burundi | (c) | | 23/06/2014(*) | 21/09/2014 |
| Cambodia | | | 05/01/1960(*) | 04/04/1960 |
| Cameroon | | | 19/02/1988(*) | 19/05/1988 |

| | | | | |
|---|---|---|---|---|
| Canada | (d) | | 12/05/1986(*) | 10/08/1986 |
| Central African Republic | (a), (c) | | 15/10/1962(*) | 13/01/1963 |
| Chile | | | 04/09/1975(*) | 03/12/1975 |
| China | (a), (c), (h) | | 22/01/1987(*) | 22/04/1987 |
| Colombia | | | 25/09/1979(*) | 24/12/1979 |
| Cook Islands | | | 12/01/2009(*) | 12/04/2009 |
| Costa Rica | | 10/06/1958 | 26/10/1987 | 24/01/1988 |
| Côte d'Ivoire | | | 01/02/1991(*) | 02/05/1991 |
| Croatia | (a), (c), (i) | | 26/07/1993(§) | 08/10/1991 |
| Cuba | (a), (c) | | 30/12/1974(*) | 30/03/1975 |
| Cyprus | (a), (c) | | 29/12/1980(*) | 29/03/1981 |
| Czech Republic | (a), (b) | | 30/09/1993(§) | 01/01/1993 |
| Democratic Republic of the Congo | | | 05/11/2014(*) | 03/02/2015 |
| Denmark | (a), (c), (f) | | 22/12/1972(*) | 22/03/1973 |
| Djibouti | (a), (c) | | 14/06/1983(§) | 27/06/1977 |
| Dominica | | | 28/10/1988(*) | 26/01/1989 |
| Dominican Republic | | | 11/04/2002(*) | 10/07/2002 |
| Ecuador | (a), (c) | 17/12/1958 | 03/01/1962 | 03/04/1962 |
| Egypt | | | 09/03/1959(*) | 07/06/1959 |
| El Salvador | | 10/06/1958 | 26/02/1998 | 27/05/1998 |
| Estonia | | | 30/08/1993(*) | 28/11/1993 |
| Fiji | | | 27/09/2010(*) | 26/12/2010 |
| Finland | | 29/12/1958 | 19/01/1962 | 19/04/1962 |
| France | (a) | 25/11/1958 | 26/06/1959 | 24/09/1959 |
| Gabon | | | 15/12/2006(*) | 15/03/2007 |
| Georgia | | | 02/06/1994(*) | 31/08/1994 |
| Germany | | 10/06/1958 | 30/06/1961 | 28/09/1961 |
| Ghana | | | 09/04/1968(*) | 08/07/1968 |
| Greece | (a), (c) | | 16/07/1962(*) | 14/10/1962 |
| Guatemala | (a), (c) | | 21/03/1984(*) | 19/06/1984 |
| Guinea | | | 23/01/1991(*) | 23/04/1991 |
| Guyana | | | 25/09/2014(*) | 24/12/2014 |
| Haiti | | | 05/12/1983(*) | 04/03/1984 |
| Holy See | (a), (c) | | 14/05/1975(*) | 12/08/1975 |
| Honduras | (a), (c) | | 03/10/2000(*) | 01/01/2001 |

| | | | | |
|---|---|---|---|---|
| Hungary | (a), (c) | | 05/03/1962(*) | 03/06/1962 |
| Iceland | | | 24/01/2002(*) | 24/04/2002 |
| India | (a), (c) | 10/06/1958 | 13/07/1960 | 11/10/1960 |
| Indonesia | (a), (c) | | 07/10/1981(*) | 05/01/1982 |
| Iran (Islamic Republic of) | (a), (c) | | 15/10/2001(*) | 13/01/2002 |
| Ireland | (a) | | 12/05/1981(*) | 10/08/1981 |
| Israel | | 10/06/1958 | 05/01/1959 | 07/06/1959 |
| Italy | | | 31/01/1969(*) | 01/05/1969 |
| Jamaica | (a), (c) | | 10/07/2002(*) | 08/10/2002 |
| Japan | (a) | | 20/06/1961(*) | 18/09/1961 |
| Jordan | | 10/06/1958 | 15/11/1979 | 13/02/1980 |
| Kazakhstan | | | 20/11/1995(*) | 18/02/1996 |
| Kenya | (a) | | 10/02/1989(*) | 11/05/1989 |
| Kuwait | (a) | | 28/04/1978(*) | 27/07/1978 |
| Kyrgyzstan | | | 18/12/1996(*) | 18/03/1997 |
| Lao People's Democratic Republic | | | 17/06/1998(*) | 15/09/1998 |
| Latvia | | | 14/04/1992(*) | 13/07/1992 |
| Lebanon | (a) | | 11/08/1998(*) | 09/11/1998 |
| Lesotho | | | 13/06/1989(*) | 11/09/1989 |
| Liberia | | | 16/09/2005(*) | 15/12/2005 |
| Liechtenstein | (a) | | 07/07/2011(*) | 05/10/2011 |
| Lithuania | (b) | | 14/03/1995(*) | 12/06/1995 |
| Luxembourg | (a) | 11/11/1958 | 09/09/1983 | 08/12/1983 |
| Madagascar | (a), (c) | | 16/07/1962(*) | 14/10/1962 |
| Malaysia | (a), (c) | | 05/11/1985(*) | 03/02/1986 |
| Mali | | | 08/09/1994(*) | 07/12/1994 |
| Malta | (a), (i) | | 22/06/2000(*) | 20/09/2000 |
| Marshall Islands | | | 21/12/2006(*) | 21/03/2007 |
| Mauritania | | | 30/01/1997(*) | 30/04/1997 |
| Mauritius | | | 19/06/1996(*) | 17/09/1996 |
| Mexico | | | 14/04/1971(*) | 13/07/1971 |
| Monaco | (a), (c) | 31/12/1958 | 02/06/1982 | 31/08/1982 |
| Mongolia | (a), (c) | | 24/10/1994(*) | 22/01/1995 |
| Montenegro | (a), (c), (i) | | 23/10/2006(§) | 03/06/2006 |
| Morocco | (a) | | 12/02/1959(*) | 07/06/1959 |
| Mozambique | (a) | | 11/06/1998(*) | 09/09/1998 |

APPENDIX 10 - UNCITRAL MODEL LAW    635

| Myanmar | | | 16/04/2013(*) | 15/07/2013 |
|---|---|---|---|---|
| Nepal | (a), (c) | | 04/03/1998(*) | 02/06/1998 |
| Netherlands | (a), (e) | 10/06/1958 | 24/04/1964 | 23/07/1964 |
| New Zealand | (a) | | 06/01/1983(*) | 06/04/1983 |
| Nicaragua | | | 24/09/2003(*) | 23/12/2003 |
| Niger | | | 14/10/1964(*) | 12/01/1965 |
| Nigeria | (a), (c) | | 17/03/1970(*) | 15/06/1970 |
| Norway | (a), (j) | | 14/03/1961(*) | 12/06/1961 |
| Oman | | | 25/02/1999(*) | 26/05/1999 |
| Pakistan | (a) | 30/12/1958 | 14/07/2005 | 12/10/2005 |
| Panama | | | 10/10/1984(*) | 08/01/1985 |
| Paraguay | | | 08/10/1997(*) | 06/01/1998 |
| Peru | | | 07/07/1988(*) | 05/10/1988 |
| Philippines | (a), (c) | 10/06/1958 | 06/07/1967 | 04/10/1967 |
| Poland | (a), (c) | 10/06/1958 | 03/10/1961 | 01/01/1962 |
| Portugal | (a) | | 18/10/1994(*) | 16/01/1995 |
| Qatar | | | 30/12/2002(*) | 30/03/2003 |
| Republic of Korea | (a), (c) | | 08/02/1973(*) | 09/05/1973 |
| Republic of Moldova | (a), (i) | | 18/09/1998(*) | 17/12/1998 |
| Romania | (a), (b), (c) | | 13/09/1961(*) | 12/12/1961 |
| Russian Federation | (b) | 29/12/1958 | 24/08/1960 | 22/11/1960 |
| Rwanda | | | 31/10/2008(*) | 29/01/2009 |
| Saint Vincent and the Grenadines | (a), (c) | | 12/09/2000(*) | 11/12/2000 |
| San Marino | | | 17/05/1979(*) | 15/08/1979 |
| Sao Tome and Principe | | | 20/11/2012(*) | 18/02/2013 |
| Saudi Arabia | (a) | | 19/04/1994(*) | 18/07/1994 |
| Senegal | | | 17/10/1994(*) | 15/01/1995 |
| Serbia | (a), (c), (i) | | 12/03/2001(§) | 27/04/1992 |
| Singapore | (a) | | 21/08/1986(*) | 19/11/1986 |
| Slovakia | (a), (b) | | 28/05/1993(§) | 01/01/1993 |
| Slovenia | (i) | | 06/07/1992(§) | 25/06/1991 |
| South Africa | | | 03/05/1976(*) | 01/08/1976 |
| Spain | | | 12/05/1977(*) | 10/08/1977 |
| Sri Lanka | | 30/12/1958 | 09/04/1962 | 08/07/1962 |

| | | | | |
|---|---|---|---|---|
| Sweden | | 23/12/1958 | 28/01/1972 | 27/04/1972 |
| Switzerland | | 29/12/1958 | 01/06/1965 | 30/08/1965 |
| Syrian Arab Republic | | | 09/03/1959(*) | 07/06/1959 |
| Tajikistan | (a), (i), (j) | | 14/08/2012(*) | 12/11/2012 |
| Thailand | | | 21/12/1959(*) | 20/03/1960 |
| The former Yugoslav Republic of Macedonia | (c), (i) | | 10/03/1994(§) | 17/11/1991 |
| Trinidad and Tobago | (a), (c) | | 14/02/1966(*) | 15/05/1966 |
| Tunisia | (a), (c) | | 17/07/1967(*) | 15/10/1967 |
| Turkey | (a), (c) | | 02/07/1992(*) | 30/09/1992 |
| Uganda | (a) | | 12/02/1992(*) | 12/05/1992 |
| Ukraine | (b) | 29/12/1958 | 10/10/1960 | 08/01/1961 |
| United Arab Emirates | | | 21/08/2006(*) | 19/11/2006 |
| United Kingdom of Great Britain and Northern Ireland | (a), (g) | | 24/09/1975(*) | 23/12/1975 |
| United Republic of Tanzania | (a) | | 13/10/1964(*) | 11/01/1965 |
| United States of America | (a), (c) | | 30/09/1970(*) | 29/12/1970 |
| Uruguay | | | 30/03/1983(*) | 28/06/1983 |
| Uzbekistan | | | 07/02/1996(*) | 07/05/1996 |
| Venezuela (Bolivarian Republic of) | (a), (c) | | 08/02/1995(*) | 09/05/1995 |
| Viet Nam | (a), (b), (c) | | 12/09/1995(*) | 11/12/1995 |
| Zambia | | | 14/03/2002(*) | 12/06/2002 |
| Zimbabwe | | | 29/09/1994(*) | 28/12/1994 |

**Parties: 153**

**Notes**

**Declarations or other notifications pursuant to article I(3) and article X(1)**

(a) This State will apply the Convention only to recognition and enforcement of awards made in the territory of another contracting State.

(b) With regard to awards made in the territory of non-contracting States, this State will apply the Convention only to the extent to which those States grant reciprocal treatment.

(c) This State will apply the Convention only to differences arising out of legal relationships, whether contractual or not, that are considered commercial under the national law.

(d) Canada declared that it would apply the Convention only to differences arising out of legal relationships, whether contractual or not, that were considered commercial under the laws of Canada, except in the case of the Province of Quebec, where the law did not provide for such limitation.

(e) On 24 April 1964, the Netherlands declared that the Convention shall apply to the Netherlands Antilles.

(f) On 10 February 1976, Denmark declared that the Convention shall apply to the Faeroe Islands and Greenland.

(g) On 24 February 2014, the United Kingdom submitted a notification to extend territorial application of the Convention to the British Virgin Islands. For the following territories, the United Kingdom has submitted notifications extending territorial application and declaring that the Convention shall apply only to the recognition and enforcement of awards made in the territory of another Contracting State: Gibraltar (24 September 1975), Isle of Man (22 February 1979), Bermuda (14 November 1979), Cayman Islands (26 November 1980), Guernsey (19 April 1985), Bailiwick of Jersey (28 May 2002).

(h) Upon resumption of sovereignty over Hong Kong on 1 July 1997, the Government of China extended the territorial application of the Convention to Hong Kong, Special Administrative Region of China, subject to the statement originally made by China upon accession to the Convention. On 19 July 2005, China declared that the Convention shall apply to the Macao Special Administrative Region of China, subject to the statement originally made by China upon accession to the Convention.

**Reservations or other notifications**

(i) This State formulated a reservation with regards to retroactive application of the Convention.

(j) This State formulated a reservation with regards to the application of the Convention in cases concerning immovable property.

# Part One

## UNCITRAL Model Law on International Commercial Arbitration

(United Nations documents A/40/17,
annex I and A/61/17, annex I)

**(As adopted by the United Nations Commission on
International Trade Law on 21 June 1985,
and as amended by the United Nations Commission
on International Trade Law on 7 July 2006)**

### CHAPTER I. GENERAL PROVISIONS

### *Article 1. Scope of application*[1]

(1) This Law applies to international commercial[2] arbitration, subject to any agreement in force between this State and any other State or States.

(2) The provisions of this Law, except articles 8, 9, 17 H, 17 I, 17 J, 35 and 36, apply only if the place of arbitration is in the territory of this State.

*(Article 1(2) has been amended by the Commission at its
thirty-ninth session, in 2006)*

(3) An arbitration is international if:

*(a)* the parties to an arbitration agreement have, at the time of the conclusion of that agreement, their places of business in different States; or

*(b)* one of the following places is situated outside the State in which the parties have their places of business:

(i) the place of arbitration if determined in, or pursuant to, the arbitration agreement;

---

[1] Article headings are for reference purposes only and are not to be used for purposes of interpretation.

[2] The term "commercial" should be given a wide interpretation so as to cover matters arising from all relationships of a commercial nature, whether contractual or not. Relationships of a commercial nature include, but are not limited to, the following transactions: any trade transaction for the supply or exchange of goods or services; distribution agreement; commercial representation or agency; factoring; leasing; construction of works; consulting; engineering; licensing; investment; financing; banking; insurance; exploitation agreement or concession; joint venture and other forms of industrial or business cooperation; carriage of goods or passengers by air, sea, rail or road.

(ii) any place where a substantial part of the obligations of the commercial relationship is to be performed or the place with which the subject-matter of the dispute is most closely connected; or

*(c)* the parties have expressly agreed that the subject matter of the arbitration agreement relates to more than one country.

(4) For the purposes of paragraph (3) of this article:

*(a)* if a party has more than one place of business, the place of business is that which has the closest relationship to the arbitration agreement;

*(b)* if a party does not have a place of business, reference is to be made to his habitual residence.

(5) This Law shall not affect any other law of this State by virtue of which certain disputes may not be submitted to arbitration or may be submitted to arbitration only according to provisions other than those of this Law.

### Article 2. Definitions and rules of interpretation

For the purposes of this Law:

*(a)* "arbitration" means any arbitration whether or not administered by a permanent arbitral institution;

*(b)* "arbitral tribunal" means a sole arbitrator or a panel of arbitrators;

*(c)* "court" means a body or organ of the judicial system of a State;

*(d)* where a provision of this Law, except article 28, leaves the parties free to determine a certain issue, such freedom includes the right of the parties to authorize a third party, including an institution, to make that determination;

*(e)* where a provision of this Law refers to the fact that the parties have agreed or that they may agree or in any other way refers to an agreement of the parties, such agreement includes any arbitration rules referred to in that agreement;

*(f)* where a provision of this Law, other than in articles 25*(a)* and 32(2) *(a)*, refers to a claim, it also applies to a counter-claim, and where it refers to a defence, it also applies to a defence to such counter-claim.

### Article 2 A. International origin and general principles
*(As adopted by the Commission at its thirty-ninth session, in 2006)*

(1) In the interpretation of this Law, regard is to be had to its international origin and to the need to promote uniformity in its application and the observance of good faith.

(2) Questions concerning matters governed by this Law which are not expressly settled in it are to be settled in conformity with the general principles on which this Law is based.

### Article 3. Receipt of written communications

(1) Unless otherwise agreed by the parties:

 (a) any written communication is deemed to have been received if it is delivered to the addressee personally or if it is delivered at his place of business, habitual residence or mailing address; if none of these can be found after making a reasonable inquiry, a written communication is deemed to have been received if it is sent to the addressee's last-known place of business, habitual residence or mailing address by registered letter or any other means which provides a record of the attempt to deliver it;

 (b) the communication is deemed to have been received on the day it is so delivered.

(2) The provisions of this article do not apply to communications in court proceedings.

### Article 4. Waiver of right to object

A party who knows that any provision of this Law from which the parties may derogate or any requirement under the arbitration agreement has not been complied with and yet proceeds with the arbitration without stating his objection to such non-compliance without undue delay or, if a time-limit is provided therefor, within such period of time, shall be deemed to have waived his right to object.

### Article 5. Extent of court intervention

In matters governed by this Law, no court shall intervene except where so provided in this Law.

### Article 6. Court or other authority for certain functions of arbitration assistance and supervision

The functions referred to in articles 11(3), 11(4), 13(3), 14, 16(3) and 34(2) shall be performed by ... [Each State enacting this model law specifies the court, courts or, where referred to therein, other authority competent to perform these functions.]

## CHAPTER II. ARBITRATION AGREEMENT

*Option I*

### Article 7. Definition and form of arbitration agreement
*(As adopted by the Commission at its thirty-ninth session, in 2006)*

(1) "Arbitration agreement" is an agreement by the parties to submit to arbitration all or certain disputes which have arisen or which may arise between them in respect of a defined legal relationship, whether contractual or not. An arbitration agreement may be in the form of an arbitration clause in a contract or in the form of a separate agreement.

(2) The arbitration agreement shall be in writing.

(3) An arbitration agreement is in writing if its content is recorded in any form, whether or not the arbitration agreement or contract has been concluded orally, by conduct, or by other means.

(4) The requirement that an arbitration agreement be in writing is met by an electronic communication if the information contained therein is accessible so as to be useable for subsequent reference; "electronic communication" means any communication that the parties make by means of data messages; "data message" means information generated, sent, received or stored by electronic, magnetic, optical or similar means, including, but not limited to, electronic data interchange (EDI), electronic mail, telegram, telex or telecopy.

(5) Furthermore, an arbitration agreement is in writing if it is contained in an exchange of statements of claim and defence in which the existence of an agreement is alleged by one party and not denied by the other.

(6) The reference in a contract to any document containing an arbitration clause constitutes an arbitration agreement in writing, provided that the reference is such as to make that clause part of the contract.

*Option II*

### Article 7. Definition of arbitration agreement
*(As adopted by the Commission at its thirty-ninth session, in 2006)*

"Arbitration agreement" is an agreement by the parties to submit to arbitration all or certain disputes which have arisen or which may arise between them in respect of a defined legal relationship, whether contractual or not.

### Article 8. Arbitration agreement and substantive claim before court

(1) A court before which an action is brought in a matter which is the subject of an arbitration agreement shall, if a party so requests not later than when submitting his first statement on the substance of the dispute, refer the parties to arbitration unless it finds that the agreement is null and void, inoperative or incapable of being performed.

(2) Where an action referred to in paragraph (1) of this article has been brought, arbitral proceedings may nevertheless be commenced or continued, and an award may be made, while the issue is pending before the court.

### Article 9. Arbitration agreement and interim measures by court

It is not incompatible with an arbitration agreement for a party to request, before or during arbitral proceedings, from a court an interim measure of protection and for a court to grant such measure.

## CHAPTER III. COMPOSITION OF ARBITRAL TRIBUNAL

### Article 10. Number of arbitrators

(1) The parties are free to determine the number of arbitrators.

(2) Failing such determination, the number of arbitrators shall be three.

### Article 11. Appointment of arbitrators

(1) No person shall be precluded by reason of his nationality from acting as an arbitrator, unless otherwise agreed by the parties.

(2) The parties are free to agree on a procedure of appointing the arbitrator or arbitrators, subject to the provisions of paragraphs (4) and (5) of this article.

(3) Failing such agreement,

*(a)* in an arbitration with three arbitrators, each party shall appoint one arbitrator, and the two arbitrators thus appointed shall appoint the third arbitrator; if a party fails to appoint the arbitrator within thirty days of receipt of a request to do so from the other party, or if the two arbitrators fail to agree on the third arbitrator within thirty days of their appointment, the appointment shall be made, upon request of a party, by the court or other authority specified in article 6;

*(b)* in an arbitration with a sole arbitrator, if the parties are unable to agree on the arbitrator, he shall be appointed, upon request of a party, by the court or other authority specified in article 6.

(4) Where, under an appointment procedure agreed upon by the parties,

*(a)* a party fails to act as required under such procedure, or

*(b)* the parties, or two arbitrators, are unable to reach an agreement expected of them under such procedure, or

*(c)* a third party, including an institution, fails to perform any function entrusted to it under such procedure,

any party may request the court or other authority specified in article 6 to take the necessary measure, unless the agreement on the appointment procedure provides other means for securing the appointment.

(5) A decision on a matter entrusted by paragraph (3) or (4) of this article to the court or other authority specified in article 6 shall be subject to no appeal. The court or other authority, in appointing an arbitrator, shall have due regard to any qualifications required of the arbitrator by the agreement of the parties and to such considerations as are likely to secure the appointment of an independent and impartial arbitrator and, in the case of a sole or third arbitrator, shall take into account as well the advisability of appointing an arbitrator of a nationality other than those of the parties.

## Article 12. Grounds for challenge

(1) When a person is approached in connection with his possible appointment as an arbitrator, he shall disclose any circumstances likely to give rise to justifiable doubts as to his impartiality or independence. An arbitrator, from the time of his appointment and throughout the arbitral proceedings, shall without delay disclose any such circumstances to the parties unless they have already been informed of them by him.

(2) An arbitrator may be challenged only if circumstances exist that give rise to justifiable doubts as to his impartiality or independence, or if he does not possess qualifications agreed to by the parties. A party may challenge an arbitrator appointed by him, or in whose appointment he has participated, only for reasons of which he becomes aware after the appointment has been made.

## Article 13. Challenge procedure

(1) The parties are free to agree on a procedure for challenging an arbitrator, subject to the provisions of paragraph (3) of this article.

(2) Failing such agreement, a party who intends to challenge an arbitrator shall, within fifteen days after becoming aware of the constitution of the arbitral tribunal or after becoming aware of any circumstance referred to in article 12(2), send a written statement of the reasons for the challenge to the arbitral tribunal. Unless the challenged arbitrator withdraws from his office or the other party agrees to the challenge, the arbitral tribunal shall decide on the challenge.

(3) If a challenge under any procedure agreed upon by the parties or under the procedure of paragraph (2) of this article is not successful, the challenging party may request, within thirty days after having received notice of the decision rejecting the challenge, the court or other authority specified in article 6 to decide on the challenge, which decision shall be subject to no appeal; while such a request is pending, the arbitral tribunal, including the challenged arbitrator, may continue the arbitral proceedings and make an award.

## Article 14. Failure or impossibility to act

(1) If an arbitrator becomes *de jure* or *de facto* unable to perform his functions or for other reasons fails to act without undue delay, his mandate terminates if he withdraws from his office or if the parties agree on the termination. Otherwise, if a controversy remains concerning any of these grounds, any party may request the court or other authority specified in article 6 to decide on the termination of the mandate, which decision shall be subject to no appeal.

(2) If, under this article or article 13(2), an arbitrator withdraws from his office or a party agrees to the termination of the mandate of an arbitrator, this does not imply acceptance of the validity of any ground referred to in this article or article 12(2).

### Article 15. Appointment of substitute arbitrator

Where the mandate of an arbitrator terminates under article 13 or 14 or because of his withdrawal from office for any other reason or because of the revocation of his mandate by agreement of the parties or in any other case of termination of his mandate, a substitute arbitrator shall be appointed according to the rules that were applicable to the appointment of the arbitrator being replaced.

## CHAPTER IV. JURISDICTION OF ARBITRAL TRIBUNAL

### Article 16. Competence of arbitral tribunal to rule on its jurisdiction

(1) The arbitral tribunal may rule on its own jurisdiction, including any objections with respect to the existence or validity of the arbitration agreement. For that purpose, an arbitration clause which forms part of a contract shall be treated as an agreement independent of the other terms of the contract. A decision by the arbitral tribunal that the contract is null and void shall not entail *ipso jure* the invalidity of the arbitration clause.

(2) A plea that the arbitral tribunal does not have jurisdiction shall be raised not later than the submission of the statement of defence. A party is not precluded from raising such a plea by the fact that he has appointed, or participated in the appointment of, an arbitrator. A plea that the arbitral tribunal is exceeding the scope of its authority shall be raised as soon as the matter alleged to be beyond the scope of its authority is raised during the arbitral proceedings. The arbitral tribunal may, in either case, admit a later plea if it considers the delay justified.

(3) The arbitral tribunal may rule on a plea referred to in paragraph (2) of this article either as a preliminary question or in an award on the merits. If the arbitral tribunal rules as a preliminary question that it has jurisdiction, any party may request, within thirty days after having received notice of that ruling, the court specified in article 6 to decide the matter, which decision shall be subject to no appeal; while such a request is pending, the arbitral tribunal may continue the arbitral proceedings and make an award.

## CHAPTER IV A. INTERIM MEASURES AND PRELIMINARY ORDERS
*(As adopted by the Commission at its thirty-ninth session, in 2006)*

### Section 1. Interim measures

### Article 17. Power of arbitral tribunal to order interim measures

(1) Unless otherwise agreed by the parties, the arbitral tribunal may, at the request of a party, grant interim measures.

(2) An interim measure is any temporary measure, whether in the form of an award or in another form, by which, at any time prior to the issuance of the award by which the dispute is finally decided, the arbitral tribunal orders a party to:

*(a)* Maintain or restore the status quo pending determination of the dispute;

*(b)* Take action that would prevent, or refrain from taking action that is likely to cause, current or imminent harm or prejudice to the arbitral process itself;

*(c)* Provide a means of preserving assets out of which a subsequent award may be satisfied; or

*(d)* Preserve evidence that may be relevant and material to the resolution of the dispute.

### *Article 17 A. Conditions for granting interim measures*

(1) The party requesting an interim measure under article 17(2)*(a)*, *(b)* and *(c)* shall satisfy the arbitral tribunal that:

*(a)* Harm not adequately reparable by an award of damages is likely to result if the measure is not ordered, and such harm substantially outweighs the harm that is likely to result to the party against whom the measure is directed if the measure is granted; and

*(b)* There is a reasonable possibility that the requesting party will succeed on the merits of the claim. The determination on this possibility shall not affect the discretion of the arbitral tribunal in making any subsequent determination.

(2) With regard to a request for an interim measure under article 17(2)*(d)*, the requirements in paragraphs (1)*(a)* and *(b)* of this article shall apply only to the extent the arbitral tribunal considers appropriate.

### *Section 2. Preliminary orders*

### *Article 17 B. Applications for preliminary orders and conditions for granting preliminary orders*

(1) Unless otherwise agreed by the parties, a party may, without notice to any other party, make a request for an interim measure together with an application for a preliminary order directing a party not to frustrate the purpose of the interim measure requested.

(2) The arbitral tribunal may grant a preliminary order provided it considers that prior disclosure of the request for the interim measure to the party against whom it is directed risks frustrating the purpose of the measure.

(3) The conditions defined under article 17A apply to any preliminary order, provided that the harm to be assessed under article 17A(1)*(a)*, is the harm likely to result from the order being granted or not.

### *Article 17 C. Specific regime for preliminary orders*

(1) Immediately after the arbitral tribunal has made a determination in respect of an application for a preliminary order, the arbitral tribunal shall give notice to

all parties of the request for the interim measure, the application for the preliminary order, the preliminary order, if any, and all other communications, including by indicating the content of any oral communication, between any party and the arbitral tribunal in relation thereto.

(2) At the same time, the arbitral tribunal shall give an opportunity to any party against whom a preliminary order is directed to present its case at the earliest practicable time.

(3) The arbitral tribunal shall decide promptly on any objection to the preliminary order.

(4) A preliminary order shall expire after twenty days from the date on which it was issued by the arbitral tribunal. However, the arbitral tribunal may issue an interim measure adopting or modifying the preliminary order, after the party against whom the preliminary order is directed has been given notice and an opportunity to present its case.

(5) A preliminary order shall be binding on the parties but shall not be subject to enforcement by a court. Such a preliminary order does not constitute an award.

## Section 3. Provisions applicable to interim measures and preliminary orders

### Article 17 D. Modification, suspension, termination

The arbitral tribunal may modify, suspend or terminate an interim measure or a preliminary order it has granted, upon application of any party or, in exceptional circumstances and upon prior notice to the parties, on the arbitral tribunal's own initiative.

### Article 17 E. Provision of security

(1) The arbitral tribunal may require the party requesting an interim measure to provide appropriate security in connection with the measure.

(2) The arbitral tribunal shall require the party applying for a preliminary order to provide security in connection with the order unless the arbitral tribunal considers it inappropriate or unnecessary to do so.

### Article 17 F. Disclosure

(1) The arbitral tribunal may require any party promptly to disclose any material change in the circumstances on the basis of which the measure was requested or granted.

(2) The party applying for a preliminary order shall disclose to the arbitral tribunal all circumstances that are likely to be relevant to the arbitral tribunal's determination whether to grant or maintain the order, and such obligation shall continue until the party against whom the order has been requested has had an opportunity to present its case. Thereafter, paragraph (1) of this article shall apply.

## Article 17 G. Costs and damages

The party requesting an interim measure or applying for a preliminary order shall be liable for any costs and damages caused by the measure or the order to any party if the arbitral tribunal later determines that, in the circumstances, the measure or the order should not have been granted. The arbitral tribunal may award such costs and damages at any point during the proceedings.

### Section 4. Recognition and enforcement of interim measures

## Article 17 H. Recognition and enforcement

(1) An interim measure issued by an arbitral tribunal shall be recognized as binding and, unless otherwise provided by the arbitral tribunal, enforced upon application to the competent court, irrespective of the country in which it was issued, subject to the provisions of article 17 I.

(2) The party who is seeking or has obtained recognition or enforcement of an interim measure shall promptly inform the court of any termination, suspension or modification of that interim measure.

(3) The court of the State where recognition or enforcement is sought may, if it considers it proper, order the requesting party to provide appropriate security if the arbitral tribunal has not already made a determination with respect to security or where such a decision is necessary to protect the rights of third parties.

## Article 17 I. Grounds for refusing recognition or enforcement[3]

(1) Recognition or enforcement of an interim measure may be refused only:

*(a)* At the request of the party against whom it is invoked if the court is satisfied that:

  (i) Such refusal is warranted on the grounds set forth in article 36(1)*(a)* (i), (ii), (iii) or (iv); or

  (ii) The arbitral tribunal's decision with respect to the provision of security in connection with the interim measure issued by the arbitral tribunal has not been complied with; or

  (iii) The interim measure has been terminated or suspended by the arbitral tribunal or, where so empowered, by the court of the State in which the arbitration takes place or under the law of which that interim measure was granted; or

---

[3] The conditions set forth in article 17 I are intended to limit the number of circumstances in which the court may refuse to enforce an interim measure. It would not be contrary to the level of harmonization sought to be achieved by these model provisions if a State were to adopt fewer circumstances in which enforcement may be refused.

*(b)* If the court finds that:

  (i) The interim measure is incompatible with the powers conferred upon the court unless the court decides to reformulate the interim measure to the extent necessary to adapt it to its own powers and procedures for the purposes of enforcing that interim measure and without modifying its substance; or

  (ii) Any of the grounds set forth in article 36(1)*(b)*(i) or (ii), apply to the recognition and enforcement of the interim measure.

(2) Any determination made by the court on any ground in paragraph (1) of this article shall be effective only for the purposes of the application to recognize and enforce the interim measure. The court where recognition or enforcement is sought shall not, in making that determination, undertake a review of the substance of the interim measure.

### Section 5. Court-ordered interim measures

### Article 17 J. Court-ordered interim measures

A court shall have the same power of issuing an interim measure in relation to arbitration proceedings, irrespective of whether their place is in the territory of this State, as it has in relation to proceedings in courts. The court shall exercise such power in accordance with its own procedures in consideration of the specific features of international arbitration.

## CHAPTER V. CONDUCT OF ARBITRAL PROCEEDINGS

### Article 18. Equal treatment of parties

The parties shall be treated with equality and each party shall be given a full opportunity of presenting his case.

### Article 19. Determination of rules of procedure

(1) Subject to the provisions of this Law, the parties are free to agree on the procedure to be followed by the arbitral tribunal in conducting the proceedings.

(2) Failing such agreement, the arbitral tribunal may, subject to the provisions of this Law, conduct the arbitration in such manner as it considers appropriate. The power conferred upon the arbitral tribunal includes the power to determine the admissibility, relevance, materiality and weight of any evidence.

### Article 20. Place of arbitration

(1) The parties are free to agree on the place of arbitration. Failing such agreement, the place of arbitration shall be determined by the arbitral tribunal having regard to the circumstances of the case, including the convenience of the parties.

(2) Notwithstanding the provisions of paragraph (1) of this article, the arbitral tribunal may, unless otherwise agreed by the parties, meet at any place it considers appropriate for consultation among its members, for hearing witnesses, experts or the parties, or for inspection of goods, other property or documents.

### Article 21. Commencement of arbitral proceedings

Unless otherwise agreed by the parties, the arbitral proceedings in respect of a particular dispute commence on the date on which a request for that dispute to be referred to arbitration is received by the respondent.

### Article 22. Language

(1) The parties are free to agree on the language or languages to be used in the arbitral proceedings. Failing such agreement, the arbitral tribunal shall determine the language or languages to be used in the proceedings. This agreement or determination, unless otherwise specified therein, shall apply to any written statement by a party, any hearing and any award, decision or other communication by the arbitral tribunal.

(2) The arbitral tribunal may order that any documentary evidence shall be accompanied by a translation into the language or languages agreed upon by the parties or determined by the arbitral tribunal.

### Article 23. Statements of claim and defence

(1) Within the period of time agreed by the parties or determined by the arbitral tribunal, the claimant shall state the facts supporting his claim, the points at issue and the relief or remedy sought, and the respondent shall state his defence in respect of these particulars, unless the parties have otherwise agreed as to the required elements of such statements. The parties may submit with their statements all documents they consider to be relevant or may add a reference to the documents or other evidence they will submit.

(2) Unless otherwise agreed by the parties, either party may amend or supplement his claim or defence during the course of the arbitral proceedings, unless the arbitral tribunal considers it inappropriate to allow such amendment having regard to the delay in making it.

### Article 24. Hearings and written proceedings

(1) Subject to any contrary agreement by the parties, the arbitral tribunal shall decide whether to hold oral hearings for the presentation of evidence or for oral argument, or whether the proceedings shall be conducted on the basis of documents and other materials. However, unless the parties have agreed that no hearings shall be held, the arbitral tribunal shall hold such hearings at an appropriate stage of the proceedings, if so requested by a party.

(2) The parties shall be given sufficient advance notice of any hearing and of any meeting of the arbitral tribunal for the purposes of inspection of goods, other property or documents.

(3) All statements, documents or other information supplied to the arbitral tribunal by one party shall be communicated to the other party. Also any expert report or evidentiary document on which the arbitral tribunal may rely in making its decision shall be communicated to the parties.

### Article 25. *Default of a party*

Unless otherwise agreed by the parties, if, without showing sufficient cause,

*(a)* the claimant fails to communicate his statement of claim in accordance with article 23(1), the arbitral tribunal shall terminate the proceedings;

*(b)* the respondent fails to communicate his statement of defence in accordance with article 23(1), the arbitral tribunal shall continue the proceedings without treating such failure in itself as an admission of the claimant's allegations;

*(c)* any party fails to appear at a hearing or to produce documentary evidence, the arbitral tribunal may continue the proceedings and make the award on the evidence before it.

### Article 26. *Expert appointed by arbitral tribunal*

(1) Unless otherwise agreed by the parties, the arbitral tribunal

*(a)* may appoint one or more experts to report to it on specific issues to be determined by the arbitral tribunal;

*(b)* may require a party to give the expert any relevant information or to produce, or to provide access to, any relevant documents, goods or other property for his inspection.

(2) Unless otherwise agreed by the parties, if a party so requests or if the arbitral tribunal considers it necessary, the expert shall, after delivery of his written or oral report, participate in a hearing where the parties have the opportunity to put questions to him and to present expert witnesses in order to testify on the points at issue.

### Article 27. *Court assistance in taking evidence*

The arbitral tribunal or a party with the approval of the arbitral tribunal may request from a competent court of this State assistance in taking evidence. The court may execute the request within its competence and according to its rules on taking evidence.

## CHAPTER VI. MAKING OF AWARD AND TERMINATION OF PROCEEDINGS

### Article 28. *Rules applicable to substance of dispute*

(1) The arbitral tribunal shall decide the dispute in accordance with such rules of law as are chosen by the parties as applicable to the substance of the dispute.

Any designation of the law or legal system of a given State shall be construed, unless otherwise expressed, as directly referring to the substantive law of that State and not to its conflict of laws rules.

(2) Failing any designation by the parties, the arbitral tribunal shall apply the law determined by the conflict of laws rules which it considers applicable.

(3) The arbitral tribunal shall decide *ex aequo et bono* or as *amiable compositeur* only if the parties have expressly authorized it to do so.

(4) In all cases, the arbitral tribunal shall decide in accordance with the terms of the contract and shall take into account the usages of the trade applicable to the transaction.

## Article 29. Decision-making by panel of arbitrators

In arbitral proceedings with more than one arbitrator, any decision of the arbitral tribunal shall be made, unless otherwise agreed by the parties, by a majority of all its members. However, questions of procedure may be decided by a presiding arbitrator, if so authorized by the parties or all members of the arbitral tribunal.

## Article 30. Settlement

(1) If, during arbitral proceedings, the parties settle the dispute, the arbitral tribunal shall terminate the proceedings and, if requested by the parties and not objected to by the arbitral tribunal, record the settlement in the form of an arbitral award on agreed terms.

(2) An award on agreed terms shall be made in accordance with the provisions of article 31 and shall state that it is an award. Such an award has the same status and effect as any other award on the merits of the case.

## Article 31. Form and contents of award

(1) The award shall be made in writing and shall be signed by the arbitrator or arbitrators. In arbitral proceedings with more than one arbitrator, the signatures of the majority of all members of the arbitral tribunal shall suffice, provided that the reason for any omitted signature is stated.

(2) The award shall state the reasons upon which it is based, unless the parties have agreed that no reasons are to be given or the award is an award on agreed terms under article 30.

(3) The award shall state its date and the place of arbitration as determined in accordance with article 20(1). The award shall be deemed to have been made at that place.

(4) After the award is made, a copy signed by the arbitrators in accordance with paragraph (1) of this article shall be delivered to each party.

## Article 32. Termination of proceedings

(1) The arbitral proceedings are terminated by the final award or by an order of the arbitral tribunal in accordance with paragraph (2) of this article.

(2) The arbitral tribunal shall issue an order for the termination of the arbitral proceedings when:

*(a)* the claimant withdraws his claim, unless the respondent objects thereto and the arbitral tribunal recognizes a legitimate interest on his part in obtaining a final settlement of the dispute;

*(b)* the parties agree on the termination of the proceedings;

*(c)* the arbitral tribunal finds that the continuation of the proceedings has for any other reason become unnecessary or impossible.

(3) The mandate of the arbitral tribunal terminates with the termination of the arbitral proceedings, subject to the provisions of articles 33 and 34(4).

## Article 33. Correction and interpretation of award; additional award

(1) Within thirty days of receipt of the award, unless another period of time has been agreed upon by the parties:

*(a)* a party, with notice to the other party, may request the arbitral tribunal to correct in the award any errors in computation, any clerical or typographical errors or any errors of similar nature;

*(b)* if so agreed by the parties, a party, with notice to the other party, may request the arbitral tribunal to give an interpretation of a specific point or part of the award.

If the arbitral tribunal considers the request to be justified, it shall make the correction or give the interpretation within thirty days of receipt of the request. The interpretation shall form part of the award.

(2) The arbitral tribunal may correct any error of the type referred to in paragraph (1)*(a)* of this article on its own initiative within thirty days of the date of the award.

(3) Unless otherwise agreed by the parties, a party, with notice to the other party, may request, within thirty days of receipt of the award, the arbitral tribunal to make an additional award as to claims presented in the arbitral proceedings but omitted from the award. If the arbitral tribunal considers the request to be justified, it shall make the additional award within sixty days.

(4) The arbitral tribunal may extend, if necessary, the period of time within which it shall make a correction, interpretation or an additional award under paragraph (1) or (3) of this article.

(5) The provisions of article 31 shall apply to a correction or interpretation of the award or to an additional award.

## CHAPTER VII. RECOURSE AGAINST AWARD

### Article 34. Application for setting aside as exclusive recourse against arbitral award

(1)  Recourse to a court against an arbitral award may be made only by an application for setting aside in accordance with paragraphs (2) and (3) of this article.

(2)  An arbitral award may be set aside by the court specified in article 6 only if:

 *(a)* the party making the application furnishes proof that:

  (i) a party to the arbitration agreement referred to in article 7 was under some incapacity; or the said agreement is not valid under the law to which the parties have subjected it or, failing any indication thereon, under the law of this State; or

  (ii) the party making the application was not given proper notice of the appointment of an arbitrator or of the arbitral proceedings or was otherwise unable to present his case; or

  (iii) the award deals with a dispute not contemplated by or not falling within the terms of the submission to arbitration, or contains decisions on matters beyond the scope of the submission to arbitration, provided that, if the decisions on matters submitted to arbitration can be separated from those not so submitted, only that part of the award which contains decisions on matters not submitted to arbitration may be set aside; or

  (iv) the composition of the arbitral tribunal or the arbitral procedure was not in accordance with the agreement of the parties, unless such agreement was in conflict with a provision of this Law from which the parties cannot derogate, or, failing such agreement, was not in accordance with this Law; or

 *(b)* the court finds that:

  (i) the subject-matter of the dispute is not capable of settlement by arbitration under the law of this State; or

  (ii) the award is in conflict with the public policy of this State.

(3)  An application for setting aside may not be made after three months have elapsed from the date on which the party making that application had received the award or, if a request had been made under article 33, from the date on which that request had been disposed of by the arbitral tribunal.

(4)  The court, when asked to set aside an award, may, where appropriate and so requested by a party, suspend the setting aside proceedings for a period of time determined by it in order to give the arbitral tribunal an opportunity to resume the arbitral proceedings or to take such other action as in the arbitral tribunal's opinion will eliminate the grounds for setting aside.

# CHAPTER VIII. RECOGNITION AND ENFORCEMENT OF AWARDS

### Article 35. Recognition and enforcement

(1) An arbitral award, irrespective of the country in which it was made, shall be recognized as binding and, upon application in writing to the competent court, shall be enforced subject to the provisions of this article and of article 36.

(2) The party relying on an award or applying for its enforcement shall supply the original award or a copy thereof. If the award is not made in an official language of this State, the court may request the party to supply a translation thereof into such language.[4]

*(Article 35(2) has been amended by the Commission at its thirty-ninth session, in 2006)*

### Article 36. Grounds for refusing recognition or enforcement

(1) Recognition or enforcement of an arbitral award, irrespective of the country in which it was made, may be refused only:

  (a) at the request of the party against whom it is invoked, if that party furnishes to the competent court where recognition or enforcement is sought proof that:

  (i) a party to the arbitration agreement referred to in article 7 was under some incapacity; or the said agreement is not valid under the law to which the parties have subjected it or, failing any indication thereon, under the law of the country where the award was made; or

  (ii) the party against whom the award is invoked was not given proper notice of the appointment of an arbitrator or of the arbitral proceedings or was otherwise unable to present his case; or

  (iii) the award deals with a dispute not contemplated by or not falling within the terms of the submission to arbitration, or it contains decisions on matters beyond the scope of the submission to arbitration, provided that, if the decisions on matters submitted to arbitration can be separated from those not so submitted, that part of the award which contains decisions on matters submitted to arbitration may be recognized and enforced; or

  (iv) the composition of the arbitral tribunal or the arbitral procedure was not in accordance with the agreement of the parties or, failing such agreement, was not in accordance with the law of the country where the arbitration took place; or

---

[4] The conditions set forth in this paragraph are intended to set maximum standards. It would, thus, not be contrary to the harmonization to be achieved by the model law if a State retained even less onerous conditions.

(v) the award has not yet become binding on the parties or has been set aside or suspended by a court of the country in which, or under the law of which, that award was made; or

*(b)* if the court finds that:

(i) the subject-matter of the dispute is not capable of settlement by arbitration under the law of this State; or

(ii) the recognition or enforcement of the award would be contrary to the public policy of this State.

(2) If an application for setting aside or suspension of an award has been made to a court referred to in paragraph (1)*(a)*(v) of this article, the court where recognition or enforcement is sought may, if it considers it proper, adjourn its decision and may also, on the application of the party claiming recognition or enforcement of the award, order the other party to provide appropriate security.

Part Two

Explanatory Note by the UNCITRAL secretariat on the
1985 Model Law on International Commercial Arbitration
as amended in 2006[1]

1. The UNCITRAL Model Law on International Commercial Arbitration ("the Model Law") was adopted by the United Nations Commission on International Trade Law (UNCITRAL) on 21 June 1985, at the end of the eighteenth session of the Commission. The General Assembly, in its resolution 40/72 of 11 December 1985, recommended "that all States give due consideration to the Model Law on International Commercial Arbitration, in view of the desirability of uniformity of the law of arbitral procedures and the specific needs of international commercial arbitration practice". The Model Law was amended by UNCITRAL on 7 July 2006, at the thirty-ninth session of the Commission (see below, paragraphs 4, 19, 20, 27, 29 and 53). The General Assembly, in its resolution 61/33 of 4 December 2006, recommended "that all States give favourable consideration to the enactment of the revised articles of the UNCITRAL Model Law on International Commercial Arbitration, or the revised UNCITRAL Model Law on International Commercial Arbitration, when they enact or revise their laws (. . .)".

2. The Model Law constitutes a sound basis for the desired harmonization and improvement of national laws. It covers all stages of the arbitral process from the arbitration agreement to the recognition and enforcement of the arbitral award and reflects a worldwide consensus on the principles and important issues of international arbitration practice. It is acceptable to States of all regions and the different legal or economic systems of the world. Since its adoption by UNCITRAL, the Model Law has come to represent the accepted international legislative standard for a modern arbitration law and a significant number of jurisdictions have enacted arbitration legislation based on the Model Law.

3. The form of a model law was chosen as the vehicle for harmonization and modernization in view of the flexibility it gives to States in preparing new arbitration laws. Notwithstanding that flexibility, and in order to increase the likelihood of achieving a satisfactory degree of harmonization, States are encouraged to make as few changes as possible when incorporating the Model Law into their legal systems. Efforts to minimize variation from the text adopted by UNCITRAL

---

[1] This note was prepared by the secretariat of the United Nations Commission on International Trade Law (UNCITRAL) for informational purposes only; it is not an official commentary on the Model Law. A commentary prepared by the Secretariat on an early draft of the Model Law appears in document A/CN.9/264 (reproduced in UNCITRAL Yearbook, vol. XVI — 1985, United Nations publication, Sales No. E.87.V.4).

are also expected to increase the visibility of harmonization, thus enhancing the confidence of foreign parties, as the primary users of international arbitration, in the reliability of arbitration law in the enacting State.

4. The revision of the Model Law adopted in 2006 includes article 2 A, which is designed to facilitate interpretation by reference to internationally accepted principles and is aimed at promoting a uniform understanding of the Model Law. Other substantive amendments to the Model Law relate to the form of the arbitration agreement and to interim measures. The original 1985 version of the provision on the form of the arbitration agreement (article 7) was modelled on the language used in article II (2) of the Convention on the Recognition and Enforcement of Foreign Arbitral Awards (New York, 1958) ("the New York Convention"). The revision of article 7 is intended to address evolving practice in international trade and technological developments. The extensive revision of article 17 on interim measures was considered necessary in light of the fact that such measures are increasingly relied upon in the practice of international commercial arbitration. The revision also includes an enforcement regime for such measures in recognition of the fact that the effectiveness of arbitration frequently depends upon the possibility of enforcing interim measures. The new provisions are contained in a new chapter of the Model Law on interim measures and preliminary orders (chapter IV A).

## A. Background to the Model Law

5. The Model Law was developed to address considerable disparities in national laws on arbitration. The need for improvement and harmonization was based on findings that national laws were often particularly inappropriate for international cases.

### *1. Inadequacy of domestic laws*

6. Recurrent inadequacies to be found in outdated national laws include provisions that equate the arbitral process with court litigation and fragmentary provisions that fail to address all relevant substantive law issues. Even most of those laws that appear to be up-to-date and comprehensive were drafted with domestic arbitration primarily, if not exclusively, in mind. While this approach is understandable in view of the fact that even today the bulk of cases governed by arbitration law would be of a purely domestic nature, the unfortunate consequence is that traditional local concepts are imposed on international cases and the needs of modern practice are often not met.

7. The expectations of the parties as expressed in a chosen set of arbitration rules or a "one-off" arbitration agreement may be frustrated, especially by mandatory provisions of applicable law. Unexpected and undesired restrictions found in national laws may prevent the parties, for example, from submitting future disputes to arbitration, from selecting the arbitrator freely, or from having the arbitral proceedings conducted according to agreed rules of procedure and with no more court involvement than appropriate. Frustration may also ensue from

non-mandatory provisions that may impose undesired requirements on unwary parties who may not think about the need to provide otherwise when drafting the arbitration agreement. Even the absence of any legislative provision may cause difficulties simply by leaving unanswered some of the many procedural issues relevant in arbitration and not always settled in the arbitration agreement. The Model Law is intended to reduce the risk of such possible frustration, difficulties or surprise.

### 2. Disparity between national laws

8.   Problems stemming from inadequate arbitration laws or from the absence of specific legislation governing arbitration are aggravated by the fact that national laws differ widely. Such differences are a frequent source of concern in international arbitration, where at least one of the parties is, and often both parties are, confronted with foreign and unfamiliar provisions and procedures. Obtaining a full and precise account of the law applicable to the arbitration is, in such circumstances often expensive, impractical or impossible.

9.   Uncertainty about the local law with the inherent risk of frustration may adversely affect the functioning of the arbitral process and also impact on the selection of the place of arbitration. Due to such uncertainty, a party may hesitate or refuse to agree to a place, which for practical reasons would otherwise be appropriate. The range of places of arbitration acceptable to parties is thus widened and the smooth functioning of the arbitral proceedings is enhanced where States adopt the Model Law, which is easily recognizable, meets the specific needs of international commercial arbitration and provides an international standard based on solutions acceptable to parties from different legal systems.

## B. Salient features of the Model Law

### 1. Special procedural regime for international commercial arbitration

10.   The principles and solutions adopted in the Model Law aim at reducing or eliminating the above-mentioned concerns and difficulties. As a response to the inadequacies and disparities of national laws, the Model Law presents a special legal regime tailored to international commercial arbitration, without affecting any relevant treaty in force in the State adopting the Model Law. While the Model Law was designed with international commercial arbitration in mind, it offers a set of basic rules that are not, in and of themselves, unsuitable to any other type of arbitration. States may thus consider extending their enactment of the Model Law to cover also domestic disputes, as a number of enacting States already have.

#### (a) Substantive and territorial scope of application

11.   Article 1 defines the scope of application of the Model Law by reference to the notion of "international commercial arbitration". The Model Law defines an arbitration as international if "the parties to an arbitration agreement have, at the time of the conclusion of that agreement, their places of business in different

States" (article 1 (3)). The vast majority of situations commonly regarded as international will meet this criterion. In addition, article 1 (3) broadens the notion of internationality so that the Model Law also covers cases where the place of arbitration, the place of contract performance, or the place of the subject-matter of the dispute is situated outside the State where the parties have their place of business, or cases where the parties have expressly agreed that the subject-matter of the arbitration agreement relates to more than one country. Article 1 thus recognizes extensively the freedom of the parties to submit a dispute to the legal regime established pursuant to the Model Law.

12. In respect of the term "commercial", the Model Law provides no strict definition. The footnote to article 1 (1) calls for "a wide interpretation" and offers an illustrative and open-ended list of relationships that might be described as commercial in nature, "whether contractual or not". The purpose of the footnote is to circumvent any technical difficulty that may arise, for example, in determining which transactions should be governed by a specific body of "commercial law" that may exist in some legal systems.

13. Another aspect of applicability is the territorial scope of application. The principle embodied in article 1 (2) is that the Model Law as enacted in a given State applies only if the place of arbitration is in the territory of that State. However, article 1 (2) also contains important exceptions to that principle, to the effect that certain articles apply, irrespective of whether the place of arbitration is in the enacting State or elsewhere (or, as the case may be, even before the place of arbitration is determined). These articles are the following: articles 8 (1) and 9, which deal with the recognition of arbitration agreements, including their compatibility with interim measures ordered by a court, article 17 J on court-ordered interim measures, articles 17 H and 17 I on the recognition and enforcement of interim measures ordered by an arbitral tribunal, and articles 35 and 36 on the recognition and enforcement of arbitral awards.

14. The territorial criterion governing most of the provisions of the Model Law was adopted for the sake of certainty and in view of the following facts. In most legal systems, the place of arbitration is the exclusive criterion for determining the applicability of national law and, where the national law allows parties to choose the procedural law of a State other than that where the arbitration takes place, experience shows that parties rarely make use of that possibility. Incidentally, enactment of the Model Law reduces any need for the parties to choose a "foreign" law, since the Model Law grants the parties wide freedom in shaping the rules of the arbitral proceedings. In addition to designating the law governing the arbitral procedure, the territorial criterion is of considerable practical importance in respect of articles 11, 13, 14, 16, 27 and 34, which entrust State courts at the place of arbitration with functions of supervision and assistance to arbitration. It should be noted that the territorial criterion legally triggered by the parties' choice regarding the place of arbitration does not limit the arbitral tribunal's ability to meet at any place it considers appropriate for the conduct of the proceedings, as provided by article 20 (2).

## (b) Delimitation of court assistance and supervision

15. Recent amendments to arbitration laws reveal a trend in favour of limiting and clearly defining court involvement in international commercial arbitration. This is justified in view of the fact that the parties to an arbitration agreement make a conscious decision to exclude court jurisdiction and prefer the finality and expediency of the arbitral process.

16. In this spirit, the Model Law envisages court involvement in the following instances. A first group comprises issues of appointment, challenge and termination of the mandate of an arbitrator (articles 11, 13 and 14), jurisdiction of the arbitral tribunal (article 16) and setting aside of the arbitral award (article 34). These instances are listed in article 6 as functions that should be entrusted, for the sake of centralization, specialization and efficiency, to a specially designated court or, with respect to articles 11, 13 and 14, possibly to another authority (for example, an arbitral institution or a chamber of commerce). A second group comprises issues of court assistance in taking evidence (article 27), recognition of the arbitration agreement, including its compatibility with court-ordered interim measures (articles 8 and 9), court-ordered interim measures (article 17 J), and recognition and enforcement of interim measures (articles 17 H and 17 I) and of arbitral awards (articles 35 and 36).

17. Beyond the instances in these two groups, "no court shall intervene, in matters governed by this Law". Article 5 thus guarantees that all instances of possible court intervention are found in the piece of legislation enacting the Model Law, except for matters not regulated by it (for example, consolidation of arbitral proceedings, contractual relationship between arbitrators and parties or arbitral institutions, or fixing of costs and fees, including deposits). Protecting the arbitral process from unpredictable or disruptive court interference is essential to parties who choose arbitration (in particular foreign parties).

## 2. Arbitration agreement

18. Chapter II of the Model Law deals with the arbitration agreement, including its recognition by courts.

### (a) Definition and form of arbitration agreement

19. The original 1985 version of the provision on the definition and form of arbitration agreement (article 7) closely followed article II (2) of the New York Convention, which requires that an arbitration agreement be in writing. If the parties have agreed to arbitrate, but they entered into the arbitration agreement in a manner that does not meet the form requirement, any party may have grounds to object to the jurisdiction of the arbitral tribunal. It was pointed out by practitioners that, in a number of situations, the drafting of a written document was impossible or impractical. In such cases, where the willingness of the parties to arbitrate was not in question, the validity of the arbitration agreement should be recognized. For that reason, article 7 was amended in 2006 to better conform to international

contract practices. In amending article 7, the Commission adopted two options, which reflect two different approaches on the question of definition and form of arbitration agreement. The first approach follows the detailed structure of the original 1985 text. It confirms the validity and effect of a commitment by the parties to submit to arbitration an existing dispute ("*compromis*") or a future dispute ("*clause compromissoire*"). It follows the New York Convention in requiring the written form of the arbitration agreement but recognizes a record of the "contents" of the agreement "in any form" as equivalent to traditional "writing". The agreement to arbitrate may be entered into in any form (e.g. including orally) as long as the content of the agreement is recorded. This new rule is significant in that it no longer requires signatures of the parties or an exchange of messages between the parties. It modernizes the language referring to the use of electronic commerce by adopting wording inspired from the 1996 UNCITRAL Model Law on Electronic Commerce and the 2005 United Nations Convention on the Use of Electronic Communications in International Contracts. It covers the situation of "an exchange of statements of claim and defence in which the existence of an agreement is alleged by one party and not denied by another". It also states that "the reference in a contract to any document" (for example, general conditions) "containing an arbitration clause constitutes an arbitration agreement in writing provided that the reference is such as to make that clause part of the contract". It thus clarifies that applicable contract law remains available to determine the level of consent necessary for a party to become bound by an arbitration agreement allegedly made "by reference". The second approach defines the arbitration agreement in a manner that omits any form requirement. No preference was expressed by the Commission in favour of either option I or II, both of which are offered for enacting States to consider, depending on their particular needs, and by reference to the legal context in which the Model Law is enacted, including the general contract law of the enacting State. Both options are intended to preserve the enforceability of arbitration agreements under the New York Convention.

20. In that respect, the Commission also adopted, at its thirty-ninth session in 2006, a "Recommendation regarding the interpretation of article II, paragraph 2, and article VII, paragraph 1, of the Convention on the Recognition and Enforcement of Foreign Arbitral Awards, done in New York, 10 June 1958" (A/61/17, Annex 2).[2] The General Assembly, in its resolution 61/33 of 4 December 2006 noted that "in connection with the modernization of articles of the Model Law, the promotion of a uniform interpretation and application of the Convention on the Recognition and Enforcement of Foreign Arbitral Awards, done in New York, 10 June 1958, is particularly timely". The Recommendation was drafted in recognition of the widening use of electronic commerce and enactments of domestic legislation as well as case law, which are more favourable than the New York Convention in respect of the form requirement governing arbitration agreements, arbitration proceedings, and the enforcement of arbitral awards. The Recommendation encourages States to apply article II (2) of the New York

---

[2] Reproduced in Part Three hereafter.

Convention "recognizing that the circumstances described therein are not exhaustive". In addition, the Recommendation encourages States to adopt the revised article 7 of the Model Law. Both options of the revised article 7 establish a more favourable regime for the recognition and enforcement of arbitral awards than that provided under the New York Convention. By virtue of the "more favourable law provision" contained in article VII (1) of the New York Convention, the Recommendation clarifies that "any interested party" should be allowed "to avail itself of rights it may have, under the law or treaties of the country where an arbitration agreement is sought to be relied upon, to seek recognition of the validity of such an arbitration agreement".

### (b) Arbitration agreement and the courts

21. Articles 8 and 9 deal with two important aspects of the complex relationship between the arbitration agreement and the resort to courts. Modelled on article II (3) of the New York Convention, article 8 (1) of the Model Law places any court under an obligation to refer the parties to arbitration if the court is seized with a claim on the same subject-matter unless it finds that the arbitration agreement is null and void, inoperative or incapable of being performed. The referral is dependent on a request, which a party may make not later than when submitting its first statement on the substance of the dispute. This provision, where adopted by a State enacting the Model Law, is by its nature binding only on the courts of that State. However, since article 8 is not limited in scope to agreements providing for arbitration to take place in the enacting State, it promotes the universal recognition and effect of international commercial arbitration agreements.

22. Article 9 expresses the principle that any interim measures of protection that may be obtained from courts under their procedural law (for example, pre-award attachments) are compatible with an arbitration agreement. That provision is ultimately addressed to the courts of any State, insofar as it establishes the compatibility between interim measures possibly issued by any court and an arbitration agreement, irrespective of the place of arbitration. Wherever a request for interim measures may be made to a court, it may not be relied upon, under the Model Law, as a waiver or an objection against the existence or effect of the arbitration agreement.

### 3. Composition of arbitral tribunal

23. Chapter III contains a number of detailed provisions on appointment, challenge, termination of mandate and replacement of an arbitrator. The chapter illustrates the general approach taken by the Model Law in eliminating difficulties that arise from inappropriate or fragmentary laws or rules. First, the approach recognizes the freedom of the parties to determine, by reference to an existing set of arbitration rules or by an ad hoc agreement, the procedure to be followed, subject to the fundamental requirements of fairness and justice. Secondly, where the parties have not exercised their freedom to lay down the rules of procedure or they have failed to cover a particular issue, the Model Law ensures, by providing a set

of suppletive rules, that the arbitration may commence and proceed effectively until the dispute is resolved.

24. Where under any procedure, agreed upon by the parties or based upon the suppletive rules of the Model Law, difficulties arise in the process of appointment, challenge or termination of the mandate of an arbitrator, articles 11, 13 and 14 provide for assistance by courts or other competent authorities designated by the enacting State. In view of the urgency of matters relating to the composition of the arbitral tribunal or its ability to function, and in order to reduce the risk and effect of any dilatory tactics, short time-periods are set and decisions rendered by courts or other authorities on such matters are not appealable.

### 4. Jurisdiction of arbitral tribunal

#### (a) Competence to rule on own jurisdiction

25. Article 16 (1) adopts the two important (not yet generally recognized) principles of "*Kompetenz-Kompetenz*" and of separability or autonomy of the arbitration clause. "*Kompetenz-Kompetenz*" means that the arbitral tribunal may independently rule on the question of whether it has jurisdiction, including any objections with respect to the existence or validity of the arbitration agreement, without having to resort to a court. Separability means that an arbitration clause shall be treated as an agreement independent of the other terms of the contract. As a consequence, a decision by the arbitral tribunal that the contract is null and void shall not entail *ipso jure* the invalidity of the arbitration clause. Detailed provisions in paragraph (2) require that any objections relating to the arbitrators' jurisdiction be made at the earliest possible time.

26. The competence of the arbitral tribunal to rule on its own jurisdiction (i.e. on the foundation, content and extent of its mandate and power) is, of course, subject to court control. Where the arbitral tribunal rules as a preliminary question that it has jurisdiction, article 16 (3) allows for immediate court control in order to avoid waste of time and money. However, three procedural safeguards are added to reduce the risk and effect of dilatory tactics: short time-period for resort to court (30 days), court decision not appealable, and discretion of the arbitral tribunal to continue the proceedings and make an award while the matter is pending before the court. In those cases where the arbitral tribunal decides to combine its decision on jurisdiction with an award on the merits, judicial review on the question of jurisdiction is available in setting aside proceedings under article 34 or in enforcement proceedings under article 36.

#### (b) Power to order interim measures and preliminary orders

27. Chapter IV A on interim measures and preliminary orders was adopted by the Commission in 2006. It replaces article 17 of the original 1985 version of the Model Law. Section 1 provides a generic definition of interim measures and sets out the conditions for granting such measures. An important innovation of the revision lies in the establishment (in section 4) of a regime for the recognition and enforcement of interim measures, which was modelled, as appropriate, on the

regime for the recognition and enforcement of arbitral awards under articles 35 and 36 of the Model Law.

28. Section 2 of chapter IV A deals with the application for, and conditions for the granting of, preliminary orders. Preliminary orders provide a means for preserving the status quo until the arbitral tribunal issues an interim measure adopting or modifying the preliminary order. Article 17 B (1) provides that "a party may, without notice to any other party, make a request for an interim measure together with an application for a preliminary order directing a party not to frustrate the purpose of the interim measure requested". Article 17 B (2) permits an arbitral tribunal to grant a preliminary order if "it considers that prior disclosure of the request for the interim measure to the party against whom it is directed risks frustrating the purpose of the measure". Article 17 C contains carefully drafted safeguards for the party against whom the preliminary order is directed, such as prompt notification of the application for the preliminary order and of the preliminary order itself (if any), and an opportunity for that party to present its case "at the earliest practicable time". In any event, a preliminary order has a maximum duration of twenty days and, while binding on the parties, is not subject to court enforcement and does not constitute an award. The term "preliminary order" is used to emphasize its limited nature.

29. Section 3 sets out rules applicable to both preliminary orders and interim measures.

30. Section 5 includes article 17 J on interim measures ordered by courts in support of arbitration, and provides that "a court shall have the same power of issuing an interim measure in relation to arbitration proceedings irrespective of whether their place is in the territory of the enacting State, as it has in relation to proceedings in courts". That article has been added in 2006 to put it beyond any doubt that the existence of an arbitration agreement does not infringe on the powers of the competent court to issue interim measures and that the party to such an arbitration agreement is free to approach the court with a request to order interim measures.

## 5. *Conduct of arbitral proceedings*

31. Chapter V provides the legal framework for a fair and effective conduct of the arbitral proceedings. Article 18, which sets out fundamental requirements of procedural justice, and article 19 on the rights and powers to determine the rules of procedure, express principles that are central to the Model Law.

### (a) *Fundamental procedural rights of a party*

32. Article 18 embodies the principles that the parties shall be treated with equality and given a full opportunity of presenting their case. A number of provisions illustrate those principles. For example, article 24 (1) provides that, unless the parties have agreed that no oral hearings be held for the presentation of evidence or for oral argument, the arbitral tribunal shall hold such hearings at an appropriate stage of the proceedings, if so requested by a party. It should be noted that article 24 (1) deals

only with the general entitlement of a party to oral hearings (as an alternative to proceedings conducted on the basis of documents and other materials) and not with the procedural aspects, such as the length, number or timing of hearings.

33. Another illustration of those principles relates to evidence by an expert appointed by the arbitral tribunal. Article 26 (2) requires the expert, after delivering his or her written or oral report, to participate in a hearing where the parties may put questions to the expert and present expert witnesses to testify on the points at issue, if such a hearing is requested by a party or deemed necessary by the arbitral tribunal. As another provision aimed at ensuring fairness, objectivity and impartiality, article 24 (3) provides that all statements, documents and other information supplied to the arbitral tribunal by one party shall be communicated to the other party, and that any expert report or evidentiary document on which the arbitral tribunal may rely in making its decision shall be communicated to the parties. In order to enable the parties to be present at any hearing and at any meeting of the arbitral tribunal for inspection purposes, they shall be given sufficient notice in advance (article 24 (2)).

*(b) Determination of rules of procedure*

34. Article 19 guarantees the parties' freedom to agree on the procedure to be followed by the arbitral tribunal in conducting the proceedings, subject to a few mandatory provisions on procedure, and empowers the arbitral tribunal, failing agreement by the parties, to conduct the arbitration in such a manner as it considers appropriate. The power conferred upon the arbitral tribunal includes the power to determine the admissibility, relevance, materiality and weight of any evidence.

35. Autonomy of the parties in determining the rules of procedure is of special importance in international cases since it allows the parties to select or tailor the rules according to their specific wishes and needs, unimpeded by traditional and possibly conflicting domestic concepts, thus obviating the earlier mentioned risk of frustration or surprise (see above, paras. 7 and 9). The supplementary discretion of the arbitral tribunal is equally important in that it allows the tribunal to tailor the conduct of the proceedings to the specific features of the case without being hindered by any restraint that may stem from traditional local law, including any domestic rule on evidence. Moreover, it provides grounds for displaying initiative in solving any procedural question not regulated in the arbitration agreement or the Model Law.

36. In addition to the general provisions of article 19, other provisions in the Model Law recognize party autonomy and, failing agreement, empower the arbitral tribunal to decide on certain matters. Examples of particular practical importance in international cases are article 20 on the place of arbitration and article 22 on the language to be used in the proceedings.

*(c) Default of a party*

37. The arbitral proceedings may be continued in the absence of a party, provided that due notice has been given. This applies, in particular, to the failure

of the respondent to communicate its statement of defence (article 25 *(b)*). The arbitral tribunal may also continue the proceedings where a party fails to appear at a hearing or to produce documentary evidence without showing sufficient cause for the failure (article 25 *(c)*). However, if the claimant fails to submit its statement of claim, the arbitral tribunal is obliged to terminate the proceedings (article 25 *(a)*).

38. Provisions that empower the arbitral tribunal to carry out its task even if one of the parties does not participate are of considerable practical importance. As experience shows, it is not uncommon for one of the parties to have little interest in cooperating or expediting matters. Such provisions therefore provide international commercial arbitration its necessary effectiveness, within the limits of fundamental requirements of procedural justice.

### 6. Making of award and termination of proceedings

#### (a) Rules applicable to substance of dispute

39. Article 28 deals with the determination of the rules of law governing the substance of the dispute. Under paragraph (1), the arbitral tribunal decides the dispute in accordance with the rules of law chosen by the parties. This provision is significant in two respects. It grants the parties the freedom to choose the applicable substantive law, which is important where the national law does not clearly or fully recognize that right. In addition, by referring to the choice of "rules of law" instead of "law", the Model Law broadens the range of options available to the parties as regards the designation of the law applicable to the substance of the dispute. For example, parties may agree on rules of law that have been elaborated by an international forum but have not yet been incorporated into any national legal system. Parties could also choose directly an instrument such as the United Nations Convention on Contracts for the International Sale of Goods as the body of substantive law governing the arbitration, without having to refer to the national law of any State party to that Convention. The power of the arbitral tribunal, on the other hand, follows more traditional lines. When the parties have not chosen the applicable law, the arbitral tribunal shall apply the law (i.e., the national law) determined by the conflict-of-laws rules that it considers applicable.

40. Article 28 (3) recognizes that the parties may authorize the arbitral tribunal to decide the dispute *ex aequo et bono* or as *amiables compositeur*. This type of arbitration (where the arbitral tribunal may decide the dispute on the basis of principles it believes to be just, without having to refer to any particular body of law) is currently not known or used in all legal systems. The Model Law does not intend to regulate this area. It simply calls the attention of the parties on the need to provide clarification in the arbitration agreement and specifically to empower the arbitral tribunal. However, paragraph (4) makes it clear that in all cases where the dispute relates to a contract (including arbitration *ex aequo et bono*) the arbitral tribunal must decide in accordance with the terms of the contract and shall take into account the usages of the trade applicable to the transaction.

### (b) Making of award and other decisions

41. In its rules on the making of the award (articles 29-31), the Model Law focuses on the situation where the arbitral tribunal consists of more than one arbitrator. In such a situation, any award and other decision shall be made by a majority of the arbitrators, except on questions of procedure, which may be left to a presiding arbitrator. The majority principle applies also to the signing of the award, provided that the reason for any omitted signature is stated.

42. Article 31 (3) provides that the award shall state the place of arbitration and shall be deemed to have been made at that place. The effect of the deeming provision is to emphasize that the final making of the award constitutes a legal act, which in practice does not necessarily coincide with one factual event. For the same reason that the arbitral proceedings need not be carried out at the place designated as the legal "place of arbitration", the making of the award may be completed through deliberations held at various places, by telephone or correspondence. In addition, the award does not have to be signed by the arbitrators physically gathering at the same place.

43. The arbitral award must be in writing and state its date. It must also state the reasons on which it is based, unless the parties have agreed otherwise or the award is "on agreed terms" (i.e., an award that records the terms of an amicable settlement by the parties). It may be added that the Model Law neither requires nor prohibits "dissenting opinions".

## 7. Recourse against award

44. The disparity found in national laws as regards the types of recourse against an arbitral award available to the parties presents a major difficulty in harmonizing international arbitration legislation. Some outdated laws on arbitration, by establishing parallel regimes for recourse against arbitral awards or against court decisions, provide various types of recourse, various (and often long) time periods for exercising the recourse, and extensive lists of grounds on which recourse may be based. That situation (of considerable concern to those involved in international commercial arbitration) is greatly improved by the Model Law, which provides uniform grounds upon which (and clear time periods within which) recourse against an arbitral award may be made.

### (a) Application for setting aside as exclusive recourse

45. The first measure of improvement is to allow only one type of recourse, to the exclusion of any other recourse regulated in any procedural law of the State in question. Article 34 (1) provides that the sole recourse against an arbitral award is by application for setting aside, which must be made within three months of receipt of the award (article 34 (3)). In regulating "recourse" (i.e., the means through which a party may actively "attack" the award), article 34 does not preclude a party from seeking court control by way of defence in enforcement proceedings (articles 35 and 36). Article 34 is limited to action before a court (i.e.,

an organ of the judicial system of a State). However, a party is not precluded from appealing to an arbitral tribunal of second instance if the parties have agreed on such a possibility (as is common in certain commodity trades).

### (b) Grounds for setting aside

46. As a further measure of improvement, the Model Law lists exhaustively the grounds on which an award may be set aside. This list essentially mirrors that contained in article 36 (1), which is taken from article V of the New York Convention. The grounds provided in article 34 (2) are set out in two categories. Grounds which are to be proven by one party are as follows: lack of capacity of the parties to conclude an arbitration agreement; lack of a valid arbitration agreement; lack of notice of appointment of an arbitrator or of the arbitral proceedings or inability of a party to present its case; the award deals with matters not covered by the submission to arbitration; the composition of the arbitral tribunal or the conduct of arbitral proceedings are contrary to the effective agreement of the parties or, failing such agreement, to the Model Law. Grounds that a court may consider of its own initiative are as follows: non-arbitrability of the subject-matter of the dispute or violation of public policy (which is to be understood as serious departures from fundamental notions of procedural justice).

47. The approach under which the grounds for setting aside an award under the Model Law parallel the grounds for refusing recognition and enforcement of the award under article V of the New York Convention is reminiscent of the approach taken in the European Convention on International Commercial Arbitration (Geneva, 1961). Under article IX of the latter Convention, the decision of a foreign court to set aside an award for a reason other than the ones listed in article V of the New York Convention does not constitute a ground for refusing enforcement. The Model Law takes this philosophy one step further by directly limiting the reasons for setting aside.

48. Although the grounds for setting aside as set out in article 34 (2) are almost identical to those for refusing recognition or enforcement as set out in article 36 (1), a practical difference should be noted. An application for setting aside under article 34 (2) may only be made to a court in the State where the award was rendered whereas an application for enforcement might be made in a court in any State. For that reason, the grounds relating to public policy and non-arbitrability may vary in substance with the law applied by the court (in the State of setting aside or in the State of enforcement).

### 8. Recognition and enforcement of awards

49. The eighth and last chapter of the Model Law deals with the recognition and enforcement of awards. Its provisions reflect the significant policy decision that the same rules should apply to arbitral awards whether made in the country of enforcement or abroad, and that those rules should follow closely the New York Convention.

### (a) Towards uniform treatment of all awards irrespective of country of origin

50. By treating awards rendered in international commercial arbitration in a uniform manner irrespective of where they were made, the Model Law distinguishes between "international" and "non-international" awards instead of relying on the traditional distinction between "foreign" and "domestic" awards. This new line is based on substantive grounds rather than territorial borders, which are inappropriate in view of the limited importance of the place of arbitration in international cases. The place of arbitration is often chosen for reasons of convenience of the parties and the dispute may have little or no connection with the State where the arbitration legally takes place. Consequently, the recognition and enforcement of "international" awards, whether "foreign" or "domestic", should be governed by the same provisions.

51. By modelling the recognition and enforcement rules on the relevant provisions of the New York Convention, the Model Law supplements, without conflicting with, the regime of recognition and enforcement created by that successful Convention.

### (b) Procedural conditions of recognition and enforcement

52. Under article 35 (1) any arbitral award, irrespective of the country in which it was made, shall be recognized as binding and enforceable, subject to the provisions of article 35 (2) and of article 36 (the latter of which sets forth the grounds on which recognition or enforcement may be refused). Based on the above consideration of the limited importance of the place of arbitration in international cases and the desire of overcoming territorial restrictions, reciprocity is not included as a condition for recognition and enforcement.

53. The Model Law does not lay down procedural details of recognition and enforcement, which are left to national procedural laws and practices. The Model Law merely sets certain conditions for obtaining enforcement under article 35 (2). It was amended in 2006 to liberalize formal requirements and reflect the amendment made to article 7 on the form of the arbitration agreement. Presentation of a copy of the arbitration agreement is no longer required under article 35 (2).

### (c) Grounds for refusing recognition or enforcement

54. Although the grounds on which recognition or enforcement may be refused under the Model Law are identical to those listed in article V of the New York Convention, the grounds listed in the Model Law are relevant not only to foreign awards but to all awards rendered in the sphere of application of the piece of legislation enacting the Model Law. Generally, it was deemed desirable to adopt, for the sake of harmony, the same approach and wording as this important Convention. However, the first ground on the list as contained in the New York Convention (which provides that recognition and enforcement may be refused if "the parties to the arbitration agreement were, under the law applicable to them, under some incapacity") was modified since it was viewed as containing an incomplete and potentially misleading conflict-of-laws rule.

Further information on the Model Law may be obtained from:

UNCITRAL secretariat
Vienna International Centre
P.O. Box 500
1400 Vienna
Austria

Telephone: (+43-1) 26060-4060
Telefax: (+43-1) 26060-5813
Internet: www.uncitral.org
E-mail: uncitral@uncitral.org

## Part Three

**Recommendation regarding the interpretation of article II, paragraph 2, and article VII, paragraph 1, of the Convention on the Recognition and Enforcement of Foreign Arbitral Awards, done in New York, 10 June 1958, adopted by the United Nations Commission on International Trade Law on 7 July 2006 at its thirty-ninth session**

*The United Nations Commission on International Trade Law,*

*Recalling* General Assembly resolution 2205 (XXI) of 17 December 1966, which established the United Nations Commission on International Trade Law with the object of promoting the progressive harmonization and unification of the law of international trade by, inter alia, promoting ways and means of ensuring a uniform interpretation and application of international conventions and uniform laws in the field of the law of international trade,

*Conscious* of the fact that the different legal, social and economic systems of the world, together with different levels of development, are represented in the Commission,

*Recalling* successive resolutions of the General Assembly reaffirming the mandate of the Commission as the core legal body within the United Nations system in the field of international trade law to coordinate legal activities in this field,

*Convinced* that the wide adoption of the Convention on the Recognition and Enforcement of Foreign Arbitral Awards, done in New York on 10 June 1958,[1] has been a significant achievement in the promotion of the rule of law, particularly in the field of international trade,

*Recalling* that the Conference of Plenipotentiaries which prepared and opened the Convention for signature adopted a resolution, which states, inter alia, that the Conference "considers that greater uniformity of national laws on arbitration would further the effectiveness of arbitration in the settlement of private law disputes",

*Bearing in mind* differing interpretations of the form requirements under the Convention that result in part from differences of expression as between the five equally authentic texts of the Convention,

*Taking into account* article VII, paragraph 1, of the Convention, a purpose of which is to enable the enforcement of foreign arbitral awards to the greatest extent, in particular by recognizing the right of any interested party to avail itself of law or treaties of the country where the award is sought to be relied upon, including where such law or treaties offer a regime more favourable than the Convention,

---

[1] United Nations, *Treaty Series*, vol. 330, No. 4739.

*Considering* the wide use of electronic commerce,

*Taking into account* international legal instruments, such as the 1985 UNCITRAL Model Law on International Commercial Arbitration,[2] as subsequently revised, particularly with respect to article 7,[3] the UNCITRAL Model Law on Electronic Commerce,[4] the UNCITRAL Model Law on Electronic Signatures[5] and the United Nations Convention on the Use of Electronic Communications in International Contracts,[6]

*Taking into account also* enactments of domestic legislation, as well as case law, more favourable than the Convention in respect of form requirement governing arbitration agreements, arbitration proceedings and the enforcement of arbitral awards,

*Considering that*, in interpreting the Convention, regard is to be had to the need to promote recognition and enforcement of arbitral awards,

1. *Recommends* that article II, paragraph 2, of the Convention on the Recognition and Enforcement of Foreign Arbitral Awards, done in New York, 10 June 1958, be applied recognizing that the circumstances described therein are not exhaustive;

2. *Recommends also* that article VII, paragraph 1, of the Convention on the Recognition and Enforcement of Foreign Arbitral Awards, done in New York, 10 June 1958, should be applied to allow any interested party to avail itself of rights it may have, under the law or treaties of the country where an arbitration agreement is sought to be relied upon, to seek recognition of the validity of such an arbitration agreement.

---

[2] *Official Records of the General Assembly, Fortieth Session, Supplement No. 17* (A/40/17), annex I, and United Nations publication, Sales No. E.95.V.18.

[3] Ibid., *Sixty-first Session, Supplement No. 17* (A/61/17), annex I.

[4] Ibid., *Fifty-first Session, Supplement No. 17* (A/51/17), annex I, and United Nations publication, Sales No. E.99.V.4, which contains also an additional article 5 bis, adopted in 1998, and the accompanying Guide to Enactment.

[5] Ibid., *Fifty-sixth Session, Supplement No. 17* and corrigendum (A/56/17 and Corr.3), annex II, and United Nations publication, Sales No. E.02.V.8, which contains also the accompanying Guide to Enactment.

[6] General Assembly resolution 60/21, annex.

# APPENDIX 11

# UNCITRAL ARBITRATION RULES

(as revised in 2010)

**Resolution adopted by the General Assembly**

[*on the report of the Sixth Committee (A/65/465)*]

**65/22. UNCITRAL Arbitration Rules as revised in 2010**

*The General Assembly*,

*Recalling* its resolution 2205 (XXI) of 17 December 1966, which established the United Nations Commission on International Trade Law with the purpose of furthering the progressive harmonization and unification of the law of international trade in the interests of all peoples, in particular those of developing countries,

*Also recalling* its resolution 31/98 of 15 December 1976 recommending the use of the Arbitration Rules of the United Nations Commission on International Trade Law,[1]

*Recognizing* the value of arbitration as a method of settling disputes that may arise in the context of international commercial relations,

*Noting* that the Arbitration Rules are recognized as a very successful text and are used in a wide variety of circumstances covering a broad range of disputes, including disputes between private commercial parties, investor-State disputes, State-to-State disputes and commercial disputes administered by arbitral institutions, in all parts of the world,

*Recognizing* the need for revising the Arbitration Rules to conform to current practices in international trade and to meet changes that have taken place over the last thirty years in arbitral practice,

*Believing* that the Arbitration Rules as revised in 2010 to reflect current practices will significantly enhance the efficiency of arbitration under the Rules,

---

[1] *Official Records of the General Assembly, Thirty-first Session, Supplement No. 17* (A/31/17), chap. V, sect. C.

*Convinced* that the revision of the Arbitration Rules in a manner that is acceptable to countries with different legal, social and economic systems can significantly contribute to the development of harmonious international economic relations and to the continuous strengthening of the rule of law,

*Noting* that the preparation of the Arbitration Rules as revised in 2010 was the subject of due deliberation and extensive consultations with Governments and interested circles and that the revised text can be expected to contribute significantly to the establishment of a harmonized legal framework for the fair and efficient settlement of international commercial disputes,

*Also noting* that the Arbitration Rules as revised in 2010 were adopted by the United Nations Commission on International Trade Law at its forty-third session after due deliberation,[2]

1. *Expresses its appreciation* to the United Nations Commission on International Trade Law for having formulated and adopted the revised provisions of the Arbitration Rules, the text of which is contained in an annex to the report of the United Nations Commission on International Trade Law on the work of its forty-third session;[3]

2. *Recommends* the use of the Arbitration Rules as revised in 2010 in the settlement of disputes arising in the context of international commercial relations;

3. *Requests* the Secretary-General to make all efforts to ensure that the Arbitration Rules as revised in 2010 become generally known and available.

*57th plenary meeting*
*6 December 2010*

## UNCITRAL Arbitration Rules

### (as revised in 2010)

### Section I. Introductory rules

*Scope of application\**

Article 1

1. Where parties have agreed that disputes between them in respect of a defined legal relationship, whether contractual or not, shall be referred to arbitration under the UNCITRAL Arbitration Rules, then such disputes shall be settled in accordance with these Rules subject to such modification as the parties may agree.

---

[2] Ibid., *Sixty-fifth Session, Supplement No. 17* (A/65/17), chap. III.
[3] Ibid., annex I.
\* A model arbitration clause for contracts can be found in the annex to the Rules.

2. The parties to an arbitration agreement concluded after 15 August 2010 shall be presumed to have referred to the Rules in effect on the date of commencement of the arbitration, unless the parties have agreed to apply a particular version of the Rules. That presumption does not apply where the arbitration agreement has been concluded by accepting after 15 August 2010 an offer made before that date.

3. These Rules shall govern the arbitration except that where any of these Rules is in conflict with a provision of the law applicable to the arbitration from which the parties cannot derogate, that provision shall prevail.

## Notice and calculation of periods of time

### Article 2

1. A notice, including a notification, communication or proposal, may be transmitted by any means of communication that provides or allows for a record of its transmission.

2. If an address has been designated by a party specifically for this purpose or authorized by the arbitral tribunal, any notice shall be delivered to that party at that address, and if so delivered shall be deemed to have been received. Delivery by electronic means such as facsimile or e-mail may only be made to an address so designated or authorized.

3. In the absence of such designation or authorization, a notice is:
   (a) Received if it is physically delivered to the addressee; or
   (b) Deemed to have been received if it is delivered at the place of business, habitual residence or mailing address of the addressee.

4. If, after reasonable efforts, delivery cannot be effected in accordance with paragraphs 2 or 3, a notice is deemed to have been received if it is sent to the addressee's last-known place of business, habitual residence or mailing address by registered letter or any other means that provides a record of delivery or of attempted delivery.

5. A notice shall be deemed to have been received on the day it is delivered in accordance with paragraphs 2, 3 or 4, or attempted to be delivered in accordance with paragraph 4. A notice transmitted by electronic means is deemed to have been received on the day it is sent, except that a notice of arbitration so transmitted is only deemed to have been received on the day when it reaches the addressee's electronic address.

6. For the purpose of calculating a period of time under these Rules, such period shall begin to run on the day following the day when a notice is received. If the last day of such period is an official holiday or a non-business day at the residence or place of business of the addressee, the period is extended until the first business day which follows. Official holidays or non-business days occurring during the running of the period of time are included in calculating the period.

## Notice of arbitration

*Article 3*

1. The party or parties initiating recourse to arbitration (hereinafter called the "claimant") shall communicate to the other party or parties (hereinafter called the "respondent") a notice of arbitration.

2. Arbitral proceedings shall be deemed to commence on the date on which the notice of arbitration is received by the respondent.

3. The notice of arbitration shall include the following:
    *(a)* A demand that the dispute be referred to arbitration;
    *(b)* The names and contact details of the parties;
    *(c)* Identification of the arbitration agreement that is invoked;
    *(d)* Identification of any contract or other legal instrument out of or in relation to which the dispute arises or, in the absence of such contract or instrument, a brief description of the relevant relationship;
    *(e)* A brief description of the claim and an indication of the amount involved, if any;
    *(f)* The relief or remedy sought;
    *(g)* A proposal as to the number of arbitrators, language and place of arbitration, if the parties have not previously agreed thereon.

4. The notice of arbitration may also include:
    *(a)* A proposal for the designation of an appointing authority referred to in article 6, paragraph 1;
    *(b)* A proposal for the appointment of a sole arbitrator referred to in article 8, paragraph 1;
    *(c)* Notification of the appointment of an arbitrator referred to in article 9 or 10.

5. The constitution of the arbitral tribunal shall not be hindered by any controversy with respect to the sufficiency of the notice of arbitration, which shall be finally resolved by the arbitral tribunal.

## Response to the notice of arbitration

*Article 4*

1. Within 30 days of the receipt of the notice of arbitration, the respondent shall communicate to the claimant a response to the notice of arbitration, which shall include:
    *(a)* The name and contact details of each respondent;
    *(b)* A response to the information set forth in the notice of arbitration, pursuant to article 3, paragraphs 3 *(c)* to *(g)*.

2. The response to the notice of arbitration may also include:
    *(a)* Any plea that an arbitral tribunal to be constituted under these Rules lacks jurisdiction;

*(b)* A proposal for the designation of an appointing authority referred to in article 6, paragraph 1;
*(c)* A proposal for the appointment of a sole arbitrator referred to in article 8, paragraph 1;
*(d)* Notification of the appointment of an arbitrator referred to in article 9 or 10;
*(e)* A brief description of counterclaims or claims for the purpose of a set-off, if any, including where relevant, an indication of the amounts involved, and the relief or remedy sought;
*(f)* A notice of arbitration in accordance with article 3 in case the respondent formulates a claim against a party to the arbitration agreement other than the claimant.

3. The constitution of the arbitral tribunal shall not be hindered by any controversy with respect to the respondent's failure to communicate a response to the notice of arbitration, or an incomplete or late response to the notice of arbitration, which shall be finally resolved by the arbitral tribunal.

*Representation and assistance*

Article 5

Each party may be represented or assisted by persons chosen by it. The names and addresses of such persons must be communicated to all parties and to the arbitral tribunal. Such communication must specify whether the appointment is being made for purposes of representation or assistance. Where a person is to act as a representative of a party, the arbitral tribunal, on its own initiative or at the request of any party, may at any time require proof of authority granted to the representative in such a form as the arbitral tribunal may determine.

*Designating and appointing authorities*

Article 6

1. Unless the parties have already agreed on the choice of an appointing authority, a party may at any time propose the name or names of one or more institutions or persons, including the Secretary-General of the Permanent Court of Arbitration at The Hague (hereinafter called the "PCA"), one of whom would serve as appointing authority.

2. If all parties have not agreed on the choice of an appointing authority within 30 days after a proposal made in accordance with paragraph 1 has been received by all other parties, any party may request the Secretary-General of the PCA to designate the appointing authority.

3. Where these Rules provide for a period of time within which a party must refer a matter to an appointing authority and no appointing authority has been

agreed on or designated, the period is suspended from the date on which a party initiates the procedure for agreeing on or designating an appointing authority until the date of such agreement or designation.

4. Except as referred to in article 41, paragraph 4, if the appointing authority refuses to act, or if it fails to appoint an arbitrator within 30 days after it receives a party's request to do so, fails to act within any other period provided by these Rules, or fails to decide on a challenge to an arbitrator within a reasonable time after receiving a party's request to do so, any party may request the Secretary-General of the PCA to designate a substitute appointing authority.

5. In exercising their functions under these Rules, the appointing authority and the Secretary-General of the PCA may require from any party and the arbitrators the information they deem necessary and they shall give the parties and, where appropriate, the arbitrators, an opportunity to present their views in any manner they consider appropriate. All such communications to and from the appointing authority and the Secretary-General of the PCA shall also be provided by the sender to all other parties.

6. When the appointing authority is requested to appoint an arbitrator pursuant to articles 8, 9, 10 or 14, the party making the request shall send to the appointing authority copies of the notice of arbitration and, if it exists, any response to the notice of arbitration.

7. The appointing authority shall have regard to such considerations as are likely to secure the appointment of an independent and impartial arbitrator and shall take into account the advisability of appointing an arbitrator of a nationality other than the nationalities of the parties.

## Section II. Composition of the arbitral tribunal

### Number of arbitrators

*Article 7*

1. If the parties have not previously agreed on the number of arbitrators, and if within 30 days after the receipt by the respondent of the notice of arbitration the parties have not agreed that there shall be only one arbitrator, three arbitrators shall be appointed.

2. Notwithstanding paragraph 1, if no other parties have responded to a party's proposal to appoint a sole arbitrator within the time limit provided for in paragraph 1 and the party or parties concerned have failed to appoint a second arbitrator in accordance with article 9 or 10, the appointing authority may, at the request of a party, appoint a sole arbitrator pursuant to the procedure provided for in article 8, paragraph 2, if it determines that, in view of the circumstances of the case, this is more appropriate.

## Appointment of arbitrators (articles 8 to 10)

*Article 8*

1. If the parties have agreed that a sole arbitrator is to be appointed and if within 30 days after receipt by all other parties of a proposal for the appointment of a sole arbitrator the parties have not reached agreement thereon, a sole arbitrator shall, at the request of a party, be appointed by the appointing authority.

2. The appointing authority shall appoint the sole arbitrator as promptly as possible. In making the appointment, the appointing authority shall use the following list-procedure, unless the parties agree that the list-procedure should not be used or unless the appointing authority determines in its discretion that the use of the list-procedure is not appropriate for the case:
   - *(a)* The appointing authority shall communicate to each of the parties an identical list containing at least three names;
   - *(b)* Within 15 days after the receipt of this list, each party may return the list to the appointing authority after having deleted the name or names to which it objects and numbered the remaining names on the list in the order of its preference;
   - *(c)* After the expiration of the above period of time the appointing authority shall appoint the sole arbitrator from among the names approved on the lists returned to it and in accordance with the order of preference indicated by the parties;
   - *(d)* If for any reason the appointment cannot be made according to this procedure, the appointing authority may exercise its discretion in appointing the sole arbitrator.

*Article 9*

1. If three arbitrators are to be appointed, each party shall appoint one arbitrator. The two arbitrators thus appointed shall choose the third arbitrator who will act as the presiding arbitrator of the arbitral tribunal.

2. If within 30 days after the receipt of a party's notification of the appointment of an arbitrator the other party has not notified the first party of the arbitrator it has appointed, the first party may request the appointing authority to appoint the second arbitrator.

3. If within 30 days after the appointment of the second arbitrator the two arbitrators have not agreed on the choice of the presiding arbitrator, the presiding arbitrator shall be appointed by the appointing authority in the same way as a sole arbitrator would be appointed under article 8.

*Article 10*

1. For the purposes of article 9, paragraph 1, where three arbitrators are to be appointed and there are multiple parties as claimant or as respondent, unless the

parties have agreed to another method of appointment of arbitrators, the multiple parties jointly, whether as claimant or as respondent, shall appoint an arbitrator.

2. If the parties have agreed that the arbitral tribunal is to be composed of a number of arbitrators other than one or three, the arbitrators shall be appointed according to the method agreed upon by the parties.

3. In the event of any failure to constitute the arbitral tribunal under these Rules, the appointing authority shall, at the request of any party, constitute the arbitral tribunal and, in doing so, may revoke any appointment already made and appoint or reappoint each of the arbitrators and designate one of them as the presiding arbitrator.

## *Disclosures by and challenge of arbitrators* ** *(articles 11 to 13)*

*Article 11*

When a person is approached in connection with his or her possible appointment as an arbitrator, he or she shall disclose any circumstances likely to give rise to justifiable doubts as to his or her impartiality or independence. An arbitrator, from the time of his or her appointment and throughout the arbitral proceedings, shall without delay disclose any such circumstances to the parties and the other arbitrators unless they have already been informed by him or her of these circumstances.

*Article 12*

1. Any arbitrator may be challenged if circumstances exist that give rise to justifiable doubts as to the arbitrator's impartiality or independence.

2. A party may challenge the arbitrator appointed by it only for reasons of which it becomes aware after the appointment has been made.

3. In the event that an arbitrator fails to act or in the event of the de jure or de facto impossibility of his or her performing his or her functions, the procedure in respect of the challenge of an arbitrator as provided in article 13 shall apply.

*Article 13*

1. A party that intends to challenge an arbitrator shall send notice of its challenge within 15 days after it has been notified of the appointment of the challenged arbitrator, or within 15 days after the circumstances mentioned in articles 11 and 12 became known to that party.

2. The notice of challenge shall be communicated to all other parties, to the arbitrator who is challenged and to the other arbitrators. The notice of challenge shall state the reasons for the challenge.

---

** Model statements of independence pursuant to article 11 can be found in the annex to the Rules.

3. When an arbitrator has been challenged by a party, all parties may agree to the challenge. The arbitrator may also, after the challenge, withdraw from his or her office. In neither case does this imply acceptance of the validity of the grounds for the challenge.

4. If, within 15 days from the date of the notice of challenge, all parties do not agree to the challenge or the challenged arbitrator does not withdraw, the party making the challenge may elect to pursue it. In that case, within 30 days from the date of the notice of challenge, it shall seek a decision on the challenge by the appointing authority.

## *Replacement of an arbitrator*

Article 14

1. Subject to paragraph 2, in any event where an arbitrator has to be replaced during the course of the arbitral proceedings, a substitute arbitrator shall be appointed or chosen pursuant to the procedure provided for in articles 8 to 11 that was applicable to the appointment or choice of the arbitrator being replaced. This procedure shall apply even if during the process of appointing the arbitrator to be replaced, a party had failed to exercise its right to appoint or to participate in the appointment.

2. If, at the request of a party, the appointing authority determines that, in view of the exceptional circumstances of the case, it would be justified for a party to be deprived of its right to appoint a substitute arbitrator, the appointing authority may, after giving an opportunity to the parties and the remaining arbitrators to express their views: *(a)* appoint the substitute arbitrator; or *(b)* after the closure of the hearings, authorize the other arbitrators to proceed with the arbitration and make any decision or award.

## *Repetition of hearings in the event of the replacement of an arbitrator*

Article 15

If an arbitrator is replaced, the proceedings shall resume at the stage where the arbitrator who was replaced ceased to perform his or her functions, unless the arbitral tribunal decides otherwise.

## *Exclusion of liability*

Article 16

Save for intentional wrongdoing, the parties waive, to the fullest extent permitted under the applicable law, any claim against the arbitrators, the appointing authority and any person appointed by the arbitral tribunal based on any act or omission in connection with the arbitration.

## Section III. Arbitral proceedings

### *General provisions*

*Article 17*

1. Subject to these Rules, the arbitral tribunal may conduct the arbitration in such manner as it considers appropriate, provided that the parties are treated with equality and that at an appropriate stage of the proceedings each party is given a reasonable opportunity of presenting its case. The arbitral tribunal, in exercising its discretion, shall conduct the proceedings so as to avoid unnecessary delay and expense and to provide a fair and efficient process for resolving the parties' dispute.

2. As soon as practicable after its constitution and after inviting the parties to express their views, the arbitral tribunal shall establish the provisional timetable of the arbitration. The arbitral tribunal may, at any time, after inviting the parties to express their views, extend or abridge any period of time prescribed under these Rules or agreed by the parties.

3. If at an appropriate stage of the proceedings any party so requests, the arbitral tribunal shall hold hearings for the presentation of evidence by witnesses, including expert witnesses, or for oral argument. In the absence of such a request, the arbitral tribunal shall decide whether to hold such hearings or whether the proceedings shall be conducted on the basis of documents and other materials.

4. All communications to the arbitral tribunal by one party shall be communicated by that party to all other parties. Such communications shall be made at the same time, except as otherwise permitted by the arbitral tribunal if it may do so under applicable law.

5. The arbitral tribunal may, at the request of any party, allow one or more third persons to be joined in the arbitration as a party provided such person is a party to the arbitration agreement, unless the arbitral tribunal finds, after giving all parties, including the person or persons to be joined, the opportunity to be heard, that joinder should not be permitted because of prejudice to any of those parties. The arbitral tribunal may make a single award or several awards in respect of all parties so involved in the arbitration.

### *Place of arbitration*

*Article 18*

1. If the parties have not previously agreed on the place of arbitration, the place of arbitration shall be determined by the arbitral tribunal having regard to the circumstances of the case. The award shall be deemed to have been made at the place of arbitration.

2. The arbitral tribunal may meet at any location it considers appropriate for deliberations. Unless otherwise agreed by the parties, the arbitral tribunal may also meet at any location it considers appropriate for any other purpose, including hearings.

## *Language*

*Article 19*

1. Subject to an agreement by the parties, the arbitral tribunal shall, promptly after its appointment, determine the language or languages to be used in the proceedings. This determination shall apply to the statement of claim, the statement of defence, and any further written statements and, if oral hearings take place, to the language or languages to be used in such hearings.

2. The arbitral tribunal may order that any documents annexed to the statement of claim or statement of defence, and any supplementary documents or exhibits submitted in the course of the proceedings, delivered in their original language, shall be accompanied by a translation into the language or languages agreed upon by the parties or determined by the arbitral tribunal.

## *Statement of claim*

*Article 20*

1. The claimant shall communicate its statement of claim in writing to the respondent and to each of the arbitrators within a period of time to be determined by the arbitral tribunal. The claimant may elect to treat its notice of arbitration referred to in article 3 as a statement of claim, provided that the notice of arbitration also complies with the requirements of paragraphs 2 to 4 of this article.

2. The statement of claim shall include the following particulars:
   *(a)* The names and contact details of the parties;
   *(b)* A statement of the facts supporting the claim;
   *(c)* The points at issue;
   *(d)* The relief or remedy sought;
   *(e)* The legal grounds or arguments supporting the claim.

3. A copy of any contract or other legal instrument out of or in relation to which the dispute arises and of the arbitration agreement shall be annexed to the statement of claim.

4. The statement of claim should, as far as possible, be accompanied by all documents and other evidence relied upon by the claimant, or contain references to them.

## Statement of defence

*Article 21*

1. The respondent shall communicate its statement of defence in writing to the claimant and to each of the arbitrators within a period of time to be determined by the arbitral tribunal. The respondent may elect to treat its response to the notice of arbitration referred to in article 4 as a statement of defence, provided that the response to the notice of arbitration also complies with the requirements of paragraph 2 of this article.

2. The statement of defence shall reply to the particulars *(b)* to *(e)* of the statement of claim (Article 20, para. 2). The statement of defence should, as far as possible, be accompanied by all documents and other evidence relied upon by the respondent, or contain references to them.

3. In its statement of defence, or at a later stage in the arbitral proceedings if the arbitral tribunal decides that the delay was justified under the circumstances, the respondent may make a counterclaim or rely on a claim for the purpose of a set-off provided that the arbitral tribunal has jurisdiction over it.

4. The provisions of article 20, paragraphs 2 to 4, shall apply to a counterclaim, a claim under article 4, paragraph 2 *(f)*, and a claim relied on for the purpose of a set-off.

## Amendments to the claim or defence

*Article 22*

During the course of the arbitral proceedings, a party may amend or supplement its claim or defence, including a counterclaim or a claim for the purpose of a set-off, unless the arbitral tribunal considers it inappropriate to allow such amendment or supplement having regard to the delay in making it or prejudice to other parties or any other circumstances. However, a claim or defence, including a counterclaim or a claim for the purpose of a set-off, may not be amended or supplemented in such a manner that the amended or supplemented claim or defence falls outside the jurisdiction of the arbitral tribunal.

## Pleas as to the jurisdiction of the arbitral tribunal

*Article 23*

1. The arbitral tribunal shall have the power to rule on its own jurisdiction, including any objections with respect to the existence or validity of the arbitration agreement. For that purpose, an arbitration clause that forms part of a contract shall be treated as an agreement independent of the other terms of the contract. A decision by the arbitral tribunal that the contract is null shall not entail automatically the invalidity of the arbitration clause.

2. A plea that the arbitral tribunal does not have jurisdiction shall be raised no later than in the statement of defence or, with respect to a counterclaim or a claim for the purpose of a set-off, in the reply to the counterclaim or to the claim for the purpose of a set-off. A party is not precluded from raising such a plea by the fact that it has appointed, or participated in the appointment of, an arbitrator. A plea that the arbitral tribunal is exceeding the scope of its authority shall be raised as soon as the matter alleged to be beyond the scope of its authority is raised during the arbitral proceedings. The arbitral tribunal may, in either case, admit a later plea if it considers the delay justified.

3. The arbitral tribunal may rule on a plea referred to in paragraph 2 either as a preliminary question or in an award on the merits. The arbitral tribunal may continue the arbitral proceedings and make an award, notwithstanding any pending challenge to its jurisdiction before a court.

## Further written statements

*Article 24*

The arbitral tribunal shall decide which further written statements, in addition to the statement of claim and the statement of defence, shall be required from the parties or may be presented by them and shall fix the periods of time for communicating such statements.

## Periods of time

*Article 25*

The periods of time fixed by the arbitral tribunal for the communication of written statements (including the statement of claim and statement of defence) should not exceed 45 days. However, the arbitral tribunal may extend the time limits if it concludes that an extension is justified.

## Interim measures

*Article 26*

1. The arbitral tribunal may, at the request of a party, grant interim measures.

2. An interim measure is any temporary measure by which, at any time prior to the issuance of the award by which the dispute is finally decided, the arbitral tribunal orders a party, for example and without limitation, to:
   (a) Maintain or restore the status quo pending determination of the dispute;
   (b) Take action that would prevent, or refrain from taking action that is likely to cause, (i) current or imminent harm or (ii) prejudice to the arbitral process itself;
   (c) Provide a means of preserving assets out of which a subsequent award may be satisfied; or

(d) Preserve evidence that may be relevant and material to the resolution of the dispute.

3. The party requesting an interim measure under paragraphs 2 *(a)* to *(c)* shall satisfy the arbitral tribunal that:
   (a) Harm not adequately reparable by an award of damages is likely to result if the measure is not ordered, and such harm substantially outweighs the harm that is likely to result to the party against whom the measure is directed if the measure is granted; and
   (b) There is a reasonable possibility that the requesting party will succeed on the merits of the claim. The determination on this possibility shall not affect the discretion of the arbitral tribunal in making any subsequent determination.

4. With regard to a request for an interim measure under paragraph 2 *(d)*, the requirements in paragraphs 3 *(a)* and *(b)* shall apply only to the extent the arbitral tribunal considers appropriate.

5. The arbitral tribunal may modify, suspend or terminate an interim measure it has granted, upon application of any party or, in exceptional circumstances and upon prior notice to the parties, on the arbitral tribunal's own initiative.

6. The arbitral tribunal may require the party requesting an interim measure to provide appropriate security in connection with the measure.

7. The arbitral tribunal may require any party promptly to disclose any material change in the circumstances on the basis of which the interim measure was requested or granted.

8. The party requesting an interim measure may be liable for any costs and damages caused by the measure to any party if the arbitral tribunal later determines that, in the circumstances then prevailing, the measure should not have been granted. The arbitral tribunal may award such costs and damages at any point during the proceedings.

9. A request for interim measures addressed by any party to a judicial authority shall not be deemed incompatible with the agreement to arbitrate, or as a waiver of that agreement.

## *Evidence*

*Article 27*

1. Each party shall have the burden of proving the facts relied on to support its claim or defence.

2. Witnesses, including expert witnesses, who are presented by the parties to testify to the arbitral tribunal on any issue of fact or expertise may be any individual, notwithstanding that the individual is a party to the arbitration or in any way related to a party. Unless otherwise directed by the arbitral tribunal, statements by witnesses, including expert witnesses, may be presented in writing and signed by them.

3. At any time during the arbitral proceedings the arbitral tribunal may require the parties to produce documents, exhibits or other evidence within such a period of time as the arbitral tribunal shall determine.

4. The arbitral tribunal shall determine the admissibility, relevance, materiality and weight of the evidence offered.

## Hearings

### Article 28

1. In the event of an oral hearing, the arbitral tribunal shall give the parties adequate advance notice of the date, time and place thereof.

2. Witnesses, including expert witnesses, may be heard under the conditions and examined in the manner set by the arbitral tribunal.

3. Hearings shall be held in camera unless the parties agree otherwise. The arbitral tribunal may require the retirement of any witness or witnesses, including expert witnesses, during the testimony of such other witnesses, except that a witness, including an expert witness, who is a party to the arbitration shall not, in principle, be asked to retire.

4. The arbitral tribunal may direct that witnesses, including expert witnesses, be examined through means of telecommunication that do not require their physical presence at the hearing (such as videoconference).

## Experts appointed by the arbitral tribunal

### Article 29

1. After consultation with the parties, the arbitral tribunal may appoint one or more independent experts to report to it, in writing, on specific issues to be determined by the arbitral tribunal. A copy of the expert's terms of reference, established by the arbitral tribunal, shall be communicated to the parties.

2. The expert shall, in principle before accepting appointment, submit to the arbitral tribunal and to the parties a description of his or her qualifications and a statement of his or her impartiality and independence. Within the time ordered by the arbitral tribunal, the parties shall inform the arbitral tribunal whether they have any objections as to the expert's qualifications, impartiality or independence. The arbitral tribunal shall decide promptly whether to accept any such objections. After an expert's appointment, a party may object to the expert's qualifications, impartiality or independence only if the objection is for reasons of which the party becomes aware after the appointment has been made. The arbitral tribunal shall decide promptly what, if any, action to take.

3. The parties shall give the expert any relevant information or produce for his or her inspection any relevant documents or goods that he or she may require of

them. Any dispute between a party and such expert as to the relevance of the required information or production shall be referred to the arbitral tribunal for decision.

4. Upon receipt of the expert's report, the arbitral tribunal shall communicate a copy of the report to the parties, which shall be given the opportunity to express, in writing, their opinion on the report. A party shall be entitled to examine any document on which the expert has relied in his or her report.

5. At the request of any party, the expert, after delivery of the report, may be heard at a hearing where the parties shall have the opportunity to be present and to interrogate the expert. At this hearing, any party may present expert witnesses in order to testify on the points at issue. The provisions of article 28 shall be applicable to such proceedings.

## *Default*

*Article 30*

1. If, within the period of time fixed by these Rules or the arbitral tribunal, without showing sufficient cause:
   *(a)* The claimant has failed to communicate its statement of claim, the arbitral tribunal shall issue an order for the termination of the arbitral proceedings, unless there are remaining matters that may need to be decided and the arbitral tribunal considers it appropriate to do so;
   *(b)* The respondent has failed to communicate its response to the notice of arbitration or its statement of defence, the arbitral tribunal shall order that the proceedings continue, without treating such failure in itself as an admission of the claimant's allegations; the provisions of this subparagraph also apply to a claimant's failure to submit a defence to a counterclaim or to a claim for the purpose of a set-off.

2. If a party, duly notified under these Rules, fails to appear at a hearing, without showing sufficient cause for such failure, the arbitral tribunal may proceed with the arbitration.

3. If a party, duly invited by the arbitral tribunal to produce documents, exhibits or other evidence, fails to do so within the established period of time, without showing sufficient cause for such failure, the arbitral tribunal may make the award on the evidence before it.

## *Closure of hearings*

*Article 31*

1. The arbitral tribunal may inquire of the parties if they have any further proof to offer or witnesses to be heard or submissions to make and, if there are none, it may declare the hearings closed.

2. The arbitral tribunal may, if it considers it necessary owing to exceptional circumstances, decide, on its own initiative or upon application of a party, to reopen the hearings at any time before the award is made.

## *Waiver of right to object*

*Article 32*

A failure by any party to object promptly to any non-compliance with these Rules or with any requirement of the arbitration agreement shall be deemed to be a waiver of the right of such party to make such an objection, unless such party can show that, under the circumstances, its failure to object was justified.

## Section IV. The award

### *Decisions*

*Article 33*

1. When there is more than one arbitrator, any award or other decision of the arbitral tribunal shall be made by a majority of the arbitrators.

2. In the case of questions of procedure, when there is no majority or when the arbitral tribunal so authorizes, the presiding arbitrator may decide alone, subject to revision, if any, by the arbitral tribunal.

### *Form and effect of the award*

*Article 34*

1. The arbitral tribunal may make separate awards on different issues at different times.

2. All awards shall be made in writing and shall be final and binding on the parties. The parties shall carry out all awards without delay.

3. The arbitral tribunal shall state the reasons upon which the award is based, unless the parties have agreed that no reasons are to be given.

4. An award shall be signed by the arbitrators and it shall contain the date on which the award was made and indicate the place of arbitration. Where there is more than one arbitrator and any of them fails to sign, the award shall state the reason for the absence of the signature.

5. An award may be made public with the consent of all parties or where and to the extent disclosure is required of a party by legal duty, to protect or pursue a legal right or in relation to legal proceedings before a court or other competent authority.

6. Copies of the award signed by the arbitrators shall be communicated to the parties by the arbitral tribunal.

## *Applicable law,* amiable compositeur

*Article 35*

1. The arbitral tribunal shall apply the rules of law designated by the parties as applicable to the substance of the dispute. Failing such designation by the parties, the arbitral tribunal shall apply the law which it determines to be appropriate.

2. The arbitral tribunal shall decide as *amiable compositeur* or *ex aequo et bono* only if the parties have expressly authorized the arbitral tribunal to do so.

3. In all cases, the arbitral tribunal shall decide in accordance with the terms of the contract, if any, and shall take into account any usage of trade applicable to the transaction.

## *Settlement or other grounds for termination*

*Article 36*

1. If, before the award is made, the parties agree on a settlement of the dispute, the arbitral tribunal shall either issue an order for the termination of the arbitral proceedings or, if requested by the parties and accepted by the arbitral tribunal, record the settlement in the form of an arbitral award on agreed terms. The arbitral tribunal is not obliged to give reasons for such an award.

2. If, before the award is made, the continuation of the arbitral proceedings becomes unnecessary or impossible for any reason not mentioned in paragraph 1, the arbitral tribunal shall inform the parties of its intention to issue an order for the termination of the proceedings. The arbitral tribunal shall have the power to issue such an order unless there are remaining matters that may need to be decided and the arbitral tribunal considers it appropriate to do so.

3. Copies of the order for termination of the arbitral proceedings or of the arbitral award on agreed terms, signed by the arbitrators, shall be communicated by the arbitral tribunal to the parties. Where an arbitral award on agreed terms is made, the provisions of article 34, paragraphs 2, 4 and 5, shall apply.

## *Interpretation of the award*

*Article 37*

1. Within 30 days after the receipt of the award, a party, with notice to the other parties, may request that the arbitral tribunal give an interpretation of the award.

2. The interpretation shall be given in writing within 45 days after the receipt of the request. The interpretation shall form part of the award and the provisions of article 34, paragraphs 2 to 6, shall apply.

## Correction of the award

### Article 38

1. Within 30 days after the receipt of the award, a party, with notice to the other parties, may request the arbitral tribunal to correct in the award any error in computation, any clerical or typographical error, or any error or omission of a similar nature. If the arbitral tribunal considers that the request is justified, it shall make the correction within 45 days of receipt of the request.

2. The arbitral tribunal may within 30 days after the communication of the award make such corrections on its own initiative.

3. Such corrections shall be in writing and shall form part of the award. The provisions of article 34, paragraphs 2 to 6, shall apply.

## Additional award

### Article 39

1. Within 30 days after the receipt of the termination order or the award, a party, with notice to the other parties, may request the arbitral tribunal to make an award or an additional award as to claims presented in the arbitral proceedings but not decided by the arbitral tribunal.

2. If the arbitral tribunal considers the request for an award or additional award to be justified, it shall render or complete its award within 60 days after the receipt of the request. The arbitral tribunal may extend, if necessary, the period of time within which it shall make the award.

3. When such an award or additional award is made, the provisions of article 34, paragraphs 2 to 6, shall apply.

## Definition of costs

### Article 40

1. The arbitral tribunal shall fix the costs of arbitration in the final award and, if it deems appropriate, in another decision.

2. The term "costs" includes only:
    *(a)* The fees of the arbitral tribunal to be stated separately as to each arbitrator and to be fixed by the tribunal itself in accordance with article 41;
    *(b)* The reasonable travel and other expenses incurred by the arbitrators;

(c) The reasonable costs of expert advice and of other assistance required by the arbitral tribunal;
  (d) The reasonable travel and other expenses of witnesses to the extent such expenses are approved by the arbitral tribunal;
  (e) The legal and other costs incurred by the parties in relation to the arbitration to the extent that the arbitral tribunal determines that the amount of such costs is reasonable;
  (f) Any fees and expenses of the appointing authority as well as the fees and expenses of the Secretary-General of the PCA.

3. In relation to interpretation, correction or completion of any award under articles 37 to 39, the arbitral tribunal may charge the costs referred to in paragraphs 2 (b) to (f), but no additional fees.

## Fees and expenses of arbitrators

*Article 41*

1. The fees and expenses of the arbitrators shall be reasonable in amount, taking into account the amount in dispute, the complexity of the subject matter, the time spent by the arbitrators and any other relevant circumstances of the case.

2. If there is an appointing authority and it applies or has stated that it will apply a schedule or particular method for determining the fees for arbitrators in international cases, the arbitral tribunal in fixing its fees shall take that schedule or method into account to the extent that it considers appropriate in the circumstances of the case.

3. Promptly after its constitution, the arbitral tribunal shall inform the parties as to how it proposes to determine its fees and expenses, including any rates it intends to apply. Within 15 days of receiving that proposal, any party may refer the proposal to the appointing authority for review. If, within 45 days of receipt of such a referral, the appointing authority finds that the proposal of the arbitral tribunal is inconsistent with paragraph 1, it shall make any necessary adjustments thereto, which shall be binding upon the arbitral tribunal.

4. (a) When informing the parties of the arbitrators' fees and expenses that have been fixed pursuant to article 40, paragraphs 2 (a) and (b), the arbitral tribunal shall also explain the manner in which the corresponding amounts have been calculated;
  (b) Within 15 days of receiving the arbitral tribunal's determination of fees and expenses, any party may refer for review such determination to the appointing authority. If no appointing authority has been agreed upon or designated, or if the appointing authority fails to act within the time specified in these Rules, then the review shall be made by the Secretary-General of the PCA;
  (c) If the appointing authority or the Secretary-General of the PCA finds that the arbitral tribunal's determination is inconsistent with the arbitral tribunal's proposal (and any adjustment thereto) under paragraph 3 or is

otherwise manifestly excessive, it shall, within 45 days of receiving such a referral, make any adjustments to the arbitral tribunal's determination that are necessary to satisfy the criteria in paragraph 1. Any such adjustments shall be binding upon the arbitral tribunal;

(d) Any such adjustments shall either be included by the arbitral tribunal in its award or, if the award has already been issued, be implemented in a correction to the award, to which the procedure of article 38, paragraph 3, shall apply.

5. Throughout the procedure under paragraphs 3 and 4, the arbitral tribunal shall proceed with the arbitration, in accordance with article 17, paragraph 1.

6. A referral under paragraph 4 shall not affect any determination in the award other than the arbitral tribunal's fees and expenses; nor shall it delay the recognition and enforcement of all parts of the award other than those relating to the determination of the arbitral tribunal's fees and expenses.

## *Allocation of costs*

*Article 42*

1. The costs of the arbitration shall in principle be borne by the unsuccessful party or parties. However, the arbitral tribunal may apportion each of such costs between the parties if it determines that apportionment is reasonable, taking into account the circumstances of the case.

2. The arbitral tribunal shall in the final award or, if it deems appropriate, in any other award, determine any amount that a party may have to pay to another party as a result of the decision on allocation of costs.

## *Deposit of costs*

*Article 43*

1. The arbitral tribunal, on its establishment, may request the parties to deposit an equal amount as an advance for the costs referred to in article 40, paragraphs 2 *(a)* to *(c)*.

2. During the course of the arbitral proceedings the arbitral tribunal may request supplementary deposits from the parties.

3. If an appointing authority has been agreed upon or designated, and when a party so requests and the appointing authority consents to perform the function, the arbitral tribunal shall fix the amounts of any deposits or supplementary deposits only after consultation with the appointing authority, which may make any comments to the arbitral tribunal that it deems appropriate concerning the amount of such deposits and supplementary deposits.

4. If the required deposits are not paid in full within 30 days after the receipt of the request, the arbitral tribunal shall so inform the parties in order that one or more of them may make the required payment. If such payment is not made, the arbitral tribunal may order the suspension or termination of the arbitral proceedings.

5. After a termination order or final award has been made, the arbitral tribunal shall render an accounting to the parties of the deposits received and return any unexpended balance to the parties.

## ANNEX

### Model arbitration clause for contracts

Any dispute, controversy or claim arising out of or relating to this contract, or the breach, termination or invalidity thereof, shall be settled by arbitration in accordance with the UNCITRAL Arbitration Rules.

*Note. Parties should consider adding:*
- *(a)* The appointing authority shall be . . . [name of institution or person];
- *(b)* The number of arbitrators shall be . . . [one or three];
- *(c)* The place of arbitration shall be . . . [town and country];
- *(d)* The language to be used in the arbitral proceedings shall be. . . .

### Possible waiver statement

*Note. If the parties wish to exclude recourse against the arbitral award that may be available under the applicable law, they may consider adding a provision to that effect as suggested below, considering, however, that the effectiveness and conditions of such an exclusion depend on the applicable law.*

*Waiver*

The parties hereby waive their right to any form of recourse against an award to any court or other competent authority, insofar as such waiver can validly be made under the applicable law.

### Model statements of independence pursuant to article 11 of the Rules

*No circumstances to disclose*

I am impartial and independent of each of the parties and intend to remain so. To the best of my knowledge, there are no circumstances, past or present, likely to give rise to justifiable doubts as to my impartiality or independence. I shall promptly notify the parties and the other arbitrators of any such circumstances that may subsequently come to my attention during this arbitration.

*Circumstances to disclose*

I am impartial and independent of each of the parties and intend to remain so. Attached is a statement made pursuant to article 11 of the UNCITRAL Arbitration Rules of *(a)* my past and present professional, business and other relationships with the parties and *(b)* any other relevant circumstances. [Include statement.] I confirm that those circumstances do not affect my independence and impartiality. I shall promptly notify the parties and the other arbitrators of any such further relationships or circumstances that may subsequently come to my attention during this arbitration.

*Note. Any party may consider requesting from the arbitrator the following addition to the statement of independence:*

I confirm, on the basis of the information presently available to me, that I can devote the time necessary to conduct this arbitration diligently, efficiently and in accordance with the time limits in the Rules.

Appendix 12

# IBA RULES ON THE TAKING OF EVIDENCE IN INTERNATIONAL ARBITRATION

*Adopted by a resolution of the IBA Council 29 May 2010*
*International Bar Association*

## About the Arbitration Committee

Established as the Committee in the International Bar Association's Legal Practice Division which focuses on the laws, practice and procedures relating to the arbitration of transnational disputes, the Arbitration Committee currently has over 2,300 members from over 90 countries, and membership is increasing steadily.

Through its publications and conferences, the Committee seeks to share information about international arbitration, promote its use and improve its effectiveness. The Committee maintains standing subcommittees and, as appropriate, establishes Task Forces to address specific issues. At the time of issuance of these revised Rules, the Committee has four subcommittees, namely the Rules of Evidence Subcommittee, the Investment Treaty Arbitration Subcommittee, the Conflicts of Interest Subcommittee, and the Recognition and Enforcement of Arbitral Awards Subcommittee; and two task forces: the Task Force on Attorney Ethics in Arbitration and the Task Force on Arbitration Agreements.

## Foreword

These IBA Rules on the Taking of Evidence in International Arbitration ('IBA Rules of Evidence') are a revised version of the IBA Rules on the Taking of Evidence in International Commercial Arbitration, prepared by a Working Party of the Arbitration Committee whose members are listed on pages i and ii.

The IBA issued these Rules as a resource to parties and to arbitrators to provide an efficient, economical and fair process for the taking of evidence in international arbitration. The Rules provide mechanisms for the presentation of documents, witnesses of fact and expert witnesses, inspections, as well as the conduct of evidentiary hearings. The Rules are designed to be used in conjunction with, and adopted together with, institutional, ad hoc or other rules or procedures governing international arbitrations. The IBA Rules of Evidence reflect procedures in use in many different legal systems, and they may be particularly useful when the parties come from different legal cultures.

Since their issuance in 1999, the IBA Rules on the Taking of Evidence in International Commercial Arbitration have gained wide acceptance within the international arbitral community. In 2008, a review process was initiated at the instance of Sally Harpole and Pierre Bienvenu, the then Co-Chairs of the Arbitration Committee. The revised version of the IBA Rules of Evidence was developed by the members of the IBA Rules of Evidence Review Subcommittee, assisted by members of the 1999 Working Party. These revised Rules replace the IBA Rules on the Taking of Evidence in International Commercial Arbitration, which themselves replaced the IBA Supplementary Rules Governing the Presentation and Reception of Evidence in International Commercial Arbitration, issued in 1983.

If parties wish to adopt the IBA Rules of Evidence in their arbitration clause, it is recommended that they add the following language to the clause, selecting one of the alternatives therein provided:

> '[In addition to the institutional, ad hoc or other rules chosen by the parties,] [t]he parties agree that the arbitration shall be conducted according to the IBA Rules of Evidence as current on the date of [this agreement/the commencement of the arbitration].'

In addition, parties and Arbitral Tribunals may adopt the IBA Rules of Evidence, in whole or in part, at the commencement of the arbitration, or at any time thereafter. They may also vary them or use them as guidelines in developing their own procedures.

The IBA Rules of Evidence were adopted by resolution of the IBA Council on 29 May 2010. The IBA Rules of Evidence are available in English, and translations in other languages are planned. Copies of the IBA Rules of Evidence may be ordered from the IBA, and the Rules are available to download at **http://tinyurl.com/iba- Arbitration-Guidelines.**

**Guido S Tawil**
**Judith Gill, QC**
*Co-Chairs, Arbitration Committee*
29 May 2010

**The Rules**

**Preamble**
1. These IBA Rules on the Taking of Evidence in International Arbitration are intended to provide an efficient, economical and fair process for the taking of evidence in international arbitrations, particularly those between Parties from different legal traditions. They are designed to supplement the legal provisions and the institutional, ad hoc or other rules that apply to the conduct of the arbitration.

2. Parties and Arbitral Tribunals may adopt the IBA Rules of Evidence, in whole or in part, to govern arbitration proceedings, or they may vary them or use them as guidelines in developing their own procedures. The Rules are not intended to limit the flexibility that is inherent in, and an advantage of, international arbitration, and Parties and Arbitral Tribunals are free to adapt them to the particular circumstances of each arbitration.
3. The taking of evidence shall be conducted on the principles that each Party shall act in good faith and be entitled to know, reasonably in advance of any Evidentiary Hearing or any fact or merits determination, the evidence on which the other Parties rely.

**Definitions**

In the IBA Rules of Evidence:

*'Arbitral Tribunal'* means a sole arbitrator or a panel of arbitrators;

*'Claimant'* means the Party or Parties who commenced the arbitration and any Party who, through joinder or otherwise, becomes aligned with such Party or Parties;

*'Document'* means a writing, communication, picture, drawing, program or data of any kind, whether recorded or maintained on paper or by electronic, audio, visual or any other means;

*'Evidentiary Hearing'* means any hearing, whether or not held on consecutive days, at which the Arbitral Tribunal, whether in person, by teleconference, videoconference or other method, receives oral or other evidence;

*'Expert Report'* means a written statement by a Tribunal- Appointed Expert or a Party-Appointed Expert;

*'General Rules'* mean the institutional, ad hoc or other rules that apply to the conduct of the arbitration;

*'IBA Rules of Evidence'* or *'Rules'* means these IBA Rules on the Taking of Evidence in International Arbitration, as they may be revised or amended from time to time;

*'Party'* means a party to the arbitration;

*'Party-Appointed Expert'* means a person or organisation appointed by a Party in order to report on specific issues determined by the Party;

*'Request to Produce'* means a written request by a Party that another Party produce Documents;

*'Respondent'* means the Party or Parties against whom the Claimant made its claim, and any Party who, through joinder or otherwise, becomes aligned with such Party or Parties, and includes a Respondent making a counter-claim;

'Tribunal-Appointed Expert' means a person or organisation appointed by the Arbitral Tribunal in order to report to it on specific issues determined by the Arbitral Tribunal; and

'Witness Statement' means a written statement of testimony by a witness of fact.

## Article 1 Scope of Application

1. Whenever the Parties have agreed or the Arbitral Tribunal has determined to apply the IBA Rules of Evidence, the Rules shall govern the taking of evidence, except to the extent that any specific provision of them may be found to be in conflict with any mandatory provision of law determined to be applicable to the case by the Parties or by the Arbitral Tribunal.
2. Where the Parties have agreed to apply the IBA Rules of Evidence, they shall be deemed to have agreed, in the absence of a contrary indication, to the version as current on the date of such agreement.
3. In case of conflict between any provisions of the IBA Rules of Evidence and the General Rules, the Arbitral Tribunal shall apply the IBA Rules of Evidence in the manner that it determines best in order to accomplish the purposes of both the General Rules and the IBA Rules of Evidence, unless the Parties agree to the contrary.
4. In the event of any dispute regarding the meaning of the IBA Rules of Evidence, the Arbitral Tribunal shall interpret them according to their purpose and in the manner most appropriate for the particular arbitration.
5. Insofar as the IBA Rules of Evidence and the General Rules are silent on any matter concerning the taking of evidence and the Parties have not agreed otherwise, the Arbitral Tribunal shall conduct the taking of evidence as it deems appropriate, in accordance with the general principles of the IBA Rules of Evidence.

## Article 2 Consultation on Evidentiary Issues

1. The Arbitral Tribunal shall consult the Parties at the earliest appropriate time in the proceedings and invite them to consult each other with a view to agreeing on an efficient, economical and fair process for the taking of evidence.
2. The consultation on evidentiary issues may address the scope, timing and manner of the taking of evidence, including:
   (a) the preparation and submission of Witness Statements and Expert Reports;
   (b) the taking of oral testimony at any Evidentiary Hearing;
   (c) the requirements, procedure and format applicable to the production of Documents;
   (d) the level of confidentiality protection to be afforded to evidence in the arbitration; and
   (e) the promotion of efficiency, economy and conservation of resources in connection with the taking of evidence.
3. The Arbitral Tribunal is encouraged to identify to the Parties, as soon as it considers it to be appropriate, any issues:

(a) that the Arbitral Tribunal may regard as relevant to the case and material to its outcome; and/or
(b) for which a preliminary determination may be appropriate.

**Article 3  Documents**
1. Within the time ordered by the Arbitral Tribunal, each Party shall submit to the Arbitral Tribunal and to the other Parties all Documents available to it on which it relies, including public Documents and those in the public domain, except for any Documents that have already been submitted by another Party.
2. Within the time ordered by the Arbitral Tribunal, any Party may submit to the Arbitral Tribunal and to the other Parties a Request to Produce.
3. A Request to Produce shall contain:
    (a) *(i)* a description of each requested Document sufficient to identify it, or
    *(ii)* a description in sufficient detail (including subject matter) of a narrow and specific requested category of Documents that are reasonably believed to exist; in the case of Documents maintained in electronic form, the requesting Party may, or the Arbitral Tribunal may order that it shall be required to, identify specific files, search terms, individuals or other means of searching for such Documents in an efficient and economical manner;
    (b) a statement as to how the Documents requested are relevant to the case and material to its outcome; and
    (c) *(i)* a statement that the Documents requested are not in the possession, custody or control of the requesting Party or a statement of the reasons why it would be unreasonably burdensome for the requesting Party to produce such Documents, and
    *(ii)* a statement of the reasons why the requesting Party assumes the Documents requested are in the possession, custody or control of another Party.
4. Within the time ordered by the Arbitral Tribunal, the Party to whom the Request to Produce is addressed shall produce to the other Parties and, if the Arbitral Tribunal so orders, to it, all the Documents requested in its possession, custody or control as to which it makes no objection.
5. If the Party to whom the Request to Produce is addressed has an objection to some or all of the Documents requested, it shall state the objection in writing to the Arbitral Tribunal and the other Parties within the time ordered by the Arbitral Tribunal. The reasons for such objection shall be any of those set forth in Article 9.2 or a failure to satisfy any of the requirements of Article 3.3.
6. Upon receipt of any such objection, the Arbitral Tribunal may invite the relevant Parties to consult with each other with a view to resolving the objection.
7. Either Party may, within the time ordered by the Arbitral Tribunal, request the Arbitral Tribunal to rule on the objection. The Arbitral Tribunal shall then, in consultation with the Parties and in timely fashion, consider the Request to Produce and the objection. The Arbitral Tribunal may order the Party to whom such Request is addressed to produce any requested Document

in its possession, custody or control as to which the Arbitral Tribunal determines that *(i)* the issues that the requesting Party wishes to prove are relevant to the case and material to its outcome; *(ii)* none of the reasons for objection set forth in Article 9.2 applies; and *(iii)* the requirements of Article 3.3 have been satisfied. Any such Document shall be produced to the other Parties and, if the Arbitral Tribunal so orders, to it.

8. In exceptional circumstances, if the propriety of an objection can be determined only by review of the Document, the Arbitral Tribunal may determine that it should not review the Document. In that event, the Arbitral Tribunal may, after consultation with the Parties, appoint an independent and impartial expert, bound to confidentiality, to review any such Document and to report on the objection. To the extent that the objection is upheld by the Arbitral Tribunal, the expert shall not disclose to the Arbitral Tribunal and to the other Parties the contents of the Document reviewed.

9. If a Party wishes to obtain the production of Documents from a person or organisation who is not a Party to the arbitration and from whom the Party cannot obtain the Documents on its own, the Party may, within the time ordered by the Arbitral Tribunal, ask it to take whatever steps are legally available to obtain the requested Documents, or seek leave from the Arbitral Tribunal to take such steps itself. The Party shall submit such request to the Arbitral Tribunal and to the other Parties in writing, and the request shall contain the particulars set forth in Article 3.3, as applicable. The Arbitral Tribunal shall decide on this request and shall take, authorize the requesting Party to take, or order any other Party to take, such steps as the Arbitral Tribunal considers appropriate if, in its discretion, it determines that *(i)* the Documents would be relevant to the case and material to its outcome, *(ii)* the requirements of Article 3.3, as applicable, have been satisfied and *(iii)* none of the reasons for objection set forth in Article 9.2 applies.

10. At any time before the arbitration is concluded, the Arbitral Tribunal may *(i)* request any Party to produce Documents, *(ii)* request any Party to use its best efforts to take or *(iii)* itself take, any step that it considers appropriate to obtain Documents from any person or organisation. A Party to whom such a request for Documents is addressed may object to the request for any of the reasons set forth in Article 9.2. In such cases, Article 3.4 to Article 3.8 shall apply correspondingly.

11. Within the time ordered by the Arbitral Tribunal, the Parties may submit to the Arbitral Tribunal and to the other Parties any additional Documents on which they intend to rely or which they believe have become relevant to the case and material to its outcome as a consequence of the issues raised in Documents, Witness Statements or Expert Reports submitted or produced, or in other submissions of the Parties.

12. With respect to the form of submission or production of Documents:
    (a) copies of Documents shall conform to the originals and, at the request of the Arbitral Tribunal, any original shall be presented for inspection;
    (b) Documents that a Party maintains in electronic form shall be submitted or produced in the form most convenient or economical to it that is reasonably usable by the recipients, unless the Parties agree otherwise

or, in the absence of such agreement, the Arbitral Tribunal decides otherwise;
  (c) a Party is not obligated to produce multiple copies of Documents which are essentially identical unless the Arbitral Tribunal decides otherwise; and
  (d) translations of Documents shall be submitted together with the originals and marked as translations with the original language identified.
13. Any Document submitted or produced by a Party or non-Party in the arbitration and not otherwise in the public domain shall be kept confidential by the Arbitral Tribunal and the other Parties, and shall be used only in connection with the arbitration. This requirement shall apply except and to the extent that disclosure may be required of a Party to fulfil a legal duty, protect or pursue a legal right, or enforce or challenge an award in bona fide legal proceedings before a state court or other judicial authority. The Arbitral Tribunal may issue orders to set forth the terms of this confidentiality. This requirement shall be without prejudice to all other obligations of confidentiality in the arbitration.
14. If the arbitration is organised into separate issues or phases (such as jurisdiction, preliminary determinations, liability or damages), the Arbitral Tribunal may, after consultation with the Parties, schedule the submission of Documents and Requests to Produce separately for each issue or phase.

**Article 4  Witnesses of Fact**
1. Within the time ordered by the Arbitral Tribunal, each Party shall identify the witnesses on whose testimony it intends to rely and the subject matter of that testimony.
2. Any person may present evidence as a witness, including a Party or a Party's officer, employee or other representative.
3. It shall not be improper for a Party, its officers, employees, legal advisors or other representatives to interview its witnesses or potential witnesses and to discuss their prospective testimony with them.
4. The Arbitral Tribunal may order each Party to submit within a specified time to the Arbitral Tribunal and to the other Parties Witness Statements by each witness on whose testimony it intends to rely, except for those witnesses whose testimony is sought pursuant to Articles 4.9 or 4.10. If Evidentiary Hearings are organised into separate issues or phases (such as jurisdiction, preliminary determinations, liability or damages), the Arbitral Tribunal or the Parties by agreement may schedule the submission of Witness Statements separately for each issue or phase.
5. Each Witness Statement shall contain:
  (a) the full name and address of the witness, a statement regarding his or her present and past relationship (if any) with any of the Parties, and a description of his or her background, qualifications, training and experience, if such a description may be relevant to the dispute or to the contents of the statement;
  (b) a full and detailed description of the facts, and the source of the witness's information as to those facts, sufficient to serve as that witness's

evidence in the matter in dispute. Documents on which the witness relies that have not already been submitted shall be provided;
   (c) a statement as to the language in which the Witness Statement was originally prepared and the language in which the witness anticipates giving testimony at the Evidentiary Hearing;
   (d) an affirmation of the truth of the Witness Statement; and
   (e) the signature of the witness and its date and place.
6. If Witness Statements are submitted, any Party may, within the time ordered by the Arbitral Tribunal, submit to the Arbitral Tribunal and to the other Parties revised or additional Witness Statements, including statements from persons not previously named as witnesses, so long as any such revisions or additions respond only to matters contained in another Party's Witness Statements, Expert Reports or other submissions that have not been previously presented in the arbitration.
7. If a witness whose appearance has been requested pursuant to Article 8.1 fails without a valid reason to appear for testimony at an Evidentiary Hearing, the Arbitral Tribunal shall disregard any Witness Statement related to that Evidentiary Hearing by that witness unless, in exceptional circumstances, the Arbitral Tribunal decides otherwise.
8. If the appearance of a witness has not been requested pursuant to Article 8.1, none of the other Parties shall be deemed to have agreed to the correctness of the content of the Witness Statement.
9. If a Party wishes to present evidence from a person who will not appear voluntarily at its request, the Party may, within the time ordered by the Arbitral Tribunal, ask it to take whatever steps are legally available to obtain the testimony of that person, or seek leave from the Arbitral Tribunal to take such steps itself. In the case of a request to the Arbitral Tribunal, the Party shall identify the intended witness, shall describe the subjects on which the witness's testimony is sought and shall state why such subjects are relevant to the case and material to its outcome. The Arbitral Tribunal shall decide on this request and shall take, authorize the requesting Party to take or order any other Party to take, such steps as the Arbitral Tribunal considers appropriate if, in its discretion, it determines that the testimony of that witness would be relevant to the case and material to its outcome.
10. At any time before the arbitration is concluded, the Arbitral Tribunal may order any Party to provide for, or to use its best efforts to provide for, the appearance for testimony at an Evidentiary Hearing of any person, including one whose testimony has not yet been offered. A Party to whom such a request is addressed may object for any of the reasons set forth in Article 9.2.

**Article 5 Party-Appointed Experts**
1. A Party may rely on a Party-Appointed Expert as a means of evidence on specific issues. Within the time ordered by the Arbitral Tribunal, (i) each Party shall identify any Party-Appointed Expert on whose testimony it intends to rely and the subject-matter of such testimony; and (ii) the Party-Appointed Expert shall submit an Expert Report.
2. The Expert Report shall contain:

(a) the full name and address of the Party- Appointed Expert, a statement regarding his or her present and past relationship (if any) with any of the Parties, their legal advisors and the Arbitral Tribunal, and a description of his or her background, qualifications, training and experience;
(b) a description of the instructions pursuant to which he or she is providing his or her opinions and conclusions;
(c) a statement of his or her independence from the Parties, their legal advisors and the Arbitral Tribunal;
(d) a statement of the facts on which he or she is basing his or her expert opinions and conclusions;
(e) his or her expert opinions and conclusions, including a description of the methods, evidence and information used in arriving at the conclusions. Documents on which the Party-Appointed Expert relies that have not already been submitted shall be provided;
(f) if the Expert Report has been translated, a statement as to the language in which it was originally prepared, and the language in which the Party-Appointed Expert anticipates giving testimony at the Evidentiary Hearing;
(g) an affirmation of his or her genuine belief in the opinions expressed in the Expert Report;
(h) the signature of the Party-Appointed Expert and its date and place; and
(i) if the Expert Report has been signed by more than one person, an attribution of the entirety or specific parts of the Expert Report to each author.

3. If Expert Reports are submitted, any Party may, within the time ordered by the Arbitral Tribunal, submit to the Arbitral Tribunal and to the other Parties revised or additional Expert Reports, including reports or statements from persons not previously identified as Party-Appointed Experts, so long as any such revisions or additions respond only to matters contained in another Party's Witness Statements, Expert Reports or other submissions that have not been previously presented in the arbitration.

4. The Arbitral Tribunal in its discretion may order that any Party-Appointed Experts who will submit or who have submitted Expert Reports on the same or related issues meet and confer on such issues. At such meeting, the Party-Appointed Experts shall attempt to reach agreement on the issues within the scope of their Expert Reports, and they shall record in writing any such issues on which they reach agreement, any remaining areas of disagreement and the reasons therefore.

5. If a Party-Appointed Expert whose appearance has been requested pursuant to Article 8.1 fails without a valid reason to appear for testimony at an Evidentiary Hearing, the Arbitral Tribunal shall disregard any Expert Report by that Party-Appointed Expert related to that Evidentiary Hearing unless, in exceptional circumstances, the Arbitral Tribunal decides otherwise.

6. If the appearance of a Party-Appointed Expert has not been requested pursuant to Article 8.1, none of the other Parties shall be deemed to have agreed to the correctness of the content of the Expert Report.

## Article 6 Tribunal-Appointed Experts

1. The Arbitral Tribunal, after consulting with the Parties, may appoint one or more independent Tribunal-Appointed Experts to report to it on specific issues designated by the Arbitral Tribunal. The Arbitral Tribunal shall establish the terms of reference for any Tribunal-Appointed Expert Report after consulting with the Parties. A copy of the final terms of reference shall be sent by the Arbitral Tribunal to the Parties.
2. The Tribunal-Appointed Expert shall, before accepting appointment, submit to the Arbitral Tribunal and to the Parties a description of his or her qualifications and a statement of his or her independence from the Parties, their legal advisors and the Arbitral Tribunal. Within the time ordered by the Arbitral Tribunal, the Parties shall inform the Arbitral Tribunal whether they have any objections as to the Tribunal-Appointed Expert's qualifications and independence. The Arbitral Tribunal shall decide promptly whether to accept any such objection. After the appointment of a Tribunal- Appointed Expert, a Party may object to the expert's qualifications or independence only if the objection is for reasons of which the Party becomes aware after the appointment has been made. The Arbitral Tribunal shall decide promptly what, if any, action to take.
3. Subject to the provisions of Article 9.2, the Tribunal- Appointed Expert may request a Party to provide any information or to provide access to any Documents, goods, samples, property, machinery, systems, processes or site for inspection, to the extent relevant to the case and material to its outcome. The authority of a Tribunal-Appointed Expert to request such information or access shall be the same as the authority of the Arbitral Tribunal. The Parties and their representatives shall have the right to receive any such information and to attend any such inspection. Any disagreement between a Tribunal-Appointed Expert and a Party as to the relevance, materiality or appropriateness of such a request shall be decided by the Arbitral Tribunal, in the manner provided in Articles 3.5 through 3.8. The Tribunal- Appointed Expert shall record in the Expert Report any non-compliance by a Party with an appropriate request or decision by the Arbitral Tribunal and shall describe its effects on the determination of the specific issue.
4. The Tribunal-Appointed Expert shall report in writing to the Arbitral Tribunal in an Expert Report. The Expert Report shall contain:
    (a) the full name and address of the Tribunal- Appointed Expert, and a description of his or her background, qualifications, training and experience;
    (b) a statement of the facts on which he or she is basing his or her expert opinions and conclusions;
    (c) his or her expert opinions and conclusions, including a description of the methods, evidence and information used in arriving at the conclusions. Documents on which the Tribunal-Appointed Expert relies that have not already been submitted shall be provided;
    (d) if the Expert Report has been translated, a statement as to the language in which it was originally prepared, and the language in which the

Tribunal-Appointed Expert anticipates giving testimony at the Evidentiary Hearing;
(e) an affirmation of his or her genuine belief in the opinions expressed in the Expert Report;
(f) the signature of the Tribunal-Appointed Expert and its date and place; and
(g) if the Expert Report has been signed by more than one person, an attribution of the entirety or specific parts of the Expert Report to each author.
5. The Arbitral Tribunal shall send a copy of such Expert Report to the Parties. The Parties may examine any information, Documents, goods, samples, property, machinery, systems, processes or site for inspection that the Tribunal-Appointed Expert has examined and any correspondence between the Arbitral Tribunal and the Tribunal-Appointed Expert. Within the time ordered by the Arbitral Tribunal, any Party shall have the opportunity to respond to the Expert Report in a submission by the Party or through a Witness Statement or an Expert Report by a Party-Appointed Expert. The Arbitral Tribunal shall send the submission, Witness Statement or Expert Report to the Tribunal-Appointed Expert and to the other Parties.
6. At the request of a Party or of the Arbitral Tribunal, the Tribunal-Appointed Expert shall be present at an Evidentiary Hearing. The Arbitral Tribunal may question the Tribunal-Appointed Expert, and he or she may be questioned by the Parties or by any Party-Appointed Expert on issues raised in his or her Expert Report, the Parties' submissions or Witness Statement or the Expert Reports made by the Party- Appointed Experts pursuant to Article 6.5.
7. Any Expert Report made by a Tribunal-Appointed Expert and its conclusions shall be assessed by the Arbitral Tribunal with due regard to all circumstances of the case.
8. The fees and expenses of a Tribunal-Appointed Expert, to be funded in a manner determined by the Arbitral Tribunal, shall form part of the costs of the arbitration.

## Article 7 Inspection

Subject to the provisions of Article 9.2, the Arbitral Tribunal may, at the request of a Party or on its own motion, inspect or require the inspection by a Tribunal-Appointed Expert or a Party-Appointed Expert of any site, property, machinery or any other goods, samples, systems, processes or Documents, as it deems appropriate. The Arbitral Tribunal shall, in consultation with the Parties, determine the timing and arrangement for the inspection. The Parties and their representatives shall have the right to attend any such inspection.

## Article 8 Evidentiary Hearing

1. Within the time ordered by the Arbitral Tribunal, each Party shall inform the Arbitral Tribunal and the other Parties of the witnesses whose appearance it requests. Each witness (which term includes, for the purposes of this Article, witnesses of fact and any experts) shall, subject to Article 8.2, appear for testimony at the Evidentiary Hearing if such person's appearance has been

requested by any Party or by the Arbitral Tribunal. Each witness shall appear in person unless the Arbitral Tribunal allows the use of videoconference or similar technology with respect to a particular witness.
2. The Arbitral Tribunal shall at all times have complete control over the Evidentiary Hearing. The Arbitral Tribunal may limit or exclude any question to, answer by or appearance of a witness, if it considers such question, answer or appearance to be irrelevant, immaterial, unreasonably burdensome, duplicative or otherwise covered by a reason for objection set forth in Article 9.2. Questions to a witness during direct and re-direct testimony may not be unreasonably leading.
3. With respect to oral testimony at an Evidentiary Hearing:
    (a) the Claimant shall ordinarily first present the testimony of its witnesses, followed by the Respondent presenting the testimony of its witnesses;
    (b) following direct testimony, any other Party may question such witness, in an order to be determined by the Arbitral Tribunal. The Party who initially presented the witness shall subsequently have the opportunity to ask additional questions on the matters raised in the other Parties' questioning;
    (c) thereafter, the Claimant shall ordinarily first present the testimony of its Party-Appointed Experts, followed by the Respondent presenting the testimony of its Party-Appointed Experts. The Party who initially presented the Party-Appointed Expert shall subsequently have the opportunity to ask additional questions on the matters raised in the other Parties' questioning;
    (d) the Arbitral Tribunal may question a Tribunal- Appointed Expert, and he or she may be questioned by the Parties or by any Party- Appointed Expert, on issues raised in the Tribunal-Appointed Expert Report, in the Parties' submissions or in the Expert Reports made by the Party-Appointed Experts;
    (e) if the arbitration is organised into separate issues or phases (such as jurisdiction, preliminary determinations, liability and damages), the Parties may agree or the Arbitral Tribunal may order the scheduling of testimony separately for each issue or phase;
    (f) the Arbitral Tribunal, upon request of a Party or on its own motion, may vary this order of proceeding, including the arrangement of testimony by particular issues or in such a manner that witnesses be questioned at the same time and in confrontation with each other (witness conferencing);
    (g) the Arbitral Tribunal may ask questions to a witness at any time.
4. A witness of fact providing testimony shall first affirm, in a manner determined appropriate by the Arbitral Tribunal, that he or she commits to tell the truth or, in the case of an expert witness, his or her genuine belief in the opinions to be expressed at the Evidentiary Hearing. If the witness has submitted a Witness Statement or an Expert Report, the witness shall confirm it. The Parties may agree or the Arbitral Tribunal may order that the Witness Statement or Expert Report shall serve as that witness's direct testimony.

5. Subject to the provisions of Article 9.2, the Arbitral Tribunal may request any person to give oral or written evidence on any issue that the Arbitral Tribunal considers to be relevant to the case and material to its outcome. Any witness called and questioned by the Arbitral Tribunal may also be questioned by the Parties.

**Article 9 Admissibility and Assessment of Evidence**
1. The Arbitral Tribunal shall determine the admissibility, relevance, materiality and weight of evidence.
2. The Arbitral Tribunal shall, at the request of a Party or on its own motion, exclude from evidence or production any Document, statement, oral testimony or inspection for any of the following reasons:
    (a) lack of sufficient relevance to the case or materiality to its outcome;
    (b) legal impediment or privilege under the legal or ethical rules determined by the Arbitral Tribunal to be applicable;
    (c) unreasonable burden to produce the requested evidence;
    (d) loss or destruction of the Document that has been shown with reasonable likelihood to have occurred;
    (e) grounds of commercial or technical confiden- tiality that the Arbitral Tribunal determines to be compelling;
    (f) grounds of special political or institutional sensitivity (including evidence that has been classified as secret by a government or a public international institution) that the Arbitral Tribunal determines to be compelling; or
    (g) considerations of procedural economy, proportionality, fairness or equality of the Parties that the Arbitral Tribunal determines to be compelling.
3. In considering issues of legal impediment or privilege under Article 9.2(b), and insofar as permitted by any mandatory legal or ethical rules that are determined by it to be applicable, the Arbitral Tribunal may take into account:
    (a) any need to protect the confidentiality of a Document created or statement or oral communication made in connection with and for the purpose of providing or obtaining legal advice;
    (b) any need to protect the confidentiality of a Document created or statement or oral communication made in connection with and for the purpose of settlement negotiations;
    (c) the expectations of the Parties and their advisors at the time the legal impediment or privilege is said to have arisen;
    (d) any possible waiver of any applicable legal impediment or privilege by virtue of consent, earlier disclosure, affirmative use of the Document, statement, oral communication or advice contained therein, or otherwise; and
    (e) the need to maintain fairness and equality as between the Parties, particularly if they are subject to different legal or ethical rules.
4. The Arbitral Tribunal may, where appropriate, make necessary arrangements to permit evidence to be presented or considered subject to suitable confidentiality protection.

5. If a Party fails without satisfactory explanation to produce any Document requested in a Request to Produce to which it has not objected in due time or fails to produce any Document ordered to be produced by the Arbitral Tribunal, the Arbitral Tribunal may infer that such document would be adverse to the interests of that Party.
6. If a Party fails without satisfactory explanation to make available any other relevant evidence, including testimony, sought by one Party to which the Party to whom the request was addressed has not objected in due time or fails to make available any evidence, including testimony, ordered by the Arbitral Tribunal to be produced, the Arbitral Tribunal may infer that such evidence would be adverse to the interests of that Party.
7. If the Arbitral Tribunal determines that a Party has failed to conduct itself in good faith in the taking of evidence, the Arbitral Tribunal may, in addition to any other measures available under these Rules, take such failure into account in its assignment of the costs of the arbitration, including costs arising out of or in connection with the taking of evidence.

APPENDIX 13

# IBA GUIDELINES ON CONFLICTS OF INTEREST IN INTERNATIONAL ARBITRATION 2014

Since their issuance in 2004, the *IBA Guidelines on Conflicts of Interest in International Arbitration* (the 'Guidelines')[1] have gained wide acceptance within the international arbitration community. Arbitrators commonly use the Guidelines when making decisions about prospective appointments and disclosures. Likewise, parties and their counsel frequently consider the Guidelines in assessing the impartiality and independence of arbitrators, and arbitral institutions and courts also often consult the Guidelines in considering challenges to arbitrators. As contemplated when the Guidelines were first adopted, on the eve of their tenth anniversary it was considered appropriate to reflect on the accumulated experience of using them and to identify areas of possible clarification or improvement. Accordingly, in 2012, the IBA Arbitration Committee initiated a review of the Guidelines, which was conducted by an expanded Conflicts of Interest Subcommittee (the 'Subcommittee'),[2] representing diverse legal cultures and a range of perspectives, including counsel, arbitrators and arbitration users. The Subcommittee was chaired by David Arias, later co-chaired by Julie Bédard, and the review process was conducted under the leadership of Pierre Bienvenu and Bernard Hanotiau.

While the Guidelines were originally intended to apply to both commercial and investment arbitration, it was found in the course of the review process that

---

[1] The 2004 Guidelines were drafted by a Working Group of 19 experts: Henri Alvarez, Canada; John Beechey, England; Jim Carter, United States; Emmanuel Gaillard, France; Emilio Gonzales de Castilla, Mexico; Bernard Hanotiau, Belgium; Michael Hwang, Singapore; Albert Jan van den Berg, Belgium; Doug Jones, Australia; Gabrielle Kaufmann-Kohler, Switzerland; Arthur Marriott, England; Tore Wiwen Nilsson, Sweden; Hilmar Raeschke-Kessler, Germany; David W. Rivkin, United States; Klaus Sachs, Germany; Nathalie Voser, Switzerland (Rapporteur); David Williams, New Zealand; Des Williams, South Africa; and Otto de Witt Wijnen, The Netherlands (Chair).

[2] The members of the expanded Subcommittee on Conflicts of Interest were: Habib Almulla, UAE; David Arias, Spain (Co-Chair); Julie Bédard, United States (Co-Chair); José Astigarraga, United States; Pierre Bienvenu, Canada (Review Process Co-Chair); Karl-Heinz Böckstiegel, Germany; Yves Derains, France; Teresa Giovannini, Switzerland; Eduardo Damião Gonçalves, Brazil; Bernard Hanotiau, Belgium (Review Process Co-Chair); Paula Hodges, England; Toby Landau, England; Christian Leathley, England; Carole Malinvaud, France; Ciccu Mukhopadhaya, India; Yoshimi Ohara, Japan; Tinuade Oyekunle, Nigeria; Eun Young Park, Korea; Constantine Partasides, England; Peter Rees, The Netherlands; Anke Sessler, Germany; Guido Tawil, Argentina; Jingzhou Tao, China; Gäetan Verhoosel, England (Rapporteur); Nathalie Voser, Switzerland; Nassib Ziadé, UAE; and Alexis Mourre. Assistance was provided by: Niuscha Bassiri, Belgium; Alison Fitzgerald, Canada; Oliver Cojo, Spain; and Ricardo Dalmaso Marques, Brazil.

uncertainty lingered as to their application to investment arbitration. Similarly, despite a comment in the original version of the Guidelines that their application extended to non-legal professionals serving as arbitrator, there appeared to remain uncertainty in this regard as well. A consensus emerged in favour of a general affirmation that the Guidelines apply to both commercial and investment arbitration, and to both legal and non-legal professionals serving as arbitrator.

The Subcommittee has carefully considered a number of issues that have received attention in international arbitration practice since 2004, such as the effects of so-called 'advance waivers', whether the fact of acting concurrently as counsel and arbitrator in unrelated cases raising similar legal issues warrants disclosure, 'issue' conflicts, the independence and impartiality of arbitral or administrative secretaries and third-party funding. The revised Guidelines reflect the Subcommittee's conclusions on these issues.

The Subcommittee has also considered, in view of the evolution of the global practice of international arbitration, whether the revised Guidelines should impose stricter standards in regard to arbitrator disclosure. The revised Guidelines reflect the conclusion that, while the basic approach of the 2004 Guidelines should not be altered, disclosure should be required in certain circumstances not contemplated in the 2004 Guidelines. It is also essential to reaffirm that the fact of requiring disclosure – or of an arbitrator making a disclosure – does not imply the existence of doubts as to the impartiality or independence of the arbitrator. Indeed, the standard for disclosure differs from the standard for challenge. Similarly, the revised Guidelines are not in any way intended to discourage the service as arbitrators of lawyers practising in large firms or legal associations.

The Guidelines were adopted by resolution of the IBA Council on Thursday 23 October 2014. The Guidelines are available for download at: **www.ibanet.org/ Publications/publications_IBA_guides_and_free_materials.aspx**
Eduardo Zuleta and Paul Friedland
Co-Chairs, Arbitration Committee

**Introduction**

1. Arbitrators and party representatives are often unsure about the scope of their disclosure obligations. The growth of international business, including larger corporate groups and international law firms, has generated more disclosures and resulted in increased complexity in the analysis of disclosure and conflict of interest issues. Parties have more opportunities to use challenges of arbitrators to delay arbitrations, or to deny the opposing party the arbitrator of its choice. Disclosure of any relationship, no matter how minor or serious, may lead to unwarranted or frivolous challenges. At the same time, it is important that more information be made available to the parties, so as to protect awards against challenges based upon alleged failures to disclose, and to promote a level playing field among parties and among counsel engaged in international arbitration.

2. Parties, arbitrators, institutions and courts face complex decisions about the information that arbitrators should disclose and the standards to apply to

disclosure. In addition, institutions and courts face difficult decisions when an objection or a challenge is made after a disclosure. There is a tension between, on the one hand, the parties' right to disclosure of circumstances that may call into question an arbitrator's impartiality or independence in order to protect the parties' right to a fair hearing, and, on the other hand, the need to avoid unnecessary challenges against arbitrators in order to protect the parties' ability to select arbitrators of their choosing.

3. It is in the interest of the international arbitration community that arbitration proceedings are not hindered by ill-founded challenges against arbitrators and that the legitimacy of the process is not affected by uncertainty and a lack of uniformity in the applicable standards for disclosures, objections and challenges. The 2004 Guidelines reflected the view that the standards existing at the time lacked sufficient clarity and uniformity in their application. The Guidelines therefore set forth some 'General Standards and Explanatory Notes on the Standards'. Moreover, in order to promote greater consistency and to avoid unnecessary challenges and arbitrator withdrawals and removals, the Guidelines list specific situations indicating whether they warrant disclosure or disqualification of an arbitrator. Such lists, designated 'Red', 'Orange' and 'Green' (the 'Application Lists'), have been updated and appear at the end of these revised Guidelines.

4. The Guidelines reflect the understanding of the IBA Arbitration Committee as to the best current international practice, firmly rooted in the principles expressed in the General Standards below. The General Standards and the Application Lists are based upon statutes and case law in a cross-section of jurisdictions, and upon the judgement and experience of practitioners involved in international arbitration. In reviewing the 2004 Guidelines, the IBA Arbitration Committee updated its analysis of the laws and practices in a number of jurisdictions. The Guidelines seek to balance the various interests of parties, representatives, arbitrators and arbitration institutions, all of whom have a responsibility for ensuring the integrity, reputation and efficiency of international arbitration. Both the 2004 Working Group and the Subcommittee in 2012–2014 have sought and considered the views of leading arbitration institutions, corporate counsel and other persons involved in international arbitration through public consultations at IBA annual meetings, and at meetings with arbitrators and practitioners. The comments received were reviewed in detail and many were adopted. The IBA Arbitration Committee is grateful for the serious consideration given to its proposals by so many institutions and individuals.

5. The Guidelines apply to international commercial arbitration and investment arbitration, whether the representation of the parties is carried out by lawyers or non-lawyers, and irrespective of whether or not non-legal professionals serve as arbitrators.

6. These Guidelines are not legal provisions and do not override any applicable national law or arbitral rules chosen by the parties. However, it is hoped that, as was the case for the 2004 Guidelines and other sets of rules and guidelines of the IBA Arbitration Committee, the revised Guidelines will find broad acceptance within the international arbitration community, and that they will assist parties,

practitioners, arbitrators, institutions and courts in dealing with these important questions of impartiality and independence. The IBA Arbitration Committee trusts that the Guidelines will be applied with robust common sense and without unduly formalistic interpretation.

7. The Application Lists cover many of the varied situations that commonly arise in practice, but they do not purport to be exhaustive, nor could they be. Nevertheless, the IBA Arbitration Committee is confident that the Application Lists provide concrete guidance that is useful in applying the General Standards. The IBA Arbitration Committee will continue to study the actual use of the Guidelines with a view to furthering their improvement.

8. In 1987, the IBA published *Rules of Ethics for International Arbitrators*. Those Rules cover more topics than these Guidelines, and they remain in effect as to subjects that are not discussed in the Guidelines. The Guidelines supersede the *Rules of Ethics* as to the matters treated here.

## Part I: General Standards Regarding Impartiality, Independence and Disclosure

### (1) GENERAL PRINCIPLE

Every arbitrator shall be impartial and independent of the parties at the time of accepting an appointment to serve and shall remain so until the final award has been rendered or the proceedings have otherwise finally terminated.

*Explanation to General Standard 1:*

A fundamental principle underlying these Guidelines is that each arbitrator must be impartial and independent of the parties at the time he or she accepts an appointment to act as arbitrator and must remain so during the entire course of the arbitration proceeding, including the time period for the correction or interpretation of a final award under the relevant rules, assuming such time period is known or readily ascertainable.

The question has arisen as to whether this obligation should extend to the period during which the award may be challenged before the relevant courts. The decision taken is that this obligation should not extend in this manner, unless the final award may be referred back to the original Arbitral Tribunal under the relevant applicable law, or relevant institutional rules. Thus, the arbitrator's obligation in this regard ends when the Arbitral Tribunal has rendered the final award, and any correction or interpretation as may be permitted under the relevant rules has been issued, or the time for seeking the same has elapsed, the proceedings have been finally terminated (for example, because of a settlement), or the arbitrator otherwise no longer has jurisdiction. If, after setting aside or other proceedings, the dispute is referred back to the same Arbitral Tribunal, a fresh round of disclosure and review of potential conflicts of interests may be necessary.

## (2) CONFLICTS OF INTEREST

(a) An arbitrator shall decline to accept an appointment or, if the arbitration has already been commenced, refuse to continue to act as an arbitrator, if he or she has any doubt as to his or her ability to be impartial or independent.

(b) The same principle applies if facts or circumstances exist, or have arisen since the appointment, which, from the point of view of a reasonable third person having knowledge of the relevant facts and circumstances, would give rise to justifiable doubts as to the arbitrator's impartiality or independence, unless the parties have accepted the arbitrator in accordance with the requirements set out in General Standard 4.

(c) Doubts are justifiable if a reasonable third person, having knowledge of the relevant facts and circumstances, would reach the conclusion that there is a likelihood that the arbitrator may be influenced by factors other than the merits of the case as presented by the parties in reaching his or her decision.

(d) Justifiable doubts necessarily exist as to the arbitrator's impartiality or independence in any of the situations described in the Non-Waivable Red List.

*Explanation to General Standard 2:*

(a) If the arbitrator has doubts as to his or her ability to be impartial and independent, the arbitrator must decline the appointment. This standard should apply regardless of the stage of the proceedings. This is a basic principle that is spelled out in these Guidelines in order to avoid confusion and to foster confidence in the arbitral process.

(b) In order for standards to be applied as consistently as possible, the test for disqualification is an objective one. The wording 'impartiality or independence' derives from the widely adopted Article 12 of the United Nations Commission on International Trade Law (UNCITRAL) Model Law, and the use of an appearance test based on justifiable doubts as to the impartiality or independence of the arbitrator, as provided in Article 12(2) of the UNCITRAL Model Law, is to be applied objectively (a 'reasonable third person test'). Again, as described in the Explanation to General Standard 3(e), this standard applies regardless of the stage of the proceedings.

(c) Laws and rules that rely on the standard of justifiable doubts often do not define that standard. This General Standard is intended to provide some context for making this determination.

(d) The Non-Waivable Red List describes circumstances that necessarily raise justifiable doubts as to the arbitrator's impartiality or independence. For example, because no one is allowed to be his or her own judge, there cannot be identity between an arbitrator and a party. The parties therefore cannot waive the conflict of interest arising in such a situation.

## (3) DISCLOSURE BY THE ARBITRATOR

(a) If facts or circumstances exist that may, in the eyes of the parties, give rise to doubts as to the arbitrator's impartiality or independence, the arbitrator shall disclose such facts or circumstances to the parties, the arbitration institution or other appointing authority (if any, and if so required by the applicable institutional rules) and the co-arbitrators, if any, prior to accepting his or her appointment or, if thereafter, as soon as he or she learns of them.

(b) An advance declaration or waiver in relation to possible conflicts of interest arising from facts and circumstances that may arise in the future does not discharge the arbitrator's ongoing duty of disclosure under General Standard 3(a).

(c) It follows from General Standards 1 and 2(a) that an arbitrator who has made a disclosure considers himself or herself to be impartial and independent of the parties, despite the disclosed facts, and therefore capable of performing his or her duties as arbitrator. Otherwise, he or she would have declined the nomination or appointment at the outset, or resigned.

(d) Any doubt as to whether an arbitrator should disclose certain facts or circumstances should be resolved in favour of disclosure.

(e) When considering whether facts or circumstances exist that should be disclosed, the arbitrator shall not take into account whether the arbitration is at the beginning or at a later stage.

*Explanation to General Standard 3:*

(a) The arbitrator's duty to disclose under General Standard 3(a) rests on the principle that the parties have an interest in being fully informed of any facts or circumstances that may be relevant in their view. Accordingly, General Standard 3(d) provides that any doubt as to whether certain facts or circumstances should be disclosed should be resolved in favour of disclosure. However, situations that, such as those set out in the Green List, could never lead to disqualification under the objective test set out in General Standard 2, need not be disclosed. As reflected in General Standard 3(c), a disclosure does not imply that the disclosed facts are such as to disqualify the arbitrator under General Standard 2. The duty of disclosure under General Standard 3(a) is ongoing in nature.

(b) The IBA Arbitration Committee has considered the increasing use by prospective arbitrators of declarations in respect of facts or circumstances that may arise in the future, and the possible conflicts of interest that may result, sometimes referred to as 'advance waivers'. Such declarations do not discharge the arbitrator's ongoing duty of disclosure under General Standard 3(a). The Guidelines, however, do not otherwise take a position as to the validity and effect of advance declarations or waivers, because the validity and effect of any advance declaration or waiver must be assessed in view of the specific text of the advance declaration or waiver, the particular circumstances at hand and the applicable law.

(c) A disclosure does not imply the existence of a conflict of interest. An arbitrator who has made a disclosure to the parties considers himself or herself to be impartial and independent of the parties, despite the disclosed facts, or else he or she would have declined the nomination, or resigned. An arbitrator making a disclosure thus feels capable of performing his or her duties. It is the purpose of disclosure to allow the parties to judge whether they agree with the evaluation of the arbitrator and, if they so wish, to explore the situation further. It is hoped that the promulgation of this General Standard will eliminate the misconception that disclosure itself implies doubts sufficient to disqualify the arbitrator, or even creates a presumption in favour of disqualification. Instead, any challenge should only be successful if an objective test, as set forth in General Standard 2 above, is met. Under Comment 5 of the Practical Application of the General Standards, a failure to disclose certain facts and circumstances that may, in the eyes of the parties, give rise to doubts as to the arbitrator's impartiality or independence, does not necessarily mean that a conflict of interest exists, or that a disqualification should ensue.

(d) In determining which facts should be disclosed, an arbitrator should take into account all circumstances known to him or her. If the arbitrator finds that he or she should make a disclosure, but that professional secrecy rules or other rules of practice or professional conduct prevent such disclosure, he or she should not accept the appointment, or should resign.

(e) Disclosure or disqualification (as set out in General Standards 2 and 3) should not depend on the particular stage of the arbitration. In order to determine whether the arbitrator should disclose, decline the appointment or refuse to continue to act, the facts and circumstances alone are relevant, not the current stage of the proceedings, or the consequences of the withdrawal. As a practical matter, arbitration institutions may make a distinction depending on the stage of the arbitration. Courts may likewise apply different standards. Nevertheless, no distinction is made by these Guidelines depending on the stage of the arbitral proceedings. While there are practical concerns, if an arbitrator must withdraw after the arbitration has commenced, a distinction based on the stage of the arbitration would be inconsistent with the General Standards.

(4) WAIVER BY THE PARTIES

(a) If, within 30 days after the receipt of any disclosure by the arbitrator, or after a party otherwise learns of facts or circumstances that could constitute a potential conflict of interest for an arbitrator, a party does not raise an express objection with regard to that arbitrator, subject to paragraphs

(b) and (c) of this General Standard, the party is deemed to have waived any potential conflict of interest in respect of the arbitrator based on such facts or circumstances and may not raise any objection based on such facts or circumstances at a later stage.

(b) However, if facts or circumstances exist as described in the Non-Waivable Red List, any waiver by a party (including any declaration or advance waiver, such as that contemplated in General Standard 3(b)), or any agreement by the parties to have such a person serve as arbitrator, shall be regarded as invalid.

(c) A person should not serve as an arbitrator when a conflict of interest, such as those exemplified in the Waivable Red List, exists. Nevertheless, such a person may accept appointment as arbitrator, or continue to act as an arbitrator, if the following conditions are met:

   (i) all parties, all arbitrators and the arbitration institution, or other appointing authority (if any), have full knowledge of the conflict of interest; and

   (ii) all parties expressly agree that such a person may serve as arbitrator, despite the conflict of interest.

(d) An arbitrator may assist the parties in reaching a settlement of the dispute, through conciliation, mediation or otherwise, at any stage of the proceedings. However, before doing so, the arbitrator should receive an express agreement by the parties that acting in such a manner shall not disqualify the arbitrator from continuing to serve as arbitrator. Such express agreement shall be considered to be an effective waiver of any potential conflict of interest that may arise from the arbitrator's participation in such a process, or from information that the arbitrator may learn in the process. If the assistance by the arbitrator does not lead to the final settlement of the case, the parties remain bound by their waiver. However, consistent with General Standard 2(a) and notwithstanding such agreement, the arbitrator shall resign if, as a consequence of his or her involvement in the settlement process, the arbitrator develops doubts as to his or her ability to remain impartial or independent in the future course of the arbitration.

*Explanation to General Standard 4:*

(a) Under General Standard 4(a), a party is deemed to have waived any potential conflict of interest, if such party has not raised an objection in respect of such conflict of interest within 30 days. This time limit should run from the date on which the party learns of the relevant facts or circumstances, including through the disclosure process.

(b) General Standard 4(b) serves to exclude from the scope of General Standard 4(a) the facts and circumstances described in the Non-Waivable Red List. Some arbitrators make declarations that seek waivers from the parties with respect to facts or circumstances that may arise in the future.

Irrespective of any such waiver sought by the arbitrator, as provided in General Standard 3(b) facts and circumstances arising in the course of the arbitration should be disclosed to the parties by virtue of the arbitrator's ongoing duty of disclosure.

(c) Notwithstanding a serious conflict of interest, such as those that are described by way of example in the Waivable Red List, the parties may wish to engage such a person as an arbitrator. Here, party autonomy and the desire to have only impartial and independent arbitrators must be balanced. Persons with a serious conflict of interest, such as those that are described by way of example in the Waivable Red List, may serve as arbitrators only if the parties make fully informed, explicit waivers.

(d) The concept of the Arbitral Tribunal assisting the parties in reaching a settlement of their dispute in the course of the arbitration proceedings is well established in some jurisdictions, but not in others. Informed consent by the parties to such a process prior to its beginning should be regarded as an effective waiver of a potential conflict of interest. Certain jurisdictions may require such consent to be in writing and signed by the parties. Subject to any requirements of applicable law, express consent may be sufficient and may be given at a hearing and reflected in the minutes or transcript of the proceeding. In addition, in order to avoid parties using an arbitrator as mediator as a means of disqualifying the arbitrator, the General Standard makes clear that the waiver should remain effective, if the mediation is unsuccessful. In giving their express consent, the parties should realise the consequences of the arbitrator assisting them in a settlement process, including the risk of the resignation of the arbitrator.

(5) SCOPE

(a) These Guidelines apply equally to tribunal chairs, sole arbitrators and co-arbitrators howsoever appointed.

(b) Arbitral or administrative secretaries and assistants, to an individual arbitrator or the Arbitral Tribunal, are bound by the same duty of independence and impartiality as arbitrators, and it is the responsibility of the Arbitral Tribunal to ensure that such duty is respected at all stages of the arbitration.

*Explanation to General Standard 5:*

(a) Because each member of an Arbitral Tribunal has an obligation to be impartial and independent, the General Standards do not distinguish between sole arbitrators, tribunal chairs, party-appointed arbitrators or arbitrators appointed by an institution.

(b) Some arbitration institutions require arbitral or administrative secretaries and assistants to sign a declaration of independence and impartiality. Whether or not such a requirement exists, arbitral or administrative secretaries and assistants to the Arbitral Tribunal are bound by the same duty of independence and impartiality (including the duty of disclosure) as arbitrators, and it is the responsibility of the Arbitral Tribunal to ensure that such duty is respected at all stages of the arbitration. Furthermore, this duty applies to arbitral or administrative secretaries and assistants to either the Arbitral Tribunal or individual members of the Arbitral Tribunal.

(6) RELATIONSHIPS

(a) The arbitrator is in principle considered to bear the identity of his or her law firm, but when considering the relevance of facts or circumstances to determine whether a potential conflict of interest exists, or whether disclosure should be made, the activities of an arbitrator's law firm, if any, and the relationship of the arbitrator with the law firm, should be considered in each individual case. The fact that the activities of the arbitrator's firm involve one of the parties shall not necessarily constitute a source of such conflict, or a reason for disclosure. Similarly, if one of the parties is a member of a group with which the arbitrator's firm has a relationship, such fact should be considered in each individual case, but shall not necessarily constitute by itself a source of a conflict of interest, or a reason for disclosure.

(b) If one of the parties is a legal entity, any legal or physical person having a controlling influence on the legal entity, or a direct economic interest in, or a duty to indemnify a party for, the award to be rendered in the arbitration, may be considered to bear the identity of such party.

*Explanation to General Standard 6:*

(a) The growing size of law firms should be taken into account as part of today's reality in international arbitration. There is a need to balance the interests of a party to appoint the arbitrator of its choice, who may be a partner at a large law firm, and the importance of maintaining confidence in the impartiality and independence of international arbitrators. The arbitrator must in principle be considered to bear the identity of his or her law firm, but the activities of the arbitrator's firm should not automatically create a conflict of interest. The relevance of the activities of the arbitrator's firm, such as the nature, timing and scope of the work by the law firm, and the relationship of the arbitrator with the law firm, should be considered in each case. General Standard 6(a) uses the term 'involve' rather than 'acting for' because the relevant connections with a party may include activities other than representation on a legal matter. Although barristers' chambers should not be equated with law firms for the purposes of conflicts, and no general standard is proffered for barristers' chambers, disclosure may be warranted in view of the relationships among barristers, parties or counsel. When a party to an arbitration is a member of a group of companies, special questions regarding conflicts of interest arise. Because individual corporate structure arrangements vary widely, a catch-all rule is not appropriate. Instead, the particular circumstances of an affiliation with another entity within the same group of companies, and the relationship of that entity with the arbitrator's law firm, should be considered in each individual case.

(b) When a party in international arbitration is a legal entity, other legal and physical persons may have a controlling influence on this legal entity, or a direct economic interest in, or a duty to indemnify a party for, the award to be rendered in the arbitration. Each situation should be assessed individually, and General Standard 6(b) clarifies that such legal persons and individuals may be considered effectively to be that party. Third-party funders and insurers in relation to the dispute may have a direct economic interest in the award, and as such may be considered to be the equivalent of the party. For these purposes, the terms 'third-party funder' and 'insurer' refer to any person or entity that is contributing funds, or other material support, to the prosecution or defence of the case and that has a direct economic interest in, or a duty to indemnify a party for, the award to be rendered in the arbitration.

(7) DUTY OF THE PARTIES AND THE ARBITRATOR

(a) A party shall inform an arbitrator, the Arbitral Tribunal, the other parties and the arbitration institution or other appointing authority (if any) of any relationship, direct or indirect, between the arbitrator and the party (or another company of the same group of companies, or an individual having a controlling influence on the party in the arbitration), or between the arbitrator and any person or entity with a direct economic interest in, or a duty to indemnify a party for, the award to be rendered in the arbitration. The party shall do so on its own initiative at the earliest opportunity.

(b) A party shall inform an arbitrator, the Arbitral Tribunal, the other parties and the arbitration institution or other appointing authority (if any) of the identity of its counsel appearing in the arbitration, as well as of any relationship, including membership of the same barristers' chambers, between its counsel and the arbitrator. The party shall do so on its own initiative at the earliest opportunity, and upon any change in its counsel team.

(c) In order to comply with General Standard 7(a), a party shall perform reasonable enquiries and provide any relevant information available to it.

(d) An arbitrator is under a duty to make reasonable enquiries to identify any conflict of interest, as well as any facts or circumstances that may reasonably give rise to doubts as to his or her impartiality or independence. Failure to disclose a conflict is not excused by lack of knowledge, if the arbitrator does not perform such reasonable enquiries.

*Explanation to General Standard 7:*

(a) The parties are required to disclose any relationship with the arbitrator. Disclosure of such relationships should reduce the risk of an unmeritorious challenge of an arbitrator's impartiality or independence based on information learned after the appointment. The parties' duty of disclosure of any relationship, direct or indirect, between the arbitrator and the party (or another company of the same group of companies, or an individual having a controlling influence on the party in the arbitration) has been extended to relationships with persons or entities having a direct economic interest in the award to be rendered in the arbitration, such as an entity providing funding for the arbitration, or having a duty to indemnify a party for the award.

(b) Counsel appearing in the arbitration, namely the persons involved in the representation of the parties in the arbitration, must be identified by the parties at the earliest opportunity. A party's duty to disclose the identity of counsel appearing in the arbitration extends to all members of that party's counsel team and arises from the outset of the proceedings.

(c) In order to satisfy their duty of disclosure, the parties are required to investigate any relevant information that is reasonably available to them. In addition, any party to an arbitration is required, at the outset and on an ongoing basis during the entirety of the proceedings, to make a reasonable effort to ascertain and to disclose available information that, applying the general standard, might affect the arbitrator's impartiality or independence.

(d) In order to satisfy their duty of disclosure under the Guidelines, arbitrators are required to investigate any relevant information that is reasonably available to them.

**Part II: Practical Application of the General Standards**

1. If the Guidelines are to have an important practical influence, they should address situations that are likely to occur in today's arbitration practice and should provide specific guidance to arbitrators, parties, institutions and courts as to which situations do or do not constitute conflicts of interest, or should or should not be disclosed. For this purpose, the Guidelines categorise situations that may occur in the following Application Lists. These lists cannot cover every situation. In all cases, the General Standards should control the outcome.

2. The Red List consists of two parts: 'a Non-Waivable Red List' (see General Standards 2(d) and 4(b)) and 'a Waivable Red List' (see General Standard 4(c)). These lists are a non-exhaustive and detail specific situations that, depending on the facts of a given case, give rise to justifiable doubts as to the arbitrator's impartiality and independence. That is, in these circumstances, an objective conflict of interest exists from the point of view of a reasonable third person having knowledge of the relevant facts and circumstances (see General Standard 2(b)). The Non-Waivable Red List includes situations deriving from the overriding principle that no person can be his or her own judge. Therefore, acceptance of such a situation cannot cure the conflict. The Waivable Red List covers situations that are serious but not as severe. Because of their seriousness, unlike circumstances described in the Orange List, these situations should be considered

waivable, but only if and when the parties, being aware of the conflict of interest situation, expressly state their willingness to have such a person act as arbitrator, as set forth in General Standard 4(c).

3. The Orange List is a non-exhaustive list of specific situations that, depending on the facts of a given case, may, in the eyes of the parties, give rise to doubts as to the arbitrator's impartiality or independence. The Orange List thus reflects situations that would fall under General Standard 3(a), with the consequence that the arbitrator has a duty to disclose such situations. In all these situations, the parties are deemed to have accepted the arbitrator if, after disclosure, no timely objection is made, as established in General Standard 4(a).

4. Disclosure does not imply the existence of a conflict of interest; nor should it by itself result either in a disqualification of the arbitrator, or in a presumption regarding disqualification. The purpose of the disclosure is to inform the parties of a situation that they may wish to explore further in order to determine whether objectively – that is from the point of view of a reasonable third person having knowledge of the relevant facts and circumstances – there are justifiable doubts as to the arbitrator's impartiality or independence. If the conclusion is that there are no justifiable doubts, the arbitrator can act. Apart from the situations covered by the Non-Waivable Red List, he or she can also act if there is no timely objection by the parties or, in situations covered by the Waivable Red List, if there is a specific acceptance by the parties in accordance with General Standard 4(c). If a party challenges the arbitrator, he or she can nevertheless act, if the authority that rules on the challenge decides that the challenge does not meet the objective test for disqualification.

5. A later challenge based on the fact that an arbitrator did not disclose such facts or circumstances should not result automatically in non-appointment, later disqualification or a successful challenge to any award. Nondisclosure cannot by itself make an arbitrator partial or lacking independence: only the facts or circumstances that he or she failed to disclose can do so.

6. Situations not listed in the Orange List or falling outside the time limits used in some of the Orange List situations are generally not subject to disclosure. However, an arbitrator needs to assess on a case-by-case basis whether a given situation, even though not mentioned in the Orange List, is nevertheless such as to give rise to justifiable doubts as to his or her impartiality or independence. Because the Orange List is a non-exhaustive list of examples, there may be situations not mentioned, which, depending on the circumstances, may need to be disclosed by an arbitrator. Such may be the case, for example, in the event of repeat past appointments by the same party or the same counsel beyond the three-year period provided for in the Orange List, or when an arbitrator concurrently acts as counsel in an unrelated case in which similar issues of law are raised. Likewise, an appointment made by the same party or the same counsel appearing before an arbitrator, while the case is ongoing, may also have to be disclosed, depending on the circumstances. While the Guidelines do not require disclosure of the fact that an arbitrator concurrently serves, or has in the past served, on the same Arbitral Tribunal with another member of the tribunal, or with one of the counsel in the

current proceedings, an arbitrator should assess on a case-by-case basis whether the fact of having frequently served as counsel with, or as an arbitrator on, Arbitral Tribunals with another member of the tribunal may create a perceived imbalance within the tribunal. If the conclusion is 'yes', the arbitrator should consider a disclosure.

7. The Green List is a non-exhaustive list of specific situations where no appearance and no actual conflict of interest exists from an objective point of view. Thus, the arbitrator has no duty to disclose situations falling within the Green List. As stated in the Explanation to General Standard 3(a), there should be a limit to disclosure, based on reasonableness; in some situations, an objective test should prevail over the purely subjective test of 'the eyes' of the parties.

8. The borderline between the categories that comprise the Lists can be thin. It can be debated whether a certain situation should be on one List instead of another. Also, the Lists contain, for various situations, general terms such as 'significant' and 'relevant'. The Lists reflect international principles and best practices to the extent possible. Further definition of the norms, which are to be interpreted reasonably in light of the facts and circumstances in each case, would be counterproductive.

## 1. NON-WAIVABLE RED LIST

1.1 There is an identity between a party and the arbitrator, or the arbitrator is a legal representative or employee of an entity that is a party in the arbitration.

1.2 The arbitrator is a manager, director or member of the supervisory board, or has a controlling influence on one of the parties or an entity that has a direct economic interest in the award to be rendered in the arbitration.

1.3 The arbitrator has a significant financial or personal interest in one of the parties, or the outcome of the case.

1.4 The arbitrator or his or her firm regularly advises the party, or an affiliate of the party, and the arbitrator or his or her firm derives significant financial income therefrom.

## 2. WAIVABLE RED LIST

2.1 Relationship of the arbitrator to the dispute

2.1.1 The arbitrator has given legal advice, or provided an expert opinion, on the dispute to a party or an affiliate of one of the parties.
2.1.2 The arbitrator had a prior involvement in the dispute.

2.2 Arbitrator's direct or indirect interest in the dispute

2.2.1 The arbitrator holds shares, either directly or indirectly, in one of the parties, or an affiliate of one of the parties, this party or an affiliate being privately held.

2.2.2 A close family member[3] of the arbitrator has a significant financial interest in the outcome of the dispute.

2.2.3 The arbitrator, or a close family member of the arbitrator, has a close relationship with a non-party who may be liable to recourse on the part of the unsuccessful party in the dispute.

2.3 Arbitrator's relationship with the parties or counsel

2.3.1 The arbitrator currently represents or advises one of the parties, or an affiliate of one of the parties.

2.3.2 The arbitrator currently represents or advises the lawyer or law firm acting as counsel for one of the parties.

2.3.3 The arbitrator is a lawyer in the same law firm as the counsel to one of the parties.

2.3.4 The arbitrator is a manager, director or member of the supervisory board, or has a controlling influence in an affiliate[4] of one of the parties, if the affiliate is directly involved in the matters in dispute in the arbitration.

2.3.5 The arbitrator's law firm had a previous but terminated involvement in the case without the arbitrator being involved himself or herself.

2.3.6 The arbitrator's law firm currently has a significant commercial relationship with one of the parties, or an affiliate of one of the parties.

2.3.7 The arbitrator regularly advises one of the parties, or an affiliate of one of the parties, but neither the arbitrator nor his or her firm derives a significant financial income therefrom.

2.3.8 The arbitrator has a close family relationship with one of the parties, or with a manager, director or member of the supervisory board, or any person having a controlling influence in one of the parties, or an affiliate of one of the parties, or with a counsel representing a party.

2.3.9 A close family member of the arbitrator has a significant financial or personal interest in one of the parties, or an affiliate of one of the parties.

3. ORANGE LIST

3.1 Previous services for one of the parties or other involvement in the case

3.1.1 The arbitrator has, within the past three years, served as counsel for one of the parties, or an affiliate of one of the parties, or has previously advised or been consulted by the party, or an affiliate of the party, making the appointment in an unrelated matter, but the arbitrator and the party, or the affiliate of the party, have no ongoing relationship.

3.1.2 The arbitrator has, within the past three years, served as counsel against one of the parties, or an affiliate of one of the parties, in an unrelated matter.

---

[3] Throughout the Application Lists, the term 'close family member' refers to a: spouse, sibling, child, parent or life partner, in addition to any other family member with whom a close relationship exists.
[4] Throughout the Application Lists, the term 'affiliate' encompasses all companies in a group of companies, including the parent company.

3.1.3 The arbitrator, has within the past three years, been appointed as arbitrator on two or more occasions by one of the parties, or an affiliate of one of the parties.[5]

3.1.4 The arbitrator's law firm has, within the past three years, acted for or against one of the parties, or an affiliate of one of the parties, in an unrelated matter without the involvement of the arbitrator.

3.1.5 The arbitrator currently serves, or has served within the past three years, as arbitrator in another arbitration involving one of the parties, or an affiliate of one of the parties.

3.2 Current services for one of the parties

3.2.1 The arbitrator's law firm is currently rendering services to one of the parties, or to an affiliate of one of the parties, without creating a significant commercial relationship for the law firm and without the involvement of the arbitrator.

3.2.2 A law firm or other legal organisation that shares significant fees or other revenues with the arbitrator's law firm renders services to one of the parties, or an affiliate of one of the parties, before the arbitral tribunal.

3.3.3 The arbitrator or his or her firm represents a party, or an affiliate of one of the parties to the arbitration, on a regular basis but such representation does not concern the current dispute.

3.3 Relationship between an arbitrator and another arbitrator or counsel

3.3.1 The arbitrator and another arbitrator are lawyers in the same law firm.

3.3.2 The arbitrator and another arbitrator, or the counsel for one of the parties, are members of the same barristers' chambers.

3.3.3 The arbitrator was, within the past three years, a partner of, or otherwise affiliated with, another arbitrator or any of the counsel in the arbitration.

3.3.4 A lawyer in the arbitrator's law firm is an arbitrator in another dispute involving the same party or parties, or an affiliate of one of the parties.

3.3.5 A close family member of the arbitrator is a partner or employee of the law firm representing one of the parties, but is not assisting with the dispute.

3.3.6 A close personal friendship exists between an arbitrator and a counsel of a party.

3.3.7 Enmity exists between an arbitrator and counsel appearing in the arbitration.

3.3.8 The arbitrator has, within the past three years, been appointed on more than three occasions by the same counsel, or the same law firm.

3.3.9 The arbitrator and another arbitrator, or counsel for one of the parties in the arbitration, currently act or have acted together within the past three years as co-counsel.

[5] It may be the practice in certain types of arbitration, such as maritime, sports or commodities arbitration, to draw arbitrators from a smaller or specialised pool of individuals. If in such fields it is the custom and practice for parties to frequently appoint the same arbitrator in different cases, no disclosure of this fact is required, where all parties in the arbitration should be familiar with such custom and practice.

3.4 Relationship between arbitrator and party and others involved in the arbitration

3.4.1 The arbitrator's law firm is currently acting adversely to one of the parties, or an affiliate of one of the parties.
3.4.2 The arbitrator has been associated with a party, or an affiliate of one of the parties, in a professional capacity, such as a former employee or partner.
3.4.3 A close personal friendship exists between an arbitrator and a manager or director or a member of the supervisory board of: a party; an entity that has a direct economic interest in the award to be rendered in the arbitration; or any person having a controlling influence, such as a controlling shareholder interest, on one of the parties or an affiliate of one of the parties or a witness or expert.
3.4.4 Enmity exists between an arbitrator and: a manager or director or a member of the supervisory board of a party; an entity that has a direct economic interest in the award; or any person having a controlling influence on one of the parties; or an affiliate of one of the parties; or a witness; or an expert.
3.4.5 If the arbitrator is a former judge, he or she has, within the past three years, heard a significant case involving one of the parties, or an affiliate of one of the parties.

3.5 Other circumstances

3.5.1 The arbitrator holds shares, either directly or indirectly, that by reason of number or denomination constitute a material holding in one of the parties, or an affiliate of one of the parties, this party or affiliate being publicly listed.
3.5.2 The arbitrator has publicly advocated a position on the case, whether in a published paper, or speech, or otherwise.
3.5.3 The arbitrator holds a position with the appointing authority with respect to the dispute.
3.5.4 The arbitrator is a manager, director or member of the supervisory board, or has a controlling influence on an affiliate of one of the parties, where the affiliate is not directly involved in the matters in dispute in the arbitration.

4. GREEN LIST

4.1 Previously expressed legal opinions

4.1.1 The arbitrator has previously expressed a legal opinion (such as in a law review article or public lecture) concerning an issue that also arises in the arbitration (but this opinion is not focused on the case).

4.2 Current services for one of the parties

4.2.1 A firm, in association or in alliance with the arbitrator's law firm, but that does not share significant fees or other revenues with the arbitrator's law firm, renders services to one of the parties, or an affiliate of one of the parties, in an unrelated matter.

4.3 Contacts with another arbitrator, or with counsel for one of the parties

4.3.1 The arbitrator has a relationship with another arbitrator, or with the counsel for one of the parties, through membership in the same professional association, or social or charitable organisation, or through a social media network.

4.3.2 The arbitrator and counsel for one of the parties have previously served together as arbitrators.

4.3.3 The arbitrator teaches in the same faculty or school as another arbitrator or counsel to one of the parties, or serves as an officer of a professional association or social or charitable organisation with another arbitrator or counsel for one of the parties.

4.3.4 The arbitrator was a speaker, moderator or organiser in one or more conferences, or participated in seminars or working parties of a professional, social or charitable organisation, with another arbitrator or counsel to the parties.

4.4 Contacts between the arbitrator and one of the parties

4.4.1 The arbitrator has had an initial contact with a party, or an affiliate of a party (or their counsel) prior to appointment, if this contact is limited to the arbitrator's availability and qualifications to serve, or to the names of possible candidates for a chairperson, and did not address the merits or procedural aspects of the dispute, other than to provide the arbitrator with a basic understanding of the case.

4.4.2 The arbitrator holds an insignificant amount of shares in one of the parties, or an affiliate of one of the parties, which is publicly listed.

4.4.3 The arbitrator and a manager, director or member of the supervisory board, or any person having a controlling influence on one of the parties, or an affiliate of one of the parties, have worked together as joint experts, or in another professional capacity, including as arbitrators in the same case.

4.4.4 The arbitrator has a relationship with one of the parties or its affiliates through a social media network.

# Appendix 14

# IBA GUIDELINES ON PARTY REPRESENTATION IN INTERNATIONAL ARBITRATION

**Adopted by a resolution of the IBA Council 25 May 2013**
**International Bar Association**

### About the IBA Arbitration Committee

Established as a Committee of the International Bar Association's Legal Practice Division, which focuses on the laws, practise and procedures relating to the arbitration of transnational disputes, the Arbitration Committee currently has over 2,600 members from 115 countries, and membership is increasing steadily.

Through its publications and conferences, the Committee seeks to share information about international arbitration, promote its use and improve its effectiveness.

The Committee has published several sets of rules and guidelines, which have become widely accepted by the arbitration community as an expression of arbitration best practises, such as the IBA Rules on the Taking of Evidence in International Arbitration, as revised in 2010, the IBA Guidelines on Conflicts of Interest in International Arbitration, which are currently under revision, and the IBA Guidelines on Drafting Arbitration Agreements. The Committee also publishes a newsletter twice a year and organises conferences, seminars and training sessions around the globe.

The Committee maintains standing subcommittees and, as appropriate, establishes task forces to address specific issues.

At the time of the issuance of these Guidelines the Committee has – in addition to its Task Force on Counsel Conduct – three subcommittees, namely, the Investment Treaty Arbitration Subcommittee, the Conflicts of Interest Subcommittee and the Young Arbitration Practitioners Subcommittee.

### The Guidelines

**Preamble**

The IBA Arbitration Committee established the Task Force on Counsel Conduct in International Arbitration (the 'Task Force') in 2008.

The mandate of the Task Force was to focus on issues of counsel conduct and party representation in international arbitration that are subject to, or informed by, diverse and potentially conflicting rules and norms. As an initial inquiry, the Task Force undertook to determine whether such differing norms and practises may undermine the fundamental fairness and integrity of international arbitral proceedings and whether international guidelines on party representation in international arbitration may assist parties, counsel and arbitrators. In 2010, the Task Force commissioned a survey (the 'Survey') in order to examine these issues. Respondents to the Survey expressed support for the development of international guidelines for party representation.

The Task Force proposed draft guidelines to the IBA Arbitration Committee's officers in October 2012. The Committee then reviewed the draft guidelines and consulted with experienced arbitration practitioners, arbitrators and arbitral institutions. The draft guidelines were then submitted to all members of the IBA Arbitration Committee for consideration.

Unlike in domestic judicial settings, in which counsel are familiar with, and subject, to a single set of professional conduct rules, party representatives in international arbitration may be subject to diverse and potentially conflicting bodies of domestic rules and norms. The range of rules and norms applicable to the representation of parties in international arbitration may include those of the party representative's home jurisdiction, the arbitral seat, and the place where hearings physically take place. The Survey revealed a high degree of uncertainty among respondents regarding what rules govern party representation in international arbitration. The potential for confusion may be aggravated when individual counsel working collectively, either within a firm or through a co-counsel relationship, are themselves admitted to practise in multiple jurisdictions that have conflicting rules and norms.

In addition to the potential for uncertainty, rules and norms developed for domestic judicial litigation may be ill-adapted to international arbitral proceedings. Indeed, specialised practises and procedures have been developed in international arbitration to accommodate the legal and cultural differences among participants and the complex, multinational nature of the disputes. Domestic professional conduct rules and norms, by contrast, are developed to apply in specific legal cultures consistent with established national procedures.

The IBA Guidelines on Party Representation in International Arbitration (the 'Guidelines') are inspired by the principle that party representatives should act with integrity and honesty and should not engage in activities designed to produce unnecessary delay or expense, including tactics aimed at obstructing the arbitration proceedings.

As with the International Principles on Conduct for the Legal Profession, adopted by the IBA on 28 May 2011, the Guidelines are not intended to displace otherwise applicable mandatory laws, professional or disciplinary rules, or agreed arbitration rules that may be relevant or applicable to matters of party representation.

They are also not intended to vest arbitral tribunals with powers otherwise reserved to bars or other professional bodies.

The use of the term guidelines rather than rules is intended to highlight their contractual nature. The parties may thus adopt the Guidelines or a portion thereof by agreement. Arbitral tribunals may also apply the Guidelines in their discretion, subject to any applicable mandatory rules, if they determine that they have the authority to do so.

The Guidelines are not intended to limit the flexibility that is inherent in, and a considerable advantage of, international arbitration, and parties and arbitral tribunals may adapt them to the particular circumstances of each arbitration.

**Definitions**

In the IBA Guidelines on Party Representation in International Arbitration:

*'Arbitral Tribunal'* or *'Tribunal'* means a sole Arbitrator or a panel of Arbitrators in the arbitration;

*'Arbitrator'* means an arbitrator in the arbitration;

*'Document'* means a writing, communication, picture, drawing, program or data of any kind, whether recorded or maintained on paper or by electronic, audio, visual or any other means;

*'Domestic Bar'* or *'Bar'* means the national or local authority or authorities responsible for the regulation of the professional conduct of lawyers;

*'Evidence'* means documentary evidence and written and oral testimony.

*'Ex Parte Communications'* means oral or written communications between a Party Representative and an Arbitrator or prospective Arbitrator without the presence or knowledge of the opposing Party or Parties;

*'Expert'* means a person or organisation appearing before an Arbitral Tribunal to provide expert analysis and opinion on specific issues determined by a Party or by the Arbitral Tribunal;

*'Expert Report'* means a written statement by an Expert;

*'Guidelines'* mean these IBA Guidelines on Party Representation in International Arbitration, as they may be revised or amended from time to time;

*'Knowingly'* means with actual knowledge of the fact in question;

*'Misconduct'* means a breach of the present Guidelines or any other conduct that the Arbitral Tribunal determines to be contrary to the duties of a Party Representative;

*'Party'* means a party to the arbitration;

*'Party-Nominated Arbitrator'* means an Arbitrator who is nominated or appointed by one or more Parties;

*'Party Representative'* or *'Representative'* means any person, including a Party's employee, who appears in an arbitration on behalf of a Party and makes submissions, arguments or representations to the Arbitral Tribunal on behalf of such Party, other than in the capacity as a Witness or Expert, and whether or not legally qualified or admitted to a Domestic Bar;

*'Presiding Arbitrator'* means an arbitrator who is either a sole Arbitrator or the chairperson of the Arbitral Tribunal;

*'Request to Produce'* means a written request by a Party that another Party produce Documents;

*'Witness'* means a person appearing before an Arbitral Tribunal to provide testimony of fact;

*'Witness Statement'* means a written statement by a Witness recording testimony.

**Application of Guidelines**

1. *The Guidelines shall apply where and to the extent that the Parties have so agreed, or the Arbitral Tribunal, after consultation with the Parties, wishes to rely upon them after having determined that it has the authority to rule on matters of Party representation to ensure the integrity and fairness of the arbitral proceedings.*
2. *In the event of any dispute regarding the meaning of the Guidelines, the Arbitral Tribunal should interpret them in accordance with their overall purpose and in the manner most appropriate for the particular arbitration.*
3. *The Guidelines are not intended to displace otherwise applicable mandatory laws, professional or disciplinary rules, or agreed arbitration rules, in matters of Party representation. The Guidelines are also not intended to derogate from the arbitration agreement or to undermine either a Party representative's primary duty of loyalty to the party whom he or she represents or a Party representative's paramount obligation to present such Party's case to the Arbitral Tribunal.*

**Comments to Guidelines 1–3**

As explained in the Preamble, the Parties and Arbitral Tribunals may benefit from guidance in matters of Party Representation, in particular in order to address instances where differing norms and expectations may threaten the integrity and fairness of the arbitral proceedings.

By virtue of these Guidelines, Arbitral Tribunals need not, in dealing with such issues, and subject to applicable mandatory laws, be limited by a choice-of-law rule or private international law analysis to choosing among national or domestic professional conduct rules. Instead, these Guidelines offer an approach designed to account for the multi-faceted nature of international arbitral proceedings.

These Guidelines shall apply where and to the extent that the Parties have so agreed. Parties may adopt these Guidelines, in whole or in part, in their arbitration agreement or at any time subsequently.

An Arbitral Tribunal may also apply, or draw inspiration from, the Guidelines, after having determined that it has the authority to rule on matters of Party representation in order to ensure the integrity and fairness of the arbitral proceedings. Before making such determination, the Arbitral Tribunal should give the Parties an opportunity to express their views.

These Guidelines do not state whether Arbitral Tribunals have the authority to rule on matters of Party representation and to apply the Guidelines in the absence of an agreement by the Parties to that effect. The Guidelines neither recognise nor exclude the existence of such authority. It remains for the Tribunal to make a determination as to whether it has the authority to rule on matters of Party representation and to apply the Guidelines.

A Party Representative, acting within the authority granted to it, acts on behalf of the Party whom he or she represents. It follows therefore that an obligation or duty bearing on a Party Representative is an obligation or duty of the represented Party, who may ultimately bear the consequences of the misconduct of its Representative.

**Party Representation**

4. Party Representatives should identify themselves to the other Party or Parties and the Arbitral Tribunal at the earliest opportunity. A Party should promptly inform the Arbitral Tribunal and the other Party or Parties of any change in such representation.
5. Once the Arbitral Tribunal has been constituted, a person should not accept representation of a Party in the arbitration when a relationship exists between the person and an Arbitrator that would create a conflict of interest, unless none of the Parties objects after proper disclosure.
6. The Arbitral Tribunal may, in case of breach of Guideline 5, take measures appropriate to safeguard the integrity of the proceedings, including the exclusion of the new Party Representative from participating in all or part of the arbitral proceedings.

**Comments to Guidelines 4–6**

Changes in Party representation in the course of the arbitration may, because of conflicts of interest between a newly-appointed Party Representative and one or more of the Arbitrators, threaten the integrity of the proceedings. In such case, the Arbitral Tribunal may, if compelling circumstances so justify, and where it has found that it has the requisite authority, consider excluding the new Representative from participating in all or part of the arbitral proceedings. In assessing whether any such conflict of interest exists, the Arbitral Tribunal may rely on the IBA Guidelines on Conflicts of Interest in International Arbitration.

Before resorting to such measure, it is important that the Arbitral Tribunal give the Parties an opportunity to express their views about the existence of a conflict, the extent of the Tribunal's authority to act in relation to such conflict, and the consequences of the measure that the Tribunal is contemplating.

**Communications with Arbitrators**

7. *Unless agreed otherwise by the Parties, and subject to the exceptions below, a Party Representative should not engage in any Ex Parte Communications with an Arbitrator concerning the arbitration.*
8. *It is not improper for a Party Representative to have Ex Parte Communications in the following circumstances:*
    *(a) A Party Representative may communicate with a prospective Party-Nominated Arbitrator to determine his or her expertise, experience, ability, availability, willingness and the existence of potential conflicts of interest.*
    *(b) A Party Representative may communicate with a prospective or appointed Party-Nominated Arbitrator for the purpose of the selection of the Presiding Arbitrator.*
    *(c) A Party Representative may, if the Parties are in agreement that such a communication is permissible, communicate with a prospective Presiding Arbitrator to determine his or her expertise, experience, ability, availability, willingness and the existence of potential conflicts of interest.*
    *(d) While communications with a prospective Party-Nominated Arbitrator or Presiding Arbitrator may include a general description of the dispute, a Party Representative should not seek the views of the prospective Party-Nominated Arbitrator or Presiding Arbitrator on the substance of the dispute.*

**Comments to Guidelines 7–8**

Guidelines 7–8 deal with communications between a Party Representative and an Arbitrator or potential Arbitrator concerning the arbitration.

The Guidelines seek to reflect best international practices and, as such, may depart from potentially diverging domestic arbitration practices that are more restrictive or, to the contrary, permit broader Ex Parte Communications.

Ex Parte Communications, as defined in these Guidelines, may occur only in defined circumstances, and a Party Representative should otherwise refrain from any such communication. The Guidelines do not seek to define when the relevant period begins or ends. Any communication that takes place in the context of, or in relation to, the constitution of the Arbitral Tribunal is covered.

Ex Parte Communications with a prospective Arbitrator (Party-Nominated or Presiding Arbitrator) should be limited to providing a general description of the dispute and obtaining information regarding the suitability of the potential Arbitrator, as described in further detail below. A Party Representative should not take the opportunity to seek the prospective Arbitrator's views on the substance of the dispute.

The following discussion topics are appropriate in pre-appointment communications in order to assess the prospective Arbitrator's expertise, experience, ability, availability, willingness and the existence of potential conflicts of interest: (a) the prospective Arbitrator's publications, including books, articles and conference papers or engagements; (b) any activities of the prospective Arbitrator and his or her law firm or organisation within which he or she operates, that may raise justifiable doubts as to the prospective Arbitrator's independence or impartiality; (c) a description of the general nature of the dispute; (d) the terms of the arbitration agreement, and in particular any agreement as to the seat, language, applicable law and rules of the arbitration; (e) the identities of the Parties, Party Representatives, Witnesses, Experts and interested parties; and (f) the anticipated timetable and general conduct of the proceedings.

Applications to the Arbitral Tribunal without the presence or knowledge of the opposing Party or Parties may be permitted in certain circumstances, if the parties so agreed, or as permitted by applicable law. Such may be the case, in particular, for interim measures.

Finally, a Party Representative may communicate with the Arbitral Tribunal if the other Party or Parties fail to participate in a hearing or proceedings and are not represented.

**Submissions to the Arbitral Tribunal**

9.  *A Party Representative should not make any knowingly false submission of fact to the Arbitral Tribunal.*
10. *In the event that a Party Representative learns that he or she previously made a false submission of fact to the Arbitral Tribunal, the Party Representative should, subject to countervailing considerations of confidentiality and privilege, promptly correct such submission.*
11. *A Party Representative should not submit Witness or Expert evidence that he or she knows to be false. If a Witness or Expert intends to present or presents evidence that a Party Representative knows or later discovers to be false, such Party Representative should promptly advise the Party whom he or she represents of the necessity of taking remedial measures and of the consequences of failing to do so. Depending upon the circumstances, and subject to countervailing considerations of confidentiality and privilege, the Party Representative should promptly take remedial measures, which may include one or more of the following:*
    *(a) advise the Witness or Expert to testify truthfully;*
    *(b) take reasonable steps to deter the Witness or Expert from submitting false evidence;*
    *(c) urge the Witness or Expert to correct or withdraw the false evidence;*
    *(d) correct or withdraw the false evidence;*
    *(e) withdraw as Party Representative if the circumstances so warrant.*

## Comments to Guidelines 9–11

Guidelines 9–11 concern the responsibility of a Party Representative when making submissions and tendering evidence to the Arbitral Tribunal. This principle is sometimes referred to as the duty of candour or honesty owed to the Tribunal.

The Guidelines identify two aspects of the responsibility of a Party Representative: the first relates to submissions of fact made by a Party Representative (Guidelines 9 and 10), and the second concerns the evidence given by a Witness or Expert (Guideline 11).

With respect to submissions to the Arbitral Tribunal, these Guidelines contain two limitations to the principles set out for Party Representatives. First, Guidelines 9 and 10 are restricted to false submissions of fact. Secondly, the Party Representative must have actual knowledge of the false nature of the submission, which may be inferred from the circumstances.

Under Guideline 10, a Party Representative should promptly correct any false submissions of fact previously made to the Tribunal, unless prevented from doing so by countervailing considerations of confidentiality and privilege. Such principle also applies, in case of a change in representation, to a newly-appointed Party Representative who becomes aware that his or her predecessor made a false submission.

With respect to legal submissions to the Tribunal, a Party Representative may argue any construction of a law, a contract, a treaty or any authority that he or she believes is reasonable.

Guideline 11 addresses the presentation of evidence to the Tribunal that a Party Representative knows to be false. A Party Representative should not offer knowingly false evidence or testimony. A Party Representative therefore should not assist a Witness or Expert or seek to influence a Witness or Expert to give false evidence to the Tribunal in oral testimony or written Witness Statements or Expert Reports.

The considerations outlined for Guidelines 9 and 10 apply equally to Guideline 11. Guideline 11 is more specific in terms of the remedial measures that a Party Representative may take in the event that the Witness or Expert intends to present or presents evidence that the Party Representative knows or later discovers to be false. The list of remedial measures provided in Guideline 11 is not exhaustive. Such remedial measures may extend to the Party Representative's withdrawal from the case, if the circumstances so warrant. Guideline 11 acknowledges, by using the term 'may', that certain remedial measures, such as correcting or withdrawing false Witness or Expert evidence may not be compatible with the ethical rules bearing on counsel in some jurisdictions.

## Information Exchange and Disclosure

*12. When the arbitral proceedings involve or are likely to involve Document production, a Party Representative should inform the client of the need to*

preserve, so far as reasonably possible, Documents, including electronic Documents that would otherwise be deleted in accordance with a Document retention policy or in the ordinary course of business, which are potentially relevant to the arbitration.
13. A Party Representative should not make any Request to Produce, or any objection to a Request to Produce, for an improper purpose, such as to harass or cause unnecessary delay.
14. A Party Representative should explain to the Party whom he or she represents the necessity of producing, and potential consequences of failing to produce, any Document that the Party or Parties have undertaken, or been ordered, to produce.
15. A Party Representative should advise the Party whom he or she represents to take, and assist such Party in taking, reasonable steps to ensure that: (i) a reasonable search is made for Documents that a Party has undertaken, or been ordered, to produce; and (ii) all non-privileged, responsive Documents are produced.
16. A Party Representative should not suppress or conceal, or advise a Party to suppress or conceal, Documents that have been requested by another Party or that the Party whom he or she represents has undertaken, or been ordered, to produce.
17. If, during the course of an arbitration, a Party Representative becomes aware of the existence of a Document that should have been produced, but was not produced, such Party Representative should advise the Party whom he or she represents of the necessity of producing the Document and the consequences of failing to do so.

**Comments to Guidelines 12–17**

The IBA addressed the scope of Document production in the IBA Rules on the Taking of Evidence in International Arbitration (*see* Articles 3 and 9). Guidelines 12–17 concern the conduct of Party Representatives in connection with Document production.

Party Representatives are often unsure whether and to what extent their respective domestic standards of professional conduct apply to the process of preserving, collecting and producing documents in international arbitration. It is common for Party Representatives in the same arbitration proceeding to apply different standards. For example, one Party Representative may consider him- or her-self obligated to ensure that the Party whom he or she represents undertakes a reasonable search for, and produces, all responsive, non-privileged Documents, while another Party Representative may view Document production as the sole responsibility of the Party whom he or she represents. In these circumstances, the disparity in access to information or evidence may undermine the integrity and fairness of the arbitral proceedings.

The Guidelines are intended to address these difficulties by suggesting standards of conduct in international arbitration. They may not be necessary in cases where Party Representatives share similar expectations with respect to their role in relation to Document production or in cases where Document production is not done or is minimal.

The Guidelines are intended to foster the taking of objectively reasonable steps to preserve, search for and produce Documents that a Party has an obligation to disclose.

Under Guidelines 12–17, a Party Representative should, under the given circumstances, advise the Party whom he or she represents to: (i) identify those persons within the Party's control who might possess Documents potentially relevant to the arbitration, including electronic Documents; (ii) notify such persons of the need to preserve and not destroy any such Documents; and (iii) suspend or otherwise make arrangements to override any Document retention or other policies/ practises whereby potentially relevant Documents might be destroyed in the ordinary course of business.

Under Guidelines 12–17, a Party Representative should, under the given circumstances, advise the Party whom he or she represents to, and assist such Party to: (i) put in place a reasonable and proportionate system for collecting and reviewing Documents within the possession of persons within the Party's control in order to identify Documents that are relevant to the arbitration or that have been requested by another Party; and (ii) ensure that the Party Representative is provided with copies of, or access to, all such Documents.

While Article 3 of the IBA Rules on the Taking of Evidence in International Arbitration requires the production of Documents relevant to the case and material to its outcome, Guideline 12 refers only to potentially relevant Documents because its purpose is different: when a Party Representative advises the Party whom he or she represents to preserve evidence, such Party Representative is typically not at that stage in a position to assess materiality, and the test for preserving and collecting Documents therefore should be potential relevance to the case at hand.

Finally, a Party Representative should not make a Request to Produce, or object to a Request to Produce, when such request or objection is only aimed at harassing, obtaining documents for purposes extraneous to the arbitration, or causing unnecessary delay (Guideline 13).

**Witnesses and Experts**

18. *Before seeking any information from a potential Witness or Expert, a Party Representative should identify himself or herself, as well as the Party he or she represents, and the reason for which the information is sought.*
19. *A Party Representative should make any potential Witness aware that he or she has the right to inform or instruct his or her own counsel about the contact and to discontinue the communication with the Party Representative.*
20. *A Party Representative may assist Witnesses in the preparation of Witness Statements and Experts in the preparation of Expert Reports.*

21. *A Party Representative should seek to ensure that a Witness Statement reflects the Witness's own account of relevant facts, events and circumstances.*
22. *A Party Representative should seek to ensure that an Expert Report reflects the Expert's own analysis and opinion.*
23. *A Party Representative should not invite or encourage a Witness to give false evidence.*
24. *A Party Representative may, consistent with the principle that the evidence given should reflect the Witness's own account of relevant facts, events or circumstances, or the Expert's own analysis or opinion, meet or interact with Witnesses and Experts in order to discuss and prepare their prospective testimony.*
25. *A Party Representative may pay, offer to pay, or acquiesce in the payment of:*
    *(a) expenses reasonably incurred by a Witness or Expert in preparing to testify or testifying at a hearing;*
    *(b) reasonable compensation for the loss of time incurred by a Witness in testifying and preparing to testify; and*
    *(c) reasonable fees for the professional services of a Party-appointed Expert.*

**Comments to Guidelines 18–25**

Guidelines 18–25 are concerned with interactions between Party Representatives and Witnesses and Experts. The interaction between Party Representatives and Witnesses is also addressed in Guidelines 9–11 concerning Submissions to the Arbitral Tribunal.

Many international arbitration practitioners desire more transparent and predictable standards of conduct with respect to relations with Witnesses and Experts in order to promote the principle of equal treatment among Parties. Disparate practises among jurisdictions may create inequality and threaten the integrity of the arbitral proceedings.

The Guidelines are intended to reflect best international arbitration practise with respect to the preparation of Witness and Expert testimony.

When a Party Representative contacts a potential Witness, he or she should disclose his or her identity and the reason for the contact before seeking any information from the potential Witness (Guideline 18). A Party Representative should also make the potential Witness aware of his or her right to inform or instruct counsel about this contact and involve such counsel in any further communication (Guideline 19).

Domestic professional conduct norms in some jurisdictions require higher standards with respect to contacts with potential Witnesses who are known to be represented by counsel. For example, some common law jurisdictions maintain a prohibition against contact by counsel with any potential Witness whom counsel knows to be represented in respect of the particular arbitration.

If a Party Representative determines that he or she is subject to a higher standard than the standard prescribed in these Guidelines, he or she may address the situation with the other Party and/or the Arbitral Tribunal.

As provided by Guideline 20, a Party Representative may assist in the preparation of Witness Statements and Expert Reports, but should seek to ensure that a Witness Statement reflects the Witness's own account of relevant facts, events and circumstances (Guideline 21), and that any Expert Report reflects the Expert's own views, analysis and conclusions (Guideline 22).

A Party Representative should not invite or encourage a Witness to give false evidence (Guideline 23).

As part of the preparation of testimony for the arbitration, a Party Representative may meet with Witnesses and Experts (or potential Witnesses and Experts) to discuss their prospective testimony. A Party Representative may also help a Witness in preparing his or her own Witness Statement or Expert Report. Further, a Party Representative may assist a Witness in preparing for their testimony in direct and cross-examination, including through practise questions and answers (Guideline 24). This preparation may include a review of the procedures through which testimony will be elicited and preparation of both direct testimony and cross-examination. Such contacts should however not alter the genuineness of the Witness or Expert evidence, which should always reflect the Witness's own account of relevant facts, events or circumstances, or the Expert's own analysis or opinion.

Finally, Party Representatives may pay, offer to pay or acquiesce in the payment of reasonable compensation to a Witness for his or her time and a reasonable fee for the professional services of an Expert (Guideline 25).

**Remedies for Misconduct**

26. *If the Arbitral Tribunal, after giving the Parties notice and a reasonable opportunity to be heard, finds that a Party Representative has committed Misconduct, the Arbitral Tribunal, as appropriate, may:*

    *(a) admonish the Party Representative;*

    *(b) draw appropriate inferences in assessing the evidence relied upon, or the legal arguments advanced by, the Party Representative;*

    *(c) consider the Party Representative's Misconduct in apportioning the costs of the arbitration, indicating, if appropriate, how and in what amount the Party Representative's Misconduct leads the Tribunal to a different apportionment of costs;*

    *(d) take any other appropriate measure in order to preserve the fairness and integrity of the proceedings.*

27. *In addressing issues of Misconduct, the Arbitral Tribunal should take into account:*

*(a)* *the need to preserve the integrity and fairness of the arbitral proceedings and the enforceability of the award;*

*(b)* *the potential impact of a ruling regarding Misconduct on the rights of the Parties;*

*(c)* *the nature and gravity of the Misconduct, including the extent to which the misconduct affects the conduct of the proceedings;*

*(d)* *the good faith of the Party Representative;*

*(e)* *relevant considerations of privilege and confidentiality; and*

*(f)* *the extent to which the Party represented by the Party Representative knew of, condoned, directed, or participated in, the Misconduct.*

## Comments to Guidelines 26–27

Guidelines 26–27 articulate potential remedies to address Misconduct by a Party Representative.

Their purpose is to preserve or restore the fairness and integrity of the arbitration.

The Arbitral Tribunal should seek to apply the most proportionate remedy or combination of remedies in light of the nature and gravity of the Misconduct, the good faith of the Party Representative and the Party whom he or she represents, the impact of the remedy on the Parties' rights, and the need to preserve the integrity, effectiveness and fairness of the arbitration and the enforceability of the award.

Guideline 27 sets forth a list of factors that is neither exhaustive nor binding, but instead reflects an overarching balancing exercise to be conducted in addressing matters of Misconduct by a Party Representative in order to ensure that the arbitration proceed in a fair and appropriate manner.

Before imposing any remedy in respect of alleged Misconduct, it is important that the Arbitral Tribunal gives the Parties and the impugned Representative the right to be heard in relation to the allegations made.

# INDEX

## LEGAL TAXONOMY
FROM SWEET & MAXWELL

This index has been prepared using Sweet and Maxwell's Legal Taxonomy. Main index entries conform to keywords provided by the Legal Taxonomy except where references to specific documents or non-standard terms (denoted by quotation marks) have been included. These keywords provide a means of identifying similar concepts in other Sweet and Maxwell publications and online services to which keywords from the Legal Taxonomy have been applied. Readers may find some minor differences between terms used in the text and those which appear in the index. Suggestions to *sweetandmaxwell.taxonomy@thomson.com*.

**All references are to paragraph number**

**Ad hoc arbitration**
   administered arbitration compared, I–009
   appointment of tribunal, 5–002
**Additional awards**
   challenges/appeals in national courts, 27–010
   form, 27–012
   generally, 27–010
   introduction, 27–001—27–002
   time limits, 27–009
   tribunal's own initiative, 27–011
**Addresses for service**
   generally, 4–008—4–009
**Administered arbitration**
   *see* **Institutional arbitration**
**"Administrative secretaries"**
   permitted in LCIA arbitrations, 34–026—34–028
**Amendments**
   requests, 1–015, 22–007
   responses, 22–007
   statements of case, 22–007
**Amiable composition**
   tribunal's powers, 22–052
**Applicable law**
   choice of law
      express choice of law, 22–048
      generally, 22–047
      mandatory rules of law, 22–051
      no express choice of law, 22–049—22–050

      generally, 14–003, 16–014—16–018
   LCIA arbitration clauses, III–023—III–024
   LCIA-MIAC, VI–020
**Appointments**
   arbitrators
      consultation as to presiding arbitrator, 13–014—13–015
      emergency arbitrators, 9–024—9–052
      expedited appointment of replacement arbitrators, 9–053—9–057
      generally, 5–041—5–043
      LCIA Court's sole power of appointment, 5–044
      nomination, 7–001—7–010
      number of arbitrators, 5–045—5–048
      President, Vice Presidents and Chairman, 5–051
      revocation, 10–001—10–028
      selection of arbitrators, 5–049—5–050
      three or more parties to arbitration, 8–001—8–005
   experts, 21–004—21–005
**Arbitrability**
   non-arbitrable disputes, III–009
**Arbitral tribunals**
   *see also* **Arbitrators**
   *see also under specific subjects*
   communications between parties and tribunal

consultation as to presiding arbitrator, 13–014—13–015
copies for arbitrators, parties and Registrar, 13–010
copies of Registrar communications, 13–009
direct communication, 13–006—13–008
introduction, 13–001—13–003
unilateral communications, 13–011—13–013
discretion, 14–015—14–018
duties, 14–011—14–014
expedited formation
  applications, 9–006—9–018
  determination of applications, 9–022—9–023
  emergency arbitrators, 9–024—9–052
  expedited appointment of replacement arbitrators, 9–053—9–057
  inadmissibility of applications, 9–019
  interim relief from national courts, 9–021
  introduction, 9–001—9–005
  prejudice to respondent, 9–020
  rejection of applications, 9–019
formation
  appointment of tribunal by LCIA Court, 5–041—5–051
  expedited formation, 9–001—9–057
  incomplete or missing request or response, 5–004
  impartiality and independence, 5–006—5–040
  introduction, 5–001—5–003
  references to "Arbitral Tribunal", 5–005
good faith, 14–017—14–018, 32–007—32–010
impartiality and independence
  arbitrators not to act as advocate, 5–017
  arbitrators not to advise a party, 5–018—5–020
  conflict of interest, 5–026—5–037
  continuing duty, 5–040
  generally, 5–006—5–011
  Green List, 5–036
  IBA Guidelines, 5–008—5–011
  impartiality and independence distinguished, 5–012—5–016
  Orange List, 5–035
  Red List, 5–033—5–034
  revocation of appointment, 10–014—10–018, 10–022—10–025
  statements of independence, 5–021—5–037
jurisdiction
  challenges to jurisdiction, 23–013—23–019
  introduction, 23–001—23–006
  self-determination by tribunal, 23–007—23–008
  separability of arbitration agreement, 23–009—23–012
language
  agreement between parties, 17–008—17–010
  determination by LCIA Court, 17–011—17–012
  determination by tribunal, 17–014
  introduction, 17–001—17–007
  language of arbitration agreement, 17–008—17–010
  non-participating or defaulting parties, 17–013
  translations, 17–015
limitation of liability, 31–001—31–004
majority power to continue deliberations, 12–001—12–007
references to "Arbitral Tribunal", 5–005
statements about arbitration, no obligation to make, 31–004

**Arbitration agreements**
ad hoc submission agreements, P–004
applicable law, 16–014—16–018
capacity to enter into arbitration agreement, III–008
challenging applicability in response, 2–010
consequences of entering into arbitration agreement, III–004—III–007
definition, P–001—P–011, III–004
form, III–004—III–005
good faith, 32–007—32–010
incorporation from other contracts, P–003—P–004
incorporation of LCIA Rules, P–008—P–010
language, 17–008—17–010
LCIA recommended clauses
  capacity to enter into arbitration agreement, III–008
  choice of law, III–023—III–024
  consequences of entering into arbitration agreement, III–004—III–006
  existing disputes, III–025—III–026
  form of arbitration agreement, III–004—III–005
  formal requirements, III–006

future disputes, III–010—III–024
initial considerations,
    III–008—III–009
introduction, III–001—III–003
language of arbitration,
    III–021—III–022
non-arbitrable disputes, III–009
number of arbitrators,
    III–015—III–017
parties bound by arbitration
    agreement, III–009
seat of arbitration, III–018—III–020
writing, III–006
nomination of arbitrators,
    1–018—1–019
non-arbitrable disputes, III–009
parties bound by arbitration agreement,
    III–009
procedural matters, 1–016—1–017
references to LCIA, P–005—P–007
references to LCIA Rules,
    P–008—P–010
separability
    generally, 23–009—23–012,
    LCIA India, V–015—V–016
severability, 32–011
spirit of the agreement,
    32–007—32–010
stand-alone agreements, P–004
terms relied on in making request,
    1–008
umbrella agreements, P–004
waiver of right to object to breach,
    32–001—32–006
written agreements, P–003—P–006,
    III–006
**Arbitration clauses**
capacity to enter into arbitration
    agreement, III–008
consequences of entering into arbitration
    agreement, III–004—III–007
existing disputes, III–025—III–026
form of arbitration agreement,
    III–004—III–005
formal requirements, III–006
future disputes
    choice of law, III–023—III–024
    introduction, III–010—III–014
    language of arbitration,
        III–021—III–022
    number of arbitrators,
        III–015—III–017
    seat of arbitration, III–018—III–020
initial considerations, III–008—III–009
introduction, III–001—III–003
non-arbitrable disputes, III–009

parties bound by arbitration agreement,
    III–009
writing, III–006
**Arbitration costs**
*see* **Costs**
**Arbitrators**
acting as advocate, 5–017
advising parties, 5–018—5–020
appointment
    consultation as to presiding arbitrator,
        13–014—13–015
    emergency arbitrators, 9–024—9–052
    expedited appointment of replacement
        arbitrators, 9–053—9–057
    generally, 5–041—5–043
    LCIA Court's sole power of
        appointment, 5–044
    nomination, 7–001—7–010
    number of arbitrators, 5–045—5–048
    President, Vice Presidents and
        Chairman, 5–051
    revocation, 10–001—10–028
    selection of arbitrators,
        5–049—5–050
    three or more parties to arbitration,
        8–001—8–005
Chairman of the LCIA Board of
    Directors, 5–051
challenges to arbitrators
    appointment of President, Vice
        President or Division,
        10–030—10–032
    costs of challenge, 10–044—10–045
    fees and expenses of arbitrator, 10–043
    form, 10–035—10–036
    introduction, 10–001—10–005,
        10–029
    nationality, 6–009
    notification, 10–030
    opportunity for other parties to
        comment, 10–038
    party-nominated arbitrators, 10–037
    repeated challenges, 33–012
    revocation of appointment,
        10–039—10–042
    time limits, 10–033—10–034
consultation as to presiding arbitrator,
    13–014—13–015
CVs, 5–021, 5–024—5–025
devoting sufficient time, diligence and
    industry, 5–021, 5–038—5–039
discretion, 14–015—14–018
duties, 14–011—14–014
emergency arbitrators
    applicability of other rules, 9–051
    awards, 9–043—9–044

conduct of proceedings,
    9–038—9–039
content of applications, 9–030
delivery of orders and awards,
    9–043—9–044
determination of applications,
    9–035—9–037
discharge of orders or awards,
    9–046—9–048
ex parte applications, 9–040
fees and expenses, 9–034, 9–045,
    34–037—34–040
grounds for appointment,
    9–031—9–033
introduction, 9–024—9–025
making applications, 9–029
national court applications for interim
    relief, 9–049—9–050
opportunity for parties to be
    consulted, 9–038—9–039
opting in/out, 9–052
orders, 9–043—9–044
powers, 9–042
revocation of orders or awards,
    9–046—9–048
special fee, 9–034, 9–045,
    34–037—34–040
threshold procedure, 9–026—9–028
time limit for conduct of proceedings,
    9–041
variation of orders or awards,
    9–046—9–048
expedited appointment of replacement
    arbitrators, 9–053—9–057
failure to act fairly and impartially,
    10–022—10–025
failure to conduct proceedings with
    reasonable efficiency, diligence and
    industry, 10–026—10–028
failure to participate in deliberations,
    12–001—12–007
fees and expenses
    amounts, 34–016—34–024
    challenges to arbitrators, 10–043
    emergency arbitrators, 9–034, 9–045,
        34–037—34–040
    generally, 5–021—5–023,
        28–005—28–006
    payments on account, 34–032
good faith, 14–017—14–018,
    32–007—32–010
illness, 10–010
impartiality and independence
    arbitrators not to act as advocate, 5–017
    arbitrators not to advise a party,
        5–018—5–020

conflict of interest, 5–026—5–037
continuing duty, 5–040
generally, 5–006—5–011
Green List, 5–036
IBA Guidelines, 5–008—5–011
impartiality and independence
    distinguished, 5–012—5–016
Orange List, 5–035
Red List, 5–033—5–034
revocation of appointment, 10–014—
    10–018, 10–022—10–025
statements of independence,
    5–021—5–037
limitation of liability, 31–001—31–004
majority power to continue
    deliberations, 12–001—12–007
nationality, 6–001—6–009
nomination
    generally, 7–001—7–010
    replacement arbitrators,
        11–001—11–004
    three or more parties to arbitration,
        8–001—8–005
number, 5–005, 5–045—5–048
panels, 5–005, 5–045—5–048
payments on account, 34–032
President of the LCIA Court,
    5–051
presiding arbitrator
    consultation, 13–014—13–015
    power to make procedural orders
        alone, 14–019
refusal to participate in deliberations,
    12–001—12–007
replacement arbitrators
    expedited appointment,
        9–053—9–057
    nomination, 11–001—11–004
resignation, 10–008—10–009
revocation of appointment
    challenges to arbitrators,
        10–039—10–042
    doubts as to impartiality or
        independence, 10–014—10–018
    grounds, 10–006—10–028
    inability to act, 10–011
    introduction, 10–001—10–005
    nomination of replacement
        arbitrators, 11–001—11–004
    refusal to act, 10–012
    resignation, 10–008—10–009
    serious illness, 10–010
    unfitness to act, 10–013,
        10–019—10–028
    violation of arbitration agreement,
        10–020—10–021

selection, 5–049—5–050
sole arbitrators, 5–005,
    5–045—5–048
statements about arbitration, no
    obligation to make, 31–004
summary of qualifications etc., 5–021,
    5–024—5–025
unfitness to act
    failure to act fairly and impartially,
        10–022—10–025
    failure to conduct proceedings with
        reasonable efficiency, diligence and
        industry, 10–026—10–028
    introduction, 10–013, 10–019
    violation of arbitration agreement,
        10–020—10–021
    Vice Presidents of the LCIA Court,
        5–051
violation of arbitration agreement,
    10–020—10–021
**Authentication**
awards, 26–019
**Authority**
challenges to jurisdiction
    decisions on jurisdictional challenges,
        23–017—23–018
    generally, 23–013—23–016
    national courts, 23–019
    introduction, 23–001—23–006
    self-determination by tribunal,
        23–007—23–008
    separability of arbitration agreement,
        23–009—23–012
**Autonomy**
principles underlying LCIA Rules,
    I–025—I–027
**Awards**
accounting details, 26–006—26–008
additional awards
    challenges/appeals in national courts,
        27–010
    form, 27–012
    generally, 27–010
    introduction, 27–001—27–002
    time limits, 27–009
    tribunal's own initiative, 27–011
authentication, 26–019
certified copies, 26–018—26–019
confidentiality, 30–006
consent awards, 26–024
contents and form, 26–004—26–009
correction
    challenges/appeals in national courts,
        27–006—27–007
    correction on tribunal's own initiative,
        27–008

errors, 27–003—27–005
form of award, 27–012
introduction, 27–001—27–002
memorandums, 27–005
time limits, 27–003
costs, 26–003, 26–006
currency, 26–010
dating, 26–005—26–006, 26–018
delivery to parties, 26–017
dissenting opinions, 26–015—26–016
electronic form, 26–020
final and binding, 26–021—26–023
interest, 26–011—26–012
introduction, 26–001—26–002
majority decisions, 26–013—26–016
multiple awards, 26–003
place of making, 26–005—26–006
publication, 30–006
reasons, 26–004—26–005
seat, 26–005
signature, 26–008, 26–014—26–016
transmission to parties,
    26–017—26–020
writing, 26–004

**Barristers**
*see* **Legal representatives**

**Capacity**
entering into arbitration agreements,
    III–008
**Chairman of the LCIA Board of
Directors**
appointment as arbitrator, 5–051
**Challenges to arbitrators**
appointment of President, Vice
    President or Division,
    10–030—10–032
costs of challenge, 10–044—10–045
fees and expenses of arbitrator, 10–043
form, 10–035—10–036
introduction, 10–001—10–005, 10–029
nationality, 6–009
notification, 10–030
opportunity for other parties to
    comment, 10–038
party-nominated arbitrators, 10–037
repeated challenges, 33–012
revocation of appointment,
    10–039—10–042
time limits, 10–033—10–034
**Choice of law**
applicable law, 14–003,
    16–014—16–018
express choice of law, 22–048
generally, 22–047

LCIA arbitration clauses,
    III–023—III–024
LCIA-MIAC, VI–020
mandatory rules of law, 22–051
no express choice of law,
    22–049—22–050
**Commencement**
*see also* **Requests for arbitration**
date of receipt of request by Registrar,
    1–025
delivery of request to all parties, 1–022
payment of registration fee, 1–020
**Communications**
communications between parties and
    LCIA Court, 3–010
communications between parties and
    tribunal
    consultation as to presiding arbitrator,
        13–014—13–015
    copies for arbitrators, parties and
        Registrar, 13–010
    copies of Registrar communications,
        13–009
    direct communication,
        13–006—13–008
    introduction, 13–001—13–003
    unilateral communications,
        13–011—13–013
ex parte communications, 33–016
written communications
    addresses for service,
        4–008—4–009
    electronic delivery, 4–010
    generally, 4–001—4–003
    modes of service, 4–006—4–007
    national laws, 4–004
    scope of rules, 4–005
**Compensation**
tribunal's power to order,
    22–021—22–022
**Concealment of evidence**
guidelines for legal representatives,
    33–015
**Confidentiality**
confidentiality undertakings,
    30–003—30–004
deliberations of tribunal, 30–005
introduction, 30–001—30–002
principles underlying LCIA Rules,
    I–037
private hearings, 19–013—19–014
publication of awards, 30–006
**Conflict of interest**
*see also* **Challenges to arbitrators**
arbitrators, 5–026—5–037
LCIA-MIAC, VI–019

legal representatives, 18–019—18–021
**Consent orders**
consent awards, 26–024
**Conservatory measures**
*see* **Interim measures**
**Consolidated proceedings**
consolidation before formation of
    tribunal, 22–043—22–044
consolidation with agreement of parties,
    22–039—22–040
consolidation without agreement of
    parties, 22–041—22–042
exercise of tribunal's powers,
    22–035—22–037
introduction, 22–003—22–004
mechanics of consolidation, 22–038
scope of tribunal's powers,
    22–033—22–034
**Correction of awards**
*see* **Awards**
**Costs**
arbitration costs
    abandonment, suspension, withdrawal
        or early conclusion, 28–020
    administrative charges,
        34–004—34–015
    agreement between parties, 28–019
    allocation between parties,
        28–009—28–010
    arbitrators' fees and expenses,
        28–005—28–006, 34–016—
        34–024, 34–032
    currency of invoices and payments,
        34–014, 34–022
    deposits, 28–021, 34–025
    determination, 28–009
    disputes, 34–033
    emergency arbitrators,
        34–037—34–040
    interim payments, 34–026—34–029
    introduction, 28–001
    joint and several liability, 28–007,
        34–034—34–036
    LCIA Court charges,
        34–010—34–011
    LCIA Court expenses, 34–013
    LCIA general overheads, 34–012
    LCIA Secretariat charges,
        34–006—34–009
    LCIA Secretariat expenses, 34–013
    non-payment, 28–007—28–008
    payments on account of arbitrators'
        fees, 34–032
    principles for ordering,
        28–015—28–018
    refund of excess deposit, 28–021

# INDEX

Registrar's authority,
    34–030—34–033
registration fee, 34–004—34–005
Schedule of Costs, 34–001—34–040
time reserved but not used, 34–020
travelling expenses, 34–019
tribunal fees and expenses, 28–002—
    28–004, 34–016—34–024
VAT, 34–015, 34–024
challenges to arbitrators,
    10–044—10–045
legal costs
    agreement between parties, 28–019
    allocation between parties, 28–012
    introduction, 28–001
    principles for ordering,
        28–015—28–018
    reasonableness, 28–013—28–014
    tribunal's power to order costs, 28–011
Schedule of Costs
    administrative charges,
        34–004—34–015
    deposits, 34–025
    emergency arbitrators,
        34–037—34–040
    interim payments, 34–026—34–029
    introduction, 34–001—34–003
    parties' liability, 34–034—34–036
    Registrar's authority,
        34–030—34–033
    tribunal fees and expenses,
        34–016—34–024

**Counsel**
*see* **Legal representatives**

**Cross-claims**
failure to submit defence to cross-claim,
    15–021
generally, 15–014—15–016
responses, 2–008, 2–011—2–012

**Cross-examination**
generally, 20–011—20–012,
    20–020—20–021

**Currencies**
arbitration costs, 34–014, 34–022
awards, 26–010

**CVs**
arbitrators, 5–021, 5–024—5–025

**Defences**
*see also* **Written statements**
responses, 2–008—2–010
statement of defence, 15–014—15–016
statement of defence to cross-claim,
    15–017—15–018

**Delivery**
*see also* **Written statements**

addresses for delivery, 4–008—4–009
electronic delivery, 4–010
introduction, 4–001—4–003
modes of delivery, 4–006—4–007
national laws, 4–004
scope of rules, 4–005
service distinguished, 4–002

**Deposits**
arbitration costs, 34–025
further deposits, 24–010
holding of deposits, 24–009
introduction, 24–001—24–004
legal status, 24–009
non-payment, 24–011—24–016
refund of surplus, 24–004, 28–021
substitute payments, 24–011—24–016
tribunal's powers, 24–005—24–008

**DIFC-LCIA**
arbitration in Dubai and UAE
    enforcement of awards, IV–009
    federal law on arbitration, IV–007
    inconsistency across courts, IV–010
    introduction, IV–006
    lengthy court process, IV–011
    procedural law, IV–008
background, IV–006—IV–017
conclusion, IV–028
demand for arbitration in Middle East,
    IV–002—IV–005
DIFC
    arbitration, IV–013—IV–014
    conversion of judgments to DIFC-
        LCIA awards, IV–016—IV–017
    courts, IV–013
    Dispute Resolution Authority, IV–015
    enforcement of awards, IV–014
    establishment, IV–012
    legal regime, IV–012
    relationship with DIFC-LCIA,
        IV–018—IV–019
DIFC-LCIA Rules,
    IV–020—IV–021
future developments,
    IV–026—IV–027
introduction, IV–001
legal regime, IV–012
other regional institutions compared,
    IV–024—IV–025
relationship with DIFC,
    IV–018—IV–019
use, IV–022—IV–023

**Disclosure**
tribunal's power to order,
    22–013—22–016

**Discontinuance**
tribunal's powers, 22–045

**Dubai International Financial Centre**
see **DIFC-LCIA**

**Electronic communications**
awards, 26–020
delivery, 4–010
emergency arbitrator applications, 9–029
expedited applications, 9–011
expedited appointment of replacement arbitrators, 9–056
requests, 1–024
responses, 2–023

**Emergency arbitrators**
applicability of other rules, 9–051
awards, 9–043—9–044
conduct of proceedings, 9–038—9–039
content of applications, 9–030
delivery of orders and awards, 9–043—9–044
determination of applications, 9–035—9–037
discharge of orders or awards, 9–046—9–048
ex parte applications, 9–040
fees and expenses, 9–034, 9–045, 34–037—34–040
grounds for appointment, 9–031—9–033
introduction, 9–024—9–025
making applications, 9–029
national court applications for interim relief, 9–049—9–050
opportunity for parties to be consulted, 9–038—9–039
opting in/out, 9–052
orders, 9–043—9–044
powers, 9–042
revocation of orders or awards, 9–046—9–048
special fee, 9–034, 9–045, 34–037—34–040
threshold procedure, 9–026—9–028
time limit for conduct of proceedings, 9–041
variation of orders or awards, 9–046—9–048

**Enforcement**
awards, I–034—I–035, 32–007—32–011

**Evidence**
see also **Experts; Witnesses**
control by tribunal, 20–010
disapplication of evidentiary rules, 22–017—22–020
disclosure, 22–013—22–016
orders for inspection, 22–012
witness statements, 20–009

*"Ex aequo et bono"*
tribunal's powers, 22–052

**Expedited applications**
see also **Emergency arbitrators**
determination, 9–022—9–023
expedited appointment of replacement arbitrators, 9–053—9–057
inadmissibility, 9–019
interim relief from national courts, 9–021
introduction, 9–001—9–005
making applications, 9–006—9–018
prejudice to respondent, 9–020
rejection, 9–019

**Expenses**
arbitrators
amounts, 34–016—34–024
challenges to arbitrators, 10–043
generally, 5–021—5–023, 28–005—28–006
payments on account, 34–032
emergency arbitrators, 9–034, 9–045, 34–037—34–040
experts, 21–009
legal expenses, 28–011—28–014
tribunal expenses, 28–002—28–004, 34–016—34–024

**Experts**
access to information, items, etc., 21–007
appointment, 21–004—21–005
fees and expenses, 21–009
impartiality and independence, 21–006
introduction, 21–001—21–003
participation in hearing, 21–008

**Extensions of time**
LCIA Court's powers, 2–006, 22–053
tribunal's powers, 22–008—22–009

**Fairness**
amiable composition, 22–052
*ex aequo et bono*, 22–052
honourable engagement, 22–052
principles underlying LCIA Rules, I–032—I–033

**False statements**
guidelines for legal representatives, 33–013—33–014

**Fees**
arbitrators
amounts, 34–016—34–024
challenges to arbitrators, 10–043
generally, 5–021—5–023, 28–005—28–006
payments on account, 34–032
emergency arbitrators, 9–034, 9–045, 34–037—34–040

INDEX 749

experts, 21–009
legal fees, 28–011—28–014
registration fee
  amount, 28–003
  arbitration costs, 34–004
  commencement of arbitration, 1–020
  payment methods, 1–021
tribunal fees, 28–002—28–004,
  34–016—34–024
**Formation of tribunal**
*see* **Arbitral tribunals**
**Freezing injunctions**
interim measures, 25–021—25–022

**Good faith**
duties of good faith, 14–017—14–018,
  32–007—32–010
**Governing law**
*see* **Applicable law**
**"Green List"**
independence and impartiality, 5–036

**Hearings**
conduct of hearings, 19–007—19–00
consultation with parties, 19–008
introduction, 19–001—19–003
LCIA-MIAC, VI–018
notice of hearings, 19–012
oral submissions, 19–010—19–011
private hearings, 19–013—19–014
questioning by tribunal,
  19–010—19–011
right to a hearing, 19–004—19–005
split hearings, 19–006
times, 19–009
venue, 19–007
video conferences/teleconferences,
  19–009
**"Honourable engagement"**
tribunal's powers, 22–052

**Ill health**
arbitrators, 10–010
**Impartiality**
arbitrators
  arbitrators not to act as advocate,
    5–017
  arbitrators not to advise a party,
    5–018—5–020
  conflict of interest, 5–026—5–037
  continuing duty, 5–040
  generally, 5–006—5–011
  Green List, 5–036
  IBA Guidelines, 5–008—5–011
  impartiality and independence
    distinguished, 5–012—5–016

Orange List, 5–035
Red List, 5–033—5–034
revocation of appointment, 10–014—
  10–018, 10–022—10–025
statements of independence,
  5–021—5–037
experts, 21–006
principles underlying LCIA Rules, I–031
**Independence**
arbitrators
  arbitrators not to act as advocate,
    5–017
  arbitrators not to advise a party,
    5–018—5–020
  conflict of interest, 5–026—5–037
  continuing duty, 5–040
  generally, 5–006—5–011
  Green List, 5–036
  IBA Guidelines, 5–008—5–011
  impartiality and independence
    distinguished, 5–012—5–016
  Orange List, 5–035
  Red List, 5–033—5–034
  revocation of appointment, 10–014—
    10–018, 10–022—10–025
  statements of independence,
    5–021—5–037
experts, 21–006
principles underlying LCIA Rules, I–031
**India**
*see* **LCIA India**
**Inquiries**
tribunal's powers, 22–010—22–011
**Inspection**
tribunal's powers, 22–012
**Institutional arbitration**
advantages, I–010
LCIA's services, I–009
**Interest**
awards, 26–011—26–012
deposits, 24–009
**Interim measures**
conservatory measures,
  25–015—25–016
exclusion of tribunal's powers, 25–010
freezing injunctions, 25–021—25–022
introduction, 25–001—25–008
LCIA India, V–012—V–013
national court measures,
  25–026—25–027
provisional measures,
  25–017—25–022
security for a claim, 25–011—25–014
security for costs, 25–023—25–025,
  25–028
tribunal's powers, 25–009—25–010

## Joinder
exercise of tribunal's discretion, 22–031—22–032
expression of contrary intent, 22–030
forced joinder, 22–027
indeterminate class of disputants, 22–028—22–029
introduction, 22–003—22–004
potential drawbacks, 22–026
scope of tribunal's powers, 22–023—22–025

## Jurisdiction
challenges to jurisdiction
  decisions on jurisdictional challenges, 23–017—23–018
  generally, 23–013—23–016
  national courts, 23–019
introduction, 23–001—23–006
self-determination by tribunal, 23–007—23–008
separability of arbitration agreement, 23–009—23–012

## Language
agreement between parties, 17–008—17–010
determination by LCIA Court, 17–011—17–012
determination by tribunal, 17–014
introduction, 17–001—17–007
language of arbitration agreement, 17–008—17–010
LCIA arbitration clauses, III–021—III–022
LCIA-MIAC, VI–017
non-participating or defaulting parties, 17–013
translations, 17–015

## LCIA
*see also* **LCIA Court; LCIA Registrar; LCIA Rules**
administration of arbitrations, I–009—I–010
aims, I–005—I–018
growth, I–002—I–004
introduction, I–001
LCIA Company, I–011—I–013
LCIA Secretariat, I–017
legal culture, I–040
organisational structure, I–005—I–018
overheads, 34–012
use, I–002—I–004
Users' Councils, I–018

## LCIA Court
addressing of communications, 3–010
charges, 34–010—34–011
determinations and decisions
  appeals or review, 29–006—29–007
  conclusive and binding, 29–001—29–005
expenses, 34–013
functions, I–011—I–016, 3–001—3–003
good faith, 32–007—32–010
limitation of liability, 31–001—31–004
no obligation to make statements about arbitration, 31–004

## LCIA India
challenges to awards, V–014
court jurisdiction in relation to arbitration proceedings, V–008
default appointment of arbitrators, V–010—V–011
demand for arbitration in India, V–002—V–005
enforcement of arbitration agreements, V–009
establishment, V–017
generally, V–017—V–018
interim relief, V–012—V–013
introduction, V–001
judicial intervention, V–007
legal framework, V–006—V–016
LCIA India Rules, V–019—V–020
Notes for Arbitrators, V–021—V–02
separability of arbitration agreements, V–015—V–016
use, V–018

## LCIA-MIAC
applicable law, VI–020
arbitration environment in Africa, VI–005—VI–007
arbitrators' duties, VI–018—VI–019
conflict of interest, VI–019
cultural diversity of Mauritius, VI–003—VI–004
development of Mauritius infrastructure, VI–008—VI–013
future developments, VI–021—VI–022
hearings, VI–018
introduction, VI–001—VI–004
language of proceedings, VI–017
LCIA Court supervisory role, VI–016
LCIA-MIAC Arbitration Centre, VI–014
LCIA-MIAC Rules, VI–015—VI–020
nomination of arbitrators, VI–017
procedure, VI–017—VI–020
replacement of arbitrators, VI–020
seat of arbitration, VI–019

## LCIA recommended clauses
*see* **Arbitration clauses**

## LCIA Registrar
addressing of communications, 3–010
functions, 3–004—3–009
good faith, 32–007—32–010
limitation of liability, 31–001—31–004
statements about arbitration, no obligation to make, 31–004

## LCIA Rules
*see also under specific subjects*
administration, I–038
confidentiality, I–037
costs, I–039
definition, P–002, P–011
efficiency, I–028—I–030
enforceability of awards, I–034—I–035
fairness, I–032—I–033
impartiality and independence, I–031
incorporation into arbitration agreements, P–008—P–010
introduction, I–019
legal culture of LCIA, I–040
neutrality, I–031
party autonomy, I–025—I–027
preamble, P–001—P–011
privacy, I–037
references to Rules in arbitration agreements, P–008—P–010
structure and organisation, I–020—I–023
underlying principles, I–024—I–035

## LCIA Secretariat
charges, 34–006—34–009
expenses, 34–013
generally, I–017

## Legal representatives
"appearing by name", 18–008—18–009
changes in representation
  notification and approval, 18–013—18–018
  withholding of approval, 18–019—18–021
complaints, 18–029
conflict of interest, 18–019—18–021
contact details, 18–009
entitlement to representation, 18–006—18–009
introduction, 18–001—18–005
LCIA Guidelines
  background, 33–001—33–003
  concealment of evidence, 33–015
  ex parte communications, 33–016
  false evidence, 33–014
  false statements, 33–013
  generally, 18–022—18–028
  intention, 33–006—33–008
  obstruction of arbitration, 33–012
  overview, 33–004
  personal application, 33–009—33–010
  sanctions for breach, 18–029, 33–017—33–021
  substantive limits, 33–011
  unfair conduct, 33–012
  utility, 33–005
powers of attorney, 18–010—18–012
proof/confirmation of authority, 18–010—18–012

## Limit of liability
LCIA Court and officers, 31–001—31–004

## London Chamber of Commerce and Industry
deemed references to LCIA, P–006

## Mauritius International Arbitration Centre
*see* **LCIA-MIAC**

## Middle East
*see* **DIFC-LCIA**

## Model arbitration clauses
capacity to enter into arbitration agreement, III–008
consequences of entering into arbitration agreement, III–004—III–007
existing disputes, III–025—III–026
form of arbitration agreement, III–004—III–005
formal requirements, III–006
future disputes
  choice of law, III–023—III–024
  introduction, III–010—III–014
  language of arbitration, III–021—III–022
  number of arbitrators, III–015—III–017
  seat of arbitration, III–018—III–020
initial considerations, III–008—III–009
introduction, III–001—III–003
non-arbitrable disputes, III–009
parties bound by arbitration agreement, III–009
writing, III–006

## Nationality
arbitrators, 6–001—6–009
parties, I–016

## Neutrality
principles underlying LCIA Rules, I–031

## Nomination (arbitrators)
generally, 7–001—7–010
LCIA-MIAC, VI–017
replacement arbitrators, 11–001—11–004

requests for arbitration, 1–018—1–019
responses, 2–013—2–020
three or more parties to arbitration,
    8–001—8–005

**Oaths**
witnesses, 20–019
**Obstruction**
guidelines for legal representatives,
    33–012
**"Orange List"**
independence and impartiality, 5–035

**Party autonomy**
*see* **Autonomy**
**Payments on account**
*see also* **Deposits**
arbitrators' fees, 34–032
**Place of arbitration**
*see also* **Seat of arbitration**
generally, 16–013, 19–007
**Pleadings**
*see* **Written statements**
**Powers of attorney**
legal representatives, 18–010—18–012
**Preservatory measures**
*see* **Interim measures**
**President of the LCIA Court**
appointment as arbitrator, 5–051
**Privacy**
*see* **Confidentiality**
**Procedure**
*see also under specific subjects*
agreed proposals, 14–006—14–010
applicable law, 14–003,
    16–014—16–018
good faith, 32–007—32–010
introduction, 14–001—14–005
presiding arbitrators' power to make
    procedural orders alone, 14–019
tribunal's discretion, 14–015—14–018
tribunal's duties, 14–011—14–014
tribunal's powers
    alteration of time limits, 22–008—
        22–009, 22–053
    amendment of statements of case,
        22–007
    amiable composition, 22–052
    choice of law, 22–047—22–051
    consolidation, 22–003—22–004,
        22–033—22–044
    disapplication of evidentiary rules,
        22–017—22–020
    disclosure orders, 22–013—22–016
    discontinuance of arbitration, 22–045
    enquiries, 22–010—22–011
    *ex aequo et bono*, 22–052
    honourable engagement, 22–052

introduction, 22–001—22–002
joinder, 22–003—22–004,
    22–023—22–032
no relief in national courts without
    permission or agreement, 22–046
orders for payment of compensation
    for breach of legal obligation,
    22–021—22–022
orders for things to be made available
    for inspection, 22–012
orders requiring parties to comply
    with legal obligation,
    22–021—22–022
production orders, 22–013—22–016
reasonable opportunity for parties to
    state views, 22–005—22–006
specific performance,
    22–021—22–022
tribunal's own initiative,
    22–005—22–006
**Production orders**
generally, 22–013—22–016

**Qualifications**
arbitrators, 5–021, 5–024—5–025

**Reasons**
awards, 26–004—26–005
**Recommended arbitration clauses**
capacity to enter into arbitration
    agreement, III–008
consequences of entering into arbitration
    agreement, III–004—III–007
existing disputes, III–025—III–026
form of arbitration agreement,
    III–004—III–005
formal requirements, III–006
future disputes
    choice of law, III–023—III–024
    introduction, III–010—III–014
    language of arbitration,
        III–021—III–022
    number of arbitrators,
        III–015—III–017
    seat of arbitration, III–018—III–020
initial considerations, III–008—III–009
introduction, III–001—III–003
non-arbitrable disputes, III–009
parties bound by arbitration agreement,
    III–009
writing, III–006
**"Red List"**
independence and impartiality,
    5–033—5–034
**Registrar**
*see* **LCIA Registrar**
**Registration fee**
*see* **Fees**

# INDEX

**Replacement of arbitrators**
*see* **Revocation (arbitrator's appointment)**
**Reply to defences**
statement of reply, 15–017—15–018
**Representatives**
*see* **Legal representatives**
**Requests for arbitration**
*see also* **Written statements**
date of receipt by Registrar, 1–025
delivery to all parties, 1–022
electronic form, 1–024
fees, 1–020—1–021, 34–004—34–005
incomplete or missing request, 5–004
introduction, 1–001—1–003
multiple claimants, 1–025
nomination of arbitrators, 1–018—1–019
parties' details, 1–006—1–007
procedural matters, 1–016—1–017
requirements, 1–004—1–005
saving provision, 1–027
statement summarising dispute
  claims advanced against each respondent, 1–014—1–015
  estimated monetary value of dispute, 1–012
  generally, 1–009
  nature and circumstances of dispute, 1–010—1–011
  transactions at issue, 1–013
submission, 1–023
terms of arbitration agreement relied on, 1–008
**Resignation**
arbitrators, 10–008—10–009
**Responses**
*see also* **Written statements**
applicability of arbitration agreement, 2–010
confirmation of delivery to relevant parties, 2–021
confirmation or denial of claims, 2–008—2–010
cross-claims, 2–008, 2–011—2–012
defences, 2–008—2–010
electronic form, 2–023
generally, 2–001—2–004
incomplete or missing response, 5–004
multiple respondents, 2–028
nomination of arbitrators, 2–013—2–020
procedural issues, 2–013—2–017
respondent's details, 2–007
saving provision, 2–029
submission, 2–022
time limits

failure to comply, 2–024—2–027
generally, 2–005—2–006
**Revocation (arbitrator's appointment)**
challenges to arbitrators, 10–039—10–042
doubts as to impartiality or independence, 10–014—10–018
grounds, 10–006—10–028
inability to act, 10–011
introduction, 10–001—10–005
LCIA-MIAC, VI–020
nomination of replacement arbitrators, 11–001—11–004
refusal to act, 10–012
resignation, 10–008—10–009
serious illness, 10–010
unfitness to act, 10–013, 10–019—10–028
violation of arbitration agreement, 10–020—10–021

**Schedule of Costs**
*see* **Costs**
**Seat of arbitration**
agreement between parties, 16–005—16–006
applicable law, 14–003, 16–014—16–018
default seat, 16–007—16–012
introduction, 16–001—16–004
LCIA-MIAC, VI–019
statement in awards, 26–005
venue for hearings and deliberations, 16–013
**Secretariat**
*see* **LCIA Secretariat**
**Security**
security for a claim, 25–011—25–014
security for costs, 25–023—25–025, 25–028
**Separability of arbitration agreements**
*see* **Severability**
**Service**
*see* **Delivery**
**Settlement**
consent awards, 26–024
costs, 28–009
return of balance of funds, 28–010
**Severability**
generally, 23–009—23–012, 32–011
LCIA India, V–015—V–016
**Signatures**
awards, 26–008, 26–014—26–016
**Slips**
challenges/appeals in national courts, 27–006—27–007
correction on tribunal's own initiative, 27–008

errors, 27–003—27–005
form of award, 27–012
introduction, 27–001—27–002
memorandums, 27–005
time limits, 27–003
**Sole arbitrators**
generally, 5–005, 5–045—5–048
**Specific performance**
tribunal's power to order, 22–021—22–022
**Split hearings**
generally, 19–006
**Statements of case**
see also **Written statements**
amendment, 22–007
statement of case, 15–009—15–013
statement of defence, 15–014—15–016
statement of defence to cross-claim, 15–017—15–018
statement of reply, 15–017—15–018

**Teleconferences**
hearings, 19–009
**Time limits**
additional awards, 27–009
alteration by LCIA Court, 22–053
alteration by tribunal, 22–008—22–009
challenges to arbitrators, 10–033—10–034
commencement, 4–013
compliance, 4–014
correction of awards, 27–003
emergency arbitration, 9–041
end, 4–014
examples, 4–015—4–016
generally, 4–011—4–012
introduction, 4–001—4–003
responses
  failure to comply, 2–024—2–027
  generally, 2–005—2–006
written submissions, 15–003
**Translations**
generally, 17–015
**Travelling expenses**
arbitration costs, 34–019
**"Truncated tribunals"**
generally, 12–001—12–002

**Unfair conduct**
guidelines for legal representatives, 33–012
**Unfitness of arbitrators**
see **Arbitrators**
**Urgent cases**

see **Emergency arbitrators; Expedited applications**
**Users' Councils**
generally, I–018

**VAT**
arbitration costs, 34–015, 34–024
**Venues**
see also **Seat of arbitration**
generally, 16–013, 19–007
**Vice Presidents of the LCIA Court**
appointment as arbitrator, 5–051
**Video conferences**
hearings, 19–009

**Waiver**
right to object to breach of arbitration agreement, 32–001—32–006
**Witnesses**
attendance, 20–011—20–013
calling by tribunal, 20–013
control of evidence by tribunal, 20–010
cross-examination, 20–011—20–012, 20–020—20–021
exchange of witness statements, 20–010
expert witnesses, 21–008
IBA Rules, 20–005—20–006
interviewing witnesses, 20–014—20–017
introduction, 20–001—20–006
notice of identity of witnesses and subject matter of testimony, 20–007—20–008
oaths, 20–019
parties giving evidence, 20–018
questioning by tribunal, 19–010—19–011, 20–020—20–021
witness preparation/coaching, 20–014—20–017
witness statements, 20–009
**Written communications**
see **Communications**
**Written statements**
accompanying documents, 15–003
additional directions where multiple claimants or respondents, 15–019
additional submissions prohibited, 15–020
cross-claims, 15–014—15–016
default procedure, 15–008
failure to submit defence or defence to cross-claim, 15–021
introduction, 15–001—15–007
memorials, 15–005—15–006
procedure following final submission, 15–022—15–023

statement of case, 15–009—15–013
statement of defence to cross-claim,
    15–017—15–018
statement of defence,
    15–014—15–016
statement of reply, 15–017—15–018
summary of timetable, 15–003
written elections
    claimants, 15–009
    respondents, 15–014